MANUAL
GREEK LEXICON

A
MANUAL
GREEK LEXICON
OF THE
NEW TESTAMENT

G. ABBOTT-SMITH

Principal of the Montreal Diocesan Theological College and
Professor of Hellenistic Greek in McGill University

T&T CLARK
EDINBURGH AND NEW YORK

T&T CLARK LTD

A Continuum imprint

59 George Street	370 Lexington Avenue
Edinburgh EH2 2LQ	New York 10017–6503
Scotland	USA
www.tandtclark.co.uk	www.continuumbooks.com

First published in paperback 1999
Reprinted 2001

ISBN 0 567 08684 4

British Library Cataloguing in Publication Data
A catalogue record for this book is available from the British Library

Printed and bound in Great Britain by MPG Books Ltd,
Bodmin, Cornwall

PREFACE TO THIRD EDITION

THE Third Edition to the Lexicon follows after two successive printings of the Second Edition, first issued in 1923. During the interval a very considerable list of corrections and additions has been collected. Many of these have been noted by various scholars who have been good enough to bring them to my attention. In this connection I am particularly indebted to Professor W. F. Howard, who on the first appearance of the Lexicon examined it carefully throughout and has from time to time since then sent me many valuable suggestions. To Professor Michaels of Emmanuel College, University of Toronto, my grateful acknowledgment is also due for several valuable lists of addenda and corrigenda.

I would here repeat the regret expressed in a Note to the Second Edition for the unintentional omission of Dr. A. T. Robertson's *Grammar* from the Bibliography. The references in the Lexicon to this very complete and comprehensive work would have been more had it come into my hands before the greater part of the manuscript was written.

The Addenda to this edition contain several references to Dr. Souter's pocket Lexicon, which appeared too late for use in the First Edition. For the help it has since given me I would extend my sincere thanks to the scholarly editor of this useful little book.

It is hoped that with the notes in the Addenda the Lexicon has been made as complete as the limits of space will allow and that the numerous corrections in the stereotype plates have made it reasonably free from error.

To correspondents in various parts of the world who have written kindly about the Lexicon I would express my thanks for their appreciation. My greatest reward for the work done is the knowledge that it has proved of some use to so many fellow-workers in New Testament studies, known and unknown to me by name. For its limitations and any errors which may still remain, I ask their kind indulgence.

G. ABBOTT-SMITH.

September, 1936.

v

3669

PREFACE

THE need of a new Greek-English Lexicon of the New Testament will hardly be questioned. Thayer's monumental work, deservedly the standard for more than thirty years past, and, supplemented by later literature, still likely to remain a standard of reference for some time to come, was rather too bulky to serve as a table companion to the New Testament for the average man. A smaller book, which would lend itself more readily to constant reference, has been a real and growing want for the student.

This want has been enhanced by the progress of lexical study during the last quarter century. The study of vernacular texts, which in recent years received a new impetus through the discovery of vast numbers of non-literary papyri, chiefly in Egypt, has removed all doubt as to the category to which the language of the New Testament belongs. It is now abundantly clear that the diction of the apostolic writers is not a peculiar isolated idiom, characteristic of Jewish Hellenists, but simply the common speech of the Greek-speaking world at the time when the New Testament books were written.

While the statement just made has come to be a commonplace, it has not been so for long. There has arisen, therefore, the need not only of the collection and arrangement in convenient form (a need which is now being supplied for the advanced scholar in Moulton and Milligan's *Vocabulary of the Greek Testament*) of the results of pioneer study in the papyri, but also of a systematic revision, in the light of recent research, of many of the views regarding the diction and vocabulary of the New Testament which were commonly accepted thirty or even twenty years ago.

The considerations therefore—so well set forth by Dr. Moulton in his *Prolegomena*—which call for an entirely new grammar of the New Testament, apply also to the work of the Lexicographer. And the materials for his work—still steadily accumulating—have been liberally furnished by the special studies of Deissmann and Thumb in Germany and Moulton and Milligan in Great Britain and have also found their way into the more recent commentaries.

The new impulse given to the study of the Septuagint by the publication of the *Oxford Concordance* by Hatch and Redpath, the Cambridge Manual Edition of the Septuagint and its accompanying Introduction by Dr. Swete, together with the *Grammar* of Mr. Thackeray, has also had its influence on New Testament studies. While Dr. Abbott's caution [1] as to the possibility of exaggerating the influence of the Septuagint still holds good, the evidence of the papyri has brought about a growing sense of its value to the student of the New Testament. More reference therefore has been made, it is believed, in this Lexicon to the usage of the Septuagint than in any previous work of the same kind, so that even where there may not appear to be any special significance in the Old Testament usage with respect to a particular word, the student will always have an idea of the extent and character of the use which was made of it in that version which was the most familiar form of the Old Testament to the writers of the New.

The books mentioned in the list which follows are, out of a larger number to which I would register here a general acknowledgement of indebtedness, those which appeared to be, on the whole, the more accessible and useful to the average reader. Among the Lexicons, an almost equal debt is owed to Liddell and Scott and to Thayer. The classification of meanings in the latter, a characteristic excellence, often defies improvement, while Preuschen, though on the whole adding little to the work of his predecessors, is often helpful in this same particular. Not a few suggestions of fresh treatment have come from Fr. Zorell, S.J., whose scholarly work is quite modern and remarkably free from any ecclesiastical bias.

Of the commentaries, besides those available to Thayer, the most helpful for lexical purposes have been those of Hort, Swete and Mayor in Macmillan's Series, also the International Critical Commentaries, especially the more recent issues. Some of Bishop Lightfoot's best lexical work is to be found in his posthumous *Notes on Epistles of St. Paul*, while Dr. Field's *Notes on the Translation of the New Testament*, contain a wealth of learning and sound judgment

[1] *Essays*, 67 ff.

such as would be hard to parallel within the limits of a single volume.

On points of grammar, references are mainly made to Dr. Moulton's *Prolegomena* and the English Translation of Blass, also, in a few instances, to Dr. A. T. Robertson's Grammar.[1]

A brief treatment is given of the more important synonyms, in the belief that while classical distinctions cannot always be pressed in late and colloquial usage, it is an advantage to know something of the distinctive features of synonymous words as traceable in their etymology and literary history.

For the text of the New Testament the standard adopted is that of Moulton and Geden's *Concordance*,[2] which, as the latest and best work of its kind, is likely to remain the recognised authority for many years to come. The Greek text followed therefore is that of Westcott and Hort, with which are compared the texts of the Eighth Edition of Tischendorf and of the English Revisers, the marginal readings of each being included. From the *Textus Receptus* as such, no reading which modern editors have rejected is as a rule recorded, except in cases where a word would otherwise be dropped from the vocabulary of the New Testament. Sometimes, also, reference is made to a reading of the *Receptus* to which some particular interest is attached.

The asterisks and daggers in the margin follow, with the kind permission of the publishers and Mr. Geden, the notation of the *Concordance*. There is, however, the one difference, that whereas in Moulton and Geden the time limit marked by the dagger is the beginning of the Christian era, it seemed better for the purpose of the Lexicon to include in the category of "late Greek" all words found only in Greek writers after the time of Aristotle[3]

It remains to express in general terms my grateful acknowledgement to colleagues and friends in McGill University with its affiliated Theological Colleges and in my own Alma Mater, the University of Bishop's College, Lennoxville, as well as to many English friends, in Cambridge and elsewhere, who have given me valued advice and encouragement.

All these will pardon me if I single out for special mention the one name of Dr. J. H. Moulton, the genial master-crafts-

---

[1] See Preface to the Third Edition and Additions to Modern Writers, pp. v and xv.

[2] *A Concordance to the Greek Testament*, by Rev. W. F. Moulton, M.A., D.D., and Rev. A. S. Geden, D.D. Second Edition. T. & T. Clark, 1899.

[3] See below, p. xvi.

man of that science to which I have sought in a humble way
to contribute what I could. At the beginning of my undertaking he took me in, a stranger, and gave me ungrudgingly
of his counsel and direction, and also my first introduction to
the publishers through whom the appearance of the work
under the best possible auspices was assured.

To the manifold assistance I have had from fellow-workers,
both by word of mouth and through the printed page I would
fain attribute most of the value which this modest effort may
possess. For its deficiencies I am alone responsible, and I
can only hope that in spite of them this book may sustain
the note sounded in the last word in the alphabetical order
of the New Testament Vocabulary—ὠφέλιμος—and may
serve in a small way to the more faithful and intelligent
study of the Book of the New Covenant of our Lord and
Saviour in the language in which it was written.

The foregoing paragraphs were written early in 1917,
when, with the last sheets of the Lexicon, they were sent
overseas for publication. The manuscript has thus been in-
accessible for revision, whence the absence of any reference
to much valuable material that has appeared, both in books
and in periodicals, during the last four years, including the
second volume of the *Grammar* of Dr. Moulton, whose tragic
death as a victim of the ruthless warfare of the submarines
was reported a few days after the earlier part of this Preface
was written. The student is recommended to supplement
the grammatical references in the body of the Lexicon by
consulting the Index to Vol. II. of Dr. Moulton's *Grammar*.

I take this opportunity of adding to the acknowledgements
already made my thanks to Professors A. R. Gordon and
S. B. Slack of McGill University and to the Rev. R. K.
Naylor, sometime classical tutor at McGill, for their kindness in proof-reading, to the publishers for their generous
enterprise at a time of unprecedented difficulty in the pro-
duction of books, and to the compositors and readers of the
Aberdeen University Press for their painstaking and accurate
performance of a difficult task.

G. ABBOTT-SMITH.

MONTREAL,
September, 1921.

LIST OF ABBREVIATIONS

I. GENERAL.

absol.	= absolute.		impv.	= imperative.
acc.	= accusative.		in l.	= in loco.
act.	= active.		indic.	= indicative.
ad fin.	= ad finem.		inf.	= infinitive.
adj.	= adjective.		infr.	= infra.
adv.	= adverb.		Ion.	= Ionic.
al.	= alibi (*elsewhere*).		l.c.	= loco citato.
aor.	= aorist.		m.	= masculine.
Apocr.	= Apocrypha.		metaph.	= metaphorically.
App.	= Appendix.		meton.	= metonymy.
Aram.	= Aramaic.		MGr.	= Modern Greek.
Att.	= Attic.		n.	= note, neuter.
bibl.	= biblical.		neg.	= negative.
bis	= twice.		nom.	= nominative.
c.	= cum (*with*).		om.	= omit, omits.
cf.	= confer (*compare*)		opp.	= opposed to.
cl.	= classics, classical.		optat.	= optative.
cogn.	= cognate.		pass.	= passive.
compar.	= comparative.		pers.	= person.
contr.	= contracted.		pf.	= perfect.
dat.	= dative.		plpf.	= pluperfect.
e.g.	= exempli gratia (*for instance*).		prep.	= preposition.
			prop.	= properly.
eccl.	= ecclesiastical.		ptcp.	= participle.
esp.	= especially.		q.v.	= quod vide.
ex.	= example.		rei	= of the thing.
exc.	= except.		s.	= sub.
f.	= and following (verse).		s.v.	= sub voce.
ff.	= „ „ (verses).		sc.	= scilicet (*that is*).
fig.	= figurative.		seq.	= sequente (*followed by*)
freq.	= frequent.		subjc.	= subjunctive.
fut.	= future.		subst.	= substantive.
gen.	= genitive.		superl.	= superlative.
Gk.	= Greek.		supr.	= supra.
Heb.	= Hebrew.		syn.	= synonym.
i.e.	= id est.		Targ.	= Targum.
ib.	= in the same place.		v.	= vide.
id.	= the same.		vb.	= verb.
impers.	= impersonal.		v.l.	= variant reading.
impf.	= imperfect.		v.s.	= vide sub.

= Equivalent to, equals.   < Derived from or related to.

II. BIBLICAL.

(a) BOOKS.

Septuagint.

Ge	= Genesis.	Ez	= Ezekiel.
Ex	= Exodus.	Da	= Daniel.
Le	= Leviticus.	Ho	= Hosea.
Nu	= Numbers.	Jl	= Joel.
De	= Deuteronomy.	Am	= Amos.
Jos	= Joshua.	Ob	= Obadiah.
Jg	= Judges.	Jh	= Jonah.
Ru	= Ruth.	Mi	= Micah.
I, II Ki	= I, II Kings (E.V., Samuel).	Na	= Nahum.
		Hb	= Habakkuk.
III, IV Ki	= III, IV Kings (E.V., I, II Kings).	Ze	= Zephaniah.
		Hg	= Haggai.
I, II Ch	= I, II Chronicles.	Za	= Zachariah.
II Es	= II Esdras (E.V., Ezra).	Ma	= Malachi.
		I Es	= I Esdras.
Ne	= Nehemiah.	To	= Tobit.
Es	= Esther.	Jth	= Judith.
Jb	= Job.	Wi	= Wisdom.
Ps	= Psalms.	Si	= Sirach.
Pr	= Proverbs.	Ba	= Baruch.
Ec	= Ecclesiastes.	Da Su	= Susannah.
Ca	= Canticles.	Da Bel	= Bel and the Dragon.
Is	= Isaiah.	Pr Ma	= Prayer of Manasseh.
Je	= Jeremiah.	I-IV Mac	= I-IV Maccabees.
La	= Lamentations.		

New Testament.

Mt	= St. Matthew.	I, II Th	= I, II Thessalonians.
Mk	= St. Mark.	I, II Ti	= I, II Timothy
Lk	= St. Luke.	Tit	= Titus.
Jo	= St. John.	Phm	= Philemon.
Ac	= Acts.	He	= Hebrews.
Ro	= Romans.	Ja	= James.
I, II Co	= I, II Corinthians.	I, II Pe	= I, II Peter.
Ga	= Galatians.	I-III Jo	= I-III John.
Eph	= Ephesians.	Ju	= Jude.
Phl	= Philippians.	Re	= Revelation.
Col	= Colossians.		

(b) VERSIONS AND EDITIONS.

Al.	= anon. version quoted by Origen.	R (in LXX refs.)	= Sixtine Ed. of LXX (1587).
Aq.	= Aquila.	Rec.	= Received Text.
AV	= Authorized version.	RV	= Revised Version.
B	= Beza.	R, txt., mg.	= R.V. text, margin.
E	= Elzevir.	Sm.	= Symmachus.
EV	= English version (A.V. and R.V.).	T	= Tischendorf.
		Th.	= Theodotion.
Gr. Ven.	= Græcus Venetus.	Tr.	= Tregelles.
L	= Lachmann.	Vg.	= Vulgate.
LXX	= Septuagint.	WH	= Westcott and Hort.

III. ANCIENT WRITERS.

(i/, ii/, etc. = 1st, 2nd century, etc.)

Ael.	= Aelian, ii/A.D.		Herm.	= Hermas, ii/A.D.
Æsch.	= Æschylus, v/B.C.		Hes.	= Hesiod, ix/B.C.?
Æschin.	= Æschines, iv/B.C.		Hipp.	= Hippocrates, v/B.C.
Anth.	= Anthology.		Hom.	= Homer, ix/B.C.?
Antonin.	= M. Aurel. Antoninus,		Inscr.	= Inscriptions.
	ii/A.D.		Luc.	= Lucian, ii/A.D.
Apoll.	= Apollonius Rhodius,		Lys.	= Lysias, v/B.C.
Rhod.	ii/B.C.		Menand.	= Menander, iv/B.C.
Arist.	= Aristotle, iv/B.C.		π.	= Papyri.
Aristoph.	= Aristophanes, v/B.C.		Paus.	= Pausanias, ii/A.D.
Ath.	= Athanasius, iv/A.D.		Phalar.	= Phalaris, Spurius Epp.?
CIG	= Corpus Inscriptionum		Philo.	= Philo Judæus, i/A.D.
	Græcarum.		Pind.	= Pindar, v/B.C.
Dio Cass.	= Dio Cassius, ii/A.D.		Plat.	= Plato, v-iv/B.C.
Diod.	= Diodorus Siculus, i/B.C.		Plut.	= Plutarch, ii/A.D.
Diog.	= Diogenes Laertius,		Polyb.	= Polybius, ii/B.C.
Laert.	ii/A.D.		Socr., HE	= Socrates, Hist. Eccl.,
Dion. H.	= Dionysius of Halicar-			v/A.D.
	nassus, i/B.C.		Soph.	= Sophocles, v/B.C.
Diosc.	= Dioscorides, i-ii/A.D.		Strab.	= Strabo, i/B.C.
Eur.	= Euripides, v/B.C.		Test. Zeb.	= Testimony of Zebedee,
Eustath.	= Eustathius, xii/A.D.			ii/A.D.
FlJ	= Flavius Josephus, i/A.D.		Theogn.	= Theognis, vi/B.C.
Greg.	= Gregory of Nazianzus,		Theophr.	= Theophrastus, iv/B.C.
Naz.	iv/A.D.		Thuc.	= Thucydides, v/B.C.
Hdt.	= Herodotus, v/B.C.		Xen.	= Xenophon, v-iv/B.C.
Heliod.	= Heliodorus, iv/A.D.			

IV. MODERN WRITERS.

Abbott, *Essays*	= Essays chiefly on the Original Texts of the Old and New Testaments, by T. K. Abbott. Longmans, 1891.
Abbott, *JG*	= Johannine Grammar, by E. A. Abbott. London, 1906.
Abbott, *JV*	= Johannine Vocabulary, by the same. London, 1905.
AR	= St. Paul's Epistle to the Ephesians, by J. Armitage Robinson. Second Edition. Macmillan, 1909.
BDB	= A Hebrew and English Lexicon of the Old Testament, by Brown, Driver, and Briggs. Oxford, 1906.
Blass, *Gosp.*	= Philology of the Gospels, by F. Blass. Macmillan, 1898.
Blass, *Gr.*	= Grammar of N.T. Greek, by F. Blass, tr. by H. St. J. Thackeray. Macmillan, 1898.
Boisacq	= Dictionnaire Étymologique de la langue Grecque, par Émile Boisacq. Paris, 1907-1914.
Burton	= New Testament Moods and Tenses, by E. de W. Burton. Third Edition. T. & T. Clark, 1898.
CGT	= Cambridge Greek Testament for Schools and Colleges.
Charles, *APOT*	= Apocrypha and Pseudepigrapha of the Old Testament, by R. H. Charles. Oxford, 1913.
CR	= Classical Review. London, 1887 ff.
Cremer	= Biblico-Theological Lexicon of N.T. Greek, by H. Cremer. Third English Edition, with Supplement. T. & T. Clark, 1886.
Dalman, *Gr.*	= Grammatik des jüdish-palästinischen Aramäisch, by G. Dalman. Leipzig, 1894.

Dalman, *Words*	= The Words of Jesus, by G. Dalman. English Edition. T. & T. Clark, 1902.
DAC	= Dictionary of the Apostolic Church, edited by J. Hastings. Vol. I. T. & T. Clark, 1915.
DB	= Dictionary of the Bible, edited by J. Hastings. 5 vols. (i-iv, *ext.* = extra vol.). T. & T. Clark, 1898-1904.
DB 1-vol.	= Dictionary of the Bible (in one volume), by J. Hastings. T. & T. Clark, 1909.
DCG	= Dictionary of Christ and the Gospels, edited by J. Hastings. 2 vols. T. & T. Clark, 1907-08.
Deiss., *BS*	= Bible Studies, by G. A. Deissmann. Second English Edition, including Bibelstudien and Neue Bibelstudien, tr. by A. Grieve. T. & T. Clark, 1909.
Deiss., *LAE*	= Light from the Ancient East, by A. Deissmann, tr. by L. R. M. Strachan. Second Edition. Hodder, 1908.
EB	= Encyclopædia Biblica. 4 vols. London, 1899-1903.
Edwards, *Lex.*	= An English-Greek Lexicon, by G. M. Edwards. Camb., 1912.
EGT	= Expositor's Greek Testament.
Ellic.	= Commentary on St. Paul's Epistles, by C. J. Ellicott. Andover, 1860-65.
Enc. Brit.	= Encyclopædia Britannica. Eleventh Edition. Camb. Univ. Press, 1910.
Exp. Times	= The Expository Times, edited by J. Hastings. T. & T. Clark, 1890 ff.
Field, *Notes*	= Notes on the Translation of the N.T., by F. Field, Camb., 1899.
Gifford, *Inc.*	= The Incarnation, by E. Gifford. Hodder, 1897.
Grimm-Thayer	= A Greek-English Lexicon of the N.T., being Grimm's Wilke's Clavis Novi Testamenti, tr. by J. H. Thayer. New York, 1897.
Hatch, *Essays*	= Essays in Biblical Greek, by Edwin Hatch. Oxford. 1889.
Hort	= Commentaries on the Greek Text of the Epistle of St. James (1^{1}-4^{7}); The First Epistle of St. Peter (1^{1}-2^{17}); and the Apocalypse of St. John (1-3), by F. J. A. Hort. Macmillan, 1898-1909.
ICC	= International Critical Commentary. T. & T. Clark.
Interp. Comm.	= Interpreter's Commentary. N.Y., Barnes & Co.
Jannaris	= A Historical Greek Grammar, by A. N. Jannaris. Macmillan, 1897.
JThS	= Journal of Theological Studies. London, 1899 ff.
Kennedy, *Sources*	= Sources of N.T. Greek, by H. A. A. Kennedy. T. & T. Clark, 1895.
Kühner³	= Ausführliche Grammatik der griechischen Sprache, by R. Kühner. Third Edition, by F. Blass and B. Gerth, 4 vols., 1890-1904.
Lft.	= Commentaries on St. Paul's Epistles to the Galatians (1892); Philippians (Third Edition, 1873); and Colossians and Philemon (1892), by J. B. Lightfoot. Macmillan. Also Apostolic Fathers, by the same. 5 vols. Macmillan, 1890.
Lft., *Notes*	= Notes on Epistles of St. Paul, by J. B. Lightfoot. Macmillan, 1895.
LS	= A Greek-English Lexicon, by H. G. Liddell and R. Scott. Seventh Edition. Harper, 1889.
Mayor	= Commentaries on the Epistle of St. James (Third Edition, 1910), and the Epistle of St. Jude and the Second Epistle of St. Peter. Macmillan, 1907.

Mayser	= Grammatik der gr. Papyri aus der Ptolemäerzeit, by E. Mayser. Leipzig, 1906.
M'Neile	= The Gospel according to St. Matthew, by A. H. M'Neile. Macmillan, 1915.
Meyer	= Critical and Exegetical Commentary on the N.T., by H. A. W. Meyer. Eng. tr., T. & T. Clark, 1883.
Milligan, *Selections*	= Selections from the Greek Papyri, by G. Milligan. Cambridge, 1910.
MM (xi-xxv)	= Lexical Notes from the Papyri, by J. H. Moulton and and G. Milligan. Expositor VII, vi, 567 ff.; VIII, iv, 561 ff.
MM (s.v.)	= The Vocabulary of the Greek Testament, by J. H. Moulton and G. Milligan. Part I (α); Part II (β-δ). Hodder, 1914-15 (remaining parts in preparation).
M, *Pr.*	= A Grammar of N.T. Greek. Vol. I, Prolegomena, by J. H. Moulton. Third Edition. T. & T. Clark, 1908.
M, *Th.*	= St. Paul's Epistles to the Thessalonians, by G. Milligan. Macmillan, 1908.
Moffatt	= James Moffatt, An Introduction to the Literature of the N.T. T. & T. Clark, 1911.
Mozley, *Ps.*	= The Psalter of the Church, by F. W. Mozley, Cambridge, 1905.
NTD	= The New Testament Documents, by G. Milligan. Macmillan, 1913.
Page	= The Acts of the Apostles, by T. E. Page. Macmillan, 1903.
Rackham	= The Acts of the Apostles, by R. B. Rackham. Methuen, 1901.
Ramsay, *St. Paul*	= St. Paul the Traveller and the Roman Citizen, by W. M. Ramsay. Hodder, 1895.
Rendall	= The Epistle to the Hebrews, by F. Rendall. Macmillan, 1911.
Rutherford, *NPhr.*	= The New Phrynichus, by W. G. Rutherford. Macmillan, 1881.
Schmidt	= J. H. Heinrich Schmidt, Synonymik der Griechischen Sprache. 4 vols. Leips., 1876-1886.
Simcox	= W. H. Simcox, the Language of the New Testament. Second Edition. Hodder, 1892.
Soph., *Lex.*	= Greek Lexicon of the Roman and Byzantine Periods, by E. A. Sophocles. Scribners, 1900.
Swete	= Commentaries on the Gospel according to St. Mark (Third Edition, 1909) and the Apocalypse of St. John, by H. B. Swete. Macmillan, 1906.
Thackeray, *Gr.*	= A Grammar of the O.T. in Greek I, by H. St. J. Thackeray. Cambridge, 1909.
Thayer	= Grimm-Thayer, q.v.
Thumb, *Handb.*	= Handbook of the Modern Greek Vernacular, by A. Thumb. Tr. from the Second German Edition by S. Angus. T. & T. Clark, 1912.
Thumb, *Hellen.*	= Die Griechische Sprache im Zeitalter des Hellenismus, von A. Thumb. Strassburg, 1901.
Tdf., *Pr.*	= Novum Testamentum Graece, C. Tischendorf. Editio octava critica maior. Vol III, Prolegomena, by C. R. Gregory. Leipzig, 1894.
Tr., *Syn.*	= Synonyms of the N.T., by R. C. Trench. Ninth Edition. Macmillan, 1880.
Vau.	= St. Paul's Epistle to the Romans, by C. F. Vaughan. Sixth Edition. Macmillan, 1885.
Veitch	= Greek Verbs, Irregular and Defective, by W. Veitch. Oxford, 1887.

Viteau	= Étude sur le grec du N.T., by J. Viteau. Vol. I, Le Verbe: Syntaxe des Propositions, Paris, 1893; Vol. II., Sujet: Complément et Attribut, 1896.
VD, *MGr.*	= E. Vincent and T. G. Dickson, A Handbook to Modern Greek. Second Edition. Macmillan, 1904.
Westc.	= Commentaries on the Gospel according to St. John, by B. F. Westcott, 2 Vols., Murray, 1908; the Epistle to the Ephesians, Macmillan, 1906; the Epistles of St. John, Third Edition, Macmillan, 1892.
WH	= The N.T. in the original Greek, by B. F. Westcott and F. J. A. Hort. Vol. II, Introduction and 'Appendix. Macmillan, 1881.
WM	= A Grammar of N.T. Greek, tr. from G. B. Winer's 7th Edition, with large additions, by W. F. Moulton. Third Edition. T. & T. Clark, 1882.
WS	= Grammatik des neutestamentlichen Sprachidioms, von G. B. Winer, 8te Aufl. von P. W. Schmiedel. Göttingen, 1894.
Zorell	= Novi Testamenti Lexicon Graecum (Cursus Scripturae Sacrae I, vii), auctore Fr. Zorell, S.J. Paris, 1911.
Gore, *Comm.*	= A New Commentary on Holy Scripture, including the Apocrypha, edited by Charles Gore, H. L. Goudge and A. Guillaume. Macmillan, 1929.
Jackson and Lake, *Beginnings*	= The Beginnings of Christianity, edited by F. J. Foakes Jackson, D.D., and Kirsopp Lake, D.D., D.Litt. Macmillan, 1933.
Lietzmann, *Handbuch*	= Handbuch zum Neuen Testament, edited by Hans Lietzmann. Tubingen, 1907-
M, *Gr.*, II	= A Grammar of New Testament Greek, by James Hope Moulton and Wilbert Francis Howard. Vol. II., Accedence and Word-Formation, with an Appendix on Semitisms in the New Testament. T. & T. Clark, 1929.
Peake, *Comm.*	= A Commentary on the Bible, edited by A. S. Peake and A. J. Grieve. London, 1920. (In one volume.)
Robertson, *Gr.*	= A Grammar of the Greek New Testament in the Light of Historical Research, by A. T. Robertson. London and New York, 1914.
Turner, *SNT*	= Studies in the New Testament, by Cuthbert Hamilton Turner. Oxford, 1920.
Zahn, *Intr.*	= Introduction to the New Testament, by Theodor Zahn. Tr. from the Third German Edition. Second Edition, New York, 1917.

---

* A single asterisk at the beginning of an article denotes (as in Moulton and Geden's Concordance) that the word to which it is attached is not found in the LXX or other Greek Versions of the O.T. and Apocrypha.

** A double asterisk similarly affixed denotes that the word occurs either in the Apocrypha or in the later Greek Versions of the O.T., but not in the LXX Version of the Hebrew Canonical books, and therefore either has, as a rule, no (known) Hebrew equivalent, or else was used in a translation not known to the N.T. writers. The later Greek versions (Aq., etc.) are cited, as a rule, only when a word is not found in LXX.

* A single asterisk placed after a list of passages from the LXX signifies that the word occurs nowhere else in that Version.

† A dagger at the beginning of an article denotes that the word is not found in Greek writers of the classical period.

† A dagger at the close of an article signifies that all the instances of the word's occurrence in the N.T. have been cited.

An inferior numeral after a biblical book (e.g. III Mac$_6$) indicates the number of times a word occurs in that book.

NOTE.

The total number of words alphabetically listed in the Lexicon is 5921. These include (1) 571 proper names; (2) 304 alternative forms of common terms, and 55 of proper names; (3) 22 letters of the alphabet. The total vocabulary of the generally accepted text of the New Testament thus contains 4969 common terms. Of these, 1018 do not occur in the LXX. The words (including proper names), of which all the N.T. examples are given, are 5254. Of 1528 of the N.T. words used in the LXX, all the instances in that and the other O.T. Greek Versions are cited.

The Lexicon is thus a complete Concordance of the N.T. with respect to 95 per cent. of its Vocabulary, and a complete Concordance of the LXX with respect to nearly 40 per cent. of the words from that version found in the N.T.

MANUAL GREEK LEXICON OF THE NEW TESTAMENT

A

A, α, ἄλφα (q.v.), τό, indecl., *alpha*, the first letter of the Greek alphabet. As a numeral, a′ = 1, a, = 1000. As a prefix, it appears to have at least two and perhaps three distinct senses: 1. ἀ- (before a vowel, ἀν-) *negative*, as in ἄ-γνωστος, ἄ-δικος. 2. ἁ-, ἀ- *copulative*, indicating community and fellowship, as in ἁ-πλοῦς, ἀ-κολουθέω, ἀ-δελφός. 3. An *intensive* force (LS, s. a), as in ἀ-τενίζω is sometimes assumed (but v. Boisacq, s.v.).

Ἀαρών (Heb. אַהֲרוֹן), indecl. (in FlJ, -ῶνος), *Aaron* (Ex 4¹⁴, al.) : Lk 1⁵, Ac 7⁴⁰, He 5⁴ 7¹¹ 9⁴.†

Ἀβαδδών (Heb. אֲבַדּוֹן, *destruction;* LXX, ἀπώλεια, only in Wisdom Lit., of the place of the ruined dead : Jb 26⁶ 28²² 31¹², Ps 88¹², Pr 15¹¹*), indecl.; in NT, *Abaddon*, the angel of the Abyss : Re 9¹¹.†

***ἀβαρής, -ές** (< βάρος), *without weight;* metaph. (MM, VGT, s.v.) *not burdensome:* II Co 11⁹.†

***†’Αββά** (T, -ᾶ), indecl. (Aram. אַבָּא, emphatic form of אַב = Heb. אָב, *father*), used in the phrase ’A. ὁ πατήρ, *Abba, Father* (v. Swete on Mk, l.c.) : Mk 14³⁶, Ro 8¹⁵, Ga 4⁶.†

Ἀβειληνή (T, Rec. ’Αβι-), -ῆς, ἡ (sc. χώρα), *Abilene*, a district in the Anti-Lebanon : Lk 3¹.†

Ἄβελ (WH, "A-), ὁ, indecl. (Heb. הֶבֶל), *Abel* (Ge 4²⁻¹⁰) : He 11⁴ 12²⁴; αἷμα "A., Mt 23³⁵, Lk 11⁵¹.†

’Αβιά (Heb. אֲבִיָּה, אֲבִיָּהוּ), ὁ, indecl. (in FlJ, ’Αβίας, -α), *Abia, Abijah.* 1. Son of Rehoboam (III Ki 14¹) : Mt 1⁷. 2. A priest of the line of Eleazar (I Ch 24³, ¹⁰) : Lk 1⁵.†

’Αβιάθαρ, ὁ, indecl. (Heb. אֶבְיָתָר), *Abiathar* (I Ki 21¹) : Mk 2²⁶.†

’Αβιληνή, v.s. ’Αβειληνή.

’Αβιούδ, ὁ, indecl. (Heb. אֲבִיהוּד), *Abiud, Abihud :* Mt 1¹³.†

’Αβραάμ (Heb. אַבְרָהָם), ὁ, indecl. (in FlJ, "Αβραμος, -ου; MM, VGT, s.v.), *Abraham* (Ge 17⁵ al.) : Mt 1¹, ² al.

1

ἄ-βυσσος, -ον (< Ion. βυσσός = βυθός), 1. in cl., *boundless, bottomless* (e.g. ἄ. πέλαγος, ἄ. πλοῦτος, Æsch.). 2. [In LXX (for תְּהוֹם, Ge 1², al.; exc. Is 44²⁷, Jb 41²² for צוּלָה, מְצוּלָה, Jb 36¹⁶ for רַחַב) and] NT, as subst. (MM, VGT, s.v.), ἡ ἄ. (sc. χώρα), *the abyss;* (a) of the sea (Ge 1²); (b) of the underworld, as the abode of the dead: Ro 10⁷ (a paraphrase of De 30¹³ LXX); as the abode of demons, Lk 8³¹, Re 9¹, ², ¹¹ 11⁷ 17⁸ 20¹, ³ (Cremer, 2).†

Ἄγαβος, -ου, ὁ, *Agabus :* Ac 11²⁸ 21¹⁰.†

*† ἀγαθοεργέω, -ῶ, *to do good, show kindness :* 1 Ti 6¹⁸ (Cremer, 8).†

ἀγαθο-ποιέω, -ῶ (= cl. ἀγαθὸν ποιεῖν, εὐεργετεῖν), [in LXX : Nu 10³², Jg 17¹³ A, Ze 1¹² (יטב hi.), To 12¹³ B, 1 Mac 11³³, 11 Mac 1² * ;] *to do good;* (a) univ.: 1 Pe 2¹⁵, ²⁰ 3⁶, ¹⁷, 111 Jo ¹¹; (b) for another's benefit : Mk 3⁴ (T, ἀγαθὸν ποιῆσαι), Lk 6⁹; (c) acc. pers., Lk 6³³, ³⁵ (Cremer, 8).†

*† ἀγαθοποιία, -ας, ἡ (< ἀγαθοποιός), *well-doing :* 1 Pe 4¹⁹.†

**† ἀγαθοποιός, -όν, = cl. ἀγαθουργός, [in LXX, of a woman who deals pleasantly in order to corrupt, Si 42¹⁴ * ;] *doing well, acting rightly* (Plut.): 1 Pe 2¹⁴ (Cremer, 8; MM, VGT, s.v.).†

ἀγαθός, -ή, -όν, [in LXX chiefly for טוֹב ;] in general, *good,* in physical and in moral sense, used of persons, things, acts, conditions, etc., applied to that which is regarded as "perfect in its kind, so as to produce pleasure and satisfaction, . . . that which, in itself good, is also at once for the good and the advantage of him who comes in contact with it" (Cremer, 3): γῆ, Lk 8⁸; δένδρον, Mt 7¹⁸; καρδία, Lk 8¹⁵; δόσις, Ja 1¹⁷; μερίς, Lk 10⁴²; ἔργον (freq. in Pl.), Phl 1⁶; ἐλπίς, 11 Th 2¹⁶; θησαυρός, Mt 12³⁵; μνεία, 1 Th 3⁶ (cf. 11 Mac 7²⁰); as subst., τὸ ἀ., that which is morally good, beneficial, acceptable to God, Ro 12²; ἐργάζεσθαι τὸ ἀ., Ro 2¹⁰, Eph 4²⁸; πράσσειν, Ro 9¹¹, 11 Co 5¹⁰; διώκειν, 1 Th 5¹⁵; μιμεῖσθαι, 111 Jo ¹¹; κολλᾶσθαι τῷ ἀ., Ro 12⁹; ἐρωτᾶν περὶ τοῦ ἀ., Mt 19¹⁷; διάκονος εἰς τὸ ἀ., Ro 13⁴; τὸ ἀ. σου, *thy favour, benefit,* Phm ¹⁴; pl., τὰ ἀ., of goods, possessions, Lk 12¹⁸; of spiritual benefits, Ro 10¹⁵, He 9¹¹ 10¹. ἀ. is opp. to πονηρός, Mt 5⁴⁵ 20¹⁵; κακός, Ro 7¹⁹; φαῦλος, Ro 9¹¹, 11 Co 5¹⁰ (cf. MM, VGT, s.v.).

SYN. : καλός, δίκαιος. κ. properly refers to goodliness as manifested in form : ἀ. to inner excellence (cf. the cl. καλὸς κἀγαθός and ἐν καρδίᾳ κ. καὶ ἀ., Lk 8¹⁵). In Ro 5⁷, where it is contrasted with δ., ἀ. implies a kindliness and attractiveness not necessarily possessed by the δίκαιος, who merely measures up to a high standard of rectitude (cf. ἀγαθωσύνη).

*† ἀγαθουργέω, -ῶ, contracted form (rare, v. WH, *App.,* 145) of ἀγαθοερ- (q.v.), *to do good :* Ac 14¹⁷.†

† ἀγαθωσύνη (on the termination, v.s. ἁγιότης, and cf. WH, *App.,* 152 ; MM, VGT, s.v.), -ης, ἡ (< ἀγαθός), [in LXX for טוֹבָה, טוֹב, טוּב, only in Heb. bks. ;] *goodness* (representing "the kindlier, as δικαιοσύνη, the sterner element in the ideal character." AR, *Eph.,* 5⁹; on its relation to χρηστότης, v. Tr., *Syn.,* § lxiii) : Ro 15¹⁴, Ga 5²², 11 Th 1¹¹.†

† ἀγαλλίασις, -εως, ἡ (< ἀγαλλιάω), [in LXX (most freq. in Pss. and

often coupled with εὐφροσύνη, as Ps 44 (45)[15]) chiefly for גִּיל;] *exulta-tion, exuberant joy* : Lk 1[44], Ac 2[46], He 1[9], Ju [24]; χαρὰ καὶ ἀ., Lk 1[14] (Cremer, 592).†

† **ἀγαλλιάω**, -ῶ, Hellenistic form of cl. ἀγάλλω, *to glorify*, mid. -ομαι, *to exult in* ; [in LXX (most freq. in Pss.) chiefly for רָנַן, גִּיל pi. ;] *to exult, rejoice greatly* : seq. ἐπί, c. dat., Lk 1[47]; c. dat. mod., 1 Pe 1[8], Re 19[7]. Mid., with same sense: Mt 5[12], Lk 10[21], Ac 2[26] 16[34], 1 Pe 4[13]; seq. ἵνα, Jo 8[56]; ἐν, Jo 5[35] (1 aor. pass. perh. as mid.; but v. Mozley, *Psalter*, 5), 1 Pe 1[6] (Cremer, 590).†

** **ἄ-γαμος**, -ον, [in LXX: IV Mac 16[9]*;] *unmarried* : 1 Co 7[8, 32]; fem. (= cl. ἄνανδρος), ib. [11, 34].†

** **ἀγανακτέω**, -ῶ (< ἄγαν, *much*, ἄχομαι, *to grieve*), [in LXX: Wi 5[22] 12[27], Da TH Bel [28], IV Mac 4[21]*;] *to be indignant, vexed* : Mt 21[15] 26[8], Mk 10[14] 14[4]; seq. περί, Mt 20[24], Mk 10[41]; seq. ὅτι, Lk 13[14] (v. MM, *VGT*, s.v.).†

** **ἀγανάκτησις**, -εως, ἡ (< ἀγανακτέω), [in LXX: Es 18[3] אֵל*;] *indig-nation, vexation* : II Co 7[11] (v. MM, *VGT*, s.v.).†

ἀγαπάω, -ῶ, [in LXX chiefly for אָהֵב;] *to love*, to feel and exhibit esteem and goodwill to a person, to prize and delight in a thing. 1. Of human affection, to men : τ. πλησίον, Mt 5[43]; τ. ἐχθρούς, ib. [44]; to Christ, Jo 8[42]; to God, Mt 22[37]; c. acc. rei, Lk 11[43], Jo 12[43]. Eph 5[25], II Tim 4[8, 10], He 1[9], 1 Pe 2[17] 3[10], II Pe 2[15], 1 Jo 2[15], Re 12[11]. 2. Of divine love ; (a) God's love : to men, Ro 8[37]; to Christ, Jo 3[35]; (b) Christ's love : to men, Mk 10[21]; to God, Jo 14[31]; c. cogn. acc., Jo 17[26], Eph 2[4]; v. *ICC* on Ga, pp. 519 ff.

SYN. : φιλέω. From its supposed etymology (Thayer, LS; but v. also Boisacq) ἀ. is commonly understood properly to denote love based on esteem (*diligo*), as distinct from that expressed by φιλέω (*amo*), spontaneous natural affection, emotional and unreasoning. If this distinction holds, ἀ. is fitly used in NT of Christian love to God and man, the spiritual affection which follows the direction of the will, and which, therefore, unlike that feeling which is instinctive and unreasoned, can be commanded as a duty. (Cf. ἀγάπη, and *v*. Tr., *Syn.*, § xii ; Cremer, 9, 592; and esp. MM, *VGT*, s.v.)

† **ἀγάπη**, -ης, ἡ, [in LXX for אַהֲבָה, which is also rendered by ἀγάπησις and φιλία;] *love, goodwill, esteem*. Outside of bibl. and eccl. books, there is no clear instance (with Deiss., *LAE*, 18₄ 70₂, cf. the same writer in *Constr. Quar.*, ii, 4; and with MM, *VGT*, s.v., cf. Dr. Moulton in *Exp. Times*, xxvi, 3, 139). In NT, like ἀγαπάω, 1. Of men's love : (a) to one another, Jo 13[35]; (b) to God, 1 Jo 2[5]. 2. Of divine love ; (a) God's love : to men, Ro 5[8]; to Christ, Jo 17[26]; (b) Christ's love to men : Ro 8[35]. 3. In pl., *love feasts* : Ju [12] (*DB*, iii, 157).

SYN. : φιλία. ἀ., signifying properly (v.s. ἀγαπάω) love which chooses its object, is taken over from LXX, where its connotation is more general, into NT, and there used exclusively to express that spiritual bond of love between God and man and between man and man, in Christ, which is characteristic of Christianity. It is thus distinct from φιλία, *friendship* (Ja 4⁴ only), στοργή, *natural affection* (in NT only in compounds, v.s. ἄστοργος) and ἔρως, *sexual love*, which is not used in NT, its place being taken by ἐπιθυμία. (Cf. ἀγαπάω; and v. Abbott, *Essays*, 70 f.; *DB*, vol. iii., 155; Cremer, 13, 593; MM, *VGT*, s.v.)

ἀγαπητός, -ή, -όν (< ἀγαπάω), [in LXX chiefly for יָחִיד, יָדִיד;] *beloved* (v. M, *Pr.*, 221); (a) by God: of Christ, Mt 3¹⁷; of men, Ro 1⁷; (b) by Christians, of one another: 1 Co 4¹⁴; freq. as form of address, ib. 10¹⁴; opp. to ἐχθρός, Ro 11²⁸ (v. AR, *Eph.*, 229; Cremer, 17; MM, *VGT*, s.v.). Used of only children (AR, l.c.; LS, *new ed.*, s.v.; *Essays Cath. and Critical*, pp. 166, 170 n.) hence perh. *only* : Mt 3¹⁷ 17⁵, Mk 1¹¹ 9⁷, Lk 3²² 9³⁵ (cf. Ge 22² LXX, but cf. also AR, l.c., on The Beloved as Messianic title).

Ἀγάρ (Rec. Ἄ-), ἡ, indecl. (in FlJ, Ἀγάρα, -ης; Heb. הָגָר), *Hagar* (Ge 16): Ga 4²⁴, ²⁵.†

*ἀγγαρεύω (from the Persian; cf. Vg. *angariare*, and the Heb. אִגֶּרֶת; on the orthogr., v. Bl., §6, 1; M, *Pr.*, 46), *to impress* into public service, employ a courier; hence, *to compel* to perform a service (prob. common in the vernac.; cf. Deiss., *BS*, 86 f., MM, *Exp.*, iv; *VGT*, s.v.): Mt 5⁴¹ 27³², Mk 15²¹.†

ἀγγεῖον, -ου, τό (< ἄγγος), [in LXX chiefly for כְּלִי;] *a vessel* (v. MM, *VGT*, s.v.): Mt 25⁴.†

ἀγγελία, -ας, ἡ (< ἄγγελος), [in LXX chiefly for שְׁמוּעָה;] *a message* : 1 Jo 1⁵ 3¹¹ (Cremer, 18; MM, *VGT*, s.v.).†

ἀγγέλλω (ἄγγελος), [in LXX for נגד hi.;] *to announce, report* : Jo 4⁵¹ (WHR omit), 20¹⁸ (MM, *VGT*, s.v.).†

ἄγγελος, -ου, ὁ, [in LXX chiefly for מַלְאָךְ;] 1. *a messenger*, one sent: Mt 11¹⁰, Ja 2²⁵. 2. As in LXX, in the special sense of *angel*, a spiritual, heavenly being, attendant upon God and employed as his messenger to men, to make known his purposes, as Lk 1¹¹, or to execute them, as Mt 4⁶. The ἄ. in Re 1²⁰ 2¹, al., is variously understood as (1) a messenger or delegate, (2) a bishop or ruler, (3) a guardian angel, (4) the prevailing spirit of each church, i.e. the Church itself. (Cf. Swete, *Ap.*, in l.; *DB*, iv, 991; Thayer, s.v.; Cremer, 18; MM, *VGT*, s.v.); on guardian angels, v. Peake, *Comm.* on Mt 18¹⁰.

ἄγγος, -εος, τό, [in LXX for כְּלוּב, כְּלִי;] *a vessel* : Mt 13⁴⁸.†

ἄγε, prop. imperat. of ἄγω, *come !* used as adv. and addressed, like φέρε, to one or more persons : Ja 4¹³ 5¹.†

ἀγέλη, -ης, ἡ (< ἄγω), [in LXX chiefly for עֵדֶר;] *a herd* : Mt 8³⁰⁻³², Mk 5¹¹, ¹³, Lk 8³², ³³.†

*†ἀγενεαλόγητος, -ον (< γενεαλογέω), *without genealogy*, i.e. without recorded pedigree (cf. Ne 7⁶⁴): He 7³ (Cremer, 152; MM, *VGT*, s.v.).

*ἀγενής, -ές (< γένος), 1. *unborn* (Plat.); 2. *of no family, ignoble, base* (opp. to ἀγαθός, Soph., *Fr.*, 105): opp. to εὐγενής, 1 Co 1²⁸ (for exx. from π., v. MM, *VGT*, s.v.).†

ἁγιάζω, Hellenistic form of ἁγίζω (< ἅγιος), *to make holy, consecrate, sanctify;* [in LXX chiefly for קָדַשׁ pi., hi. ;] 1. *to dedicate, separate, set apart for God ;* of things: Mt 23[17, 19], II Ti 2[21]; of persons: Christ, Jo 10[36] 17[19]. 2. *to purify,* make conformable in character to such dedication: forensically, to free from guilt, I Co 6[11], Eph 5[26], He 2[11] 10[10, 14, 29] 13[12]; internally, by actual sanctification of life, Jo 17[17, 19], Ac 20[32] 26[18], Ro 15[16], I Co 1[2] 7[14], I Th 5[23], Re 22[11]; of a nonbeliever influenced by marriage with a Christian, I Co 7[14]. 3. In the intermediate sense of ceremonial or levitical purification: (*a*) of things, II Ti 2[21]; (*b*) of persons, He 9[13]. 4. *to treat as holy:* Mt 6[9], Lk 11[2], I Pe 3[15] (Cremer, 53, 602; MM, *VGT*, s.v.).†

† ἁγιασμός, -οῦ, ὁ (< ἁγιάζω), [in LXX: Ez 45[4] (מִקְדָּשׁ), Si 7[31], etc. ;] as an active verbal noun in -μός, it signifies properly the process τὸ ἁγιάζειν, rather than the resultant state, ἁγιωσύνη, hence, 1. *consecration;* 2. *sanctification:* so strictly in Ro 6[19, 22] (but v. Meyer), I Co 1[30], I Th 4[3, 7], II Th 2[13]. He 12[14], I Pe 1[2]. Elsewhere it perhaps (Ellic.; but v. Milligan, *Th.*, 48) inclines to the resultant state: I Th 4[4], I Ti 2[15] (Cremer, 55, 602).†

ἅγιος, -α, -ον (< τὸ ἅγος, *religious awe; ἅζω, to venerate*), [in LXX chiefly for קֹדֶשׁ ;] primarily, *dedicated to the gods, sacred* (Hdt.; rare in Att., never in Hom., Hes. and Trag., who use ἁγνός), hence, *holy,* characteristic of God, separated to God, worthy of veneration. 1. Its highest application is to God himself, in his purity, majesty, and glory: Lk 1[49], Jo 17[11], Re 4[8]. Hence (*a*) of things and places which have a claim to reverence as sacred to God, e.g. the Temple: Mt 24[15], He 9[1]; (*b*) of persons employed by him, as angels: I Th 3[13]; prophets, Lk 1[70]; apostles, Eph 3[5]. 2. Applied to persons as separated to God's service: (*a*) of Christ, Mk 1[24], Jo 6[69], Ac 4[30]; (*b*) of Christians, Ac 9[13], Ro 1[7], He 6[10], Re 5[8]. 3. In the moral sense of sharing God's purity: Mk 6[20], Jo 17[11], Ac 3[14], Re 3[7]. 4. Of pure, clean sacrifices and offerings: I Co 7[14], Eph 1[4].

SYN.: ἁγνός, *pure,* both in ceremonial and spiritual sense; ἱερός (*sacer*), *sacred,* that which is inviolable because of its (external) relation to God; ὅσιος (*sanctus* as opp. to *nefas*), that which is based on everlasting ordinances of right. (Cf. Tr., *Syn.*, §lxxxviii; *DB*, ii, 399 f.; Cremer, 34, 594-601; MM, *VGT*, s.v.)

**† ἁγιότης, -ητος, ἡ (< ἅγιος), [in LXX: II Mac 15[2 *];] *sanctity, holiness,* regarded, properly, as an abstract quality (v. next word, and cf. Lft., *Notes,* 49; MM, *VGT*, s.v.): II Co 1[12], He 12[10].†

† ἁγιωσύνη (cf. ἀγαθωσύνη), -ης, ἡ (< ἅγιος), [in LXX: Ps 29 (30)[4] 96 (97)[12] (קֹדֶשׁ), 95 (96)[6] (עֹז), 144 (145)[5] (הוֹד), II Mac 3[12 *];] *holiness,* the state in man resulting from ἁγιασμός, q.v.: Ro 1[4], II Co 7[1], I Th 3[13] (Cremer, 52; MM, *VGT*, s.v.).†

ἀγκάλη, -ης, ἡ (< ἄγκος, *a bend*), [in LXX for אֲצִיל, חֵיק ;] *the bent arm:* Lk 2[28] (cf. ἐναγκαλίζομαι).†

ἄγκιστρον, -ου, τό (< ἄγκος, *a bend*), [in LXX for חַכָּה, etc.;] *a fishhook:* Mt 17[27].†

** ἄγκυρα, -ας, ἡ (< ἄγκος, *a bend*), [in Sm.: Je 52¹⁸ *;] *an anchor:* Ac 27²⁹, ³⁰, ⁴⁰; fig. (MM, *VGT*, s.v.), He 6¹⁹.†

*† ἄγναφος, -ον (= ἄγναπτος, < γνάπτω, late form of κνάπτω, *to card wool*), *uncarded, undressed,* i.e. new (MM, *VGT*, s.v.): Mt 9²⁶, Mk 2²¹.†

ἁγνεία (WH, ἁγνία), [in LXX for טָהֳרָה, נָזִיר, גֵּזֶר, etc.;] *purity:* ı Ti 4¹² 5² (Cremer, 58. For exx. of ceremonial use in π., v. MM, *Exp.*, iv).†

ἁγνίζω (< ἁγνός), [in LXX always ceremonially, chiefly for קָדַשׁ;] *to purify, cleanse from defilement;* (a) ceremonially: Jo 11⁵⁵, Ac 21²⁴, ²⁶ 24¹⁸; (b) morally: Ja 4⁸, ı Pe 1²², ı Jo 3³.†
SYN.: καθαρίζω, q.v. (and v.s. ἁγνός).

† ἁγνισμός, -οῦ, ὁ (< ἁγνίζω), [in LXX: Nu 6⁵ (גֶּזֶר) 8⁷ 19¹⁷ (חַטָּאת), etc.;] *purification*: in ceremonial sense, Ac 21²⁶ (LXX).†

ἀγνοέω, -ῶ, [in LXX for שָׁגָה, שָׁגַג, אָשָׁם, etc.;] 1. *to be ignorant, not to know:* absol., ı Ti 1¹³, He 5²; c. acc., Ac 13²⁷ 17²³, Ro 10³, II Co 2¹¹; ἐν οἷς, II Pe 2¹²; seq. ὅτι, Ro 2⁴ 6³ 7¹, ı Co 14³⁸; οὐ θέλω ὑμᾶς ἀγνοεῖν, a Pauline phrase: c. acc., Ro 11²⁵; seq. ὑπέρ, II Co 1⁸; περί, ı Co 12¹, ı Th 4¹³; ὅτι, Ro 1¹³, ı Co 10¹ (for similar usage in π., v. MM, *VGT*, s.v.). Pass.: ı Co 14³⁸, II Co 6⁹, Ga 1²². 2. *not to understand:* c. acc., Mk 9³², Lk 9⁴⁵.†

† ἀγνόημα, -τος, τό (< ἀγνοέω), [in LXX: Ge 43¹² (מִשְׁגֶּה), To 3³, Jth 5²⁰, Si 23² 51¹⁹, ı Mac 13³⁹ *;] *a sin of ignorance* (so in π.; v. MM, *VGT*, s.v.): He 9⁷.†

ἄγνοια, -ας, ἡ (< ἀγνοέω), [in LXX chiefly for שְׁגָנָה, אָשָׁם;] *ignorance:* Ac 3¹⁷ 17³⁰, Eph 4¹⁸ (with sense of wilful blindness; cf. MM, *VGT*, s.v.), ı Pe 1¹⁴.†

ἁγνός, -ή, -όν (< ἅγος, v.s. ἅγιος), [in LXX chiefly for טָהוֹר (Pss. and Pr. only), also II Mac 13⁸, IV Mac 18⁷, al.;] 1. *free from ceremonial defilement,* in a condition prepared for worship (for exx. of pagan usage, v. MM, *VGT*, s.v.). 2. *holy, sacred, venerable* (II Mac, l.c.). 3. As in OT (cl.), *pure, chaste, undefiled, guiltless;* (a) of persons: II Co 7¹¹ 11¹², ı Ti 5²², Tit 2⁵, ı Jo 3³; (b) of things: Phl 4⁸, Ja 3¹⁷, ı Pe 3².†
SYN.: εἰλικρινής (q.v.), *pure,* primarily as winnowed, purged, first found in ethical sense in NT (*sincere*). On the equivalence of ἁ. and καθαρός (q.v.), v. *DCG*, ii, 459ª, though Westc. (*Epp. Jo.*, 101) notes a distinction between them.

*† ἁγνότης, -τητος, ἡ (< ἁγνός), *purity, chastity* (cf. ἁγιότης): II Co 6⁶ 11³.†

* ἁγνῶς (< ἁγνός), adv., *purely, with pure motives:* Phl 1¹⁷.†

ἀγνωσία, -ας, ἡ (< γινώσκω), [in LXX: Jb 35¹⁶ (בְּלִי־דַעַת), Wi 13¹, III Mac 5²⁷ *;] *ignorance* (opp. to γνῶσις): ı Co 15³⁴, ı Pe 2¹⁵ (v. Hort in l.; MM, *VGT*, s.v.).†

** ἄγνωστος, -ον (< γινώσκω), [in LXX: Wi 11¹⁸ 18³, II Mac 1¹⁹ 2⁷ (Cremer, 157) *;] *unknown:* Ac 17²³ (cf. MM, *VGT*, s.v.).†

ἀγορά, -ᾶς, ἡ (< ἀγείρω, to bring together), [in LXX for עִזְּבוֹן, שׁוּק;]
1. an assembly (Hom., Xen., al.). 2. a place of assembly, a public place
or forum, a market-place (Hom., Thuc., al.; LXX): Mt 11¹⁶ 20³ 23⁷,
Mk 6⁵⁶ (cf. MM, VGT, s.v., ἀγυιά) 7⁴ (Bl., § 46, 7) 12³⁸, Lk 7³² (Bl., l.c.)
11⁴³ 20⁴⁶, Ac 16¹⁹ 17¹⁷ (Cremer, 59; MM, VGT, s.v.).†

ἀγοράζω (< ἀγορά), [in LXX chiefly for שָׁבַר, קָנָה;] 1. to frequent
the ἀγορά (Hdt., al.). 2. to buy in the market, purchase (Xen., al.;
LXX; in π. very common in deeds of sale, v. MM, VGT, s.v.): absol.,
Mt 21¹², Mk 11¹⁵; c. acc. rei, Mt 13⁴⁴, ⁴⁶, al.; seq. παρά, c. gen. pers.,
Re 3¹⁸ (LXX, Polyb.); ἐκ, Mt 27⁷; c. gen. pret., Mk 6³⁷, al.; metaph.,
ι Co 6²⁰ 7²³, ιι Pe 2¹, Re 5⁹ 14³, ⁴.

* ἀγοραῖος, -ον (< ἀγορά), 1. frequenting the ἀγορά, a lounger in the
ἀγορά (Xen., al.); an agitator (Lake, Earlier Epp. of St. Paul, p. 69):
Ac 17⁵. 2. In the late writers (Strab., al.), proper to the ἀγορά: ἀγοραῖοι
(sc. ἡμέραι) ἄγονται (cf. Lat. conventus agere), court-days are kept, Ac 19³⁸
(for exx. of both usages, v. MM, VGT, s.v.).†

* ἄγρα, -ας, ἡ (< ἄγω), 1. the chase, a hunting or catching: Lk 5⁴.
2. that which is taken, a catch: of fish, Lk 5⁹.†

* ἀγράμματος, -ον (< γράφω), without learning (γράμματα), un-
lettered (in π. freq. in formula used by one who signs for an illiterate;
MM, VGT, s.v.): Ac 4¹³ (but cf. Thayer, s.v.).†

* ἀγραυλέω, -ῶ (< ἄγραυλος, dwelling in the field; < ἀγρός, αὐλή),
to live in the fields: Lk 2⁸.†

ἀγρεύω (ἄγρα), [in LXX: Jb 10¹⁶, Pr 5²² 6²⁵, ²⁶, Ho 5² (לקח ni.,
שׁוטם, etc.)*;] to catch or take by hunting or fishing; metaph.,
Mk 12¹³.†

* ἀγρι-έλαιος, -ον, 1. of the wild olive (Anth.). 2. As subst., the
wild olive: Ro 11¹⁷, ²⁴ (CGT, in l.; MM, VGT, s.v.).†

ἄγριος, -a, -ον (< ἀγρός), [in LXX for שָׂדֶה, etc.;] 1. living in
fields, wild: μέλι. Mt 3⁴, Mk 1⁶. 2. savage, fierce: Ju ¹³. (Cf. usage
in π. of a malignant wound; MM, VGT, s.v.)†

Ἀγρίππας, -a (Bl., § 7, 2), ὁ, Agrippa (II): Ac 25¹³, ²², ²³, ²⁴, ²⁶
26¹, ², ¹⁹, ²⁷, ²⁸, ³². (For Agrippa I, v.s. Ἡρώδης, 3.)†

ἀγρός, -οῦ, ὁ, [in LXX chiefly for שָׂדֶה]; 1. a field: Mt 6²⁸, al.
2. the country: Mk 15²¹, al.; pl., country places, farms: Mk 5¹⁴ 6³⁶, ⁵⁶,
Lk 8³⁴ 9¹². 3. = χωρίον, a piece of ground: Mk 10²⁹, Ac 4²⁷, al. (On
the occurrence of this word as compared with χώρα, χωρίο˙˙, v. MM,
VGT, s.v.)

ἀγρυπνέω, -ῶ (< ἄγρυπνος, seeking sleep; < ἀγρεύω, ὕπνος), [in
LXX chiefly for שָׁקַד;] to be sleepless, wakeful (Theogn., Xen., al.);
metaph. (LXX) = cl. ἐγρήγορα, to be watchful, vigilant: Mk 13³³,
Lk 21³⁶, Eph 6¹⁸, He 13¹⁷.†

SYN.: γρηγορέω, q.v.; νήφω, associated with γ. in ι Pe 5⁸, expressing a wariness which results from self-control, a condition of
moral, not merely mental alertness (v. M, Th., I, 5⁶).

** ἀγρυπνία, -ας, ἡ (v. supr.), [in LXX: Si ₉, ιι Mac 2²⁶ *;] sleepless-
ness, watching: ιι Co 6⁵ 11²⁷. (Plat., Hdt.; for exx. in π., v. MM,
VGT, s.v.)†

ἀγυιά, v.s. ἀγορά, [in LXX: III Mac 1²⁰ 4³ *].

ἄγω, [in LXX for בוֹא hi., לְקָח, נהַג, etc.;] 1. *to lead, bring, carry*: c. acc., seq. ἐπί, εἰς, ἕως, πρός and simple dat.; metaph., *to lead, guide, impel*: Jo 10¹⁶, Ro 2⁴, He 2¹⁰, II Ti 3⁶, al. 2. *to spend* or *keep* a day: Lk 24²¹, Ac 19³⁸ 3. Intrans., *to go*: subjunc., ἄγωμεν, Mt 26⁴⁶, al. (Cremer, 61; MM, *VGT*, s.v.).

ἀγωγή, -ῆς, ἡ (< ἄγω), [in LXX: Es 2²⁰ 10³, II Mac 4¹⁶ 6⁸ 11²⁴, III Mac 4¹⁰ *;] 1. *a carrying away.* 2. *a leading, guiding;* metaph., *training;* hence, from the expression ἀ. τοῦ βίου, absol., *conduct, way of life:* II Ti 3¹⁰ (Cremer, 61; MM, *VGT*, s.v.).†

ἀγών, -ῶνος, ὁ (< ἄγω), [in LXX: Is 7¹³ (לאה), Es 4¹⁷, Wi 4² 10¹², II Mac ₆, IV Mac ₅ *;] 1. *a gathering*, esp. for games. 2. *a place of assembly.* 3. *a contest, struggle, trial;* metaph. (MM, *VGT*, s.v.), (*a*) of the Christian life as a contest and struggle: Phl 1³⁰, I Th 2², I Ti 6¹², II Ti 4⁷, He 12¹; (*b*) *solicitude, anxiety:* Col 2¹.†

** ἀγωνία, -ας, ἡ (< ἀγών), [in LXX: II Mac 3¹⁴, ¹⁶ 15¹⁹ *;] 1. *a contest, wrestling* (Eur., Xen.). 2. Of the mind, *great fear, agony, anguish* (Dem., Arist.): Lk 22⁴⁴ (cf. Field, *Notes*, 77 f.; Abbott, *Essays*, 101 f.; MM, *VGT*, s.v.).†

ἀγωνίζομαι (< ἀγών), [in LXX: Da TH 6¹⁴ (בְּל שׂוּם), Si 4²⁸, I, II, IV Mac ₅ *;] 1. *to contend for a prize:* I Co 9²⁵. 2. *to fight, struggle, strive:* Jo 18³⁶; metaph. (MM, *VGT*, s.v.), Col 1²⁹ 4¹², I Ti 4¹⁰ 6¹², II Ti 4⁷; c. inf. (Field, *Notes*, 66), Lk 13²⁴ (Cremer, 609).†

Ἀδάμ, ὁ, indecl. (Heb. אָדָם), *Adam:* Lk 3³⁸, Ro 5¹⁴, I Co 15²², ⁴⁵, I Ti 2¹³, ¹⁴, Ju ¹⁴; Christ ὁ ἔσχατος Ἀ., I Co 15⁴⁵.†

* ἀδάπανος, -ον (< δαπάνη), *without expense, free of charge:* I Co 9¹⁸.†

Ἀδδεί (Rec. Ἀδδί), ὁ, indecl., *Addei:* Lk 3²⁸.†

ἀδελφή, -ῆς, ἡ (< ἀδελφός), [in LXX for אָחוֹת;] *a sister:* Mt 19²⁹, al.; metaph. (MM, *VGT*, s.v.), of a member of the Christian community: Ro 16¹, I Co 7¹⁵, Ja 2¹⁵, al.

ἀδελφός, -οῦ, ὁ (< ἀ- copul., δελφύς, *womb*), in cl., *a brother*, born of the same parent or parents. [In LXX (Hort, *Ja.*, 102 f.), for אָח;] 1. lit. of a brother (Ge 4², al.). 2. Of a neighbour (Le 19¹⁷). 3. Of a member of the same nation (Ex 2¹⁴, De 15³). In NT in each of these senses (1. Mt 1², al.; 2. Mt 7³; 3. Ro 9³) and also, 4. of a fellow-Christian: I Co 1¹, Ac 9³⁰. This usage finds illustration in π., where ἀ. is used of members of a pagan religious community (M, *Th.*, I, 1⁴; MM, *VGT*, s.v.). The ἀδελφοὶ τ. Κυρίου (Mt 12⁴⁶⁻⁴⁹ 13⁵⁵ 28¹⁰, Mk 3³¹⁻³⁴, Lk 8¹⁹⁻²¹, Jo 2¹² 7³, ⁵, ¹⁰ 20¹⁷, Ac 1¹⁴, I Co 9⁵) may have been sons of Joseph and Mary (Mayor, *Ja.*, Intr. vi ff.; *DB*, i, 320 ff.) or of Joseph by a former marriage (Lft., *Gal.*, 252 ff.; *DCG*, i, 232 ff.), but the view of Jerome, which makes ἀ. equivalent to ἀνεψιός, is inconsistent with Greek usage. (Cremer, 66.)

**† ἀδελφότης, -ητος, ἡ (< ἀδελφός), [in LXX: I Mac 12¹⁰, ¹⁷, IV Mac ₅ *;] 1. abstract, *brotherhood, brotherly affection* (LXX). 2. Concrete, *the brotherhood*, the Christian community: I Pe 2¹⁷ 5⁹ (MM, *VGT*, s.v.).†

ἄ-δηλος, -ον (< δῆλος), [in LXX : Ps 50 (51)⁶ (בַּטֻּחוֹת) ;] 1. *unseen, unobserved, not manifest* (Ps, l.c.): Lk 11⁴⁴. 2. *uncertain, indistinct :* I Co 14⁸.†

**† ἀδηλότης, -ητος, ἡ (< ἄδηλος), *uncertainty :* I Ti 6¹⁷.†

* ἀδήλως (< ἄδηλος), adv., *uncertainly :* of direction, I Co 9²⁶.†

** ἀδημονέω, -ῶ (on the derivation, v. MM, VGT, s.v.), [in Aq.: Jb 18²⁰; Sm.: Ps 60 (61)³ 115² (116¹¹), Ec 7¹⁷ ⁽¹⁶⁾, Ez 3¹⁵ *;] *to be troubled, distressed* (MM, l.c.) : Mt 26³⁷, Mk 14³³, Phl 2²⁶.†

ᾅδης, -ου, ὁ, [in LXX chiefly for שְׁאוֹל, also for דּוּמָה, מָוֶת, etc. ;] 1. in Hom., *Hades* (Pluto), the god of the underworld. 2. *the abode of Hades, the underworld ;* in NT, the abode of departed spirits, *Hades :* ἐν τ. ᾅ., Lk 16²³ ; εἰς ᾅ., Ac 2²⁷, ³¹ ; πύλαι ᾅδου, Mt 16¹⁸ ; κλεῖς τοῦ ᾅ., Re 1¹⁸ ; metaph., ἕως ᾅ., Mt 11²³, Lk 10¹⁵ ; personified, Re 6⁸ 20¹³, ¹⁴ (Cremer, 67, 610 ; MM, VGT, s.v.).†

ἀ-διά-κριτος, -ον (< διακρίνω), [in LXX : Pr 25¹ *;] 1. *not to be parted, mixed, undistinguishable* (cf. Pr, l.c., and v. Lft., *Ignat. Eph.,* § 3). 2. *without uncertainty* or *indecision* (Hort, in l., but v. MM, VGT, s.v.) : Ja 3¹⁷.†

**† ἀδιάλειπτος, -ον (< διαλείπω), *unremitting, incessant :* Ro 9², II Ti 1³. (For exx., v. MM, VGT, s.v.)†

**† ἀδιαλείπτως (v. supr.), adv., [in LXX : I Mac 12¹¹, II Mac ₄, III Mac 6³³ *;] *unremittingly, incessantly :* Ro 1⁹, I Th 1³ 2¹³ 5¹⁷.†

ἀδικέω, -ῶ (< ἄδικος), [in LXX for עָשַׁק, עָוָה, etc. ;] 1. intrans., *to be ἄδικος, do wrong, act wickedly* or *criminally :* Ac 25¹¹, I Co 6⁸, II Co 7¹², Col 3²⁵, Re 22¹¹ ; *to do hurt,* Re 9¹⁹. 2. Trans. (a) *to do* some *wrong :* ὃ ἠδίκησεν, Col 3²⁵ ; *to wrong* some one, Mt 20¹³, Ac 7²⁶, ²⁷ 25¹⁰, II Co 7², Ga 4¹², Phm 1⁸, II Pe 2¹³ ; pass., Ac 7²⁴, II Co 7⁷ ; mid., I Co 6⁷ (*suffer . . . to be wronged ;* WM, § 38, 3 ; but v. Bl., § 54, 5 ; and cf. ἀποστερέω); (b) *to injure, hurt :* Lk 10¹⁹, Re 2¹¹ 6⁶ 7², ³ 9⁴, ¹⁰ 11⁵.†

ἀδίκημα, -τος, τό (< ἀδικέω), [in LXX for עָוֹן, פֶּשַׁע, etc.;] *a wrong, injury, misdeed* (MM, VGT, s.v.) : Ac 18¹⁴ 24²⁰, Re 18⁵.†

ἀδικία, -ας, ἡ (< ἄδικος), [in LXX for עָוֹן, פֶּשַׁע, עָוֶל, etc.;] 1. *injustice :* Lk 18⁶, Ro 9¹⁴. 2. *unrighteousness, iniquity :* Jo 7¹⁸, Ac 8²³, Ro 1¹⁸, ²⁹ 2⁸ 6¹³, II Ti 2¹⁹, I Jo 1⁹ 5¹⁷; opp. to ἀλήθεια, I Co 13⁶, II Th 2¹² ; τὸ δικαιοσύνη, Ro 3⁵; ἀπάτη τῆς ἀ., II Th 2¹⁰ ; μισθὸς ἀδικίας, Ac 1¹⁸, II Pe 2¹³, ¹⁵ ; ἐργάται τῆς ἀ., Lk 13²⁷ ; μαμωνᾶς τῆς ἀ., Lk 16⁹ ; κόσμος τῆς ἀ., Ja 3⁶ ; οἰκονόμος τῆς ἀ., Lk 16⁸. 3. = ἀδίκημα, *an un-righteous act :* ironically, a favour, II Co 12¹³ ; pl., He 8¹² (Cremer, 201 ; MM, VGT, s.v.).†

ἄδικος, -ον (< δίκη), [in LXX for שֶׁקֶר, עָוֶל, etc. ;] 1. *unjust :* Ro 3⁵, He 6¹⁰. 2. *unrighteous, wicked :* Lk 16¹¹ 18¹¹, Ac 24¹⁵, I Co 6¹, ⁹, I Pe 3¹⁸ ; opp. to δίκαιος, Mt 5⁴⁵ ; to εὐσεβής, II Pe 2⁹ ; to πιστός, Lk 16¹⁰ (Cremer, 200).†

ἀδίκως, adv. (< ἄδικος), [in LXX for שֶׁקֶר, עָוֶל, etc. ;] *unjustly, undeservedly :* I Pe 2¹⁰.†

Ἀδμείν (WH, mg., Ἀδάμ), ὁ, indecl., *Admin. :* Lk 3³³.†

ἀ-δόκιμος, -ον, [in LXX : Pr 25⁴, Is 1²² (סִיג)* ;] 1. of things (prop of metals : LXX, ll. c.), *not standing the test, rejected :* γῆ, He 6⁸. 2. Of persons, *rejected after testing, reprobate :* Ro 1²⁸, I Co 9²⁷, II Co 13⁵⁻⁷, II Ti 3⁸, Tit 1¹⁶ (Cremer, 212).†

* ἄ-δολος, -ον, 1. *guileless* (Pind., Thuc.). 2. Of liquids (Æsch., Eur., and late prose writers), *genuine, pure* (in π. and in MGr. of wine, also of corn : MM, *VGT*, s.v.; Milligan, *NTD*, 77): of milk, metaph., I Pe 2².†

SYN. : ἀκέραιος (q.v.), ἄκακος, ἁπλοῦς.

Ἀδραμυντηνός (T, Rec. Ἀδραμυττηνός), -ή, -όν, *of Adramyttium*, a seaport of Mysia : Ac 27².†

Ἀδρίας (T, Rec. Ἀδρίας), -ου, ὁ, the *Adriatic* sea, in later Greek usage extended to take in all the waters between Greece and Italy : Ac 27²⁷.†

* ἁδρότης, -τος, ἡ (< ἁδρός, thick, well-grown), 1. *thickness, vigour.* 2. *abundance, bounty :* II Co 8²⁰.†

ἀδυνατέω, -ῶ (< ἀδύνατος), [in LXX : De 17⁸, Za 8⁶ (פלא ni.), Jb 42² (בצר ni.), al. ;] *to be unable* (cl., Philo ; π. and LXX, of persons, v. MM, *VGT*, s.v.). 2. In LXX and NT, of things (Kennedy, *Sources*, 124 ; Hatch, *Essays*, 4 ; Field, *Notes*, 46 f.), *to be impossible :* Mt 17²⁰, Lk 1³⁷.†

ἀ-δύνατος. -ον, [in LXX for אֶבְיוֹן, דַּל, etc. ;] 1. of persons, *unable, incapable,powerless :* Ac 14⁸ ; fig., Ro 15¹ (MM, *VGT*, s.v.). 2. Of things, *impossible :* Mt 19²⁶, Mk 10²⁷, Lk 18²⁷, Ro 8³ (v. *ICC*, in l.), He 6⁴, ¹⁸ 10⁴ 11⁶.†

ᾄδω (Attic form of Ion. and poët. ἀείδω), [in LXX chiefly for שִׁיר ;] *to sing*, (*a*) intrans., c. dat. (MM, *VGT*, s.v.), of praise to God : Eph 5¹⁹, Col 3¹⁶ ; (*b*) trans., c. cogn. acc. : ᾠδήν, Re 5⁹ 14³ 15³.†

ἀεί, adv., [in LXX : Is 42¹⁴ (מֵעוֹלָם) 51¹² (תָּמִיד), Ps 94 (95)¹⁰, al. ;] *ever ;* 1. of continuous time, *unceasingly, perpetually :* Ac 7⁵¹, 2 Co 4¹¹ 6¹⁰, Tit 1¹², He 3¹⁰. 2. Of successive occurrences, *on every occasion* (MM, *VGT*, s.v.) : I Pe 3¹⁵, II Pe 1¹².†

ἀετός, -οῦ, ὁ, [in LXX for נֶשֶׁר ;] *an eagle :* Re 4⁷ 8¹³ (Rec. ἀγγέλου) 12¹⁴. Where carrion is referred to, ἀ. is probably a *vulture* (cf. Jb 39³⁰, Pr 30¹⁷) : Mt 24²⁸, Lk 17³⁷ (MM, *VGT*, s.v.).†

ἄζυμος, -ον (< ζύμη), [in LXX for מַצָּה ; τὰ ἄ. (sc. λάγανα, *cakes*) = הַמַּצּוֹת ;] *unleavened :* ἡ ἑορτὴ τῶν ἄ. (הַג הַמַּצּוֹת), the *paschal feast* (also called τὰ ἄ., Mk 14¹), Lk 22¹ ; ἡμέρα τῶν ἄ., Mt 26¹⁷, Mk 14¹², Lk 22⁷ ; ἡμέραι, Ac 12³ 20⁶. Fig., of Christians, *free from corruption :* I Co 5⁷ ; exhorted to keep festival, ἐν ἀζύμοις (sc. ἄρτοις, λάγανοις, or, indefinitely, "unleavened elements"), ib. ⁸ (Cremer, 724),†

Ἀζώρ, ὁ, indecl., *Azor :* Mt 1¹³, ¹⁴.†

Ἄζωτος, -ου, ἡ (Heb. אַשְׁדּוֹד), *Azotus*, a Philistine city : Ac 8⁴⁰.†

ἀηδία, -ας, ἡ (< ἀ- neg., ἥδος, *pleasure*), [in LXX : Pr 23²⁹ (שִׂיחַ)* ;] 1. of things or persons, *unpleasantness, odiousness* (Hipp., Dem., al.); 2. *dislike* (Plat.). *disagreement* (MM, *VGT*, s.v.) : Lk 23¹² D.†

ἀήρ, ἀέρος, ὁ, [in LXX: II Ki 22¹² (= Ps 17 (18)¹¹, רֶּחַשׁ), Wi 8;] in Hom., Hes., the lower air which surrounds the earth, as opp. to the purer αἰθήρ of the higher regions; generally, *air* (MM, *VGT*, s.v.): Ac 22²³, I Th 4¹⁷, Re 9² 16¹⁷; of the air as the realm of demons, Eph 2²; ἀ. δέρειν, of striving to no purpose, I Co 9²⁶; εἰς ἀ. λαλεῖν, of speaking without effect, not being understood, I Co 14⁹.†

** ἀθανασία, -ας, ἡ (< ἀ-θάνατος, *undying*; v. MM, *VGT*, s.v.), [in LXX: Wi 3⁴ 4¹ 8¹³, ¹⁷ 15³, IV Mac 14⁵ 16¹³ *;] *immortality*: I Co 15⁵³, ⁵⁴, I Ti 6¹⁶ (cf. Cremer, 285 f.).†

** ἀ-θέμιτος (late form of ἀθέμιστος, LS, MM, *VGT*, s.v.), -ον (< θέμις, *custom, right*), [in LXX: II Mac 6⁵ 7¹ 10³⁴, III Mac 5²⁰ *;] (*a*) of persons, *lawless* (III Mac, l.c.); (*b*) of things, *lawless, unlawful*: Ac 10²⁸, I Pe 4³.†

SYN.: v.s. ἄθεσμος.

* ἄ-θεος, -ον, 1. in cl. (*a*) *slighting* or *denying the gods* (Plat.; cf. MM, *VGT*, s.v.); (*b*) *godless, ungodly* (Pind.); (*c*) *abandoned by the gods* (Soph.) 2. In the NT (cf. Lft. on *Ign. ad Trall.*, § 3), of the heathen, *without God, not knowing God* (Cremer, 281): Eph 2¹².†

**† ἄ-θεσμος, -ον (< θεσμός, *law, custom*), [in LXX: III Mac 5¹² 6²⁶ *;] *lawless*, esp. of those who violate the law of nature and conscience (cf. MM, *VGT*, s.v.): II Pe 2⁷ 3¹⁷.†

SYN.: ἀθέμιτος, ἄνομος, κακός, πονηρός, φαῦλος (v. Tr., *Syn.*, § lxxxiv; *DCG*, ii, 821ᵇ).

† ἀθετέω, -ῶ (< τίθημι), [in LXX for seventeen different words, פשׁע, מרד, בגד, מעל, etc., often meaning, as I Ki 13³ (Heb., al.), *to revolt*]; properly, *to make ἄθετον*, or *do away with what has been laid down* (v. *DCG*, i, 453 f.). 1. *to set aside, disregard* (in Gramm., *to reject as spurious*): διαθήκην, Ga 3¹⁵; ἐντολήν, Mk 7⁹; νόμον, He 10²⁸; πίστιν, I Ti 5¹². 2. *to nullify, make void*: Lk 7³⁰ (v. Field, *Notes*, 59), I Co 1¹⁹, Ga 2²¹. 3. *to reject* (or *break faith with*, Swete, Peake, *Comm.* in l., MM, *VGT*, s.v.): Mk 6²⁶ (Field, op. cit., 30), Lk 10¹⁶, Jo 12⁴⁸, I Th 4⁸, Ju ⁸ (for exx. in π., v. MM, *VGT*, s.v.).†

† ἀθέτησις, -εως, ἡ (< ἀθετέω), [in LXX, usually of unfaithful, rebellious action: I Ki 24¹² (פשׁע), Je 12¹ (בֶּגֶד), Da TH 9⁷ (מַעַל), II Mac 14²⁸ *;] *a disannulling, setting aside*: He 7¹⁸ 9²⁶. (For similar usage in π., v. Deiss., *BS*, 228 f.; MM, *VGT*, s.v.)†

Ἀθῆναι, -ῶν, αἱ (plural because consisting of several parts), *Athens*: Ac 17¹⁵, ¹⁶ 18¹, I Th 3¹.†

Ἀθηναῖος, -αία, -αῖον, *Athenian*: Ac 17²¹, ²².†

* ἀθλέω, -ῶ (in cl. also ἀθλεύω, < ἆθλος, *a contest*, in war or in sport), *to contend* in games, *wrestle, combat*: II Ti 2⁵.†

*† ἄθλησις, -εως, ἡ (< ἀθλέω), *a contest, combat*, esp. of athletes; fig., *a struggle*: He 10³² (for exx., v. MM, *VGT*, s.v.).†

ἀθροίζω (< ἀθρόος, *assembled in crowds*, MM, *VGT*, s.v.; < θρόος, *a noise, tumult*), [in LXX chiefly for קבץ;] *to gather, assemble*: Lk 24³³.†

ἀθυμέω, -ῶ (ἄ-θυμος, *without heart*), [in LXX for חרה, etc.;] *to be disheartened*: Col 3²¹.†

ἀθῷος (Rec. wrongly, -ῶος; LS, s.v.; Mayser, 131), -ον (< θωή, a penalty), [in LXX chiefly for נקה ni., pi., נָקִי;] 1. unpunished (MM, VGT, s.v.). 2. innocent: Mt 27⁴ (WH, R, mg., δίκαιον) 27²⁴.†

αἴγειος (WH, -γιος), -α, -ον (< αἴξ, a goat), [in LXX for עֵז;] of a goat: He 11³⁷ (MM, VGT, s.v.).†

αἰγιαλός, -οῦ, ὁ (on the derivation, v. Boisacq, s.v.), [in LXX: Jg 5¹⁷ (חוֹף), Si 24¹⁴*;] the sea-shore, beach (cf. Field, Notes, 146; DCG, i, 175 f.; MM, VGT, s.v.): Mt 13², ⁴⁸, Jo 21⁴, Ac 21⁵ 27³⁹, ⁴⁰.†

Αἰγύπτιος, -α, -ον, Egyptian: Ac 7²², ²⁴, ²⁸ 21³⁸, He 11²⁹,†

Αἴγυπτος, -ου, ἡ, Egypt: Mt 2¹³⁻¹⁵, ¹⁹, Ac 2¹⁰ 7⁹⁻³⁹, He 3¹⁶ 11²⁶, ²⁷; γῆ Αἴ., Ac 7⁴⁰ 13¹⁷, He 8⁹, Ju⁵ (cf. Ex 5¹², al.); ἡ Αἴ., Ac 7¹¹; fig., of Jerusalem as hostile to God, Re 11⁸.†

** ἀΐδιος, -ον (< ἀεί), [in LXX: Wi 7²⁶, iv Mac 10¹⁵*;] everlasting (freq. in Inscr.; MM, VGT, s.v.): Ro 1²⁰, Ju⁶.†

SYN.: αἰώνιος, also freq. in Inscr. (Deiss., BS, 363₄). The etymological distinction between the meanings of the two words seems not to be retained in late Greek (v. Thayer, s.v., αἰώνιος; cf. Cremer, 79, 611).

** αἰδώς (-όος), -οῦς, ἡ, [in LXX: iii Mac 1¹⁹ 4⁵*;] a sense of shame, modesty: i Ti 2⁹ (for exx., v. MM, VGT, s.v.).†

SYN.: αἰσχύνη (v. Thayer, 14; Tr., Syn., § xix; Cremer, 611 f.; CGT on i Ti, l.c.).

Αἰθίοψ, -οπος, ὁ (< αἴθω, to burn, ὤψ, face; i.e. swarthy), [in LXX for כּוּשִׁי;] Ethiopian: Ac 8²⁷.†

Αἰλαμίτης, v.s. Ἐλαμείτης.

αἷμα, -τος, τό, [in LXX for דָּם;] blood. 1. In the ordinary sense: Mk 5²⁵, Lk 8⁴³, ⁴⁴ 22⁴⁴, Jo 19³⁴, Ac 15²⁰, ²⁹ 21²⁵, Re 8⁷, ⁸ 11⁶ 16³, ⁴, ⁶ 19¹³. 2. In special senses: (a) of generation, origin, kinship (cl.): Jo 1¹³ (v. MM, VGT, s.v.); (b) as in OT (AR on Eph., l.c.), in the phrase σάρξ καὶ αἷ. (αἷ. κ. σ.), to indicate human nature as opp. to God and created spirits: Mt 16¹⁷, i Co 15⁵⁰, Ga 1¹⁶, Eph 6¹², He 2¹⁴; (c) of things in colour resembling blood: Ac 2¹⁹, ²⁰, Re 6¹² 14¹⁸⁻²⁰; (d) of bloodshed, a bloody death (cl.): Mt 23³⁰, ³⁵ 27⁴, ⁶, ⁸, ²⁴, ²⁵, Lk 11⁵⁰, ⁵¹ 13¹, Ac 1¹⁹ 5²⁸ 18⁶ 20²⁶ 22²⁰, He 12⁴, Re 6¹⁰ 17⁶ 18²⁴ 19²; αἷ. ἐκχέειν (Deiss., LAE, 428; MM, VGT, s.v., αἷ.), Ro 3¹⁵, Re 16⁶; (e) of sacrificial blood, as an expiation: He 9⁷, ¹², ¹³, ¹⁸⁻²², ²⁵ 10⁴ 11²⁸ 13¹¹; of the blood of Christ, Mt 26²⁸, Mk 14²⁴, Lk 22²⁰, Jo 6⁵³, ⁵⁴, ⁵⁶, Ac 20²⁸, Ro 3²⁵ 5⁹, i Co 10¹⁶ 11²⁵, ²⁷, Eph 1⁷ 2¹³, Col 1²⁰, He 9¹², ¹⁴ 10¹⁹, ²⁹ 12²⁴ 13²⁰, i Pe 1², ¹⁹, i Jo 1⁷ (cf. 5⁶, ⁸), Re 1⁵ 5⁹ 7¹⁴ 12¹¹. (Cremer, 69 f., 612 f.)†

*† αἱματεκχυσία, -ας, ἡ (< αἷμα, ἐκ, χέω), shedding of blood (Eccl.; Cremer, 71): He 9²².†

αἱμορροέω, (< αἷμα, ῥέω), [in LXX: Le 15³³ (זָבָה)*;] to lose blood, suffer from a flow of blood (Hipp.): Mt 9²⁰.†

Αἰνέας, -ου, ὁ, Æneas: Ac 9³³, ³⁴.†

† **αἴνεσις**, -εως, ἡ (< αἰνέω), [in LXX chiefly for תּוֹדָה, תְּהִלָּה;] praise (Eccl.) : θυσία αἰνέσεως (Le 7¹², זֶבַח תּוֹדָה), He 13¹⁵.†

αἰνέω, -ῶ (< αἶνος), poët., Ion. and late prose (MM, VGT, s.v.) for cl. ἐπαινέω, [in LXX chiefly for הלל, ידה;] to praise : c. acc., τ. θεόν, Lk 2¹³, ²⁰ 19³⁷ 24⁵³, Ac 2⁴⁷ 3⁸, ⁹, Ro 15¹¹ ; c. dat., τ. θεῷ (Je 20¹³, al. for הַלֵּל לְ; v. Field, Notes, 245), Re 19⁵.†

SYN. : ἐξομολογέω, εὐλογέω, εὐχαριστέω, μακαρίζω (v. DCG, i, 211).

αἴνιγμα, -τος, τό (< αἰνίσσομαι, to speak in riddles ; < αἰνός = δεινός, dread, strange), [in LXX for חִידָה, Nu 12⁸ and always exc. De 28³⁷ (שַׁמָּה);] a dark saying, riddle : 1 Co 13¹² (cf. Nu, l.c.).†

αἶνος, -ου, ὁ, [in LXX for הלל pi, עֹז;] poët. and Ion., 1. = μῦθος, a tale (Hom., al.). 2. = Att. ἔπαινος, praise (Hom., al.) : Mt 21¹⁶ ⁽ᴸˣˣ⁾, Lk 18⁴³. 3. In π., a decree (MM, VGT, s.v.).†

Αἰνών, ἡ, indecl. (cf. Heb. עַיִן, a spring), Aenon : Jo 3²³.†

αἵρεσις, -εως, ἡ (< αἱρέω, -ομαι), [in LXX for נְדָבָה,] 1. capture. 2. choosing, choice (v. MM, VGT, s.v.). 3. that which is chosen, hence, opinion; esp. a peculiar opinion, heresy : 1 Co 11¹⁹, Ga 5²⁰, II Pe 2¹, R, txt. 4. In late writers (MM, VGT), of a set of persons professing particular principles or opinions, a school, sect, party, faction : Ac 5¹⁷ 15⁵ 24⁵, ¹⁴ 26⁵ 28²², 1 Co, Ga, II Pe, l.c., R, mg. (Cremer, 614).†

αἱρετίζω, [in LXX chiefly for בחר (v. Cremer, 615);] = αἱρέομαι (Hipp., Inscr.), to choose : Mt 12¹⁸ (LXX, ἀντιλήμψομαι).†

**αἱρετικός, -ή, -όν (< αἱρέομαι), 1. capable of choosing (Plat.). 2. causing division, heretical, factious (Cremer, 614) : Tit 3¹⁰.†

αἱρέω, [in LXX for אמר hi., בחר, etc.;] to take ; Mid., -ομαι (M, Pr., 158 f.; MM, VGT, s.v.), to choose : Phl 1²², II Th 2¹³, He 11²⁵. (Cf. ἀν-, ἀφ-, δι-, ἐξ-, καθ-, περι-, προ-αιρέω.)†

αἴρω, [in LXX chiefly for נשׂא, also for לקח, etc.;] 1. to raise, take up, lift or draw up : Jo 8⁵⁹ 11⁴¹, Ac 27¹⁷, al. 2. to bear, carry : Mt 4⁶ 16²⁴, al. 3. to bear or take away, carry off, remove : Mt 21²¹, Jo 19³¹, 1 Co 5¹² 6¹⁵ (v. Lft., Notes, 216), al.; of the taking away sin by Christ, Jo 1²⁹, 1 Jo 3⁵. (Cf. ἀπ-, ἐξ-, ἐπ-, μετ-, συν-, ὑπερ-αίρω. For exx. from π., v. MM, VGT, s.v.)

αἰσθάνομαι, [in LXX for בין, חפז, ידע;] to perceive : c. acc. rei (Bl., § 36, 5; MM, VGT, s.v.), Lk 9⁴⁵ (Cremer, 619 f.).†

αἴσθησις, -εως, ἡ (< αἰσθάνομαι), [in LXX chiefly for דַּעַת;] perception (MM, VGT, s.v.) : Phl 1⁹.†

SYN.: ἐπίγνωσις, q.v. (cf. Cremer, 620).

αἰσθητήριον, -ου, τό (< αἰσθάνομαι), [in LXX : Je 4¹⁹ (קִיר), IV Mac 2²² *;] sense, organ of perception : He 5¹⁴ (MM, VGT, s.v.).†

**αἰσχροκερδής, -ές (< αἰσχρός, κέρδος), greedy of base gains : 1 Ti 3⁸, Tit 1⁷.†

*† αἰσχροκερδῶς, adv., *from eagerness for base gain:* 1 Pe 5² (here only).†

* αἰσχρολογία, -ας, ἡ (< αἰσχρός, λέγω), *abusive language, abuse* (Lft., *ICC*, in l.; MM, *VGT*, s.v.) : Col 3⁸.†

αἰσχρός, -ά, -όν (< αἶσχος, *shame, disgrace*), [in LXX : Ge 41³ ᵃˡ. (רָע, רֹעַ), Jth 12¹², al. ;] *base, shameful :* 1 Co 11⁶ 14³⁵, Eph 5¹², Tit 1¹¹ (MM, *VGT*, s.v.).†

* αἰσχρότης, -ητος, ἡ (< αἰσχρός), *baseness :* Eph 5⁴.†

αἰσχύνη, -ης, ἡ (< αἶσχος, *shame, disgrace*), [in LXX chiefly for בֹּשֶׁת ;] *shame* (MM, *VGT*, s.v.) : subjectively, Lk 14¹⁹, ii Co 4² ; objectively, Phl 3¹⁹, He 12² ; as something to be ashamed of, Re 3¹⁸ ; pl. (Bl., § 32, 6), *shameful deeds*, Ju ¹³.†

SYN. : αἰδώς, q.v.

αἰσχύνω (< αἶσχος, *shame*), [in LXX chiefly for בּוֹשׁ ;] 1. *to disfigure* (Hom.). 2. *to dishonour* (Pr 29¹⁵). 3. *to make ashamed* (Si 13⁷). Pass., *to be put to shame, be ashamed :* ii Co 10⁸ ; Phl 1²⁰, 1 Pe 4¹⁶, 1 Jo 2²⁸ ; c. inf. (M, *Pr.*, 205), Lk 16³ (cf. ἐπ- (-ομαι), κατ-αισχύνω).†

αἰτέω, -ῶ, [in LXX chiefly for שָׁאַל ;] *to ask, request :* absol., Mt 7⁷, Ja 1⁶ ; c. acc. pers., Mt 5⁴², Lk 6³⁰ ; c. acc. rei, seq. ἀπό, Mt 20²⁰, 1 Jo 5¹⁵ ; id. seq. παρά, Ac 3², Ja 1⁵ ; c. dupl. acc., Mt 7⁹, Mk 6²², Jo 16²³. Mid. (on the distinction bet. mid. and act., v. M, *Pr.*, 160 ; MM, *VGT*, s.v. ; *Exp.*, viii, iii (1912), pp. 522-7) : absol., Mk 15⁸, Jo 16²⁶, Ja 4³ ; c. acc. rei, Mt 14⁷, Mk 6²⁴, al. ; c. acc. pers., Mt 27²⁰, Lk 23²⁵ ; c. acc. rei, seq. παρά, Ac 9² ; c. acc. et inf., Lk 23²³ ; c. inf., Ac 7⁴⁶, Eph 3¹³ (cf. ἀπ-, ἐξ-, ἐπ-, παρ-, προσ-αιτέω).

SYN. : ἐρωτάω, q.v., πυνθάνομαι. On the proper distinction between these words, v. Tr., *Syn.*, § xl, Thayer, s.v. αἰ. In late Gk., however, αἰ. and ἐ. seem to have become practically synonymous (cf. Ac 3², ³ ; v. Field, *Notes*, 101 f. ; M, *Th.*, I, 4¹ ; M, *Pr.*. 66ₙ ; MM, *VGT*, s.v.).

αἴτημα, -τος, τό (< αἰτέω), [in LXX chiefly for שְׁאֵלָה ;] *that which has been asked for, a petition, request :* Lk 23²⁴, Phl 4⁶, 1 Jo 5¹⁵.†

SYN. : v.s. δέησις.

αἰτία, -ας, ἡ, [in LXX : Ge 4¹³ (עָוֹן), Pr 28¹⁷ (עָשַׁק), and freq. in Wi, ii, iii Mac ;] 1. *cause, reason, occasion, case :* Mt 19³, Lk 8⁴⁷, Ac 10²¹ 22²⁴ 28²⁰, ii Ti 1⁶, ¹², Tit 1¹³, He 2¹¹ ; εἰ οὕτως ἐστὶν ἡ αἰ. (cf. Lat. *si ita res se habet*, and v. MM. *VGT*, s.v.), Mt 19¹⁰. 2. In forensic sense, (a) *accusation :* Ac 25¹⁸, ²⁷ ; (b) *cause for punishment, crime :* Mt 27³⁷, Mk 15²⁶, Jo 18³⁸ 19⁴, ⁶, Ac 13²⁸ 23²⁸ 28¹⁸.†

SYN. : ἔλεγχος, a charge, whether moral or judicial, which has been proven. αἰ. is an accusation simply, false or true.

αἰτίαμα, -τος, τό, v.s. αἰτίωμα.

* αἴτιον, -ου, τό, v.s. αἴτιος.

αἴτιος, -α, -ον (< αἰτία), [in LXX : 1 Ki 22²² (סָבַב), Da LXX Bel 41, TH ib. 42, Su 53, ii Mac 4⁴⁷ 13⁴, iv Mac 1¹¹ * ;] 1. *causative of, responsible*

for ; as subst., ὁ αἴ., *the cause, author :* He 5⁹ ; τὸ αἴ., *the cause,* Ac 19⁴⁰.
2. *blameworthy, culpable ;* as subst., ὁ αἴ., *the culprit, the accused*
(Lat. *reus*) ; τὸ αἴ. (= αἰτιά, 3), *the crime,* Lk 23⁴, ¹⁴, ²².†
*†αἰτίωμα (Rec. αἰτίαμα, the usual form ; v. MM, *VGT*, s.v.), -τος,
τό (< αἰτιάομαι, αἰτία), *a charge, accusation :* Ac 25⁷.†
**αἰφνίδιος (in Lk, l.c., ἐφν- WH ; v. M, *Pr.*, 35), -ον (< αἴφνης =
ἄφνως, *suddenly*), [in LXX : Wi 17¹⁵, ɪɪ Mac 14¹⁷, ɪɪɪ Mac 3²⁴ * ;] *sudden,
unexpected :* Lk 21³⁴, ɪ Th 5³.†

†αἰχμαλωσία, -ας, ἡ (< αἰχμάλωτος), [in LXX chiefly for שְׁבִי,
גּוֹלָה ;] *captivity* (Diod., al.) : Re 13¹⁰ ; pl., abstr. for concr., = αἰχμά-
λωτοι, Eph 4⁸ (ᴸˣˣ).†

†αἰχμαλωτεύω (< αἰχμάλωτος), [in LXX chiefly for שׁבה ;] = αἰχμα-
λωτίζω, q.v., *to lead captive :* Eph 4⁸ (ᴸˣˣ).†

†αἰχμαλωτίζω (< αἰχμάλωτος), [in LXX chiefly for שׁבה ;] in late
writers = cl. αἰχμάλωτον ποιῶ (ἄγω), *to take* or *lead captive :* seq. εἰς,
Lk 21²⁴ (cf. To 1¹⁰) ; metaph., Ro 7²³, ɪɪ Co 10⁵, ɪɪ Ti 3⁶.†

αἰχμάλωτος, -ον (< αἰχμή, *a spear*, ἀλίσκομαι, *to be taken*), [in LXX
chiefly for שָׁבָה, גּוֹלָה ;] *captive :* Lk 4¹⁸ (ᴸˣˣ).†

αἰών, -ῶνος, ὁ, [in LXX chiefly for עוֹלָם, עַד ;] 1. in cl., like Lat.
aevum (LS, MM, *VGT*, s.v.), *a space of time,* as, a lifetime, generation,
period of history, an indefinitely long period ; in NT of an indefinitely
long period, *an age, eternity,* usually c. prep. (MM, *VGT*) ; (*a*) of the
past : ἀπ' αἰ. (cf. Heb. מֵעוֹלָם), Lk 1⁷⁰ ; (*b*) of the future : εἰς τ. αἰ. (cf.
לְעוֹלָם), *forever,* Mt 21¹⁹ ; id., c. neg., *never,* Jo 4¹⁴ ; more strongly, εἰς
τὸν αἰ. τοῦ αἰ., He 1⁸ (ᴸˣˣ) ; εἰς τοὺς αἰ., Mt 6¹³ ; εἰς τοὺς αἰ. τῶν αἰ. (cf.
Is 45¹⁷, עַד־עוֹלְמֵי עַד), Ro 16²⁷, LT ; cf. also Eph 3²¹, ɪɪ Pe 3¹⁸, Ju ²⁵,
Re 14¹¹. 2. οἱ αἰ., *the worlds, the universe,* "the sum of the periods of
time, including all that is manifested in them" : He 1² 11³ (cf. ɪ Ti 1¹⁷,
where τῶν αἰ. are prob. "the ages or world-periods which when
summed up make eternity"). 3. *the present age* (Heb. הָעוֹלָם הַזֶּה) :
ὁ αἰ., Mt 13²² ; ὁ αἰ. οὗτος, Mt 12³² ; ὁ νῦν αἰ., ɪ Ti 6¹⁷ ; ὁ ἐνεστὼς αἰ., Ga 1⁴ ;
similarly, of the time after Christ's second coming (הָעוֹלָם הַבָּא), ὁ αἰ.
ἐκεῖνος, Lk 20³⁵ ; ὁ αἰ. μέλλων, Mt 12³² ; ὁ αἰ. ὁ ἐρχόμενος, Mk 10³⁰.
SYN.: κόσμος, *the ordered universe, the scheme of material things ;*
οἰκουμένη, *the inhabited earth ;* in contrast with both of which αἰ. is the
world under aspects of time (cf. Westc. on He 1² ; Tr., *Syn.*, § lix ;
Thayer, s.v., αἰ. ; Cremer, 74, 620 ; MM, *VGT*).

αἰώνιος, -ον (as usual in Attic), also -α, -ον : ɪɪ Th 2¹⁶, He 9¹² ;
(< αἰών), [in LXX chiefly for עוֹלָם ;] *age-long, eternal,* (*a*) of that which
is without either beginning or end : Ro 16²⁶, He 9¹⁴ ; (*b*) of that
which is without beginning : Ro 16²⁵, ɪɪ Ti 1⁹, Tit 1² ; (*c*) of that which
is without end (MM, *VGT*, s.v.) : σκηναί, Lk 16⁹ ; οἰκία, ɪɪ Co 5¹ ;
διαθήκη, He 13²⁰ ; εὐαγγέλιον, Re 14⁶ ; παράκλησις, ɪɪ Th 2¹⁶ ; λύτρωσις,

He 9¹²; κληρονομία, ib.¹⁵; κόλασις, Mt 25⁴⁶; κρίμα, He 6²; κρίσις, Mk 3²⁹; ὄλεθρον, II Th 1⁹; πῦρ, Mt 18⁸; freq. c. ζωή, q.v.; v. *ICC* on Ga, pp. 426 ff. *SYN.* : ἀίδιος, q.v.

ἀκαθαρσία, -ας, ἡ (< ἀκάθαρτος), [in LXX chiefly for טֻמְאָה, טָמֵא;] *uncleanness, impurity,* (*a*) physical (MM, *VGT*, s.v.) : Mt 23²⁷; (*b*) moral : Ro 1²⁴ 6¹⁹, II Co 12²¹, Ga 5¹⁹, Eph 4¹⁹ 5³, Col 3⁵, I Th 2³ 4⁷.†

*†ἀκαθάρτης, -τος, ἡ, *uncleanness* : Re 17⁴, Rec. (for τ. ἀκάθαρτα).†

ἀκάθαρτος, -ον (< ἀ- neg., καθαίρω), [in LXX chiefly for טָמֵא;] *unclean, impure;* (*a*) physically (LS, MM, *VGT*, s.v.) ; (*b*) ceremonially : Ac 10¹⁴, ²⁸ 11⁸, I Co 7¹⁴, II Co 6¹⁷, Re 18²; (*c*) morally : Eph 5⁵, Re 17⁴; c. πνεῦμα, as always in Gosp., Mt 10¹ 12⁴³, Mk 1²³, ²⁶, ²⁷ 3¹¹, ³⁰ 5², ⁸, ¹³ 6⁷ 7²⁵ 9²⁵, Lk 4³³, ³⁶ 6¹⁸ 8²⁹ 9⁴² 11²⁴, Ac 5¹⁶ 8⁷, Re 16¹³ (cf. Cremer, 320).†

*†ἀκαιρέομαι, -οῦμαι (< ἄκαιρος, *unseasonable*), *to have no opportunity* (opp. to εὐκαιρέω) : Phl 4¹⁰.†

** ἀκαίρως, adv. (< ἄκαιρος, *unseasonable*), [in LXX : Si 35 (32)⁴ *;] *out of season, unseasonably :* opp. to εὐκαίρως (q.v.), II Ti 4² (cf. Cremer, 740; MM, *VGT*, s.v.).†

ἄ-κακος, -ον, [in LXX for פֶּתִי, תָּם, etc. ;] (*a*) as in cl. (Æsch., Plat., al.), of persons, *simple, guileless :* Ro 16¹⁸, He 7²⁶ (cf. Cremer, 327) ; (*b*) of things, *undamaged* (? MM, *VGT*, s.v.).†

ἄκανθα, -ης, ἡ (< ἀκή, a point), [in LXX chiefly for קוֹץ, also for סִיר, שַׁיִת, etc.;] *a prickly plant, thorn, brier;* in NT always pl. : Mt 7¹⁶ 13⁷, ²² 27²⁹, Mk 4⁷, ¹⁸, Lk 6⁴⁴ 8⁷, ¹⁴, Jo 19², He 6⁸ (v. MM, *VGT*, s.v.).†

ἀκάνθινος, -ον (< ἄκανθα), [in LXX : Is 34¹³ (סִיר) *;] 1. *of thorns :* Mk 15¹⁷, Jo 19⁵. 2. *of acantha-wood* (Hdt.; π. ap. MM, *VGT*, s.v.).†

ἄ-καρπος, -ον, [in LXX : Je 2⁶ (צְלָמָוֶת), Wi 15⁴, IV Mac 16⁷ *;] *unfruitful, barren :* fig., Mt 13²², Mk 4¹⁹, I Co 14¹⁴, Eph 5¹¹, Tit 3¹⁴, II Pe 1⁸, Ju 12.†

**†ἀ-κατά-γνωστος, -ον (< καταγίνωσκω), [in LXX : II Mac 4⁴⁷ *;] *not open to just rebuke, irreprehensible :* Tit 2⁸ (v. Cremer, 676; and for other exx., MM, *VGT*, s.v.).†

†ἀ-κατα-κάλυπτος, -ον (< κατακαλύπτω), [in LXX : Le 13⁴⁵ A (פָּרוּעַ) *;] *uncovered, unveiled :* I Co 11⁵, ¹³.†

*†ἀ-κατά-κριτος, -ον (< κατακρίνω), 1. *uncondemned* (EV) : Ac 16³⁷ 22²⁵. 2. = cl. ἄκριτος, *without trial, not yet tried* (MM, *VGT*, s.v.) Ac, ll. cc.†

**†ἀ-κατά-λυτος, -ον (< καταλύω), [in LXX : IV Mac 10¹¹ *;] *indissoluble :* He 7¹⁶.†

*†ἀκατάπαστος (v. Mayor, II Pe, cxcvii; WH, *App.*, 170; MM. *VGT*, s.v.), -ον, a form otherwise unknown, prob. colloq. for -παυστος (q.v.) : II Pe 2¹⁴, L., Tr. mg., WH.†

*†ἀκατάπαυστος, -ον (< καταπαύω), *that cannot cease, not to be restrained :* c. gen. rei, II Pe 2¹⁴, T, Tr. txt.†

† **ἀκαταστασία**, -ας, ἡ (< ἀκατάστατος), [in LXX: Pr 26²⁸ (מִדְהֵה)], To 4¹³ * ;] *instability* (MM, *VGT*, s.v.) ; hence, *confusion, tumult, disorder :* i Co 14³³, Ja 3¹⁶ ; pl. (Bl., § 32, 6), Lk 21⁹, ii Co 6⁵ 12²⁰ (Polyb., al. ; v. Cremer, 739).†

ἀ-κατά-στατος, -ον (< καθίστημι), [in LXX: Is 54¹¹ (סֹעֲרָה) ;] *unsettled, unstable, disorderly :* Ja 1⁸ 3⁸.†

† **ἀκατάσχετος**, -ον (< κατέχω), [in LXX: Jb 31¹¹, iii Mac 6¹⁷ * ;] *that cannot be restrained :* Ja 3⁸ Rec. (for -στατος, q.v.).†

Ἀκελδαμά, -δαμάχ, v.s. Ἀχελδαμάχ.

** **ἀκέραιος**, -ον (< κεράννυμι), [in LXX: Es 8¹³ * ;] *unmixed, pure,* hence, metaph. (cf. MM, *VGT*, s.v.), *guileless, simple :* Mt 10¹⁶, Ro 16¹⁹, Phl, 2¹⁵.†

SYN.: ἄδολος, ἄκακος, ἁπλοῦς (cf. Ellic. on Phl., l.c. ; Tr., *Syn.*, § lvi).

** **ἀκλινής**, -ές (< κλίνω), [in LXX: iv Mac 6⁷ 17³ * ;] *unbending, firm :* metaph. (MM, *VGT*, s.v.), He 10²³.†

** **ἀκμάζω** (< ἀκμή), [in LXX: iv Mac 2³ * ;] *to be at the prime ;* of produce of the ground, *to be ripe* (Thuc.) : Re 14¹⁸ (MM, *VGT*, s.v.).†

* **ἀκμήν**, acc. of ἀκμή, *a point,* used as adv., *at the present point of time, even now, even yet :* Mt 15¹⁶ ; v. MM, *VGT*, s.v.†

ἀκοή, -ῆς, ἡ (< ἀκούω), [in LXX: Ex 15²⁶, al. for שֵׁמַע, its parts and derivatives, exc. De 11²² (שֵׁמֶר) ;] 1. *hearing, the sense of hearing :* i Co 12¹⁷, ii Pe 2⁸ ; "Hebraic dative," ἀκοῇ ἀκούειν (freq. in LXX ; v. M, *Pr.*, 14, 75), Mt 13¹⁴, Ac 28²⁶. 2. *organ of hearing, the ear* (Arist., al. ; MM, *VGT*, s.v.) : ii Ti 4³,⁴ ; pl., Mk 7³⁵, Lk 7¹, Ac 17²⁰, He 5¹¹. 3. *a thing heard,* i.e., (a) *a message, teaching :* Jo 12³⁸ and Ro 10¹⁶,¹⁷ (LXX), Ga 3²,⁵ R, mg. ; λόγος ἀκοῆς, i Th 2¹³, He 4² ; (b) *a report, rumour :* c. gen. pers., Mt 4²⁴ 14¹ 24⁶, Mk 1²⁸ 13⁷ (Cremer, 82, 623 ; MM, *VGT*, s.v.).†

ἀκολουθέω, -ῶ (< ἀκόλουθος, *following ;* < ἀ- cop., κέλευθος, poët., *away*), [in LXX chiefly for הלךְ ;] *to accompany, follow :* Mt 4²⁵, al. Metaph., *of discipleship :* Mt 9⁹, Mk 9³⁸, Jo 12²⁶, al. Absol. : Mt 8¹⁰ ; more freq., c. dat. (cl.), Mt 8¹, al. ; seq. μετά, c. gen. (cl. ; Rutherford, *N.Phr.*, 458 f.), Lk 9⁴⁹ ; ὀπίσω, c. gen. (Heb. הלךְ אַחֲרֵי), Mt 10³⁸ (cf. ἐξ-, ἐπ-, κατ-, παρ-, συν-ἀκολουθέω).

SYN.: (cl.) ἕπομαι, not in NT (v. Cremer, 80 ; MM, *VGT*, s.v.).

ἀκούω, [in LXX chiefly for שֵׁמַע ;] *to hear, listen, attend, perceive by hearing, comprehend by hearing.* 1. Intrans.: Mk 4³ 7³⁷, Ja 2⁵, Re 2⁷, al. ; τ. ὠσίν, Mt 13¹⁵ (LXX) ; c. cogn. dat., ἀκοῇ ἀ. (v.s. ἀκοή), Mt 13¹⁴, Ac 28²⁶ (LXX) ; ὁ ἔχων ὦτα (οὓς) ἀκούειν, ἀκουσάτω, Mt 11¹⁵, Mk 4²³, Re 2⁷, al. 2. Trans., prop. c. acc. rei, of thing heard, gen. pers., from whom heard (LS, s.v.) : Ac 1⁴ ; c. acc. rei, Mt 12¹⁹, Jo 3⁸ (Abbott, *JG*, 76), Ac 22⁹, al. ; c. dupl. acc., Jo 12¹⁸, i Co 11¹⁸ ; c. gen. rei, Jo 7⁴⁰ (Abbott, *JV*, 116) ; τ. φωνῆς (cf. Heb. שָׁמַע בְּקוֹל, Ex 18¹⁹), Jo 5²⁵,²⁸, Ac 9⁷ (on the distinction bet. this and ἀ. φωνήν, ib.⁴, v. M, *Pr.*, 66 ; Field, *Notes*, 117 ; Abbott, *Essays*, 93 f.) ; of God answering

2

prayer, Jo 9³¹, 1 Jo 5¹⁴, ¹⁵; c. acc. rei, seq. παρά, Jo 8²⁶, ⁴⁰, Ac 10²²,
II Ti 2²; id. seq. ἀπό, 1 Jo 1⁵; c. gen. pers. seq. ptcp., Mk 14⁵⁸,
Lk 18³⁶, al. (On NT usage generally, v. Bl., § 36, 5; Cremer, 82.)
** ἀκρασία, -ας, ἡ (< ἀκρατής, q.v.), [in LXX : 1 Mac 6²⁶ *;] in Arist.
and later writers = ἀκράτεια (Lft., *Notes*, 222 f.), *want of power*, hence
want of self-control, incontinence : Mt 23²⁵, 1 Co 7⁵.†

ἀκρατής, -ές (< κράτος), [in LXX : Pr 27²⁰ *;] (a) *powerless, impotent ;* (b) in moral sense, *lacking self-control, incontinent :* II Ti 3³.†

ἄκρατος, -ον (< κεράννυμι), [in LXX : Ps 74 (75)⁸ (חמר), Je 32¹
(25¹⁵) (המה), III Mac 5² *] ; *unmixed, pure :* οἶνος, Re 14¹⁰.†

ἀκρίβεια, -ας, ἡ (< ἀκριβής), [in LXX : Da LXX TH 7¹⁶ (יציב),
Wi 12²¹, Si 16²⁵ 42⁴ *;] *exactness, precision* (for exx., v. MM, *VGT*, s.v.) :
Ac 22³.†

ἀκριβής, -ές, [in LXX : Da LXX 2⁴⁵ 6¹² (יציב) 4²⁵, Es 4⁵, Si 18²⁹
19²⁵ 34 (31)²⁴ 35 (32)³ *;] *exact, precise, careful,* of things and persons :
superl., Ac 26⁵.†

** ἀκριβόω, -ῶ (< ἀκριβής), [in Aq. : Is 30⁸ 49¹⁶ *;] *to enquire with
exactness, learn carefully :* Mt 2⁷, ¹⁶ (for similar ex., v. MM, *VGT*,
s.v.).†

ἀκριβῶς, adv. (< ἀκριβής), [in LXX : De 19¹⁸ (יטב), Da TH 7¹⁹
(יצב), Ez 39¹⁴, Wi 19¹⁸, Si 18²⁹ *;] *with exactness, carefully :* Mt 2⁸,
Lk 1³, Ac 18²⁵, Eph 5¹⁵, 1 Th 5² (M, *Th.,* in l.).   Compar., ἀκριβέστερον
(Milligan, *NTD,* 111; MM, *VGT,* s.v.), Ac 18²⁶ 23¹⁵, ²⁰ 24²².†

ἀκρίς, -ίδος, ἡ, [in LXX chiefly for אַרְבֶּה, also for חָגָב, etc.;]
a locust : Mt 3⁴, Mk 1⁶, Re 9³, ⁷.†

*† ἀκροατήριον, -ου, τό (< ἀκροάομαι, *to listen*), *a place of audience :*
Ac 25²³ (Plut.).†

ἀκροατής, οῦ, ὁ (v. supr.), [in LXX : Is 3³ (לָחַשׁ), Si 3²⁹ *;] *a hearer :*
Ro 2¹³, Ja 1²², ²³, ²⁵.†

† ἀκροβυστία, -ας, ἡ (perh. an Alexandrian form of cl. ἀκροποσθία;
cf. MM, *VGT,* s.v.), [in LXX for עָרְלָה;] *the prepuce, foreskin* (LXX),
hence abstr., *uncircumcision :* Ac 11³, Ro 2²⁵⁻²⁷ 3³⁰ 4¹⁰⁻¹², 1 Co 7¹⁸, ¹⁹,
Ga 5⁶ 6¹⁵, Col 2¹³ 3¹¹.   By meton., *the uncircumcised :* Ro 4⁹, Ga 2⁷,
Eph 2¹¹.†

† ἀκρο-γωνιαῖος, -αία, -αῖον (< ἄκρος, γωνία, *an angle*), [in LXX :
Is 28¹⁶ (פִּנָּה)*;] = Attic γωνιαῖος (freq. in Inscr.; MM, *VGT,* s.v. ἀ.), *at
the extreme angle :* ὁ ἀ., *the corner foundation stone,* Eph 2²⁰, 1 Pe 2⁶.†

* ἀκροθίνιον, -ου, τό (< ἄκρος, θίς, *a heap*), prop., *the top of a heap,*
hence, in pl., 1. *first-fruits* (Xen.; MM, *VGT,* s.v.).   2. In war, *the
choicest spoils* (cf. Hdt., viii, 121 f.) : He 7⁴.†

ἄκρον, -ου, τό, v.s. ἄκρος.

ἄκρος, -α, -ον, [in LXX for קָצֶה, בֹּהֶן, etc.;] *highest, extreme ;* as
subst., τὸ ἄ., *the top, extremity :* Mk 13²⁷, Lk 16²⁴, He 11²¹; pl. (cf.
MM, *VGT,* s.v.), Mt 24³¹.†

'Ακύλας, -ου (and -α; MM, *VGT*, s.v.), ὁ (Lat.), *Aquila*: Ac 18², ¹⁸, ²⁶, Ro 16³, ι Co 16¹⁹, ιι Ti 4¹⁹.†

**†ἀκυρόω, -ῶ (< κῦρος, *authority*), [in LXX : ι Es 6³², ιν Mac₆*;] *to revoke, invalidate* (MM, *VGT*, s.v.) : Mt 15⁶, Mk 7¹³, Ga 3¹⁷ (Plut.).†

** ἀκωλύτως, adv. (< κωλύω), [in Sm. : Jb 34³¹*;] *without hindrance* (so freq. in legal documents; MM, *VGT*, s.v.) : Ac 28³¹.†

ἄκων (Attic contr. for ἀέκων), -ουσα, -ον (< ἀ- neg., ἔκων, *willing*), [in LXX : Jb 14¹⁷, ιν Mac 11¹²*;] *unwilling* : ι Co 9¹⁷.†

ἀλάβαστρον, -ου, τό (also -ος, ὁ, ἡ; colloq. and κοινή for ἀλάβαστος), [in LXX : ιν Ki 21¹³ (צְלֹחַת)*;] *a box of alabaster* (ἀλαβαστίτης) for ointment : Mt 26⁷, Mk 14³, Lk 7³⁷ (v. *DCG*, i, 41ᵇ; MM, *VGT*, s.v.).†

** ἀλαζονία (Rec. -εία, the earlier form), -ας, ἡ (< ἀλαζών), [in LXX : Wi 5⁸ 17⁷, ιι, ιν Mac₅*;] *the character of an* ἀλαζών, *boastfulness, vainglory, vaunting* : Ja 4¹⁶ (Mayor, in l.), ι Jo 2¹⁶.†

ἀλαζών, -όνος, ὁ, ἡ (< ἄλη, *wandering*), [in LXX : Jb 28⁸ (שַׁחַץ), Hb 2⁵ (יָהִיר), Pr 21²⁴ (יָלִיץ)*;] prop. *a vagabond*, hence, *an impostor, a boaster* : Ro 1³⁰, ιι Ti 3².†

SYN. : ὑβριστής, ὑπερήφανος (v. Tr., *Syn.*, § xxix; Lft., *Notes*, 256).

ἀλαλάζω (onomat. from the battle-cry ἀλαλά), [in LXX chiefly for רוע hi., ילל;] prop. *to raise a war-cry, shout with triumph or joy* ; rarely of grief, *to wail* : Mk 5³⁸ (cf. Je 4⁸) ; of a cymbal, ἀλαλάζον (RV. *clanging*), ι Co 13¹ (cf. ὀλολύζω).†

*†ἀ-λάλητος, -ον (< λαλέω), *inexpressible, not to be uttered* : Ro 8²⁶.†

ἄ-λαλος, -ον (< λάλος, *talkative*), [in LXX : Ps 30 (31)¹⁸ (אִלֵּם ni.) 37 (38)¹³ (אָלֵם) *;] *dumb, speechless* : Mk 7³⁷ 9¹⁷,²⁵.†

ἅλας (T, ἅλα), -ατος, τό, late form of cl. ἅλς, -ός, ὁ (MM, *VGT*, s.v.), [in LXX chiefly for מֶלַח;] *salt*, lit. and fig.: Mt 5¹³, Mk 9⁵⁰, Lk 14³⁴; like cl. ἅλες, *wit*, of wisdom and grace in speech : Col 4⁶.†

ἁλεεύς, v.s. ἁλιεύς.

ἀλείφω (cf. λίπος, *oil*), [in LXX : Ge 31¹³, Ex 40¹⁵, Nu 3³ (מָשַׁח), Ez 13¹⁰ ᶠᶠ (טוח), Ru 3³, ιι Ki 12²⁰ 14², ιν Ki 4², ιι Ch 28¹⁵, Mi 6¹⁵, Da LXX τη 10³ (סוּךְ), Es 2¹², Jth 16⁸*;] *to anoint*, festally or in homage : c. acc. rei or pers., Mt 6¹⁷, Jo 12³, Mk 16¹; seq. dat., ἐλαίῳ, Mk 6¹³, Ja 5¹⁴; μύρῳ, Lk 7³⁸,⁴⁶, Jo 11².†

SYN. : χρίω, μυρίζω (against the distinction made bet. ἀ. and χ. in Tr., *Syn.*, § xxxviii, v. MM, *VGT*, s.v., ἀ.).

*†ἀλεκτοροφωνία, -ας, ἡ (< ἀλέκτωρ, φωνή), *cock-crowing*, i.e. the third watch in the night : Mk 13³⁵.†

ἀλέκτωρ, -ορος, ὁ (poët. form of ἀλεκτρυών; v. MM, *VGT*, s.v.), [in LXX : Pr 24⁶⁶ (30³¹) (זַרְזִיר); BDB, *Lex.*, 267)*;] *a cock* : Mt 26³⁴,⁷⁴,⁷⁵, Mk 14³⁰,⁶⁸,⁷², Lk 22³⁴,⁶⁰,⁶¹, Jo 13³⁸ 18²⁷.†

'Αλεξανδρεύς, -έως, ὁ, *an Alexandrian* : Ac 6⁹ 18²⁴.†

'Αλεξανδρινός (Rec. -δρῖνος; v. Kühner³, II, 296), -ή, -όν, *Alexandrian* : Ac 27⁶ 28¹¹.†

Ἀλέξανδρος, -ου, ὁ, *Alexander*. 1. Son of Simon of Cyrene: Mk 15²¹. 2. A kinsman of the High Priest: Ac 4⁶. 3. A certain Jew: Ac 19³³. 4. A coppersmith: 1 Ti 1²⁰. 5. Perh. = 4 (v. Ellic. on ɪ Ti, l.c.): ɪɪ Ti 4¹⁴.†

ἄλευρον, -ου, τό (< ἀλεύω, *to grind*), [in LXX for קֶמַח, Nu 5¹⁵, al. ;] *meal* : Mt 13³³, Lk 13²¹.†

ἀλήθεια, -ας, ἡ (< ἀληθής), [in LXX chiefly for אֶמֶת (on which, v. Cremer, 627 f.), אֱמוּנָה ;] *truth* (v. *DB*, iv, 818 f.). 1. Objectively, "the reality lying at the basis of an appearance; the manifested, veritable essence of a matter" (Cremer, 86): Ro 9¹, al. ; of religious truth, Ro 1²⁵, al. ; esp. of Christian doctrine, Ga 2⁵, al. ; ἀ. θεοῦ, Ro 15⁸. 2. Subjectively, *truthfulness, truth*, not merely verbal (cl.), but sincerity and integrity of character : Jo 8⁴⁴, ɪɪɪ Jo³. 3. In phrases (MM, *VGT*, s.v.) : ἐπ' ἀληθείας, Mk 12¹⁴, al. ; ἀ. λέγειν (εἰπεῖν, λαλεῖν), Ro 9¹, ɪɪ Co 12⁶, Eph 4²⁵, al. ; ἀ. ποιεῖν, Jo 3²¹, ɪ Jo 1⁶ (cf. *DB*, iv, 818 b, ff.).

ἀληθεύω (< ἀληθής), [in LXX : Ge 20¹⁶ (יכח) 42¹⁶ (אָמַת), Pr 21³ (מִשְׁפָּט), Is 44²⁶ (שׁלם), Si 31 (34)⁴ * ;] *to speak the truth* (R, mg., *deal truly ;* Field, *Notes*, 192) : Ga 4¹⁶, Eph 4¹⁵.†

ἀληθής, -ές (< λήθω = λανθάνω, hence primarily, *unconcealed, manifest ;* hence, *actual, real*), [in LXX for אֶמֶת, etc. ;] (*a*) of things, *true*, conforming to reality : Jo 4¹⁸ 5³¹, ³² 6⁵⁵ (= ἀληθινός, q.v.) 8¹³, ¹⁴, ¹⁷ 10⁴¹ 19³⁵ 21²⁴, Ac 12⁹, Phl 4⁸, Tit 1¹³, ɪ Pe 5¹², ɪɪ Pe 2²², ɪ Jo 2⁸, ɪɪɪ Jo 12 ; (*b*) of persons, *truthful* : Mt 22¹⁶, Mk 12¹⁴, Jo 3³³ 7¹⁸ 8²⁶, Ro 3⁴, ɪɪ Co 6⁸.†

SYN. : ἀληθινός, *real, genuine, ideal*, as opp. to spurious or imperfect. ἀληθής, *true to fact*, as opp. to false, lying, denotes the actuality of a thing: ἀληθινός, its relation to the corresponding conception. (Cf. Tr., *Syn.*, § viii ; Cremer, 84 f., 631 ; Abbott, *JV*, 234 f. ; *DB*, iv, 818 f. ; MM, *VGT*, s.vv.)

ἀληθινός, -ή, -όν (< ἀληθής), [in LXX for אֶמֶת ;] *true*, in the sense of real, ideal, genuine : Lk 16¹¹, Jo 1⁹ 4²³, ³⁷ 6³² 7²⁸ 8¹⁶ 15¹ 17³ 19³⁵, ɪ Th 1⁹, He 8² 9²⁴ 10²², ɪ Jo 2⁸ 5²⁰, Re 3⁷, ¹⁴ 6¹⁰ 15³ 16⁷ 19² ; = ἀληθής, Re 19⁹ 21⁵ 22⁶ (MM, *VGT*, s.v.).†

SYN. : ἀληθής, q.v.

† ἀλήθω (κοινή form of the Attic ἀλέω), [in LXX for טחן ;] *to grind* : Mt 24⁴¹, Lk 17³⁵.†

ἀληθῶς, adv. (< ἀληθής), [in LXX (Je 35 (28)⁶, Ps 57 (58)¹, al.) chiefly for אֱמֶת and cogn. forms;] *truly, surely* : Mt 14³³ 26⁷³ 27⁵⁴, Mk 14⁷⁰ 15³⁹, Lk 9²⁷ 12⁴⁴ 21³, Jo 1⁴⁸ 4⁴² 6¹⁴ 7²⁶, ⁴⁰ 8³¹ 17⁸, Ac 12¹¹, ɪ Th 2¹³, ɪ Jo 2⁵.†

ἁλιεύς (pl. -ιεῖς. Rec. In later usage dissimulated pl. -εεῖς is found, v. M, *Pr.*, 45 ; M, *Gr.*, pp. 76, 90, 142), -έως, ὁ (< ἅλς, *the sea*), [in LXX for דַּיָּג, דַּיָּג ;] *a fisherman*. Pl. -εεῖς (v. supr.): Mt 4¹⁸, ¹⁹, Mk 1¹⁶, ¹⁷, Lk 5².†

† ἁλιεύω (< ἁλιεύς), [in LXX : Je 16¹⁶ (דיג) * ;] *to fish* : Jo 21³ (MM, *VGT*, s.v.).†

ἁλίζω (< ἅλς), [in LXX for מלח;] *to salt, season with salt*: Mt 5¹³, Mk 9⁴⁹.†

*†ἁλίσγημα, -τος, τό, (< late ἁλισγέω, *to pollute*), *pollution*: Ac 15²⁰.†

ἀλλά (ἀλλ' usually bef. α and υ, often bef. ε and η, rarely bef. ο and ω, never bef. ι; Tdf., *Pr.*, 93 f.; WH, *App.*, 146), adversative particle, stronger than δέ; prop. neuter pl. of ἄλλος, used adverbially, with changed accent; hence prop. *otherwise, on the other hand* (cf. Ro 3³¹); 1. opposing a previous negation, *but*: οὐ (μή) . . . ἀ., Mt 5¹⁵, ¹⁷, Mk 5³⁹, Jo 7¹⁶, al.; rhetorically subordinating but not entirely negativing what precedes, οὐ . . . ἀ., *not so much . . . as*, Mk 9³⁷, Mt 10²⁰, Jo 12⁴⁴, al.; with ellipse of the negation, Mt 11⁷⁻⁹, Ac 19², ι Co 3⁶ 6¹¹ 7⁷, ιι Co 7¹¹, Ga 2³, al.; in opposition to a foregoing pos. sentence, ἀ. οὐ, Mt 24⁶, ι Co 10²³; οὐ μόνον . . . ἀ. καί, Jo 5¹⁸, Ro 1³², al.; elliptically, after a negation, ἀ. ἵνα, Mk 14⁴⁹, Jo 1⁸ 9³, al.; = εἰ μή (Bl., § 77, 13; M, *Pr.*, 241; but cf. WM, § iii, 10), Mt 20²³, Mk 4²². 2. Without previous negation, to express opposition, interruption, transition, etc., *but*: Jo 16²⁰ 12²⁷, Ga 2¹⁴; before commands or requests, Ac 10²⁰ 26¹⁶, Mt 9¹⁸, Mk 9²², al.; to introduce an accessory idea, ιι Co 7¹¹; in the apodosis after a condition or concession with εἰ, ἐάν, εἴπερ, *yet, still, at least*, Mk 14²⁹, ι Co 9², ιι Co 4¹⁶, Col 2⁵, al.; after μέν, Ac 4¹⁷, Ro 14²⁰, ι Co 14¹⁷; giving emphasis to the following clause, ἀλλ' ἔρχεται ὥρα, *yea*, etc., Jo 16²; so with neg., ἀλλ' οὐδέ, *nay, nor yet*, Lk 23¹⁵. 3. Joined with other particles (a practice which increases in late writers; Simcox, *LNT*, 166), ἀ. γε, *yet at least*, Lk 24²¹, ι Co 9²; ἀ. ἤ, *save only, except*, Lk 12⁵¹, ιι Co 1¹³; ἀ. μὲν οὖν, Phl 3⁸ (on this usage, v. MM, *VGT*, s.v.).

ἀλλάσσω (< ἄλλος), [in LXX chiefly for חלף, מור hi., etc.;] 1. *to change*: Ac 6¹⁴, Ga 4²⁰. 2. *to transform*: ι Co 15⁵¹, ⁵², He 1¹². 3. *to exchange*: c. acc., seq. ἐν (= בְּ, Ps 105 (106)²⁰) instead of simple gen. (Bl., § 36, 8), Ro 1²³ (cf. ἀπ-, δι-, κατ-, ἀπο-κατ-, μετ-, συν-αλλάσσω; v. MM, *VGT*, s.v.).†

**ἀλλαχόθεν, adv. (< ἄλλος), [in LXX: iv Mac 1⁷*;] = ἄλλοθεν (v. MM, *VGT*, s.v.), *from another place*: Jo 10¹.†

*ἀλλαχοῦ, adv. (< ἄλλος), = ἄλλοσε (MM, *VGT*, s.v.), *elsewhere*: Mk 1³⁸.†

*†ἀλληγορέω, -ῶ (< ἄλλος, ἀγορεύω), *to speak allegorically* (Cremer, 96 ff.): Ga 4²⁴.†

†ἀλληλουιά (Rec. ἀλληλούϊα; Heb. הַלְלוּיָהּ, *praise the Lord*), [in LXX in the titles of certain Pss (104 (105), al.), and at the end of Ps 150; also To 13¹⁸, ιιι Mac 7¹³;] *hallelujah, alleluia*: Re 19¹, ³, ⁴, ⁶.†

ἀλλήλων (gen. pl.), dat. -οις, -αις, acc. -ους, -ας, -α (no nom.), recipr. pron. (< ἄλλος), *of one another, mutually*: Mt 25³², Mk 4⁴¹, Jo 13²², al.

†ἀλλογενής, -ές (< ἄλλος, γένος), [in LXX chiefly for זָר, נֵכָר;] *of another race, a foreigner* (= ἀλλόφυλος; Cremer, 150; MM, *VGT*, s.v.): Lk 17¹⁸.†

ἅλλομαι, [in LXX for צלח דלג, pi., etc. ;] *to leap :* Ac 3⁸ 14¹⁰ ; of water, *to spring up,* Jo 4¹⁴ (MM, *VGT*, s.v.).†

ἄλλος, -η, -ο, (cf. Lat. *alius*, Eng. *else*), [in LXX for אַחֵר, אַחָד, etc. ;] *other, another :* absol., Mt 20³, al. ; ἅ. δέ, 1 Co 3¹⁰ 12⁸ ; pl., Mk 6¹⁵ ; attached to a noun, Mt 2¹² 4²¹, al. ; c. art., ὁ ἅ., *the other,* Mt 5³⁹, Jo 19³² (Bl., § 47, 8) ; οἱ ἅ., *the others, the rest,* Jo 20²⁵, 1 Co 14²² ; ἅ. πρὸς ἄλλον = πρὸς ἀλλήλους (Bl., § 48, 10), Ac 2¹² ; ἀλλ' (i.e. ἄλλο) ἤ (Bl., § 77, 13), Lk 12⁵¹ ; seq. πλήν, Mk 12³² ; εἰ μή, Jo 6²² ; παρά c. acc., 1 Co 3¹¹ ; v. *ICC* on Ga, pp. 420 ff.

SYN.: ἕτερος, q.v. ἅ. denotes numerical, ἕ. qualitative difference (Cremer, 89). ἅ. generally " denotes simply distinction of individuals, ἕ. involves the secondary idea of difference in kind " (v. Lft., Meyer, Ramsay, on Ga 1⁶, ⁷ ; Tr., *Syn.*, § xcv ; Bl., § 51, 6 ; M, *Pr.*, 79 f., 246 ; MM, *VGT*, s.vv.).   As to whether the distinction can be maintained in 1 Co 12⁸, ¹⁰, v. *ICC*, in l., and on He 11³⁵ᶠ, v. Westc., in l.

* ἀλλοτρι-επίσκοπος (Rec. ἀλλοτριοεπ-), -ου, ὁ, *one who meddles in things alien to his calling :* 1 Pe 4¹⁵ (v. *ICC*, in l. ; Deiss., *BS*, 224₄ ; MM, *VGT*, s.v.).†

ἀλλότριος, -α, -ον (< ἄλλος), [in LXX for זָר, נֵכָר, אַחֵר ;] 1. *belonging to another, not one's own* (opp. to ἴδιος) : Lk 16¹², Ro 14⁴ 15²⁰ (Field, *Notes*, 165 f.), II Co 10¹⁵, ¹⁶, 1 Ti 5²², He 9²⁵.   2. *foreign, strange, alien* (opp. to οἰκεῖος ; v. MM, *VGT*, s.v.) : Mt 17²⁵, ²⁶, Jo 10⁵, Ac 7⁶, He 11⁹, ³⁴.†

ἀλλόφυλος, -ον (ἄλλος, φῦλον, *a tribe*), [in LXX chiefly for פְּלֶשֶׁת ;] *foreign, of another race* (MM, *VGT*, s.v.) ; as opp. to a Jew, *a Gentile :* Ac 10²⁸.†

ἄλλως, adv. (< ἄλλος), *otherwise :* 1 Ti 5²⁵.†

ἀλοάω, -ῶ (< ἅλως, v.s. ἄλων ; and cf. MM, *VGT*, s.v.), [in LXX chiefly for דּוּשׁ ;] *to thresh :* 1 Co 9⁹, ¹⁰, 1 Ti 5¹⁸.†

ἄ-λογος, -ον, [in LXX : Ex 6¹² (עֲרַל שְׂפָתַיִם), Nu 6¹² (נמל), Jb 11¹², Wi 11¹⁵, ¹⁶, IV Mac ₃* ;] 1. *without reason, irrational :* ζῷα, II Pe 2¹², Ju¹⁰.   2. *contrary to reason :* Ac 25²⁷ (v. MM, *VGT*, s.v.).†

† ἀλόη, -ης, ἡ, [in LXX : Ca 4¹⁴ א (אֲהָלוֹת) * ;] *the aloe, aloes* (the powder of a fragrant wood) : Jo 19³⁹.†

ἅλς, ἁλός, ὁ, variant for ἅλας (q.v.) : Mk 9⁴⁹, Rec. WH, mg., R, mg.†

ἁλυκός, -ή, -όν (< ἅλς), [in LXX for מֶלַח, שׂדִים ;] *salt :* Ja 3¹².†

* ἄλυπος, -ον (< λύπη), *free from grief :* Phl 2²⁸.†

** ἄλυσις, -εως, ἡ, [in LXX : Wi 17¹⁷ * ;] *a chain, bond :* Mk 5³, ⁴, Lk 8²⁹, Ac 12⁶, ⁷ 21³³ 28²⁰, Eph 6²⁰, II Ti 1¹⁶, Re 20¹.†

* ἀ-λυσιτελής, -ές (cf. λυσιτελέω), *unprofitable :* He 13¹⁷.†

Ἄλφα, τό, indecl. (v.s. A), *Alpha :* Re 1⁸ 21⁶ 22¹³ (v. Swete, in ll.).†

Ἀλφαῖος (WH, Ἀλ-), -ου, ὁ (Aram. חַלְפַּי), *Alphæus.* 1. Father of Levi : Mk 2¹⁴.   2. Father of James : Mt 10³, Mk 3¹⁸, Lk 6¹⁵, Ac 1¹³.†

ἅλων, -ωνος (for Attic ἅλως, -ω, v. MM, *VGT*, s.v.), ἡ, [in LXX chiefly for גֹּרֶן ;] *a threshing-floor :* Mt 3¹², Lk 3¹⁷ (here prob. by meton, = the grain on the threshing-floor).†

ἀλώπηξ, -εκος, ἡ, [in LXX for שׁוּעָל ;] *a fox :* Mt 8²⁰, Lk 9⁵⁸ ; metaph., of Herod, Lk 13³².†

ἅλωσις, -εως, ἡ (< ἁλίσκομαι), [in LXX : Je 27 (50)⁴⁶ (תָּפַשׂ ni.)* ;] *a taking, capture :* ii Pe 2¹².†

ἅμα, adv., *at once* (Lat. *simul*) : Ac 24²⁶ 27⁴⁰, Ro 3¹² (*one and all* = יַחְדָּו, Ps 14³), Col 4³, i Ti 5¹³, Phm ²² ; seq. σύν, i Th 4¹⁷ 5¹⁰ ; as prep. c. dat., *together with :* Mt 13²⁹ (v. MM, VGT, s.v.) ; also, c. adv., ἅ. πρωΐ (cl., ἅ. ἕω, etc.), *early in the morning :* Mt 20¹.†

** ἀμαθής, -ές (< μανθάνω), [in Sm. : Ps 48 (49)¹¹ * ;] *unlearned, ignorant :* ii Pe 3¹⁶ (on the rareness of this word, v. MM, VGT, s.v.).†

*† ἀμαράντινος, -ον (< ἀμάραντος), *of amaranth* (Inscr.) ; hence *unfading :* i Pe 5⁴.†

**† ἀμάραντος, -ον (< μαραίνομαι), [in LXX : Wi 6¹² (σοφία)* ;] *unfading* (whence ὁ ἀ., *the amaranth*, an unfading flower) : i Pe 1⁴ (cf. MM, VGT, s.v.).†

ἁμαρτάνω (pres. formed from aor. ἁμαρτεῖν), [in LXX for חָטָא, also for אָשַׁם, רָשַׁע, etc. ;] 1. *to miss the mark* (Hom., Æsch., al.), hence metaph. (Hom., al.), *to err, do wrong.* 2. In. LXX and NT, *to violate God's law, to sin* (for non-Christian exx., v. MM, VGT, s.v.) : absol., Mt 18²⁵ 27⁴, Lk 17³, Jo 5¹⁴ 8⁽¹¹⁾ 9²,³, Ro 2¹² 3²³ 5¹²,¹⁴,¹⁶ 6¹⁵, i Co 7²⁸,³⁶ 15³⁴, Eph 4²⁶, i Ti 5²⁰, Tit 3¹¹, He 3¹⁷ 10²⁶, i Pe 2²⁰, ii Pe 2⁴, i Jo 1¹⁰ 2¹ 3⁶,⁸,⁹ 5¹⁸ ; c. cogn. acc., ἁ. ἁμαρτίαν (cf. Ex 32³⁰, חָטָא חֲטָאָה), i Jo 5¹⁶ ; seq. εἰς, Mt 18²¹, Lk 15¹⁸,²¹ 17⁴, Ac 25⁸ (Καίσαρα), i Co 6¹⁸ 8¹² (Field, *Notes*, 173) ; ἐνώπιον, Lk 15¹⁸,²¹ ; πρὸς θάνατον (cf. Nu 18²², חֵטְא לָמוּת), i Jo 5¹⁶ (Cremer, 98, 633) ; v. ICC on Ga, pp. 436 ff.

ἁμάρτημα, -τος, τό (< ἁμαρτεῖν, v. supr.), [in LXX for חַטָּאת, עָוֹן, etc. ;] *an act of disobedience to divine law* (Lft., *Notes*, 273), *a sinful deed, a sin :* Mk 3²⁸,²⁹, Ro 3²⁵, i Co 6¹⁸, ii Pe 1⁹, WH, mg. ; αἰώνιον ἀ. (DCG, i, 788ᵃ), Mk 3²⁹ (for exx. from π., v. MM, VGT, s.v.).†

SYN.: ἀγνόημα, ἁμαρτία, ἀνομία, ἀσέβεια, ἥττημα, παράβασις, παρακοή, παρανομία, παράπτωμα (v. Cremer, 100 ; Tr., *Syn.*, § lxvi ; DB, iv, 532 ; DCG, l.c. ; Westc, *Eph.*, 165 f.).

ἁμαρτία, -ας, ἡ (< ἁμαρτάνω, q.v.), [in LXX chiefly for חַטָּאת and cogn. forms, also for עָוֹן, פֶּשַׁע, etc. ;] prop. *a missing the mark ;* in cl. (v. reff. to CR in MM, VGT, s.v.); (*a*) *guilt, sin* (Plat., Arist., al.) ; (*b*) more freq., from Æsch. down, *a fault, failure.* In NT (as LXX) always in ethical sense ; 1. as a principle and quality of action, = τὸ ἁμαρτάνειν, *a sinning, sin :* Ro 5¹²,¹³,²⁰ ; ὑφ' ἁμαρτίαν εἶναι, Ro 3⁹ ; ἐπιμένειν τῇ ἁ., Ro 6¹ ; ἀποθνήσκειν, νεκρὸν εἶναι τῇ ἁ., Ro 6²,¹¹ ; τὴν ἁ. γινώσκειν, Ro 7⁷ ; σῶμα τῆς ἁ., Ro 6⁶ ; ἀπάτη τῆς ἁ., He 3¹³ ; personified as a ruling principle, ἁ. βασιλεύει, κυριεύει, etc., Ro 5²¹

6¹², ¹⁴ 7¹⁷, ²⁰; δουλεύειν τῇ ἁ., Ro 6⁶; δοῦλος τῆς ἁ., ib. ¹⁷; νόμος τῆς ἁ., Ro
7²³ 8²; δύναμις τῆς ἁ., 1 Co 15⁵⁶ (cf. Ge 4⁷). 2. As a generic term
(disting. fr. the specific terms ἁμάρτημα, q.v., etc.) for concrete wrong-
doing, violation of the divine law, sin: Jo 8⁴⁶, Ja 1¹⁵, al.; ποιεῖν
(τὴν) ἁ., Jo 8³⁴, 11 Co 11⁷, 1 Jo 3⁸; ἔχειν ἁ., Jo 9⁴¹ 15²², ²⁴ 19¹¹, 1 Jo 1⁸;
in pl. ἁμαρτίαι, sin in the aggregate, 1 Th 2¹⁶ (v. Milligan, in l.); ποιεῖν
ἁμαρτίας, Ja 5¹⁵; πλῆθος ἁμαρτιῶν, Ja 5²⁰, 1 Pe 4⁸; ἄφεσις ἁμαρτιῶν,
Mt 26²⁸, Mk 1⁴, al.; ἐν ἁμαρτίαις εἶναι, 1 Co 15¹⁷; collectively,
αἴρειν τὴν ἁ. τ. κόσμου, Jo 1²⁹; ἀποθνήσκειν ἐν τῇ ἁ., Jo 8²¹. 3. = ἁμάρτημα, a sinful deed, a sin: Mt 12³¹, Ac 7⁶⁰, 1 Jo 5¹⁶.
SYN.: v.s. ἁμάρτημα.

* ἁμάρτυρος, -ον (< μάρτυς), without witness: Ac 14¹⁷.†
ἁμαρτωλός, -όν (< ἁμαρτάνω), [in LXX chiefly for רשע;] sinful, a
sinner: of all men, 1 Ti 1¹⁵; of those especially wicked, 1 Ti 1⁹, 1 Pe
4¹⁸; pl., Mt 9¹⁰, ¹¹, ¹³ 11¹⁹ 26⁴⁵, al. (v. MM, VGT, s.v.; Cremer, 102,
634).

* ἄμαχος, -ον (< μάχη); 1. invincible (freq. in cl.). 2. abstaining
from fighting, non-combatant (Xen.). Metaph. (cf. MM, VGT, s.v.),
not contentious: 1 Ti 3³, Tit 3².†

* ἀμάω, -ῶ (in cl. chiefly poët.), to reap: Ja 5⁴.†
ἀμέθυστος, -ου, ἡ (acc. to Plut., < ἀ- μεθύω, being regarded as an
antidote against drunkenness), [in LXX: Ex 28¹⁹ 36¹⁹ (39¹²) (אחלמה),
Ez 28¹³ *;] amethyst, a purple quartz: Re 21²⁰.†

ἀμελέω, -ῶ (< μέλει), [in LXX: Je 4¹⁷ (מרה) 38 (31)³² (בעל), Wi
3¹⁰, 11 Mac 4¹⁴ *;] (a) absol., to be careless, not to care: Mt 22⁵; (b) c.
gen., to be careless of, to neglect: 1 Ti 4¹⁴, He 2³ 8⁹ (v. MM, VGT,
s.v.).†

ἀ-μεμπτος, -ον (< μέμφομαι), [in LXX chiefly for תם ;]‎ blameless,
free from fault (in π. of a marriage-contract; M, Th., I, 3¹³; cf. MM,
VGT, s.v.): Lk 1⁶, Phl 2¹⁵ 3⁶, 1 Th 3¹³ (WH, mg., -ως) He 8⁷.†
SYN.: ἄμωμος, ἀνέγκλητος, ἀνεπίλημπτος, q.v. (Tr., Syn., § ciii).
ἀ-μέμπτως, adv. (< ἄμεμπτος), [in LXX: Es 3¹³ *;] blamelessly
(Lft., Notes, 28, 89; MM, VGT, s.v. -ος): 1 Th 2¹⁰ 3¹³, WH, mg., 5²³.†

** ἀμέριμνος, -ον (< μέριμνα), [in LXX: Wi 6¹⁵ 7²³ *;] free from
anxiety or care: Mt 28¹⁴, 1 Co 7³² (for exx., v. MM, VGT, s.v.).†

**† ἀ-μετάθετος, -ον (< μετατίθημι), [in LXX: 111 Mac 5¹, ¹² *;] im-
mutable: He 6¹⁸; as subst., τὸ ἁ., immutability, ib.¹⁷ (v. MM, VGT,
s.v.).†

* ἀ-μετα-κίνητος, -ον (< μετακινέω), immovable, firm: 1 Co 15⁵⁸.†
* ἀ-μεταμέλητος, -ον (< μεταμέλομαι), not repented of, unregretted:
Ro 11²⁹, 11 Co 7¹⁰.†

*† ἀμετανόητος, -ον (< μετανοέω), 1. impenitent: Ro 2⁵. 2. = ἀμετα-
μέλητος (π., Philo, al.; v. Deiss., BS, 257; MM, VGT, s.v.).†

* ἄμετρος, -ον (< μέτρον), without measure: adverbially, εἰς τὰ ἄ.,
excessively, 11 Co 10¹³, ¹⁵.†

† ἀμήν, indecl. (Heb. אָמֵן, verbal adj. fr. אמן, to prop, ni., be firm),
[in LXX: 1 Ch 16³⁶, 1 Es 9⁴⁶, Ne 5¹³ 8⁶, To 8⁸ 14¹⁵, 111 Mac 7²³,

ιν Mac 18²⁴ (elsewhere "א is rendered ἀληθινός, Is 65¹⁶; ἀληθῶς, Je 35 (28)⁶; γένοιτο, Nu 5²², De 27¹⁵ ᶠᶠ·, ιιι Ki 1³⁶, Ps 40 (41)¹³ 71 (72)¹⁹ 105 (106)⁴⁸, Je 11⁵)*·] 1. As adj. (cf. Is, l.c.), ὁ ἁ., Re 3¹⁴. 2. As adv., (a) in solemn assent to the statements or prayers of another (Nu, Ne, etc., ll. c.): τὸ ἁ., ι Co 14¹⁶; (b) similarly, at the end of one's own prayer or ascription of praise: Ro 1²⁵ 15³³, Ga 1⁵, ι Ti 1¹⁷; (c) in the Gospels, exclusively, introducing solemn statements of our Lord, truly, verily: Mt 5¹⁸, ²⁶, Mk 3²⁸ (v. Swete, in l.), Lk 4²⁴, al.; ἁ. ἁ., always in Jo 1⁵² 3³ 5¹⁹, al.; τὸ ναί, καὶ . . . τὸ ἁ., ιι Co 1²⁰ (on usage in π., v. MM, VGT, s.v.).

* ἀμήτωρ, -ορος, ὁ, ἡ (< μήτηρ), without a mother (freq. in Gk. writers of the gods): ἀπάτωρ ἁ., of one without recorded genealogy, He 7³ (cf. MM, VGT, s.v.).

** ἀ-μίαντος, -ον (< μιαίνω), [in LXX: Wi 3¹³ 4² 8²⁰, ιι Mac 14³⁶ 15³⁴ *;] undefiled, free from contamination (in π., of αἰθήρ; MM, VGT, s.v.): He 7²⁶ 13⁴, ι Pe 1⁴, Ja 1²⁷.†
SYN.: ἄμωμος, ἄσπιλος (Cremer, 784).

Ἀμιναδάβ, ὁ, indecl. (Heb. עַמִּינָדָב), Amminadab: Mt 1⁴, Lk 3³³ (WH om.).†

ἄμμος, -ου, ἡ, [in LXX chiefly for חוֹל;] sand, sandy ground: Mt 7²⁶, Ro 9²⁷, He 11¹², Re 12¹⁸ 20⁸.†

ἀμνός, -οῦ, ὁ, [in LXX chiefly for כֶּבֶשׂ;] a lamb: fig., of Christ (DCG, ii, 620b), Jo 1²⁹, ³⁶, Ac 8³² (LXX), ι Pe 1¹⁹ (cf. ἀρνίον; Cremer, 102, 635).†

** ἀμοιβή, -ῆς, ἡ (< ἀμείβομαι, to repay); [in Aq., Sm.: Pr 12¹⁴, al.;] requital, recompense: ι Ti 5⁴ (for illustration from π., v. MM, VGT, s.v.).†

ἄμπελος, -ου, ἡ, [in LXX for גֶּפֶן;] vine: Mt 26²⁹, Mk 14²⁵, Lk 22¹⁸, Ja 3¹²; fig., of Christ, Jo 15¹, ⁴, ⁵; of his enemies (on the usage here, v. MM, VGT, s.v.): Re 14¹⁸, ¹⁹.†

ἀμπελουργός, -οῦ, ὁ, ἡ, [in LXX for כֹּרֵם;] a vine dresser: Lk 13⁷.†

ἀμπελών, -ῶνος, ὁ (< ἄμπελος), [in LXX for כֶּרֶם;] a vineyard: Mt 20¹ ᶠᶠ· 21²⁸ ᶠᶠ·, Lk 13⁶ 20⁹ ᶠᶠ·, ι Co 9⁷. (Æschin., 49, 13; Diod., al.; v. MM, VGT, s.v.; LS, s.v. ἀμπελουργεῖον.)

Ἀμπλιᾶτος (T, -ίατος; Rec. Ἀμπλιᾶς; v. MM, VGT, s.v.), -ου, ὁ, Ampliatus: Ro 16⁸.†

ἀμύνω, [in LXX (mid.): Jos 10¹³ (נקם), Ps 117 (118)¹⁰⁻¹² (מול hi.), Is 59¹⁶ (ישע hi.), Wi 11³, al.;] to ward off, etc. Mid. (a) to defend oneself against; (b) to requite; (c) = act., to defend, assist (Is, l.c.): c. acc. pers., Ac 7²⁴ (MM, VGT, s.v.).†

ἀμφιάζω (< ἀμφί, on both sides: v. M, Pr., 100), Hellenistic for ἀμφιέννυμι (cf. MM, VGT, s.v.), [in LXX for לבש, etc.;] to clothe: Lk 12²⁸ (T, -έζει).†

ἀμφι-βάλλω (v. supr.), [in LXX: Hb 1¹⁷ *;] = περιβάλλω, to throw around, as a garment: absol. (MM, VGT, s.v.), of casting a net: Mk 1¹⁶ (Rec. βάλλοντας ἀμφίβληστρον).†

ἀμφίβληστρον, -ου, τό (< ἀμφιβάλλω), [in LXX chiefly for חֵרֶם ;]
something thrown around, as a garment ; spec., *a casting-net :* Mt 4¹⁸.†
SYN. : δίκτυον, σαγήνη. ἀ. is a casting-net, σ. a drag-net, δ. is
the more general term—a net of any kind (Tr., *Syn.,* § lxiv).
ἀμφιέζω, v.s. ἀμφιάζω.
ἀμφιέννυμι (< ἔννυμι, *to clothe*), *to clothe :* Mt 6³⁰ 11⁸, Lk 7²⁵
(cf. ἀμφιάζω).†
Ἀμφίπολις, -εως, ἡ, *Amphipolis,* in Macedonia, so called because
the river Strymon flowed around it : Ac 17¹.†
ἄμφοδον, -ου, τό (< ἀμφί, ὁδός), [in LXX for אַרְמְנוֹת (Je 17²⁷
30¹⁶ (49²⁷)) * ;] prop., *a road around* anything (RV, *the open street*) :
Mk 11⁴, Ac 19²⁸, WH, mg.†
ἀμφότεροι, -αι, -α (replaces ἄμφω in κοινή, v. M, *Pr.,* 57 ; used of
more than two, ib. 80 ; MM, *VGT,* s.v.), *both of two :* Mt 9¹⁷, al.
* ἀ-μώμητος, -ου (< μωμάομαι), *blameless :* ii Pe 3¹⁴.†
SYN. : ἄμεμπτος (q.v.), ἀνέγκλητος, ἀνεπίλημπτος.
* ἄμωμον, -ου, τό, *amomum,* a fragrant plant of India (RV, *spice*) :
Re 18¹³.†
ἄ-μωμος, -ον (< μῶμος, q.v.), [in LXX chiefly for תָּמִים] ; of sacrificial victims, *without blemish :* of Christ, He 9¹⁴, i Pe 1¹⁹ ; ethically,
unblemished, faultless : Eph 1⁴ 5²⁷, Phl 2¹⁵, Col 1²², Ju²⁴, Re 14⁵
(Cremer, 425, 788 ; MM, *VGT,* s.v.).†
SYN. : ἀμίαντος, ἄσπιλος.
Ἀμών, ὁ, indecl. (Heb. אָמוֹן), *Amon,* King of Judah : Mt 1¹⁰
(Rec.).†
Ἀμώς, ὁ, indecl. (Heb. אָמוֹץ, Is 1¹ ; עָמוֹס, Am 1¹ ; אָמוֹן, iv Ki
21¹⁸ ff. B) ; 1. as in iv Ki, l.c. B (A. Ἀμμών ; Jos., Ἀμμών, Ἄμωσος),
Amon : Mt 1¹⁰. 2. *Amos :* Lk 3²⁵.†
ἄν, conditional particle, which cannot usually be separately
translated in English, its force depending on the constructions which
contain it (see further, LS, s.v. ; WM, § xlii ; M, *Pr.,* 165 ff. ; MM,
VGT, s.v.). 1. In apodosis, (i) c. indic. impf. or aor., expressing what
would be or would have been if (εἰ c. impf., aor. or plpf.) some condition were or had been fulfilled : Lk 7³⁹ 17⁶, Jo 5⁴⁶, Ga 1¹⁰, Mt 12⁷
24⁴³, i Co 2⁸, Ac 18¹⁴, i Jo 2¹⁹, al. The protasis is sometimes understood (as also in cl.) : Mt 25²⁷, Lk 19²³. In hypothetical sentences,
expressing unreality, ἄν (as often in late writers, more rarely in cl.) is
omitted : Jo 8³⁰ 15²⁴ 19¹¹, Ro 7⁷, Ga 4¹⁵ ; (ii) c. opt., inf., ptcp. (cl. ;
v. LS, s.v. ; M, *Int.,* § 275 ; M, *Pr.,* 167₄). 2. In combination with
conditional, relative, temporal, and final words ; (i) as in cl., c. subj.,
(*a*) in protasis with εἰ, in Attic contr. ἐάν, q.v. ; (*b*) in conditional,
relative, and temporal clauses (coalescing with ὅτε, ἐπεί, etc. ; v.s. ὅταν,
ἐπάν, etc.), *ever, soever ;* (*a*) c. pres., ἡνίκα ἄν, ii Co 3¹⁵ ; ὃς ἄν,
Ro 9¹⁵ (LXX) 16², al. ; ὅσοι ἄν, Lk 9⁵ ; ὡς ἄν, Ro 15²⁴ (M, *Pr.,* 167) ;
(β) c. aor., ὃς ἄν, Mt 5²¹, ²², ³¹ ; ἕως ἄν, *until,* Mt 2¹³, Mk 6¹⁰, al. ; ὡς ἄν,
as soon as (M, *Pr.,* 167), i Co 11³⁴, Phl 2²³. On the freq. use of ἐάν

for ἄν with the foregoing words, v.s. ἐάν; (ii) in late Gk., when some actual fact is spoken of, c. indic.: ὅταν (q.v.); ὅπου ἄν, Mk 6⁵⁶ (M, Pr., 168); καθότι ἄν, Ac 2⁴⁵ 4³⁵; ὡς ἄν, 1 Co 12². 3. In iterative construction, c. impf. and aor. indic. (M, Pr., 167): Ac 2⁴⁵ 4³⁵, 1 Co 12². 4. c. optat., giving a potential sense to a question or wish: Ac 8³¹ 26²⁹. 5. Elliptical constructions: εἰ μή τι ἄν (M, Pr., 169), 1 Co 7⁵; ὡς ἄν, c. inf., as it were (op. cit. 167), 11 Co 10⁹.

ἄν, contr. from ἐάν, q.v.

ἀνά, prep. (the rarest in NT; M, Pr., 98; MM, VGT, s.v.), prop., upwards, up, always c. acc. 1. In phrases: ἀ. μέσον, among, between, c. gen., Mt 13²⁵, Mk 7³¹, 1 Co 6⁵ (M, Pr., 99), Re 7¹⁷ [so in LXX for בָּתוֹךְ]; ἀ. μέρος, in turn, 1 Co 14²⁷ (both found in Polyb.; cf. MGr. ἀνάμεσα). 2. Distrib., apiece, by: Mt 20⁹, ¹⁰, Lk 9³ (WH om.), ib. ¹⁴ 10¹, Jo 2⁶, Re 4⁸. 3. Adverbially ("a vulgarism," Bl., § 51, 5; cf. Deiss., BS, 139f.), ἀ. εἰς ἕκαστος, Re 21²¹. As prefix, ἀ. signifies (a) up: ἀναβαίνειν; (b) to: ἀναγγέλλειν; (c) anew: ἀναγεννᾶν; (d) back: ἀνακάμπτειν.†

ἀνα-βαθμός, -οῦ, ὁ (< ἀναβαίνω), [in LXX for מַעֲלָה: 111 Ki 10¹⁹, ²⁰, iv Ki 9¹³ 20⁹ ff., 11 Ch 9¹⁸, ¹⁹, Is 38⁸, Ez 40⁶, ⁴⁹; ᾠδὴ τῶν ἀ., tit. Pss 119 (120)-133 (134) *;] 1. a going up, an ascent (Pss, ll. c.?). 2. a step (LXX); pl., a flight of stairs: Ac 21³⁵, ⁴⁰. (On the formation -θμός, v. MM, VGT, s.v.)†

ἀνα-βαίνω, [in LXX chiefly for עלה;] to go up, ascend, (a) of persons: ἐπὶ συκομωρέαν, Lk 19⁴; εἰς τ. πλοῖον, Mk 6⁵¹; εἰς Ἱεροσόλυμα, Mt 20¹⁷; εἰς τ. ἱερόν, c. inf. (M, Pr., 205), Lk 18¹⁰; with mention of place of departure, Mt 3¹⁶ (ἀπό), Ac 8³⁹ (ἐκ); (b) of things, to rise, spring up, come up: a fish, Mt 17²⁷; smoke, Re 8⁴; plants growing, Mt 13⁷; metaph., of things coming up in one's mind (as Heb. עָלָה אֶל לֵב; iv Ki 12⁴, al.), Lk 24³⁸, 1 Co 2⁹; of prayers, Ac 10⁴; messages, Ac 21³¹ (for late exx., v. MM, VGT, s.v.).

ἀνα-βάλλω, [in LXX: Ps 77 (78)²¹ 88 (89)³⁸ (עבר), 1 Ki 28¹⁴, Ps 103 (104)² (עטה);] to defer, put off (MM, VGT, s.v.): mid., Ac 24²².†

ἀνα-βιβάζω (causal of ἀναβαίνω), [in LXX chiefly for עלה hi., also for רכב hi., etc.;] to make go up, draw up, as a ship (Xen.): σαγήνην, Mt 13⁴⁸ (metaph., MM, VGT, s.v.).†

ἀνα-βλέπω, [in LXX chiefly for נשא;] 1. to look up: Mk 8²⁴, al.; seq. εἰς, Mt 14¹⁹, al. (Xen., Plat.). 2. to recover sight (Plat., Aristoph.; cf. MM, VGT, s.v.): Mt 11⁵, Jo 9¹¹, al.

ἀνά-βλεψις, -εως, ἡ (< ἀναβλέπω), [in LXX: Is 61¹ (פְּקַח־קוֹחַ)*;] recovery of sight: Lk 4¹⁸ (LXX).†

ἀνα-βοάω, -ῶ, [in LXX for צעק, זעק, קרא, etc.;] to cry out: Mt 27⁴⁶ (WH, ἐβόησεν; v. MM, VGT, s.v.).†

ἀναβολή, -ῆς, ἡ (< ἀ ἁ ὁάλλω), [in LXX for כנף, etc.;] delay: Ac 25¹⁷ (for exx. of other meanings, v. MM, VGT, s.v.).†

* ἀνάγαιον (Rec. ἀνώγεον; on the form, v. Rutherford, NPhr.,

357 f.; MM, *VGT*, s.v.), -ου, τό (< ἀνά, γῆ), *an upper room :* Mk 14¹⁵, Lk 22¹².†
SYN. : ὑπερῷον.

ἀν-αγγέλλω, [in LXX chiefly for נגד hi.;] 1. *to bring back word, report* (Æsch., Thuc., al.): Jo 5¹⁵ (WH, εἶπεν), Ac 14²⁷ 15⁴, II Co 7⁷ 2. Later, = ἀπαγγέλλω (MM, *VGT*, s.v.), *to announce, declare* (LXX; Cremer, 24): Mt 28¹¹ (WH, ἀπ-), Jo 4²⁵ 16¹³⁻¹⁵, Ac 19¹⁸ 20²⁰,²⁷, Ro 15²¹, I Pe 1¹², I Jo 1⁵.†

†ἀνα-γεννάω, -ῶ, [in LXX: Si prol.¹⁷ א* (ABא° παρα-)*;] *to beget again :* metaph., *of spiritual birth,* I Pe 1³,²³ (cf. Cremer, 147; MM, *VGT*, s.v.).†

ἀνα-γινώσκω (Attic ἀναγιγν-), [in LXX chiefly for קרא ;] 1. *to know certainly, know again, recognize.* 2. *Of written characters, to read :* Mt 24¹⁵, Mk 13¹⁴, Ac 15³¹ 23³⁴, Eph 3⁴; c. acc. rei, Mt 22³¹, Mk 12¹⁰, Lk 6³, Jo 19²⁰, Ac 8³⁰,³², II Co 1¹³, Re 1³; c. acc. pers., Ἠσαΐαν τ. προφήτην, Ac 8²⁸,³⁰; seq. ἐν, Mt 12⁵ 21⁴², Mk 12²⁶ (sc. ἐν τ. νόμῳ), Lk 6³, Jo 19²⁰, II Co 1¹³; c. acc. pers., Ἠσαΐαν τ. προφήτην, Ac 8²⁸,³⁰; seq. ἐν, Mt 12⁵ 21⁴², Mk 12²⁶ (sc. ἐν τ. νόμῳ), Lk 10²⁶; seq. ὅτι, Mt 19⁴ 21¹⁶; τί ἐποίησε, Mt 12³, Mk 2²⁵; pass. II Co 3²; *of reading aloud :* Lk 4¹⁶, Ac 8³⁰,³² 13²⁷ 15²¹, Re 1³ (v. *ICC* in l.), (MM, *VGT*, s.v.).

ἀναγκάζω (< ἀνάγκη), [in LXX: Pr 6⁷ (שטר), I Es 3²⁴, I Mac 2²⁵, al.;] *to necessitate, compel* by force or persuasion, *constrain :* c. acc., II Co 12¹¹; id. c. inf., Mt 14²², Mk 6⁴⁵, Lk 14²³, Ac 26¹¹ (on the impf. here, v. Field, *Notes,* 141; M, *Pr.,* 128 f., 247), Ga 2¹⁴ 6¹²; pass., c. inf., Ac 28¹⁹, Ga 2³ (for exx., v. MM, *VGT*, s.v.).†

ἀναγκαῖος, -αία, -αῖον (< ἀνάγκη), [in LXX: Es 8¹³, Wi 16³, Si prol.²², II Mac 4²³ 9²¹, IV Mac 1²*;] 1. *necessary :* Ac 13⁴⁶, I Co 12²², II Co 9⁵, Phl 2²⁵, Tit 3¹⁴, He 8³; comp. -αιότερον, Phl 1²⁴. 2. *Of persons connected by bonds of nature or friendship, near, intimate* (Field, *Notes,* 118; MM, *VGT*, s.v.): ἀ. φίλοι, Ac 10²⁴.†

* ἀναγκαστῶς, adv., *necessarily* or *by constraint :* opp. to ἑκουσίως, 1 Pe 5² (rare).†

ἀνάγκη, -ης, ἡ, [in LXX chiefly for מָצוֹק, צַר ;] 1. *necessity :* ἔχειν ἀ., c. inf., *to be compelled,* Lk 14¹⁸ 23¹⁷ (Rec., R, mg.), I Co 7³⁷, Ju³, He 7²⁷; ἐξ ἀ., κατ᾽ ἀ., *of necessity,* II Co 9⁷, He 7¹², Phm ¹⁴; ἀ. μοι ἐπίκειται, *n. is laid on me,* I Co 9¹⁶; c. inf. (= ἀναγκαῖόν ἐστι), Mt 18⁷, Ro 13⁵, He 9¹⁶,²³. 2. *force, violence,* hence *pain, distress* (Diod., al.; LXX; v. M, *Th.,* 41; MM, *VGT*, s.v.; cf. θλίψις): Lk 21²³, I Co 7²⁶, I Th 3⁷; pl. (v. Bl., § 32, 6; Swete, *Mk.,* 153), ἐν ἀ., II Co 6⁴ 12¹⁰.†

ἀνα-γνωρίζω, [in LXX: Ge 45¹ (ידע hith.)*;] *to recognize :* Ac 7¹³ (WH, txt., ἐγνωρίσθη).†

ἀνά-γνωσις, -εως, ἡ, [in LXX: Ne 8⁸ (מִקְרָא), I Es 9⁴⁸, Si prol.⁹,¹³*;] 1. *recognition* (Hdt.). 2. *reading* (Plat., al.): *of the public reading of Scripture* (Milligan, *NTD,* 173ₙ, 210 f.): Ac 13¹⁵, II Co 3¹⁴, I Ti 4¹³ (Cremer, 158; MM, *VGT*, s.v.).†

ἀν-άγω, [in LXX chiefly for עלה hi.;] *to lead* or *bring up :* seq. εἰς, c. acc. loc., Mt 4¹, Lk 2²² 4⁵ (WH om. εἰς, κ.τ.λ.), Ac 9³⁹ 16³⁴; *of raising the dead* (cl.), ἐκ νεκρῶν, Ro 10⁷, He 13²⁰; *to produce and set before,*

r. λαῷ, Ac 12⁴ (MM, *VGT*, s.v.); in sacrificial sense (MM, l.c.), *to offer*, θυσίαν Ac 7⁴¹. Mid., in nautical sense (Hom., Hdt., Thuc., al.), *to put to sea*: Lk 8²², Ac 13¹³ 16¹¹ 18²¹ 20³, ¹³ 21¹, ² 27², ⁴, ¹², ²¹ 28¹⁰, ¹¹ (cf. ἐπ-ανάγω).†

ἀνα-δείκνυμι, [in LXX: Hb 3² (ידע), Da LXX 1¹¹ (מנה), 1²⁰ (מצא), I Es 6, II, III Mac 9*;] 1. *to lift up and show, show forth, declare* (cf. II Mac 2⁸, v. MM, *VGT*, s.v.): Ac 1²⁴. 2. *to consecrate, set apart*, (Strab., Plut., Anth.): Lk 10¹.†

**† ἀνά-δειξις, -εως, ἡ (< ἀναδείκνυμι), [in LXX: Si 43⁶ *;] *a shewing forth, announcement*: Lk 1⁸⁰.†

** ἀνα-δέχομαι, [in LXX: II Mac 6¹⁹ 8³⁶ *;] 1. *to assume, undertake* (in π. freq. as legal term: MM, *VGT*, s.v.): ἐπαγγελίας, He 11¹⁷. 2. = cl. ὑποδέχομαι, *to receive*: (so perh. He, l.c.); of guests, Ac 28⁷.†

** ἀνα-δίδωμι, [in LXX: Si 1²², II Mac 13¹⁵ *;] 1. *to give forth, send up*, as of plants (Hdt., al.). 2. *to give up, yield, hand over* (MM, *VGT*, s.v.): Ac 23³³.†

**† ἀνα-ζάω, -ῶ, [in Al.: Ge 45²⁷ *;] *to live again, regain life* (cf. cl. ἀναβιόω; Cremer, 722; and for other exx., v. MM, *VGT*, s.v.): metaph. of moral revival, Lk 15²⁴ (WH, mg., ἔζησεν); of sin, Ro 7⁹.†

ἀνα-ζητέω, -ῶ, [in LXX: Jb 3⁴ (דרש), 10⁶ (בקש pi.), II Mac 13²¹ *;] *to look for or seek carefully* ("specially of searching for human beings, with an implication of difficulty": MM, *VGT*, s.v.): Lk 2⁴⁴, ⁴⁵, Ac 11²⁵.†

† ἀνα-ζώννυμι, [in LXX: Jg 18¹⁶, Pr 29³⁵ (31¹⁷) (חגר)*;] *to gird up*: fig., τ. ὀσφύας τ. διανοίας, I Pe 1¹³.†

** ἀνα-ζωπυρέω, -ῶ (< ζωός, πῦρ), [in LXX: I Mac 13⁷ *;] *to kindle afresh*, or *keep in full flame*: metaph., II Ti 1⁶ (for vernac. exx., v. MM, *VGT*, s.v.).†

ἀνα-θάλλω (< θάλλω, *to flourish*), [in LXX: Ps 27 (28)⁷ (עלה), Ez 17²⁴ (פרח hi.), Ho 8⁹, Wi 4⁴, Si 5*;] *to revive*: Phl 4¹⁰ (cf. MM, *VGT*, s.v.).

† ἀνάθεμα, -τ ɩ, τό (< ἀνατίθημι), Hellenistic for Attic ἀνάθημα (Bl., § 27, 2); 1. prop. = τὸ ἀνατιθεμένον, *that which is laid by* to be kept, *a votive offering* (as ἀνάθημα in II Mac 2¹³, Lk 21⁵—where LT read -θεμα, v. M, Pr., 46). 2. [As equiv. in LXX for חֵרֶם,] *devoted, a thing devoted to God* (v Driver, *De*., 98 f., and cf. Le 27²⁸, ²⁹), hence; (a) of the sentence pronounced (De 13¹⁵), *a curse*: Ac 23¹⁴; (b) of the object on which the curse is laid, *accursed* (De 7²⁶): Ro 9³, I Co 12³ 16²², Ga 1⁸, ⁹ (v. *ICC* on *Ro.*; Lft., *Ga.*, ll. c.; Cremer, 547; Tr., *Syn.*, § v; MM, *VGT*, s.v.).†

† ἀνα-θεματίζω (< ἀνάθεμα), [in LXX chiefly for חרם hi. (Nu 21², I Ki 15³, al.), I Mac 5⁵;] *to devote to destruction, declare* or *invoke anathema*: absol., Mk 14⁷¹; ἑαυτόν, *to bind* oneself *under a curse*: Ac 23¹², ¹⁴, ²¹. (Cf. καταναθεματίζω, and on the occurrence of the word in π., v. Deiss., *LAE*, 92 f.; MM, *VGT*, s.v.).†

*† ἀνα-θεωρέω, -ῶ, *to observe carefully, consider well*: Ac 17²³, He 13⁷ (Diod., al.).†

** ἀνάθημα, -τος, τό (cf. ἀνάθεμα, and v. MM, *VGT*, s.v.), [in LXX often as v.l. for ἀνάθεμα (חֵרֶם), and in Nu 21³, Jg 1¹⁷ for חָרְמָה, but prop. in III Mac 3¹⁷, al.;] *a gift set up in a temple, a votive offering:* Lk 21⁵ (LT, -θεμα).†

** **ἀναιδία** (Rec. -εία, as in cl.), -ας, ἡ (< αἰδώς), [in LXX: Si 25²² *;] *shamelessness, importunity:* Lk 11⁸ (for exx. from π., v. MM, VGT, s.v.).†

ἀν-αίρεσις, -εως, ἡ (< ἀναιρέω), [in LXX: Nu 11¹⁵ (הרג), Jg 15¹⁷ (רמה), Jth 15⁴, II Mac 5¹³ *;] 1. *a taking up* or *away* (Thuc.). 2. *a destroying, slaying, murder* (Field, *Notes*, 116; MM, VGT, s.v.): Ac 8¹.†

ἀν-αιρέω, -ῶ, [in LXX for הרג hi., מָת hi., נכה hi., etc.;] 1. *to take up:* mid., Ac 7²¹. 2. *to take away, make an end of, destroy* (for late exx. of various senses, v. MM, VGT, s.v.); (*a*) of things (as freq. in cl. of laws, etc.): He 10⁹; (*b*) of persons, *to kill:* Mt 2¹⁶, Lk 22² 23³², Ac 2²³ 5³³, ³⁶ 7²⁸ 9²³, ²⁴, ²⁹ 10³⁹ 12² 13²⁸ 16²⁷ 22²⁰ 23¹⁵, ²¹, ²⁷ 25³ 26¹⁰, II Th 2⁸, WH, txt., R, txt.†

ἀν-αίτιος, -ον (< αἰτία), [in LXX: De 19¹⁰, ¹³ 21⁶, ⁹ (נָקִי), Da LXX TH Su ⁶², always of αἷμα (cf. MM, VGT, s.v.)*;] *guiltless, innocent:* Mt 12⁵, ⁷.†

* **ἀνα-καθ-ίζω** (v.s. καθίζω); 1. trans., *to set up.* 2. Intrans., *to sit up:* Lk 7¹⁵ (WH, mg., ἐκάθισεν), Ac 9⁴⁰ (freq. in medical writings: MM, VGT, s.v.).†

ἀνα-καινίζω (< καινός), [in LXX: II Ch 15⁸, Ps 102(103)⁵ 103 (104)³⁰, La 5²¹ (חדש pi., hith)., Ps 38(39)² (עכר ni.), I Mac 6⁹*;] *to renew:* He 6⁶ (Isocr., Plut.).†

*†**ἀνα-καινόω**, -ῶ = ἀνακαινίζω (cf. MM, VGT, s.v.), *to make new:* II Co 4¹⁶, Col 3¹⁰ (v. Cremer, 323).†

*†**ἀνακαίνωσις**, -εως, ἡ (< ἀνακαινόω), *renewal:* Ro 12², Tit 3⁵ (Cremer, 324; MM, VGT, s.v.).†

SYN.: παλινγενεσία, in NT, *new birth*, of which ἀ. is the consequent renewal or renovation, in which man as well as God takes part (v. Tr., *Syn.*, § xviii).

ἀνα-καλύπτω, [in LXX chiefly for גלה ni., pi.;] *to unveil:* metaph. of removing hindrance to perception of spiritual things, II Co 3¹⁴, ¹⁸.†

ἀνα-κάμπτω, [in LXX: I Ch 19⁵, Je 3¹, al. (שוב), Je 15⁵ (סור);] 1. trans., *to bend* or *turn back.* 2. Intrans., *to return:* Mt 2¹², Ac 18²¹, He 11¹⁵; metaph. (cf. MM, VGT, s.v.), Lk 10⁶.†

** **ἀνά-κειμαι**, [in LXX: I Es 4¹⁰, To 9⁶ א*;] 1. in cl., as pass. of ἀνατίθημι, *to be laid up, laid:* Mk 5⁴⁰ Rec. 2. In late writers (cf. MM, VGT, s.v.) = κεῖσθαι, κατακεῖσθαι, *to recline at table:* Mt 26²⁰; part. ἀνακείμενος, Mt 9¹⁰ 22¹⁰, ¹¹ 26⁷, Mk 6²⁶ 14¹⁸ 16[¹⁴], Lk 22²⁷, Jo 6¹¹ 12² 13²³, ²⁸.†

SYN.: ἀνακλίνω, ἀναπίπτω, the latter denoting an act rather than a state and thus in Jo 13²⁵ differing from ἀνάκειμαι (v.²³) by indicating a change of position.

** **ἀνα-κεφαλαιόω**, ῶ (v.s. κεφαλαιόω), [in Th., Al.: Ps 71(72)²⁰ *;] *to sum up, gather up*, present as a whole: mid., Ro 13⁹, Eph 1¹⁰ (on wh. v. Lft., *Notes*, 321 f.; AR, in l.; Cremer, 354, 748).†

** ἀνα-κλίνω, [in LXX: III Mac 5¹⁶*;] *to lay upon, lean against,* hence, (*a*) *to lay down :* Lk 2⁷; (*b*) *to make to recline :* Mk 6³⁹, WH, mg., Lk 12³⁷. Pass., *to lie back, recline :* Mt 8¹¹ 14¹⁹, Lk 13²⁹.†

SYN. : ἀνάκειμαι (q.v.), ἀναπίπτω.

ἀνα-κράζω, [in LXX for קרא, etc. ;] *to cry out, shout :* Mk 1²³ 6⁴⁹, Lk 4³³ 8²⁸ 23¹⁸.†

ἀνα-κρίνω, [in LXX: I Ki 20¹² (חקר), Da LXX Su ¹³, ib. LXX, ᾽Η ⁴⁸, ⁵¹*;] *to examine, investigate, question* (Lft., *Notes,* 181 f.) : Ac 17¹¹, I Co 2¹⁴, ¹⁵ 4³, ⁴ 9³ 10²⁵, ²⁷ 14²⁴; in forensic sense (MM, *VGT,* s.v.; esp. of examination by torture; v. Field, *Notes,* 120 f.), Lk 23¹⁴, Ac 4⁹ 12¹⁹ 24⁸ 28¹⁸.†

SYN. : v.s. ἐξετάζω.

˙ ἀνά-κρισις, -εως, ἡ, [in LXX: III Mac 7⁵;] *an examination :* spec. of legal preliminary investigation, Ac 25²⁶ (v. MM, *VGT,* s.v.).†

*ἀνα-κυλίω, (*a*) *to roll up ;* (*b*) *to roll back :* Mk 16⁴ (Rec. ἀποκ-).†

ἀνα-κύπτω [in LXX: Jb 10¹⁵ (נשׂא ראשׁ), Da LXX, Su ³⁵*;] *to lift oneself up ;* (*a*) bodily; Lk 13¹¹, Jo 8⁽⁷, ¹⁰⁾; (*b*) mentally, *to be elated :* Lk 21²⁸ (cf. MM, *VGT,* s.v.).†

ἀνα-λαμβάνω, [in LXX chiefly for נשׂא, also for לקח, etc. ;] 1. *to take up, raise :* Mk 16⁽¹⁹⁾, Ac 1², ¹¹, ²² 10¹⁶, I Ti 3¹⁶. 2. *to take up, take to oneself :* Ac 7⁴³ 20¹³, ¹⁴ 23³¹, Eph 6¹³, ¹⁶, II Ti 4¹¹ (for late exx., v. MM, *VGT,* s.v.).†

* ἀνά-λημψις, -εως, ἡ, (κοινή form of ἀνάληψις ; v. Th., *Gr.*, 108 f.), *a taking up :* Lk 9⁵¹ (MM, *VGT,* s.v.).†

ἀνά-ληψις, -εως, ἡ, Rec. for ἀνάλημψις, q.v.

ἀν-αλίσκω (on the etymology, v. MM, *VGT,* s.v.), [in LXX chiefly for אכל, also for כלה, etc. ;] 1. *to expend.* 2. *to consume, destroy :* Lk 9⁵⁴, Ga 5¹⁵, II Th 2⁸, Rec. WH, mg; all these forms are from late pres. -όω.†

** ἀναλογία, -ας, ἡ (< λόγος), [in Al. : Le 27¹⁸*;] *proportion* (MM, *VGT,* s.v.) : Ro 12⁶ (cf. Cremer, 397).†

** ἀνα-λογίζομαι, [in LXX: Wi 17¹³ א, II Mac 12⁴³ A, III Mac 7⁷*;] *to consider :* He 12³ (MM, *VGT,* s.v.).†

** ἄναλος, -ον (< ἅλς), [in Aq. : Ez 13¹⁰, ¹¹, ¹⁵ 22²⁸*;] *saltless, insipid :* Mk 9⁵⁰.†

ἀναλόω, v.s. ἀναλίσκω.

* ἀνά-λυσις, -εως, ἡ (< ἀναλύω), *a loosing,* e.g. of a vessel from its moorings or of a soldier striking his tent, hence, *departure :* from life, II Ti 4⁶.†

** ἀνα-λύω, [in LXX: I Es 3³, To 2⁹, Jth 13¹, Si 3¹⁵, Wi ₃, II, III Mac ₁₀*;] 1. *to unloose.* 2. *to unloose for departure, depart* (MM, *VGT,* s.v.) : from life, Phl 1²³. 3. *to return,* Lk 12³⁶.†

ἀναμάρτητος, -ον (< ἁμαρτεῖν), [in LXX: Dt 29¹⁹ ⁽¹⁸⁾ (צמא), II Mac 8⁴ 12⁴²*;] 1. *without missing, unerring* (Xen.). 2. In moral sense, *faultless* (Plat.), *without sin :* Jo 8⁽⁷⁾ (v. Cremer, 102, 634 ; MM, *VGT,* s.v.).†

ἀνα-μένω, [in LXX for קוה pi. ;] *to await* "one whose coming is expected, perhaps with the added idea of patience and confidence" : c. acc., I Th 1¹⁰ (v. M, *Th.*, in l. ; MM, *VGT,* s.v.).†

ἀνα-μιμνήσκω, [in LXX for זכר hi.;] *to remind, call to one's remembrance:* c. acc. rei, ι Co 4¹⁷; c. inf., ιι Ti 1⁶. Pass., *to remember, call to mind:* Mk 11²¹ 14⁷², ιι Co 7¹⁵, He 10³².†

ἀνάμνησις, -εως, ἡ (< ἀναμιμνήσκω), [in LXX : Ps 37 (38), 69 (70) tit. (זכר hi.), Le 24⁷ (אַזְכָּרָה), Nu 10¹⁰ (זִכָּרוֹן), Wi 16⁶ *;] *remembrance:* εἰς τ. ἐμὶν ἀ., Lk 22¹⁹ (WH om.), ι Co 11²⁴, ²⁵; ἀ. ἁμαρτιῶν, He 10³ (v. Abbott, *Essays,* 122 ff. ; *DCG,* ii, 74ª).†
  SYN.: ὑπόμνησις (v. Tr., *Syn.,* § cvii).

ἀνα-νεόω, -ῶ (< νέος), [in LXX : Jb 33²⁴, Es 3¹³, ι, ιν Mac ₈ *;] *to renew:* pass., Eph 4²³ (v. Cremer, 428; MM, *VGT,* s.v.).†
  * ἀνα-νήφω, *to return to soberness:* metaph., ιι Ti 2²⁶ (cf. ἐκνήφω).†
  Ἀνανίας (WH, Ἀναν-), -α, ὁ (Heb. חֲנַנְיָה), *Ananias;* 1. of Jerusalem : Ac 5¹, ³, ⁵. 2. Of Damascus : Ac 9¹⁰, ¹², ¹³, ¹⁷ 22¹². 3. High Priest : Ac 23² 24¹.†

**† ἀν-αντί-ρητος (T, -ρρητος), -ον (< ῥητός, *spoken*), [in Sm. : Jb 11² 33¹³ *;] *not to be contradicted, undeniable:* Ac 19³⁶ (MM, *VGT,* s.v.).†
  * ἀν-αντι-ρήτως (T, -ρρήτως), adv., *without contradiction:* Ac 10²⁹.†
  ἀν-άξιος, -ον (ἀ- neg., ἄξιος), [in LXX : Je 15¹⁹ א² (זלל), Es 8¹³, Si 25⁸ *;] *unworthy:* c. gen., ι Co 6² (MM, *VGT,* s.v.).†
  ** ἀναξίως (v. supr.), adv., [in LXX : ιι Mac 14⁴² *;] *in an unworthy manner:* ι Co 11²⁷.†

ἀνά-παυσις, -εως, ἡ (ἀναπαύω), [in LXX chiefly for נוח and its derivatives, שַׁבָּת and its cognates (Ex, Le) ;] *cessation, rest, refreshment:* Mt 11²⁹ 12⁴³, Lk 11²⁴, Re 4⁸ 14¹¹.†
  SYN.: ἄνεσις (lit. the relaxation of the strings of a lyre), prop. signifies the rest or ease which comes from the relaxation of unfavourable conditions, as, e.g. affliction : ἀνάπ., the rest which comes from the temporary cessation of labour (v. Tr., *Syn.,* § xl ; Cremer, 827 ; MM, *VGT,* s.v.).

ἀνα-παύω, [in LXX for fourteen different words, chiefly נוח, also שָׁכַן, רָבַץ, etc. ;] *to give intermission from labour, to give rest, refresh:* Mt 11²⁸, ι Co 16¹⁸, Phm ²⁰; pass., Phm ⁷, ιι Co 7¹³. Mid., *to take rest, enjoy rest:* Mt 26⁴⁵, Mk 6³¹ 14⁴¹, Lk 12¹⁹, Re 6¹¹ 14¹³ ; as in Heb. of Is 11² (עַל נוּחַ), τὸ πνεῦμα ἐφ᾽ ὑμᾶς ἀ., ι Pe 4¹⁴. (In π. this word is used as a technical agricultural term ; v. MM, *VGT,* s.v. ; and cf. Le 26³⁴ ᵗ. ; Cremer, 826.)†

ἀνα-πείθω, [in LXX : Je 36 (29)⁸ (נשׁא hi.), ι Mac 1¹¹ *;] *to persuade, incite:* Ac 18¹³ (cf. MM, *VGT,* s.v.).†
  * ἀνάπειρος, v.s. ἀνάπηρος.
  * ἀνα-πέμπω, 1. *to send up,* (a) to a higher place (Æsch., Plat., al.) ; (b) to a higher authority (Deiss., *BS,* 229 ; MM, *VGT,* s.v. ; cf. also Field, *Notes,* 140): Lk 23⁷, ¹⁵, Ac 25²¹. 2. *to send back* (Pind.): Lk 23¹¹, Phm ¹¹.†
  ἀνα-πηδάω, -ῶ (< πηδάω, *to leap*), [in LXX : ι Ki 20³⁴ (קום) 25¹⁰, Es 5¹, To ₄ *;] *to leap up:* Mk 10⁵⁰ (Rec. ἀναστάς).†

** ἀνά-πηρος (WH, -ειρος; v. Field, *Notes*, 67), *-ον* (πηρός, *maimed*), [in LXX: To 14² א, II Mac 8²⁴ *;] *maimed, crippled* : Lk 14¹³, ²¹.†

ἀνα-πίπτω, [in LXX: Ge 49⁹ (כרע) To 2¹ 7³, Jth 12¹⁶, Si 25¹⁸ 35 (32)², Da TH Su ³⁷ *;] 1. (cl.) *to fall back*. 2. In late writers = ἀνακλίνομαι, *to recline* for a repast (MM, *VGT*, s.v.) : at table, Lk 11³⁷ 14¹⁰ 17⁷ 22¹⁴, Jo 13¹² 21²⁰; on the ground, Mt 15³⁵, Mk 6⁴⁰ 8⁶, Jo 6¹⁰; *to lean back*, Jo 13²⁵ (T, ἐπιπεσών; v.s. ἀνάκειμαι, ad fin.).†

SYN. : ἀνάκειμαι (q.v.), ἀνακλίνομαι.

ἀνα-πληρόω, -ῶ, [in LXX chiefly for מלא, Le 12⁶, al.; also שלם (Ge 15¹⁶, III Ki 7⁵¹, Is 60²⁰), etc.;] 1. *to fill up, make full* (in π. of completing contracts and making up rent; cf. MM, *VGT*, s.v.) : τόπον, *take one's place* (cf. Heb. מָלֵא מָקוֹם), I Co 14¹⁶; ἁμαρτίας, *complete the number*, I Th 2¹⁶; τ. νόμον, *observe perfectly*, Ga 6²; pass., προφητεία, *fulfilled*, Mt 13¹⁴. 2. *to supply* : τὸ ὑστέρημα, I Co 16¹⁷, Phl 2³⁰ (Cremer, 838).†

*† ἀναπολόγητος, *-ον* (< ἀπολογέομαι), *without excuse, inexcusable* (in Polyb., al., as a forensic term; v. Lft., *Notes*, 252): Ro 1²⁰ 2¹.†

ἀνα-πτύσσω, [in LXX for פרש, etc.;] *to unroll* : τ. βιβλίον, Lk 4¹⁷ (WH, R, ἀνοίξας).†

ἀν-άπτω, [in LXX chiefly for יצת;] *to kindle* : Lk 12⁴⁹, Ja 3⁵ (MM, *VGT*, s.v.).†

ἀν-αρίθμητος, *-ον*, (< ἀριθμέω), [Jb 31²⁵, al.], *innumerable* : He 11¹².†

** ἀνα-σείω, [in Aq.: I Ki 26¹⁹, Jb 2³; Aq., Sm.: Is 36¹⁸ *;] 1. *to shake out, shake back, move to and fro* (Thuc., al.). 2. In late writers (Diod., al.; v. MM, *VGT*, s.v.), *to stir up;* metaph., *to excite* : τ. ὄχλον, Mk 15¹¹; τ. λαόν, Lk 23⁵.†

* ἀνα-σκευάζω (< σκεῦος, *a vessel*), prop. *to pack up baggage*, hence, *to dismantle, ravage, destroy;* metaph., *to unsettle, subvert* (MM, *VGT*, s.v.) : ψυχάς, Ac 15²⁴.†

ἀνα-σπάω, -ῶ, [in LXX for עלה hi. ;] *to draw up*: Lk 14⁵, Ac 11¹⁰ (in π. of pulling up barley; MM, *VGT*, s.v.).†

ἀνά-στασις, *-εως, ἡ* (< ἀνίστημι), [in LXX: Ze 3⁸ (קום), La 3⁶³ (קִימָה), Ps 65 (66) tit., Da LXX 11²⁰, II Mac 7¹⁴ 12⁴³ *;] 1. *a raising up, awakening, rising* (in Inscr. of the erection of a monument, v. MM, *VGT*, s.v.): Lk 2³⁴. 2. *a rising from the dead* (v. *DCG*, ii, 605ᵇ); (*a*) of Christ: Ac 1²² 2³¹ 4³³, Ro 6⁵, Phl 3¹⁰, I Pe 3²¹; ἐξ ἀ. νεκρῶν, Ro 1⁴ (*ICC*, in l.) ; ἐκ νεκρῶν, I Pe 1³; (*b*) of persons in OT hist. (e.g. III Ki 17¹⁷ff.) : He 11³⁵; (*c*) of the general resurrection : Mt 22²³, ²⁸, ³⁰, Mk 12¹⁸, ²³, Lk 20²⁷, ³³, ³⁶, Jo 11²⁴, Ac 17¹⁸ 23⁸ 24¹⁵, II Ti 2¹⁸; ἀ. ἐκ νεκρῶν, Lk 20³⁵, Ac 4²; τῶν νεκρῶν, Mt 22³¹, Ac 17³² 23⁶, 24²¹ 26²³, I Co 15¹², ¹³, ²¹, ⁴², He 6²; ἀ. ζωῆς, resurrection to life (cf. II Mac 7¹⁴, ἀ. εἰς ζωήν) and ἀ. τ. κρίσεως, r. to judgment, Jo 5²⁹; ἀ. τ. δικαίων, Lk 14¹⁴; κρείττων ἀ., He 11³⁵; on ἡ ἀ. ἡ πρώτη, Re 20⁵, ⁶, v. Swete, in l., Westc. on Jo 5, but v. also Thayer, s.v.; by meton. of Christ as Author of ἀ., Jo 11²⁵ (v. *DB*, iv, 231; Cremer, 307).†

† ἀνα-στατόω, ῶ (< ἀνάστατος, *driven from home;* < ὀνίστημι), [in

3

LXX: Da 7²³ (דּוּשׁ;* also in Aq., and in π. (v. Deiss., *LAE*, 80 f.; MM, *VGT*, s.v.),] *to stir up, excite, unsettle :* c. acc.; (*a*) *to tumult and sedition :* Ac 17⁶ 21³⁸; (*b*) *by false teaching :* Ga 5¹² (v. Milligan, *NTD*, 73 f.).†

*ἀνα-σταυρόω; 1. *to impale* (Hdt.). 2. *to raise on a cross, crucify* (Polyb., al.). 3. *to crucify again :* He 6⁶ (v. Westc., in l.).†

ἀνα-στενάζω, [in LXX: La 1⁴ (אנח ni.), Si 25¹⁸ ⁽¹⁷⁾, Da TH Su ²², II Mac 6³⁰ *;] *to sigh deeply :* Mk 8¹².†

ἀνα-στρέφω, [in LXX chiefly for שׁוּב;] 1. *to overturn :* Jo 2¹⁵. 2. *to turn back, return :* Ac 5²² 15¹⁶. 3. *to turn hither and thither ;* pass., *to turn oneself about, sojourn, dwell :* Mt 17²² Rec.; metaph. (like Heb. הלך, in κοινή writers and in π.; v. Deiss., *LAE*, 315; *BS*, 88, 194; MM, *VGT*, s.v.), *to conduct oneself, behave, live :* II Co 1¹², Eph 2³, I Ti 3¹⁵, He 10³³ 13¹⁸, I Pe 1¹⁷, II Pe 2¹⁸.†

SYN. : περιπατέω (Hellenistic), πολιτεύω.

** ἀνα-στροφή, -ῆς, ἡ (< ἀναστρέφομαι), [in LXX: To 4¹⁴, II Mac 5⁸ 6²³ *;] 1. *a turning down* or *back, a wheeling about* (Soph., Thuc., al.). 2. In late writers (Polyb., al.; v.s. ἀναστρέφω, and cf. Hort on Ja 3¹³; MM, *VGT*, s.v.), *manner of life, behaviour, conduct :* Ga 1¹³, Eph 4²², I Ti 4¹², He 13⁷, Ja 3¹³, I Pe 1¹⁵, ¹⁸ 2¹² 3¹, ², ¹⁶, II Pe 2⁷ 3¹¹.†

*† ἀνα-τάσσομαι, [in LXX only as v.l. (Ald.) in Ec 2²⁰;] *to arrange in order, bring together from memory* (Blass., *Phil. Gosp.*, 14 ff.; MM, *VGT*, s.v.) : Lk 1¹.†

ἀνα-τέλλω, [in LXX for צמח, פרח, זרח, etc.;] 1. trans., *to cause to rise :* Mt 5⁴⁵. 2. Intrans., *to rise :* φῶς, Mt 4¹⁶ (= Is 9¹); ὁ ἥλιος, Mt 13⁶, Mk 4⁶ 16², Ja 1¹¹; νεφέλη, Lk 12⁵⁴; φωσφόρος, II Pe 1¹⁹; ὁ Κύριος, prob. with ref. to metaph. of sun or star, He 7¹⁴ (cf. ἐξ-ανατέλλω).†

ἀνα-τίθημι, [in LXX chiefly for חרם (Cremer, 546);] *to lay upon, set up,* etc. Mid. -εμαι, in late writers (Plut., al.; v. also MM, *VGT*, s.v.), *to set forth, declare :* Ac 25¹⁴, Ga 2².†

ἀνατολή, -ῆς, ἡ (< ἀνατέλλω), [in LXX chiefly for מזרח, קדים;] 1. *a rising :* of light, Lk 1⁷⁸. 2. *the sun-rising, the east* (MM, *VGT*, s.v.) : Mt 2², ⁹, Re 21¹³; ἀ. ἡλίου, Re 7² 16¹² (WH, pl.); pl., Mt 2¹ 8¹¹ 24²⁷, Lk 13²⁹, Mk 16 [alt. ending].†

ἀνα-τρέπω, [in LXX for דחה, הדף, etc.;] *to overturn, destroy :* Jo 2¹⁵, WH, txt.; metaph., *to subvert* (MM, *VGT*, s.v.) : II Ti 2¹⁸, Tit 1¹¹.†

** ἀνα-τρέφω, [in LXX: Wi 7⁴ B, IV Mac 10² 11¹⁵ א *;] *to nurse up, nourish, educate, bring up :* Lk 4¹⁶, WH, mg., Ac 7²⁰, ²¹, 22³.†

ἀνα-φαίνω, [in LXX for צדק hi., נבט;] *to bring to light, make to appear :* ἀναφάναντες τ. Κύπρον, i.e. *having sighted* C.: Ac 21³ WH; pass., *to appear, be made manifest :* Lk 19¹¹.†

ἀνα-φέρω, [in LXX chiefly for עלה hi., also for קטר hi., etc.;] 1. *to carry* or *lead up :* c. acc. pers., Mt 17¹, Mk 9²; pass., Lk 24⁵¹ (WH, reject, R, mg. omits); ἀ. τ. ἁμαρτίας ἐπὶ τ. ξύλον (v. Deiss., *BS*, 88 f.;

ICC, in l.; MM, *VGT*, s.v.): I Pe 2²⁴. 2. In LXX and NT, *to bring to the altar, to offer* (v. Hort on I Pe, l.c.): θυσίας, etc., He 7²⁷ 13¹⁵, I Pe 2⁵; ἐπὶ τ. θυσιαστήριον, Ja 2²¹ (v. Mayor, in l.). 3. *to bear, sustain* (cf. Nu 14³³, Is 53¹²): He 9²⁸.†

ἀνα-φωνέω, -ῶ, [in LXX for שמע hi., זכר hi. ;] *to cry out, exclaim :* Lk 1⁴² (Arist., al.).†

*† ἀνά-χυσις, -εως, ἡ (< ἀναχέω, *to pour out*), *a pouring out, over-flowing, excess :* metaph., I Pe 4⁴ (MM, *VGT*, s.v.).†

ἀνα-χωρέω, -ῶ, [in LXX for ברח, נוס, etc. ;] 1. *to go back.* 2. *to withdraw :* Mt 9²⁴; freq. in sense of avoiding danger (MM, *VGT*, s.v.), Mt 2¹² (but v. Thayer), ¹³, ¹⁴, ²² 4¹² 12¹⁵ 14¹³ 15²¹ 27⁵, Mk 3⁷, Jo 6¹⁵, Ac 23¹⁹ 26³¹.†

ἀνά-ψυξις, -εως ἡ (< ἀναψύχω), [in LXX : Ex 8¹⁵ ⁽¹¹⁾ (רְוָחָה)* ;] *a refreshing :* Ac 3¹⁹.†

ἀνα-ψύχω, [in LXX for נפש ni., חיה, etc. (freq. in sense of *revive, refresh oneself*);] *to refresh :* c. acc. pers., II Ti 1¹⁶ (MM, *VGT*, s.v.; Cremer, 588).†

* ἀνδραποδιστής, -οῦ, ὁ (< ἀνδράποδον, *a slave*, captured in war), *a slave-dealer, kidnapper :* I Ti 1¹⁰ (v. MM, *VGT*, s.v.).†

Ἀνδρέας, -ου, ὁ, *Andrew*, the Apostle : Mt 4¹⁸ 10², Mk 1¹⁶, ²⁹ 3¹⁸ 13³, Lk 6¹⁴, Jo 1⁴¹, ⁴⁵ 6⁸ 12²², Ac 1¹³.†

ἀνδρίζω, [in LXX for חזק, אמץ (Jos 1⁶ff., I Ch 22¹⁹, al.; in II Ki 10¹², Ps 27¹⁴ 31²ᵉ, combined with κρατιοῦσθαι, as in I Co, l.c.) ;] *to make a man of.* Mid., *to play the man* (cf. MM, *VGT*, s.v.) : I Co 16¹³.†

Ἀνδρόνικος, -ου, ὁ, *Andronicus :* Ro 16⁷.†

** ἀνδρο-φόνος, -ου, ὁ, [in LXX : II Mac 9²⁸ * ;] *a man-slayer :* I Ti 1⁹ (cf. φονεύς, and v. MM, *VGT*, s.v.).†

** ἀν-έγκλητος, -ον (< ἀ-, ἐγκαλέω), [in LXX : III Mac 5³¹ * ;] *not to be called to account, unreprovable, irreproachable, blameless :* I Co 1⁸, Col 1²², I Ti 3¹⁰, Tit 1⁶, ⁷.†

SYN. : ἄμεμπτος, ἀνεπίλημπτος (v. Tr., *Syn.*, § ciii ; Cremer, 742 ; MM, *VGT*, s.v.).

*† ἀν-εκδιήγητος, -ον (< ἀ-, ἐκδιηγέομαι), *inexpressible :* II Co 9¹⁵ (MM, *VGT*, s.v.).†

*† ἀν-εκ-λάλητος, -ον (< ἀ-, ἐκλαλέω), *unspeakable :* I Pe 1⁸.†ι

* ἀνέκλειπτος, -ον (< ἀ-, ἐκλείπω), *unfailing :* Lk 12³³ (MM, *VGT*, s.v.).†

* ἀν-εκτός, -όν (also in late Gk. -ή, -όν; < ἀνέχομαι), *tolerable :* compar., -ότερος, Mt 10¹⁵ 11²², ²⁴, Lk 10¹², ¹⁴.†

ἀν-ελεήμων, -ον (< ἀ-, ἐλεήμων), [in LXX for אַכְזָר ;] *without mercy :* Ro 1³¹.†

*† ἀν-έλεος, -ον (Attic ἀνηλεής, ἀνελεήμων; MM, *VGT*, s.v.), *merciless :* Ja 2¹³.†

*† ἀνεμίζω = Attic ἀνεμόω (< ἄνεμος) ; pass., *to be driven by the wind :* Ja 1⁶.†

ἄνεμος, -ου, ὁ, [in LXX for רוּחַ ;] *wind :* Mt 11⁷ 14²⁴, ³⁰, ³², Mk 4³⁷, ³⁹, ⁴¹ 6⁴⁸, ⁵¹, Lk 7²⁴, 8²³, ²⁴, Jo 6¹⁸, Ac 27⁷, ¹⁴, ¹⁵, Ja 3⁴, Re 6¹³ 7¹ ; pl.,

Mt 7²⁵, ²⁷ 8²⁶, ²⁷, Lk 8²⁵, Ac 27⁴, Ju ¹² ; οἱ τέσσαρες ἄ. τῆς γῆς, Re 7¹ ; hence the four quarters of the heavens (v. Deiss., *BS*, 248 ; MM, *VGT*, s.v.), Mt 24³¹, Mk 13²⁷ ; metaph., of variable teaching, Eph 4¹⁴.†

SYN.: πνεῦμα, πνοή (and cf. θύελλα, λαῖλαψ).

*⁺ ἀν-ένδεκτος, -ον (< ἀ- neg., ἔνδεκτος ; < ἐνδέχομαι), *impossible, inadmissible* : Lk 17¹.†

** ἀνεξεραύνητος (Rec. -εύνητος, as in Attic ; M, *Pr.*, 46), -ον (< ἐξ- ερευνάω), [in Sm. (-ευ-) : Pr., 25³ * ;] *unsearchable* : Ro 11³³.†

*⁺ ἀνεξί-κακος, -ον (< fut., ἀνέξομαι, κακός), *patiently forbearing* (cf. ἀνεξικακία, Wi 2¹⁹ ; and v. MM, *VGT*, s.v.) : ιι Ti 2²⁴.†

⁺ ἀνεξιχνίαστος, -ον (< ἀ- neg., ἐξιχνιάζω, *to track out* ; < ἴχνος), [in LXX : Jb 5⁹ 9¹⁰ 34²⁴ (אֵין חֵקֶר)* ;] *that cannot be traced out* : Ro 11³³, Eph 3⁸ (MM, *VGT*, s.v.).†

*⁺ ἀν-επ-αίσχυντος, -ον (< ἐπαισχύνομαι), *not to be put to shame* : ιι Ti 2¹⁵.†

* ἀν-επί-λημπτος (Rec. -ληπτος ; Bl., § 6, 8), -ον (< ἀ-, ἐπιλαμβάνω), *without reproach* : ι Ti 3² 5⁷ 6¹⁴.†

SYN.: ἄμεμπτος, ἀνέγκλητος. It is stronger than these, for it implies not only that the man is of good report, but that he is deservedly so (cf. MM, *VGT*, s.v.).

ἀν-έρχομαι, [in LXX : ιιι Ki 13¹² (הָלַךְ)* ;] *to go up* : Jo 6³, Ga 1¹⁷, ¹⁸ (cf. ἐπανέρχ- ; and on its use of "going up" to the capital, MM, *VGT*, s.v.).†

ἄνεσις, -εως, ἡ (< ἀνίημι), [in LXX : ιι Es 4²² (שְׁלָא), ιι Ch 23¹⁵, ι Es 4⁶², Wi 13¹³, Si 15²⁰ 26¹⁰ * ;] *a loosening, relaxation* : Ac 24²³ (RV, *indulgence* ; cf. MM, *VGT*, s.v.) ; by St. Paul, opp. to θλίψις, expressed or understood, *relief* : ιι Co 2¹³ 7⁵ 8¹³, ιι Th 1⁷.†

SYN.: ἀνάπαυσις (q.v.).

⁺ ἀν-ετάζω (< ἀνά, ἐτάζω, *to examine* ; v. MM, *VGT*, s.v.), [in LXX : Jg 6²⁹ (דָּרַשׁ), Es 2²³ (בָּקַשׁ), Da ᴛʜ Su ¹⁴ * ;] *to examine judicially* : Ac 22²⁴, ²⁹.†

ἄνευ, prep. c. gen. (rarer than χωρίς, q.v. ; cf. Ellic. on Eph 2¹² ; MM, *VGT*, 42), *without* : Mt 10²⁹, ι Pe 3¹ 4⁹.†

*⁺ ἀν-εύ-θετος, -ον (v. MM, *VGT*, s.v.), *not well placed, not fit* : Ac 27¹².†

** ἀν-ευρίσκω (ἀνά, εὑρίσκω), [in LXX : ιν Mac 3¹⁴ * ;] *to find out* by search, *discover* (v. Field, *Notes*, 47 f.) : Lk 2¹⁶, Ac 21⁴.†

ἀν-έχω, [in LXX chiefly for אָפַק hithp. ;] *to hold up* ; in NT always mid., *to bear with, endure* : in cl. most freq. c. acc., but in NT c. gen. pers., Mt 17¹⁷, Mk 9¹⁹, Lk 9⁴¹, ιι Co 11¹, ¹⁹, Eph 4², Col 3¹³ ; seq. μικρόν τι, c. gen. pers. and c. gen. rei, ιι Co 11¹ ; c. dat. rei, ιι Th 1⁴ (v M, *Th.*, in l.) ; seq. εἴ τις, ιι Co 11²⁰ ; absol., ι Co 4¹², ιι Co 11⁴ ; *to bear with = to listen to*, c. gen. pers., Ac 18¹⁴ ; c. gen. rei, ιι Ti 4³, He 13²² (cf. προσανέχω and MM, *VGT*, s.v.).†

ἀνεψιός, -οῦ, ὁ (cf. Lat. *nepos*), [in LXX : Nu 36¹¹ (בֶּן דּוֹד), To 7² 9⁶ א * ;] *a cousin* : Col 4¹⁰ (MM, *VGT*, s.v.).†

* ἄνηθον, -ου, τό, *anise :* Mt 23²³.†

ἀν-ήκω (ἀνά, ἥκω), [in LXX : Jos 23¹⁴ (בּוֹא), 1 Ki 27⁸, Si. prol. ¹⁰, I, II Mac₆*;] prop., *to have come up to ;* in later writers, impers. *it is due, it is befitting :* in ethical sense (MM, *VGT*, s.v.), Eph 5⁴, Col 3¹⁸ ; τὸ ἀνῆκον, Phm ⁸.†

* ἀν-ήμερος, -ον (ἀ-, ἥμερος), *not tame, savage* (MM, *VGT*, s.v.) : II Ti 3³.†

ἀνήρ, ἀνδρός, ὁ, [in LXX chiefly for אִישׁ, freq. אֱנוֹשׁ, also אָדָם, etc. ;] *a man,* Lat. *vir.* 1. As opp. to a woman, Ac 8¹², I Ti 2¹² ; as a *husband,* Mt 1¹⁶, Jo 4¹⁶, Ro 7², Tit 1⁶. 2. As opp. to a boy or infant, I Co 13¹¹, Eph 4¹³, Ja 3². 3. In appos. with a noun or adj., as ἀ. ἁμαρτωλός, Lk 5⁸ ; ἀ. προφήτης, 24¹⁹ ; freq. in terms of address, as ἀ. ἀδελφοί, Ac 1¹⁶ ; and esp. with gentilic names, as ἀ. Ἰουδαῖος, Ac 22³ ; ἀ. Ἐφέσιοι, 19³⁵. 4. In general, *a man, a male person :* = τις, Lk 8⁴¹, Ac 6¹¹.

SYN. : ἄνθρωπος, q.v. (cf. MM, *VGT*, s.v.).

ἀνθ-ίστημι (ἀντί, ἵστημι), [in LXX for עמד, יצב, etc.;] 1. in pres., impf., fut. and 1 aor. act., causal, *to set against.* 2. In mid. and pass., also pf. and 2 aor. act., *to withstand, resist, oppose :* c. dat., Mt 5³⁹, Lk 21¹⁵, Ac 6¹⁰ 13⁸, Ro 9¹⁹ 13², Ga 2¹¹, Eph 6¹³, II Ti 3⁸ 4¹⁵, Ja 4⁷, I Pe 5⁹.†

ἀνθ-ομολογέομαι, -οῦμαι (ἀντί, ὁμολογέομαι), [in LXX : Ps 78 (79) ¹³ (יָדָה), Da LXX 4³⁴ (שְׁבַח), I Es 8⁰¹, Si 20², III Mac 6³³ *;] 1. *to make a mutual agreement* (Dem., Polyb.). 2. *to* *acknowledge fully, confess* (Diod., Polyb., cf. I Es, l.c.). 3. C. dat. pers., *to declare one's praises,* speak fully in prayer or thanksgiving, *give thanks to* (cf. Ps, l.c.) : Lk 2³⁸ (Cremer, 771 ; MM, *VGT*, s.v.).†

ἄνθος, -εος, τό, [in LXX for צִיץ, etc. ;] *a flower :* Ja 1¹⁰, ¹¹, I Pe 1²⁴ (LXX).†

** ἀνθρακιά, -ᾶς, ἡ (< ἄνθραξ), [in LXX : Si 11³², IV Mac 9²⁰ *;] *a heap of burning coals :* Jo 18¹⁸ 21⁹.†

ἄνθραξ, -ακος, ὁ, [in LXX chiefly for גַּחֶלֶת ;] *coal, charcoal :* ἀ. πυρός, *a burning coal,* Ro 12²⁰.†

† ἀνθρωπ-άρεσκος, -ον (ἄνθρωπος, ἀρεσκος, *pleasing*), [in LXX : Ps 52 (53) ⁵ *;] *studying to please men :* Eph 6⁶, Col 3²² (Cremer, 642 ; MM, *VGT*, s.v.).†

ἀνθρώπινος, -η, ον (< ἄνθρωπος), [in LXX for אָדָם, אֱנוֹשׁ ;] *human,* belonging to man : χεῖρες, Ac 17²⁵ ; σοφία, I Co 2¹³ ; φύσις, Ja 3⁷ ; κτίσις, I Pe 2¹³ (MM, *VGT*, s.v.) ; ἀ. ἡμέρα, opp. to ἡ ἡμ. (3¹³, God's Judgment-Day), *human judgment,* I Co 4³ (v. Lft., *Notes,* 198) ; πειρασμὸς ἀ., *temptation such as man can bear* (AV, *such as is common to man,* v. Field, *Notes,* 175), I Co 10¹³ ; ἀνθρώπινον λέγω, *I speak in human fashion,* with words not properly weighed, Ro 6¹⁹ (v. Field, *Notes,* 156).†

*ἀνθρωποκτόνος, -ον (< κτείνω, to kill), a murderer, manslayer
(Eur.; v. MM, VGT, s.v.): Jo 8⁴⁴, 1 Jo 3¹⁵.†
   SYN.: φονεύς, ἀνδροφόνος (v. Tr., Syn. § lxxxiii).
ἄνθρωπος, -ου, ὁ, [in LXX chiefly for אָדָם, אִישׁ, also for אֱנוֹשׁ,
etc.;] man: 1. generically, a human being, male or female (Lat.
homo): Jo 16²¹; c. art., Mt 4⁴ 12³⁵, Mk 2²⁷, Jo 2²⁵, Ro 7¹, al.;
disting. from God, Mt 19⁶, Jo 10³³, Col 3²³, al.; from animals, etc.,
Mt 4¹⁹, Lk 5¹⁰, Re 9⁴, al.; implying human frailty and imperfection,
1 Co 3⁴; σοφία ἀνθρώπων, 1 Co 2⁵; ἀνθρώπων ἐπιθυμίαι, 1 Pe 4²; κατὰ
ἄνθρωπον περιπατεῖν, 1 Co 3³; κατὰ ἄ. λέγειν (λαλεῖν), Ro 3⁵, 1 Co 9⁸;
κατὰ ἄ- λέγειν, Ga 3¹⁵ (cf. 1 Co 15³², Ga 1¹¹); by meton., of man's
nature or condition, ὁ ἔσω (ἔξω) ἄ., Ro 7²², Eph 3¹⁶, 11 Co 4¹⁶ (cf.
1 Pe 3⁴); ὁ παλαιὸς, καινὸς, νέος ἄ., Ro 6⁶, Eph 2¹⁵ 4²², ²⁴, Col 3⁹, ¹⁰;
joined with another subst., ἄ. ἔμπορος, a merchant, Mt 13⁴⁵ (WH,
txt. om. ἄ.); οἰκοδεσπότης, Mt 13⁵²; βασιλεύς, 18²³; φάγος, 11¹⁹; with
name of nation, Κυρηναῖος, Mt 27³²; Ἰουδαῖος, Ac 21³⁹; Ῥωμαῖος,
Ac 16³⁷; pl. οἱ ἄ., men, people: Mt 5¹³, ¹⁶, Mk 8²⁴, Jo 4²⁸; οὐδεὶς
ἀνθρώπων, Mk 11², 1 Ti 6¹⁶. 2. Indef., ἄ. = τις, some one, a man:
Mt 17¹⁴, Mk 12¹, al.; τις ἄ., Mt 18¹², Jo 5⁵, al.; indef. one (Fr. on),
Ro 3²⁸, Ga 2¹⁶, al.; opp. to women, servants, etc., Mt 10³⁶ 19¹⁰,
Jo 7²², ²³. 3. Definitely, c. art., of some particular person; Mt 12¹³,
Mk 3⁵, al.; οὗτος ὁ ἄ., Lk 14³⁰; ὁ ἄ. οὗτος, ἐκεῖνος, Mk 14⁷¹, Mt 12⁴⁵;
ὁ ἄ. τ. ἀνομίας, 11 Th 2³; ἄ. τ. θεοῦ (of Heb. אִישׁ אֱלֹהִים), 1 Ti 6¹¹,
11 Ti 3¹⁷, 11 Pe 1²¹; ὁ υἱὸς τοῦ ἀ., v.s. υἱός.
   SYN.: ἀνήρ, q.v. (and cf. MM, VGT, 44; Cremer, 103, 635).
*†ἀνθ-υπατεύω (see next word), to be proconsul: Ac 18¹² Rec.
(v.s. ἀνθύπατος).†
   *ἀνθ-ύπατος, -ου, ὁ (ἀντί, ὕπατος, altern. for ὑπέρτατος, supreme), a
consul, one acting in place of a consul, a proconsul, the administrator
of a senatorial province (cf. ἡγεμών, and v. MM, VGT, 44): Ac 13⁷, ⁸, ¹²
18¹² 19³⁸.†
   ἀν-ίημι (ἀνά, ἵημι), [in LXX for רפה, נשׂא, etc.;] 1. to send up,
produce, to send back. 2. to let go, leave without support: He 13⁵
(cf. De 31⁶; Hom., Il., ii, 71). 3. to relax, loosen (v. Field, Notes,
124 f.): Ac 16²⁶ 27⁴⁰; hence, metaph., to give up, desist from : Eph 6⁹.†
   ἀν-ίλεως, -ων, v.s. ἀνέλεος.
   *ἄνιπτος, -ον (ἀ-neg., νίπτω), unwashed: Mt 15²⁰, Mk 7² (5 Rec.).†
   ἀν-ίστημι (ἀνά, ἵστημι), [in LXX chiefly for קום;] 1. causal, in put.
and 1 aor. act., c. acc., to raise up: Ac 9⁴¹; from death, Jo 6³⁹,
Ac 2³²; to raise up, cause to be born or appear: Mt 22²⁴, Ac 3²², ²⁶.
2. Intrans., in mid. and 2 aor act.; (a) to rise: from lying, Mk 1³⁵;
from sitting, Lk 4¹⁶; to leave a place, Mt 9⁹; pleonastically, as Heb.
קום, before verbs of going, Mk 10¹, al. (v. Dalman, Words, 23;
M, Pr., 14); of the dead, Mt 17²³, Mk 8³¹; seq. ἐκ νεκρῶν, Mt 17⁹,
Mk 9⁹; (b) to arise, appear: Ac 5³⁶, Ro 15¹² (cf. ἐπ-, ἐξ- ἀνίστημι, and
v. Cremer, 306, 738; MM, VGT, s.v.).
   SYN.: ἐγείρω.

Ἄννα, -ας, ἡ (Heb. חַנָּה), *Anna*, a prophetess: Lk 2³⁶.†

Ἄννας, -α (FlJ, Ἄνανος, -ου), ὁ (Heb. חָנָן), *Annas*, the high priest: Lk 3², Jo 18¹³, ²⁴, Ac 4⁶.†

ἀ-νόητος, -ον (ἀ- neg., νοητός; < νοέω), [in LXX: Pr 17²⁸ (אֱוִיל)], Si 42⁸, al. ;] 1. *not thought on, not understood* (Hom., Plat.). 2. *not understanding, foolish* (Hdt., al., LXX): Lk 24²⁵, Ro 1¹⁴, Ga 3¹, ³, ι Ti 6⁹, Tit 3³ (Cremer, 438, 790; MM, *VGT*, s.v.) ; cf. Ramsay, *Hist. Comm.* on Ga 3¹.†

SYN.: ἀσύνετος (v. Tr., *Syn.*, § lxxv).

ἄνοια, -ας, ἡ (< ἄ-νοος, *without understanding*), [in LXX: Pr 14⁸ 22¹⁵ (אִוֶּלֶת), Wi 15¹⁸, al. ;] *folly, foolishness*: ιι Ti 3⁹; expressed in violent rage (cf. Plat., *Tim.*, 86Β): Lk 6¹¹.†

ἀν-οίγω (ἀνά, οἴγω = οἴγνυμι), [in LXX chiefly for פתח ;] *to open*; 1. trans., c. acc.; a door or gate, Ac 5¹⁹ 12¹⁴, Re 4¹; pass., Ac 12¹⁰ 16²⁶, ²⁷; metaph. of opportunity or welcome, Ac 14²⁷, Col 4³, Re 3²⁰; pass., ι Co 16⁹, ιι Co 2¹², Re 3⁸; absol. (sc. θύραν), Ac 5²³ 12¹⁶; c. dat. pers., Lk 12³⁶, Jo 10³; metaph., Mt 7⁷, ⁸ 25¹¹, Lk 11⁹, ¹⁰ 13²⁵, Re 3⁷; θησαυρούς (Si 43¹⁴), Mt 2¹¹; τ. μνημεῖα, Mt 27⁵²; τάφος, Ro 3¹³; τ. φρέαρ, Re 9²; of heaven, Mt 3¹⁶, Lk 3²¹, Ac 10¹¹, Re 11¹⁹ 15⁵ 19¹¹; σφραγῖδα, Re 5⁹ 6¹ ff. 8¹; βιβλίον, βιβλαρίδιον, Lk 4¹⁷, Re 5²⁻⁵ 10², ⁸ 20¹²; τ. στόμα, Mt 17²⁷; id. Hebraistically (Nu 22²⁸, Jb 3¹, Is 50⁵, al.), of beginning to speak, Mt 5², Ac 8³², ³⁵ 10³⁴ 18¹⁴; seq. εἰς βλασφημίας, Re 13⁶; ἐν παραβολαῖς (Ps 77 (78)²), Mt 13³⁵; of recovering speech, Lk 1⁶⁴; of the earth opening, Re 12¹⁶; τ. ὀφθαλμούς, Ac 9⁸, ⁴⁰; id. c. gen. pers., of restoring sight, Mt 9³⁰ 20³³, Jo 9¹⁰ ff. 10²¹ 11³⁷; metaph., Ac 2⁶ʲ¹⁸; ἀκοάς, c. gen. pers., of restoring hearing, Mk 7³⁵. 2. Intrans. in 2 pf., ἀνέῳγα (M, *Pr.*, 154); heaven, Jo 1⁵¹; τ. στόμα, seq. πρός, of speaking freely, ιι Co 6¹¹ (cf. δι-ανοίγω and v. MM, *VGT*, 45).†

ἀν-οικς-δομέω, -ῶ, [in LXX for בנה, גדר ;] *to build again, rebuild* (MM, *VGT*, s.v.): Ac 15¹⁶.†

* ἄνοιξις, -εως, ἡ (< ἀνοίγω), *an opening* (in MGr., *springtime*): ἐν ἀ., *as often as I open*, Eph 6¹⁹.†

ἀνομία, -ας, ἡ (< ἄνομος), [in LXX for עָוֹן, רֶשַׁע, פֶּשַׁע, תּוֹעֵבָה, etc. ;] *lawlessness, iniquity*: Mt 7²³ 13⁴¹ 23²⁸ 24¹², Ro 6¹⁹, ιι Co 6¹⁴, ιι Th 2³, ⁷, Tit 2¹⁴, He 1⁹, ι Jo 3⁴; in pl. (as LXX, Ps 31¹, al.; v. Bl., § 32, 6; Swete, *Mk.*, 153), of acts or manifestations of lawlessness: Ro 4⁷ (LXX), He 10¹⁷.†

SYN.: v.s. ἁμάρτημα, ἄνομος.

ἄ-νομος, -ον (ἀ-neg., νόμος), [in LXX for עָוֹן, פֶּשַׁע, רֶשַׁע, etc. ;] 1. *lawless, wicked*: Mk 15²⁸, Lk 22³⁷, Ac 2²³, ι Ti 1⁹, ιι Pe 2⁸; ὁ ἄ., ιι Th 2⁸ (= ὁ ἄνθρωπος τῆς ἀνομίας, ib. 2³). 2. *without law* (= οἱ μὴ ὑπὸ νόμον, Ro 2¹⁴): ι Co 9²¹ (MM, *VGT*, s.v.).†

SYN.: v.s. ἄθεσμος.

** ἀνόμως, adv., [in LXX: ιι Mac 8¹⁷ *;] 1. *lawlessly* (ιι Mac, l.c.). 2. = χωρὶς νόμου, *without law*: Ro 2¹².†

ἀν-ορθόω, -ῶ (ἀνά, ὀρθόω, *to set straight, set up*), [in LXX chiefly for

בּוּן hi.;] *to set upright or straight again, restore :* of persons, Lk 13¹³, He 12¹²; of things, σκηνήν, Ac 15¹⁶ (MM, *VGT*, s.v.; Cremer, 807).†

ἀν-όσιος, -ον (ἀ- neg., ὅσιος), [in LXX : Ez 22⁹ (זִמָּה), Wi 12⁴, II Mac 7³⁴ 8³², III Mac 2² 5⁷, IV Mac 12¹¹ *;] *unholy, profane* (Cremer, 464) : I Ti 1⁹, II Ti 3² (MM, *VGT*, s.v.).†

** ἀνοχή, -ῆς, ἡ (< ἀνέχω, -ομαι), [in LXX : I Mac 12²⁵ (RV, *respite*)* ;] 1. in cl., *a holding back, delaying* (MM, *VGT*, s.v.). 2. *forbearance*, delay of punishment : Ro 2⁴ 3²⁶.†

SYN.: μακροθυμία, ὑπομονή. ἀ., *forbearance*, is the result and expression of μ., which involves the idea of tolerance, *long-suffering*, as God with sinners. ὑ. expresses patience with respect to things, as μ. with persons; it is active as well as passive, denotes not merely *endurance* but *perseverance* (v. Tr., *Syn.*, § liii; Lft., *Notes*, 259, 273; *DB*, ii, 47).

** ἀντ-αγωνίζομαι, depon., [in LXX : IV Mac 17¹⁴*;] *to struggle against :* seq. πρός, c. acc., He 12⁴.†

ἀντ-άλλαγμα, -τος, τό (ἀντί, ἄλλαγμα; < ἀλλάσσω), [in LXX chiefly for מְחִיר;] *an exchange*, the price received as an equivalent for an article of commerce : Mt 16²⁶, Mk 8³⁷ (cf. Si 26¹⁴; and v. Swete, *Mk.*, l.c.; Cremer, 90).†

* ἀντ-ανα-πληρόω, -ῶ (ἀντί, ἀναπληρόω), *to fill up in turn :* Col 1²⁴ (v. Lft., in l.; MM, *VGT*, s.v.).†

ἀντ-απο-δίδωμι (ἀντί, ἀποδίδωμι), [in LXX for שׁלם pi., גָּמַל, שׁוּב hi., etc.;] *to give back as an equivalent, recompense, requital* (the ἀντί expressing the idea of full, complete return; v. Lft., *Notes*, 46) ; (*a*) in favourable sense : Lk 14¹⁴, Ro 11³⁵, I Th 3⁹; (*b*) in unfavourable sense : Ro 12¹⁹, II Th 1⁶, He 10³⁰.†

† ἀντ-από-δομα, -τος, τό (< ἀνταποδίδωμι), [in LXX chiefly for גְּמוּל;] (= cl. -δοσις, q.v.), *requital;* (*a*) in favourable sense : Lk 14¹²; (*b*) in unfavourable sense : Ro 11⁹.†

ἀντ-από-δοσις, -εως, ἡ (v. supr.), [in LXX chiefly for גְּמוּל, שׁלּוּם;] *recompense :* Col 3²⁴ (MM, *VGT*, s.v.).†

† ἀντ-απο-κρίνομαι (ἀντί, ἀποκρίνω), [in LXX : Jg 5²⁹, Jb 16⁹ ⁽ ⁸ ⁾ 32¹² (ענה)* ;] *to answer again, reply against :* seq. πρός, c. acc. rei, Lk 14⁶ ; c. dat. pers., Ro 9²⁰.†

ἀντ-εῖπον (ἀντί, εἶπον), [in LXX for שׁוּב hi., דבר pi., ענה etc.;] 2 aor., without present in use, *to speak against, gainsay :* Lk 21¹⁵, Ac 4¹⁴.†

ἀντ-έχω (ἀντί, ἔχω), [in LXX for חָזַק hi., etc.;] 1. trans., *to hold against*. 2. Intrans., *to withstand*. Mid. 1. in cl., *to hold out against*. 2. (cf. MM, *VGT*, s.v.), *to hold firmly to, cleave to :* c. gen. (v. Bl., § 36, 2), Mt 6²⁴, Lk 16¹³, I Th 5¹⁴ (v. M, *Th.*, in l.), Tit 1⁹.†

ἀντί (the ι is elided only in ἀνθ' ὧν), prep. c. gen. (cf. MM, *VGT*, s.v.); 1. prop. in local sense, *over against, opposite*, hence ; 2. *instead of, in place of, for* (Hom., etc.) : Mt 5³⁸ 17²⁷, Lk 11¹¹, I Co 11¹⁵, He 12²; c. artic. inf. (cl.), Ja 4¹⁵; of succession, Mt 2²²; χάριν ἀ. χάριτος, Jo 1¹⁶ (M, *Pr.*, 100) ; of price in exchange, He 12¹⁶; λύτρον ἀ. πολλῶν, Mt 20²⁸, Mk 10⁴⁵ (M, *Pr.*, 105) ; of requital, Ro 12¹⁷, 1 Th 5¹⁵, ι Pe 3⁹ (cf. Wi 11¹⁵); ἀνθ' ὧν, *because*, Lk 1²⁰ 19⁴⁴, Ac 12²³, ιι Th 2¹⁰ (cl., LXX for תחת אשר); id. *therefore* (cl., LXX), Lk 12³; ά. τούτου (LXX for על־בן), Eph 5³¹. As a prefix, ἀντι- (before vowels ἀντ-, ἀνθ'-), denotes (a) *over against*, ἀντιπέραν; (b) *co-operation*, ἀντιβάλλειν; (c) *requital*, ἀντιμισθία; (d) *opposition*, ἀντίχριστος; (e) *substitution*, ἀνθύπατος. Compounds of ά. usually govern dat. (Bl., § 37, 7).†

** ἀντι-βάλλω, [in LXX : ιι Mac 11¹³ *;] *to throw in turn, exchange* : metaph., λόγους (cf. Lat. *conferre sermones;* v. Field,*Notes*, 81), Lk 24¹⁷.†

*† ἀντι-δια-τίθημι, in mid. *to place oneself in opposition, oppose* : ιι Ti 2²⁵ (EV; but v. Field, *Notes*, 215 f.; cf. MM, *VGT*, s.v.).†

ἀντίδικος, -ον (< δίκη), [in LXX for ריב;] as subst., *an opponent in a lawsuit, adversary* : Mt 5²⁵, Lk 12⁵⁸ 18³, ι Pe 5⁸ (Cremer, 696; MM, *VGT*, s.v.).†

* ἀντί-θεσις, -εως, ἡ (< τίθημι), *opposition* : ι Ti 6²⁰.†

ἀντι-καθ-ίστημι, [in LXX : De 31²¹ (ענה), Jos 5⁷, Mi 2⁸ (קום) *;] 1. causal in pres. impf. fut. and 1 aor.; *to replace, oppose.* 2. Intrans. in pass. and 2 aor. act.; (a) *to supersede;* (b) *to resist* : He 12⁴.†

* ἀντι-καλέω, -ῶ, *to invite in turn* : Lk 14¹².†

ἀντί-κειμαι, [in LXX for איב, צור, שׂטן, etc.;] 1. *to lie opposite to.* 2. *to oppose, withstand, resist* : c. dat., Lk 13¹⁷ 21¹⁵, Ga 5¹⁷, ι Ti 1¹⁰; as participial subst. (ὁ) ἀντικείμενος, ι Co 16⁹, Phl 1²⁸, ιι Th 2⁴, ι Ti 5¹⁴ (Cremer, 746).†

** ἄντικρυς (Tr. -ύς, Rec. ἀντικρύ), adv. (< ἀντί), [in LXX : Ne 12⁸ (לנגד), ιιι Mac 5¹⁶ *;] in cl., *outright;* in κοινή (= cl. καταντικρύ), *over against* : Ac 20¹⁵ (v. Bl., § 5, 4; 40, 7; Rutherford, *NPhr.*, 500 f.; MM, *VGT*, s.v.).†

ἀντι-λαμβάνω, [freq. in LXX for חזק hi., תמך, etc.;] *to take instead of* or *in turn.* Mid., c. gen., *to take hold of;* (a) of persons, *to help* (v. MM, *VGT*, s.v.) : Lk 1⁵⁴, Ac 20³⁵; (b) of things, *to partake of* : ι Ti 6² (v. Field, *Notes*, 210; Cremer, 386; and cf. συν-αντιλαμβάνω).†

ἀντι-λέγω, [in LXX : Ho 4⁴ (ריב hi.), Is 50⁵(סות ni.) 22²² 65², Si 4²⁵, ιιι Mac 2²⁸, ιv Mac 4⁷ 8² *;] *contradict, oppose, resist* (v. Field, *Notes*, 106; MM, *VGT*, s.v.); absol.: Ac 28¹⁹, Ro 10²¹, Tit 1⁹ 2⁹; c. dat., Jo 19¹², Ac 13⁴⁵; c. acc. et inf., Lk 20²⁷ T; pass., Lk 2³⁴, Ac 28²².†

ἀντί-λημψις, (Rec. -ληψις; v. MM, *VGT* s.v.; M, *Pr.*, 56), -εως, ἡ (< ἀντιλαμβάνομαι), [in LXX for עז, זרוע, etc., freq. in Pss and ιι, ιιι Mac.; freq. also in π. in petitions to the Ptolemies in sense of βοήθεια (v. Deiss., *LAE*, 107; *BS*, 92, 223);] 1. cl., *a laying hold of, an exchange.* 2. Hellenistic (LXX, π.), *help* : pl. of ministrations of deacons; ι Co 12²⁸ (*DB*, ii, 347 f.; Cremer, 386).†

ἀντί-ληψις, v.s. ἀντίλημψις.

ἀντιλογία, -ας, ἡ (< ἀντιλέγω), [in LXX chiefly for ריב;] *gainsaying, strife* (the latter sense being found in π.; v. MM, *VGT*, s.v.; cf. Field, *Notes*, 106) : He 6¹⁶ 7⁷ 12³, Ju ¹¹.†

* ἀντι-λοιδορέω, -ῶ, to revile in turn : 1 Pe 2²³.†
**† *ἀντί-λυτρον,* -ον, τό, [in Al. : Ps 48 (49)⁹ *;] a ransom : 1 Ti 2⁶
(v. *CGT,* in l. ; and cf. λύτρον).†
*† *ἀντι-μετρέω, -ῶ,* to measure in return : Lk 6³⁸ (WH, mg.,
μετρέω).†
*† *ἀντιμισθία,* -ας, ἡ (< ἀντίμισθος, for a reward), a reward, requital :
in good sense, II Co 6¹³ ; in bad sense, Ro 1²⁷ (MM, *VGT,* s.v.).†
Ἀντιόχεια, -ας, ἡ, Antioch ; 1. in Syria : Ac 11¹⁹, ²⁰, ²², ²⁶, ²⁷ 13¹ 14²⁶
15²², ²³, ³⁰, ³⁵ 18²², Ga 2¹¹. 2. In Pisidia : Ac 13¹⁴ 14¹⁹, ²¹, II Ti 3¹¹.†
Ἀντιοχεύς, -έως, ὁ, a citizen of Antioch, an Antiochian : Ac 6⁵.†
**† *ἀντι-παρ-έρχομαι,* [in LXX : Wi 16¹⁰ *;] to pass by opposite to :
Lk 10³¹, ³² (MM, *VGT,* s.v.).†
Ἀντίπας (T, *Ἀντείπας*), -α (in some MSS. it appears to be indecl. ;
but v. M, *Pr.,* 12 ; it is abbrev. from *Ἀντίπατρος*), ὁ, Antipas : Re 2¹³.†
Ἀντιπατρίς, -ίδος, ἡ, Antipatris, bet. Joppa and Caesarea :
Ac 23³¹.†
*† *ἀντί-περα* (Rec. ἀντιπέραν, LTr. ἀντιπέρα), adv., = cl. ἀντιπέρας
(MM, *VGT,* 49), on the opposite side : c. gen., Lk 8²⁶.†
ἀντι-πίπτω, [in LXX : Ex 26⁵ (קבל), ib. ¹⁷ (שלב), Nu 27¹⁴ (מְרִיבָה),
Jb 23¹³ (שׁוּב hi.) *;] 1. to fall against or upon (Arist., Polyb.). 2. to
strive against, resist (Arist.) : c. dat., Ac 7⁵¹.†
* ἀντι-στρατεύομαι, to make war against : c. dat., Ro 7²³.†
ἀντι-τάσσω (Att., -ττω), [in LXX for לִרִיץ hi., נשׂא, etc. ;] to range
in battle against ; mid., to set oneself against, resist : absol., Ac 18⁶ ;
c. dat., Ro 13², Ja 4⁶ 5⁶, 1 Pe 5⁵ (MM, *VGT,* s.v.).†
** *ἀντί-τυπος,* -ον (v.s. τύπος), [in LXX : Es 3¹³ A *;] 1. act. striking
back ; metaph., resisting, adverse. 2. Pass. struck back ; metaph., corresponding to (MM, *VGT,* s.v.) ; (a) as impression of a seal or copy of
an archetype (τύπος) (RV, like in pattern), He 9²⁴ ; (b) as the reality (of
which τύπος is the copy or adumbration) (RV, after a true likeness),
1 Pe 3²¹ (Cremer, 357).†
*† *ἀντί-χριστος,* -ον, ὁ, Antichrist, "one who assuming the guise of
Christ opposes Christ" (Westc., *Epp. Jo.,* 70) : 1 Jo 2¹⁸, ²² 4³, II Jo⁷ ;
pl. 1 Jo 2¹⁸ (cf. ψευδόχριστος, and v. MM, *VGT,* s.v.).†
ἀντλέω, -ῶ (< ἄντλος, bilge-water in a hold), [in LXX for שׁאב,
etc. ;] 1. prop., to bale out. 2. Generally, to draw water : absol., Jo 2⁸
4¹⁵ ; ὕδωρ, Jo 2⁹ 4⁷ (on its use of the water made wine, v. *DCG,* ii,
815ᵃ ; MM, *VGT,* s.v. ; Field, *Notes,* 84 f.).†
*† *ἄντλημα,* -τος, τό (< ἀντλέω), (a) prop., what is drawn (Diosc.) ;
(b) a vessel to draw with, a bucket (Plut. ; v. Abbott, *Essays,* 88) :
Jo 4¹¹.†
**† *ἀντοφθαλμέω, -ῶ* (ἀντί, ὀφθαλμός), [in LXX : Wi 12¹⁴ *;] to look in
the face, look straight at (Polyb.). Metaph., to face, withstand (Wi,
l.c., Polyb.) : c. dat., ἀ. τ. ἀνέμῳ, as nautical term, to beat up against
the wind (v. *DB,* ext., 366 f. ; MM, *VGT,* s.v.) : Ac 27¹⁵.†
ἄνυδρος, -ον (< ἀ- neg., ὕδωρ), [in LXX for צִיָּה, יְשִׁימוֹן (γῆ ἄ.),

etc.;] *waterless:* τόποι, Mt 12⁴³, Lk 11²⁴; πηγαί, II Pe 2¹⁷; νεφέλαι, Ju¹² (MM, *VGT*, s.v.).†

**ἀν-υπόκριτος, -ον (< ἀ- neg., ὑποκρίνομαι), [in LXX : Wi 5¹⁸ 18¹⁶ *;] *unfeigned:* Ro 12⁹, II Co 6⁶, I Ti 1⁵, II Ti 1⁵, Ja 3¹⁷, I Pe 1²² (Cremer, 380 ; MM, *VGT*, s.v.).†

**† ἀνυπότακτος, -ον (< ἀ- neg., ὑποτάσσω), [in Sm. : I Ki 2¹² 10²⁷ (for LXX, λοιμός, בְּנֵי בְלִיַּעַל)*;] of things, *not subject to rule:* He 2⁸; of persons, *unruly:* I Ti 1⁹, Tit 1⁶, ¹⁰ (MM, *VGT*, s.v.).†

ἄνω, adv. (< ἀνά), (a) *up, upwards:* Jo 11⁴¹, He 12¹⁵; (b) *above* (opp. to κάτω): Ac 2¹⁹; with art. ἡ, Ga 4²⁶, Phl 3¹⁴; τά, Jo 8²³, Col 3¹, ²; ἕως ἅ. (*up to the brim*), Jo 2⁷ (Cremer, 106; MM, *VGT*, s.v.).†

ἀνώγαιον, ἀνώγεον, v.s. ἀνάγαιον.

ἄνωθεν, adv. (< ἄνω), (a) *from above:* ἀπὸ ἅ., Mt 27⁵¹, Mk 15³⁸; ἐκ τῶν ἅ., Jo 19²³; meaning, from heaven: Jo 3³¹ 19¹¹, Ja 1¹⁷ 3¹⁵, ¹⁷; (b) *from the first, from the beginning:* Lk 1³, Ac 26⁵; whence (c) *anew, again:* Jo 3³, ⁷, (so most, but v. Meyer, in l.; cf. Field, *Notes*, 86 f.); πάλιν ἅ., Ga 4⁹ (MM, *VGT*, s.v.).†

* ἀνωτερικός, -ή, -όν (< ἀνώτερος), *upper:* Ac 19¹.†

ἀνώτερος, α, -ον, [in LXX : Ne 3²⁵ (עֶלְיוֹן), Ez 41⁷ (מַעַל), To 8³ *;] only in neut., as adv. (cf. ἐξώτερος), (a) of motion, *higher:* Lk 14¹⁰; (b) of rest, *above, before:* He 10⁸.†

ἀν-ωφελής, -ές (ἀ- neg., ὄφελος), [in LXX: Is 44¹⁰ (בִּלְתִּי הוֹעִיל), Je 2⁸ (לֹא הוֹעִיל), Pr 28³, Wi 1¹¹ *;] *unprofitable:* Tit 3⁹; neut. as subst., *unprofitableness:* He 7¹⁸.†

ἀξίνη, -ης, ἡ, [in LXX for גַּרְזֶן, קַרְדֹּם;] *an axe:* Mt 3¹⁰, Lk 3⁹.†

ἄξιος, -α, -ον (< ἄγω, in sense, *to weigh*), [in LXX for בֶּ (De 25²), שָׁוָה מָלֵא; freq. in Wi, II Mac;] (a) *of weight, worth* (often c. gen., cf. Pr 3¹⁵ 8¹¹), seq. πρός: Ro 8¹⁸ (v. Field, *Notes*, 157); (b) *befitting, meet:* c. gen., Mt 3⁸, Lk 3⁸ 23⁴¹, Ac 26²⁰, I Co 16⁴ (v. M, *Pr.*, 216); absol., II Th 1³; (c) of persons, *worthy;* (α) in good sense : c. gen. rei, Mt 10¹⁰, Lk 7⁴ 10⁷, Ac 13⁴⁶, I Ti 1¹⁵ 4⁹ 5¹⁸ 6¹; c. aor. inf. (v. M, *Pr.*, 203): Lk 15¹⁹, ²¹, Ac 13²⁵, Re 4¹¹ 5², ⁴, ⁹, ¹²; seq. ἵνα: Jo 1²⁷; ὅς, Lk 7⁴; absol., but of what understood: Mt 10¹¹, ¹³ 22⁸, Re 3⁴; c. gen. pers., Mt 10³⁷, ³⁸, He 11³⁸; (β) in bad sense; c. gen. rei, Lk 12⁴⁸ 23¹⁵, Ac 23²⁹ 25¹¹, ²⁵ 26³¹, Ro 1³²; absol., Re 16⁶ (MM, *VGT*, s.v.).†

ἀξιόω, -ῶ (< ἄξιος), [in LXX chiefly for בָּעָא, בִּקֵּשׁ; freq. in Wi, I, II Mac;] (a) *to deem worthy:* c. acc. et inf. (v. MM, *VGT*, s.v., and cf. κατ-αξιόω), Lk 7⁷; id. et gen. rei, II Th 1¹¹; pass. c. gen. rei, I Ti 5¹⁷, He 3³ 10²⁹; (b) *to think fit:* c. inf. (v. M, *Pr.*, 205), Ac 15³⁸ 28²².†

** ἀξίως, adv., [in LXX: Wi 7¹⁵ 16¹, Si 14¹¹ *;] *worthily:* Ro 16², Eph 4¹, Phl 1²⁷; c. gen. (freq. in Inscr.; Deiss., *BS*, 248; MM, *VGT*, 51), ἀ. τ. Κυρίου, Col 1¹⁰; τ. θεοῦ, I Th 2¹², III Jo⁶.†

ἀόρατος, -ον (< ὁράω), [in LXX: Ge 1² (תֹהוּ), Is 45³ (מִסְתָּר), II Mac 9⁵ *;] *unseen, invisible:* Ro 1²⁰, Col 1¹⁵, ¹⁶, I Ti 1¹⁷, He 11²⁷.†

ἀπ-αγγέλλω, [in LXX chiefly for נגד hi. ;] of a messenger, speaker, or writer, *to report, announce, declare :* c. acc. rei, Ac 4²³, al.; c. dat. pers., Mt 2⁸, al. ; seq. ὅτι, Lk 18³⁷; πῶς, Lk 8³⁶; περί, Lk 7¹⁸ 13¹, Ac 28²¹, ι Th 1⁹ ; λέγων, Ac 22²⁶ ; c. acc. et inf., Ac 12¹⁴ ; seq. εἰς, Mk 5¹⁴, Lk 8³⁴ (MM, *VGT*, s.v.; Cremer, 25).

ἀπ-άγχω (< ἄγχω, *to press, strangle*), [in LXX : ιι Ki 17²³ (חנק), To 3¹⁰ *;] *to strangle ;* mid., *to hang oneself* (or, *to choke;* v. M, *Pr.*, 155) : Mt 27⁵.†

ἀπ-άγω, [in LXX for נהג, הלך hi., etc. ;] *to lead away :* Lk 13¹⁵, Ac 23¹⁷ 24⁷ (R, mg.), ι Co 12² ; esp. of leading to trial (so as law term in Attic), prison and death (MM, *VGT*, s.v.) : Mt 26⁵⁷ 27², ³¹, Mk 14⁴⁴, ⁵³ 15¹⁶, Lk 21¹² 22⁶⁶ 23²⁶, Ac 12¹⁹ ; of the direction of a way : Mt 7¹³,¹⁴ (cf. συν-απ-άγω).†

ἀ-παίδευτος, -ον (< παιδεύω), [in LXX for בָּסִיל, etc., chiefly in Wi. lit. ;] *uninstructed, ignorant :* ιι Ti 2²³.†

ἀπ-αίρω, [in LXX chiefly for נסע ;] *to lift off*, hence, *to take away ;* pass. : Mt 9¹⁵, Mk 2²⁰, Lk 5³⁵.†

ἀπ-αιτέω, -ῶ, [in LXX : De 15², ³, al. (נשׁה), Si 20¹⁵, Wi 15⁸, al. ;] *to ask back, demand back :* Lk 6³⁰ 12²⁰ (MM, *VGT*, s.v.).†

* ἀπ-αλγέω, -ῶ, 1. prop., *to cease to feel pain for* (Thuc., ii, 61). 2. In late Gk. (*a*) *to despair* (Polyb., i, 35, 5) ; (*b*) *to become callous, reckless* (Polyb., xvi, 12, 7 ; MM, *VGT*, s.v.) : Eph 4¹⁹.†

ἀπ-αλλάσσω, [in LXX for סור hi., etc. ;] *to remove, release :* He 2¹⁵ ; pass., *to depart :* Ac 19¹² ; in legal sense (MM, *VGT*, s.v.), seq. ἀπό, c. gen. pers., *to be quit of :* Lk 12⁵⁸ (Cremer, 90, 632).†

ἀπ-αλλοτριόω, -ῶ, [in LXX for זוּר נזר, etc. ;] *to alienate, estrange ;* pass. : Eph 2¹² 4¹⁸, Col 1²¹ (MM, *VGT*, s.v. ; Cιemer, 95, 633).†

ἀπαλός, -ή, -όν, [in LXX for רַךְ ;] *tender :* Mt 24³², Mk 13²⁸.†

ἀπαντάω, -ῶ, [in LXX chiefly for פגע ;] 1. *to go to meet.* 2. *to meet ;* c. dat. : Mk 14¹³, Lk 17¹² (WH, mg., ὑπ- ; in Rec. freq. as v.l. for ὑπ-, q.v.).†

ἀπάντησις, -εως, ἡ (< ἀπαντάω), [in LXX chiefly for לִקְרַאת ;] usually with v.l., ὑπ- ; *a meeting ;* εἰς ἀ., c. gen. or dat., *to meet :* Mt 25⁶ 27³² (WH, txt., omits), Ac 28¹⁵, ι Th 4¹⁷ (v. M, *Th.*, in l.; M, *Pr.*, 14, 242 ; MM, *VGT*, s.v. ; Lft., *Notes*, 69).†

ἅπαξ, adv., [in LXX for אֶחָד פַּעַם ;] (*a*) *once :* ιι Co 11²⁵, He 9²⁶, ²⁷ ; ἔτι ἅ., He 12²⁶, ²⁷ ; ἅ. τ. ἐνιαυτοῦ, He 9⁷ ; καὶ ἅ. κ. δίς, *twice :* Phl 4¹⁶, ιι Th 2¹⁸ ; (*b*) *once for all :* He 6⁴ 9²⁸ 10², ι Pe 3¹⁸, Ju ³, ⁵ (MM, *VGT*, s.v.).†

*† ἀ-παρά-βατος, -ον (< παραβαίνω), *inviolable*, and so unchangeable : He 7²⁴ (v. Westc., in l.; Cremer, 653 ; MM, *VGT*, s.v.).†

* ἀ-παρα-σκεύαστος, -ον (< παρασκευάζω), *unprepared :* ιι Co 9⁴.†

ἀπ-αρνέομαι (-οῦμαι), depon., [in LXX : Is 31⁷ (מאס) *;] *to deny*, i.e. to refuse to recognize, to ignore : c. acc., of oneself (*DCG*, ii, 598 f.), Mt 16²⁴, Mk 8³⁴ (MM, *VGT*, s.v.), Lk 9²³ (WH, mg., txt., ἀρν-) ; of Peter's denials of Christ, Mt 26³⁴, ³⁵, ⁷⁵, Mk 14³⁰, ³¹, ⁷², Lk 22³⁴, ⁶¹, pass., Lk 12⁹ (Cremer, 111).†

* ἀπάρτι (WH, ἀπ' ἄρτι; cl., ἀπαρτί, v. MM, *VGT*, s.v.); adv., [not in LXX, where מֵעַתָּה is rendered by ἀπὸ τοῦ νῦν;] *from now, henceforth*: Jo 13¹⁹ 14⁷, Re 14¹³.†

*† ἀπαρτισμός, -οῦ, ὁ (< ἀπαρτίζω, *to finish*), *completion*: Lk 14²⁸ (cf. MM, *VGT*, s.v.).†

ἀπ-αρχή, -ῆς, ἡ (< ἀπάρχομαι, *to make a beginning* in sacrifice, *offer first fruits*), [in LXX chiefly for תְּרוּמָה, רֵאשִׁית;] 1. *the beginning of a sacrifice.* 2. *first fruits*: τοῦ φυράματος (cf. Nu 15²⁰), Ro 11¹⁶. Metaph., ἀ. τοῦ πνεύματος: Ro 8²³; of Christians: Ro 16⁵, ι Co 16¹⁵, ιι Th 2¹³ (WH, mg., R, mg., txt., ἀπ' ἀρχῆς; v. Lft., *Notes*, 119 f.), Ja 1¹⁸, Re 14⁴; of Christ: ι Co 15²⁰, ²³ (Cremer, 117; MM, *VGT*, s.v.).†

ἅπας, -ασα, -αν (strengthened form of πᾶς, v.s. ἅ-), *all, the whole, altogether*: bef. subst. with art., as Lk 3²¹; or after, as Mk 16[15]; absol., in masc., as Lk 5²⁶; in neut., as Ac 2⁴⁴; ἅ. οὗτοι, Ac 2⁷ (LT); ἅ. ὑμεῖς, Ga 3²⁸ (TTr.). Most freq. in Lk, Ac (v. MM, *VGT*, s.v.).

**† ἀπ-ασπάζομαι, depon., [in LXX: To 10¹³ א *;] *to take leave of*: c. acc.: Ac 21⁶.†

ἀπατάω, -ῶ (< ἀπάτη), [in LXX for פתה, נשׁא hi., etc.;] *to deceive*: c. acc., Ja 1²⁶; c. acc. pers., dat. rei, Eph 5⁶; pass., ι Ti 2¹⁴ (on its infrequency in late writers, v. MM, *VGT*, s.v.; cf. ἐξαπατάω).†

ἀπάτη, -ης, ἡ, [in LXX: Ec 9⁶ א (no Heb. equiv.), Jth 9³, ¹⁰, ¹³ 16⁸, ιv Mac 18⁸ *;] *deceit, deceitfulness*: Col 2⁸; τοῦ πλούτου, Mt 13²², Mk 4¹⁹ (MM, *VGT*, s.v.); τῆς ἀδικίας, ιι Th 2¹⁰; τῆς ἁμαρτίας, He 3¹³; αἱ ἐπιθυμίαι τῆς ἀ., Eph 4²². Pl., ἀπάται (v. M, *Th.*, l.c.; *NTD*, 75; MM, l.c.): ιι Pe 2¹³ (WH, mg., R., txt., ἐν ἀγάπαις).†

* ἀπάτωρ, -ορος, ὁ, ἡ (< ἀ- neg., πατήρ); 1. *fatherless.* 2. *without father* (MM, *VGT*, s.v.), i.e., with no recorded genealogy: He 7³.†

**† ἀπ-αύγασμα, -τος, τό (< αὐγή, *brightness*, whence ἀπαυγάζω, *to radiate* or *reflect*), [in LXX: Wi 7²⁶ *;] of light beaming from a luminous body, *radiance, effulgence*: He 1³.†

ἀπ-εῖδον (WH, ἀφ-, v. Bl., § 4, 3), 2 aor. without present in use (cf. εἶδον), serving as aor. to ἀφοράω, q.v.

** ἀπείθεια (WH, -θία, exc. He, ll. c.), -ας, ἡ (< ἀπειθής), [in LXX ιv Mac 8⁹, ¹⁸ 12⁴ *;] *disobedience* (MM, *VGT*, s.v.): Ro 11³⁰, ³², He 4⁶, ¹¹; υἱοὶ τῆς ἀ. (gen. of definition, v. M, *Pr.*, 73 f.), Eph 2² 5⁶, Col 3⁶ (T, WH, R, mg., omit).†

ἀπειθέω, -ῶ (< ἀπειθής), [in LXX for מרה, סרר, etc.;] as in cl. (MM, *VGT*, s.v.); *to disobey, be disobedient*: absol., Ac 14² 19⁹, Ro 10²¹ 11³¹ 15³¹, He 3¹⁸ 11³¹, ι Pe 3²⁰; c. dat., Jo 3³⁶, Ro 2⁸ 11³⁰, ι Pe 2⁸ 3¹ 4¹⁷ (Cremer, 475).†

ἀπειθής, -ές (< πείθομαι), [in LXX for מרה, מְרִי, סרר;] *disobedient*: absol., Lk 1¹⁷, Tit 1¹⁶ 3³; c. dat., Ac 26¹⁹, Ro 1³⁰ ιι Ti 3².†

ἀπειθία, -ας, ἡ, v.s. ἀπείθεια.

ἀπειλέω, -ῶ (ἀπειλή), [in LXX: Na 1⁴ (גער), Is 66¹⁴ (זעם), Si 19¹⁷, al.;] *to threaten*: 1 Pe 2²³; mid., Ac 4¹⁷ (v. MM, *VGT*, s.v., and cf. προσαπειλέω).†

ἀπειλή, -ῆς, ἡ, [in LXX for גְּעָרָה, etc.;] *threatening, threat*: Ac 4²⁹ 9¹, Eph 6⁹.†

ἄπ-ειμι (εἰμί, *sum*), [in LXX for כֻּחֵד ni., נדח ni.;] *to be absent*: 1 Co 5³, 11 Co 10¹⋅¹¹ 13²⋅¹⁰, Phl 1²⁷, Col 2⁵.†

* ἄπ-ειμι (εἶμι, *ibo*), *to depart*: Ac 17¹⁰ (*went their way*, RV; cf. Blass, *Comm.*, 17 f.).†

ἀπ-εῖπον, 2 aor. without present in use, [in LXX for מאס, אמר, etc.;] 1. *to tell out*. 2. *to forbid* (111 Ki 11²). 3. *to renounce*: 1 aor. mid. (WH, *App.*, 164; MM, *VGT*, s.v.), 11 Co 4².†

*† ἀπείραστος, -ον (< πειράζω; for cl. ἀπείρητος, < πειράω), *untempted untried, without experience*: Ja 1¹³ (v. Hort, in l.; MM, *VGT*, s.v.).†

ἄπειρος, -ον (< ἀ- neg., πεῖρα, *trial*), [in LXX: Nu 14²³, Za 11¹ᶜ (אֱוִילִי), Je 2⁶ (עֲרָבָה) *;] *without experience of*: c. gen. rei, He 5¹³ (MM, *VGT*, s.v.).†

*† ἀπ-εκ-δέχομαι, depon., *to await* or *expect eagerly* (Lft., *Notes*, 149; MM, *VGT*, s.v.): absol., 1 Pe 3²⁰; c. acc. rei, Ro 8¹⁹⋅²³⋅²⁵, 1 Co 1⁷, Ga 5⁵; c. acc. pers., Phl 3²⁰, He 9²⁸.†

*† ἀπ-έκ-δυσις, -εως, ἡ (ἀπεκδύω), *a putting* or *stripping off*: Col 2¹¹ (MM, *VGT*, s.v.).†

*† ἀπ-εκ-δύω, *to strip off* clothes or arms; mid., *to strip off from oneself*: Col 3⁹; *to strip, despoil* (mid. for act., ICC, in l.; but cf. Lft., Ellic.), Col 2¹⁵.†

ἀπ-ελαύνω, [in LXX for נצל, שלח;] *to drive away*: Ac 18¹⁶ (MM, s.v.).†

*† ἀπ-ελεγμός, -οῦ, ὁ (< ἀπελέγχω, *to convict, refute*), *refutation, disrepute*: ἐλθεῖν εἰς ἀ., Ac 19²⁷ (not elsewhere; v. MM, s.v.).†

* ἀπ-ελεύθερος, -ου, ὁ, ἡ, *a freedman*: τ. κυρίου (MM, s.v.), 1 Co 7²².†

Ἀπελλῆς, -οῦ, acc. -ῆν (MM, s.v.), ὁ, *Apelles*: Ro 16¹⁰.†

† ἀπ-ελπίζω, [in LXX: Is 29¹⁹ (אֶבְיוֹן), Jth 9¹¹, Es 4¹⁷, Si 22²¹ 27²¹, 11 Mac 9¹⁸ *;] 1. *to give up in despair, despair of* (Polyb., Diod., LXX); Lk 6³⁵ (RV). With μηδένα (T, WH, mg.) this must be the meaning. In either case, the lexical evidence is all in its favour. 2. *To hope to receive from* or *in return* (Field, *Notes*, 59; Cremer, 712; Soph., *Lex.*, s.v.): c. acc. (M, *Pr.*, 65; MM, s.v.), Lk 6³⁵.†

† ἀπ-έναντι, adv. c. gen. (Hellenistic, common in LXX); 1. *over against* (MM, s.v.): Mt 27⁶¹, Mk 12⁴¹, WH, mg. 2. *before, in the presence of*: Mt 27²⁴ (WH, mg.), Ac 3¹⁶, Ro 3¹⁸. 3. *against*: Ac 17⁷.†

ἀπέραντος, -ον (< περαίνω, *to complete, finish*), [in LXX: Jb 36²⁶ (אֵין חֵקֶר), 111 Mac 2⁹ *;] *endless, interminable*: 1 Ti 1⁴.†

*† ἀπερισπάστως, adv. (< περισπάω; the adj. occurs in Wi 16¹¹ Si 41¹); *without distraction*: 1 Co 7³⁵.†

† ἀ-περί-τμητος, -ον (< περιτέμνω), [in LXX chiefly for עָרֵל;] *uncircumcised*; metaph. (τ.) καρδίαις (cf. Je 9²⁶, al.): Ac 7⁵¹. (ἄσημος, found in π., appears to have been the word used by Greek-speaking Egyptians: v. Deiss., *BS*, 153; cf. also Cremer, 885; MM, s.v.)†

ἀπ-έρχομαι, [in LXX chiefly for הלך;] 1. *to go away, depart* (also, in late writers, with "perfective" force, *to arrive* at a destination, the thought being carried on to the goal; M, *Pr.*, 111 f., 247; MM, s.v.); (*a*) absol.: Mt 13²⁵, al.; ptcp., ἀπελθών, used pleonastically with other verbs as in Heb. (Dalman, *Words*, 21), Mt 13²⁸, al.; (*b*) with mention of place or person: εἰς, Mt 14¹⁵; ἐπί, Lk 24²⁴; πρός, Re 10⁹; ἀπό, Lk 1³⁸; ἔξω, Ac 4¹⁵; ἐκεῖ, Mt 2²². 2. As in LXX, seq. ὀπίσω, c. gen. (Heb. הָלַךְ אַחֲרֵי), *to go after, follow:* Mk 1²⁰, Jo 12¹⁹; metaph., Mk 1⁴², Re 21¹.

ἀπ-έχω, [in LXX chiefly for רחק;] 1. trans., (*a*) *to hold back, keep off;* (*b*) *to have in full, to have received* (on the "perfective" force of the compound, v. M, *Pr.*, 112 f., 247): c. acc., Mt 6², ⁵, ¹⁶, Lk 6²⁴, Phl 4¹⁸, Phm ¹⁵ (for illustr. from π., where it is used in receipts, v. Deiss., *BS*, 229; *LAE*, 110 f.; MM, s.v.); impers., ἀπέχει (Field, *Notes*, 39), *it is enough* (so Vg., Hesych., and v. Field, s.v. But here perh., as under 2: *far from it*, Gore, *Comm.* in l. Cf. also MM, *VGT* and Souter, s.v.): Mk 14⁴¹. 2. Intrans., *to be away, distant:* absol., Lk 15²⁰; seq. ἀπό, Mt 14²⁴ 15⁸, Mk 7⁶, Lk 7⁶ 15²⁰ 24¹³. Mid., *to abstain:* c. gen., Ac 15²⁹, ɪ Ti 4³, ɪ Pe 2¹¹; seq. ἀπό, Ac 15²⁰, ɪ Th 4³ 5²².†

** ἀπιστέω, -ῶ (< ἄπιστος), [in LXX: Wi 1² 10⁷ 12¹⁷ 18¹³, Si 1²⁷, ɪɪ Mac 8¹³ *;] *to disbelieve, be faithless:* Mk 16¹¹, ¹⁶, Lk 24¹¹, ⁴¹, Ac 28²⁴, ɪ Pe 2⁷; so prob. also Ro 3³, ɪɪ Ti 2¹³ (*ICC, CGT*, in ll.; MM, s.v.). 2. = ἀπειθέω (Hdt.; on this sense in Ro, ɪɪ Ti, ll. c., v. Vaughan on Ro, l.c.; Lft., *Notes*, 265; Thayer, s.v.).†

** ἀπιστία, -ας, ἡ (< ἄπιστος), [in LXX: Wi 14²⁵, ɪᴠ Mac 12⁴ *;] *want of faith, unbelief:* Mt 13⁵⁸, Mk 6⁶ 9²⁴ 16¹⁴, Ro 3³ (but v.s. ἀπιστέω) 4²⁰ 11²⁰, ²³, ɪ Ti 1¹³, He 3¹², ¹⁹ (*DCG*, ii, 775ª; Cremer, 492).†

ἄ-πιστος, -ον (< ἀ- neg., πιστός), [in LXX: Pr 17⁶ 28²⁵, Is 17¹⁰ *;] (*a*) of things, *incredible:* Ac 26⁸; (*b*) of persons, *without faith* or *trust, unbelieving:* Mt 17¹⁷, Mk 9¹⁹, Lk 9⁴¹ 12⁴⁶, Jo 20²⁷, Tit 1¹⁵, Re 21⁸; specif., of unbelievers as opp. to Christians: ɪ Co 6⁶ 7¹²⁻¹⁵ 10²⁷ 14²²⁻²⁴, ɪɪ Co 4⁴ 6¹⁴, ¹⁵, 1 Ti 5⁸ (cf. Lft., *Notes*, 265; Cremer, 491).†

ἁπλότης, -ητος, ἡ (< ἁπλοῦς), [in LXX: ɪɪ Ki 15¹¹ (תֹּם), ɪ Ch 29¹⁷ (יֹשֶׁר לֵבָב, ἀ. τῆς καρδίας, cf. Col 3²², where v. Lft.), Wi 1¹, al.;] *simplicity, sincerity:* Ro 12⁸, ɪɪ Co 11³, Eph 6⁵, Col. 3²²; as manifested in generous, unselfish giving, *liberality, graciousness:* ɪɪ Co 8² 9¹¹, ¹³ (v. *ICC*, Ro., 12⁸; Hort, *Ja.*, 1⁵, and v.s. ἁπλῶς).†

ἁπλόος, v.s. ἁπλοῦς.

ἁπλοῦς, -ῆ, -οῦν (contr. fr. -óος; < ἁ- cop., πλόος), [in LXX: Pr 11²⁵ *;] *simple, single:* in a moral sense (*DCG*, ii, 628 f.), ὀφθαλμός, Mt 6²², Lk 11³⁴. (In π. of a marriage dowry, v. MM, s.v.).†

SYN.: ἄδολος, ἄκακος, ἀκέραιος (Tr., *Syn.*, § lvi; Cremer, 107, 639).

ἁπλῶς, adv. (< ἁπλοῦς), [in LXX: Pr 10⁹ (בַּתֹּם), Wi 16²⁷, ɪɪ Mac 6⁶ *;] *simply, sincerely, graciously:* Ja 1⁵. ("Later writers comprehend under the one word the whole magnanimous and honourable type of character in which . . . singleness of mind is the central feature"—Hort, *Ja.*, l.c.)†

ἀπό (on the freq. neglect of elision bef. vowels, v. Tdf., *Pr.*, 94,

WH, *App.*, 146), prep. c. gen. (WM, 462 ff.; on its relation to ἐκ, παρά, ὑπό, ib. 456 f.), [in LXX for מִן, בְּ, לְ;] *from* (i.e. from the exterior). 1. Of separation and cessation; (1) of motion from a place : Mt 5²⁹, ³⁰ 7²³, Lk 5² 22⁴¹, al.; (2) in partitive sense (M, *Pr.*, 72, 102, 245; MM, s.v.; Bl., § 40, 2), Mt 9¹⁶ 27²¹, Jo 21¹⁰, Ac 5², al.; also after verbs of eating, etc.; (3) of alienation (cl. gen. of separation), after such verbs as λούω (Deiss., *BS*, 227), λύω, σώζω, παύω, etc.; ἀνάθεμα ά., Ro 9³; ἀποθνήσκειν ά., Col 2²⁰; σαλευθῆναι, ιι Th 2², καθαρός, -ίζειν, ά. (Deiss., *BS*, 196, 216), Ac 20²⁶, ιι Co 7¹, He 9¹⁴; (4) of position, Mt 23³⁴ 24³¹, al.; after μακράν, Mt 8³⁰; transposed before measures of distance, Jo 10¹⁸ 21⁸, Re 14²⁰ (Abbott, *JG*, 227); (5) of time, ἀπὸ τ. ὥρας, ἡμέρας, etc., Mt 9²², Jo 19²⁷, Ac 20¹⁸, Phl 1⁵, al.; ἀπ' αἰῶνος, Lk 1⁷⁰, al.; ἀπ' ἀρχῆς, etc., Mt 19⁴, Ro 1²⁰; ἀπὸ βρέφους, ιι Ti 3¹⁵; ἀφ' ἧς, *since*, Lk 7⁴⁵, al.; ἀπὸ τ. νῦν, Lk 1⁴⁸, al.; ἀπὸ τότε, Mt 4¹⁷, al.; ἀπὸ πέρυσι, *a year ago*, ιι Co 8¹⁰ 9²; ἀπὸ πρωί, Ac 28²³; (6) of order or rank, ἀπὸ διετοῦς, Mt 2¹⁶; ἀπὸ Ἀβραάμ, Mt 1¹⁷; ἕβδομος ἀπὸ Ἀδάμ, Ju ¹⁴; ἀπὸ μικροῦ ἕως μεγάλου, Ac 8¹⁰, He 8¹¹; ἄρχεσθαι ἀπό, Mt 20⁸, Jo 8⁹, Ac 8³⁵, al.; ἀφ' οὗ, v.s. ὅς. 2. Of origin; (1) of birth, extraction, and hence, in late writers, (*a*) of local extraction (cl. ἐξ; Abbott, *JG*, 227 ff.), Mt 21¹¹, Mk 15⁴³, Jo 1⁴⁵, Ac 10³⁸, al.; οἱ ἀπὸ Ἰταλίας (WM, § 66, 6; M, *Pr.*, 237; Westc., Rendall, in l.), He 13²⁴; (*b*) of membership in a community or society (Bl., § 40, 2), Ac 12¹, al.; (*c*) of material (= cl. gen.; Bl. l.c.; M, *Pr.*, 102), Mt 3⁴ 27²¹; (*d*) after verbs of asking, seeking, etc., Lk 11⁵⁰,⁵¹, ι Th 2⁶ (Milligan, in l.); (2) of the cause, instrument, means or occasion (freq. = ὑπό, παρά, and after verbs of learning, hearing, knowing, etc.; Bl., § 40, 3), Mt 7¹⁶ 11²⁹, Lk 22⁴⁵, Ac 2²² 4³⁶ 9¹³ 12¹⁴, ι Co 11²³, Ga 3², al.; ἀπὸ τ. ὄχλου, Lk 19³ (cf. Jo 21⁶, Ac 22¹¹); ἀπὸ τ. φόβου, Mt 14²⁶, al. (cf. Mt 10²⁸ 13⁴⁴). 3. Noteworthy Hellenistic phrases : φοβεῖσθαι ἀπό (M, *Pr.*, 102, 107); προσέχειν ἀπό (M, *Pr.*, ll. c.; Milligan, *NTD*, 50); ἀπὸ νότου (Heb. מִגֶּנֶב), Re 21¹³; ἀπὸ προσώπου (מִפְּנֵי), ιι Th 1⁹ (Bl., § 40, 9); ἀπὸ τ. καρδιῶν (בְּלֵב), Mt 18³⁵; ἀπὸ ὁ ὤν (WM, § 10, 2; M, *Pr.*, 9), Re 1⁴. For Semetic influence on constructions with ἀπό, see further M, *Gr.*, ιι, pp. 460 ff. 4. In composition, ἀπό denotes separation, departure, origin, etc. (ἀπολύω, ἀπέρχομαι, ἀπογράφω); it also has a perfective force (M, *Pr.*, 112, 247), as in ἀφικνεῖσθαι, ἀπολούεσθαι, q.v.

ἀπο-βαίνω, [in LXX for היה, etc.;] *to step off, disembark* : Lk 5², Jo 21⁹; metaph., of events, *to issue, turn out* (Field, *Notes*, 74) : Lk 21¹³, Phl 1¹⁹ (MM, s.v.).†

ἀπο-βάλλω, [in LXX : Is 1³⁰ (נבל) and elsew. without Heb. equiv.;] *to throw off* : Mk 10⁵⁰; metaph., *to lose, let go* (Field, *Notes*, 231 f.; MM, s.v.) : He 10³⁵.†

ἀπο-βλέπω, [in LXX for פנה, etc.;] *to look away from all else at one object;* hence, *to look steadfastly* : He 11²⁶ (cf. ἀφοράω).†

** ἀπό-βλητος, -ον (< ἀποβάλλω), [in Aq. : Le 7¹⁸, al.; Sm. : Ho 9³ (טמא);] *to be thrown away, rejected* : ι Ti 4⁴ (Hom., Plut.).†

* ἀπο-βολή, -ῆς, ἡ (< ἀποβάλλω); 1. *a throwing away, rejection :* opp. to πρόσλημψις, Ro 11¹⁵. 2. *a losing, loss :* Ac 27²².†

** ἀπο-γίνομαι (cl. -γίγν-) [in LXX : Da TH 2¹*;] 1. *to be away, removed from*. 2. *to depart life, to die* (MM, s.v.) : τ. ἁμαρτίαις, i.e. with ref. to sins, I Pe 2²⁴ (Cremer, 149, 668).†

ἀπο-γραφή, -ῆς, ἡ (ἀπογράφω), [in LXX : Da LXX 10²¹ (כְּתָב), I Es 8³⁰, AB, II Mac 2¹, III Mac 2³² 4¹⁵, ¹⁷ 7²² *;] 1. *a written copy*. 2. As law term, *a deposition* (Demos.). 3. In late writers, *a register, enrolment, census* (MM, s.v.; Deiss., *LAE*, 160, 268 f.) : Lk 2², Ac 5³⁷.†

ἀπο-γράφω, [in LXX : Jg 8¹⁴, Pr 22²⁰ (כְּתַב), I Es 8³⁰, III Mac 2²⁹ 4¹⁴ 6³⁴, ³⁸ *;] 1. *to write out, copy*. 2. *to enrol;* mid., *to enrol oneself :* Lk 2¹ (M, *Pr*., 162; but. v. *ICC*, in l.), ib.³, ⁵; pass., He 12²³ (v. reff., s.v. ἀπογραφή).†

ἀπο-δείκνυμι, [in LXX : Es 2⁹ (רָאָה), al.;] 1. *to bring out, show forth, exhibit* (Lft., *Notes*, 200; *ICC*, in l.): I Co 4⁹. 2. *to declare, show :* Ac 2²². 3. *to prove :* Ac 25⁷. 4. As freq. in late Gk., *to proclaim to an office :* seq. ὅτι, II Th 2⁴ (Milligan, in l.; MM, s.v.; Lft., *Notes*. 113.)†

** ἀπό-δειξις, -εως, ἡ (< ἀποδείκνυμι), [in LXX : III Mac 4²⁰, IV Mac 3¹⁹, 13¹⁰*;] 1. *a showing off*. 2. As used by Gk. philosophers, *demonstration, certain proof :* I Co 2⁴ (v. *ICC*, in l.; MM, s.v.; Lft., *Notes*, 173).†

*† ἀπο-δεκατεύω = ἀποδεκατόω, q.v., *to tithe, pay a tenth of :* Lk 18¹².†

† ἀπο-δεκατόω, [in LXX for עָשַׂר, in both senses foll., e.g. (1) Ge 28²² (2) I Ki 8¹⁵] 1. c. acc. rei, *to tithe, pay a tenth of :* Mt 23²³, Lk 11⁴². 2. C. acc. pers., *to exact tithes from :* He 7⁵. 3. *to decimate* (Socr., *HE*, 573 A; v. Kennedy, *Sources*, 117).†

*† ἀπό-δεκτος, -ον (< ἀποδέχομαι), *acceptable :* I Ti 2³ 5⁴.†

** ἀπο-δέχομαι, [in LXX : To 7¹⁷, Jth 13¹³, I-IV Mac ₁₀*;] *to accept gladly, welcome, receive :* Lk 8⁴⁰ 9¹¹, Ac 18²⁷ 21¹⁷ 28³⁰; metaph., c. acc. rei, Ac 2⁴¹ 24³ (MM, s.v.; Cremer, 688).†

ἀπο-δημέω, -ῶ (< ἀπόδημος), [in LXX : Ez 19³ A*;] *to be or go abroad* (M, *Pr*., 130 ₂) : Mt 21³³ 25¹⁴, ¹⁵, Mk 12¹, Lk 15¹³ 20⁹.†

* ἀπό-δημος, -ον, *gone abroad* (RV, *sojourning in another country*) : Mk 13³⁴.†

ἀπο-δίδωμι, [in LXX for מָכַר, שׁוּב hi., נָתַן, שָׁלַם pi., etc.;] *to give up or back, restore, return :* Mt 27⁵⁸, Lk 4²⁰ 9⁴² 19⁸; esp. of wages, debts, oaths, etc. (MM, s.v.), *to render* what is due, *to pay* (Deiss., *LAE*, 334 f.) : absol., Mt 18²⁵, ²⁸, Lk 7⁴²; c. acc., Mt 5²⁶ 18²⁹, ³⁰, ³⁴ 20⁸ 21⁴¹ 22²¹, Mk 12¹⁷, Lk 10³⁵ 12⁵⁹ 20²⁵, Ro 13⁷, He 12¹¹, Re 22²; ὅρκους, Mt 5³³ (cf. Nu 30³, De 23²¹ al.); of conjugal duty, τ. ὀφειλήν, I Co 7³; ἀμοιβάς, I Ti 5⁴; μαρτύριον, *to give* (as in duty bound) *testimony*, Ac 4³³; λόγον, *to render account*, Mt 12³⁶, Lk 16², Ac 19⁴⁰, He 13¹⁷, I Pe 4⁵; hence of requital, recompense, both in good and bad sense, Mt 6⁴, ⁶, ¹⁸ 16²⁷, Ro 2⁶, II Ti 4⁸, ¹⁴, Re 18⁶ 22¹²; κακὸν ἀντὶ κακοῦ, Ro 12¹⁷, I Th 5¹⁵, I Pe 3⁹. Mid., *to give up of one's own, hence to sell* (fr. Hdt. on) : c. acc. rei, Ac 5⁸, He 12¹⁶; c. acc. pers., Ac7⁹ (cf. ἀντ-αποδίδωμι).†

* ἀπο-δι-ορίζω (< διορίζω, < ὅρος, *a limit*), *to mark off*, hence metaph. *to make separations :* Ju ¹⁹ (Cremer, 806).†

ἀπο-δοκιμάζω, [in LXX: Ps 117 (118)²², al. (מָאַס);] *to reject:*
Mt 21⁴² (LXX), Mk 8³¹ 12¹⁰ (LXX), Lk 9²² 17²⁵ 20¹⁷ (LXX), He 12¹⁷,
I Pe 2⁴, ⁷ (LXX) (Cremer, 701; MM, s.v.).†

*ἀπο-δοχή, -ῆς, ἡ (< ἀποδέχομαι), *acceptance, approbation* (Field,
Notes, 203) : I Ti 1¹⁵ 4⁹ (Cremer, 686 ; MM, s.v.).†

*ἀπό-θεσις, -εως, ἡ (< ἀποτίθημι), *a putting away:* I Pe 3²¹,
II Pe 1¹⁴.†

ἀπο-θήκη, -ης, ἡ (< ἀποτίθημι), [in LXX for אֹצָר, מָנָא, etc.;] *a
storehouse, granary:* Mt 3¹² 6²⁶ 13³⁰, Lk 3¹⁷ 12¹⁸,²⁴.†

**† ἀπο-θησαυρίζω, [in LXX: Si 3⁴*;] *to treasure up, store away:*
I Ti 6¹⁹.†

ἀπο-θλίβω, [in LXX for לחץ, Nu 22²⁵*;] *to press hard:* Lu 8⁴⁵.†

ἀπο-θνήσκω, [in LXX chiefly for מות;] *to die:* of natural death,
Mk 5³⁵, al. ; of violent death (pass. of ἀποκτείνω), esp. of Christ, Mt 26³⁵,
Jo 12³³, He 10²⁸, al. ; of spiritual death, Jo 6⁵⁰, Ro 8¹³, al. ; c. dat.
ref., Ro 6², ¹⁰ 14⁷, ⁸, Ga 2¹⁹; acc., ὅ, Ro 6¹⁰; seq. ἐν, Mt 8³², Jo 8²¹, ²⁴,
ι Co 15²², He 11³⁷, Re 14¹³; seq. ὑπέρ, περί, Jo 11⁵⁰, ⁵¹ 18¹⁴, Ro 5⁶⁻⁸
14¹⁵, ι Co 15³, ιι Co 5¹⁵, ι Th 5¹⁰, 1 Pe 3¹⁸; ἀπό, Col 2²⁰; ἐκ, Re 8¹¹;
fig., ι Co 15³¹ (cf. συν-αποθνήσκω, and v. Milligan, *NTD*, 258 f.; *DCG*,
i, 791ᵇ; Cremer, 286; MM, s.v.; on the perfective force of this verb,
M, *Pr.*, 112, 114; and on the distinction bet. pres. and aor., ib. 113 f.).

ἀπο-καθ-ιστάνω, ἀποκαθιστάω, see next word.

ἀπο-καθ-ίστημι (ἀποκαθιστάω, Mk 9¹², Rec., -ιστάνω, LTTr.; cf. Ac
1⁶; -κατιστάνω, WH), [in LXX chiefly for שׁוּב] 1. *to restore,* i.e. to a
former condition: of health, Mt 12¹³, Mk 3⁵ 8²⁵, Lk 6¹⁰; of social or
political affairs, Mt 17¹¹, Mk 9¹², Ac 1⁶. 2. *to give back, bring back:*
He 13¹⁹ (so in π., MM, s.v.; cf. also Cremer, 312).†

ἀπο-καλύπτω, [in LXX chiefly for גלה;] 1. in general sense (cl.),
to reveal, uncover, disclose, (a) of things: Mt 10²⁶, Lk 2³⁵ 12², ι Co
3¹³; (b) of persons: pass., Christ, Lk 17³⁰; Antichrist, ιι Th 2³, ⁶, ⁸.
2. In LXX and NT, in special sense of divine revelation: Mt 11²⁵ (on
the tense, v. M, *Pr.*, 136), ib. ²⁷ 16¹⁷, Lk 10²¹, ²², Jo 12³⁸, Ro 1¹⁷, ¹⁸, 8¹⁸,
ι Co 2¹⁰ 14³⁰, Ga 1¹⁶ 3²³, Eph 3⁵, Phl 3¹⁵, ι Pe 1⁵, ¹² 5¹ (Westc., *Eph.*,
178 f.; M, *Th.*, 149 f.; *ICC* on Ga, pp. 433 ff.).†
SYN.: φανερόω (v. Thayer, 62; Cremer, 342).

† ἀπο-κάλυψις, -εως, ἡ (< ἀποκαλύπτω), [in LXX: ι Ki 20³⁰ (עֶרְוָה),
Si 11²⁷ 22²² 42¹*;] *an uncovering, laying bare* (Plut.). Metaph., *a reveal-
ing, revelation:* a disclosure of divine truth, or a manifestion from God:
Lk 2³², Ro 2⁵, 8¹⁹ 16²⁵, ι Co 1⁷ 14⁶, ²⁶, ιι Co 12¹, ⁷, Ga 1¹², 2², Eph 1¹⁷ 3³,
ιι Th 1⁷, ι Pe 1⁷, ¹³ 4¹³, Re 1¹.†
SYN.: ἐπιφάνεια, παρουσία, φανέρωσις (v. Tr., *Syn.*, xciv; Lft.,
Notes, 102, 178; Westc., *Eph.*, 178 f.; M, *Th.*, 145 ff.; Cremer, 343).

*† ἀπο-καραδοκία, -ας, ἡ (< ἀποκαραδοκέω, used by Aq. in Ps 36 (37)⁷ for
התחלל; < ἀπό, κάρα, the head, δοκέω, in Ion., to watch, to watch with
outstretched head, watch anxiously), strained expectancy, eager longing:
(Polyb., π.; v. Deiss., *LAE*, 374₅, 377 f.), Ro 8¹⁹, Phl 1²⁰ (Lft., in l.;
Cremer, 177); see further, Moulton, *Gr.*, ιι, iii, § 105.†

*† ἀπο-κατ-αλλάσσω (cf. καταλλάσσω : ἀπό here signifies *completely*, v. Lft., *Col.*, l.c. ; Ellic., *Eph.*, l.c. ; but also Mey., *Eph.*, l.c.), *to reconcile completely :* Eph 2¹⁶, Col 1²⁰, ²¹.†

* ἀπο-κατά-στασις, -εως, ἡ (< ἀποκαθίστημι), *restoration :* Ac 3²¹ (in π. of repairs and restorations of temples, v. MM, s.v.).† ἀπο-κατ-ιστάνω, v. ἀποκαθίστημι.

ἀπό-κειμαι, [in LXX : Ge 49¹⁰ (שִׁילֹה), Jb 38²³ (חָשַׂךְ), II Mac 12⁴⁵, IV Mac 8¹¹ * ;] *to be laid up, in store, laid away :* Lk 19²⁰. Metaph., c. dat. pers., *to be reserved* (Dem., Plat. ; and v. MM, s.v.) : Col 1⁵, II Ti 4⁸, He 9²⁷.†

† ἀπο-κεφαλίζω (< ἀπό, κεφαλή), [in LXX : Ps 151⁷ * ;] *to behead :* Mt 14¹⁰, Mk 6¹⁶, ²⁸, Lk 9⁹.†

ἀπο-κλείω, [in LXX chiefly for סגר ;] *to shut fast :* Lk 13²⁵.†

ἀπο-κόπτω, [in LXX for קצץ, כרת, etc. ;] *to cut off :* Mk 9⁴³, ⁴⁵, Jo 18¹⁰, ²⁶, Ac 27³². Mid., *to mutilate oneself, have oneself mutilated :* Ga 5¹² (cf. De 23¹ LXX ; and v. Cremer, 751 ; MM, s.v.).†

*† ἀπό-κριμα, -τος, τό (< ἀποκρίνω) ; 1. prop., *a judicial sentence :* II Co 1⁹, R, mg. 2. *an answer* (v. Thayer, s.v.) : II Co, l.c., R, txt. (In FlJ, *Ant.*, xiv, 10, 6, of a rescript of the Senate ; in Inscr. of an official decision, Deiss., *BS*, 257 ; a reply to a deputation, MM, s.v. : cf. also Cremer, 375).†

ἀπο-κρίνω, [in LXX chiefly for ענה ;] in cl., 1. *to separate, distinguish.* 2. *to choose.* Mid., *to answer :* Mt 27¹², Mk 14⁶¹, Lk 3¹⁶ 23⁹, Jo 5¹⁷, ¹⁹, Ac 3¹². In late Gk. the pass. also is used in this sense, and pass. forms are the more freq. in NT (M, *Pr.*, 39, 161 ; MM, s.v.) ; (*a*) in general sense : absol., Mk 12³⁴ ; c. acc. rei, Mt 22⁴⁶ ; c. dat. pers., Mt 12³⁸ : seq. πρός, Ac 25¹⁶ ; (*b*) Hebraistically (i) like ענה, *to begin to speak, take up the conversation* (Kennedy, *Sources*, 124 f.) : Mt 11²⁵, al., (ii) redundant, as in the Heb. phrase וַיַּעַן וַיֹּאמֶר (Dalman, *Words*, 24 f., 38 ; M, *Pr.*, 14 ; Bl., § 58, 4 ; 74, 2 ; Cremer, 374 ; M, *Gr.*, II, pp. 453 f.) : ἀποκριθεὶς εἶπε, Mt 4⁴ ; ἔφη, 8⁸ ; λέγει, Mk 3³³ ; in Jo most freq. ἀπεκ. κ. εἶπε, 1⁴⁸.

ἀπό-κρισις, -εως, ἡ (< ἀποκρίνομαι), [in LXX for דבר, etc. ;] *an answering, an answer :* Lk 2⁴⁷ 20²⁶, Jo 1²² 19⁹.†

ἀπο-κρύπτω, [in LXX chiefly for סתר ;] *to hide, conceal, keep secret :* c. acc., Lk 10²¹ ; pass., I Co 2⁷, Eph 3⁹, Col 1²⁶ (MM, s.v.).†

ἀπόκρυφος, -ον (< ἀποκρύπτω), [in LXX chiefly for סֵתֶר ;] *hidden :* Mk 4²², Lk 8¹⁷, Col 2³ (v. Lft., in l. ; MM, s.v.).†

ἀπο-κτείνω (also in late forms -κτέννω, Mt 10²⁸, al., LTTr., -κτεννύω, Mk 12⁵, WH), [in LXX for הרג, מות ;] *to kill :* Mt 14⁵, al. ; seq. instr. ἐν (q.v.), Eph 2¹⁶, Re 2²³, al. Metaph. : Ro 7¹¹ ; τ. ἔχθραν, Eph 2¹⁶ ; τὸ γράμμα ἀποκτείνει, II Co 3⁶ (on the perfective force of this verb v. M, *Pr.*, 114 ; on the tense forms v. Moulton, *Gr.*, II, ii, p. 245).

** ἀπο-κυέω (Rec. -κύω), -ῶ (< ἀπό, κυέω or κύω, *to be pregnant*), [in LXX : IV Mac 15¹⁷ * ;] prop., " the medical word for birth as the close of pregnancy " (Hort, *Ja.*, 26 f.). In κοινή, " an ordinary syn. of τίκτω, but definitely ' perfectivised ' (M, *Pr.*, 111 ff. ; MM, s.v.) by the ἀπό, and so implying safe delivery," *to bring forth, give birth to :* Ja 1¹⁵, ¹⁸.†

† ἀπο-κυλίω (v.s. κυλίω), [in LXX : Ge 29³, ⁸, ¹⁰ (בָּלַל), Jth 13⁹ * ;] *to roll away :* Mt 28², Mk 16³, Lk 24².†

ἀπο-λαμβάνω, [in LXX : Nu 34¹⁴ (לָקַה (De, 26⁵ A, Is 5¹⁷, II Mac 4⁴⁶ 6²¹ 8⁶, IV Mac 18²³ * ;] 1. *to receive from* another; absol., *to receive as one's due :* Lk 16²⁵ 18³⁰ (v.l. λάβῃ) 23⁴¹, Ro 1²⁷, Ga 4⁵, Col 3²⁴, II Jo ⁸. 2. *to receive back :* Lk 6³⁴ 15²⁷. 3. *to take apart* or *aside :* Mk 7³³ (cf. use in π. of the recluses of the Serapeum ; MM, s.v.).†

** ἀπόλαυσις, -εως, ἡ (< ἀπολαύω, *to take of, enjoy* a thing), [in LXX : III Mac 7¹⁶ * ;] *enjoyment :* I Ti 6¹⁷, He 11²⁵ (for late exx., v. MM, s.v.).†

ἀπο-λείπω, [in LXX for חָדַל, יָתַר, etc. ;] 1. *to leave, leave behind* (in π. a *term. techn.* in wills; v. MM, s.v.) : II Ti 4¹³, ²⁰, Tit 1⁵ ; pass., *to be reserved, remain :* He 4⁶, ⁹ 10²⁶. 2. *to desert, abandon :* Ju ⁶.†

† ἀπο-λείχω (for ἐπιλ-, q.v.), *to lick up :* Lk 16²¹, Rec.†

ἀπ-όλλυμι and ἀπολλύω, [in LXX for אָבַד, etc. (38 words in all)]. 1. Act., (1) *to destroy utterly, destroy, kill :* Mk 1²⁴ 9²², al. ; τ. ψυχήν, Mt 10²⁸, al. ; (2) *to lose utterly :* Mt 10⁴², al. ; metaph., of failing to save, Jo 6³⁹ 18⁹; (3) in pf. intrans., *to perish :* Mt 10⁶. 2. Mid., (1) *to perish ;* (a) of things : Mt 5²⁹, Jo 6¹², He 1¹¹ (LXX), al. ; (b) of persons : Mt 8²⁵, al. Metaph., of loss of eternal life, Jo 3¹⁵, ¹⁶ 10²⁸ 17¹², Ro 2¹², I Co 8¹¹ 15¹⁸, II Pe 3⁹. In οἱ ἀπολλύμενοι, *the perishing,* contrasted in I Co 1¹⁸, al., with οἱ σωζόμενοι, the "perfective" force of the verb, wh. "implies the *completion* of the process of destruction," is illustrated (v. M, *Pr.*, 114 f. ; M, *Th.*, ii, 2¹⁰) ; (2) *to be lost :* Lk 15⁴ 21¹⁸. Metaph., on the basis of the relation between shepherd and flock, of spiritual destitution and alienation from God : Mt 10⁶ 15²⁴, Lk 19¹⁰ (MM, s.v.; *DCG*, i, 191 f., ii, 76, 554; Cremer, 451).

Ἀπολλύων, -οντος, ὁ (pres. ptcp. of ἀπολλύω), *Apollyon,* i.e. the Destroyer : Re 9¹¹ (cf. Ἀβάδδων). (Cremer, 453 ; *DB*, i, 125, 172.)†

Ἀπολλωνία, -ας, ἡ, *Apollonia,* a city of Macedonia : Ac 17¹.†

Ἀπολλώς, -ώ, ὁ (contr. from Ἀπολλώνιος, Ac 18²⁴ D), *Apollos :* Ac 18²⁴ 19¹, I Co 1¹² 3⁴⁻⁶, ²² 4⁶ 16¹², Tit 3¹³.†

ἀπολογέομαι, -οῦμαι (< ἀπό, λόγος), [in LXX : Je 12¹ (רִיב) 38 (31)⁶, II Mac 13²⁶ * ;] 1. *to defend :* Ro 2¹⁵. 2. *to defend one's self :* ¹absol., Lk 21¹⁴, Ac 26¹ ; seq. ὅτι, Ac 25⁸ ; τί, *to adduce something in one's defence,* Lk 12¹¹, Ac 26²⁴ (ταῦτα) 24¹⁰ (τὰ περὶ ἐμαυτοῦ) ; περί, c. gen. rei, and ἐπί, c. gen. pers., Ac 26² ; c. dat. pers., Ac 19³³, II Co 12¹⁹.†

** ἀπολογία, -ας, ἡ (< ἀπολογέομαι), [in LXX : Wi 6¹⁰ * ;] *a speech in defence :* Ac 25¹⁶, II Co 7¹¹, Phl 1⁷, ¹⁶, II Ti 4¹⁶ ; c. dat. pers., I Co 9³, I Pe 3¹⁵ ; seq. πρός, Ac 22¹.†

ἀπο-λούω, in [LXX : Jb 9³⁰ (רָחַץ) * ;] *to wash off, wash away ;* mid., metaph., c. acc. rei, *to wash off oneself :* ἁμαρτίας, Ac 22¹⁶; absol., ἀπελούσασθε, *ye washed yourselves clean* (cf. Cremer, 406), I Co 6¹¹ ; on mid., see further M, *Pr.*, 156, and on "perfective" force of ἀπο-, ib., 112, 247.

† ἀπο-λύτρωσις, -εως, ἡ (< ἀπολυτρόω, *to release on payment of*

ransom, cf. λύτρον), [in LXX: Da (LXX) 4³⁰ᶜ *;] *release effected by payment of ransom, redemption, deliverance;* metaph., He 11³⁵; of deliverance thr. Christ from evil and the consequences of sin: Lk 21²⁸, Ro 3²⁴ (Vau., in l.) 8²³, ι Co 1³⁰, Eph 1⁷, ¹⁴ 4³⁰, Col 1¹⁴, He 9¹⁵. (On the extent to wh. the word retains the sense of *ransom*, v. *ICC*, *Ro.*, 3²⁴, Westc., *He.*, 297 ff.; v. also *ICC*, *Eph.*, 11; *DCG*, ii, 605; Cremer, 410; Deiss., *LAE*, 331; Lft., *Notes*, 271, 316; Tr., *Syn.*, § lxxvii.)†

ἀπο-λύω, [in LXX for שׁוּב, etc., freq. in ι-ιν Mac;] 1. *to set free, release:* Lk 13¹², Jo 19¹⁰, al.; a debtor, Mt 18²⁷; metaph., of forgiveness, Lk 6³⁷. 2. *to let go, dismiss* (Field, *Notes*, 9 f.): Mt 15²³, Lk 2²⁹ 9¹², Ac 19⁴¹, al.; of divorce, τ. γυναῖκα: Mt 1¹⁹ 5³¹, ³² 19³, ⁸, ⁹, Mk 10², ⁴, ¹¹, Lk 16¹⁸; with ref. to Gk. and Rom. (not Jewish) custom, τ. ἄνδρα: Mk 10¹². Mid., *to depart:* Ac 28²⁵ (MM, s.v.).

** ἀπο-μάσσω (< μάσσω, Att. -ττω, *to touch, handle*), [in LXX: To 7¹⁷ *;] *to wipe off, wipe clean:* mid., Lk 10¹¹.†

ἀπο-νέμω (< νέμω, *to distribute*), [in LXX: De 4¹⁹ (חלק), ιιι Mac 1⁷ 3¹⁶ *;] *to assign, apportion:* ι Pe 3⁷. (In π. of a Prefect who renders to all their dues; v. MM, s.v.)†

ἀπο-νίπτω, [in LXX for שׁטף, רחץ, מחה;] *to wash off:* mid. (reflex.), τ. χεῖρας, Mt 27²⁴.†

ἀπο-πίπτω, [in LXX for מלל, נפל, etc.;] *to fall off:* Ac 9¹⁸.†

ἀπο-πλανάω, -ῶ, [in LXX for נדח hi., נטה hi., שׁוּב pil.;] *to cause to go astray;* metaph., of leading into error: Mk 13²²; pass., *to be led astray:* ι Ti 6¹⁰.†

* ἀπο-πλέω, -ῶ, *to sail away:* Ac 13⁴ 14²⁶ 20¹⁵ 27¹ (Burton, 159).†

ἀπο-πλύνω, [in LXX chiefly for כבם pi.;] *to wash off:* v.l. for πλύνω, Lk 5², Rec.†

ἀπο-πνίγω, [in LXX: Na 2¹² ⁽¹³⁾ (חנק pi.), To 3⁸ *;] *to choke:* Mt 13⁷, Lk 8⁷; pass., of drowning (= καταποντίζομαι), Lk 8³³.†

ἀπορέω, -ῶ (< ἄπορος, ἀ- neg., πόρος, *a way, resource*), [in LXX for צרר, מוּך, etc.;] *to be at a loss, be perplexed:* absol., Mk 6²⁰ (ἐποίει, R, mg.); mid., *be in doubt:* absol., ιι Co 4⁸; c. acc., Ac 25²⁰; seq. περί, Lk 24⁴; ἐν, Ga 4²⁰; περὶ τίνος λέγει, Jo 13²².†

SYN.: διαπορέω, διακρίνομαι, διστάζω, μετεωρίζομαι (v. *DCG*, i, 491).

ἀπορία, -ας, ἡ (< ἀπορέω), [in LXX for בְּהָלָה, etc.;] *perplexity:* Lk 21²⁵ (MM, s.v.; on the construction, v. Field, *Notes*, 74 f.).†

ἀπο-ρίπτω (Rec. -ρρίπτω, cl.), [in LXX for שׁלך hi., etc.;] *to throw away, cast forth:* reflexively, Ac 27⁴³ (RV, *cast themselves overboard;* v. MM, s.v.).†

* ἀπ-ορφανίζω (< ἀπό, ὀρφανός), *to be bereaved* (prop., *of a parent*, Lft., *Notes*, 36); metaph., ι Th 2¹⁷ (where Field thinks it = χωρισθέντες, *Notes*, 199).†

ἀπο-σκευάζω, [in LXX: Le 14³⁶ (פנה pi.) *;] *to pack and carry off;* mid., *to pack and remove one's goods:* Ac 21¹⁵, Rec. (v. ἐπισ-).†

*† ἀπο-σκίασμα, -τος, τό (< ἀποσκιάζω, *to cast a shadow;* v.s. σκία), *a shadow:* Ja 1¹⁷ (MM, s.v.).†

ἀπο-σπάω, -ῶ, [in LXX for נתק ni., hi., etc. ;] *to draw off* or *away,
tear away* (MM, s.v.): Ac 20³⁰; μάχαιραν, draw a sword, Mt 26⁵¹;
pass., *to be parted* or *withdrawn* (Field, *Notes*, 134; but v. Thayer,
s.v.), Lk 22⁴¹, Ac 21¹.†

† ἀποστασία, -ας, ἡ (< ἀφίστημι), [in LXX for מַעַל, etc. ;] *defection,
apostasy, revolt;* in late Gk. (MM, *Exp.*, viii; Lft., *Notes*, 111; Cremer,
308) for cl. ἀπόστασις, freq. in sense of political revolt, in LXX (e.g.
Jos 22²², ii Ch 29¹⁹, Je 2¹⁹) and NT always of religious apostasy:
Ac 21²¹, ii Th 2³.†

ἀποστάσιον, -ου, τό (< ἀφίστημι), [in LXX : De 24¹, ³, Je 3⁸, Is 50¹
(בְּרִיתֻת, כְּרִיתֻת) *;] 1. in cl., only in phrase ἀποστασίου δίκη, an action
against a freedman for forsaking his προστάτης (Dem.).   2. In LXX,
βιβλίον ἀποστασίου, *a bill of divorce:* Mt 19⁷, Mk 10⁴; in same sense
ἀ. alone (MM, s.v.), Mt 5³¹ (for other late exx., v. MM, l.c.; Kennedy,
Sources, 121).†

** ἀπο-στεγάζω (< στέγη), [in Sm.: Je 49¹⁰ (29¹¹)* ;] *to unroof:*
Mk 2⁴.†

ἀπο-στέλλω, [in LXX very freq., almost always for שׁלח ;] prop.,
to send away, to dispatch on service; 1. *to send* with a commission, or
on service; (a) of persons: Christ, Mt 10⁴⁰; the apostles, 10¹⁶;
servants, Mk 12²; angels, 13²⁷; (b) of things: ὄνος, Mt 21³; τὸ δρέπανον, Mk 4²⁹; τ. λόγον, Ac 10³⁶; τ. ἐπαγγελίαν (i.e. the promised Holy
Spirit), Lk 24⁴⁹, Rec.; seq. εἰς, Mt 20², Lk 11⁴⁹, Jo 3¹⁷; ὀπίσω, Lk 19¹⁴;
ἔμπροσθεν, Jo 3²⁸; πρὸ προσώπου, Mt 11¹⁰; πρός, Mt 21³⁴; with ref. to
sender or place of departure: ἀπό, Lk 1²⁶ (Rec. ὑπό); παρά, Jo 1⁶;
ἐκ, ib. 1¹⁹; ὑπό, Ac 10¹⁷ (Rec. ἀπό); seq. inf., Mk 3¹⁴, al.; ἵνα, Mk 12²,
al.; εἰς (of purpose), He 1¹⁴; without direct obj.: seq. πρός, Jo 5³³;
λέγων, Jo 11³; ἀποστείλας, c. indic., Mt 2¹⁶, Ac 7¹⁴, Re 1¹. 2. *to send
away, dismiss:* Lk 4¹⁸, Mk 5¹⁰ 8²⁶ 12³ (cf. ἐξ-, συν-αποστέλλω).
SYN.: πέμπω, the general term. ἀ. " suggests official or authori-
tative sending" (v. Thayer, s.v. πέμπω; Westc., *Jo.*, 298; *Epp. Jo.*,
125; Cremer, 529; MM, s.v.).

ἀπο-στερέω, -ῶ (< στερέω, *to rob*), [in LXX : Ex 21¹⁰ (גָּרַע), De 24¹⁴
(עָשַׁק), Ma 3⁵, Si 4¹ 29⁶, ⁷ 31 (34)²¹, ²² *;] *to defraud, deprive of, despoil*
(in cl. chiefly of the misappropriation of trust funds, Field, *Notes*, 33;
cf. MM, s.v.): absol., Mk 10¹⁹, i Co 6⁸; c. acc. pers., i Co 7⁵. Mid.,
endure deprivation: i Co 6⁷ (WM, § 38, 3; but v. Bl., § 54, 5; M, *Pr.*,
162); pass., ἀπεστερημένοι, *bereft of:* i Ti 6⁵.†

ἀπο-στολή, -ῆς, ἡ (< ἀποστέλλω), [in LXX : De 22⁷, iii Ki 4³⁴ 9¹⁶,
Ps 77 (78)⁴⁹, Ec 8⁸, Ca 4¹³ (for שׁלח and its cognates), i Es 9⁵¹, ⁵⁴,
Je 39 (32)³⁶, Ba 2²⁵, i Mac 2¹⁸, ii Mac 3² *.] 1. In cl., *a sending away*
(MM, s.v.), as, an expedition (Hdt.). 2. In LXX (a) *discharge, dis-
missal* (Ec 8⁸); (b) *a gift* (iii Ki 9¹⁶, i Mac 2¹⁸). 3. In NT, the office
of an Apostle of Christ, *apostleship:* Ac 1²⁵, Ro 1⁵, i Co 9², Ga 2⁸
(Cremer, 530).†

ἀπόστολος, -ου, ὁ (< ἀποστέλλω), [in LXX : iii Ki 14⁶ A (שָׁלִיחַ) *;]

1. *a fleet, an expedition* (Dem.). 2. *a messenger, one sent on a mission* (Hdt., LXX, l.c., and π.; v. M, *Pr.*, 37 f.; MM, s.v.; M, *Th.*, i, 2⁷ and reff.): Jo 13¹⁶, ii Co 8²³, Phl 2²⁵. 3. In NT, *an Apostle* of Christ (*a*) with special ref. to the Twelve: Mt 10², Mk 3¹⁴, Lk 11⁴⁹, Eph 3⁵, Re 18²⁰, al., equality with whom is claimed by St. Paul, Ga 1¹, ¹¹ff., i Ti 2⁷, al.; (*b*) in a wider sense of prominent Christian teachers, as Barnabas, Ac 14¹⁴, apparently also Silvanus and Timothy, i Th 2⁶, and perhaps Andronicus and Junias (Junia?), Ro 16⁷ (v. *ICC*, in l.); of false teachers, claiming apostleship: ii Co 11⁵, ¹³, Re 2². (On the different uses of the term in NT, v. Lft., *Gal.*, 92-101; Cremer, 530; *DB*, i, 126; *DCG*, i, 105; *Enc. Br.*, ii, 196 ff.)

* **ἀποστοματίζω** (< στόμα), 1. In cl., *to speak from memory, to dictate* to a pupil (Plat.). 2. In late Gk., *to catechize, question*: Lk 11⁵³ (MM, s.v.).†

ἀπο-στρέφω, [in LXX chiefly for שׁוּב;] trans., c. acc., (*a*) *to turn away, remove*: Ro 11²⁶, ii Ti 4⁴; metaph., to turn away from allegiance, *pervert*: Lk 23¹⁴; (*b*) *to turn back, return*: μάχαιραν, Mt 26⁵². Pass., reflex., *to turn oneself away from*: c. acc., Mt 5⁴², ii Ti 1¹⁵, Tit 1¹⁴, He 12²⁵; so act., absol., Ac 3²⁶ (cf. Si 8⁵; Bl., § 53, 1; Cremer, 880).†

* **ἀπο-στυγέω**, -ῶ (< στυγέω, to hate), *to abhor*: Ro 12⁹.†

*† **ἀποσυνάγωγος**, -ον (< συναγωγή), *expelled from the congregation* (Field, *Notes*, 96), *excommunicated*: Jo 9²² 12⁴² 16² (Cremer, 64, 607).†

ἀπο-τάσσω, [in LXX: Ec 2²⁰ (יאשׁ pi.), i Es 6²⁷, Je 20², i Mac₄ *;] *to set apart*. Mid., in late Gk. (Bl., § 37, 1; Swete, *Mk.*, 136 f.; MM, s.v.), c. dat., (*a*) *to take leave of*: Mk 6⁴⁶, Lk 9⁶¹, Ac 18¹⁸, ²¹, ii Co 2¹³; (*b*) *to forsake*: Lk 14³³.†

** **ἀπο-τελέω**, -ῶ, [in LXX: i Es 5⁷³, ii Mac 15³⁹ *;] *to bring to an end, complete, accomplish, bring to maturity* (cf. MM, s.v.): Lk 13³², Ja 1¹⁵ (*ICC* on Ja, l.c.).†

ἀπο-τίθημι, in [LXX chiefly for נוח hi.;] *to put off* or *aside;* in NT always mid., (*a*) *to put off from oneself* as a garment: τ. ἱμάτια, Ac 7⁵⁸; metaph., in ethical sense, *to put off, lay aside*: Ro 13¹², Eph 4²², ²⁵, Col 3⁸, He 12¹, Ja 1²¹, i Pe 2¹; (*b*) *to stow away, put: ἐν τ. φυλακῇ* (MM, s.v.), Mt 14³.†

ἀπο-τινάσσω, [in LXX: Jg 16²⁰ A (נער ni.), i Ki 10² (נשׁט), La 2⁷ (נאר pi.) *;] *to shake off*: Lk 9⁵, Ac 28⁵.†

ἀπο-τίνω (or -τίω), [in LXX chiefly for שׁלם pi.;] *to pay off, repay*: Phm ¹⁹ (MM, s.v.).†

* **ἀπο-τολμάω**, -ῶ, *to be quite bold, make a bold venture*: Ro 10²⁰.†

† **ἀποτομία, -ας, ἡ (< ἀποτέμνω, to cut off), [in Sm.: Je 51 (28)³⁵, Na 3¹ *;] *steepness, sharpness;* metaph., *severity* (MM, s.v.): Ro 11²².†

** **ἀποτόμως**, adv., [in LXX: Wi 5²² *;] *abruptly, curtly, hence sharply, severely*: ii Co 13¹⁰, Ti 1¹³ (MM, s.v.).†

** **ἀπο-τρέπω**, [in LXX: Si 20²⁹ 48¹⁸, iii Mac 1²³, iv Mac 1³³ 16¹² *;] *to turn away;* mid., *to turn oneself away from*: c. acc., ii Ti 3⁵.†

* **ἀπουσία**, -ας. ἡ (< ἄπειμι); 1. *absence* (Æsch., Thuc.): Phl 2¹². 2. *deficiency, waste* (MM, s.v.).†

ἀπο-φέρω, [in LXX for הלך, etc.;] *to carry off, bear,* or *lead away:* c. acc., Mk 15[1], 1 Co 16[3], Re 17[3] 21[10].   Pass., Lk 16[22], Ac 19[12].†

** ἀπο-φεύγω, [in LXX: Si 22[22] *;] *to flee from, escape:* c. acc., 11 Pe 2[18, 20]; c. gen., 11 Pe 1[4].†

† ἀπο-φθέγγομαι, [in LXX for נבא, etc.;] *to speak forth, give utterance:* Ac 2[4, 14] 26[25] (MM, s.v.).†

*† ἀπο-φορτίζομαι (< φορτίζω, *to load*), *to discharge a cargo* (Field, *Notes*, 134), *to unlade:* c. acc., τ. γόμον, Ac 21[3].†

*† ἀπό-χρησις, -εως. ἡ (< ἀποχράομαι, *to use to the full, abuse*), *abuse, misuse:* Col 2[22] (MM, s.v.).†

ἀπο-χωρέω, -ῶ, [in LXX: Je 26 (46)[5] (סונ), 11 Mac 4[33], 111 Mac 2[33] *;] *to go away, depart, withdraw:* seq. ἀπό, Mt 7[23], Lk 9[39], Ac 13[13] (absol., Lk 20[20], Tr., mg.).†

ἀπο-χωρίζω, [in LXX: Ez 43[21] (מפקד)* ;] *to separate, part asunder:* pass., Re 6[14]; reflexively, *to separate oneself:* Ac 15[39].†

** ἀπο-ψύχω, [in LXX: IV Mac 15[18] *;] 1. *to breathe out life, expire* (Thuc.; LXX, l.c.).   2. *to leave off breathing, faint* (Hom., *Od.*, xxiv, 348): seq. ἀπό, Lk 21[26].†

Ἄππιος, -ου, ὁ, *Appius;* Ἀππίου Φόρον, *Appii Forum* (Market of Appius), a town in Italy: Ac 28[15].†

*† ἀ-πρόσ-ιτος, -ον (< πρόσειμι, *to go to*), *unapproachable:* φῶς, 1 Ti 6[16].†

**† ἀπρόσκοπος, -ον (< προσκόπτω), [in LXX: Si 35 (32)[21], 111 Mac 3[8] *;] 1. act., *not causing to stumble:* metaph., of not leading others into si·, 1 Co 10[32].   2. Pass., *not stumbling, without offence, blameless:* Ac 24[16], Phl 1[10] (for exx., v. MM, s.v.).†

*† ἀπροσωπολήμπτως (Rec. -λήπτως, cl.), adv. (< α- neg., προσωπολήμπτης), *without respect of persons, impartially:* 1 Pe 1[17].†

** ἄ-πταιστος, -ον (< πταίω), [in LXX: 111 Mac 6[39] *;] *without stumbling, sure-footed:* metaph. (MM, s.v.), Ju 24.†

ἅπτω, [in LXX chiefly for נבע ;] prop., *to fasten to;* hence, of fire, *to kindle, light:* Lk 8[16] 11[33] 15[8], Ac 28[2].   Mid., c. gen., *to fasten oneself to, cling to, lay hold of* (so in π.; MM, s.v.): Mt 8[3, 15], Jo 20[17], al.; of carnal intercourse, 1 Co 7[1]; with reference to levitical and ceremonial prohibitions, 11 Co 6[17], Col 2[21]; of hostile action, 1 Jo 5[18] (cf. ἀν-, καθ-, περι- ἅπτω).

SYN.: θιγγάνω, ψηλαφάω.   ἅ. is the stronger, θ., *to touch*, the lighter term.   ψ. is *to feel*, as in search of something (Tr., *Syn.*, § xvii; Lft., *Col.*, 201 f.).

Ἀπφία, -ας, ἡ, *Apphia:* Phm ² (MM, s.v.).†

ἀπ-ωθέω, -ῶ, [in LXX for זנח, מאם, etc.;] *to thrust away.* Mid., *to thrust away from oneself, refuse,* reject: c. acc. pers. (MM, s.v.), Ac 7[27, 39] 13[46], Ro 11[1, 2], 1 Ti 1[19].†

ἀπώλεια, -ας, ἡ (< ἀπόλλυμι), [in LXX (Cremer, 797) for אבד, איד, etc.;] *destruction, waste, loss, perishing* (in π., of money, v. MM, s.v.): Mt 26[8], Mk 14[4], Ac 8[20], Ro 9[22], 1 Ti 6[9], 11 Pe 2[1]; in special sense of the loss of eternal life, *perdition*, the antithesis of σωτηρία: Mt 7¹³, Jo 17¹², Phl 1²⁸ 3¹⁹, ΙΙ Th 2³, He 10³⁹, ΙΙ Pe 2³ 3⁷, ¹⁶, Re 17⁸, ¹¹ (*DB*, iii, 744).†

Ἄρ, indecl., Re 16¹⁶, v.s., Ἀρμαγεδών.

ἄρα, illative particle, expressing a more subjective or informal inference than οὖν, *then*: prop. (as in cl.), the second word in the sentence, Ro 7²¹ 8¹, Ga 3⁷; ἐπεὶ ἄρα, ι Co 7¹⁴ (with another word between) 5¹⁰; as the first word, Lk 11⁴⁸, Ac 11¹⁸, Ro 10¹⁷, ι Co 15¹⁸, ΙΙ Co 5¹⁵ 7¹², He 4⁹; so prop. in apodosis after protasis with εἰ, Mt 12²⁸, Lk 11²⁰, Ga 2²¹ 3²⁹ 5¹¹, He 12⁸ (κενὸν ἄρα), ι Co 15¹⁴; often in interrogations, direct and indirect, τίς (τί) ἄρα, Mt 18¹ 19²⁵, ²⁷ 24⁴⁵, Mk 4⁴¹, Lk 1⁶⁶ 8²⁵ 12⁴² 22²³, Ac 12¹⁸; εἰ ἄρα, Mk 11¹³, Ac 8²²; εἴπερ ἄρα, ι Co 15¹⁵; οὐκ ἄρα, Ac 21³⁸; μήτι ἄρα, ΙΙ Co 1¹⁷; in strengthened forms, ἄρα γε, ἄραγε, Mt 7²⁰ 17²⁶, Ac 17²⁷, and more freq. ἄρα οὖν (Epp. Paul.), *so then*, Ro 5¹⁸ 7³, ²⁵ 8¹² 9¹⁶, ¹⁸ 14¹², ¹⁹, Ga 6¹⁰, Eph 2¹⁹, ι Th 5⁶, ΙΙ Th 2¹⁵ (Bl., § 77, 2; 78, 5; MM, s.v.).†

ἆρα, interrog. particle, implying anxiety or impatience, "quite rare and only in Luke and Paul, therefore a literary word" (Bl., § 77, 2). 1. (*num igitur*) expecting a neg. reply, Lk 18⁸; ἆρά γε, Ac 8³⁰. 2. (*ergone*) in apodosis, expecting an affirm. reply, Ga 2¹⁷ (Bl., l.c.; Lft., *Ga.*, in l.; MM, s.v.).†

ἀρά, -ᾶς, ἡ, [in LXX chiefly for אלה]; 1. *a prayer* (MM, s.v.). 2. (as in Homer) *a curse, malediction*: Ro 3¹⁴ (LXX).†

Ἀραβία, -ας, ἡ, *Arabia*: Ga 1¹⁷ 4²⁵.†

ἀραβών, v.s. ἀρραβών.

ἄραγε, v.s. ἄρα.

ἆράγε, v.s. ἆρα.

Ἀράμ, indic. (Heb. רָם), *Aram*: Mt 1³, ⁴, Lk 3³³ (R, txt., WH, Ἀρνεί).†

*ἄραφος, -ον (Rec. ἄρραφος, < ῥάπτω, to sew) *without seam*: Jo 19²³.†

Ἄραψ, -αβος, ὁ, *an Arabian*: Ac 2¹¹.†

ἀργέω, -ῶ (< ἀργός), [in LXX: ΙΙ Es 4²⁴, Ec 12³ (בטל), ι Es 2³⁰, Si 30³⁶ (33²⁷), ΙΙ Mac 5²⁵*;] *to be idle; τὸ κρίμα . . . ἀ., lingers* (cf. MGr. ἀργά, *late*: MM, s.v.): ΙΙ Pe 2³.†

ἀργός, -όν (in late Gk., incl. NT, -ή, -όν; < ἀ- neg., ἔργον), [in LXX: ΙΙΙ Ki 6⁷ (מַסָּע?), Wi 14⁵ 15¹⁵, Si 37¹¹ 38²⁸*;] *inactive, idle*: Mt 20³, ⁶, ι Ti 5¹³, Tit 1¹², ΙΙ Pe 1⁸. Metaph., of things, *inactive, ineffective, worthless*: ῥῆμα, Mt 12³⁶; πίστις, Ja 2²⁰ (v. Cremer, 259 f.).†

SYN.: βραδύς, *slow*; νωθρός, *sluggish* (Tr., *Syn.*, § civ).

ἀργύρεος (v. MM, s.v.), -οῦς, -ᾶ, -οῦν (< ἄργυρος), [in LXX for כֶּסֶף;] *of silver*: Ac 19²⁴ (WH, br.), ΙΙ Ti 2²⁰, Re 9²⁰.†

ἀργύριον, -ου, τό (< ἄργυρος), [in LXX for כֶּסֶף (Ge 13², al.), exc. La 4¹ (כֶּתֶם);] prop., *a piece of silver* (Lft., *Notes*, 191); in NT, (*a*) *silver*: Ac 3⁶ 7¹⁶ 19¹⁰ 20³³, ι Co 3¹², ι Pe 1¹⁸; (*b*) *money*:

Mt 25¹⁸,²⁷, Mk 14¹¹, Lk 9³ 19¹⁵,²³ 22⁵, Ac 8²⁰; (c) a silver coin: pl.,
Mt 26¹⁵ 27³,⁵,⁶,⁹ 28¹²,¹⁵, where the value is that of a shekel or
tetradrachm; ἀργυρίου μυριάδες πέντε (prob. drachmas; MM, s.v.),
Ac 19¹⁹.†

† ἀργυροκόπος, -ου, ὁ (< ἄργυρος, κόπτω, to beat), [in LXX: Jg 17⁴,
Je 6²⁹ (צָרַף) *;] a silversmith: Ac 19²⁴ (Plut.; π., v. MM, s.v.).†

ἄργυρος, -ου, ὁ (< ἀργός, shining), [in LXX for בָּסֶף;] silver (on its
relation to ἀργύριον, v. MM, s.v.): Mt 10⁹, Ac 17²⁹, Ja 5⁵, Re 18¹².†

Ἄρειος Πάγος (T, Ἄριος Π.), -ου, ὁ, Hill of Ares or Mars,
Areopagus; also, the Court of Areopagus, the highest tribunal of
Athens: Ac 17¹⁹,²².†

Ἀρεοπαγίτης (T, -είτης), -ου, ὁ (v. supr.), a judge of the Court of
Areopagus: Ac 17³⁴.†

ἀρεσκία (Rec. -εία), -ας, ἡ (< ἀρέσκω), [in LXX (-εία): Pr 31³⁰
(חֵן) *;] pleasing, desire to please: Col 1¹⁰. In Gk. writers (Arist.,
Polyb.), most freq. in bad sense, but in π., Inscr., and in Philo, as
above (v. Deiss., BS, 224; MM, s.v.; Cremer, 642).†

ἀρέσκω, [in LXX chiefly for טוֹב ;] 1. to please (Hom., Hdt., al.):
c. dat. pers., Mt 14⁶, Mk 6²², Ro 8⁸ 15², ι Th 2¹⁵ 4¹, ι Co 7³²,³³,³⁴,
Gal 1¹⁰, ιι Ti 2⁴; seq. ἐνώπιον (= Heb. בְּעֵינֵי, Bl., § 37, 1; 40, 7).
Ac 6⁵. 2. In late Gk., esp. in Inscr., to render service to (v. M, Th.,
ICC, ι Co., ll. c.; Cremer, 640 f.); Ro 15¹,³, ι Co 10³³, ι Th 2⁴.†

ἀρεστός, -ή, -όν (< ἀρέσκω), [in LXX for יָשָׁר, etc.;] pleasing,
agreeable (Hdt., Xen., and later writers; v. Cremer, 641 f.; MM,
s.v.): c. dat. pers., Jo 8²⁹, Ac 12³; seq. ἐνώπιον, c. gen. (Bl., § 37, 1; 40,
7), ι Jo 3²²; ἀρεστόν ἐστιν, c. acc. et inf (Bl., § 69, 5; 72, 5), Ac 6².†

Ἀρέτας (WH, Ἁρ.; Intr., 313), -α, ὁ, Aretas, an Arabian king:
ιι Co 11³² (Deiss., BS, 183 f., thinks the proper spelling Ἀρέθας was
changed, as Schürer suggests, "by desire to Hellenise a barbaric
name by assimilation to ἀρετή").†

ἀρετή, -ῆς, ἡ, [in LXX, in sing.: Hb 3³, Za 6¹³ (הוֹד), in pl.:
Is 42⁸,¹² 43²¹ 63⁷ (תְּהִלָּה), Es 14¹⁰, Wi 4¹ 5¹³ 8⁷, ιι-ιv Mac ₂₂ *;] prop.,
whatever procures pre-eminent estimation for a person or thing, in
Hom. any kind of conspicuous advantage. Later confined by philos.
writers to intrinsic eminence—moral goodness, virtue; (a) of God:
ιι Pe 1³; (b) of men: Phl 4⁸, ιι Pe 1⁵; pl. (Is, Es, ll. c.), excellencies:
ι Pe 2⁹ (the usage appears to be a survival of an early comprehensive
sense in which the original idea is blended with the impression which
it makes on others, i.e. praise, renown; v. Hort, ι Pe., 129. Deiss.,
BS, 95 f., thinks it means manifestations of divine power, as in
current Gk. speech; cf. also MM, s.v.)†

ἀρήν, ἀρνός, ὁ (nom. not in use, exc. in early times: v. MM,
s.v.), [in LXX for מָרִיא, כֶּבֶשׂ, etc.;] a lamb: Lk 10³.†

ἀριθμέω, -ῶ, [in LXX for סָפַר pi., פָּקַד pi., etc.;] to number
(esp. for payment; MM, s.v.): Mt 10³⁰, Lk 12⁷, Re 7⁹.†

ἀριθμός, -οˆ, ὁ, [in LXX chiefly for מִסְפָּר ;] *number, a number* :
Lk 22³, Jo 6¹⁰, Ac 4⁴ 5³⁶ 6⁷ 11²¹ 16⁵, Ro 9²⁷, Re 5¹¹ 7⁴ 9¹⁶ 13¹⁷, ¹⁸ 15²
20⁸ (for exx. of mystical use in π., v. MM, s.v.).†

'Αριμαθεία (WH, 'Αρ.), -ας, ἡ, [in LXX : 'Αρμαθάιμ, 1 Ki 1¹, al.
(רָמָתַיִם) ;] *Arimathœa* : Mt 27⁵⁷, Mk 15⁴³, Lk 23⁵¹, Jo 19³⁸.†

Ἄριος, v.s. Ἄρειος.

'Αρίσταρχος, -ου, ὁ (< ἄριστος, ἀρχός; i.e. *best-ruling*), *Aristarchus* :
Ac 19²⁹ 20⁴ 27², Col 4¹⁰, Phm ²⁴.†

ἀριστάω, -ῶ (< ἄριστον), [in LXX : Ge 43²⁵ (אָכַל לֶחֶם), 1 Ki 14²⁴
(לֶחֶם), III Ki 13⁷ (סָעַד), To 2¹ *;] 1. prop., *to breakfast* : Jo 21¹², ¹⁵.
2. In late Gk., *to take a meal, dine* : Lk 11³⁷.†

ἀριστερός, -ά, -όν, [in LXX for שְׂמֹאל ;] *left, on the left* : ὅπλα,
II Co 6⁷ ; ἡ ἀ. (sc. χείρ), Mt 6³ ; ἐξ ἀριστερῶν, *on the left* (MM, s.v.) :
Mk 10³⁷, Lk 23³³.†

'Αριστόβουλος, -ου, ὁ (< ἄριστος, βουλή, i.e. *best-counselling*),
Aristobulus, a Christian : Ro 16¹⁰.†

ἄριστον, -ου, τό, [in LXX : III Ki 3¹ (לֶחֶם), To 2¹, ⁴, al.;] 1. prop.,
breakfast. 2. In late Gk. = cl. δεῖπνον, *dinner* : Mt 22⁴, Lk 11³⁸ 14¹².†

**† ἀρκετός, -ή, -όν (< ἀρκέω), [in Aq. : De 25² *;] *sufficient* : Mt 6³⁴
(on the neut., v. Bl., § 31, 2) ; seq. ἵνα (M, *Pr.*, 210), Mt 10²⁵ ; c. inf.,
1 Pe 4³ (for exx., v. Deiss., *BS*, 257; MM, s.v.).†

ἀρκέω, -ῶ, [in LXX for חוּן, etc.;] 1. *to keep off* ; c. dat., *to assist.*
2. *to suffice* : c. dat. pers., Jo 6⁷, II Co 12⁹ ; impers., Mt 25⁹, Jo 14⁸
(MM, s.v.). Pass., *to be satisfied* : c. dat. rei, Lk 3¹⁴, 1 Ti 6⁸, He 13⁵ ;
seq. ἐπί, III Jo ¹⁰.†

ἄρκος (Rec. (cl.) ἄρκτος), [in LXX for דֹּב ;] -ου, ὁ, ἡ, *a bear* : Re 13².
(This form is also found in late Inscr.; MM, s.v.)†

ἅρμα, -τος, τό (< ἀραρίσκω, *to join*), [in LXX for רֶכֶב ;] *a chariot* :
Ac 8²⁸, ²⁹, ³⁸, Re 9⁹.†

'Αρμαγεδών (WH, Ἀρ Μαγεδών; Rec. 'Αρμαγεδδών, prop. = הַר
מְגִדּוֹ), cf. LXX, Μαγεδών, II Ch 35²², Μαγεδώ, Jg 1²⁷ ; *Har-Magedon*
(AV, *Armageddon*) : Re 16¹⁶ (v. Swete, in l., but also Thayer, s.v.).†

ἁρμόζω (< ἁρμός), [in LXX for אָמַן, etc.;] 1. *to fit, join.* 2. *of
marriage, to betroth.* Mid., (*a*) *to join to oneself, marry, take to wife ;*
(*b*) *to give in marriage :* II Co 11² (for this there is no direct parallel.
But v. M, *Pr.*, 160; MM, s.v.).†

** ἁρμός, -οῦ, ὁ, [in LXX : Si 27², IV Mac 10⁵ *;] *a joining, joint* :
He 4¹².†

ἄρνας, v.s. ἀρήν.

'Αρνεί (Rec. 'Αράμ), ὁ, indecl., *Arnei* : Lk 3³³.†

ἀρνέομαι, -οῦμαι, depon., [in LXX : Ge 18¹⁵ (כָּחַשׁ pi.), Wi 12²⁷ 16¹⁶
17¹⁰, IV Mac 8⁷ 10¹⁵ *;] 1. *to deny, say no*, opp. to εἰπεῖν : absol., Mt 26⁷⁰,
Lk 8⁴⁵ ; seq. ὅτι, 1 Jo 2²² ; c. inf., He 11²⁴. 2. In late Gk. (MM, s.v.),
c. acc. pers., *to deny, refuse to acknowledge, disown* : Ac 3¹⁴ 7³⁵ ;

Ἰησοῦν, Mt 10³³, ΙΙ Ti 2¹², ι Jo 2²², Ju⁴; ἑαυτόν, Lk 9²³, ΙΙ Ti 2¹³ (*prove false to*). 3. C. acc. rei (in cl. *to refuse*), *to deny, abjure*: ι Ti 5⁸, Tit 2¹², ΙΙ Ti 3⁵ (cf. ἀπαρνέομαι).

ἀρνίον, -ου, τό (dimin. of ἀρήν; v. MM, s.v.), [in LXX: Ps 113 (114)⁴, ⁶ (pl., בְּנֵי עֹאן), Je 11¹⁹ (כְּבֶשׂ), 27 (50)⁴⁵ (צָעִיר) *;] *a little lamb, a lamb*: Jo 21¹⁵, Re ₂₇.†

†ἀροτριάω, -ῶ (< ἄροτρον), [in LXX: De 22¹⁰, al. (חָרַשׁ), Is 7²⁵ (עֲדָד);] later form of ἀρόω, *to plough* (MM, s.v.): Lk 17⁷, ι Co 9¹⁰.†

ἄροτρον, -ου, τό (< ἀρόω, *to plough*), [in LXX chiefly for אֵת;] *a plough*: Lk 9⁶².†

ἁρπαγή, -ῆς, ἡ (< ἁρπάζω), [in LXX (as also ἅρπαγμα) for גָּזֵל, etc.;] *pillage, plundering, robbery*: Mt 23²⁵, Lk 11³⁹, He 10³⁴.†

*†ἁρπαγμός, οῦ, ὁ (< ἁρπάζω); 1. prop., acc. to the rule of its formation (Bl., § 27, 2), actively, *the act of seizing, robbery* (Plut., *de Puer. Educ.*, p. 12ᴀ), Phl 2⁶, AV (Waterland, *Works*, II, 108; Cremer, 649 f.; Meyer, in l.; cf. also *JThS*, July, 1909, April, 1911; MM, s.v.). 2. Passively = ἅρπαγμα (Ez 22²⁵, of a lion's prey, טֶרֶף), *a thing seized*, hence, *a prize*: Phl, l.c., RV (Lft., Ellic., *ICC*, in l.; Donaldson, *NCrat.*, 450 ff.; and esp. Gifford, *The Incarnation*, 59-71, and reff. in *DB*, ii, 835 ᴮ). The lexical data favour the active meaning, but as they also admit the possibility of the alternative, most modern expositors have accepted the latter as seeming to suit the logic of the passage better. The lexical difficulty, however, remains (MM, s.v., esp. the last ref.). As to the usage of St. Paul, he seems inclined to adopt the -μα form where it is appropriate (e.g. Ro 11⁹, where cf. LXX; ι Co 13⁹, ΙΙ Co 1⁹), and there is certainly a presumption in favour of the active meaning here from the fact that he does not use the LXX ἅρπαγμα. Suggestions looking to a fresh exegesis are given in *JThS*, ll. c.†

ἁρπάζω, [in LXX chiefly for גָּזַל, טֶרֶף;] *to seize, catch up, snatch away, carry off by force*: c. acc. rei, Mt 12²⁹ 13¹⁹, Jo 10¹², ²⁸, ²⁹; τ. βασιλείαν τ. θεοῦ, Mt 11¹²; c. acc. pers., Jo 6¹⁵, Ac 8³⁹ 23¹⁰, Ju²³; pass., seq. ἕως, ΙΙ Co 12²; εἰς, ib. 12⁴, ι Th 4¹⁷; πρός, Re 12⁵ (cf. δι-, συν-αρπάζω, and v. MM, s.v.).†

ἅρπαξ, -αγος, ὁ, ἡ (< ἁρπάζω), [in LXX: Ge 49²⁷ (טרף) *;] *rapacious*: Mt 7¹⁵, Lk 18¹¹; as subst., *a swindler, an extortioner* (MM, s.v.), ι Co 5¹⁰, ¹¹ 6¹⁰.†

ἀρραβών (T, ἀραβ-: ΙΙ Co, ll. c.), -ῶνος, ὁ, [in LXX: Ge 38¹⁷, ¹⁸, ²⁰ (עֵרָבוֹן) *;] *an earnest*, part payment in advance for security, a first instalment: ΙΙ Co 1²² 5⁵, Eph 1¹⁴. (The word is found in cl. and was prob. brought to Greece by the Phœnicians (AR, *Eph.*, l.c.). It is found in π. with both spellings (v. Milligan, *NTD*, 73). In MGr. ἀρραβῶνα is an *engagement ring*; v. MM, s.v.)†

ἄρραφος, v.s. ἄραφος.

ἄρρην, v.s. ἄρσην.

** ἄρρητος, -ον (< ἀ- neg., ῥητός, ῥέω), [in Sm. : Le 18²³ * ;] 1. *unspoken* (Hom., al.). 2. *unspeakable* (Hdt., al.; freq. in Inscr.; MM, s.v.) : II Co 12⁴.†

ἄρρωστος, -ον (< ἀ- neg., ῥώννυμι), [in LXX : III Ki 14⁵A, Ma 1⁸ (חלה), Si 7³⁵ * ;] *feeble, sickly* : Mt 14¹⁴, Mk 6⁵, ¹³ 16[¹³], I Co 11³⁰.†

*† ἀρσενοκοίτης, -ου, ὁ (< ἄρσην, κοιτή), *a sodomite* : I Co 6⁹, I Ti 1¹⁰.†

ἄρσην (ἄ̩ρρην, T, in Ro 1²⁷ ; Rec. in Re 12⁵, ¹³), -ενος, ὁ, ἡ, ἄρσεν, τό (old Attic for ἄρρην, v. supr.; both forms are found in π.; MM, s.v.), [in LXX chiefly for זָכָר ;] *male* : Mt 19⁴, Mk 10⁶, Lk 2²³, Ro 1²⁷, Ga 3²⁸, Re 12⁵, ¹³.†

Ἀρτεμᾶς, -ᾶ, ὁ, *Artemas* : Tit 3¹².†

Ἄρτεμις, -ιδος, ἡ, *Artemis*, an Asiatic goddess, to be disting. from the Gk. goddess of the same name : Ac 19²⁴, ²⁷, ²⁸, ³⁴, ³⁵.†

*† ἀρτέμων, -ωνος (Rec. -ονος), ὁ (< ἀρτάω, *to fasten to*), *a fore-sail* or *top-sail* : Ac 27⁴⁰ (v. *DB, ext.*, 366ᵇ, 399ᵃ ; MM, s.v.).†

ἄρτι, [in LXX : Da LXX 9²² 10¹¹ (עַתָּה), al. ;] adv. of coincidence, denoting strictly present time, as contrasted with past or future, *just, just now, this moment* : Mt 3¹⁵ 9¹⁸ 26⁵³, Jo 13⁷, Ga 4²⁰, I Th 3⁶ (v. Lft., *Notes*, 44 ; Milligan, in l.), Re 12¹⁰ ; opp. to past time, Jo 9¹⁹, ²⁵ 13³³, I Co 16⁷, Ga 1⁹, ¹⁰ ; to future, Jo 13³⁷ 16¹², ³¹, I Co 13¹², II Th 2⁷, I Pe 1⁶, ⁸ ; ἄχρι τῆς ἄ. ὥρας, I Co 4¹¹ ; ἕως ἄ., Mt 11¹², Jo 2¹⁰ 5¹⁷ 16²⁴, I Co 4¹³ 8⁷ 15⁶ I Jo 2⁹ ; ἀπ' ἄ., v.s. ἀπάρτι (v. Rutherford, *NPhr.*, 70 f ; MM, s.v.).†

SYN. : νῦν, *now*, "the objective, immediate present; ἤδη, *now*, already, "the subjective present, with a suggested reference to some other time or to some expectation". (Thayer, 75.)

*† ἀρτι-γέννητος, -ον (< ἄρτι, γεννάω), *new-born* : I Pe 2² (Luc.).†

* ἄρτιος, -α, -ον, *fitted, complete* : II Ti 3¹⁷ (MM, s.v.).†

ἄρτος, -ου, ὁ, [in LXX chiefly for לֶחֶם ;] *bread, a loaf* : Mt 4³, ⁴, Mk 3²⁰, al.; ἄρτοι τ. προθέσεως, *bread of the setting forth*, i.e. the shewbread. Metaph., ὁ ἄ. τ. θεοῦ, τ. ζωῆς, ref. to Christ, Jo 6³³, ³⁵ ; in general, *food* : Mt 6¹¹, al.; ἄ. φαγεῖν (Heb. אָכַל לֶחֶם), *to eat* (MM, s.v.), Lu 14¹, al.

** ἀρτύω, [in Sm. : Ca 8² * ;] 1. *to arrange, make ready* (Hom.). 2. Of food (as in comic writers), *to season* (MM, s.v.) : Mk 9⁵⁰, Lk 14³⁴, Col 4⁶.†

Ἀρφαξάδ, ὁ (Heb. אַרְפַּכְשַׁד), *Arphaxad* : Lk 3³⁶.†

*† ἀρχ-άγγελος, -ου, ὁ (< ἄρχι-, ἄγγελος), *archangel*, a chief angel : I Th 4¹⁶, Ju ⁹ (Cremer, 24 ; MM, s.v.).†

ἀρχαῖος, -αία, -αῖον (< ἀρχή), [in LXX chiefly for קֶדֶם ;] *original, ancient* : Mt 5²¹, ³³, Lk 9⁸, ¹⁹, Ac 15⁷, ²¹ 21¹⁶, II Co 5¹⁷, II Pe 2⁵, Re 12⁹ 20².†

SYN. : παλαιός, *old*, without the reference to beginning and origin contained in ἀ. The distinction is observed in π. (MM, s.v.). ἀ. is the antithesis to καινός : παλ. to νέος (v. Westc., *He.*, 223 ; Cremer, 116).

Ἀρχέλαος, -ov, ὁ, *Archelaus*, son of Herod the Great, King of Judæa, Samaria and Idumæa : Mt 2²².†

ἀρχή, -ῆς, ἡ, [in LXX for קֶדֶם, ראֹשׁ, רֵאשִׁית, etc. ;] 1. *beginning, origin ;* (*a*) absol., of the beginning of all things : of God as the Eternal, the First Cause, Re 21⁶ (cf. 1⁸) ; similarly, of Christ, Re 22¹³ ; of Christ as the uncreated principle, the active cause of creation, Re˙ 3¹⁴ ; in his relation to the Church, Col 1¹⁸ ; ἐν ἀ., Jo 1¹, ² ; ἀπ᾽ ἀ. (and ἀπ᾽ ἀ. κτίσεως), Mt 19⁴, ⁸ 24²¹, Mk 10⁶ 13¹⁹, Jo 8⁴⁴, II Th 2¹³, II Pe 3⁴, I Jo 1¹ 2¹³, ¹⁴ 3⁸ ; κατ᾽ ἀρχάς, He 1¹⁰ ; (*b*) relatively : He 7³ ; ἀ. ὠδίνων, Mt 24⁸, Mk 13⁸ ; τ. σημείων, Jo 2¹¹ ; τ. ὑποστάσεως, He 3¹⁴ ; τ. λογίων, 5¹² ; ὁ τ. ἀρχῆς τ. Χριστοῦ λόγος, the account of the beginning, the elementary view of Christ, He 6¹ ; ἀρχὴν λαμβάνειν, to begin, He 2³ ; ἐξ ἀ., Jo 6⁶⁴ 16⁴ ; ἀπ᾽ ἀ., Lk 1², Jo 15²⁷, I Jo 2⁷, ²⁴ 3¹¹, II Jo 5, ⁶ ; ἐν ἀ., Ac 11¹⁵ 26⁴, Phl 4¹⁵ ; τὴν ἀρχήν, adverbially, *at all* (Hdt., al. ; v. MM, s.v.) : Jo 8²⁵. 2. *an extremity, a corner :* Ac 10¹¹ 11⁵. 3. *sovereignty, principality, rule* (cf. *DB*, i, 616 f.) : Lk 12¹¹ 20²⁰, Ro 8³⁸, I Co 15²⁴, Eph 1²¹ 3¹⁰ 6¹², Col 1¹⁶ 2¹⁰, ¹⁵, Tit 3¹, Ju ⁶ (Cremer, 113).†

ἀρχηγός, -όν, [in LXX for ראֹשׁ, נָשִׂיא, etc. ;] *beginning, originating :* more freq., as subst. ; 1. *founder, author* (Lat. *auctor ;* so sometimes in π., v. MM, s.v. ; Milligan, *NTD*, 75) : Ac 3¹⁵ (R, mg.), He 2¹⁰ (R, txt. ; but v. Westc., in l., and Page, *Ac.*, l.c.). 2. *prince, leader* (so in MGr., v. Kennedy, *Sources*, 153) : Ac 3¹⁵ (R, txt.) 5³¹, He 2¹⁰ (cf. R, mg.) 12² (Cremer, 117).†

ἀρχι- (< ἄρχω), insep. prefix, denoting high office and dignity, freq. in Alex. and Byzant. Gk. (MM, s.v.).

*†ἀρχ-ιερατικός, -ή, -όν (< ἀρχιερεύς), *high-priestly :* Ac 4⁶ (MM, s.v.).†

ἀρχ-ιερεύς, -έως, ὁ, [in LXX for כֹּהֵן, כּ׳ הַגָּדֹול, כ׳ הָרֹאשׁ ;] 1. *high-priest :* Mk 2²⁶ 14⁴⁷, al. ; of Christ : He 2¹⁷ 3¹, al. 2. In pl., *chief priests,* including ex-high-priests and members of high-priestly families : Mt 2⁴, Mk 8³¹, al. (Cremer, 294 ; *DCG*, i, 297 f. ; MM, s.v.).

**†ἀρχι-ποίμην, -ενος, ὁ, [in Sm. : IV Ki 3⁴ * ;] found on an Egyptian mummy label (Deiss., *LAE*, 97 ff. ; cf. MM, s.v.) ; used by modern Greeks of tribal chiefs ; *chief shepherd* . of Christ, I Pe 5⁴.†

Ἄρχιππος, -ov, ὁ, *Archippus :* Col 4¹⁷, Phm ².†

*†ἀρχισυνάγωγος, -ov, ὁ (< συναγωγή), *ruler of a synagogue,* an administrative officer, supervising the worship (ראֹשׁ הַכְּנֶסֶת) : Mk 5²², ³⁵, ³⁶, ³⁸, Lk 8⁴⁹ 13¹⁴, Ac 13¹⁵ 18⁸, ¹⁷ (Inscr., v. MM, s.v. ; cf. also *DB*, ext., 101).†

ἀρχι-τέκτων, -ονος, ὁ (< τέκτων), [in LXX : Is 3³ (חָרָשׁ), Si 38²⁷, II Mac 2²⁹ * ;] *a master-builder, architect :* I Co 3¹⁰ (in π. of building contractors, MM, s.v.).†

*†ἀρχι-τελώνης, -ov, ὁ, *a chief tax-collector, chief publican :* Lk 19².†

*†ἀρχι-τρίκλινος, -ov, ὁ (< τρί-κλινος or -ov, *a room with three couches*) *the superintendent of a banquet,* whose duty it was to arrange the tables and food (*DB*, ii, 253) : Jo 2⁸, ⁹.†

ἄρχω, [in LXX for חלל, משל, etc.;] 1. *to begin.* 2. *to rule* (v. *DCG*, ii, 538 b.) : c. gen., Mk 10⁴², Ro 15¹². Mid., *to begin* : seq. ἀπό, Mt 16²¹ 20⁸, Lk 14¹⁸ 23⁵ 24²⁷, ⁴⁷, Jo 8⁹, Ac 1²² 8³⁵ 10³⁷, I Pe 4¹⁷ ; c. inf., an Aramaic pleonasm, Mk 1⁴⁵ 2³³ 5¹⁷, Lk 3⁸, al. (v. M, *Pr.*, 14 f.; Dalman, *Words*, 27 ; MM, s.v ; M, *Gr.*, II, pp. 451 ff.).

ἄρχων, -οντος, ὁ (pres. ptcp. of ἄρχω), [in LXX for נשׂיא, ראשׁ, שׂר, etc.;] *a ruler, chief:* Jesus, Re 1⁵; rulers of nations, Mt 20²⁵, Ac 4²⁶ 7³⁵; magistrates, Ac 23⁵, Ro 13³ ; judges, Lk 12⁵⁸, Ac 7²⁷, ³⁵ 16¹⁹; members of the Sanhedrin, Lk 14¹ 23¹³, ³⁵ 24²⁰, Jo 3¹ 7²⁶, ⁴⁸ 12⁴², Ac 3¹⁷ 4⁵, ⁸ 13²⁷ 14⁵; rulers of synagogues, Mt 9¹⁸, ²³, Lk 8⁴¹ 18¹⁸; οἱ ἄ. τ. αἰῶνος τούτου, I Co 2⁶, ⁸; of the devil: ἄ. τῶν δαιμονίων, Mt 9³⁴ 12²⁴, Mk 3²², Lk 11¹⁵; ὁ ἄ. τοῦ κόσμου, Jo 12³¹ 14³⁰ 16¹¹; ἄ. τ. ἐξουσίας τ. ἀέρος, Eph 2² (MM, s.v.; *DB*, iii, 838; *Ext.*, 99 f; *DCG*, ii, 419; *DCB*, s.v. Archon).†

ἄρωμα, -τος, τό, [in LXX for בֹּשֶׂם ;] *spice:* Mk 16¹, Lk 23⁵⁶ 24¹, Jo 19⁴⁰.†

Ἀσά, v.s. Ασάφ.

ἀσαίνω, v.s. σαίνω.

ἀ-σάλευτος, -ον (< σαλεύω), [in LXX: Ex 13¹⁶, De 6⁸ 11¹⁸ (מוֹפֵת)*;] *unmoved, immovable:* Ac 27⁴¹; metaph., He 12²⁸.†

Ἀσάφ, ὁ, indecl. (Heb. אָסָף), *Asaph,* an obvious error for Ἀσά, found in the best texts, and adopted by LTTr. and WH, R, mg.: Mt 1⁷, ⁸.†

ἄ-σβεστος, -ον (<σβέννυμι), [in LXX for לֹא נִכְבֶּה, Jb 20²⁶ א ³ A (ἄκαυστον, א ² B)*;] *unquenched, unquenchable:* πῦρ, Mt 3¹², Mk 9⁴³, Lk 3¹⁷.†

ἀσέβεια, -ας, ἡ (< ἀσεβής), [in LXX for פֶּשַׁע, רֶשַׁע, etc.;] *ungodliness, impiety:* Ro 1¹⁸ 11²⁶, II Ti 2¹⁶, Tit 2¹²; ἔργα ἀσεβείας, ungodly deeds, Ju ¹⁵; ἐπιθυμίαι τ. ἀσεβειῶν, *desires for ungodly things* or *deeds,* Ju ¹⁸ (*DB*, iv, 532; Cremer, 523; MM, s.v.).†

ἀσεβέω, -ῶ (< ἀσεβής), [in LXX for פָּשַׁע, רָשַׁע;] *to be ungodly, act profanely:* II Pe 2⁶; c. cogn. acc. (MM, s.v.), Ju ¹⁵.†

ἀσεβής, -ές (σέβω, *to reverence*), [in LXX chiefly for רָשָׁע;] *ungodly, impious:* Ro 4⁵ 5⁶, I Ti 1⁹, I Pe 4¹⁸, II Pe 2⁵, ⁶ 3⁷, Ju ⁴, ¹⁵.†

** ἀσέλγεια, -ας, ἡ (< ἀσελγής, *licentious;* v. MM, s.v.), [in LXX: Wi 14²⁶, III Mac 2²⁶ *;] *licentiousness, wantonness, excess:* Mk 7²², Ro 13¹³, II Co 12²¹, Ga 5¹⁹ (Lft., in l.), Eph 4¹⁹, I Pe 4³, II Pe 2², ⁷, ¹⁸, Ju ⁴.†

SYN.: ἀσωτία, *profligacy, prodigality* (v. Tr., *Syn.*, § xvi; *DB*, iii, 46).

ἄσημος, -ον (< σῆμα, *a mark*), [in LXX: Ge 30⁴² (עֲטֻף), Jb 42¹¹, III Mac 1³ *;] *without mark* (in π. of an uncircumcised boy: Deiss., *BS*, 153; MM, s.v.). Metaph. (MM, s.v.), *unknown, obscure:* litotes, οὐκ ἄ. (Eur., al.), πόλις, Ac 21³⁹.†

Ἀσήρ, ὁ, indecl. (Heb. אָשֵׁר), *Asher:* Lk 2³⁶, Re 7⁶.†

ἀσθένεια, -ας, ἡ (< ἀσθενής), [in LXX for כְּשֹׁל, etc.;] *weakness, frailty, sickness:* Lk 13¹¹, ¹², Jo 11⁴, Ac 28⁹, Ro 6¹⁹ 8²⁶, II Co 11³⁰ 13⁴, Ga 4¹³ (MM, s.v.), He 5² 7²⁸ 11³⁴; ἐν ἀ., Jo 5⁵, I Co 2³ 15⁴³, II Co 12⁹; pl., Mt 8¹⁷, Lk 5¹⁵ 8², II Co 12⁵, ⁹, ¹⁰, I Ti 5²³, He 4¹⁵.†
    SYN.: μαλακία, νόσος (v. *DB*, iii, 323ᵃ).

ἀσθενέω, -ῶ (< ἀσθενής), [in LXX chiefly for כְּשֹׁל;] *to be weak, feeble:* Ac 20³⁵, Ro 8³, II Co 11²¹ 12¹⁰ 13⁴, ⁹; c. dat., πίστει (Cremer, 527), Ro 4¹⁹ 14¹; same implied, Ro 14², ²¹, I Co 8¹¹, ¹², II Co 11²⁹; εἰς, II Co 13³. Specif., of bodily debility, *to be sick:* Mt 25³⁶, ³⁹, Lk 4⁴⁰, Jo 4⁴⁶ 5³, ⁷, ¹³ 11¹⁻³, ⁶, Ac 9³⁷, Phl 2²⁶, ²⁷, II Ti 4²⁰, Ja 5¹⁴; οἱ ἀσθενοῦντες, *the sick:* Mt 10⁸ (MM, s.v.), Mk 6⁵⁶, Lk 9², Ac 19¹².†

* ἀσθένημα, -τος, τό (< ἀσθενής), *an infirmity* (MM, s.v.): Ro 15¹.†
ἀσθενής, -ές (< ἀ- neg., σθένος, strength), [in LXX for עָנִי, etc.;] *without strength, weak, feeble:* I Co 1²⁷ 4¹⁰ 12²², II Co 10¹⁰, Ga 4⁹, I Th 5¹⁴, He 7¹⁸, 1 Pe 3⁷. Rhetorically, τὸ ἀ. τ. θεοῦ, God's action of apparent weakness: I Co 1²⁵; of bodily debility, *sick, sickly:* Mt 25³⁹ (Rec.) ⁴³, ⁴⁴, Lk 9² (Rec.) 10⁹, Ac 4⁹ 5¹⁵, ¹⁶. In moral and spiritual sense (MM, s.v.; Cremer, 526), Mt 26⁴¹, Mk 14³⁸, Ro 5⁶, I Co 8⁷, ⁹, ¹⁰ 9²² 11³⁰.†

Ἀσία, -ας, ἡ, *Asia,* the Roman province: Ac 2⁹ 6⁹ 16⁶ 19¹, ¹⁰, ²², ²⁶ (M, *Pr.,* 73), ib.²⁷ 20⁴, ¹⁶, ¹⁸ 21²⁷ 24¹⁸ 27², Ro 16⁵, I Co 16¹⁹, II Co 1⁸, II Ti 1¹⁵, I Pe 1¹, Re 1⁴.†

Ἀσιανός, -ή, -όν, *Asian, of Asia, Asiatic;* as subst., ὁ (οἱ) Ἀ.: Ac 20⁴.†

*†Ἀσιάρχης, -ου, ὁ, *an Asiarch,* one of ten officers elected by the various cities in the province of Asia whose duty it was to celebrate at their own charges the public games and festivals: Ac 19³¹ (Strab., Inscr.; *DB*, s.v.).†

* ἀσιτία, -ας, ἡ (< ἄσιτος), *fasting, abstinence from food:* Ac 27²¹.†
    SYN.: νηστεία (MM, ut infr.).

* ἄσιτος, -ον (< ἀ- neg., σῖτος), *fasting, without eating* (cf. MM, s.v.): Ac 27³³.†

** ἀσκέω, -ῶ, [in LXX: II Mac 15⁴ *;] 1. *to adorn* (poët.). 2. *to practise, exercise* (Hdt., Xen.). 3. *to endeavour* (Xen., al.): c. inf., Ac 24¹⁶.†

ἀσκός, -οῦ, ὁ, [in LXX for חֵמַת, נֹאד, נֵבֶל;] *a leather bottle, wineskin:* Mt 9¹⁷, Mk 2²², Lk 5³⁷, ³⁸.†

** ἀσμένως, adv. (< ἥδομαι, *to be glad*), [in LXX: II Mac 4¹² 10³³, III Mac 3¹⁵ 5²¹ *;] *gladly:* Ac 21¹⁷.†

ἄ-σοφος, -ον, [in LXX: Pr 9⁸ א ² A *;] *unwise, foolish:* Eph 5¹⁵.†

ἀσπάζομαι, depon., [in LXX: Ex 18⁷, Jg 18¹⁵ (שָׁאַל לְשָׁלוֹם), Es 5²,
I Mac 7²⁹, al.;] *to welcome, greet, salute:* c. acc. pers., Mt 5⁴⁷, Mk 9¹⁵, Ac 21⁷, al.; id. seq. ἐν φιλήματι, Ro 16¹⁶, I Co 16²⁰, II Co 13¹², I Th 5²⁶, I Pe 5¹⁴; τ. ἐκκλησίαν (Deiss., *BS*, 257), Ac 18²²; as *term. tech.* for conveying greetings at the end of a letter (MM, s.v.), used by an amanuensis (Milligan, *NTD*, 23), Ro 16²² (on the aoristic pres., here

and elsewhere, v. M, *Pr.*, 119; Bl., § 56, 4); κατήντησαν . . . ἀσπασά-μενοι (on this constr., v. Bl., § 58, 4; M, *Pr.*, 132, 238), Ac 25¹³ (cf. ἀπ-ασπάζομαι).

*ἀσπασμός, -οῦ, ὁ (< ἀσπάζομαι), a *salutation* (so always in RV), *greeting:* oral, Mt 23⁷, Mk 12³⁸, Lk 1²⁹, ⁴¹, ⁴⁴ 11⁴³ 20⁴⁶; written, ɪ Co 16²¹, Col 4¹⁸, ɪɪ Th 3¹⁷.†

**† ἄ-σπιλος, -ον (< ἀ- neg., σπῖλος), [in Sm.: Jb 15¹⁵ (LXX, καθαρός)*;] *spotless, unstained:* ɪ Pe 1¹⁹; metaph., 1 Ti 6¹⁴, Ja 1²⁷, ɪɪ Pe 3¹⁴ (for exx., v. MM, s.v.).†
 SYN.: ἀμίαντος, ἄμωμος.

ἀσπίς, -ίδος, ἡ, [in LXX for פֶּתֶן, etc.;] *an asp:* Ro 3¹³.†

* ἄσπονδος, -ον (< σπονδή, a *libation*); 1. *without truce* (Thuc.). 2. *admitting of no truce, implacable* (Dem., al.): ɪɪ Ti 3³.†

**† ἀσσάριον, -ου, τό (dim. of Lat. *as*), *an assarion, a farthing,* one-tenth of a drachma: Mt 10²⁹, Lk 12⁶ (MM, s.v.; *DB,* iii, 428; *DCG,* ii, 200).†

* ἄσσον (Rec., after Vg., Ἄσσον), adv. (compar. of ἄγχι, *near*), *nearer:* Ac 27¹³ (RV, *close in shore;* v. Bl., § 11, 3; 44, 3; poets, Ion. and late prose).†

Ἄσσος, -ου (also Ἀσσός, -οῦ), ἡ, *Assos,* a city on the E. coast of Asia Minor: Ac 20¹³, ¹⁴ (v.s. ἄσσον).†

**† ἀστατέω, -ῶ (< ἄστατος, *unstable*), [in Aq.: Is 58⁷ (LXX, ἄστε-γος)*;] *to be unsettled, be homeless, lead a vagabond life* (Cremer, 738 MM, s.v.): ɪ Co 4¹¹.†

ἀστεῖος, -ον (< ἄστυ, a *city*), [in LXX: Ex 2² (טוֹב), Nu 22³² (οὐκ ἀ. יָרַט), Jg 3¹⁷ (בָּרִיא), Jth 11²³, Da LXX, Su⁷, ɪɪ Mac 6²³ *;] 1. *of the town.* 2. (Like Lat. *urbanus*), (*a*) *courteous,* (*b*) *elegant* (in π., of clothing, MM, s.v.), *comely, fair* (as in Ex, l.c), He 11²³, Ac 7²⁰.†

ἀστήρ, -έρος, ὁ, [in LXX chiefly for כּוֹכָב;] *a star:* Mt 2², ⁷, ⁹, ¹⁰ 24²⁹, Mk 13²⁵, ɪ Co 15⁴¹, Re 6¹³ 8¹⁰, ¹¹, ¹² 9¹ 12¹, ⁴; metaph., ὁ ἀ. ἁ πρωϊνός, Re 2²⁸ 22¹⁶; ἀ. πλανῆται, Ju¹³; ἀ. ἑπτά, symbolizing the angeli of the seven churches, Re 1¹⁶, ²⁰ 2¹ 3¹ (cf. ἄστρον, and v. *DCG*, ii, 674 f., MM, s.v.).†

*† ἀ-στήρικτος, -ον (< στηρίζω), *unstable, unsettled:* ɪɪ Pe 2¹⁴ 3¹⁶.†

* ἄστοργος, -ον (< στοργή, *family affection, love of kindred,* v.s. ἀγάπη), *without natural affection:* Ro 1³¹, ɪɪ Ti 3³ (MM, s.v.).†

**† ἀστοχέω, -ῶ (στόχος, a *mark*), [in LXX: Si 7¹⁹ 8⁹*;] *to miss the mark, fail:* c. gen., ɪ Ti 1⁶ (so in π., MM, s.v.); seq. περί, ɪ Ti 6²¹, ɪɪ Ti 2¹⁸.†

ἀστραπή, -ῆς, ἡ, [in LXX for בָּרָק;] *lightning:* Mt 24²⁷ 28³, Lk 10¹⁸ 17²⁴; pl., Re 4⁵ 8⁵ 11¹⁹ 16¹⁸; of a lamp, *shining brightness,* Lk 11³⁶.†

ἀστράπτω, [in LXX for ברק;] *to lighten, flash forth:* Lk 17²⁴ 24⁴ (MM, s.v.).†

ἄστρον, -ου, τό, [in LXX chiefly for כּוֹכָב;] (*a*) mostly in pl. (as

5

in cl.), *the stars*: Lk 21²⁵, Ac 27²⁰, He 11¹²; (*b*) in sing. (Xen., al.), only of some noted star: the symbol or image of a star, Ac 7⁴³ (cf. ἀστήρ, and v. MM, s.v.).†

Ἀσύγκριτος, v.s. Ἀσύνκριτος.

** ἀ-σύμφωνος, -ον, [in LXX: Wi 18¹⁰, Da, LXX, Bel ¹⁵ *;] *dissonant, discordant*; metaph., *at variance*: πρὸς ἀλλήλους, Ac 28²⁵.†

ἀ-σύνετος, -ον [in LXX: De 32²¹ (נָבָל), Jb 13² (נפל), Ps 91 (92)⁶ (בְּמִיל), Ps 75 (76)⁵, Wi ₂, Si ₆*;] *without understanding* or *discernment*: Mt 15¹⁶, Mk 7¹⁸ (Swete, in l.), Ro 1²¹, ³¹ 10¹⁹ (for an ex. of its use in the moral sense, v. MM, s.v.).†

SYN.: ἀνόητος, q.v.

ἀ-σύν-θετος, -ον (< συντίθεμαι; v. M, *Pr.*, 222; MM, s.v.), [in LXX: Je 3⁷, ⁸, ¹⁰, ¹¹ (בגד)*;] *false to engagements, not keeping covenant faithless* (MM, s.v.): Ro 1³¹.†

Ἀσύνκριτος (Rec. Ἀσύγκρ.), -ον, ὁ, *Asyncritus*: Ro 16¹⁴.†

ἀσφάλεια, -ας, ἡ (< ἀσφαλής), [in LXX for בֶּטַח, etc.;] 1. *firmness*. 2. *certainty*: Lu 1⁴. 3. *security*: Ac 5²³, 1 Th 5³. (In π. it is used as a law-term, *proof, security; v.* MM, s.v.; M, *Th.*, l.c.)†

ἀσφαλής, -ές (< ἀ- neg., σφάλλω, *to trip up*), [in LXX for אשר pu., etc.;] *certain, secure, safe*: Ac 21³⁴ 22³⁰ 25²⁶, Phl 3¹, He 6¹⁹ (MM, s.v.).†

† ἀσφαλίζω (< ἀσφαλής), [in LXX: Ne 3¹⁵ (חזק hi.), Is 41¹⁰ (תמך), Wi 4¹⁷ 10¹² 13¹⁵ *;] *to make firm, secure*: mid., Mt 27⁶⁵, ⁶⁶, Ac 16²⁴; pass., Mt 27⁶⁴ (MM, s.v.).†

ἀσφαλῶς, adv., [in LXX: Ge 34²⁵ (בֶּטַח), To 6⁴ Wi 18⁶, Ba 5⁷, 1 Mac 6⁴⁰, III Mac 7⁶ *;] (*a*) *safely*: Mk 14⁴⁴, Ac 16²³; (*b*) *assuredly*· Ac 2³⁶.†

ἀσχημονέω, -ῶ (< ἀσχήμων), [in LXX: Ez 16⁷, ²², ³⁹23 ²⁹ (עֶרְיָה); De 25³ (קלה ni.)*;] *to act unbecomingly, behave dishonourably*: 1 Co 13⁵; seq. ἐπί, ib. 7³⁶ (MM, s.v.).†

ἀσχημοσύνη, -ης, ἡ (< ἀσχήμων), [in LXX chiefly for עֶרְוָה;] *unseemliness*: Ro 1²⁷ (MM, s.v.); euphemism for ἡ αἰσχύνη, as freq. in LXX, *shame, nakedness*: Re 16¹⁵.†

ἀσχήμων, -ον (< ἀ- neg., σχῆμα), [in LXX: Ge 34⁷ (נְבָלָה), De 24¹ (עֶרְוָה), Wi 2²⁰, Da τη Su ⁶³, II Mac 9² *;] 1. *shapeless*. 2. *uncomely, unseemly*: 1 Co 12²³.†

ἀσωτία, -ας, ἡ (< ἀ- neg., σώζω), [in LXX: Pr 28⁷ (זלל), II Mac 6⁴*;] *prodigality, wastefulness, profligacy*: Eph 5¹⁸, Tit 1⁶, 1 Pe 4⁴ (MM, s.v.).†

SYN.: ἀσέλγεια, q.v.

* ἀσώτως, adv. (< ἄσωτος, *prodigal, wasteful*), [in LXX for סרר, Pr 7¹¹ *;] *wastefully*: Lk 15¹³ (EV, *in riotous living;* but not necessarily dissolute; cf. MM, ut supr.; Milligan, *NTD*, 79).†

* ἀτακτέω, -ῶ (< ἄτακτος), primarily, of soldiers marching, *to be out of order, to quit the ranks;* hence, metaph., *to be remiss, fail in the performance of duty* (in π., of truancy on the part of an apprentice): II Th 3⁷ (on ἀ. and its cognates, v. M, *Th.*, 152 ff.; MM, s.vv.).†

** ἄ-τακτος, -ον (< τάσσω), [in LXX: III Mac 1¹⁹ *;] *out of order, out of place* (Lat. *inordinatus*), freq. of soldiers not keeping the ranks, or an army in disarray (cf. III Mac, l.c.); hence, metaph., *irregular, disorderly* (v. previous word): I Th 5¹⁴.†

** ἀ-τάκτως, adv., [in Sm.: IV Ki 9²⁰ *;] *disorderly, irregularly:* II Th 3⁶, ¹¹.†

ἄτεκνος, -ον (< τέκνον), [in LXX: Ge 15², Le 20²⁰, ²¹ (עֲרִירִי), Is 49²¹, Je 18²¹ (שַׁכֻּל), Si 16³ *;] *childless:* Lk 20²⁸, ²⁹.†

** ἀτενίζω (< ἀτενής, *strained, intent;* < τείνω), [in LXX: I Es 6²⁸, III Mac 2²⁶ *;] *to look fixedly, gaze* (MM, s.v.): c. dat. pers., *gaze upon:* Lk 4²⁰ 22⁵⁶, Ac 3¹² 10⁴ 14⁹ 23¹; seq. εἰς, c. acc. pers., Ac 3⁴ 6¹⁵ 13⁹; metaph., Ac 1¹⁰ 7⁵⁵ 11⁶, II Co 3⁷, ¹³.†

** ἄτερ, prep., [in LXX: II Mac 12¹⁵ *;] in cl. most freq. in poets; *without, apart from:* c. gen., Lk 22⁶, ³⁵ (for exx. from π., v. MM, s.v.).†

ἀτιμάζω (< ἄτιμος), [in LXX for בוז, קלה, etc.;] *to dishonour, insult:* Mk 12⁴, TTr., mg., WH, Lk 20¹¹, Jo 8⁴⁹, Ro 2²³, Ja 2⁶; pass.: Ac 5⁴¹, Ro 1²⁴ (cf ἀτιμάω).†

* ἀ-τιμάω, -ῶ (< τιμή), *to dishonour, despise:* c. acc. pers., Mk 12⁴, LTr., txt. (cf. ἀτιμάζω).†

ἀτιμία, -ας, ἡ (ἄτιμος), [in LXX for כְּלִמָּה, קָלוֹן, etc.;] *dishonour, disgrace:* I Co 11¹⁴, II Co 6⁸; εἰς ἀ., Ro 9²¹, II Ti 2²⁰; ἐν ἀ., I Co 15⁴³, κατ ἀ., II Co 11²¹; πάθη ἀτιμίας, *base passions,* Ro 1²⁶.†

ἄτιμος, -ον (< τιμή), [in LXX: Is 3⁵ (קלה ni.), 53³ (בזה), Jb 30⁴, ⁸ (בְּלִי-שֵׁם), Wi ₅, Si ₁*;] *without honour, dishonoured, despised:* Mt 13⁵⁷, Mk 6⁴, I Co 4¹⁰; comp., I Co 12²³.†

ἀτιμόω, -ῶ (< ἄτιμος), [in LXX chiefly for בזה;] = ἀτιμάζω, *to dishonour, treat with indignity:* Mk 12⁴, Rec.†

ἀτμίς, -ίδος, ἡ, [in LXX for עָנָן, תִּימָרָה, etc.;] *vapour:* Ja 4¹⁴; ἀ. καπνοῦ, Ac 2¹⁹ (LXX).†

** ἄ-τομος, -ον (< τέμνω), [in Sm.: Is 54⁸ (MM, s.v.) *;] *indivisible;* of time, ἄτομον, a *moment:* ἐν ἀ., I Co 15⁵².†

ἄ-τοπος, -ον (< τόπος), [in LXX: Jb 4⁸ 11¹¹, Pr 30²⁰ (24⁵⁵), al., for אָוֶן, etc.;] 1. *out of place, not befitting.* 2. *marvellous, strange* (of symptoms, Hipp.): Ac 28⁶; hence, in late Greek, with ethical sense, 3. *improper, unrighteous* (so in LXX, and for exx. from π., v. M, *Th.,* l.c.; MM, s.v.): Lk 23⁴¹, Ac 25⁵, II Th 3².†

Ἀτταλία (Rec. -άλεια), -ας, ἡ, *Attalia,* a city of Pamphylia: Ac 14²⁵.†

αὐγάζω (< αὐγή), [in LXX: Le 13²⁴⁻²⁶, ²⁸, ³⁸ 14⁵⁶ (בָּהֶרֶת) 13³⁹ (כֵּהָה)*;] 1. Trans. (cl.), *to irradiate.* 2. Intrans. (a) (poët.), *to see clearly* (so perh. II Co, l.c.; MM, s.v.); (b) as in LXX, *to shine forth:* II Co 4⁴ (cf. δι-, κατ-αυγάζω).†

αὐγή, -ῆς, ἡ, [in LXX: Is 59⁹ (נְגֹהָה), II Mac 12⁹ *;] 1. *brightness.*

2. Later (as in MGr.; MM, s.v.), *daylight, dawn:* Ac 20¹¹ (Cremer, 118).†

SYN.: φέγγος (v. Thayer, s. φ.; *DB,* iii, 44ª; Tr., *Syn.,* § xlvi).

Αὔγουστος, -ου, ὁ (Lat.), *Augustus,* the Roman Emperor: Lk 2¹ (cf. Σεβαστός; and v. MM, s.v.).†

αὐθάδης, -ες (< αὐτός, ἥδομαι), [in LXX: Ge 49³, ⁷ (עַז), Pr 21²⁴ (יָהִיר)*;] *self-pleasing, arrogant:* Tit 1⁷, II Pe 2¹⁰ (Cremer, 654).†

SYN.: φίλαυτος (v. Tr., *Syn.,* § xciii).

** αὐθαίρετος, -ον (< αὐτός, αἱρέομαι), [in Sm.: Ex 35⁵, ²² *;] 1. *self-chosen.* 2. *of one's own accord:* II Co 8³, ¹⁷.†

*† αὐθεντέω, -ῶ (< αὐθέντης, i.e. αὐτο- ἕντης, *one who acts on his own authority,* in π., *an autocrat;* cf. Wi 12⁶; cf. -ία, III Mac 2²⁹; -ικος is freq. in vernacular, MM, s.v.), *to govern, exercise authority, have mastery, lord it over:* I Ti 2¹².†

** αὐλέω, -ῶ (< αὐλός), [in Al.: III Ki 1⁴⁰ *;] *to play on a flute, to pipe:* mid., Mt 11¹⁷, Lk 7³², I Co 14⁷.†

αὐλή, -ῆς, ἡ, [in LXX chiefly for חָצֵר;] 1. in Hom., *an open courtyard* before a house, hence, *an enclosure in the open, a sheepfold:* Jo 10¹, ¹⁶. 2. *the court, courtyard,* round which a house is built. Mt 26³, ⁵⁸, ⁶⁹, Mk 14⁵⁴, ⁶⁶ 15¹⁶, Lk 11²¹ 22⁵⁵, Jo 18¹⁵; *τ. ναοῦ,* Re 11² 3. *a dwelling, a palace* (so, acc. to Grimm-Th., s.v.): Mt 26³, ⁵⁸, Mk 14⁵⁴ 15¹⁶, Lk 11²¹, Jo 18¹⁵ (but v. MM, s.v.; cf. also *DB,* ii, 25, 287).†

* αὐλητής, -οῦ, ὁ (< αὐλέω), *a flute-player:* Mt 9²³, Re 18²² (MM, s.v.).†

αὐλίζομαι (< αὐλή), [in LXX chiefly for לוּן, לִין;] 1. prop., *to lodge in a courtyard.* 2. *to lodge in the open.* 3. *to pass the night, lodge* (LXX; MM, s.v.): Mt 21¹⁷, Lk 21³⁷.†

αὐλός, -οῦ, ὁ (< ἄω, *to blow*), [in LXX chiefly for חָלִיל;] *a pipe:* I Co 14⁷.†

αὐξάνω (and the earlier form αὔξω, Eph 2²¹, Col 2¹⁹; MM, s.v.), [in LXX chiefly for פרה;] 1. trans., *to make to grow:* I Co 3⁶, ⁷, II Co 9¹⁰. Pass., *to grow, increase, become greater:* Mt 13³², Mk 4⁸, II Co 10¹⁵, Col 1⁶; *τῇ ἐπιγνώσει τ. θεοῦ,* Col 1¹⁰; *εἰς σωτηρίαν,* I Pe 2². 2. In later Gk. (but nowhere in LXX), intrans., *to grow, increase:* of plants, Mt 6²⁸, Lk 12²⁷ 13¹⁹; of infants, Lk 1⁸⁰ 2⁴⁰; of a multitude, Ac 7¹⁷; of the increase of the Gospel: *ὁ λόγος ηὔξανε,* Ac 6⁷ 12²⁴ 19²⁰; of Christ as a leader, Jo 3³⁰; of Christian character: *εἰς Χριστόν,* Eph 4¹⁵; *εἰς ναόν,* Eph 2²¹; *ἐν χάριτι,* II Pe 3¹⁸; *τὴν αὔξησιν τ. θεοῦ,* Col 2¹⁹ (cf. συν-, ὑπερ-αυξάνω).†

** αὔξησις, -εως, ἡ (< αὔξω), [in LXX: II Mac 5¹⁶ *;] *increase, growth:* Eph 4¹⁶, Col 2¹⁹.†

αὔξω, v.s. αὐξάνω.

αὔρα, *a breeze:* τ. πνεούσῃ (sc. αὔρᾳ), Ac 27⁴⁰.†

αὔριον, adv., [in LXX for מָחָר;] *to-morrow:* Mt 6³⁰, Lk 12²⁸, Ac 23²⁰ 25²², I Co 15³², Lk 13³², ³³, Ja 4¹³; *ἡ αὔ.* (sc. ἡμέρα, MM, s.v.),

Mt 6³⁴, Ac 4³; ἐπὶ τὴν αὔ., Lk 10³⁵, Ac 4⁵; τὸ (WH om.) τῆς αὔ., Ja 4¹⁴.†

**αὐστηρός, -ά, -όν (< αὔω, to dry up), [in LXX: 11 Mac 14³⁰ *;] prop., *stringent, harsh* to the taste. Metaph., in Inscr., of a rough country; of disposition and manners, *strict, severe* (as in π., of an inspector; MM, s.v.) : Lk 19²¹, ²².†
SYN.: σκληρός (Tr., § xiv).

*αὐτάρκεια, -ας, ἡ (< αὐτάρκης, q.v.), (a) *sufficiency* (MM, s.v.) : in subjective sense (v. Milligan, *NTD,* 57), 11 Co 9⁸; (b) *contentment :* ι Ti 6⁶.†

αὐτάρκης, -ες (< αὐτός, ἀρκέω), [in LXX: Pr 24³¹ (30⁸) (פֹק), Si 5¹ 11²⁴ 34 (31)²⁸ 40¹⁸, ιν Mac 9⁹ *;] as in cl., in philosophical sense, *self-sufficient, independent ;* subjectively, *contented :* Phl 4¹¹ (in non-lit. π., the word means simply *enough, sufficient ;* MM, s.v.).†

*†αὐτο-κατά-κριτος, -ον (< αὐτός, κατακρίνω), *self-condemned :* Tit 3¹¹ (Eccl., Cremer, 377 ; MM, s.v.).†

αὐτόματος, -ον, and -η, -ον (etym. doubtful ; v. Boisacq, Prellwitz, s.v.), [in LXX, Le 25⁵, ¹¹, ιν Ki 19²⁹ (סָפִיח), Jos 6⁵, Jb 24²⁴, Wi 17⁶ *;] 1. of persons, *acting of one's own will.* 2. Of inanimate things and natural agencies, *of itself, of its own accord :* γῆ, Mk 4²⁸ (MM, s.v.); πύλη, Ac 12¹⁰.†

*αὐτόπτης, -ου, ὁ, *an eye-witness :* Lk 1².†
αὐτός, -ή, -ό, determinative pron., in late Gk. much more freq. than in cl. (WM, 178 f. ; Jannaris, *HGG,* § 1399). 1. Emphatic (so usually in nom., but at times without emphasis) ; (1) *self (ipse),* expressing opposition, distinction, exclusion, etc., αὐ. ἐκχυθήσεται, Lk 5³⁷ ; αὐ. ἐγίνωσκεν. Jo 2²⁵ ; αὐ. ὑμεῖς, Jo 3²⁸ ; καὶ αὐ. ἐγώ, Ro 15¹⁴ ; αὐ. Ἰησοῦς, Jo 2²⁴ ; αὐ. καὶ οἱ μετ' αὐτοῦ, Mk 2²⁵ ; ὑμεῖς αὐ., Mk 6³¹ ; esp. (as freq. in cl.) αὐ. ὁ, Mt 3⁴, Mk 6¹⁷, Jo 16²⁷, ι Th 3¹¹, al. ; in late Gk., sometimes weakened, ἐν αὐτῇ τ. ὥρα, *in that hour,* Lk 10²¹ (M, *Pr.,* 91 ; MM, s.v.) ; (2) emphatic, *he, she, it* (M, *Pr.,* 86 ; Bl., § 48, 1, 2, 7), Mt 1²¹ 12⁵⁰, Lk 6³⁵, al. ; pointing to some one as master (cl.), Mt 8²⁴, Mk 4³⁸, al. ; αὐ. καὶ αὐ. = οὗτος, ὁ δὲ (Bl., § 48, 1), Mt 14², Mk 14¹⁵, ⁴⁴, Lk 1²² 2²⁸, al. 2. In oblique cases (cl.), for the simple pron. of 3rd pers., *he, she, it,* Mt 7⁹ 10¹² 26⁴⁴, al. ; with ptcp. in gen. absol., Mt 9¹⁸, Mk 13¹, al. (for irreg. constructions, v. Bl., § 74, 5) ; pleonastically after the relative (cf. Heb. לֹ . . . אֲשֶׁר; WM, 184 ff. ; Bl., § 50, 4 ; MM, s.v. ; M, *Gr.,* 11, pp. 431 f., 434 f.), Mk 7⁻⁵, Re 3⁸ 7², al. ; in constr. ad sensum, without proper subject expressly indicated, Mt 4²³, Ac 8⁵, 11 Co 2¹³, al. ; gen. αὐτοῦ = ἐκείνου, Ro 11¹¹, ι Th 2¹⁹, Tit 3⁵, He 2⁴. 3. ὁ, ἡ, τὸ αὐ., *the same :* He 1¹² 13⁸; τὸ αὐ. ποιεῖν, Mt 5⁴⁶, ⁴⁷, al. ; φρονεῖν, Ro 12¹⁶ 15⁵, Phl 2², al. ; τὰ αὐ., Ac 15²⁷, Ro 2¹, al. ; κατὰ τὸ (τὰ) αὐ. (MM, s.v.), Ac 14¹, Lk 6²³, al. ; ἐπὶ τὸ αὐ., *together* (MM, s.v.), Mt 22³⁴, Ac 1¹⁵, al. ; ἐν κ. τὸ αὐ., ι Co 11⁵ 12¹¹; c. dat. (cl.), ι Co 11⁵; with a noun, λόγος, Mk 14³⁹; μέτρος, Phl 1³⁰; πνεῦμα, ι Co 12⁴.

αὐτοῦ, adv., prop. neut. gen. of αὐτός, [in LXX for פֹּה, בָּזֶה ;]

there, here : Mt 26³⁶, Mk 6³³, WH, mg., Lk 9²⁷, Ac 15³⁴, WH, mg., R mg., 18¹⁹ 21⁴.†
αὐτοῦ, -ῆς, -οῦ, = ἑαυτοῦ (q.v.), Mt 6³⁴, Lk 12¹⁷, al. (MM, s.v.).
** αὐτόφωρος, -ον (< αὐτός, φώρ, *a thief*), [in Sm. : Jb 34¹¹ * ;] prop. with ref. to theft, then generally, *in the very act :* as freq., neut. dat. after ἐπί, Jo 8⁴ (Rec., ἐπαυτοφώρῳ).†
* αὐτό-χειρ, -ρος, ὁ, ἡ (< αὐτός, χείρ), *with one's own hand :* Ac 27¹⁹.†
* αὐχέω, -ῶ (< αὔχη, *boasting*), *to boast :* c. acc. (MM, s.v.), μεγάλα αὐχεῖ (Rec. μεγαλαυχεῖ, q.v.), Ja 3⁵.†
* αὐχμηρός, -ά, -όν (< αὐχμός, *drought*); 1. *dry.* 2. *squalid, dismal :* II Pe 1¹⁹ (MM, s.v.).†
ἀφ-αιρέω, -ῶ, [in LXX (Cremer, 615 f.) for סוּר, עבר, רוּם, כָּרַת, etc. (35 words in all) ;] *to take from, take away, take off :* c. acc., τὸ ὠτίον, Mt 26⁵¹, Mk 14⁴⁷ (ὠτάριον, WH), Lk 22⁵⁰ (οὖς) ; ὄνειδος, Lk 1²⁵ ; seq. ἀπό, Re 22¹⁹, Lk 16³ (mid.) ; pass., c. gen., Lk 10⁴² ; ἁ. ἁμαρτίας, He 10⁴, Ro 11²⁷ (mid.) (MM, s.v.).†
ἀφανής, -ές (< φαίνω), [in LXX : Ne 4⁸ ⁽²⁾, Jb 24²⁰, Si 20³⁰ 41¹⁴, II Mac 3³⁴ * ;] *unseen, hidden :* He 4¹³.†
ἀφανίζω, (< ἀφανής), [in LXX for שָׁמֵם ni., שָׁמַד hi., etc. ;] 1. *to make unseen, hide from sight* (Xen., al.). 2. Later (MM, s.v.), (*a*) *to destroy :* Mt 6¹⁹, ²⁰ ; (*b*) *to disfigure :* Mt 6¹⁶. Pass., *to vanish :* Ja 4¹⁴ ; *to perish :* Ac 13⁴¹ ⁽ᴸˣˣ⁾.†
ἀφανισμός, -οῦ, ὁ (< ἀφανίζω), [in LXX chiefly for שַׁמָּה, שְׁמָמָה ;] *vanishing, obliteration, destruction :* He 8¹³ (v. Rendall in l.).†
* ἄφαντος, -ον (< φαίνομαι), poët. and late prose (MM, s.v.), *invisible, hidden :* Lk 24³¹.†
*† ἀφεδρών, -ῶνος, ὁ (cf. ἄφεδρος, Le 12⁵) = cl. ἄφοδος (MM, s.v.), *a privy, drain :* Mt 15¹⁷, Mk 7¹⁹ (ὀχετόν, WH, mg.).†
* ἀφειδία (L, -εία), -ας, ἡ (< ἀφειδής, *unsparing*) ; 1. *extravagance.* 2. *unsparing treatment, severity :* Col 2²³.†
ἀφεῖδον, v.s. ἀπεῖδον.
*† ἀφελότης, -ητος, ἡ = cl. ἀφέλεια (v. MM, s.v.), *simplicity :* Ac 2⁴⁶.†
ἄφεσις, -εως, ἡ (< ἀφίημι), [in LXX for יוֹבֵל, דְּרוֹר, etc. (v. Deiss., *BS*, 98 ff. ; MM, s.v.) ;] 1. *dismissal, release :* Lk 4¹⁸. 2. Metaph., of sins (never in LXX), *pardon, remission* of penalty : ἁμαρτιῶν, Mt 26²⁸, Mk 1⁴, Lk 1⁷⁷ 3³ 24⁴⁷, Ac 2³⁸ 5³¹ 10⁴³ 13³⁸ 26¹⁸, Col 1¹⁴ ; παραπτωμάτων, Eph 1⁷ ; absol., Mk 3²⁹, He 9²² 10¹⁸ (cf. *DB*, ii, 56 ; *DCG*, i, 437, ii, 605 ; Cremer, 297 f.).†
SYN. : πάρεσις, q.v. (and cf. Tr., § xxxiii).
ἀφή, -ῆς, ἡ (< ἅπτω, *to fasten, fit*), [in LXX for נֶגַע, freq. in Le ;] *a joint* (MM, s.v.) : Eph 4¹⁶, Col 2¹⁹ (Lft., in l.).†
**† ἀφθαρσία, -ας, ἡ (< ἄφθαρτος), [in LXX : Wi 2²³ 6¹⁹, IV Mac 9²² 17¹² * ;] *incorruptibility, immortality :* Ro 2⁷, I Co 15⁴², ⁵⁰, ⁵³, ⁵⁴, II Ti 1¹⁰ ; ἀγαπώντων . . . ἐν ἁ., Eph 6²⁴ (v. AR, in l.).†

** ἄ-φθαρτος, -ον (< φθείρω), [in LXX : Wi 12¹ 18⁴ * ;] *imperishable, immortal ;* (*a*) of things : 1 Co 9²⁵, 1 Pe 1⁴, ²³ 3⁴ ; (*b*) of persons : of men, 1 Co 15⁵² ; of God, Ro 1²³, 1 Ti 1¹⁷ (MM, s.v.), Mk 16 [alt. ending].†

† **ἀ-φθορία**, -ας, ἡ (< φθείρω), [in LXX : Hg 2¹⁸ ⁽¹⁷⁾ (שְׁדָפוֹן)* ;] *un-corruptness :* Tit 2⁷ (Rec. ἀφθαρσία).†

ἀφ-ίημι, [in LXX for נשׂא, נוח hi., נתן, סלח ni., עזב, etc. ;] 1. *to send forth, send away, let go :* of divorce (*DB*, iii, 274ᵃ), τ. γυναῖκα (Hdt.), 1 Co 7¹¹⁻¹³ ; of death, τ. πνεῦμα (Ge 35¹⁸, Hdt., al.), Mt 27⁵⁰ ; φωνήν, *to utter a cry,* Mk 15³⁷ ; of debts, *to remit, forgive* (cl.), τ. δανεῖον, Mt 18²⁷ ; τ. ὀφειλήν, Mt 18³² ; esp. of sins (Cremer 296 f.), τ. ἁμαρτίας, ἁμαρτήματα, ἀνομίας, Mt 9², Ro 4⁷ ⁽ᴸˣˣ⁾, 1 Jo 1⁹, al. ; punctiliar and iterative pres. (M, *Pr.*, 119), Mk 2⁵, Lk 11⁴ ; Ion. pf., ἀφέωνται (M, *Pr.*, 38), Lk 5²³. 2. *to leave alone, leave, neglect, forsake :* Mt 4¹¹ 5²⁴ 15¹⁴, Mk 1²⁰, ³¹, Lk 13³⁵, Jo 4³, ²⁸, al. ; τ. ἐντολὴν τ. θεοῦ, Mk 7⁸ ; τὸν τ. ἀρχῆς τ. Χριστοῦ λόγον, He 6¹ ; τ. ἀγάπην τ. πρώτην, Re 2⁴ ; ptcp., ἀφείς, pleonastic (as in Aram.; M, *Pr.*, 14; Dalman, *Words*, 21 f.), Mt 13³⁶ 22²², Mk 8¹³, al. 3. *to let, suffer, permit :* Mt 3¹⁵ ; c. acc., Mt 3¹⁵, 19¹⁴, al. ; c. acc. rei et dat. pers., Mt 5⁴⁰ ; c. inf. pres., Mt 23¹⁴, al. ; aor., Mk 5³⁷, al. ; in late Gk. (M, *Pr.*, 175 f.), seq. ἵνα, Mk 11¹⁶, Jo 12⁷ ; c. subjunct. (M, *Pr.*, l.c. ; Bl., § 64, 2), Mt 7⁴ 27⁴⁹, Mk 15³⁶, Lk 6⁴² (see further MM, s.v.).

ἀφ-ικνέομαι, -οῦμαι, [in LXX for בוא, etc. ;] perfective of ἱκνέομαι, *to come* (M, *Pr.*, 247), *to arrive at, come to, reach :* metaph. (MM, s.v.), Ro 16¹⁹.†

*† ἀ-φιλ-άγαθος, -ον, *without love of good :* 11 Ti 3³ (not elsewhere in Gk. lit., but v. MM, s.v.).†

*† ἀ-φιλ-άργυρος, -ον, *without love of money, not avaricious ;* 1 Ti 3³, He 13⁵. (For other instances, v. MM, s.v.)†

** ἄφ-ιξις, -εως, ἡ (< ἀφικνέομαι), [in LXX : 111 Mac 7¹⁸ * ;] in cl. usually, *arrival ;* rarely, *departure :* Ac 20²⁹ (so in π., cf. MM, s.v. ; M, *Pr.*, 26, n.).†

ἀφ-ίστημι, [in LXX for מעל, סור, etc. (41 words in all) ;] 1. trans. in pres., impf., fut., 1 aor., *to put away, lead away ;* metaph., *to move to revolt :* Ac 5³⁷. 2. Intrans. in pf., plpf., 2 aor., *to stand off, depart from, withdraw from :* c. gen., Lk 2³⁷ ; seq. ἀπό, Lk 4¹³ 13²⁷, Ac 5³⁸ 12¹⁰, 15³⁸ 19⁹ 22²⁹, 11 Co 12⁸ ; metaph., ἀπὸ ἀδικίας, 11 Ti 2¹⁹ ; ἀπὸ θεοῦ, (*fall away, apostatize*), He 3¹². Mid. (exc. 1 aor., wh. is trans.), *to withdraw oneself from, absent oneself from :* Lk 2³⁷ ; metaph., *fall away, apostatize :* absol., Lk 8¹³ ; c. gen., 1 Ti 4¹ (MM, s.v. ; Cremer, 308).†

ἄφνω, adv., [in LXX for פתאם ;] *suddenly :* Ac 2² 16²⁶ 28⁶.†

ἀφόβως, adv. (< φόβος), [in LXX : Pr 1³³ (מפחד), Wi 17⁴ * ;] *without fear :* Lk 1⁷⁴, Phl 1¹⁴, 1 Co 16¹⁰, Ju 12.†

** ἀφ-ομοιόω, -ῶ, [in LXX : Wi 13¹⁴, Ep. Je ⁵, ⁶³, ⁷¹ * ;] *to make like :* pass, He 7³.†

ἀφ-οράω, -ῶ, [in LXX : ιν Mac 17¹⁰ (εἰς θεόν)* ;] (*a*) *to look away* *from all else at, fix one's gaze upon :* metaph. (MM, s.v.), He 12² ; (b) simply, *to see :* ἀφίδω (v.s. ἀπεῖδον, and Lft., *Phl.,* in l.; MM, s.v.), Phl 2²³ (v. Ellic., in l.).†

ἀφ-ορίζω, [in LXX (Cremer, 805 f.) for בָּדַל hi., סָגַר hi., נוּף hi., רוּם hi., etc. ;] (a) *to mark off by boundaries* from, *separate* from : c. acc., Ac 19⁹, Ga 2¹² ; id. seq. ἐκ (ἀπό), Mt 13⁴⁹ 25³² (MM, s.v.) ; of excommunication, Lk 6²². Pass., absol., II Co 6¹⁷ ; (b) *to set apart,* devote to a special purpose (seq. εἰς) : c. acc., Ga 1¹⁵. Mid., Ac 13², Ro 1¹ (*DB,* iii, 588).†

ἀφ-ορμή, -ῆς, ἡ, [in LXX : Ez 5⁷ (הָמֹן?), Pr 9⁹, III Mac 3² * ;] prop., *a starting-point ;* in war, *a base of operations ;* metaph., *an occasion, incentive, opportunity* (MM, s.v.) : II Co 11¹², Ga 5¹³ ; ἀφ. λαμβάνειν, Lk 11²⁴, WH, mg., Ro 7⁸, ¹¹ ; ἀφ. διδόναι, II Co 5¹², I Ti 5¹⁴.†

* ἀφρίζω (< ἀφρός), *to foam at the mouth :* Mk 9¹⁸, ²⁰.†

* ἀφρός, -οῦ, ὁ, *foam :* Lk 9³⁹ (MM, s.v.).†

ἀφροσύνη, -ης, ἡ (< ἄφρων), [in LXX for אִוֶּלֶת, נְבָלָה, etc. ;] *foolishness :* Mk 7²², II Co 11¹, ¹⁷, ²¹.†

ἄφρων, -ον, gen. -ονος (< φρήν), [in LXX for כְּסִיל, נָבָל, etc. ;] *without reason, senseless, foolish,* expressing " want of mental sanity and sobriety, a reckless and inconsiderate habit of mind " (Hort ; cf. MM, s.v.) : Lk 11⁴⁰ 12²⁰, Ro 2²⁰, I Co 15³⁶, II Co 11¹⁶ 12⁶, ¹¹, I Pe 2¹⁵ ; opp. to φρόνιμος, II Co 11¹⁹ ; to συνιέντες, Eph 2¹⁷.†

**† ἀφ-υπνόω, -ῶ (< ὑπνόω, *to put to sleep*), [in Al. : Ge 28¹¹ * ;] 1. *to awake from sleep* (Anth.). 2. = cl. καθυπνόω (MM, s.v.), *to fall asleep :* Lk 8²³.†

† ἀφ-υστερέω, -ῶ, [in LXX : Ne 9²⁰ (מנע), Si 14¹⁴ * ;] 1. as in cl., *to be late* (Polyb., Si, l.c.). 2. Trans., *to keep back* (Ne, l.c. ; v. Mayor, Ja., 157 f.) : pass., Ja 5⁴ (MM, s.v.).†

ἄφωνος, -ον (φωνή), [in LXX : Is 53⁷ (אלם ni.), Wi 4¹⁹, II Mac 3²⁹ * ;] *dumb, speechless :* Ac 8³² (LXX) ; of idols (MM, s.v.), I Co 12² ; of beasts, II Pe 2¹⁶ ; τοσαῦτα γένη φωνῶν καὶ οὐδὲν ἄ.—so many kinds of voices and none voiceless, i.e. without signification, *unintelligible :* I Co 14¹⁰.†

Ἄχαζ (WH, Ἄχας), ὁ (Heb. אָחָז), *Ahaz :* Mt 1⁹.†

Ἀχαία (T, Ἀχαΐα), -ας, ἡ (Bl., § 46, 11), *Achaia,* the Roman province : Ac 18¹², ²⁷ 19²¹ Ro 15²⁶, I Co 16¹⁵, II Co 1¹ 9² 11¹⁰, I Th 1⁷, ⁸.†

Ἀχαϊκός, -οῦ, ὁ, *Achaicus :* I Co 16¹⁷.†

** ἀχάριστος, -ον (< χαρίζομαι), [in LXX : Wi 16²⁹, Si 29¹⁷, ²⁵, IV Mac 9¹⁰ * ;] (a) *ungracious, unpleasing ;* (b) *ungrateful, thankless :* Lk 6³⁵, II Ti 3².†

Ἄχας, v.s. Ἄχαζ.

Ἀχείμ, ὁ, *Achim :* Mt 1¹⁴.†

*† ἀ-χειρο-ποίητος, -ον (< χειροποίητος), *not made by hands :* Mk 14⁵⁸, II Co 5¹ ; metaph., περιτομή ἀ. (i.e. *spiritual,* Col 2¹¹ (MM, s.v.).†

Ἀχελδαμάχ (T, Ἀχ-; Rec. Ἀκελδαμά, WH, Ἁκελδαμάχ), indecl.
(Aram. אָדְקַל חֲקֵל, field of blood), Akeldama (AV, Aceldama) : Ac 1¹⁹.†

** ἀχλύς, -ύος, ἡ, [in Aq.: Ez 12⁷; Sm.: Jb 3⁵ *;] a mist, esp. a
dimness of the eyes : Ac 13¹¹ (v. Tr., Syn., § c).†

ἀ-χρεῖος, -ον (< χρεῖος, useful), [in LXX: ii Ki 6²² (שָׁפָל), Ep.
Je ¹⁷ *;] useless, unprofitable : Mt 25³⁰, Lk 17¹⁰ (MM, s.v.).†

† ἀχρεόω (Rec. -ειόω, Polyb., LXX), -ῶ (< ἄχρεος = ἀχρεῖος), [in
LXX (-ειόω) for אלח ni., etc.;] to make useless, unprofitable : pass., Ro
3¹² (LXX).†

ἄ-χρηστος, -ον, [in LXX: Ho 8⁸ (אֵין חֵפֶץ), Wi 2¹¹, Si 16¹, al. ;]
useless, unserviceable : opp. to εὔχρηστος, Phm ¹¹.†

ἄχρι (and Epic ἄχρις, bef. vowel (v. MM, s.v.), Ro 11²⁵ T, Ga 3¹⁹
T, WH, mg., He 3¹³); 1. adv., utterly (Hom.). 2. Prep. c. gen.,
until, unto, as far as ; (a) of time : Ac 3²¹ 22²², Ro 1¹³ 5¹³, i Co 4¹¹,
ii Co 3¹⁴, Ga 4², Phl 1⁶; ἄ. καιροῦ, Lk 4¹³, Ac 13¹¹; ἄ. ἧς ἡμέρας,
Mt 24³⁸, Lk 1²⁰ 17²⁷, Ac 1² (τῆς ἡ. ἧς), ib.²²; ἄ. ταύτης τ. ἡμέρας (τ. ἡ.
ταύτης), Ac 2²⁹ 23¹ 26²²; ἄ. ἡμερῶν πέντε, Ac 20⁶; ἄ. αὐγῆς, Ac 20¹¹; ἄ.
τοῦ νῦν, Ro 8²², Phl 1⁵; ἄ. τέλους, He 6¹¹, Re 2²⁶; (b) of space : Ac 11⁵
13⁶ 20⁴ (R, txt., WH, mg.) 28¹⁵, ii Co 10¹³, ¹⁴, He 4¹², Re 14²⁰ 18⁵;
(c) of measure or degree : ἄ. θανάτου, Ac 22⁴, Re 2¹⁰ 12¹¹. 3. As conj.,
until ; (a) ἄχρι alone : c. subj. aor., Ga 3¹⁹ (ἄ. οὖ T, WH, mg.); id.
without ἄν (Bl., § 65, 10), Re 7³ 15⁸ 20³, ⁵; c. indic. fut., Re 17¹⁷;
(b) ἄ. οὖ (i.e. ἄ. τούτου ᾧ) : c. indic. aor., Ac 7¹⁸; impf., 27³³; c. subj.
aor. (Bl., ut supr.), Lk 21²⁴, Ro 11²⁵, i Co 11²⁶ 15²⁵, Ga 3¹⁹, T, WH,
mg.; id. with ἄν, Re 2²⁵; c. indic. pres., while, He 3¹³ (cf. μέχρι).†

ἄχυρον, -ου, τό, [in LXX chiefly for תֶּבֶן;] chaff : Mt 3¹², Lk 3¹⁷.†

** ἀ-ψευδής, -ές (< ψεῦδος), [in LXX: Wi 7¹⁷ *;] free from falsehood, truthful : Tit 1².†

*† ἄψινθος, -ου, ἡ (also ἀψίνθιον, τό; ἀψινθία, ἡ), wormwood : as a
proper name, Re 8¹¹.†

** ἄψυχος, -ον (< ψυχή), [in LXX: Wi 13¹⁷ 14²⁹ *;] inanimate,
lifeless : i Co 14⁷.†

B

B, β, βῆτα, τό, indecl., beta, b, the second letter. As a numeral,
β′ = 2; β, = 2000.

Βάαλ (Rec. Βαάλ), ὁ, ἡ, indecl. (Heb. בַּעַל, lord), Baal : Ro
11⁴ (LXX). The fem. art. here agrees with the usage of LXX, where,
following a similar Hebrew practice (בֹּשֶׁת for בַּעַל), αἰσχύνη appears
to have been substituted in reading for the written Βάαλ (cf. iii Ki
18¹⁹), and to account for the freq. use of the fem. art. bef. B. The
usage, however, is not general, and in the passage cited in Ro (iii Ki
19¹⁸), LXX reads τῷ B.†

Βαβυλών, -ῶνος, ἡ (בָּבֶל, Heb. form of Assyr. Bab-ili, *Gate of God*), *Babylon* : Mt 1¹¹,¹²,¹⁷, Ac 7⁴³ (LXX); symbolically, of *Rome* : Re 14⁸ 16¹⁹ 17⁵ 18²,¹⁰,²¹, and prob. also ι Pe 5¹³.†

βαθέως, v.s. βαθύς.

† βαθμός, -οῦ, ὁ, Ion. form of βασμός (< βαίνω, *to step*), [in LXX ι Ki 5⁵ (מִפְתָּן), ιν Ki 20⁹,¹⁰,¹¹ (מַעֲלָה), Si 6³⁶ *;] *a step* (ιν Ki, l.c., of *degrees* of a dial); metaph., a *degree, standing* : ι Ti 3¹³ (on this form see further, MM, *VGT*, s.v., and reff. there).†

βάθος, -εος (-ους), τό, [in LXX for תַּחְתִּי, מְצוּלָה, etc.;] *depth* : Mt 13⁵, Mk 4⁵, Ro 8³⁹, Eph 3¹⁸; τὸ β., *the deep* sea : Lk 5⁴; metaph., β. πλούτου . . . Θεοῦ, Ro 11³³; τὰ β. τ. Θεοῦ (the Divine counsels), ι Co 2¹⁰; ἡ κατὰ βάθους πτωχεία, *deep poverty*, ιι Co 8².†

βαθύνω (< βαθύς), [in LXX for עמק : Ps 91 (92)⁵ Je 29 (49)⁸ 30 (49)³⁰ *;] *to deepen* : Lk 6⁴⁸.†

βαθύς (gen. -έως, vernac., Lk, l.c.; Bl., § 8, 5), -εῖα, -ύ, [in LXX chiefly for עמק ;] *deep* : Jo 4¹¹; metaph., ὄρθρου βαθέως (v. supr.), *early dawn*, Lk 24¹; ὕπνος, Ac 20⁹; τὰ β. τοῦ Σατανᾶ, Re 2²⁴.†

**† βαΐον, ον, τό (also βάϊον, another form of βαΐς, from the Egyptian), [in LXX: ι Mac 13⁵¹ *;] (freq. in Egyptian π., v. MM, *Exp.*, x); a *palm-branch* : Jo 12¹³ (*DB*, i, 314).†

Βαλαάμ, ὁ, indecl. (Heb. בִּלְעָם), as in LXX (FlJ has ὁ Βάλαμος); *Balaam* (Nu 22-24): ιι Pe 2¹⁵, Ju¹¹, Re 2¹⁴.†

Βαλάκ, ὁ, indecl. (Heb. בָּלָק), *Balak* (Nu 22²): Re 2¹⁴.†

βαλλάντιον (Rec. βαλά-), -ου, τό, [in LXX: Jb 14¹⁷ (צְרוֹר), Pr 1¹⁴ (כִּים), To 1¹⁴ 8², Si 18³³ א ² *;] *a purse* : Lk 10⁴ 12³³ 22³⁵,³⁶.†

βάλλω, [in LXX for נפל, שׂום, ידד, etc.;] prop., of a weapon or missile; then generally, of things and persons, lit. and metaph., *to throw, cast, put, place* : c. acc., seq. εἰς, Mt 4¹⁸, and freq. ἐπί, Mt 10³⁴; κάτω, Mt 4⁶; ἔξω, Mt 5¹³; ἀπό, Mt 5²⁹; ἐκ, Mk 12⁴⁴; δρέπανον, Re 14¹⁹; μάχαιραν, Mt 10³⁴; κλῆρον, Mt 27³⁵; of fluids, *to pour* : Mt 9¹⁷, Jo 13⁵; pass., *to be laid, to lie ill* : Mt 9²; ἐβλήθη (timeless aor., M, *Pr.*, 134), Jo 15⁶; intrans., *to rush* (Bl., § 53, 1): Ac 27¹⁴. Metaph., β. εἰς τ. καρδίαν, Jo 13² (cf. usage in π., without idea of violence; also of liquids; MM, *Exp.*, x; v. also Cremer, 120, 657; cf. ἀμφι-, ἀνα-, ἀντι-, ἀπο-, δια-, ἐκ-, ἐμ-, παρ-εμ-, ἐπι-, κατα-, μετα-, παρα-, περι-, προ-, συμ-, ὑπερ-, ὑπο-βάλλω).

βαπτίζω (< βάπτω), [in LXX: ιν Ki 5¹⁴ (טבל), Is 21⁴, Jth 12⁷, Si 31 (34)³⁰ *;] *to dip, immerse, sink* ; 1. generally (in Polyb., iii, 72, of soldiers wading breast-deep; in i, 51, of the sinking of ships); metaph., *to overwhelm* (Is, l.c.; cf. MM, *Exp.*, x); c. cogn. acc., βάπτισμα β., Mk 10³⁸,³⁹, Lk 12⁵⁰. Mid., 2. *to perform ablutions, wash oneself, bathe* (Ki, Jth, Si, ll. c.): Mk 7⁴; aor. pass. in same sense, Lk 11³⁸. 3. Of ablution, immersion, as a religious rite, *to baptize* ; (a) absol.; Mk 1⁴, Jo 1²⁵,²⁶,²⁸ 3²²,²³,²⁶ 4² 10⁴⁰, ι Co 1¹⁷; ὁ βαπτίζωι (= ὁ βαπτιστής, M, *Pr.*, 127), Mk 6¹⁴,²⁴; c. acc., Jo 4¹, Ac 8³⁸, ι Co

1¹⁴, ¹⁶; c. cogn. acc., τὸ βάπτισμα, Ac 19⁴ (cf. Mk 10³⁸, supr.); pass., *to be baptized, receive baptism :* Mt 3¹³, ¹⁴, ¹⁶, Mk 16¹⁶, Lk 3⁷, ¹², ²¹ 7²⁹ (τ. βάπτισμα) ib. ³⁰, Ac 2⁴¹ 8¹², ¹³, ³⁶ 9¹⁸ 10⁴⁷ 16¹⁵, ³³ 18⁸; mid., 22¹⁶ (M, *Pr.,* 163); (*b*) with prepositions : ἐν, of the element, Mt 3⁶, ¹¹, Mk 1⁴, ⁵, ⁸, Lk 3¹⁶, Jo 1²⁶, ³¹, ³³ 3²³, Ac 1⁵ 2³⁸ 10⁴⁸ 11¹⁶, ɪ Co 10²; εἰς, of the element, purpose or result (Lft., *Notes,* 155), Mt 3¹¹ 28¹⁹, Mk 1⁹, Ac 8¹⁶ 19³, ⁵, Ro 6³, ɪ Co 1¹³, ¹⁵ 10² 12¹³, Ga 3²⁷; c. dat., ὕδατι, Lk 3¹⁶, Ac 1⁵ 11¹⁶; ὑπὲρ τῶν νεκρῶν, perh. to fulfil the wish of a dead friend, ɪ Co 15²⁹ (v. *ICC,* in l.; cf. *DB,* i, 238 ff.; *DCG,* i, 169 ª; ii, 605 ᵇ; Cremer, 126); on ɪ Co 15²⁹ v. Peake, *Comm.,* in l., Leitzmann, *Handbuch,* ɪɪɪ, p. 152.†

*†βάπτισμα, -τος, τό (< βαπτίζω), prop., the result of the act, τὸ βαπτίζειν, as distinct from βαπτισμός, the act itself, *immersion, baptism ;* 1. metaph., of affliction : Mk 10³⁸, ³⁹, Lk 12⁵⁰. 2. Of the religious rite of baptism ; (*a*) of John's baptism : Mt 3⁷ 21²⁵, Mk 11³⁰, Lk 7²⁹ 20⁴, Ac 1²² 10³⁷ 18²⁵ 19³; β. μετανοίας, Mk 1⁴, Lk 3³, Ac 13²⁴ 19⁴; (*b*) of Christian baptism ; Ro 6⁴, Eph 4⁵, Col 2¹² (Tr., -μῷ, q.v.), ɪ Pe 3²¹ (cf. Cremer, 130; Tr., *Syn.* § xcix).†

*†βαπτισμός, -οῦ, ὁ (< βαπτίζω), prop., the act of which βάπτισμα is the result ; 1. *a dipping, washing, lustration :* Mk 7⁴; of Jewish ceremonial, He 9¹⁰; in He 6², βαπτισμῶν διδαχήν (-ῆς), "the pl. and the peculiar form seem to be used to include Christian baptism with ᴐther lustral rites" (Westc., in l.). 2. *baptism :* FlJ, *Ant.,* 18, 5, 2 (of John's baptism), and some Fathers (v. Soph., s.v.). Not so in NT, unless ἐν τ. βαπτισμῷ, *in the act of baptism,* Col 2¹², be read with Tr. (Rec., WH, R, -ματι).†

*†βαπτιστής, -οῦ, ὁ (< βαπτίζω), *a baptizer :* of John the Baptist, Mt 3¹ 11¹¹, ¹² 14², ⁸ 16¹⁴ 17¹³, Mk 6²⁵ 8²⁸, Lk 7²⁰, ³³ 9¹⁹.†

βάπτω, [in LXX chiefly for טָבַל ;] (*a*) *to dip :* Lk 16²⁴, Jo 13²⁶ (ἐμβ-, L) ; (*b*) *to dip in dye, to dye :* Re 19¹³ (Rec. ; ῥεραντισμένον, WH ; περιρεραμμένον, T ; ῥεραμμένον, Swete, in l., q.v.).†

βάρ (Aram. : בַּר), *son,* indecl. : β. Ἰωνᾶ, *son of Jonah,* Mt 16¹⁷, Rec. (L, T, WH, Βαριωνᾶ, q.v.).†

Βαραββᾶς, -ᾶ, ὁ (Aram. בַּר־אַבָּא, lit., *son of a father,* i.e. acc. to Jerome, *filius magistri*), *Barabbas :* Mt 27¹⁶, ¹⁷, ²⁰, ²¹, ²⁶, Mk 15⁷, ¹¹, ¹⁵, Lk 23¹⁸, Jo 18⁴⁰. (In Mt 27¹⁶, some MSS. read Ἰησοῦν B. ; v. WH, *App.,* 19 f.)†

Βαράκ, ὁ, indecl. (Heb. בָּרָק), *Barak* (Jg 4⁶) : He 11³².†

Βαραχίας, -ου, ὁ (Heb. בֶּרֶכְיָה), *Barachiah :* Mt 23³⁵, v.s. Ζαχαρίας.†

βάρβαρος, -ον (prob. onomatop., descriptive of unintelligible sounds), [in LXX : Ps 113 (114)¹ (לֹעֵז), Ez 21³¹ ⁽³⁶⁾ (בַּעַר), ɪɪ Mac 2²¹ 4²⁵ 10⁴, ɪɪɪ Mac 3²⁴ * ;] *barbarous, barbarian,* strange to Greek language and culture (and also, after the Persian war, with the added sense of *brutal, rude*) : Ac 28², ⁴, Ro 1¹⁴, ɪ Co 14¹¹, Col 3¹¹ (v. Lft., in l., and *Notes,* 249).†

βαρέω, -ῶ (later form of βαρύνω, q.v.), [in LXX : Ex 7¹⁴ (כָּבֵד),

ιι Mac 13⁹ * ;] to depress, weigh down, burden. In NT, in pass. only: Mt 26⁴³, Lk 9³² 21³⁴, ιι Co 1⁸ 5⁴, ι Ti 5¹⁶.†

βαρέως, adv. (< βαρύς), [in LXX : β. φέρειν, Ge 31³⁵ (בעיני חרה); β. ἀκούειν, Is 6¹⁰ (כבד hi.)* ;] heavily, with difficulty : Mt 13¹⁵, Ac 28²⁷ (LXX).†

Βαρθολομαῖος, -ου, ὁ (Aram. בַּר־תַּלְמַי, son of Tolmai), Bartholomew, the Apostle (v.s. Ναθαναήλ) : Mt 10³, Mk 3¹⁸, Lk 6¹⁴, Ac 1¹³.†

Βαρ-ιησοῦς, -οῦ, ὁ (Aram. בַּר־יֵשׁוּעַ, son of Joshua), Bar-Jesus : Ac 13⁶ (v.s. Ἐλύμας).†

Βαριωνᾶς, -ᾶ, ὁ (Aram. בַּר־יוֹנָה, son of Jonah), Bar-Jonah, a surname of Peter : Mt 16¹⁷.†

Βαρ-νάβας, -α, ὁ (Aram. בַּר, son, as prefix to another word interpreted in Ac 4³⁶, τῆς παρακλήσεως, perh. נְבוּאָה, wh., however, should be rendered by προφητεία as in ιι Es 6¹⁴, LXX. Deiss., BS, 309 f., thinks B. may be a variant of the name Βαρνεβοῦς, son of Nebo, found in a Syrian Inscr., altered with a view to disguising its origin; v. also Milligan, NTD, iii; Dalman, Gr., 142), Barnabas : Ac 4³⁶ 9²⁷ 11²², ³⁰ 12²⁵ 13-15, ι Co 9⁶, Ga 2¹, ⁹, ¹³, Col 4¹⁰.†

βάρος, -εος, τό, [in LXX : Jg 18²¹ (כבד), Jth 7⁴, Si 13², ιι Mac 9¹⁰, ιιι Mac 5⁴⁷ * ;] weight ; (a) a weight, burden, lit. and metaph. : Mt 20¹², Ac 15²⁸, ιι Co 4¹⁷, Re 2²⁴ ; ἀλλήλων τὰ β., one another's faults, Ga 6² ; ἐν β., burdensome : ι Th 2⁷, R, txt., but v. infr.; (b) in late Gk. (Soph., Lex., s.v.), dignity, authority : ἐν βάρει, ι Th 2⁶ (R, mg.; v. Milligan, ICC, in l.).†

SYN.: ὄγκος, an encumbrance ; φορτίον, a burden, that which is borne.

Βαρσαββᾶς (Rec. -αβᾶς), -ᾶ (Aram., son of Sabba), Barsabbas : 1. the surname of one Joseph : Ac 1²³. 2. The surname of one Judas : Ac 15²².†

Βαρτίμαιος, -ου, ὁ (-μαῖος, T; perh. Aram. בַּר־טָמָאִי, v. DB, iv, p. 762), Bartimæus : Mk 10⁴⁶.†

βαρύνω, to weigh down = βαρέω (q.v.) : Lk 21³⁴, Rec.†

βαρύς, -εῖα, ύ, [in LXX chiefly for כָּבֵד ;] heavy : Mt 23⁴. Metaph., burdensome : ἐντολή, ι Jo 5³ ; severe (perh. impressive) : ἐπιστολή, ιι Co 10¹⁰ ; weighty : τὰ βαρύτερα τ. νόμου, Mt 23²³ ; αἰτιώματα, Ac 25⁷ ; violent, cruel (EV, grievous) : λύκος, Ac 20²⁹.†

* βαρύτιμος, -ον (< βαρύς, τιμή), of great value, very costly : Mt 26⁷ (T, πολυτίμου).†

βασανίζω (< βάσανος), [in LXX : ι Ki 5³, Si 4¹⁷, and freq. in Wi, ιι, ιν Mac ;] 1. prop., to rub on the touchstone, put to the test. 2. to examine by torture, hence, generally, to torture, torment, distress : Mt 8⁶, ²⁹ 14²⁴, Mk 5⁷ 6⁴⁸, Lk 8²⁸, ιι Pe 2⁸, Re 9⁵ 11¹⁰ 12² 14¹⁰ 20¹⁰.†

** βασανισμός, -οῦ, ὁ (< βασανίζω), [in LXX : ιν Mac 9⁶ 11² * ;] torture, torment : Re 9⁵ 14¹¹ 18⁷, ¹⁰, ¹⁵.†

*βασανιστής, -οῦ, ὁ (< βασανίζω), prop., *a torturer;* used of a gaoler, Mt 18³⁴.†

βάσανος, -ου, ὁ (of Oriental origin), [in LXX chiefly for אֶשָּׁם, כַּלְמָה, and freq. in IV Mac ;] 1. prop., *touchstone,* a dark stone used in testing metals. 2. *examination by torture.* 3. *torment, torture:* Mt 4²⁴, Lk 16²³, ²⁸.†

βασιλεία, -ας, ἡ (< βασιλεύω), [in LXX chiefly for מַלְכוּת, מַמְלָכָה ;] 1. prop. abstract, *sovereignty, royal power, dominion:* Lk 1³³ 22²⁹, Jo 18³⁶, Ac 1⁶, He 1⁸, ι Co 15²⁴; λαβεῖν β., Lk 19¹², ¹⁵, Re 17¹²; δοῦναι τὴν β., ib. ¹⁷; ἔχειν β., ib. ¹⁸; ἔρχεσθαι ἐν τ. (εἰς τὴν) β., Mt 16²⁸, Lk 23⁴²; β. τ. θεοῦ, Re 12¹⁰. 2. By meton., concrete (MM, *Exp.*, x), (a) a *kingdom,* the territory or people over whom the king rules (Es 5³, al.): Mt 4⁸ 12²⁵, ²⁶ 24⁷, Mk 3²⁴ 6²³, Lk 4⁵, He 11³³, al.; (b) *the royal majesty* (cf. our phrase *His Majesty*), *the king* himself (τ. σπέρμα τῆς β., IV Ki 11¹). 3. In LXX (Wi 6⁵, To 13¹, al.), Targ. and NT, of the Messianic rule and kingdom, ἡ β. τ. θεοῦ, τ. οὐρανῶν (Heb. מַלְכוּת שָׁמַיִם, Aram. מַלְכוּתָא דִשְׁמַיָּא ; v. Dalman, *Words,* 91-147; Cremer, 132, 658), *the kingdom of God* (on the equivalence of the two phrases, v. Dalman, *op. cit.*, 93, 218 f.); τ. θεοῦ, Mt 6³³ 12²⁸, al.; τ. οὐρανῶν, Mt 3² 4¹⁷, al.; τ. Χριστοῦ (מַלְכוּת דִמְשִׁיחָא, Targ. Jon. on Is 53¹⁰), Eph 5⁵; τ. κυρίου, ιι Pe 1¹¹, Re 11¹⁵; τ. Δαυείδ, Mk 11¹⁰; absol., ἡ β., Mt 4²³, Ja 2⁵, al. The kingdom is regarded as present: Mt 11¹², Lk 17²¹, Ro 14¹⁷, al.; as that which is to be consummated in the future, Mt 6¹⁰, Mk 9¹, Jo 3⁵, ιι Pe 1¹¹, al. Noteworthy phrases are : ζητεῖν τὴν β., Mt 6³³; δέχεσθαι, Mk 10¹⁵; κληρονομεῖν, Mt 25³⁴; διδόναι, Lk 12³²; παραλαμβάνειν, He 12²⁸; αὐτῶν (τοιούτων) ἐστὶν ἡ β., Mt 5³, ¹⁰ 19¹⁴, Mk 10¹⁴, Lk 18¹⁶; διὰ τὴν β., Mt 19¹²; ἕνεκεν τῆς β., Lk 18²⁹; εὐαγγελίζεσθαι, κηρύσσειν, διαγγέλλειν τὴν β., Lk 4⁴³ 9², ⁶⁰; ἤγγικεν ἡ β., Mt 3², Mk 1¹⁵; κλεῖς τῆς β., Mt 16¹⁹; κλείειν τὴν β., Mt 23¹⁴; υἱοὶ τῆς β., Mt 8¹² 13³⁸ (cf. Cremer, 132, 658).

βασίλειον, -ου, τό (< βασίλειος, q.v.), [in LXX for הֵיכָל (Na 2⁶, Da 6¹⁸ *), מַמְלָכָה (III Ki 3¹ 14⁸, IV Ki 15¹⁹ *), etc. ;] 1. a *capital* city. 2. Freq. in pl., τὰ β., a *palace :* Lk 7²⁵ (LXX), (but v. infr.).†

βασίλειος, -ον (also -α, -ον ; < βασιλεύς), [in LXX : Ex 19⁶, De 3¹⁰ (מַמְלָכָה), Ex 23²², Wi 18¹⁵, III Mac 3²⁸, IV Mac 3⁸ * ;] *royal :* Lk 7²⁵ (LXX) (among *royal persons or courtiers,* but v. supr.), ι Pe 2⁹ (LXX, v. Hort, in l.).†

βασιλεύς, -έως, ὁ, [in LXX chiefly for מֶלֶךְ ;] a *king :* Mt 1⁶ 2¹; used by courtesy of Herod the Tetrarch, Mt 14⁹; of the Roman Emperor, as freq. in κοινή (Deiss., *LAE*, p. 367), ι Pe 2¹³, ¹⁷; of the Christ, in the phrase ὁ β. τ. Ἰουδαίων, Mt 2², al.; τοῦ Ἰσραήλ, Mk 15³², Jo 1⁵⁰ 12¹³; of God, Mt 5³⁵, ι Ti 1¹⁷, Re 15³; β. βασιλέων, Re 17¹⁴ 19¹⁶; β. τ. βασιλευόντων, ι Ti 6¹⁵ (on the associations of the word to Jewish Hellenists, v. *Cl. Rev.*, i, 7).†

βασιλεύω, (< βασιλεύς), [in LXX for מלך, its parts and derivatives, exc. IV Ki 15⁵ (ישב);] to be king, to reign, rule: I Ti 6¹⁵; c. gen. (cl.), Mt 2²²; seq. ἐπί, c. acc. (= Heb. מלך על; Bl., § 36, 8), Lk 1³³ 19¹⁴, ²⁷, Ro 5¹⁴; ἐπὶ τ. γῆς, on earth, Re 5¹⁰; of God, Re 11¹⁵, ¹⁷ 19⁶; of Christ, Lk 1³³, I Co 15²⁵, Re 11¹⁵; of Christians, Re 5¹⁰ 20⁴ (constative aor., M, Pr., 130), ib.⁶ 22⁵. Metaph., Christians, Ro 5¹⁷, I Co 4⁸; θάνατος, Ro 5¹⁴, ¹⁷; ἁμαρτία, Ro 5²¹ 6¹². Ingressive aor. (M, Pr., 109), to begin to reign : I Co 4⁸, Re 11¹⁷ 19⁶ (Cremer, 137).†

βασιλικός, -ή, -όν (< βασιλεύς), [in LXX for מֶלֶךְ and its cognates;] royal, belonging to a king : χώρα, Ac 12²⁰; ἐσθής, Ac 12²¹; νόμος β., a supreme law, " a law which governs other laws and so has a specially regal character" (Hort), or because made by a king (LAE, p. 367 ³), Ja 2⁸; τις, one in the service of a king, a courtier, Jo 4⁴⁶, ⁴⁹ (WH, mg., βασιλίσκος).†

† βασιλίσκος, -ου, ὁ (dim. of βασιλεύς), [in LXX a basilisk : Ps 90 (91) ¹³ (פֶּתֶן), Is 59⁵ (אֶפְעֶה) *;] prop., a petty king : Jo 4⁴⁶, ⁴⁹, WH, mg. (v.s. βασιλικός).†

βασίλισσα, -ης, ἡ (in Attic, βασίλεια, βασιλίς), [in LXX chiefly for מַלְכָּה;] a queen : Mt 12⁴², Lk 11³¹, Ac 8²⁷, Re 18⁷.†

βάσις, -εως, ἡ (< βαίνω), [in LXX chiefly for אֶרֶן;] 1. a step (Æsch., al.). 2. Hence, a foot (Plat.; Wi 13¹⁸) : Ac 3⁷.†

βασκαίνω, [in LXX : De 28⁵⁴, ⁵⁶ (רעע), Si 14⁶, ⁸ *;] 1. to slander (Dem.). 2. to blight by the evil eye, to fascinate, bewitch : Ga 3¹.†

βαστάζω, [in LXX : Jg 16³⁰ (נטה), Ru 2¹⁶, II Ki 23⁵, IV Ki 18¹⁴ and Jb 21³ (נשא), Si 6²⁵, Da TH Bel ³⁶ *;] 1. to take up with the hands, to lift : λίθους, Jo 10³¹. 2. to bear, to carry, as a burden, and metaph., to endure : Mt 3¹¹ 20¹², Mk 14¹³, Lk 7¹⁴ 10⁷ 11²⁷ 14²⁷ 22¹⁰, Jo 16¹² 19¹⁷, Ac 3² 9¹⁵ 15¹⁰ 21³⁵, Ro 11¹⁸ 15¹, Ga 5¹⁰ 6², ⁵, ¹⁷, Re 2², ³ 17⁷. 3. In late writers (MM, Exp., ii, iii, x), (a) to take away : Mt 8¹⁷ (Is 53⁴, Heb.) ; (b) to carry off, take away : Jo 20¹⁵ ; (c) to steal (Polyb., FlJ, π.) : Jo 12⁶ ; (d) to take off (Vernac., v. MM, VGT, s.v.; but v. supr., l. 4) : Mt 3¹¹.†

βάτος, -ου, ὁ, ἡ, [in LXX (always masc., as in Attic) : Ex 3²⁻⁴, De 33¹⁶ (סְנֶה), Jb 31⁴⁰ (בָּאְשָׁה) *;] a bramble-bush : Lk 6⁴⁴, Ac 7³⁰, ³⁵; ἐπὶ τοῦ (τῆς) β., in the place concerning the bush : Mk 12²⁶, Lk 20³⁷.†

† βάτος, -ου, ὁ (Heb. בַּת), [in LXX (also βαίθ, βάδος) : II Es 7²² *;] bath, a Jewish liquid measure, = μετρητής (q.v.), or about 8¾ gals. : Lk 16⁶.†

βάτραχος, -ου, ὁ, [in LXX : Ex 8, Ps 77 (78) ⁴⁵ 104 (105)³⁰ (צְפַרְדֵּעַ), Wi 19¹⁰ *;] a frog : Re 16¹³.†

*† βατταλογέω, -ῶ (Rec. βαττολ-, D, βλαττ- = βατταρίζω, prob. onomatop.; v. MM, s.v.; DCG, ii, 499 ᵇ, 790 ᵃ) ; to stammer, repeat idly : Mt 6⁷ (Cremer, 765 ; M, Gr., II, 272).†

† βδέλυγμα, -τος, τό (< βδελύσσω), [in LXX chiefly for תּוֹעֵבָה; שֶׁקֶץ;] an abomination, a detestable thing : Lk 16¹⁵, Re 17⁴, ⁵ 21²⁷ ; τὸ

β. τ. ἐρημώσεως (Da LXX 12¹¹, cf. 1 Mac 1⁵⁴; DB, i, 12 f.; DCG, i, 6 f.), Mk 13¹⁴. Mt 24¹⁵ (Cremer, 138).†

† βδελυκτός, ή, -όν (< βδελύσσω), [in LXX: Pr 17¹⁵ (תּוֹעֵבָה), Si 41⁵, II Mac 1²⁷ *;] abominable, detestable: Tit 1¹⁶ (Cremer, 137).†

βδελύσσω (< βδέω, to stink), [in LXX chiefly for תעב, שׁקץ;] in cl., mid. only (Attic, -ττομαι); to make foul; pass., Re 21⁸; mid., to turn away in disgust from, to detest: Ro 2²² (Cremer, 137).†

** βέβαιος, -ον (also -α, -ον; < βαίνω), [in LXX: Es 3¹³, Wi 7²³, III Mac 5³¹ 7⁷, IV Mac 17⁴ *;] firm, secure: ἄγκυρα, He 6¹⁹; metaph., sure (esp. "in the sense of legally guaranteed security," Deiss., BS, 109; cf. two foll. words): ἐπαγγελία, Ro 4¹⁶; ἐλπίς, II Co 1⁶; λόγος, He 2²; παρρησία, He 3⁶; ἀρχή (τ. ὑποστάσεως), He 3¹⁴; διαθήκη, He 9¹⁷; κλῆσις κ. ἐκλογή, II Pe 1¹⁰; comp. (-ότερος), προφητικὸς λόγος, II Pe 1¹⁹.†

βεβαιόω, -ῶ (< βέβαιος), [in LXX: Ps 40 (41)¹² (נצב hi.), 118 (119)²⁸ (קום pi.), III Mac 5⁴² *;] to confirm, establish, secure, of things (cl.): λόγον, Mk 16 [²⁰]; ἐπαγγελίας, Ro 15⁸; of persons (DCG, ii, 605): I Co 1⁸, II Co 1²¹. Pass., I Co 1⁶, Col 2⁷, He 2³ 13⁹ (as an Attic legal term, to guarantee the validity of a purchase, establish or confirm a title; v. next word, Cremer, 139; cf. δια-β.).†

βεβαίωσις, -εως, ή (< βεβαιόω, q.v.), [in LXX: Le 25²³ (צְמִיתֻת), Wi 6¹⁹ *;] confirmation: τ. εὐαγγελίου, Phl 1⁷; εἰς β., He 6¹⁶, a phrase freq. in π. of guarantee in a business transaction (Deiss., BS, 104 ff.; Cremer, 140).†

βέβηλος, -ον (< βαίνω, whence βηλός, a threshold), [in LXX chiefly for חלל;] 1. permitted to be trodden, accessible (v. DCG, ii, 422ʰ), hence, 2. (opp. to ἱερός) unhallowed, profane: of things, I Ti 4⁷ 6²⁰, II Ti 2¹⁶; of men, I Ti 1⁹, He 12¹⁶ (cf. κοινός; Cremer, 140).†

† βεβηλόω, -ῶ (< βέβηλος), [in LXX chiefly for חלל;] to profane: τ. σάββατον, Mt 12⁵; τ. ἱερόν, Ac 24⁶ (Cremer, 141).†

SYN.: κοινόω, q.v.

Βεελζεβούλ (WH, App., 159, Rec., βεελζεβούλ), ὁ, indecl. (Heb. בַּעַל, lord, and the Talmudic זְבוּל, from זֶבֶל, dung (Dalman, Gr., 137ₙ), or perh. זְבֻל, habitation, but, v. DB, iv, 409 f.; DCG, i, 181). The AV, RV, Beelzebub, comes through Vg. from IV Ki 1², בַּעַל זְבוּב, lord of flies (LXX, Βάαλ μυῖα, Sm., βεελζεβούβ), Beelzebul, Beelzebub, a name of Satan: Mt 10²⁵ 12²⁴, ²⁷, Mk 3²², Lk 11¹⁵, ¹⁸, ¹⁹.†

Βελίαλ, ὁ, indecl. (Heb. בְּלִיַּעַל, worthlessness, but v. DB, i, 268), Belial, a name of Satan: II Co 6¹⁵, Rec. See next word.†

Βελίαρ, ὁ, indecl. (another form of previous word, "due to harsh Syriac pronunciation," or else < Heb. בַּל יַעַר, lord of the forest), Beliar, a name of Satan: II Co 6¹⁵ (v. DB, i, 269).†

* βελόνη, -ης, ή (< βέλος), 1. a sharp point, as of a spear. 2. a needle: Lk 18²⁵ (Rec. ῥαφίς, q.v.).†

βέλος, -εος, τό (< βάλλω), [in LXX chiefly for חֵץ;] a missile, a dart: Eph 6¹⁶.†

βελτίων, -ον (gen. -ονος), comp. of ἀγαθός, [in LXX chiefly for טוֹב;] neut. as adv., better, very well: II Ti 1¹⁸ (also Ac 10²⁸ D). On elative use in these passages, v. M, Pr., 78, 236.†

Βενιαμείν, (Rec. -μίν), ὁ, indecl. (Heb. בִּנְיָמִין), Benjamin: Ac 13²¹, Ro 11¹, Phl 3⁵, Re 7⁸.†

Βερνίκη (elsewhere Βερενίκη, Macedonian form of Φερενίκη, cf. Veronica, Victoria), -ης, ἡ, Bernice, Berenice, dau. of Herod Agrippa I: Ac 25¹³, ²³ 26³⁰.†

Βέροια, -ας, ἡ, Berœa, a city of Macedonia: Ac 17¹⁰, ¹³.†
Βεροιαῖος, -α, -ον, Berœan: Ac 20⁴.†

Βεώρ, ὁ, indecl. (Heb. בְּעוֹר), Beor, father of Balaam: II Pe 2¹⁵ (Rec. Βοσόρ).†

Βηθαβαρά, -ᾶς (Rec. -ρᾶ, indecl.; Heb. עֲבָרָה בֵּית, place of crossing; -αραβᾷ, R, mg.), Bethabara: Jo 1²⁸, Rec. (WH, R, Βηθανία).†

Βηθανία, -ας (also -ιά, indecl., Lk 19²⁹ and in B*, Mk 11¹), ἡ, (Heb. עֲנִיָּה בֵּית, house of affliction, acc. to Jerome, or perh., house of dates, cf. Bethphage), Bethany; 1. a village fifteen furlongs from Jerusalem, the modern El Azeriyeh: Mt 21¹⁷ 26⁶, Mk 8²² (WH, mg.) 11¹, ¹¹, ¹² 14³, Lk 19²⁹ 24⁵⁰, Jo 11¹, ¹⁸ 12¹.   2. A place on E bank of Jordan: Jo 1²⁸ (R, mg., Βηθαβαρά, q.v.).†

Βηθεσδά, ἡ, indecl. (deriv. uncertain, v. Westc. on Jo 5², and DB, i, 279), Bethesda, a pool in Jerusalem: Jo 5², Rec. (Βηθζαθά, WH, Βηθσαϊδά, WH, mg.).†

Βηθζαθά, ἡ, indecl. (perh. Aram. זַיְתָא בֵּית, house of olives) Bethzatha: Jo 5², WH (Rec. Βηθεσδά, q.v.).†

Βηθλεέμ, ἡ, indecl. (Heb. לֶחֶם בֵּית, house of bread), Bethlehem, a town 6 m. S. of Jerusalem: Mt 2¹, ⁵, ⁶, ⁸, ¹⁶, Lk 2⁴, ¹⁵, Jo 7⁴².†

Βηθσαιδά (Rec. -σαϊδά), and -δάν (Mt, Mk, ll. c.), ἡ, indecl. (Syr., house of fish), Bethsaida, a town on NE. shore of the Sea of Galilee: Lk 9¹⁰. It is generally supposed that a second B. on the W. shore is referred to in Mt 11²¹, Mk 6⁴⁵ 8²², Lk 10¹³, Jo 1⁴⁵ 12²¹ (DB, i, 282 f.; but v. Swete on Mk 6⁴⁵).   2. v.l. for Βηθζαθά, Βηθεσδά, Jo 5².†

Βηθφαγή (L, -γῆ), ἡ, indecl. (Aram. בֵּית־פַּגֵּי, house of unripe figs; Dalman, Gr., 191), Bethphage: Mt 21¹, Mk 11¹, Lk 19²⁹.†

βῆμα, -τος, τό (< βαίνω), [in LXX: De 2⁵ (מִדְרָךְ), Ne 8⁴ (מִגְדָּל), I Es 9⁴², Si 19³⁰ 45⁹, II Mac 13²⁶ *;] 1. a step, stride, pace: Ac 7⁵.   2. a raised place, a platform reached by steps, originally that in the Pnyx at Athens from which orations were made; freq. of the tribune or tribunal of a Roman magistrate or ruler: Mt 27¹⁹, Jo 19¹³, Ac 12²¹, 18¹², ¹⁶, ¹⁷ 25⁶, ¹⁰, ¹⁷; β. τοῦ θεοῦ, Ro 14¹⁰; τ. Χριστοῦ, II Co 5¹⁰.†

**† βήρυλλος, -ου, ὁ, ἡ, [in LXX: To 13¹⁷ (-ύλλιον in Ex 28²⁰, שֹׁהַם)*;] *beryl,* a jewel of sea-green colour : Re 21²⁰.†

βία, -ας, ἡ, [in LXX for פֶּרֶךְ, etc.;] *strength, force, violence :* Ac 5²⁶ 21³⁵ 24⁷ 27⁴¹.†

βιάζω (< *βία*), and depon. -ομαι, [in LXX for פָּרַץ, פָּצַר, etc.;] *to force, constrain,* rare in act. (poët. and late prose), but found in cl. in pass., and so perh. *βιάζεται, suffereth violence,* Mt 11¹², EV (but v. infr.), whether (*a*) in good sense, of disciples (Thayer, al.), or (*b*) in bad sense, of the enemies of the kingdom (Meyer, in l.; Dalman, *Words,* 139 ff.; Cremer, 141 ff.). Mid., *advanceth violently,* Mt, l.c. (Deiss., *BS.,* 258; Banks, v. ref. in *DCG,* ii, 803 f.); seq. εἰς, *to press violently,* or *force one's way into,* Lk 16¹⁶ (v. *ICC,* in l., and in Mt, l.c.; cf. παραβιάζομαι and v. MM, s.v.).†

βίαιος, -α, -ον (< *βία*), [in LXX for אַנְשֵׁי, עַז, צַר, etc.;] *violent :* Ac 2².†

*† βιαστής, -οῦ, ὁ (< *βιάζω*), late form of βιατάς ; 1. *strong, forceful.* 2. *violent* (McNeile in l. notes that Kohn and Westland edit βίας τῶν in *Agr.,* 19) : Mt 11¹² (see βιάζω).†

*† βιβλαρίδιον, -ου, τό (dim. of βιβλάριον, dim. of βίβλος), *a littl(book :* Re 10², ⁸ (WH, βιβλίον, Τ², ⁷ βιβλιδάριον)⁹, ¹⁰. Not hithert(found elsewhere.†

βιβλιδάριον, -ου, τό, v.s. βιβλαρίδιον.

βιβλίον, -ου, τό (dim. of βίβλος, q.v.), [in LXX also in th(alternat. form βυβ-, chiefly for סֵפֶר and the most freq. of the cognate forms;] 1. *a paper, letter, written document :* β. ἀποστασίου, *bill of divorce,* Mt 19⁷, Mk 10⁴. 2. *a book, a roll :* Lk 4¹⁷, ²⁰, Jo 20³⁰ 21²⁵, Ga 3¹⁰, II Ti 4¹³, He 9¹⁹ 10⁷, Re 1¹¹ 5¹·⁹ 6¹⁴ 10⁸ 20¹² 22⁷⁻¹⁹; β. τ. ζωῆς., Re 13⁸ 17⁸ 20¹² 21²⁷.†

βίβλος, -ου, ἡ (variant form of βύβλος, the Egyptian *papyrus, paper* made from its fibrous coat), [in LXX for סֵפֶר, the form βύβ- being sometimes used;] *a book, a roll,* used much less freq. than βιβλίον, and with a "connotation of sacredness and veneration" (MM, *Exp.,* x), Mt 1¹, Mk 12²⁶, Lk 3⁴ 20⁴² Ac 1²⁰ 7⁴² 19¹⁹; β. τ. ζωῆς, Phl 4³, Re 3⁵ 20¹⁵.†

βιβρώσκω, poët. and late prose, [in LXX for אָכַל;] *to eat :* Jo 6¹³.†

Βιθυνία, -ας, *Bithynia,* a province in Asia Minor : Ac 16⁷, I Pe 1¹.†

βίος, -ου, ὁ, [in LXX chiefly for יָמִים;] 1. *period* or *course of life, life :* Lk 8¹⁴, I Ti 2², II Ti 2⁴, I Jo 2¹⁶. 2. *living, livelihood, means* (in Pr 31¹⁴ for לֶחֶם; v. *DCG,* ii, 39ᵃ) : Mk 12⁴⁴, Lk 8⁴³ 15¹², ³⁰ 21⁴, I Jo 3¹⁷.†

SYN.: ζωή, is life *intensive,* "vita quâ vivimus," the vital principle; βίος, life *extensive,* "vita quam vivimus," (1) the period of life, (2) the means by which it is sustained. Hence, in cl., ζ., being confined to the physical life common to men and animals, is the

6

inferior word (cf. *zoology, biography*).   In NT, ζωή is elevated into the ethical and spiritual sphere (cf. Tr., *Syn.*, § xxvii).

βιόω, -ῶ (< βίος), [in LXX: Pr 7² 9⁶ (חיה), Jb 29¹⁸, Wi 4⁴ א¹, 12²³, Si 40²⁸, iv Mac 5²² 17¹⁸*;] *to spend life, to live:* τ. χρόνον βιῶσαι (cl., more freq. 2 aor., -ναι), ι Pe 4² (cf. Jb, l.c.).†
  SYN.: ζάω (q.v.).

**† βίωσις, -εως, ἡ (< βιόω), [in LXX: Si *prol.*¹²*;] *manner of life:* Ac 26⁴.†

* βιωτικός, -ή, -όν (< βίος), *pertaining to life,* hence, *worldly* (Field, *Notes,* 171): Lk 21³⁴, ι Co 6³, ⁴.†

βλαβερός, -ά, -όν (< βλάπτω), [in LXX: Pr 10²⁶*;] *hurtful:* ι Ti 6⁹.†

βλάπτω, [in LXX: Pr 25²⁰, To 12², Wi 10⁸ 18², ιι Mac 12²², iv Mac 9⁷*;] *to hurt, injure:* c. acc., Mk 16[18], Lk 4³⁵.†

βλαστάνω, -άω (v. M, *Gr.*, ιι, 231), [in LXX for צמח, etc.;] 1. *ti sprout:* Mt 13²⁶, Mk 4²⁷, He 9⁴. 2. In late Gk., causal, *to make to grow, produce:* c. acc., Ja 5¹⁸.†

Βλάστος, -ου, ὁ, *Blastus,* chamberlain of Agrippa: Ac 12²⁰.†

βλασφημέω, -ῶ (< βλάσφημος), [in LXX: iv Ki 19⁴ (יכח hi.) ib.⁶, ²² (גדף pi.), Is 52⁵ (נאץ hith.), Da LXX 3²⁹ ⁽⁹⁶⁾ (שלח אמר), To 1¹⁸, Da ΤΗ Bel⁹, ιι Mac ₂ *;] 1. *to speak lightly or profanely of sacred things* (in cl., opp. of εὐφημέω), esp. *to speak impiously of God, to blaspheme, speak blasphemously:* absol., Mt 9³ 26⁶⁵, Mk 2⁷, Jo 10³⁶, Ac 26¹¹, ι Ti 1²⁰, ιι Pe 2¹²; τ. θεόν, Ac 19³⁷, Re 16¹¹, ²¹; τὸ ὄνομα τ. θεοῦ, Re 13⁶ 16⁹; δόξας, Ju⁸, ιι Pe 2¹⁰; εἰς τὸ πνεῦμα τὸ ἅγιον, Mk 3²⁹, Lk 12¹⁰. 2. *to revile, rail at, slander:* absol., Lk 22⁶⁵, Ac 13⁴⁵ 18⁶, ι Pe 4⁴; c. acc., Mt 27³⁹, Mk 3²⁸ 15²⁹, Lk 23³⁹, Tit 3², Ja 2⁷, Ju¹⁰. P₂ss.: Ro 2²⁴ 3⁸ 14¹⁶, ι Co 10³⁰, ι Ti 6¹, Tit 2⁵, ιι Pe 2² (Cremer, 570).†

βλασφημία, -ας, ἡ (< βλάσφημος), [in LXX: Ez 35¹² (נאצה), Da ΤΗ 3²⁹ ⁽⁹⁶⁾ (שלה), To 1¹⁸, ι Mac 2⁶, ιι Mac 8⁴ 10³⁵ 15²⁴*;] (*a*) *railing, slander:* Mt 12³¹ 15¹⁹, Mk 3²⁸ 7²², Eph 4³¹, Col 3⁸, ι Ti 6⁴, Ju⁹, Re 2⁹·; (*b*) spec., *impious speech against God, blasphemy:* Mt 26⁶⁵, Mk 14⁶⁴, Lk 5²¹, Jo 10³³, Re 13⁵; ὄνομα βλασφημίας, Re 13¹ 17³; c. gen. obj., Mt 12³¹; πρὸς τ. θεόν, Re 13⁶ (Cremer, 570; *DB*, i, 305; *DCG*, ii, 423).†

βλάσφημος, -ον (< βλασ-, of uncertain deriv., v. Thayer, Boisacq; + φήμη, speech; v. also M, *Gr.*, ιι, 272; MM, *VGT*, s.v.), [in LXX: Is 66³ (אָוֶן מְבָרֵךְ), Wi 1⁶, Si 3¹⁶, ιι Mac 9²⁸ 10⁴, ³⁶*;] (*a*) *evil-speaking, slanderous, blasphemous:* Ac 6¹¹, ιι Ti 3², ιι Pe 2¹¹ (cf. Ju⁹); (*b*) as subst., *a blasphemer:* ι Ti 1¹³ (Cremer, 570).†

* βλέμμα, -τος, τό (< βλέπω), *a look, a glance:* βλέμματι καὶ ἀκοῇ, ιι Pe 2⁸, *sight and hearing,* a sense not found for β. in Gk. lit., but perh. recognized in the vernacular (*ICC,* in l.)†

βλέπω, [in LXX chiefly for ראה, also for פנה, etc.;] 1. of bodily sight; (*a*) *to see, have sight* (opp. to τυφλὸς εἶναι): Mt 12²², Jo 9⁷, Ac 9⁹, Ro 11⁸, Re 3¹⁸, al.; (*b*) *to perceive, look* (*at*), *see:* absol.,

Ac 1⁹; c. acc., Mt 7³, Mk 5³¹, Lk 6⁴¹, Jo 1²⁹, al.; ὅραμα, Ac 12⁹; γυναῖκα, Mt 5²⁸; βιβλίον, Re 5³,⁴; τ. βλεπόμενα, II Co 4¹⁸. 2. Metaph., of mental vision; (a) to see, perceive, discern: absol., Mt 13¹³, Lk 8¹⁰; δι᾽ ἐσόπτρου, I Co 13¹²; c. acc., He 2⁹ 10²⁵; seq. ὅτι, He 3¹⁹, Ja 2²²; (b) to consider, look to, take heed: absol., Mk 13²³,³³; c. acc., I Co 1²⁶, al.; seq. πῶς, c. indic., Lk 8¹⁸, I Co 3¹⁰, Eph 5¹⁵; seq. τί, c. indic., Mk 4²⁴; seq. εἰς πρόσωπον, of partiality, Mt 22¹⁶, Mk 12¹⁴. Colloq. (for ex. from π., v. Deiss., LAE, 122; M, Pr., 107; MM, Exp., x; Milligan, NTD, 50), β. ἑαυτόν: Mk 13⁹; seq. ἵνα μή, II Jo ⁸; β. ἀπό, Mk 8¹⁵ 12³⁸; seq. μή (cl. ὁρᾶν μή), c. fut. indic., Col 2⁸, He 3¹²; id. c. aor. subj., Mt 24⁴, Mk 13⁵. 3. Of situation and direction (Lat. specto), t> look, face (towards), places, etc. (seq. πρός, Xen, Hell., vii, 1, 17; Ez 40²³,²⁴): seq. κατά, c. acc., Ac 27¹² (cf. ἀνα-, ἀπο-, δια-, ἐμ-, ἐπι-, περ-, προ-βλέπω), v. DCG, i, 446; ii, 596.

*† βλητέος, -α, -ον (gerundive of βάλλω), (that which) one must put: Lk 5³⁸.†

Βοάζ, v.s. Βοός.

Βοανηργές, indecl. (on the derivation, v. Dalman, Gr., 144; Words, 42; Swete, Mk., l.c.; DCG, i, 216), Boanerges: Mk 3·⁷.†

βοάω, -ῶ (< βοή), [in LXX chiefly for זעק, צעק, קרא;] 1. absol., to cry, call out: Mt 3³, 27⁴⁶, Mk 1³ 15³⁴, Lk 3⁴ 9³⁸ 18³⁸, Jo 1²³, Ac 8¹ 17⁶ 25²⁴, Ga 4²⁷. 2. C. dat., to call on for help (Heb. זעק על, Ho 7¹⁴, al.), Lk 18⁷.†

SYN.: καλέω, to call, invite, summon; κράζω, to cry, harshly cr inarticulately, as animals; κραυγάζω, intensive of κράζω. βοάω expresses emotion, whether joy, fear, etc.

Βοές, ὁ, v.s. Βοός.

βοή, ῆς, ἡ, [in LXX for זְעָקָה, etc.;] a cry: Ja 5⁴.†

βοήθεια, -ας, ἡ (v.s. βοηθέω), [in LXX for עֵזֶר, etc.;] help: He 4¹⁶; pl., helps, "frapping," a technical nautical term (MM, Exp., x; DB, ext., 367): Ac 27¹⁷.†

βοηθέω, -ῶ (< βοή + θέω, to run), [in LXX chiefly for עזר;] to come to aid, to help, succour: absol., Ac 21²⁸; c. dat., Mt 15²⁵, Mk 9²²,²⁴, Ac 16⁹, II Co 6² (LXX), He 2¹⁸, Re 12¹⁶.†

βοηθός, -όν (v.s. βοηθέω), [in LXX chiefly for עזר;] 1. (poët. -όος), hasting to the war-cry (Hom.). 2. helping, auxiliary; as subst. (Hdt.), a helper: He 13⁶ (LXX).†

βόθυνος, -ου, ὁ (= βόθρος, more freq. in cl.), [in LXX chiefly for פחת;] a pit: Mt 12¹¹ 15¹⁴, Lk 6³⁹ (cf. DB, iii, 885; DCG, ii, 367).†

βολή, -ῆς, ἡ (< βάλλω), [in LXX: Ge 21¹⁶ (מחה), II Mac 5³, III Mac 5²⁶*;] a throw; λίθου β. (Thuc., v, 65, 2), a stone's throw: Lk 22⁴¹.†

*† βολίζω (< βολίς, in sense of sounding-lead), to heave the lead, take soundings: Ac 27²⁸.†

† βολίς, ίδος, ἡ (< βάλλω), [in LXX for חִץ, יָרָה, etc.;] a dart, javelin: He 12²⁰, Rec. (LXX).†

84   MANUAL GREEK LEXICON OF THE NEW TESTAMENT

Boós and Boés (RV, Boáζ, Rec. Boóζ), ὁ, indecl. (Heb. בֹּעַז), *Boaz*
(Ru 2¹): Mt 1⁵, Lk 3³².†

βόρβορος, -ου, ὁ, [in LXX: Je 45 (38)⁶ (טִיט)*;] *mud, filth:* II Pe
2²².†

βορρᾶς, -ᾶ (Attic contr. of Βορέας, *the North wind* personified), [in
LXX for צָפוֹן;] 1. *Boreas, the North wind.* 2. *the north:* Lk 13²⁹,
Re 21¹³.†

βόσκω, [in LXX for רָעָה;] prop., of a herdsman, *to feed:* Mt 8³³,
Mk 5¹⁴, Lk 8³⁴ 15¹⁵; metaph., of Christian pastoral care, Jo 21¹⁵, ¹⁷.
Pass., of cattle, *to feed, graze:* Mt 8³⁰, Mk 5¹¹, Lk 8³².†
  SYN.: ποιμαίνειν, *to tend, shepherd,* a wider term, including over-
sight as well as feeding (v. Tr., *Syn.,* § xxv).
  Βοσόρ, v. Βεώρ.

βοτάνη, -ης, ἡ (< βόσκω), [in LXX for עֵשֶׂב, דֶּשֶׁא, חָצִיר;] 1.
grass, fodder. 2. *green herb:* He 6⁷.†
  SYN.: λάχανον, *a garden herb,* a vegetable.

βότρυς, -υος, ὁ, [in LXX for אֶשְׁכֹּל;] *a cluster of grapes:* Re 14¹⁸
(cf. σταφυλή).†

βουλευτής, -οῦ, ὁ (< βουλεύω), [in LXX: Jb 3¹⁴ 12¹⁷ (יָעַץ)*;] *a
councillor, a senator;* of a member of the Sanhedrin: Mk 15⁴³, Lk
23⁵⁰.†

βουλεύω (< βουλή), [in LXX chiefly for יָעַץ;] *to take counsel,
deliberate, resolve.* In mid., 1. *to take counsel with oneself, consider:*
seq. εἰ, Lk 14³¹. 2. *to determine with oneself, resolve:* c. inf., Ac 5³³
27³⁹; c. acc., II Co 1¹⁷; seq. ἵνα, Jo 11⁵³ 12¹⁰ (cf. παρα-, συμ-).†

βουλή, -ῆς, ἡ (< βούλομαι), [in LXX freq. for עֵצָה;] *counsel,
purpose* (in cl., esp. of the gods): Lk 23⁵¹, Ac 4²⁸ 5³⁸ 19¹ 27¹², ⁴²;
pl., I Co 4⁵; of the Divine purpose, He 6¹⁷; τ. βουλὴν τ. θελήματος
αὐτοῦ, Eph 1¹¹; β. τ. θεοῦ, Lk 7³⁰, Ac 2²³ 13³⁶ 20²⁷.†

βούλημα, -τος, τό (< βούλομαι), [in LXX: Pr 9¹⁰ (דַּעַת), II Mac
15⁵, IV Mac 8¹⁸ *;] *purpose, will:* Ac 27⁴³, Ro 9¹⁹, I Pe 4³.†
  SYN.: θέλημα.

βούλομαι, [in LXX for חָפֵץ, אָבָה, יָעַץ, etc.;] *to will, wish, desire,
purpose, be minded,* implying more strongly than θέλω (q.v.), the
deliberate exercise of volition (v. Hort on Ja 1¹⁸): c. inf. (M, *Pr.,* 205;
Bl., § 69, 4), Mk 15¹⁵, Ac 5²⁸, ³³ 12⁴ 15³⁷ 17²⁰ 18¹⁵, ²⁷ 19³⁰ 22³⁰ 23²⁸ 27⁴ᵗ
28¹⁸, II Co 1¹⁵, I Ti 6⁹, He 6¹⁷, II Jo¹², III Jo¹⁰, Ju⁵; c. acc., II Co 1¹⁷;
c. acc. et inf., Phl 1¹², I Ti 2⁸ 5¹⁴, Tit 3⁸, II Pe 3⁹; of the will making
choice between alternatives, Mt 1¹⁹ 11²⁷, Lk 10²², Ac 25²⁰, I Co 12¹¹,
Ja 3⁴ 4⁴; εἰ βούλει (cl., a courteous phrase = θέλεις, colloq.; Bl., § 21,
8; LS, s.v.), Lk 22⁴²; c. subjc., adding force to a question of delibera-
tion (Bl., § 64, 6), Jo 18³⁹; βουληθείς, *of set purpose* (v. Hort, in l.),
Ja 1¹⁸; impf., ἐβουλόμην (= cl. βουλοίμην ἄν; Bl., § 63, 5; Lft., *Phm.* ¹³),
Ac 25²². Phm ¹³ (v. also Cremer, 143).†

βουνός, -οῦ, ὁ (a Cyrenaïc word, Hdt., iv, 199), [in LXX chiefly for גִּבְעָה;] a hill : Lk 3⁵ (LXX) 23³⁰.†

βοῦς, βοός, ὁ, ἡ, [in LXX chiefly for בָּקָר;] an ox, a cow : Lk 13¹⁵ 14⁵, ¹⁹, Jo 2¹⁴, ¹⁵, ɪ Co 9⁹ (LXX), ɪ Ti 5¹⁸.†

* βραβεῖον, -ου, τό (< βραβεύς, an umpire), a prize in the games : ɪ Co 9²⁴; metaph., of the Christian's reward, Phl 3¹⁴.†

** βραβεύω (< βραβεύς, an umpire), [in LXX : Wi 10¹² *;] (a) prop., to act as umpire ; hence, (b) generally, to arbitrate, decide (Isocr., Dem.; Lft., Col., l.c.; MM, s.v.): Col 3¹⁵; (c) in some late writers, to direct, rule, control (so in Col., l.c., acc. to Thayer, s.v., Meyer, in l.), (cf. κατα-βραβεύω).†

βραδύνω (< βραδύς), [in LXX : Ge 43¹⁰ (מהה hith.), De 7¹⁰, Is 46¹³ (אחר pi.), Si 32 (35)¹⁸ *;] 1. trans., to retard (Soph., Is, l.c.). 2. More freq. intrans., to be slow, to tarry : ɪ Ti 3¹⁵, ɪɪ Pe 3⁹.†

*† βραδυπλοέω, -ῶ (< βραδύς, πλοῦς), to sail slowly : Ac 27⁷.†

* βραδύς, -εῖα, -ύ, slow : εἰς τὸ λαλῆσαι, Ja 1¹⁹; metaph., of the understanding : β. τ. καρδίᾳ, assoc. with ἀνόητος, Lk 24²⁵.†

* βραδυτής, -ῆτος, ἡ, slowness : ɪɪ Pe 3⁹.†

βραχίων, -ονος, ὁ, [in LXX, β. Κυρίου, freq. for זְרוֹעַ יְהוָה;] the arm ; as in OT, β. κυρίου, metaph., for the Divine power : Lk 1⁵¹, Jo 12³⁸ (LXX), Ac 13¹⁷.†

βραχύς, -εῖα, -ύ, [in LXX chiefly for מְעַט;] short ; (a) of time ; short, little : βραχύ, Ac 5³⁴; μετὰ β., Lk 22⁵⁸; β. τι, a short time, He 2⁷, ⁹, RV, mg. ; (b) of distance : Ac 27²⁸; (c) of quantity or value, little, few : Jo 6⁷, He 2⁷, ⁹, RV, txt. ; pl., διὰ βραχέων, in few words, He 13²².†

** βρέφος, -ους, τό, [in LXX : Si 19¹¹, ɪ Mac 1⁶¹, ɪɪ Mac 6¹⁰, ɪɪɪ Mac 5⁴⁹, ɪv Mac 4²⁵ *;] 1. an unborn child : Lk 1⁴¹, ⁴⁴. 2. a new-born child, a babe : Lk 2¹², ¹⁶ 18¹⁵, Ac 7¹⁹, ɪ Pe 2²; ἀπὸ βρέφους, from infancy, ɪɪ Ti 3¹⁵.†

βρέχω, [in LXX chiefly for מטר;] 1. to wet : Lk 7³⁸, ⁴⁴. 2. In late Gk. writers and vernac. = ὕειν, to send rain, to rain (Kennedy, Sources, 39, 155): Mt 5⁴⁵; trop., β. πῦρ κ. θεῖον, Lk 17²⁹; impers., βρέχει, it rains : Ja 5¹⁷; with ὑετός as subj., Re 11⁶.†

βροντή, -ῆς, ἡ, [in LXX for רַעַם;] thunder : Mk 3¹⁷, Jo 12²⁹, Re 4⁵ 6¹ 8⁵ 10³, ⁴ 11¹⁹ 14² 16¹⁸ 19⁶.†

† βροχή, -ῆς, ἡ (< βρέχω), [in LXX : Ps 67 (68)⁹, 104 (105)³² (גֶּשֶׁם) *;] 1. = βροχετός, a wetting (in π., of irrigation in Egypt; Deiss., LAE, 77). 2. As in MGr. (Kennedy, Sources, 153), = ὑετός, rain : Mt 7²⁵, ²⁷.†

βρόχος, -ου, ὁ, [in LXX : Pr 6⁵ (יָד) 7²¹ (חֵלֶק) 22²⁵ (מוֹקֵשׁ), ɪɪɪ Mac 4⁸ *;] a noose, a slip-knot, a halter : metaph., a restraint (not, as AV, R, txt., a snare) : ɪ Co 7³⁵.†

βρυγμός, -οῦ, ὁ (< βρύχω), [in LXX: Pr 19¹² (נָהַם), Si 51³ *;] a biting, a gnashing of teeth : Mt 8¹² 13⁴², ⁵⁰ 22¹³ 24⁵¹ 25³⁰, Lk 13²⁸.†

βρύχω (Attic, βρύκω), [in LXX: Jb 16¹⁰ ⁽⁹⁾, Ps 34 (35)¹⁶ 36 (37)¹² 111 (112)¹⁰, La 2¹⁶ (חרק) *;] 1. to bite or eat greedily. 2. to gnash, grind, with the teeth : Ac 7⁵⁴.†

* βρύω, poët., late prose and vernac., to be full to bursting; 1. of the earth producing vegetation. 2. Of plants putting forth buds. 3. Of springs, to gush with water : Ja 3¹¹.†

βρῶμα, -τος, τό (cf. βιβρώσκω), [in LXX chiefly for אֹכֶל;] food : Ro 14¹⁵, ²⁰, ı Co 8⁸, ¹³ 10³; pl., Mt 14¹⁵, Mk 7¹⁹, Lk 3¹¹ 9¹³, ı Co 6¹³, ı Ti 4³, He 9¹⁰ 13⁹; trop., of spiritual food, Jo 4³⁴, ı Co 3² (cf. βρῶσις).†

βρώσιμος, -ον (< βρῶσις), [in LXX: Le 19²³, Ne 9²⁵, Ez 47¹² (מַאֲכָל) *;] eatable : Lk 24⁴¹.†

βρῶσις, -εως, ἡ (cf. βιβρώσκω), [in LXX chiefly for parts and derivatives of אכל;] 1. eating : β. καὶ πόσις, Ro 14¹⁷, Col 2¹⁶ (v. Lft., ICC, in l.); c. gen. obj., ı Co 8⁴; metaph., corrosion, rust : Mt 6¹⁹, ²⁰. 2. As also in cl. (Hom., al.) = βρῶμα, food : Jo 6²⁷ᵃ, ıı Co 9¹⁰, Col 2¹⁶ (EV, but v. supr.), He 12¹⁶; metaph., of spiritual nourishment, Jo 4³² 6²⁷ᵇ, ⁵⁵.†

** βυθίζω (< βυθός), [in LXX: ıı Mac 12⁴ *;] trans., to cause to sink, to sink : metaph., εἰς ὄλεθρον, ı Ti 6⁹; pass., to sink, intrans. : Lk 5⁷.†

βυθός, -οῦ, ὁ, [in LXX: Ex 15⁵, Ne 9¹¹ (מְצוֹלָה), Ps 67 (68)²² 68 (69)², ¹⁵ 106 (107)²⁴ (מְצוּלָה) *;] 1. the bottom. 2. the depth of the sea, the deep sea : ıı Co 11²⁵.†

*† βυρσεύς, -έως, ὁ (< βύρσα, a hide), late form for βυρσοδέψης, a tanner : Ac 9⁴³ 10⁶, ³².†

βύσσινος, -η, -ον (< βύσσος), [in LXX chiefly for שֵׁשׁ, בּוּץ, etc.;] made of βύσσος, fine linen : Re 18¹², ¹⁶ 19⁸, ¹⁴.†

βύσσος, -ου, ἡ (cf. Heb. בּוּץ), [in LXX chiefly for שֵׁשׁ, בּוּץ;] byssus, a fine species of flax, also the linen made from it : Lk 16¹⁹.†

βωμός, -οῦ, ὁ (< βαίνω), [in LXX (Hex.) for מִזְבֵּחַ, in Proph., chiefly for בָּמָה;] 1. any raised place, a platform. 2. an altar : Ac 17²³ (cf. θυσιαστήριον and v. DB, i, 75).†

Γ

Γ, γ, γάμμα, τό, indecl., gamma, g, the third letter. As a numeral, γ′ = 3; ,γ = 3000.

Γαββαθά (Rec. -θᾶ), ἡ, indecl., Gabbatha, the Greek transliteration of an uncertain Aramaic word (DB, s.v.; Dalman, Words, 7), used as the equivalent of λιθόστρωτον, stone pavement : Jo 19¹³.†

Γαβριήλ, ὁ, indecl. (Heb. גַּבְרִיאֵל, hero of God), the archangel Gabriel : Lk 1¹⁹, ²⁶.†

*† γάγγραινα, -ης, ἡ, a gangrene, an eating sore, which leads to mortification : ιι Ti 2¹⁷.†

Γάδ, ὁ, indecl. (Heb. גָּד), Gad (Ge 30¹¹ 49¹³, al.) : Re 7⁵.†

Γαδαρηνός, -ή, -όν (< Γαδαρά, Gadara, the capital of Peræa), Gadarene, of Gadara : Mt 8²⁸ (Rec. Γεργεσηνῶν), Mk 5¹, Rec. (Edd., Γερασηνῶν), Lk 8²⁶, ³⁷, Rec. (Edd., Γερασηνῶν).†

Γάζα -ης, ἡ (Heb. עַזָּה), Gaza, in OT, one of the five chief cities of the Philistines : Ac 8²⁶.†

† γάζα, -ης, ἡ (a Persian word), [in LXX for גִּנְזִין, ιι Es 5¹⁷ 6¹ 7²⁰, ²¹, Es 4⁷ ; גִּנְבַּר, ιι Es 7²¹ ; Is 39² * ;] treasure : Ac 8²⁷.†

† γαζο-φυλάκιον, -ου, τό (< γάζα, φυλακή), [in LXX chiefly for לִשְׁכָּה, נִשְׁכָּה (ιν Ki 23¹¹, al.), once for גְּנָזִים (Es 3⁹) ; τὸ γ., τὰ γ., of a temple treasury, Ne 10³⁷, ιι Mac 3⁶, al. ;] treasury : also, apparently, the trumpet-shaped chests into which the peoples' temple-offerings were thrown (DB, iv, 96 ; DCG, ii, 748) : Mk 12⁴¹, ⁴³, Lk 21¹, Jo 8²⁰.†

Γαῖος, -ου, ὁ (Γάϊος, Rec.), Gaius, the name of a Christian ; 1. of Macedonia : Ac 19²⁹. 2. Of Derbe : Ac 20⁴. 3. Of Corinth : Ro 16²³, ι Co 1¹⁴. 4. The one to whom ιιι Ep. Jo is addressed : ιιι Jo ¹.†

γάλα, -ακτος, τό, [in LXX for חָלָב ;] milk : ι Co 9⁷. Metaph., of elementary Christian teaching : ι Co 3², He 5¹², ¹³ ; τὸ λογικὸν ἄδολον γ., the rational (spiritual) genuine milk (v. Hort, in l.), ι Pe 2² (in support of AV, milk of the word, v. ICC, in l.).†

Γαλάτης, -ου, ὁ (originally syn. with cl. Κέλτης ; cf. ι Mac 8², and v. next word), a Galatian : Ga 3¹.†

Γαλατία, -ας, ἡ, Galatia ; 1. a gentilic region in Asia Minor, settled by Gauls (iii/B.C.). 2. A Roman Province which included this region (DB, ii, 85 ff.) : ι Co 16¹, Ga 1², ιι Ti 4¹⁰ (T, Tr., mg., Γαλλίαν ; but even reading Γαλατίαν, the ref. here may be to Gaul ; cf. ICC on Ga, p. xvii), ι Pe 1¹.†

Γαλατικός, -ή, -όν (v. previous word), Galatian, belonging to Galatia : Ac 16⁶ 18²³.†

* γαλήνη, -ης, ἡ, a calm : Mt 8²⁶, Mk 4³⁹, Lk 8²⁴.†

Γαλιλαία, -ας, ἡ (Heb. הַגָּלִיל, the circle, district), Galilee, the name of the northern region of Palestine in NT times : Γ. τῶν ἐθνῶν, Mt 4¹⁵ (LXX) ; θάλασσα τῆς Γ., Mt 15²⁹ (cf. Jo 6¹).

Γαλιλαῖος, -αία, -αῖον, Galilæan : Mt 26⁶⁹, Mk 14⁷⁰, Lk 13¹, ² 22⁵⁹, 13⁶, Jo 4⁴⁵, Ac 1¹¹ 2⁷ 5³⁷.†

Γαλλία, -ας, ἡ, Gaul : T., Tr., mg., for Γαλατία, ιι Ti 4¹⁰.†

Γαλλίων, -ωνος, ὁ, Gallio, proconsul of Achaia : Ac 18¹², ¹⁴, ¹⁷.†

Γαμαλιήλ, ὁ (Heb. גַּמְלִיאֵל), Gamaliel the elder, a Pharisee and Doctor of the Law : Ac 5³⁴ 22³.†

** γαμέω, -ῶ, [in LXX : Es 10³, ιι Mac 14²⁵, ιν Mac 16⁹ * ;] to marry ; 1. of the man, to marry, take to wife (ducere) : absol., Mt 19¹⁰ 22²⁵, ³⁰ 24³⁸, Mk 12²⁵, Lk 17²⁷, 20³⁴, ³⁵, ι Co 7²⁸, ³³ ; c. acc. : Mt 5³² 19⁹, Mk 6¹⁷ 10¹¹, Lk 14²⁰ 16¹⁸. 2. Of the woman, (a) mid. (and in late writers, pass.), *to give oneself in marriage, marry (nubere)* : 1 Co 7³⁹; (*b*) in Hellenistic (M, *Pr.*, 159), act. (as of the man), *to marry* : absol., 1 Co 7²⁸, ³⁴, 1 Ti 5¹¹, ¹⁴ ; c. acc., Mk 10¹². (3) Of both sexes : absol., 1 Ti 4³, 1 Co 7⁹, ¹⁰, ³⁶.†

*†γαμίζω (< γάμος), *to give in marriage*, a daughter : 1 Co 7³⁸. Pass., Mt 22³⁰ 24³⁸, Mk 12²⁵, Lk 17²⁷ 20³⁵ (WH, mg., γαμίσκονται; cf. ἐκγαμίζω); 1 Co 7³⁸ : for the view that γ. here = γαμέω, v. Leitzmann, *Handbuch*, Peake, *Comm.*, in l., D. Smith, *Life and Letters of St. Paul*, p. 269, in which case ὑπέρακμος = *excessively virile*, of the man.

*γαμίσκω, = γαμίζω, q.v. : Lk 20³⁴, ³⁵, WH, mg. (Arist.).†

γάμος, -ου, ὁ, [in LXX for מִשְׁתֶּה ;] 1. *a wedding*, esp. *a weddingfeast* : Mt 22⁸, ¹⁰, ¹¹, ¹², Jo 2¹⁻³, Re 19⁷, ⁹ ; pl. (Field, *Notes*, 16), Mt 22²⁻⁴, ⁹ 25¹⁰, Lk 12³⁶ 14⁸. 2. *marriage* : He 13⁴ (Cremer, 666).†

γάρ, co-ordinating particle, contr. of γε ἄρα, *verily then*, hence, *in truth, indeed, yea, then, why*, and when giving a reason or explanation, *for*, the usage in NT being in general accord with that of cl.; 1. explicative and epexegetic : Mt 4¹⁸ 19¹², Mk 1¹⁶ 5⁴² 16⁴, Lk 11³⁰, Ro 7¹, 1 Co 16⁵, al. 2. Conclusive, in questions, answers and exclamations : Mt 9⁵ 27²³, Lk 9²⁵ 22²⁷, Jo 9³⁰, Ac 8³¹ 16³⁷ 19³⁵, Ro 15²⁶, 1 Co 9¹⁰, Phl 1¹⁸ (Ellic., in l.), 1 Th 2²⁰, al. 3. Causal : Mt 1²¹ 2², ⁵, ⁶, 3²³, Mk 1²² 9⁶, Lk 1¹⁵, ¹⁸, Jo 2²⁵, Ac 2²⁵, Ro 1⁹, ¹¹, 1 Co 11⁵, Re 1³, al.; giving the reason for a command or prohibition, Mt 2²⁰ 3⁹, Ro 13¹¹, Col 3³, 1 Th 4³, al.; where the cause is contained in an interrog. statement, Lk 22²⁷, Ro 3³ 4³, 1 Co 10²⁹ ; καὶ γάρ, *for also*, Mk 10⁴⁵, Lk 6³², 1 Co 5⁷, al.; id. as in cl. = *etenim*, where the καί loses its connective force (Bl., § 78, 6 ; Kühner³, ii, 854 f.), Mk 14⁷⁰, Lk 1⁶⁶ 22³⁷, II Co 13⁴. The proper place of γάρ is after the first word in a clause, but in poets it often comes third or fourth, and so in late prose : II Co 1¹⁹. Yet "not the number but the nature of the word after which it stands is the point to be noticed" (v. Thayer, s.v.).

γαστήρ, -τρός, ἡ, [in LXX for בֶּטֶן, ἐν γ. ἔχειν for הָרָה, ἐν γ. λαμβάνειν for חָרָה;] 1. *the belly* : metaph., *a glutton*, Tit 1¹². 2. *the womb* : ἐν γ. ἔχειν, *to be with child*, Mt 1¹⁸, ²³ (LXX) 24¹⁹, Mk 13¹⁷, Lk 21²³, 1 Th 5³, Re 12² ; ἐν γ. συλλαμβ., *to conceive*, Lk 1³¹.†

γε, enclitic postpositive particle, rarer in κοινή than in cl., giving special prominence to the word to which it is attached, distinguishing it as the least or the most important (Thayer, s.v.), *indeed, at least, even* (but not always translatable into English); 1. used alone : Lk 11⁸ 18⁵ Ro 8³². 2. More freq. with other particles : ἀλλά γε, Lk 24²¹, 1 Co 9² ; ἄρα γε, Mt 7²⁰ 17²⁶, Ac 17²⁷ ; ἆρά γε, Ac 8²⁰ ; εἴ γε (Rec. εἴγε), II Co 5³, Ga 3⁴, Eph 3² 4²¹, Col 1²³ (v. Meyer, Ellic., on Ga, Eph, ll. c.; Lft., on Ga, Col, ll. c.); εἰ δὲ μήγε, following an affirmation, Mt 6¹, Lk 10⁶ 13⁹ ; a negation, Mt 9¹⁷, Lk 5³⁶, ³⁷ 14³², II Co 11¹⁶ ; καί γε (Rec. καίγε, cl. καὶ . . . γε), Lk 19⁴² (WH om.), Ac 2¹⁸ 17²⁷ ; καίτοιγε (L καίτοι γε, Tr. καί τοι γε), Jo 4² ; μενοῦνγε (v. s.v.); μήτι γε, v.s. μήτι; ὄφελόν γέ, 1 Co 4⁸.†

Γεδεών, ὁ, indecl. in LXX and NT, in FlJ, *Ant.*, v. 6, 3 and 4 -ῶνος (Heb. גִּדְעוֹן), *Gideon* (Jg 6-8) : He 11³².†

✝γέεννα (γέενα, Mk 9⁴⁵, Rec.), -ης, ἡ (perh. through Aram. גֵּיהִנָּם, from Heb. גֵּי הִנֹּם, Ne 11³⁰; גֵּי בֶן־הִנֹּם, Jo 18¹⁵; גֵּי בְּנֵי־הִנֹּם, iv Ki 23¹⁰; valley of (the son, sons of) lamentation); [in LXX the nearest approach to γ. is γαίεννα, Jos 18¹⁶ (Γαὶ 'Οννόμ, A), elsewhere φάραγξ 'Ονόμ (Jos 15⁸, al.), v. Swete on Mk 9⁴³;] Gehenna, a valley W. and S. of Jerusalem, which as the site of fire-worship from the time of Ahaz, was desecrated by Josiah and became a dumping-place for the offal of the city. Later, the name was used as a symbol of the place of future punishment, as in NT: Mt 5²⁹, ³⁰ 10²⁸, Mk 9⁴³, ⁴⁵, ⁴⁷, Lk 12⁵, Ja 3⁶; γ. τ. πυρός, Mt 5²² 18¹⁹, prob. with ref. to fires of Moloch (DB, ii, 119 ᵇ); υἱὸς γεέννης, Mt 23¹⁵; κρίσις γεέννης, 23³³.✝

Γεθσημανεί (Rec. -νῆ, LTr. -νεί) indecl. (Heb. גַּת שְׁמָנֵי, oil-press), Gethsemane: called in Jo 18¹ a κῆπος, but named only in Mt 26³⁶, Mk 14³².✝

γείτων, -ονος, ὁ, ἡ (< γῆ), [in LXX chiefly for שָׁכֵן;] a neighbour: Lk 14¹² 15⁶, ⁹, Jo 9⁸.✝

γελάω, -ῶ, [in LXX chiefly for צָחַק, שָׂחַק;] to laugh: Lk 6²⁵; fut., γελάσω (M, Pr., 154), ib. ²¹ (cf. κατα-γελάω).✝

γέλως, -ωτος, ὁ, [in LXX chiefly for שְׂחוֹק;] laughter: Ja 4⁹.✝

γεμίζω (< γέμω), [in LXX: Ge 45¹⁷ (טָעַן), iii Mac 5⁴⁷, iv Mac 3¹⁴ *;] to fill; 1. properly, of a ship (Thuc., al.): Mk 4³⁷ (pass.). 2. In late writers, generally (MGr., v. Kennedy, Sources, 155), c. acc., seq. gen., Mk 15³⁶, Jo 2⁷ 6¹³, Re 15⁸; ἀπό, Lk 15¹⁶, Rec. WH, mg.; ἐκ, Lk 15¹⁶, WH, Re 8⁵. Pass., absol.: Lk 14²³.✝

γέμω (used only in pres. and impf.), [in LXX for מָלֵא, נָשָׂא;] to be full; 1. properly, of a ship (Xen.). 2. Generally (Plat., al.), (a) c. gen. rei: Mt 23²⁷, Lk 11³⁹, Ro 3¹⁴ (LXX), Re 4⁶, ⁸ 5⁸ 15⁷ 17³ (Rec) ⁴ 21⁹; (b) seq. ἐκ: Mt 23²⁵; (c) c. acc. rei (called a solecism in WM, 251; Bl., § 36, 4), as in later Gk. from Byz. to Mod. times (Jannaris, Gr., 1319): Re 17³.✝

γενεά, -ᾶς, ἡ (< γίγνομαι), [in LXX chiefly for דּוֹר, דֹּר (Cremer, 148);] 1. race, stock, family (in NT, γέννημα, q.v.). 2. generation; (a) of the contemporary members of a family: pl., Mt 1¹⁷ (cf. Ge 31³, מֹלֶדֶת); metaph., of those alike in character, in bad sense, Mt 17¹⁷, Mk 9¹⁹, Lk 9⁴¹ 16⁸, Ac 2⁴⁰; (b) of all the people of a given period: Mt 24³⁴, Mk 13³⁰, Lk 21³², Phl 2¹⁵; pl., Lk 1⁴⁸; esp. of the Jewish people, Mt 11¹⁶ 12³⁹, ⁴¹, ⁴², ⁴⁵ 16⁴ 23³⁶, Mk 8¹², ³⁸, Lk 7³¹ 11²⁹, ³⁰⁻³², ⁵⁰, ⁵¹ 17²⁵, Ac 13³⁶, He 3¹⁰ (LXX); τὴν γ. αὐτοῦ τίς διηγήσεται, Ac 8³³ (LXX); (c) the period covered by the life-time of a generation, used loosely in pl. of successive ages: Ac 14¹⁶ 15²¹, Eph 3⁵, Col 1²⁶; εἰς γενεὰς καὶ γ. (= לְדוֹר וָדוֹר, Is 34¹⁷, al.), Lk 1⁵⁰; εἰς πάσας τὰς γ. τοῦ αἰῶνος τῶν αἰώνων, Eph 3²¹ (Ellic., in l.; DCG, i, 639 f.).✝

γενεαλογέω, -ῶ (< γενεά, λέγω), [in LXX: i Ch 5¹ (יחש) *;] to trace ancestry, reckon genealogy; pass., seq. ἐκ: He 7⁶.✝

*γενεαλογία, -ας, ἡ (v. previous word); 1. *the making of a pedigree.*
2. *a genealogy:* pl., ι Ti 1⁴, Tit 3⁹ (v. *CGT*, in l., and ib. *Intr.*, xlix ff.;
DB, ii, p. 141).†

*γενέσια, -ων, τά, neut. pl. of adj. -ιος, -ον, *relating to birth*
(< γένεσις) ; 1. in Attic Gk., *a commemoration of the dead.* 2. In late
Gk., *a birthday feast* (= cl. γενέθλια; so in π., v. MM, *Exp.*, x; cf.
also Rutherford, *NPhr.*, 184) : Mt 14⁶, Mk 6²¹.†

γένεσις, -εως, ἡ (< γίγνομαι), [in LXX chiefly for תּוֹלֵדֹת;] 1. *origin,*
lineage: βίβλος γενέσεως (as in Ge 2⁴ᵃ 5¹), Mt 1¹. 2. *birth:* Mt 1¹⁸,
Lk 1¹⁴ (Rec. γέννησις) ; πρόσωπον τῆς γ., *face of his birth* ("what God
made him to be," Hort., in l.), Ja 1²³; ὁ τροχὸς τῆς γ., *the wheel
(course) of birth* or *creation* ("the wheel of man's nature according to
its original Divine purpose," Hort), Ja 3⁶ ; but v. *ICC* on Ja, ll.c.†

γενετή, -ῆς, ἡ = γενεή, Ion. for γενεά, [in LXX : Le 25⁴⁷ (עָקַר
מִשְׁפָּחָה), Es 4¹⁷ * ;] *birth:* ἐκ γ., Jo 9¹.†

† γένημα, -τος, τό (< γίγνομαι), [in LXX chiefly for תְּבוּאָה;] a form
not found in cl., but used in LXX, NT and π. (Bl., § 3, 10; M,
Pr., 45; Deiss., *BS*, 184), as distinct from γέννημα, q.v., of *fruit,
produce* of the earth : Mt 26²⁹, Mk 14²⁵, Lk 12¹⁸ 22¹⁸, ιι Co 9¹⁰ (Rec.
γέννημα).†

γεννάω, -ῶ (< γέννα, poët. for γένος), [in LXX chiefly for ילד;] 1.
of the father, *to beget:* c. acc., Mt 1¹⁻¹⁶, Ac 7⁸, ²⁹; seq. ἐκ, Mt 1³, ⁵, ⁶.
2. Of the mother, *to bring forth, bear:* Lk 1¹³, ⁵⁷ 23²⁹, Jo 16²¹; εἰς
δουλείαν, Ga 4²⁴. Pass. (1) *to be begotten:* Mt 1²⁰; (2) *to be born:* Mt
2¹, ⁴ 19¹² 26²⁴, Mk 14²¹, Lk 1³⁵, Jo 3⁴, Ac 7²⁰, Ro 9¹¹, He 11²³; seq. ἐκ,
Jo 16²¹ 18³⁷, ιι Pe 2¹²; ἐν, Ac 2⁸ 22³, (ἁμαρτίαις), Jo 9³⁴; ἀπό, He 11¹²
(WH, mg., ἐγεν-) ; ἐκ, Jo 1¹³ 3⁶ 8⁴¹; c. adj., τυφλὸς γ., Jo 9²; [Ῥωμαῖος],
Ac 22²⁸; κατὰ σάρκα: κ. πνεῦμα : Ga 4²⁹. Metaph.; μάχας, ιι Ti 2²³;
ὑμᾶς ἐγέννησα, ι Co 4¹⁵, (ὅν), Phm ¹⁰; in quotation, Ps 2⁷ (LXX), Ac
13³³, He 1⁵ 5⁵; of Christians as begotten of God, born again : Jo 1¹³
3³, ⁵⁻⁸, ι Jo 2²⁹ 3⁹ 4⁷ 5¹, ⁴, ¹⁸ (cf. ἀνα-γεννάω) ; (Cremer, 146).†

γέννημα, -τος, τό (< γεννάω), [in LXX chiefly for תְּבוּאָה;] *offspring* of men or animals : ἐχιδνῶν, Mt 3⁷ 12³⁴ 23³³, Lk 3⁷ (and elsewhere in Rec. for γένημα, q.v.).†

Γεννησαρέτ (Rec. Γεννησ-, Mk, l.c.; Targ. גְּנֵיסַר), [in LXX :
Γεννησάρ (as in some MSS. Mt, Mk), ι Mac 11⁶⁷ * ;] *Gennesaret*, a
fertile plain on W. shore of the Sea of Galilee; ἡ γῆ Γ., Mt 14³⁴, Mk
6⁵³; ἡ λίμνη Γ. (יָם כִּנֶּרֶת, Nu 34¹¹, elsewhere ἡ θάλασσα τ. Γαλιλαίας,
Mk 1¹⁶ ; ἡ θ. τ. Τιβεριάδος, Jo 6¹), Lk 5¹.†

γέννησις, -εως, ἡ (< γεννάω), [in LXX : ι Ch 4⁸ (מִשְׁפָּחָה), Ec 7²
(ילד ni.; γένεσις, Aא), Wi 3¹³ אı (γένεσις, ABא²), Si 22³ * ;] 1. *a
begetting.* 2. *birth:* Mt 1¹⁸, Lk 1¹⁴, Rec.†

γεννητός, -ή, -όν (< γεννάω), [in LXX : Jb 11², ¹² 14¹ 15¹⁴ 25⁴

(ילד)* ;] *begotten, born:* pl., γ. γυναικῶν (cf. אִשָּׁה יְלוּד, Jb 14¹), periphrasis for mankind, Mt 11¹¹, Lk 7²⁸ (Cremer, 147).†

γένος, -ους, τό (< γίγνομαι), [in LXX for עַם, מִין, זֶרַע, etc. ;] 1. *family:* Ac 4⁶ 7¹³ 13²⁰. 2. *offspring:* Ac 17²⁸, ²⁹, Re 22¹⁶. 3. *race, nation:* Mk 7²⁶, Ac 4³⁶ 7¹⁹ 18², ²⁴, II Co 11²⁶, Phl 3⁵, Ga 1¹⁴, 1 Pe 2⁹ 4. *kind, sort, class:* Mt 13⁴⁷ 17²¹, Rec., Mk 9²⁹, I Co 12¹⁰, ²⁸, 14¹⁰.†

Γερασηνός, -ή, -όν, *Gerasene, of Gerasa,* not the G. of Decapolis, 30 m. S.E. of the Lake, but a Gerasa or Gergesa (perh. the mod. *Kersa*) on E. shore ; as subst., pl. οἱ Γ., Mk 5¹, Lk 8²⁶, ³⁷ (Γεργεσηνῶν, RV, mg. ¹; Γαδαρηνῶν, RV, mg. ²).†

Γεργεσηνός, -ή, -όν, *Gergesene:* Lk 8²⁶, ³⁷, TR, mg. ¹ (LTr., WH, R, txt., Γερασηνῶν ; R, mg. ², Γαδαρηνῶν).†

γερουσία, -ας, ἡ (< γέρων), [in LXX (Hex. only in OT) for זָקֵן ;] a *council of elders, senate;* in NT, of the Sanhedrin (*Cl. Rev.,* i, 43 f.; *DB, ext.,* 99) : Ac 5²¹.†

γέρων, -οντος, ὁ, [in LXX for זָקֵן ;] *an old man:* Jo 3⁴.†

γεύω, [in LXX chiefly for טָעַם ;] *to make to taste.* Mid., *to taste, eat:* absol., Ac 10¹⁰ 20¹¹, Col 2²¹ ; c. gen., Mt 27³⁴, Lk 14²⁴, Ac 23¹⁴ ; c. acc. (not cl., but v. Westc., *Heb.,* l.c.; M, *Pr.,* 66, 245), Jo 2⁹. Metaph., He 6⁴ ; ῥῆμα θεοῦ, He 6⁵ (on case, v. supr., and cf. Milligan, *NTD,* 68) ; θανάτου (cf. Talmudic טְעַם מִיתָה), Mt 16²⁸, Mk 9¹, Lk 9²⁷, Jo 8⁵², He 2⁹ ; seq. ὅτι, I Pe 2³ (Cremer, 148).†

γεωργέω, -ῶ (< γεωργός), [in LXX : I Ch 27²⁶ (עָשָׂה מְלֶאכֶת הַשָּׂדֶה), I Es 4⁶, I Mac 14⁸ * ;] *to till* the ground : pass., He 6⁷.†

† γεώργιον, -ου, τό (< γεωργός), [in LXX, freq. in Pr., for שָׂדֶה, etc.;] 1. *a field* (Pr 24⁵, ³⁰, Strabo). 2. *cultivation, husbandry, tillage* (Pr 6⁷ גִּיל, Je 28²³, Si 27⁶) : I Co 3⁹.†

γεωργός, -οῦ, ὁ (< γῆ, ἔργω = ἔρδω, *to do*), [in LXX for אִכָּר, etc.;] 1. *a husbandman:* II Ti 2⁶, Ja 5⁷. 2. *a vine-dresser* (cf. ἀμπελουργός, Lk 13⁷) : Mt 21³³⁻³⁵, ³⁸, ⁴⁰, ⁴¹, Mk 12¹, ², ⁷, ⁹, Lk 20⁹, ¹⁰, ¹⁴, ¹⁶, Jo 15¹.†

γῆ, γῆς, ἡ, [in LXX for אֶרֶץ, אֲדָמָה, etc.;] 1. *the earth, world:* Lk 21³⁵, Ac 1⁸, He 11¹³, Re 3¹⁰, al.; opp. to οὐρανός, Mt 5¹⁸ 11²⁵, Mk 13²⁷, al. 2. *land;* (*a*) opp. to sea or water : Mk 4¹, Lk 5³, Jo 6²¹, al. ; (*b*) as subject to cultivation : Mt 13⁵, Mk 4⁸, Lk 13⁷, He 6⁷, al. ; (*c*) *the ground :* Mt 10²⁹, Mk 8⁶, Lk 24⁵, Jo 8⁶, al. ; (*d*) *a region, country :* Lk 4²⁵, Ro 9²⁸, Ja 5¹⁷ ; γῆ Ἰσραήλ, Mt 2²⁰, ²¹ ; Χαλδαίων, Ac 7⁴ ; ἡ Ἰουδαία γῆ, Jo 3²² ; c. gen. pers., Ac 7³.

γῆρας, Attic, gen. (-αος) -ως, dat. ᾳ; Ion. and κοινή, -εος (-ους), dat. -ει, τό, [in LXX for שֵׂיבָה, etc. ;] *old age:* ἐν γήρει, Lk 1³⁶.†

γηράσκω (also γηράω ; < γῆρας), [in LXX chiefly for זָקֵן ;] *to grow old :* Jo 21¹⁸, He 8¹³.†

SYN.: παλαιοῦμαι.

γίγνομαι, v.s. γίνομαι.

γίνομαι, Ion. and κοινή for Att. γίγν- (M, Pr., 47; Bl., § 6, 8; Mayser, 166 f.), [in LXX chiefly for היה;] 1. of persons, things, occurrences, to come into being, be born, arise, come on: Jo 1¹⁵ 8⁵⁸, 1 Co 15³⁷; a first appearance in public, Mk 1⁴, Jo 1⁶, al.; seq. ἐκ (of birth), Ro 1³, Ga 4⁴; διά, Jo 1³; βροντή, Jo 12²⁹; σεισμός, Re 6¹²; γογγυσμός, Ac 6¹; χαρά, Ac 8⁸, and many other similar exx.; ἡμέρα, Lk 22⁶⁶, al.; ὀψέ, Mk 11¹⁹; πρωΐα, Mt 27¹; νίξ, Ac 27²⁷. 2. Of events, to come to pass, take place, happen: Mt 5¹⁸, Mk 5¹⁴, Lk 1²⁰ 2¹⁵, Ac 4²¹, II Ti 2¹⁸, al.; μὴ γένοιτο [LXX for חלילה, Jo 22²⁹, al.], far be it, God forbid: Ro 3⁴ (ICC, in l.), 1 Co 6¹⁵ and freq. in Pl.; καὶ ἐγένετο, ἐγένετο δέ ([in LXX for ויהי;] v. Burton, 142 f.; M, Pr., 16 f.; M, Gr., II, pp. 425 ff.; Dalman, Words, 32 f.; Robertson, Gr., 1042 f.), c. indic., Mt 7²⁶, Lk 1⁸, al.; seq. καί et indic., Lk 8¹, Ac 5⁷, al.; c. acc. et inf., Mk 2²³, Lk 3²¹, al.; ὡς δὲ ἐγένετο, seq. τοῦ c. inf., Ac 10²⁵; c. dat. pers., to befall one: c. inf., Ac 20¹⁶; c. acc. et inf., Ac 22⁶; c. adv., εἴ, Eph 6³; τί ἐγένετο αὐτῷ (Field, Notes, 115), Ac 7⁴⁰ (LXX); seq. εἰς, Ac 28⁶. 3. to be made, done, performed, observed, enacted, ordained, etc.: Mt 6¹⁰ 19⁸, Mk 2²⁷ 11²³, Ac 19²⁶, al.; seq. διά c. gen., Mk 6², Ac 2⁴³; ὑπό, Lk 13¹⁷; εἰς, Lk 4²³; ἐν, 1 Co 9¹⁵; ἀπογραφή, Lk 2²; ἀνάκρισις, Ac 25²⁶; ἄφεσις, He 9²²; ἵ νόμος, Ga 3¹⁷; τὸ πάσχα, Mt 26². 4. to become, be made, come to be: c. pred., Mt 4³, Lk 4³, Jo 2⁹, 1 Co 13¹¹, al.; seq. ὡς, ὡσεί, Mt 10²⁵, Mk 9²⁶; εἰς (M, Pr., 71 f.), Mk 12¹⁰, al.; c. gen., Re 11¹⁵; id., of age, Lk 2⁴²; c. dat., γ. ἀνδρί ([LXX for היה לאיש, Ru 1¹², al.;] v. Field, Notes, 156), Ro 7³˒⁴; seq. ἐν, Ac 22¹⁷, Re 1¹⁰, al.; ἐπάνω, Lk 19¹⁹; μετά, c. gen., Mk 16[¹⁰], Ac 9¹⁹; seq. εἰς, ἐπί (Field, Notes, 135), κατά (ib., 62), c. acc. of place, Ac 20¹⁶ 21³⁵ 27⁷, al.; seq. ἐκ, Mk 9⁷, Lk 3²², II Th 2⁷, al. Aoristic pf. γέγονα (M, Pr., 52, 145 f.; Field, Notes, 1 f.), Mt 25⁶, Lk 10³⁶, al. Aor. ἐγενήθη (for ἐγένετο, M, Pr., 139 f.; Mayser, 379), Mt 11²³, al. (Cf. ἀπο-, δια-, ἐπι-, παρα-, συμ- παρα-, προ-.)

γινώσκω (= γιγν-: v. previous word. So also vulgar Attic, in Inscr., v. Thumb, MGV, 207), [in LXX chiefly for ידע;] to be taking in knowledge, come to know, recognize, perceive, understand; in past tenses to know, realize; pass., to become known: c. acc., Mt 22¹⁸, Mk 5⁴³, Col 4⁸, 1 Th 3⁵, al. Pass., Mt 10²⁶, Phl 4⁵, al.; seq. ὅτι, Mt 21⁴⁵, Jo 4¹, al.; τί, Mt 6³; ἀπό, Mk 15⁴⁵; ὅ, Ro 7¹⁵; τ. λεγόμενα, Lk 18³⁴; τ. θέλημα, Lk 12⁴⁷; τ. καρδίας, Lk 16¹⁵; c. acc. pers., of recognition by God, 1 Co 8³, Ga 4⁹; by Christ, neg., Mt 7²³; freq. of the knowledge of divine things, of God and Christ: τ. θεόν, Ro 1²¹, Ga 4⁹; τ. πατέρα, Jo 8⁵⁵; τ. κύριον, He 8¹¹ (LXX); νοῦν κυρίου, Ro 11³⁴; Χριστόν, Jo 17³, 1 Jo 3⁶; τὰ τοῦ πνεύματος, 1 Co 2¹⁴; τ. πνεῦμα, 1 Jo 4⁶; τ. ἀλήθειαν, Jo 8³²; of Christ's knowledge of the Father (ἐπιγ.), Mt 11²⁷ (Dalman, Words, 282 ff.). In Hellenistic writers [LXX for Heb. ידע, Ge 4¹, al.], of sexual intercourse, to know carnally: Mt 1²⁵, Lk 1³⁴ (Cremer, 153).

SYN.: γ., to know by observation and experience is thus prop. disting. from οἶδα, to know by reflection (a mental process, based on intuition or information); cf. also ἐφίστημι, συνίημι. (Cf. ἀνα-, δια-, ἐπι-, κατα-, προ-γινώσκω.)

γλεῦκος (-εος), -ους, τό, [in LXX for יַיִן, Jb 32¹⁹ *;] *must, sweet new wine* (Arist.) : Ac 2¹³.†

γλυκύς, -εῖα, -ύ, [in LXX chiefly for מָתוֹק;] Ja 3¹¹, ¹²; opp. to πικρόν, ἁλυκόν, Re 10⁹, ¹⁰.†

γλῶσσα, -ης, ἡ, [in LXX chiefly for לָשׁוֹן;] 1. *the tongue,* as the organ of speech : Mk 7³³, ³⁵, Lk 1⁶⁴ 16²⁴, Ac 2²⁶ (LXX), Ro 3¹³ (LXX) 14¹¹ (LXX), 1 Co 14⁹, Phl 2¹¹, Ja 1²⁶ 3⁵, ⁶, ⁸, 1 Pe 3¹⁰ (LXX), 1 Jo 3¹⁸, Re 16¹⁰ ; of a tongue-like object, Ac 2³. 2. *a tongue, language :* Ac 2¹¹; joined with φυλή, λαός, ἔθνος, freq. in pl., Re 5⁹ 7⁹ 10¹¹ 11⁹ 13⁷ 14⁶ 17¹⁵ ; of unintelligible sounds uttered in spiritual ecstasy, λαλεῖν ἑτέραις γ., Ac 2⁴ ; γ. λαλεῖν καιναῖς, WH, txt. (RV, mg., omit καιναῖς), Mk 16¹⁷ ; λαλεῖν γλώσσαις, γλώσσῃ (v. *ICC,* ll. c. ; *DB,* iv, 793 ff.), Mk 16¹⁷, WH, txt., R, mg., Ac 10⁴⁶ 19⁶, 1 Co 12³⁰ 13¹ 14², ⁴⁻⁶, ¹³, ¹⁸, ²³, ²⁷, ³⁹ ; γλῶσσαι (= λόγοι ἐν γλώσσῃ, 1 Co 14¹⁹), 1 Co 13⁸ 14²² ; γένη γλωσσῶν, 1 Co 12¹⁰, ²⁸ ; προσεύχεσθαι γλώσσῃ, 1 Co 14¹⁴ ; γλῶσσαν ἔχειν, 1 Co 14²⁶ (Cremer, 163, 679).†

†**γλωσσόκομον**, -ου, τό, vernac. form of cl. γλωσσοκομεῖον (< γλῶσσα, κομέω), [in LXX for אָרוֹן, II Ki 6¹¹, II Ch 24⁸, ¹⁰, ¹¹ *;] 1. = cl. -εῖον (v. supr.), *a case* for holding the reeds or tongues of musical instruments. 2. As in LXX, π. (MM, s.v.), *a box, chest :* Jo 12⁶ 13²⁹.†

γναφεύς, -έως, ὁ, Ion. and κοινή form of Att. κναφεύς (< κνάπτω, *to card* wool), [in LXX for כָּבַם, IV Ki 18¹⁷, Is 7³ 36² *;] *a fuller, cloth-dresser :* Mk 9³.†

γνήσιος, -α, -ον (< γίγνομαι), [in LXX: Si 7¹⁸, III Mac 3¹⁹ *;] 1. prop., *lawfully begotten, born in wedlock* (in π., γυνὴ γ., *a lawful wife ;* MM, s.v.). 2. *true, genuine, sincere :* Phl 4³, 1 Ti 1², Tit 1⁴ ; as subst., τὸ γ. = ἡ γνησιότης, *sincerity,* II Co 8⁸.†

γνησίως, adv., [in LXX : II Mac 14⁸, III Mac 3²³ *;] *sincerely, honourably :* Phl 2²⁰ (for a parallel in π., v. MM, s.v.).†

γνόφος, -ου, ὁ (later form of δν-), [in LXX for אָפֵל, עֲרָפֶל, etc. ;] *darkness, gloom* (including "an element of tempest," Tr., *Syn.,* § c) : He 12¹⁸.†

SYN. : ἀχλύς, ζόφος, σκότος (Tr., l.c. ; *DB,* i, 457ᵃ).

γνώμη, -ης, ἡ (< γιγνώσκω), [in LXX : Da TH 2¹⁵ (דָּת), Ps 82 (83)³ (סוֹד), elsewhere, chiefly II Es, for טַעַם ;] 1. *a means of knowing, a token* (Theogn.). 2. In Attic writers, *the mind,* its operations and results (v. Edwards, *Lex., App.,* A) ; (a) *mind, understanding ;* (b) *purpose, intention :* Ac 20³ ; (c) *judgment, opinion :* 1 Co 1¹⁰, Re 17¹³ ; (d) *counsel, advice :* 1 Co 7²⁵, ⁴⁰, II Co 8¹⁰, Phm ¹⁴ ; (e) *royal purpose, decree* (as in Da, I and II Es) : Re 17¹⁷ (Cremer, 671).†

γνωρίζω (< γιγνώσκω), [in LXX chiefly for ידע hi. ;] 1. as most commonly in cl., *to come to know, discover, know :* Phl 1²² (but cf. R,

mg.).   2. *to make known:* c. acc., Ro 9²²,²³; c. acc. rei dat. pers.,
Lk 2¹⁵, Jo 15¹⁵ 17²⁶, Ac 2²⁸ (LXX), ı Co 15¹, ıı Co 8¹, Ga 1¹¹, Eph 1⁹ 6¹⁹,²¹,
Col 4⁷,⁹, ıı Pe 1¹⁶; c. dat., seq. ὅτι, ı Co 12³; seq. τί, Col 1²⁷; περί,
Lk 2¹⁷.   Pass., Ac 7¹³, Ro 16²⁶, Eph 3³,⁵,¹⁰, Phl 4⁶ (Cremer, 677; cf.
ἀνα-, δια-γνωρίζω).†

γνῶσις, -εως, ἡ (< γιγνώσκω), [in LXX chiefly for דַּעַת;] 1. *a
seeking to know, inquiry, investigation.*   2. *knowledge,* in NT, specially
of the kn. of spiritual truth : absol., Lk 11⁵², Ro 2²⁰ 15¹⁴, ı Co 1⁵ (Lft.,
Notes, 147) 8¹,⁷,¹⁰,¹¹ 13²,⁸ 14⁶, ıı Co 6⁶ 8⁷ 11⁶, Eph 3¹⁹, Col 2³, ı Pe 3⁷,
ıı Pe 1⁵,⁶; c. gen. obj., σωτηρίας, Lk 1⁷⁷; τ. δόξης τ. θεοῦ, ıı Co 4⁶; τ.
θεοῦ, ıı Co 2¹⁴ 10⁵; Χριστοῦ Ἰησοῦ, Phl 3⁸ (v. Deiss., *LAE,* 383₈), ıı Pe
3¹⁸; c. gen. subjc., θεοῦ, Ro 11³³; λόγος γνώσεως, ı Co 12⁸; ψευδωνύμου
γνώσεως, ı Ti 6²⁰.†

SYN.: σοφία, φρόνησις (cf. ἐπί-γνωσις and v. Lft. on Col 2³;
Cremer, 156).

†γνώστης, -ου, ὁ (< γιγνώσκω), [in LXX chiefly for יִדְּעֹנִי;] *one who
knows, an expert :* Ac 26³.†

γνωστός, -ή, -όν, later form of γνωτός (< γιγνώσκω), [in LXX for
various parts of ידע;] *known :* Ac 9⁴²; c. dat., Jo 18¹⁵,¹⁶ (Rec.), Ac 1¹⁹ 2¹⁴
4¹⁰ 13³⁸ 15¹⁸ 19¹⁷ 28²²,²⁸; γ. σημεῖον, a *notable* (EV) *sign,* one that is
matter of knowledge, Ac 4¹⁶; γνωστὸν ποιεῖν, Ac 15¹⁷,¹⁸; τὸ γνωστὸν τ.
θεοῦ, Ro 1¹⁹; in pl., as subst., γνωστοί, *acquaintances,* Lk 2⁴⁴ 23⁴⁹; so
in sing., Jo 18¹⁶ (WH).†

†γογγύζω, [in LXX chiefly for לוּן;] *to mutter, murmur :* ı Co
10¹⁰; seq. κατά, Mt 20¹¹; πρός, Lk 5³⁰; περί, Jo 6⁴¹,⁶¹; μετ' ἀλλήλων, Jo
6⁴³; c. acc., seq. περί, Jo 7³² (cf. δια-γογγύζω).†

†γογγυσμός, -οῦ, ο (< γογγύζω), [in LXX: Is 58⁹ (אָנֵן), Ex 16 ⁷⁻⁹,
Nu 17⁵,¹⁰ (תְּלוּנָה), Wi 1¹⁰,¹¹, Si 46⁷ *;] *a murmuring, muttering :*
Jo 7¹², Ac 6¹; ἄνευ γ., ı Pe 4⁹; pl., χωρὶς γ., Phl 2¹⁴.†

**†γογγυστής, -οῦ, ὁ (< γογγύζω); [in Sm.: Pr 26²², Is 29²⁴; Th.: Pr
26²⁰ *;] *a murmurer :* Ju¹⁶.†

*γόης, -ητος, ὁ (γοάω, to wail); 1. *a wailer.*   2. *a wizard.*   3. *an
impostor* (cf. γοητεία, *trickery,* ıı Mac 12²⁴) : ıı Ti 3¹³.†

Γολγοθά (Rec. -θᾶ; WH, mg., Γολγόθ, Jo, l.c., Aram. גָּלְגָּלְתָּא
= Heb. גֻּלְגֹּלֶת, LXX, κρανίον, Jg 9⁵³, ıı Ki 9³⁵); indecl. (exc. Mk 15²²,
-άν), *Golgotha,* the place of the crucifixion : Mt 27³³, Mk 15²², Jo 19¹⁷.†

Γόμορρα, -ας, ἡ, and **-ων, τά** (Heb. עֲמֹרָה), *Gomorrah,* one of the
cities of the plain (Ge 19) : Mt 10¹⁵, Ro 9²⁹ (LXX), ıı Pe 2⁶, Ju⁷.†

γόμος, -ου, ὁ (< γέμω), [in LXX : Ex 23⁵, ıv Ki 5¹⁷ (מַשָּׂא) *;]   *a
ship's freight, cargo :* Ac 21³, Re 18¹¹,¹².†

γονεύς, -έως, ὁ (< γίγνομαι), [in LXX for אָב, אֵם;] *a begetter, a
father ;* mostly in pl., οἱ γ., *parents :* Lk 2⁴¹,⁴³ 8⁵⁶ 21¹⁶, Jo 9²,³,²⁰,²²,²³,

Ro 1³⁰, II Co 12¹⁴, Eph 6¹, Col 3²⁰, II Ti 3² ; acc. pl. (Hellenistic, v. Thackeray, *Gr.*, i, 148), γονεῖς, Mt 10²¹, Mk 13¹², Lk 2²⁷ 18²⁹, Jo 9¹⁸.†

γόνυ, -ατος, τό, [in LXX chiefly for בֶּרֶךְ ;] *the knee :* He 12¹² ; of a suppliant, προσπίπτειν τοῖς γ., Lk 5⁸ ; so also τιθέναι τὰ γ., *to kneel :* Lk 22⁴¹, Ac 7⁶⁰ 9⁴⁰ 20³⁶ 21⁵ ; in mockery, Mk 15¹⁹ ; κάμπτειν τὰ γ., *to bend the knee :* Ro 11⁴ ⁽ᴸˣˣ⁾ 14¹¹ ⁽ᴸˣˣ⁾, Eph 3¹⁴, Phl 2¹⁰.†

*†γονυπετέω, -ῶ (< γόνυ, πίπτω) ; 1. *to fall on the knees :* seq. ἔμπροσθεν, Mt 27²⁹. 2. *to fall down before* one : c. acc., Mt 17¹⁴, Mk 1⁴⁰, R, txt., 10¹⁷.†

γράμμα, -τος, τό (< γράφω), [in LXX for סֵפֶר, etc. ;] 1. *that which is traced* or *drawn, a picture.* 2. *that which is written ;* (1) *a character, letter :* Ga 6¹¹ ; (2) *a writing, a written document ;* (*a*) *a bill* or *account :* Lk 16⁶, ⁷ ; (*b*) *a letter :* Ac 28²¹ ; (*c*) τὰ ἱερὰ γ., *the sacred writings,* i.e. the OT : II Ti 3¹⁵ (so in Philo, *Vit. Mos.*, iii, 39) ; (*d*) τὸ γ., *the letter,* the written word as an external authority in contrast with the direct influence of the Spirit as manifested in the new Covenant : Ro 2²⁷, ²⁹ 7⁶, II Co 3⁶, ⁷ ; (3) τὰ γ., *letters,* i.e. *learning :* Jo 7¹⁵, Ac 26²⁴. (In π. an illiterate person is very frequently referred to as γράμματα μὴ εἰδότος, and this "never means anything else than inability to write" : MM, *Exp.*, x ; but v. also Cremer, 166 ; *DCG*, i, 202 ; ii 584.)†

γραμματεύς, -έως (acc. pl., -εῖς, v. Bl., § 8, 2), ὁ (< γράμμα), [in LXX always for שֹׁטֵר in Hex., elsewhere chiefly for סֹפֵר] 1. *a secretary ;* γ. τ. πόλεως, a state-clerk : Ac 19³⁵. 2. In π., of a military officer (Deiss., *BS*, 110 f.). So Jg 5¹⁴, IV Ki 25¹⁹ (סֹפֵר), al. 3. *a scribe, a biblical scholar, teacher of the law* (so first in I Es 8³, II Es 7⁶ ; in Lk 5¹⁷, νομοδιδάσκαλος ; in Lk 10²⁵, νομικός) : Mt 7²⁹, Mk 1²², and freq. in Gosp. γ. καὶ ἀρχιερεῖς, Mt 2⁴, et al. ; γ. κ. Φαρισαῖοι, Mt 5²⁰, et al. ; γ. μαθητευθεὶς τῇ βασιλείᾳ τ. οὐρ., Mt 13⁵² ; ποῦ σοφός ; ποῦ γ., I Co 1²⁰ (Cremer, 167 ; *DB*, iv, 420, 800).

γραπτός, -ή, -όν (< γράφω), [in LXX for מִכְתָּב ;] 1. *painted.* 2. *written :* Ro 2¹⁵.†

γραφή, -ῆς, ἡ (< γράφω), [in LXX chiefly for כָּתָב ;] 1. *a drawing, painting.* 2. (*a*) *writing ;* (*b*) *that which is written, a writing :* πᾶσα γ., II Ti 3¹⁶ ; γ. ἅγιαι, Ro 1² ; προφητικαί, Ro 16²⁶ ; αἱ γ. τ. προφητῶν, Mt 26⁵⁶ ; ἡ γ., αἱ γ., *the sacred writings, the Scriptures* (i.e. the OT ; v. Milligan, *NTD*, 205) ; in pl., when the sacred writings as a whole are meant, e.g. Mt 21⁴² 26⁵⁴, Jo 5³⁹, Ro 15⁴ ; in sing., when a particular passage is referred to, as in Lk 4²¹, Jo 19²⁴, Ro 4³ 9¹⁷ 10¹¹ 11², Ja 2²³ (Cremer, 165 ; *DCG*, iii, 584).

γράφω, [in LXX chiefly for כתב] ; 1. *to scrape, graze* (Hom.), and later (Hdt.) *to sketch, draw.* 2. *to write ;* (*a*) of forming or tracing letters on writing material : Jo 8⁽⁶⁾, Ga 6¹¹, II Th 3¹⁷ ; (*b*) to express in writing, commit to writing, record : Lk 1⁶³, Jo 19²¹, ²², Re 1¹¹, ¹⁹, al. ; of scripture as a standing authority (Deiss., *BS*, 112 ff.), γέγραπται, *it stands written* (Luther), Mt 4⁴, Mk 7⁶, Lk 4⁸, Ro 1¹⁷, ι Co 1³¹, al.; id. seq. ἐν, Mk 1², Ac 1²⁰, al.; c. acc., *to write of:* Jo 1⁴⁶, Ro 10⁵; seq. περί, Mt 26²⁴, Mk 14²¹, Jo 5⁴⁶, al.; c. dat. (WM, § 31, 4), Lk 18³¹; id. seq. ἵνα (M, *Pr.*, 207 f.), Mk 12¹⁹, Lk 20²⁸; κατὰ τ. γεγραμμένον, ιι Co 4¹³; γεγραμμένον ἐστί, Jo 2¹⁷; ἐγράφη δι' ἡμᾶς, Ro 4²⁴; ἐπ' αὐτῷ γεγραμμένα, Jo 12¹⁶; (*c*) of writing directions or information, c. dat. pers.: Ro 15¹⁵, ιι Co 7¹², al.; (*d*) of that which contains the record or message: βιβλίον, Mk 10⁴, Jo 21²⁵, Re 5¹; τίτλον, Jo 19¹⁹; ἐπιστολήν, Ac 23²⁵; ἐντολήν, Mk 10⁵ (cf. ἀπο-, ἐγ-, ἐπι-, κατα-, προ-).

† γραώδης, -ες (γραῦς, *an old woman*, εἶδος), *anile, old-womanish:* ι Ti 4⁷.†

γρηγορέω, -ῶ, = Attic ἐγρήγορα, pf. of ἐγείρω, q.v., [in LXX (later bks. only) chiefly for שָׁקַד;] 1. *to be awake;* metaph., of being alive, ι Th 5¹⁰. 2. *to watch:* Mt 24⁴³ 26³⁸, ⁴⁰, Mk 13³⁴ 14³⁴, ³⁷, Lk 12³⁷, ³⁹; metaph., Mt 24⁴² 25¹³ 26⁴¹, Mk 13³⁵, ³⁷ 14³⁸, Ac 20³¹, ι Co 16¹³, ι Th 5⁶, ι Pe 5⁸, Re 3², ³ 16¹⁵; seq. ἐν, Col 4². (Cf. δια-γρηγορέω.)†

SYN.: v.s. ἀγρυπνέω.

** γυμνάζω (< γυμνός), [in LXX: ιι Mac 10¹⁵ *;] 1. properly, *to exercise naked.* 2. Generally, *to exercise, train* the body or mind: ι Ti 4⁷, He 5¹⁴ 12¹¹, ιι Pe 2¹⁴.†

** γυμνασία, -ας, ἡ (< γυμνάζω), [in LXX: ιν Mac 11²⁰ *;] *exercise:* ι Ti 4⁸.†

*† γυμνιτεύω (Rec. γυμνητ-, v. Tdf., *Pr.*, 81), *to be naked* or *scantily clad:* ι Co 4¹¹ (cf. ἐν ψύχει κ. γυμνότητ·, ιι Co 11²⁷; γυμνοί, Ja 2¹⁵. In κοινή writers, γ. also means *to go light-armed.*)†

γυμνός, -ή, -όν, [in LXX chiefly for עָרוֹם;] *naked, without clothing,* and sometimes (as freq. in cl.) *scantily* or *poorly clad* (Is 20² ᶠᶠ·, To 1¹⁶, ιι Mac 11¹²): Mt 25³⁶, ³⁸, ⁴³, ⁴⁴, Mk 14⁵², Jo 21⁷, Ac 19¹⁶, Ja 2¹⁵, Re 3¹⁷ 16¹⁵, 17¹⁶; as subst., τὸ γ., *the naked body,* Mk 14⁵¹. Metaph., of things exposed, He 4¹³; of the soul without a body (Plat., *Crat.*, c., 20, and cf. Deiss., *LAE*, 293), ιι Co 5³; of seed, *bare,* ι Co 15³⁷ (Cremer, 168).†

† γυμνότης, -ητος, ἡ (< γυμνός), [in LXX for עָרוֹם, De 28⁴⁸ *;] *nakedness:* Ro 8³⁵, ιι Co 11²⁷, Re 3¹⁸.†

* γυναικάριον, -ου, τό (dim. of γυνή), *a little woman;* contemptuously, *a silly woman* (EV), *a poor weak woman:* ιι Ti 3⁶.†

γυναικεῖος, -α, -ον (< γυνή), [in LXX chiefly for אִשָּׁה;] *female:* ι Pe 3⁷.†

γυνή, -αικός, ἡ, [in LXX for אִשָּׁה;] 1. *a woman,* married or un-married: Mt 11¹¹ 14²¹, al.; ὕπανδρος γ., Ro 7²; γ. χήρα, Lk 4²⁶; in vocat., γύναι implies neither reproof nor severity, but is used freq. as a term of respect and endearment, Mt 15²⁸, Jo 2⁴, 4²¹ 19²⁶. 2. *a wife:* Mt 1²⁰, ι Co 7³, ⁴, al.; γ. ἀπολύειν, Mk 10², al.; γ. ἔχειν, Mk 6¹⁸; γ. λαβεῖν, Mk 12¹⁹; γ. γαμεῖν, Lk 14²⁰. 3. *a deaconess,* ι Ti 3¹¹ (*CGT,* in l.).

Γώγ, ὁ (Heb. גּוֹג), indecl., *Gog,* assoc. with Magog (q.v): Re 20⁸.†

γωνία, -ας, ἡ (< γόνυ), [in LXX chiefly for פִּנָּה;] an angle, a corner: Mt 6⁵, Ac 26²⁶; τ. τέσσαρας γ. τ. γῆς, Re 7¹, 20⁸; κεφαλὴ γωνίας (רֹאשׁ פִּנָּה, Ps 117 (118)²², LXX), Mt 21⁴², Mk 12¹⁰, Lk 20¹⁷, Ac 4¹¹, I Pe 2⁷.†

Δ

Δ, δ, δέλτα, τό, indecl., the fourth letter. As a numeral, δ′ = 4, δ = 4000.

Δαβίδ, v.s. Δαυείδ.

**δαιμονίζομαι (in cl. also δαιμονάω; < δαίμων), [in Aq.: Ps 90 (91)⁶*;] to be under the power of a δαίμων (δαιμόνιον, q.v.), to be possessed: Mt 15²²; elsewhere always ptcp., -ιζόμενος, -ισθείς: Mt 4²⁴ 8¹⁶, ²⁸, ³³ 9³² 12²², Mk 1³² 5¹⁵, ¹⁶, ¹⁸, Lk 8³⁶, Jo 10²¹ (Cremer, 171).†

δαιμόνιον, -ου, τό (neut. of δαιμόνιος, -α, -ον, divine), [in LXX (so also in π.; v. MM, Exp., x) for שֵׁד, אֱלִיל (freq. in To);] 1. as in cl.; (a) the Divine power, Deity (Hdt., Plat., al.); (b) an inferior divinity, deity or demon (as in magical π., Deiss., BS, 281; MM, Exp., x): ξένα δ., Ac 17¹⁸. 2. (a) In OT, heathen deities, false gods (e.g. De 32¹⁷, Ps 95 (96)⁵); (b) evil spirits, demons: θύουσιν δαιμονίοις, I Co 10²⁰; διδασκαλίαι δαιμονίων, I Ti 4¹; προσκυνεῖν τὰ δ., Re 9²⁰; ἄρχων τῶν δ., Mt 9³⁴; especially (syn. with πνεῦμα ἀκάθαρτον) as operating upon and "possessing" (cf. δαιμονίζομαι) men: Mt 11¹⁸, et al.; εἰσέρχεσθαι δ. εἰς . . ., Lk 8³⁰; δ. ἔχειν, Lk 4³³; δ. ἐκβάλλειν, Mt 7²². In the phrase πνεῦμα δαιμονίου ἀκαθάρτου, Lk 4³³, the wider cl. usage (1. b) is recognised, ἀκ. being elsewhere in NT, the epithet of πν., and δ. = πν. ἀκ. (v. ICC, in 1; Cremer, 168).

**†δαιμονιώδης, -ες (< δαιμόνιον, εἶδος), [in Sm.: Ps 90 (91)⁶*;] demon-like: Ja 3¹⁵ (Cremer, 171).†

δαίμων, -ονος, ὁ, ἡ, [in LXX for גַּד, Is 65¹¹ (א; δαιμονίῳ, AB)*;] in cl. and NT = δαιμόνιον; a demon: Mt 8³¹.†

δάκνω, [in LXX for נָשַׁךְ, Ge 49¹⁷, al., exc. De 8¹⁵ (שָׂרַף);] to bite: metaph., Ga 5¹⁵.†

δάκρυον (poët. form δάκρυ), -ου, τό, [in LXX for דִּמְעָה;] a tear: Mk 9²⁴ (WH, txt., R, txt. omit), Ac 20¹⁹, ³¹, II Co 2⁴, II Ti 1⁴, He 5⁷ 12¹⁷, Re 7¹⁷ 21⁴; metaphl. dat. pl., δάκρυσι (La 2¹¹, Thuc., vii, 75; Bl., § 9, 3), Lk 7³⁸, ⁴⁴.†

δακρύω, [in LXX for בָּכָה, etc.;] to weep, shed tears: Jo 11³⁵.†

SYN.: κλαίω, of audible weeping, to cry; ὀδύρομαι, of grief expressed verbally, to lament; θρηνέω, of formal lamentation, to sing a dirge; ἀλαλάζω, to wail in Oriental fashion; στενάζω, of grief expressed by inarticulate sounds, to groan.

δακτύλιος, -ου, ὁ (< δάκτυλος), [in LXX chiefly for טַבַּעַת;] a ring: Lk 15²².†

7

δάκτυλος, -ου, ὁ, [in LXX chiefly for אֶצְבַּע;] a finger : Mt 23⁴, Mk 7³³, Lk 11⁴⁶ 16²⁴, Jo 8⁶,⁸ 20²⁵,²⁷; metaph., δ. θεοῦ (cf. Ex 8¹⁹), Lk 11²⁰.†

Δαλμανουθά, ἡ, indecl., Dalmanutha, an unidentified place near the Sea of Galilee: ⸀Mk⸀8¹⁰ (cf. Μαγαδάν). For conjecture on textual corruption, v. Burkitt in AJTh, xv (1911), p. 174.

Δαλματία (L, Δελ-), -ας, ἡ, Dalmatia, a part of Illyria on E. coast of the Adriatic : II Ti 4¹⁰.†

δαμάζω, [in LXX: Da 2⁴⁰ (חֲשַׁל) *;] to tame, subdue : Mk 5⁴, Ja 3⁷; metaph., τ. γλῶσσαν, Ja 3⁸ (Field, Notes, 237 f.).†

δάμαλις, -εως, ἡ (fem. of δαμάλης, a bullock), [in LXX chiefly for עֶגְלָה, פָּרָה;] a heifer, He 9¹³.†

Δάμαρις, -ιδος, ἡ (< δάμαρ, poët., a wife), Damaris : Ac 17³⁴.†

Δαμασκηνός, -ή, -όν, of Damascus, Damascene : II Co 11³².†

Δαμασκός, -οῦ, ἡ (Heb. דַּמֶּשֶׂק), Damascus : Ac 9² ff. 22⁵ ff. 26¹²,²⁰, II Co 11³², Ga 1¹⁷.†

δανείζω, v. δανίζω.

δάνειον, v. δάνιον.

δανειστής, v. δανιστής.

δανίζω (late form of cl. -είζω, Rec., Bl., § 3; Thackeray, Gr., 85 f.), [in LXX chiefly for לוה (Pr 19¹⁷);] to lend money on interest : Lk 6³⁴,³⁵; mid., to borrow : Mt 5⁴².†

SYN. : κίχρημι (v.s. χράω), to lend in a friendly way.

Δανιήλ, ὁ, indecl. (Heb. דָּנִיֵּאל, God is my Judge), Daniel, the prophet : Mt 24¹⁵.†

δάνιον, -ου, τό (late form of δάνειον, Rec.; v.s. δανίζω), [in LXX : De 24¹¹ (נָשָׁה) 15⁸,¹⁰ (עבט hi.), IV Mac 2⁸ *;] a loan : Mt 18²⁷.†

δανιστής, -οῦ, ὁ (late form of -ειστής, Rec.; v.s. δανείζω), [in LXX : IV Ki 4¹, Ps 108 (109)¹¹ (נשׁה), Pr 29¹³ (רָשׁ), Si 29²⁸ *;] a money-lender : Lk 7⁴¹.†

** δαπανάω, -ῶ, [in LXX : To 1⁷, I Mac 14³², al.;] 1. to spend, expend . c. acc., Mk 5²⁶; seq. ἐπί, c. dat. pers., Ac 21²⁴; ὑπέρ, II Co 12¹⁵. 2. to consume, squander : Lk 15¹⁴; ἐν τ. ἡδοναῖς (on the constr. with ἐν, v. Hort, Mayor, in l.), Ja 4³ (cf. ἐκ-, προσ- δ.).†

δαπάνη, -ης, ἡ, [in LXX : II Es 6⁴,⁸ (נִפְקָא), Da LXX Bel ²¹, al.;] expense, cost : Lk 14²⁸.†

Δαυείδ (Rec. Δαβίδ), ὁ, indecl. (Heb. דָּוִד), David, King of Israel : Mt 1⁶ 12³, et al. ; σκηνὴ Δ., Ac 15¹⁶; κλεὶς Δ., Re 3⁷; θρόνος Δ., Lk 1³²; ῥίζα Δ., Re 5⁵; βασιλεία Δ., Mk 11¹⁰; υἱὸς Δ., the Messiah (Ps. Sol., 17²³; for other reff. in Jewish lit., v. Dalman, Words, 317), Mt 1¹ 9²⁷, et al.; ἐν Δ., i.e. the Psalter, He 4⁷.

δέ (before vowels δ'; on the general neglect of the elision in NT, v. WH, App., 146; Tdf., Pr., 96), post-positive conjunctive particle;

1. copulative, *but, in the next place, and, now* (Abbott, *JG*, 104):
Mt 1² ff., 11 Co 6¹⁵,¹⁶, 11 Pe 1⁵⁻⁷; in repetition for emphasis, Ro 3²¹,²²
9³⁰, 1 Co 2⁶, Ga 2², Phl 2⁸; in transition to something new, Mt 1¹⁸ 2¹⁹,
Lk 13¹, Jo 7¹⁴, Ac 6¹, Ro 8²⁸, 1 Co 7¹ 8¹, al.; in explanatory parenthesis
or addition, Jo 3¹⁹, Ro 5⁸, 1 Co 1¹², Eph 2⁴ 5³², al.; ὡς δέ, Jo 2⁹; καὶ
. . . δέ, *but also*, Mt 10¹⁸, Lk 1⁷⁶, Jo 6⁵¹, Ro 11²³, al.; καὶ ἐὰν δέ, *yea
even if*, Jo 8¹⁶. 2. Adversative, *but, on the other hand*, prop., answering
to a foregoing μέν (q.v.), and distinguishing a word or clause from one
preceding (in NT most freq. without μέν; Bl., § 77, 12): ἐὰν δέ, Mt
6¹⁴,²³, al.; ἐγὼ (σὺ, etc.) δέ, Mt 5²² 6⁶, Mk 8²⁹, al.; ὁ δέ, αὐτὸς δέ, Mk
1⁴⁵, Lk 4⁴⁰, al.; after a negation, Mt 6¹⁹,²⁰, Ro 3⁴, 1 Th 5²¹, al.

δέησις, -εως, ἡ (< δέομαι), [in LXX for תְּחִנָּה, רִנָּה, תְּפִלָּה, etc.;]
1. *a wanting, need* (so Ps 21 (22)²⁵). 2. *an asking, entreaty, supplication;* in NT always addressed to God: Lk 1¹³, 11 Co 1¹¹, Phl 1¹⁹, 11 Ti
1³, Ja 5¹⁶, 1 Pe 3¹² (LXX); with νηστεῖαι, Lk 2³⁷; προσευχή, -αί, Eph 6¹⁸,
Phl 4⁶, 1 Ti 2¹ 5⁵; ἱκετηρίαι, He 5⁷; προσκαρτέρησις, Eph 6¹⁸; ἐντεύξεις,
1 Ti 2¹; δ. ποιεῖσθαι (Deiss., *BS*, 250), Lk 5³³, Phl 1⁴ (pl.), 1 Ti 2¹;
seq. ὑπέρ, 11 Co 9¹⁴, Phl 1⁴; περί, Eph 6¹⁸; πρός, Ro 10¹.†
  SYN.: προσευχή, used of *prayer* in general, while δ. gives prominence to the sense of need; on the other hand, δ. is used as well of
requests from man to man, while π. is limited to prayer to God.
ἔντευξις, in the papyri, is the regular word for *petition* to a superior
(Deiss., *BS*, 250); cf. the Pauline ἐντυγχάνειν, *to entreat*). Cf. also
εὐχή (Ja 5¹⁵), αἴτημα, ἱκετηρία (Tr., *Syn.*, § li; Cremer, 73, 174, 684).

δεῖ, impersonal (δέω), [in LXX chiefly for infin. with לְ;] *one
must, it is necessary:* c. inf., Mt 26⁵⁴, Mk 13⁷, Ac 5²⁹, al.; c. acc. et
inf., Mt 16²¹, Mk 8³¹, Jo 3⁷, Ac 25¹⁰, al.; with ellipse of acc., Mt 23²³;
of acc. and inf., Mk 13¹⁴, Ro 1²⁷ 8²⁶; οὐ (μὴ) δεῖ (*non licet*), *ought not, must
not:* Ac 25²⁴, 11 Ti 2²⁴; impf., ἔδει, of necessity or obligation in past
time regarding a past event (Bl., § 63, 4), Mt 18³³, Lk 15³², Jo 4⁴,
Ac 27²¹, al.; periphr., δέον ἐστίν (as in Attic, χρεών ἐστι = χρή, v.s.
δέον), Ac 19³⁶; id., with ellipse of ἐστίν, 1 Pe 1⁶; τὰ μὴ δέοντα (= ἃ οὐ
δεῖ), 1 Ti 5¹³.
  SYN.: ὀφείλει, expressing moral obligation, as distinct from δεῖ,
denoting logical necessity and χρή, a need which results from the fitness
of things (v. Tr., *Syn.*, § cvii, 10; Westc. on He 2¹, 1 Jo 2⁶; Hort on
Ja 3¹⁰).

*δεῖγμα, -τος, τό (< δείκνυμι); 1. (cl.) *a thing shown, a specimen*.
2. = cl. παράδ- (cf. ὑπόδ-, 11 Pe 2⁶), *an example* (a warning): Ju 7.†
†δειγματίζω (< δεῖγμα), a rare word (*ICC*, ll. c.), *to make a show
of, to expose:* Mt 1¹⁹ (Rec. παραδ-, q.v.), Col 2¹⁵.†
  δείκνυμι, δεικνύω (v. Bl., § 23, 1; Veitch, s.v.), [in LXX chiefly
for רָאָה hi.;] *to show*, c. acc. rei (pers.), dat. pers.; (*a*) *to show, exhibit:*
Mt 4⁸ 8⁴, Mk 1⁴⁴ 14¹⁵, Lk 4⁵ 5¹⁴ 20²⁴ 22¹² 24⁴⁰, Jo 2¹⁸ 5²⁰ 10³² 20²⁰,
Ac 7³ (LXX), 1 Ti 6¹⁵, Re 17¹ 21⁹,¹⁰ 22¹,⁸, pass., He 8⁵ (LXX); (*b*) *to make
known:* Mt 16²¹, Jo 14⁸,⁹, Ac 10²⁸, 1 Co 12³¹, Re 1¹ 4¹, 22⁶; (*c*) *to
prove:* Ja 2¹⁸ 3¹³.†

δειλία, -ας, ἡ (< δειλός), [in LXX for אֵימָה, מְחִתָּה, etc.;]
cowardice, timidity (never in good sense): II Ti 1⁷.†

SYN.: φόβος, *fear*, in general, good or bad; εὐλάβεια (q.v.),
apprehension generally, but chiefly *pious fear*, "that careful and
watchful reverence which pays regard to every circumstance in that
with which it has to deal" (cf. Tr., *Syn.*, § x).

† δειλιάω, -ῶ (< δειλία), [in LXX for חתת ni., פחד, etc.;] = the
more freq. ἀποδ-, *to be cowardly, timid, fearful*: Jo 14²⁷.†

δειλός, -ή, όν (< δέος), [in LXX for רך, etc.;] *cowardly, fearful*:
Mt 8²⁶, Mk 4⁴⁰, Re 21⁸.†

** δεῖνα, ὁ, ἡ, τό (gen. -νος, dat. -νι, acc. -να), [in Aq.: Ru 4¹, I Ki
21² (3) (Sm. also), IV Ki 6⁸ *;] *such an one, a certain one*, whom one
cannot or will not name: Mt 26¹⁸.†

δεινῶς, adv. (< δέος), [in LXX: Jb 10¹⁶, Wi 17³, al.;] 1. *terribly*:
Mt 8⁶.   2. *vehemently*: Lk 11⁵³.†

δειπνέω, -ῶ (< δεῖπνον, q.v.), [in LXX: Pr 23¹ (לחם), To 7⁸ 8¹,
Da LXX 11²⁷ *;] to take the chief meal of the day, *to dine, to sup*:
Lk 17⁸ 22²⁰ (WH, br., R, mg. omits), I Co 11²⁵; metaph., Re 3²⁰.†

δεῖπνον, -ου, τό, [in LXX chiefly for פַּת־בַּג (Da);] the chief meal
of the day, *dinner, supper*: Mt 23⁶, Mk 12³⁹, Lk 14¹⁷, ²⁴ 20⁴⁶, Jo 13², ⁴
21²⁰, I Co 11²¹; δ. ποιεῖν, Mk 6²¹, Lk 14¹², ¹⁶, Jo 12²; κυριακὸν (q.v.) δ.,
I Co 11²⁰; metaph. (Dalman, *Words*, 118), δ. τ. γάμου τ. ἀρνίου, Re 19⁹;
δ. τ. μέγα τ. Θεοῦ, Re 19¹⁷.†

*† δεισιδαιμονία, -ας, ἡ (< δεισιδαίμων, q.v.); 1. *fear of the gods;*
(*a*) *piety, religion;* (*b*) *superstition.*   2. Objectively, *a religion*: Ac
25¹⁹ (Cremer, 72, 682).†

* δεισι-δαίμων, -ον (< δείδω, *to fear;* δαίμων, *deity*), *reverent to the
deity, religious;* compar. -μονεστέρους (AV, *too superstitious*, R, txt.,
somewhat superstitious, a sense in wh. the word is sometimes used;
cf. Field, *Notes*, 125), *more religious, God-fearing*, than others, *quite
religious* (Abbott, *Essays*, 105 ff.; Deiss., *LAE*, 285): Ac 17²².†

SYN.: εὐσεβής (q.v.), θεοσεβής, θρῆσκος (Cremer, 681; *DB, ext.*,
142 ª).

δέκα, οἱ, αἱ, τά, *ten*: Mt 20²⁴, al.; θλίψις ἡμερῶν δ., i.e. of brief
duration: Re 2¹⁰.

† δεκα-δύο, Rec. for δώδεκα: Ac 19⁷ 24¹¹.†

† δεκα-έξ, = ἑκκαίδεκα, *sixteen* (Jannaris, *Gr.*, § 645): Re 13¹⁸,
L, mg. (for ἑξήκοντα ἕξ; v. Swete, in l.).†

† δεκα-οκτώ, T for δέκα ὀκτώ, *eighteen*: Lk 13⁴.†

† δεκα-πέντε, [in LXX: Ex 27¹⁵, I Mac 10⁴⁰, al.;] late form of
πεντεκαίδεκα, *fifteen*: Jo 11¹⁸, Ac 27⁵, WH, mg., ib. ²⁸, Ga 1¹⁸.†

Δεκά-πολις, -εως, ἡ, *Decapolis*, a region east of the Jordan containing ten cities: Mt 4²⁵, Mk 5²⁰ 7³¹.†

† δεκατέσσαρες, -ων, οἱ, αἱ, -α, τά, [in LXX: Ge 31⁴¹, To 8¹⁹, al.;]
= cl. τεσσαρεσκαίδεκα, more freq. in later Gk. than the older form and
in MGr. (for thirteen and upwards) universal, *fourteen*: Mt 1¹⁷, II Co
12², Ga 2¹ (cf. τεσσαρεσκαιδέκατος).†

δεκάτη, -ης, ἡ, prop. fem. (sc. μερίς) of δέκατος, -η, -ον, [in LXX for מַעֲשֵׂר: Ge 14²⁰, Ne 12⁴⁴, et al.;] a tenth part, a tithe: He 7², ⁴, ⁸, ⁹ (for a curious inversion of the Biblical use, v. MM, s.v.).†

δέκατος, -η, -ον (< δέκα), [in LXX for מַעֲשֵׂר and cognate forms;] tenth: Jo 1⁴⁰, Ac 19⁹ (WH, txt., RV omit), Re 11¹³ 21²⁰.†

† δεκατόω, -ῶ, = cl. -τεύω (< δεκάτη), [in LXX: Ne 10³⁷ (³⁸) (עשׂר pi.) * ;] to take tithe of: c. acc. pers., He 7⁶; pass. to pay tithe: He 7⁹.†

† δεκτός, -ή, -όν, verbal adj. of δέχομαι, [in LXX chiefly for רָצוֹן: Pr 11¹, al.;] acceptable: Lk 4¹⁹ (LXX) ²⁴, Ac 10³⁵, II Co 6² (LXX), Phl 4¹⁸ (cf. εὐπροσδ-).†

*δελεάζω (< δέλεαρ, a bait), to allure by a bait: metaph., to allure, entice: c. acc., II Pe 2¹⁴, ¹⁸; pass., Ja 1¹⁴.†

Δελματία, v. Δαλματία.

δένδρον, -ου, τό, [in LXX for עֵץ, etc.;] a tree: Mt 3¹⁰, al.; δ. ἀγαθόν, Mt 7¹⁷, ¹⁸; δ. καλόν, Mt 12³³, Lk 6⁴³; δ. σαπρόν, Mt 7¹⁷, ¹⁸ 12³³, Lk 6⁴³; γίνεσθαι δ., Mt 13³²; γ. εἰς δ., Lk 13¹⁹.

*† δεξιο-βόλος, -ου, ὁ (< δεξιός, βάλλω), one who throws with the right hand: L for δεξιολάβος, Ac 23²³.†

* δεξιολάβος, -ου, ὁ (< δεξιός, λαμβάνω), a kind of soldier, prob. a spearman (Vg., lancearius) or slinger: Ac 23²³.†

δεξιός, -ά, -όν, [in LXX chiefly for יָמִין;] the right: Mt 5²⁹, Jo 18¹⁰, al.; ὅπλα δ., weapons carried in the right hand, i.e. for offence, II Co 6⁷; ἡ δ. χείρ, Mt 5³⁰, Lk 6⁶, al.; ἡ δ. (sc. χείρ), Mt 6³, al.; ἐπὶ τὴν δ., in the right hand (R, txt., on R, mg.), Re 5¹; διδόναι τὴν δ., in friendship (Deiss., BS, 251), Ga 2⁹; metaph. of power, τῇ δ. αὐτοῦ, Ac 2³³ 5³¹; τὰ δ., the right side, Mk 16⁵; ἐκ δεξιῶν, on the right hand, c. gen., Mt 25³³, ³⁴, Mk 15²⁷, Lk 1¹¹, al.; of a place of honour in the Messianic Kingdom (cf. III Ki 2¹⁹, Ps 44 (45)¹⁰), καθίσαι ἐκ δεξιῶν, Mt 20²¹, Mk 10³⁷; of the heavenly session of Christ, Mt 26⁶⁴, Mk 14⁶², He 1¹³ (Cremer, 172).

δέομαι (mid. of δέω, II, q.v., as depon.), [in LXX for חנן, etc.;] to want for oneself; 1. to want, need: (a) absol.; (b) c. gen. 2. to beg, request, beseech, pray; (i) in general: absol., Ac 26³, WH; c. gen. pers., Lk 5¹² 8²⁸, ³⁸ (ἐδεῖτο; T, ἐδέετο, cf. Veitch, s.v. δέω) 9³⁸, Ac 8³⁴ 21³⁹, II Co 5²⁰, Ga 4¹²; seq. ἵνα, Lk 9⁴⁰; seq. τό, c. inf., II Co 10²; c. gen. pers. et rei, II Co 8⁴; (ii) of prayer to God: absol., Ac 4³¹; seq. εἰ πως, Ro 1¹⁰; ἵνα, Lk 21³⁶ 22³²; εἰς τό, I Th 3¹⁰; ὑπὲρ ἐμοῦ πρὸς τ. κύριον, ὅπως, Ac 8²⁴; c. gen., τοῦ κυρίου, ὅπως, Mt 9³⁸, Lk 10²; τοῦ Θεοῦ, Ac 10²; seq. εἰ ἄρα, Ac 8²².†

SYN.: αἰτέω, and cf. δέησις.

δέον, -οντος, τό (neut. part. of δεῖ, used as subst.), [in LXX · Si prol. ³, ⁴, I Mac 12¹¹, II Mac 1¹⁸ *; pl. τὰ δ., for לֶחֶם, Ex 16²², III Ki 4²² (5²), Pr 24³¹ (30⁸); שְׁאָר, Ex 21¹⁰; פַּת־בָּג, Da TH 11²⁶; To 5¹⁴, ιι Mac 13²⁰ *;] *that which is needful, due, proper* : δ. ἐστίν (periphr. for δεῖ, q.v.), Ac 19³⁶, with ellipse of ἐστίν, ι Pe 1⁶; τὰ μὴ δ., ι Ti 5¹³.†

δέος, -ους, τό (< δείδω), [in LXX : ιι Mac 3¹⁷, ³⁰ 12²² 13¹⁶ 15²³ *;] *fear, awe, reverence* : μετὰ εὐλαβείας καὶ δ., He 12²⁸.†

SYN.: δειλία, φόβος.

Δερβαῖος, -α, -ον, *of Derbe* : Ac 20⁴.†

Δέρβη, -ης, ἡ, *Derbe,* a city of Lycaonia : Ac 14⁶, ²⁰ 16¹.†

δέρμα, -τος, τό (< δέρω), [in LXX for עוֹר;] *the skin, hide* of beasts : ἐν αἰγίοις δ., He 11³⁷.†

δερμάτινος, -η, -ον (< δέρμα), [in LXX for עוֹר;] *of skin, leathern* : Mt 3⁴, Mk 1⁶ (cf. ιν Ki 1⁸).†

δέρρις, -εως, ἡ (< δέρος = δέρμα), [in LXX : Ex 26⁷ *ᵃ·* (וְרִיעָה), Za 13⁴ (אַדֶּרֶת), etc.;] *a skin :* Mk 1⁶ (D, from Za, l.c.; Swete, in l.; Rec., Edd. τρίχας; cf. MM, *Exp.,* x).†

δέρω, [in LXX : Le 1⁶, ιι Ch 29³⁴ 35¹¹ (פָּשַׁט hi.) *;] 1. *to skin, flay.* 2. (cf. Eng. slang, *hide) to beat, thrash :* c. acc., Mt 21³⁵, Mk 12³, ⁵, Lk 20¹⁰, ¹¹ 22⁶³, Jo 18²³, Ac 5⁴⁰ 16³⁷ 22¹⁹; ὡς ἀέρα δέρων, ι Co 9²⁶; εἰς πρόσωπον δ., ιι Co 11²⁰. Pass., Mk 13⁹, Lk 12⁴⁷, ⁴⁸ (δαρήσεται πολλάς, ὀλίγας, sc. πληγάς).†

δεσμεύω (< δεσμός), [in LXX for אסר (Jg 16¹¹, al.), אלם pi. (Ge 37⁷, al.), etc.;] 1. *to put in chains :* Lk 8²⁹, Ac 22⁴. 2. *to bind, tie together :* φορτία, Mt 23⁴.†

δεσμέω, -ῶ, Rec. for δεσμεύω, q.v. : Lk 8²⁹.†

δέσμη (Rec. δεσμή), -ης, ἡ (< δέω), [in LXX for אֲגֻדָּה, Ex 12²² *;] *a bundle :* δήσατε αὐτὰ εἰς δέσμας (D, Orig., omit εἰς, and Blass thinks original reading, δέσμας δέσμας; v. Deiss., *LAE,* 125₄), Mt 13³⁰.†

δέσμιος, -ον (also -α, -ον ; < δεσμός), [in LXX for אסר;] 1. *binding.* 2. *bound, captive;* ὁ δ., as subst., *a prisoner :* Mt 27¹⁵, ¹⁶, Mk 15⁶, Ac 16²⁵, ²⁷ 23¹⁸ 25¹⁴, ²⁷ 28¹⁶ (Rec.) ¹⁷, He 10³⁴ 13³ ; ὁ δ. τοῦ Χριστοῦ, Eph 3¹, ιι Ti 1⁸, Phm ¹, ⁹ ; ὁ δ. ἐν κυρίῳ, Eph 4¹.†

δεσμός, -οῦ, ὁ (< δέω), [in LXX chiefly for אסר;] *a band, bond :* metaph., Lk 13¹⁶; ὁ δεσμὸς τ. γλώσσης, Mk 7³⁵ (for this expression in π., v. Deiss., *LAE,* 306 ff.; of actual bonds, v. Ruth., *Gr.,* 9). Pl., δεσμοί, Phl 1¹³; δεσμά (as also in cl.), Lk 8²⁹, Ac 16²⁶ 20²³; gen., dat., Ac 23²⁹ 26²⁹, ³¹, Phl 1⁷, ¹⁴, ¹⁷, Col 4¹⁸, ιι Ti 2⁹, Phm ¹⁰, He 11³⁶, Ju ⁶; ἐν τοῖς δ. τοῦ εὐαγγελίου, Phm ¹³.†

***†δεσμο-φύλαξ, -κος, ὁ** (δεσμός, φύλαξ), *a prison-keeper, gaoler :* Ac 16²³, ²⁷, ³⁶ (cf. ἀρχιδ-, Ge 39²¹).†

δεσμωτήριον, -ου, τό, [in LXX for בֵּית הַסֹּהַר (Ge), אָסִיר;] *a prison :* Mt 11², Ac 5²¹, ²³ 16²⁶.†

δεσμώτης, -ου, ὁ, [in LXX for אסר, מִסְגֵּר;] *a prisoner :* Ac 27¹, ⁴².†

δεσπότης, -ου, ὁ, [in LXX chiefly for אָדוֹן, אֲדֹנָי; in Jth 9¹⁷, δ. τ. οὐρανῶν κ. τ. γῆς]; *a master, lord,* correlative of δοῦλος, οἰκέτης : ι Ti 6¹, ², ιι Ti 2²¹, Tit 2⁹, ι Pe 2¹⁸ ; as title of God, voc., δέσποτα (so usually in

LXX), Lk 2²⁹, Ac 4²⁴; ὁ δ. = voc. δέσποτα (cf. Bl., § 33, 4), Re 6¹⁰; of Christ, II Pe 2¹, Ju ⁴, R, txt. (but cf. mg.).†

SYN.: κύριος (q.v.), implying limitation of authority and a more general relation than δ., which "denoted absolute ownership and uncontrolled power" (Thayer).

δεῦρο, adv., [in LXX chiefly for לְךָ, לְכָה;] 1. of place; (a) hither, with verbs of motion; (b) (in cl. chiefly poët.) as an imperat., here! come!: Mt 19²¹, Mk 10²¹, Lk 18²², Jo 11⁴³, Ac 7³ (LXX), ³⁴ (LXX), Re 17¹ 21⁹. 2. Of time, hitherto, now: Ro 1¹³.†

δεῦτε, adv., as pl. of δεῦρο, 1. (b), q.v., [in LXX chiefly for לְכוּ;] come on! come here! come!: c. imperat., Mt 25³⁴ 28⁶, Jo 4²⁹ 21¹², Re 19¹⁷; c. subjc., Mt 21³⁸, Mk 12⁷; seq. ὀπίσω, Mt 4¹⁹, Mk 1¹⁷; πρός, Mt 11²⁸; εἰς, Mt 22⁴, Mk 6³¹.†

*δευτεραῖος, -α, -ον (< δεύτερος), adj. with adverbial sense; on the second day: δευτεραῖοι ἤλθομεν, Ac 28¹³.†

*†δευτερό-πρωτος, -ον, second-first (in what sense, there is no satisfactory explanation. The reading is prob. not original, v. ICC, in l.; DCG, i, 411; ii, 541, 724, and for Burkitt's suggestion of dittography, v. MM, VGT, s.v.): Lk 6¹, WH, mg., R, mg.†

δεύτερος, -α, -ον, second in order, with or without idea of time: Mt 22²⁶, ³⁹, al.; θάνατος, Re 2¹¹ 20¹⁴ 21⁸; χάρις, II Co 1¹⁵. In neut. as adv., secondly, a second time; opp. to πρῶτον: Jo 3⁴ 21¹⁶, I Co 12²⁸, Re 19³; τὸ δ., II Co 13², Ju ⁵; ἐν τ. δ., at the second time: Ac 7¹³; in later usage (as I Mac 9¹), ἐκ δ., Mk 14⁷², Jo 9²⁴, Ac 11⁹, He 9²⁸.

δέχομαι, depon. mid., [in LXX chiefly for לקח;] to receive, accept; 1. c. acc. rei, of taking or accepting what is offered: γράμματα, Lk 16⁶, ⁷; id. in different sense, Ac 28²¹; ποτήριον, Lk 22¹⁷; παιδίον (εἰς τ. ἀγκάλας), Lk 2²⁸; περικεφαλαίαν, μάχαιραν, Eph 6¹⁷; ἐπιστολάς, Ac 22⁵; τ. βασιλείαν τ. θεοῦ, Mk 10¹⁵, Lk 18¹⁷; λογία ζῶντα, Ac 7³⁸; εὐαγγέλιον, II Co 11⁴; τ. χάριν τ. θεοῦ, II Co 6¹; metaph., of mental acceptance, Mt 11¹⁴; τ. λόγον, Lk 8¹³, Ac 8¹⁴ 11¹ 17¹¹, I Th 1⁶ 2¹³, Ja 1²¹; τὰ τ. πνεύματος, I Co 2¹⁴; τ. παράκλησιν, II Co 8¹⁷; τ. ἀγάπην τ. ἀληθείας, II Th 2¹⁰. 2. C. acc. pers., of receiving kindly or hospitably, Mt 10¹⁴, ⁴⁰, ⁴¹, Mk 6¹¹, Lk 9⁵, ⁵³ 10⁸, ¹⁰, Jo 4⁴⁵, II Co 7¹⁵ 11¹⁶, Ga 4¹⁴, Col 4¹⁰, He 11³¹; παιδίον, Mt 18⁵, Mk 9³⁷, Lk 9⁴⁸; εἰς οἴκους, σκηνάς, Lk 16⁴, ⁹; δέξαι τ. πνεῦμά μου, Ac 7⁵⁹; ὃν δεῖ οὐρανὸν δέξασθαι, Ac 3²¹ (cf. ἀνα-, ἀπο-, δια-, εἰσ-, ἐκ-, ἀπ-εκ-, ἐν-, ἐπι-, παρα-, προσ-, ὑπο-δέχομαι; Cremer, 174).†

δέω (I), [in LXX chiefly for אסר;] to tie, bind, fasten; (1) c. acc. rei, seq. εἰς δεσμάς, Mt 13³⁰; of an ass, Mt 21², Mk 11²,⁴, Lk 19³⁰. (2) c. acc. pers., of swathing a dead body, ὀθονίοις, Jo 19⁴⁰; δεδομένος τ. πόδας . . . κειρίαις (Bl., § 34, 6; Kühner³, iii, 125), Jo 11⁴⁴; of binding with chains, ἀγγέλους, Re 9¹⁴; a demoniac, πέδαις κ. ἀλύσεσι, Mk 5³,⁴; captives, Mt 12²⁹ 14³ 22¹³ 27², Mk 3²⁷ 6¹⁷ 15¹,⁷, Jo 18¹²,²⁴, Ac 9²,¹⁴,²¹ 21¹¹,¹³ 22⁵,²⁹ 24²⁷, Col 4³, Re 20²; ἀλύσεσι, Ac 12⁶ 21³³. Metaph., ὁ λόγος τ. θεοῦ, II Ti 2⁹; of Satan binding by disease (MM, s.v.), Lk 13¹⁶; of constraint or obligation, Ac 20²²; of the marriage bond

1 Co 7³⁹; id. c. dat. pers., ἀνδρί, Ro 7²; γυναικί, 1 Co 7²⁷; in Rabbinic lang. (Dalman, *Words*, 213 f.), *to forbid, declare forbidden*, Mt 16¹⁹ 18¹⁸ (cf. κατα-, περι-, συν-, ὑπο-δέω; Cremer, 82).†

δέω (II), Attic, *to want, miss*; mid., δέομαι, q.v.

δή, consecutive co-ordinating particle with no exact equiv. in Eng., giving greater exactness and emphasis to the word or words to which it is attached; sometimes translatable as *now therefore, then, verily, certainly*. 1. With verbs: imperat., Ac 6³ (WH, mg.) 13², 1 Co 6²⁰; hort. subjc., Lk 2¹⁵, Ac 15³⁶; indic., δή που (T, δήπου, q.v.), He 2¹⁶. 2. With pronouns: ὃ δή, *now this is he who*, Mt 13²³.†

*† δηλαυγῶς, adv. (< δῆλος, αὐγή), *clearly* : Mk 8²⁵, T, WH, mg. (for τηλαυγῶς, q.v.).†

δῆλος, -η, -ον, [in LXX for אוּר, etc. ;] 1. *visible*. 2. *clear* to the mind, *evident* : Mt 26⁷³; δ. (sc. ἐστίν), seq. ὅτι, 1 Co 15²⁷, Ga 3¹¹.†

SYN.: φανερός, with ref. to outward appearance, *manifest* as opp. to concealed; δ. with ref. to inner perception, *evident*, known, understood.

δηλόω, -ῶ, [in LXX chiefly for ידע ;] *to make plain, declare* : c. acc., 1 Co 3¹³, Col 1⁸, He 9⁸ 12²⁷; c. dat. pers., II Pe 1¹⁴; c. dat. pers., seq. περί (pass.), 1 Co 1¹¹; seq. εἰς, 1 Pe 1¹¹.†

SYN.: ἐμφανίζω, *to make manifest*, render visible to the sight; δ. to render evident to the mind.

Δημᾶς, ὁ (perh. contracted from Δημήτριος), *Demas*, a companion of St. Paul : Col 4¹⁴, Phm ²⁴, II Ti 4¹⁰.†

δημηγορέω, -ῶ (< δῆμος, ἀγορεύω, *to speak in the assembly*), [in LXX : Pr 24⁶⁶ (30³¹), IV Mac 5¹⁵ * ;] *to deliver an oration* : Ac 12²¹.†

Δημήτριος, -ου, ὁ, *Demetrius* ; 1. a silversmith, Ac 19²⁴, ³⁸. 2. A Christian disciple, III Jo ¹².†

** δημιουργός, -οῦ, ὁ (< δῆμος, ἔργον), [in LXX: II Mac 4¹ * ;] 1. *one who works for the people*. 2. Univ., *an author, builder, maker* ; *the maker* of the world (Xen., *Mem.*, I, 4, 9, al.), He 11¹⁰.†

SYN.: κτίστης, *creator*, τεχνίτης, *craftsman, designer*. In He, l.c., τ. has reference to the plan, δ. to its execution.

δῆμος, -ου, ὁ, [in LXX chiefly for מִשְׁפָּחָה ;] 1. *a district, country*. 2. *the common people, the people* generally; esp. *the people assembled* : Ac 12²² 17⁵ 19³⁰, ³³.†

SYN.: λαός, *the people* at large : δ., the people as a body politic; opp. to δ. is ὄχλος, the unorganized *multitude*. ἔθνος, in sing., means in NT as in Gk. writers generally, *a nation*, but in pl. denotes the rest of mankind apart from the Jews : *Gentiles*. λ. also, rare in cl. (Att. λεώς), is freq. in LXX and NT, and usually limited to the chosen people, Israel (cf. *Cl. Rev.*, i, 42 f.; Cremer, 689).

** δημόσιος, -α, -ον (< δῆμος), [in LXX : II Mac 6¹⁰, III Mac 2²⁷ 4⁷ * ;] *belonging to the people, public* : Ac 5¹⁸; dat. fem. used adverbially (cl.); (*a*) *at the public expense, by public consent; (b) publicly* : Ac 16³⁷ 18²⁸ 20²⁰.†

*† δηνάριον, -ου, τό, the Lat. *denarius*, a Roman coin, nearly equal

to the δραχμή, q.v.: Mt 18²⁸ 20³, ⁹, ¹³ 22¹⁹, Mk 6³⁷ 12¹⁵ 14⁵, Lk 7⁴¹ 10³⁵ 20²⁴, Jo 6⁷ 12⁵, Re 6⁶; τὸ ἀνὰ δ., Mt 20¹⁰.†

δή-ποτε, indef. adv. (also written δή ποτε), with generalizing force; 1. absol., sometime. 2. With adv. or relat., -soever : ᾧ δ., Jo 5[⁴] (L, οἰῳδηποτοῦν).†

*δή-που (WH, δή που), indef. adv., mostly in sense of surely, of course, we know : He 2¹⁶ T (WH, δή που).†

Δία, acc. of Ζεύς, q.v.

διά (before a vowel δι᾽, exc. Ro 8¹⁰, 11 Co 5⁷, and in pr. names; Tdf., Pr., 94), prep. c. gen., acc., as in cl.; 1. c. gen., through; (i) of Place, after verbs of motion or action : Mt 2¹² 12⁴³, Mk 2²³, Lk 4³⁰, Jo 4⁴, 11 Co 11³³, al.; σώζεσθαι (διασ-) δ. πυρός, ὕδατος, 1 Co 3¹⁵, 1 Pe 3²⁰; βλέπειν δ. ἐσόπτρου, 1 Co 13¹²; metaph., of a state or condition : Ro 14²⁰, 11 Co 2⁴ 5⁷, ¹⁰; δ. γράμματος, ἀκροβυστίας (Lft., Notes, 263, 279), Ro 2²⁷ 4¹¹; δι᾽ ὑπομονῆς, Ro 8²⁵. (ii) Of Time; (a) during which : Mt 26⁶¹, Mk 14⁵⁸, Lk 5⁵; δ. παντὸς τοῦ ζῆν, He 2¹⁵; δ. παντός (διαπαντός in Mk 5⁵, Lk 24⁵³), always, continually, Mt 18¹⁰, Ac 2²⁵ (LXX) 10² 24¹⁶, Ro 11¹⁰ (LXX), 11 Th 3¹⁶, He 9⁶ 13¹⁵; (b) within which: Ac 1³; δ. νυκτός, Ac 5¹⁹ 16⁹ 17¹⁰ 23³¹; (c) after which (Field, Notes, 20; Abbott, JG, 255 f.): Mk 2¹, Ac 24¹⁷, Ga 2¹. (iii) Of the Means or Instrument; (1) of the efficient cause (regarded also as the instrument) : of God, Ro 11³⁶, 1 Co 1⁹, Ga 4⁷, He 2¹⁰ 7²¹; of Christ, Ro 1⁸ 5¹, ¹⁷, 1 Co 15²¹, 1 Pe 4¹¹, al.; δ. τ. ὑμῶν δεήσεως, Ro 1¹², 11 Co 1⁴, Ga 4²³, al.; (2) of the agent, instrument or means; (a) c. gen. pers., Mt 11², Lk 1⁷⁰, Jo 1¹⁷, Ac 1¹⁶, Ro 2¹⁶, 1 Co 1²¹, Eph 1⁵, He 2¹⁴, Re 1¹, al; ὑπὸ τ. κυρίου δ. τ. προφήτου (δ. τ. κυρίου, 1 Th 4² (M, Th., in l.); Lft., Rev., 121 f.), Mt 1²² 2¹⁵, Ro 1²; δ. ἐπιστολῆς ὡς δ. ἡμῶν (Field, Notes, 202), 11 Th 2²; δ. Σ. (NTD, 22), 1 Pe 5¹²; (b) c. gen. rei (where often the simple dat. is used in cl.; Jannaris, Gr., 375), Jo 11⁴, Ac 5¹²; δ. τ. πίστεως, Ro 3³⁰; δ. λόγου θεοῦ, 1 Pe 1²³; δ. παραβολῆς, Lk 8⁴; δουλεύειν δ. τ. ἀγάπης, Ga 5¹³; δ. ἐπαγγελίας, Ga 3¹⁸. 2. C. acc.; (i) rarely, as c. gen., through (Hom), δ. μέσον Σαμαρίας (ICC, in l.; Bl., § 42, 1; Robertson, Gr., 581), Lk 17¹¹. (ii) by reason of, because of, for the sake of; (a) c. acc. pers. (M, Pr., 105), Mk 2²⁷, Jo 6⁵⁷ 11⁴², Ro 8²⁰; (b) c. acc. rei, δ. φθόνον, Mt 27¹⁸, Mk 15¹⁰; δ. φόβον, Jo 7¹³ 20¹⁹; δ. ἀγάπην, Eph 2⁴; δ. τοῦτο, freq., for this cause, therefore, Mt 6²⁵, Mk 6¹⁴, Lk 11⁴⁹, Jo 6⁶⁵, al.; id. seq. ὅτι, Jo 5¹⁶ 10¹⁷, al.; δ. τί, why, Mt 9¹¹, ¹⁴, Mk 2¹⁸, Jo 7⁴⁵, al.; δ. τό, c. inf., Mk 5⁴, Lk 9⁷, Ja 4². 3. In composition, (1) through, as in διαβαίνω; (2) of separation, asunder, as in διασπάω; (3) of distribution, abroad, as in διαγγέλλω; (4) of transition, as διαλλάσσω; (5) of "perfective" action (M, Pr., 112 f., 115 f.), as διαφύγω, διακαθαρίζω.

δια-βαίνω, [in LXX chiefly for עבר] 1. to make a stride. 2. to step across, cross over; (a) trans.: τ. θάλασσαν, He 11²⁹; (b) intrans.: seq. εἰς, Ac 16⁹; πρός, Lk 16²⁶.†

δια-βάλλω, [in LXX: Da LXX 3⁸, ΤΗ 3⁸ 6²⁴ ⁽²⁵⁾ (אֲכַל קְרַץ), 11 Mac 3¹¹, IV Mac 4¹*;] 1. to throw across. 2. To slander, defame, accuse falsely or maliciously, also, in general, to accuse (MM, VGT, s.v.) : Lk 16¹ (Cremer, 120).†

*δια-βεβαιόομαι, -οῦμαι, to affirm confidently : Tit 3⁸ ; seq. περί, 1 Ti 1⁷ (Cremer, 140).†

*δια-βλέπω ; 1. to look straight before one. 2. to see clearly : Mt 7⁵, Mk 8²⁵, Lk 6⁴² (cf. διάβλεψις, Aq., Is 61¹, for LXX ἀνάβ-).†

διάβολος, -ον (< διαβάλλω, q.v.), [in LXX for שָׂטָן (as Jb 1⁶), exc. Es 7⁴ 8¹ (צָר, צָרַר);] slanderous, accusing falsely. As subst., ὁ, ἡ, δ.; (a) generally (cf. Es, ll. c.), a slanderer, false accuser : 1 Ti 3⁶, ⁷ (CGT, in l., but v. infr.) 3¹¹, 11 Ti 3³, Tit 2³ ; (b) as chiefly in LXX, of Satan, the Accuser, the Devil : Mt 4¹, ⁵, ⁸, ¹¹ 13³⁹ 25⁴¹, Lk 4², ³, ⁶, ¹³ 8¹², Jo 13², Ac 10³⁸, Eph 4²⁷ 6¹¹, 1 Ti 3⁶, ⁷ (but v. supr.), 11 Ti 2²⁶, He 2¹⁴, Ja 4⁷, 1 Pe 5⁸, Ju ⁹, Re 2¹⁰ 12⁹, ¹² 20², ¹⁰ ; εἶναι ἐκ τοῦ δ., Jo 8⁴⁴, 1 Jo 3⁸ ; τέκνα τοῦ δ., 1 Jo 3¹⁰ ; υἱὸς, Ac 13¹⁰ ; metaph., of Judas, Jo 6⁷⁰ (Cremer, 121 ; DCG, ii, 605).†

δι-αγγέλλω, [in LXX for ספר pi., etc.;] to publish abroad, proclaim : c. acc., Lk 9⁶⁰, Ac 21²⁶, Ro 9¹⁷ (LXX).†

διά-γε (WH, διά γε), v.s. γέ.

**δια-γίνομαι (Ion. and late Gk. for διαγίγν-), [in LXX, 11 Mac 11²⁶ *;] 1. to go through, to pass, e.g. τ. νύκτα; absol., to live. 2. Of time, to intervene, elapse : ptcp., c. ἡμερῶν τινῶν, Ac 25¹³ ; ἱκανοῦ χρόνου, ib. 27⁹ ; τ. σαββάτου, Mk 16¹.†

δια-γινώσκω (v. previous word), [in LXX chiefly for ידע, and cf. 11 Mac 9¹⁵ ;] 1. to distinguish, ascertain exactly : Ac 23¹⁵. 2. As Athen. law-term, to determine : τὰ καθ᾽ ὑμᾶς, your case, Ac 24²² (Cremer, 673).†

*†δια-γνωρίζω, to publish abroad : Lk 2¹⁷, Rec. (ἐγνώρισεν, Edd.).† ᵢ

**διά-γνωσις, -εως, ἡ (< διαγιγνώσκω), [in LXX : Wi 3¹⁸ *;] 1. a distinguishing, also as medical term. 2. As law-term (Lat. cognitio), determination, decision : Ac 25²¹ (Cremer, 674).†

†δια-γογγύζω, [in LXX chiefly for לין, לון, as Ex 16², and cf. Si 34 (31)²⁴ ;] of a number, to murmur or mutter among themselves : Lk 15² 19⁷.†

*†δια-γρηγορέω, -ῶ, (a) prop., to remain awake (R, mg.) ; (b) to be fully awake (R, txt.) : Lk 9³².†

δι-άγω, [in LXX for עבר hi., etc. ;] 1. to carry over. 2. Of time, to pass : βίον, 1 Ti 2² ; absol., to live, seq. ἐν, Tit 3³.†

δια-δέχομαι, [in LXX for מִשְׁנֶה (Deiss., BS, 115), פַּרְבָּר ;] to receive through another, receive in turn : Ac 7⁴⁵ (RV, in their turn ; v. Field, Notes, 116).†

διάδημα, -τος, τό (< διαδέω, to bind round), [in LXX for כֶּתֶר (as Es 1¹¹), etc. ;] the band round the τιάρα of a Persian king ; a diadem, the badge of royalty : Re 12³ 13¹ 19¹².†

SYN. : στέφανος, the badge of " victory, of valour, of nuptial joy, of festal gladness" (but v. M, Th., i, 2¹⁹ ; cf. DB, i, 530, 604).

δια-δίδωμι, [in LXX for חלק pi., etc. ;] 1. tc hand over, deliver : Re 17¹³, Rec. 2. to distribute : Lk 11²² 18²², Jo 6¹¹, Ac 4³⁵.†

διά-δοχος, -ου, ὁ, ἡ (< διαδέχομαι), [in LXX: I Ch 18¹⁷ (לְיָד), II Ch 26¹¹ (שָׂר) 28⁷ (מִשְׁנֶה), Si 46¹ 48⁸, II Mac 4²⁹ 14²⁶ *;] *a successor*: Ac 24²⁷ (for usage in LXX and π. in sense of court official, v. Deiss., *BS*, 115).†

διά-ζώννυμι, (also -ννύω), [in LXX for חָגוֹר, Ez 23¹⁵ A*;] *to gird round*: ἑαυτόν, Jo 13⁴; pass., ib. 13⁵; mid., *to gird oneself with*: c. acc., Jo 21⁷.†

διαθήκη, -ης, ἡ (< διατίθημι), [freq. in LXX, and nearly always for בְּרִית;] 1. as usually in cl., *a disposition, testament, will* (Plat., al.): Ga 3¹⁵ (R, mg., but v. Lft., in l.), He 9¹⁶, ¹⁷ (R, txt.; MM, *Exp.*, xi,; Milligan, *NTD*, 75; Abbott, *Essays*, 107; Deiss., *LAE*, 341; but v. infr.). 2. As in LXX (for בְּרִית) = cl. συνθήκη, *a convention, arrangement, covenant* (exc. in the disputed cases mentioned above, always bet. God and man, "perhaps with the feeling that the δια- compound was more suitable than the συν- for a covenant with God—συνθ. might suggest equal terms," MM, *Exp.*, l.c.): Ga 3¹⁵ (R, txt., but v. supr., and cf. Thayer, s.v.), He 9¹⁶, ¹⁷ (R, mg., Westc., in l.; Hatch, *Essays*, 47; but v. supr.), Mt 26²⁸, Mk 14²⁴, Lk 1⁷², Ac 3²⁵ 7⁸, Ro 11²⁷(LXX), II Co 3¹⁴, Ga 3¹⁷, He 7²² 8⁶, ib. 9, 10 (LXX) 9⁴, 15, ib. 20 (LXX) 10¹⁶ (LXX), 29 12²⁴ 13²⁰, Re 11¹⁹; καινὴ δ., Mt 26²⁸, and Mk 14²⁴ (R, mg.), Lk 22²⁰. I Co 11²⁵, II Co 3⁶, He 8⁸ (LXX) 9¹⁵; pl., Ro 9⁴, Ga 4²⁴, Eph 2¹² (v. *ICC* on Ga, pp. 496 ff.).†

δι-αίρεσις, -εως, ἡ (< διαιρέω), [in LXX chiefly for מַחֲלֹקֶת;] 1. *a distinction, difference*. 2. *a division, distribution*: I Co 12⁴⁻⁶ (cf. διαιρέω; Cremer, 616).†

δι-αιρέω, -ῶ, [in LXX for בתר (as Ge 15¹⁰), חלק (as Jos 18⁵), etc.;] 1. *to divide into parts, cut asunder*. 2. *to distribute*: c. acc. rei, dat. pers., Lk 15¹², I Co 12¹¹.†

*διά-καθαίρω, *to cleanse thoroughly*: Lk 3¹⁷.†

*†διά-καθαρίζω = -θαίρω: Mt 3¹².†

*†διά-κατ-ελέγχομαι, *to confute completely*: Ac 18²⁸.†

*διακονέω, ῶ (< διάκονος); 1. generally, *to minister, serve, wait upon*, especially at table, *to do one a service, care for one's needs*: absol., Mt 20²⁸, Mk 10⁴⁵, Lk 10⁴⁰ 22²⁶, ²⁷, Jo 12², I Pe 4¹¹; ὅσα διηκόνησεν, II Ti 1¹⁸; c. dat. pers., Mt 4¹¹ 8¹⁵ 25⁴⁴ 27⁵⁵, Mk 1¹³, ³¹ 15⁴¹, Lk 4³⁹ 8³ 12³⁷ 17⁸, Jo 12²⁶, Ac 6² 19²², Ro 15²⁵, Phm 13, He 6¹⁰. 2. *to serve as deacon*: I Ti 3¹⁰, ¹³. 3. C. acc. rei, *to minister, supply, supply by ministration*: I Pe 1¹² 4¹⁰; pass., II Co 3³ 8¹⁹, ²⁰.†
SYN.: λειτουργέω, q.v. (Cremer, 179).

διακονία, -ας, ἡ (< διάκονος), [in LXX for נַעַר, שָׁרַת pi.: Es 6³, ⁵ A; I Mac 11⁵⁸ *;] *the office and work of a διάκονος, service, ministry;* (a) of domestic duties (Field, *Notes*, 63): Lk 10⁴⁰; (b) spec. of religious ministration, and the exercise of ministerial functions in the Church: Ac 1¹⁷, ²⁵ 6¹, ⁴ 11²⁹ 12²⁵ 20²⁴ 21¹⁹, Ro 11¹³ 12⁷ 15³¹, I Co 16¹⁵, II Co 4¹ 6³ 8⁴ 9¹, ¹³, Eph 4¹², Col 4¹⁷, I Ti 1¹², II Ti 4⁵, ¹¹, He 1¹⁴, Re 2¹⁹; δ. τ.

θανάτου, II Co 3⁷ ; τ. πνεύματος, ib. ⁸ ; τ. κατακρίσεως, τ. δικαιοσύνης, ib. ⁹ ; τ. καταλλαγῆς, ib. 5¹⁸ ; τ. λειτουργίας, ib. 9¹² ; c. obj. gen., τὴν ὑμῶν δ., ib. 11⁸ ; pl., I Co 12⁵.†

διάκονος, -ου, ὁ, ἡ (derivation unknown), [in LXX for נַעַר, שָׁרַת pi. : Es 6³,⁵, א B 1¹⁰, 2², Pr 10⁴, 4 Mac 9¹⁷*;] 1. in general, a servant, attendant, minister : Mt 20²⁶ 22¹³ 23¹¹, Mk 9³⁵ 10⁴³, Jo 2⁵,⁹, I Co 3⁵, Ga 2¹⁷, Eph 6²¹, Col 4⁷ ; δ. θεοῦ, Ro 13⁴, II Co 6⁴, I Th 3² ; δ. Χριστοῦ, II Co 11²³, Col 1⁷, I Ti 4⁶ ; cf. ὁ δ. ὁ ἐμός, Jo 12²⁶ ; δ. περιτομῆς, Ro 15⁸ ; δ. καινῆς διαθήκης, II Co 3⁶ ; δ. δικαιοσύνης, II Co 11¹⁵ ; δ. [εὐαγγελίου], Eph 3⁷, Col 1²³ ; δ. [ἐκκλησίας], Col 1²⁵. 2. As technical term for Church officer (so in pre-Christian times, v. M, Th., ι, 3²), a deacon : Phl 1¹, I Ti 3⁸,¹² ; fem. (cf. Eccl. διακονίσσα), Ro 16¹ (cf. I Ti 3¹¹, and CGT, in l., also M, Th., l.c.).†

SYN.: δοῦλος, bondman ; θεράπων, servant acting voluntarily ; ὑπηρέτης, servant, attendant, by etymol. suggesting subordination. All these imply relation to a person, in distinction from which δ. represents rather the servant in relation to his work. Cf. also λειτουργός, a public servant, in which the idea of service to the community is prominent ; οἰκέτης, a house servant.

διακόσιοι, -αι, -α, two hundred : Mk 6³⁷, et al.

δι-ακούω, [in LXX : De 1¹⁶ (שָׁמַע), Jb 9³³ (שִׁית יָד hi.)*;] to hear through, hear fully ; technically, to hear judicially (as De, l.c.; cf. Deiss., BS, 230) : Ac 23³⁵.†

δια-κρίνω, [in LXX for שָׁפַט, דִּין, etc.;] 1. to separate, hence, to distinguish, discriminate, discern : μηδὲν δ., Ac 11¹² ; οὐδὲν δ. μεταξύ, Ac 15⁹ ; σε, I Co 4⁷ ; τὸ σῶμα, I Co 11²⁹. 2. to settle, decide, judge, arbitrate : Mt 16³, I Co 6⁵ 11²⁹ (ICC, in l.), ib. ³¹ 14²⁹. Mid. and pass. ; 1. to get a decision, contend, dispute : seq. πρός, Ac 11² ; c. dat. (but v. ICC, in l.), Ju ⁹ ; absol., Ju ²² (R, mg.). 3. Hellenistic (NT and Eccl., but not LXX), to be divided in one's mind, to hesitate, doubt : Mt 21²¹, Ro 14²³, Ja 1⁶ ; ἐν ἑαυτῷ, Ja 2⁴ ; ἐν τ. καρδίᾳ, Mk 11²³ ; μηδὲν δ., Ac 10²⁰ ; δ. τ. ἀπιστίᾳ, Ro 4²⁰, Ju ²² (R, txt.).†

διά-κρισις, -εως, ἡ (< διακρίνω), [in LXX for מִפְלָשׂ, Jb 37¹⁶*;] the act of judgment, discernment : Ro 14¹, I Co 12¹⁰, He 5¹⁴.†

**δια-κωλύω, [in LXX : Jth 4⁷ 12⁷*;] to hinder, prevent : c. acc., Mt 3¹⁴.†

**δια-λαλέω, -ῶ, [in Sm. : Ps 50 (51)¹⁶, et al.;] 1. to talk with : πρός, Lk 6¹¹. 2. to talk over : pass., Lk 1⁶⁵.†

δια-λέγομαι (mid. of διαλέγω, to pick out, distinguish, as depon.), [in LXX : Ex 6²⁷, Is 63¹ (דָּבַר pi.), Jg 8¹ (רִיב), I Es 8⁴⁶, Es 5², Si 14²⁰, II Mac 11²⁰*;] to converse with, discourse (v. Cl. Rev., i, 45), discuss, argue : Ac 18⁴ 19⁸,⁹ 20⁹ ; c. dat. pers., Ac 17¹⁷ 18¹⁹ 20⁷, He 12⁵ ; seq. πρός, Mk 9³⁴, Ac 17¹⁷ 24¹² ; περί, Ac 24²⁵, Ju ⁹ ; ἀπὸ τ. γραφῶν, Ac 17².†

δια-λείπω, [in LXX for חָדַל (as I Ki 10⁸), etc.;] to intermit, leave off for a time : Lk 7⁴⁵.†

διά-λεκτος, -ου, ἡ (< διαλέγομαι), [in LXX: Da LXX 1⁴ (לָשׁוֹן),
Es 9²⁶ *;] 1. *conversation, discourse, speech* (Plat., Dem., al.). 2. As
in Polyb. and later writers, the *language* or *dialect* of a particular
country or district: Ac 1¹⁹ 2⁶,⁸ 21⁴⁰ 22² 26¹⁴.†

†δια-λιμπάνω, [in LXX: To 10⁷*]; *to intermit, cease:* Ac 8²⁴,
WH, mg.†

δι-αλλάσσω, [in LXX: 1 Ki 29⁴ (רָצָה hithp.), 1 Es 4³¹, al.;] 1. *to
change, exchange.* 2. *to change enmity for friendship, to reconcile:*
pass., c. dat. pers., Mt 5²⁴. "The word denotes mutual concession
after mutual hostility, an idea absent from καταλλ-," q.v. (Lft., *Notes*,
288; cf. Deiss., *LAE*, 178₁₅; Cremer, 91, 632).†

δια-λογίζομαι, depon., [in LXX chiefly for חָשַׁב, freq. in Pss.;]
1. *to balance accounts* (Dem.). 2. *to consider, reason* (Isocr.): Lk 1²⁹
5²¹; ἐν τ. καρδίᾳ, Mk 2⁶,⁸, Lk 5²²; περί, Lk 3¹⁵; ἐν ἑαυτῷ (-οῖς), Mt 16⁷,⁸,
Mk 2⁸, Lk 12¹⁷; πρὸς ἑ., Mk 9³³ 11³¹, Lk 20¹⁴; παρ' ἑ., Mt 21²⁵ (ἐν ἑ.,
T, WH, mg.); πρὸς ἀλλήλους, Mk 8¹⁶; ὅτι, Mk 8¹⁷, Jo 11⁵⁰, Rec. (*DB*, i,
611; Cremer, 400).†

δια-λογισμός, -οῦ, ὁ (< διαλογίζομαι), [in LXX chiefly for
מַחֲשָׁבָה;] a *thought, reasoning, inward questioning:* Mt 15¹⁹, Mk 7²¹,
Lk 2³⁵ 5²² 6⁸ 9⁴⁶,⁴⁷ 24³⁸, Ro 1²¹ 14¹, 1 Co 3²⁰ (LXX), Phl 2¹⁴; κριταὶ δ.
πονηρῶν, gen. of qual. (cf. Pr 12⁵), Ja 2⁴; χωρὶς ὀργῆς καὶ δ. (where
perh. δ., like מְזִמָּה, in Ps 138 (139)²⁰, al., implies evil intention), 1 Ti 2⁸
(v. Hort, in l.; cf. Cremer, 400).†

δια-λύω, [in LXX for אבה, חבל, etc.;] *to part asunder,
dissolve;* of an assembly, pass., *to disperse:* Ac 5³⁶.†

δια-μαρτύρομαι, depon., of Ionic origin, intensive of the simple
μαρτύρομαι, q.v., [in LXX chiefly for עוד hi., usually c. dat. pers., De
4²⁶ 8¹⁹, 1 Ki 8⁹, al.;] *solemnly to protest:* Lk 16²⁸, Ac 2⁴⁰ 8²⁵ 10⁴² 18⁵
20²¹,²³,²⁴ 23¹¹ 28²³, 1 Th 4⁶, He 2⁶; in adjuration, seq. ἐνώπιον τ. θεοῦ,
1 Ti 5²¹, 11 Ti 2¹⁴ 4¹ (Cremer, 415).†

δια-μάχομαι, [in LXX for לחם ni., Da LXX 10²⁰; Si 8¹,³ 38²⁸
51¹⁹ *;] 1. *to struggle against.* 2. In argument, *to contend:* Ac 23⁹.†

δια-μένω, [in LXX for עמד, etc.;] *to remain, continue:* Lk 1²²
22²⁸, Ga 2⁵, He 1¹¹ (LXX), 11 Pe 3⁴.†

δια-μερίζω, [in LXX chiefly for חלק pi.;] 1. *to distribute:* c. dat.
pers., Ac 2⁴⁵; seq. εἰς, Lk 22¹⁷, pass., Ac 2³. Mid. *to distribute
among themselves:* Mt 27³⁵, Mk 15²⁴, Lk 23³⁴; with redundant ἑαυτοῖς,
Jo 19²⁴ (LXX) (v. M, *Pr*., 157). 2. *to divide, separate:* pass., seq. ἐπί,
c. acc., Lk 11¹⁷,¹⁸; ἐπί, c. dat., Lk 12⁵²,⁵³.†

δια-μερισμός, -οῦ, ὁ (< διαμερίζω), [in LXX: Ez 48²⁹ (מַחֲלֹקֶת), Mi
7¹² *;] a *division:* opp. to εἰρήνη, Lk 12⁵¹.†

δια-νέμω, [in LXX for חלק, De 29²⁶ (²⁵) *;] *to distribute, divide:*
pass., *to be spread about*, Ac 4¹⁷.†

†δια-νεύω, [in LXX: Ps 34 (35)¹⁹ (קרץ), Si 27²² *;] *to wink at,
nod to, beckon to:* Lk 1²².†

δια-νόημα, -τος, τό (< διανοέομαι, to think), [in LXX for מַחֲשָׁבָה, etc., Is 55⁹, al., freq. in Si;] a thought : Lk 11¹⁷.†

διάνοια, -ας, ἡ, [in LXX chiefly for לֵב, לֵבָב;] the understanding, mind : Lk 1⁵¹, Eph 4¹⁸, Col 1²¹, I Pe 1¹³, II Pe 3¹, I Jo 5²⁰; pl., Eph 2³; in quotations from LXX, Mt 22³⁷, Mk 12³⁰, Lk 10²⁷, He 8¹⁰ 10¹⁶ (Cremer, 79, 438).†

δι-αν-οίγω, [in LXX for פטר (Ex, Nu), פקח, פתח, etc.;] to open up completely, to open : Lk 2²³ (LXX); pass., Mk 7³⁴, Ac 7⁵⁶. Metaph., δ. τ. νοῦν, Lk 24⁴⁵, τ. καρδίαν, Ac 16¹⁴, pass., οἱ ὀφθαλμοί, Lk 24³¹; of explaining, τ. γραφάς, Lk 24³², Ac 17³.†

δια-νυκτερεύω (cf. διημερεύω, to pass the day), [in LXX: Jb 2⁹*;] to pass the night : seq. ἐν τ. προσευχῇ, Lk 6¹².†

**δι-ανύω, [in LXX: II Mac 12¹⁷*;] 1. to accomplish fully, finish, complete : Ac 21⁷ (EV). 2. In late writers (Xen., al., Clem., I ad Cor., xxv, 3), to continue : Ac, l.c. (Field, Notes, 134 f.).†

δια-παντός, v. διά, c. gen.

*†δια-παρα-τριβή, -ῆς, ἡ (< παρατριβή, friction, irritation), mutual irritation (Field, Notes, 211), wrangling : I Ti 6⁵ (Rec. παραδιατριβή).†

δια-περάω, -ῶ, [in LXX : De 30¹³, Is 23² (עבר), I Mac 6*;] to pass over, cross over : Mt 9¹; seq. ἐπὶ τ. γῆν, Mt 14³⁴, Mk 6⁵³; εἰς, Mk 5²¹, Ac 21²; πρὸς ἡμᾶς, Lk 16²⁶.†

*δια-πλέω, -ῶ, to sail across : Ac 27⁵.†

δια-πονέω, -ῶ, [in LXX : Ec 10⁹ (עצב ni.), II Mac 2²⁸; in Aq.: Ge 6⁶, I Ki 20³*;] to work out with labour. Pass., to be worn out, sore troubled : Mk 14⁴ (WH, mg.), Ac 4² 16¹⁸.†

δια-πορεύω, [in LXX for עבר, הלך, etc.;] to carry over. Pass., to pass across, journey through : absol., Lk 18³⁶, Ro 15²⁴; seq. κατὰ πόλεις κ. κώμας, Lk 13²²; διά, c. gen., Mk 2²³, Lk 6¹ (cf. Pr 9¹²ᶜ, Wi 3¹); c. acc., Ac 16⁴.†

**δι-απορέω, -ῶ, [in Sm.: Ps 76 (77)⁵, Da 2¹*;] to be quite at a loss, be in great perplexity : absol., Ac 2¹²; seq. διὰ τό, c. inf., Lk 9⁷; περί, Ac 5²⁴; ἐν ἑαυτῷ, Ac 10¹⁷.†

*δια-πραγματεύομαι, "perfective compound" (v. M, Pr., 118); 1. to examine thoroughly (Plat.). 2. In late writers (Dion. Hal.), to gain by trading : Lk 19¹⁵.†

δια-πρίω, [in LXX: I Ch 20³ (שׂור)*;] to saw asunder. Pass., metaph. (vernacular ?), EV, cut to the heart : Ac 5³³; seq. τ. καρδίαις αὐτῶν, Ac 7⁵⁴.†

δι-αρπάζω, [in LXX for בזז, גזל, שׁסם, etc.;] to plunder : Mt 12²⁹, Mk 3²⁷.†

δια-ρήσσω (so WH, exc. Ac, l.c.), δια-ρρήσσω (poetic and late form of διαρρήγνυμι), [in LXX chiefly for קרע;] to break asunder, burst, rend : δεσμά, Lk 8²⁹; pass., δίκτυα, Lk 5⁶; ἱμάτια, χιτῶνας, in grief or anger (as Ge 37²⁹, al.), Mt 26⁶⁵, Ac 14¹⁴, Mk 14⁶³.†

δια-σαφέω, -ῶ (< σαφής, clear), [in LXX : De 1⁵ (באר pi.), Da LXX, 2⁶ (חוה aph.), I-III Mac 9*;] to make clear, explain fully : c. acc. rei, dat. pers., Mt 13³⁶ 18³¹.†

δια-σείω, [in LXX: Jb 4¹⁴ (פחד hi.), III Mac 7²¹*;] *to shake violently;* metaph., *to intimidate:* Lk 3¹⁴.†

†|δια-σκορπίζω, [in LXX for פוץ, זרה, etc.;] *to scatter abroad, disperse:* of sheep, Mt 26³¹ = Mk 14²⁷ (LXX); of persons, Lk 1⁵¹, Ac 5³⁷, opp. to συνάγω, Jo 11⁵²; of winnowing grain, Mt 25²⁴, ²⁶; metaph., of property, *to squander, waste:* Lk 15¹³ 16¹.†

δια-σπάω, -ῶ, [in LXX chiefly for נתק, as Jg 16⁹;] *to break or tear asunder:* pass., ἀλύσεις, Mk 5⁴; Παῦλος, Ac 23¹⁰.†

δια-σπείρω, [freq. in LXX for פוץ, etc.;] *to scatter abroad, disperse:* Ac 8¹, ⁴ 11¹⁹.†

δια-σπορά, -ᾶς, ἡ (< διασπείρω), [in LXX of Israelites dispersed and exiled in foreign lands, as De 28²⁵ (זעוה) 30⁴ (נדח ni.), Is 49⁶ (נער); by meton., of the exiles themselves (as Ps 146 (147)², II Mac 1²⁷);] *a dispersion:* δ. τῶν Ἑλλήνων, Jo 7³⁵; metaph., of Christians (*DB*, iii, 782 f.), Ja 1¹, I Pe 1¹ (v. Hort, in ll.).†

δια-στέλλω, [in LXX for בדל hi. (De 10⁸, al.), זהר hi. (Ez 3¹⁸, ¹⁹, al.), and 19 other words]; 1. *to divide, distinguish, define.* 2. *to command, charge expressly:* pass., τὸ διαστελλόμενον, He 12²⁰. Mid. in late Gk. with same sense (so Ez, l.c.; et al. in LXX; MM, s.v.); c. dat. pers., Mk 8¹⁵, Ac 15²⁴; seq. ἵνα, Mt 16²⁰, Mk 5⁴³ 7³⁶ 9⁹.†

διάστημα, -τος, τό (< διίστημι), [in LXX for רוח, etc.;] *an interval, space:* of time (Si, *prol.* ²⁴), Ac 5⁷.†

δια-στολή, -ῆς, ἡ (< διαστέλλω), [in LXX for פדות: Ex 8²³ ⁽¹⁹⁾, etc.;] 1. *a separation.* 2. *a distinction, difference:* Ro 3²² 10¹², I Co 14⁷.†

δια-στρέφω, [in LXX for הפך, עקש, etc.;] *to distort, twist;* metaph., *to distort, pervert:* Lk 23², Ac 13⁸, ¹⁰; διεστραμμένος, *perverse:* Mt 17¹⁷, Lk 9⁴¹, Ac 20³⁰, Phl 2¹⁵.†

δια-σώζω, [in LXX for מלט, ישע, etc.;] *to bring safely through* a danger: Lk 7³, Ac 27⁴³; seq. πρός, Ac 23²⁴. Pass., *to come safe through:* Ac 28¹; ἐπὶ τ. γῆν, Ac 27⁴⁴; ἐκ τ. θαλάσσης, Ac 28⁴; δι᾽ ὕδατος, I Pe 3²⁰; of sickness, *to recover:* Mt 14³⁶.†

† δια-ταγή, -ῆς, ἡ (< διατάσσω), [in LXX: II Es 4¹¹ (פרשגן)*;] in late writers (Deiss., *LAE*, 86 ff.) for cl. διάταξις (wh., however, is found in LXX, Ps 118 (119)⁹¹, al.); (*a*) *disposition* (cf. διάταξις for צבא; Sm., IV Ki 23⁴, Je 8² 19¹³); εἰς διαταγὰς ἀγγέλων, AV, *by the disposition of angels* (Alf., in l., Field, *Notes*, 116; but v. infr.): Ac 7⁵³; (*b*) *ordinance* (C. I. 3465): Ro 13², Ac 7⁵³, R, txt. (and v. mg.; Page and *EGT*, in l.; but also v. supr.).†

† διά-ταγμα, -τος, τό (< διατάσσω), [in LXX: II Es 7¹¹ (נשתון), Es 3¹³, Wi 11⁷*;] *an edict, mandate:* He 11²³.†

** δια-ταράσσω, [in Sm.: III Ki 20 (21)⁴³*;] *to agitate greatly* (Lat. *perturbare*): Lk 1²⁹.†

δια-τάσσω, [in LXX for שׂים שׂוּם, שׂמר, etc.;] *to charge, give orders to, appoint, arrange, ordain*: c. dat., Mt 11¹, I Co 9¹⁴ 16¹; seq. inf., Lk 8⁵⁵, Ac 18². Mid., I Co 7¹⁷, Ac 20¹³; c. acc., I Co 11³⁴; c. dat., Tit 1⁵; seq. inf., Ac 7⁴⁴ 24²³. Pass., τὸ διατεταγμένον, Lk 3¹³, Ac 23³¹; τὰ διαταχθέντα, Lk 17⁹, ¹⁰; διαταγείς, Ga 3¹⁹.†

δια-τελέω, -ῶ, [in LXX: De 9⁷ (היה), Je 20⁷, ¹⁸ (כלה), Es 8¹³, II Mac 5²⁷*;] prop. trans., *to accomplish;* used with ellipse of obj. as intrans. (Bl., § 81, 1), and joined to participles (in Ac, l.c., to adj.; v. Bl., § 73, 4) with adverbial sense (= *continuously*), *to continue*: Ac 27³³.†

δια-τηρέω, -ῶ, [in LXX for שׁמר, נצר, etc.; seq. ἀπό (for מן), as in Ps 11 (12)⁸;] *to keep carefully*: Lk 2⁵¹; seq. ἐκ, Ac 15²⁹.†

δια-τί, Τ, Rec. for διὰ τί, v.s. διά.

δια-τίθημι, [in LXX chiefly for כרת, freq. δ. διαθήκην (כָּרַת בְּרִית);] *to place separately, arrange, dispose*. Mid. only in NT; 1. (*a*) in general, *to dispose of;* c. dat. pers., *to assign to* one, Lk 22²⁹; (*b*) *to dispose of by a will, make a testament* (in cl., δ. διαθήκην also in this sense): He 9¹⁶, ¹⁷ (but cf. R, mg., and v.s. διαθήκη). 2. δ. διαθήκην, *to make a covenant* (Aristoph.): c. dat. pers., He 8¹⁰ (LXX); seq. πρός, c. acc. pers., Ac 3²⁵, He 10¹⁶ (LXX) (cf. ἀντι-διατίθημι).†

δια-τρίβω, [in LXX Le 14⁸ (ישׁב), Je 42 (35)⁷ (גּוּר), To 11⁸, ¹², Jth 10², II Mac 14²³*;] *to rub hard, rub away, consume;* δ. χρόνον, ἡμέρας, *to spend* time: Ac 14³, ²⁸ 16¹², 20⁶ 25⁶, ¹⁴. Intransitively with ellipse of object (Bl., § 81, 1), *to spend time, stay*: Jo 3²² 11⁵⁴ 15³⁵, Ac 12¹⁹.†

** δια-τροφή, ῆς, ἡ (< διατρέφω, *to support, sustain*), [in LXX: I Mac 6⁴⁹*;] *food, nourishment*: I Ti 6⁸.†

**† δι-αυγάζω, [in Aq.: Jb 25⁵*;] *to shine through, to dawn*: II Pe 1¹⁹ (cf. ἕως οὗ διαπνεύσῃ ἡ ἡμέρα, Ca 2¹⁷).†

** διαυγής, -ές (< αὐγή), [in Aq.: Pr 16²*;] *transparent*: Re 21²¹.†

διαφανής, -ές (< διαφαίνω *to show through, shine through*), [in LXX: Ex 30³⁴ (זָךְ), Is 3²¹ (²³) (גִּלָּיוֹן), Es 1⁶*;] *transparent*: Re 21²¹ (Rec.; v. διαυγής).†

δια-φέρω, [in LXX for שָׂנֵא (Da 7 only); I Ki 17³⁹, Es 3¹³, al.;] 1. trans., (*a*) *to carry through*: seq. διά, Mk 11¹⁶; (*b*) *to carry about, spread abroad*: pass., Ac 13⁴⁹ 27²⁷. 2. Intrans., (*a*) *to differ*: τὰ διαφέροντα, Ro 2¹⁸, Phl 1¹⁰ (R, mg., but v. infr.); impers., διαφέρει, *it makes a difference, it matters*: Ga 2⁶; (*b*) *to excel*: c. gen. Mt 6²⁶ 10³¹ 12¹², Lk 12⁷, ²⁴, I Co 15⁴¹, Ga 4¹; τὰ διαφέροντα, Ro 2¹⁸, Phl 1¹⁰ (R, txt.; for discussion and reff. v. *ICC* on Ro, Phl, ll. c.).†

δια-φεύγω, [in LXX: Jos 8²² (פָּלִיט), ib. 10²⁸ (שָׂרִיד), etc.;] *to flee through, escape*: Ac 27⁴².†

*† δια-φημίζω, in late writers only, *to spread abroad*: τ. λόγν (= הַדָּבָר, *the matter*), Mk 1⁴⁵, Mt 28¹⁵; c. acc. pers., *to spread abroad one's fame*: Mt 9³¹.†

δια-φθείρω, [in LXX chiefly for שׁחת hi. ;] 1. *to destroy utterly:* Lk 12³³, Re 11¹⁸; pass., *to be destroyed, disabled:* Re 8⁹, II Co 4¹⁶. 2. In moral sense, *to corrupt, deprave:* τ. γῆν, Re 11¹⁸; pass., διεφθαρμένοι τ. νοῦν, I Ti 6⁵.†

δια-φθορά, -ᾶς, ἡ (< διαφθείρω), [in LXX chiefly for שׁחת, and cogn. forms;] 1. *destruction.* 2. *corruption* (physical or moral): of the grave, Ac 2²⁷ (LXX), 31 13³⁴⁻³⁷.†

διά-φορος, -ον (< διαφέρω), [in LXX for שׁנא (Da 7⁷, ¹⁹); also as in Polyb., IV, 18⁸, al., τὸ δ., τὰ δ., *money:* Si 27¹ 42⁵, II Mac 3⁶;] 1. *different:* Ro 12⁶, He 9¹⁰. 2. *excellent:* compar., -ώτερος, He 1⁴ 8⁶.†

δια-φυλάσσω, [in LXX chiefly for שׁמר (as Ps 90 (91)¹¹);] *to guard carefully* (M, Pr., 116), *defend:* c. acc., Lk 4¹⁰ (LXX).†

*δια-χειρίζω (< χείρ), *to have in hand, conduct, manage.* Mid. (a) = act.; (b) in late writers (Polyb., FlJ, al.), *to lay hands on, kill:* c. acc., Ac 5³⁰ 26²¹.†

*δια-χλευάζω, intensive of χλευάζω, *to scoff, mock:* (a) c. acc.; (b) absol., Ac 2¹³.†

δια-χωρίζω, [in LXX: Ge 1⁴ᵃˡ. בדל hi.), 13⁹ᵃˡ. (פרד ni.), etc.;] *to separate entirely.* Mid., *to separate oneself, depart:* seq. ἀπό, Lk 9³³.†

*†διδακτικός, -ή, -όν (= cl. διδασκαλικός), *apt at teaching:* I Ti 3², II Ti 2²⁴.†

διδακτός, -ή, -όν (< διδάσκω), [in LXX: Is 54¹³ (למּד), I Mac 4⁷ *;] 1. *that can be taught.* 2. *taught;* c. gen., of source of teaching (in cl., poët. only); (a) of persons: δ. θεοῦ, Jo 6⁴⁵ (LXX); (b) of things, λόγοις δ. πνεύματος, I Co 2¹³.†

διδασκαλία, -ας, ἡ (< διδάσκω), [in LXX: Pr 2¹⁷ (אלּוּף), Is 29¹³ (למּד pu.), Si 24³³ 39⁸ *;] *teaching, instruction,* in both active and objective senses, most freq. the latter: Ro 12⁷ 15⁴, Eph 4¹⁴, I Ti 4⁶, ¹³, ¹⁶ 5¹⁷ 6¹, ³, II Ti 3¹⁰, ¹⁶, Tit 2⁷, ¹⁰; ὑγιαινοῦσα δ., I Ti 1¹⁰, II Ti 4³, Tit 1⁹ 2¹; pl., δ. τ. ἀνθρώπων, Col 2²²; δ. δαιμονίων, I Ti 4¹; δ. διδάσκειν, Mt 15⁹, Mk 7⁷ (LXX) (Cremer, 182).†

SYN.: διδαχή.

**διδάσκαλος, -ου, ὁ (< διδάσκω), [in LXX: Es 6¹, II Mac 1¹⁰ *;] given as rendering of Heb. רבּי, רבּון (NT, Ῥαββεί, Ῥαββουνεί, q.v.); *a teacher:* Jo 1³⁹ 20¹⁶; of Jewish teachers, Lk 2⁴⁶, Jo 3¹⁰, cf. Ro 2²⁰, ²¹; of John Baptist, Lk 3¹²; of Jesus, Jo 3², ¹⁰ 8[⁴] 11²⁸ 13¹³, ¹⁴, and often in *Syn.,* most freq. in voc., as title of address, as Mt 8¹⁹, Mk 4³⁸; of Jesus by himself, Mt 23⁸; of an apostle, I Ti 2⁷, II Ti 1¹¹; of Christians, I Co 12²⁸, ²⁹, Eph 4¹¹, Ac 13¹, Ja 3¹; of false teachers, II Ti 4³ (Cremer, 181; *DB,* i, 609, iii, 294, iv, 691).

SYN.: παιδευτής, q.v.

διδάσκω, [in LXX chiefly for למד pi., also for ידע hi., ירה hi., etc.;] *to teach* (i.e. *instruct*) a person, *teach* a thing; 1. trans.: c. acc.

S

pers., Mt 5², Mk 1²², al.; seq. ὅτι, Mk 8³¹; περί, ι Jo 2²⁷; c. inf., Lk
11¹; c. acc. rei, Mk 6³⁰ 12¹⁴; c. cogn. acc., Mt 15⁹ ⁽ᴸˣˣ⁾; c. dupl. acc.,
Mk 4², Jo 14²⁶; pass., Ga 1¹², ιι Th 2¹⁵; c. dat. pers. (like Heb., cf.
Jb 21²², but prob. a vernac. usage, v. Swete, in l.), Re 2¹⁴. 2. Absol.,
to teach, give instruction : Mt 4²³, Mk 1²¹, and often in Gosp., Ro 12⁷,
ι Co 4¹⁷, ι Ti 2¹², al.
    SYN.: παιδεύω (cf. Westc., *Heb.,* 402; Cremer, 180).
    διδαχή, -ῆς, ἡ (< διδάσκω), [in LXX: Ps 59 (60) *tit.* (למד pi.); Sm.:
De 33⁸ *;] 1. objectively, *teaching, doctrine,* that which is taught: Mk
1²⁷, Jo 7¹⁶, Ac 17¹⁹, Ro 6⁷ 16¹⁷, ιι Jo 2²⁴; c. gen. poss., Mt 7²⁸
16¹² 22³³, Mk 1²² 11¹⁸, Lk 4³², Jo 18¹⁹, Ac 5²⁸, Re 2¹⁴, ¹⁵; ἡ δ., of
Christ, Jo 7¹⁷, Ac 13¹², ιι Jo⁹; cf. τὴν δ., Tit 1⁹; c. gen. obj., βαπτισμῶν δ., He 6²; pl., He 13⁹. 2. Actively, *teaching :* Ac 2⁴², ιι Ti 4²;
ἐν τ. δ., *in the course of his teaching :* Mk 4² 12³⁸; λαλεῖν ἐν δ., ι Co 14⁶;
ἔχειν δ., ib. ²⁶ (*DCG,* i, 485; Cremer, 181).†
    SYN.: διδασκαλία.
    †δίδραχμος, -ον (< δίς, δραχμή), *worth two drachmae ;* τὸ δ. (sc.
νόμισμα, *coin*), [in LXX chiefly for שֶׁקֶל (Ge 23¹⁵, al.), also for בֶּקַע:
Ge 20¹⁶, De 22²⁹ ;] a *double drachma,* nearly equal to the Jewish *half-
shekel,* the amount of the Temple tax: Mt 17²⁴ (*DB,* iii, 428).†.
    Δίδυμος, -ου, ὁ (prop. name from δίδυμος, -η, -ον, *double,* sc. παῖς,
twin), *Didymus,* surname of the apostle Thomas: Jo 11¹⁶ 20²⁴ 21².†
    δίδωμι, [in LXX chiefly for נתן (53 words in all);] *to give*—in
various senses, acc. to context—*bestow, grant, supply, deliver, commit,
yield :* absol., Ac 20³⁵; c. acc. rei et dat. pers., Mt 4⁹ 5³¹, Jo 1¹², al.
mult.; c. dat. pers., seq. ἐκ, Mt 25⁸; id. c. gen. part., Re 2¹⁷; c. acc.
pers., Jo 3¹⁶, Re 20¹³, al.; δεξιάς, Ga 2⁹; φίλημα, Lk 7⁴⁵; γνῶσιν,
Lk 1⁷⁷; κρίσιν, Jo 5²²; of seed yielding fruit, Mk 4⁷, ⁸; ἐργασίαν (Deiss.,
LAE, 117 f.), Lk 12⁵⁸; c. inf. fin., Mt 27³⁴, Mk 5⁴³, Lk 8⁵⁵, Jo 6⁵², al.;
c. dat. pers. et inf., Lk 1⁷⁴, al.; c. acc. et inf., Ac 2²⁷; c. dupl. acc., Mt
20²⁸, Mk 10⁴⁵, Eph. 1²² 4¹¹, ιι Th 3⁹, ι Ti 2⁶, al.; ἑαυτὸν δ. εἰς (Polyb.,
al.), Ac 19³¹; c. dat. pers., seq. κατά (MM, *Exp.,* xi), Re 2²³ ⁽ᴸˣˣ⁾; δ. ἵνα,
Re 3⁹; δίδωκα ἐνώπιόν σου θύραν ἀνεῳγμένην, Re 3⁸; on possible Hebraisms
and Latinisms, v. MM, *VGT,* s.v., *ICC* on Re 3⁸ (on the Hebraisms in these
passages, v. *ICC* on Re in ll. and ib., p. cxlviii; on vernac. and late usage,
v. MM, *VGT,* s.v.; on tense forms v. M, *Gr.,* ιι, pp. 75, 83, 210 f., 218, 233.
    SYN.: δωρέομαι.
    **δι-εγείρω, [in LXX: Jth 1⁴, Es 1¹, ιι Mac 7²¹ 15¹⁰, ιιι Mac 5¹⁵ *;]
to arouse completely, arouse as from rest or sleep: Lk 8²⁴; pass.,
Mk 4³⁹, Lk 8²⁴; of the sea, Jo 6¹⁸. Metaph., of the mind: ἐν ὑπομ-
νήσει, ιι Pe 1¹³ 3¹.†
    *†δι-ενθυμέομαι, -οῦμαι, depon., *to consider, reflect :* seq. περί, Ac
10¹⁹.†
    δι-έξ-οδος, -ον, ἡ, [in LXX chiefly for תּוֹצָאוֹת, as Nu 34⁴ ᶠᶠ, and
freq. in Jos ;] in π. of the *conclusion* of a trial (MM, *Exp.,* xi); *a way
out through, an outlet ;* pl., δ. τῶν ὁδῶν, RV, *the partings of the high-
ways :* Mt 22⁹.†
    *†δι-ερμηνευτής, -οῦ, ὁ (< διερμηνεύω), *an interpreter :* ι Co 14²⁸.†

*† δι-ερμηνεία, ας, ἡ, *interpretation :* 1 Co 12¹⁰, L, txt. (not elsewhere).†

**† δι-ερμηνεύω, [in LXX: II Mac 1³⁶ *;] intensive of ἑρμηνεύω, *to interpret ;* (*a*) *to explain, expound :* c. acc., Lk 24²⁷; absol., 1 Co 12³⁰ 14⁵,¹³,²⁷; (*b*) *to translate :* Ac 9³⁶.†

δι-έρχομαι, [in LXX for אבר, הלך, בוא, etc.;] 1. *to go through, pass through ;* (*a*) of things : Mt 19²⁴, Mk 10²⁵, Lk 2³⁵, al.; (*b*) of persons : Lk 19⁴; c. acc. loc., Lk 19¹, He 4¹⁴, Ac 12¹⁰; seq. διά, c. gen. loc., Mt 12⁴³, 1 Co 10¹; seq. εἰς, Mk 4³⁵; ἕως, Lk 2¹⁵. 2. *to go about :* Lk 9⁶, Ac 20²⁵; of a report, *to spread, go abroad* (Thuc.), Lk 5¹⁵.

* δι-ερωτάω, -ῶ, *to find by inquiry :* c. acc., Ac 10¹⁷.†

** διετής, -ές (< δίς, ἔτος), [in LXX: II Mac 10³ *;] 1. *lasting two years.* 2. *two years old :* ἀπὸ δ. (sc. παιδός, or neuter; cf. 1 Ch 27²³, ἀπὸ εἰκοσαετοῦς), Mt 2¹⁶.†

† διετία, -ας, ἡ (< διετής), [in LXX (*Grœc. Ven.*) : Ge 41¹ 45⁵ *;] *the space of two years :* Ac 24²⁷ 28³⁰.†

δι-ηγέομαι, -οῦμαι, [in LXX chiefly for ספר pi.;] *to set out in detail, recount, describe :* absol., He 11³²; c. acc. rei, Ac 8³³; c. dat. pers., seq. πῶς, Mk 5¹⁶, Ac 9²⁷ 12¹⁷; ἃ εἶδον, Mk 9⁹; ὅσα ἐποίησε, -αν, Lk 8³⁹ 9¹⁰.†

δι-ήγησις, -εως, ἡ (< διηγέομαι), [in LXX : Jg 7¹⁵ (מְסָפֵר), Hb 2⁶ (חִידָה), freq. in Si (6³⁵, al.), II Mac 2³² 6¹⁷;] *a narrative :* Lk 1¹ (cf. Milligan, *NTD*, 130).†

** δι-ηνεκής, -ές (< διήνεγκα, aor. of διαφέρω), [in Sm. : Ps 47 (48)¹⁵ 88 (89)³⁰;] *unbroken, continuous :* adverbially, εἰς τὸ δ., *continually* (EV), *perpetually, forever* (Westc., Rendall, on He 10¹), (for exx., v. Deiss., *BS*, 251), He 7³ 10¹,¹²,¹⁴.†

*† δι-θάλασσος, -ον (δίς, θάλασσα); 1. *divided into two seas* (as the Euxine, Strab., ii, 5²²). 2. *dividing the sea :* τόπον δ., *a tongue of land, or reef, running out into the sea :* Ac 27⁴¹.†

δι-ικνέομαι (Rec. διϊκ-), -οῦμαι, [in LXX for ברח hi., Ex 26²⁸ *;] *to go through, penetrate :* He 4¹².†

δι-ίστημι (Rec. διϊσ-), [in LXX: Ez 5¹ חלק pi.), Pr 17⁹ פרד hi.), etc.;] *to set apart, separate ;* of time (or space), *to make an interval, intervene :* διαστάσης ὥρας μιᾶς, Lk 22⁵⁹; βραχὺ διαστήσαντες, Ac 27²⁸. In pass., mid. and 2 aor., pf. and plpf. act., *to part, withdraw :* Lk 24⁵¹.†

* δι-ισχυρίζομαι (T, Rec. διϊσ-), depon.; 1. *to lean upon.* 2. *to affirm confidently :* c. ptcp., Lk 22⁵⁹; c. acc. et inf. (Bl., § 70, 3), Ac 12¹⁵.†

δικάζω, *to judge :* Lk 6³⁷ (Tr., mg.; v.s. καταδ-; Cremer, 199).†

*† δικαιοκρισία, -ας, ἡ, *righteous judgment :* Ro 2⁵ (cf. τ. δικαίας κρίσεως, II Th 1⁵; τὴν δ. κ., Jo 7²⁴. For use in π., v. Deiss., *LAE*, 89 f.).†

δίκαιος, -α, -ον (< δίκη), [in LXX chiefly for צַדִּיק (for rendering of צַדִּיק in sense of *correct*, v. Deiss., *BS*, 115 f.); sometimes for נָקִי, as Pr 1¹¹, al.;] in early Gk. writers, (*a*) of persons, observant of δίκη, custom, rule, right, *righteous* in performing duties to gods and men; (b) of things, *righteous*, in accordance with right.   In NT : 1. *righteous*, chiefly in the broad sense, as above, of the person or thing corresponding to the Divine standard of right; (a) of persons : of God, Ro 3²⁶, 1 Jo 2²⁹ 3⁷; of Christ, Ac 3¹⁴ 7⁵² 22¹⁴, 1 Pe 3¹⁸, 1 Jo 2¹; of men, Mt 1¹⁹ (Abbott, *Essays*, 75 f.) 10⁴¹ 13¹⁷, ⁴³, ⁴⁹, Lk 1⁶, ¹⁷, Ro 5⁷, 1 Ti 1⁹, Ja 5⁶, 1 Pe 3¹², 1 Jo 3⁷, Re 22¹¹, al.; δ. καὶ εὐλαβής, Lk 2²⁵; ἅγιος, Mk 6²⁰; ἀγαθός, Lk 23⁵⁰; φοβούμενος τ. θεόν, Ac 10²²; opp. to ἁμαρτωλοὶ καὶ ἀσεβεῖς, 1 Pe 4¹⁸; ἄδικοι, Mt 5⁴⁵, Ac 24¹⁵; δ. ἐκ πίστεως, Ro 1¹⁷, Ga 3¹¹, He 10³⁸ (LXX); δ. παρὰ τ. θεῷ, Ro 2¹³; (b) of things : ἔργα δ., opp. to πονηρά, 1 Jo 3¹²; ἐντολή, Ro 7¹²; metaph., αἷμα, Mt 23³⁵; τὸ δ., Lk 12⁵⁷; δ. ἐστιν, Ac 4¹⁹, Eph 6¹, Phl 1⁷; ὅ, Mt 20⁴; ὅσα, Phl 4⁸.   2. In narrower sense; (a) of persons, as in later cl. writers, *just*, rendering to each his due : Tit 1⁸, 1 Jo 1⁹; δ. κριτής, II Ti 4⁸; (b) of things : τὸ δ., Col 4¹; δ., sc. ἐστιν, II Th 1⁶; κρίσις δ., Jo 5³⁰; ὁδοί, Re 15³.

SYN. : ἀγαθός (q.v.), καλός, χρηστός (Cremer, 183, 690).

δίκαιος, -οσύνη, -όω, v. ICC on Ga, pp. 460 ff.

δικαιοσύνη, -ης, ἡ (< δίκαιος), [in LXX chiefly for צֶדֶק, and cognates, Ge 15⁶, al., rarely for חֶסֶד, Ge 19¹⁹;] the character of ὁ δίκαιος (q.v.); 1. in broad sense, *righteousness*, conformity to the Divine will in purpose, thought and action : Mt 5⁶, Jo 16⁸, Ac 13¹⁰, Ro 4³; λόγος δικαιοσύνης, *teaching of r*., He 5¹³; βασιλεὺς δ. (cf. FlJ, BJ, vi, 10, β. δίκαιος), He 7²; ὅπλα δ., Ro 6¹³; ὁδὸς δ., Mt 21³²; θώραξ τῆς δ., Eph 6¹⁴; διάκονοι δ., II Co 11¹⁵; ὁσιότης καὶ δ., Lk 1⁷⁵, cf. Eph 4²⁴; ἀγαθωσύνη καὶ δ., Eph 5⁹; δ. κ. εἰρήνη κ. χαρά, Ro 14¹⁷; δ. κ. ἁγιασμός, 1 Co 1³⁰; opp. to ἁμαρτία, Ro 8¹⁰; ἀνομία, II Co 6¹⁴; ἀδικία, Ro 3⁵; ποιεῖν τὴν δ., 1 Jo 2²⁹ 3⁷; id. as an inclusive term for the active duties of the religious life (*ICC*, in l.; Abbott, *Essays*, 73 ff), Mt 6¹; ἐργάζεσθαι δ., Ac 10³⁵; διώκειν δ., 1 Ti 6¹¹; πληροῦν πᾶσαν δ., Mt 3¹⁵; ζῆν τῇ δ., 1 Pe 2²⁴; δ. θεοῦ, a righteousness divine in its character and origin, Mt 6³³, Ja 1²⁰, Ro (where it also includes the idea of God's personal r.; v. ICC, on 1¹⁷) 1¹⁷ 3⁵, ²¹⁻²⁶ 10³, II Co 5²¹, Phl 3⁹; ἡ δ. τ. πίστεως, Ro 4¹¹; ἡ ἐκ π. δ., Ro 9³⁰; ἡ κατὰ π. δ., He 11⁷; opp. to this is ἡ ἐκ νόμου δ., Ro 10⁵; ἡ δ. ἐν ν., Phl 3⁶; ἡ ἰδία δ., Ro 10³, cf. Phl 3⁹. 2. In narrower sense (cf. δίκαιος), *justice* : Ac 17³¹, II Pe 1¹, Re 19¹¹ (*DCG*, ii, 529 ff.; Cremer, 190, 690).

δικαιόω, -ῶ (< δίκαιος), [in LXX chiefly for צָדֵק pi., hi., (1) as Ez 16⁵¹, Je 3¹¹ (cf. NT usage); (2) as De 25¹, Ex 23⁷, Is 50⁸;] 1. in cl., (a) c. acc. rei, *to deem right;* (b) c. acc. pers., *to do one justice;* pass., δικαιοῦσθαι, *to be treated rightly*, opp. to ἀδικεῖσθαι. 2. In NT, as in LXX, and as usual with verbs in -όω from adjectives of moral meaning; (1) *to show to be righteous* : Mt 11¹⁹, Lk 7³⁵, Ro 3⁴ (LXX), 1 Ti 3¹⁶; (2) *to declare, pronounce righteous* : Lk 7²⁹ 10²⁹ 16¹⁵ 18¹⁴, Ro 2¹³ 3²⁴, ²⁶, ²⁸ 4⁵ 8³⁰, ³³, Tit 3⁷; seq. ἀπό, Mt 11¹⁹, Lk 7³⁵, Ac 13³⁹, Ro 6⁷; ἐκ πίστεως, Ro 3³⁰ 5¹, Ga 2¹⁶ 3⁸, ²⁴; ἐξ ἔργων, Ro 3²⁰ (LXX) 4², Ga 2¹⁶, Ja 2²¹, ²⁴, ²⁵; ἐκ τ. λόγων, Mt 12³⁷; διὰ τ. πίστεως, Ro 3³⁰; c. dat., Ro 3²⁴, ²⁸ Tit 3⁷; seq. ἐν, Ac 13³⁹, Ro 3⁴ 5⁹, 1 Co 4⁴ 6¹¹, Ga 2¹⁷ 3¹¹ 5⁴, 1 Ti 3¹⁶ (v. Cremer, 193, 693; *DB*, ii, 826 ff.).†

δικαίωμα, -τος, τό (< δικαιόω), [in LXX most freq. for חֹק, in Ez, chiefly for מִשְׁפָּט, in Pss, τὰ δ., freq. for פִּקֻּדִים;] a concrete expression of righteousness, the expression and result of the act of δικαίωσις, "a declaration that a thing is δίκαιον, or that a person is δίκαιος," hence, (a) an ordinance: δ. τ. θεοῦ, Ro 1³²; τ. κυρίου, Lk 1⁶; τ. νόμου, Ro 2²⁶ 8⁴; λατρείας, He 9¹; σαρκός, He 9¹⁰; (b) a sentence: of acquittal, Ro 5¹⁶ (also 5¹⁸; ICC, in l.), or of condemnation; (c) a righteous act: Ro 5¹⁸ (RV), Re 15⁴ 19⁸ (on the usage of π., v. MM, Exp., iii, xi).†

δικαίως, adv. (< δίκαιος, q.v.), [in. LXX for צֶדֶק, etc.;] 1. righteously: 1 Co 15³⁴, 1 Th 2¹⁰, Tit 2¹². 2. justly: Lk 23⁴¹, 1 Pe 2²³.†

δικαίωσις, -εως, ἡ (< δικαιόω), [in LXX for מִשְׁפָּט, Le 24²² *;] the act of pronouncing righteous, justification, acquittal: Ro 4²⁵ 5¹⁸ (Cremer, 199).†

δικαστής, -οῦ, ὁ (< δικάζω), [in LXX for שֹׁפֵט;] a judge: Ac 7²⁷, ³⁵ (LXX).†

SYN.: κριτής, wh. "gives prominence to the mental process" (Thayer). δ. is the forensic term. In Attic law, the δικασταί were jurors, with a κριτής as presiding officer (LS, s.v.; Enc. Brit.¹¹, xii, 504 f.).

δίκη, -ης, ἡ, [in LXX for נקם, ריב, etc.;] 1. custom. 2. right. 3. a judicial hearing; hence its result, the execution of a sentence, punishment: δ. τίνειν, II Th 1⁹; δ. ὑπέχειν, Ju⁷. 4. Personified (cf. Lat. Justitia), justice, vengeance: Ac 28⁴.†

δίκτυον, -ου, τό, [in LXX chiefly for רֶשֶׁת, שְׂבָכָה;] general term for a net: Mt 4²⁰, ²¹, Mk 1¹⁸, ¹⁹, Lk 5², ⁴·⁶, Jo 21⁶, ⁸, ¹¹.†

SYN.: ἀμφίβληστρον (q.v.), σαγήνη.

*† **δίλογος**, -ον (< δίς, λέγω), 1. in sense of διλογεῖν, -ία (Xen.), given to repetition. 2. In NT, prob. (cf. δίγλωσσος, Pr 11¹³, Si 5⁹) double-tongued: 1 Ti 3⁸.†

διό, conjunct. for δι' ὅ, wherefore, on which account: Mt 27⁸, Lk 7⁷, Ac 15¹⁹, Ro 1²⁴, al.; δ. καί, Lk 1³⁵, Ac 10²⁹ 24²⁶, Ro 4²² 15²², II Co 1²⁰ 4¹³ 5⁹, Phl 2⁹, He 11¹² 13¹² (v. Ellic. on Ga 4³¹).

† **δι-οδεύω**, [in LXX chiefly for עבר;] 1. to travel through: c. acc., Ac 17¹. 2. to travel along (Ba 4², 1 Mac 12³², ³³): Lk 8¹.†

Διονύσιος, -ου, ὁ, Dionysius, an Athenian: Ac 17³⁴.†

** **διό-περ**, conjunct. (διό, q.v., strengthened by πέρ), [in LXX: Jth 8¹⁷, II Mac₅ *;] for which very reason: 1 Co 8¹³ 10¹⁴.†

* **διοπετής** (written also διïπ-), -ές (< δῖος, πίπτω, v. Page on Ac, l.c.; DB, i, 605, n., ext., 112ᵃ; Field, Notes, 130 f.), fallen from heaven (R, mg.): τὸ δ. (sc. ἄγαλμα, statue, image), Ac 19³⁵.†

* **διόρθωμα**, -τος, τό (< διορθόω, to make straight, set right), a correction, reform: Ac 24³.†

* διόρθωσις, -εως, ἡ (v. supr.), 1. *a making straight.* 2. *a reforming, reformation* (used in late writers of laws, etc.): He 9¹⁰ (Cremer, 807).†

δι-ορύσσω, [in LXX: Jb 24¹⁶, Ez 12⁵,⁷,¹², (חתר)*;] *to dig through:* c. acc., of house-breaking (as in π.; MM, *Exp.*, xi), Mt 24⁴³, Lk 12³⁹; absol., Mt 6¹⁹,²⁰.†

Διόσ-κουροι, -ων, οἱ (Ion. and κοινή form of Att., **Διόσκοροι**; < **Διός**, gen. of Ζεύς + κόρος, a son), *the Dioscuri* (Castor and Pollux), twin sons of Zeus and Leda (RV, *The Twin Brothers*): Ac 28¹¹.†

δι-ότι, conjunct., for διὰ τοῦτο, ὅτι (Lat. *propterea quod*), *because:* Lk 1¹³ 2⁷ 21²⁸, Ac 13³⁵ 18¹⁰ 20²⁶ 22¹⁸, Ro 1¹⁹,²¹ 3²⁰ 8⁷,²¹, 1 Co 15⁹, Phl 2²⁶, 1 Th 2⁸,¹⁸ (Lft., *Notes*, 37) 4⁶, He 11⁵,²³, Ja 4³, 1 Pe 1¹⁶,²⁴ 2⁶. It is usually stronger than ὅτι, but sometimes, as in Lk 1¹³, Ro 1¹⁹, 1 Th 2¹⁸, approximates to MGr. sense, *for;* cf. Milligan, *Th.*, l.c.†

Διοτρέφης (Rec. -τρεφής), -ες (< **Διός**, gen. of Ζεύς + τρέφω: *cherished by Zeus*), as pr. name, *Diotrephes:* III Jo 9.†

διπλόος (poët., **διπλός**, whence comp. -ότερον), -όη, -όον (-οῦς, -ῆ, -οῦν), [in LXX for כפל, מִשְׁנֶה, and cognates;] *twofold, double:* 1 Ti 5¹⁷, Re 18⁶; διπλότερον, *in twofold measure:* Mt 23¹⁵.†

* διπλόω, -ῶ (< διπλόυς), *to double:* δ. τὰ διπλᾶ, Re 18⁶.†

δίς, adv., *twice:* Mk 14³⁰,⁷²; δ. τ. σαββάτου, Lk 18¹²; καὶ ἅπαξ κ. δ., Phl 4¹⁶, 1 Th 2¹⁸; δ. ἀποθανόντα, Ju¹² (v. Mayor, *ICC*, in l.); δ. μυριάδες, Re 9¹⁶.†

Δίς, old nom. for Ζεύς (q.v.), whence gen. **Διός**, acc. **Δία**: Ac 14¹²,¹³.†

**† δισ-μυριάς, -άδος, ἡ, [in LXX: II Mac ₆*;] *twice ten thousand* Re 9¹⁶ (LT; δὶς μυριάδες, WH; δύο μ., Rec.).†

* διστάζω (< δίς), *to doubt, hesitate:* Mt 14³¹ 28¹⁷.†

SYN.: ἀπορέω, διαπορέω, διακρίνομαι, μετεωρίζομαι (v. *DCG*, i, 491).

δίστομος, -ον (< δίς, στόμα), [in LXX: Jg 3¹⁶, Ps 149⁶, Pr 5⁴ (פֵּיּוֹת), Si 21³*;] 1. of rivers and roads, *double-mouthed, double branching.* 2. Of swords (Eur.; LXX, ll. c.), *two-edged:* He 4¹², Re 1¹⁶ 2¹².†

δισ-χίλιοι, -αι, -α, *two thousand:* Mk 5¹³.†

δι-υλίζω (< δια, ὑλίζω, to strain), [in LXX: Am 6⁶*;] 1. *to strain thoroughly* (Archytas; Am., l.c.). 2. Later, *to strain out:* fig., Mt 23²⁴.†

** διχάζω (δίχα, *apart*), [in Aq.: Le 1¹⁷, De 14⁶ *;] *to cut apart, divide in two;* metaph., *to set at variance:* Mt 10³⁵.†

** διχοστασία, -ας, ἡ (< διχοστατέω, to stand apart), [in LXX: 1 Mac 3²⁹*;] *standing apart, dissension:* Ro 16¹⁷, Ga 5²⁰.†

διχοτομέω, -ῶ (< διχοτόμος, < δίχα, τέμνω), [in LXX: Ex 29¹⁷ (נתח pi.);] *to cut in two, cut asunder:* perh. metaph. of severe scourging (but v. Meyer on Mt, l.c., and cf. 1 Ki 15³³, 11 Ki 12³¹, He 11³⁷), Mt 24⁵¹, Lk 12⁴⁶ (cf. MM, *VGT*, s.v.; *EGT* in l.; and *Exp.*, VIII, 129 (Sept., 1921) for suggestion that δ. here may be rendering of Aram. *pasak*, (1) *to cut off*, (2) *to single out, set aside*).†

διψάω, -ῶ (< δίψα, *thirst*), [in LXX chiefly for צמא;] *to thirst:*

absol., Mt 25³⁵, ³⁷, ⁴², ⁴⁴, Jo 4¹³, ¹⁵ 19²⁸, Ro 12²⁰ (LXX), ι Co 4¹¹; fig., Jo 4¹⁴ 6³⁵ 7³⁷, Re 7¹⁶ 21⁶ 22¹⁷; c. acc. (= cl. c. gen.), τ. δικαιοσύνην, Mt 5⁶.†

δίψος, -εος (-ους), τό, (late form of δίψα), [in LXX chiefly for צָמָא and cognates;] *thirst:* ιι Co 11²⁷.†

*† δίψυχος, -ον (< δίς, ψυχή), *of two minds, wavering:* Ja 1⁸ 4⁸ (Cremer, 588; *DB,* iv, 528).†

διωγμός, -οῦ, ὁ (< διώκω), [in LXX : Pr 11¹⁹ (רדף pi.), La 3¹⁹ (מָרוֹד), ιι Mac 12²³ *;] *persecution:* Mt 13²¹, Mk 4¹⁷ 10³⁰, Ac 8¹ 13⁵⁰, Ro 8³⁵, ιι Co 12¹⁰, ιι Th 1⁴, ιι Ti 3¹¹.†

*† διώκτης, -ου, ὁ (< διώκω), *a persecutor:* ι Ti 1¹³.†

διώκω, [in LXX chiefly for רדף;] 1. *to put to flight, drive away:* Mt 23³⁴. 2. *to pursue;* (*a*) of persons; c. acc., without hostility, *to follow after:* Lk 17²³; with hostile purpose: Ac 26¹¹, Re 12¹³. Hence, *to persecute:* Mt 5¹⁰⁻¹², ⁴⁴ 10²³, Lk 11⁴⁹ 21¹², Jo 5¹⁶ 15²⁰, Ac 7⁵² 9⁴, ⁵ 22⁴, ⁷, ⁸ 26¹⁴, ¹⁵, Ro 12¹⁴, ι Co 4¹² 15⁹, ιι Co 4⁹, Ga 1¹³, ²³ 4²⁹ 5¹¹ 6¹², Phl 3⁶, ιι Ti 3¹²; (*b*) metaph., c. acc. rei, of seeking eagerly after: Ro 9³⁰, ι Ti 6¹¹, ιι Ti 2²²; νόμον δικαιοσύνης, Ro 9³¹; τ. φιλοξενίαν, Ro 12¹³; εἰρήνην, He 12¹⁴, ι Pe 3¹¹; τὰ τῆς εἰ., Ro 14¹⁹; τ. ἀγάπην, ι Co 14¹; τὸ ἀγαθόν, ι Th 5¹⁵; absol., *to follow on, drive,* or *speed on* (Æsch.), Phl 3¹², ¹⁴.†

δόγμα, -τος, τό (< δοκέω), [in LXX chiefly for דָּת, טְעֵם;] 1. *an opinion.* 2. A public *decree, ordinance:* of Roman rulers, Lk 2¹, Ac 17⁷; of the Jewish law, Eph 2¹⁵, Col 2¹⁴; of the Apostles, Ac 16⁴ (Cremer, 205).†

† δογματίζω, [in LXX : Es 3⁹ (כָּתַב ni.), Da LXX, 2¹³, ¹⁵ (דְּתָא, דָּת), ι Es 6³⁴, ιι Mac 10⁸ 15³⁶, ιιι Mac 4¹¹ *;] *to decree.* Mid., *to subject oneself to an ordinance:* Col 2²⁰.†

δοκέω, -ῶ (< δόκος, opinion, < δέκομαι, Ion. form of δέχ-), [in LXX for מזב, נדב, etc.;] 1. *to be of opinion, suppose:* Mt 24⁴⁴, Lk 12⁴⁰, He 10²⁹; c. inf., Mt 3⁹, Lk 8¹⁸ 24³⁷, Jo 5³⁹ 16², Ac 12⁹, 27¹³, ι Co 3¹⁸ 7⁴⁰ 8² 10¹² 14³⁷, Ga 6³, Phl 3⁴, Ja 1²⁶; c. acc. et inf., ι Co 12²³, ιι Co 11¹⁶; seq. ὅτι, Mt 6⁷ 26⁵³, Mk 6⁴⁹, Lk 12⁵¹ 13², ⁴ 19¹¹, Jo 5⁴⁵ 11¹³, ³¹ 13²⁹ 20¹⁵, ι Co 4⁹, ιι Co 12¹⁹, Ja 4⁵. 2. *to seem, be reputed:* Ac 25²⁷; c. inf., Mk 10⁴², Lk 10³⁶ 22²⁴, Ac 17¹⁸ 26⁹, ι Co 11¹⁶ 12²², ιι Co 10⁹, Ga 2⁶, ⁹, He 4¹ 12¹¹; οἱ δοκοῦντες, *those of repute,* Ga 2². Impers., *it seems,* c. dat. pers.; (*a*) *to think:* Mt 17²⁵, 18¹² 21²⁸ 22¹⁷, ⁴² 26⁶⁶, Jo 11⁵⁶, He 12¹⁰; (*b*) *to please, seem good to:* c. inf., Lk 1³, Ac 15²², ²⁵, ²⁸, ³⁴.†

SYN. (δοκέω 1.): ἡγέομαι², νομίζω², οἴομαι; ἡ. and ν. properly express belief resting on external proof, ἡ. denoting the more careful judgment; δ. and οἴ. imply a subjective judgment which in the case of οἴ. is based on feeling, in δ. on thought (v. Schmidt, c. 17).

(δοκέω 2.): φαίνομαι; φ., from the standpoint of the object, "expresses how a matter phenomenally shows and presents itself"; δ., from the standpoint of the observer, expresses one's subjective judgment about a matter (v. Tr., *Syn.,* § lxxx; Cremer, 204).

δοκιμάζω (< δόκιμος), [in LXX chiefly for בחן ;] 1. primarily of metals (Pr 8¹⁰ 17³, Si 2⁵, Wi 3⁶), *to test, try, prove* (in the hope and expectation that the test will prove successful, v. reff. s. *Syn.*): χρυσίον, ι Pe 1⁷; other things, Lk 12⁵⁶ 14¹⁹, ιι Co 8⁸, Ga 6⁴, ι Th 2⁴ 5²¹; τὰ διαφέροντα, Ro 2¹⁸, Phl 1¹⁰ (R, mg., but v. infr.); πνεύματα, ι Jo 4¹; of men, ι Ti 3¹⁰ (pass.); ἑαυτόν, ι Co 11²⁸, ιι Co 13⁵; seq. subst. clause, Ro 12², ι Co 3¹³, Eph 5¹⁰. 2. As the result of trial, *to approve, think fit*: Ro 1²⁸ 14²², ι Co 16³, ιι Co 8²², ι Th 2⁴ (δεδοκιμάσμεθα); τὰ διαφέροντα, Ro 2¹⁸, Phl 1¹⁰, R, txt. (but v. supr.; cf. διαφέρω).†
SYN.: πειράζω (v. Tr., *Syn.*, lxxiv; Cremer, 494 ff., 699 ff.).

**δοκιμασία, -ας, ἡ (< δοκιμάζω), [in LXX: Si 6²¹ *;] a *testing, proving*: He 3⁹ (LXX).†

**†δοκιμή, -ῆς, ἡ (< δόκιμος), [in Sm.: Ps 67 (68)³¹ *;] 1. the process of trial, *proving, test*: ιι Co 8² 9¹³. 2. The result of trial, *approval, approvedness, proof*: Ro 5⁴, ιι Co 2⁹ 13³, Phl 2²² (Cremer, 212, 701).†

δοκίμιον, -ον, τό, [in LXX : Pr 17³ 27²¹ (מצרף) *;] usually regarded as a variant form of δοκιμεῖον, a *test*, and so perh. Ja 1³ (v. Mayor, in l.), but see next word (cf. Cremer, 212, 702).†

†δοκίμιος, -α, -ον (< δοκιμή), [in LXX : ἀργύριον δ. (עָלִיל), Ps 11 (12)⁶; and as v.l. for δόκιμος (B), ἀργυρίου δ. (זקק pu.), ι Ch 29⁴ (Bᵃᵇ); εἰ δ. ἐστιν (יָקָר), Za 11¹³ א ᶜ ᵃ ᵛⁱᵈ, Q *)*;] = δόκιμος, *tested, approved*: τὸ δ. ὑμῶν τ. πίστεως, *that which is approved in your faith*, ι Pe 1⁷ (where Hort suggests the v.l. δόκιμος, found in some cursives), Ja 1³ (but v. Mayor, in l. For full discussion of this word, not hitherto found in a Gk. Lexicon, and for exx. of its use in π., v. Deiss. (to whom is due the credit of its discovery), *BS*, 259 ff.; MM, *Exp.*, xi; cf. also Milligan, *NTD*, 76).†

δόκιμος, -ον (< δέκομαι = δέχομαι), [in LXX for זקק pu., etc.;] primarily of metals, *tested, accepted, approved*: of persons, Ro 14¹⁸, 16¹⁰, ι Co 11¹⁹, ιι Co 10¹⁸ 13⁷, ιι Ti 2¹⁵, Ja 1¹² (Cremer, 212, 697).†

δοκός, -οῦ, ἡ (δέχομαι), [in LXX for קֹרָה, etc.;] a *beam* of timber: Mt 7³⁻⁵, Lk 6⁴¹, ⁴² (*DCG*, i, 176).†

δόλιος, -α, -ον (< δόλος), [in LXX—chiefly in Pss, Pr, Si—for מִרְמָה, etc.;] *deceitful*: ιι Co 11¹³.†

†δολιόω (< δόλιος), [in LXX: Nu 25¹⁸, Ps 104 (105)²⁵ (נכל), Ps 5⁹ (חלק hi.) *;] *to deceive*: ἐδολιοῦσαν (-σαν, freq. in κοινή Gk. for impf. 3rd pers. pl.), Ro 3¹³ (LXX).†

δόλος, -ον, ὁ, [in LXX chiefly for מִרְמָה ;] 1. in Hom., a *bait*. 2. a *snare*. 3. In the abstract, *craft, deceit*: Mt 26⁴, Mk 7²² 14¹, Jo 1⁴⁷, Ac 13¹⁰, Ro 1²⁹, ιι Co 12¹⁶, ι Th 2³, ι Pe 2¹, ²² 3¹⁰ (LXX) (λαλῆσαι δ.).†

δολόω, -ῶ (δόλος), [in LXX: Ps 14 (15)³ (רגל), 35 (36)² (חלק hi.) *;] 1. *to ensnare*. 2. As of wine, *to adulterate, corrupt*: τ. λόγον τ. θεοῦ, ιι Co 4².†
SYN.: καπηλεύω, q.v.

δόμα, -τος, τό (< δίδωμι), [in LXX for מַתָּנָה, etc.;] *a gift:* Mt 7¹¹, Lk 11¹³, Eph 4⁸ (LXX), Phl 4¹⁷.†

SYN.: δόσις, δῶρον, δωρεά, δώρημα.

δόξα, -ης, ἡ (< δοκέω), [in LXX very freq. for כָּבוֹד, also for תִּפְאָרֶת, הוֹד, etc., 25 words in all;] in cl., 1. *expectation, judgment, opinion* (IV Mac 5¹⁸). 2. *opinion, estimation* in which one is held, *repute ;* in NT, always *good opinion,* hence *reputation, praise, honour, glory :* Lk 14¹⁰, Jo 12⁴³, He 3³ ; opp. to αἰσχύνη, Phl 3¹⁹; to ἀτιμία, II Co 6⁸; δ. κ. τιμή, Ro 2⁷, ¹⁰, I Pe 1⁷, II Pe 1¹⁷; ζητεῖν δ., Jo 5⁴⁴ 7¹⁸ 8⁵⁰, I Th 2⁶ ; λαμβάνειν, Jo 5⁴¹, II Pe 1¹⁷, Re 5¹²; διδόναι δ. τ. θεῷ (cf. נָתַן כָּבוֹד לַיהוָה, Je 13¹⁶, al.), Lk 17¹⁸, Jo 9²⁴, Ac 12²³, Ro 4²⁰, Re 4⁹; εἰς (τ.) δ. θεοῦ, Ro 3⁷ 15⁷, Phl 1¹¹, al.; in doxologies, τ. θεῷ (ᾧ) ἡ δ., Lk 2¹⁴, Ro 11³⁶ 16²⁷, Ga 1⁵, Eph 3²¹, al. 3. Later also (not cl.) as in LXX (= הוֹד, Jb 39²⁰, I Ch 29²⁵; כָּבוֹד, Jb 19⁹, Es 5¹¹, al.), visible *brightness, splendour, glory :* of light, Ac 22¹¹; of heavenly bodies, I Co 15⁴⁰ ᶠˡ.; esp. that wh. radiates from God's presence, as manifested in the pillar of cloud and in the Holy of Holies (= כָּבוֹד, Ex 16¹⁰ 25²² 40³⁴, al.; and new Heb. שְׁכִינָה, II Mac 2⁸; v. DB, iv, 489b), Ro 9⁴, Ja 2¹ (v. Hort, Mayor, in l.); hence of the manifested glory of God, Ro 1²³, Col 1¹¹, Eph 1⁶, ¹², ¹⁷ 3¹⁶; of the same as communicated to man through Christ, II Co 3¹⁸ 4⁶; and of the glorious condition into which Christians shall enter hereafter, Ro 8¹⁸, ²¹ 9²³, II Ti 2¹⁰, al.

SYN.: ἔπαινος, τιμή (v. Hort on I Pe 1⁷).

δοξάζω (< δόξα), [in LXX chiefly for כבד ni., pi., also for פאר, etc.;] 1. *to think, suppose, hold an opinion* (Æsch., Plat., al.). 2. To *bestow δόξα* (q.v.) *on,* to *magnify, extol, praise* (Thuc., iii, 45; Plut., al.): c. acc., Mt 5¹⁶, Mk 2¹², Jo 8⁵⁴, Ro 15⁶, I Pe 2¹², al.; id. seq. ἐπί, Lk 2²⁰; ἐν, Ga 1²⁴, I Pe 4¹⁶. 3. In LXX and NT (v.s. δόξα, 3), *to clothe with splendour, glorify* (Ex 34²⁹, ³⁰, Ps 36 (37)²⁰, Is 44²³, Es 3¹, al.): Ro 8³⁰, II Co 3¹⁰, II Th 3¹, I Pe 1⁸, al.; of Christ, Jo 7³⁹ 8⁵⁴, al. (on the Johannine use, v. Cremer, 211; Westc., Jo., Intr.); of the Father, Jo 13³¹, ³², I Pe 4¹¹, al. (cf. ἐν-, συν-δοξάζω).

Δορκάς, -άδος, ἡ (δορκάς, *a gazelle*), *Dorcas,* also called Ταβειθά, q.v.: Ac 9³⁶, ³⁹.†

δόσις, -εως, ἡ (δίδωμι), [in LXX for חֵלֶק (Ge 47²²), מַתָּן, מַתַּת (Pr 21¹⁴ 25¹⁴), freq. in Si.;] 1. properly, the act of *giving :* Phl 4¹⁵. 2. Objectively, *a gift :* Ja 1¹⁷.†

SYN.: v.s. δόμα.

†δότης, -ου, ὁ (< δίδωμι), [in LXX: Pr 22⁸ * ;] = δοτήρ, *a giver :* II Co 9⁷ (LXX) (not elsewhere).†

*†δουλαγωγέω, -ῶ (< δοῦλος, ἄγω), to *make a slave, bring into bondage :* I Co 9²⁷ (Cremer, 703).†

δουλεία (T, -λία), -ας, ἡ (< δουλεύω), [in LXX, as Ex 13³, for עֶבֶד and cognates;] *slavery, bondage :* Ro 8¹⁵, ²¹, Ga 4²⁴ 5¹, He 2¹⁵.†

δουλεύω (< δοῦλος), [in LXX for עבד, as Ge 14⁴, exc. Da TH
7¹⁴, ²⁷ (פְּלַח), Is 56⁶ (שָׁרַת pi.);] to be a slave, be subject to, serve.
absol., Ro 7⁶, Ga 4²⁵, ι Ti 6²; c. dat pers., Mt 6²⁴, Lk 15²⁹ 16¹³,
Ro 9¹² (LXX); of nations, Jo 8³³, Ac 7⁷ (LXX); θεῷ, τ. κυρίῳ, Mt 6²⁴,
Lk 16¹³, Ac 20¹⁹, Ro 12¹¹ (R, mg., καιρῷ) 16¹⁸, Eph 6⁷, Col 3²⁴,
ι Th 1⁹; τ. Χριστῷ, Ro 14¹⁸, Col 3²⁴; νόμῳ θεοῦ, Ro 7²⁵; τ. θεοῖς,
Ga 4⁸; τ. καιρῷ, Ro 12¹¹ (R, mg. for κυρίῳ); ἀλλήλοις, Ga 5¹³; σὺν ἐμοί,
Phl 2²²; τ. ἁμαρτίᾳ, Ro 6⁶; νόμῳ ἁμαρτίας, Ro 7²⁵; ἐπιθυμίαις κ. ἡδοναῖς,
Tit 3³; τ. κοιλίᾳ, Ro 16¹⁸; μαμωνᾷ, Mt 6²⁴, Lk 16¹³; τ. στοιχείοις τ.
κόσμου, Ga 4⁹ (Cremer, 217).†
    δούλη, ἡ, v.s. δοῦλος.
    δοῦλος, -η, -ον, [in LXX, ὁ. δ. nearly always for עֶבֶד; ἡ δ. chiefly
for אָמָה, שִׁפְחָה;] 1. in bondage to, subject to: Ro 6¹⁹. 2. As subst.,
ὁ, ἡ δ., a slave; (a) fem., ἡ δ., a female slave, bondmaid (Cremer, 702;
DB, iii, 215): Lk 1³⁸, ⁴⁸, Ac 2¹⁸ (LXX); (b) masc., ὁ δ., a slave, bondman: Mt 8⁹ 18²³, al.; opp. to ἐλεύθερος, ι Co 7²² 12¹³, Ga 3²⁸, Eph 6⁸,
Col 3¹¹, Re 6¹⁵ 13¹⁶ 19¹⁸; opp. to κύριος, δεσπότης, οἰκοδεσπότης, Mt 10²⁴
13²⁷, ²⁸, Lk 12⁴⁶, Jo 15¹⁵, Eph 6⁵, Col 3²² 4¹, al.; metaph., δ. Χριστοῦ,
τοῦ Χρ., Ιησοῦ Χρ., Ro 1¹, ι Co 7²², Ga 1¹⁰, Eph 6⁶, Phl 1¹, Col 4¹²,
ι Pe 2¹⁶, Re 7³ 15³; δ. τ. θεοῦ, τ. κυρίου, Ac 16¹⁷, ιι Ti 2²⁴, Tit 1¹,
ι Pe 2¹⁶, Re 7³ 15³; δ. πονηρός, ἀχρεῖος, κακός, Mt 18³² 24⁴⁸ 25²⁶, ³⁰,
Lk 17¹⁰ 19²²; δ. ἁμαρτίας, Jo 8³⁴, Ro 6¹⁷, ²⁰; τ. φθορᾶς, ιι Pe 2¹⁹.
    SYN.: διάκονος (q.v.), θεράπων, ὑπηρέτης (v. DB, iii, 377; iv, 461,
469; DCG, i, 221; ii, 613; Cremer, 215, 702).
    δουλόω, -ῶ (< δοῦλος), [in LXX for עבד;] to enslave, bring into
bondage: Ac 7⁶ (LXX), ιι Pe 2¹⁹; metaph., ι Co 9¹⁹; pass., seq. ἐν, ib.
7¹⁵; τ. θεῷ, Ro 6²²; τ. δικαιοσύνῃ, Ro 6¹⁸; οἴνῳ, Tit 2³; ὑπὸ τὰ στοιχεῖα
τ. κόσμου, Ga 4³ (Cremer, 217).†
    δοχή, -ῆς, ἡ (< δέχομαι), [in LXX: Ge 21⁸, Es 1², al. (מִשְׁתֶּה), Da
LXX 5¹ (לְחֶם);] a feast, banquet, reception: Lk 5²⁹ 14¹³.†
    δράκων, -οντος, ὁ, [in LXX chiefly for תַּנִּין;] a dragon, a mythical
monster: fig., of Satan, Re 12³⁻¹⁷ 13², ⁴, ¹¹ 16¹³ 20².†
    δράμω, obsol., to run, v.s. τρέχω.
    δράσσομαι, [in LXX for נשׂא pi., Ps 2¹²; elsewhere קמץ, as Le 2²;]
to grasp with the hand, to lay hold of: metaph., c. acc. (M, Pr., 65),
ι Co 3¹⁹ (LXX).†
    δραχμή, -ῆς, ἡ (< δράσσομαι), [in LXX: in Hex. for בֶּקַע, שֶׁקֶל;
in ιι Es for אֲדַרְכּוֹן, דַּרְכְּמוֹן;] a drachma, nearly equal to the Roman
denarius (v.s. δηνάριον): Lk 15⁸, ⁹ (DCG, ii, 200).†
    δρέπανον, -ου, τό (later form of Attic δρεπάνη, < δρέπω, to pluck),
[in LXX for מַזְמֵרָה, חֶרְמֵשׁ, etc.;] a sickle, pruning-hook: Mk 4²⁹,
Re 14¹⁴⁻¹⁹.†

δρόμος, -ου, ὁ (< δραμεῖν, v.s. τρέχω), [in LXX chiefly for מְרוּצָה;] *a course, race :* fig., of life or ministry, Ac 13²⁵ 20²⁴, II Ti 4⁷.†

Δρούσιλλα (Rec. Δρουσίλλα), ης, ἡ, *Drusilla,* wife of Felix: Ac 24²⁴.†

δύναμαι, depon., [in LXX chiefly for יָכֹל;] *to be able, have power,* whether by personal ability, permission, or opportunity: c. inf. (M, Pr., 205; WM, § 44, 3) pres., Mt 6²⁴, Mk 2⁷, Jo 3², I Co 10²¹, al.; c inf. aor., Mt 3⁹, Mk 1⁴⁵, Jo 3³, ⁴, Ro 8³⁹, al.; c. acc., *to be able to do* something: Mk 9²³, Lk 12²⁶, II Co 13⁸; absol., *to be able, capable, powerful :* I Co 3² 10¹³.

δύναμις, -εως, ἡ (< δύναμαι), [in LXX for חַיִל (חֵיל), צָבָא, גְּבוּרָה, עֹז, etc.; 35 words in all;] *power, might, strength;* relatively, *ability, power* to perform: Mt 25¹⁵, Ac 3¹², He 11¹¹; κατὰ δ., II Co 8³; παρὰ δ., ib.; ὑπὲρ δ., II Co 1⁸; of pecuniary ability, II Co 8³, Re 18³; absol., *power, might :* Lk 24⁴⁹, Ac 1⁸; opp. to ἀσθένεια, I Co 15⁴³; ἡ δ. τ. ἁμαρτίας, I Co 15⁵⁶; of power in action, Ro 1¹⁶, ²⁰, I Co 1¹⁸, Phl 3¹⁰, al.; ἡ δ. τ. θεοῦ, Mt 22²⁹, Mk 12²⁴, Ro 1²⁰, al.; opp. to μόρφωσις, II Ti 3⁵; in doxologies, Re 4¹¹ 7¹², al.; ἐν δ., Mk 9¹, Lk 4³⁶, Ro 1⁴, al.; of the power of performing miracles, Ac 6⁸, II Th 2⁹; pl., Mt 13⁵⁴, Mk 6¹⁴, Ga 3⁵, al.; of the *force* or *meaning* of a word (Plat., al.), I Co 14¹¹. By meton., of persons or things; (*a*) of God, Mt 26⁶⁴, Mk 14⁶² (Dalman, *Words,* 200 ff.); (*b*) of angels, Ro 8³⁸, Eph 1²¹, I Pe 3²²; (*c*) of armies, pl. [LXX for צְבָאוֹת], metaph., of the stars, Mt 24²⁹, Mk 13²⁵, Lk 21²⁶; (*d*) of that wh. manifests God's power: Christ, I Co 1²⁴; τ. εὐαγγέλιον, Ro 1¹⁶; ἡ δ. τ. κυρίου, I Co 5⁴; (*e*) of mighty works (Tr., *Syn.,* § xci), δ. ποιεῖν, Mk 6⁵ 9³⁹; pl., Mt 7²², Mk 6², Lk 10¹³, al.; σημεῖα κ. δ., Ac 8¹³; δ. κ. τέρατα κ. σημεῖα, Ac 2²², II Co 12¹².

SYN.: βία, ἐνέργεια, ἐξουσία, ἰσχύς, κράτος (v. Tr., l.c.; Cremer, 218, 236; *DB,* i, 616; iv, 29; *DCG,* i, 607; ii, 188).

† δυναμόω, -ῶ (< δύναμις), [in LXX for עוּז, Ps 51 (52)⁷ 67 (68)²⁸; גְּבַר pi., hi., Ec 10¹⁰, Da TH 9²⁷ *;] *to make strong, strengthen :* Eph 6¹⁰ (WH, mg.; ἐνδυν-, WH, txt., RV), Col 1¹¹, He 11³⁴.†

δυνάστης, -ου, ὁ (< δύναμαι), [in LXX for גִּבּוֹר, עָרִיץ, בַּיִת, etc.;] *a prince, ruler, potentate :* Lk 1⁵²; of God (Si 46⁵, ¹⁶, II Mac 15³), I Ti 6¹⁵; of a high official (cf. δυνάσται Φαραώ, Ge 50⁴), Ac 8²⁷ (Cremer, 221).†

*† δυνατέω, -ῶ (< δυνατός), *to be able, be powerful, mighty :* c. inf., Ro 14⁴, II Co 9⁸; absol., opp. to ἀσθενῶ, II Co 13³.†

δυνατός, -ή, -όν (< δύναμαι), [in LXX for גִּבּוֹר, חַיִל, etc.;] 1. *strong, mighty, powerful :* absol., Lk 1⁴⁹, I Co 1²⁶; οἱ δ., the chief men, Ac 25⁵; of spiritual strength, Ro 15¹, II Co 12¹⁰ 13⁹; seq. ἐν, Lk 24¹⁹, Ac 7²² 18²⁴; πρός, II Co 10⁴. 2. C. inf., *able to do :* Lk 14³¹, Ac 11¹⁷, Ro 4²¹ 11²³, II Ti 1¹², Tit 1⁹, He 11¹⁹, Ja 3². 3. Neut., δυνατόν, *possible :* Mt 19²⁶, Mk 9²³ 10²⁷ 14³⁶, Lk 18²⁷, Ac 2²⁴ 20¹⁶; εἰ δ. (ἐστι),

Mt 24²⁴ 26³⁹, Mk 13²² 14³⁵, Ro 12¹⁸, Ga 4¹⁵; τὸ δ. (= ἡ δύναμις) αὐτοῦ, Ro 9²².†

δύνω, Ion. and trag. form of δύω, [in LXX chiefly for בּוֹא;] to enter, sink into; of the sun (sc. πόντον), set: Mk 1³², Lk 4⁴⁰ (cf. ἐκ-, ἀπ-εκ-, ἐν-, ἐπ-εν-, παρ-εισ-, ἐπι-δύνω).†

δύο, numeral, indecl. exc. in dat., δυσί, δυσίν (Attic δυοῖν), two: Mt 19⁶, Mk 10⁸, Jo 2⁶, al.; with pl. noun, Mt 9²⁷ 10¹⁰, al.; οἱ, τῶν, τοὺς δ., Mt 19⁵ 20²⁴, Mk 10⁸, Eph 2¹⁵, al.; δ. ἐξ, Lk 24¹³; distrib., ἀνά, κατὰ δ., two and two, two apiece: Lk 10¹ (WH, ἀνὰ δ. [δύο]), Jo 2⁶, I Co 14²⁷; δύο δύο (= ἀνὰ δ., as LXX, Ge 6¹⁹ for שְׁנַיִם שְׁנַיִם, but not merely "Hebraism," cf. μυρία μυρία, Æsch., Pers., 981, and for usage in π. and MGr., v. M, Pr., 21, 97), Mk 6⁷; εἰς δ. (two and two, Xen., Cyr., 7, 5, 17), into two parts, Mt 27⁵¹, Mk 15³⁸.

δυσ-, inseparable prefix, opp. to εὖ, like un-, mis- (in unrest, mischance), giving the idea of difficulty, opposition, injuriousness, etc.

† δυσ-βάστακτος, -ον (< βαστάζω), [in LXX for נָמֵל, Pr 27³ *;] hard to be borne, difficult to carry: Mt 23⁴ (om. WH, txt., R, mg.), Lk 11⁴⁶.†

* δυσεντερία, -ας, ἡ, Rec. for δυσεντέριον (q.v.), Ac 28⁸.†

*† δυσεντέριον, -ον, τό (ἔντερον, intestine), late form of δυσεντερία (Rec., l.c.), dysentery: Ac 28⁸.†

*† δυσερμήνευτος, -ον (< ἑρμηνεύω), hard of interpretation: He 5¹¹.†

δύσις, -εως, ἡ (< δύνω), [in LXX: Ps 103 (104)¹⁹ (מָבוֹא) *;] 1. a sinking, setting, as of the sun (Æsch.): Mk 16 [alt. ending]. 2. the sunsetting, the west (Thuc.).†

δύσκολος, -ον (< κόλον, food), [in LXX for אַיִר, Je 29⁹ (49⁸) (cf. δυσκολία, Jb 34³⁰; εὔκολος, II Ki 15³) *;] 1. properly, of persons, hard to satisfy with food, hence, generally, hard to please (Eur., Plat.). 2. Of things, difficult, hard (Arist.): Mk 10²⁴.†

* δυσκόλως, adv., with difficulty: Mt 19²³, Mk 10²³, Lk 18²⁴.†

δυσμή, -ῆς, ἡ (= δύσις, < δύνω), [in LXX for בּוֹא, עֲרָבָה, etc.;] mostly in pl., opp. to ἀνατολαί; 1. a setting, as of the sun (acc. to Thayer, s.v., so perhaps in Lk 12⁵⁴). 2. the quarter of sunset, the West: anarth., Mt 8¹¹ 24²⁷, Lk 12⁵⁴ 13²⁹, Re 21¹³.†

* δυσνόητος, -ον (< νοέω), hard to understand: II Pe 3¹⁶.†

** δυσφημέω, -ῶ (< δύσφημος, slanderous), [in LXX: I Mac 7⁴¹ *;] 1. intrans., to use evil words (Æsch.). 2. Trans., to speak ill of, defame (Soph.): pass., I Co 4¹³.†

** δυσφημία, -ας, ἡ (< δύσφημος, slanderous), [in LXX: I Mac 7³⁸, III Mac 2²⁶ *;] evil-speaking, defamation: opp. to εὐφημία, II Co 6⁸.†

δύω, v.s. δύνω.

δώδεκα, οἱ, αἱ, τά, indecl. numeral, twelve: Mt 9²⁰ 10¹, al.; οἱ δ., the apostles, Mt 10⁵, Mk 4¹⁰, al.; in Ac 19⁷ 24¹¹, for Rec. δεκαδύο.

δωδέκατος, -η, -ον, twelfth: Re 21²⁰.†

*† δωδεκά-φυλος, -ον (< δώδεκα, φυλή), of twelve tribes: as subst. neut., τὸ δ. (cf. λαὸς ὁ δ., Sibyll. Orac.), the twelve tribes, Ac 26⁷.†

δῶμα, -τος, τό (< δέμω, to build), [in LXX for גַּג;] chiefly in poets and late (not Attic) prose; 1. *a house, hall.* 2. In LXX (and Hom., *Od.*, x, 554; cf. MGr., *terrace*), *house-top: ἐπὶ τ. δῶμα*, Lk 5¹⁹, Ac 10⁹ ; *ἐπὶ τ. δώματος, -άτων*, Mt 10²⁷ 24¹⁷, Mk 13¹⁵, Lk 12³ 17³¹.†

δωρεά, -ᾶς, ἡ (< δίδωμι), [in LXX chiefly (-άν) for חִנָּם, as Ge 29¹⁵ ;] *a gift:* Ac 11¹⁷, Ro 5¹⁵, He 6⁴ ; δ. τ. θεοῦ, Jo 4¹⁰, Ac 8²ᶜ ; τ. Χριστοῦ, Eph 4⁷ ; τ. πνεύματος, Ac 2³⁸ 10⁴⁵ ; τ. δικαιοσύνης, Ro 5¹⁷; τ. χάριτος, Eph 3⁷ ; ἀνεκδιηγήτῳ δ., II Co 9¹⁵. Acc., δωρεάν, adverbially (as freq. in LXX), (*a*) *freely, as a gift:* Mt 10⁸, Ro 3²⁴, II Co 11⁷, II Th 3⁸, Re 21⁶ 22¹⁷ ; (*b*) *in vain, uselessly:* Jo 15²⁵ (LXX), Ga 2²¹.†
SYN.: v.s. δόμα.
δωρεάν, v.s. δωρεά.

δωρέω, -ῶ, [in LXX: Ge 30²⁰ (זבר), Es 8¹, Pr 4² (נתן), Le 7⁵ (15) (קרבן), I Es 1⁷ 8¹⁴, ⁵⁵, Si 7²⁵ *;] *to present, bestow.* As depon. (with same sense), -έομαι, -οῦμαι : Mk 15⁴⁵, II Pe 1³,⁴.†
SYN.: δίδωμι, q.v.
** δώρημα, -τος, τό (< δωρέω), [in LXX: Si 31 (34)¹⁸ *;] *a gift, boon, benefaction* (poët.) : Ro 5¹⁶, Ja 1¹⁷.†
SYN.: v.s. δόμα.

δῶρον, -ου, τό (< δίδωμι), [in LXX chiefly for קָרְבָּן, also for מִנְחָה, etc. ;] *a gift, present:* Mt 2¹¹, Re 11¹⁰ ; of gifts and sacrifices to God, Mt 5²³, ²⁴ 8⁴ 15⁵ 23¹⁸, ¹⁹, Mk 7¹¹, Lk 21¹, ⁴, He 5¹ 8³, ⁴ 9⁹ 11⁴ ; δ. θεοῦ, Eph 2⁸.†
SYN.: s.v. δόμα.
*δωροφορία, -ας, ἡ, *a bringing of presents:* LTr., mg., for διακονία, Ro 15³¹.†

E

E, ε, ἒ ψιλόν (ἐψῖλον), τό, indecl., *epsilon*, ĕ, the fifth letter. As a numeral, ε′ = 5, ε, = 5000.
ἔα, interj., expressing surprise, indignation, fear (in cl. chiefly in poët.), *ah ! ha !:* Lk 4³⁴.†
ἐάν, contr. fr. εἰ ἄν, conditional particle, representing something as "under certain circumstances actual or liable to happen," but not so definitely expected as in the case of εἰ c. ind. (Bl., § 65, 4 ; cf. Jo 13¹⁷, I Co 7³⁶), *if haply, if ;* 1. c. subjc. (cl.) ; (*a*) pres. : Mt 6²², Lk 10⁶, Jo 7¹⁷, Ro 2²⁵, ²⁶, al. ; (*b*) aor. (= Lat. fut. pf.) : Mt 4⁹ 16²⁶ (cf. ptcp. in Lk 9²⁵ ; M, *Pr.*, 230), Mk 3²⁴, Lk 14³⁴, Jo 5⁴³, Ro 7², al. ; = cl. εἰ, c. opt., Jo 9²² 11⁵⁷, Ac 9² ; as Heb. אִם = ὅταν, Jo 12³² 14³, I Jo 2²⁸ 3², He 3⁷ (LXX). 2. C. indic. (as in late writers, fr. Arist. on ; v. WH, *App.*, 171 ; VD, *MGr.*², *App.*, § 77 ; Deiss., *BS*, 201 f., *LAE*, 155, 254 ; M, *Pr.*, 168, 187 ; Bl., § 65, 4) ; (*a*) fut. : Mt 18¹⁹ T, Lk 19⁴⁰,

Ac 7⁷; (b) pres.: ι Th 3⁸ (v. Milligan, in l.).   3. With other particles: ἐ. καί (Bl., § 65, 6), Ga 6¹; ἐ. μή (M, Pr., 185, 187; Bl., l.c.), c. subjc. pres., Mt 10¹³, ι Co 8⁸, Ja 2¹⁷, ι Jo 3²¹; aor., Mt 6¹⁵, Mk 3²⁷, Jo 3³, Ro 10¹⁵, Ga 2¹⁶ (v. Lft., Ellic., in ll.); ἐ. τε . . . ἐ. τε, [in LXX for אִם . . . אִם, Es 19¹³, al.,] Ro 14⁸.   4. = cl. ἄν (q.v.), after relat. pronouns and adverbs (Tdf., Pr., 96; WH, App., 173; M, Pr., 42 f.; Bl., § 26, 4; Mayser, 152 f.; Deiss., BS, 202 ff.): ὅς ἐ., Mt 5¹⁹, Mk 6²², ²³, Lk 17³³, ι Co 6¹⁸, al.; ὅπου ἐ., Mt 8¹⁹; ὁσάκις ἐ., Re 11⁶; οὗ ἐ., ι Co 16⁶; καθὸ ἐ., ιι Co 8¹²; ὅστις ἐ., Ga 5¹⁰; καὶ ἐ., Ga 1⁸ (v. ICC in l.).

ἑαυτοῦ, -ῆς, -οῦ, dat. -ῷ, etc., acc. -όν, etc., pl. -ῶν, etc. (Att. contr. αὑτοῦ, etc); reflex pron.; 1. prop. of 3rd person (Lat. sui, sibi, se), of himself, herself, itself, etc.: Mt 27⁴², Mk 15³¹, Lk 23³⁵, al.; added to a middle verb, διεμερίσαντο ἑαυτοῖς, Jo 19²⁴; to an active verb, Ac 14¹⁴ (M, Pr., 157); ἀφ' ἑαυτοῦ, Lk 12⁵⁷ 21³⁰, Jo 5¹⁹, al. (v.s. ἀπό); δι' ἑαυτοῦ, Ro 14¹⁴; ἐν ἑ., Mt 3⁹, Mk 5³⁰, al.; εἰς ἑ., Lk 15¹⁷; καθ' ἑαυτόν, Ac 28¹⁶, Ja 2¹⁷; παρ' ἑαυτῷ, at his own house, ι Co 16²; πρὸς ἑ., with, to himself, Lk 18¹¹; pl., to their own homes, Jo 20¹⁰; ἐφ' ἑ., ιι Co 10⁷; as poss. pron. (with emphasis weakened; v. M, Pr., 87 f.), τ. ἑαυτῶν νεκρούς, Lk 9⁶⁰.   2. As reflective 1st and 2nd pers. (so also freq. in cl., chiefly poetry), Mt 23³¹, Mk 9⁵⁰, Ro 8²³, ι Th 2⁸, al.   3. In pl., for reciprocal pron., ἀλλήλων, -οις, -ους, of one another, etc.: Mt 21³⁸, Mk 16³, Eph 5¹⁹, al.

ἐάω, -ῶ, [in LXX for רפה hi., etc.;] 1. to let, permit: c. acc., c. inf., c. acc. et inf. (M, Pr., 205): Mt 24⁴³, Lk 4⁴¹ 22⁵¹, Ac 14¹⁶ 16⁷ 19³⁰ 23³² 27³² 28⁴, ι Co 10¹³.   2. to let alone, leave: ἀγκύρας, Ac 27⁴⁰ (cf. προσ-εάω).†

ἑβδομήκοντα, οἱ, αἱ, τά, indecl. (< ἑπτά), seventy: Lk 10¹, ¹⁷, Ac 7¹⁴ 23²³ 27³⁷.†

† ἑβδομηκοντάκις, adv., [in LXX for שִׁבְעִים, Ge 4²⁴ *;] seventy times: ἐ. ἑπτά, seventy times seven, Mt 18²² (R, txt., ICC, in l.), or seventy-seven times (R, mg.; cf. M, Pr., 98; WM, 314; Meyer, in l.).†

ἕβδομος, -η, -ον (< ἑπτά), [in LXX chiefly for שְׁבִיעִי;] seventh: Jo 4⁵², He 4⁴ (LXX), Ju ¹⁴, Re 8¹ 10⁷ 11¹⁵ 16¹⁷ 21²⁰.†

Ἔβερ (Rec. Ἐβέρ), ὁ, indecl. (Heb. עֵבֶר, Ge 10²⁴), Eber (OT, Heber): Lk 3³⁵.†

*† Ἑβραϊκός, -ή, -όν, Hebrew: Lk 23³⁸, Rec.†

† Ἑβραῖος (WH, Ἑβ-), -α, -ον (Aram. עִבְרָי), as subst., ὁ Ε., [in LXX for עֶבֶר, עִבְרִי;] a Hebrew. 1. In OT, of Israelites in contrast with those of another race (Ge 14¹³, Ex 1¹⁵, De 15¹², al.).   2. In NT as the correlative of Ἑλληνιστής, a Jew who had adopted, in greater or less degree, Greek culture and Greek language.   The distinction was not merely linguistic (DB, ii, 325); as far as it was so, Συριστής would be a more correct Greek term for the Jew of Semitic speech (v.s. Ἑβραΐς, and cf. Dalman, Words, 7): Ac 6¹, ιι Co 11²², Phl 3⁵.†

**† Ἑβραΐς (WH, Ἑβ-), -ίδος (Aram. עִבְרָי), peculiar form of Ἑβραϊκός,

[in LXX, ἡ 'E. φωνή, iv Mac 12⁷ 16¹⁵ * ;] in NT, ἡ 'E. διάλεκτος, *Hebrew*, i.e. the Aramaic vernacular of Palestine : Ac 21⁴⁰ 22² 26¹⁴.†
**† Ἑβραϊστί (WH, Ἑβ-), adv., [in LXX : Si *prol.* ¹³ * ;] *in Hebrew* : Re 9¹¹ ; elsewhere, *in Aramaic* (v. supr.) : Jo 5² 19¹³, ¹⁷, ²⁰ 20¹⁶, Re 16¹⁶.†
ἐγγίζω (< ἐγγύς), [in LXX for נגש, קרב, etc. ;] 1. trans., *to bring near* : Ge 48¹⁰, Is 5⁸. 2. Intrans., *to come near* : absol., Mt 26⁴⁶, Mk 14⁴², Lk 18⁴⁰ 19⁴¹ 21²⁰, ²⁸ 24¹⁵, Ac 21³³ 23¹⁵ ; c. adv., ὅπου, Lk 12³³ ; c. dat., Lk 7¹² 15¹, ²⁵ 22⁴⁷, Ac 9³ 10⁹ 22⁶ ; τ. θεῷ, He 7¹⁹, Ja 4⁸ ; seq. εἰς, Mt 21¹, Mk 11¹, Lk 18³⁵ 19²⁹ 24²⁸ ; πρός, c. dat., Lk 19³⁷ ; μέχρι θανάτου, Phl 2³⁰ ; of time, ὥρα, Mt 26⁴⁵ ; ἡμέρα, Ro 13¹², He 10²⁵ ; καιρός, Mt 21³⁴, Lk 21⁸ ; χρόνος, Ac 7¹⁷ ; ἑορτή, Lk 22¹ ; παρουσία, Ja 5⁸ ; τέλος, 1 Pe 4⁷ ; ἐρήμωσις, Lk 21²⁰ ; ἀπολύτρωσις, Lk 21²⁸ ; ἤγγικεν ἡ βασιλεία (for similar expressions in Targ., v. Dalman, 106), Mt 3² 4¹⁷ 10⁷, Mk 1¹⁵, Lk 10⁹ (ἐφ᾽ ὑμᾶς) 10¹¹ (cf. προσ-εγγίζω, and v. Cremer, 224).†
ἔγγιστος, v.s. ἐγγύς.
ἐγ-γράφω, v.s. ἐνγράφω.
** ἔγγυος, -ου, ὁ, ἡ, [in LXX : Si 29¹⁵, ¹⁶, ii Mac 10²⁸ * ;] *a surety* : He 7²² (exx. from π., v. MM, *Exp.*, xi ; cf. Cremer, 222).†
ἐγγύς, adv., [in LXX chiefly for קרוב ;] *near ;* 1. of place : Jo 19²⁰, ⁴² ; as prep. c. gen. (M, *Pr.*, 99), Lk 19¹¹, Jo 3²³ 6¹⁹, ²³ 11¹⁸, ⁵⁴, Ac 1¹² ; c. dat., Ac 9³⁸ 27⁸ ; superl., ἔγγιστα, Mk 6³⁶, WH, mg.; metaph., οἱ ἐ., opp. to οἱ μακράν, Eph 2¹⁷ ; ἐ. γίνεσθαι, Eph 2¹³ ; ἐ. σου τὸ ῥῆμα, Ro 10⁸ (LXX). 2. Of time : Mt 24³² 26¹⁸, Mk 13²⁸, ²⁹, Lk 21³⁰, ³¹, Jo 2¹³ 6⁴ 7² 11⁵⁵, Re 1³ 22¹⁰ ; ὁ κύριος ἐ., Phl 4⁵ ; seq. ἐπὶ θύραις, Mt 24³³ ; compar., ἐγγύτερον (neut. of adj. -ος, used adverbially), Ro 13¹¹ (cf. R, txt.) ; as prep. c. gen., ἐ. κατάρας, He 6⁸ ; ἀφανισμοῦ, He 8¹³ (cf. Cremer, 223).†
ἐγγύτερος, v.s. ἐγγύς.
ἐγείρω, [in LXX for קום, etc. ;] trans. (imperat. ἔγειρε used intransitively, Mt 9⁵, Mk 2¹¹, al.) ; 1. *to awaken, arouse from sleep* : Mk 4³⁸, Ac 12⁷ ; metaph., of spiritual awakening, Ro 13¹¹ (pass.), Eph 5¹⁴ ; pass., *to be aroused, wake up* : Mt 25⁷, Mk 4²⁷ ; ἀπὸ τ. ὕπνου, Mt 1²⁴. 2. Freq. in NT, *to raise* from the dead : νεκρούς, Jo 5²¹, Ac 26⁸, ii Co 1⁹ ; ἐκ νεκρῶν, Jo 12¹, Ac 3¹⁵, Ro 8¹¹, al. ; pass., *rise from death* : Mt 11⁵, Lk 7²², Jo 2²², Ro 6⁹, al. ; ἀπὸ τ. νεκρῶν, Mt 14², al. 3. In late Gk., (*a*) *to raise*, from sitting, lying, sickness ; mid. and pass., *to rise* : Mt 9⁵, ⁷, Mk 1³¹ 9²⁷ 10⁴⁹, al. ; redundant, like Heb. קום, Mt 2¹⁵ 9¹⁹, Re 11¹ (v. Dalman, 23 f.) ; (*b*) *to raise up, cause to appear* : Ac 13²² (cf. Jg 2¹⁸) ; τέκνα, Mt 3⁹ ; pass., *to appear* : Mt 11¹¹, Mk 13²², al. 4. *to rouse, stir up ;* pass., *to rise against* : Mt 24⁷, Mk 13⁸. 5. Of buildings, *to raise* : τ. ναόν, Jo 2¹⁹, ²⁰ (cf. De 16²², Si 49¹³) ; (cf. δι-, ἐξ-, ἐπ-, συν-εγείρω, and v. Cremer, 224).
ἔγερσις, -εως, ἡ (< ἐγείρω, -ομαι), [in LXX : Jg 7¹⁹, Ps 138 (139)² (קום), i Es 5⁶² * ;] 1. *a rousing* (Plat.). 2. *a rising* (Ps, l.c.) : from death, Mt 27⁵³.†
ἐγκάθετος, v.s. ἐνκ-.
ἐγκα'νια, v.s. ἐνκ-.

ἐγκαινίζω, v.s. ἐνκ-.

ἐγκακέω, v.s. ἐνκ-.

ἐγκαλέω, -ῶ, [in LXX for אמר, etc.; c. dat., Za 1⁴ (קְרָא אֶל), Wi 12¹², Si 46¹⁹;] 1. *to call in*, *demand*. 2. *to bring a charge against*, *accuse*: c. dat. pers. (as in cl.), Ac 19³³ 23²⁸; seq. κατά, c. gen. pers., Ro 8³³. Pass., *to be accused*: c. gen. rei; στάσεως, Ac 19⁴⁰; ὧν (perh. by attraction = ἅ), Ac 26²; seq. περί, c. gen. rei, Ac 23²⁹ 26⁷ (Cremer, 743).†

SYN.: αἰτιάομαι (q.v.), διαβάλλω, ἐπικαλέω, κατηγορέω.

ἐγ-κατα-λείπω, [in LXX chiefly for עזב;] 1. *to leave behind*: ἡμῖν σπέρμα, Ro 9²⁹ (LXX). 2. *to abandon, desert, forsake*: c. acc. pers., Mt 27⁴⁶ (LXX), Mk 15³⁴ (ib.), Ac 2²⁷ (LXX) (WH, ἐνκ-), II Ti 4¹⁰, ¹⁶, He 13⁵ (LXX); τ. ἐπισυναγωγήν (cf. MM, *Exp*., xi), He 10²⁵. Pass., Ac 2³¹ (WH, ἐνκ-), II Co 4⁹.†

ἐγ-κατ-οικέω, v.s. ἐνκ-.

ἐγ-καυχάομαι, v.s. ἐνκ-.

ἐγ-κεντρίζω, v.s. ἐνκ-.

* ἔγκλημα, -τος, τό (< ἐγκαλέω), *an accusation, charge*: Ac 23²⁹ 25¹⁶ (Cremer, 743).†

*† ἐγ-κομβόομαι, -οῦμαι (< κόμβος, a knot, whence ἐγκόμβωμα, a garment tied on over others, used especially of a frock or apron worn by slaves), *to put on oneself*, as a garment, *gird on*: ἀλλήλοις τ. ταπεινοφροσύνην (as for service, RV, cf. Thayer, s.v., but cf. also *ICC*, in l.), I Pe 5⁵.†

ἐγ-κοπή, v.s. ἐνκ-.

ἐγ-κόπτω, v.s. ἐνκ-.

** ἐγκράτεια, -ας, ἡ (< ἐγκρατής), [in LXX: Si 18¹⁵, ³⁰, IV Mac 5³⁴*;] 1. prop., *mastery, control*. 2. (sc. ἑαυτοῦ) *self-control*: Ac 24²⁵, Ga 5²³, II Pe 1⁶ (v. *DB*, iv, 558ᵇ, 695ᵃ; Page on Ac, l.c.).†

ἐγκρατεύομαι, depon., [in LXX for אפק, Ge 43³¹, I Ki 13¹², Es 5¹⁰ א³*;] *to exercise self-control*: I Co 7⁹; c. acc., πάντα (v. Bl., 91), I Co 9²⁵.†

** ἐγκρατής, -ές (< κράτος), [in LXX: Wi 8²⁰, Si 6²⁷ 15¹ 26¹⁵ 27³⁰, al.;] 1. strong, powerful. 2. C. gen. rei, *master of*, hence, 3. (sc. ἑαυτοῦ), *self-controlled, exercising self-control*: Tit 1⁸.†

SYN.: σώφρων (v. reff. s. ἐγκράτεια).

ἐγ-κρίνω, v.s. ἐνκ-.

ἐγ-κρύπτω, [in LXX for טמן, etc.;] *to conceal in*: c. acc., seq. εἰς, Mt 13³³.†

ἔγκυος, v.s. ἐνκ-.

ἐγ-χρίω, [in LXX: Je 4³⁰ (קרע), To 2¹⁰ 6⁸ 11⁷*;] *to rub in*, *anoint*: mid., c. dupl. acc., Re 3¹⁸.†

ἐγώ, gen., etc., ἐμοῦ, ἐμοί, ἐμέ (enclitic μου, μοι, με), pl., ἡμεῖς, -ῶν, -ῖν, -ᾶς, pers. pron. *I*. (a) The nom. is usually emphatic, when expressed as subjc., as in Mt 3¹¹, Mk 1⁸, Lk 3¹⁶, al. But often there is no apparent emphasis, as Mt 10¹⁶, Jo 10¹⁷; ἰδοὺ ἐ. (= Heb. הִנְנִי, cf. I Ki 3⁸), Ac 9¹⁰; ἐ. (like Heb. אֲנִי), *I am*, Jo 1²³ (LXX), Ac 7³² (LXX).

(*b*) The enclitic forms (v. supr.) are used with nouns, adjectives, verbs, adverbs, where there is no emphasis: ἐν τ. πατρί μου, Jo 14²⁰; μου τ. λόγους, Mt 7²⁴; ὀπίσω μου, Mt 3¹¹; ἰσχυρότερός μου, ib.; λέγει μοι, Re 5⁵; also with the prep. πρός, as Mk 9¹⁹, al. The full forms (ἐμοῦ, etc.) are used with the other prepositions, as δι' ἐμοῦ, ἐν ἐμοί, εἰς ἐμέ, etc., also for emphasis, as Lk 10¹⁶, Jo 7²³, Mk 14⁷, al. (*c*) The gen. μου and ἡμῶν are often used for the poss. pronouns ἐμός, ἡμέτερος : τ. λαόν μου, Mt 2⁶; μου τῇ ἀπιστίᾳ, Mk 9²⁴. (*d*) τί ἐμοὶ καὶ σοί (= Heb. מַה־לִּי וָלָךְ, Jg 11¹², al.), i.e. *what have we in common*: Mt 8²⁹, Mk 1²⁴ 5⁷, Lk 8²⁸, Jo 2⁴; τί γάρ μοι, 1 Co 5². (*e*) The interchange of ἐγώ and ἡμεῖς, common in π., appears in Pauline Epp. (v. M, *Pr.*, 86 f., M, *Th.*, 131 f.). (*f*) κἀγώ (= καὶ ἐγώ), *and I, even I, I also*: Mt 2⁸, Lk 2⁴⁸, Jo 6⁵⁶, Ro 3⁷, 1 Co 7⁴⁰, al.; κἀγώ . . . καί, *both . . . and*, Jo 7²⁸.

ἐδαφίζω (< ἔδαφος) [in LXX chiefly for רשש pu.;] 1. *to beat level like a threshing floor* (Theophr.). 2. *to dash to the ground* (Field, *Notes*, 74): Lk 19⁴⁴ (cf. Ps 136 (137)⁹, Ho 14¹).†

ἔδαφος, -εος (-ους), τό, [in LXX for עָפָר, קַרְקַע, etc.;] *bottom, pavement, ground*: Ac 22⁷.†

** ἑδραῖος, -ον (< ἕδρα, a seat), [in Sm.: Ps 32 (33)¹⁴, al.;] 1. *sitting, seated.* 2. *steadfast, firm*; metaph., of moral fixity: 1 Co 7³⁷ 15⁵⁸, Col 1²³.†

*† ἑδραίωμα, -τος, τό (< ἑδραῖος), *a support, bulwark, stay* (Vg. *fermamentum*): 1 Ti 3¹⁵ (eccl.).†

Ἐζεκίας (Rec. Ἐζ-), -ου, ὁ (Heb. חִזְקִיָּה, *strength of Jehovah*), *Hezekiah*, King of Judah: Mt 1⁹, ¹⁰.†

*† ἐθελο-θρησκία (Rec. -εία), -ας, ἡ, *self-imposed worship*: Col 2²³ (eccl.; cf. *DB*, iv, 923ᵃ; Cremer, 733).†

ἐθέλω, v.s. θέλω.

** ἐθίζω (< ἔθος), [in LXX: Si 23⁹, ¹³, 11 Mac 14³⁰;] *to accustom*: pass. pf. ptcp., τὸ εἰθισμένον, *the established custom*, Lk 2²⁷.†

*†† ἐθνάρχης, -ου, ὁ (< ἔθνος, ἄρχω), [in LXX: 1 Mac 14⁴⁷ 15¹, ² *;] *an ethnarch*, a provincial governor (cf. 1 Mac, ll. c.; FlJ, *Ant.*, xiii, 6, 6; Dalman, 332): 11 Co 11³².†

*†† ἐθνικός, -ή, -όν (< ἔθνος), [in Al.: Le 21⁷ *;] 1. *national* (Polyb.). 2. *foreign* (gramm.); in NT, as subst., ὁ ἐ., *the Gentile* (the adj. "describes character rather than mere position"; cf. ἔθνος, and v. Cremer, 228): Mt 5⁴⁷ 6⁷ 18¹⁷, 111 Jo⁷.†

*† ἐθνικῶς, adv., *in Gentile fashion*: Ga 2¹⁴.†

ἔθνος, -ους, τό, [in LXX chiefly for גּוֹי, עַם;] 1. *a multitude, a company*, whether of beasts or men (Hom.). 2. *a nation, people*: Mt 21⁴³ 24⁷, Mk 13⁸, Lk 22²⁵, Ac 10³⁵, al.; in sing., of the Jewish people, Lk 7⁵ 23², Jo 11⁴⁸, ⁵⁰⁻⁵³ 18³⁵, Ac 10²² 24³, ¹⁰ 26⁴ 28¹⁹. 3. In pl., as in OT, τὰ ἔ. (like Heb. הַגּוֹיִם), *the nations*, as distinct from Israel,

9

Gentiles : Mt 4¹⁵ 6³², Ac 26¹⁷, Ro 3²⁰ 11¹¹ 15¹⁰, Ga 2⁸, al.; of Gentile Christians, Ro 11¹³ 15²⁷ 16⁴, Ga 2¹², ¹⁴, Eph 3¹.
SYN.: λαός (v. *DCG,* ii, 229; Cremer, 226).

** ἔθος, -εος (-ους), τό (< ἔθω), [in LXX : Wi 14¹⁶, Da TH Bel¹⁵, I Mac 10⁸⁹, II Mac 11²⁵ 13⁴, IV Mac 18⁵ אR *;] *habit, custom :* Lk 22³⁹, Jo 19⁴⁰, Ac 16²¹ 25¹⁶, He 10²⁵; in Lk 1⁹ 2⁴², Ac 6¹⁴ 15¹ 21²¹ 26³ 28¹⁷, almost in the narrower sense of law (Deiss., *BS,* 251 f.).†

ἔθω, pf. with pres. sense εἴωθα, [in LXX : Nu 24¹ (כְּפַעַם־בְּפַעַם), Da LXX Su¹³, Si 37¹⁴, IV Mac 1¹² *;] *to be accustomed, wont :* Mt 27¹⁵, Mk 10¹; ptcp., τὸ εἰωθός, *custom :* κατὰ τὸ εἰ. (Nu, l.c.), Lk 4¹⁶, Ac 17².†

εἰ, conjunctive particle, used in conditions and in indirect questions. I. Conditional, *if ;* 1. c. indic., expressing a general assumption; (*a*) pres. : seq. indic. pres., Mt 11¹⁴, Ro 8²⁵, al.; seq. imperat., Mk 4²³ 9²², Jo 15¹⁸, I Co 7⁹, al.; seq. fut. indic., Lk 16³¹, Ro 8¹¹, al.; seq. pf. or aor., with negation in apodosis, Mt 12²⁶, Ro 4¹⁴, al.; similarly, seq. impf., Lk 17⁶, Jo 8³⁹; seq. quæst., Mt 6²³, Jo 5⁴⁷ 7²³ 8⁴⁶, I Pe 2²⁰; (*b*) fut. : Mt 26³³, I Pe 2²⁰; (*c*) pf. : Jo 11¹², Ro 6⁵, al.; (*d*) aor. : Lk 16¹¹ 19⁸, Jo 13³², 18²³, Re 20¹⁵, al.   2. Where the assumption is certain = ἐπεί : Mt 12²⁸, Jo 7⁴, Ro 5¹⁷, al.   3. Of an unfulfilled condition, c. indic. impf., aor. or plpf., seq. ἄν, c. imp. or aor. (v.s. ἄν, I, i).   4. C. indic., after verbs denoting wonder, etc., sometimes, but not always, coupled with an element of doubt : Mk 15⁴⁴, I Jo 3¹³, al.   5. C. indic., as in LXX (Nu 14³⁰, I Ki 14⁴⁵, al. = Heb. אִם), in oaths, with the formula of imprecation understood in a suppressed apodosis (WM, 627; Burton, § 272; M, *Gr.,* II, pp. 268 ff.) : Mk 8¹², He 3¹¹ (LXX) 4³ (LXX) (v. II, 2, infr.).   6. Rarely (cl.) c. optat., to express a merely possible condition : Ac 24¹⁹ 27³⁹, I Co 14¹⁰ 15³⁷, I Pe 3¹⁴, ¹⁷.

II. Interrogative, *if, whether.*   1. As in cl., in indir. questions after verbs of seeing, asking, knowing, saying, etc : c. indic. pres., Mt 26⁶³, Mk 15³⁶, Ac 19², II Co 13⁵, al.; fut., Mk 3², Ac 8²², al.; aor., Mk 15⁴⁴, I Co 1¹⁶, al.; c. subjc. aor. (M, *Pr.,* 194), Phl 3¹².   2. As in LXX (= Heb. אִם and interrog. הֲ, Ge 17¹⁷, al.; v. WM, 639 f.; Viteau, i, 22), in direct questions : Mk 8²³ (Tr., WH, txt.), Lk 13²³, 22⁴⁹, Ac 19², al.   (In this usage εἰ prob. = ἦ (vernac. εἴ). So also in I, 5, supr., cf. III, 7, infr.)

III. With other particles.   1. εἰ ἄρα, εἴγε, εἰ δὲ μήγε, v.s. ἄρα, γε.   2. εἰ δὲ καί, *but if also :* Lk 11¹⁸; *but even if,* I Co 4⁷, II Co 4³ 11⁶.   3. εἰ δὲ μή, *but if not, but if otherwise :* Mk 2²¹, ²², Jo 14², Re 2⁵, al.   4. εἰ καί, *if even, if also, although :* Mk 14²⁹, Lk 11⁸, I Co 7²¹, II Co 4¹⁶, Phl 2¹⁷, al.   5. καὶ εἰ, *even if,* v.s. καί.   6. εἰ μή, *if not, unless, except, but only :* Mt 24²², Mk 2²⁶ 6⁵, Jo 9³³, I Co 7¹⁷ (*only*), Ga 1¹⁹ (cf. ἐὰν μή, 2¹⁶; v. Hort., *Ja.,* xvi); ἐκτὸς εἰ μή, pleonastic (Bl., § 65, 6), I Co 14⁵ 15², I Ti 5¹⁹.   7. εἰ μήν = cl. ἦ μήν (M, *Pr.,* 46), in oaths, *surely* (Ez 33²⁷, al.) : He 6¹⁴.   8. εἰ πως, *if haply :* Ac 27¹², Ro 1¹⁰.   9. εἴτε . . . εἴτε, *whether . . . or :* Ro 12⁶⁻⁸, I Co 3²² 13⁸, al.   10. εἴπερ, emphatic, *if indeed :* Ro 3³⁰, al.

εἰδέα (Rec. ἰδ-, as in cl.; v. Tdf., *Pr.,* 81), -ας, ἡ (< εἶδον), [in

LXX (v.l. ἰδ-): Ge 5³ (דְּמוּת), Da TH 1¹³, ¹⁵ (מַרְאָה), Ep. Je ⁶³, II Mac 3¹⁶ *;] *form, appearance, look :* Mt 28³.†
εἶδον, v.s. ὁράω.

εἶδος, -ους, τό, [in LXX for תֹּאַר, מַרְאֶה, etc. ;] 1. *that which is seen, appearance, external form :* Lk 3²² 9²⁹, Jo 5³⁷, II Co 5⁷ (*ICC* in l.). 2. *form, sort, kind :* I Th 5²².†

†εἰδώλιον (Rec. -εῖον), -ου, τό (< εἴδωλον), [in LXX : Da LXX 1² (בֵּית אוֹצַר אֱלֹהִים), Bel ⁹, I Es 2¹⁰, I Mac 1⁴⁷ 10⁸³ *;] *an idol's temple :* I Co 8¹⁰ (cf. Ἀσταρτεῖον, I Ki 31¹⁰ ; v. *ICC*, in I Co, l.c.).†

**†εἰδωλόθυτος, -ον (< εἴδωλον, θύω), [in LXX : IV Mac 5² *;] *sacrificed to idols :* τό, τὰ εἰ., Ac 15²⁹ 21²⁵, I Co 8¹, ⁴, ⁷, ¹⁰ 10¹⁹, Re 2¹⁴, ²⁰.†

*†εἰδωλο-λατρία (-εία, Rec.), -ας, ἡ (< εἴδωλον, λατρεία), *idolatry :* I Co 10¹⁴, Ga 5²⁰, Col 3⁵ ; pl. (Bl., § 32, 6), I Pe 4³ (Cremer, 390).†

*†εἰδωλολάτρης, -ου, ὁ (< εἴδωλον + λάτρις, *a hireling*), *an idolator :* I Co 5¹⁰, ¹¹ 6⁹ 10⁷, Eph 5⁵, Re 21⁸ 22¹⁵ (Cremer, 709).†

εἴδωλον, -ου, τό (< εἶδος), [in LXX for אֱלוֹהַּ, גִּלּוּלִים, etc. ;] 1. in cl. (*a*) *a phantom, image, likeness ;* (*b*) *an image in the mind, an idea, fancy.* 2. In LXX and NT, (*a*) *an image of a god, an idol* (cf. Polyb., xxxi, 3, 13) : Ac 7⁴¹, I Co 12², Re 9²⁰ ; (*b*) *the false god* or *idol* worshipped in an image (*ICC*, on I Th, l.c.) : Ac 15²⁰, Ro 2²², I Co 8⁴, ⁷ 10¹⁹, II Co 6¹⁶, I Th 1⁹, I Jo 5²¹.†

εἰκῇ (-ῆ, Rec., as in cl.), adv., [in LXX : Pr 28²⁵ (εἰκῇ)* ;] 1. *without cause* or *reason :* Mt 5²² (R, mg.), Col 2¹⁸ (*ICC*). 2. *vainly, fruitlessly, to no purpose :* Ro 13⁴, I Co 15², Ga 3⁴ 4¹¹, Col 2¹⁸ ; on this form, v. Moulton, *Gr.*, II, i, p. 84.†

εἴκοσι (never -ιν in WH, cf. Bl., § 5, 3, and note), indecl., οἱ, αἱ, τά, *twenty :* Lk 14³¹, Jo 6¹⁹, Ac 1¹⁵ 27²⁸, I Co 10⁸, Re 4⁴, ¹⁰ 5⁸ 11¹⁶ 19⁴.†

εἴκω, [in LXX : II Ki 12⁷ (עָנָה), Wi 18²⁵, IV Mac 1⁶ *;] *to yield :* Ga 2⁵ (cf. ὑπ-είκω).†

εἴκω (obsolete pres.), v.s. ἔοικα.

εἰκών, -όνος, ἡ (cf. ἔοικα), [in LXX chiefly for צֶלֶם ;] *an image, likeness :* Mt 22²⁰, Mk 12¹⁶, Lk 20²⁴, Ro 1²³, I Co 15⁴⁹, Re 13¹⁴, ¹⁵ 14⁹, ¹¹ 15² 16² 19²⁰ 20⁴ ; opp. to σκιά, He 10¹ ; of man, εἰ. θεοῦ, I Co 11⁷ ; of the regenerate, εἰ. τ. θεοῦ, Col 3¹⁰ (v. Lft., in l.) ; εἰ. τ. υἱοῦ τ. θεοῦ, Ro 8²⁹, II Co 3¹⁸ ; of Christ, εἰ. τ. θεοῦ, II Co 4⁴, Col 1¹⁵.†

SYN. : ὁμοίωμα, denoting resemblance, which may however be merely accidental. εἰ. is a *derived* likeness and like the head on a coin or the parental likeness in a child, implies an archetype. Cf. also εἶδος, *appearance*, not necessarily based on reality ; σκιά, a shadowed resemblance ; χαρακτήρ, the *impress* of a stamp ; μόρφη (q.v.), the *form* as indicative of the inner being.

** εἰλικρινής, -ές, [in LXX : Wi 7²⁵ אB *;] *unalloyed, pure* (Lat. *sincerus ;* v. *DCG*, ii, 635ᵃ) : (*a*) of unmixed substances ; (*b*) of abstract ideas ; (*c*) of ethical purity : Phl 1¹⁰, II Pe 3¹.†

SYN. : ἁγνός (q.v.), καθαρός, cf. Tr., *Syn.*, § lxxxv ; *DB*, iv, 176ᵃ ; Cremer, 378 ; Westc. on I Jo 3³.

εἰλικρινία (Rec., cl., -κρινεία), -ας, ἡ (< εἰλικρινής), [in LXX : Wi 7²⁵ A *;] *sincerity, purity :* I Co 5⁸, II Co 1¹² 2¹⁷.†

εἰλίσσω, v.s. ἑλίσσω.

εἰμί, with various uses and significations, like the English verb *to be.* I. As substantive verb. 1. Of persons and things, *to be, exist :* Ac 17²⁸, Jo 1¹ 8⁵⁸ 17⁵, al; ὁ ὢν καὶ ὁ ἦν (for past ptcp.), Re 1⁴, ⁸ 4⁸ 11¹⁷ 16⁵ (v. Swete, *Ap.*, 5; M, *Pr.*, 228); τὰ (μὴ) ὄντα, Ro 4¹⁷, I Co 1²⁸. 2. Of times, events, etc., *to be, happen, take place :* Mt 24³, Mk 14² 15⁴², Lk 21²³, Jo 4⁶, ²³ 5¹⁰, al. 3. *to be present, be* in a place, *have come :* Mt 2¹³, ¹⁵, Mk 1⁴⁵ 5²¹ 15⁴⁰, Lk 1⁸⁰ 5²⁹, Jo 7³⁰, al.; seq. εἰς, Mk 2¹; seq. ἐκ (ἐξ), Mt 1²⁰ 21²⁵, Mk 11³⁰, Jo 3³¹, al. 4. Impers., ἔστι, ἦν, etc.; (*a*) *there is* (Fr. *il y a*), *was*, etc.: Mt 16²⁸, Lk 16¹⁹, Jo 3¹ 5², Ro 3¹⁰, al.; c. dat. (of the possessor; Bl., § 37, 3), Mt 16²², Lk 1⁷, Jo 18¹⁰, Ro 9², al.; ἔστιν ὅς, ὅστις (chiefly in pl.), Mt 16²⁸ 19², Mk 9¹, al.; (*b*) c. inf., = ἔξεστιν (q.v.), *it is possible :* He 9⁵, I Co 11²⁰, RV (but v. *ICC*, in l.). II. As copula uniting subject and predicate. 1. Expressing simply identity or equivalence : Mt 5¹³ 14¹⁵, Lk 1¹⁸, ¹⁹, Jo 1¹ 4¹⁹, Re 3⁹, al. mult. 2. Explicative, as in parable, figure, type, etc.: Mt 13¹⁹ *ff.*, I Co 9² 10⁴ 11²⁵, Ga 4²⁴, Re 17¹⁵, al.; τοῦτ᾽ ἔστιν, Mt 27⁴⁶, Mk 7², Ro 7¹⁸, al.; ὅ ἐστιν, Mk 3¹⁷, Col 1²⁴, He 7², al.; akin to this is the sacramental usage : Mt 26²⁶, ²⁸, Mk 14²², ²⁴, Lk 22¹⁹, I Co 11²⁴ (v. *ICC* on Mk, I Co, ll. c.; *DB*, iii, 148 f.). 3. C. gen.: qual., etc., Mk 5⁴², Lk 3²³, I Co 14³³, He 12¹¹, al.; part., I Ti 1²⁰, II Ti 1¹⁵; poss., Mt 5³, ¹⁰, Mk 12⁷, Lk 4⁷; of service or partisanship, Ro 8⁹, I Co 1¹², II Co 10⁷, II Ti 2¹⁹. 4. C. dat. (Bl., § 37, 3): Ac 1⁸ 9¹⁵, Ro 4¹², I Co 1¹⁸ 2¹⁴, Re 21⁷, al. 5. C. ptcp., as a periphrasis for the simple verb (Bl., § 62, 1, 2; M, *Pr.*, 225 ff.); (*a*) c. ptcp. pf. (cl.): Mt 10³⁰, Lk 9³², Jo 3²⁴, Ac 21³³, I Co 15¹⁹, al; (*b*) c. ptcp. pr. (esp. in impf., as in Heb. and Aram.; Dalman, *Words*, 35 f.), Mt 7²⁹, Mk 1²², Lk 4³¹ 14¹, Ac 1¹⁰, al. mult., id. for imper. (M, *Pr.*, 180 f., 182 f.), with ellipsis of εἰμί, Ro 12⁹, ¹⁰, He 13⁵, al.; (*c*) c. ptcp. aor. (cl.), Lk 23⁹. 6. Seq. εἰς (cf. Heb. הָיָה לְ), a vernac. usage (M, *Pr.*, 71): Mt 19⁵, Mk 10⁸, He 8¹⁰, al. 7. C. adv.: Mt 19²⁰, Mk 4²⁶, Lk 18¹¹, al. 8. Ellipses; (*a*) of the copula (Bl., § 30, 3): Mt 8²⁹ 24³², Jo 21²², ²³, He 6⁴, al.; (*b*) of the predicate: ἐγώ εἰμι, Mt 14²⁷, Mk 6⁵⁰, al.; absol. (cf. De 32³⁹: אֲנִי הוּא), Mk 13⁶, Jo 4²⁶, al. (cf. ἀπ-, ἐν-, πάρ-, συμ-πάρ-, σύν-ειμι).

εἴνεκεν, v.s. ἕνεκα.

εἴ-περ, v.s. εἰ.

εἶπον, 2 aor. of obsol. pres. ἔπω (cf. Veitch), used as aor. of λέγω, q.v.

εἴ-πως, v.s. εἰ.

εἰρηνεύω (< εἰρήνη), [in LXX chiefly for שׁלם, שׁקט ;] 1. *to bring to peace, reconcile* (so I Mac 6⁶⁰). 2. *to keep peace, be at peace :* Mk 9⁵⁰, Ro 12¹⁸, II Co 13¹¹, I Th 5¹³ (cf. Si 28⁹; Cremer, 246).†

εἰρήνη, -ης, ἡ, [in LXX chiefly for שׁלום ;] *peace ;* 1. of public peace, freedom from war: Lk 14³², Ac 12²⁰ 24²; of the church, Ac

9³¹. 2. Of peace between persons, concord, agreement: Mt 10³⁴, Lk 12⁵¹, Ro 14¹⁷, ɪ Co 7¹⁵, Ga 5²², Ja 3¹⁸; ζητεῖν εἰ., ɪ Pe 3¹¹; διώκειν, ɪɪ Ti 2²²; ib. seq. μετὰ πάντων, He 12¹⁴; by meton., of him who brings peace, Eph 2¹⁴. 3. As in LXX (= Heb. שָׁלוֹם, Aram. שְׁלָם), of a state of security and safety: Jo 16³³, Ro 2¹⁰, ɪ Th 5³; whence the formulæ, ὕπαγε (πορεύου) εἰς εἰ., Mk 5³⁴, Lk 7⁵⁰ (cf. ɪ Ki 1¹⁷, al.; לְכִי לְשָׁלוֹם); εἰ. ὑμῖν (בָּכֶם שָׁלוֹם), Jo 20¹⁹, ²¹, ²⁶; ἀπολύειν ἐν εἰ., Lk 2²⁹, cf. ɪ Co 16¹¹; ἡ εἰ. ὑμῶν, Mt 10¹³ Lk 10⁶; υἱὸς εἰρήνης, ib. 4. Of spiritual peace, the peace of Christ's kingdom (DCG, ii, 330 f.): Lk 1⁷⁹ 2¹⁴, Jo 16³³, Ro 2¹⁰ 5¹ 8⁶, al.; ὁ κύριος τῆς εἰ., ɪɪ Th 3¹⁶; ὁ θεὸς τῆς εἰ., Ro 15³³ 16²⁰, ɪɪ Co 13¹¹, al.; in epistolary salutations, Ro 1⁷, ɪ Co 1³, Ga 1³, ɪ Th 1¹, ɪ Pe 1², ɪɪ Jo ³, Re 1⁴, al. (v. Cremer, 244); v. ICC on Ga, pp. 424 ff.

εἰρηνικός, -ή, -όν (< εἰρήνη), [in LXX for שָׁלוֹם and cognates;] peaceful: He 12¹¹, Ja 3¹⁷.†

† **εἰρηνο-ποιέω, -ῶ,** [in LXX: Pr 10¹⁰ *;] to make peace: Col 1²⁰.†

* **εἰρηνοποιός, -όν,** peace-making, a peacemaker: Mt 5⁹.†

εἴρω (fut. ἐρῶ), v.s. λέγω, p. 496.

εἰς, prep. c. acc., expressing entrance, direction, limit, into, unto, to, upon, towards, for, among (Lat. in, c. acc.). I. Of place. 1. After verbs of motion; (a) of entrance into: Mt 8²³ 9⁷, Mk 1⁴⁵, Lk 2¹⁵ 8³¹, al.; (b) of approach, to or towards: Mk 11¹, Lk 6⁸ 19²⁸, Jo 11³¹ 21⁶, al.; (c) before pl. and collective nouns, among: Mk 4⁷ 8¹⁹, ²⁰, Lk 11⁴⁹, Jo 21²³, al; (d) of a limit reached, unto, on, upon: Mt 8¹⁸ 21¹, Mk 11¹ 13¹⁶, Lk 14¹⁰, Jo 6³ 11³², al.; c. acc. pers. (as in Ep. and Ion.), Ac 23¹⁵, Ro 5¹² 16¹⁹, ɪɪ Co 10¹⁴; (e) elliptical: ἐπιστολαὶ εἰς Δαμασκόν, Ac 9²; ἡ διακονία μου ἡ εἰς Ἰ., Ro 15³¹; metaph., of entrance into a certain state or condition, or of approach or direction towards some end (Thayer, B, i, 1; ii, 1), εἰς τ. ὄνομα, M, Pr., 200. 2. Of direction; (a) after verbs of seeing: Mt 6²⁶, Mk 6⁴¹, Lk 9¹⁶, ⁶², Jo 13²², al.; metaph., of the mind, He 11²⁶ 12², al.; (b) after verbs of speaking: Mk 13¹⁰ 14⁹, ɪ Th 2⁹, al. 3. After verbs of rest; (a) in "pregnant" construction, implying previous motion (cl.; v. WM, 516; Bl., § 39, 3; M, Pr., 234 f.): Mt 2²³ 4¹³, ɪɪ Th 2⁴, ɪɪ Ti 1¹¹, He 11⁹, al.; (b) by an assimilation general in late Gk (v. Bl., M, Pr., ll. c.) = ἐν: Lk 1⁴⁴ 4²³, Ac 20¹⁶ 21¹⁷, Jo 1¹⁸ (but v. Westc., in l.), al. II. Of time, for, unto; 1. accentuating the duration expressed by the acc.: εἰς τ. αἰῶνα, Mt 21¹⁹; εἰς γενεὰς καὶ γ., Lk 1⁵⁰; εἰς τ. διηνεκές, He 7³, al. 2. Of a point or limit of time, unto, up to, until: Mt 6³⁴, Ac 4³, 25²¹, Phl 1¹⁰ 2¹⁶, ɪ Th 4¹⁵, ɪɪ Ti 1¹²; of entrance into a future period, εἰς τὸ μέλλον (v.s. μέλλω), next (year), Lk 13⁹ (but v. ICC, in l.); εἰς τ. μεταξὺ σάββατον, on the next Sabbath, Ac 13⁴²; εἰς τὸ πάλιν (v.s. πάλιν), ɪɪ Co 13². III. Of result, after verbs of changing, joining, dividing, etc.: στρέφειν εἰς, Re 11⁶; μετασ-, Ac 2²⁰, Ja 4⁹; μεταλλάσσειν, Ro 1²⁶; σχίζειν εἰς δύο, Mt 27⁵¹, al.; predicatively with εἶναι, Ac 8²³. IV. Of relation, to, towards, for, in regard to (so in cl., but more freq. in late Gk., εἰς encroaching on the simple dat., which it has wholly displaced in MGr.; Jannaris, *Gr.*, § 1541; Robertson, *Gr.*, 594; Deiss., *BS*, 117 f.): Lk 7³⁰, Ro 4²⁰ 15², ²⁶, ɪ Co 16¹, Eph 3¹⁶, al.; ἀγάπη εἰς, Ro 5⁸, al.; χρηστός, Eph 4³²; φρονεῖν εἰς, Ro 12¹⁶; θαρρεῖν, ɪɪ Co 10¹. V. Of the end or object: εὔθετος εἰς, Lk 14³⁴; σόφος, Ro 16¹⁹; ἰσχύειν, Mt 5¹³; εἰς τοῦτο, Mk 1³⁸, al.; ἀφορίζειν εἰς, Ro 1¹; indicating purpose, εἰς φόβον, Ro 8¹⁵; εἰς ἔνδειξιν, Ro 3²⁵; εἰς τό, c. inf. (= ἵνα or ὥστε; Bl., § 71, 5; M, *Pr.*, 218 ff.): Mt 20¹⁹, Ro 1¹¹, ɪ Co 9¹⁸, al. VI. Adverbial phrases: εἰς τέλος, εἰς τὸ πάλιν, etc. (v.s. τέλος, πάλιν, etc.). VII. εἰς c. acc. in place of predicative nom. or acc. (v. M, *Gr.*, ɪɪ, pp. 462 f.): with γίνεσθαι, Mt 21⁴² (LXX), Lk 13¹⁹, al.; with εἶναι, Mt 19⁵ (LXX), al.

εἷς, μία, ἕν, gen. ἑνός, μιᾶς, ἑνός, cardinal numeral, *one*; 1. *one*, as opp. to many: Mt 25¹⁵, Ro 5¹², ɪ Co 10⁸, al.; as subst., Ro 5¹⁵, Eph 2¹⁴; id. c. gen. partit., Mt 5¹⁹, al.; seq. ἐκ (ἐξ), Mk 14¹⁸, Jo 6⁸, al.; metaph., of union and concord, Jo 10³⁰ 17¹¹, Ro 12⁴, ⁵, Phl 1²⁷; ἀπὸ μιᾶς (Bl., § 44, 1), Lk 14¹⁸; c. neg., εἷς . . . οὐ (μή), more emphatic than οὐδείς, *no one, none* (cl.), Mt 5¹⁸ 10²⁹, Lk 11⁴⁶ 12⁶. 2. Emphatically, to the exclusion of others; (*a*) *a single* (*one*): Mt 21²⁴, Mk 8¹⁴; absol., ɪ Co 9²⁴, al.; οὐδὲ εἷς, Mt 27¹⁴, Jo 1³, Ro 3¹⁰, al.; (*b*) *one, alone*: Mk 2⁷ 10¹⁸, Lk 18¹⁹; (*c*) *one and the same*: Ro 3³⁰, ɪ Co 3⁸ 11⁵ 12¹¹, ɪ Jo 5⁸. 3. In late Gk., with weakened force, = τις or indef. art. (cf. Heb. אֶחָד, Ge 22¹³, al.; v. Bl., § 45, 2; M, *Pr.*, 96 f.): Mt 8¹⁹, 19⁶, Re 8¹³, al.; εἷς τις (Bl., l.c.), Lk 22⁵⁰, Jo 11⁴⁹. 4. Distributively: εἷς ἕκαστος (cl.), Lk 4⁴⁰, Ac 2⁶, al.; εἷς . . . καὶ εἷς (cl., εἷς μὲν . . . εἷς δέ), Mt 17⁴, Mk 9⁵, Jo 20¹², al. (cf. LXX and use of Heb. אֶחָד, Ex 17¹², al.); ὁ εἷς . . . ὁ ἕτερος (ἄλλος) = cl. ὁ μὲν (ἕτερος) . . . ὁ δέ (ἕτερος), Mt 6²⁴, Lk 7⁴¹, Re 17¹⁰; καθ᾽ εἷς, εἷς κ. εἷς (in which καθ᾽ is adverbial, or the expression formed from the analogy of ἕν καθ᾽ ἕν; M, *Pr.*, 105), *one by one, severally*: Mk 14¹⁹, Ro 12⁵, al.; εἷς τὸν ἕνα = ἀλλήλους (Bl., § 45, 2; M, *Pr.*, 246), ɪ Th 5¹¹. 5. As ordinal = πρῶτος (like Heb. אֶחָד; Bl., § 45, 1; M, *Pr.*, 95 f.), *first*: Mt 28¹, Mk 16², al.

εἰσ-άγω, [in LXX chiefly for בּוֹא hi.;] *to bring in*: c. acc., Lk 2²⁷, Jo 18¹⁶, Ac 7⁴⁵; seq. εἰς, Lk 22⁵⁴, Ac 9⁸ 21²⁸, ²⁹, ³⁷ 22²⁴, He 1⁶; ὧδε, Lk 14²¹.†

εἰσ-ακούω, [in LXX chiefly for שָׁמַע, also for עָנָה, etc.;] *to listen to*, in two senses; (*a*) *to obey*: ɪ Co 14²¹ (cf. De 1⁴³, Si 3⁶); (*b*) *to listen, assent to*; pass., *to be heard*: of persons praying, Mt 6⁷, He 5⁷; of the prayer offered, Lk 1¹³, Ac 10³¹ (cf. Ps 4², Si 31 (34)²⁹ (²⁶); v. Cremer, 624).†

εἰσ-δέχομαι, [in LXX for קָבַץ;] *to admit, receive*: ɪɪ Co 6¹⁷ (LXX) (Cremer, 687).†

εἴσ-ειμι, [in LXX for בּוֹא;] *to go in, enter*: seq. εἰς, Ac 3³ 21²⁶, He 9⁶; πρὸς Ἰάκωβον, Ac 21¹⁸.†

εἰσ-έρχομαι, [in LXX chiefly for בּוֹא;] *to go in or into, enter*: Mt 9²⁵, Lk 7⁴⁵, al.; seq. εἰς, Mt 10¹², Mk 2¹, al.; seq. διά (πύλης, θύρας, etc.), Mt 7¹³, Jo 10¹, al.; ὑπὸ τ. στέγην, Mt 8⁸; c. adv.: ὅπου, Mk 14¹⁴, He 6²⁰; ὧδε, Mt 22¹², ἔσω, Mt 26⁵⁸; seq. πρός, c. acc. pers., Mk 15⁴³, Lk 1²⁸, Ac 10³ 11³ 16⁴⁰ 17² 28⁸, Re 3²⁰; of demons taking possession, Mk 9²⁵, Lk 8³⁰

22³, Jo 13²⁷; of food, Mt 15¹¹, Ac 11⁸. Metaph., of thoughts, Lk 9⁴⁶; εἰς κόπον, Jo 4³⁸; εἰς πειρασμόν, Mt 26⁴¹, Lk 22⁴⁰,⁴⁶; of hope as an anchor, He 6¹⁹; βοαί, Ja 5⁴; πνεῦμα ζωῆς, Re 11¹¹; εἰς τ. κόσμον (cf. Wi 2²⁴ 14¹⁴, Jo 18³⁷), Ro 5¹², He 10⁵; in counterparts of Jewish Aram. phrases relating to the theocracy (cf. Dalman, *Words*, 116 ff.): εἰς τ. γάμους, Mt 25¹⁰; εἰς τ. χάραν τ. κυρίου, Mt 25²¹,²³; εἰς τ. ζωήν, Mt 18⁸,⁹ 19¹⁷, Mk 9⁴³,⁴⁵; εἰς τ. βασιλ. τ. οὐρανῶν (τ. θεοῦ), Mt 5²⁰ 7²¹, al. (v.s. βασιλεία); εἰς τ. κατάπαυσιν, He 3¹¹,¹⁸ 4¹ ᶠᶠ·; εἰς τ. δόξαν, Lk 24²⁶; εἰσ. καὶ ἐξέρχ., *to go in and out* (like Heb. וְצֵאת בֹּא, De 28⁶, etc.), of familiar intercourse, Ac 1²¹; fig., of moral freedom, Jo 10⁹ (cf. ἐπ-, παρ-, συν-εισέρχομαι).

* εἰσ-καλέω, -ῶ, to call in: mid., c. acc. pers., Ac 10²³.†

εἴσ-οδος, -ου, ἡ (< ὁδός), [in LXX chiefly for בֹּא;] 1. *a means of entering, place of entrance:* He 10¹⁹, II Pe 1¹¹ (cf. Westc., *He.*, l.c.; MM, *Exp.*, xii; but v. infr.). 2. *a going in, entrance:* Ac 13²⁴; c. gen. loc., He 10¹⁹ (Thayer, s.v.; but v. supr.); seq. εἰς, II Pe 1¹¹ (Mayor, in l.; Thayer; but v. supr.); πρός, I Th 1⁹ 2¹.†

εἰσ-πηδάω, -ῶ, [in LXX: Am 5¹⁹ (בֹּא), Da TH Su ²⁶ *;] *to spring in, rush in:* Ac 14¹⁴ (Rec.), 16²⁹ (for exx. from π., v. MM, *Exp.*, xii).†

εἰσ-πορεύομαι, [in LXX chiefly for בֹּא;] *to go into, enter:* Lk 8¹⁶ 11³³ 19³⁰; seq. εἰς, Mk 1²¹ 6⁵⁶ 11², Lk 22¹⁰, Ac 3²; πρός, c. acc. pers., Ac 28³⁰; ὅπου, Mk 5⁴⁰; κατὰ τ. οἴκους, *house after house*, Ac 8³; of things (food), Mt 15¹⁷, Mk 7¹⁵,¹⁸,¹⁹. Metaph. (cf. εἰσέρχομαι, 2), Mk 4¹⁹, Lk 18²⁴; εἰσ. καὶ ἐκπορ., *to associate with*, seq. μετά (cf. εἰσέρχομαι), Ac 9²⁸.†

*** εἰσ-τρέχω, [in LXX: II Mac 5²⁶ *;] *to run in:* Ac 12¹⁴.†

εἰσ-φέρω, [in LXX chiefly for בֹּא hi.;] *to bring in, into:* c. acc. pers., Lk 5¹⁸,¹⁹; seq. εἰς, Mt 6¹³, Lk 11⁴; ἐπί, Lk 12¹¹; c. acc. rei, seq. εἰς, I Ti 6⁷; pass., He 13¹¹.†

εἶτα, adv., denoting sequence; 1. of time; *then, next:* Mk 8²⁵, Lk 8¹², Jo 13⁵ 19²⁷ 20²⁷, I Ti 3¹⁰, Ja 1¹⁵; seq. gen. abs., Mk 4¹⁷; in enumerations, I Co 15⁵,⁷,²⁴, I Ti 2¹³. 2. In argument; (a) *therefore, then*; (b) *furthermore:* He 12⁹ (cf. εἶτεν).†

εἶτε, v.s. εἰ.

** εἶτεν, Ion. and Hellenistic for εἶτα (q.v.), *then:* Mk 4²⁸.†

εἴωθα, v.s. ἔθω.

ἐκ (ἐξ), prep. c. gen., *from out of, from* (see Addendum, p. 492).

ἕκαστος, -η, -ον, [in LXX chiefly for אִישׁ;] *each, every* (Lat. *quisque*); (a) with a noun: Lk 6⁴⁴, Jo 19²³; seq. κατά, He 3¹³, Re 22²; εἰς ἕ., Eph 4¹⁶; (b) without a noun: Ac 4³⁵, Ro 2⁶, al.; (c) partit. gen., Ro 14¹², I Co 1¹², al.; in sing. with pl. verb, Lk 2³, Ac 11²⁹, al.; in apposition with pl. noun or pron., Lk 2³, Jo 16³², Ac 2⁸ 3²⁶, al.; εἰς ἕ. (Lat. *unusquisque*), Ac 2⁶ 21²⁶, Col 4⁶, al.; ἕ. τ. ἀδελφῷ (= Heb. אִישׁ לְאָחִיו, Ge 26³¹), Mt 18³⁵ (cf. He 8¹¹); ἕ. μετὰ τοῦ πλησίον (= אִישׁ אֶל־רֵעֵהוּ, Jg 6²⁹, al.), Eph 4²⁵.

** ἑκάστοτε, adv., *each time, always:* II Pe 1¹⁵.†

ἑκατόν, οἱ, αἱ, τά, indecl., a hundred: Mt 13⁸, ²³, Lk 15⁴, al.; κατὰ ἑ., Mk 6⁴⁰ ; εἰς, ἐν ἑ., Mk 4⁸, ²⁰.

ἑκατονταετής (Rec. -έτης), -ές (< ἑκατόν, ἔτης), [in LXX for בֶּן מְאָה שָׁנָה, Ge 17¹⁷ * ;] a hundred years old : Ro 4¹⁹.†

ἑκατονταπλασίων, -ον, [in LXX : ΙΙ Ki 14³ (מְאָה פְעָמִים) * ;] a hundred-fold : Mt 19²⁹ (R, mg.), Mk 10³⁰, Lk 8⁸.†

ἑκατοντάρχης (-άρχος, Mt 8⁵, ⁸ 27⁵⁴, Lk 7², Ac 22²⁵ 28¹⁶; cf. M, Pr., 48); -ου (< ἑκατόν, ἄρχω,), [in LXX for שַׂר מֵאוֹת ;] a centurion : Mt 8¹³, Lk 7⁶ 23⁴⁷, Ac 10¹, ²² 21³² 22²⁶ 23¹⁷, ²³ 24²³ 27¹, ⁶, ¹¹, ³¹, ⁴³ (cf. κεντυρίων).†

ἐκ-βαίνω, [in LXX for עלה ;] to go out : He 11¹⁵.†

ἐκ-βάλλω, [in LXX chiefly for גרשׁ pi., also for שׁלך hi., יצא hi., ירשׁ hi., etc. ;] 1. to drive, cast or send out, to expel : c. acc. rei, mid. (σῖτον), seq. εἰς, Ac 27³⁸ ; pass., Mt 15¹⁷ ; c. acc. pers., Mt 21¹², Mk 11¹⁵, al.; δαιμόνια, Mt 7²², Mk 1³⁴, al. ; id. seq. ἐκ, Mk 7²⁶ ; παρά, Mk 16[9] ; ἐν, Mk 3²² ; (ἐν) τ. ὀνόματι, Mt 7²², Mk 9³⁸ ; λόγῳ, Mt 8¹⁶ ; seq. ἔξω, Jo 6³⁷ ; id. c. gen., Mk 12⁸, al. ; of expulsion from home, Ga 4³⁰ ; from the Church, ΙΙΙ Jo ¹⁰.   2. In LXX and NT (like Heb. הוֹצִיא and Aram. הַנְפֵּק), to command or cause to depart : Mt 9³⁸, Mk 1¹² (v. Swete, in l.), ib. ⁴³ 5⁴⁰, Lk 10², Ja 2²⁵ ; τ. κρίσιν εἰς νῖκος (to cause to proceed to its goal), Mt 12²⁰ (LXX).   3. to reject (cl.) : τ. ὄνομα ὑμῶν ὡς πονηρόν (cf. De 25¹⁴), Lk 6²² ; to leave out, Re 11². 4. to take, draw or pluck out; (a) with violence : Mt 7⁵, Mk 9⁴⁷, Lk 6⁴² ; (b) to bring forth or out of : Mt 12³⁵, Lk 10³⁵.

** ἔκ-βασις, -εως, ἡ (< ἐκβαίνω), [in LXX : Wi 2¹⁷ 8⁸ 11¹⁴ * ;] 1. a way out (Hom., Xen.) : I Co 10¹³.   2. the issue (Menand.) : He 13⁷.†

ἐκ-βολή, -ῆς (< ἐκβάλλω), [in LXX : Ex 11¹ (גרשׁ), Jos 1⁵ (ἐκβολὴν ποιεῖσθαι, מול hi.), Ez 47⁸ (יצא) * ;] 1. a throwing out.   2. a jettison, a throwing overboard of cargo : Ac 27¹⁸ (cf. Jos, l.c. ; and v. Field, Notes, 144 f.).†

*† ἐκ-γαμίζω, Rec. for γαμίζω, q.v. : Mt 22³⁰ 24³⁸, Lk 17²⁷, I Co 7³⁸. Not elsewhere.†

*† ἐκ-γαμίσκω, Rec. for γαμίσκω, q.v. : Lk 20³⁴, ³⁵.   Not elsewhere.†

ἔκ-γονος, -ον (< ἐκγίγνομαι, to be born of), [in LXX for פְּרִי (neut.), בֵּן, etc. ;] 1. c. gen., born of.   2. As subst., ὁ, ἡ ἔ., a child, son or daughter; in pl., descendants : τέκνα ἢ ἔ., children or grandchildren, I Ti 5⁴.†

*† ἐκ-δαπανάω, -ῶ, strengthened form of δαπανάω, to spend wholly; pass., with reflexive force, to spend oneself wholly : seq. ὑπέρ, II Co 12¹⁵.†

ἐκ-δέχομαι, [in LXX for ערב, קבץ, etc. ;] 1. to take or receive from (Hom., Hdt., al.).   2. (Rare in cl.), to expect, await : c. acc. rei, Jo 5[3], He 11¹⁰, Ja 5⁷ ; c. acc. pers., Ac 17¹⁶, I Co 11³³ 16¹¹ ; seq. ἕως, He 10¹³ (Cremer, 687).†

** ἔκ-δηλος, -ον (< δῆλος), [in LXX : ΙΙΙ Mac 3¹⁹ 6⁵ * ;] strengthened form of δῆλος, q.v., quite clear, evident : II Ti 3⁹.†

* ἐκ-δημέω, -ῶ (< ἔκδημος, *from home;* cf. *-ία,* III Mac 4¹¹) *; *to be from home, absent:* II Co 5⁶; seq. ἀπό, ib.⁸; seq. ἐκ, ib.⁹ (cf. ἀπο-, ἐνδημέω).†

ἐκ-δίδωμι, [in LXX for נתן, etc.;] 1. *to surrender, give up, give out.* 2. *to let out for hire* (Hdt.); mid. (as freq. in π.; v. MM, *Exp.,* xii); *to let out to one's advantage,* Mt 21³³, ⁴¹, Mk 12¹, Lk 20⁹.†

ἐκ-δι-ηγέομαι, -οῦμαι, depon., [in LXX chiefly for ספר, pi.;] *to tell in detail, relate, declare:* Ac 13⁴¹ (LXX) 15³.†

† ἐκδικέω, -ῶ (< ἔκδικος), [in LXX for פקד, נקם, שׁפט, etc.;] 1. *to vindicate:* c. acc. pers., Lk 18³, ⁵. 2. *to avenge:* c. acc. pers., ἑαυτούς, Ro 12¹⁹; c. acc. rei, παρακοήν, II Co 10⁶; αἷμα, Re 6¹⁰ 19² (Cremer, 203; for exx. from π. in both senses, v. MM, *Exp.,* xii).†

† ἐκ-δίκησις, -εως, ἡ (< ἐκδικέω), [in LXX chiefly for נקם;] *vengeance, vindication:* Lk 21²², Ro 12¹⁹ (v. MM, *Exp.,* xii), He 10³⁰ (LXX), II Co 7¹¹; of the injured person, c. gen., Lk 18⁷, ⁸; c. dat., Ac 7²⁴; of the offender, c. gen. obj., I Pe 2¹⁴; c. dat., II Th 1⁸ (cf. Si 12⁶).†

** ἔκδικος, -ον (< δίκη), [in LXX: Wi 12¹², Si 30⁶, IV Mac 15²⁹ *;] 1. *without law, unjust.* 2. *exacting penalty from;* as subst., *an avenger:* Ro 13⁴; seq. περί, I Th 4⁶ (in π., *a legal representative;* Milligan, *Th.,* l.c.).†

ἐκ-διώκω, [in LXX for ברח hi., צמת, רדף, etc.;] *to chase away, drive out:* I Th 2¹⁵ (cf. De 6¹⁹, Jl 2²⁰).†

** ἔκ-δοτος, -ον (< ἐκδίδωμι), [in LXX: Da TH Bel²² *;] *given up, delivered over:* Ac 2²³ (for construction, v. Field, *Notes,* 111 f.).†

* ἐκ-δοχή -ῆς, ἡ (< ἐκδέχομαι); 1. in cl., (*a*) *a receiving from, succession;* (*b*) *an interpretation.* 2. In NT, = προσδοκία, *expectation:* He 10²⁷ (cf. Field, *Notes,* 231; Cremer, 688).†

ἐκ-δύω, [in LXX chiefly for פשׁט;] *to take off, strip off, strip:* c. acc. pers. (sc. clothing), Mt 27²⁸; c. acc. pers. et rei, Mt 27³¹, Mk 15²⁰, Lk 10³⁰; mid., *to put off:* fig., of the body, II Co 5⁴.†

ἐκεῖ, adv., [in LXX chiefly for שׁם;] 1. properly, of place, *there:* Mt 2¹³ 5²⁴, al.; οἱ ἐ., Mt 26⁷¹; οὗ . . . ἐ., Mt 6²¹ 18²⁰ 24²⁸, Mk 6¹⁰, Lk 12³⁴; pleonastic, ὅπου . . . ἐ. (= שׁם אֲשֶׁר, De 4⁵, al.), Re 12⁶, ¹⁴ (cf. Bl., § 50, 4). 2. As often in cl. (Hdt., Thuc., al.), with verbs of motion, for ἐκεῖσε, *thither:* Mt 2²² 17²⁰ 24²⁸ 26³⁶, Mk 6³³, Lk 12¹⁸ 17³⁷ 21², Jo 11⁸ 18², ³, Ro 15²⁴.

ἐκεῖθεν, adv., [in LXX chiefly for מִשָּׁם;] 1. of place, *thence:* Mt 4²¹, Mk 6¹, al. 2. Of time, *thereafter* (v.s. κἀκεῖθεν).

ἐκεῖνος, -η, -ο (< ἐκεῖ), [in LXX chiefly for הוּא, הַהוּא, and cogn. forms;] demonstr. pron., *that* person or thing (*ille*), implying remoteness as compared with οὗτος (*hic*); 1. absol., emphatic *he, she, it:* opp. to οὗτος, Lk 18¹⁴, Ja 4¹⁵; ἡμεῖς, He 12²⁵; ὑμεῖς, Mt 13¹¹, Mk 4¹¹; ἄλλοι, Jo 9⁹; ἐγώ, Jo 3³⁰; to persons named, Mk 16[10, 13, 20], Jo 2²¹; of one (absent) who is not named, contemptuously (Abbott, *JG,* §§ 2385,

2732), Jo 7¹¹ 9²⁸; with respect, of Christ, I Jo 2⁶ 3³, al.; referring to a preceding noun, Mk 16[¹⁰], Jo 7⁴⁵; resumption of a participial subject, Jo 1³³ 9³⁷ 10¹, Ro 14¹⁴, al. (on its reference in Jo 19³⁵, v. Westc., in l.; Moffatt, *Intr.*, 568; Sanday, *Fourth Gospel*, 77 ff.).   2. As adj., joined, like οὗτος, to a noun with the article: Mt 7²⁵, Mk 3²⁴, Jo 18¹⁵, al.; esp. of time, past or future: ἐν τ. ἡμέραις ἐ., Mt 3¹, Mk 1⁹, Ac 2¹⁸ (LXX), al.; ἐν ἐ. τ. ἡμέρᾳ, esp of the Parousia, Mt 7²², Lk 6²³, II Th 1¹⁰, II Ti 1¹²; adverbially, ἐκεινής (sc. ὁδοῦ) = cl. ἐκεινῇ (Bl., § 36, 13), *that way*, Lk 19⁴.

ἐκεῖσε, adv., [in LXX: Jb 39²⁹ (מִשָּׁם)*;] *thither*: Ac 21³; constr. pregn. (MM, *Exp.*, xii; Field, *Notes*, 134), τοὺς ἐ. ὄντας, Ac 22⁵.†

†**ἐκ-ζητέω**, -ῶ, [in LXX chiefly for דרשׁ, also for נצר, בקשׁ, etc.;] 1. *to seek out* or *after, search for*: c. acc. pers. (I Mac 9²⁶); fig., τ. κύριον, θεόν (cf. Ps 13 (14)², Am 5⁴, al.), Ac 15¹⁷, Ro 3¹¹, He 11⁶; εὐλογίαν, He 12¹⁷; ἐξεζήτησαν κ. ἐξηραύνησαν (as in I Mac, l.c.), *sought and searched out*: I Pe 1¹⁰.   2. As in II Ki 4¹¹, Ez 3¹⁸, ²⁰, al. (דרשׁ), *to demand, require*: Lk 11⁵⁰, ⁵¹.†

*†**ἐκ-ζήτησις**, -εως, ἡ (< ἐκζητέω), *a questioning* (RV), *subject for dispute*: I Ti 1⁴.†

†ἐκ-θαμβέω, -ῶ (< ἔκθαμβος), [in LXX: Si 30⁹*;] 1. *to be amazed*.   2. *to amaze, terrify* (Si, l.c.).   Pass., *to be amazed, terrified*: Mk 9¹⁵ 14³³, 16⁵, ⁶.†

†ἔκ-θαμβος**, -ον (< θάμβος), [in LXX: Wi 10¹⁹, Da ᴛʜ 7⁷ (*dreadful, terrible*: אֵימְתָנִי)*;] *amazed* (cf. Polyb., xx, 10, 9): Ac 3¹¹.†

†ἐκ-θαυμάζω, [in LXX: Si 27²³ 43¹⁸, iv Mac 17¹⁷*;] strengthened form of θαυμ-; *to wonder greatly*: Mk 12¹⁷.†

** ἔκ-θετος**, -ον (< ἐκτίθημι), [in Al.: Ez 42³*;] *cast out*: ποιεῖν ἐ. = ἐκτιθέναι, Ac 7¹⁹.†

ἐκ-καθαίρω, [in LXX for בער, etc.;] 1. *to cleanse thoroughly, cleanse out*: c. acc., ἑαυτόν, II Ti 2²¹; of the impurity removed, ζυμήν, I Co 5⁷.†

ἐκ-καίω, [in LXX chiefly for בער;] 1. *to burn up*.   2. *to kindle*. Pass., *to burn*: metaph., of the passions (cf. Si 16⁶, Jb 3¹⁷), Ro 1²⁷.†

ἐκκακέω, -ῶ, v.s. ἐνκακέω.

ἐκ-κεντέω, -ῶ, [in LXX chiefly for דקר;] 1. *to prick out, put out* (Arist.).   2. *to pierce* (Polyb., LXX): c. acc. pers., Jo 19³⁷ (LXX), Re 1⁷.†

ἐκ-κλάω, -ῶ, [in LXX: Le 1¹⁷ (שׁסע pi.)*;] *to break off*: pass., Ro 11¹⁷, ¹⁹, ²⁰.†

ἐκ-κλείω, [in LXX: ἐ. κρίσιν, for נטה hi., Ex 23² (also as v.l., Jb 34²⁰, Ps 67 (68)³⁰)*;] *to shut out*: Ga 4¹⁷.   Pass., Ro 3²⁷.†

ἐκκλησία, -ας, ἡ (< ἐκ-καλέω), [in LXX chiefly for קָהָל, otherwise for one of its cogn. forms;] 1. prop., *an assembly* of citizens regularly convened (in Thuc., ii, 22, opp. to σύλλογος, *a concourse*): Ac 19³², ³⁹, ⁴¹. 2. In LXX of *the assembly, congregation, community* of Israel (De 4¹⁰ 23², al.): Ac 7³⁸, He 2¹² (LXX).   3. In NT, esp. of an assembly or company of Christians, *a (the) church*; (a) of gatherings for worship:

ι Co 11¹⁸ 14¹⁹, ³⁴, ³⁵; (b) of local communities : Ac 8³, ι Co 4¹⁷; with name added, Ac 8¹, Ro 16¹, ι Th 1¹, al.; pl., Ac 15⁴¹, ι Co 7¹⁷; τ. Χριστοῦ, Ro 16¹⁶; τ. Ἀσίας, ι Co 16¹⁹; τ. ἁγίων, ι Co 14³³; εἰπὸν τ. ἐκκλησίᾳ, Mt 18¹⁷ (but v. Hort, Ecclesia, 10); of a house-congregation (DB, i, 431ª), Ro 16⁵, ι Co 16¹⁹, Col 4¹⁵, Phm ²; (c) of the whole body of Christians : Mt 16¹⁸, ι Co 12²⁸, Eph 1²², Phl 3⁶, al,; τ. θεοῦ, Ac 20²⁸ (Κυρίου, T, R, mg.), ι Co 15⁹, Ga 1¹³, ι Ti 3¹⁵; ἐ. προτοτόκων ἀπογεγραμμένων ἐν οὐρανοῖς, He 12²³; v. ICC on Ga, pp. 417 ff.
SYN.: συναγωγή, q.v. (v. Tr., Syn., § i; DB, i, 426; Hort, Ecclesia, esp. 4 ff., 107 ff.; Hamilton, People of God, ii, 37 ff.; reff. s.vv. "Church," "Congregation," in DB and DCG; Cremer, 332).

ἐκ-κλίνω, [in LXX for נָטָה, סוּר, etc.;] intrans., to turn aside, turn away : metaph., from the right path, absol., Ro 3¹² (LXX); from evil, absol., ι Pe 3¹¹; seq. ἀπό, c. gen. pers., Ro 16¹⁷.†

* ἐκ-κολυμβάω, -ῶ, to swim out of : Ac 27⁴².†

* ἐκ-κομίζω, to carry out : as freq., a corpse for burial, Lk 7¹².†

** ἐκ-κοπή, -ῆς, ἡ, [in Aq.: Is 51¹ *;] in T for ἐνκοπή (q.v.): ι Co 9¹².†

ἐκ-κόπτω, [in LXX for כרת, etc.;] to cut out, cut off, cut down : of a hand, foot, Mt 5³⁰ 18⁸; a tree, Mt 3¹⁰ 7¹⁹, Lk 3⁹ 13⁷, ⁹; fig., of a branch, Ro 11²²; seq. ἐκ, Ro 11²⁴; metaph., τ. ἀφορμήν (cf. Jb 19¹⁰, ἐλπίδα), ιι Co 11¹².†

ἐκ-κρέμαννυμι, [in LXX for קשׁר, Ge 44³⁰ *;] to hang from or upon ; mid., ἐκκρέμαμαι : fig., ἐξεκρέματο αὐτοῦ ἀκούων (Rec.; WH read ἐξεκρέμετο, which implies a pres. ἐκκρέμομαι, otherwise unknown; cf. Veitch, s.v. κρέμαμαι), Lk 19⁴⁸.†

† ἐκ-κρέμομαι, Lk 19⁴⁸ (WH, v.s. ἐκκρέμαννυμι).†

** ἐκ-λαλέω, -ῶ, [in LXX: Jth 11⁹ *;] to speak out, divulge : Ac 23²².†

ἐκ-λάμπω, [in LXX for אור hi., etc.;] to shine forth : Mt 13⁴³.†

** ἐκ-λανθάνω, [in Sm.: Ps 12 (13)² *;] to escape notice utterly ; mid., to forget utterly : He 12⁵.†

ἐκ-λέγω, [in LXX chiefly for בחר;] to pick out, choose.   In NT always mid. (exc. Lk 9³⁵, ἐκλελεγμένος, WH, ἀγαπητός, R, mg.), to pick out for oneself, choose (cf. M, Pr., 157 f.) : c. acc. rei, Lk 10⁴² 14⁷; c. acc. pers., Ac 6⁵ 15²², ²⁵; of Christ (v. supr.), Lk 9³⁵; of Christ's choice of disciples, Lk 6¹³, Jo 6⁷⁰ 13¹⁸ 15¹⁶, ¹⁹, Ac 1²; of the Divine choice : of persons, Mk 13²⁰, Ac 1²⁴ 13¹⁷ 15⁷, Eph 1⁴, Ja 2⁵; of things, ι Co 1²⁷, ²⁸ (Cremer, 402, 773).†

ἐκ-λείπω, [in LXX for כלה, כרת ni., תמם, etc., 47 different words in all;] 1. trans., to leave out, pass over.   2. Intrans., to leave off, cease, fail : μαμωνᾶς, Lk 16⁹; πίστις, Lk 22³²; ἔτη, He 1¹² (LXX); of the sun in an eclipse, Lk 23⁴⁵.†

ἐκ-λεκτός, -ή, -όν (< ἐκλέγω), [in LXX for בחר (so prob. in Is 28¹⁶, Pr 17³, for MT בחן), בָּרִיא, etc.;] 1. choice, select (cl., rarely; Thuc., Plat., al.), hence, eminent : Ro 16¹³ (cf. Ez 27²⁴).   2. As in

Inscr. (MM, *Exp.*, xii), *chosen;* esp. as in LXX, of Israel, *elect, chosen* of God (Is 65⁹, Ps 104 (105)⁴³, al.); so in NT; (*a*) of Christ: Lk 23³⁵ (cf. Is 42¹); fig., λίθος, 1 Pe 2⁴,⁶ (LXX); (*b*) of holy angels: 1 Ti 5²¹; (*c*) of Christians: Mt 24²²,²⁴, Mk 13²⁰,²²,²⁷, 11 Ti 2¹⁰, 1 Pe 1¹; τ. θεοῦ, Lk 18⁷, Ro 8³³, Col 3¹², Tit 1¹; τ. Χριστοῦ, Mt 24³¹; ἐ. κυρία, 11 Jo¹; ἀδελφή, ib.¹³; γένος, 1 Pe 2⁹ (LXX); κλητοὶ καὶ ἐ. κ. πιστοί, Re 17¹⁴; opp. to κλητός (not so in Epp.; v. Lft. on Col 3¹²), Mt 20¹⁶ (T, WH, txt., R, omit) 22¹⁴ (Cremer, 405, 775).†

** ἐκλογή, -ῆς, ἡ (< ἐκλέγω), [in Aq.: Is 22⁷; Sm., Th.: ib. 37²⁴ *;] *a choice, selection;* in NT, always of the Divine choice (EV, *election*): σκεῦος ἐκλογῆς, gen. qual., *a chosen vessel; κατ' ἐ.*, Ro 9¹¹ 11⁵,²⁸; c. gen. pers., 1 Th 1⁴, 11 Pe 1¹⁰; by meton., ἡ ἐ. = οἱ ἐκλεκτοί, Ro 11⁷.†

ἐκ-λύω, [in LXX for רפה, etc.;] 1. *to loose, release.* 2. *to unloose,* as a bow-string, *to relax, enfeeble;* pass., *to be faint, grow weary :* Mt 15³², Mk 8³; of mental weariness, Ga 6⁹, He 12³,⁵ (LXX).†

** ἐκ-μάσσω, [in LXX: Si 12¹¹, Ep. Je¹³,²⁴ *;] *to wipe off :* c. acc., Lk 7³⁸,⁴⁴, Jo 11² 12³ 13⁵.†

† ἐκ-μυκτηρίζω, [in LXX: Ps 2⁴ 21 (22)⁷ 34 (35)¹⁶ (לעג), 1 Es 1⁵¹ A *;] *to hold up the nose in derision at, scoff at :* c. acc., Lk 16¹⁴ 23³⁵.†

ἐκ-νεύω, [in LXX: Jg 4¹⁸ (סור) 18²⁶, IV Ki 2²⁴ 23¹⁶ (פנה), Mi 6¹⁴ (סוה hi.), III Mac 3²² *;] 1. *to bend the head aside* (Xen.). 2. (*a*) *to shun, avoid* (Diod.); (*b*) *to withdraw :* Jo 5¹³.†

† ἐκ-νήφω, [in LXX: Ge 9²⁴, Hb 2⁷ (יקץ), Jl 1⁵, Hb 2¹⁹ (קיץ hi.), 1 Ki 25³⁷ (יצא), Si 34 (31)²*;] *to become sober* after drunkenness: metaph., of sobriety of mind, 1 Co 15³⁴.†

ἑκούσιος, -ον (< ἑκών), [in LXX chiefly for נְדָבָה, as Nu 15³ (κατ' ἐ.);] usually of actions, *voluntary : κατὰ ἐ., of free will* (Lft., in l.), Phm ¹⁴.†

ἑκουσίως, adv., [in LXX: Ps 53 (54)⁶ (בִּנְדָבָה), 11 Mac 14³, al.;] *voluntarily, willingly :* He 10²⁶, 1 Pe 5².†

*† ἐκ-πάλαι, adv. (of a class of compound adverbs common in late Gk.; v. Mayor on 11 Pe, l.c.), *for a long time, from of old :* 11 Pe 2³ 3⁵.†

† ἐκ-πειράζω, [in LXX: De 6¹⁶ 8²,¹⁶, Ps 77 (78)¹⁸ (נסה pi.) *;] = cl. ἐκπειράομαι, *to put to the proof* or *test, make trial of, tempt :* c. acc., of God, Mt 4⁷ (LXX), Lk 4¹² (ib.), 1 Co 10⁹; of Christ, Lk 10²⁵ (Cremer, 497).†

ἐκ-πέμπω, [in LXX for שלח;] *to send forth :* Ac 13⁴ 17¹⁰.†

*† ἐκ-περισσῶς, adv., *more exceedingly :* Mk 14³¹ (cf. ὑπερπερ-).†

ἐκ-πετάννυμι, [in LXX chiefly for פרש, as Is 65² (hithp.);] *to spread out* (as a sail), *stretch forth :* Ro 10²¹ (LXX).†

ἐκ-πηδάω, -ῶ, [in LXX: De 33²² (זנק), etc.;] *to spring forth :* εἰς τ. ὄχλον (cf. Ju 14¹⁷), Ac 14¹⁴ (for ex. in π., v. MM, *Exp.*, xii).†

ἐκ-πίπτω, [in LXX: Is 40⁸ 28¹,⁴ (נבל), Jb 14² (מלל, v. RV. mg.), Jb 15³⁰ (סור), Jb 15³³ (שלך hi.), etc.;] *to fall out of, fall from, fall off*: seq. ἐκ τ. χειρῶν, Ac 12⁷; absol., Ac 27³²; of the withering of flowers (as LXX, ll. c.), Ja 1¹¹, 1 Pe 1²⁴ (LXX); of navigators falling off from a straight course, Ac 27¹⁷, ²⁶, ²⁹. Metaph., c. gen. rei: Ga 5⁴, II Pe 3¹⁷; absol., *fall from its place, fail, perish*: Ro 9⁶.†

* ἐκ-πλέω, -ῶ, *to sail away*: Ac 20⁶; seq. εἰς, Ac 15³⁹ 18¹⁸.†

** ἐκ-πληρόω, [in LXX: II Mac 8¹⁰, III Mac 1², ²² *;] 1. *to fill full, make up* a number. 2. *to fulfil* (MM, *Exp.*, xii; Cremer, 839), Ac 13³².†

**† ἐκ-πλήρωσις, -εως, ἡ, [in LXX: II Mac 6¹⁴ *;] *a completion, fulfilment*: Ac 21²⁶.†

ἐκ-πλήσσω (Attic -ττω, Ac 13¹²), [in LXX: (pass.) Ec 17¹⁶ (¹⁷, (שמם hithp.), Wi 13⁴, II Mac 7¹², IV Mac 8⁴ 17¹⁶ *;] 1. prop., *to strike out, drive away*. 2. *to strike with panic or shock, to amaze, astonish*: pass., Mt 13⁵⁴ 19²⁵, Mk 6² 7³⁷ 10²⁶, Lk 2⁴⁸; seq. ἐπί, c. dat. rei, Mt 7²⁸ 22³³, Mk 1²² 11¹⁸, Lk 4³² 9⁴³, Ac 13¹².†

SYN.: "πτωεῖν, *to terrify*, agitate with fear; τρεμεῖν, *to tremble*, predominantly physical; φοβεῖν, *to fear*, the general term," Thayer; cf. also φρίσσω, *to shudder*, and v.s. δειλία.

* ἐκ-πνέω, -ῶ, *to breathe out; sc. βίον, ψυχήν* (expressed in cl., Æsch., al.; cf. LS, s.v.), *to breathe one's last, expire*: Mk 15³⁷, ³⁹, Lk 23⁴⁶. For force of aorist, v. Swete, *Mk.*, l.c.†

ἐκ-πορεύω, [in LXX chiefly for יצא;] *to make to go out;* pass. and mid., *to go forth*: Lk 3⁷, Ac 25⁴; of demons leaving one possessed, Mt 17²¹ (WH om.), Ac 19¹²; of excrement, Mk 7¹⁹; seq. ἀπό, Mt 20²⁹, Mk 10⁴⁶; ἐκ, Mk 13¹ (of the dead rising, Jo 5²⁹); ἐκεῖθεν, Mk 6¹¹; ἔξω, Mk 11¹⁹; εἰς, Mk 10¹⁷, Jo 5²⁹; ἐπί, c. acc. pers., Re 16¹⁴; πρός, c. acc. pers., Mt 3⁵, Mk 1⁵; εἰσπορ- (q.v.) καὶ ἐ., Ac 9²⁸; metaph., *to come forth, proceed*: of feelings, etc., Mk 7²³; seq. ἐκ, Mt 15¹¹, ¹⁸, Mk 7¹⁵, ²⁰, ²¹, Lk 4²², Eph 4²⁹; ῥῆμα, seq. διά, Mt 4⁴ (LXX); of lightning and flame, Re 4⁵ 9¹⁷, ¹⁸ 11⁵; a river, Re 22¹; a sword, Re 1¹⁶ 19¹⁵; a rumour, seq. εἰς, Lk 4³⁷; of the Holy Spirit, seq. παρά, Jo 15²⁶.†

† ἐκ-πορνεύω, [in LXX chiefly for זנה, freq. of spiritual un-faithfulness;] strengthened form of πορνεύω, implying excessive indulgence; mid. *to give oneself up to fornication*: Ju⁷.†

* ἐκ-πτύω, 1. *to spit out*. 2. *to spit at* in disgust, *to abominate, loathe* (= cl. ἀποπτ-, καταπτ-): Ga 4¹⁴.†

† ἐκ-ριζόω, -ῶ, [in LXX: Jg 5¹⁴ (שֹׁרֶשׁ), Je 1¹⁰ (נתש), Ze 2⁴ (גרשׁ A, עקר BS), Da TH 7⁸ (עקר), Da LXX 4¹¹, ²³, Wi 4⁴, Si 3⁹ 49⁷, 1 Mac 5⁵¹, II Mac 12⁷ *;] *to root out, pluck up by the roots*: c. acc. rei, Mt 13²⁹ 15¹³ Lk 17⁶, Ju 1².†

ἔκ-στασις, -εως, ἡ (ἐξίστημι), [in LXX: Ga 27³³, 1 Ki 14¹⁵, Ez 26¹⁶, al. (חֲרָדָה); II Ch 14¹⁴ (13) 17¹⁰ 20²⁹ (פחד), al.;] 1. *a displacement* (Arist.). 2. An abnormal condition of the mind, in which the subject passes out of his usual self-control (Hippocr.); in NT (Kennedy, *Sources*, 121 f.); (a) *a trance*: Ac 10¹⁰ 11⁵ 22¹⁷; (b) *amazement*: Mk 5⁴² 16⁸, Lk 5²⁶, Ac 3¹⁰.†

ἐκ-στρέφω, [in LXX: De 32²⁰, Am 6¹³ (12), Ez 16³⁴ A (הפך), Za

11¹⁶ (פרק pi.), Ez 13²⁰ (צדד pil.)*;] 1. *to turn out of* (Hom.). 2. *to turn inside out;* metaph., *to change entirely, pervert* (Aristoph.): Tit 3¹¹.†

* **ἐκ-σώζω**, *to preserve from danger, bring safe:* Ac 27³⁹ (ἐξῶσαι, WH, mg., R, txt., v.s. ἐξωθέω).†

ἐκ-ταράσσω, [in LXX: Ps 17 (18)⁴ (בעת pi.), 87 (88)¹⁶ (צמת), Wi 17³, ⁴ 18¹⁷ *;] *to throw into great trouble, agitate:* Ac 16²⁰.†

ἐκ-τείνω, [in LXX for שלח, נטה, etc.;] *to stretch out* or *forth:* τ. χεῖρα (as often in LXX), Mt 8³ 12¹³ 14³¹, 26⁵¹, Mk 1⁴¹ 3⁵, Lk 5¹³ 6¹⁰, Jo 21¹⁸, Ac 26¹; seq. ἐπί, c. acc. pers., *towards,* Mt 12⁴⁹; *against,* Lk 22⁵³; εἰς ἴασιν, Ac 4³⁰; of anchors, *to cast,* Ac 27³⁰.†

ἐκ-τελέω, -ῶ, [in LXX: De 32⁴⁵ (כלה), ii Ch 4⁵, Da TH 3⁽⁴⁰⁾, ii Mac 15⁹*;] *to bring to an end, finish, complete:* Lk 14²⁹, ³⁰.†

†ἐκ-τένεια, -ας, ἡ (< ἐκτενής), [in LXX: Jth 4⁹, ii Mac 14³⁸, iii Mac 6⁴¹*;] *zeal, intentness, earnestness* (cf. Deiss., *BS*, 262): Ac 26⁷.†

ἐκτενής, -ές (< ἐκτείνω), [in LXX: iii Mac 3¹⁰ 5²⁹*;] *stretched, strained.* Metaph., *earnest, zealous:* i Pe 4⁸.†

ἐκτενῶς, adv., [in LXX: Jh 3⁸ (בחזקה), Jl 1¹⁴, Jth 4¹², iii Mac 5⁹*;] *fervently, earnestly:* Ac 12⁵, i Pe 1²²; compar., Lk 22⁴⁴ (WH br., R, mg., omits).†

ἐκ-τίθημι, [in LXX for נתן ni., etc.;] *to set out, expose:* Ac 7²¹. Metaph., *to set forth, expound:* Ac 11⁴ 28²³; c. acc. rei, 18²⁶.†

ἐκ-τινάσσω, [in LXX for נער ni., pi., etc.;] *to shake off:* κονιορτόν, Mt 10¹⁴; χοῦν, Mk 6¹¹. Mid.: κονιορτόν, Ac 13⁵¹; ἱμάτια, Ac 18⁶ (cf. MM, *Exp.*, iii).†

ἕκτος, -η, -ον, *the sixth:* Mt 20⁵, al.

ἐκτός, adv., [in LXX: Jg 8²⁶ 20¹⁵, iii Ki 10¹³, al. (מלבד, לבד מן), Jg 5²⁸ (בעד), Ca 4¹, ³ (למבעד ל), al.;] 1. as adv., *outside, beyond:* τὸ ἐ., c. poss. gen., *the outside,* Mt 23²⁶; in late Gk. (v. Deiss., *BS*, 118), pleonastic, ἐκτὸς εἰ μή, i Co 14⁵ 15², i Ti 5¹⁹. 2. With force of prep., c. gen.; (*a*) *outside of:* i Co 6¹⁸, ii Co 12²; (*b*) *beyond, besides, except:* Ac 26²², i Co 15²⁷.†

ἐκ-τρέπω, [in LXX for הפך, Am 5⁸*;] *to turn out of the course, turn aside,* c. acc. Pass., with middle sense, intrans., *to turn aside:* He 12¹³ (R, txt., for *be put out of joint,* R, mg., v. Thayer, s.v. Westc., in l.); fig., seq. εἰς, i Ti 1⁶; ἐπί, ii Ti 4⁴; ὀπίσω, i Ti 5¹⁵; c. acc., *to shun, avoid:* i Ti 6²⁰.†

ἐκ-τρέφω, [in LXX for גדל, etc.;] 1. prop., of children, *to nurture, bring up:* Eph 6⁴. 2. *to nourish:* Eph 5²⁹.†

†ἔκτρομος, -ον, = ἔντρομος, *exceedingly terrified:* He 12²¹ (for exx. from π., v. Deiss., *BS*, 290; *LAE*, 254).†

ἔκ-τρωμα, -τος, τό (< ἐκτιτρώσκω, *to miscarry*), [in LXX: Jb 3¹⁶, Ec 6³ (נפל); also in Aq., Ps 57 (58)⁹, Nu 12¹² (מות)*;] *an abortion, an untimely birth* (v. Field, *Notes*, 179): i Co 15⁸.†

ἐκ-φέρω, [in LXX chiefly for יצא hi. ;] 1. *to carry out, bring out :*
c. acc. rei, Lk 15²², ɪ Ti 6⁷; c. acc. pers., Mk 8²³, Ac 5¹⁵; of the dead
for burial (cf. κομίζω), Ac 5⁶˒ ⁹˒ ¹⁰. 2. *to bring forth ;* (*a*) of women
(Hipp., Arist., al.); (*b*) of the ground (Hdt.) : He 6⁸.†

ἐκ-φεύγω, [in LXX for נוס, etc. ;] *to flee away, escape :* absol.,
Ac 16²⁷, ɪ Th 5³, He 2³; seq. ἐκ, Ac 19¹⁶; c. acc. pers., He 12²⁵; c.
acc. rei, Lk 21³⁶, Ro 2³; τ. χεῖρας αὐτοῦ, ɪɪ Co 11³³.†

ἐκ-φοβέω, -ῶ, [in LXX chiefly for חָרַד hi. ;] *to frighten away,
terrify :* c. acc. pers., ɪɪ Co 10⁹.†

ἔκφοβος, -ον, [in LXX : ἔ. εἶναι for יָגֹר, De 9¹⁹; also ɪ Mac 13² * ;]
affrighted, terrified : Mk 9¹⁶, He 12²¹.†

** ἐκ-φύω, [in OT (Sm.) Ps 103 (104)¹⁴; (Al.) Is 61¹¹ * ;] *to cause to
grow out, put forth* (leaves) : Mt 24³², Mk 13²⁸.†

ἐκ-χέω, also Hellenistic, ἐκχύνω (in Th. : ɪɪ Ki 14¹⁴ *), and ἐκχύννω
(q.v.), [in LXX chiefly for שָׁפַךְ ;] *to pour out :* φιάλην, Re 16¹⁻⁴, ⁸, ¹⁰, ¹², ¹⁷ ;
κέρματα, Jo 2¹⁵; αἷμα, Mt 23³⁵ (cf. MM, *Exp.*, xii), Lk 11⁵⁰, Ac 22²⁰,
Ro 3¹⁵ ⁽ᴸˣˣ⁾, Re 16⁶. Pass., αἷμα, Mt 26²⁸, Mk 14²⁴, Ac 22²⁰; οἶνος,
Mt 9¹⁷, Lk 5³⁷; σπλάγχνα, Ac 1¹⁸. Metaph., τ. πνεῦμα, Ac 2¹⁷, ¹⁸ ⁽ᴸˣˣ⁾, ³³
10⁴⁵, Tit 3⁶; ἀγάπη, Ro 5⁵ (cf. Si 33 (36)⁸, ὀργήν); pass., of persons (like
Lat. *effundor*), *to give oneself up to* (RV, *ran riotously in*) : Ju ¹¹.†

**† ἐκ-χύννω, Hellenistic form of ἐκχέω, q.v. (Bl., § 17) : Mt 23³⁵ 26²⁸,
Mk 14²⁴, Lk 5³⁷ 11⁵⁰ 22²⁰, Ac 1¹⁸ 10⁴⁵ 22²⁰, Ro 5⁵, Ju ¹¹.†

ἐκ-χωρέω, -ῶ [in LXX : Nu 16⁴⁵ (17¹⁰) (רוּם ni.), Jg 7³ (צפר),
Am 7¹² (ברח), ɪ Es 4⁴⁴, ⁵⁷, ɪ Mac 9⁶² * ;] *to depart, withdraw :* Lk
21²¹.†

ἐκ-ψύχω, [in LXX : Jg 4²¹ A (עוּף), Ez 21⁷ ⁽¹²⁾ (כָּהָה pi.) * ;] *to expire,
breathe one's last :* Ac 5⁵, ¹⁰ 12²³ (cf. ἐκπνέω; Cremer, 906).†

ἑκών, -οῦσα, -όν, [in LXX : Ex 21¹³, Jb 36¹⁹ * ;] *willing, of one's
own free will :* Ro 8²⁰, ɪ Co 9¹⁷ (Cremer, 246).†

ἐλαία (Attic, ἐλάα), -ας, ἡ, [in LXX for זַיִת ;] *an olive tree :* Ro
11¹⁷, ²⁴, Re 11⁴; τ. ὄρος τῶν ἐ. (הַר הַזֵּיתִים, Za 14⁴), *the Mount of Olives :*
Mt 21¹ 24³ 26³⁰, Mk 11¹ (for τῶν ἐ., WH, mg., reads τὸ ἐ., in which case
ἐ. prob. = ἐλαιών, q.v.) 13³ 14²⁶, Lk 19³⁷ 22³⁹; τὸ καλούμενον ἐ. (T:
ἐλαιών, q.v.), Lk 19²⁹ 21³⁷. 2. *an olive* (Aristoph.) : Ja 3¹².†

ἔλαιον, -ου, τό, [in LXX chiefly for שֶׁמֶן ;] *olive-oil :* Lk 16⁶,
Re 6⁶ 18¹³; for lamps, Mt 25³, ⁴, ⁸; for healing, Mk 6¹³, Lk 10³⁴,
Ja 5¹⁴; for anointing at feasts, Lk 7⁴⁶, He 1⁹ ⁽ᴸˣˣ⁾.†
SYN. : μύρον, *ointment,* v. Tr., *Syn.,* 135.

† ἐλαιών, -ῶνος, ὁ (< ἐλαία), [in LXX for זַיִת ;] *olive-grove, olive-
garden* (so in FlJ and in π.; Deiss., *BS,* 208 ff.; MM, *Exp.,* iii ;
M, *Pr.,* 49, 69, 235) : Mk 11¹ (v. supr., s.v. ἐλαία, and cf. Swete, in l.),
Lk 19²⁹ 21³⁷ (WH, -ῶν; v. their *App.,* 158; Field, *Notes,* 73; Bl.,
§ 10, 5; 33, 1; Thayer, s.v.), Ac 1¹² (where Bl., ll. c., proposes the
conjectural emendation ἐλαιῶν for -ῶνος).†

Ἐλαμείτης (Rec. -αμίτης), -ου, ὁ (Heb. עֵילָם;) [in LXX (cl.)
Ἐλυμαῖος, Ἔλαμος: Jth 1⁶; Ἀιλαμείτης (vv.ll. Ἐλ-, -αμίτης; Bl.,
§ 3, 7) : Is 11¹¹ 21² 22⁶);] an Elamite : Ac 2⁹.†

ἐλάσσων (-ττων, He 7⁷, WH, ɪ Ti 5⁹), -ον (formed, with superl.
ἐλάχιστος, from the epic ἐλαχύς, little, and serving as compar. of
μικρός), [in LXX for מְעַט, etc.;] less, in age, rank or quality : Jo 2¹⁰,
Ro 9¹² (LXX), He 7⁷; neut., -ον, adverbially : ɪ Ti 5⁹.†

† ἐλαττονέω, -ῶ (< ἔλαττον), [in LXX (with -όω) chiefly for
חָסֵר;] to be less (RV, had no lack) : ɪɪ Co 8¹⁵ (LXX) (a rare word; cf.
MM, Exp., xii).†

ἐλαττόω, -ῶ (< ἐλάττων), [in LXX (where also -σσῶ) chiefly for
חָסֵר, and very freq. in Si;] to make less : He 2⁷ (LXX); pass., Jo 3³⁰,
He 2⁹.†

ἐλαύνω, [in LXX : Is 41⁷ (הָלַם) 33²¹ (שַׁיִט), etc.;] to drive : of
the wind, Ja 3⁴, ɪɪ Pe 2¹⁷; of sailors rowing or sailing a boat, Mk 6⁴⁸,
Jo 6¹⁹; of demons, Lk 8²⁹ (cf. ἀπ-, συν-ελαύνω).†

*† ἐλαφρία, -ας, ἡ, lightness, levity : ɪɪ Co 1¹⁷.†

ἐλαφρός, -ά, -όν, [in LXX chiefly for קַל, קָלַל;] light in weight₎
easy to bear : Mt 11³⁰; θλῖψις (EV, our light affliction), ɪɪ Co 4¹⁷.†

ἐλάχιστος, -η, -ον (v.s. ἐλάσσων), smallest, least : as proper
superlat., ɪ Co 15⁹; elsewhere, as usually in late Gk., intensive (Bl.,
§ 11, 3); Mt 2⁶ (LXX) 25⁴⁰, ⁴⁵, Lk 12²⁶ 16¹⁰ 19¹⁷, ɪ Co 4³ 6², Ja 3⁴; ἐ. ἐν
τ. βασιλείᾳ τ. οὐρανῶν, Mt 5¹⁹ (v. Dalman, Words, 113). Compar.,
ἐλαχιστότερος (for corresp. superl., v. LS; v. also Bl., § 44, 3); less
than the least : Eph 3⁸.†

Ἐλεάζαρ (Heb. אֶלְעָזָר), ὁ, indecl., Eleazar : Mt 1¹⁵.†

† ἐλεάω, later form of ἐλεέω, q.v., [in LXX as v.l. in To 13², Ps
36 (37)²⁶, al.;] in NT : Ro 9¹⁶, Ju ²³, WH.†

† ἐλεγμός, -οῦ, ὁ (< ἐλέγχω), [in LXX : Ps 37 (38)¹⁴ 38 (39)¹¹
(תּוֹכַחַת), Si 20²⁹ 21⁶ 41⁴, al.;] reproof : ɪɪ Ti 3¹⁶.†

† ἔλεγξις, -εως, ἡ (< ἐλέγχω), [in LXX : Jb 21⁴ 23² (שִׂיחַ)*;] rebuke : ɪɪ Pe 2¹⁶.†

ἔλεγχος, -ον, ὁ (ἐλέγχω), [in LXX : freq. in Pr, Jb (תּוֹכַחַת),
Wi ₅, Si ₃, etc.;] a proof, test : He 11¹.†

ἐλέγχω, [in LXX chiefly for יכח hi.;] 1. in Hom., to treat with
contempt. 2. to convict : c. acc., Mt 18¹⁵ (RV, show him his fault),
Tit 1⁹; seq. περί, Jo 8⁴⁶ 16⁸, Ju ¹⁵; pass., Ja 2⁹. 3. to reprove, rebuke : ɪ Ti 5²ᶜ, ɪɪ Ti 4², Tit 1¹³ 2¹⁵, Re 3¹⁹; pass., seq. περί, Lk 3¹⁹;
ὑπό, He 12⁵ (LXX). 4. to expose : Eph 5¹¹; pass., Jo 3²⁰, ɪ Co 14²⁴
(RV reprove, mg. convict), Eph 5¹³ (RV, as ɪ Co, l.c., cf. AR on Eph
5¹¹; MM, Exp., xii; cf. ἐξ-, δια-κατ-ελέγχομαι).†

SYN. : ἐπιτιμῶ, expressing simply rebuke, which may be un-
deserved (Mt 16²²) or ineffectual (Lk 23⁴⁰), while ἐλ. implies rebuke
which brings conviction (v. Tr., Syn., § iv).

ἐλεεινός, -ή, -όν (< ἔλεος; in Re, l.c., WH have the Attic poëtic form, ἐλεινός), *pitiable, miserable :* Re 3¹⁷; comparat., 1 Co 15¹⁹.†

ἐλεέω (in Ro 9¹⁶, Ju²², -άω, q.v.), -ῶ (< ἔλεος), [in LXX (Hex, Pss, Pr) chiefly for חנן, also freq. in Proph. for רחם, etc.;] *to have pity* or *mercy on, to show mercy :* absol., Ro 9¹⁶ 12⁸; c. acc., Mt 9²⁷ 15²² 17¹⁵ 18³³ 20³⁰, ³¹, Mk 5¹⁹ 10⁴⁷, ⁴⁸, Lk 16²⁴ 17¹³ 18³⁸, ³⁹, Ro 9¹⁵, ¹⁸ 11³², Phl 2²⁷, Ju²². Pass., *to have pity* or *mercy shown one* (EV, *obtain mercy*): Mt 5⁷, Ro 11³⁰, ³¹, 1 Co 7²⁵, 11 Co 4¹, 1 Ti 1¹³, ¹⁶, 1 Pe 2¹⁰.†

SYN.: οἰκτείρω (v. Tr., *Syn.*, § xlvii; Thayer, s.v. ἐλεέω; Cremer, 249).

† ἐλεημοσύνη, -ης, ἡ (< ἐλεέω), [in LXX chiefly for חֶסֶד, צְדָקָה;] 1. *mercy, pity.* 2. *almsgiving, alms* (like the German *Almosen*, a corruption of the Greek word ἐ.) : Mt 6⁴; ποιεῖν ἐ., Mt 6², ³, Ac 9³⁶ 10² 24¹⁷; ἐ. διδόναι, Lk 11⁴¹ (cf. Mt 23³⁶; Dalman, *Words*, 62 f.) 12³³; αἰτεῖν, Ac 3²; λαβεῖν, Ac 3³; πρὸς (in order to ask) ἐ., Ac 3¹⁰; pl., Ac 10⁴, ³¹ (Cremer, 711).†

ἐλεήμων, -ον, [in LXX chiefly for חַנּוּן;] *merciful :* Mt 5⁷, He 2¹⁷.†

ἐλεινός, v.s. ἐλεεινός.

Ἐλεισάβετ (T, Rec. Ἐλισ-; v. WH, *App.*, 155), ἡ, indecl. (Heb. אֱלִישֶׁבַע), *Elizabeth :* Lk 1⁵ᵃ·.†

ἔλεος, -ους, τό (cl. -ον, ὁ, and so Rec., Mt 9¹³ 12⁷ 23²³, Tit 3⁵, He 4¹⁶; on the Hellenistic form τὸ ἔ., v. WH, *App.*, 158; M, *Pr.*, 60; Mayser, 277; Kühner, i, 515), [in LXX chiefly for חֶסֶד;] *mercy, pity, compassion ;* 1. of men : Mt 9¹³ (LXX) 12⁷ 23²³; ποιεῖν ἔ. (and id. seq. μετά, c. gen.; cf. Heb. עִם חֶסֶד עָשָׂה, Ge 21²³, al.), Lk 10³⁷, Ja 2¹³ 3¹⁷. 2. Of God: Lk 1⁵⁰, ⁵⁴, ⁵⁸, Ro 15⁹, Eph 2⁴, 11 Ti 1¹⁶, ¹⁸, Tit 3⁵, He 4¹⁶, 1 Pe 1³; esp. in benedictions, Ga 6¹⁶, 1 Ti 1², 11 Ti 1², 11 Jo³, Ju²; σκευὴ ἐλέους, Ro 9²³; σπλάγχνα ἐλέους, Lk 1⁷⁸; ποιεῖν ἔ. (v. supr.), Lk 1⁷²; τ. ὑμετέρῳ ἐλέει, Ro 11³¹. 3. Of Christ : Ju²¹.†

SYN.: οἰκτιρμός (v.s. ἐλεέω).

ἐλευθερία, -ας, ἡ, [in LXX: Le 19²⁰ (חֻפְשָׁה), 1 Es 4⁴⁹, ⁵³, Si 7²¹ 30³⁴ (33²⁵), 1 Mac 14²⁷, 111 Mac 3²⁸ *;] *liberty :* with reference to the religious life, 1 Co 10²⁹, 11 Co 3¹⁷, Ga 2⁴ 5¹, 1 Pe 2¹⁶, 11 Pe 2¹⁹; ὁ νόμος τῆς ἐ., Ja 1²⁵ 2¹²; ἡ ἐ. τῆς δόξης, Ro 8²¹; ἐπ' ἐ., Ga 5¹³ (on which formula, cf. Deiss., *LAE*, 327 ff.; Cremer, 251).†

ἐλεύθερος, -α, -ον, [in LXX chiefly for חָפְשִׁי;] *free ;* (*a*) in civil sense, not a slave: Jo 8³³, 1 Co 7²¹, ²² 12¹³, Ga 3²⁸, Eph 6⁸, Col 3¹¹, Re 6¹⁵ 13¹⁶ 19¹⁸; fem., Ga 4²², ²³, ³⁰; (*b*) as regards restraint and obligation n general : Mt 17²⁶, 1 Co 9¹; seq. ἐκ, 1 Co 9¹⁹; ἀπό, Ro 7³; c. inf., 1 Co 7³⁹; from the law, Ga 4²⁶, 1 Pe 2¹⁶; from sin, Jo 8³⁶; τῇ δικαιοσύνῃ, as regards righteousness, Ro 6²⁰ (Cremer, 249).†

ἐλευθερόω, -ῶ, [in LXX: Pr 25¹⁰, 11 Mac 1²⁷ 2²² *;] *to make free :*

from sin, Jo 8³²,³⁶; seq. ἀπό, Ro 6¹⁸,²² 8²,²¹; τ. ἐλευθερία (dat. commodi), Ga 5¹ (on the "punctiliar" force of this verb, v. M, *Pr.* 149; cf. also Cremer, 251).†

*† ἔλευσις, -εως, ἡ, *a coming :* Ac 7⁵².†

ἐλεφάντινος, -η, -ον (< ἐλέφας, *ivory*), [in LXX for שֵׁן;] *of ivory :* Re 18¹².†

Ἐλιακείμ (Heb. אֶלְיָקִים), *Eliakim,* an ancestor of Jesus : Mt 1¹³, Lk 3³⁰.†

* ἕλιγμα, -τος, τό (< ἑλίσσω), *a roll :* Jo 19³⁹, WH, txt. (μῖγμα, Rec. ; μίγμα, WH, mg., R, txt.).†

Ἐλιέζερ (Heb. אֱלִיעֶזֶר), ὁ, indecl., *Eliezer,* an ancestor of Jesus : Lk 3²⁹.†

Ἐλιούδ, ὁ, indecl., *Eliud,* an ancestor of Jesus : Mt 1¹⁴,¹⁵.†
Ἐλισάβετ, v.s. Ἔλεισ-.

Ἐλισαῖος (Rec. Ἐλισσαῖος; T, Ἐλισ-), -ου, ὁ (Heb. אֱלִישָׁע), *Elisha,* the prophet : Lk 4²⁷.†

ἑλίσσω, [in LXX : Is 34⁴ (בָּלַל ni.), Ps 101 (102)²⁶ (חלף hi.), etc. ;] *to roll, roll up :* He 1¹² (LXX), Re 6¹⁴.†

ἕλκος, -εος (-ους), τό [in LXX : Ex 9⁹⁻¹¹, Le 13¹⁸⁻²⁷, ιν Ki 20⁷, Jb 2⁷ (שְׁחִין);] 1. *a wound* (Hom.). 2. *a sore, an ulcer* (Thuc., al.): Lk 16²¹, Re 16²,¹¹.†

* ἑλκόω, -ῶ ; 1. *to wound.* 2. *to ulcerate;* pass., *to suffer from sores :* pf. ptcp., εἱλκωμένος (Rec. ἡλκ-), EV, *full of sores,* Lk 16²⁰.†
ἑλκύω, v.s. ἕλκω.

ἕλκω (Hellenistic forms in fut. and aor. from ἑλκύω, in Jo, ll. c., Ac 16¹⁹), [in LXX for מָשַׁךְ, etc. ;] *to draw :* c. acc. rei, Jo 18¹⁰ 21⁶; c. acc. pers., seq. ἔξω, Ac 21³⁰ ; εἰς, Ac 16¹⁹, Ja 2⁶. Metaph., *to draw, lead, impel :* Jo 6⁴⁴, 12⁵². (For discussion of ἑ. in *Oxyrh. Log.,* v. Deiss., *LAE,* 437 ff.)†

Ἑλλάς, -άδος, ἡ, [in LXX : Is 66¹⁹, Ez 27¹³ (יָוָן), ι Mac 1¹ 8⁹ *;] with varying usage as to geographical limits; in NT = Ἀχαία (cf. Ac 18¹²), *Greece :* Ac 20².†

Ἕλλην, -ηνος, ὁ, [in LXX : Jl 3 (4)⁶, Za 9¹³ (יָוָן), etc. ; ι Mac 1¹⁰, al. ;] *a Greek ;* opp. to βάρβαρος, Ro 1¹⁴; usually in NT of Greek Gentiles, opp. to Ἰουδαῖοι : Jo 7³⁵, Ac 11²⁰ 14¹ 16¹,³ 18⁴ 19¹⁰,¹⁷ 20²¹ 21²⁸, Ro 1¹⁶ 2⁹,¹⁰ 3⁹ 10¹², ι Co 1²², ²⁴ 10³² 12¹³, Ga 2³ 3²⁸, Col 3¹¹; of proselytes, Jo 12²⁰, Ac 17⁴.†

Ἑλληνικός, -ή, -όν, [in LXX : Je 26 (46)¹⁶ 27 (50)¹⁶ (יוֹנָה : aliter in Heb.), ιι Mac 4¹⁰,¹⁵ 6⁹ 11²⁴ 13², ιν Mac 8⁸ *;] *Greek :* τ. Ἑλληνικῇ (sc. γλωσσῇ), Re 9¹¹.†

** Ἑλληνίς, -ίδ.ς, ἡ, [in LXX : ιι Mac 6⁸ A *;] *a Greek* (i.e. *Gentile*) *woman :* Mk 7²⁶, Ac 17¹².†

*† Ἑλληνιστής, -οῦ, ὁ (< Ἑλληνίζω, *to Hellenize, affect Greek customs*), *a Hellenist* (RV, *Grecian Jew*): Ac 6¹ 9²⁹ 11²⁰.†

*'Ελληνιστί, adv., *in Greek :* Jo 19²⁰; 'E. (sc. λαλεῖν) γινώσκεις, Ac 21³⁷ (cf. Field, *Notes*, 135).†

*† ἐλλογάω, -ῶ (a κοινή word, elsewhere usually -έω; cf. Bl., § 22, 2), *to charge to one's account, impute :* Phm ¹⁸ (on parallels, cf. Deiss., *LAE*, 79 f., 335 f.; Milligan, *NTD*, 73; MM, *Exp.*, xii); of sin, Ro 5¹³ (Cremer, 400).†

'Ελμαδάμ (L, 'Ελ-; Rec. -μωδάμ), ὁ, indecl., *Elmadam*, an ancestor of Jesus : Lk 3²⁸.†

ἐλπίζω, [in LXX chiefly for בָּטַח, also for חָסָה, יָחַל pi., hi., etc.;] *to look for, expect, hope (for) :* c. acc. rei, Ro 8²⁴,²⁵, ι Co 13⁷, He 11¹; c. dat. rei (τ. τύχῃ, Thuc., iii, 97, 2), Mt 12²¹; seq. καθώς, ιι Co 8⁵; c. inf., Lk 6³⁴ 23⁸, Ac 26⁷, Ro 15²⁴, ι Co 16⁷, ιι Co 5¹¹, Phl 2¹⁹,²³, ι Ti 3¹⁴, ιι Jo 12, ιιι Jo 14; seq. ὅτι, c. pres., Lk 24²¹; c. fut., Ac 24²⁶, ιι Co 1¹³ 13⁶, Phm ²². As in LXX (WM, § xxxiii, d; and esp. in the pf., Ellic. on ι Ti 4¹⁰; Bl., § 59, 2), c. prep.; εἰς, Jo 5⁴⁵ (v. Ellic. l.c.), ι Pe 3⁵; seq. ὅτι, ιι Co 1¹⁰; ἐπί, c. dat., Ro 15¹²(LXX), ι Ti 4¹⁰ 6¹⁷; ἐν, ι Co 15¹⁹; c. acc., ι Pe 1¹³ (aor. imper. v. Bl., § 58, 2); τ. θεόν, ι Ti 5⁵ (cf. ἀπ-, προ-ελπίζω, v. Cremer, 255).†

ἐλπίς, (ἐλ-, Ro 8²⁰, WH, v. Bl., § 4, 3; M, *Pr.*, 44), -ίδος, ἡ, [in LXX for בָּטַח and its derivatives, תִּקְוָה (freq. in Jb), etc.;] *expectation* (in cl., rarely of evil, mostly of good, and so always in NT), *hope ;* 1. of hope in general : ιι Co 1⁶; c. gen. obj., Ac 16¹⁹; art. inf., Ac 27²⁰, ι Co 9¹⁰; παρ' ἐλπίδα, Ro 4¹⁸; ἐπ' ἐλπίδι, ι Co 9¹⁰. 2. Of religious hope : ἐπ' ἐλπίδι, Ac 2²⁶ 26⁶, Ro 4¹⁸ 8²⁰, Tit 1²; τῇ ἐ. ἐσώθημεν, Ro 8²⁴; κατ' ἐλπίδα ζωῆς αἰωνίου, Tit 3⁷; of the Messianic hope of Israel, Ac 23⁶ 26⁶,⁷ 28²⁰; of Christian hope, Ro 5²,⁴,⁵ 12¹² 15⁴,¹³, ι Co 13¹³, ιι Th 2¹⁶, He 3⁶ 6¹¹ 7¹⁹ 10²³, ι Pe 1³,²¹ 3¹⁵; c. gen. obj., Ro 5², Col 1²⁷, ι Th 1³ 5⁸, Tit 1²; c. gen. of that on which the hope is based, Ac 26⁶, Eph 1¹⁸ 4⁴, Col 1²³; ὁ θεὸς τῆς ἐ., Ro 15¹³; ἔχειν ἐ. (= cl. ἐλπίζειν), Ac 24¹⁵, Ro 15⁴, ιι Co 3¹² 10¹⁵, Eph 2¹², ι Th 4¹³; seq. ἐπί, c. dat., ι Jo 3³; εἰς, Ac 24¹⁵; ὅτι, Ro 8²⁰, Phl 1²⁰,²¹. Meton., (*a*) of the author or ground of hope (cl.) : ι Th 2¹⁹, ι Ti 1¹; c. gen. obj., Col 1²⁷; (*b*) of the thing hoped for : Ga 5⁵, Col 1⁵, Tit 2¹³, He 6¹⁸ (Cremer, 252, 712).†

'Ελύμας, -α, ὁ (< Aram. or Arab., cf. *DB*, i, 246 b), *Elymas :* Ac 13⁸.†

ἐλωί (-ί Rec.; ἐλωί LT; Aram. אֱלָהִי), *Eloi :* Mt 27⁴⁶, Mk 15³⁴(LXX).†

ἐμαυτοῦ, -ῆς, -οῦ, reflex pron. of first pers., used only in gen., dat. and acc. sing., *of myself :* Lk 7⁷, al.; ἀπ' ἐ., Jo 5³⁰ 7¹⁷,²⁸ 8²⁸,⁴² 10¹⁸ 14¹⁰; ὑπ' ἐμαυτόν, Mt 8⁹, Lk 7⁸.

ἐμ-βαίνω, [in LXX for עלה, etc.;] *to step into :* Jo 5⁴ (WH, RV omit); εἰς πλοῖον, *to embark :* Mt 8²³ 9¹ 13² 14²² 15³⁹, Mk 4¹ 5¹⁸ 6⁴⁵ 8¹⁰,¹³, Lk 5³ 8²²,³⁷, Jo 6¹⁷,²⁴ 21³, Ac 21⁶.†

ἐμ-βάλλω, [in LXX for שׂוּם, etc.;] *to cast into :* seq. εἰς, Lk 12⁵ (cf. MM, *Exp.*, vii, 93).†

*ιἐμ-βάπτω, *to dip in :* τ. χεῖρα ἐν τ. τρυβλίῳ, Mt 26²³; mid., seq. εἰς, Mk 14²⁰.†

148   MANUAL GREEK LEXICON OF THE NEW TESTAMENT

ἐμβατεύω, [in LXX: c. acc., Jos 19⁴⁹ (נחל), 19⁵¹ (חלק pi.); seq. εἰς,
I Mac 12²⁵ 13²⁰ 14³¹ 15⁴⁰; metaph., II Mac 2³⁰*;] (< ἐμβάτης
< ἐμβαίνω); 1. to step in or on (Soph.), hence (a) to frequent, haunt,
dwell in (Æsch., Eur.); metaph., Col 2¹⁸ (dwelling in, R, txt.; taking his
stand upon, R, mg.); (b) to invade (I Mac, ll. c.; metaph., Col, l.c.). 2. to
enter on, come into possession of (Eur., Dem.; LXX, Jos, ll. c.); on the
difficulties of reading and interpretation in this passage, v. Lft, Col., 194 f.,
252; ICC, 268 ff.; Field, Notes, 197; Milligan, NTD, 177; and for exx.
from π., MM, Exp., xii (cf. κενεμβ.), MM, VGT, s.v., and reff. there, which
make unnecessary the emendation formerly proposed. ἐ., as term. tech.
of the mystery religions, is quoted here to denote the entrance (setting
foot on) of the initiated to the new life.†

ἐμ-βιβάζω, [in LXX: IV Ki 9²⁸ (רכב hi.), Pr 4¹¹ (דרך hi.)*;] 1.
to set in, put in. 2. to put on board ship, embark: c. acc. pers., seq.
εἰς, Ac 27⁶.†

ἐμ-βλέπω, [in LXX for ראה (III Ki 8⁸, al.), פנה (Jb 6²⁸ A, al.);
metaph., Is 51¹ (נבט hi.), Si 2¹⁰, etc.;] to look at: c. acc. rei, Mk 8²⁵;
c. dat. pers. (part., seq. λέγει, εἶπεν, cf. Xen., Cyr., i, 3, 2), Mt 19²⁶, Mk
10²¹·²⁷ 14⁶⁷, Lk 20¹⁷ 22⁶¹ (ἐνέβλεψεν), Jo 1³⁶·⁴³; absol., to look, Ac 22¹¹;
metaph., to consider: Mt 6²⁶.†

ἐμ-βριμάομαι (T, -έομαι; Bl., § 22, 1), -ῶμαι (< βρίμη, strength,
bulk, whence βριμάομαι, to snort with anger), depon., with aor. mid.
and pass., [in LXX (Hatch, Essays, 25): Da LXX 11³⁰ (also Aq., Ps
7¹²; Sm., Is 17¹³)*;] to snort in (of horses, Æsch.), hence, to speak
or act with deep feeling (DCG, i, 62ᵇ); (a) to be moved with anger
(cf. ἐμβρίμημα, La 2⁶): c. dat., Mk 14⁵, Jo 11³³; ἐν ἑαυτῷ, Jo 11³⁸;
(b) to admonish sternly: c. dat., Mt 9³⁰, Mk 1⁴³.†

ἐμέω, -ῶ, [in LXX: Is 19¹⁴ (קיא)*;] to vomit: fig., Re 3¹⁶.†

*† ἐμ-μαίνομαι, depon., to rage against: c. dat., Ac 26¹¹.†

†'Εμμανουήλ, ὁ (Heb. עִמָּנוּ אֵל, Is 7¹⁴), Immanuel: Mt 1²³ (LXX).†

'Εμμαούς, ἡ, Emmaus, a place 60 furlongs from Jerusalem: Lk
24¹³.†

ἐμμένω, [in LXX chiefly for קום;] 1. to abide in: Ac 28³⁰. 2.
to abide by, be true to: seq. ἐν; τ. πίστει, Ac 14²²; τ. διαθήκῃ, He
8⁹ (LXX); c. dat., τ. γεγραμμένοις (dat. ptcp. as in legal formula; cf.
Deiss., BS, 248; MM, Exp., xii): Ga 3¹⁰ (LXX).†

'Εμμώρ (T, 'Εμμώρ, Rec. -όρ, indecl. (Heb. חֲמוֹר), Emmor (Ge
33¹⁹): Ac 7¹⁶.†

ἐμός, -ή, -όν, poss. pron. of first pers., representing the emphasized gen. ἐμοῦ, mine, subjectively and objectively, i.e. belonging
to, proceeding from or related to me: Mt 18²⁰, Mk 8³⁸, Jo 3²⁹ (most
freq. in this gospel), al.; absol., τὸ ἐμόν, τὰ ἐμά, Mt 20¹⁵ 25²⁷, Lk 15³¹,
Jo 10¹⁴ 16¹⁴·¹⁵ 17¹⁰; = gen. obj. (cl.), εἰς τ. ἐμὴν ἀνάμνησιν, Lk 22¹⁹,
I Co 11²⁴·²⁵; c. gen. expl., τ. ἐμῇ χειρὶ Παύλου, I Co 16²¹, Col 4¹⁸,
II Th 3¹⁷.

*† ἐμπαιγμονή, -ῆς, ἡ (< ἐμπαίζω, q.v.), mockery: II Pe 3³.†

†ἐμ-παιγμός, -οῦ, ὁ (< ἐμπαίζω, q.v.), [in LXX: Ez 22⁴ (קַלָּסָה), Ps 37 (38)⁷ B אֲ¹ (קלח ni.), Wi 12²⁵, Si 27²⁸, II Mac 7⁷, III Mac 5²² * ;] a mocking: He 11³⁶.†

ἐμ-παίζω, [in LXX for עלל hithp., שׂחק, etc.;] = Attic προσ-, καταπαίζω, to mock at, mock (Hdt.): c. dat., Mt 27²⁹, ³¹, Mk 15²⁰, Lk 14²⁹ 22⁶³ 23³⁶; pass., Mt 2¹⁶, Lk 18³²; absol., Mt 20¹⁹ 27⁴¹, Mk 10³⁴ 15³¹, Lk 23¹¹.†

†ἐμ-παίκτης, -ου, ὁ (< ἐμπαίζω, q.v.), [in LXX: Is 3⁴ (תַעֲלוּלִים) * ;] a mocker: II Pe 3³, Ju 18.†

ἐμ-περι-πατέω, -ῶ, v.s. ἐνπ-.

ἐμ-πίπλημι (on ἐμπίμπ-, v. LS, s.v., Bl., § 6, 8), and ἐμπιπλάω (Ac 14¹⁷), [in LXX chiefly for מלא, שׂבע ;] to fill full, fill up, satisfy: c. acc. pers. et gen. rei, Lk 1⁵³, Ac 14¹⁷; pass., Lk 6²⁵, Jo 6¹²; metaph., c. gen. pers., to take one's fill of: Ro 15²⁴ (cf. Da LXX Su ³²).†

ἐμ-πίπρημι, ἐμπρήθω (for the form, v.s. ἐμπίπλημι, and cf. Veitch, s.v. πίμπρημι), [in LXX chiefly for שׂרף ;] to set on fire: πόλιν, Mt 22⁷; pass., of the body, to become inflamed: Ac 28⁶ (T; πίμπρημι, WH, q.v.).†

ἐμ-πίπτω, [in LXX chiefly for נפל ;] to fall into: seq. εἰς, Mt 12¹¹, Lk 6³⁹ 10³⁶; metaph., εἰς κρίμα, I Ti 3⁶; ὀνειδισμόν, ib. 3⁷; πειρασμόν, ib. | 6⁹; εἰς χεῖρας θεοῦ (cf. II Ki 24¹⁴, I Ch 21¹³, Si 2¹⁸), He 10³¹.†

ἐμ-πλέκω, [in LXX: Pr 28¹⁸ (נפל), II Mac 15¹⁷ * ;] to weave in, entwine; pass., metaph., to be involved, entangled in: II Ti 2⁴, II Pe 2²⁰.†

*†ἐμ-πλοκή, -ῆς, ἡ (< ἐμπλέκω), a braiding: τριχῶν, I Pe 3³.†

ἐμ-πνέω, -ῶ, v.s. ἐνπ-.

ἐμ-πορεύομαι, depon. (< ἔμπορος), [in LXX chiefly for סחר ;] 1. to travel, esp. for business. 2. to traffic, trade: Ja 4¹³. 3. C. acc. rei (a) to traffic in; (b) to import: (Ho 12¹, for יבל hoph.). 4. C. acc. pers., to make a gain of: II Pe 2³.†

ἐμπορία, -ας, ἡ (< ἔμπορος), [in LXX for סחר, רכל, etc.;] commerce, business, trade: Mt 22⁵.†

ἐμπόριον, -ου, τό (ἔμπορος), [in LXX: De 33¹⁹ (שׂפן), Ez 27³ (רכל); ἐ. εἶναι, Is 23¹⁷ (זנה) * ;] a trading-place, exchange: οἶκος ἐμπορίου, Jo 2¹⁶.†

ἔμ-πορος, -ου, ὁ (< πόρος, a journey), [in LXX chiefly for סחר, רכל ;] 1. a passenger on shipboard, one on a journey. 2. a merchant: Mt 13⁴⁵, Re 18³, ¹¹, ¹⁵, ²³.†

ἐμ-πρήθω, v.s. ἐμπίπρημι.

ἔμ-προσθεν, adv. of place (in cl. also of time), [in LXX chiefly for לִפְנֵי ;] 1. adverbially, before, in front: Lk 19²⁸; εἰς τὸ ἔ., ib. ⁴; opp. to ὄπισθεν, Re 4⁶; opp. to τὰ ὀπίσω, τὰ ἔ., Phl 3¹³. 2. As prep., c. gen., before; (a) in front of: Mt 5²⁴ 6² 7⁶ 11¹⁰ 27²⁹, Lk 5¹⁹ 7²⁷ 14², Jo 3²⁸ 10⁴, Re 19¹⁰ 22⁸; (b) in the presence of: Mt 27¹¹, Ga 2¹⁴, I Th 1³ 2¹⁹ 3⁹, ¹³; ὁμολογεῖν, ἀρνεῖσθαι (Dalman, Words, 210), Mt 10³², ³³ 26⁷⁰, Lk 12⁸; in forensic sense, Mt 25³² 27¹¹, Lk 21³⁶, Ac 18¹⁷, II Co 5¹⁰, I Th 2¹⁹, I Jo

150 MANUAL GREEK LEXICON OF THE NEW TESTAMENT

3¹⁹; εὐδοκία (θέλημά) ἐστι ἕ. θεοῦ (a targumic formula; Dalman, *Words*, 211), Mt 11²⁶ 18¹⁴, Lk 10²¹; (c) in the sight of: Mt 5¹⁶ 6¹ 17² 23¹⁴, Mk 2¹² 9², Lk 19²⁷, Jo 12³⁷, Ac 10⁴; (d) of rank and dignity (Dem., Plat., al.; LXX, Ge 48²⁰): Jo 1¹⁵,³⁰.†

ἐμ-πτύω, [in LXX: seq. εἰς, Nu 12¹⁴ A, De 25⁹ (ירק) *;] = cl., καταπτύω (Ruth., *NPhr.*, 66), to spit upon: c. dat., Mk 10³⁴ 14⁶⁵ 15¹⁹; seq. εἰς, Mt 26⁶⁷ 27³⁰. Pass., Lk 18³².†

ἐμφανής, -ές (< ἐμφαίνω, to show in, exhibit), [in LXX: Mi 4¹, Is 2² (כה ni.), Wi 6²² 7²¹ 14¹⁷; ἕ. γίνεσθαι, Ex 2¹⁴ (ידע ni.), Is 65¹ (דרש ni.) *;] manifest: Ac 10⁴⁰; metaph., Ro 10²⁰ (LXX) (v.s. ἐπιφανής).†

ἐμφανίζω, [in LXX for ידע hi., etc.;] 1. to manifest, exhibit: ἑαυτόν, c. dat pers., Jo 14²¹,²² (*DCG*, ii, 112ᵇ). Pass. and mid., to show oneself, appear: Mt 27⁵³, He 9²⁴ (cf. MM, *Exp.*, xii). 2. to declare, make known: seq. ὅτι, He 11¹⁴; c. dat. pers., Ac 23¹⁵; c acc. rei, seq. πρός, Ac 23²²; κατά, c. gen. pers., Ac 24¹ 25²; περί, Ac 25¹⁵.†

SYN.: δηλόω, q.v.

** ἔμ-φοβος, [in LXX: Si 19²⁴, 1 Mac 13² *;] 1. terrible. 2. in fear (of Godly fear, Si, l.c.), terrified: Lk 24⁵,³⁷, Ac 10⁴ 24²⁵, Re 11¹³.†

ἐμ-φυσάω, -ῶ (< φυσάω, to blow), [in LXX for נפח, etc.;] to breathe into (cf. Ge 2⁷, Wi 15¹¹, al.), breathe upon: Jo 20²².†

** ἔμ-φυτος, -ον (< ἐμφύω, to implant), [in LXX: ἕ. ἡ κακία αὐτῶν, Wi 12¹⁰ *;] 1. innate (Wi, l.c.). 2. rooted, implanted: Ja 1²¹ (v. Mayor, in l.).†

ἐν, prep. (the most freq. of all in NT), c. dat. (= Heb. בְּ, Lat. in, c. abl.). I. Of place, c. dat. rei, pers., in, within, on, at, by, among: ἐν τ. πόλει, Lk 7³⁷; τ. ὀφθαλμῷ, Mt 7³; τ. κοιλίᾳ, Mt 12⁴⁰; τ. θρόνῳ, II Pe 1¹⁸; τ. θρόνῳ, Re 3²¹; τ. δεξιᾷ τ. θεοῦ, Ro 8³⁴; ἐν ὑμ̄ν, Lk 1¹; of books, ἐν τ. βιβλίῳ, Ga 3¹⁰; τ. νόμῳ, Mt 12⁵, al.; ἐν τοῖς τ. Πατρός μου, in my Father's house (RV; cf. M, *Pr.*, 103), Lk 2⁴⁹; trop., of the region of thought or feeling, ἐν τ. καρδίᾳ (-αις), Mt 5²⁸, II Co 4⁶, al.; τ. συνειδήσεσιν, II Co 5¹¹; after verbs of motion, instead of εἰς (constructio prægnans, a usage extended in late Gk. beyond the limits observed in cl.; cf. Bl., § 41, 1; M, *Th.*, 12), ἀποστέλλω . . . ἐν, Mt 10¹⁶; δέδωκεν ἐν τ. χειρί (cf. τιθέναι ἐν χερσί, Hom., *Il.*, i, 441, al.), Jo 3³⁵; id. after verbs of coming and going (not in cl.), εἰσῆλθε, Lk 9⁴⁶; ἐξῆλθεν, Lk 7¹⁷. II. Of state, condition, form, occupation, etc.: ἐν ζωῇ, Ro 5¹⁰; ἐν τ. θανάτῳ, I Jo 3¹⁴; ἐν πειρασμοῖς, I Pe 1⁶; ἐν εἰρήνῃ, Mk 5²⁵; ἐν δόξῃ, Phl 4¹⁹; ἐν πραΰτητι, Ja 3¹³; ἐν μυστηρίῳ, I Co 2⁷; ἐν τ. διδαχῇ, Mk 4²; of a part as contained in a whole, ἐν τ. ἀμπέλῳ, Jo 15⁴; ἐν ἑνὶ σώματι, Ro 12⁴; of accompanying objects or persons (simple dat. in cl.), with, ἐν αἵματι, He 9²⁵; ἐν δέκα χιλιάσιν, Lk 14³¹ (cf. Ju ¹⁴, Ac 7¹⁴); similarly (cl.), of clothing, armour, arms, ἐν στολαῖς, Mk 12³⁸; ἐν ἐσθῆτι λαμπρᾷ, Ja 2²; ἐν μαχαίρῃ, Lk 22⁴⁹ classify under III; ἐν ῥάβδῳ, I Co 4²¹ (cf. ἐν τόξοις, Xen., *Mem.*, 3, 9, 2); of manner (cl.), ἐν τάχει (= ταχέως), Lk 18⁸ (cf. Bl., § 41, 1); of spiritual influence, ἐν πνεύματι, Ro 8⁹; ἐν π. ἀκαθάρτῳ, Mk 1²³; of the mystical relation of the Christian life and the believer himself, to God and Christ (cf. *ICC*, *Ro.*, 160 f.;

Mayor on Ju¹; M, *Pr.*, 103): ἐν Χριστῷ ('Iησοῦ), ἐν κυρίῳ, Ro 3²⁴ 6¹¹, ι Co 3¹ 4¹⁰, ιι Co 12², Ga 2¹⁷, Eph 6²¹, Col 4⁷, ι Th 4¹⁶, al. III. Of the agent, instrument or means (an extension of cl. ἐν of instr.—v. LS, s.v. III—corresponding to similar use of Heb. בְּ), *by, with :* ἐν ὑμῖν κρίνεται ὁ κόσμος (= cl. παρά, c. dat.), ι Co 6²; ἐν τ. ἄρχοντι τ. δαιμονίων, Mt 9³⁴; ἐν αἵματι, He 9²²; ἐν ὕδατι, Mt 3¹¹, al.; ἐν μαχαίρᾳ ἀποκτενεῖ (cf. the absol. ἐν ῥάβδῳ, supr., II, which some would classify here), Re 13¹⁰ (cf. 6⁸), cf. Lk 22⁴⁹. Allied to this usage and distinctly Semitic are the following (v. M, *Gr.*, II, pp. 463 f.): ἠγόρασας . . . ἐν τ. αἵματι σου (cf. *BDB*, s.v. בְּ, III, 3), Re 5⁹; ὁμολογεῖν ἐν (= Aram. בְּ אֹדִי; cf. McNeile on Mt, l.c.; M, *Pr.*, 104), Mt 10³², Lk 12⁸; ὀμνύναι ἐν (= cl. acc., so Ja 5¹²), Mt 5³⁴, al.; also *at the rate of, amounting to,* Mk 4⁸ (WH; vv. ll., εἰς, ἐν), Ac 7¹⁴ (LXX). IV. Of time, (a) *in* or *during* a period: ἐν τ. ἡμέρᾳ (νυκτί), Jo 11⁹, al.; ἐν σαββάτῳ, Mt 12², al.; ἐν τῷ μεταξύ, *meanwhile,* Jo 4³¹; (b) *at* the time of an event: ἐν τ. παρουσίᾳ, ι Co 15²³; ἐν τ. ἀναστάσει, Mt 22²⁸; (c) c. art. inf., (a) pres. (so sometimes in cl., but not as in NT = ἕως; v. M, *Pr.*, 215), *while :* Mt 13⁴, Mk 6⁴⁸, Ga 4¹⁸, al.; (β) aor., *when, after :* Lk 9³⁶, al.; (d) *within* (cl.) : Mt 27⁴⁰. V. In composition : (i) meaning : (a) with adjectives, it signifies usually the possession of a quality, as ἐνάλιος, ἔνδοξος; (b) with verbs, continuance in (seq. ἐν) or motion into (seq. εἰς), as ἐμμένω, ἐμβαίνω. (ii) Assimilation : ἐν becomes ἐμ- before β, μ, π, φ, ψ; ἐγ- before γ, κ, ξ, χ; ἐλ- before λ. But in the older MSS of NT, followed by modern editions, assimilation is sometimes neglected, as ἐνγράφω, ἐνκαινίζω, etc.

† **ἐν-αγκαλίζομαι** (< ἀγκάλη), [in LXX for חבק pi., Pr 6¹⁰ 24⁴⁸ (33) *;] *to take into one's arms :* Mk 9³⁶ 10¹⁶.†

* **ἐν-άλιος, -ον** (also -α, -ον; < ἅλς, *the sea*), *of the sea :* τὰ ἐ., *marine creatures,* Ja 3⁷.†

† **ἔν-αντι,** adv., a κοινή word (MM, *Exp.*, xii), *before;* as prep., c. gen.: Lk 1⁸, Ac 7¹⁰ (WH, ἐναντίον), 8²¹.†

ἐν-αντίος, -α, -ον (< ἀντίος, *set against*), [in LXX: ἐξ ἐναντίας, for נֶגֶד, etc.; ἐναντίον, for לִפְנֵי, etc.;] *over against, opposite, contrary :* ἄνεμος, Mt 14²⁴, Mk 6⁴⁸, Ac 27⁴; ἐξ ἐναντίας (ellipse obscure, v. Bl., § 44, 1; Mozley, *Ps.*, 42), c. gen., Mk 15³⁹. Metaph., *opposed, hostile :* ι Th 2¹⁵, Ac 26⁹ 28¹⁷; ὁ ἐξ ἐ., Tit 2⁸. Neut., -ίον, adv., as prep. c. gen., *before, in the presence of :* Lk 1⁶ 20²⁶ 24¹⁹, Ac 7¹⁰ (ἔναντι, T), 8³² (LXX).†

ἐν-άρχομαι, [in LXX chiefly for חלל hi.;] *to begin, make a beginning :* Ga 3³, Phl 1⁶.†

ἔνατος, (Rec. ἔνν-), -η, -ον, *ninth :* Re 21²⁰; of the ninth hour (3 o'clock, p.m.), Mt 20⁵, 27⁴⁵,⁴⁶, Mk 15³³,³⁴, Lk 23⁴⁴, Ac 3¹ 10³,³⁰.†

ἐν-γράφω (L, Tr., ἐγγ-), [in LXX chiefly for כתב;] *to inscribe, write in :* pass., seq. ἐν, ιι Co 3²,³. 2. *to enter in a register, enrol :* pass., Lk 10²⁰ (cf. ι Mac 13⁴⁰; and v. Dalman, *Words,* 209).†

ἐνδεής, -ές (< ἐνδέω, *to lack*), [in LXX for חָסֵר, אֶבְיוֹן, etc.;] *in want, needy :* Ac 4³⁴.†

* ἔν-δειγμα, -τος (< ἐνδείκνυμι), a plain token, proof: II Th 1⁵ (cf. ἔνδειξις, which refers rather to the "act of proving"; ἕ., with the passive formation, to the thing proved, v. Lft., Notes, 100; M, Th., l.c.).†

SYN.: τεκμήριον.

ἐν-δείκνυμι, [in LXX for לכד, גמל, ראה hi.;] to mark, point out. Mid., 1. to show forth, prove: c. acc. rei, Ro 2¹⁵ 9²², Eph 2⁷, Tit 2¹⁰ 3², He 6¹¹; seq. ἐν, c. dat. pers., Ro 9¹⁷ (LXX), I Ti 1¹⁶; seq. εἰς, He 6¹⁰ (c. cogn. acc.), II Co 8²⁴. 2. to manifest (by act): c. acc. rei et dat. pers., II Ti 4¹⁴ (cf. Ge 50¹⁵, ¹⁷, and v. MM, Exp., xiii).†

* ἔν-δειξις, -εως, ἡ (< ἐνδείκν υμι), a pointing out, showing forth, proof (v.s. ἔνδειγμα): Ro 3²⁵, ²⁶, II Co 8²⁴, Phl 1²⁸.†

ἔν-δεκα, οἱ, αἱ, τά, indecl., eleven: of the eleven apostles, οἱ ἕ., Mt 28¹⁶, Mk 16 [14], Lk 24⁹, ³³, Ac 1²⁶ 2¹⁴.†

ἐν-δέκατος, -η, -ον, eleventh: Mt 20⁶, ⁹, Re 21²⁰.†

ἐν-δέχομαι, [in LXX: Ps 118 (119)¹²² (ערב), II Mac 11¹⁸ *;] 1. to admit, approve. 2. to be possible; impers., ἐνδέχεται, it is possible: c. acc. et inf., Lk 13³³ (Cremer, 687).†

* ἐνδημέω, -ῶ (< ἔνδημος, living in a place), to live in a place, be at home: ἐν τ. σώματι, II Co 5⁶, ⁹; πρὸς τ. Κύριον, ib. ⁸.†

† ἐνδιδύσκω, [in LXX: II Ki 1²⁴ 13¹⁸, Pr 31²¹ (לבש), Jth 9¹ 10³, Si 50¹¹ *;] to put on: c. dupl. acc., Mk 15¹⁷ (ἐνδύουσι, Rec.). Mid., to put on oneself, be clothed in: c. acc. rei, Lk 16¹⁹ (cf. MM, Exp., xii).†

* ἔνδικος, -ον (< δίκη), righteous, just: Ro 3⁸, He 2² (Cremer, 204).†

ἐν-δόμησις, -εως, ἡ, v.s. ἐνδώμ-.

† ἐν-δοξάζω, [in LXX for כבד ni., Ex 14⁴, ¹⁷, ¹⁸, Ez 28²², etc.; for ערץ, Ps 88 (89)⁷; Si 38⁶, al.;] to glorify: pass., II Th 1¹⁰, ¹².†

ἔνδοξος, -ον (< δόξα), [in LXX for כבד, etc.;] 1. held in honour, of high repute: I Co 4¹⁰. 2. glorious, splendid: of deeds, τὰ ἕ., Lk 13¹⁷; of clothing, Lk 7²⁵. Metaph., ἐκκλησία, Eph 5²⁷ (cf. παράδοξος).†

† ἔνδυμα, -τος, τό (< ἐνδύω), [in LXX chiefly for לבוש;] raiment, clothing, a garment: Mt 3⁴ 6²⁵, ²⁸ 7¹⁵ 22¹¹, ¹² 28³, Lk 12²³.†

† ἐν-δυναμόω, -ῶ, [in LXX: Jg 6³⁴, I Ch 12¹⁸ A (לבש), Ps 51 (52)⁷ (עזז) *;] to make strong, strengthen: c. acc. pers., Phl 4¹³, I Ti 1¹², II Ti 4¹⁷. Pass., Ac 9²²; c. dat., Ro 4²⁰; seq. ἐν, II Ti 2¹ (ἐν Κυρίῳ), Eph 6¹⁰ (Cremer, 221).†

ἐν-δύνω, v.s. ἐνδύω.

ἔν-δυσις, -εως, ἡ (< ἐνδύω), [in LXX: Jb 41⁴ (5) (לבוש), Es 5¹ *;] a putting on: ἱματίων, I Pe 3³.†

ἐν-δύω (ἐνδύνω, II Ti 3⁶), [in LXX chiefly for לבש;] c. acc. pers., Mt 27²⁸ (WH, mg., R, mg.); c. dupl. acc., Mt 27³¹, Mk 15²⁰, Lk 15²²; mid., to put on oneself, be clothed with: c. acc. rei, Mt 6²⁵, Mk 6⁹, Lk 8²⁷ 12²², Ac 12²¹; ptcp., Mt 22¹¹, Mk 1⁶, II Co 5³, Re 1¹³ 15⁶ 19¹⁴; of armour (fig.): Ro 13¹², Eph 6¹¹, ¹⁴, I Th 5⁸; metaph., δύναμιν, Lk 24⁴⁹; ἀφθαρσίαν, ἀθανασίαν, I Co 15⁵³, ⁵⁴; τ. καινὸν ἄνθρωπον, Eph 4²⁴, Col 3¹⁰; σπλάγχνα οἰκτιρμοῦ, Col 3¹²; Ἰησ. Χριστόν, Ro 13¹⁴, Ga 3²⁷. 2. to enter, press into: II Ti 3⁶ (cf. ἐπ-ενδύω).†

*† ἐν-δώμησις (Rec. -δόμησις), -εως, ἡ (< δωμάω, to build), a building in : ἡ ἐ. τ. τείχους αὐτῆς ἴασπις, its wall had jasper built into it, Re 21¹⁸ (v. MM, Exp., xiii; Swete, Ap., l.c.; Charles (ICC in l.) quotes the only two other instances of this word (FlJ, Inscr.), and thinks it means here materials or fabric. Souter, s.v., suggests roofing, coping.) †

ἐν-έδρα, -ας, ἡ (< ἕδρα, a seat), [in LXX: Jos 8⁷, ⁹, Ps 9²⁹ (10⁸) (ארב)*;] a lying in wait, an ambush: Ac 23¹⁶ (Rec. ἔνεδρον, a form freq. in LXX), 25³.†

ἐνεδρεύω (< ἐνέδρα), [in LXX chiefly for ארב;] to lie in wait for : c. acc. pers., Lk 11⁵⁴, Ac 23²¹.†

ἔνεδρον, -ου, τό, v.s. ἐνέδρα.

ἐν-ειλέω, -ῶ, [in LXX: 1 Ki 21⁹ ⁽¹⁰⁾ (לוט) *;] to roll in, wind in : c. acc. pers. et dat. rei, Mk 15⁴⁶.†

ἔν-ειμι, 1. to be in, within (Jb 27³, al.) : ptcp. pl., τὰ ἐνόντα, Lk 11⁴¹ (R, txt., cf. MM, Exp., xii). 2. to be possible : Lk, l.c. (R, mg.).†

ἕνεκα (so Mt 19⁵, Lk 6²², Ac 19³² 26²¹; elsewhere, prop. only before a vowel, ἕνεκεν; εἵνεκεν, originally Ionic: Lk 4¹⁸ 18²⁹, Ac 28²⁰, II Co 3¹⁰), prep. c. gen., on account of, because of : Mt 5¹⁰, ¹¹ 16²⁵ 19²⁹, Mk 8³⁵, Lk 6²², Ac 28²⁰, Ro 8³⁶, II Co 3¹⁰; ἕ. τούτου, Mt 19⁵; τούτων, Ac 26²¹; τίνος ἕ., Ac 19³²; seq. τοῦ, c. inf., II Co 7¹²; οὗ ἕν., Lk 4¹⁸.

ἐνενήκοντα (Rec. ἐννεν-), οἱ, αἱ, τά, indecl., ninety : Mt 18¹², ¹³, Lk 15⁴, ⁷.†

ἐνεός (Rec. ἐνν-), -ά, -όν, [in LXX: Is 56¹⁰ (אִלֵּם), Ep Je 41; ἐ. ποιεῖν, Pr 17²⁸ *;] dumb, speechless : Ac 9⁷.†

** ἐνέργεια, -ας, ἡ (< ἐνεργής), [in LXX: Wi 7¹⁷, ²⁶ 13⁴ 18²², II Mac 3²⁹, III Mac 4²¹ 5¹², ²⁸ *;] operative power (as distinct from δύναμις, potential power), working : of God, Eph 1¹⁹ 3⁷ 4¹⁶, Phl 3²¹, Col 1²⁹ 2¹²; of Satan, II Th 2⁹, ¹¹ (cf. M, Th., l.c.; AR, Eph., 241 ff.; Cremer, 261).†

ἐνεργέω, -ῶ, [in LXX: Nu 8²⁴ B (צָבָא בַּעֲבֹדַת), Is 41⁴, Pr 21⁶ (פָּעַל), 31¹² (גָּמַל), 1 Es 2²⁰, Wi 15¹¹ 16¹⁷ *;] (for full lexical treatment, v. AR, Eph., 243 ff.); 1. intrans., to be at work or in action, to operate (opp. to ἀργέω) : seq. ἐν, c. dat. pers., Mt 14² (here perh. representing Aram. עֲבַד, to act; pass. to be wrought, the Aram. in this passage being are wrought by him, v. Exp., Sept., 1921, p. 237), Mk 6¹⁴, Eph 2²; c. dat. pers., seq. εἰς (Lft., in l.), Ga ̄2⁸. 2. Trans., to work, effect, do : c. acc. rei, 1 Co 12¹¹, Eph 1¹¹; id. seq. ἐν, c. dat. pers., 1 Co 12⁶, Ga 3⁵, Phl 2¹³; ἐ. ἐνέργειαν, Eph 1¹⁹, ²⁰. Pass. (taken as mid. by Lft., Ga., 204 f.; but v. AR, Eph., l.c.; Milligan, Th., 28 f.; Mayor, Ja., 177 ff.), in NT, "always used of some principle or power at work" (Meyer), to be actuated, set in operation : II Th 2⁷; seq. ἐν, Ro 7⁵, II Co 1⁶ 4¹², Eph 3²⁰, Col 1²⁹, 1 Th 2¹³; seq. διά, c. gen. rei, Ga 5⁶; ἐνεργουμένη (M, Pr., 156), Ja 5¹⁶ (Cremer, 262).†

*† ἐνέργημα, -τος, τό (< ἐνεργέω), effect, operation (Polyb.) : pl., 1 Co 12⁶, ¹⁰ (Cremer, 262, 713).†

* ἐνεργής, -ές (late form of ἐνεργός, on wh. cf. AR, Eph., 241), at work, active, effective : 1 Co 16⁹, Phm ⁶, He 4¹² (Cremer, 261).†

† ἐν-ευλογέω, -ῶ, [in LXX chiefly for בָּרַךְ;] to bless : pass., seq. ἐν, Ac 3²⁵ ⁽ᴸˣˣ⁾, Ga 3⁸ ⁽ᴸˣˣ⁾ (Cremer, 770).†

ἐν-έχω, [in LXX: Ge 49²³ (שׂטם), Ez 14⁴˒⁷, III Mac 6¹⁰ *;] 1. *to hold in;* pass., *to be held, entangled:* c. dat. rei; fig., ζυγῷ δουλείας, Ga 5¹ (cf. MM, *Exp.*, xii); θλίψεσιν, II Th 1⁴ (cf. ἀσεβείαις, III Mac, l.c.). 2. *to set oneself against, be urgent against* (as Ge, l.c.; for construction, v. Swete, *Mk.*, l.c.): Mk 6¹⁹, Lk 11⁵³.†

** ἐνθά-δε, adv., [in LXX: II Mac 12²⁷, III Mac 6²⁵ *;] (a) *here:* Lk 24⁴¹, Ac 10¹⁸ 16²⁸ 17⁶ 25²⁴; (b) *hither:* Jo 4¹⁵˒¹⁶, Ac 25¹⁷.†

ἔνθεν, adv., [in LXX for מְזֶה, מִפֹּה, etc.;] *hence:* Mt 17²⁰, Lk 16²⁶.†

ἐνθυμέομαι, -οῦμαι (< θυμός), [in LXX for דמה pi., etc.;] *to reflect on, ponder:* c. acc. rei, Mt 1²⁰ 9⁴.†

** ἐνθύμησις, -εως, ἡ (< ἐνθυμέομαι), [in Sm.: Jb 21²⁷, Ez 11²¹ *;] *consideration, pondering* (EV, *device*): Ac 17²⁹; pl., *thoughts, feelings:* Mt 9⁴ 12²⁵, He 4¹².†

SYN.: ἔννοια, the action of the reason; while ἐνθ. is rather that of the affections (cf. Westc., *Heb.*, l.c.).

** ἔνι, Ionic form of ἐν (ἐνί), with strengthened accent; [in LXX: Si 37², IV Mac 4²² *;] = ἔνεστι, *is in, has place, can be:* I Co 6⁵, Ga 3²⁸ ⁽ᵗʳⁱˢ⁾, Col 3¹¹, Ja 1¹⁷ (cf. Lft., *Ga.*; Hort and Mayor, *Ja.*, ll. c.).†

ἐνιαυτός, -οῦ, ὁ, [in LXX for שׁנה;] 1. prop., *a cycle of time.* 2. = ἔτος, *a year:* Jo 11⁴⁹˒⁵¹ 18¹³, Ac 11²⁶ 18¹¹, Ja 5¹⁷, Re 9¹⁵; pl., of sabbatical years, Ga 4¹⁰; ποιεῖν ἐ., to spend a year, Ja 4¹³; ἅπαξ τοῦ ἐ., He 9⁷; κατ᾽ ἐ., He 9²⁵ 10¹˒³; ἐ. δεκτόν, Lk 4¹⁹ ⁽ᴸˣˣ⁾.†

ἐν-ίστημι, [in LXX: IV Ki 13⁶ A (עמד), III Ki 12²⁴, I Es 5⁴⁷ 9⁶, Es 3¹³, I-IV Mac ₉ *;] *to place in;* in pf., plpf., 2 aor. and in mid., intrans.; (a) *to be at hand, impend, threaten:* II Ti 3¹; (b) *to be present:* II Th 2² (but v. Thayer, s.v.); pf. ptcp., *present:* I Co 7²⁶, Ga 1⁴, He 9⁹; pl., Ro 8³⁸, I Co 3²² (Cremer, 309).†

ἐνίστημι, ἐνεστώς, v. *ICC* on Ga, pp. 432 f.

ἐν-ισχύω, [in LXX for חזק, etc.;] *to strengthen:* in spiritual sense, Lk 22 ⁽⁴³⁾; pass., Ac 9¹⁹ (Rec. ἐνισχύσεν, became strong, as in LXX, Ge 12¹⁰ 48², al.).†

ἐνκάθετος (Rec. ἐγκ-), -ον (< ἐγκαθίημι), [in LXX: Jb 31⁹ (ארב), 19¹² *;] *suborned to lie in wait, lying in wait:* as subst., Lk 20²⁰.†

† ἐνκαίνια (Rec. ἐγκ-), -ων, τά (< ἐν, καινός), [in LXX for חֲנֻכָּה, II Es 6¹⁶˒¹⁷, Ne 12²⁷, Da ᵀᴴ 3² (and cf. ἐγκαινισμός, Nu 7¹⁰, al., -ισις, Nu 7⁸⁸) *;] *dedication* (anniversary of the cleansing of the Temple from the defilements of Antiochus Epiphanes): Jo 10²².†

† ἐν-καινίζω (Rec. ἐγκ-, v.s. ἐν), [in LXX: (to renew) I Ki 11¹⁴, II Ch 15⁸, Ps 50 (51)¹⁰ (חדשׁ pi.); (to dedicate) De 20⁵, II Ch 7⁵ (חנך); Is 16¹¹ 41¹ 45¹⁶ (aliter in Heb.), Si 33 (36)⁶, I Mac 4³⁶˒⁵⁴˒⁵⁷ 5¹, II Mac 2³⁹ *;] 1. *to innovate* (Eust.). 2. *to renew* (LXX ut supr.). 3. *to initiate, inaugurate, dedicate* (LXX ut supr.): διαθήκην, He 9¹⁸; ὁδόν, ib. 10²⁰ (Cremer, 323).†

**† ἐν-κακέω, -ῶ (LTr., ἐγκ-; Rec. ἐκκ-; cf. WH, *Notes*, 157 f.; < κακός, cowardly), [in Sm.: Ge 27⁴⁶, Nu 21⁵, Pr 3¹¹, Is 7¹⁶ *;] *to lose heart:* Lk 18¹, II Co 4¹˒¹⁶, Ga 6⁹, Eph 3¹³, II Th 3¹³ (Cremer, 330).†

*ἐν-κατοικέω, -ῶ (Rec. ἐγκ-, v.s. ἐν), *to dwell among:* seq. ἐν, II Pe 2⁸.†

†ἐν-καυχάομαι (Rec. ἐγκ-, v.s. ἐν), -ῶμαι, [in LXX: Ps 51 (52)¹ 96 (97)⁷ (הלל hithp.); Ps 73 (74)⁴ (שאג); Ps 105 (106)⁴⁷ (שבח) *;] *to take pride in, glory in:* seq. ἐν, II Th 1⁴.†

**ἐν-κεντρίζω (Rec. ἐγκ-, v.s. ἐν; < κεντρίζω, *to graft*), [in LXX: Wi 16¹¹ *;] *to ingraft, graft in:* fig., c. acc. pers., Ro 11¹⁷, ¹⁹, ²³, ²⁴.†

*†ἐν-κοπή (Rec. ἐγκ-, v.s. ἐν; Τ, ἐκκ-), -ῆς, ἡ (< ἐγκόπτω); 1. *an incision, a cutting, break.* 2. Metaph., *an interruption, a hindrance:* I Co 9¹².†

* ἐν-κόπτω (Rec. ἐγκ-, v.s. ἐν; and in I Pe, l.c., ἐκκ-); 1. *to cut into* (as in breaking up a road), hence, 2. *to hinder:* c. acc., Ac 24⁴, I Th 2¹⁸; c. inf., Ga 5⁷; seq. τοῦ, c. inf., Ro 15²²; εἰς τό, c. inf., I Pe 3⁷.†

* ἐν-κρίνω (Rec. ἐγκ-, v.s. ἐν), *to reckon among:* ἑαυτούς, II Co 10¹².†

**ἔγκυος (Rec. ἐγκ-, v.s. ἐν), -ον (< κύω, *to conceive*), [in LXX: Si 42¹⁰ *;] *pregnant, big with child:* Lk 2⁵.†

ἐννέα, οἱ, αἱ, τά, indecl., *nine:* Lk 17¹⁷; ἐνενήκοντα ἐ., Mt 18¹², ¹³, Lk 15⁴, ⁷.†

ἐννενήκοντα, v.s. ἐνεν-.

ἐννεός, v.s. ἐνεός.

ἐν-νεύω, [in LXX: Pr 6¹³ 10¹⁰ (קרץ), Si 27²² A *;] *to nod to, make a sign to:* c. dat. pers., Lk 1⁶².†

ἔννοια, -ας, ἡ (< νοῦς), [in LXX: Pr 1⁴ 2¹¹ 3²¹ 4¹ 5² 8¹² 16²² 18¹⁵ 19⁷ 23⁴, ¹⁹ 24⁷ (מְזִמָּה, etc.), Wi 2¹⁴, Da TH Su 28 *;] 1. *thinking, consideration.* 2. *a thought, purpose, design:* He 4¹², I Pe 4¹.†
SYN.: ἐνθύμησις, q.v. (Cremer, 439).

**ἔν-νομος, -ον, [in LXX: Si, prol. ¹² *;] 1. *lawful, legal* (MM, Exp., xiii): Ac 19³⁹. 2. Of persons, (a) *law-abiding;* (b) *under law:* ἔ. Χριστοῦ, in relation to Christ, I Co 9²¹ (Cremer. 435).†

*†ἔννυχα, v.s. ἔννυχος.

ἔννυχος, -ον (< νύξ), [in LXX: III Mac 5⁵ *;] (in cl. poët.; prose in late Gk. only) *nightly.* Neut., adverbially, ἔννυχα (Rec. -χον), *by night:* Mk 1³⁵.†

ἐν-οικέω, -ῶ, [in LXX chiefly (²⁹/₃₆) for ישב;] *to dwell in;* metaph., seq. c. dat. pers: ὁ θεός, II Co 6¹⁶; τ. πνεῦμα, Ro 8¹¹, II Ti 1¹⁴; ὁ λόγος, Col 3¹⁶; πίστις, II Ti 1⁵; ἁμαρτία, Ro 7¹⁷.†

†ἐν-ορκίζω, [in LXX: Ne 13²⁵ A (שבע hi.) *;] *to adjure:* c. dupl. acc. (like ὁρκίζω, q.v.), ὑμᾶς τ. κύριον, I Th 5²⁷.†

* ἐνότης, -ητος, ἡ (< εἷς), *unity, unanimity:* Eph 4³, ¹³.†

ἐν-οχλέω, -ῶ (< ὄχλος), [in LXX for חלה;] *to trouble:* c. acc., He 12¹⁵ (LXX) (De 29¹⁸. B reads ἐνχολῇ; v. ICC on He in l.). Pass., seq. ἀπό, Lk 6¹⁸.†

ἔνοχος, -ον (= ἐνεχόμενος), (in LXX for ישע hi., etc.;] 1. *held in, bound by:* c. gen. (cl. c. dat.), δουλείας, He 2¹⁵. 2. In law-phrases; (a) *liable* to a charge or action (cl. c. dat., of crime): c. dat., of the tribunal (MM, Exp., xiii), Mt 5²¹, ²²; seq. εἰς (Field, Notes, 4 f.), ib. ²². (b) c. gen., of the punishment (Ge 26¹¹): θανάτου, Mt 26⁶⁶, Mk 14⁶⁴; (c) c. gen. (cl. c. dat., rarely c. prep.; MM, Exp., xiii), of the crime

(II Mac 13⁶) : Mk 3²⁹; (d) c. gen., of the thing injured, *guilty* (absol., in cl.) : I Co 11²⁷, Ja 2¹⁰ (cf. Is 54¹⁷; *DB*, ii, 268ᵃ).†

† ἐν-περι-πατέω, -ῶ (Rec. ἐμπ-, v.s. ἐν), [in LXX : Le 26¹² Jb 1⁷, al. (הלּךְ hithp.), Wi 19²¹;] *to walk about in* or *among :* seq. ἐν., dat. pers., II Co 6¹⁶ (LXX).†

ἐν-πνέω, -ῶ (Rec. ἐμπ-, v.s. ἐν), [in LXX : De 20¹⁶, Jos 10²⁸ ff. 11¹¹, ¹⁴ (ptcp. neut., for נֶפֶשׁ, נְשָׁמָה), Wi 15¹¹ *;] 1. *to breathe on.* 2. *to breathe;* (a) absol.; (b) c. gen. part. : fig., ἀπειλῆς κ. φόνου, Ac 9¹.†

† ἔνταλμα, -τος, τό (< ἐντέλλω), [in LXX : Jb 23¹¹ (אָשׁוּר) ¹², Is 29¹³ (מִצְוָה), 55¹¹ (aliter in Heb.) *;] *a precept :* pl., Mt 15⁹ (LXX), Mk 7⁷, Col 2²².†

† ἐνταφιάζω, [in LXX : Ge 50² (חנט; cf. ἐνταφιαστής, ib., for רֹפֵא; v. Deiss., *BS*, 120 f.; MM, *Exp.*, xiii)*;] a κοινή word (Deiss., *LAE*, 72₃), *to prepare for burial :* Mt 26¹², Jo 19⁴⁰.†

*† ἐνταφιασμός, -οῦ (< ἐνταφιάζω), *preparation for burial :* Mk 14⁸, Jo 12⁷.†

ἐν-τέλλω, [in LXX, as in NT (and mostly in Hdt.), always mid., chiefly for צוה pi.;] -ομαι, *to command, enjoin, instruct :* seq. περί, He 11²²; c. inf., Mt 19⁷; c. dat. pers., Mk 10³, Jo 15¹⁴, ¹⁷, Ac 1²; οὕτως, Ac 13⁴⁷; καθώς, Jo 14³¹ (ἐντολὴν ἔδωκεν, WH); seq. λέγων, Mt 17⁹; c. inf., Jo 8 [5]; ἵνα, Mk 13³⁴; c. acc. rei, Mt 28²⁰, Mk 10³, Jo 15¹⁴, ¹⁷; seq. περί, c. gen. pers., Mt 4⁶ and Lk 4¹⁰ (LXX); διαθήκην ἐ. πρός, c. acc. pers., He 9²⁰ (LXX) (cf. Si 45³).†

SYN. : κελεύω, *to command,* of verbal orders in general; παραγγέλλω, *to charge,* esp. of the transmitted orders of a military commander; ἐντέλλω points rather to the contents of the command (v. Thayer, s.v. κελεύω).

ἐντεῦθεν, adv. (< ἔνθεν), [in LXX chiefly for מִזֶּה;] 1. *of place, hence :* Lk 4⁹ 13³¹, Jo 2¹⁶ 7³ 14³¹ 18³⁶; ἐ. καὶ ἐ. (for cl. ἔνθεν κ. ἔνθεν), *on this side and on that, on each side,* Jo 19¹⁸; similarly, ἐ. καὶ ἐκεῖθεν, Re 22². 2. *Of time, thereupon.* 3. *Causal; hence, therefore :* Ja 4¹.†

** ἔν-τευξις, -εως, ἡ (< ἐντυγχάνω, q.v.), [in LXX : II Mac 4⁸ *;] 1. *a lighting upon, meeting with.* 2. *conversation.* 3. *a petition* (in this sense common in π.; cf. Deiss., *BS*, 121 f., 146; MM, *Exp.*, xiii) : I Ti 4⁵; pl., ib. 2¹.†

SYN. : δέησις (q.v.).

ἔντιμος, -ον (< τιμή), [in LXX for הֹד, etc.;] *honoured, prized, precious :* of persons, Lk 7², Phl 2²⁹; compar., Lk 14⁸; of things, metaph., λίθος, I Pe 2⁴, ⁶ (LXX).†

ἐντολή, -ῆς, ἡ (< ἐντέλλω, q.v.), [in LXX chiefly for מִצְוָה; in pl. freq. in Pss for פִּקּוּדִים;] 1. generally, *a charge, injunction, order, command :* Lk 15²⁹, Jo 10¹⁸ 11⁵⁷ 12⁴⁹, ⁵⁰ 14³¹, Ac 17¹⁵, Col 4¹⁰; ἐ. σαρκίνη, He 7¹⁶, ¹⁸. 2. Esp. *of religious precepts and commandments;* (a) of God's commandments : in OT, Mt 15³ 22³⁶, ³⁸, ⁴⁰, Mk

7⁸,⁹ 10⁵,¹⁹ 12²⁸,³¹, Eph 2¹⁵, He 9¹⁹; esp. of the decalogue, Mt 5¹⁹ 19¹⁷, Mk 10¹⁹, Lk 18²⁰ 23⁵⁶, Ro 7⁸⁻¹³ 13⁹, Eph 6²; of God's commandments in general, Lk 1⁶, ι Co 7¹⁹, ι Jo 2³⁻⁸ 3²²⁻²⁴ 4²¹ 5²,³, Re 12¹⁷ 14¹²; collectively, ἡ ἐ. (cf. τ. ἔργον τ. θεοῦ, Jo 6²⁹), ι Ti 6¹⁴, ιι Pe 2²¹ 3²; (b) of things commanded Christ by the Father: Jo 12⁴⁹,⁵⁰ 14³¹ 15¹⁰; (c) of the precepts of Christ: Jo 13³⁴ 14¹⁵,²¹ 15¹⁰,¹², ι Co 14³⁷. 3. Phrases: seq. ἵνα, Jo 13³⁴ 15¹², ι Jo 3²³ 4²¹, ιι Jo⁶; ἐντολὴν (ἂς) παραβαίνειν, Mt 15³; ἀκυροῦν, Mt 15⁶ Rec.; τηρεῖν, Mt 19¹⁷, Jo 15¹⁰, al.; ποιεῖν, ι Jo 5²; διδόναι, Jo 11⁵⁷; λαμβάνειν, Jo 10¹⁸, ιι Jo⁴; ἔχειν, Jo 14²¹, He 7⁵; ἐ. καὶ δικαιώματα, Lk 1⁶; ἐντολαὶ ἀνθρώπων (of Jewish tradition), Tit 1¹⁴; ἐ. καινή, Jo 13³⁴, ι Jo 2⁷, ιι Jo⁵.†

* ἐντόπιος, -ον (< τόπος), of a place, resident : Ac 21¹².†

ἐντός (< ἐν), adv., [in LXX: Jb 18²⁰, Ps 38 (39)³ 108 (109)²², Ca 3¹⁰; ὁ, τὸ, τὰ ἐ., Ps 102 (103)¹, Is 16¹¹, Da ᴛʜ 10¹⁶, Si 19²⁶, ι Mac 4⁴⁸*;] within : c. gen., ἐ. ὑμῶν, within you (i.e. in your hearts, R, txt.), or among you (R, mg.), Lk 17²¹ (cf. Field, Notes, 71; Thayer, s.v.; ICC, Lk, l.c.; Dalman, Words, 145 ff.); τὸ ἐ., Mt 23²⁶.†

ἐν-τρέπω, [in LXX for כנע ni., כלם ni., etc.;] to turn about; metaph., put to shame : c. acc., ι Co 4¹⁴; pass., ιι Th 3¹⁴, Tit 2⁸; mid., to reverence : c. acc. pers. (cl. c. gen.), Mt 21³⁷, Mk 12⁶, Lk 18²,⁴ 20¹³, He 12⁹ (cf. MM, Exp., iii, xiii).†

* ἐν-τρέφω, to train up, nurture; pass., metaph., τοῖς λόγοις τ. πίστεως, ι Ti 4⁶.†

† ἔν-τρομος, -ον, [in LXX: Da ᴛʜ 10¹¹ (רעד hi.); ἐ. γίγνεσθαι, Ps 17 (18)⁷ 76 (77)¹⁸ (רעש), Wi 17¹⁰, ι Mac 13²*;] trembling with fear (Plut.): Ac 7³² 16²⁹, He 12²¹ (ἔκτρ-, WH, mg.).†

ἐν-τροπή, -ῆς, ἡ, [in LXX: Jb 20³, Ps 34 (35)²⁶ 43 (44)¹⁵ 68 (69)⁷,¹⁹ 70 (71)¹³ 108 (109)²⁹ (כלמה)*;] 1. c. gen. pers., respect, reverence (Soph., Polyb., al.). 2. Absol., shame (Hipp.): ι Co 6⁵ 15³⁴.†

ἐν-τρυφάω, -ῶ, [in LXX: Is 55² 57⁴ (ענג hith.), Hb 1¹⁰ (קלם hith.), ιν Mac 8⁸, etc.;] to revel in : ἐν τ. ἀπάταις, ιι Pe 2¹³ (v. Mayor, in l.).†

ἐν-τυγχάνω, [in LXX: Da ᴛʜ 6¹² ⁽¹³⁾ (קרב), Wi 8²⁰ 16²⁸, ιι Mac 2²⁵ 4³⁶ 6¹² 15³⁹, ιιι Mac 6³⁷; seq. κατά, ι Mac 8³² 10⁶¹,⁶³,⁶⁴ 11²⁵*;] 1. to fall in with. 2. to meet with in order to converse. 3. to petition, make petition : c. dat. pers., seq. ὑπέρ c. gen. pers., Ac 25²⁴ (cf. Field, Notes, 140), He 7²⁵, Ro 8²⁷,³⁴ (θεῷ, not expressed); seq. κατά, against : Ro 11² (cf. ἔντευξις, ὑπερ-εντυγχάνω).†

* ἐν-τυλίσσω, to wrap up (LS), roll or coil about (DCG, ii, 227ª, 507ª) : c. acc. et dat., Mt 27⁵⁹ (ἐν, Tr. [WH], cf. similar sentence in π.; MM, Exp., xiii), Lk 23⁵³; pass., Jo 20⁷.†

ἐν-τυπόω, -ῶ (< τύπος), [in LXX for פתח, Ex 36³⁹ (39³⁰) A*;] to imprint, engrave : pass. ptcp., c. dat., ιι Co 3⁷.†

** ἐν-υβρίζω, [in OT (Al.), Le 24¹¹*;] to insult, mock at : He 10²⁹.†

ἐνυπνιάζω (< ἐνύπνιον), [in LXX, as in NT, -ομαι, depon., chiefly for חלם;] to dream : ἐνυπνίοις ἐ., Ac 2¹⁷ ⁽ᴸˣˣ⁾; pres. ptcp., Ju⁸.†

ἐνύπνιον, -ου, τό (< ὕπνος), [in LXX chiefly for חֲלוֹם;] *a dream*: pl., Ac 2¹⁷.†

† ἐνώπιος, -ον (< ὤψ), [in LXX for פָּנֶה, etc.;] *face to face, in sight* (Theocr.; ἄρτοι ἐ., Ex 25²⁹): neut., ἐνώπιον, in vernacular, with force of prep. c. gen. [in LXX for לִפְנֵי, לְעֵינֵי, etc., cf. Dalman, *Words*, 31 f., 209 f., and Deiss., *BS.*, 213], בְ NT, most freq. in Lk, Ac, Re, never in Mt, Mk, *before, in the presence of:* Lk 1¹⁹ 4⁷, Ac 4¹⁰ 6⁵, Re 1⁴ 2¹⁴, al.; esp. ἐ. κυρίου (θεοῦ), in the sight of God, or with God as witness or as judge, Ro 14²², I Co 1²⁹, I Ti 2³, Ja 4¹⁰, I Pe 3⁴, al.

Ἐνώς (Heb. אֱנוֹשׁ), ὁ, *Enos* (Ge 4²⁶): Lk 3³⁸.†

† ἐνωτίζομαι (< οὖς), depon. mid., [in LXX chiefly for אזן hi.;] *to give ear to, hearken to:* c. acc., Ac 2¹⁴.†

Ἐνώχ (Heb. חֲנוֹךְ), ὁ, *Enoch* (Ge 5¹⁸): Lk 3³⁷, He 11⁵, Ju ¹⁴.†

ἐξ, v.s. ἐκ.

ἕξ, οἱ, αἱ, τά, indecl., *six:* Mt 17¹, Lk 13¹⁴, al.

ἐξ-αγγέλλω, [in LXX chiefly for ספר pi.;] *to tell out, proclaim:* I Pe 2⁹ [Mk 16, "shorter conclusion"] (Cremer, 29).†

† ἐξ-αγοράζω, [in LXX: καιρὸν ὑμεῖς ἐξαγοράζετε (זְבַן), Da LXX TH 2⁸*;] 1. *to redeem, ransom* (esp. of slaves): metaph., Ga 3¹³ 4⁵.   2. *to buy up;* mid., *to buy up for oneself:* τ. καιρόν, Eph 5¹⁶, Col 4⁵ (Cremer, 60).†

ἐξ-άγω, [in LXX chiefly for יָצָא hi.;] *to lead out:* c. acc., Mk 15²⁰, Jo 10³, Ac 5¹⁹ 7³⁶ 16³⁷, ³⁹; seq. ἔξω, Lk 24⁵⁰; ἐκ, Ac 7⁴⁰ 12¹⁷ 13¹⁷, He 8⁹; εἰς, Ac 21³⁸.†

ἐξ-αιρέω -ῶ, [in LXX chiefly for נצל hi.;] *to take out:* c. acc., ὀφθαλμόν, Mt 5²⁹ 18⁹; mid. (*a*) *to take out for oneself, choose:* Ac 26¹⁷ (Thayer, s.v.; Page, *Ac.*, l.c., but v. infr.); (*b*) *to deliver:* Ac 7¹⁰, ³⁴ (LXX) 12¹¹ 23²⁷ 26¹⁷ (EV, but v. supr.), Ga 1⁴.†

ἐξ-αίρω, [in LXX for נסע, ירשׁ hi., כרת ni., סור, בער pi., etc.;] *to lift up, lift off the earth, remove:* I Co 5¹³ (LXX).†

* ἐξ-αιτέω, -ῶ, *to ask from;* mid., *to ask for oneself, demand:* aor., ἐξῃτήσατο, c. acc. (*obtained you by asking*, R, mg.), Lk 22³¹ (v. Field, *Notes*, 76; Cremer, 73).†

ἐξ-αίφνης (WH, ἐξέφνης, exc. Ac 22⁶; v. App., p. 151, and cf. M, *Pr.*, 35), adv. (< ἄφνω), [in LXX chiefly for פִּתְאֹם;] *suddenly:* Mk 13³⁶, Lk 2¹³ 9³⁹, Ac 9³ 22⁶.†

† ἐξ-ακολουθέω, -ῶ, [in LXX: Am 2⁴, Je 2² (הָלַךְ אַחַר), Is 56¹¹ (פנה), Jb 31⁹ (פתה ni.), Si 5², Da LXX TH, 3⁽⁴¹⁾*;] *to follow, follow up* (in various senses): metaph., II Pe 1¹⁶ 2², ¹⁵.†

ἑξακόσιοι, -αι, -α, *six hundred:* Re 13¹⁸ 14²⁰.†

ἐξ-αλείφω, [in LXX for מחה, Le 14⁴², al.; metaph., מחה, שׁחת,

etc.;] 1. *to plaster, wash over* (LXX). 2. *to wipe off, wipe out :*
δάκρυον, Re 7¹⁷ 21⁴; metaph., χειρόγραφον, Col 2¹⁴; τ. ὄνομα, seq. ἐκ,
Re 3⁵ (MM, *Exp.*, xiii); pass., ἀμαρ·ίαι (ἐξαλιφθῆι αι, WH), Ac 3¹⁹ (cf.
Ps 50 (15)¹¹ 108 (109)¹³, Is 43²⁵, Si 46²⁰ (ἁμ. ἀπαλ-), III Mac 2¹⁹).†

ἐξ-άλλομαι, [in LXX for קלל (Hb 1⁸), etc.;] *to leap up :* Ac 3⁸.†

* **ἐξ-ανάστασις, -εως, ἡ** (< ἐξανίστημι), *a rising again :* ἐκ τ. νεκρῶν,
Phl 3¹¹ (Cremer, 308).†

ἐξ-ανα-τέλλω, [in LXX : Ge 2⁹, Ps 103 (104)¹⁴ 131 (132)¹⁷ 146 (147)⁸
(צמח hi.); Ps 111 (112)⁴ (זרח) *;] 1. trans., *to cause to spring up* (LXX).
2. Intrans. (as ἀνατέλλω, Ge 3¹⁸), *to spring up :* Mt 13⁵, Mk 4⁵.†

ἐξ-ανίστημι, [in LXX chiefly for קום;] 1. trans., *to raise up :* σπέρμα
(cf. Ge 38⁸), Mk 12¹⁹, Lk 20²⁸. 2. In 2 aor. act., intrans., *to rise :*
Ac 15⁵.†

ἐξ-απατάω, -ῶ, strengthened form of ἀπατάω, [in LXX : Ex 8²⁹ ⁽²⁵⁾
(תלל hi.), Da ΤΗ Su ⁵⁶ *;] *to deceive :* c. acc., Ro 7¹¹ 16¹⁸, ι Co 3¹⁸,
II Co 11³, II Th 2³; pass., ι Ti 2¹⁴.†

† **ἐξάπινα** = ἐξαπίνης, ἐξαίφνης (q.v.), [in LXX for פתאם, etc.;]
suddenly : Mk 9⁸.†

† **ἐξ-απορέω, -ῶ,** [in LXX, pass., for פוך, Ps 87 (88)¹⁵ *;] so in NT,
depon. pass., *to be utterly at a loss, be in despair :* absol. (as Ps, l.c.),
II Co 4⁸; τοῦ ζῆν, II Co 1⁸.†

ἐξ-απο-στέλλω, [in LXX freq., chiefly for שלח pi.;] 1. *to send
forth :* c. acc. pers., Ac 7¹² 12¹¹, Ga 4⁴; τ. ἐπαγγελίαν, Lk 24⁴⁹; τ. πνεῦμα,
Ga 4⁶; [τ. κήρυγμα, Mk 16, "shorter conclusion," WH;] seq. εἰς,
Ac 22²¹; pass., ὁ λόγος, Ac 13²⁶. 2. *to send away :* c. acc. pers., seq.
εἰς, Ac 9³⁰; seq. ἕως, Ac 11²²; c. inf., Ac 17¹⁴; κενόν, Lk 1⁵³ 20¹⁰, ¹¹.†

† **ἐξ-αρτίζω** (< ἄρτιος), [in LXX : Ex 28⁷ (חבר pu.) *;] 1. *to complete, finish :* τ. ἡμέρας, Ac 21⁵. 2. *to furnish, supply :* pass., II Ti 3¹⁷
(for exx., v. MM, *Exp.*, xiii ; Cremer, 651).†

† **ἐξ-αστράπτω,** [in LXX : Nu 3³ (ברק), Ez 1⁴ (לקח hithp.) 1⁷
Da LXX 10⁶ (קלל) *;] *to flash like lightning, gleam, be radiant :*
ἱματισμός, Lk 9²⁹.†

* **ἐξ-αυτῆς** (a κοινή word, = ἐξ αὐτῆς τ. ὥρας), *at once, forthwith :*
Mk 6²⁵, Ac 10³³ 11¹¹ 21³² 23³⁰, Phl 2²³.†

ἐξ-εγείρω, [in LXX for עור ni., hi., etc.;] *to raise up :* Ro 9¹⁷ (cf.
ICC, in l.); from the dead, ι Co 6¹⁴.†

ἔξ-ειμι (< εἶμι), *to go forth :* Ac 13⁴² 17¹⁵ 20⁷; seq. ἐπί, c. acc.,
Ac 27⁴³.†

ἔξ-ειμι (< εἰμί), v.s. ἔξεστι.

ἐξ-ελέγχω, [in LXX : Pr 24²⁹ (30⁶), Mi 4³, Is 2⁴ (יכח hi.), Wi 12¹⁷,
IV Mac 2¹² *;] *to convict :* Ju ¹⁵, Rec. (for ἐλέγχω, WH, q.v.).†

ἐξ-έλκω, [in LXX : Ge 37²⁸ (משׁך), etc.;] *to draw out* or *away :*
metaph., ὑπὸ τ. ἐπιθυμίας, Ja 1¹⁴ (v. Mayor, in l.).†

*† **ἐξέραμα, -τος, τό** (< ἐξεράω, *to evacuate, disgorge*), *a vomit :*
II Pe 2²² ⁽ᴸˣˣ⁾.†

ἐξ-εραυνάω (Rec. ἐξερευνάω), **-ῶ,** [in LXX for חקר, נצר, etc.;] *to
search out, search carefully :* seq. περί, ι Pe 1¹⁰.†

ἐξερευνάω, v.s. ἐξεραυνάω.

ἐξ-έρχομαι, [in LXX chiefly and very freq. for יָצָא, also for בּוֹא, עָלָה, etc.;] depon., *to go*, or *come out of*: Mt 10¹¹, Mk 1³⁵, Jo 13³⁰, al.; c. inf., Mt 11⁸, Mk 3²¹, Lk 7²⁵, ²⁶, Ac 20¹, Re 20⁸; id. seq. ἐπί, Mt 26⁵⁵, al.; εἰς, Mk 1³⁸; ἵνα, Re 6²; ἐ. seq. ἐκ (cl. c. gen. loc.), Mk 5², Jo 4³⁰, al.; ἐξω, c. gen., Mt 21¹⁷, Mk 14⁶⁸, Ac 16¹³, He 13¹³; ἀπό. Mk 11¹², Lk 9⁵, Phl 4¹⁵; ἐκεῖθεν, Mt 15²¹, Mk 6¹, Lk 9⁴, al.; of demons expelled, seq. ἐκ (ἀπό), c. gen. pers., Mk 1²⁵, ²⁶ 5⁸, Lk 4³⁵, al.; of prisoners released, Mt 5²⁶, Ac 16⁴⁰; ptcp., ἐξελθών, c. indic. of verb of departure (cf. Dalman, *Words*, 20 f.), Mt 8³² 15²¹ 24¹, Mk 16⁸, Lk 22³⁹, Ac 12⁹, ¹⁷, al. Metaph., (*a*) of persons : II Co 6¹⁷, I Jo 2¹⁹; of birth or origin, Mt 2⁶ (LXX), He 7⁵ (cf. Ge 35¹¹); of escape from danger, ἐκ τ. χειρὸς αὐτῶν, Jo 10³⁹; of public appearance, I Jo 4¹; (*b*) of things : Mt 24²⁷; esp. of utterances, reports, proclamations : φωνή, Re 16¹⁷ 19⁵; φήμη, Mt 9²⁶, Lk 4¹⁴; ἀκοή, Mk 1²⁸; λόγος, Jo 21²³; δόγμα, Lk 2¹ (cf. δι-εξέρχομαι).

ἔξ-εστι (< εἰμί), impers. verb., *it is permitted, lawful* : Mk 2²⁴, Ac 8³⁷ (R, mg.), I Co 10²³; c. inf.. Mt 12², ¹⁰, ¹² 14⁴ 15²⁶ 19³ 22¹⁷ 27⁶, Mk 3⁴ 12¹⁴, Lk 6², ⁹ 14³, Jo 5¹⁰; seq. acc., Mk 2²⁶, Lk 6⁴ 20²²; c. dat. pers. et inf., Mt 20¹⁵, Mk 6¹⁸ 10², Jo 18³¹, Ac 16²¹ 21³⁷ 22²⁵ (inf. understood), I Co 6¹²; ἐξόν (sc. ἐστί), Ac 2²⁹, II Co 12⁴; ἐξὸν ἦν, Mt 12⁴.†

ἐξ-ετάζω (< ἐτάζω (rare), *to examine*), [in LXX : De 13¹⁴ ⁽¹⁵⁾ 19¹⁸, I Ch 28⁹ A (דָּרַשׁ), Ps 10 (11)⁵, ⁶ (בָּחַן), Wi 6³, Si 3²¹, al.;] *to examine closely, inquire carefully (of)* : seq. περί (c. ἀκριβῶς), Mt 2⁸; seq. τίς, Mt 10¹¹; c. acc. pers., Jo 21¹².†

SYN.: ἀνακρίνω, ἐραυνάω (v. DCG, ii, 594ᵇ).

ἐξέφνης, v.s. ἐξαίφνης.

ἐξ-ηγέομαι, -οῦμαι, [in LXX chiefly for סָפַר pi.;] *to lead, show the way;* metaph., *to unfold, narrate, declare* : c. acc. rei, Lk 24³⁵, Ac 21¹⁹; c. dat. pers., Ac 10⁸; θεόν (understood), Jo 1¹⁸; seq. ὅσα, Ac 15¹²; καθώς, Ac 15¹⁴.†

ἑξήκοντα, οἱ, αἱ, τά, indecl., *sixty* : Mt 13⁸, ²³, Mk 4⁸, ²⁰, Lk 24¹³, I Ti 5⁹, Re 11³ 12⁶ 13¹⁸.†

ἑξῆς, adv. (< ἔχω), *in order, successively, next* : τῇ ἐ. ἡμέρᾳ, Lk 9³⁷; ἐν τῷ ἐ. (sc. χρόνῳ), *soon after*, Lk 7¹¹; τῇ ἐ. (sc. ἡμέρᾳ), Ac 21¹ 25¹⁷ 27¹⁸.†

† ἐξ-ηχέω, -ῶ, [in LXX : Jl 3 (4)¹⁴ (הָמוֹן), Si 40¹³, III Mac 3² *;] *to sound forth* (as a trumpet, or thunder; v. M, *Th.*, l.c.): pass., I Th 1⁸.†

ἕξις, -εως, ἡ (< ἔχω), [in LXX, cf. Si, prol. ⁹;] *habit, use, experience* : He 5¹⁴.†

ἐξ-ίστημι (also in Hellenistic -ιστάνω, Ac 8⁹), [in LXX for חָרַד, etc. (29 words in all);] 1. causal in pres., impf., fut., 1 aor., *to put out of its place;* metaph., ἐ. τινὰ φρενῶν (Eur.), *to drive one out of his senses*, hence, absol., *to confound, amaze* : c. acc. pers., Lk 24²², Ac 8⁹, ¹¹. 2. Intr. in pass. and mid., also in 2 aor., pf., plpf. act., seq. ἐκ or c. gen., *to stand aside from, retire from;* esp. τ. φρενῶν, *to lose one's senses* (Eur.), hence, absol.; (*a*) *to be beside oneself, be mad*: Mk 3²¹, II Co 5¹³ (opp. to σωφρονεῖν); (*b*) *to be amazed, confounded*: Mt 12²³, Mk 2¹² 5⁴² 6⁵¹, Lk 2⁴⁷ 8⁵⁶, Ac 2⁷, ¹² 8¹³ 9²¹ 10⁴⁵ 12¹⁶ (Cremer, 309).†

**† ἐξ-ισχύω, [in LXX: Si 7⁶ *;] *to have strength enough, to be quite able*: c. inf., Eph 3¹⁸.†

ἔξ-οδος, -ου, ὁ (< ὁδός), [in LXX chiefly for מוֹצָא, also חֻדִּין, etc.;] *a going out, departure*: He 11²²; of death, Lk 9³¹, II Pe 1¹⁵.†

† ἐξ-ολεθρεύω (so best MSS. and WH; also read -οθρεύω), [in LXX freq. (rare in Gk. writers) for כרת ni., hi., etc.;] *to destroy utterly*: seq. ἐκ τ. λαοῦ, Ac 3²³ (LXX).†

† ἐξ-ομολογέω, -ῶ, and depon. mid., -έομαι, -οῦμαι, [as always in LXX chiefly for ידה hi.;] 1. act. = cl. ὁμολογέω, *to profess* or *agree to do* (Field, *Notes*, 75): Lk 22⁶. 2. Mid., *to acknowledge, confess* (MM, *Exp.*, xiv): τ. ἁμαρτίας, Mt 3⁶, Mk 1⁵, Ja 5¹⁶; τ. πράξεις, Ac 19¹⁸; seq. ὅτι, Phl 2¹¹; c. dat. pers., *to make acknowledgment to one's honour, to praise, give praise to* (as in LXX; Kennedy, *Sources*, 118): Ro 14¹¹ (LXX) 15⁹ (LXX); seq. ὅτι, Mt 11²⁵, Lk 10²¹ (Cremer, 771).†

ἐξ-όν, v.s. ἔξεστι.

ἐξ-ορκίζω (later form of ἐξορκόω), [in LXX: Jg 17² (אלה), Ge 24³, III Ki 22¹⁶ (שבע hi.) *;] 1. *to administer an oath to* (Dem., Polyb., al.). 2. *to adjure*: c. acc. pers., seq. κατά, c. gen. (as freq. in magic π.; MM, *Exp.*, xiv), Mt 26⁶³.†

**† ἐξ-ορκιστής, -οῦ, ὁ (< ἐξορκίζω), 1. *one who administers an oath*. 2. *an exorcist*: Ac 19¹³.†

ἐξ-ορύσσω, [in LXX: Pr 29²²; ὀφθαλμόν (-ούς), Jg 16²¹, I Ki 11² (נקר) *;] 1. *to dig out, dig up*: στέγην, Mk 2⁴; metaph., ὀ φθαλμούς (cf. LXX, ll. c.; Herod., viii, 116), Ga 4¹⁵.†

† ἐξ-ουδενέω (Rec. -όω; T, -θενόω), -ῶ, [in LXX (with vv. ll. -όω, -θενέω, -θενόω) for בוז, בזה, מאס, בזם, etc.;] *to despise, set at nought*: Mk 9¹² (cf. ἐξουθενέω).†

ἐξ-ουδενόω, v.s. ἐξουδενέω.

† ἐξ-ουθενέω, -ῶ (<οὐθείς, q.v.), [in LXX (v.s. ἐξουδενέω): I Ki 2³⁰, al., and as v.l. for -δενέω, -όω, -θενόω;] *to set at nought, despise utterly, treat with contempt*: c. acc. pers., Lk 18⁹ 23¹¹, Ro 14³, ¹⁰, I Co 16¹¹; c. acc. rei, Ga 4¹⁴, I Th 5²⁰; pass., of persons: Mk 9¹² (T, -όω), I Co 6⁴; of things: λίθος, Ac 4¹¹ (LXX ἀπεδοκίμασαν); λόγος, II Co 10¹⁰; τὰ ἐξουθενημένα, I Co 1²⁸.†

SYN.: ἀθετέω, καταφρονέω (v. DCG, i, 453ᵇ).

† ἐξουθενόω, -ῶ, v.l. for -έω (q.v.): Mk 9¹² T.†

ἐξουσία, -ας, ἡ (< ἔξεστι), [in LXX: IV Ki 20¹³, Ps 113 (114)² 135 (136)⁸, ⁹, Is 39², Je 28 (51)²⁸ (מֶמְשָׁלָה), freq. in Da for Aram. שָׁלְטָן, etc., Wi 10¹⁴, Si 9¹³, al.;] 1. prop., *liberty* or *power to act, freedom to exercise the inward force or faculty* expressed by δύναμις (q.v.): I Co 9¹²; ἐ. ἔχειν, II Th 3⁹; id. seq. inf., Jo 10¹⁸, I Co 9⁴, ⁵; c. gen. obj., Ro 9²¹; seq. ἐπί, c. acc., Re 22¹⁴; περί, I Co 7³⁷. 2. Later (cf. Milligan, *Th.*, 114; MM, *Exp.*, xiv), of the power of *right*, *authority*: Mt 21²³, Mk 11²⁸, Lk 20²; of Messianic authority, Mt 9⁶, Mk 2¹⁰, al.; of apostolic authority, II Co 10⁸ 13¹⁰; of the authority of government: Mt 8⁹ 28¹⁸, Ju ²⁵, Re 12¹⁰, al.; esp. of judicial authority, Lk 20²⁰, Jo 19¹⁰,¹¹. 3. Meton., (*a*) *jurisdiction*: Lk 23⁷ (cf. I Mac 6¹¹, Is 39²); (*b*) *a ruler* or *magistrate*: Ro 13¹⁻³; pl., Lk 12¹¹, Ro 13¹, Tit 3¹; (*c*) of supramundane powers (syn. with ἀρχή, δύναμις, θρόνος, κυριότης): I Co 15²⁴, Eph 1²¹ 3¹⁰, Col 2¹⁰, I Pe 3²², al. (Cremer, 236). *SYN.*: v.s. δύναμις.

ἐξουσιάζω (< ἐξουσία), [in LXX (freq. in Ec) chiefly for שׁלט;] 1. *to exercise authority* (Arist.). 2. Trans., *to exercise authority over*: c. gen. pers., Lk 22²⁵; c. gen. rei, I Co 7⁴; pass., *to be held under authority* (v. Lft., *Notes*, 214): seq. ὑπό, I Co 6¹².†

ἐξοχή, -ῆς, ἡ (< ἐξέχω, *to stand out*), [in LXX for שׁוֹע, Jb 39²⁸ *;] 1. *a projection* (ἐ. πέτρας, Jb, l.c.). 2. Metaph., *eminence, excellence*: οἱ κατ᾽ ἐ., *the chief men*, Ac 25²³.†

†ἐξ-υπνίζω, [in LXX: Jg 16¹⁴,²⁰, III Ki 3¹³ (יקץ), Jb 14¹² (עוּר ni.)*;] *to awaken out of sleep* (= ἀφυπνίζω): c. acc. pers., Jo 11¹¹.†

**†ἔξ-υπνος, -ον (< ὕπνος), [in LXX: I Es 3³ *;] *roused out of sleep*: Ac 16²⁷.†

ἔξω, adv. (< ἐξ), [in LXX for חוּץ;] 1. *outside, without; (a)* adverbially: Mt 12⁴⁶, Mk 3³¹ 11⁴, Lk 8²⁰, Jo 18¹⁶, al.; c. art., ὁ ἔ., *he who is without;* metaph., in pl., οἱ ἔ., of those outside the Church, I Co 5¹²,¹³, Col 4⁵ (Lft., in l.), I Th 4¹²; ὁ ἔ. ἄνθρωπος, II Co 4¹⁶; αἱ ἔ. πόλεις, Ac 26¹¹; (*b*) as prep. c. gen.: Lk 13³³, Ac 21⁵, He 13¹¹,¹². 2. After verbs of motion; (*a*) adverbially, *forth, out:* Mt 5¹³ 26⁷⁵, Mk 14⁶⁸, Lk 22⁶², Jo 6³⁷ 19⁴,¹³, Ac 9⁴⁰, al.; (*b*) as prep. c. gen., *out of:* Mt 21¹⁷, Mk 11¹⁹ 12⁸, Lk 4²⁹, Ac 7⁵⁸, He 13¹³, al.

ἔξωθεν, adv. (< ἔξω; opp. to ἔσωθεν), [in LXX for חוּץ;] 1. prop. (in answer to the question, *Whence?*), *from without:* Mk 7¹⁸. 2. More often (= ἔξω; cf. Bl., § 25, 3), *without:* Mt 23²⁷,²⁸, Mk 7¹⁸, II Co 7⁵; τὸ ἔ., Mt 23²⁵, Lk 11³⁹,⁴⁰; οἱ ἔ., I Ti 3⁷, Mk 4¹¹ (WH, mg.); ὁ ἔ. κόσμος, I Pe 3³; ἐκβάλλειν ἔ., Re 11². As prep. c. gen.: Mk 7¹⁵, Re 11² 14²⁰ (cf. Robertson, *Gr.*, 548).†

ἐξ-ωθέω, -ῶ, [in LXX chiefly for נדה hi.;] 1. *to thrust out:* Ac 7⁴⁵. 2. *to drive out of the sea, drive on shore:* Ac 27³⁹ (WH, txt., ἐκσῶσαι).†

†ἐξώτερος, -α, -ον (compar., from ἔξω; opp. to ἐσώτερος), [in LXX chiefly for חִיצוֹן;] *outer:* σκότος, Mt 8¹² 22¹³ 25³⁰.†

ἔοικα, pf. with pres. sense, [Jb 6³,²⁵ ;*] *to be like:* c. dat., Ja 1⁶,²³.†

ἑορτάζω (< ἑορτή), [in LXX for חגג;] *to keep festival:* I Co 5⁸.†

ἑορτή, -ῆς, ἡ, [in LXX for חַג (chiefly), מוֹעֵד;] *a feast, festival:* Lk 2⁴², Jo 5¹ 6⁴ 7³⁷, Col 2¹⁶; ἡ ἑ. τοῦ πάσχα, Lk 2⁴¹, Jo 13¹; τ. ἀζύμων, Lk 22¹; ἡ σκηνοπηγία, Jo 7² (Deiss., *LAE*, 116); ἐν τ. ἑ., Mt 26⁵, Mk 14², Jo 4⁴⁵ 7¹¹ 12²⁰ (εἶναι ἐν ἑ.), ib. 2²³; εἰς τ. ἑ. (*for the feast*),

Jo 13²⁹; ἀναβαίνειν, ἔρχεσθαι εἰς τ. ἐ., Jo 4⁴⁵ 7⁸, ¹⁰ 11⁵⁶ 12¹²; τῆς ἐ. μεσούσης, Jo 7¹⁴; κατὰ ἐ. (at each feast), Mt 27¹⁵, Mk 15⁶, Lk 23¹⁷, R, mg.; τ. ἐ. ποιεῖν, Ac 18²¹; κατὰ τὸ ἔθος τῆς ἐ., Lk 2⁴².†

ἐπ-αγγελία, -ας, ἡ (< ἐπαγγέλλω), [in LXX: Ps 55 (56)⁸ (סְפָרָה‎)), etc.;] 1. a summons (as Attic law-term, Dem., al.). 2. a promise (Dem., Arist., al.): Ac 23²¹; esp. in NT of the divine promises, Ac 7¹⁷, Ro 4¹⁴, ¹⁶ 9⁴, Ga 3¹⁷, ¹⁸, ²¹ 4²³, He 8⁶ 11⁹, ¹⁷, II Pe 3⁹; c. inf., He 4¹; γίνεται, etc., c. dat. pers., Ac 2³⁹, Ro 4¹³, Ga 3¹⁶; seq. πρός, Ac 13³² 26⁶; ἐπαγγέλεσθαι τὴν ἐ., I Jo 2²⁵; ἔχειν ἐπαγγελίας, He 7⁶, II Co 7¹; εἶναι ἐν ἐπαγγελίᾳ, Eph 6²; ἡ γῆ τῆς ἐ., He 11⁹; τὰ τέκνα τῆς ἐ., Ro 9⁸, Ga 4²⁸; τ. πνεῦμα τῆς ἐ. τ. ἅγιον, Eph 1¹³; αἱ διαθῆκαι τῆς ἐ., Eph 2¹²; ἡ ἐ. τ. θεοῦ, Ro 4²⁰; pl., II Co 1²⁰; αἱ ἐ. τ. πατέρων, Ro 15⁸; c. gen. obj., τ. ζωῆς (v. Dalman, Words, 103), I Ti 4⁸; τ. παρουσίας αὐτοῦ, II Pe 3⁴; κατ᾽ ἐπαγγελίαν, Ac 13²³, Ga 3²⁹, II Ti 1¹; δι᾽ ἐπαγγελίας, Ga 3¹⁸; συμμέτοχα τῆς ἐ., Eph 3⁶; λόγος ἐπαγγελίας, Ro 9⁹. By meton. (cf. ἐλπίς), of a promised blessing: Lk 24⁴⁹, Ac 1¹⁴, Ga 3²², He 6¹², ¹⁵, ¹⁷ 10³⁶ 11¹³, ³³, ³⁹; c. gen. epexeg., Ac 2³³, Ga 3¹⁴, He 9¹⁵ (Cremer, 27).†

ἐπ-αγγέλλω, [in LXX: Es 4⁸ (אמר‎), Pr 13¹², Wi 2¹³, al.;] 1. to announce, proclaim. 2. (a) to promise; (b) to profess. Mid., also freq. in both these senses; (c) to promise: c. dat. pers., He 6¹³; c. acc. rei, Ro 4²¹, Tit 1²; c. dat pers. et acc. rei, Ja 1¹² 2⁵, II Pe 2¹⁹; ἐπαγγελίαν, I Jo 2²⁵; c. inf., Mk 14¹¹, Ac 7⁵; seq. λέγων, He 12²⁶; ptcp., He 10²³ 11¹¹; (d) to profess: θεοσέβειαν, I Ti 2¹⁰; γνῶσιν, ib. 6²¹. Pass., Ga 3¹⁹ (cf. προ-επαγγέλλω; and v. Cremer, 26).†

*ἐπ-άγγελμα, -τος, τό (< ἐπαγγέλλω), a promise: II Pe 1⁴ 3¹³.†

ἐπ-άγω, [in LXX for בֹּוא‎ hi., etc. (29 words in all);] to bring upon: c. dat. et acc., II Pe 2⁵; ἑαυτοῖς ἐ. (for cl. mid., v. Mayor, in l.), ib. 2¹; ἐ. τὸ αἷμα (cf. Ge 20⁹), Ac 5²⁸.†

*†ἐπ-αγωνίζομαι, depon.; 1. to contend with (Plut.). 2. to contend for (C.I., 2335, 19): c. dat. rei, Ju ³.†

*†ἐπ-αθροίζω, to assemble besides (Plut.): pass., Lk 11²⁹.†

Ἐπαίνετος (Rec. -τός), -ου, ὁ, Epænetus, a Christian of Rome: Ro 16⁵.†

ἐπ-αινέω, -ῶ, [in LXX for הלל‎ pi., שבח‎ pi.;] to praise: c. acc., Ro 15¹¹, I Co 11²²; seq. ὅτι, Lk 16⁸, I Co 11²; absol., seq. ὅτι, I Co 11¹⁷.†

ἔπ-αινος, -ου, ὁ, [in LXX for תְּהִלָּה‎, etc.;] praise: Ro 2²⁹ 13³, I Co 4⁵, II Co 8¹⁸, Eph 1⁶, ¹², ¹⁴, Phl 1¹¹ 4⁸, I Pe 17 2¹⁴.†

ἐπ-αίρω, [in LXX for נשא‎, רוּם‎, etc.;] to lift up, raise: τ. ἀρτέμονα, Ac 27⁴⁰; χεῖρας, Lk 24⁵⁰, I Ti 2⁸; κεφαλάς, Lk 21²⁸; ὀφθαλμούς, Mt 17⁸, Lk 6²⁰ 16²³ 18¹³, Jo 4³⁵ 6⁵ 17¹; φωνήν, Lk 11²⁷, Ac 2¹⁴ 14¹¹ 22²²; τ. πτέρναν (fig.), Jo 13¹⁸. Pass., Ac 1⁹; metaph., to be lifted up with pride: II Co 10⁵ 11²⁰.†

ἐπ-αισχύνομαι, [in LXX: Jb 34¹⁹ (נשא‎), Ps 118 (119)⁶ (בּוּשׁ‎), Is 12⁹ A (חָפֵר‎)*;] to be ashamed (of): absol., II Ti 1¹²; c. acc. pers., Mk 8³⁸, Lk 9²⁶; c. acc rei, Ro 1¹⁶, II Ti 1⁸, ¹⁶; ἐπί, c. dat. rei, Ro 6²¹; c. inf., He 2¹¹; c. acc. pers. et inf., He 11¹⁶.†

ἐπ-αιτέω, -ῶ, [in LXX: Ps 108(109)[10] (שָׁאַל), Si 40[28]*;] to ask besides. 2. to beg (as a mendicant; cf. MM, Exp., xiv): Lk 16³ 18³⁵ (Cremer, 74).†

ἐπ-ακολουθέω, -ῶ, [in LXX (chiefly metaph.) for אַחַר, הָלַךְ, etc.;] to follow after; in NT metaph.; absol.: Mk 16[20] (illustrated by use in verifying accounts; v. MM, Exp., xiv; Milligan, NTD, 78); c. dat. pers., of sins, ι Ti 5²⁴ (cf. Ellic. and CGT, in l.); τ. ἴχνεσιν, ι Pe 2²¹; ἔργῳ ἀγαθῷ, ι Ti 5¹⁰.†

ἐπ-ακούω, [in LXX for שָׁמַע, עָנָה, etc.;] 1. to listen to. 2. to hearken to, hear with favour (one's prayer): c. gen. pers., ιι Co 6² (LXX).†

* ἐπ-ακροάομαι, -ῶμαι, to listen attentively: Ac 16²⁵ (cf. Page, in l.).†

† ἐπ-άν, conj. (< ἐπεί, q.v., ἄν), later form of ἐπήν, after, when: c. subjc. pres., Lk 11³⁴; c. subjc. aor., Mt 2⁸, Lk 11²².†

* ἐπανάγκης, -ες (< ἀνάγκη), only in neut.; 1. ἐπάναγκες (sc. ἐστί), it is compulsory, necessary. 2. As adv., of necessity: Ac 15²⁸.†

ἐπ-αν-άγω, [in LXX: Za 4¹² (רוּק hi.), Si 17²⁶ 26²⁸, ιι Mac 9²¹ 12⁴*;] to bring up or back (sc. ναῦς); to put out to sea (DB, iii, 63ᵇ): Lk 5³,⁴; intrans., to return: Mt 21¹⁸.†

* ἐπ-ανα-μιμνήσκω, to remind again: c. acc. pers., Ro 15¹⁵.†

ἐπ-ανα-παύω, [in LXX, mid., for נוּחַ, שָׁעַן ni.;] to refresh, cause to rest (upon); mid., to rest upon: metaph., c. dat., Ro 2¹⁷; seq. ἐπί, c. acc., Lk 10⁶ (Cremer, 827).†

ἐπ-αν-έρχομαι, [in LXX for שׁוּב, etc.;] to return: Lk 10³⁵ 19¹⁵.†

ἐπ-αν-ίστημι, [in LXX chiefly for קוּם;] to raise up against; mid., to rise up against: seq. ἐπί, c. acc. pers., Mt 10²¹, Mk 13¹².†

** ἐπ-αν-όρθωσις, -εως, ἡ (< ἐπανορθόω, to correct, restore; cf. ιι Mac 2²²), [in LXX: ι Es 8⁵², ι Mac 14³⁴*;] correction: of life, ιι Ti 3¹⁶ (cf. MM, Exp., xiv).†

ἐπ-άνω, adv., [in LXX for מַעְלָה, עַל, מֵעַל, etc.;] above; 1. adverbially; (a) of place: Lk 11⁴⁴; (b) of number, more than: Mk 14⁵, ι Co 15⁶. 2. As prep. c. gen.; (a) of place: Mt 2⁹ 5¹⁴ 21⁷ 23¹⁸, ²⁰, ²² 27³⁷ 28², Lk 4³⁹ 10¹⁹, Re 6⁸ 20³; (b) of pre-eminence: Lk 19¹⁷, ¹⁹, Jo 3³¹.†

* ἐπ-άρατος, -ον (< ἐπαράομαι, to imprecate), accursed: Jo 7⁴⁹ (for exx. from π., v. MM, Exp., xiv; cf. Cremer, 108).†

** ἐπ-αρκέω, -ῶ, [in LXX: ι Mac 8²⁶ 11³⁵*;] 1. to be strong enough for. 2. to ward off. 3. to aid, relieve: c. dat. pers., ι Ti 5¹⁰, ¹⁶ (mid., WH, mg.).†

† ἐπαρχεία (Rec. -χία, v. Bl., § 3, 5), -ας, ἡ (< ἔπαρχος, a prefect), [in LXX: Es 4¹¹ (מְדִינָה), Jth 3⁶ A*;] the jurisdiction of a prefect, a province: Ac 23³⁴ 25¹.†

*† ἐπάρχειος, -ον, of a prefect: ἡ ἐ. (sc. ἐξουσία) = ἐπαρχεία, q.v., Ac 25¹ (WH, mg.).†

ἔπ-αυλις, -εως, ἡ (< αὐλή), [in LXX for חָצֵר, טִירָה, (l.c.), etc.;] a dwelling, habitation: Ac 1²⁰ (LXX).†

† ἐπ-αύριον, adv., [in LXX for מָחָר, Ge 30³³, elsewhere, Ex 9⁶, al., for מׇחֳרׇת;] on the morrow: in NT, ἡ ἐ. (sc. ἡμέρα), Mt 27⁶², Mk 11¹², Jo 1²⁹, Ac 10⁹, al.

Ἐπαφρᾶς, -ᾶ (Bl., § 7, 4), ὁ, Epaphras: Col 1⁷ 4¹², Phm ²³.†

*† ἐπ-αφρίζω, to foam up: metaph., τ. αἰσχύνας, Ju ¹³.†

Ἐπαφρόδιτος, -ου, ὁ (i.e. charming); Epaphroditus: Phl 2²⁵ 4¹⁸.†

ἐπ-εγείρω, [in LXX for עוּר hi., קוּם hi., etc.;] to rouse up, excite: c. acc. rei, διωγμόν, Ac 13⁵⁰; ψυχάς, ib. 14².†

ἐπεί, conj. (ἐπί, εἰ), when, since; 1. of time, when, after: Lk 7¹ (Rec., WH, mg.). 2. Of cause, since, because: Mt 18³² 21⁴⁶ 27⁶, Mk 15⁴², Lk 1³⁴, Jo 13²⁹ 19³¹, Ac 13⁴⁶ (Rec., WH, mg.), ɪ Co 14¹², ɪɪ Co 11¹⁸ 13³, He 5², ¹¹ 6¹³ 9¹⁷ 11¹¹; ἐ. οὖν, He 2¹⁴ 4⁶. With ellipsis, otherwise, else: Ro 11⁶, ²², He 9²⁶; ἐ. ἄρα, ɪ Co 5¹⁰ 7¹⁴; introducing a question, Ro 3⁶, ɪ Co 14¹⁶ 15²⁹, He 10² (cf. ɪv Mac 1³³ 2⁷, ¹⁹ 4²⁴, ²⁶).†

ἐπει-δή, conj.; 1. of time, when now, after that: Lk 7¹ (WH, txt.). 2. Of cause, seeing that, forasmuch as: Lk 11⁶, Ac 13⁴⁶ (WH, txt., RV) 14¹² 15²⁴, ɪ Co 1²¹, ²² 14¹⁶ 15²¹, Phl 2²⁶.†

* ἐπει-δή-περ, conj., forasmuch as ("a stately compound," freq. in cl. and suitable for the formal introduction of Lk): Lk 1¹.†

ἐπ-εῖδον, 2 aor. without pres. in use; [in LXX chiefly for ראה;] to regard with attention, look upon (in cl., of the gods); 1. with a view to bless: c. inf., Lk 1²⁵ (cf. DB, 136ᵇ). 2. To punish: seq. ἐπί, Ac 4²⁹.†

ἔπ-ειμι, [in LXX: Ex 8²² ⁽¹⁸⁾ (עמד), Si 42¹⁹, etc.;] 1. to come upon, approach. 2. Of time, to come on or after; mostly as ptcp., ἐπιών, -οῦσα, όν, next, following: τῇ ἐ. (sc. ἡμέρᾳ, as freq. in late Gk.), Ac 16¹¹ 20¹⁵ 21¹⁸; ἡμέρᾳ (as usual in cl.), Ac 7²⁶; νυκτί, Ac 23¹¹.†

ἐπεί-περ, conj., since indeed: Ro 3³⁰ (Rec.; εἴπερ, WH).†

* ἐπ-εισ-αγωγή, -ῆς, ἡ, a bringing in besides or in addition (Hipp., FlJ, al.): He 7¹⁹ (cf. MM, Exp., xiv).†

ἐπ-εισ-έρχομαι, [in LXX: ɪ Mac 16¹⁶ (c. dat.)*;] to come in upon: seq. ἐπί, Lk 21³⁵.†

ἔπειτα, adv. of sequence, [in LXX: Nu 19¹⁹ A, Is 16², ɪv Mac 6³ *;] thereupon, thereafter, then: Lk 16⁷, Ga 1²¹, Ja 4¹⁴; seq. μετὰ τοῦτο, Jo 11⁷; μετὰ ἔτη τρία, Ga 1¹⁸; διὰ δεκατεσσάρων ἐτῶν, Ga 2¹; πρῶτον . . . ἔ., ɪ Co 15⁴⁶, ɪ Th 4¹⁷, He 7²; πρότερον . . . ἔ., He 7²⁷; ἀπαρχὴ . . . ἔ., ɪ Co 15²³; εἶτα . . . ἔ., ɪ Co 15⁵, ⁶ (WH, txt.); ἔ. . . . ἔ., ɪ Co 15⁵⁻⁷ (WH, mg.); τρίτον . . . ἔ. (bis), ɪ Co 12²⁸.†

ἐπ-έκεινα, adv. (= ἐπ' ἐκεῖνα), [in LXX: Le 22²⁷, Nu 32¹⁹, al. (הָלְאָה), etc.;] beyond; c. gen., Ac 7⁴³ (LXX).†

* ἐπ-εκ-τείνω, to extend: mid., to stretch forward: c. dat., Phl 3¹³.†

ἐπενδύτης, -ου, ὁ (< ἐπενδύω), [in LXX for מְעִיל, Le 8⁷ A (Aq. ἐπένδυμα), ι Ki 18⁴ A, ιι Ki 13¹⁸ *;] an outer tunic (RV, coat) : Jo 21⁷.†

*† ἐπ-εν-δύω = -δύνω (Hdt.), to put on over; pass. (Plut., al.), to have on over, be clothed upon : ιι Co 5²˒⁴.†

ἐπ-έρχομαι, [in LXX for בּוֹא, עבר, etc. ;] 1. to come to, arrive, come on : seq. ἀπό, c. gen. loc., Ac 14¹⁹ (ἐπῆλθαν; cf. M, Pr., 65; Deiss., BS, 191); of time, Eph 2⁷. 2. to come upon (as in Hom.) : of calamities, Lk 21²⁶, Ac 8²⁴ 13⁴⁰, Ja 5¹; of an enemy, Lk 11²²; of the Holy Spirit, Lk 1³⁵, Ac 1⁸, [in LXX : γίγνομαι ἐπί, Jg 14⁶, ι Ki 11⁶, al.].†

ἐπ-ερωτάω, -ῶ, [in LXX chiefly for שָׁאַל, also for דרשׁ, etc. ;] to inquire of, consult, question : c. acc. pers., Mk 12³⁴, Lk 2⁴⁶, al. ; c. dupl. acc., Mk 7¹⁷ 11²⁹, Lk 20⁴⁰, al.; c. acc. pers., seq. λέγων, Mt 12¹⁸, Mk 9¹¹; εἰ, Mk 8²³, Lk 23⁶, al.; ἐ. θεόν, Ro 10²⁰ (LXX). 2. In late Gk., to beg of, demand of : c. acc. pers. et inf., Mt 16¹ (cf. ἐρωτάω; and v. Cremer, 716).

** ἐπ-ερώτημα, -τος, τό, [in LXX : Da TH 4¹⁴ (שְׁאֵלָא), Si 36 (33)³ *;] 1. a question, an inquiry (Hdt., Thuc.). 2. a demand : ι Pe 3²¹ (v. ICC, in l.).†

ἐπ-έχω, [in LXX for חדל, etc.; also Si 8¹ 31 (34)², ιι Mac 5²⁵ 9²⁵, al.;] 1. to hold upon. 2. Like παρέχω (as in Hom., al.), to hold out, offer : λόγον ζωῆς, Phl 2¹⁶. 3. to hold or direct towards, sc. νοῦν; (a) absol., to intend, purpose ; (b) to observe, give attention to (v. MM, Exp., xiv) : seq. πῶς, Lk 14⁷; c. dat. pers., Ac 3⁵, ι Ti 4¹⁶. 4. to stay, wait : Ac 19²² (in legal phrase, MM, Exp., l.c.).†

* ἐπηρεάζω (< ἐπήρεια, spiteful abuse), to revile : c. acc. pers., Lk 6²⁸; c. acc. rei (but v. ICC, in l.), ι Pe 3¹⁶.†

ἐπί (before a smooth breathing ἐπ', before a rough breathing ἐφ'), prep. c. gen., dat., acc. (acc. most freq. in NT), with primary sense of superposition, on, upon. I. C. gen., 1. of place, answering the question, where? (a) of the place on which, on, upon: ἐπί (τ.) γῆς, Mt 6¹⁰˒¹⁹, al.; τ. κεφαλῆς, ι Co 11¹⁰; τ. νεφελῶν, Mt 24³⁰, al.; like ἐν, in constr. prægn. after verbs of motion : βάλλειν, Mk 4²⁶; σπείρειν, ib. ³¹; ἔρχεσθαι, He 6⁷, al.; fig., ἐπ' ἀληθείας (MM, s.v. ἀ.); of the subject of thought or speech, Ga 3¹⁶; of power or authority, over, πάντων, Ro 9⁵; τ. γάζης, Ac 8²⁷; ἐξουσία ἐπί, Re 2²⁶ 11⁶ 20⁶; (b) of vicinity, at, by : τ. θαλάσσης, Jo 6¹⁹; τ. ὁδοῦ, Mt 21¹⁹; τοῦ βάτου, Mk 12²⁶ (v. Swete, in l.); c. gen. pers., in the presence of, before, Mt 28¹⁴, Ac 23³⁰, ι Co 6¹, al. 2. Of time, (a) c. gen. pers., in the time of : ἐπὶ Ἐλισαίου, Lk 4²⁷; ἐπὶ Κλαυδίου, Ac 11²⁸; ἐπὶ Ἀβιάθαρ ἀρχιερέως, when A. was high priest, Mk 2²⁶; (b) c. gen. rei, at, at the time of : Mt 1¹¹, He 1², ιι Pe 3³; ἐπὶ τ. προσευχῶν μου (ἡμῶν), Ro 1¹⁰, Eph 1¹⁶, ι Th 1², Phm ⁴. II. C. dat., of place, answering the question, where? (a) lit., on, upon : Mt 9¹⁶, 14⁸, al.; after verbs of motion (v. supr., ι, 1, (a)), Mt 9¹⁶ Ac 8¹⁶; above, Lk 23³⁸; at, by, Mk 13²⁹, Jo 5², Ac 5⁹, al.; (b) metaph., upon, on the ground of, Lk 4⁴ (LXX); in the matter of, Mk 6⁵² (v. Swete, in l.); upon, of, concerning, Ac 5³⁵˒⁴⁰; of the ground, reason or motive (Bl., § 38, 2; 43, 3), Mt 18⁵ 19⁹, Ro 12¹², al.; ἐφ' ᾧ, for the reason that, *because*, Ro 5¹², ɪɪ Co 5⁴; after verbs of motion, *over*, Mt 18¹³, Ro 16¹⁹, al.; of a condition (cl.), Ro 8²⁰, ɪ Co 9¹⁰; ἐπὶ δυσὶ μάρτυσιν (v. Westc. on He 9¹⁰), He 10²⁸; of purpose or aim, Eph 2¹⁰, Phl 4¹⁰; of authority, *over*, Mt 24⁴⁷, Lk 12⁴⁴; of hostility, c. dat. pers. (cl.), *against*, Lk 12⁵²; *in addition to* (cl.), ɪɪ Co 7¹³; of an adjunct, *in, at, on*, Phl 1³ 2¹⁷. III. C. acc., 1. of place of motion upon or over, answering the question, whither? (*a*) lit., *upon, over :* Mt 14²⁸,²⁹, Lk 5¹⁹, al. mult.; in NT also, answering the question, where? (as c. gen., dat.), Mk 4³⁸ 11², Lk 2²⁵, Jo 1³²; ἐπὶ τ. αὐτό, Ac 1¹⁵ 2¹, al.; of motion to a vicinity, *to*, Mk 16², Ac 8³⁶, al.; (*b*) metaph. (in wh. "the acc. is more widely prevalent than it strictly should be," Bl., § 43, 1); of blessings, evils, etc., coming upon one, c. acc. pers., Mt 10¹³ 12²⁸, Ac 2¹⁷, Jo 18⁴, Eph 5⁶, al.; of addition (dat. in cl.), λύπη ἐπὶ λύπην, Phl 2²⁷; ἐπικαλεῖν ὄνομα ἐπί (v.s. ἐπικαλέω), Ac 15¹⁷, Ja 2⁷; καλεῖν ἐπί, *to call after*, Lk 1⁵⁹; of number or degree: ἐπὶ τρίς (cl. εἰς τ.), *thrice*, Ac 10¹⁶ 11¹⁰; ἐπὶ πλεῖον, *the more, further*, Ac 4¹⁷, ɪɪ Ti 2¹⁶ 3⁹ (v. also infr., 2, (*a*)); ἐφ' ὅσον (v. infr., ib.), *forasmuch as*, Mt 25⁴⁰,⁴⁵, Ro 11¹³; of power, authority, control, Lk 1³³, Ac 7¹⁰, Ro 5¹⁴, He 3⁶, al.; of the direction of thoughts and feelings, *unto, towards*, Lk 1¹⁷ 23²⁸, Ac 9³⁵,⁴², Ro 11²², Ga 4⁹, Eph 2⁷, ɪ Ti 5⁵, al.; of purpose, *for*, Mt 3⁷, Lk 23⁴⁸; ἐφ' ὃ πάρει (Rec. ἐφ' ᾧ), Mt 26⁵⁰; of hostility, *against*, Mt 24⁷, Mk 3²⁴·²⁶ 10¹¹ 13⁸, Lk 9⁵, Jo 13¹⁸, Ac 7⁵⁴, ɪ Co 7³⁶, ɪɪ Co 1²³; of reference, *concerning, for* (cl. usually dat.), Mk 9¹² 15²⁴, Jo 19²⁴, Ro 4⁹. 2. Of time, (*a*) *during, for :* Lk 4²⁵ (WH, txt., omits ἐπί), Ac 13³¹ 16¹⁸, He 11³⁰, al.; ἐφ' ὅσον (χρόνον), *as long as, for so long time as*, Mk 9¹⁵, Ro 7¹, al. (for ἐφ' ὅ. in another sense, v. supr., 1, (*b*)); ἐφ' ἱκανόν (v.s. *i.*), Ac 20¹¹; ἐπὶ πλεῖον (v. supr., 1, (*b*)), *yet longer, further*, Ac 20⁹ 24⁴; (*b*) *on, about, towards* (cl. εἰς): Lk 10³⁵ Ac 3¹ 4⁵. IV. In composition, ἐπί signifies: *up*, ἐπαίρω; *upon*, ἐπίγειος, ἐπιδημέω, ἐπικαθίζω; *towards*, ἐπιβλέπω, ἐπεκτείνω; *over* (of superintendence), ἐπιστάτης; *again, in addition*, ἐπαιτέω, ἐπισυνάγω; *against*, ἐπιορκέω, ἐπιβουλή.

ἐπι-βαίνω, [in LXX chiefly for רכב;] 1. *to get up on, mount :* seq. ἐπί, c. acc., Mt 21⁵ (LXX); *to embark in* (a boat), *go aboard :* c. dat., Ac 27²; seq. εἰς, Ac 21⁶ (Rec.); absol., Ac 21². 2. *to go up to, go on to, enter :* seq. εἰς, Ac 20¹⁸ 21⁴; c. dat., Ac 25¹.†

ἐπι-βάλλω, [in LXX for שלח, שית, etc.;] 1. trans., *to cast, lay* or *put upon :* c. acc. et dat., Mk 11⁷, ɪ Co 7³⁵; c. acc., seq. ἐπί c. acc., Re 18¹⁹, WH, mg.; τ. χεῖρα (-ας) ἐπί (Bl., § 37, 7), of seizing a prisoner, Mt 26⁵⁰, Lk 20¹⁹ 21¹², Jo 7³⁰, Ac 5¹⁸ 21²⁷; c. dat. (Polyb.), Mk 14⁴⁶, Ac 4³; c. inf., Ac 12¹; τὴν χ. ἐπ' ἄροτρον, Lk 9⁶²; ἐπίβλημα ἐπὶ ἱμάτιον, Lk 5³⁶; ἐπὶ ἱματίῳ, Mt 9¹⁶. 2. Intrans. (*a*) *to throw oneself* or *rush upon :* τ. κύματα εἰς τ. πλοῖον, Mk 4³⁷; metaph.. *to put one's mind upon* (but v. Field, *Notes*, 41 ff.), ἐπιβαλὼν ἔκλαιεν, *when he thought thereon* (sc. τ. ῥήματι), *he wept* (EV, txt.; R, mg., *he began to weep ;* cf. M, *Pr.*, 131, *he set to and wept ;* cf. MM, *VGT*, s.v., *ICC* in l.): Mk 14⁷² (v. also Swete, in l.); (*b*) *to fall to one's share :* τὸ ἐπιβάλλον (sc. dat.; Hdt., al., a technical formula freq. in π.; Deiss., *BS*, 230, *LAE*, 152), Lk 15¹².†

*† ἐπι-βαρέω, -ῶ, to put a burden on, be burdensome : fig., absol., II Co 2⁵; c. acc. pers., I Th 2⁹, II Th 3⁸ (cf. M, Th., I, 2⁹).†

ἐπι-βιβάζω, [in LXX chiefly for רכב hi.;] to place upon : c. acc. pers., Lk 10³⁴ 19³⁵, Ac 23²⁴.†

ἐπι-βλέπω, [in LXX for נבט hi., פנה, ראה, etc.;] to look upon. In NT, as in LXX (I Ki 1¹¹ 9¹⁶, Ps 24 (25)¹⁶, To 3³, al.), to look on with favour : seq. ἐπί, c. acc. pers., Lk 1⁴⁸ 9³⁸, Ja 2³.†

ἐπί-βλημα, -τος, τό, [in LXX: Is 3²²; in Sm.: Jos 9¹¹ ⁽⁵⁾;] 1. that which is thrown over, a cover. 2. a tapestry, hanging (Is, l.c.). 3. that which is put on ; (a) embroidery ; (b) a patch (Jos, l.c.) : Mt 9¹⁶, Mk 2²¹, Lk 5³⁶.†

ἐπι-βοάω, -ῶ, to cry out : Ac 25²⁴ (Rec., for βοάω, q.v.).†

ἐπι-βουλή, -ῆς, ἡ, [in LXX: Es 2²², I Es 5⁷³, II Mac 5⁷, al.;] a plan against, a plot : Ac 9²⁴ 20³, ¹⁹ 23³⁰.†

† ἐπι-γαμβρεύω (< γαμβρός, a connection by marriage), [in LXX: Ge 34⁹, I Ki 18²¹ ff., II Ch 18¹, II Es 9¹⁴ (חתן hithp.), Ge 38⁸ R (יבם pi.), I Mac 10⁵⁴, ⁵⁶ *;] 1. to enter into affinity with : c. dat. (LXX, ll. c., exc. Ge 38⁸). 2. to marry (as deceased husband's next of kin, cf. Ge 38⁸) : c. acc., Mt 22²⁴.†

* ἐπί-γειος, -ον (< ἐπί, γῆ), of the earth, earthly : τὰ ἐ., Jo 3¹², Phl 2¹⁰ 3¹⁹ (anarth.); σώματα, I Co 15⁴⁰; οἰκία, II Co 5¹; σοφία, Ja 3¹⁵ (Cremer, 153).†

** ἐπι-γίνομαι (v.s. γίνομαι), [in LXX: Ep. Je ⁴⁷, III Mac 2⁵ *;] to arrive, arise, come on : Ac 28¹³.†

ἐπι-γινώσκω, [in LXX chiefly for נכר hi., also for ידע, etc.;] "directive" of γινώσκω (AR, Eph., 249), as in cl.; 1. to observe, perceive, discern, recognize ; (a) absol.: Ac 25¹⁰, I Co 13¹²; seq. ὅτι, Lk 1²²; τ. πνεύματι, seq. ὅτι, Mk 2⁸; (b) c. acc. rei: Lk 1⁴ 5²², Ac 12¹⁴ 27³⁹, Ro 1³², II Co 1¹³, Col 1⁶, I Ti 4³; ἐν ἑαυτῷ, Mk 5³⁰; seq. ὅτι, I Co 14³⁷; (c) c. acc. pers.: Mt 11²⁷ 14³⁵ 17¹², Mk 6³³ (T, αὐτούς, but LTr., WH, R, omit the pron., and LTr., WH, txt., read ἔγνωσαν), ib. ⁵⁴, Lk 24¹⁶, ³¹, I Co 16¹⁸, Co 1¹⁴; seq. ἀπό, c. gen. rei, Mt 7¹⁶, ²⁰; seq. ὅτι, Ac 3¹⁰ 4¹³, II Co 13⁵; pass., I Co 13¹²; opp. to ἀγνοούμενοι, II Co 6⁹. 2. to discover, ascertain, determine : Ac 9³⁰; seq. ὅτι, Lk 7³⁷ 23⁷, Ac 19³⁴ 22²⁹ 24¹¹ 28¹; c. acc. rei, seq. quæst., Ac 23²⁸; δι' ἣν αἰτίαν, Ac 22²⁴; παρά, c. gen. pers., seq. περί, c. gen. rei, Ac 24⁸; τ. ὁδὸν τῆς δικαιοσύνης, II Pe 2²¹ (cf. Lft., Col., 136; Cremer, 159; M, Pr., 113; AR, Eph., 248 ff.).†

† ἐπί-γνωσις, -εως, ἡ (< ἐπιγνώσκω, q.v.), [in LXX: III Ki 7¹⁴ (B. γν-), Pr 2⁵, Ho 4¹, ⁶ 6⁷ ⁽⁶⁾ (דעת), Jth 9¹⁴, II Mac 9¹¹ *;] acquaintance, discernment, recognition (Plut., al.) : Phl 1⁹, Col 3¹⁰; c. gen. rei, Col 1⁹ 2², Phm ⁶; τ. ἀληθείας, I Ti 2⁴, II Ti 2²⁵ 3⁷, Tit 1¹, He 10²⁶; τ. ἁμαρτίας, Ro 3²⁰; c. gen. pers., of God : Eph 1¹⁷, Col 1¹⁰, II Pe 1², ³; of Christ : Eph 4¹³, II Pe 1⁸ 2²⁰; of God and Christ : II Pe 1²; κατ' ἐ., Ro 10²; ἔχειν ἐν ἐ., Ro 1²⁸ (v. AR, Eph., 248 ff.; and for a somewhat different view, Thayer, s.v.; Lft. on Col, 1⁹; Tr., Syn., lxxv; Cremer, 159 f.; cf. αἴσθησις).†

*ἐπι-γραφή, -ῆς, ἡ (< ἐπιγράφω), an inscription : Mt 22²⁰, Mk 12¹⁶ 15²⁶, Lk 20²⁴ 23³⁸.†

ἐπι-γράφω, [in LXX for כתב, Nu 17² ⁽¹⁷⁾; fig., Je 38 (31)³³, al.;] to write upon, inscribe : Mk 15²⁶, Ac 17²³, Re 21¹²; fig., He 8¹⁰ (LXX) 10¹⁶ (ib.).†

ἐπι-δείκνυμι, [in LXX : Pr 12¹⁷ (פוח hi.), Is 37²⁶ (בוא hi.), Ep. Je ⁵⁹, II Mac 15³², al.;] 1. to show, exhibit, display : c. acc. et dat., Mt 16¹ 22¹⁹ 24¹, Lk 17¹⁴. Mid., to display for oneself or as one's own (but cf. Bl., § 55, 1): Ac 9³⁹. 2. to show, point out, prove : c. acc., He 6¹⁷; c. acc. et inf., Ac 18²⁸ (cf. MM, Exp., xiv).†

** ἐπι-δέχομαι, [in LXX : Jth 13¹³ B², I Mac 10¹ 14²³, Si 51²⁶, al. ;] 1. in cl., of things, to allow of, admit of (Dem., Arist., al.). In late writers, 2. to accept besides (Polyb.), to accept (in π. of the terms of a lease; v. ICC, on III Jo, l.c.): III Jo ⁹. 3. (a) to receive besides (Menand.); (b) to receive hospitably (I Mac, Si, ll. c.): III Jo ¹⁰.†

* ἐπι-δημέω, -ῶ (< δῆμος); 1. to be at home (Thuc., Plat., al.), 2. to stay in a place, sojourn (Plat., Xen., al.; and v. MM, Exp., xiv): Ac 2¹⁰ 17²¹; seq. ἐν, ib. 18²⁷ (WH, mg.).†

*† ἐπι-δια-τάσσομαι, to add provisions to a document : Ga 3¹⁵ (cf. ἐπιδιαθήκη, a second will, FlJ, BJ, ii, 2, 3; the word is used of wills in π., cf. Deiss., LAE, 87).†

ἐπι-δίδωμι, [in LXX for נתן, etc.;] 1. to give over, to hand : c. acc. rei et dat. pers., Mt 7⁹, ¹⁰, Lk 11¹¹, ¹² 24³⁰, ⁴², Ac 15³⁰; pass. c. dat. pers., Lk 4¹⁷. 2. to give in, give way : absol., Ac 27¹⁵.†

*† ἐπι-δι-ορθόω, to set in order further : Tit 1⁵ (Inscr.; Cremer, 808).†

ἐπι-δύω, [in LXX : De 24¹⁵, Jos 8²⁹, Je 15⁹ (בוא) *;] to go down, set (of the sun) : Eph 4²⁶.†

ἐπιείκεια, v.s. ἐπιεικία.

ἐπιεικής, -ές (< εἰκός, likely), [in LXX : Ps 85 (86)⁵ (סלָּח), Es 8¹³ *;] 1. seemly, fitting (Hom.). 2. equitable, fair, moderate : I Ti 3³, Tit 3², I Pe 2¹⁸, Ja 3¹⁷; τὸ ἐ. (Thuc., i, 76), Phl 4⁵ (cf. Mayor, Ja, l.c., and v.s. ἐπιεικία).†

ἐπιεικία (Rec. -είκεια), -ας, ἡ (< ἐπιεικής), [in LXX : Wi 2¹⁹ 12¹⁸, Ba 2²⁷, Da LXX 3⁽⁴²⁾ 4²⁴, TH 3⁽⁴²⁾, II Mac 2²² 10⁴, III Mac 3¹⁵ 7⁶ *;] fairness, moderation, gentleness ("sweet reasonableness," Matthew Arnold): Ac 24⁴; c. πραΰτης, II Co 10¹.†

SYN. : πραΰτης (v. Tr., Syn., § xliii).

ἐπι-ζητέω, -ῶ, [in LXX chiefly for דרש, IV Ki 8⁸, Is 62¹², al.; also for בקש, I Ki 20¹, Ec 7²⁹ ⁽²⁸⁾, Ho 3⁵; פקד, II Ki 3⁸;] "directive" of ζητέω (MM, Exp., xiv), to inquire for, seek after, wish for : c. acc. rei, Mt 6³² 12³⁹ 16⁴, Lk 12³⁰, Ac 19³⁹, Ro 11⁷, Phl 4¹⁷, He 11¹⁴ 13¹⁴; c. acc. pers., Lk 4⁴², Ac 12¹⁹; c. inf., Ac 13⁷.†

** ἐπιθανάτιος, -ον, [in LXX : Da Bel ³¹ *;] condemned to death : I Co 4⁹.†

ἐπί-θεσις, -εως, ἡ (< ἐπιτίθημι), [in LXX : II Ch 25²⁷ (קשָׁר), Ez

170 MANUAL GREEK LEXICON OF THE NEW TESTAMENT

23¹¹ (עֲנָבָה) II Mac 4⁴¹ 5⁵ 14¹⁵ *;] 1. *a laying on :* χειρῶν, Ac 8¹⁸, I Ti
4¹⁴, II Ti 1⁶, He 6² (cf. Westc., *He.*, l.c.; *CGT* on I Ti, l.c.).   2. *an
attack, assault* (II Mac, ll.c.).†

ἐπιθυμέω, -ῶ (< θυμός), [in LXX chiefly for אוה pi., hithp.; also
for חמד, etc.;] *to set one's heart upon, desire, lust after, covet :*
absol., Ja 4², Ro 7⁷ 13⁹ (LXX), I Co 10⁶ (cf. IV Mac 2⁶); seq. κατά
(against, in opposition to), Ga 5¹⁷; prop. (as in cl.) c. gen., Ac 20³³,
I Ti 3¹; in late Gk. also c. acc. (M, *Pr.*, 65), Mt 5²⁸ (Rec. αὐτῆς;
T omits; cf. Ex 20¹⁷, Mi 2², Wi 16³, al.); c. inf., Mt 13¹⁷, Lk 15¹⁶
16²¹ 17²², I Pe 1¹², Re 9⁶; c. acc. et inf., He 6¹¹; as in Hebrew,
ἐπιθυμίᾳ ἐπεθύμησα, Lk 22¹⁵.†

SYN.: ὀρέγω (cf. Field, *Notes*, 204), θέλω (*DCG.* i, 453ª).

ἐπιθυμητής, -οῦ, ὁ (< ἐπιθυμέω), [in LXX: Nu 11³⁴ (אוה hithp.);
εἶναι ἐ., Pr 1²² (חמד) *;] *one longing for, lustful after :* κακῶν, I Co
10⁶.†

ἐπιθυμία, -ας, ἡ (< ἐπιθυμέω), [in LXX chiefly for תַּאֲוָה, אַוָּה; also
for חָמַד, etc.;] *desire, longing :* Lk 22¹⁵ (v.s. ἐπιθυμέω), Phl 1²³, I Th
2¹⁷, Re 18¹⁴; pl., Mk 4¹⁹; esp. with ref. to forbidden things, *desire,
lust, passionate longing* (Vg., *concupiscentia*) : Ro 7⁷, ⁸, Ja 1¹⁴, ¹⁵, II Pe 1⁴;
pl., Ga 5²⁴, I Ti 6⁹, II Ti 2²² 4³, I Pe 1¹⁴ 4²; πάθος ἐπιθυμίας, I Th 4⁵; ἐ. κακή,
Col 3⁵; c. gen., μιασμοῦ, II Pe 2¹⁰ (v. Mayor, in l.); τ. καρδιῶν, Ro 1²⁴; τ.
κόσμου (aroused by the world), I Jo 2¹⁷; τ. σώματος, Ro 6¹²; τ. ἀπάτης,
Eph 4²² (v. *ICC*, in l.); τ. σαρκός, I Jo 2¹⁶, II Pe 2¹⁸ (without art.), Ga
5¹⁶; τ. ὀφθαλμῶν, I Jo 2¹⁶; σαρκικαὶ ἐ., I Pe 2¹¹ (cf. IV Mac 1³²);
κοσμικαί, Tit 2¹²; εἰς ἐπιθυμίας, Ro 13¹⁴; ποιεῖν τὰς ἐ., Jo 8⁴⁴; ὑπακούειν
ταῖς ἐ., Ro 6¹²; δουλεύειν, ἄγεσθαι, ἐπιθυμίαις, Tit 3³, II Ti 3⁶; πορεύεσθαι
ἐν ἐ., I Pe 4³; κατά, Ju ¹⁶,¹⁸, II Pe 3³; ἀναστρέφεσθαι ἐν ταῖς ἐ., Eph 2³.†

SYN.: πάθος (q.v.), ὄρεξις.

ἐπι-καθ-ίζω, [in LXX for רכב, etc.;] *to sit upon :* Mt 21⁷.†

ἐπι-καλέω, -ῶ, [in LXX chiefly for קרא;] 1. *to call, name, surname :* c. acc. (cl.), Mt 10²⁵; pass., Ac 1²³ 4³⁶ 10⁵,¹⁸,³² 11¹³
12¹²,²⁵, He 11¹⁶; τ. ὄνομα, seq. ἐπί (denoting possession, as Heb.
עַל . . (נִקְרָא שֵׁם), Ac 15¹⁷ (LXX), Ja 2⁷ (v. *CB* on Am 9¹²).   2. Mid.
(so also act.; cl., LXX), *to call upon, invoke, appeal to* (θεόν, θεούς,
Hdt., Xen., al.; cf. Deiss., *LAE*, 426): Καίσαρα (Σεβαστόν, Ac 25²⁵),
Ac 25¹¹,¹²,²¹ 26³² 28¹⁹; sc. τ. Κύριον Ἰησοῦν, Ac 7⁵⁹; μάρτυρα (cl.) τ.
θεόν, II Co 1²³; πατέρα, I Pe 1¹⁷; τ. κύριον, Ro 10¹², II Ti 2²²; τ. ὄνομα
κυρίου (μου, σου; like Heb. קָרָא בְּשֵׁם יְהוָה, Ac 2²¹ (LXX) 9¹⁴,²¹ 22¹⁶, Ro
10¹³,¹⁴ (LXX), I Co 1² (Cremer, 335, 742).†

ἐπι-κάλυμμα, -τος, τό (< ἐπικαλύπτω), [in LXX: Ex 26¹⁴
39²¹ (³⁴) (מִכְסֶה), II Ki 17¹⁹ (מָסָךְ), Jb 19²⁹ (aliter in Heb.) *;] *a cover,
veil :* metaph., τ. κακίας, I Pe 2¹⁶.†

ἐπι-καλύπτω, [in LXX for כסה, etc.;] *to cover over, cover up :*
metaph., Ro 4⁷ (LXX).†

† ἐπι-κατ-άρατος, -ον (< ἐπικαταράομαι, to imprecate curses on), [in LXX for אָרוּר, also Wi 3¹² 14⁸, iv Mac 2¹⁹;] accursed: Ga 3¹⁰ (LXX) 13 (LXX κεκαταραμένος) (Cremer, 109).†

ἐπι-κείμαι, [in LXX: Ex 36⁴⁰ (39³¹) (נתן), Jb 19³ (הכר hi.) 21²⁷ (חמם), i Mac 6⁵⁷, ii Mac 1²¹, iii Mac 1²² *;] to be placed, lie on: Jo 21⁹; seq. ἐπί, c. dat., ib. 11³⁸; fig., He 9¹⁰; ἀνάγκη, i Co 9¹⁶; χειμῶν, to threaten, come on: Ac 27²⁰; of persons, to press upon, insist: Lk 5¹ 23²³.†

* ἐπι-κέλλω, of a ship, to run ashore: c. acc., Ac 27⁴¹.†

* ἐπι-κεφάλαιον, -ου, τό, a poll-tax: Mk 12¹⁴ (WH, mg., for κῆνσον, as in D, Syrr. Sin. pesh., 124, etc.).†

** ἐπικουρία, -ας, ἡ (< ἐπικουρέω to be an ἐπίκουρος, an ally), [in LXX: Wi 13¹⁸ *;] aid, assistance: Ac 26²².†

† Ἐπικούριος, -α, -ον, belonging to Epicurus, Epicurean: Ac 17¹⁸; as subst., -ου, ὁ, an Epicurean.†

** ἐπι-κρίνω, [in LXX: ii Mac 4⁴⁷, iii Mac 4² *;] to decree, give sentence: c. acc. et inf., Lk 23²⁴.†

ἐπι-λαμβάνω, [in LXX for חזק hi., אחז, etc.;] always mid. in LXX and NT (v. Cremer, 758), to lay hold of: c. gen. pers., Mt 14³¹, Ac 17¹⁹ 21³⁰, ³³; c. acc. pers. (not cl.), Lk 9⁴⁷ 14⁴ 23²⁶ (WH, but v. Bl., 101₅), Ac 9²⁷ 16⁹ 18¹⁷; c. gen. rei, Mk 8²³, Ac 23¹⁹, He 8⁹ (LXX); c. gen. pers. et rei, Lk 20²⁰, ²⁶; τ. αἰωνίου (ὄντως) ζωῆς, i Ti 6¹², ¹⁹. Metaph. (as in Si 4¹¹), He 2¹⁶ (v. Westc., in l.).†

ἐπι-λανθάνομαι (alternative mid. form of ἐπιλήθω, to cause to forget), [in LXX chiefly for שכח;] to forget, neglect: c. inf., Mt 16⁵, Mk 8¹⁴; c. gen., He 6¹⁰ 13², ¹⁶; c. acc. (as occasionally in cl.; MM, Exp., xiv), Phl 3¹³; ὁποῖος ἦν, Ja 1²⁴; pass. ptcp. (cf. Is 23¹⁶, Si 3¹⁴ 23¹⁴, Wi 2⁴), Lk 12⁶.†

ἐπι-λέγω, [in LXX chiefly for בחר;] 1. to say in addition (Hdt.). 2. to call by name, to call: Jo 5². 3. to choose; mid., to choose for oneself: Ac 15⁴⁰.†

ἐπι-λείπω, [in LXX: Ob 1⁵ אֱלוֹ¹R (שאר hi.) *;] to fail: c. acc. pers., He 11³².†

*† ἐπι-λείχω, to lick over: c. acc., Lk 16²¹ (cf. MM, Exp., xiv).†

**† ἐπι-λησμονή, -ῆς, ἡ (< ἐπιλήθω), [in LXX: Si 11²⁷ *;] forgetfulness: ἀκροατὴς ἐ. (gen. of qual.), Ja 1²⁵.†

ἐπί-λοιπος, -ον (< λοιπός), [in LXX for יתר, שאר;] still left, remaining: χρόνος, i Pe 4².†

** ἐπί-λυσις -εως, ἡ (< ἐπιλύω), [in Aq.: Ge 40⁸; Sm.: Ho 3⁴ *;] 1. release. 2. solution, interpretation: ii Pe 1²⁰.†

** ἐπι-λύω, [in Aq.: Ge 40⁸ 41⁸, ¹²; Th.: Ho 3⁴ *;] 1. to loose, release. 2. to solve, settle, explain: Mk 4³⁴, Ac 19³⁹.†

* ἐπι-μαρτυρέω, -ῶ, to bear witness to: c. acc. et. inf., i Pe 5¹².†

ἐπιμέλεια, -ας, ἡ (< ἐπιμελέομαι), [in LXX: Pr 3⁸ (שְׁקוּי), Wi 13¹³, i Es 6¹⁰, i Mac 16¹⁴, al.;] attention, care: Ac 27³ (v. Field, Notes, 143).†

ἐπι-μελέομαι, -οῦμαι, [in LXX: Ge 44²¹ (שִׂים עַיִן), i Es 6²⁷,

Pr 27²⁵, Si 33¹³ (30²⁵), ι Mac 11³⁷*;] *to take care of:* c. gen., Lk 10³⁴,³⁵, ι Ti 3⁵.†

ἐπιμελῶς, adv., [in LXX for רֵק, etc.;] *carefully:* Lk 15⁸.†

ἐπι-μένω, [in LXX: Ex 12³⁹ (מהה hith.)*;] *to stay on, tarry* or *abide still:* seq. ἐν, ι Co 16⁸; αὐτοῦ, *there,* Ac 15³⁴ (WH, txt., RV, txt., omit) 21⁴; c. dat., τ. σαρκί, Phl 1²⁴; seq. παρά, c. dat. pers., Ac 28¹⁴; πρός, c. acc. pers., ι Co 16⁷, Ga 1¹⁸; c. acc. temp., Ac 10⁴⁸, 21⁴,¹⁰ 28¹²,¹⁴, ι Co 16⁷. Metaph., *to continue in a pursuit or state:* c. dat., τ. ἁμαρτίᾳ, Ro 6¹; τ. ἀπιστίᾳ, ib. 11²³; τ. πίστει, Col 1²³; αὐτοῖς (v. CGT, in l.), ι Ti 4¹⁶; τ. χρηστότητι, Ro 11²²; c. ptcp. (cf. Bl., § 73, 4; 76, 2), Jo 8⁽⁷⁾, Ac 12¹⁶.†

ἐπι-νεύω, [in LXX: Pr 26²⁴ (נכר ni.), ι Mac 6⁵⁷, ιι Mac 4¹⁰ 11¹⁵ 14²⁰*;] *to nod* in command or approval, *to nod approval, consent:* Ac 18²⁰.†

ἐπίνοια, -ας, ἡ (< ἐπινοέω, *to contrive*), [in LXX: Je 20¹⁰, Wi 6¹⁶ 9¹⁴ 14¹² 15⁴, Si 40², ιι Mac 12⁴⁵, ιν Mac 17²*;] *a thought, design:* Ac 8²².†

** ἐπιορκέω, -ῶ (< ἐπίορκος), [in LXX: ι Es 1⁴⁸, Wi 14²⁸*;] *to swear falsely, forswear oneself:* Mt 5³³.†

ἐπί-ορκος, -ον, [in LXX: Za 5³ (שבע ni.)*;] 1. of oaths, *sworn falsely.* 2. Of persons, *perjured;* as subst., *a perjurer, false swearer:* ι Ti 1¹⁰.†

ἐπιοῦσα, v.s. ἔπειμι.

*† ἐπιούσιος, -ον (cf. περιούσιος, [in LXX for סְגֻלָּה, De 7⁶, etc.]), found only in the phrase ἄρτος ἐ., EV, *daily;* R, mg., *for the coming day:* Mt 6¹¹ Lk 11³. Several derivations find support, each pointing to a different meaning. 1. < ἐπιοῦσα (sc. ἡμέρα) (or, < ἐπὶ τὴν ἰοῦσαν (sc. ἡμέραν), Zorell, s.v.), hence, *for the morrow* or *for the coming day* (R, mg.). 2. (a) < ἐπί + οὐσία, hence, *for subsistence, needful* (Am. R, mg.); (b) < ἐπί + εἶναι in fem. ptcp. form, hence, *pertaining to* (the day).) For renderings of versions and views of various writers, v. reff. in *DB, ext.,* 36 f.; *DCG,* ii, 58 f., 62ª; *ICC* on Lk, l.c.; McNeile on Mt, l.c.; Nestle in *Exp. T.,* xxi, p. 43. The EV, *daily,* is based on the Vg. (Lk; OL, Mt, Lk, *quotidianus*). "It is difficult not to think that τὸν ἐ. rests upon misunderstanding of an original Aramaic phrase, or upon a Greek corruption" (*ICC* on Mt, l.c.; cf. also Cremer, 239).†

ἐπι-πίπτω, [in LXX chiefly for נפל;] *to fall upon* (Field, *Notes,* 25): c. dat. pers., Mk 3¹⁰ (v. Swete, in l.), Ac 20¹⁰; seq. ἐπὶ τ. τράχηλον (as Ge 46²⁹, To 11⁸, ιιι Mac 5⁴⁹, al.), Lk 15²⁰, Ac 20³⁷. Metaph., φόβος, Lk 1¹², Ac 19¹⁷, Re 11¹¹; ὀνειδισμοί, Ro 15³ ⁽ᴸˣˣ⁾; of the Holy Spirit: seq. ἐπί, c. dat., Ac 8¹⁶; ἐπί, c. acc., Ac 10⁴⁴ 11¹⁵; absol., Ac 23⁷.†

* ἐπι-πλήσσω, 1. *to strike at, to punish.* 2. *to rebuke, reprove:* ι Ti 5¹.†

ἐπι-ποθέω, -ῶ, [in LXX for ערג יאב, כסף hi., etc.;] *to long for, desire:* c. inf., Ro 1¹¹, ιι Co 5², ι Th 3⁶, ιι Ti 1⁴, Phl 2²⁶ (WH, [txt.]);

c. acc. rei, 1 Pe 2². ; c. acc. pers., 11 Co 9¹⁴, Phl 1⁸ 2²⁶ (WH, mg.); absol., Ja 4⁵ (v. Mayor, in l.).†

**† ἐπι-πόθησις, -εως, ἡ, [in Aq.: Ez 23¹¹*;] longing: 11 Co 7⁷, ¹¹.†

*† ἐπι-πόθητος, -ον, greatly desired, longed for : Phl 4¹.†

*† ἐπιποθία (WH, -πόθεια), -ας, ἡ = ἐπιπόθησις, longing: Ro 15²³.†

† ἐπι-πορεύομαι, [in LXX: Le 26³³ (אָחַר), Ez 39¹⁴ (עבר), Ep. Je ⁶², 11 Mac 2²⁸, 111 Mac 1⁴*;] to travel, journey to: seq. πρός, c. acc. pers., Lk 8⁴.†

*† ἐπι-ράπτω (Rec. -ρράπτω), to sew upon : seq. ἐπί, c. acc., Mk 2²¹.†

ἐπι-ρίπτω (Rec. -ρρίπτω, as in cl.), [in LXX chiefly for שָׁלַךְ hi.;] 1. to cast at. 2. to cast or place upon: c. acc. seq. ἐπί, c. acc., Lk 19³⁵; metaph., τ. μέριμιαν, 1 Pe 5⁷ (LXX).†

ἐπίσημος, -ον (< σῆμα, a mark), [in LXX: Ge 30⁴² (קָשַׁר), Es 5⁴ B¹³, 1 Mac 11³⁷ 14⁴⁸, 11 Mac 15³⁶, 111 Mac 6¹*;] 1. bearing a mark ; of money, stamped, coined. 2. Metaph., (a) in good sense, notable, illustrious : Ro 16⁷; (b) in bad sense, notorious : Mt 27¹⁶.†

ἐπισιτισμός, -οῦ, ὁ (< ἐπισιτίζομαι, to supply with provisions), [in LXX: Ge 42²⁵, al. (צֵדָה), Jth 2¹⁸ 4⁵;] 1. a foraging. 2. provisions, food : Lk 9¹².†

ἐπι-σκέπτομαι (late form of ἐπισκοπέω, q.v.), [in LXX very freq., chiefly for פָּקַד;] 1. to inspect, examine. 2. (a) to visit: c. acc., Ac 7²³ 15³⁶ (cf. Jg 15¹); especially, the sick and afflicted (as in MGr. and sometimes in cl.), Mt 25³⁶, ⁴³, Ja 1²⁷ (cf. Si 7³⁵); (b) in LXX and NT (as פָּקַד in Ge 21¹, Ex 4³¹, Ps 8⁵, al.), to visit with help, to care for : Lk 1⁶⁸, ⁷⁸ 7¹⁶, Ac 15¹⁴, He 2⁶ ; (c) to visit with punishment (Je 9²⁵, Ps 88 (89)³³, al.; cf. MM, Exp., xiv; Cremer, 863).†

ἐπι-σκευάζω, [in LXX for חָזַק pi., etc.;] to equip, make ready ; mid., to make one's preparations : Ac 21¹⁵.†

*† ἐπι-σκηνόω, -ῶ, to tent upon, spread a tabernacle over : metaph., seq. ἐπ᾽ ἐμέ (RV, rest upon, cover), 11 Co 12⁹.†

ἐπι-σκιάζω, [in LXX: Ex 40²⁹ (³⁵) (שָׁכַן), Ps 90 (91)⁴ 139 (140)⁷ (סָכַךְ), Pr 18¹¹*;] to throw a shadow upon, overshadow : c. dat., Ac 5¹⁵; of a shining (Mt, l.c., and cf. Ex 40²⁹ ³⁵, 11 Mac 2⁸) cloud, c. dat., Mk 9⁷; c. acc., Mt 17⁵, Lk 9³⁴; metaph. (cf. Pss, Pr, ll.c.), of the Holy Spirit, Lk 1³⁵.†

ἐπι-σκοπέω, -ῶ, [in LXX for פָּקַד ni., etc.;] 1. to look upon, observe, examine : seq. μή, He 12¹⁵. 2. As ἐπισκέπτομαι in LXX, NT, to visit, care for : 1 Pe 5² (R, txt.; WH om.; Cremer, 527).†

† ἐπι-σκοπή, -ῆς, ἡ, [in LXX chiefly for פָּקַד, פְּקֻדָּה;] 1. a visiting, visitation (εἰς ἐ. τοῦ παιδός, Lucian, dial. deor., 20, 6); as in LXX (after Heb.), of God's visitation in mercy, or in judgment (Le 19²⁰, Jb 10¹², Je 6¹⁵, Wi 2²⁰, al.): Lk 19⁴⁴, 1 Pe 2¹² (v. Hort, in l.). 2. office, charge, oversight, esp. office of an ἐπίσκοπος (q.v.): Ac 1²⁰ (LXX), 1 Ti 3¹ (Cremer, 527 f., 864; DCG, ii, 809ᵇ).†

ἐπί-σκοπος, -ου, ὁ (< σκοπός, a watcher), [in LXX for פָּקִיד, its
parts and derivatives, Nu 4¹⁶ 31¹⁴, Jg 9²⁸, iv Ki 11¹⁵, ¹⁸, ii Ch 34¹², ¹⁷,
Ne 11⁹, ¹⁴, ²²; אֵל, Jb 20²⁹; נֹגֵשׂ, Is 60¹⁷; Wi 1⁶, i Mac 1⁵¹ *;] a
superintendent, guardian, overseer (cl.; for exx. v. LS, s.v.): Ac 20²⁸,
i Pe 2²⁵ (ICC, in l.); as technical term for a religious office (Deiss.,
BS, 230 f.), in later Paul. epp. of the head or heads of a church (Vg.
episcopus), a bishop : Phl 1¹ (v. Lft, in l.), i Ti 3², Tit 1⁷ (v. reff. s.v.
ἐπισκοπή) ; v. also reff. s.v. πρέσβυς.†
    ἐπι-σπάω, -ῶ, [in LXX: Is 5¹⁸ (מָשַׁךְ), etc.;] to draw on: mid.,
in peculiar sense of effacing signs of Judaism (cf. i Mac 1¹⁵, FlJ, Ant.,
xii, 5, i; v. Thayer, s.v.), to become as uncircumcised: i Co 7¹⁸.†
    * ἐπι-σπείρω, to sow upon or besides : ἀνὰ μέσον, Mt 13²⁵.†
    ἐπίσταμαι (prob. an old mid. of ἐφίστημι, q.v.), [in LXX chiefly
for יָדַע;] to know, know of, understand : c. acc. pers., Ac 19¹⁵; c.
ptcp., ib. 24¹⁰; c. acc. rei, Mk 14⁶⁸, Ac 18²⁵, i Ti 6⁴, Ja 4¹⁴, Ju ¹⁰; seq.
περί, Ac 26²⁶; ὅτι, ib. 15⁷ 19²⁵ 22¹⁹; ὡς, ib. 10²⁸; πῶς, ib. 20¹⁸; ποῦ, He
11⁸; on the reading c. gen. rei in Ja 4¹⁴, v. ICC, in l.†
    SYN.: γινώσκω (q.v.), οἶδα.
    ** ἐπί-στασις, -εως, ἡ (< ἐφίστημι), [in LXX: ii Mac 6³ *;] 1. a
stopping, halting (as of soldiers): ὄχλου, collecting a crowd (v. Rackham, Acts, l.c.): Ac 24¹² (WH, Rec. ἐπισύστασις). 2. superintendence,
attention (but v. Thayer, s.v.; Field, Notes, 185 f.): ii Co 11²⁸ (WH,
Rec. ut supr.).†
    ἐπιστάτης, -ου, ὁ (< ἐφίστημι), [in LXX: iv Ki 25¹⁹, Je 36 (29)²⁶
52²⁵ (פָּקִיד), ii Ch 31¹² (נָגִיד), ii Mac 5²², etc.;] a chief, commander,
master : Lk 5⁵ 8²⁴, ⁴⁵ 9³³, ⁴⁹ 17¹³ (cf. Dalman, Words, 336 ff.).†
    ἐπι-στέλλω, [in LXX: iii Ki 5⁸ ⁽²²⁾, Ne 6¹⁹ (שָׁלַח), Jth 15⁴, i Mac
10²⁵ 12⁷ 13¹⁸ (in each case with v.l. ἀποσ-) *;] 1. to send to. 2. to
send a message by letter, to write word (MM, Exp., xiv): c. dat. pers.,
Ac 21²⁵, He 13²²; seq. τοῦ, c. inf., Ac 15²⁰.†
    ἐπιστήμων, -ον, gen., -ονος (ἐπίσταμαι), [in LXX: De 1¹³ 4⁶,
Is 5²¹ (בִּין ni.), i Es 8⁴⁴, Si 10²⁵ 21¹⁵, etc.;] knowing, skilled : Ja 3¹³.†
    ἐπι-στηρίζω, [in LXX for סָמַךְ, etc.;] to make stronger, confirm :
c. acc., Ac 14²² 15³², ⁴¹.†
    ἐπι-στολή, -ῆς, ἡ (< ἐπιστέλλω), [in LXX for אִגֶּרֶת, etc.; freq.
in Mac;] 1. a message. 2. a letter, an epistle: Ac 9², i Co 5⁹, al.;
pl., Ac 22⁵, i Co 16³, al.; ἐ. συστατικαί, ii Co 3¹ (cf. Milligan, NTD,
254 f.). (On the NT ἐπιστολαί, cf. Milligan, Th., 121 ff.; NTD,
85 ff.; Deiss., BS, 3 ff.; St. Paul, 8 ff.)
    * ἐπι-στομίζω (< στόμα), to bridle ; metaph., to stop the mouth, to
silence : Tit 1¹¹.†
    ἐπι-στρέφω, [very freq. in LXX, chiefly for שׁוּב, in its various
senses, also for פָּנָה, etc.;] 1. trans., to turn about, round or towards,
hence metaph., to turn, cause to return (to God, virtue, etc.): Lk
1¹⁶, ¹⁷ (cf. Ma 3²⁴), Ja 5¹⁹, ²⁰. 2. Intrans., (a) to turn, turn oneself
around : Ac 16¹⁸; c. inf., Re 1¹²; seq. πρός. Ac 9⁴⁰; so also pass. (cl.),

Mk 5³⁰ 8³³, Jo 21²⁰; metaph., of turning to God (v. Field, *Notes*, 246 ff.), ἐπὶ τ. κύριον (θεόν), Ac 9³⁵ 11²¹ 14¹⁵ 15¹⁹ 26²⁰; πρὸς τ. θεόν, ι Th 1⁹, ιι Co 3¹⁶; ἀπὸ σκότους εἰς φῶς, Ac 26¹⁸; pass., ι Pe 2²⁵; (b) to *return* (as in MGr.): Lk 8⁵⁵, Ac 15³⁶; seq. ὀπίσω, c. inf., Mt 24¹⁸; seq. εἰς, Mt 12⁴⁴, Mk 13¹⁶, Lk 2³⁹ 17³¹; ἐπί, ιι Pe 2²²; metaph., seq. ἐπί, Ga 4⁹; πρός, Lk 17⁴; of moral reform, Mt 13¹⁵, Mk 4¹², Lk 22³², Ac 3¹⁹ 28²⁷; pass., Mt 10¹³ (Cremer, 531, 881).†

ἐπι-στροφή, -ῆς, ἡ (ἐπιστρέφω), [in LXX: Ez 47⁷ (שׁוּב), Si 18²¹ 49², etc. ;] a *turning about*; metaph., *conversion* (Field, *Notes*, 246): Ac 15³.†

* **ἐπι-συν-άγω**, [in LXX for אסף, קבץ, etc. (Cremer, 65);] 1. *to gather together*: Mt 23³⁷ 24³¹, Mk 13²⁷, Lk 13³⁴; pass., Mk 1³³, Lk 12¹ 17³⁷. (cf. Ps 101 (102)²³ 105 (106)⁴⁷, ιι Mac 1²⁷, al.). 2. *to gather together against* (Mi 4¹¹, Za 12³, ι Mac 3⁵⁸, al.).†

† ἐπι-συν-αγωγή, -ῆς, ἡ (< ἐπισυνάγω), [in LXX: ιι Mac 2⁷*;] a *gathering together, assembly*: He 10²⁵; seq. ἐπί, ιι Th 2¹ (cf. ιι Mac, l.c.).†

*† **ἐπι-συν-τρέχω**, to *run together again*: Mk 9²⁵ (v. Swete, in l.).†

† ἐπι-σύστασις, -εως, ἡ (< ἐπισυνίστημι), [in LXX: Nu 16⁴⁰ (עֵדָה) 26⁹ (נצה hi.), ι Es 5⁷³ A*;] a *gathering, a riotous throng*: Rec. (for ἐπίστασις, q.v.), Ac 24¹², ιι Co 11²⁸.†

** **ἐπισφαλής, -ές** (< σφάλλω, to *cause to fall*), [in LXX: Wi 9¹⁴ (cf. -ῶς, ib. 4⁴)*;] 1. *prone to fall* (Plat.). 2. *dangerous* (Hipp., Plut., al.): Ac 27⁹.†

** **ἐπι-ισχύω**, [in LXX: Si 29¹, ι Mac 6⁶*;] 1. *to make stronger* (Si, l.c.). 2. *to grow stronger*; metaph., *be more urgent*: Lk 23⁵.†

† ἐπι-σωρεύω, [in Sm.: Jb 14¹⁷, Ca 2⁴*;] *to heap together*; metaph., διδασκάλους, ιι Ti 4³.†

† ἐπι-ταγή, -ῆς, ἡ (< ἐπιτάσσω), [in ꝈXX: Da LXX 3¹⁶ (פִּתְגָם), ι Es 1¹⁸, Wi 14¹⁶ 18¹⁶ 19⁶, ιιι Mac 7²⁰*;] = cl., ἐπίταγμα, a *command*, Ro 16²⁶, ι Co 7⁶, ²⁵, ιι Co 8⁸, ι Ti 1¹, Tit 1³ (for use in Inscr. of divine commands, v. MM, *Exp.*, xiv); μετὰ πάσης ἐ., *with all authority*: Tit 2¹⁵.†

ἐπι-τάσσω, [in LXX for אמר, צוה, etc.;] *to command, charge*: c. acc. rei, Lk 14²²; c. dat. pers., Mk 1²⁷ 9²⁵, Lk 4³⁶ 8²⁵; id. c. acc. rei, Phm ⁸; id. c. inf., Mk 6³⁹, Lk 8³¹, Ac 23²; id. c. imperat., Mk 9²⁵; c. acc. et inf., Mk 6²⁷.†

SYN. : κελεύω.

ἐπι-τελέω, -ῶ, [in LXX for כלה, עשׂה, etc. ;] *to complete, accomplish, execute* : c. acc. rei, Ro 15²⁸, ιι Co 7¹ 8⁶, ¹¹, Phl 1⁶, He 8⁵; of religious services (cf. Hdt., ii, 37, al.), He 9⁶; art. inf., ιι Co 8¹¹. Mid., (a) *to complete for oneself, make an end* (R, mg.; pass., R, txt; cf. Meyer, in l.): Ga 3³; (b) *to pay in full, pay the tax, be subject to*: c. acc. (cf. Xen., *Mem.*, iv, 8, 8), ι Pe 5⁹ (pass., RV, etc.; cf. Thayer, s.v.; *ICC*, in l).†

ἐπιτήδειος, -α, -ον, [in LXX: ι Ch 28², Wi 4⁵, ι Mac 4⁴⁶, al.;] 1. *suitable, convenient*. 2. *useful, necessary*: τὰ ἐ., *necessaries*, Ja 2¹⁶.†

ἐπι-τίθημι, [in LXX for נתן, שׂום, etc. ;] 1. *to lay, set* or *place upon :* c. acc. rei, seq. ἐπί, c. acc. rei, Mt 23⁴, Lk 15⁵, Jo 9⁶ (WH, txt.), 15, Ac 15¹⁰ 28³ ; ἐπί, c. gen. rei, Mt 27²⁹ ; ἐν, ib. ; c. dat. pers., σταυρόν, Lk 23²⁶ ; στέφανον, Jo 19² ; ὄνομα, Mk 3¹⁶, ¹⁷ ; πληγάς, Lk 10³⁰, Ac 16²³ ; ἐπί, c. acc. pers., Re 22¹⁸ ; of the laying on of hands, τ. χεῖρα (-ας), seq. ἐπί, c. acc. pers., Mt 9¹⁸, Mk 16⁽¹⁸⁾, Ac 8¹⁷ 9¹⁷ ; c. dat. pers., Mt 19¹³, ¹⁵, Mk 5²³ 6⁵ 7³² 8²³, Lk 4⁴⁰ 13¹³, Ac 6⁶ 8¹⁹ 9¹² 13³ 19⁶ 28⁸, ι Ti 5²². Mid., (a) *to provide :* Ac 28¹⁰ (RV, *put on board ;* cf. Field, *Notes*, 149) ; (b) *to throw oneself upon, attack :* c. dat. pers., Ac 18¹⁰. 2. *to add to :* Re 22¹⁸ (v. supr., and cf. Swete, in l.).†

ἐπι-τιμάω, -ῶ, [in LXX for בְּעַר, Ge 37¹⁰, Ps 9⁵, Za 3³ ⁽²⁾ ; Si 11⁷, al. ;] 1. *to honour.* 2. *to raise in price.* 3. *to mete out due measure ;* (a) *to award ;* (b) *to censure, rebuke, admonish :* absol., ιι Ti 4² ; c. dat., Mt 8²⁶ 17¹⁸ 19¹³, Mk 4³⁹ 8³² 10¹³, Lk 4³⁹, ⁴¹ 8²⁴ 9²¹, ⁴², ⁵⁵ 17³ 18¹⁵ 19³⁹, Ju ⁹ ; seq. ἵνα, *warn* (and for sense *forbid* in Mk 3¹² 8³⁰, v. Barton in *JBL*, xli (1923), pp. 233 ff.), Mt 12¹⁶ 16²⁰ 20³¹, Mk 3¹² 8³⁰ 10⁴⁸, Lk 18³⁹ ; seq. λέγων, λέγει, etc., Mt 16²², Mk 1²⁵ 8³³ 9²⁵, Lk 4³⁵ 23⁴⁰.†
SYN.: ἐλέγχω, q.v.

ἐπιτιμία, -ας, ἡ (< ἐπιτιμάω), [in LXX: Wi 3¹⁰ * ;] 1. *citizenship, franchise.* 2. As in Inscr. (LS, s.v.), LXX, l.c. (= cl. τὸ ἐπιτίμιον), *punishment, penalty :* ιι Co 2⁶.†

ἐπι-τρέπω, [in LXX (usually with v.l. ἐπιστρ-) : Ge 39⁶ (עזב), etc. ;] 1. *to turn to, commit, entrust.* 2. *to yield, permit :* ι Co 16⁷, He 6³ ; c. dat. pers., Mk 5¹³, Jo 19³⁸ ; id. c. inf. (cf. M, *Pr.*, 205), Mt 8²¹ 19⁸, Lk 8³² 9⁵⁹, ⁶¹, Ac 21³⁹, ⁴⁰ 27³, ι Ti 2¹² ; c. inf., Mk 10⁴. Pass., c. dat. et inf., Ac 26¹ 28¹⁶, ι Co 14³⁴.†

* ἐπιτροπεύω (< ἐπίτροπος, *a procurator*), *to govern :* Lk 3¹ (WH, mg., for ἡγεμονεύοντος, an obvious correction for precision).†

** ἐπι-τροπή, -ῆς, ἡ (< ἐπιτρέπω), [in LXX : ιι Mac 13¹⁴ * ;] *power to decide, authority, commission :* Ac 26ⁱ².†

** ἐπίτροπος, -ου, ὁ (< ἐπιτρέπω), [in LXX : ιι Mac 11¹ 13² 14² * ;] 1. *an administrator, a steward :* Mt 20⁸, Lk 8³. 2. *a guardian* (c. gen. pers., ιι Mac, ll. c.) : Ga 4².†

ἐπι-τυγχάνω, [in LXX : Ge 39² (צלח hi.), Pr 12²⁷ (חרךּ) * ;] 1. *to light upon.* 2. *to obtain, attain to :* Ja 4², c. gen. rei (as in cl.), He 6¹⁵ 11³³ ; c. acc. (late Gk.), Ro 11⁷ (Rec. τούτου).†

ἐπι-φαίνω, [in LXX for אור hi., etc. ;] 1. *to show forth.* 2. (= pass. in cl.) *to appear :* Ac 27²⁰ ; c. dat. pers., Lk 1⁷⁹ ; metaph., Tit 3⁴ ; c. dat., ib. 2¹¹ (Cremer, 567).†

ἐπιφάνεια, -ας, ἡ (< ἐπιφανής), [in LXX: ιι Ki 7²³ (נורא), Es 5¹, Am 5²², ιι Mac 2²¹ 3²⁴ 5⁴ 12²² 14¹⁵ 15²⁷, ιιι Mac 2⁹ 5⁸, ⁵¹ * ;] (in late Gk. and Inscr., freq. of deities, v. MM, *Exp.*, xiv), *a manifestation, appearance :* ιι Th 2⁸, ι Ti 6¹⁴, ιι Ti 1¹⁰ 4¹, ⁸, Tit 2¹³ (cf. M, *Th.*, 148 f.).†

ἐπιφανής, -ές (< ἐπιφαίνω), [in LXX (v. Thayer, s.v.) for נורא, etc., Jg 13⁶, Jl 2¹¹, ³¹, al. ; ιι Mac 6²³, ιιι Mac 5³⁵, al. ;] *renowned, illustrious, notable :* Ac 2²⁰ ⁽LXX⁾ (cf. MM, *Exp.*, xiv).†

† ἐπι-φαύσκω (variant form of ἐπιφώσκω, q.v.), [in LXX : Jb 25⁵

(אהל hi.) 31²⁶ 41⁹ ⁽¹⁰⁾ (הלל hi.) *;] *to shine forth :* fig., c. dat., Eph 5¹⁴ (on v.l. -ψαύσει, v. ICC, Westc., AR, in l.).†

ἐπι-φέρω, [in LXX chiefly for שלם;] 1. *to bring upon* or *against :* κρίσιν, Ju ⁹. 2. *to impose, inflict :* Ro 3⁵.†

** ἐπι-φωνέω, -ῶ, [in LXX : ι Es 9⁴⁷ AR, ιι Mac 1²³, ιιι Mac 7¹³ *;] *to call out, shout :* c. acc. rei, Ac 21³⁴ ; c. dat. pers., ib. 22²⁴ ; seq. λέγοντες, Lk 23²¹ ; orat. rect., Ac 12²².†

ἐπι-φώσκω, [in LXX for הלל hi., Jb 41⁹ ⁽¹⁰⁾ A (Bא, ἐπιφαύσκ-) *;] 1. *to let shine.* 2. *to dawn* (cf. MM, Exp., xiv): Lk 23⁵⁴ ; seq. εἰς, Mt 28¹.†

ἐπιχειρέω, -ῶ (< χείρ), [in LXX for חשב, Es 9²⁵ ; גמל, ιι Ch 20¹¹, al.;] 1. *to put one's hand to.* 2. *to take in hand, attempt :* c. inf., Lk 1¹, Ac 9²⁹ 19¹³.†

ἐπι-χέω, [in LXX chiefly for יצק, Ge 28¹⁸, al.;] *to pour upon :* Lk 10³⁴.†

** ἐπι-χορηγέω, -ῶ, [in LXX : Si 25²², ιι Mac 4⁹ A *;] *to supply, provide :* c. acc. rei, ιι Pe 1⁵ ; id. c. dat. pers., ιι Co 9¹⁰, Ga 3⁵ ; pass., Col 2¹⁹, ιι Pe 1¹¹ (cf. χορηγέω, and v. MM, Exp., xiv).†

*† ἐπι-χορηγία, -ας, ἡ (< ἐπιχορηγέω), a *supply :* Eph 4¹⁶, Phl 1¹⁹.†

** ἐπι-χρίω, [in Sm. : Ez 13¹⁰ 22²⁸ *;] *to spread on, anoint :* c. acc., Jo 9¹¹ ; id. seq. ἐπί, c. acc., Jo 9⁶ (cf. MM, Exp., xiv).†

* ἐπ-οικοδομέω, -ῶ, in NT, always metaph., of the spiritual life regarded as a building (Cremer, 449); 1. *to build upon :* ι Co 3¹⁰, ¹², ¹⁴ ; pass., Eph 2²⁰. 2. *to build up :* Col 2⁷, ι Pe 2⁵ (T, οἰκοδ- WH, Rec.), Ju ²⁰.†

ἐπ-ονομάζω, [in LXX chiefly for קרא;] *to name, call by a name, surname :* pass., Ro 2¹⁷.†

** ἐπ-οπτεύω, [in Sm. : Ps 9³⁵ (10¹⁴) 32 (33)¹³ *;] *to watch* (in Hom., as an overseer ; cf. Ps, ll. c.), *look upon :* ι Pe 2¹² 3².†

** ἐπόπτης, -ου, ὁ, [in LXX (of God): Es 5¹, ιι Mac 3³⁹ 7³⁵, ιιι Mac 2²¹ *;] 1. *an overseer* (LXX, ll. c.). 2. *a spectator :* ιι Pe 1¹⁶ (of ἐ. as applied to God, v. parallels in Inscr., MM, Exp., xiv; of the use of this term in the mysteries, v. Mayor on ιι Pe, l.c.; Thayer, s.v.).†

ἔπος, -εος (-ους), τό, [in LXX : Za 7³, Si 44⁵ *;] *a word :* ὡς ἔ. εἰπεῖν (cl.), *so to speak :* He 7⁹.†

SYN. : λόγος, *reasoned speech ;* ῥῆμα, *mere articulated utterance ;* ἔ., the articulated expression of a thought.

ἐπουράνιος, -ον (< οὐρανός), [in LXX : Ps 67 (68)¹⁴ (שַׁדַּי), Da ΤΗ 4²³ A (שְׁמַיָּא), ιι Mac 3³⁹, ιιι Mac 6²⁸ 7⁶, ιv Mac 4¹¹ AR, 11³ א *;] *in* or *of heaven, heavenly* (in Hom., of the Gods): οἱ ἐ., opp. to ἐπίγειοι and καταχθόνιοι, Phl 2¹⁰ ; to χοϊκός, ι Co 15⁴⁸, ⁴⁹ ; σώματα (v. Lft., Col., 376), ι Co 15⁴⁰ ; βασιλεία, ιι Ti 4¹⁸ ; πατρίς, He 11¹⁶ ; Ἰερουσαλήμ, He 12²² ; κλῆσις (cf. Lft. on Phl 3¹⁴), He 3¹ ; τὰ ἐ., He 8⁵ 9²³ ; opp. to ἐπίγειος, Jo 3¹² ; id., of the heavenly regions, *in the heavenly sphere,* Eph 1³, ²⁰ 2⁶ 3¹⁰ 6¹² ; ἡ δωρεὰ ἡ ἐ., He 6⁴ (Cremer, 468).†

ἑπτά, οἱ, αἱ, τά, indecl., *seven :* Mt 12⁴⁵ 18²² (cf. ἑβδομηκοντάκις), Mk 8⁵, al. ; οἱ ἑ., Ac 21⁸.

ἑπτάκις, adv., *seven times :* Mt 18²¹,²², Lk 17⁴.†

ἑπτακισχίλιοι, -αι, -α, *seven thousand :* Ro 11⁴.†

ἑπταπλασίων, -ον, gen., -ονος, [in LXX for שִׁבְעָתַיִם, Ps 78 (79)¹², al. ;] *sevenfold :* Lk 18³⁰ (WH, mg., for πολλαπλ- WH, txt., RV; v. WH, *Notes,* 62).†

Ἔραστος, -ου, ὁ, *Erastus ;* 1. a companion of St. Paul, Ac 19²², and prob. II Ti 4²⁰.   2. The treasurer of Corinth, Ro 16²³.†

ἐραυνάω, -ῶ, late form of ἐρευνάω (Rec., ll. c.; cf. Bl., § 6, 1; M, *Pr.,* 46), [in LXX, ἐρευν- (exc. I Ch 19³ A), for חָפַשׂ pi., חָקַר, etc. ;] *to search, examine :* Jo 7⁵²; c. acc. rei, Jo 5³⁹, Ro 8²⁷, I Co 2¹⁰, Re 2²³ ; seq. orat. obliq., I Pe 1¹¹.†
SYN. : v.s. ἐξετάζω.

ἐργάζομαι (< ἔργον), [in LXX for עָבַד, פָּעַל, עָשָׂה, etc. ;] 1. intrans., (a) *to work, labour :* Mt 21²⁸, Lk 13¹⁴, Jo 5¹⁷ 9⁴ᵇ, Ac 18³, I Co 9⁶, II Th 3¹⁰⁻¹²; τ. χερσίν, I Co 4¹², I Th 4¹¹; νυκτὸς κ. ἡμέρας, I Th 2⁹, II Th 3⁸; of working for pay, Mt 21²⁸; for reward, Ro 4⁴,⁵; (b) *to work at a trade* or *business, to trade :* seq. ἐν (Dem.), Mt 25¹⁶.   2. Trans., (a) *to work, work out, do, produce, perform :* c. acc., II Co 7¹⁰, Col 3²³, II Th 3¹¹, Ja 1²⁰, II Jo ⁸, seq. εἰς, III Jo ⁵; ἔργον, Ac 13⁴¹ (LXX); id. seq. εἰς, Mt 26¹⁰; ἐν, Mk 14⁶; ἔργα, Jo 3²¹; τὰ ἔ. τ. θεοῦ, Jo 6²⁸ 9⁴; τὸ ἔ. κυρίου, I Co 16¹⁰; τ. ἀγαθόν, Ro 2¹⁰, Eph 4²⁸ (v. AR, *Eph.,* 190); id. seq. πρός, Ga 6¹⁰; κακόν, seq. dat. pers. (more freq. dupl. acc. in cl.), Ro 13¹⁰; δικαιοσύνην, Ac 10³⁵, He 11³³; ἀνομίαν, Mt 7²³; ἁμαρτίαν, Ja 2⁹; σημεῖον, Jo 6³⁰; τ. ἱερά, I Co 9¹³; τ. θάλασσαν (*work the sea,* i.e. make one's living from it), Re 18¹⁷; (b) *to work for, earn by working* (cl.) : Jo 6²⁷ (cf. κατ-, περι-, προσ-εργάζομαι ; Cremer, 258; on the force of the aorist of this verb, v. M, *Pr.,* 116).†

ἐργασία, -ας, ἡ (< ἔργον), [in LXX for מְלָאכָה, עֲבֹדָה, etc. ;] 1. *work, business :* Ac 16¹⁶,¹⁹ 19²⁴,²⁵; δὸς ἐ. (Lat. *da operam*), Lk 12⁵⁸.   2. *working, performance :* Eph 4¹⁹.†

ἐργάτης, -ου, ὁ (< ἐργάζομαι, q.v.), [in LXX : Wi 17¹⁷, Si 19¹ 40¹⁸, I Mac 3⁶ * ;] 1. prop., *a field labourer, husbandman :* Mt 9³⁷,³⁸ 20¹,²,⁸, Lk 10², Ja 5⁴ (cf. Wi, l.c.). 2. Generally, *a workman, labourer :* Mt 10¹⁰, Lk 10⁷, Ac 19²⁵ (opp. tὸ τεχνίτης), I Ti 5¹⁸; of Christian teachers, II Co 11¹³, Phl 3², II Ti 2¹⁵. 3. *a worker, doer :* τ. ἀδικίας, Lk 13²⁷ (cf. I Mac, l.c.).†

ἔργον, -ου, τό (originally Ϝέργον, *work*), [very freq. in LXX, chiefly for מַעֲשֶׂה, מְלָאכָה, also for עֲבֹדָה, פֹּעַל, etc. ;] 1. *work, task, employment :* Mk 13³⁴, Jo 4³⁴ 17⁴, Ac 13², Phl 1²² 2³⁰, I Th 5¹³, al.; of an enterprise or undertaking (De 15¹⁰, Wi 2¹²), Ac 5³⁸.   2. *a deed, action :* Tit 1¹⁶, Ja 1²⁵; disting. from λόγος, Lk 24¹⁹, Ro 15¹⁸, II Th 2¹⁷, I Jo 3¹⁸; ἐν λόγοις κ. ἔ., Ac 7²²; of acts of God, Jo 9³, Ac 13⁴¹ (LXX), He 4¹⁰, Re 15³; of Christ, Mt 11²; esp. in Jo, e.g. 5²⁰,³⁶ 7³ 10³⁸ 14¹¹,¹² 15²⁴; in ethical sense, of human actions (AR, *Eph.,* 190), bad or good,

Mt 23³, Lk 11⁴⁸, Jo 3²⁰,²¹, Ja 2¹⁴ᶠ. 3¹³, Re 2⁵ 3⁸; τὸ ἔ., collectively, Ga 6⁴, Ja 1⁴, ι Pe 1¹⁷, Re 22¹²; τὸ ἔ. τ. νόμου, Ro 2¹⁵; ἔ. ἀγαθόν, Ro 2⁷, Col 1¹⁰, ιι Th 2¹⁷, Tit 1¹⁶, al.; καλόν, Mt 26¹⁰, Mk 14⁶; pl. (as freq. in cl.), Mt 5¹⁶, ι Ti 5¹⁰,²⁵, He 10²⁴; ἔ. πίστεως, ι Th 1³, ιι Th 1¹¹; ἔ. πονηρά, Col 1²¹, ιι Jo ¹¹; νέκρα, He 6¹ 9¹⁴; ἄκαρπα, Eph 5¹¹; ἔ. ἀσεβείας, Ju ¹⁵; τ. σκότους, Ro 13¹², Eph 5¹¹; ἔ. νόμου, Ro 3²⁰,²⁸, Ga 2¹⁶ 3², ⁵, ¹⁰. 3. *that which is wrought* or *made, a work :* ι Co 3¹³⁻¹⁵; τ. χειρῶν, Ac 7⁴¹; of the works of God, He 1¹⁰; γῆ κ. τὰ ἐν αὐτῇ ἔ., ιι Pe 3¹⁰; τὸ ἔ. τ. θεοῦ, Ro 14²⁰.

ἐρεθίζω, [in LXX: Da LXX 11¹⁰,²⁵ (גרה hithp.), ι Mac 15⁴⁰, ιι Mac 14¹⁷, etc.;] 1. *to stir up, provoke* (as in cl.): Col 3²¹. 2. In good sense (cf. ἐρεθισμός, *excitement*, in MGr.), *to stir up, stimulate :* ιι Co 9².†

ἐρείδω (chiefly in poets and late prose for ἐρυγγάνω), [in LXX for תמך (Pr 4⁴ 5⁵ 11¹⁶, al.), etc.;] *to prop, fix firmly :* act., as mid., ἐρείσασα, of a ship driving ashore (RV, *struck*), Ac 27⁴¹.†

ἐρεύγομαι, [in LXX chiefly for שאג, Ho 11¹⁰, Am 3⁴,⁸, al.; also for נבע, Ps 18 (19)², etc.;] 1. *to spit* or *spue out.* 2. Prop., of oxen (Hom.), *to bellow, roar ;* whence, as in LXX, *to speak aloud, utter :* Mt 13³⁵ (LXX). (For other examples of softened force of words in late Gk., cf. σκύλλω, τρώγω, χορτάζω.) †

ἐρευνάω, -ῶ. v.s. ἐραυνάω.

ἐρημία, -ας, ἡ (<ἔρημος), [in LXX : Is 60²⁰, Ez 35⁴ (חָרֵב, חָרְבָּה), ib. 35⁹ (שְׁמָמָה), Wi 17¹⁷, Si 47¹⁷, Ba 4³³, ιν Mac 18⁸ *;] *a solitude, wilderness :* Mt 15³³, Mk 8⁴, ιι Co 11²⁶, He 11³⁸.†

ἔρημος (in older Gk. ἐρῆμος), -ον, [in LXX chiefly for מִדְבָּר;] *solitary, lonely, desolate, deserted :* (*a*) of persons, γυνή, Ga 4²⁷ (LXX); (*b*) of places, Mt 14¹³,¹⁵ 23³⁸ (WH, om.), Mk 1³⁵ 6³², Lk 4⁴² 9¹², al.; as subst., ἡ ἔ. (sc. χώρα; as in Hdt., ii, 32, al.), *the desert,* Mt 3¹,³, Mk 1³,⁴, Jo 3¹⁴, al.; pl., αἱ ἔ., *desert places,* Lk 1⁸⁰ 5¹⁶ 8²⁹.

ἐρημόω, -ῶ (<ἔρημος), [in LXX for חָרַב hi., שָׁמֵם ni., etc.;] *to desolate, lay waste :* Mt 12²⁵, Lk 11¹⁷, Re 17¹⁶ 18¹⁶,¹⁹.†

†ἐρήμωσις, -εως, ἡ (<ἐρημόω), [in LXX for שמם, Le 26³⁴,³⁵, Ps 72 (73)¹⁹, Da 9²⁷ 11³¹ 12¹¹, al.; חָרְבָּה, Je 7³⁴ 22⁵, al.;] *a making desolate, laying waste :* Lk 21²⁰; βδέλυγμα ἐρημώσεως (Da, ll. c., ι Mac 1⁵⁴), Mt 24¹⁵ (LXX), Mk 13¹⁴ (ib.).†

ἐρίζω (<ἔρις), [in LXX for מרה, etc.;] *to wrangle, strive :* Mt 12¹⁹ (LXX, κεκράξεται).†

**ἐριθία, (T, cl., -εία), -ας, ἡ, [in Sm.: Ez 23¹¹ *;] (on the origin and history of the word, v. Hort, *Ja.,* 81 ff.; Ellic. on Ga 5²⁰; Cremer, 262; see further MM, *VGT,* s.v., and reff. there), *ambition, self-seeking, rivalry :* Ja 3¹⁴,¹⁶; κατ᾽ ἐριθίαν, Phl 2³; οἱ ἐξ ἔ., Ro 2⁸, Phl 1¹⁷; pl. (Bl., § 32, 6; WM, 220; Swete, *Mk.,* 153), ιι Co 12²⁰, Ga 5²⁰.†

ἔριον, -ου, τό, [in LXX for צֶמֶר, Le 13⁴⁷, Is 1¹⁸, al.;] *wool :* He 9¹⁹, Re 1¹⁴.†

ἔρις, -ιδος, acc., ἔριν (on the declension, v. Bl., § 8, 3; WH, *App.*, 157), ἡ, [in LXX: Ps 138 (139)²⁰, Si 28¹¹ 40⁵, ⁹ *;] *strife, wrangling, contention:* Ro 1²⁹ 13¹³, 1 Co 3³, 11 Co 12²⁰, Ga 5²⁰, Phl 1¹⁵, 1 Ti 6⁴, Tit 3⁹; pl. (v.s. ἐριθία), Ro 13¹³, WH, mg., 1 Co 1¹¹, Ga, l.c., WH, mg.†

**† ἐρίφιον, -ου, τό (dim. of ἔριφος, q.v.), [in LXX: To 2¹³ *;] Mt 25³³, Lk 15²⁹ (ἔριφον, WH, txt.).†

ἔριφος, -ου, [in LXX chiefly for גְּדִי;] *a kid:* Mt 25³², Lk 15²⁹, WH, txt.†

Ἑρμᾶς, -ᾶ, acc., -ᾶν (Doric form of Ἑρμῆς), *Hermas,* a Christian: Ro 16¹⁴.†

ἑρμηνεία, v.s. ἑρμηνία.

ἑρμηνευτής, -οῦ, ὁ (< ἑρμηνεύω), [in LXX for לִיץ hi., Ge 42²³ *;] *an interpreter:* 1 Co 14²⁸ (WH, mg.).†

ἑρμηνεύω, [in LXX: 11 Es 4⁷ (תִּרְגָּם), Es 10³ Jb 42¹⁸ *;] 1. *to explain.* 2. *to interpret:* Lk 24²⁷ (WH, mg.), Jo 1³⁹, ⁴³ 9⁷, He 7².†

ἑρμηνία (T, cl., -εία), -ας, ἡ (< ἑρμηνεύω), [in LXX (-εία), Si, prol. ¹⁴ 47¹⁷, Da LXX 5¹ *;] *interpretation:* 1 Co 12¹⁰ 14²⁶.†

Ἑρμῆς, -οῦ, acc., Ἑρμῆν, ὁ, *Hermes;* (*a*) the Greek god (Lat. *Mercurius*): Ac 14¹²; (*b*) a Christian: Ro 16¹⁴.†

Ἑρμογένης, -ους, ὁ, *Hermogenes,* a Christian: 11 Ti 1¹⁵.†

ἑρπετόν, -οῦ, τό (< ἕρπω, *to crawl*), [in LXX chiefly for רֶמֶשׂ, שֶׁרֶץ;] *a creeping thing, reptile:* Ac 10¹² 11⁶, Ro 1²³, Ja 3⁷.†

ἐρυθρός, -ά, -όν, [in LXX for אָדֹם, Is 63²; ἐ. θάλασσα for יַם־סוּף, Ex 10¹⁹, al.;] *red:* ἡ ἐ. θάλασσα, *the Red Sea,* Ac 7³⁶, He 11²⁹.†

ἔρχομαι, [in LXX very freq. for בּוֹא, also for הָלַךְ ni., אָתָה, etc., 34 words in all;] 1. *to come;* (*a*) of persons, either as arriving or returning from elsewhere: Mt 8⁹, Mk 6³¹, Lk 7⁸, Jo 4²⁷, Ro 9⁹, al.; seq. ἀ ρό, Mk 5³⁵ 7¹, Jo 3², al.; ἐκ, Lk 5¹⁷, Jo 3³¹, al.; εἰς, Mk 1²⁹, al.; διά seq. εἰς, Mk 7³¹; ἐν (Cremer, 263 f., but v.s. ἐν), Ro 15²⁹, 1 Co 4²¹; ἐπί, c. acc., Mk 6⁵³ 11¹³, Jo 19³³, al.; κατά, c. acc., Lk 10³³ Ac 16⁷; παρά, c. gen., Lk 8⁴⁹; c. acc., Mt 15²⁹, Mk 9¹⁴, al.; c. dat. comm., incomm. (M, *Pr.,* 75, 245), Mt 21⁵, Re 2⁵, ¹⁶; with adverbs: πόθεν, Jo 3⁸, al.; ἄνωθεν, Jo 3³¹; ὄπισθεν, Mk 5²⁷; ὧδε, Mt 8²⁹; ἐκεῖ, Jo 18³; ποῦ, He 11⁸; seq. ἕως, Lk 4⁴²; ἄχρι, Ac 11⁵; with purpose expressed by inf., Mk 5¹⁴, Lk 1⁵⁹, al.; by fut. ptcp., Mt 27⁴⁹; ἵνα, Jo 12⁹; εἰς τοῦτο, ἵνα, Ac 9²¹; διά, c. acc., Jo 12⁹; before verbs of action, ἔρχεται καί, ἦλθε καί, etc.: Mk 2¹⁸, Jo 6¹⁵, al.; ἔρχου καὶ ἴδε, Jo 1⁴⁷ 11³⁴; ἐλθών (redundant; Dalman, *Words,* 20 f.), Mt 2⁸ 8⁷, Mk 7²⁵, Ac 16³⁹, al.; similarly ἐρχόμενος, Lk 15²⁵, al.; of coming into public view: esp. of the Messiah (ὁ ἐρχόμενος, Mt 11³, al.; v. Cremer, 264), Lk 3¹⁶, Jo 4²⁵; hence, of Jesus, Mt 11¹⁹, Lk 7³⁴, Jo 5⁴³, al.; of the second coming, Mt 10²³, Ac 1¹¹, 1 Co 4⁵, 1 Th 5², al.; (*b*) of time: ἔρχονται ἡμέραι (pres. for fut.: Bl., § 56, 8), Lk 23²⁹, He 8⁸ ⁽ᴸˣˣ⁾; fut., Mt 9¹⁵, Mk 2²⁰, al.; ἔρχεται ὥρα, ὅτε, Jo 4²¹, ²³, al.; ἦλθεν, ἐλήλυθε ἡ ὥρα, Jo 13¹ 16³² 17¹; ἡ ἡμέρα τ. κυρίου, 1 Th 5²; καιροί, Ac 3¹⁹; (*c*) of things and events: κατακλυσμός, Lk 17²⁷; λιμός, Ac 7¹¹; ἡ ὀργή, 1 Th 1¹⁰; ὁ λύχνος, Mk 4²¹ (v. Swete, in l.). Metaph., τ. ἀγαθά, Ro 3⁸; τ. τέλειον, 1 Co 13¹⁰; ἡ πίστις, Ga 3²³,²⁵; ἡ ἐντολή, Ro 7⁹; with prepositions : ἐκ τ. θλίψεως, Re 7¹⁴; εἰς τ. χεῖρον, Mk 5²⁶; εἰς πειρασμόν, ib. 14³⁸, al. 2. to go : ὀπίσω, c. gen. (Heb. הָלַךְ אַחֲרֵי), Mt 16²⁴, Mk 8³⁴, Lk 9²³; σύν, Jo 21³; ὁδόν, Lk 2⁴⁴. (Cf. ἀν-, ἐπ-αν-, ἀπ-, δι-, εἰς, ἐπ-εισ-, παρ-εισ-, συν-εισ-, ἐξ-, δι-εξ-, ἐπ-, κατ-, παρ-, ἀντι-παρ-, περι-, προ-, προσ-, συν-έρχομαι.)

SYN.: πορεύομαι, χωρέω (v. Thayer, s.v. ἔρχομαι).

ἐρῶ, v.s. λέγω, p. 496.

ἐρωτάω (-έω; v. M, Gr., ii, p. 238), -ῶ, [in LXX chiefly for שָׁאַל·] 1. to ask, question (cl.): absol., Lk 19³¹ 22⁶⁸, Jo 8 [7]; c. acc. pers., Jo 9²¹ 16¹⁹, ³⁰ 18²¹; seq. λέγων, Mt 16¹³, Lk 23³, Jo 1¹⁹, ²¹ 5¹² 9¹⁹ 16⁵; c. dupl. acc. (WM, § 32, 4a), Mt 21²⁴, Mk 4¹⁰, Lk 20³, Jo 16²³ (M, Pr., 66ₙ); c. acc. pers., seq. περί, Lk 9⁴⁵, Jo 18¹⁹. 2. In late Gk. (Milligan, NTD, 51; not, as Cremer, 716, Thayer, s.v., a "Hebraism"), = αἰτέω (q.v.), to ask, request : c. acc. pers., Jo 14¹⁶; seq. imperat., Lk 14¹⁸,¹⁹, Phl 4³; λέγων, Mt 15²³, Jo 12²¹; seq. ἵνα (M, Pr., 208), Mk 7²⁶, Lk 7³⁶ 16²⁷, Jo 4⁴⁷ 17¹⁵ 19³¹,³⁸, 1 Th 4¹, ii Jo 5; ὅπως, Lk 7³ 11³⁷, Ac 23²⁰; c. inf., Lk 5³ 8³⁷, Jo 4⁴⁰, Ac 3³ 10⁴⁸ 23¹⁸, 1 Th 5¹²; c. acc. pers., seq. περί, Lk 4³⁸, Jo 17⁹,²⁰, 1 Jo 5¹⁶; ὑπέρ, ii Th 2¹,²; τὰ (WH, txt., om. τὰ) πρὸς εἰρήνην, Lk 14³² (cf. δι-, ἐπ-ερωτάω).

SYN.: v.s. αἰτέω.

** ἐσθής, -ῆτος, ἡ (< ἕννυμι, to clothe; hence, ἐσθής, Lk, ll. c., Elz.), [in LXX: 1 Es 8⁷¹,⁷³, ii Mac 8³⁵ 11⁸ *;] clothing, raiment : Lk 23¹¹ 24⁴, Ac 10³⁰ 12²¹, Ja 2²,³.†

** ἔσθησις, -εως, ἡ, [in LXX: pl., ii Mac 3³³, iii Mac 1¹⁶ *;] clothing : pl., Ac 1¹⁰.†

ἐσθίω, and (poët. and late prose) ἔσθω, [in LXX chiefly for אָכַל;] to eat; (a) absol.: Mt 14²⁰,²¹, Mk 6³¹, Jo 4³¹, al.; ἐν τ. φαγεῖν (on this aor. form, v. M, Pr., 111), 1 Co 11²¹; διδόναι φαγεῖν, c. dat. pers., Mk 5⁴³, al.; ἐ. καὶ πίνειν, Mt 6²⁵,³¹, Lk 10⁷, al.; of ordinary use of food and drink, 1 Co 9⁴ 11²²; of partaking of food at table, Mk 2¹⁶, Lk 5³⁰, al.; opp. to fasting, Mt 11¹⁸, Lk 5³³, al.; of revelling, Mt 24⁴⁹, Lk 12⁴⁵; (b) c. acc. rei : Mt 6²⁵, Mk 1⁶, Jo 6³¹, Ro 14², al.; ἄρτον (Heb. אָכַל לֶחֶם), Mt 15², Mk 3²⁰, al.; τὸν ἑαυτοῦ ἄ., ii Th 3¹²; ἄ. seq. παρά, c. gen. pers., ii Th 3⁸; τά seq. id., Lk 10⁷; τ. πάσχα, Mt 26¹⁷, Mk 14¹², al; τ. κυριακὸν δεῖπνον, 1 Co 11²⁰; τ. θυσίας, 1 Co 10¹⁸; seq. ἐκ (= cl. part. gen.), Jo 6²⁶,⁵⁰,⁵¹, 1 Co 11²⁸; ἀπό (cf. Heb. אָכַל מִן), Mt 15²⁷, Mk 7²⁸; metaph., to devour, consume : He 10²⁷, Ja 5³, Re 17¹⁶ (cf. κατ-, συν-εσθίω).

Ἐσλεί (Rec. Ἐσλί, v. WH, Notes, 155), ὁ, Esli, an ancestor of Jesus : Lk 3²⁵.†

** ἔσοπτρον, -ου, τό, [in LXX: Wi 7²⁶, Si 12¹¹ *;] a mirror : 1 Co 13¹², Ja 1²³.†

ἑσπέρα, -ας, ἡ (prop. fem. of ἕσπερος), [in LXX chiefly for עֶרֶב;]

(a) (sc. ὥρα), *evening*: Lk 24²⁹, Ac 4³ 20¹⁵ 28²³; (b) (sc. χώρα), *the west.*†

ἑσπερινός, -ή, -όν (= the more freq. ἑσπέριος, -α, -ον), [in LXX for עֶרֶב, iv Ki 16¹⁵, Ps 140 (141)², al.;] *of the evening, evening*: Lk 12³⁸ (WH, ⊣ mg. ⊢).†

Ἑσρώμ (Ἑσρών, Lk, l.c.; Rec. Ἐσρ-), ὁ (Heb. חֶצְרוֹן, Ge 46¹², Nu 26²¹, I Ch 2⁵, al.), [in LXX both forms, ut supr. (cf. *ICC*, on Mt, l.c.; WH, § 408);] *Esrom* (AV), *Hezron* (RV), an ancestor of Jesus: Mt 1³, Lk 3³³.†

Ἑσρών, Ἐσρ-, v.s. Ἑσρώμ.

ἔσχατος, -η, -ον, [in LXX chiefly for אַחֲרִית אַחֲרוֹן;] *last, utmost, extreme*; (a) of place: of the lowest or least honoured place, Lk 14⁹, ¹⁰; τ. ἔσχατον, c. gen. part., Ac 1⁸ 13⁴⁷; (b) of time: Mt 20¹², ¹⁴, Mk 12⁶, ²², opp. to πρῶτος, Mt 20⁸, I Co 15⁴⁵, Re 2¹⁹, al.; τὰ ἔ. καὶ τ. πρῶτα, Mt 12⁴⁵, Lk 11²⁶, II Pe 2²⁰; of the Eternal, ὁ πρῶτος καὶ ὁ ἔ., Re 1¹⁷ 2⁸ 22¹³; in phrases relating to the Messianic age and the consummation of the Kingdom of God: ἐπ' ἐσχάτου (-ων) τ. ἡμερῶν, He 1², II Pe 3³; τ. χρόνων, I Pe 1²⁰; ἔ. ὥρα, I Jo 2¹⁸; ἐπ' ἐ. χρόνου, Ju ¹⁸; ἐν ἐ. ἡμέραις, Ac 2¹⁷, Ja 5³, II Ti 3¹; neut., ἔσχατον, as adv., Mk 12²², I Co 15⁸; (c) of rank: Mk 9³⁵, I Co 4⁹.

*** ἐσχάτως,** adv., *extremely, utterly*; ἐ. ἔχειν (= Lat. *in extremis esse*), only in late writers (cf. ἐν ἐσχάτοις εἶναι, FlJ, *Ant*., ix, 8, 6), *to be at the point of death*: Mk 5²³.†

ἔσω, Ion. and old Att. form of εἴσω (< εἰς), adv., [in LXX for פְּנִימָה, etc.;] 1. prop., after verbs of motion (*to*) *within, into*: Mt 26⁵⁸, Mk 14⁵⁴; c. gen., Mk 15¹⁶. 2. As freq. in cl. (= cl. ἔνδον), after verbs of rest, *within*: Jo 20²⁶, Ac 5²³; οἱ ἔ. (opp. to οἱ ἔξω), I Co 5¹²; ὁ ἔ. ἄνθρωπος, Ro 7²², II Co 4¹⁶, Eph 3¹⁶.†

ἔσωθεν (< ἔσω), adv., [in LXX for בְּבַיִת, לִפְנֵי and cognate forms;] 1. *from within*: Mk 7²¹, ²³, Lk 11⁷. 2. *within*: Mt 7¹⁵ 23²⁵, ²⁷, ²⁸, II Co 7⁵, Re 4⁸ 5¹; τὸ ἔ., Lk 11⁴⁰; id. c. gen., ib. ³⁹.†

ἐσώτερος, -α, -ον (compar. of ἔσω), [in LXX chiefly for פְּנִימִי and cognate forms;] *inner*: Ac 16²⁴; τὸ ἐ., He 6¹⁹.†

ἑταῖρος, -ου, ὁ, [in LXX chiefly for רֵעַ and cognate forms, also Si 11⁶ 37²ᶠ, al.;] *a companion, comrade*: Mt 11¹⁶ (WH, ἑτέροις); voc., as term of address, *my friend*: Mt 20¹³ 22¹² 26⁵⁰.†

**† ἑτερό-γλωσσος (Att. -ττος), -ον, [in Aq.: Ps 113 (114)¹, Is 33¹⁹ *;] *of alien speech, of another tongue* (v. Cremer, 681) · I Co 14²¹ (aliter in LXX).†

*† ἑτεροδιδασκαλέω, -ῶ, *to teach other* or *different doctrine*: I Ti 1³ 6³ (cf. *CGT*, in l.; Milligan, *NTD*, 102).†

*† ἑτερο-ζυγέω, -ῶ, [in LXX cf. ἑτερόζυγος, Le 19¹⁹ (כִּלְאַיִם) *;] *to be unequally yoked*: metaph., c. dat. pers., II Co 6¹⁴.†

ἕτερος, -α, -ον, [in LXX chiefly for אַחֵר ;] distributive pron.,
prop. dual (Bl., § 13, 5; 51, 6), denoting the second of a pair, but in
late Gk. encroaching on ἄλλος (M, Pr., 79 f.); 1. of number, other ;
c. art., the other ; (a) of two, Lk 5⁷ 9⁵⁶, al.; opp. to ὁ πρῶτος, Mt 21³⁰;
ὁ εἷς, Mt 6²⁴, Lk 7⁴¹, Ac 23⁶, al.; ἕ. μὲν . . . ἕ. δέ, the one . . . the
other : I Co 15⁴⁰; the next : Lk 6⁶ 9⁵⁶ (sc. ἡμέρα, Xen.), Ac 20¹⁵ 27³ ;
= ὁ πλησίον, one's neighbour : Ro 2¹ 13⁸, I Co 6¹, al.; (b) of more
than two, another : Mt 8²¹ 11³, Lk 6⁶ 22⁶⁵, Jo 19³⁷, Ro 8³⁹, al.; pl., Ac
2¹³ ; οἱ μὲν . . . ἄλλοι δὲ . . . ἕ. δέ, Mt 16¹⁴; τινὲς . . . ἕ. δέ, Lk 11¹⁶.
2. Of kind or quality, other, another, different (Plat., Dem., al.) : Mk
16 [12], Lk 9²⁹, Ac 2⁴, I Co 14²¹, II Co 11⁴, Ga 1⁶, al. (cf. ἑτερό-γλωσσος,
-διδασκαλέω, -ζυγέω) ; v. ICC on Ga, p. 420 ff.
SYN. : ἄλλος, q.v. (v. reff. ut supr., also Robertson, Gr., 748 ff.).
ἑτέρως, adv., differently, otherwise : Phl 3¹⁵.†
ἔτι, adv., yet, as yet, still ; 1. of time; (a) of the present
(adhuc) : Mk 5³⁵, I Co 3³ 15¹⁷, Ga 1¹⁰, al.; (b) of the past, mostly c.
impf. : Mt 12⁴⁶, Lk 8⁴⁹ 15²⁰, Jo 20¹, Ac 9¹, Ro 5⁶, ⁸, II Th 2⁵, He 7¹⁰
9⁸, al.; (c) of the future : Lk 1¹⁵, II Co 1¹⁰; (d) with a neg. : Mt 5¹³,
Lk 16² 20³⁶, He 10², Re 3¹² 20³, al. 2. Of degree, even, yet, still,
further : c. compar., Phl 1⁹, He 7¹⁵ ; of what remains, Mk 12⁶, Jo 4³⁵
7³³, al.; of what is added, Mt 18¹⁶ 26⁶⁵, He 11³² 12²⁶, ²⁷; of continuance apart from the idea of time, Ro 3⁷ 6² 9¹⁹, Ga 5¹¹ ; ἔτι δέ, Ac
2²⁶ (LXX), He 11³⁶ ; ἔτι τε καί, Lk 14²⁶, Ac 21²⁸.
ἑτοιμάζω (< ἕτοιμος), [in LXX chiefly for כּוּן hi. (Hatch, Essays,
51 ff.) ;] to prepare, make ready ; (a) absol., of hospitable preparation :
Mk 14¹⁵, Lk 9⁵² 12⁴⁷ 22⁹, ¹² ; c. inf., Mt 26¹⁷; ἵνα, Mk 14¹² ; (b) c. acc.
rei : Mt 22⁴ 26¹⁹, Mk 14¹⁶, Lk 12²⁰ 17⁸ 22⁸, ¹³ 23⁵⁶ 24¹, Jo 14², ³, Phm ²²
Re 9⁷ 16¹² ; seq. εἰς, II Ti 2²¹; of God's ordaining coming events
(Dalman, Words, 128) ; of blessing, Mt 20²³ 25³⁴, Mk 10⁴⁰, Lk 2³¹,
I Co 2⁹, He 11¹⁶, Re 12⁶ ; of judgment, Mt 25⁴¹ ; of preparation for the
Messiah, τ. ὁδὸν κυρίου, Mt 3³, Mk 1³, Lk 1⁷⁶ 3⁴ (LXX); (c) c. acc. pers. :
Lk 1¹⁷, Ac 23²³, Re 19⁷, seq. ἵνα, Re 8⁶ ; εἰς, II Ti 2²¹, Re 9⁷, ¹⁵ 21².†
ἑτοιμασία, -ας, ἡ (< ἑτοιμάζω, q.v.), [in LXX for כּוּן hi., כֵּן, מָכוֹן ,
and cognate forms, II Es 2⁶⁸ 3³, Ps 9³⁸ (10¹⁷) 64 (65)⁹ 88 (89)¹⁴,
Na 2³ (4), Za 5¹¹, Ez 43¹¹, Da TH 11⁷, ²⁰, ²¹, Wi 13¹² * ;] 1. = ἑτοιμότης,
(a) readiness (Hipp.); (b) preparation (LXX; e.g. ἑ. τ. καρδίας, Ps
9³⁸ (10¹⁷)) : Eph 6¹⁵, EV. 2. foundation, firm footing (Ps 88 (89)¹⁴) :
Eph, l.c. (Hatch, Essays, 55 ; Exp. Times, ix, 38 ; but v. also Abbott,
Essays, 95).†
ἕτοιμος, -ον, also (in cl. after Thuc.) -η (II Co 9⁵, I Pe 1⁵), -ον, [in
LXX chiefly for נָכוֹן, מָכוֹן (cf. Hatch, Essays, 51 ff.) ;] prepared, ready ;
(a) of things : Mt 22⁴, ⁸, Mk 14¹⁵, II Co 9⁵ 10¹⁶, I Pe 1⁵; ἔρχεσθε ὅτι
ἤδη ἕτοιμά ἐστιν (Field, Notes, 67), Lk 14¹⁷; ὁ καιρός, Jo 7⁶; (b) of
persons : Mt 24⁴⁴ 25¹⁰, Lk 12⁴⁰, Ac 23²¹; seq. πρός, Tit 3¹, I Pe 3¹⁵;
c. inf., Lk 22²³; τοῦ, c. inf. (WM, § 44, 4a ; Robertson, Gr., 1068),
Ac 23¹⁵ ; ἐν ἑ. ἔχω (MM, Exp., xiv), c. inf., II Co 10⁶.†

ἑτοίμως, adv., [in LXX: ΙΙ Es 7¹⁷ ᶠ., Da LXX τη 3¹⁵ *;] *readily:*
ι Pe 4⁵; ἑ. ἔχω, *to be ready* (Deiss., *BS*, 252; MM, *Exp.*, xiv): c. inf.,
Ac 21¹³, ιι Co 12¹⁴.†

ἔτος, -ους, τό, [in LXX for שָׁנָה;] *a year:* Lk 3¹, He 1¹², Re 20³,
al.; ἔτη ἔχειν, Jo 5⁵ 8⁵⁷; εἶναι, γίνεσθαι, ἐτῶν, Mk 5⁴², Lk 2⁴², Ac 4²²,
ι Ti 5⁹; dat. pl. of space of time, Jo 2²⁰, Ac 13²⁰; acc. in ans. to *how
long?* Mt 9²⁰, Mk 5²⁵, Lk 2³⁶, Ac 7⁶, He 3⁹, al.; preceded by a prep.:
ἀπό, Lk 8⁴³, Ro 15²³; διά, c. gen. (v.s. διά), Ac 24¹⁷, Ga 2¹; ἐκ, Ac 24¹⁰;
εἰς, Lk 12¹⁹; ἐπί, c. acc., Ac 19¹⁰; μετά, c. acc., Ga 1¹⁸ 3¹⁷; πρό, c. gen.,
ιι Co 12²; κατ᾽ ἔτος, *yearly*, Lk 2⁴¹.
    SYN.: ἐνιαυτός, q.v.; cf. LS, s.v. ἐνιαυτός.

εὖ, adv. (prop. neuter of old Epic ἐΰς, *good, noble*), [in LXX, εὖ
γίγνεσθαι, εὖ ποιεῖν (יטב);] *well :* εὖ γιν., Eph 6³ (LXX); εὖ ποιεῖν, c. dat.
(cf. Si 12¹, ²), *to do good*, Mk 14⁷ (where Nestle suggests εὐποιεῖν, q.v.);
εὖ πράσσειν, *to fare well*, Ac 15²⁹; in replies (= εὖγε), *good! well done!*
Mt 25²¹, ²³, Lk 19¹⁷ (εὖγε, WH, txt.).†

    Εὖα (WH, Εὔα, § 408; Rec. Εὔα; S (in ι Ti), Εὔα), -ας, ἡ (Heb.
חַוָּה, Ge 3²⁰), *Eve*, wife of Adam: ιι Co 11³, ι Ti 2¹³.†

    εὐαγγελίζω, [in LXX for בשׂר pi., hith.; for good news in
general: ι Ki 31⁹, al.; of God's loving kindness, Ps 39 (40)¹⁰ 95 (96)²,
and esp. of Messianic blessings, Is 40⁹ 60⁶, al.;] *to bring* or *announce
glad tidings;* 1. act. (only in late writers): c. acc. pers., Re 10⁷; seq.
ἐπί, c. acc. pers., Re 14⁶; pass., of things, *to be proclaimed as glad
tidings:* Lk 16¹⁶, Ga 1¹¹, ι Pe 1²⁵; impers., ι Pe 4⁶; of persons, *to
have glad tidings proclaimed* to one: Mt 11⁵, Lk 7²², He 4², ⁶. 2.
Depon. mid. (cl.), *to proclaim glad tidings*, in NT esp. of the Christian
message of salvation: absol., Lk 9⁶, Ro 15²⁰, al.; c. dat. pers., Lk
4¹⁸ (LXX), Ro 1¹⁵, al.; in same sense c. acc. pers. (not cl.), Lk 3¹⁸,
Ac 16¹⁰, Ga 1⁹, ι Pe 1¹²; c. acc. rei, εἰρήνην, Ac 10³⁶, Ro 10¹⁵ (LXX);
τ. βασιλείαν τ. θεοῦ, Lk 8¹; c. dat. pers., Lk 1¹⁹ 4⁴³, Eph 2¹⁷ 3⁸; αὐτῷ
τ. Ἰησοῦν, Ac 8³⁵ 17¹⁸; c. dupl. acc., Ac 13³²; c. acc. pers. et inf., Ac
14¹⁵; τ. κώμας (πολεῖς), Ac 8²⁵, ⁴⁰ 14²¹ (cf. προ-ευαγγελίζομαι).

    εὐαγγέλιον, -ου, τό, [in LXX for בְּשׂוֹרָה בְּשׂרָה, ιι Ki 4¹⁰
18²², ²⁵ *;] 1. in cl., (*a*) *a reward for good tidings* (Hom.; pl., LXX,
ιι Ki 4¹⁰); (*b*) in pl., εὐ. θύειν, *to make a thank-offering for good
tidings* (Xen., al.). 2. Later (Luc., Plut., al.), *good tidings, good news;*
in NT of the good tidings of the kingdom of God and of salvation
through Christ, *the gospel:* Mk 1¹⁵, Ac 15⁷, Ro 1¹⁶, Ga 2², ι Th 2⁴,
al.; c. gen. obj., τ. βασιλείας, Mt 4²³; τ. Χριστοῦ, Ro 15¹⁹, al.; τ. κυρίου
ἡμῶν Ἰησοῦ, ιι Th 1⁸; τ. υἱοῦ τ. θεοῦ, Ro 1⁹; τ. δόξης τ. μακαρίου θεοῦ,
ι Ti 1¹¹; τ. δόξης τ. Χριστοῦ, ιι Co 4⁴; of the author, τ. θεοῦ, Ro 15¹⁶,
al.; of the teacher, ἡμῶν, Ro 2¹⁶, ιι Co 4³, ι Th 1⁵, ιι Ti 2⁸; of the
taught, τ. περιτομῆς, τ. ἀκροβυστίας, Ga 2⁷; ἡ ἀλήθεια τοῦ εὐ., Ga 2⁵, ¹⁴,
Col 1⁵; ἡ ἐλπὶς (πίστις) τοῦ εὐ., Col 1²³, Phl 1²⁷ (v. Cremer, 31 ff.; and
on the later eccl. use of the word, M, *Th.*, 143 f.); v. *ICC* on Ga, p. 422 ff.

    *†εὐαγγελιστής, -οῦ, ὁ, *an evangelist;* (*a*) in NT, a preacher of

the gospel: Ac 21⁸, Eph 4¹¹, ɪɪ Ti 4⁵; (b) later, a writer of a gospel (eccl.).†

εὐαρεστέω, -ῶ, [in LXX chiefly for הלך hith., Ge 5²², ²⁴, Ps 25 (26)³ 55 (56)¹³, al., Si 44¹⁶;] to be well-pleasing: τ. θεῷ (LXX, ll. c.), He 11⁵, ⁶. Pass., to be well pleased: c. dat., He 13¹⁶.†

**† εὐ-άρεστος, -ον, [in LXX: Wi 4¹⁰ 9¹⁰ *;] well-pleasing, acceptable: Ro 12²; c. dat. pers., Ro 12¹ 14¹⁸, ɪɪ Co 5⁹, Eph 5¹⁰, Phl 4¹⁸; id. seq. ἐν, Tit 2⁹ (κυρίῳ), Col 3²⁰; ἐνώπιον, He 13²¹ (for ex. in Inscr., v. Deiss., BS, 215).†

* εὐ-αρέστως, adv., acceptably: τ. θεῷ, He 12²⁸.†

Εὔβουλος, -ον, ὁ., Eubulus, a Christian: ɪɪ Ti 4²¹.†

εὖ-γε, adv., in replies, well! good! well done!: Lk 19¹⁷ (WH for Rec. εὖ, q.v.).†

εὐγενής, -ές (< εὖ, γένος), [in LXX: Jb 1³ (גָּדוֹל), ɪɪ Mac 10¹³ R, ɪᴠ Mac 6⁵ 9¹³, ²³, ²⁷ 10³, ¹⁵ *;] 1. well born, of noble race: Lk 19¹², ɪ Co 1²⁶. 2. noble-minded: compar., -έστερος, Ac 17¹¹.†

** εὐδία, -ας, ἡ, [in LXX: Si 3¹⁵ *;] (< εὔδιος, calm), fair weather: Mt 16² (Rec., R, txt.).†

† εὐ-δοκέω, -ῶ (on the derivation, v. Bl., § 28, 6), [in LXX chiefly for רצה, also for אבה, חפץ, etc.;] 1. c. inf. (Polyb., al.), to be well pleased, to think it good, to give consent (so freq. in π. in legal documents; Milligan, Th., 22 f.): Lk 12³², Ro 15²⁶, ²⁷, ɪ Co 1²¹, Ga 1¹⁵, Col 1¹⁹, R, mg. (ICC, in l., but v. infr.), ɪ Th 2⁸ 3¹; μᾶλλον εὖ., ɪɪ Co 5⁸; c. acc. et inf. (Polyb., i, 8, 4), Col, l.c., R, txt. (Lft., in l.). 2. to be well pleased or take pleasure with or in a person or thing; (a) c. dat. (Polyb., al.; ɪ Mac 1⁴³, ɪ Es 4³⁹): ɪɪ Th 2¹²; (b) as freq. in LXX, (a) c. acc.: Mt 12¹⁸, He 10⁶, ⁸ (LXX); (β) seq. ἐν (cf. Heb. רָצָה בְּ, Ps 149⁴): Mt 3¹⁷ 17⁵, Mk 1¹¹, Lk 3²² (on the tense, v. M, Pr., 134 f.; DCG, i, 308 b), ɪ Co 10⁵, ɪɪ Co 12¹⁰, He 10³⁸ (LXX); (c) seq. εἰς: ɪɪ Pe 1¹⁷. (Cf. συν-ευδοκέω, and v. Cremer, 213 f.; Field, Notes, 48 f.; DCG, i, 355ᵃ.) †

† εὐδοκία, -ας, ἡ (< εὐδοκέω, q.v.), [in LXX: Ps 5¹², al. (רָצוֹן), freq. in Si; in Inscr. (I.G., 5960), LXX, and NT = εὐδόκησις (Diod.);] good pleasure, good-will, satisfaction, approval: Mt 11²⁶, Lk 10²¹, Ro 10¹, Eph 1⁵, ⁹, Phl 1¹⁵ 2¹³; c. gen. obj., ɪɪ Th 1¹¹ (v. Milligan, in l.); ἐν ἀνθρώποις εὐδοκία, Rec., R, mg., WH, mg. (v. Field, Notes, 48 f.), Lk 2¹⁴; -ας, men with whom God is well pleased, Lk, l.c., R, txt., WH, txt. (v. ICC, in l.; WH, App., in l.).†

εὐεργεσία, -ας, ἡ (< εὐεργέτης), [in LXX: Ps 77 (78)¹¹ (עֲלִילָה), Wi 16¹¹, ²⁴, ɪɪ Mac 6¹³ 9²⁶, ɪᴠ Mac 8¹⁷ *;] a good deed, kindness, benefit: ɪ Ti 6²; c. gen. pers. (εὐ. πόλεως, Plat., leg., 805b), Ac 4⁹.†

εὐεργετέω, -ῶ (< εὐεργέτης), [in LXX: Ps 12 (13)⁶ (גָּמַל), Wi 3⁵, al.;] to do good, bestow benefit: Ac 10³⁸.†

** εὐεργέτης, -ον, ὁ, [in LXX: Es 8¹³, Wi 19¹⁴, ɪɪ Mac 4², ɪɪɪ Mac 3¹⁹ 6²⁴ *;] a benefactor: Lk 22²⁵ (for contemp. usage, v. Deiss., LAE, 248).†

εὔ-θετος, -ον (< τίθημι), [in LXX: Ps 31 (32)⁶ (מָצָא), Da ᴛʜ

Su [15]*;] *ready for use, fit:* of things, c. dat., He 6[7]; seq. εἰς, Lk 14[35]; of persons, c. dat., Lk 9[62] (for rabbinic parallels, v. Dalman, *Words,* 119 f.).†

εὐθέως, adv. (< εὐθύς), [in LXX: Jb 5[3] (פִּתְאֹם), Wi 5[12], ı Mac 11[12], al.;] *straightway, at once, directly:* Ga 1[16], Ja 1[24], ııı Jo[14] (cf. Dalman, *Words,* 28 f.), Re 4[2], and freq. in Mt, Lk, Jo, Ac (in Mk, εὐθύς, q.v.).

*†εὐθυδρομέω, -ῶ, of ships, *to run a straight \course* (Philo): Ac 16[11] 21[1].†

**εὐθυμέω, -ῶ (< εὔθυμος), [in Sm.: Ps 31 (32)[11], Pr 15[15]*;] 1. trans., *to make cheerful* (Æsch.). 2. Intrans. (Eur., Plut.; so mid. in Xen., Plat.), *to be of good cheer:* Ac 27[22, 25], Ja 5[13].†

**εὔ-θυμος, -ον, [in LXX: ıı Mac 11[26]*;] 1. *kind* (Hom.). 2. *of good cheer* (Æsch., al.): Ac 27[36].†

* εὐθύμως, adv., *cheerfully:* Ac 24[10].†

εὐθύνω (< εὐθύς), [in LXX: Nu 22[23], Jo 24[23] (נטה hi.), Jg 14[7], ı Ki 18[20, 26] (יֹשֶׁר), Pr 20[24], Si 2[2, 6], al.;] 1. *to direct:* Ja 3[4]. 2. *to make straight:* Jo 1[23] (LXX, ἑτοιμάσατε).†

εὐθύς, -εῖα, -ύ, [in LXX chiefly for יָשָׁר;] 1. *straight, direct:* τρίβοι, Mt 3[3], Mk 1[3], Lk 3[4] (LXX); εἰς εὐθείας, (sc. ὁδούς), Lk 3[5]; εὐ. ὁδός; fig., Ac 13[10], ıı Pe 2[15]; as pr. name of a street, Ac 9[11]. 2. In moral sense, *straightforward, right:* καρδία, Ac 8[21] (cf. Ps 7[11] 31 (32)[11], al.).†

εὐθύς, adv., [in LXX (more freq. than εὐθέως) chiefly for יָשָׁר;] = εὐθέως, *straightway, directly:* Mt 3[16] 13[20, 21] 14[27] 21[2, 3] 26[74], Lk 6[49], Jo 13[30, 32] 19[34], Ac 10[16] and 42 (41) times in Mk.†

εὐθύτης, -ητος, ἡ (< εὐθύς), [in LXX chiefly for מִישׁוֹר, יֹשֶׁר, and cognate forms;] *uprightness:* He 1[8] (LXX).†

*†εὐκαιρέω, -ῶ (= cl., εὖ σχολῆς ἔχειν; used by Polyb. and Philo; cf. Rutherford, *NPhr.,* 205; MM, *Exp.,* xiv), *to have leisure* or *opportunity:* ı Co 16[12]; c. inf., Mk 6[31]; seq. εἰς, *to devote one's leisure to,* Ac 17[21].†

εὐκαιρία, -ας, ἡ (< εὔκαιρος), [in LXX: Ps 9[10] (v. Soph., *Lex.,* s.v.) 9[22] (10[1]) 144 (145)[15] (עֵת), Si 38[24], ı Mac 11[42]*;] *fitting time, opportunity:* seq. ἵνα, Mt 26[16]; τοῦ, c. inf., Lk 22[6].†

εὔ-καιρος, -ον, [in LXX: Ps 103 (104)[27] (עֵת), ıı Mac 14[29] 15[20, 21], ııı Mac 4[11] 5[44]*;] *timely, seasonable, suitable* (Cremer, 740): ἡμέρα, Mk 6[21] (or *empty, festal,* as in Byz. and MGr.; v. MM, *Exp.,* xiv; *Exp. T.,* xxxiv, 7 (April, 1923), p. 332 f.); βοήθεια, He 4[16].†

**εὐκαίρως, adv., [in LXX: Si 18[22]*;] *seasonably, in season:* Mk 14[11]; opp. to ἀκ- (Kühner[3], iv, 346 d), ıı Ti 4[2].†

**†εὔ-κοπος, -ον, [in LXX: Si 22[15], ı Mac 3[18]*;] *with easy labour, easy:* compar., -ώτερόν ἐστι, c. inf., Mt 9[5], Mk 2[9], Lk 5[23]; c. acc. et inf., Mt 19[24], Mk 10[25], Lk 16[17] 18[25] (Polyb.; the adv. -ως occurs in Aristoph., *Fr.,* 615).†

εὐλάβεια, -ας, ἡ (< εὐλαβής), [in LXX: Jo 22²⁴ (דְּאָגָה), Pr 28¹⁴, Wi 17⁸*;] 1. *caution, discretion* (Soph., Plat., al.). 2. In later Gk. (Diod., Plut., al.), also *reverence, godly fear :* He 5⁷ 12²⁸.†
SYN.: δειλία (q.v.), φόβος (cf. Cremer, 387 f., 759; *DB*, ii, 222).

εὐλαβέομαι, -οῦμαι, [in LXX: Pr 24²⁸ (30⁵), Na 1⁷ (חסה), al., for 15 different Heb. words in all; also Si 7²⁹ 41³, al.;] 1. *to be cautious, to beware :* Ac 23¹⁰ (Rec.; φοβηθείς, WH, RV). 2. *to reverence :* He 11⁷ (cf. Cremer, 388).†

εὐλαβής, -ές (< εὖ, λαβεῖν), [in LXX: Mi 7² AB² (חָסִיד); εὐ. ποιεῖν, Le 15³¹ (נזר) hi.), Si 11⁷ א²*;] 1. *cautious, circumspect.* 2. *devout, religious, reverent :* Ac 2⁵ 8² 22¹²; δίκαιος καὶ εὐ., Lk 2²⁵.†

εὐλογέω, -ῶ, [in LXX chiefly for בָּרַךְ pi.;] 1. *to speak well of, praise* (cl.; LXX De 8¹⁰, al.): τ. θεόν, Lk 1⁶⁴ 2²⁸ 24⁵¹, ⁵³ (αἰνοῦντες, T, WH, mg.), Ja 3⁹; absol., *to give praise,* Mt 14¹⁹ 26²⁶ (v. Swete on Mk 14²²), Mk 6⁴¹ 14²² (v. Swete, in l.), Lk 24³⁰, ι Co 14¹⁶. 2. As in LXX (= בָּרַךְ pi.); (*a*) *to bless, invoke blessings on* (Ge 24⁶⁰, Nu 23²⁰, al.): absol., ι Co 4¹², ι Pe 3⁹; c. acc. pers., Lk 2³⁴ 6²⁸ 24⁵⁰, ⁵¹, Ro 12¹⁴, He 7¹, ⁶, ⁷, 11²⁰, ²¹; εὐλογημένος (= בָּרוּךְ; v. Lft., *Notes,* 310; *DCG,* i, 189), *blessed,* Mt 21⁹ 23³⁹ (LXX), Mk 11⁹, ¹⁰, Lk 13³⁵ 19³⁸ (LXX), Jo 12¹³; c. acc. rei, Mk 8⁷, Lk 9¹⁶, ι Co 10¹⁶; (*b*) with God as subject (Ps 44³, al.), *to bless, prosper, bestow blessings on :* c. acc. pers., Ac 3²⁶, Ga 3⁹, Eph 1³ (Lft., *Notes,* 311), He 6¹⁴; εὐλογημένος, Lk 1²⁸ (WH, txt., R, txt., omit) ib.⁴²; εὐλογημένοι τ. πατρός (cf. Is 61⁹), Mt 25³⁴; pass., Ac 3²⁵ (cf. ἐν-, κατ-ευλογέω).†
SYN.: v.s. αἰνέω, and cf. *DCG,* i, 189, 211; Cremer, 766.

† εὐλογητός, -όν (< εὐλογέω), [in LXX chiefly for בָּרוּךְ;] *blessed ;* (*a*) of men (Ge 12² A, De 7¹⁴, Jg 17² B, Ru 2²⁰, ι Ki 15¹³); (*b*) of God (Lft., *Notes,* 310 f.), as chiefly in LXX (Ge 9²⁶, Ex 17¹⁰, Ps 17 (18)⁴⁶, al.): Lk 1⁶⁸, Ro 1²⁵ 9⁵ (*ICC,* in l.), ιι Co 1³ 11³¹, Eph 1³, ι Pe 1³, absol., ὁ εὐλογητός (Dalman, *Words,* 200; *JThS,* v, 453), Mk 14⁶¹ (Cremer, 769).†

εὐλογία, -ας, ἡ [in LXX chiefly for בְּרָכָה;] 1. *fair speaking, flattering speech :* χρηστολογίας καὶ εὐ., Ro 16¹⁸. 2. *praise :* of God (as in late Inscr.; LS, s.v.) and Christ, Re 5¹², ¹³ 7¹². 3. In LXX and NT: *blessing, benediction ;* (*a*) the act of blessing: ι Co 10¹⁶, He 12¹⁷, Ja 3¹⁰; (*b*) concrete, *a blessing :* Ro 15²⁹, ιι Co 9⁵, ⁶, Ga 3¹⁴, Eph 1³, He 6⁷, ι Pe 3⁹ (cf. De 11²⁶, Si 7³², al.).†

*†εὐ-μετά-δοτος, -ον (< εὖ, μεταδίδωμι), *ready to impart :* assoc. with κοινωνικός (for the distinction bet. the two, v. Field, *Notes,* 213; *CGT,* in l.), ι Ti 6¹⁸.†

Εὐνίκη (Rec. -νείκη), -ης, *Eunice,* Timothy's mother : ιι Ti 1⁵.†

εὐ-νοέω, -ῶ (< εὔνοος, *friendly*), [in LXX: Es 8¹³ Bא¹, Da LXX 2⁴³, ιιι Mac 7¹¹*;] *to be favourable, kindly disposed :* c. dat., Mt 5²⁵.†

εὔνοια, -ας, ἡ (< εὔνοος), [in LXX: Es 2²³, al.;] goodwill: Eph 6⁷ (of slaves; cf. MM, Exp., xiv).†

*†εὐνουχίζω (< εὐνοῦχος), to make a eunuch of, castrate: pass., Mt 19¹²; metaph., εὐ. ἑαυτόν, ib.†

εὐνοῦχος, -ου, ὁ (i.e. ὁ τὴν εὐνὴν (bed) ἔχων), [in LXX for סָרִים (perhaps not of necessity an actual eunuch; DB, s.v.), Ge 39¹, al., Wi 3¹⁴, Si 20⁴ 30²⁰;] an emasculated man, a eunuch: Mt 19¹²; one such holding, as was common, high office, as of chamberlain, at court, Ac 8²⁷, ³⁴, ³⁶, ³⁸, ³⁹; metaph., of one naturally incapacitated for or voluntarily abstaining from wedlock, Mt 19¹².†

Εὐοδία (Rec. -ωδία), -ας, ἡ, Euodia (not as AV, Euodias), a Christian woman: Phl 4².†

εὐ-οδόω, -ῶ (< ὁδός), [in LXX chiefly for צָלַח hi.;] to help on one's way (Soph., al.). Pass., to have a prosperous journey; metaph. (Hdt., al.), to prosper, be prospered, be successful: III Jo ², Ro 1¹⁰, I Co 16² (on the tense, v. M, Pr., 54; ICC, in l.).†

*† εὐ-πάρ-εδρος, -ον (< εὖ, πάρεδρος, sitting near; cf. Wi 9⁴), constantly attendant or waiting on: τ. κυρίῳ, I Co 7³⁵ (Rec. εὐπρόσ-).†

** εὐ-πειθής, ές (< εὖ, πείθομαι), [in LXX: IV Mac 12⁶ AR*;] ready to obey, compliant: Ja 3¹⁷.†

*† εὐ-περί-στατος, -ον (< εὖ, περιΐστημι), easily encircling; of sins readily besetting: He 12¹ (on form and sense of the word, v. Westc. in l.).†

† εὐ-ποιέω, ῶ, = εὖ ποιέω, to do good (whence εὐποιία, q.v.): εὐποιῆσαι, Mk 14⁷ B (also Is 41²³ B, al.; v. Nestle, in Exp. T., xxiii, 7).†

*† εὐ-ποιία (Rec. -ΐα), -ας, ἡ; 1. beneficence, doing good: He 13¹⁶. 2. a benefit (FlJ, Ant., ii, 11, 2, al.).†

εὐ-πορέω, -ῶ (< εὔπορος, well provided for), [in LXX: Le 25²⁶, ⁴⁹ נשׂיג hi.), ib. ²⁸ (v.l.), Wi 10¹⁰*;] to prosper, be well off: Ac 11²⁹.†

εὐ-πορία, -ας, ἡ (< εὔπορος), [in LXX for חַיִל, IV Ki 25¹⁰ A (freq. in Aq.)*;] 1. facility. 2. plenty, wealth: Ac 19²⁵.†

εὐ-πρέπεια, -ας, ἡ (< εὐπρεπής, comely), [in LXX for הֶדֶר, etc.;] goodly appearance, comeliness: Ja 1¹¹.†

*† εὐ-πρόσ-δεκτος, -ον (< εὖ, προσδέχομαι), more usual than δέκτος, q.v., acceptable: Ro 15¹⁶, ³¹, II Co 6² 8¹², I Pe 2⁵.†

*† εὐ-πρόσ-εδρος, -ον, Rec. for εὐπάρεδρος, q.v.: I Co 7³⁵.†

**† εὐ-προσωπέω, -ῶ (< εὐπρόσωπος, fair of face), [in Al.: Ps 140 (141)⁶, v.l. for -ίζω*;] to look well, make a fair show: metaph. (as in π.; v. Deiss., LAE, 96), Ga 6¹².†

† Εὐρ-ακύλων (Rec. εὐροκλύδων, q.v.), -ωνος (< Εὖρος, the East wind, and Lat. Aquilo; Vg., Euroaquilo), the Euraquilo, a N.E. wind (i.e. between Eurus and Aquilo): Ac 27¹⁴.†

εὑρίσκω, [in LXX chiefly for מצא, also for נשׂיג hi., etc.;] to find, with or without previous search: absol., opp. to ζητέω, Mt 7⁷, ⁸, Lk 11⁹, ¹⁰; c. acc., Mt 2⁸, Mk 1³⁷, Ac 13²², II Ti 1¹⁷, al.; pass., οὐχ εὑ., of disappearance, He 11⁵, Re 16²⁰, al.; γῆ κ. τὰ ἐν αὐτῇ ἔργα εὑρεθήσεται (for conjectures as to the meaning of this reading, v. Mayor, ICC, in l.), ɪ Pe 3¹⁰, WH, R, mg. Metaph., *to find, find out* by inquiry, *learn, discover :* Lk 19⁴⁸, Ac 4²¹; αἰτίαν, Jo 18³⁸, Ac 13²⁸, al.; pass., Mt 1¹⁸, Lk 17¹⁸, Ro 7¹⁰, ɪ Co 4², Ga 2¹⁷, ɪ Pe 1⁷, Re 5⁴, al.; of attaining to the knowledge of God, εὐ. θεόν, Ac 17²⁷; pass., Ro 10²⁰ ⁽ᴸˣˣ⁾. Mid., *to find for oneself, gain, procure, obtain :* c. acc. rei, λύτρωσιν, He 9¹²; act. in same sense (so cl. poets, but not in Attic prose), Mt 10³⁹ 11²⁹, Lk 1³⁰, Ac 7⁴⁶, ɪɪ Ti 1¹⁸, al. (cf. ἀν-ευρίσκω).

† **εὐρο-κλύδων** (G, εὐρυκλ-), -ωνος, ὁ (< Εὖρος (v.l. < εὐρύς, *broad*), κλύδων), *Euroclydon* (prob. a sailor's corruption of Εὐρακύλων, q.v.) : Ac 27¹⁴, Rec.†

εὐρύ-χωρος, -ον, (< εὐρύς, *broad* + χώρα), [in LXX for רחב ni., and cognate forms (Is 30²³, al.), exc. ɪɪ Ch 18⁹ (בֶּרֶן;] *spacious, broad :* Mt 7¹³.†

εὐ-σέβεια, -ας, ἡ (< εὐσεβής, q.v.), [in LXX : Pr 1⁷, Is 33⁶ (יִרְאָה), Pr 13¹¹ (aliter in Heb.), Is 11² (יִרְאַת יְהוָה), ɪ Es 1²³, Wi 10¹², Si 49³, and very freq. in ɪᴠ Mac;] 1. *piety, reverence* (towards parents and others). 2. *piety towards God, godliness :* Ac 3¹², ɪ Ti 2² ⁴⁷,⁸ 6⁵,⁶,¹¹, ɪɪ Pe 1³,⁶,⁷; τὸ τῆς εὐ. μυστήριον, ɪ Ti 3¹⁶; ἡ κατ᾽ εὐ. διδασκαλία, ɪ Ti 6³; ἡ ἀλήθεια ἡ κατ᾽ εὐ., Tit 1¹; μόρφωσις εὐσεβείας, ɪɪ Ti 3⁵; pl. (v. Bl., § 32, 6; Mayor on Ja 2¹), ɪɪ Pe 3¹¹ (on the use of εὐ. and cognates in Past. Epp., v. *CGT*, on ɪ Ti 2²; cf. also Cremer, 524).†

** **εὐ-σεβέω**, -ῶ (< εὐσεβής, q.v.), [in LXX : Da LXX Su ⁶⁴, ɪᴠ Mac 9⁶ אR, 11⁵,⁸,²³ 18²*;] *to reverence, show piety towards ;* c. acc. (elsewhere more freq. seq. εἰς, περί, πρός) : οἶκον, ɪ Ti 5⁴; θεόν, Ac 17²³ (Cremer, 525).†

εὐσεβής, -ές (< εὖ, σέβομαι), [in LXX : Pr 12¹², Is 24¹⁶ 26⁷ (צַדִּיק), Mi 7² (חָסִיד), Is 32⁸ (נָדִיב), and freq. in Si and ɪᴠ Mac;] *pious, godly, devout :* Ac 10²,⁷, ɪɪ Pe 2⁹.†

SYN. : θεοσεβής, θρῆσκος (v. Tr., *Syn.*, § xlviii; *DB*, ii, 221 f.; Cremer, 524 f., 858).

** **εὐσεβῶς**, adv., [in LXX : ɪᴠ Mac 7²¹*;] *piously, religiously :* ɪɪ Ti 3¹², Tit 2¹².†

εὔσημος, -ον (< εὖ + σῆμα, a *sign*), [in LXX for בָּרָה, Ps 80 (81)³ (-ως, Da LXX 2¹⁹)*;] 1. *conspicuous* (cf. Ps, l.c.). 2. *clear to the understanding, distinct :* ɪ Co 14⁹.†

** **εὔσπλαγχνος**, -ον (εὖ, σπλάγχνον, q.v.), [in Pr Ma⁷ (*Camb. Manual LXX*, iii, 825);] 1. in Hippocr., as medical term (LS, s.v.). 2. Metaph. (cf. εὐσπλαγχνία, Eurip., *Rhes.*, 192), in NT, *tenderhearted, compassionate :* Eph 4³², ɪ Pe 3⁸.†

* **εὐσχημόνως**, adv. (< εὐσχήμων), *decorously, becomingly :* ɪ Co 14⁴⁰; περιπατεῖν, Ro 13¹³, ɪ Th 4¹².†

** **εὐσχημοσύνη** (< εὐσχήμων), [in LXX : ɪᴠ Mac 6²*;] *seemliness, comeliness :* ɪ Co 12²³.†

εὐσχήμων, -ον (εὖ, σχῆμα), [in LXX : Pr 11²⁵*;] 1. *elegant, graceful, comely* (Eur., Plat., al.) : τὰ εὐ. ἡμῶν (opp. to τὰ ἀσχ- ἡμ-),

1 Co 12²⁴; in moral sense, *seemly, becoming,* 1 Co 7³⁵. 2. Also in late Gk. (v. Swete, *Mk.,* l.c.; MM, *Exp.,* xiv), *wealthy, influential* (RV, *of honourable estate*): Mk 15⁴³, Ac 13⁵⁰ 17¹².†

εὐτόνως, adv. (< εὖ, τείνω), [in LXX for בְּשׁוֹפְרוֹת, Jos 6⁷ ⁽⁸⁾ *;] *vigorously, vehemently :* Lk 23¹⁰, Ac 18²⁸.†

* **εὐτραπελία,** -ας, ἡ (< εὖ, τρέπω), 1. *versatility, wit, facetiousness* (Hippocr., Plat., al.). 2. = βωμολογία, *coarse jesting, ribaldry* (Abbott, *Essays,* 93): Eph 5⁴.†
SYN.: μωρολογία, v. Tr., *Syn.,* § xxxiv.

Εὔτυχος, -ου, ὁ (εὖ, τυχή), *Eutychus,* a young man : Ac 20⁹.†

** **εὐφημία,** -ας, ἡ (< εὔφημος), [in Sm.: Ps 41 (42)⁵ 46 (47)² 99 (100)² 125 (126)² *;] *good report, praise, good reputation* (MM, *VGT,* s.v.): opp. to δυσφημία, 11 Co 6⁸.†

* **εὔφημος,** -ον (εὖ, φήμη), [in Sm. : Ps 62 (63)⁶;] primarily, *uttering words* or *sounds of good omen,* hence, 1. *avoiding ill-omened words, religiously silent.* 2. *fair-sounding, auspicious, well reported of* (R, mg., *gracious*) : Phl 4⁸.†

* **εὐ-φορέω,** -ῶ, *to be fruitful :* Lk 12¹⁶.†

εὐφραίνω, [in LXX chiefly for שָׂמַח, qal, pi.;] *to cheer, gladden :* c. acc. pers., opp. to λυπεῖν, 11 Co 2². Pass., *to be happy, rejoice, make merry :* Lk 15³², Ac 2²⁶ ⁽ᴸˣˣ⁾, Ro 15¹⁰ ⁽ᴸˣˣ⁾, Ga 4²⁷ ⁽ᴸˣˣ⁾, Re 11¹⁰ 12¹²; seq. ἐν, Ac 7⁴¹; ἐπί, c. dat., Re 18²⁰; of merry-making at a feast (III Ki 4²⁰; cf. Kennedy, *Sources,* 155; Field, *Notes,* 69 f.), Lk 12¹⁹ 15²³, ²⁴, ²⁹ ⁽ᴸˣˣ⁾ (λαμπρῶς) 16¹⁹.†

Εὐφράτης, -ου, ὁ, the river *Euphrates :* Re 9¹⁴ 16¹².†

εὐφροσύνη, -ης, ἡ (< εὔφρων, *cheerful*), [in LXX chiefly for שִׂמְחָה;] *rejoicing, gladness :* Ac 2²⁸ ⁽ᴸˣˣ⁾ 14¹⁷.†

** **εὐχαριστέω,** -ῶ, [in LXX: Jth 8²⁵ Wi 18², 11 Mac 1¹¹ 10⁷ A 12³¹ R, III Mac 7¹⁶ *;] *to be thankful, give thanks* (chiefly in late writers and Inscr.; cf. Milligan, *Th.,* 5; Ellic. on Col 1¹²; Lft., *Notes,* 9) : Ro 1²¹, 1 Co 14¹⁷, 1 Th 5¹⁸; of giving thanks before meat, Mt 15³⁶ 26²⁷, Mk 8⁶ 14²³, Lk 22¹⁷, ¹⁹, Jo 6¹¹, ²³, 1 Co 11²⁴; c. dat. pers., τ. θεῷ, Lk 17¹⁶, Ac 27³⁵ 28¹⁵, Ro 14⁶ 16⁴, 1 Co 14¹⁸, Phl 1³, Col 1³, ¹², Phm ⁴; seq. διὰ Ἰ. Χριστοῦ, Ro 1⁸ 7²⁵, R, WH, mg., Col 3¹⁷; ἐν ὀνόματι Χρ., Eph 5²⁰; seq. περί, 1 Th 1², 11 Th 1³; ὅτι, Ro 1⁸, 11 Th 2¹³; ἐπί, c. dat. rei, 1 Co 1⁴; ὑπέρ, 1 Co 10³⁰, Eph 1¹⁶ 5²⁰; ὅτι, Lk 18¹¹, Jo 11⁴¹, 1 Co 1¹⁴, 1 Th 2¹³, Re 11¹⁷; pass. (Deiss., *BS,* 122 f.), *is received with thanks,* 11 Co 1¹¹.†
SYN.: v.s. αἰνέω; and cf. Cremer, 903 f.

** **εὐχαριστία,** -ας, ἡ (< εὐχάριστος), [in LXX: Es 8¹³, Wi 16²⁸, Si 37¹¹, 11 Mac 2²⁷ *;] 1. *thankfulness, gratitude* (Polyb.; Es, Si, 11 Mac, ll. c.): Ac 24³. 2. *giving of thanks, thanksgiving* (so in π. and Inscr.; M, *Th.,* 41 f.): 1 Co 14¹⁶, 11 Co 4¹⁵, Eph 5⁴, Phl 4⁶, Col 2⁷ 4², 1 Th 3⁹, 1 Ti 4³, ⁴, Re 4⁹ 7¹²; c. dat. pers., 11 Co 9¹¹ (cf. τ. θεοῦ, Wi, l.c.); pl., 11 Co 9¹², 1 Ti 2¹ (Cremer, 904).†

εὐχάριστος, -ον (< εὖ, χαρίζομαι), [in LXX for חֵן, Pr 11¹⁶ *;] 1. = εὔχαρις, *winning, gracious, agreeable* (Pr, l.c.). 2. *grateful, thankful :* Col 3¹⁵.†

εὐχή, -ῆς, ἡ (< εὔχομαι), [in LXX chiefly for נֶדֶר;] 1. *a prayer:*
Ja 5¹⁵. 2. *a vow:* Ac 18¹⁸ 21²³.†
    SYN.: v.s. δέησις.
εὔχομαι, [in LXX chiefly for נדר, also for עתר hi., etc.;] *to*
pray: c. acc. rei, ΙΙ Co 13⁹; c. dat. pers., τ. θεῷ, Ac 26²⁹; seq. πρὸς τ.
θεόν, ΙΙ Co 13⁷; c. acc. et inf., Ac 27²⁹, ΙΙΙ Jo²; seq. ὑπέρ, Ja 5¹⁶;
ηὐχόμην εἶναι (on impf. here, v. *ICC,* in l., Lft., *Philem.*¹³), Ro 9³
(Cremer, 718).†
    εὔ-χρηστος, -ον (εὔ, χράομαι), [in LXX: Pr 31¹³ (חֵפֶץ), Wi 13¹³ *;]
useful, serviceable: c. dat. pers., ΙΙ Ti 2²¹; id. seq. εἰς, c. dat. rei,
ΙΙ Ti 4¹¹; opp. to ἄχρηστος, Phm ¹¹.†
    *† εὐψυχέω, -ῶ (< εὔψυχος, *courageous*), *to be of good courage:* Phl
2¹⁹.†
    εὐωδία, -ας, ἡ (< εὐώδης, *fragrant;* < ὄζω), [in LXX for נִיחֹחַ,
Ge 8²¹, al. (ὀσμὴ εὐωδίας); Si 20⁹ 24¹⁵, al.;] *fragrance:* metaph.,
Χριστοῦ εὐ., ΙΙ Co 2¹⁵; ὀσμὴ εὐωδίας (a metaphor of sacrifice, most freq.
in Pent. and Ez.), Eph 5², Phl 4¹⁸.†
    Εὐωδία, -ας, ἡ, Phl 4², Rec. (for Εὐοδία, q.v.).†
    εὐώνυμος, -ον (εὔ, ὄνομα), [in LXX chiefly for שְׂמֹאל;] 1. *of good*
name or *omen, well-named,* to avoid the ill-omen attaching to the left.
2. Euphemistic for ἀριστερός, *left:* Ac 21³, Re 10²; ἐξ εὐωνύμων, *on the*
left: Mt 20²¹, ²³ 25³³, ⁴¹ 27³⁸, Mk 10⁴⁰ 15²⁷.†
    ἐφάλλομαι, [in LXX for צָלַח, ι Ki 10⁶ 11⁶ 16¹³ *;] *to leap upon:*
seq. ἐπί, c. acc. pers. Ac 19¹⁶.†
    * ἐφ-άπαξ, adv., 1. *once for all* (Eupol.): Ro 6¹⁰, He 7²⁷ 9¹² 10¹⁰.
2. *at once:* ι Co 15⁶.†
    ἐφεῖδον, v.s. ἐπεῖδον.
    Ἐφεσῖνος, -η, -ον, *Ephesian:* Re 2¹, Rec. (ἐν Ἐφέσῳ, WH, RV).†
    Ἐφέσιος, -α, -ον, *Ephesian:* Ac 18²⁷ 19²⁸, ³⁴, ³⁵ 21²⁹.†
    Ἔφεσος, -ου, ἡ, *Ephesus,* a city in Asia Minor: Ac 18¹⁹, ²¹, ²⁴, ²⁷
19¹, ¹⁷, ²⁶ (on the gen., v. M, *Pr.,* 73) 20¹⁶, ¹⁷, ι Co 15³² 16⁸, Eph 1¹,
ι Ti 1³, ΙΙ Ti 1¹⁸ 4¹², Re 1¹¹ 2¹.†
    * ἐφ-ευρετής, -οῦ, ὁ (< ἐφευρίσκω, *to find out*), *an inventor, con-*
triver: κακῶν (cf. κακίας εὑρετής, ΙΙ Mac 7³¹), Ro 1³⁰.†
    † ἐφ-ημερία, -ας, ἡ (< ἐφήμερος), [in LXX chiefly for מִשְׁמֶרֶת,
מַחֲלֹקֶת;] 1. *a course of daily services* (Ne 13³⁰, ι Ch 25⁸, al.). 2. *a*
class or *course* of priests detailed for service in the temple (ι Ch 23⁶,
al.): Lk 1⁵, ⁸ (cf. MGr., ἐφημέριος, *priest*).†
    * ἐφ-ήμερος, -ον (ἐπί, ἡμέρα), 1. *lasting for a day.* 2. *daily, for*
the day: Ja 2¹⁵.†
    ἔφιδε, v.s. ἐπεῖδον.
    ** ἐφ-ικνέομαι, -οῦμαι, [in LXX: Si 43²⁷, ³⁰ R (ἀφικ- ABא) *;] *to*
come to, to reach: seq. ἄ‚ρι, ΙΙ Co 10¹³; εἰς, ib. ¹⁴.†
    ἐφ-ίστημι, [in LXX for נצב ni., שׁית, נתן, etc.;] 1. causal in
pres., impf., fut., 1 aor., *to set upon* or *by, set up,* etc. (Æsch., Hdt.,

Arist., al). 2. Intrans. in mid. and in pf. and 2 aor. act.; (a) *to stand upon ;* (b) *to be set over ;* (c) *to stand by, be present, be at hand, come on* or *upon :* Lk 2³⁸ 10⁴⁰ 20¹, Ac 6¹² 12⁷ 22¹³, ²⁰ 23²⁷, II Ti 4²; c. dat. pers., Lk 2⁹ 24⁴, Ac 4¹ 23¹¹; c. dat. loc., Ac 17⁵; seq. ἐπί, c. acc., Ac 10¹⁷ 11¹¹; seq. ἐπάνω, Lk 4³⁹; of rain, Ac 28²; of evils impending, c. dat. pers., I Th 5³; seq. ἐπί (Wi 6ʸ), Lk 21³⁴; of time, II Ti 4⁶ (cf. κατ-, συν-εφίστημι).†

ἐφνίδιος, v.s. αἰφνίδιος.

'Εφραίμ (-ίμ, Tr.), *Ephraim,* a town near Jerusalem : Jo 11⁵⁴.†

† ἐφφαθά (Aram. אֶתְפְּתַח, v. Abbott, *Essays,* 142 ff.; *DCG,* i, 522), *ephphatha, be opened :* Mk 7³⁴.†

ἐχθές (Rec. χθές), adv., [in LXX for תְּמוֹל, etc.;] *yesterday :* Jo 4⁵², Ac 7²⁸, He 13⁸ (on the form, v. Rutherford, *NPhr.,* 370 f.).†

ἔχθρα, -ας, ἡ (< ἐχθρός), [in LXX for אֵיבָה, שִׂנְאָה, etc.;] *enmity :* Lk 23¹², Ro 8⁷, Ga 5²⁰, Eph 2¹⁵, ¹⁶, Ja 4⁴.†

ἐχθρός, -ά, -όν (< ἔχθος, *hatred*), [in LXX chiefly for אוֹיֵב, also for צַר, etc.;] 1. *hated, hateful* (Hom.) : opp. to ἀγαπητός, Ro 11²⁸. 2. Actively, *hating, hostile :* Ro 5¹⁰, I Co 15²⁵, II Th 3¹⁵; c. gen. pers. (cl.), Ja 4⁴; τ. διανοίᾳ, Col 1²¹; ἐ. ἄνθρωπος, Mt 13²⁸; as subst., ὁ ἐ., *an enemy,* I Co 15²⁶; the devil, Mt 13³⁹, Lk 10¹⁹; c. gen. pers., Mt 22⁴⁴, Mk 12³⁶, Lk 20⁴³, Ac 2³⁵, I Co 15²⁵, He 1¹³ 10¹³ (LXX); Mt 5⁴³, ⁴⁴ 10³⁶ 13²⁵, Lk 1⁷¹, ⁷⁴ 6²⁷, ³⁵ 19²⁷, ⁴³, Ro 12²⁰, Ga 4¹⁶, Re 11⁵, ¹²; c. gen. rei, Ac 13¹⁰, Phl 3¹⁸.†

** ἔχιδνα, -ης, ἡ, [in OT (Aq.), Is 59⁵ *;] *a viper :* Ac 28³; metaph., γεννήματα ἐχιδνῶν, Mt 3⁷ 12³⁴ 23³³, Lk 3⁷.†

ἔχω, [in LXX for אָצַל (ἐχόμενος), בַּעַל, יֵשׁ, etc., 59 words in all;] (on the *Aktionsart* of the various tenses, v. M, *Pr.,* 110, 145, 150, 183), *to have,* as in cl., in various senses and constructions. I. Trans.; 1. *to have, hold, hold fast,* etc.; (a) *to hold,* as, in the hand : Re 5⁸ 14⁶, al.; ἐν τ. χειρί, Re 1¹⁶ 10², al.; (b) of arms and clothing, = φέρω, φορέω, *to bear, wear :* Mt 3⁴ 22¹², al.; so freq. pres. ptcp. (LS, s.v., A, I, 6; Bl., § 74, 2), Mk 11¹³, Jo 18¹⁰, Re 9¹⁷, al.; (c) of a woman, ἐν γαστρὶ ἔ. (κοίτην ἔ.), *to be with child :* Mk 13¹⁷, Ro 9¹⁰; (d) *to hold fast, keep :* Lk 19²⁰; metaph., of the mind and conduct, Mk 16⁸ (cf. Jb 21⁶, Is 13⁸; Deiss., *BS,* 293; Field, *Notes,* 44 f.), Jo 14²¹, Ro 1²⁸, I Ti 3⁹, II Ti 1¹³, Re 6⁹, al.; (e) *to involve :* He 10³⁵ (LXX), Ja 1⁴, I Jo 4¹⁸; (f) = Lat. *habere* (Bl., § 34, 5; 73, 5), *to hold, consider :* c. acc. et predic. ptcp., Lk 14¹⁸; c. acc., seq. ὡς, Mt 14⁵; εἰς (Hebraism), Mt 21⁴⁶; ὅτι (Bl., § 70, 2), Mk 11³². 2. *to have, possess ;* (a) in general, c. acc. rei : Mt 19²², Mk 10²², Lk 12¹⁹, Jo 10¹⁶, I Co 11²², al.; of wealth or poverty, absol., ἔχειν (neg. οὐκ, μή), Mt 13¹² 25²⁹, II Co 8¹²; ἐκ τ. ἔχειν, *according to your means,* II Co 8¹¹; (b) of relationship, association, etc. : πατέρα, Jo 8⁴¹; γυναῖκα (MM, xiv), I Co 7²; φίλον, Lk 11⁵; βασιλέα, Jo 19¹⁵; ποιμένα, Mt 9³⁶; c. dupl. acc, Mt 3⁹, al.; (c) of parts or members : ὦτα, Mt 9¹⁵; μέλη, Ro 12⁴; θεμελίους, He 11¹⁰;

(d) c. acc., as periphrasis of verb: μνείαν ἔ. (= μεμνῆσθαι), 1 Th 3⁶; ἀγάπην, Jo 13³⁵; γνῶσιν, 1 Co 8¹; πεποίθησιν, 11 Co 3⁴; θλίψιν, Jo 16³³, etc. (Thayer, s.v., I, 2, f., g.); (e) of duty, necessity, etc.: ἀνάγκην, 1 Co 7³⁷; νόμον, Jo 19⁷; ἐπιταγήν, 1 Co 7²⁵; ἀγῶνα, Phl 1³⁰; κρίμα, 1 Ti 5¹²; (f) of complaints and disputes; κατά, c. gen. pers., Mt 5²³, Mk 11²⁵; id. seq. ὅτι, Re 2⁴, ²⁰; c. acc. seq. πρός, Ac 24¹⁹, al.; (g) c. inf., (a) (cl.) to be able (Field, Notes, 14): Mt 18²⁵, Mk 14⁸ (sc. ποιῆσαι), Lk 12⁴, Ac 4¹⁴, al.; (β) of necessity (Bl., § 69, 4): Lk 12⁵⁰, Ac 23¹⁷⁻¹⁹ 28¹⁹. II. Intrans. (Bl., § 53, 1), to be in a certain condition: ἑτοίμως ἔ., c. inf., Ac 21¹³, 11 Co 12¹⁴; ἐσχάτως (q.v.), Mk 5²³; κακῶς, to be ill, Mt 4²⁴, al.; καλῶς, Mk 16·[18]; κομψότερον, Jo 4⁵²; πῶς, Ac 15³⁶; impers., ἄλλως ἔχει, it is otherwise, 1 Ti 5²⁵; οὕτως, Ac 7¹, al.; τὸ νῦν ἔχον, as things now are (To 7¹¹), Ac 24²⁵. III. Mid., -ομαι, to hold oneself fast, hold on or cling to, be next to: c. gen., τ. ἐχόμενα σωτηρίας, He 6⁹ (Rendall, in l.); ptcp., ὁ ἐχόμενος, near, next: of place, Mk 1³⁸; of time, τ. ἐχομένῃ (ἡμέρᾳ, expressed or understood), Lk 13³³, Ac 20¹⁵ 21²⁶; σαββάτῳ, Ac 13⁴⁴. (Cf. ἀν-, προσ-αν-, ἀντ-, ἀπ-, ἐν-, ἐπ-, κατ-, μετ-, παρ-, περι-, προ-, προσ-, συν-, ὑπερ-, ὑπ-έχω.)

ἕως, relative particle (Lat. donec, usque), expressing the terminus ad quem (cf. Burton, § 321 ff.). I. As conjunction; 1. till, until; (a) of a fact in past time, c. indic.: Mt 2⁹, al. (Wi 10¹⁴, al.); (b) ἕως ἄν, c. subjc. aor.: Mt 2¹³ 5¹⁸, Mk 6¹⁰, al.; without ἄν (M. Pr., 168 f.; Lft., Notes, 115), Mk 14³² (Burton, § 325), Lk 12⁵⁹, 11 Th 2⁷, al.; (c) c. indic. pres. (Burton, § 328; Bl., § 65, 10): Mk 6⁴⁵, Jo 21²², ²³, 1 Ti 4¹³. 2. C. indic., as long as, while (Burton, § 327): Jo 9⁴ (Plat., Phaedo, 89 c). II. As an adverb (chiefly in later writers). 1. Of time, until, unto; (a) as prep. c. gen. (Bl., § 40, 6; M, Pr., 99): τ. ἡμέρας, Mt 26²⁹, Lk 1⁸⁰, Ro 11⁸, al.; ὥρας, Mt 27⁴⁵, al.; τέλους, 1 Co 1⁸, 11 Co 1¹³; τ. νῦν, Mt 24²¹, Mk 13¹⁹ (1 Mac 2³³); ἐτῶν ὀγ. (Field, Notes, 49 f.), Lk 2³⁷; τ. ἐλθεῖν, Ac 8⁴⁰; before names and events, Mt 1¹⁷ 2¹⁵, Lk 11⁵¹, Ja 5⁷, al.; (b) seq. οὗ, ὅτου, with the force of a conjc. (Burton, § 330; M, Pr., 91); (a) ἔ. οὗ (Hdt., ii, 143; Plut., al.): c. indic., Mt 1²⁵ (WH br., οὗ) 13³³, al.; c. subjc. aor., Mt 14²², al.; (β) ἔ. ὅτου: c. subjc., Lk 13⁸; c. indic., Mt 5²⁵ (until), Jo 9¹⁸; (c) c. adv. (ἔ. ὀψέ, Thuc., iii, 108): ἄρτι, Mt 11¹², Jo 2¹⁰, 1 Co 4¹³, al.; πότε (M, Pr., 107), Mt 17¹⁷, Mk 9¹⁹, Jo 10²⁴, al. 2. Of place, as far as, even to, unto (Arist., al.); (a) as prep. c. gen. (v. supr.): Mt 11²³, Lk 10¹⁵, al.; (b) c. adv. (Bl., § 40, 6): ἄνω, Jo 2⁷; ἔσω, Mk 14⁵⁴; κάτω, Mt 27⁵¹, Mk 15³⁸; ὧδε, Lk 23⁵; (c) c. prep.: ἔξω, Ac 21⁵; πρός, Lk 24⁵⁰ (Field, Notes, 83). 3. Of quantity, measure, etc.: Mt 18²¹, Mk 6²³, Lk 22⁵¹, al.

Z

Z, ζ, ζῆτα, τό, zeta, the sixth letter. As a numeral, ζ' = ἑπτά, ἕβδομος ζ, = 7000.

Ζαβουλών, ὁ, indecl. (Heb. זְבֻלוּן, v. Ge 30²⁰), Zebulun, Jacob's tenth son: the tribe of Z., Mt 4¹³, ¹⁵, Re 7⁸.†

Ζακχαῖος, -ου, ὁ (Heb. זַכָּי, cf. Ne 7¹⁴, 1 Es 2⁹, LXX Ζακχού), *Zaccai, Zacchaeus*, a publican : Lk 19², ⁵, ⁸ (cf. 11 Mac 10¹⁹).†

Ζαρά, ὁ, indecl. (Heb. זֶרַח, Ge 38³⁰), *Zerah*, an ancestor of Jesus : Mt 1³.†

ζαφθανεί (cf. Heb. עֲזַבְתָּנִי), *zaphthanei* : Mt 27⁴⁶ (WH, mg., for Rec. σεβαχθανεί, q.v.; " probably an attempt to reproduce the Heb. as disting from Aram. forms," WH, *Notes*, 21; cf. also Dalman, *Words*, 53 f.).†

Ζαχαρίας, -ου, ὁ (Heb. זְכַרְיָה, זְכַרְיָהוּ); 1. *Zacharias*, father of John the Baptist : Lk 1⁵, ¹², ¹³, ¹⁸, ²¹, ⁴⁰, ⁵⁹, ⁶⁷ 3². 2. *Zechariah*, the son of Jehoiada (in txt. wrongly called *son of Barachiah ;* cf. 11 Ch 24¹⁹ ᶠᶠ·) : Mt 23³⁵, Lk 11⁵¹.†

ζάω, -ῶ, [in LXX chiefly for חיה (most freq. ptcp., ζῶν, inf., ζῆν, for חַי) ;] 1. prop., *to live, be alive* (v. Syn., s.v. βίος ; in cl. usually of animal life, but sometimes of plants, as Arist., *Eth. N*, i, 7, 12) : Ac 20¹², Ro 7¹⁻³, 1 Co 7³⁹, Re 19²⁰, al. ; ἐν αὐτῷ ζῶμεν, Ac 17²⁸ ; ἐμοὶ τὸ ζῆν Χριστός, Phl 1²¹ ; διὰ παντὸς τοῦ ζῆν (M, *Pr*., 215, 249), He 2¹⁵ ; ὃ δὲ νῦν ζῶ ἐν σαρκί, Ga 2²⁰ ; ζῇ ἐν ἐμοὶ Χριστός, Ga 2²⁰ ; (ὁ) ζῶν, of God (אֵל חַי) and cognate phrases, Jos 3¹⁰, Ho 2¹ (1¹⁰), Is 37⁴, al. ; v. *DCG*, ii, 39ᵃ), Mt 16¹⁶, Jo 6⁵⁷, Ro 9²⁶, 1 Th 1⁹, He 3¹², Re 7², al. ; in juristic phrase, ζῶ ἐγώ (חַי־אָנִי, Nu 14²¹, al.), *as I live*, Ro 14¹¹ ; ζῆν ἐπ᾽ ἄρτῳ, Mt 4⁴, al. ; ἐκ, 1 Co 9¹⁴ ; of coming to life, Mk 16⁽¹¹⁾, Ro 6¹⁰ 14⁹, 11 Co 13⁴ ; opp. to νεκρός, Re 1¹⁸ 2⁸ ; metaph., Lk 15³² ; ζῆν ἐκ νεκρῶν, Ro 6¹³ ; of the spiritual life of Christians, Lk 10²⁸, Jo 5²⁵, Ro 1¹⁷ 8¹³ ; εἰς τ. αἰῶνα, Jo 6⁵¹, ⁵⁸ ; σὺν Χριστῷ, 1 Th 5¹⁰ ; ὄνομα ἔχεις ὅτι ζῇς, Re 3¹. 2. As sometimes in cl., = βιόω, *to live, pass one's life* : Lk 2³⁶, Ac 26⁵, Ro 7⁹, Col 2²⁰ ; ἐν πίστει, Ga 2²⁰ ; ἐν τ. ἁμαρτίᾳ, Ro 6² ; εὐσεβῶς, 11 Ti 3¹² ; ἀσώτως, Lk 15¹³ ; c. dat. (cl.), ἑαυτῷ (Field, *Notes*, 164), Ro 14⁷, 11 Co 5¹⁵ ; τ. θεῷ, Lk 20³⁸, Ro 6¹⁰, ¹¹, Ga 2¹⁹ ; τ. Χριστῷ, 11 Co 5¹⁵ ; τ. δικαιοσύνῃ, 1 Pe 2²⁴ ; πνεύματι, Ga 5²⁵ ; κατὰ σάρκα, Ro 8¹², ¹³. 3. Of inanimate things, metaph. : ὕδωρ ζῶν (i.e. springing water, as opp. to still water), in a spiritual sense, Jo 4¹⁰, ¹¹ 7³⁸ (*DCG*, ii, 39 f.) : ἐλπὶς ζῶσα, 1 Pe 1³ ; ὁδὸς ζῶσα, He 10²⁰ (cf. ἀνα-, συν-ζάω ; Cremer, 270, 721).

ζέννυμι, for σβ-, 1 Th 5¹⁹ T (v. WH, *Notes*, 148).†

Ζεβεδαῖος, -ου, ὁ (Heb. זְבַדְיָה; LXX : Ζαβδειά, 11 Es 8⁸ 10²⁰; Ζαβαδαίας, 1 Es 9³⁵ ; Ζαβδαῖος, ib. ²¹), *Zebedee*, father of James and John the Apostles : Mt 4²¹ 10² 20²⁰ 26³⁷ 27⁵⁶, Mk 1¹⁹, ²⁰ 3¹⁷ 10³⁵, Lk 5¹⁰, Jo 21².†

**†ζεστός, -ή, -όν (ζέω), [in Aq. : Le 6²¹ ⁽¹⁴⁾ ; in Al. : ib. 7¹² *;] *boiling hot* (Strab., al.) : metaph., Re 3¹⁵, ¹⁶.†

ζεῦγος, -εος (-ους), τό (< ζεύγνυμι, *to yoke*), [in LXX chiefly for צֶמֶד, Jg 19³, al.;] 1. *a yoke* of beasts : Lk 14¹⁹. 2. *a pair* of anything, Lk 2²⁴ ⁽ᴸˣˣ⁾.†

*† **ζευκτήριος**, -α -ον (< ζεύγνυμι), *fit for joining.* As subst., (a) ζευκτήριον, τό = ζυγόν, *a yoke;* (b) ζευκτηρία, -ας, ἡ = ζεύγλη, *the cross-bar* of a double rudder : Ac 27⁴⁰ (found nowhere else).†

Ζεύς, gen., Διός, dat., Διΐ, acc., Δία (Δίαν, D, al.), *Zeus* (Lat. *Jupiter*): Ac 14¹², ¹³.†

ζέω, [in LXX for רוּם, רתח, metaph., iv Mac 18²⁰;] *to boil, be hot;* metaph., of anger, love, zeal : ptcp., *fervent :* τ. πνεύματι, Ac 18²⁵, Ro 12¹¹.†

* **ζηλεύω**, late and rare form of ζηλόω, q.v.; 1. *to envy, be jealous.* 2. *to be zealous :* Re 3¹⁹.†

ζῆλος, -ου, ὁ, and in late Gk., also -εος, τό (ii Co 9², Phl 3⁶), [in LXX for קִנְאָה, Nu 25¹¹, al.;] 1. *zeal :* ii Co 7¹¹ 9²; κατὰ ζῆλος, Phl 3⁶; c. gen. obj., Jo 2¹⁷ (LXX), Ro 10²; seq. ὑπέρ, ii Co 7⁷; c. gen. subj., θεοῦ, ii Co 11²; πυρός, He 10²⁷ (cf. Is 26¹¹, Wi 5¹⁸, and cf. Westc., in l.). 2. *jealousy :* Ro 13¹³, i Co 3³, ii Co 12²⁰, Ga 5²⁰ (WH, txt, RV), Ja 3¹⁴,¹⁶; πλησθῆναι ζήλου Ac 5¹⁷ 13⁴⁵; pl., ζῆλοι (v. Bl., § 32, 6), Ga 5²⁰, WH, mg.†

ζηλόω, -ῶ, [in LXX chiefly for קנא pi.;] 1. *to burn with envy* or *jealousy, to be jealous :* absol., Ac 7⁹ 17⁵, i Co 13⁴, Ja 4² (R, mg., cf. Mayor, in l.). 2. *to seek* or *desire eagerly :* c. acc. rei, i Co 12³¹ 14¹, ³⁹ (cf. Si 50¹⁸, Wi 1¹²); c. acc. pers., ii Co 11², Ga 4¹⁷; pass., Ga 4¹⁸.†

ζηλωτής, -οῦ, ὁ (< ζηλόω), [in LXX for קַנָּא (θεὸς ζ.), Ex 20⁵ 34¹⁴, De 4²⁴ 5⁹ 6¹⁵; קַנּוֹא, Na 1² (θεός); pl., i Es 8⁷²; ζ. τῶν νόμων, ii Mac 4²; τὸν ζ. Φινεές, iv Mac 18¹² (cf. Nu 25¹¹)*;] 1. in cl. *an emulator, zealous admirer* (Plat., al.). 2. *eagerly desirous, zealous;* (a) absol., as in OT, ll. c.; (b) c. gen. obj. : (zealous to acquire or to defend), i Co 14¹², Tit 2¹⁴, i Pe 3¹³; τ. νόμου (ii Mac, l.c.), Ac 21²⁰; παραδόσεων, Ga 1¹⁴; c. gen. pers., θεοῦ, Ac 22³. 3. In FlJ, NT, *a Zealot,* member of the Jewish party so called : as surname of the Apostle Simon, Lk 6¹⁵, Ac 1¹³.†

ζημία, -ας, ἡ, [in LXX for עֹנֶשׁ ni. and cognate forms;] *damage, loss :* Ac 27¹⁰, ²¹, Phl 3⁸; opp. to κέρδος, ib.⁷.†

ζημιόω, -ῶ (< ζημία), [in LXX chiefly for ענשׁ;] *to damage.* Pass., *to suffer loss, forfeit, lose :* absol., i Co 3¹⁵; seq. ἐν, ii Co 7⁹; c. acc. rei (v. Bl., § 34, 6), τ. ψυχήν, Mt 16²⁶, Mk 8³⁶; ἑαυτόν, Lk 9²⁵; τ. πάντα, Phl 3⁸.†

Ζηνᾶς, -ᾶ, acc. -ᾶν (contr. from Ζηνόδωρος), *Zenas :* Tit 3¹³.†

ζητέω, -ῶ, [in LXX chiefly for בקשׁ pi., also for דרשׁ, etc.;] 1. *to seek, seek for :* Mt 7⁷, ⁸, Lk 11⁹, ¹⁰; c. acc. pers., Mk 1²⁷, Lk 2⁴⁸, Jo 6²⁴, al.; id. seq. ἐν, Ac 9¹¹; c. acc. rei, Mt 13⁴⁵, Lk 19¹⁰; seq. ἐν, Lk 13⁶, ⁷; ψυχήν, of plotting against one's life (Ex 4¹⁹, al.), Mt 2²⁰, Ro 11³ (LXX). Metaph., *to seek* by thinking, *search after, inquire into :* Mk 11¹⁸, Lk 12²⁹, Jo 16¹⁹; τ. θεόν, Ac 17²⁷. 2. *to seek* or *strive after, desire :* Mt 12⁴⁶, Mk 12¹², Lk 9⁹, Jo 5¹⁸, Ro 10³, al.; τ. θάνατον, Re 9⁶; τ. βασιλείαν τ. θεοῦ, Mt 6³³ (Dalman, *Words,* 121 f.); τὰ ἄνω, Col 3¹;

εἰρήνην, I Pe 3¹¹ (LXX). 3. *to require, demand :* c. acc. rei, Mk 8¹², Lk 11²⁹, I Co 1²², II Co 13³ ; seq. παρά, Mk 8¹¹, al. ; ἵνα, I Co 4² (cf. ἀνα-, ἐκ-, ἐπι-, συν-ζητέω).

ζήτημα, -τος, τό (< ζητέω), [in LXX: ζ. τίθεσθαι (שׂוּם דָּ ni.), Ez 36³⁷ A * ;] *an inquiry, question :* Ac 15² 18¹⁵ 23²⁹ 25¹⁹ 26³.†

*ζήτησις, -εως, ἡ (< ζητέω). 1. *a seeking, search.* 2. *a questioning, inquiry, debate :* Ac 15²,⁷, II Ti 2²³, Tit 3⁹; seq. περί, Jo 3²⁵, Ac 25²⁰, I Ti 6⁴.†

*ζιζάνιον, -ου, τό (in Talmud זוּנִין), *zizanium* (EV, *tares*), a kind of darnel, resembling wheat : Mt 13²⁵⁻²⁷, ²⁹, ³⁰, ³⁶, ³⁸, ⁴⁰ (cf. *DB*, s.v. "Tares").†

Ζμύρνα, -ης, ἡ, Re 1¹¹ 2⁸ T, for Σμ-, q.v. (cf. Bl., § 3, 9; Mayser, 204).†

Ζοροβάβελ (FlJ, Ζοροβάβηλος, -ου), ὁ, indecl. (Heb. זְרֻבָּבֶל), *Zerubbabel* (I Ch 3¹⁹, al.) : Mt 1¹², ¹³, Lk 3²⁷.†

**ζόφος, -ου, ὁ (akin to γνόφος, q.v.), [in Sm.: Ex 10²², Jb 28³, Ps 10 (11)² 90 (91)⁶, Is 59⁹*;] in Hom. *the gloom of the under-world;* hence, *darkness, deep gloom* (poët. and late prose writers) : He 12¹⁸, II Pe 2⁴, ¹⁷, Ju ⁶, ¹³.†

ζυγός (in cl. more freq. τὸ ζυγόν), -οῦ, ὁ (< ζεύγνυμι), [in LXX for עֹל, מֹאזְנַיִם, etc.;] 1. *a yoke;* metaph., of bondage or submission to authority : Mt 11²⁹, ³⁰, Ac 15¹⁰, Ga 5¹, I Ti 6¹. 2. *a balance :* Re 6⁵ (cf. Is 40¹², al.).†

ζύμη, -ης, ἡ, [in LXX for חָמֵץ, Ex 12¹⁵ 13³ 23¹⁸ 34²⁵, De 16³; שְׂאֹר, Ex 12¹⁵, ¹⁹ 13⁷, Le 2¹¹, De 16⁴*;] *leaven :* Mt 13³³, Lk 13²¹; τ. ἄρτου, Mt 16¹². Metaph., of a moral influence or tendency, always, exc. in the Parable of the Leaven (Mt 13³³, Lk 13²¹), for evil: I Co 5⁶⁻⁸, Ga 5⁹; ζ. τ. Φαρισαίων, Mt 16⁶, ¹¹, Mk 8¹⁵, Lk 12¹ (Cremer, 723).†

ζυμόω, -ῶ (< ζύμη), [in LXX for חָמֵץ, Ex 12³⁴, ³⁹, Le 6¹⁷ (¹⁰) 23¹⁷, Ho 7⁴*;] *to leaven :* Mt 13³³, Lk 13²¹, I Co 5⁶, Ga 5⁹.†

ζωγρέω, -ῶ (< ζωός, *alive,* + ἀγρεύω), [in LXX chiefly for חיה hi.;] *to catch alive, take captive :* metaph., Lk 5¹⁰; pass., II Ti 2²⁶ (on the meaning and construction, v. Ellic., *CGT*, in l.).†

ζωή, -ῆς, ἡ (ζάω), [in LXX chiefly for חַיִּים;] *life* (in Hom., Hdt., = βίος, q.v.; later, *existence, vita quâ vivimus,* as distinct from βίος, *vita quam vivimus ;* opp. to θάνατος) ; 1. of natural life : Lk 16²⁵, Ac 8³³, I Co 15¹⁹, I Ti 4⁸, He 7³, Ja 4¹⁴; πνεῦμα ζωῆς, Re 11¹¹; ψυχὴ ζωῆς (Ge 1³⁰), Re 16³; of the life of one risen from the dead, Ro 5¹⁰, He 7¹⁶. 2. Of the life of the kingdom of God, the present life of grace and the life of glory which is to follow (Dalman, *Words,* 156 ff. ; Westc., *Epp. Jo.,* 214 ff. ; Cremer, 272 ff.) : Jo 6⁵¹, ⁵³, Ro 7¹⁰ 8⁶, ¹⁰, Phl 2¹⁶, Col 3⁴, II Pe 1³; αἰώνιος (reff. supr.; *DCG,* i, 538ᵃ, ii, 30 f.), Jo 4³⁶ 12⁵⁰ 17³, I Jo 1², al.; τ. φῶς τῆς ζ., Jo 8¹²; ὁ Λόγος τ. ζ., I Jo 1¹; ὁ ἄρτος τ. ζ. Jo 6³⁵, ⁴⁸; δικαίωσις ζωῆς, Ro 5¹⁸; μετάνοια εἰς ζ., Ac 11¹⁸; ἐν αὐτῷ ζ. ἦν.

Jo 1⁴; ζ. ἡ ἐν. X. 'Ι., ΙΙ Ti 1¹; τὰ πρὸς ζωήν, ΙΙ Pe 1³, al.; στέφανος τῆς ζ., Ja 1¹²; Re 2¹⁰; χάρις ζωῆς (gen. expl.), ι Pe 3⁷; ζ. καὶ εἰρήνη, Ro 8⁶; ζ. καὶ ἀφθαρσία, ΙΙ Ti 1¹⁰; ἀνάστασις ζωῆς, Jo 5²⁹; βίβλος ζωῆς, Phl 4³, Re 3⁵; ξύλον ζωῆς, Re 2⁷; ὕδωρ ζωῆς, Re 22¹⁷; meton., of that which has life: τ. πνεῦμα, Ro 8¹⁰; ῥήματα, Jo 6⁶³; of one who gives life, Jo 11²⁵ 14⁶, ι Jo 1²; ἡ ἐντολή, Jo 12⁵⁰.
SYN.: v.s. βίος.

ζώνη, -ης, ἡ (ζώννυμι), [in LXX for אַבְנֵט, חֲגוֹרָה, etc.;] a belt, girdle: Mt 3⁴, Mk 1⁶, Ac 21¹¹, Re 1¹³ 15⁶; as a receptacle for money, Mt 10⁹, Mk 6⁸.†

ζώννυμι and ζωννύω, [in LXX chiefly for חגר;] to gird: c. acc. pers., Jo 21¹⁸. Mid., to gird oneself: Ac 12⁸ (cf. ἀνα-, δια-, περι-, ὑπο-ζώννυμι).†

ζωογονέω, -ῶ (< ζωός, alive, γένεσθαι), [in LXX: Ex 1¹⁷, ¹⁸, ²², Jg 8¹⁹, ι Ki 2⁶ 27⁹, ¹¹, ΙΙΙ Ki 21 (20)³¹, ιν Ki 7⁴ (חיה pi., hi.), Le 11⁴⁷ (חָיָה) *;] 1. in cl., to engender, produce alive, endue with life. 2. In LXX and NT, to preserve alive (DCG, ii, 606ᵃ; Cremer, 274): Lk 17³³, Ac 7¹⁹, ι Ti 6¹³ (RV, quickeneth; R, mg., preserveth).†

ζῷον (Rec. ζῶον, v. LS, s.v.), -ου, τό (< ζωός, alive), [in LXX for חַיָּה (chiefly) and cognate forms; freq. in Wi;] a living creature, an animal: Re 4⁶⁻⁹ 5⁶ ᶠᶠ· 6¹ ᶠᶠ· 7¹¹ 14³ 15⁷ 19⁴; ζῴων τ. αἷμα, He 13¹¹; ἄλογα ζ., ΙΙ Pe 2¹², Ju 10.†
SYN.: θηρίον, in which the brutal, bestial element is emphasized, and which is never used of sacrificial animals. On the other hand, ζ. is the more comprehensive, as expressing the vital element common to the whole animal creation (v. Tr., Syn., lxxxi; Cremer, 274).

ζωο-ποιέω, ῶ, [in LXX for חיה pi., hi., Jg 21¹⁴, ιν Ki 5⁷, Ne 9⁶, Jb 36⁶, Ps 70²⁰, Ec 7¹³ (12) *;] 1. in cl. (= ζωογονέω), to produce alive. 2. In LXX and NT, to make alive, cause to live, quicken (DCG, ii, 606ᵃ; Cremer, 275): Jo 5²¹ 6⁶³, Ro 4¹⁷ 8¹¹, ι Co 15⁴⁵, ΙΙ Co 3⁶, Ga 3²¹. Pass., ι Co 15²², ³⁶, ι Pe 3¹⁸.†

H

H, η, ἦτα, τό, indecl., eta, the seventh letter. As a numeral, η΄ = 8; η, = 8000.

ἤ, disjunctive and comparative particle (Bl., § 36, 12; 77, 11); 1. disjunctive, or; (a) between single words: Mt 5¹⁷, Mk 6⁵⁶, Lk 2²⁴, Jo 6¹⁹, Ro 1²¹, al.; (b) before a sentence expressing a variation, denial or refutation of a previous statement, freq. in interrog. form: Mt 7⁴, ⁹, Mk 12¹⁴, Lk 13⁴, Ro 3²⁹ 6³ 9²¹, ι Co 6⁹, ¹⁶ 9⁶, ΙΙ Co 11⁷; ἤ . . . ἤ, either . . . or, Mt 6²⁴, Lk 16¹³, ι Co 14⁶; (c) in a disjunctive question (as Lat. an after utrum): Mt 9⁵, Mk 2⁹, Lk 7¹⁹, al.; after πότερον, Jo 7¹⁷; μή, ι Co 9⁸; μήτι, ΙΙ Co 1¹⁷; ἤ . . . ἤ . . . ἤ, Mk 13³⁵. 2. Comparative, than: after comparatives, Mt 10¹⁵, Lk 9¹³, Jo 3¹⁹, Ro 13¹¹, al.; after ἕτερον, Ac 17²¹; θέλω (Kühner³, iv, 303), ι Co 14¹⁹; πρὶν ἤ,

before, seq. acc. et inf., Mt 1¹⁸, Mk 14³⁰; after a positive adj. or a verb, = *more than* (Ge 49¹²; cf. Robertson, *Gr.*, 661; M, *Gr.*, ii, pp. 441 f.), Mt 18⁸, ⁹, Mk 3⁴ 9⁴³, ⁴⁵, ⁴⁷, Lk 15⁷. 3. With other particles: ἀλλ' ἤ, v.s. ἀλλά; ἢ γάρ, v.s. γάρ; ἢ καί, *or even, or also*, Mt 7¹⁰, Lk 11¹¹, ¹², Ro 2¹⁵, 4⁹, al.; ἤτοι . . . ἤ, Ro 6¹⁶ (cf. Wi 11¹⁹).
ἤ (μήν), v.s. εἰ, iii, 7.

* **ἡγεμονεύω** (< ἡγεμών), 1. *to lead the way*. 2. *to lead* in war, *command* (cf. Ramsay, *Was Christ born at Bethlehem ?; DCG*, ii, 463 f.). 3. *to be governor* of a province: c. gen. loc., Lk 2² 3¹.†

ἡγεμονία, -ας, ἡ (< ἡγεμών), [in LXX: Ge 36³⁰ (אַלּוּף), Nu 1⁵² 2¹⁷ (דֶּגֶל), Si 7⁴ 10¹, iv Mac 6³³ 13⁴ *;] *rule, sovereignty*: Lk 3¹.†

ἡγεμών, -όνος, ὁ (ἡγέομαι), [in LXX for אַלּוּף, שַׂר, etc.;] 1. *a leader, guide*. 2. *a commander*. 3. *a governor* of a province (proconsul, propraetor, legate, or procurator; but cf. ἀνθύπατος): Mt 10¹⁸, Mk 13⁹, Lk 21¹², i Pe 2¹⁴; of the Procurator of Judæa, Mt 27², ¹¹, ¹⁴, ¹⁵, ²¹, ²⁷ 28¹⁴, Lk 20²⁰, Ac 23²⁴, ²⁶, ³³ 24¹, ¹⁰ 26³⁰. 4. For Heb. אַלֻּף (LXX, χίλιαι) misread אַלֻּף, *leaders*: Mt 2⁶ ⁽ᴼᵀ⁾.†

ἡγέομαι, -οῦμαι, depon. mid., [in LXX (chiefly pres. ptcp.) for נָגִיד, רֹאשׁ, שַׂר, etc.;] 1. *to lead; (a) to guide, go before; (b) to rule, be leader*: pres. ptcp., ἡγούμενος, *a ruler, leader* (MM, *Exp.*, xiv), Mt 2⁶ ⁽ᴸˣˣ⁾, Lk 22²⁶, Ac 7¹⁰ 14¹² 15²², He 13⁷, ¹⁷, ²⁴. 2. *to suppose, believe, consider, think* (Hdt., Soph., al.; cf. Lat. *duco*): c. dupl. acc., Ac 26², Phl 2³, ⁶ 3⁷, i Ti 1¹² 6¹, He 10²⁹ 11¹¹, ²⁶, ii Pe 1¹³ 2¹³ 3⁹, ¹⁵; c. acc. seq. ὡς, c. acc., ii Th 3¹⁵; c. acc. seq. adv., i Th 5¹³; ὅταν, Ja 1²; ἀναγκαῖον, c. inf., ii Co 9⁵, Phl 2²⁵; δίκαιον, c. inf., ii Pe 1¹³; c. acc. et inf., Phl 3⁸ (cf. δι-, ἐκ-δι-, ἐξ-, προ-ηγέομαι).†
SYN.: v.s. δοκέω.

ἡδέως, adv. (< ἡδύς, *sweet*), [in LXX: Pr 3²⁴ (עָרֵב), etc.;] *gladly, with pleasure*: Mk 6²⁰ 12³⁷, ii Co 11¹⁹; superlat., ἥδιστα, *very gladly* (Bl., § 11, 3), ii Co 12⁹, ¹⁵.†

ἤδη, adv., in NT, always of time; *now, already*: Mt 3¹⁰, Mk 4³⁷, Lk 7⁶, Jo 4³⁶, al.; νῦν . . . ἤ., *now already*, i Jo 4³; ἤ. ποτέ, *now at length*, c. fut., Ro 1¹⁰ (cf. ἄρτι).

ἥδιστα, v.s. ἡδέως.

ἡδονή, -ῆς, ἡ (< ἥδομαι, *to be glad*), [in LXX: Nu 11⁸ (טַעַם), Pr 17¹, Wi 7² 16²⁰, and freq. in iv Mac;] *pleasure*: ii Pe 2¹³; pl., Lk 8¹⁴, Tit 3³, Ja 4¹, ³.†

* **ἡδύ-οσμος**, -ον (< ἡδύς, ὀσμή), *sweet-smelling*; as subst., τὸ ἡ., *mint*: Mt 23²³, Lk 11⁴².†

** **ἦθος**, -εος (-ους), τό, [in LXX: Si, prol.²⁷ 20²⁶ ⁽²⁵⁾, iv Mac 1²⁹ 2⁷, ²¹ 5²⁴ 13²⁷ *;] 1 *a haunt, abode*. 2. = ἔθος, *custom, manner*: pl., i Co 15³³.†

ἥκω, [in LXX chiefly for בּוֹא;] pf. with pres. meaning (hence impf. = plpf.), *to have come, be present*: Mt 24⁵⁰, Mk 8³ (late pf., ἧκα, v. Swete, in l.; WH, *App.*, 169), Lk 12⁴⁶ 15²⁷, Jo 8⁴², He 10⁷, ⁹, ³⁷, i Jo

5²⁰, Re 2²⁵ 3³, ⁹ 15⁴; seq. ἀπό, c. gen. loc., Mt 8¹¹, Lk 13²⁹; ἐκ, Ro 11²⁶; id. seq. εἰς, Jo 4⁴⁷; μακρόθεν, Mk 8³; ἐπί, c. acc., Re 3³. Metaph., of discipleship: Jo 6³⁷; of time and events: absol., Mt 24¹⁴, Jo 2⁴, II Pe 3¹⁰, Re 18⁸; seq. ἐπί, c acc. pers., Mt 23³⁶, Lk 19⁴³ (cf. ἀν-, καθ-ήκω).†

†ἤλει (Rec. ἠλί, L, ἠλί; Heb. אֵלִי), *Eli, my God:* Mt 27⁴⁶ (cf. ἐλωΐ).†

Ἡλεί (Rec. Ἡλί; RV, Ἡλί), ὁ, indecl., *Heli,* Joseph's father: Lk 3²³.†

Ἡλείας (Rec. Ἡλίας; LTr., Ἡλίας; T, Ἡλείας; cf. WH, *App.,* 155, *Intr.,* § 408), -ου (-α, Lk 1¹⁷, WH), ὁ (Heb. אֵלִיָּה, אֵלִיָּהוּ), *Elijah* (III Ki 17, al.): Mt 11¹⁴ 16¹⁴ 17³, ⁴, ¹⁰⁻¹² 27⁴⁷, ⁴⁹, Mk 6¹⁵ 8²⁸ 9⁴, ⁵, ¹¹⁻¹³ 15³⁵, ³⁶, Lk 1¹⁷ 4²⁵, ²⁶ 9⁸, ¹⁹, ³⁰, ³³, ⁵⁴, Jo 1²¹, ²⁵, Ja 5¹⁷; ἐν Ἡ., in the portion concerning E., Ro 11².†

ἡλικία, -ας, ἡ (< ἧλιξ, *of the same age, mature*), [in LXX: Ez 13¹⁸ (קוֹמָה), Jb 29¹⁸, Wi 4⁹, Si 26¹⁷, freq. in II-IV Mac; always of age or maturity]; "a stage of growth whether measured by age or stature"; 1. (*a*) *age:* Mt 6²⁷, Lk 12²⁵ (R, mg.), He 11¹¹; (*b*) *full age, maturity:* Jo 9²¹, ²³, Eph 4¹³. 2. *stature:* Lk 2⁵² 19³ (Mt 6²⁷, Lk 12²⁵, AV, R, txt.; but the prevailing usage in LXX and π. favours the former meaning in these doubtful passages; cf., Ellic., *ICC,* AR, on Eph, l.c.; Milligan, *NTD,* 74 f., and esp., MM, *Exp.,* xv; e contra, Field, *Notes,* 6).†

*ἡλίκος, -η, -ον, 1. prop., *as big as, as old as.* 2. As indirect interrog., *what sized, what, how great, how small* (the sense to be determined by the context): Col 2¹, Ja 3⁵, Ga 6¹¹ (WH, mg.; πηλ-, WH, txt., RV).†

ἥλιος, -ου, ὁ, [in LXX chiefly for שֶׁמֶשׁ;] *the sun:* with art. (Bl., § 46, 5), Mt 5⁴⁵ 13⁴³ 17² 24²⁹, Mk 1³² 4⁶ 13²⁴ 16², Lk 4⁴⁰, Ac 2²⁰ (LXX) 26¹³, Eph 4²⁶, Ja 1¹¹, Re 1¹⁶ 6¹² 8¹² 9² 10¹ 12¹ 16⁸ 19¹⁷ 21²³; βλέπειν τὸν ἥ., Ac 13¹¹; οὐδὲ μὴ πέσῃ ἐπ' αὐτοὺς ὁ ἥ., Re 7¹⁶; without art., Mt 13⁶, Lk 21²⁵ 23⁴⁵, Ac 27²⁰, I Co 15⁴¹, Re 7² 16¹² 22⁵.†

ἧλος, -ου, ὁ, [in LXX: Is 41⁷ (מַסְמְרִים), etc.;] *a nail:* Jo 20²⁵.†

ἡμεῖς, v.s. ἐγώ.

ἡμέρα, -ας, ἡ, [in LXX chiefly (very freq.) for יוֹם;] *day;* 1. as distinct from night: gen. ἡμέρας, *by day* (WM, § 30, 11), Lk 21²⁵; ἡ. κ. νυκτός (ν. κ. ἡ.), Ac 9²⁴, I Th 2⁹, II Th 3⁸, Re 4⁸ (Bl., § 36, 13); ἡμέρας μέσης, *at mid-day,* Ac 26¹³; acc. durat., τ. ἡμέρας, Lk 21³⁷; ὅλην τὴν ἡ., Ro 8³⁶; ἐν ἡμέρᾳ, Jo 11⁹, Ro 13¹³; ἡμέρας ὁδός, *a day's journey,* Lk 2⁴⁴; ἡ. γίνεται, Lk 4⁴² 22⁶⁶; κλίνει, Lk 9¹², al.; metaph., Jo 9⁴, Ro 13¹², I Th 5⁴, ⁵, ⁸, II Pe 1¹⁹. 2. Of a civil day of 24 hours, incl. night: Mt 6³⁴, Mk 6²¹, Lk 13¹⁴, al.; τρίτῃ ἡ., Mt 16²¹; ἡμέρᾳ κ. ἡ. (cf. יוֹם בְּיוֹם, Es 3⁴), II Co 4¹⁶; ὅλην τ. ἡ., Ro 8³⁶ 10²¹; pl., Jo 2¹², Ac 9¹⁹, al.; ἡ. τῶν ἀζύμων, Ac 12³; τ. σαββάτου, Lk 13¹⁴, ¹⁶; ἡ κυριακὴ ἡ., Re 1¹⁰. 3. In Messianic sense, of the last day: ἡ ἡ. (ἐκείνη, τ. κυρίου, etc.), Mt 7²², Lk 6²³, Ro 13¹², ι Co 1⁸, ι Th 5², ιι Th 2², ιι Pe 3¹⁰, al.; by meton., as compared with the divine judgment on that day, ἡ. ἀνθρωπίνη, of a human *tribunal*, ι Co 4³ (EV, *man's judgment*). 4. As in Heb. (also in Gk. writers; Bl., § 46, 9; M, *Pr.*, 81), of time in general: Jo 8⁵⁶ 14²⁰, ιι Co 6², Eph 6¹³, ιι Pe 3¹⁸; pl., Ac 15⁷, Eph 5¹⁶, He 10³²; πᾶσας τὰς ἡ. (cf. כָּל־הַיָּמִים, De 4⁴⁰, al.; MM, *Exp.*, xv), Mt 28²⁰; ἐλεύσονται ἡ. ὅταν (ὅτε), Mt 9¹⁵, Mk 2²⁰, Lk 5³⁵ 17²²; αἱ ἡ., c. gen. pers. (Ge 26¹, al.), Mt 2¹, Lk 1⁵, Ac 7⁴⁵, ι Pe 3²⁰; ἀρχὴ ἡμερῶν, He 7³.

ἡμέτερος, -α, -ον (ἡμεῖς), poss. pron. of first pers., *our*: Ac 2¹¹ 24⁶ 26⁵, Ro 15⁴, ιι Ti 4¹⁵, ι Jo 1³ 2²; τὸ ἡ., Lk 16¹², WH, txt., R, mg. (τὸ ὑμ., Rec., WH, mg., R, txt.); οἱ ἡ., *our* (people), Tit 3¹⁴.†

ἤ μήν, v.s. ἦ.

†ἡμιθανής, -ές (< ἥμι, *half* + θνήσκω), [in LXX: ιv Mac 4¹¹ *;] *half-dead*: Lk 10³⁰.†

ἥμισυς, -εια, -υ, gen., -ους (late, as in π., for cl., -εος; Bl., § 8, 4; Mayser, 294), n. pl., ἡμίσια (Rec., cl., -εια), [in LXX for חֲצִי, מַחֲצִית;] *half*; 1. as adj., agreeing in gender and number with the substantive following, τὰ ἡμίσια τ. ὑπαρχόντων, Lk 19⁸. 2. As neut. subst., τὸ ἥμισυ, *the half*; ἥ. (anarth.), *a half*: c. gen., ἥ. καιροῦ, Re 12¹⁴; ἕως ἡμίσους τ. βασιλείας μου, Mk 6²³; after a cardinal number, ἡμέρας τρεῖς κ. ἥμισυ, Re 11⁹, ¹¹.†

†ἡμίωρον (Rec. -ιον), -ου, τό (ἥμι, *half* + ὥρα), *half an hour*: Re 8¹.†

ἡνίκα, rel. adv. of time, *at which time, when*; seq. ἄν, c. subjc., *whensoever*: ιι Co 3¹⁵, ¹⁶.†

ἤπερ, v.s. ἤ.

ἤπιος, -α, -ον, *mild, gentle*: ι Th 2⁷ (WH, R, mg., νήπιος); seq. πρός, ιι Ti 2²⁴.†

Ἤρ (L, Ἦρ), ὁ, indecl. (Heb. עֵר), *Er*, an ancestor of Jesus: Lk 3²⁸.†

†ἤρεμος, -ον, [in LXX: Es 3¹³ A *;] *quiet, tranquil* (Luc., al.): ι Ti 2².†

SYN.: ἡσύχιος, q.v.

Ἡρώδης (Rec. -ώδης), -ου, ὁ, *Herod*; 1. *Herod the Great*: Mt 2, Ac 23³⁵. 2. *Herod Antipas* (ὁ τετραάρχης, Mt 14¹): Mt 14¹, ³, ⁶, Mk 6 8¹⁵, Lk 1⁵ 3¹, ¹⁹ 8³ 9⁷, ⁹, 13³¹ 23, Ac 4²⁷ 13¹. 3. *Herod Agrippa I*: Ac 12¹, ⁶, ¹¹, ¹⁹, ²¹ (cf. Ἀγρίππας (II)).†

Ἡρῳδιανοί (Rec. Ἡρω-), -ῶν, οἱ, *Herodians*, partisans of Herod (cf. τοὺς τὰ Ἡρῴδου φρονοῦντας, FlJ, *Ant.*, xiv, 15, 10): Mt 22¹⁶, Mk 3⁶ 12¹³.†

Ἡρῳδιάς (Rec. Ἡρω-), -άδος, ἡ, *Herodias*, granddaughter of Herod the Great: Mt 14³, ⁶, Mk 6¹⁷, ¹⁹, ²², Lk 3¹⁹.†

Ἡρῳδίων (Rec. Ἡρω-), -ωνος, ὁ, *Herodion*: Ro 16¹¹.†

Ἡσαίας (Rec. Ἡσαίας), -ου, ο (Heb. יְשַׁעְיָהוּ), *Isaiah*, the prophet:

Mt 3³ 4¹⁴ 8¹⁷ 12¹⁷ 13¹⁴,³⁵ 15⁷, Mk 7⁶, Lk 3⁴ 4¹⁷, Jo 1²³ 12³⁸,³⁹,⁴¹, Ac 8²⁸ 28²⁵, Ro 9²⁷,²⁹ 10¹⁶,²⁰ 15¹²; ἀνεγίνωσκεν τ. προφήτην 'H., Ac 8³⁰; ἐν τ. 'H., Mk 1².†

'Hσαῦ, ὁ, indecl. (Heb. עֵשָׂו, Ge 25²⁵), Esau: Ro 9¹³ (LXX), He 11²⁷ 12¹⁶.†

ἡσσόω (v. M, Gr., II, p. 240).

ἥσσων (Rec. ἥττ-, the Attic literary form), ἧσσον, inferior, less; neut., τὸ ἧ., adverbially, less: II Co 12¹⁵; εἰς τὸ ἧ., for the worse (opp. to κρεῖττον): I Co 11¹⁷.†

ἡσυχάζω, [in LXX chiefly for שָׁקַט;] to be still; (a) to rest from labour: Lk 23⁵⁶; (b) to live quietly: I Th 4¹¹; (c) to be silent: Lk 14⁴, Ac 11¹⁸ 21¹⁴ (cf. Jb 32⁷, Ne 5⁸).†
SYN.: σιγάω (q.v.), σιωπάω.

ἡσυχία, -ας, ἡ (< ἡσύχιος, q.v.), [in LXX for אִישׁוֹן, שֶׁלִי, etc.;] 1. quietness: II Th 3¹². 2. stillness, silence: Ac 22², I Ti 2¹¹,¹².†

ἡσύχιος, -α, -ον (= the more freq. ἥσυχος; cf. Wi 18¹⁴, Si 25²⁰), [in LXX: Is 66² (נְכֵה־רוּחַ)*;] quiet, tranquil: I Ti 2², I Pe 3⁴.†
SYN.: ἤρεμος, of tranquillity arising from without; ἡ., from within (v. Ellic. on I Ti, l.c.; but also v. CGT, ib.).

ἤτοι, disjunct. part., whether: Ro 6¹⁶.†

ἡττάω, -ῶ (ἥσσ-, II Co 12¹³, v.s. ἥσσων), [in LXX for חתת, etc.;] pass., 1. to be inferior: seq. ὑπέρ, II Co 12¹³. 2. to be overcome: absol., II Pe 2²⁰; c. dat., ib.¹⁹.†

† ἥττημα, -τος, τό, [in LXX for מַם, Is 31⁹ (8) *;] defect, loss, defeat: Ro 11¹² (cf. Is, l.c.), I Co 6⁷ (cf. Field, Notes, 160 f., 171 f.; Lft., Notes, 212).†

ἥττων, v.s ἥσσων.

ἠχέω, -ῶ (< ἦχος), [in LXX for המה, etc.;] to sound: I Co 13¹ (cf. ἐξ-, κατ-ηχέω).†

ἦχος, -ου, ὁ (also in late and MGr., -εος, τό, Lk 21²⁵), [in LXX for הָמוֹן, etc.;] 1. a noise, sound: Ac 2²; ἧ. θαλάσσης, Lk 21²⁵; σάλπιγγος, He 12¹⁹. 2. a report: seq. περί, Lk 4³⁷.†

Θ

Θ, θ and ϑ, θῆτα, τό, indecl., theta, the eighth letter. As a numeral, θ′ = 9, θ, = 9000.

Θαδδαῖος, -ου, ὁ (Aram. תַּדַּאי, תַּדִּי), Thaddæus: Mt 10³, Mk 3¹⁸ (WH, mg., Λεββαῖος, q.v.).†

θάλασσα, -ης, ἡ, [in LXX chiefly for יָם;] the sea: Mt 23¹⁵, Mk 11²³, Lk 21²⁵, Ro 9²⁷, He 11¹², Ja 1⁶, Ju ¹³, Re 7¹, al.; τὸ πέλαγος τῆς θ. (v. Tr., ut infr.), Mt 18⁶; ὁ οὐρανὸς κ. ἡ γῆ κ. ἡ θ., of the whole world,

Ac 4²⁴, al. (Hg 2⁷); θ. ὑαλίνη, Re 4⁶ 15²; of the Mediterranean, Ac 10⁶, ³² 17¹⁴; of the Red Sea, ἐρυθρὰ θ., Ac 7³⁶, ι Co 10¹, ², He 11²⁹; of an inland lake (as Heb. יָם), θ. τ. Γαλιλαίας, Mt 4¹⁸ 15²⁹, Mk 1¹⁶ 7³¹; τ. Τιβεριάδος, Jo 21¹; τ. Γ. τ. Τ., Jo 6¹; of the same, simply ἡ θ., Mt 4¹⁵, Mk 2¹³, al.

SYN.: πέλαγος, "the vast expanse of open water"; θ., "the sea as contrasted with the land" (Tr., *Syn.*, xiii).

θάλπω, [in LXX for סכן, etc.;] *to heat, warm;* metaph., (*a*) *to inflame* (Trag.); (*b*) *to foster, cherish:* Eph 5²⁹, ι Th 2⁷.†

Θάμαρ (Tr., Θαμάρ), ἡ (Heb. תָּמָר, Ge 38⁶), *Tamar:* Mt 1³.†

θαμβέω, -ῶ (θάμβος), [in LXX for בעת ni., pi., etc.;] 1. *to be amazed.* 2. In late Gk., *to astonish, terrify* (ιι Ki 22⁵): pass., Mk 1²⁷ 10³²; seq. ἐπί, c. dat. rei, Mk 10²⁴; on Mk 10³², v. Turner, *SNT*, p. 62.†

θάμβος, -ους, τό, [in LXX for פַּחַד, etc.;] *amazement:* Lk 4³⁶ 5⁹, Ac 3¹⁰.†

* θανάσιμος, -ον (< θάνατος), *deadly:* Mk 16 [18].†

θανατη-φόρος, -ον (< θάνατος, φέρω), [in LXX: Nu 18²² (מוּת), Jb 33²³, ιv Mac 8¹⁸, ²⁶ 15²⁶ *;] *deadly, death-bringing:* Ja 3⁸.†

θάνατος, -ου, ὁ (θνήσκω), [in LXX chiefly for מוּת, מָוֶת, sometimes for דֶּבֶר;] *death;* 1. of the death of the body, whether natural or violent: Jo 11¹³, Phl 2²⁷, He 7²³, al; opp. to ζωή, Ro 8³⁸, Phl 1²⁰; of the death of Christ, Ro 5¹⁰, Phl 3¹⁰, He 2⁹; ῥύεσθαι (σώζειν) ἐκ θ., ιι Co 1¹⁰, He 5⁷; περίλυπος ἕως θανάτου, Mt 26³⁸, Mk 14³⁴; μέχρι (ἄχρι) θ., Phl 2⁸, Re 2¹⁰; πληγὴ θανάτου, a deadly wound, Re 13³; ἰδεῖν θάνατον, Lk 2²⁶, He 11⁵; γενέσθαι θανάτου, Mk 9¹; ἔνοχ·s θανάτου, Mk 14⁶⁴; θανάτῳ τελευτᾶν (Ex 21¹⁷, מוֹת יוּמָת), Mk 7¹⁰; death personified, Ro 6⁹, ι Co 15²⁶, Re 21⁴; pl., of deadly perils, ιι Co 11²³. 2. Of spiritual death: Jo 5²⁴ 8⁵¹, Ro 7¹⁰, Ja 1¹⁵, 5²⁰, ι Jo 3¹⁴ 5¹⁶, al.; of eternal death, Ro 1³² 7⁵, al.; ὁ θ. ὁ δεύτερος, Re 2¹¹ 21⁸ (cf. Cremer, 283 ff.; *DB*, iii, 114 ff.; *DCG*, i, 791 f.).

. θανατόω, -ῶ, [in LXX chiefly for מוּת hi., ho., also for הרג, etc.;] *to put to death:* c. acc., Mt 10²¹ 26⁵⁹ 27¹, Mk 13¹² 14⁵⁵, Lk 21¹⁶, ιι Co 6⁹, ι Pe 3¹⁸; pass., Ro 8³⁶. Metaph.: Ro 8¹³; pass., c. dat, (in relation to), Ro 7⁴.†

θάπτω, [in LXX chiefly for קבר;] *to bury:* c. acc., Mt 8²¹, ²² 14¹², Lk 9⁵⁹, ⁶⁰, Ac 5⁶, ⁹, ¹⁰; pass., Lk 16²², Ac 2²⁹, ι Co 15⁴.†

Θαρά (Rec. Θάρα), ὁ, indecl. (Heb. תֶּרַח), *Terah* (Ge 11): Lk 3³⁴.†

θαρρέω, -ῶ (later form of θαρσέω), [in LXX: Pr 1²¹, Ba 4²¹, ²⁷, Da LXX 6¹⁶ (17), ιv Mac 13¹¹ 17⁴ *;] *to be of good cheer* or *courage, to be confident:* ιι Co 5⁶, ⁸, He 13⁶; τ. πεποιθήσει, ιι Co 10²; seq. εἰς, ιι Co 10¹; ἐν, ib. 7¹⁶.†

SYN.: τολμάω. "θ. has reference more to the character, τ. to its manifestation" (Thayer, s.v. τολμάω).

θαρσέω, -ῶ (v.s. θαρρέω), [in LXX chiefly for יָרֵא, c. neg. ;] *to be of good courage:* imperat., θάρσει, -εῖτε, Mt 9², ²² 14²⁷, Mk 6⁵⁰ 10⁴⁹, Jo 16³³, Ac 23¹¹.†

θάρσος, -ους, τό, *courage:* Ac 28¹⁵.†

θαῦμα, -τος, τό, [in LXX: Jb 17⁸ 18²⁰ 20⁸ 21⁵ (שַׁעַר, etc.) * ;] 1. *a wonder:* II Co 11¹⁴. 2. *wonder:* Re 17⁶.†

θαυμάζω, [in LXX for נָשָׂא, etc. ;] *to marvel, wonder, wonder at:* absol., Mt 8¹⁰, ²⁷ 9³³ 15³¹ 21²⁰ 22²² 27¹⁴, Mk 5²⁰ 15⁵, Lk 1²¹ (R, txt.; *ICC*, in l., but v. infr.), ib. ⁶³ 8²⁵ 11¹⁴ 24⁴¹, Jo 5²⁰ 7¹⁵, Ac 2⁷ 4¹³ 13⁴¹, Re 17⁷, ⁸; c. acc. pers., Lk 7⁹; c. acc. rei, Lk 24¹² (WH, R, mg. om.), Jo 5²⁸, Ac 7³¹; θαῦμα μέγα, Re 17⁶; πρόσωπον (LXX for נָשָׂא פָנִים, De 10¹⁷, al.), Ju ¹⁶; seq. διά, c. acc., Mk 6⁶, Jo 7²¹; seq. ἐν, c. dat. obj., Lk 1²¹ (? R, mg., but v. supr.); seq. ἐπί, c. dat. rei, Lk 2³³ 4²² 9⁴³, 20²⁶, Ac 3¹²; περί, Lk 2¹⁸; ὀπίσω, Re 13³; ὅτι, Lk 11³⁸, Jo 3⁷ 4²⁷, Ga 1⁶; εἰ, Mk 15⁴⁴, I Jo 3¹³. Pass. (Si 38³, Wi 8¹¹): seq. ἐν, c. dat. pers., II Th 1¹⁰ (cf. ἐκ-θαυμάζω).†

θαυμάσιος, -α, -ον (< θαῦμα), [in LXX chiefly for פָּלָא ni. (n. pl. = נִפְלָאוֹת) ;] *wonderful;* n. pl., *wonders:* Mt 21¹⁵.†

θαυμαστός, -ή, -όν (< θαυμάζω), [in LXX for פָּלָא and cogn. forms (Ps 117 (118)²², ²³ 118 (119)¹²⁹, Is 25¹, al.), יָרֵא ni. (Ex 15¹¹, Ps 64 (65)⁵, al.), אַדִּיר (Ps 8¹, ⁹ 92 (93)⁴), etc. ;] *wonderful, marvellous:* Mt 21⁴² (LXX), Mk 12¹¹ (ib.), Jo 9³⁰, I Pe 2⁹, Re 15¹, ³.†

* θεά, -ᾶς, ἡ (fem. of θεός, q.v.), *a goddess:* Ac 19²⁷.†

θεάομαι, -ῶμαι, [in LXX: II Ch 22⁶ (רָאָה), To 2² 13⁶, ¹⁴, Jth 15⁸, II Mac 2⁴ 3³⁶, III Mac 5⁴⁷ * ;] *to behold, look upon, contemplate, view* (in early writers with a sense of *wondering*), in NT apparently always in literal, physical sense of "careful and deliberate vision which interprets . . . its object": c. acc. rei, Mt 11⁷, Lk 7²⁴ 23⁵⁵, Jo 1¹⁴, ³² 4³⁵ 11⁴⁵, Ac 22⁹, I Jo 1¹; c. acc. pers., Mt 22¹¹, Ac 21²⁷, Ro 15²⁴, I Jo 4¹²; c. ptcp., Mk 16 [14], Lk 5²⁷, Jo 1³⁸, Ac 1¹¹; seq. ὅτι, Jo 6⁵, I Jo 4¹⁴; pass., Mt 6¹ 23⁵, Mk 16 [11].†

SYN.: v.s. θεωρέω.

*†θεατρίζω (< θέατρον), *to make a spectacle of, expose to contempt* (eccl.; ἐκθ-, Polyb.): pass., He 10³³.†

* θέατρον, -ου, τό (< θεάομαι), 1. *a theatre* (used also as a place of assembly): Ac 19²⁹, ³¹. 2. Collective for οἱ θεαταί, the *spectators.* 3. = θέα, θέαμα, *a spectacle, show:* metaph., I Co 4⁹.†

θεῖον, -ου, τό, [in LXX: Ge 19²⁴, De 29²³ (22), Jb 18¹⁵, Ps 10 (11)⁷, Is 30³³ 34⁹, Ez 38²² (גָּפְרִית), III Mac 2⁵ * ;] *brimstone:* Lk 17²⁹ (LXX), Re 9¹⁷, ¹⁸ 14¹⁰ 19²⁰ 20¹⁰, 21⁸.†

θεῖος, -εία, -εῖον (< θεός), [in LXX: Ex 31³ 35³¹, Jb 27³ 33⁴, Pr 2¹⁷ (אֵל, אֱלוֹהַּ, אֱלֹהִים), Si 6³⁵, II Mac ₃, III Mac ₁, IV Mac ₂₅ * :] *divine:*

δύναμις, II Pe 1³; φύσις (for parallel in π., v. MM, *Exp.*, xv), ib.⁴; τὸ θ., *the Deity* (so in cl.; of God, in Philo and FlJ), Ac 17²⁹.†

**† θειότης, -ητος, ἡ (< θεῖος), [in LXX: Wi 18⁹*;] *divine nature, divinity*: Ro 1²⁰ (for ex. from π., v. MM, *Exp.*, xv).†

SYN.: θεότης, *deity, godhead*, divine personality. θει. = divine nature and properties, a summary term for the attributes of deity, differing from θεότης as quality or attribute from essence.

*† θειώδης, -ες (< θεῖον), *of brimstone, sulphureous*: Re 9¹⁷.†

† θέλημα, -τος, τό (< θέλω), [in LXX chiefly for חֵפֶץ, also for רָצוֹן, etc.;] *will*, (a) objectively = that which is willed: Mt 18¹⁴, Lk 12⁴⁷, Jo 5³⁰, I Co 7³⁷, I Th 5¹⁸, II Ti 2²⁶, He 10¹⁰, Re 4¹¹; θ. τ. θεοῦ, Ac 22¹⁴, Ro 2¹⁸ 12², Eph 1⁹, Col 1⁹ 4¹², I Pe 4²; τ. κυρίου, Eph 5¹⁷; pl., of precepts, Mk 3³⁵, WH, mg., Ac 13²² (LXX); ἐστιν τὸ θ., c. gen. pers., seq. ἵνα, Jo 6³⁹,⁴⁰, I Co 16¹²; c. inf., I Pe 2¹⁵; c. acc. et inf., I Th 4³; (b) subjectively = τὸ θέλειν (cf. θέλησις): Lk 23²⁵, Jo 1¹³, I Pe 3¹⁷, II Pe 1²¹; ποιεῖν, Mt 7²¹ 12⁵⁰ 21³¹, Mk 3³⁵ (pl., WH, mg., v. supr.), Jo 4³⁴ 6³⁸ 7¹⁷ 9³¹, Eph 6⁶, He 10⁷,⁹,³⁶ 13²¹, I Jo 2¹⁷; γίνεσθαι, Mt 6¹⁰ 26⁴², Lk 22⁴², Ac 21¹⁴; ἡ εὐδοκία (βουλὴ) τοῦ θ., Eph 1⁵,¹¹; ἐν τῷ θ. τοῦ θεοῦ, Ro 1¹⁰; διὰ θ. θεοῦ, Ro 15³², I Co 1¹, II Co 1¹ 8⁵, Eph 1¹, Col 1¹, II Ti 1¹; κατὰ τὸ θ. τ. θεοῦ, Ga 1⁴, I Pe 4¹⁹, I Jo 5¹⁴; pl., Eph 2³ (Cremer, 728).†

† θέλησις, -εως, ἡ (θέλω), [in LXX: II Ch 15¹⁵, Pr 8³⁵ (רָצוֹן), Ez 18²³ (חֵפֶץ), Da LXX 11⁴⁵ (צְבִי), To 12¹⁸, Wi 16²⁵, II Mac 12¹⁶, III Mac 2²⁶*;] in colloq. and MGr. = τὸ θέλειν, *will*: He 2⁴.†

θέλω (the strengthened form ἐθέλω is found in Hom., and is the more freq. in Attic; v. Rutherford, *NPhr.*, 415 f.), [in LXX for אבה, חפץ; c. neg., מאן pi., etc.;] *to will, be willing, wish, desire* (more freq. than βούλομαι, q.v., in vernac. and late Gk., also in MGr.; for various views as to its relation to β., v. Thayer, 286; but v. also Bl., § 24, s.v.): absol., Ro 9¹⁶, I Co 4¹⁹ 12¹⁸, Ja 4¹⁵; τ. θεοῦ θέλοντος, Ac 18²¹; c. acc. rei, Mt 20²¹, Mk 14³⁶, Jo 15⁷, Ro 7¹⁵,¹⁶, I Co 4²¹ 7³⁶, Ga 5¹⁷; c. inf., Mt 5⁴⁰, Mk 10⁴³, Jo 6²¹,⁶⁷, Ro 7²¹, Ga 4⁹; c. acc. et inf., Mk 7²⁴, Lk 1⁶², Jo 21²²,²³, Ro 16¹⁹, I Co 14⁵, Ga 6¹³; οὐ θέλω, Mt 18³⁰, al.; id. c. inf., Mt 2¹⁸, Mk 6²⁶, Jo 5⁴⁰, I Co 16⁷; seq. ἵνα, Mt 7¹², Mk 6²⁵, Jo 17²⁴; opp. to ποιέω, πράσσω, ἐνεργέω, Ro 7¹⁵,¹⁹, II Co 8¹⁰,¹¹, Phl 2¹³; seq. ἤ (ICC, in l.; Deiss., *LAE*, 179₂₄), I Co 14¹⁹; θέλων ἐν ταπεινοφροσύνῃ (*of his own mere will, by humility*, R, mg.), Col. 2¹⁸; (cf. ICC, in l.; Lft., tr., θ. ἐν, *taking delight in*; v. also Peake, *Comm.*, in l.; Zahn, *Intr.*, I, 477₇; Lietzmann, *Handbuch*, III, ii, p. 83; Souter renders *fixing one's will on*); of things, τί θέλει, what does it mean (Hdt., al.; cf. Lat. *quid sibi vult*), Ac 17²⁰; with comp. particle ἤ, I Co 14¹⁹ (M, *Gr.*, II, p. 442); in OT quotations, for Heb. חפץ, c. acc. pers., Mt 27⁴³; c. acc. rei, Mt 9¹³ 12⁷, He 10⁵,⁸; c. inf., I Pe 3¹⁰; for אמר, c. inf., Ac 7²⁸ (v. Cremer, 726 ff.).

θεμέλιος, -ον (< τίθημι), [in LXX for אַרְמוֹן, מוֹסָד, etc. ;] of or for a foundation; as subst., ὁ θ. (sc. λίθος), a foundation stone, foundation: Lk 6⁴⁸, ⁴⁹ 14²⁹ (but v. Deiss., BS, 123 ; pl., οἱ θ. (cl.), He 11¹⁰, Re 21¹⁴, ¹⁹ ; neut., τὸ θ. (Arist., Phys., vi, 6, 10, LXX and later writers), Ac 16²⁶ ; metaph., Ro 15²⁰, ι Co 3¹⁰⁻¹², Eph 2²⁰, ι Ti 6¹⁹, ιι Ti 2¹⁹, He 6¹.†

θεμελιόω, -ῶ, [in LXX chiefly for יסד;] to lay the foundation of, to found : c. acc., τ. γῆν, He 1¹⁰ (LXX); pass., Mt 7²⁵, Lk 6⁴⁸; metaph., ι Pe 5¹⁰ (R, mg., settle); pass., Eph 3¹⁸, Col 1²³.†

*† θεο-δίδακτος, -ον, taught of God (cf. διδακτοὶ θεοῦ, Jo 6⁴⁵) : ι Th 4⁹.†

* θεο-λόγος, -ου, ὁ, 1. one who treats of the Divine nature (applied in cl. to the old poets and philosophers). 2. In eccl., a theologian, divine : Re, tit., Rec.†

** θεομαχέω, -ῶ (< θεομάχος), [in LXX : ιι Mac 7¹⁹ *;] to fight against God : Ac 23⁹ (Rec.).†

**† θεομάχος, -ον, [in Sm. : Jb 26⁵, Pr 9¹⁸ 21¹⁶ *;] fighting against God : Ac 5³⁹.†

*† θεόπνευστος, -ον (< θεός, πνέω), inspired by God : ιι Ti 3¹⁶.†

θεός, -οῦ, ὁ, ἡ (Ac 19³⁷ only; v. M, Pr., 60, 244), late voc., θεέ (Mt 27⁴⁶ ; cf. De 3²⁴, al.), [in LXX chiefly for אֱלֹהִים, also for אֵל and other cognate forms, יהוה, etc. ;] a god or deity, God. 1. In polytheistic sense, a god or deity : Ac 28⁶, ι Co 8⁴, ιι Th 2⁴, al. ; pl., Ac. 14¹¹ 19²⁶, Ga 4⁸, al. 2. Of the one true God ; (a) anarthrous : Mt 6²⁴, Lk 20³⁸, al. ; esp. c. prep. (Kühner ³, iii, 605), ἀπὸ θ., Jo 3² ; ἐκ, Ac 5³⁹, ιι Co 5¹, Phl 3⁹ ; ὑπό, Ro 13¹ ; παρὰ θεοῦ, Jo 1⁶ ; παρὰ θεῷ, ιι Th 1⁶, ι Pe 2⁴ ; κατὰ θεόν, Ro 8²⁷, ιι Co 7⁹, ¹⁰ ; also when in gen. dependent on an anarth. noun (Bl., § 46, 6), Mt 27⁴³, Lk 3², Ro 1¹⁷, ι Th 2¹³ ; as pred., Lk 20³⁸, Jo 1¹, and when the nature and character rather than the person of God is meant, Ac 5²⁹, Ga 2⁶, al. (M, Th., 14) ; (b) more freq., c. art. : Mt 1²³, Mk 2⁷, al. mult. ; c. prep., ἀπὸ τ. θ., Lk 1²⁶ ; ἐκ, Jo 8⁴², al. ; παρὰ τοῦ θ., Jo 8⁴⁰ ; π. τῷ θ., Ro 9¹⁴ ; ἐν, Col 3³ ; ἐπὶ τῷ θ., Lk 1⁴⁷ ; ἐπὶ τὸν θ., Ac 15¹⁹ ; εἰς τ. θ., Ac 24¹⁵ ; πρὸς τ. θ., Jo 1² ; c. gen. pers., Mt 22³², Mk 12²⁶, ²⁷, Lk 20³⁷, Jo 20¹⁷, al. ; ὁ θ. μου, Ro 1⁸, Phl 1³, al. ; ὁ θ. κα πατήρ κ.τ.λ., Ro 15⁶, Eph 1³, Phl 4²⁰, al. ; c. gen. rei, Ro 15⁵, ¹³, ³³, ιι Co 1³, ι Th 5²³ ; τὰ τ. θεοῦ, Mt 16²³, Mk 12¹⁷, ι Co 2¹¹ ; τὰ πρὸς τὸν θ., Ro 15¹⁷, He 2¹⁷ 5¹ ; τ. θεῷ, as a superl. (LXX, Jos 3³), Ac 7²⁰, ιι Co 10⁴ ; Hebraistically, of judges (Ps 81 (82)⁶), Jo 10³⁴ (LXX), ³⁵.

θεοσέβεια, -ας, ἡ (< θεοσεβής), [in LXX : Ge 20¹¹ (יִרְאַת אֱלֹהִים), Jb 28²⁸ (אֲדֹנָי id.), Si 1²⁴, Ba 5⁴, ιν Mac 7⁶, ²² א 15²⁸ א 17¹⁵ *;] fear of God, godliness : ι Ti 2¹⁰.†

θεοσεβής, -ές (< θεός, σέβομαι), [in LXX for יְרֵא אֱלֹהִים, Ex 18²¹, al.;] God-fearing, godly : Jo 9³¹.†

SYN. : εὐσεβής (q.v.), θρῆσκος.

* θεοστυγής, -ές (< θεός, στυγέω), 1. passive, as freq. in cl., hateful to God : Ro 1³⁰ (R, txt., cf. Lft., Notes, 256). 2. Active, hating God : ib. (R, mg., cf. ICC, in l.).†

†θεότης. -ητος, ἡ, *deity, Godhead :* Col 2⁹.†
SYN. : θειότης, q.v.

Θεόφιλος, -ου (θεός, φίλος), *Theophilus :* Lk 1³, Ac 1¹.†

θεραπεία, -ας, ἡ (θεραπεύω), [in LXX for עֲבָדִים, Ge 45¹⁶ (cf. Es 5²),
etc.;] 1. *service, care, attention.* 2. *medical service, healing :* Lk 9¹¹
(Field, *Notes*, 60), Re 22². 3. Collective (concrete for abstract, as Lat.
servitum), *household attendants, servants :* Lk 12⁴² (LXX, ll. c.).†

θεραπεύω, [in LXX for יָשַׁב, etc.;] 1. *to do service, serve :* c. acc.
pers., pass., Ac 17²⁵. 2. As medical term, *to treat* (MM, *Exp.*, xv),
cure, heal : Mt 12¹⁰, Mk 6⁵, Lk 6⁷, al.; c. acc. pers., Mt 4²⁴, Mk 1³⁴,
al.; seq. ἀπό, Lk 5¹⁵ 6¹⁸ 7²¹ 8², ⁴³; θ. νόσον (μαλακίαν), Mt 4²³, al.
SYN. : ἰάομαι (cf. MM, *VGT*, s.v. ἰ., Field, *Notes*, p. 60).

θεράπων, -οντος, ὁ, [in LXX chiefly for עֶבֶד;] *an attendant
servant :* He 3⁵ (LXX).†
SYN. : v.s. διάκονος.'

θερίζω (< θέρος), [in LXX chiefly for קָצַר;] *to reap :* Mt 6²⁶, Lk
12²⁴, Ja 5⁴; fig., Mt 25²⁴, ²⁶, Lk 19²¹, ²², Jo 4³⁶⁻³⁸, II Co 9⁶, Ga 6⁷, ⁹,
Re 14¹⁵ ; c. acc., τ. σαρκικά, I Co 9¹¹ ; φθοράν, ζωὴν αἰώνιον, Ga 6⁸ ; τ. γῆν,
Re 14¹⁶.†

θερισμός, -οῦ, ὁ (< θερίζω), [in LXX chiefly for קָצִיר;] *harvest ;*
(*a*) the act : Jo 4³⁵ ; (*b*) the time : fig., Mt 13³⁰, ³⁹, Mk 4²⁹ (*c*) the crop :
fig., Mt 9³⁷, ³⁸, Lk 10², Re 14¹⁵.†

**θεριστής, -οῦ, ὁ (< θερίζω), [in LXX : Da LXX Bel ³², TH ib.³³ *;]
a reaper : Mt 13³⁰, ³⁹.†

θερμαίνω (< θερμός), [in LXX chiefly for חָמַם;] *to warm, heat ;*
mid., *to warm oneself :* Mk 14⁵⁴, ⁶⁷, Jo 18¹⁸, ²⁵, Ja 2¹⁶.†

θέρμη, -ης, ἡ, [in LXX : Jb 6¹⁷, Ps 18 (19)⁶, Ec 4¹¹ (חָמַם and
derivatives), Si 38²⁸ *;] *heat :* Ac 28³.†

θέρος, -ους, τό (θέρω, *to heat*), [in LXX chiefly for קַיִץ;] *summer :*
Mt 24³², Mk 13²⁸, Lk 21³⁰.†

Θεσσαλονικεύς, -έως, ὁ, *a Thessalonian :* Ac 20⁴ 27², I Th 1¹, II Th
1¹.†

Θεσσαλονίκη, -ης, ἡ, *Thessalonica*, a city of Macedonia : Ac
17¹, ¹¹, ¹³, Phl 4¹⁶, II Ti 4¹⁰.†

Θευδᾶς (perh. contr. from Θεόδωρος, but v. MM, *Exp.*, xv), -ᾶ, ὁ,
Theudas : Ac 5³⁶.†

θεωρέω, -ῶ (< θεωρός, *a spectator*, < θεάομαι), [in LXX chiefly for
רָאָה, חָזָה;] (pres. and impf. only, exc. Jo 7³ (fut.), Mt 28¹, Lk 23⁴⁸, Jo
8⁵¹, Re 11¹² (aor.); Bl., § 24); 1. (cl.), *to look at, gaze, behold :* absol.,
Mt 27⁵⁵, Mk 15⁴⁰, Lk 23³⁵; seq. πῶς, Mk 12⁴¹; ποῦ, Mk 15⁴⁷; c. acc.
pers., Jo 6⁴⁰, ⁶² 12⁴⁵ 16¹⁰⁻¹⁹, Ac 3¹⁶ 20³⁸ 25²⁴, Re 11¹¹, ¹²; id. c. ptcp.,
Mk 5¹⁵, Lk 10¹⁸, Jo 6¹⁹ 10¹² 20¹², ¹⁴, I Jo 3¹⁷; c. acc. rei, Mt 28¹, Lk
14²⁹ 21⁶ 23⁴⁸, Jo 2²³ 6² 7³, Ac 4¹³ 8¹³; id. c. ptcp., Jo 20⁶, Ac 7⁵⁶ 10¹¹;
seq. ὅτι, Ac 19²⁶. 2. In popular lang. (Kennedy, *Sources*, 155; Bl.,
§ 24, s.v. ὁρᾶν), in pres. and impf. = ὁράω, *to see, perceive, discern :* seq.
ὅτι, Mk 16⁴, Jo 4¹⁹ 12¹⁹, Ac 19²⁶ 27¹⁰; πόσαι, Ac 21²⁰; πηλίκος, He 7⁴;
c. acc. rei, Mk 5³⁸; id. c. ptcp., Ac 17¹⁶ 28⁶; c. acc. pers., Mk 3¹¹, Jo
14¹⁹, Ac 9⁷ 17²²; πνεῦμα, Lk 24³⁷; τὸ π., Jo 14¹⁷; seq. ὅτι, Jo 9⁸; c.

ptcp., Lk 24³⁹. 3. Hebraistically, *to experience, partake of :* τ. θάνατον, Jo 8⁵¹ (cf. Ps 88 (89)⁴⁹) ; τ. δόξαν, Jo 17²⁴ (cf. ἀνα-, παρα-θεωρέω).†

θεωρία, -ας, ἡ (v.s. θεωρέω), [in LXX: Da LXX 5⁷, ιι Mac 5²⁶ 15¹², ιιι Mac 5²⁴ *;] 1. *a viewing.* 2. = θεώρημα, *a spectacle, sight :* Lk 23⁴⁸ (both senses in cl.).†

θήκη, -ης, ἡ (< τίθημι), [in LXX: Ex 25²⁶ ⁽²⁷⁾ (בַּיִת), Is 6¹³ (מַצֶּבֶת), ib. 3²⁶ *;] *a receptacle, chest, case :* of the *sheath* of a sword, Jo 18¹¹.†

θηλάζω (< θηλή, *a breast*), [in LXX chiefly for יָנַק hi. ;] 1. of the mother, *to suckle :* Mt 24¹⁹, Mk 13¹⁷, Lk 21²³. 2. Of the young, *to suck :* Mt 21¹⁶ ; μαστούς, Lk 11²⁷ (cf. Jb 3¹², Ca 8¹, al.).†

θῆλυς, -εια, -υ, [in LXX chiefly for נְקֵבָה ;] *female :* as subst., ἡ θ., *a female, a woman :* Ro 1²⁶, ²⁷ ; τὸ θ., Mt 19⁴, Mk 10⁶, Ga 3²⁸.†

θήρα, -ας, ἡ, [in LXX for צַיִד, טֶרֶף, רֶשֶׁת, and cogn. forms ;] 1. *a hunting, chase* (Hdt., Xen., al.). 2. *prey, game* (cl.). 3. As in Ps 34 (35)⁸ = רֶשֶׁת, *a net :* Ro 11⁹ (but v. Thayer, s.v.).†

θηρεύω (< θήρα), [in LXX for צוּד, etc. ;] *to hunt, ensnare, catch :* metaph., Lk 11⁵⁴.†

*† θηριομαχέω, -ῶ (< θηρίον, μάχομαι), *to fight with wild beasts* (Diod., al.) : ι Co 15³².†

θηρίον, -ου, τό (dimin. of θήρ), [in LXX chiefly for חַיָּה ;] *a wild beast, beast :* Mk 1¹³, Ac 11⁶ 28⁴, ⁵, Tit 1¹², He 12²⁰, Ja 3⁷, Re 6⁸; of Antichrist, Re 11⁷ 13-20.†

θησαυρίζω, [in LXX for צָפַן, etc. ;] *to lay up, store up :* of riches, Ja 5³; id. c. dat. pers., Lk 12²¹, ιι Co 12¹⁴; c. acc. rei, ι Co 16²; θησαυροὺς ἑαυτῷ, Mt 6¹⁹, ²⁰; pass., ιι Pe 3⁷; metaph., ὀργὴν ἑαυτῷ, Ro 2⁵ (cf. Pr 1¹⁸, Pss. Sol 9⁹).†

θησαυρός, -οῦ, ὁ (< τίθημι), [in LXX chiefly for אוֹצָר ;] 1. *a place of safe keeping;* (a) *a casket :* Mt 2¹¹; (b) *a treasury* (ι Mac 3²⁹ and freq. in cl.); (c) *a storehouse* (Ne 13¹², De 28¹², al.): Mt 13⁵²; metaph., of the soul, Mt 12³⁵; τ. καρδίας, Lk 6⁴⁵. 2. *a treasure :* Mt 6¹⁹⁻²¹ 13⁴⁴, Lk 12³³, ³⁴, He 11²⁶; θ. ἐν οὐρανῷ (v. Dalman, *Words*, 206 ff.), Mt 19²¹, Mk 10²¹, Lk 18²²; of the knowledge of God through Christ, ιι Co 4⁷; τ. σοφίας κ. γνώσεως, Col 2³.†

θιγγάνω, [in LXX for נָגַע, Ex 19¹² *;] 1. *to touch, handle :* Col 2²¹, He 12²⁰ ⁽ᴸˣˣ⁾. 2. *to injure* (like Heb. נָגַע, and as in Eur., *Iph. Aul.*, 1351): c. gen., He 11²⁸.†

SYN.: v.s. ἅπτω.

θλίβω, [in LXX chiefly (ὁ θλίβων) for צַר ;] *to press :* c. acc. pers., Mk 3⁹; ὁδὸς τεθλιμμένη, *a narrow (compressed) way,* Mt 7¹⁴. Metaph. (as freq. in LXX), *to oppress, afflict, distress :* c. acc. pers., ιι Th 1⁶; pass. (Vg., *tribulor, tribulationem patior*), ιι Co 1⁶ 4⁸ 7⁵, ι Th 3⁴, ιι Th 1⁷, ι Ti 5¹⁰, He 11³⁷ (cf. ἀπο-, συν-θλίβω).†

θλίψις (LTr., θλῖψις), -εως, ἡ (< θλίβω), [in LXX for צָרָה, etc. ;]

pressure (Arist.). In LXX and NT metaph., *tribulation, affliction, distress* : Mt 24⁹, ²¹, ²⁹, Mk 13¹⁹, ²⁴, Jo 16²¹, Ac 7¹¹ 11¹⁹, Ro 12¹², ɪɪ Co 1⁴, ⁸ 4¹⁷ 6⁴ 7⁴ 8², ¹³, Phl 4¹⁴, ɪɪ Th 1⁶, Ja 1²⁷, Re 1⁹ 2⁹, ²² 7¹⁴; c. ἀνάγκη (q.v.), ɪ Th 3⁷; στενοχωρία (which from the order of the words would appear to be the stronger term), Ro 2⁹ 8³⁵; διωγμός, Mt 13²¹, Mk 4¹⁷, ɪɪ Th 1⁴; θ. ἔχω, Jo 16³³, ɪ Co 7²⁸, Re 2¹⁰; ἔρχεσθαι ἐπί, Ac 7¹¹; ἐν θλίψει, ɪ Th 1⁶; pl., Ac 7¹⁰ 14²² 20²³, Ro 5³, Eph 3¹³, ɪ Th 3³, He 10³³; τ. Χριστοῦ, Col 1²⁴; θ. τῆς καρδίας, ɪɪ Co 2⁴; θ. ἐγείρειν, Phl 1¹⁷.†

SYN. : ἀνάγκη, διωγμός, στενοχωρία (v. supr., and cf. Tr., *Syn*, § lv; Lft., *Notes*, 45).

θνήσκω, [in LXX chiefly for מוּת;] *to die;* pf. (M, *Pr*., 114), *to be dead* : Mt 2²⁰, Mk 15⁴⁴, Lk 7¹² 8⁴⁹, Jo 11⁴⁴ 19³³, Ac 14¹⁹ 25¹⁹; metaph., of spiritual death, ɪ Ti 5⁶ (cf. ἀπο-, συν-απο-θνήσκω).†

θνητός, -ή, -όν (< θνήσκω), [in LXX : Pr 3¹³ 20²⁴ (אָדָם), Jb 30²³ (חַי), Is 51¹² (מוּת), Wi 9¹⁴ 15¹⁷, ɪɪ Mac 9¹², ɪɪɪ Mac 3²⁹*;] *subject to death, mortal* : Ro 6¹² 8¹¹, ɪ Co 15⁵³, ⁵⁴ ɪɪ Co 4¹¹ 5⁴.†

†*θορυβάζω** (< θόρυβος), = τυρβάζω (q.v.), *to disturb, trouble* : pass., Lk 10⁴¹.†

θορυβέω, -ῶ (< θόρυβος), [in LXX : Na 2³ ⁽⁴⁾ (רָעַל ho.), Da LXX 8¹⁷ (בָּעַת ni.), Jg 3²⁶, Wi 18¹⁹, Si 40⁶*;] 1. *to make a noise* or *uproar* : mid., of loud and ostentatious lamentation, Mt 9²³, Mk 5³⁹, Ac 20¹⁰. 2. Trans., *to trouble, throw into confusion* : τ. πόλιν, Ac 17⁵.†

θόρυβος, -ου, ὁ, [in LXX for הָמוֹן, etc.;] *a noise, uproar, tumult*, as of an excited mob : Mt 26⁵ 27²⁴, Mk 14², Ac 20¹ 21³⁴ 24¹⁸; of mourners, = ὄχλος θορυβούμενος, Mk 5³⁸.†

θραύω, [in LXX for רָצַץ (De 28³³, Is 42⁴ 58⁶), etc.;] *to break in pieces, shatter;* metaph., *to break down* : Lk 4¹⁸ ⁽LXX⁾.†

*****θρέμμα, -τος, τό** (τρέφω); 1. *a nurseling*, esp. of animals (Eur., Plat., al.). 2. *cattle* : Jo 4¹².†

θρηνέω, -ῶ (< θρῆνος), [in LXX chiefly for יָלַל hi., also for קִין pil., etc.;] 1. intrans., *to lament, wail* : Mt 11¹⁷, Lk 7³², Jo 16²⁰. 2. Trans., *to bewail* : c. acc. pers., Lk 23²⁷.†

SYN. : κλαίω, κόπτομαι, λυπέομαι, πενθέω (v. Tr., *Syn*., § lxv).

θρῆνος, -ου, ὁ, [in LXX chiefly for קִינָה;] *a lamentation* : Mt 2¹⁸, Rec.†

†θρησκεία** (-κία, T), **-ας, ἡ** (< θρῆσκος), [in LXX : Wi 14¹⁸, ²⁷, Si 22⁵ A, ɪv Mac 5⁶, ¹³*;] *religion in its external aspect* (MM, *Exp*., xv), *worship* : Ac 26⁵, Ja 1²⁶, ²⁷; θ. τῶν ἀγγέλων, Col 2¹⁸.†

SYN. : v.s. θρῆσκος.

*****θρῆσκος** (-κός, WH), **-ου, ὁ**, *religious*, careful of the outward forms of divine service (see previous word)· : Ja 1²⁶.†

SYN. : εὐσεβής, θεοσεβής, δεισιδαίμων (v. Tr., *Syn*., § xlviii).

†*θριαμβεύω** (< θρίαμβος, 1. *a festal hymn to Bacchus*. 2. The Roman *triumphus*), 1. *to triumph* (and rarely, c. acc., *to triumph over ;* so perh. Col 2¹⁵, but v. infr.). 2. *to lead in triumph* : c. acc.

pers., II Co 2¹⁴; hence, generally, *to make a spectacle* or *show of:* Col 2¹⁵ (but v. supr.; cf. MM, *Exp.*, xv; and esp. Field, *Notes*, 181).†

θρίξ, τριχός, ἡ, [in LXX chiefly for שֵׂעָר;] *hair;* (*a*) of the head: Mt 3⁴ 5³⁶ 10³⁰, Lk 7³⁸, ⁴⁴ 12⁷ 21¹⁸, Jo 11² 12³, Ac 27³⁴, I Pe 3³, Re 1¹⁴; (*b*) of animals: Mk 1⁶, Re 9⁸.†

θροέω, -ῶ (< θρόος, *a noise, tumult*), [in LXX: Ca 5⁴ (הָמָה) *;*] in cl., 1. *to cry aloud, make an outcry.* 2. *to utter aloud.* 3. In NT (and LXX), pass., *to be troubled*, as by an alarm, *alarmed :* Mt 24⁶, Mk 13⁷, Lk 24³⁷ (WH, mg.), II Th 2² (cf. Kennedy, *Sources*, 126).†

*** θρόμβος, -ου, ὁ** (< τρέφω, in primary sense *to thicken*), *a lump, a clot* of blood (*DCG*, ii, 685ᵇ): αἵματος, Lk 22⁴⁴ (WH, R, mg. omit the passage, v. WH, *App.*, 64 ff.).†

θρόνος, -ου, ὁ [in LXX chiefly for כִּסֵּא, Ex 11⁵, al.;] in Hom., a *seat, chair.* Later, *a throne, chair* of state, *seat* of authority; of kings: metaph., of God, Mt 5³⁴, Ac 7⁴⁹ (LXX), Re 1⁴, al.; by meton., for *kingly power, sovereignty*, Lk 1³², ⁵², Ac 2³⁰; for an angelic hierarchy, Col 1¹⁶; of Christ, Mt 19²⁸, Re 3²¹, al.; of Satan, Re 2¹³; τ. θηρίου, ib. 16¹⁰; of the Apostles, Mt 19²⁸, Lk 22³⁰, cf. Re 20⁴; of πρεσβύτεροι, Re 4⁴ 11¹⁶ (on θ. τῆς χάριτος, He 4¹⁶, v. Westc., in l.; Deiss., *BS*, 135).

Θυάτειρα, -ων, τά (-ας, ἡ, Re 1¹¹ L; cf. WH, *App.*, 156), *Thyatira*, a city of Lydia: Ac 16¹⁴, Re 1¹¹ 2¹⁸, ²⁴.†

θυγάτηρ, -τρός, ἡ (for use of vocat., cf. M, *Pr.*, 71; WH, *App*, 158), [in LXX for בַּת (Ge 5⁴, al.), exc. Jg 21¹⁴ B, II Ch 21¹⁷ (אִשָּׁה);] *a daughter :* Mt 9¹⁸ 10³⁵, ³⁷ 14⁶ 15²², ²⁸, Mk 5³⁵ 6²² 7²⁶, ²⁹, Lk 2³⁶ 8⁴², ⁴⁹ 12⁵³, Ac 2¹⁷ (LXX) 7²¹ 21⁹, He 11²⁴. In NT, as in OT, not in cl.; (*a*) as a form of friendly address (cf. Ru 2², ²², al.): Mt 9²², Mk 5³⁴, Lk 8⁴⁸; (*b*) metaph.: sc. κυρίου, II Co 6¹⁸ (cf. Is 43⁶); (*c*) of posterity: θ. 'Ααρών, Lk 1⁵; 'Αβραάμ, ib. 13¹⁶ (cf. Is 16², IV Mac 15²⁸, al.); (*d*) of habitation: θ. Σιών, 'Ιερουσαλήμ, Mt 21⁵ (LXX), Lk 23²⁸, Jo 12¹⁵ (cf. Is 1⁸, Za 9⁹, al.).†

*** θυγάτριον, -ου, τό** (dimin. of θυγάτηρ), *a little daughter*, a term of endearment used in late Gk. (cf. Bl., § 27, 4): Mk 5²³ 7²⁵.†

θύελλα, -ης, ἡ (< θύω). [in LXX. De 4¹¹ 5²² (19) (עֲרָפֶל), Ex 10²² *;*] (poët. in cl.), *a hurricane, cyclone, whirlwind :* He 12¹⁸.†
SYN.: λαῖλαψ (q.v.).

**† θύϊνος (usually θύϊνος, as Rec.), -η, -ον (< θυΐα, θύα, an African aromatic tree, with ornamentally veined wood of varying colour, = Lat. *citrinus*), [in Sm.: III Ki 10¹¹ (אַלְמֻגִּים) *;*] *thyine :* ξύλον, Re 18¹² (Diosc.).†

θυμίαμα, -τος, τό (< θυμιάω), [in LXX chiefly for קְטֹרֶת;] *fragrant stuff* for burning, *incense :* ἡ ὥρα τοῦ θ., Lk 1¹⁰; θυσιαστήριον τοῦ θ. (Ex 30²⁷, al.), ib.¹¹; pl., Re 5⁸ 8³, ⁴ 18¹³.†

θυμιατήριον, -ου, τό (< θυμιάω), [in LXX: II Ch 26¹⁹, Ez 8¹¹

14

(מְקַטֶּרֶת), iv Mac 7¹¹ *;] 1. as in cl. (Hdt., iv, 162; Thuc., vi, 46) and LXX, *a censer:* He 9⁴ (but v. infr., and cf. Westc., in l.). 2. As in Philo., *rer. div.*, § 46, FlJ, *Ant.*, iv, 2, 4, al., *the altar of incense:* He, l.c. (but v. supr. and cf. MM, *Exp.*, xv).†

θυμιάω, -ῶ (< θύω), [in LXX (with -άζω) chiefly for קְטֹר pi., hi.;] *to burn incense:* Lk 1⁹.†

*† θυμομαχέω, -ῶ (θυμός, μάχομαι), *to fight desperately, have a hot quarrel:* c. dat. pers., Ac 12²⁰.†

θυμός, -οῦ, ὁ (< θύω), [in LXX most freq. for אַף, also for חֵמָה, חָרוֹן, etc., 30 words in all;] *passion, hot anger, wrath:* He 11²⁷; ὀργὴ καὶ θ., Ro 2⁸, cf. Col 3⁸; πικρία κ. θ., Eph 4³¹; πλησθῆναι, πλήρης θυμοῦ, Lk 4²⁸, Ac 19²⁸; θ. ἔχειν, Re 12¹²; οἶνος τ. θυμοῦ τ. πορνείας (cf. Je 28 (51)⁷), Re 14⁸ 18³ (cf. 17²); οἶνος τ. θ. τ θεοῦ, ib. 14¹⁰; id., τ. ὀργῆς τ. θεοῦ, ib. 16¹⁹ 19¹⁵; ὁ θ. τ. θεοῦ, ib. 14¹⁹ 15¹,⁷ 16¹; pl., *impulses* or *outbursts of anger:* ἔρις, ζῆλος, θυμοί, ἐριθίαι, II Co 12²⁰, Ga 5²⁰ (Cremer, 287, 733).†

SYN.: ὀργή, παροργισμός.

θυμόω, -ῶ (θυμός), [in LXX (chiefly in pass.) for חרה, אַף חרה, חָרָה אַף hith., etc.;] (no act. in Attic.); pass. (and mid.), *to be wroth* or *very angry:* Mt 2¹⁶.†

θύρα, -ας, ἡ, [in LXX chiefly for פֶּתַח, also for דַּל, דֶּלֶת, etc.;] *a door:* κλείειν (ἀποκ-) τὴν θ., Mt 6⁶, Lk 13²⁵; pass., Mt 25¹⁰, Lk 11⁷, Jo 20¹⁹,²⁶, Ac 21³⁰; ἀνοίγειν, Ac 5¹⁹; pass., Ac 16²⁶,²⁷; κρούειν, Ac 12¹³; διὰ τῆς θ., Jo 10¹,²; πρὸς τὴν θ., Mk 1³³ 11⁴ (WH om. τήν), Ac 3²; τὰ πρὸς τὴν θ., the space by the door, Mk 2²; πρὸς τῇ θ., Jo 18¹⁶; ἐπὶ τῇ θ, Ac 5⁹; πρὸ τῆς θ., Ac 12⁶; ἐπὶ τῶν θ., Ac 5²³; ἡ θ. τ. μνημείου, Mt 27⁶⁰, Mk 15⁴⁶ 16³. Metaph., of Christ, ἡ θ. τ. προβάτων, Jo 10⁷,⁹; of the Kingdom of Heaven, Lk 13²⁴; of opportunities, θ. πίστεως, Ac 14²⁷; θ. μεγάλη, I Co 16⁹; θ. τ. λόγου, Col 4³; θ. ἀνεῳγμένη (ἠνεῳγ-), II Co 2¹², Re 3⁸ 4¹; of Christ, ἑστηκὼς ἐπὶ τὴν θ. καὶ κρούων, Re 3²⁰; of his second coming, ἐπὶ θύραις εἶναι, Mt 24³³, Mk 13²⁹; πρὸ θυρῶν ἑστηκέναι, Ja 5⁹.†

θυρεός, -οῦ, ὁ (< θύρα), [in LXX for מָגֵן, צִנָּה;] 1. in Hom., *a door-stone.* 2. In late Gk. (Polyb., Plut.), the *scutum,* a large oblong *shield:* θ. τ. πίστεως, Eph 6¹⁶ (cf. Wi 5²⁰, where ὁσιότης is likened to the ἀσπίς, the *clypeus* or small round shield of the light-armed soldier).†

θυρίς, -ίδος, ἡ (dim. of θύρα), [in LXX chiefly for חַלּוֹן;] *a window:* Ac 20⁹, II Co 11³³.†

θυρωρός, -οῦ, ὁ, ἡ (< θύρα, + οὖρος, *a guardian*), [in LXX: iv Ki 7¹¹ (שׁוֹעֵר), Ez 44¹¹ (פְּקֻדָּה), II Ki 4⁶, I Es₇ *;] *a door-keeper, porter:* ὁ, Mk 13³⁴, Jo 10³; ἡ, Jo 18¹⁶,¹⁷.†

θυσία, -ας, ἡ (θύω), [in LXX chiefly for מִנְחָה, זֶבַח;] 1. actively, *an offering, sacrifice* (Hdt., al.). 2. Objectively, that which is offered, *a sacrifice*: Mt 9¹³ 12⁷ ⁽ᴸˣˣ⁾, Mk 9⁴⁹ (WH, mg.), Eph 5², He 10⁵, ²⁶; pl. (as usually in cl.), Mk 12³³, Lk 13¹, He 9²³ 10¹, ⁸ (θ. καὶ προσφοράς); θ. ἀνάγειν, Ac 7⁴¹; ἀναφέρειν, He 7²⁷; προσφέρειν, Ac 7⁴²; He 5¹ 8³ (δῶρά τε καὶ θ.) 10¹¹, ¹² 11⁴; δοῦναι, Lk 2²⁴; pass., He 9⁹; διὰ τῆς θ. αὐτοῦ, He 9²⁶; ἐσθίειν τὰς θ. (Le 7¹⁵ ᵃ.), ɪ Co 10¹⁸. Metaph., Phl 4¹⁸, He 13¹⁶; θ. πνευματικαί, ɪ Pe 2⁵; θ. ζῶσα, Ro 12¹; θ. αἰνέσεως, He 13¹⁵; θ. . . . τ. πίστεως, Phl 2¹⁷.†

† θυσιαστήριον, -ου, τό (< θυσιάζω, to sacrifice), [in LXX (where the word first appears) very freq., nearly always for מִזְבֵּחַ;] *an altar*: (*a*) generally, Ja 2²¹; pl., Ro 11³ ⁽ᴸˣˣ⁾; metaph., He 13¹⁰ (v. Westc., in l., and esp. his add. note on the history of the word, 455 ff.); (*b*) of the altar of burnt-offering in the Temple, Mt 5²³, ²⁴ 23¹⁸⁻²⁰, ³⁵, Lk 11⁵¹, ɪ Co 9¹³ 10¹⁸, He 7¹³, Re 11¹; (*c*) of the altar of incense in the sanctuary (Ex 30¹, al.), Lk 1¹¹; symbolically in Heaven, Re 6⁹ 8³, ⁵ 9¹³ 14¹⁸ 16⁷ (Cremer, 292).†

θύω, [in LXX chiefly for זבח, also for שחט, etc.;] as in cl.; 1. *to offer* first fruits to a god. 2. *to sacrifice* by slaying a victim, *offer sacrifice*: Ac 14¹³; c. dat. pers., ib.¹⁸; id. c. acc. rei, ɪ Co 10²⁰. 3. *to slay, kill*: Jo 10¹⁰, Ac 10¹³ 11⁷; c. acc. rei, Lk 15²³, ²⁷, ³⁰; pass., Mt 22⁴; τὸ πάσχα (Ex 12²¹), Mk 14¹²; pass., Lk 22⁷, ɪ Co 5⁷.†

Θωμᾶς, -ᾶ, ὁ (Heb. תְּאוֹם, *a twin;* cf. δίδυμος), *Thomas* the Apostle: Mt 10³, Mk 3¹⁸, Lk 6¹⁵, Jo 11¹⁶ 14⁵ 20²⁴⁻²⁸ 21², Ac 1¹³.†

θώραξ, -ακος, ὁ, [in LXX chiefly for שִׁרְיוֹן and cogn. forms;] *a breastplate*: Re 9⁹, ¹⁷; θ. τ. δικαιοσύνης, Eph 6¹⁴ (cf. Is 59¹⁷, Wi 5¹⁸ ⁽¹⁹⁾); θ. πίστεως, ɪ Th 5⁸.†

I

Ι, ι, ἰῶτα, τό, indecl., *iota*, the ninth letter. As a numeral, ι′ = 10, ι, = 10,000.

Ἰάειρος, -ου, ὁ (Heb. יָאִיר, Nu 32⁴¹), *Jairus*: Mk 5²², Lk 8⁴¹.†

Ἰακώβ, ὁ, indecl. (Heb. יַעֲקֹב), *Jacob;* 1. The patriarch: Mt 1² 8¹¹, Jo 4⁵, ⁶, Ac 7⁸, al.; as in Heb. (cf. Nu 23⁷, Is 41⁸, Si 23¹², al.), of his descendants, Ro 11²⁶ ⁽ᴸˣˣ⁾. 2. The father-in-law of Mary: Mt 1¹⁵, ¹⁶ (on the form as distinct from that of the next word, v. Deiss., *BS*, 316₁).

Ἰάκωβος, -ου, ὁ (Heb., v. previous word), *James;* 1. Son of Zebedee: Mt 4²¹, Mk 1¹⁹, ²⁹, Ac 1¹³ 12², al. 2. Son of Alphæus: Mt 10³, Mk 2¹⁴, al.; commonly identified with Ἰ. ὁ μικρός, *James the little*, son of Mary (v.s. Μαρία, 3; Κλωπᾶς), Mt 27⁵⁶, Mk 15⁴⁰ 16¹ (cf. Jo 19·⁵). 3. The Lord's brother (v.s. ἀδελφός): Mt 13⁵⁵ Mk 6³, Ac 12¹⁷, al., ɪ Co 15⁷ (probably), Ga 1¹⁹ 2⁹, ¹², Ja 1¹, Ju¹. 4. The father of the apostle, Ἰούδας Ἰακώβου: Lk 6¹⁶, Ac 1¹³.

ἴαμα, -τος, τό (< ἰάομαι), [in LXX for מַרְפֵּא (ɪɪ Ch 36¹⁶, Ec 10⁴,

Je 40 (33)⁶), etc.;] 1. most freq. in cl., *a means of healing, remedy* (Thuc., al.; Wi 11⁴ 10⁹). 2. = ἴασις (q.v.), *a healing* (Plat.; Je, l.c.): pl., ι Co 12⁹, ²⁸, ³⁰.†

Ἰαμβρῆς, ὁ, *Jambres* (cf. Ex 7¹¹, ¹²): ιι Ti 3⁸.†

Ἰανναί, (Rec. -νά), ὁ, *Jannai :* Lk 3²⁴.†

Ἰαννῆς, ὁ, *Jannes* (cf. Ἰαμβρῆς): ιι Ti 3⁸.†

ἰάομαι, -ῶμαι, [in LXX for רפא (Ge 20¹⁷, al.), exc. Is 30²⁶ 61¹ (חבּשׁ);] *to heal :* c. acc. pers., Lk 5¹⁷ 6¹⁹ 9², ¹¹, ⁴² 14⁴ 22⁵¹, Jo 4⁴⁷, Ac 9³⁴ 10³⁸ 28⁸; pass., Mt 8⁸, ¹³ 15²⁸, Lk 7⁷ 8⁴⁷ 17¹⁵, Jo 5¹³; id. seq. ἀπό, Mk 5²⁹, Lk 6¹⁷; fig., of spiritual healing, Mt 13¹⁵, Jo 12⁴⁰, Ac 28²⁷ (LXX); pass., He 12¹³, Ja 5¹⁶, ι Pe 2²⁴.†

SYN.: θεραπεύω, q.v.

Ἰάρετ (Rec. -ρέδ, L, Ἰάρεθ), ὁ (Heb. יֶרֶד, LXX Ἰάρεδ, FlJ, Ἰάρεδος), *Jared* (Ge 5¹⁵): Lk 3³⁷.†

ἴασις, -εως, ἡ (< ἰάομαι), [in LXX chiefly for מַרְפֵּא;] *a healing, cure :* Ac 4²², ³⁰; pl., Lk 13³².†

SYN.: v.s. θεραπεία, 2; ἴαμα, 2.

ἴασπις, -ιδος, ἡ (a Phœnician word; v. MM, *VGT*, s.v., Boisacq., p. 364), [in LXX: Ex 28¹⁸ 36¹⁸ (39¹¹) (יַהֲלֹם), Is 54¹² (כַּדְכֹד), Ez 28¹³ (יָשְׁפֵה, v. BDB, *Lex.*, s.v.) *;] jasper,* apparently not the modern stone of that name, but a translucent stone (*DB,* s.v.) : Re 4³ 21¹¹, ¹⁸, ¹⁹.†

Ἰάσων, -ονος, ὁ, *Jason :* Ac 17⁵⁻⁷, ⁹; perhaps the same, Ro 16²¹.†

ἰατρός, -οῦ, ὁ (< ἰάομαι), [in LXX for רֹפֵא;] *a physician :* Mt 9¹², Mk 2¹⁷ 5²⁶, Lk 4²³ 5³¹, 8⁴³ (om. WH, R, mg.), Col 4¹⁴ (on the status of physicians, v. MM, *Exp.,* xv.).†

ἴδε (Attic ἰδέ; the "later" accentuation is also found in Hom.; Veitch, 215), 1. prop., 2 aor. imperat. of ὁράω, q.v. 2. As interjection, apart from the construction of the sentence, and used where one or many are addressed, *see! behold! lo! :* Mt 25²⁰, ²², ²⁵, Mk 2²⁴ 3³⁴ 11²¹ 13¹, ²¹ 15⁴, ³⁵ 16⁶, Jo 1²⁹, ³⁶, ⁴⁸ 3²⁶ 5¹⁴ 7²⁶ 11³, ³⁶ 12¹⁹ 16²⁹ 18²¹ 19⁴, ¹⁴, ²⁶, ²⁷, Ga 5².†

ἰδέα, -ας, ἡ, v.s. εἰδέα.

ἴδιος, -α, -ον (in Attic usually -ος, -ον), [in LXX chiefly for pers. suff., also for לָהֶם, etc.; (τὰ ἴ.) (בֵּיתוֹ;] 1. *one's own ;* (*a*) of that which is private and personal (in cl. opp. to κοινός, δημόσιος; cf. infr. 3); (*b*) of property, friends, home, country, etc. (in cl. opp. to ἀλλότριος; in late writers often, like ἑαυτοῦ, with weakened sense, v. M, *Pr.,* 87 ff.; Deiss., *BS,* 123 f.) : Lk 6⁴¹, Jo 1⁴² 5⁴³, Ac 2⁶ 20²⁸, ι Co 11²¹, Ga 6⁵, ιι Ti 1⁹, He 7²⁷, Ju ⁶, al.; πράσσειν τὰ ἴ., ι Th 4¹¹; κατὰ τὰς ἰ. ἐπιθυμίας, ιι Ti 4³; οἱ ἴδιοι, Jo 1¹¹ (M, *Pr.,* 90 f.; Fiel I, *Notes,* 84) 13¹, Ac 4²³, ι Ti 5⁸; τὰ ἴδια, one's *home* (Field, *Notes,* l.c.), Lk 18²⁸, Jo 1¹¹ 16³² 19²⁷. 2. *peculiar, distinct, appropriate, proper :* τὸ ἴ. σῶμα, ι Co 15³⁸; ἐν τ. ἰ. τάγματι, ι Co 15²³; εἰς τ. τόπον τ. ἴ., Ac 1²⁵; = αὐτοῦ (v. Deiss., ut. supr.), Mt 22⁵, Jo 1⁴² (cf. Wi 10¹). 3. Adverbially (v. supr., 1 (*a*);

and cf. WM, 739₂); (a) ἰδίᾳ, severally, separately : I Co 12¹¹ ; (b) κατ' ἰδίαν, apart, privately, in private : Mt 14¹³,²³ 20¹⁷, Mk 4³⁴ 7³³, Lk 10²³, Ac 23¹⁹, al.

ἰδιώτης, -ου, ὁ (< ἴδιος), [in LXX : Pr 6⁸ (no Heb.) *;] 1. a private person, as opp. to the State or an official (βασιλεῖς κ. ἰδιῶται, Pr, l.c.; and cf. MM, Exp., xv). 2. one without professional knowledge, unskilled, uneducated, unlearned : I Co 14¹⁶,²³,²⁴ (R, mg., without gifts) ; ἀγράμματοι κ. ἰ., Ac 4¹³ ; c. dat. (= cl. c. gen. rei), λόγῳ, II Co 11⁶.†

ἰδού, [in LXX chiefly for הִנֵּה,] prop. imperat. 2 aor. mid. of ὁράω, used as a demonstrative particle, with frequency much greater in LXX and NT than in cl. (v. M, Pr., 11), lo, behold, see : Mt 10¹⁶ 11⁸ 13³, Mk 3³², Lk 2⁴⁸, I Co 15⁵¹, Ja 5⁹, Ju¹⁴, Re 1⁷, al.; after gen. absol., Mt 1²⁰ 2¹,¹³ 12⁴⁶, al.; καὶ ἰδού, Mt 2⁹ (and freq.), Lk 1²⁰ 10²⁵, Ac 12⁷, al.; in elliptical sentences, taking the place of copula or predicate (like הִנֵּה in Heb.), Mt 3¹⁷, Lk 5¹² 22³¹,⁴⁷, Ac 8²⁷,³⁶, al.

'Ιδουμαία, -ας, ἡ (Heb. אֱדוֹם), [in LXX : II Ki 8¹⁴, al.; elsewhere, as Ge 25³⁰, 'Εδώμ ;] Idumæa : Mk 3⁸.†

ἰδρώς (Tr. -ῶς), -ῶτος, ὁ, [in LXX : Ge 3¹⁹ (זֵעָה), II Mac 2²⁶, IV Mac 7⁸ *;] sweat : Lk 22⁴⁴ (WH, omit).†

'Ιεζάβελ (L, 'Ιεζ-; Tr. -βέλ; Rec. -βήλ) ἡ, indecl. (Heb. אִיזֶבֶל; LXX as txt.; FlJ, 'Ιεζαβέλη), Jezebel (III Ki 16³¹, al.) : symbolically, Re 2²⁰ (v. Swete, in l.).†

'Ιεράπολις (WH, 'Ιερὰ Πόλις), -εως, ἡ, Hierapolis : a city in the Lycus valley in the Province of Asia : Col 4¹³.†

ἱερατεία (WH, -ία), -ας, ἡ (< ἱερατεύω), [in LXX for כֹּהֵן pi., כְּהֻנָּה (Ex 29⁹, al.), exc. Ho 3⁴ (אֵפוֹד);] priesthood, office of priest : Lk 1⁹, He 7⁵.†

†ἱεράτευμα, -τος, τό (< ἱερατεύω), [in LXX : βασίλειον ἱ., Ex 19⁶ (מַמְלֶכֶת כֹּהֲנִים) 23²², II Mac 2¹⁷ *;] a priesthood, body of priests : ἱ. ἅγιον, I Pe 2⁵ ; βασ. ἱ., ib. ⁹ (LXX, Ex, l.c.).†

ἱερατεύω (cl. = ἱεράομαι), [in LXX chiefly for כֹּהֵן pi.;] to be a priest, officiate as a priest : Lk 1⁸ (the word is freq. in Inscr.; v. LS, s.v.; Deiss., BS, 215; LAE, 70; Cremer, 734).†

'Ιερειχώ (T, 'Ιερ-; Rec. 'Ιεριχώ; cf. Bl., § 3, 4, 4; WH, App., 155), ἡ, indecl. (Heb. יְרִיחוֹ, יְרֵחוֹ), Jericho : Mt 20²⁹, Mk 10⁴⁶, Lk 10³⁰ 18³⁵ 19¹, He 11³⁰.†

'Ιερεμίας (T, Rec. 'Ιερ-; v. WH, § 408), -ου, ὁ (Heb. יִרְמְיָה, יִרְמְיָהוּ), Jeremiah the prophet : Mt 2¹⁷ 16¹⁴ 27⁹ (a ref. to Za 11¹³).†

ἱερεύς, -έως, ὁ (< ἱερός), [in LXX for כֹּהֵן;] a priest : ἱ. τ. Διός, Ac 14¹³; of Jewish priests, Mt 8⁴ 12⁴,⁵, Mk 1⁴⁴ 2²⁶, Lk 1⁵ 5¹⁴, Jo 1¹⁹,

He 8⁴, al.; of Christ, He 5⁶ ⁽ᴸˣˣ⁾ 10²¹; of Christians, Re 1⁶ 5¹⁰ 20⁶ (Cremer, 293; on the acc. pl., ἱερεῖς, v. Thack., *Gr.*, 147 f.; Bl., § 8, 2).

ἱεριχώ, v.s. Ἱερειχώ.

*** ἱερόθυτος,** -ον (< ἱερός, θύω), *offered in sacrifice:* ι Co 10²⁸ (Rec. εἰδωλοθ-).†

ἱερόν, -οῦ, τό, v.s. ἱερός.

**** ἱεροπρεπής,** -ές (< ἱερός, πρέπει), [in LXX: ιv Mac 9²⁵ 11²⁰ *;] *suited to a sacred character, reverend* (RV, *reverent*): Tit 2³ (cf. Tr., *Syn.*, § xcii).†

ἱερός, -ά, όν, [in LXX: Ez 28¹⁸ (שֶׁקְדָּשׁ); τὸ ἱ., ι Ch 29⁴ (בַּיִת), Ez 45¹⁹ (עֲזָרָה); very freq. in ι Es, ι-ιv Mac;] 1. in Hom., *marvellous, mighty, divine.* 2. (Also in Hom. and later cl.) *consecrated to the deity, sacred:* pl., ἱ. γράμματα, ιι Ti 3¹⁵. 3. As subst., (*a*) (so in Hom.), τὰ ἱ., *sacrifices, sacred rites, sacred things:* ι Co 9¹³; (*b*) later, τὸ ἱ., *a consecrated* or *sacred place, a temple:* τ. Ἀρτέμιδος, Ac 19²⁷; of the temple at Jerusalem, i.e. the entire precincts or some part thereof (as distinct from ὁ ναός, q.v., the *Sanctuary* proper): ι Co 9¹³, and freq. in Gosp. and esp. in Ac, Mt 12⁶, Mk 13³, Ac 4¹, al. (on the use of ἱ. in Imperial Inscr., v. Deiss., *LAE*, 380 f.).

Ἱεροσόλυμα (WH, Ἱερ-, v. *Intr.*, § 408), -ων, τά (on πᾶσα Ἱ., Mt 2³, v. WM, 79₄; M, *Pr.*, 48, 244; Thayer, s.v.), and **Ἱερουσαλήμ** (WH, Ἱερ-), ἡ., indecl., as always in LXX exc. some parts of Apocr. (Heb. יְרוּשָׁלֵם, יְרוּשָׁלַיִם), the former always in FlJ, Mk, Jo ᵉᵛ· and Mt (exc. 27³⁷), and most freq. in Lk, the latter always in He, Re, and by St. Paul (exc. Ga 1¹⁷, ¹⁸ 2¹), *Jerusalem:* Mt 2¹, Mk 3⁸, Jo 1¹⁹, al.; its inhabitants, Mt 2³ 3⁵ 23³⁷, Lk 13³⁴. Symbolically, ἡ ἄνω Ἱ., Ga 4²⁶, contrasted with ἡ νῦν Ἱ., ib.²⁵; Ἱ. ἐπουράνιος, He 12²²; ἡ καινὴ Ἱ., Re 3¹² 21², ¹⁰.

Ἱεροσολυμείτης (WH, Ἱερ-; Rec. -μίτης), -ου, ὁ, [in LXX: Si 50²⁷ ⁽²⁹⁾, ιι Mac 4²², ³⁹ (V* -μήτης) 18⁵ *;] *an inhabitant of Jerusalem:* Mk 1⁵, Jo 7²⁵.†

**** ἱερο-συλέω,** -ῶ (< ἱερόσυλος, q.v.), [in LXX: ιι Mac 9² *;] *to rob a temple* (*commit sacrilege*, R, mg.): Ro 2²².†

**** ἱερόσυλος,** -ον (< ἱερόν, συλάω), [in LXX: ιι Mac 4⁴² (cf. -λημα, ib.³⁹; -λία, 13⁶) *;] *robbing temples:* Ac 19³⁷.†

**** ἱερουργέω,** -ῶ (< ἱερουργός, *a sacrificing priest*), [in LXX: ιv Mac 7⁸ R (cf. -γία, ib. 3³⁰ אR) *;] *to perform sacred rites;* c. acc., *to minister in priestly service* (*minister in sacrifice*, R, mg.), τὸ εὐαγγέλιον, Ro 15¹⁶.†

Ἱερουσαλήμ, v.s. Ἱεροσόλυμα.

ἱερωσύνη, -ης, ἡ (< ἱερός), [in LXX: ι Ch 29²² (כֹּהֵן), ι Es 5³⁸, Si 45²⁴, ι Mac 2⁵⁴ 3⁴⁹ 7⁹, ²¹, ιv Mac 5³⁵ 7⁶ *;] *priesthood:* He 7¹¹, ¹², ²⁴.†

Ἱεσσαί (FlJ, -σσαῖος), ὁ (Heb. יִשַׁי, Ru 4¹⁷, al.), *Jesse:* Mt 1⁵, ⁶, Lk 3³², Ac 13²² ⁽ᴸˣˣ⁾, Ro 15¹² ⁽ᴸˣˣ⁾.†

Ἰεφθάε (FlJ, -θάς, -οῦ), ὁ (Heb. יִפְתָּח), *Jephthah* : He 11³².†

Ἰεχονίας, -ου, ὁ (Heb. יְהוֹיָכִין, *Jehoiakin*), *Jechoniah* : Mt 1¹¹, ¹².†

Ἰησοῦς, -οῦ, dat., voc. -οῦ, acc., -οῦν (Heb. יְהוֹשׁוּעַ, יְהוֹשֻׁעַ, יֵשׁוּעַ), 1. Jesus: Mt 1²¹, al.; ὁ Ἰ., ib. 3¹³, al.; Ἰ. Χριστός, ib. 1¹, Mk 1¹, al.; Χρ. Ἰ., Ro 2²⁶, al.; κύριος Ἰ., Ac 28³¹, al.; Ἰησοῦ, voc., Mk 1²⁴, al. 2. *Joshua* : Ac 7⁴⁵, He 4⁸. 3. *Jesus*, son of Eliezer: Lk 3²⁹. 4. *Jesus*, surnamed *Justus* : Col 4¹¹. 5. v.s. Βαραββᾶς.

ἱκανός, -ή, -όν (< ἵκω, ἱκάνω, to reach, attain), [in LXX for דַּי, etc.;] 1. of persons, *sufficient, competent, fit* : c. inf., Mt 3¹¹, Mk 1⁷, Lk 3¹⁶, 1 Co 15⁹, 11 Co 3⁵, 11 Ti 2² ; seq. πρός, 11 Co 2¹⁶ ; seq. ἵνα, Mt 8⁸, Lk 7⁶. 2. Of things, in number, quantity or size, *sufficient, enough, much, many* : absol., ἱκανοί, Lk 7¹¹ (WH, R, omit) 8³², Ac 12¹² 14²¹ 19¹⁹, 1 Co 11³⁰ ; ὄχλος ἱ., Mk 10⁴⁶, Lk 7¹², Ac 11²⁴, ²⁶ 19²⁶ ; κλαυθμός, Ac 20³⁷ ; ἀργύρια, Mt 28¹² ; λαμπάδες, Ac 20⁸ ; λόγοι, Lk 23⁹ ; φῶς, Ac 22⁶ ; ἱ. ἐστιν (cf. רַב לָכֶם, LXX ἱκανούσθω, De 3²⁶), Lk 22³⁸ ; τὸ ἱ. ποιεῖν (Lat. *satisfacere* ; cf. Je 31 (48)³⁰), Mk 15¹⁵ ; τὸ ἱ. λαμβάνειν (Lat. *satis accipere* ; v. M, *Pr.*, 20 f.), Ac 17⁹ ; of time, ἡμέραι ἱ., Ac 9²³, ⁴³ 18¹⁸ 27⁷ ; ἱ. χρόνος, Lk 8²⁷, Ac 8¹¹ 14³ 27⁹ ; pl., Lk 20⁹ ; ἐκ χρόνων ἱ., Lk 23⁸ ; ἀπὸ ἱ. ἐτῶν, Ro 15²³ (WH) ; ἐφ' ἱκανόν (cf. 11 Mac 8²⁵), Ac 20¹¹.†

*ἱκανότης, -ητος, ἡ (< ἱκανός), *sufficiency, ability* (Plat.): 11 Co 3⁵.†

†ἱκανόω, -ῶ (< ἱκανός), [in LXX chiefly for רַב;] to *make sufficient, render fit* : c. dupl. acc., 11 Co 3⁶ ; c. acc. pers. seq. εἰς, Col 1¹².†

ἱκετήριος, -α, -ον (< ἱκέτης, a *suppliant*), [in LXX : Jb 40²² ⁽²⁷⁾, 11 Mac 9¹⁸ * ;] of a *suppliant* ; as subst., ἡ ἱ. (sc. ῥάβδος), 1. in cl., an *olive-branch*, carried by a suppliant. 2. In late Gk. = ἱκεσία, *supplication* : pl., δεήσεις κ. ἱ., He 5⁷.†

SYN. : v.s. δέησις.

ἱκμάς, -άδος, ἡ, [in LXX. Je 17⁸ (יוּבַל), Jb 26¹⁴ (שֶׁמֶץ) * ;] *moisture* : Lk 8⁶.†

Ἰκόνιον, -ου, τό, *Iconium*, a city of the province of Galatia : Ac 13⁵¹ 14¹, ¹⁹, ²¹ 16², 11 Ti 3¹¹.†

ἱλαρός, -ά, -όν (< ἵλαος = ἵλεως, q.v.), [in LXX : Pr 19¹² (רָצוֹן) 22⁸, Es 5¹, Jb 33²⁶, Si 13²⁶ 26⁴, 111 Mac 6³⁵ * ;] *cheerful, joyous* : 11 Co 9⁷ (Pr 22⁸ ⁽⁹⁾ ⁽LXX⁾).†

†ἱλαρότης, -ητος, ἡ (< ἱλαρός), [in LXX : Pr 18²² (רָצוֹן) * ;] *cheerfulness* : Ro 12⁸.†

ἱλάσκομαι (< ἵλαος = ἵλεως), [in LXX (cf. Westc., *Epp. Jo.*, 85 f.) for סלח, ιν Ki 5¹⁸ 24⁴, Ps 24 (25)¹¹, La 3¹², Da ΤΗ 9¹⁹; כפר pi., Ps 64 (65)³ 77 (78)³⁸ 78 (79)⁹ ; נחם ni., Ex 32¹⁴, Es 4¹⁷ * ;] 1. in cl., c. acc. pers., to *conciliate, appease, propitiate* (= ἐξιλάσκομαι, Ge 32²⁰, Pr 16¹⁴, Ma 1⁹, al.). 2. In LXX (Thackeray, *Gr.*, 270 f.), Inscr. (Deiss., *BS*,

224 f.), and NT, *to be propitious, merciful* (c. dat. rei, Ps 78 (79)[9], al.) : c. dat pers. (iv Ki 5[18]), Lk 18[13]. 3. As in Philo (= ἐξιλάσκ-, in LXX : Ez 43[22], al.), *to expiate, make propitiation for :* τ. ἁμαρτίας, He 2[17] (Cremer, 301 ff., 735).†

† **ἱλασμός**, -οῦ (< ἱλάσκομαι), [in LXX : Le 25[9], Nu 5[8] (כִּפֻּרִים), Ps 129 (130)[4], Da TH 9[9] (סְלִיחָה), Am 8[14] (אַשְׁמָה), Ez 44[27] (חַטָּאת), ι Ch 28[20], Si 18[20] A, ιι Mac 3[33] * ;] 1. *an appeasing* (Plut.). 2. *a means of appeasing, propitiation* (Philo ; Nu, Ez, ll.c.) : ι Jo 2[2] 4[10]. 3. In LXX also *forgiveness* (Ps, Da TH, ll.c.).†

† **ἱλαστήριος**, -α, -ον (< ἱλάσκομαι), [in LXX : iv Mac 17[22]; neut., Ex 25[16 (17) ff.] 31[7] 35[12] 38[5] (37[6]) ff., Le 16[2, 13 ff.], Nu 7[89] (כַּפֹּרֶת), Ez 43[14, 17, 20] (עֲזָרָה), Am 9[1] (on the original here, v. Deiss., *BS*, 127) * ;] *propitiatory* (μνῆμα, FlJ, *Ant.*, xvi, 7, 1 ; θάνατις, ιι Mac, l.c.) : of Christ, Ro 3[25] ; as subst., τὸ ἱ. (sc. ἐπίθεμα, Ex 25[16, 17], where the word first occurs in LXX and where ἱ. ἐ. = כַּפֹּרֶת (q.v. in BDB, s.v.), elsewhere rendered simply τὸ ἱ.; cf. Deiss., 124 ff.; Westc., *He.*, in l.), He 9[5].†

ἵλεως, -ων (Att. for ἵλαος), [in LXX for חָלִיל, ι Ki 14[45], ιι Ki 20[20], al.; ἱ. εἶναι, סלח, ιιι Ki 8[30 ff.], Je 38 (31)[34], al.;] *propitious, merciful:* τ. ἀδικίαις, He 8[12] (Je, l.c.; cf. ιιι Ki, l.c.); ἱ. σοι (sc. ἔστω ὁ θεός), Mt 16[22] (cf. ι Ki, l.c.).†

Ἰλλυρικόν, -οῦ, τό, *Illyricum*, a region bordering on the Adriatic Sea : Ro 15[19].†

ἱμάς, -άντος, ὁ, [in LXX : Is 5[27] (שְׂרוֹךְ), Si 30[35] (33[26]), iv Mac 9[11], al;] *a thong, strap :* for binding prisoners (Ma, Si, ll. c.), Ac 22[25] ; for fastening sandals, Mk 1[7], Lk 3[16], Jo 1[27].†

*† **ἱματίζω** (< ἱμάτιον), *to clothe :* Mk 5[15], Lk 8[35] (elsewhere only in π.; cf. MM, *Exp.*, xv; Deiss., *LAE*, 78 f.).†

ἱμάτιον, -ου, τό (dim. of εἷμα, *a garment*), [in LXX chiefly for בֶּגֶד, also for שִׂמְלָה, שַׂלְמָה, etc.;] *a garment*, but in usage always (exc. in pl., v. infr.) of an outer garment, *a mantle, cloak* (thrown over the χιτών; v. Rutherford, *NPhr.*, 22 ; *DCG*, i, 499[a]) : Mt 9[16, 20, 21], Mk 2[21] 5[27, 28, 30], Jo 19[2], Ac 12[8], al.; opp. to χιτών, Mt 5[40], Lk 6[29], Ac 9[39]; pl., *garments, clothes* (i.e. the cloak and the tunic), Mt 17[2] 26[65] 27[31, 35], Mk 5[30] 15[20, 24], Jo 19[23, 24], Ja 5[2], al.

† **ἱματισμός**, -οῦ (< ἱματίζω), [in LXX : Ge 24[53], ιι Ch 18[29], Ez 16[18], al. (בֶּגֶד) ; Ex 3[22] 12[35], Ru 3[3], al. (שִׂמְלָה), etc.;] *clothing, apparel* (usually of sumptuous attire; v. Tr., *Syn.*, § 1) : Lk 7[25] 9[29], Jo 19[24] (Ps 21[18] (22[19]), LXX for לְבוּשׁ), Ac 20[33], ι Ti 2[9].†

ἱμείρω, [in LXX : Jb 3[21] B[3]R (ABא, ὁμ-) ;] ι Th 2[8 (Rec.)], v.s. ὁμείρομαι.

ἵνα, I. adverb (poët., Hom., al.), 1. of place, *where, whither*. 2. of circumstance, *when*. II. Conjunction, 1. prop., final, denoting purpose or end (cl.), *that, in order that*, usually the first word in the clause, but sometimes (cl. also) preceded by an emphatic word (Ac 19⁴, Ro 11³¹ (?), Ga 2¹⁰, al.); (*a*) c. optat. (so in cl. after historic tenses): after a pres., Eph 1¹⁷ (but WH, mg., subjc.; v. Burton, § 225, Rem., 2); (*b*) c. subjc.: after a pres., Mk 4²¹, Lk 6³⁴, Jo 3¹⁵, Ac 2²⁵, Ro 1¹¹, al.; after a pf., Mt 1²², Jo 5²³, ι Co 9²², al.; after an imperat. (pres. or aor.), Mt 7¹, Mk 11²⁵, Jo 10³⁸, ι Co 7⁵, al.; after a delib. subjc., Mk 1³⁸, al.; after a fut., Lk 16⁴, Jo 14³, ι Co 15²⁸, al.; after historic tenses (where optat. in cl.; WM, 359 f.; M, *Pr.*, 196 f.), Mk 6⁴¹ (impf.), Jo 4⁸ (plpf.), Mk 3¹⁴ (aor.), al.; (*c*) in late writers (M, *Pr.*, 35; Burton, §§ 198, 199), c. indic. fut: Lk 20¹⁰, ι Pe 3¹, al.; (*d*) as often in eccl. writers (Thayer, s.v.), c. indic. pres.: ι Co 4⁶, Ga 4¹⁷, al. (?; but v. Burton, § 198, Rem.); (*e*) εἰς (διὰ) τοῦτο, ἵνα: Jo 18³⁷, ι Ti 1¹⁶, al.; τούτου χάριν, Tit 1⁵; (*f*) elliptical constructions: omission of the principal verb, Jo 1⁸, ιι Th 3⁹, ι Jo 2¹⁹, al.; of the final verb, Ro 4¹⁶, ιι Co 8¹³, al.   2. In late writers, definitive, = inf. (WM, 420; Bl., § 69, 1), *that;* (*a*) after verbs of wishing, caring, striving, etc.: θέλω, Mt 7¹², al.; ζητῶ, ι Co 4² 14¹²; ζηλόω, ι Co 14¹, al.; (*b*) after verbs of saying, asking, exhorting: εἰπεῖν, Mt 4³, al.; ἐρωτῶ, Mk 7²⁶, al.; παρακαλῶ, Mt 14³⁶, ι Co 1¹⁰, al., etc.; (*c*) after words expressing expediency, etc.: συμφέρει, Mt 18⁶, Jo 11⁵⁰, al.; ἱκανός, Mt 8⁸, Lk 7⁶; χρείαν ἔχω, Jo 2²⁵, al, etc.; (*d*) after substantives, adding further definition: ὥρα, Jo 12²³ 13¹; χρόνος, Re 2²¹; συνήθεια, Jo 18³⁹; μισθός, ι Co 9¹⁸.   3. In late writers, ecbatic, denoting the result, = ὥστε, *that,* *so that* (M, *Pr.*, 206 ff.; WM, 572; Bl., § 69, 3; Burton, § 223): Ro 11¹¹, ι Co 7²⁹, ι Th 5⁴, al. (but v. Thayer, s.v.); so with the formula referring to the fulfilment of prophecy, ἵνα πληρωθῇ, Mt 1²² 2¹⁴ 4¹⁴, Jo 13¹⁸, al. But on the telic force of the word in these passages v. M'Neile on Mt 1²², M, *Gr.*, ιι, 469 f.   On ἵνα μή, Jo 12⁴⁰, v. M, *Gr.*, p. 470.

ʼ**Ιόππη** (FlJ, id., and also Ἰόπη), -ης, ἡ, (Heb. יָפוֹ), *Joppa :* Ac 9, 10, 11.†

ʼ**Ιορδάνης,** -ου, ὁ (Heb. יַרְדֵּן), *the Jordan :* Mt 3⁵, Mk 1⁵, al.

ἰός, -οῦ, ὁ, [in LXX: Ez 24⁶, ¹¹, ¹² (חֶלְאָה), Ps 139, (140)³ (חֵמָה), al.;] 1. *an arrow.* 2. *rust* (Ez, l.c.): Ja 5³ (cf. MM, *Exp.*, xv).   3. *poison :* fig., Ro 3¹³ (Ps. l.c.), Ja 3⁸.†

ʼ**Ιούδα,** v.s. Ἰούδας.

ʼ**Ιουδαία,** -ας, ἡ, v.s. Ἰουδαῖος.

†ʼ**Ιουδαΐζω** (< Ἰουδαῖος), [in LXX: Es 8¹⁷ (יהד hith.) *;*] *to conform to Jewish practice, to Judaize :* Ga 2¹⁴.†

†ʼ**Ιουδαϊκός,** -ή, -όν, [in LXX: ιι Mac 8¹¹ V, 13²¹ *;*] *Jewish :* Tit 1¹⁴.†

*†ʼ**Ιουδαϊκῶς,** adv.; *in Jewish fashion :* Ga 2¹⁴.†

ʼ**Ιουδαῖος,** -αία, -αιον (< Ἰούδας), *Jewish :* ἀνήρ, Ac 10²⁸ 22³; ἄνθρωπος, Ac 21³⁹; ψευδοπροφήτης, 13⁶; ἀρχιερεύς, 19¹⁴; γυνή, 16¹ 24²⁴; γῆ, Jo 3²²; χώρα, Mk 1⁵. Substantively, (*a*) Ἰουδαῖος, ὁ, *a Jew :* Jo 4⁹ Ac 18²⁴, Ro 2²⁸; pl., Re 2⁹ 3⁹; οἱ Ἰ., Mt 2², Mk 7³, Jo 2⁶, al.; ʼΙ. τε καὶ Ἕλληνες, Ac 14¹, al.; κ. προσήλυτοι, Ac 2¹⁰; ἔθνη τε κ. Ἰ., Ac 14⁵; οἱ κατὰ τὰ ἔθνη Ἰ., Ac 21²¹; of Jewish Christians, Ga 2¹³; of the ruling class who opposed Jesus, Jo 1¹⁹ 2¹⁸ 5¹⁰ 11⁸ 13³³, al.; (b) 'Ιουδα΄α, -ας, ἡ (sc. γῆ, χώρα, cf. Jo 3²², Mk 1⁵), (Heb. יְהוּדָה), Judæa: Mt 2¹, Lk 1⁵, Jo 4³, al.

†'Ιουδαϊσμός, -οῦ, ὁ (< 'Ιουδαΐζω), [in LXX: ii Mac 2²¹ 8¹ 14³⁸, iv Mac 4²⁶ *;] Judaism, the observance of Jewish rites: Ga 1¹³,¹⁴.†

'Ιούδας, -α, dat. -ᾳ, acc. -αν (so in LXX, and also rarely, 'Ιουδά, indecl.; cf. Thack., Gr., 163), (Heb. יְהוּדָה); 1. Judah, son of Jacob: Mt 1²,³, Lk 3³³; φυλή 'Ι., Re 5⁵ 7⁵; by meton., of the tribe, He 7¹⁴; of its confines, γῆ 'Ι., Mt 2⁶; πόλις 'Ι., Lk 1³⁹. 2. Judah (unknown): Lk 3³⁰. 3. Judas Iscariot (v.s. 'Ισκαριώτης): Mt 10⁴, Mk 3¹⁹, Lk 6¹⁶, Jo 6⁷¹ 13², al. 4. Judas, the Lord's brother (v.s. ἀδελφός): Mt 13⁵⁵, Mk 6³ (prob.), Ju¹. 5. Judas the Apostle, son of James (v.s. Θαδδαῖος): Lk 6¹⁶, Jo 14²², Ac 1¹³. 6. Judas, of Damascus: Ac 9¹¹. 7. Judas, surnamed Βαρσαββᾶς (q.v.): Ac 15²²,²⁷,³². 8. Judas the Galilean: Ac 5³⁷.

'Ιουλία, -ας, ἡ, Julia: Ro 16¹⁵.†

'Ιούλιος, -ου, ὁ, Julius: Ac 27¹,³.†

'Ιουνίας, -α, ὁ (or 'Ιουνία, -ας, ἡ, Junia; AV, R, mg.), Junias: Ro 16⁷.†

'Ιοῦστος, -ου, ὁ, Justus, the surname of, 1. Joseph Barsabbas: Ac 1²³. 2. Titus, of Corinth: Ac 18⁷. 3. Jesus, a Christian of Rome: Col 4¹¹.†

ἱππεύς, -έως (on acc. pl., -εῖς, v. Bl., § 8, 2; Thack., Gr., 148), ὁ (< ἵππος), [in LXX chiefly for פָּרָשׁ;] a horseman: Ac 23²³,³².†

**ἱππικός, -ή, -όν (< ἵππος), [in LXX: i Mac 15³⁸, iii Mac 1¹ *;] of a horse or of horsemen, equestrian; as subst., τὸ ἱ. (sc. στράτευμα), cavalry: Re 9¹⁶†

ἵππος, -ου, ὁ, [in LXX chiefly for סוּס, sometimes for פָּרָשׁ, רֶכֶב;] a horse: Ja 3³, Re 6² ff. 9⁷ ff. 14²⁰ 18¹³ 19¹¹ ff.†

ἶρις, -ιδος, ἡ, [in LXX: Ex 30²⁴ (קִדָּה)*, (קֶשֶׁת, Ge 9¹³, Ez 1²⁸, is rendered by τόξον);] 1. Iris, the messenger of the gods. 2. a rainbow or halo: Re 4³ 10¹. 3. The plant Iris (cf. Ex., l.c.).†

'Ισαάκ (in MSS. sometimes -σάκ; cf. Deiss., BS, 189; Thack., Gr., 100), ὁ, indecl. (in FlJ, 'Ισακος, -ου), (Heb. יִצְחָק), Isaac (Ge 17¹⁹, al.): Mt 1², Ro 9¹⁰, al.

*†ἰσάγγελος, -ον (< ἴσος, ἄγγελος), like or equal to angels: Lk 20³⁶.†

'Ισασχάρ, 'Ισαχάρ, v.s. 'Ισσαχάρ.

'Ισκαριώθ, ὁ, indecl. (Mk 3¹⁹ 14¹⁰, Lk 6¹⁶, elsewhere -ιώτης; v. infr.) and 'Ισκαριώτης, -ου (Heb. prob. אִישׁ קְרִיּוֹת; v. Swete, Mk., 3¹⁹), Iscariot: surname of Judas, ll. c. supr., also Mt 10⁴ 26¹⁴, Mk 14⁴³ (WH, R, omit), Lk 22³, Jo 12⁴ 13² 14²²; of his father Simon, Jo 6⁷¹ 13²⁶.†

ἴσος (epic ἶσος, so sometimes Rec.), -η, -ον, [in LXX for כְּ, Jb

5¹⁴ 10¹⁰, al.; אֶחָד, Ez 40⁵ ff.; II Mac 9¹⁵, IV Mac 13²⁰, ²¹, al.;] *equal,*
the same in size, number, quality, etc.: δωρεά, Ac 11¹⁷; μαρτυρίαι,
Mk 14⁵⁶, ⁵⁹; ἴ. ποιεῖν, c. acc. et dat., Mt 20¹²; ἑαυτὸν τ. θεῷ, Jo 5¹⁸;
τὰ ἴ. ἀπολαβεῖν, Lk 6³⁴, n. pl., ἴσα, adverbially, Re 21¹⁶; τ. θεῷ, Phl 2⁶.†
ἰσότης, -ητος, ἡ (< ἴσος), [in LXX: Jb 36³⁰, Za 4⁷ *;] 1. *equality:*
II Co 8¹³, ¹⁴. 2. *equity, fairness:* τὸ δίκαιον κ. τὴν ἴ., Col 4¹ (for distinction bet. τὸ δ. and ἡ ἴ., v. *ICC,* in l.).†
*† ἰσότιμος, -ον, (< ἴσος, τιμή), *equally privileged, held in equal*
honour: πίστις, II Pe 1¹ (R, mg., *equally precious,* but v. Field, *Notes,*
240; Mayor, in l.).†
ἰσόψυχος -ον (< ἴσος, ψυχή), [in LXX: Ps 54 (55)¹³ (כְּעֶרְכִּי)*;]
1. *of equal spirit* (Æsch., *Agam.,* 1470). 2. *like-minded:* Phl 2²⁰.†
'Ισραήλ (FlJ, 'Ισράηλος, -ου), ὁ, indecl. (Heb. יִשְׂרָאֵל, Ge 32²⁸),
Israel: ὁ οἶκος 'Ι., Ac 7⁴² (LXX), al.; λαός, Ac 4¹⁰; υἱοί, ib. 5²¹, al.;
αἱ φυλαὶ τοῦ 'Ι., Mt 19²⁸, al. By meton., for the Israelites, Mt 2⁶, Lk 1⁵⁴,
Ro 11², al.; ὁ λαὸς 'Ι., Ac 4¹⁰; γῇ 'Ι., Mt 2²⁰, ²¹; βασιλεὺς 'Ι., Mt 27⁴²,
Jo 1⁵⁰; ἡ ἐλπὶς τοῦ 'Ι., Ac 28²⁰; ὁ 'Ι. τοῦ θεοῦ (of Christians), Ga 6¹⁶;
ὁ 'Ι. κατὰ σάρκα, I Co 10¹⁸.
'Ισραηλείτης (Rec. -λίτης), ου, ὁ, [in LXX: Nu 25⁸ (יִשְׂרָאֵל), III
Ki 20 (21)¹ (יִזְרְעֵאלִי); Luc. 'Ιεζραηλίτης), etc.;] *an Israelite,* the name
expressive of theocratic privilege (v.s. 'Εβραῖος): Ro 9⁴ 11¹, II Co 11²²;
ἀληθῶς 'Ι., Jo 1⁴⁸; ἄνδρες 'Ι., Ac 2²² 3¹² 5³⁵ 13¹⁶ 21²⁸.†
'Ισσαχάρ (Rec. 'Ισαχ-, 'Ισασχ- (Elz.), T, -άχαρ), ὁ, indecl. (FlJ,
'Ισάχαρις, 'Ισάσχ-) (Heb. יִשָּׂשכָר, Ge 30¹⁸), *Issachar:* Re 7⁷.†
ἵστημι, and in late writers, also ἱστάνω, ἱστάω (Veitch, s.v.; Bl.,
§ 23, 2; M, *Pr.,* 55), [in LXX chiefly for עָמַד, קוּם, also for נָצַב ni., hi.,
יָצַב hith., etc.]. I. Trans. in pres., impf., fut. and 1 aor. act. and in the
tenses of the pass. 1. *to make to stand, to place, set, set up, establish,*
appoint: c. acc. pers., Mk 7⁹, Ac 1²³ 6¹³ 17³¹, He 10⁹; id. seq. ἐπί, c.
acc. loc., Mt 4⁵, Lk 4⁹; ἐν μέσῳ, Mt 18², Mk 9³⁶, Jo 8[3]; ἐνώπιον, Ac
6⁶; παρ' ἑαυτῷ, Lk 9⁴⁷; ἐκ δεξιῶν, Mt 25³³; mid., *to place oneself, to*
stand: Re 18¹⁵; so also pass., *to be made to stand, to stand:* Mt 2⁹,
Lk 11¹⁸ 19⁸, II Co 13¹, al. 2. *to set in a balance, to weigh* (cl.; LXX
for שָׁקַל, Is 46⁶, al.): Mt 26¹⁵. II. Intrans., in pf., plpf. (with sense
of pres. and impf.; M, *Pr.,* 147 f.) and 2 aor. act., *to stand, stand by,*
stand still: Mt 20³² 26⁷³, Mk 10⁴⁹, Lk 8⁴⁴, Jo 1³⁵ 3²⁹, Ac 16⁹, al.; seq.
ἐν, Mt 6⁵, al.; ἐνώπιον, Ac 10³⁰, al.; πρός, c. dat. loc., Jo 18¹⁶; ἐπί, c.
gen. loc., Lk 6¹⁷, Ac 5²³ 25¹⁰, al.; ἔμπροσθεν, Mt 27¹¹; κύκλῳ, Re 7¹¹;
ἐκ δεξιῶν, Lk 1¹¹; ἐπί, c. acc., Mt 13², Re 3²⁰; παρά, Lk 5²; ἐκεῖ, Mk
11⁵; ὧδε, Mk 9¹; ὅπου, Mk 13¹⁴; ἔξω, Mt 12⁴⁶; μακρόθεν, Lk 18¹³;
πόρρωθεν, Lk 17¹². Metaph., *to stand ready, stand firm, be steadfast:*
I Co 7³⁷ 10¹², Eph 6¹¹, ¹³, ¹⁴, Col 4¹²; τ. πίστει, Ro 11²⁰; ἐν τ. ἀληθείᾳ,
Jo 8⁴⁴; ἐν τ. χάριτι, Ro 5²; ἐν τ. εὐαγγελίῳ, I Co 15¹ (cf. ἀν-, ἐπ-αν-,
ἐξ-αν-, ἀνθ-, ἀφ-, δι-, ἐν-, ἐξ-, ἐπ- (-μαι), ἐφ-, κατ-εφ-, συν-εφ-, καθ-,
ἀντι-καθ-, ἀπο-καθ-, μεθ-, παρ-, περι-, προ-, συν-ίστημι).

** ἱστορέω, -ῶ (< ἵστωρ, *one learned* or *skilled in*), [in LXX: 1 Es 1³³,⁴² *;] 1. c. acc. rei, *to inquire into, learn by inquiry.* 2. C. acc. pers., *to inquire of* or *about.* 3. *to narrate, record.* 4. In late writers, *to visit, become acquainted with :* Ga 1¹⁸ (v. Ellic., in l., and cf. MM, *Exp.*, xv).†

ἰσχυρός, -ά, -όν (< ἰσχύω), [in LXX for אֵל, גִּבּוֹר, עָצוּם, חָזָק, etc.;] *strong, mighty, powerful ;* (*a*) of persons, as to body or spirit : Mt 12²⁹, Mk 3²⁷, Lk 11²¹,²², 1 Co 4¹⁰ (opp. to ἀσθενής), He 11³⁴ (ἐν πολέμῳ), Re 5² 10¹ 18²¹ 19¹⁸ ; οἱ πλούσιοι κ. οἱ ἰ., ib. 6¹⁵ ; τὰ ἰ = οἱ ἰ. (cf. IV Ki 24¹⁵), 1 Co 1²⁷ ; of God (cf. De 10¹⁷), Re 18⁸ ; compar., Mt 3¹¹, Mk 1⁷, Lk 11²², 1 Co 1²⁵ (τὸ ἀσθενὲς τ. θεοῦ) 10²² ; (*b*) of things : λιμός, Lk 15¹⁴ ; ἐπιστολαί (βαρεῖαι κ. ἰ.), II Co 10¹⁰ ; κραυγή, He 5⁷ ; φωνή, Re 18² ; παράκλησις, He 6¹⁸ ; πόλις, Re 18¹⁰ ; βρονταί, ib. 19⁶.†

ἰσχύς, -ύος, ἡ, [in LXX chiefly for כֹּחַ, also for חַיִל, עֹז, גְּבוּרָה, etc.;] *strength, might, power, force, ability :* Re 5¹² 7¹² ; ἰ. κ. δύναμις, II Pe 2¹¹ ; τ. κράτος τῆς ἰ. (Is 40²⁶), Eph 1¹⁹ 6¹⁰ ; ἡ δόξα τῆς ἰ., II Th 1⁹ ; ἐξ ἰ., I Pe 4¹¹ ; ἐν ὅλῃ τ. ἰ., Mk 12³⁰, ³³ (LXX), Lk 10²⁷ (LXX).†

SYN.: δύναμις (q.v., and cf. *ICC*, Phl 4¹³) ; κράτος (cf. M, *Th.*, I, 1⁹).

ἰσχύω (< ἰσχύς), [in LXX for חָזָק, גִּבּוֹר, עָצַם, etc.;] 1. *to be strong in body:* Mt 9¹², Mk 2¹⁷. 2. *to be powerful, have power, prevail :* Ac 19²⁰, Re 12⁸ ; seq. κατά, c. gen. pers., Ac 19¹⁶ ; c. inf., *to be able* (MM, *Exp.*, xv) : Mt 8²³ 26⁴⁰, Mk 5⁴ 9¹⁸ (inf. understood) 14³⁷, Lk 6⁴⁸ 8⁴³ 13²⁴ 14⁶, ²⁹, ³⁰ 16³ 20²⁶, Jo 21⁶, Ac 6¹⁰ 15¹⁰ 25⁷ 27¹⁶ ; c. acc., Phl 4¹³, Ja 5¹⁶ ; of things, *to avail, be serviceable* (MM, *Exp.*, l.c.) : Mt 5¹³, Ga 5⁶, He 9¹⁷ (cf. ἐν-, ἐξ-, ἐπ-, κατ-ισχύω).†

ἴσως (< ἴσος), adv., [in LXX for אוּלַי, אַךְ, הֵן, Ge 32²⁰, Je 5⁴, al.;] 1. *equally.* 2. *perhaps :* Lk 20¹³.†

Ἰταλία, -ας, ἡ, *Italy :* ἡ Ἰ. (v. Bl., § 46, 11), Ac 18² 27¹, ⁶, He 13¹⁴.†

Ἰταλικός, -ή, -όν (< Ἰταλία), *Italian :* σπεῖρα Ἰ., Ac 10¹.†

Ἰτουραία, v.s. Ἰτουραῖος.

Ἰτουραῖος, -αία, -αῖον, [in LXX: 1 Ch 5¹⁹ A (יְטוּר) *;] *Iturœan* (in cl. always ὁι Ἰ., *the Iturœans*) · χώρα (ἡ Ἰτουραίων ὀρεινή, τὰ τῶν Ἰ. μέρη, Strabo, XVI, ii, 16, 20), Lk 3¹ (cf. *Exp.* (1894), ix, 51 ff., 143 ff., 288 ff.).†

* ἰχθύδιον, -ου, τό (dimin. of ἰχθύς), *a little fish :* Mt 15³⁴, Mk 8⁷.†

ἰχθύς, -ύος, ὁ, [in LXX for דָּג, דָּגָה;] *a fish :* Mt 7¹⁰, Mk 6³⁸, al.

ἴχνος, -εος (-ους), τό, [in LXX for כַּף, etc.;] *a track, footstep :* metaph. (as freq. in cl.), στοιχεῖν τοῖς ἰ., Ro 4¹² ; περιπατεῖν τοῖς ἰ., II Co 12¹⁸ ; ἐπακολουθεῖν τοῖς ἰ., I Pe 2²¹ (cf. MM, *Exp.*, xv).†

Ἰωάθαμ (WH, -θάμ), ὁ, indecl. (Heb. יוֹתָם), *Jotham,* King of Judah : Mt 1⁹.†

Ἰωάνα (TR, -ννα; v. WH, *App.*, 159), -ης, ἡ (Aram. יוֹחָן), *Joanna:*
Lk 8³ 24¹⁰.†

Ἰωανάν (Rec. Ἰωαννᾶς, -ᾶ), ὁ, indecl. (Heb. יוֹחָנָן), *Joanan* (cf.
Ἰωάνης): Lk 3²⁷.†

Ἰωάνης (Rec. -ννης, q.v.; cf. Dalman, *Gr.*, 142; Tdf., *Pr.*, 79;
WH, *App.*, 159; Bl., § 3, 10; 10, 2), -ου, dat., -ῃ (b¹it in Mt 11⁴,
Lk 7¹⁸, ²², Re 1¹, -ει), acc., -ην, ὁ (Heb. יוֹחָנָן, LXX: Ἰωανάν, ii Ch 23¹,
al.; -ννάν, Je 47 (40)⁸, al., Aq.), Hellenized form of Ἰωανάν, *John* (i Es
8³⁸ (⁴¹)*), viz., 1. *John* the Baptist: Mt 3¹, al. 2. *John* the Apostle,
son of Zebedee: Mt 4²¹, Mk 1¹⁹, Lk 5¹⁰, Ac 1¹³, al. 3. The father of
St. Peter: Jo 1⁴³ 21¹⁵⁻¹⁷. 4. *John* surnamed Mark: Ac 12¹², ²⁵ 13⁵, ¹³
15³⁷. 5. The writer of the Apocalypse, traditionally identified with
2: Re 1¹, ⁴, ⁹.

Ἰωάννης (D, Ἰωνάθας; v. MM, *Exp.*, xv; Bl., § 10, 2), ὁ, *John:*
Ac 4⁶ 13⁵, Tr., WH, Re 22⁸ (cf. Ἰωάνης).†

Ἰώβ, ὁ (Heb. אִיּוֹב), *Job:* Ja 5¹¹.†

Ἰωβήδ (WH, -βήλ, Lk, l.c.; Rec., RV, Ὠβήδ), ὁ, indecl., *Jobed*
(*Obed*): Mt 1⁵, Lk 3³².†

Ἰωβήλ, v.s. Ἰωβήδ.

Ἰωδά (Rec. Ἰούδα), *Joda:* Lk 3²⁶.†

Ἰωήλ, ὁ, indecl. (Heb. יוֹאֵל), *Joel:* Ac 2¹⁶.†

Ἰωνάθας, v.s. Ἰωάννης.

Ἰωνάμ (Rec. -άν), *Jonam:* Lk 3³⁰.†

Ἰωνᾶς, -ᾶ, ὁ (Heb. יוֹנָה), *Jonah,* the prophet: Mt 12³⁹⁻⁴¹ 16⁴
Lk 11²⁹, ³⁰, ³².†

Ἰωράμ, ο, indecl. (Heb. יְחוֹרָם), *Joram, Jehoram:* Mt 1⁸.†

Ἰωρείμ, ὁ, indecl., *Jorim:* Lk 3²⁹.†

Ἰωσαφάτ, ὁ, indecl. (Heb. יְהוֹשָׁפָט), *Jehoshaphat:* Mt 1⁸.†

Ἰωσείας (-σίας, Rec.), -ου, ὁ (Heb. יֹאשִׁיָּהוּ), *Josiah:* Mt 1¹⁰, ¹¹.†

Ἰωσή, v.s. Ἰωσῆς.

Ἰωσῆς, -ῆ (Rec. -ή, Lk 3²⁹; AV, *Jose;* v.s. Ἰησοῦς, 3), and -ῆτος
(Mk, ll. c.), ὁ, *Joses;* 1. brother of our Lord: Mk 6³, Mt 13⁵⁵ (Rec.,
v.s. Ἰωσήφ). 2. Son of Mary: Mt 27⁵⁶ (-σήφ, WH, txt), Mk 15⁴⁰, ⁴⁷.
3. v.s. Βαρνάβας.†

Ἰωσήφ, ὁ, indecl. (FlJ, Ἰώσηπος, -ου), (Heb. יוֹסֵף), *Joseph;* 1. the
Son of Jacob: Jo 4⁵, Ac 7⁹, ¹³, ¹⁴, ¹⁸, He 11²¹, ²², Re 7⁸. 2. In the
genealogy of our Lord, (a) the son of Matthias: Lk 3²⁴; (b) the son
Joram: ib. ³⁰. 3. The husband of Mary, the Lord's mother: Mt 1¹⁶ ff.,
Lk 1²⁷, Jo 1⁴⁶, al. 4. One of the brethren of our Lord (v.s. ἀδελφός):
Mt 13⁵⁵. 5. Son of Mary: Mt 27⁵⁶ (-σῆς, WH, mg., RV). 6. *Joseph*
of Arimathæa: Mt 27⁵⁷, ⁵⁹, Mk 15⁴³, ⁴⁵, Lk 23⁵⁰, Jo 19³⁸. 7. v.s.
Βαρνάβας. 8. v.s. Βαρσαββᾶς.

'Ιωσήχ, *Josech* : Lk 3²⁶.†
'Ιωσίας, v.s. 'Ιωσείας.
ἰῶτα, τό, *iota* (Heb. י , i.e. the smallest letter) : Mt 5¹⁸.†

K

K, κ, κάππα, τό, indecl., *kappa*, *k*, the tenth letter. As a numeral, κ´ = 20; κ, = 20,000.
κἀγώ, v.s. ἐγώ.
καθά, adv. (for καθ' ἅ), [in LXX : Ge 7⁹ 19⁸, al. (כְּ, כַּאֲשֶׁר), Is 58¹¹, Wi 3¹⁰, al.;] *just as, according as* : Mt 27¹⁰ (LXX), Lk 1², D (cf. Bl., § 78, 1; *Phil. Gosp.*, 8 f.).†
καθ-αίρεσις, -εως, ἡ (< καθαιρέω), [in LXX : Ex 23²⁴ (הֶרֶם), 1 Mac 3⁴³ *;] a pulling down, destruction* : fig., κ. ὀχυρωμάτων, 11 Co 10⁴; opp. to οἰκοδομή, ib. ⁸ 13¹⁰.†
καθ-αιρέω, -ῶ, [in LXX for נתץ, פרק, ירד, etc.;] 1. *to take down* : c. acc. pers. (the technical term for removal after crucifixion, Field, *Notes*, 44), Mk 15³⁶, ⁴⁶, Lk 23⁵³, Ac 13²⁹. 2. *to put down by force, pull down, destroy* : ἀποθήκας, Lk 12¹⁸ (opp. to οἰκοδομεῖν); δυνάστας, Lk 1⁵²; ἔθνη, Ac 13¹⁹; pass., Ac 19²⁷ (*diminished*, Field, *Notes*, 129 f.) ; fig., *to refute* : λογισμούς, 11 Co 10⁵.†
καθαίρω (< καθαρός), [in LXX : Is 28²⁷ (דּוּשׁ ho.), 11 Ki 4⁶, Je 28 (51)³⁹ א *;] to cleanse* : of pruning, Jo 15² (cf. καθαρίζω).†
καθάπερ (for καθ' ἅπερ = καθά), adv., [in LXX for כַּאֲשֶׁר, Ge 12⁴, Ex 7⁶, al. ;] *just as, even as* : Ro 3⁴ 4⁶ 9¹³ 10¹⁵ 11⁸ 12⁴, 1 Co 10¹⁰ 12¹², 11 Co 1¹⁴, 3¹³, ¹⁸ 8¹¹, 1 Th 2¹¹ 3⁶, ¹² 4⁵, He 4².†
＊＊καθ-άπτω, [in Sm. : Ca 1⁶ *;] 1. *to fasten on, put upon*, c. acc 2. Act. for mid. (cf. Bl., § 53, 3), *to lay hold of, attack* : c. gen., χειρός, Ac 28³.†
† καθαρίζω (Hellenistic—FlJ, Inscr.—for Attic καθαίρω, q.v., on the vulgar -ερ-, Mt 8³, Mk 1⁴², v. Bl., § 6, 1; Thackeray, *Gr.*, 74), [in LXX chiefly for טָהַר;] *to cleanse, make clean.* 1. In physical sense : c. acc. rei, fig., Mt 23²⁵, ²⁶, Lk 11³⁹; of disease (leprosy), c. acc. pers., Mt 8², ³ 10⁸ 11⁵, Mk 1⁴⁰⁻⁴², Lk 4²⁷ 5¹², ¹³ 7²² 17¹⁴, ¹⁷; ἡ λέπρα ἐκαθερίσθη (on the spelling v. supr.), Mt 8³. 2. In ethical sense : τ. καρδίας, Ac 15⁹ (cf. Si 38¹⁰); τ. χεῖρας, Ja 4⁸; λαὸν ἑαυτῷ, Tit 2¹⁴; τ. ἐκκλησίαν, Eph 5²⁶; c. acc. pers. (rei), seq. ἀπό (Bl., § 36, 9; Deiss., *BS*, 216 f.), 11 Co 7¹, He 9¹⁴, 1 Jo 1⁷, ⁹. 3. In ceremonial sense : Mk 7¹⁹, Ac 10¹⁵ 11⁹, He 9²², ²³ 10² (cf. δια-καθαρίζω).†
† καθαρισμός, -οῦ, ὁ (< καθαρίζω), [in LXX for טָהֳרָה, טׇהֳרָה, etc. ;] *cleansing, purification* : Jo 3²⁵; c. gen. subj., τ. 'Ιουδαίων, Jo 2⁶; c. gen. obj., of women after childbirth, Lk 2²²; of lepers, Mk 1⁴⁴, Lk 5¹⁴; c. gen. rei, τ. ἁμαρτιῶν, He 1³, 11 Pe 1⁹ (Cremer, 319).†

καθαρός, -ά, -όν, [in LXX chiefly for טָהוֹר;] *pure, clean.* 1. Physically: Mt 23²⁶ 27⁵⁹, Jo 13¹⁰, ¹¹ (fig.), 15³ (fig., as of a vine cleansed by pruning), He 10²², Re 15⁶ 19⁸, ¹⁴ 21¹⁸, ²¹. 2. Ceremonially: Lk 11⁴¹, Ro 14²⁰, Tit 1¹⁵. 3. Ethically; (*a*) of persons: Jo 13¹⁰, Ac 18⁶, Tit 1¹⁵; ὁ κ. τῇ καρδίᾳ (καθαρὸς χείρας, Hdt., i, 35), Mt 5⁸; seq. ἀπό (cl. c. gen. simp.; Bl., § 36, 11; Deiss., *BS*, 196; MM, *Exp.*, xv), Ac 20²⁶; (*b*) of things: καρδία, ι Ti 1⁵, ιι Ti 2²²; συνείδησις, ι Ti 3⁹, ιι Ti 1³; θρησκεία, Ja 1²⁷.†

SYN.: v.s. ἁγνός.

καθαρότης, -ητος, ἡ (< καθαρός), [in LXX: Ex 24¹⁰ (טֹהַר), Wi 7²⁴*;] *purity, cleanness:* c. gen., He 9¹³.†

καθ-έδρα, -ας, ἡ (< κατά, + ἕδρα, *a seat*), [in LXX for מוֹשָׁב and cogn. forms;] *a chair, seat:* Mt 21¹², Mk 11¹⁵; of teachers, Mt 23².†

καθ-έζομαι, [in LXX: Le 12⁵, al. (יָשַׁב), Jb 39²⁸ (שָׁכַן);] *to sit down, sit:* Jo 20¹²; seq. ἐν, Mt 26⁵⁵, Lk 2⁴⁶, Jo 11²⁰, Ac 6¹⁵; seq. ἐπί, c. gen., Ac 20⁹; id. c. dat., Jo 4⁶ (cf. παρα-καθέζ-, κάθημαι).†

καθ' εἷς, v.s. εἷς.

*†καθ-εξῆς (= cl. ἐξῆς, ἐφεξῆς), adv., 1. *successively, in order:* Lk 1³, Ac 11⁴ 18²³; τῶν κ. (*those that succeeded* him), Ac 3²⁴. 2. *afterwards:* ἐν τῷ κ. (sc. χρόνῳ), Lk 8¹.†

καθεύδω, [in LXX chiefly for שָׁכַב, Ge 28¹³, Ps 87 (88)⁵, al.; also for יָשֵׁן, Ca 5², Da LXX ᴛʜ 12², al.; for יָשַׁב, ι Ki 19⁹;] *to sleep:* Mt 8²⁴ 9²⁴ 13²⁵ 25⁵ 26⁴⁰, ⁴³, ⁴⁵, Mk 4²⁷, ³⁸ 5³⁹ 14³⁷, ⁴⁰, ⁴¹, Lk 8⁵² 22⁴⁶, ι Th 5⁷. Metaph., (*a*) of death (as Ps, Da, ll. c.): ι Th 5¹⁰ (cf. Mt 9²⁴, Mk 5³⁹, Lk 8⁵², and v. Swete, *Mk.*, l.c.); (*b*) of moral and spiritual insensibility: Mk 13³⁶, Eph 5¹⁴, ι Th 5⁶.†

SYN.: κοιμάω.

* καθηγητής, -οῦ, ὁ (< καθηγέομαι, *to go before, guide*), 1. prop. *a guide.* 2. *a master, teacher* (MGr. *professor*): Mt 23¹⁰.†

καθ-ήκω, [in LXX: impers., Le 5¹⁰, Ez 21²⁷ (³²), al. (מִשְׁפָּט); τὰ κ., Ex 5¹³, al. (דָּבָר), etc.;] 1. *to come down, come to.* 2. *to be fit, proper:* impers., c. acc. et inf., Ac 22²² (on the tense, v. Bl., § 63, 4); τὰ μὴ καθήκοντα, Ro 1²⁸.†

κάθ-ημαι, [in LXX chiefly for יָשַׁב;] in cl. pres. and impf. only (prop. pf. and plpf. of καθέζομαι; cf. Bl., § 24), in LXX and NT fut. also, *to sit, be seated:* Mt 11¹⁶ 22⁴⁴ (ʟxx), Mk 2⁶, Jo 6³, Ac 2², Ja 2³ (on the vulgar imper. κάθου, v. Kennedy, *Sources*, 162), Re 4³, al.; seq. prep. c. acc., ἐπί, Mt 9⁹, Mk 2¹⁴, Jo 12¹⁵; παρά, Mt 13¹, Mk 10⁴⁶; περί, Mk 3³², ³⁴; πρός, Lk 22⁵⁶; ὑπό, Ja 2³; εἰς, Mk 13³; μετά, c. gen. pers., Mt 26⁵⁸; ἐκ δεξιῶν, Mt 22⁴⁴; ἐπάνω, c. gen., Mt 28²; ἀπέναντι, c. gen., Mt 27⁶¹; ἐπί, c. dat., Ac 3¹⁰; id. c. gen., Ac 8²⁸; ἐκεῖ, Mt 15²⁹; pleonastic (M, *Pr.*, 230, 241; Dalman, *Words*, 22), Mt 13², Ac 23³, Re 18⁷; metaph., Mt 4¹⁶, Lk 1⁷⁹ (ʟxx); of one's domicile (Ne 11⁶, Si 50²⁶; Hdt., v, 63), Lk 21³⁵, Ac 2², Re 14⁶ (cf. συν-κάθημαι).

†καθημερινός, -ή, -όν (< καθ' ἡμέραν), [in LXX: Jth 12¹⁵ *;] *daily* (MGr. καθημερνός) : Ac 6¹.†

καθ-ίζω, [in LXX chiefly for יָשַׁב;] 1. causal, *to make to sit down, set, appoint :* Ac 2³⁰, ι Co 6⁴, Eph 1²⁰. 2. Intrans., *to sit down, be seated, sit :* Mt 5¹, Mk 9³⁵, Lk 7¹⁵, Jo 8², al.; c. inf. tel., ι Co 10⁷; seq. εἰς, ιι Th 2⁴; ἐπί, c. acc., Mk 11², Jo 12¹⁴; id. c. gen., Jo 19¹³, Ac 12²¹; ὧδε, Mk 14³²; αὐτοῦ, Mt 26³⁶; ἐν δεξιᾷ, He 1³; ἐκ δεξιῶν, Mt 20²¹, ²³; ἐν, Re 3²¹; καθίσας pleonastic (M, *Pr.*, 14; Dalman, *Words*, 22), Mt 13⁴⁸, Lk 5³ 14³¹ 16⁶; of settling in a place (ἐς χωρίον, Thuc., iv, 93), seq. ἐν, Lk 24⁴⁹ (cf. ἀνα-, ἐπι-, παρα-, περι-, συν-καθίζω).

καθ-ίημι, [in LXX: Ex 17¹¹ (נוּחַ hi.), and v.l., ι Ch 21²⁷, Za 11¹³, Je 39 (32)¹⁴ *;] *to send* or *let down :* seq. εἰς, Lk 5¹⁹; διά, c. gen., ib., Ac 9²⁵; ptcp., seq. ἐπί, c. gen., Ac 10¹¹; ἐκ, Ac 11⁵.†

καθ-ίστημι (and καθιστάνω, Ac 17¹⁵), [in LXX for פָּקַד, קוּם, שׂוּם, etc., 24 words in all ;] 1. (*a*) *to set down ;* (*b*) *to bring down* to a place (Hom., Xen., al.; ιι Ch 28¹⁵, ι Ki 5³): Ac 17¹⁵. 2. *to set in order, appoint, make, constitute :* Tit 1⁵, ιι Pe 1⁸; c. dupl. acc., κριτήν, Lk 12¹⁴; ἡγούμενον, Ac 7¹⁰; ἄρχοντα, ib. ²⁷, ³⁵ (LXX); ἀρχιερεῖς, He 7²⁸; seq. ἐπί, c. gen., Mt 24⁴⁵ 25²¹, ²³, Lk 12⁴², Ac 6³; id. c. dat., Mt 24⁴⁷, Lk 12⁴⁴; id. c. acc., He 2⁷ (LXX) (WH, R, mg. omit); pass. (v. Mayor, *Ja.*, 115 f.), Ro 5¹⁹, Ja 3⁶ 4⁴; seq. εἰς c. inf., He 8³; τὰ πρὸς τ. θεόν, He 5¹ (cf. ἀντι-, ἀπο-καθίστημι).†

καθό (= καθ' ὅ), adv., [in LXX: Le 9⁵, ¹⁵ (אֲשֶׁר), ι Es 1⁵⁰, Si 16²⁰, Ba 1⁶ ιι Mac 4¹⁶ *;] *as, according as :* Ro 8²⁶, ιι Co 8¹², ι Pe 4¹³.†

*καθολικός, -ή, -όν (< καθόλου), *catholic, general :* tit. Epp. Ja, Pe, Jo, Ju (Rec.) (v. Mayor, *Ja.*, ccxc).†

καθόλου (= καθ' ὅλου and so in cl. bef. Arist.), adv., [in LXX: Ex 22¹¹ (10), Am 3³, ⁴; Ez 13³, ²² 17¹⁴ (τὸ κ. μή = לְבִלְתִּי), Da LXX TH 3⁵⁰ *;] *on the whole, in general :* μὴ κ., *not at all*, Ac 4¹⁸.†

καθ-οπλίζω, [in LXX: Je 26 (46)⁹ (תפש), Mac₉*;] *to arm fully :* pass., Lk 11²¹.†

καθ-οράω, -ῶ, [in LXX: Nu 24² (ראה), Jb 10⁴ 39²⁶, ιιι Mac 3¹¹ *;] 1. *to look down*. 2. *to discern clearly :* Ro 1²⁰.†

καθότι (= καθ' ὅ τι), adv., [in LXX: Ex 1¹², ¹⁷ (כַּאֲשֶׁר), To 1¹², Jth 2¹³, al.;] 1. in cl., *according as, just as* (Ex, l.c.) : Ac 2⁴⁵ 4³⁵. 2. In late Gk. = διότι (To, l.c.), *because :* Lk 1⁷ 19⁹, Ac 2²⁴ 17³¹.†

καθώς, (i.e. καθ' ὡς), Hellenistic for καθά, q.v., καθάπερ, καθό, καθοτι (Mayser, 485; Rutherford, *NPhr.*, 495; Bl., § 78, 1), *according as, even as, just as, as :* Lk 1² (v.s. καθά), 24³⁹, Jo 5²³, Ac 7⁴⁸, ι Co 8², Ga 3⁶, al.; seq. οὕτως, Lk 11³⁰, Jo 3¹⁴, ιι Co 1⁵, Col 3¹³, ι Jo 2⁶, al.; seq. καί, Jo 15⁹, ι Co 15⁴⁹, ι Jo 2¹⁸, al.; οὕτως . . . κ., Lk 24²⁴; id. with ellipsis of οὕτως, Mt 21⁶, Mk 16⁷, Ro 1¹³, al.; with other elliptical constructions, Jo 6⁵⁸ 17²¹, ²², Ac 15⁸, ι Th 2¹³, ι Ti 1³, ι Jo 3², ³, ¹²; καθὼς γέγραπται (Deiss., *BS*, 249), Mt 26²⁴, Mk 9¹³, Ro 1¹⁷, al.; introducing subst. clause as object of verb (as in Heb.), Mt 21⁶, Mk 11⁶,

Lk 5¹⁴, al.; after verbs of speaking, Ac 15¹⁴; of proportion and degree, Mk 4³³, 1 Co 12¹¹, ¹⁸, al.; of time (Ne 5⁶, 11 Mac 1³¹), Ac 7¹⁷.

*καθώσπερ (Tr. καθώς περ), adv. (v.s. καθώς), *even as :* 11 Co 3⁸ (WH, mg.), He 5⁴.†

καί, conj., *and.* I. Copulative. 1. Connecting single words; (*a*) in general : Mt 2¹⁸ 16¹, Mk 2¹⁵, Lk 8¹⁵, He 1¹, al. mult.; repeated before each of the terms in a series, Mt 23²³, Lk 14²¹, Ro 7¹² 9⁴, al.; (*b*) connecting numerals (WM, § 37, 4) : Jo 2²⁰, Ac 13²⁰; (*c*) joining terms which are not mutually exclusive, as the part with the whole : Mt 8³³ 26⁵⁹, Mk 16¹⁷, Ac 5²⁹, al. 2. Connecting clauses and sentences : Mt 3¹², Ac 5²¹, al. mult.; esp. (*a*) where, after the simplicity of the popular language, sentences are paratactically joined (WM, § 60, 3 ; M, *Pr.*, 12; Deiss., *LAE*, 128 ff.) : Mt 1²¹ 7²⁵, Mk 9⁵, Jo 10³, al.; (*b*) joining affirmative to negative sentences : Lk 3¹⁴, Jo 4¹¹, 111 Jo ¹⁰; (*c*) consecutive, *and so :* Mt 5¹⁵, 23³², He 3¹⁹, al.; after imperatives, Mt 4¹⁹, Lk 7⁷, al.; (*d*) = καίτοι, *and yet :* Mt 3¹⁴ 6²⁶, Mk 12¹², Lk 18⁷ (Field, *Notes*, 72), 1 Co 5², al.; (*e*) beginning an apodosis (= Heb. וְ; so sometimes δέ in cl.), *then :* Lk 2²¹ 7¹², Ac 1¹⁰; beginning a question (WM, § 53, 3 a) : Mk 10²⁶, Lk 10²⁹, Jo 9³⁶. 3. Epexegetic, *and, and indeed, namely* (WM, § 53, 3 c) : Lk 3¹⁸, Jo 1¹⁶, Ac 23⁶, Ro 1⁵, 1 Co 3⁵, al. 4. In transition : Mt 4²³, Mk 5¹, ²¹, Jo 1¹⁹, al.; so, Hebraistically, καὶ ἐγένετο (וַיְהִי; also ἐγένετο δέ), Mk 1⁹ (cf. Lk 5¹; v. Burton, §§ 357-60; M, *Pr.*, 14, 16). 5. καὶ . . . καί, *both . . . and* (for τε . . . καί, v.s. τε); (*a*) connecting single words : Mt 10²⁸, Mk 4⁴¹, Ro 11³³, al.; (*b*) clauses and sentences : Mk 9¹³, Jo 7²⁸, 1 Co 1²², al. II. Adjunctive, *also, even, still :* Mt 5³⁹, ⁴⁰, Mk 2²⁸, al. mult.; esp. c. pron., adv., etc., Mt 20⁴, Jo 7⁴⁷, al.; ὡς κ., Ac 11¹⁷; καθὼς κ., Ro 15⁷; οὕτω κ., Ro 6¹¹; διὸ κ., Lk 1³⁵; ὁ κ. (Deiss., *BS*, 313 ff.), Ac 13⁹; pleonastically, μετὰ κ. (Bl., § 77, 7; Deiss., *BS*, 265 f.), Phl 4³; τί κ., 1 Co 15²⁹; ἀλλὰ κ., Lk 14²², Jo 5¹⁸, al.; καίγε (M, *Pr.*, 230; Burton, § 437), Ac 17²⁷; καίπερ, He 5⁸; κ. ἐάν, v.s. ἐάν; εἰ, *even if,* 1 Pe 3¹ (cf. Thayer, s.v. εἰ, 111, 7). On the use of καὶ in paratactic sentences (l. 9) see further, M, *Gr.*, p. 420 f.

Καιάφας (T, Καϊ-), -α ὁ, *Caiaphas* (on the name, v. *Exp. Times*, x, 185) : Mt 26³, ⁵⁷, Lk 3², Jo 11⁴⁹, 18¹³, ¹⁴, ²⁴, ²⁸, Ac 4⁶.†

Καίν (T, Κάϊν), ὁ, indecl. (in FlJ, Κάϊς, -ιος), (Heb. קַיִן; Ge 4¹), *Cain :* He 11⁴, 1 Jo 3¹², Ju ¹¹.†

Καινάμ (T, Καϊ-; Rec. Καϊνάν), ὁ, indecl. (Heb. קֵינָן), *Cainam, Cainan ;* 1. son of Enos (Ge 5⁹) : Lk 3³⁷. 2. Son of Arphaxad (Ge 10²⁴ (LXX)) : Lk 3³⁶.†

καινός, -ή, -όν, [in LXX (Ez 11¹⁹, al.) for חָדָשׁ, exc. Is 65¹⁵ (אַחֵר);] of that which is unused or unaccustomed, *new* in respect to form or quality, *fresh, unused, novel :* opp. to παλαιός, ἀρχαῖος, Mt 9¹⁷ 13⁵², Mk 2²¹, ²², Lk 5³⁶, ³⁸, 11 Co 5¹⁷, Eph 4²⁴; πλήρωμα, Mk 2²¹; μνημεῖον, Mt 27⁶⁰, Jo 19⁴¹; διαθήκη (T, WH, R, txt., omit), Lk 22²⁰, 1 Co 11²⁵, 11 Co 3⁶, He 8⁸ (LXX), ¹³ 9¹⁵; οὐρανοί, γῆ, 11 Pe 3¹³, Re 21¹ (LXX);

Ἱερουσαλήμ, Re 3¹² 21²; ἄνθρωπος, Eph 2¹⁵ (cf. Ez 18³¹); πάντα, Re
21⁵; γέννημα τ. ἀμπέλου, Mt 26²⁹, Mk 14²⁵; διδαχή, Mk 1²⁷, Ac 17¹⁹;
ἐντολή, Jo 13³⁴, ɪ Jo 2⁷, ⁸, ɪɪ Jo ⁵; ὄνομα, Re 2¹⁷ (ᴸˣˣ); ᾠδή, Re 5⁹ 14³
(cf. Ps 143 (144)⁹); κτίσις, ɪɪ Co 5¹⁷, Ga 6¹⁵; γλῶσσαι, Mk 16[17];
compar., Ac 17²¹.†

SYN.: νέος, "the new primarily in reference to time, the young,
recent; κ. . . . the new primarily in reference to quality, the fresh,
unworn". Cf. Tr., Syn., § lx (the distinction, however, is less marked
in late Gk.; cf. He 12²⁴ with He, ll. c. supr., and v. MM, Exp., xv).

καινότης, -ητος, ἡ (< καινός), [in LXX: ɪɪɪ Ki 8⁵³, Ez 47¹² *;]
1. novelty (Thuc., Isocr., LS, s.v.).   2. freshness, newness: ἐν κ. ζωῆς
(v. Lft., Notes, 296), Ro 6⁴; ἐν κ. πνεύματος, Ro 7⁶.†

καίπερ, concessive particle, [in LXX: Pr 6⁸, Wi 11⁹, Jh 1¹³,
ɪɪ-ɪv Mac ₁₁ *;] although: c. ptcp., Phl 3⁴, He 5⁸ 7⁵ 12¹⁷, ɪɪ Pe 1¹².†

καιρός, -οῦ, ὁ, [in LXX chiefly for עֵת, also for מוֹעֵד, etc.;]
1. due measure, fitness, proportion (Eur., Xen., al.).   2. Of Time
(cl. also) in the sense of a fixed and definite period, time, season
(Kennedy, Sources, 153): Mt 11²⁵, Mk 1¹⁵, Lk 21⁸, Ro 13¹¹, Eph 6¹⁸,
He 11¹⁵, ɪ Pe 1⁵, ¹¹, Re 1³, al.; c. gen., πειρασμοῦ, Lk 8¹³; τ. καρπῶν,
Mt 21³⁴; σύκων, Mk 11¹³; pl., Mt 21⁴¹; χρόνοι ἢ (καὶ) κ., Ac 1⁷, ɪ Th 5¹;
ἐθνῶν, Lk 21²⁴; of opportune or seasonable time, Ac 24²⁵, Ga 6¹⁰,
Eph 5¹⁶, Col 4⁵; c. inf., He 11¹⁵; ὁ κ. οὗτος, Mk 10³⁰, Lk 18³⁰; ὁ νῦν κ.
(Dalman, Words, 148), Ro 8¹⁸; ὁ κ. ὁ ἐμός, Jo 7⁶; κ. δεκτῷ, ɪɪ Co
6² (ᴸˣˣ); δουλεύειν τῷ κ., Ro 12¹¹, R, mg.; τ. σημεῖα τῶν κ., Mt 16³;
adverbial usages: ἐν κ., Mt 24⁴⁵, ɪ Pe 5⁶ (cf. καιρῷ, Lk 20¹⁰; τῷ κ., Mk
12²); ἄχρι καιροῦ, Lk 4¹³, Ac 13¹¹; πρὸς καιρόν, Lk 8¹³, ɪ Co 7⁵; κατὰ
καιρόν, Ro 5⁶; πρὸ καιροῦ, Mt 8²⁹. (On Mk 4²⁹—for καρπός—v. Turner,
SNT, pp. 61 f.)

SYN.: χρόνος, time in the sense of duration.

Καῖσαρ, -αρος, ὁ, Cæsar: Mt 22¹⁷, Lk 2¹, Jo 19¹², Ac 25⁸ ⁴⁰, al.

Καισαρία (Rec. -άρεα), -ας, ἡ, Cæsarea; 1. Cæsarea Philippi, at
the foot of Lebanon: Mt 16¹³, Mk 8²⁷.   2. Cæsarea of Palestine, on
the sea-coast: Ac 8⁴⁰ 9³⁰ 10¹, ²⁴ 11¹¹ 12¹⁹ 18²² 21⁸, ¹⁶ 23²³, ³³ 25¹, ⁴, ⁶, ¹³.†

** καίτοι (= καί τοι, and so also written in cl.), concessive particle,
[in LXX: ɪv Mac 2⁶ *;] and yet, although: Ac 14¹⁷; c. ptcp., He 4³.†

* καίτοιγε, strengthened form of καίτοι, q.v. (and v.s. γε): Jo 4².†

Καϊφας, for Καιάφας, q.v.: Lk 3² (L).

καίω, [in LXX for בָּעַר, יָקַד, שָׂרַף, etc.;] 1. to kindle, light:
c. acc., λύχνον, Mt 5¹⁵; pass., to be lighted, to burn: ptcp., Lk 12³⁵,
Re 4⁵ 8¹⁰ 19²⁰; πυρί, He 12¹⁸, Re 8⁸ 21⁸; metaph., Lk 24³², Jo 5³⁵.
2. to burn, destroy by fire: pass., Jo 15⁶, ɪ Co 13³.†

κἀκεῖ (by crasis for καὶ ἐκεῖ, and so sometimes written, v. infr.),
and there, there also: Mt 5²³ (κ. ἐ., Tr., mg.) 10¹¹ 28¹⁰ (κ. ἐ., T),
Mk 1³⁵ (κ. ἐ., L) ³⁸ (κ. ἐ., WH) 14¹⁵ (κ. ἐ., WH), Jo 11⁵⁴, Ac 14⁷
17¹³ 22¹⁰ 25²⁰, 27⁶.†

κἀκεῖθεν (by crasis for καὶ ἐκεῖθεν, and so sometimes written, v.s.
ἐκεῖθεν), 1. of place, and from thence, and thence: Mk 9³⁰, Lk 11⁵³,
Ac 7⁴ 14²⁶ 16¹² 20¹⁵ 21¹ 27⁴ 28¹⁵.   2. of time, and thereafter: Ac 13²¹.†

κἀκεῖνος, -είνη, -εῖνο (by crasis for καὶ ἐκεῖνος, and so sometimes written, v.s. ἐκεῖνος), *and he, she* or *it ; he, she* or *it also :* Mt 15¹⁸ 23²³, Mk 12⁴, ⁵ 16[¹¹, ¹³], Lk 11⁷, ⁴² 20¹¹ 22¹², Jo 6⁵⁷ 7²⁹ 10¹⁶ 14¹² 17²⁴ 19³⁵, Ac 5³⁷ 15¹¹ 18¹⁹, Ro 11²³, ɪ Co 10⁶, ɪɪ Ti 2¹², He 4².†

κακία, -ας, ἡ (< κακός), [in LXX chiefly for רָעָה;] 1. *badness* in quality (opp. to ἀρετή, *excellence*). 2. *wickedness, depravity, malignity :* Ac 8²², Ro 1²⁹, ɪ Co 5⁸ 14²⁰, Eph 4³¹, Col 3⁸, Tit 3³, Ja 1²¹, ɪ Pe 2¹, ¹⁶. 3. In late Gk., *evil, trouble, affliction* (Am 3⁶, ɪ Ki 6⁹, Ec 7¹⁵, Si 19⁶, al.): Mt 6³⁴ (cf. MM, *Exp.*, xv).†
SYN. : πονηρία.

** κακοήθεια (WH, -θία), -ας, ἡ (< κακός, ἦθος), [in LXX: Es 8¹³, ɪɪɪ Mac 3²² 7³ A, ɪᴠ Mac 1⁴ 3⁴ *;] *malignity, malevolence :* Ro 1²⁹ (Cremer, 329).†

κακολογέω, -ῶ (< κακολόγος, *slanderous*), [in LXX: Ex 21¹⁶ 22²⁸, ɪ Ki 3¹³, Pr 20²⁰, Ez 22⁷ (קלל pi., hi.), ɪɪ Mac 4¹ *;] *to speak ill of, revile, abuse :* c. acc. pers., Mt 15⁴, Mk 7¹⁰ (ʟxx) 9³⁰; c. acc. rei, Ac 19⁹.†

κακοπάθεια (WH, -θία), -ας, ἡ (< κακοπαθής, *suffering*), [in LXX: Ma 1¹³ (תְּלָאָה), ɪɪ Mac 2²⁶, ²⁷, ɪᴠ Mac 9⁸ *;] *distress, affliction :* Ja 5¹⁰.†

κακοπαθέω, -ῶ, [in LXX: Jh 4¹⁰ (עמל) *;] *to suffer evil, endure affliction :* ɪɪ Ti 2⁹ 4⁵, Ja 5¹³.†

κακο-ποιέω, -ῶ, [in LXX chiefly for רעע hi.;] *to do harm, to do evil :* Mk 3⁴, Lk 6⁹, ɪ Pe 3¹⁷, ɪɪɪ Jo ¹¹ (Cremer, 329).†

κακοποιός, -όν (< κακόν, ποιέω), [in LXX: Pr 12⁴ (בּוֹשׁ hi.) 24¹⁹ (רעע hi.) *;] *doing evil ;* as susbt., *an evil-doer :* ɪ Pe 2¹², ¹⁴ 4¹⁵.†

κακός, -ή, -όν, [in LXX chiefly for רַע, רָעָה;] 1. in general, opp. to ἀγαθός, καλός, in various senses, *bad, mean, base, worthless* (cl.). 2. In ethical sense, *base, evil, wicked :* of persons, Mt 21⁴¹ 24⁴⁸, Phl 3²; Re 2²; διαλογισμοί, Mk 7²¹; ὁμιλίαι, ɪ Co 15³³; ἐπιθυμία (Pr 12¹²); Col 3⁵; ἔργον, Ro 13³; neut., κακόν, τὸ κ., *evil :* Jo 18²³, Ac 23⁹, Ro 7²¹ 14²⁰ 16¹⁹, ɪ Co 13⁵, He 5¹⁴, ɪ Pe 3¹⁰, ¹¹, ɪɪɪ Jo ¹¹; pl., Ro 1³⁰, ɪ Co 10⁶, ɪ Ti 6¹⁰, Ja 1¹³; κ. (τὸ, τὰ κ.) ποιεῖν (πράσσειν), Mt 27²³, Mk 15¹⁴, Lk 23²², Jo 18³⁰, Ro 3⁸ 7¹⁹ 13⁴, ɪɪ Co 13⁷, ɪ Pe 3¹²; κατεργάζεσθαι, Ro 2⁹; of wrongs inflicted, Ac 9¹³, Ro 12¹⁷, ²¹ 13¹⁰, ɪ Th 5¹⁵, ɪɪ Ti 4¹⁴, ɪ Pe 3⁹. 3. *pernicious, harmful, evil :* Lk 16²⁵, Ac 16²⁸ 28⁵, Tit 1¹², Ja 3⁸, Re 16² (Cremer, 325, 741).†
SYN. : v.s. ἄθεσμος.

κακοῦργος, -ον (contr. from epic κακόεργος), [in LXX. Pr 21¹⁵ (פֹּעַל אָוֶן), Es 8¹³, Si 11³³ 30³⁵ (33²⁶) *;] *a malefactor, criminal :* Lk 23³², ³³, ³⁹, ɪɪ Ti 2⁹.†

† κακουχέω, -ῶ (< κακόν, ἔχω), [in LXX: ɪɪɪ Ki 2²⁶ 11³⁹ (ענה pi., hith.) *;] *to ill-treat, hurt, torment :* pass. ptcp., He 11³⁷ 13³.†

κακόω, -ῶ (< κακός), [in LXX chiefly for רעע hi., ענה pi.;] 1. *to ill-treat, afflict, distress :* c. acc. pers., Ac 7⁶, ¹⁹ 12¹ 18¹⁰, ɪ Pe 3¹³. 2. (not in cl.), *to embitter* (Ps 105 (106)³²) : Ac 14².†

κακῶς (< κακός), adv., [in LXX: Wi 18¹⁹, ιν Mac 6¹⁷, al.; κ. εἰπεῖν, ἐρεῖν (קלל אַרר pi.), Ex 22²⁸ ⁽²⁷⁾, Le 19¹⁴, Is 8²¹; κ. ἔχειν (חלה), Ez 34⁴, al.;] badly, ill; (a) in physical sense: κ. ἔχειν, to be ill, Mt 4²⁴ 8¹⁶ 9¹², 14³⁵ 17¹⁵, Mk 1³²,³⁴ 2¹⁷ 6⁵⁵, Lk 5³¹ 7²; πάσχειν, Mt 17¹⁵ (WH, mg.); δαιμονίζεσθαι, Mt 15²²; κακοὺς κ. ἀπολέσει (as freq. in cl., v. LS, s.v.; MM, Exp., xv), evil that they are, he will evilly, etc., Mt 21⁴¹; (b) in moral sense, wrongly (ι Mac 7⁴², ιν Mac, l.c., al.): κ. λαλεῖν, Jo 18²³; εἰπεῖν, c. acc. pers., Ac 23⁵; αἰτεῖσθαι, Ja 4³.†

κάκωσις, -εως, ἡ (κακόω), [in LXX (for עֲנִי, רָעָה, etc.): Ex 3⁷, Je 2²⁸, Wi 3², al.;] ill-treatment: Ac 7³⁴ (LXX).†

καλάμη, -ης, ἡ (cf. κάλαμος), [in LXX chiefly for קַשׁ, Ex 5¹², Is 5²⁴, al.;] a stalk of corn, stubble: ι Co 3¹².†

κάλαμος, -ου, ὁ, [in LXX chiefly for קָנֶה, Is 42³, Ez 40³ ᶠᶠ., al.;] a reed: Mt 11⁷ 12²⁰ (LXX), Lk 7²⁴; hence, acc. to its various uses, (a) a reed-pipe, flute; (b) a reed-staff, staff (cf. ιν Ki 18²¹, ῥάβδος καλαμίνη): Mt 27²⁹, ³⁰, ⁴⁸, Mk 15¹⁹, ³⁶; (c) a measuring reed or rod (Ez, l.c.): Re 11¹ 21¹⁵, ¹⁶; (d) a writing reed, a pen: ιιι Jo ¹³ (cf. Milligan, NTD, 9, 7).†

καλέω, -ῶ, [in LXX chiefly for קרא;] 1. to call, summon: c. acc. pers., Mt 20⁸ 25¹⁴, Mk 3³¹, Lk 19¹³, Ac 4¹⁸; seq. ἐκ, Mt 2¹⁵ (LXX); metaph., ι Pe 2⁹. 2. to call to one's house, invite: Lk 14¹⁶, ι Co 10²⁷, Re 19⁹; εἰς τ. γάμους, Mt 22³, ⁹, Lk 14⁸, ⁹, Jo 2²; ὁ καλέσας, Lk 7³⁹; οἱ κεκλημένοι, Mt 22⁸; metaph., of inviting to partake of the blessings of the kingdom of God (Dalman, Words, 118 f.): Ro 8³⁰ 9²⁴, ²⁵, ι Co 7¹⁷, ¹⁸; seq. εἰς, ι Co 1⁹, ι Th 2¹², ι Ti 6¹²; ὁ καλῶν (καλέσας), of God, Ga 1⁶ 5⁸, ι Th 5²⁴, ι Pe 1¹⁵, ιι Pe 1³; οἱ κεκλημένοι, He 9¹⁵; seq. ἐν (ἐπί), ι Co 7¹⁵, Ga 5¹³, Eph 4⁴, ι Th 4⁷; κλήσει, Eph 4¹, ιι Ti 1⁹. 3. to call, name, call by name: pass., Mt 2²³, Lk 1³², al.; καλούμενος, Lk 7¹¹, Ac 7⁵⁸, al.; ὁ κ. (Deiss., BS, 210), Lk 6¹⁵ 22³ 23³³, Ac 10¹, Re 12⁹, al.; c. pred. nom., Mt 5⁹, Lk 1³⁵, Ro 9²⁶, Ja 2²³, ι Jo 3¹. (Cf. ἀντι-, ἐν-, εἰσ- (-μαι), ἐπι-, μετα-, παρα-, συν-παρα-, προ-, προσ-, συν-καλέω.)

* καλλιέλαιος, ου, ἡ, the garden olive (opp. to ἀγριέλ-): Ro 11²⁴.†

καλλίων, -ον, compar. of καλός, v.s. καλῶς.

*† καλο-διδάσκαλος, -ου, ὁ, a teacher of that which is good: Tit 2³.†

Καλοὶ Λιμένες, Fair Havens, a harbour in Crete: Ac 27⁸.†

† καλο-ποιέω, -ῶ, [in LXX: Le 5⁴ F (καλῶς π., B)*;] to do well, act honourably: ιι Th 3¹³ (cf. Ga 6⁹ τὸ καλὸν π.).†

καλός, -ή, -όν, [in LXX chiefly for טוֹב, טוֹבָה, also for יָפֶה, etc.;] 1. primarily, of outward form ("related to . . . ἀγαθός as the appearance to the essence," Cremer, 339), fair, beautiful: λίθοι (EV, goodly), Lk 21⁵. 2. In reference to use, of that which is well adapted to its ends, good, excellent: of fish, τ. καλά (opp. to σαπρά), Mt 13⁴⁸; σπέρμα, Mt 13²⁴, ²⁷, ³⁷, ³⁸; καρπός, Mt 3¹⁰ 7¹⁷⁻¹⁹ 12³³, Lk 3⁹ [WH] 6⁴³; δένδρον (opp. to σαπρόν), Mt 12³³, Lk 6⁴³; γῆ, Mt 13⁸, ²³, Mk 4⁸, ²⁰, Lk 8¹⁵; τ. ἅλας, Mk 9⁵⁰, Lk 14³⁴; ὁ νόμος, Ro 7¹⁶, ι Ti 1⁸; διδασκαλία, ι Ti 4⁶;

καρδία κ. καὶ ἀγαθή, Lk 8¹⁵; παραθήκη, II Ti 1¹⁴; μέτρον, Lk 6³⁸; βαθμός, I Ti 3¹³; θεμέλιος, I Ti 6¹⁹; τὸ κ., I Th 5²¹; μαργαρῖται, Mt 13⁴⁵; οἶνος, Jo 2¹⁰; ποιμήν, Jo 10¹¹,¹⁴; διάκονος, I Ti 4⁶; οἰκονόμος, I Pe 4¹⁰; στρατιώτης, II Ti 2³; στρατεία, I Ti 1¹⁸; ἀγών, I Ti 6¹², II Ti 4⁷; ὁμολογία, I Ti 6¹²,¹³; ἔργον, Mt 26¹⁰, Mk 14⁶, Jo 10³³, I Ti 3¹; pl., Jo 10³²; καλόν ἐστιν, c. inf. et dat., Mt 18⁸,⁹, I Co 7¹,²⁶ 9¹⁵; id. c. acc. et inf., Mt 17⁴, Mk 9⁵,⁴³,⁴⁵,⁴⁷, Lk 9³³, He 13⁹; seq. εἰ, Mt 26²⁴, Mk 9⁴² 14²¹; ἐάν, I Co 7⁸. 3. Ethically, *good*, in the sense of right, fair, noble, honourable: Ga 4¹⁸, He 5¹⁴; ἔργα, Mt 5¹⁶, I Ti 5¹⁰,²⁵ 6¹⁸, Tit 2⁷,¹⁴ 3⁸,¹⁴ (Field, *Notes*, 223 f.), He 10²⁴, I Pe 2¹²; ἀναστροφή, Ja 3¹³, I Pe 2¹²; συνείδησις, He 13¹⁸; seq. ἐνώπιον, Ro 12¹⁷, II Co 8²¹, I Ti 2³; τὸ κ. ποιεῖν (κατεργάζεσθαι), Ro 7¹⁸,²¹, II Co 13⁷, Ga 6⁹, Ja 4¹⁷; καλόν ἐστιν, c. inf., Mt 15²⁶ (T, ἔξεστιν), Mk 7²⁷, Ro 14²¹, Ga 4¹⁸; μαρτυρία, I Ti 3⁷; ὄνομα, Ja 2⁷; καύχημα, I Co 5⁶ (neg.); θεοῦ ῥῆμα, He 6⁵. κ. does not occur in Re.†

SYN.: v.s. ἀγαθός.

κάλυμμα, -τος, τό (< καλύπτω), [in LXX: Nu 3²⁵ 4⁸ ff. (מִכְסֶה), Ex 34³³ ff. (מַסְוֶה), etc.;] *a covering, veil*: II Co 3¹³⁻¹⁶.†

καλύπτω, [in LXX almost always for כסה pi.;] in cl., rare in prose, *to cover*: c. acc. pers., Lk 23³⁰; c. acc. rei et dat., Lk 8¹⁶; pass., Mt 8²⁴; metaph., *to veil, conceal*: pf. ptcp. pass., Mt 10²⁶, II Co 4³; of the forgiveness of sins (cf. Ps 31 (32)⁵ 84 (85)²; *DB*, ii, 56ᵇ): I Pe 4⁸, Ja 5²⁰; (v.l. for καιομένη, WH, mg., Lk 24³²).†

καλῶς, adv. (< καλός), [in LXX for parts and derivatives of יטב;] *finely, rightly, well*: Lk 6⁴⁸, I Co 14¹⁷, Ga 4¹⁷ 5⁷, Ja 2³; λέγειν, λαλεῖν, etc., Mt 15⁷, Mk 7⁶ 12²⁸, Lk 6²⁶ 20³⁹, Jo 4¹⁷ 8⁴⁸ 13¹³ 18²³, Ac 28²⁵; as exclamation of approval, Mk 12³², Ro 11²⁰; κ. ποιεῖν, Mt 12¹², I Co 7³⁷,³⁸, Ja 2⁸,¹⁹; c. dat. pers. (cl. acc.; WM, § 32, 1 β), Lk 6²⁷; c. acc. rei, Mk 7³⁷; c. ptcp., Ac 10³³ (M, *Pr.*, 131), Phl 4¹⁴, II Pe 1¹⁹, III Jo ⁶; προΐστάναι (-ασθαι), I Ti 3⁴,¹² 5¹⁷; διακονεῖν, I Ti 3¹³; ἀνατρέφεσθαι, He 13¹⁸; ironically, Mk 7⁹, II Co 11⁴ (but v. *CGT*, in l.); κ. ἔχειν, *to be well*: Mk 16⁽¹⁸⁾. Compar., κάλλιον (for superl., Bl., § 44, 3), *very well*: Ac 25¹⁰.†

κἀμέ = καὶ ἐμέ, v.s. ἐγώ.

κάμηλος, -ου, ὁ, ἡ, [in LXX for גָּמָל;] *camel*: Mt 3⁴, Mk 1⁶; in proverbs, Mt 19²⁴ 23²⁴, Mk 10²⁵, Lk 18²⁵ (on the v.l. κάμιλος, v. WH, *Notes*, 151).†

κάμιλος, v.s κάμηλος, and cf. Thayer; LS, s.v.

κάμινος, -ου, ἡ, [in LXX: Ge 19²⁸, Ex 19¹⁸, Is 48¹⁰, al. (כּוּר, כִּבְשָׁן), Da LXX TH 3⁶ ff. (אַתּוּן);] *a furnace*: Mt 13⁴²,⁵⁰, Re 1¹⁵ 9².†

καμμύω (syncopated form of καταμύω, used by Ep. and κοινή writers; Rutherford, *NPhr.*, 426 f.), [in LXX: Is 6¹⁰ (שׁעע hi.) 29¹⁰ 33¹⁵ (עצם), La 3⁴⁴ AR *;] *to shut the eyes*: τ. ὀφθαλμούς, Mt 13¹⁵, Ac 28²⁷ (Is, l.c.).†

κάμνω, [in LXX: Jb 10¹ (קוט ni.) 17², Wi 4¹⁶ 15⁹, IV Mac 3⁸

7¹³ *;] 1. *to work;* hence, from the effect of continued work, 2. *to be weary:* He 12³. 3. *to be sick:* Ja 5¹⁵.†

κάμοι = καὶ ἐμοί, v.s. ἐγώ.

κάμπτω, [in LXX chiefly for כרע, IV Ki 1¹³, II Ch 29²⁹, Is 45²⁴ ⁽²³⁾, al.;] *to bend, bow:* c. acc. rei, γόνυ, τὰ γ.; c. dat. pers., τῇ Βάαλ, Ro 11⁴ ⁽ᴸˣˣ⁾; πρὸς τ. πατέρα, Eph 3¹⁴; by meton., πᾶν γόνυ for πᾶς, Ro 14¹¹ ⁽ᴸˣˣ⁾, Phl 2¹⁰ (cf. ἀνα-, συν-κάμπτω).†

κἄν, by crasis for καὶ ἄν (= ἐάν; WH, *App.*, 145ᵇ; Thayer, s.v.), c. subjunc., 1. *and if:* Mk 16⁽¹⁸⁾, Lk 12³⁸, Jo 8⁵⁵, I Co 13²ˑ³, Ja 5¹⁵; c. ellips., Lk 13⁹. 2. Concessive, *even if:* Mt 21²¹ 26³⁵, Jo 8¹⁴ 10³⁸ 11²⁵, He 12²⁰. 3. As intensive of simple καί (M, *Pr.*, 167; WM, 730; Jannaris, *Gr.*, 598), *even, at least:* Mk 5²⁸ 6⁵⁶, Ac 5¹⁵, II Co 11¹⁶.†

Κανά (Rec. -νᾶ), ἡ, indecl., *Cana,* of Galilee: Jo 2¹ˑ ¹¹ 4⁴⁶ 21².†

Καναναῖος, -ου, ὁ (late Heb. קַנְאָנָא), *a Cananæan* or *Zealot* (cf. ζηλωτής): Mt 10⁴, Mk 3¹⁸ (Rec. -νίτης).†

Κανανίτης, v.s. Καναναῖος.

Κανδάκη, -ης, ἡ, *Candace:* Ac 8²⁷.†

κανών, -όνος, ὁ (cf. κάννα, and Heb. קָנֶה, *a reed*), [in LXX: Mi 7⁴, Jth 13⁶, IV Mac 7²¹ (and in Aq., Ps 18 (19)⁵, Jb 38⁵) *;] 1. *a rod* or *bar* (Jth, l.c.). 2. *a measuring rule;* hence, metaph, 3. *a rule* or *standard:* Ga 6¹⁶. 4. *a limit* (RV, *province*): II Co 10¹³ˑ ¹⁵ˑ ¹⁶. (For the history of the word and esp. its later meanings, v. Westc., *Canon, App. A;* cf. also MM, *Exp.,* xv; Cremer, 744.)†

Καπερναούμ, v.s. Καφαρναούμ.

* καπηλεύω (<κάπηλος, *a huckster,* cf. Is 1²² ⁽ᴸˣˣ⁾, Si 26²⁹), *to make a trade of* (RV, mg., *make merchandise of*), or perhaps (cf. Is, l.c.) *to corrupt* (RV, txt.): II Co 2¹⁷.†

καπνός, -οῦ, ὁ, [in LXX for עָשָׁן;] *smoke:* Re 8⁴ 9²ˑ ³ˑ ¹⁷ˑ ¹⁸ 14¹¹ 15⁸ 18⁹ˑ ¹⁸ 19³; ἀτμὶς καπνοῦ, Ac 2¹⁹ ⁽ᴸˣˣ⁾.†

Καππαδοκία, -ας, ἡ, *Cappadocia,* a province of Asia Minor: Ac 2⁹, I Pe 1¹.†

καρδία, -ας, ἡ, [in LXX chiefly for לֵב, לֵבָב;] *the heart,* 1. the bodily organ which is regarded as the seat of life (II Ki 18¹⁴, IV Ki 9²⁴, al.). 2. In a psychological sense, the seat of man's collective energies, the focus of personal life, the seat of the rational as well as the emotional and volitional elements in human life, hence that wherein lies the moral and religious condition of the man (*DB*, ii, 317 f.; *DCG*, ii, 344ᵃ); (*a*) of the seat of physical life (Jg 19⁵, Ps 101 (102)⁵ 103 (104)¹⁵): Ac 14¹⁷, Ja 5⁵; (*b*) of the seat of spiritual life: Mt 5⁸, Mk 7¹⁹, Lk 1⁵¹, Ac 5³, Ro 10⁹ˑ ¹⁰, Eph 6⁵, al.; pl., Mt 9⁴, Mk 2⁶, al.; opp. to στόμα, χείλεα, πρόσωπον, Mt 15⁸, Mk 7⁶, Ro 10⁸ˑ ⁹, II Co 5¹²; περιτομὴ καρδίας, Ro 2²⁹; ἐκ κ., Ro 6¹⁷, I Pe 1²²; ἀπὸ τῶν κ., Mt 18³⁵; ἐν ὅλῃ (ἐξ ὅλης) τ. κ., Mt 22³⁷, Mk 12³⁰ ⁽ᴸˣˣ⁾; γινώσκειν (ἐρευνᾶν, δοκιμάζειν) τὰς κ., Lk 16¹⁵, Ro 8²⁷, I Th 2⁴; to think, etc., ἐν τ. κ., Mt 9⁴, Mk 2⁶, Lk 12⁴⁵, Ro 10⁶; συνιέναι (νοεῖν) τῇ κ., Mt 13¹⁵, Jo 12⁴⁰; ἐπαχύνθη ἡ κ.,

Mt 13¹⁵ (LXX); πωροῦν τὴν κ., Jo 12⁴⁰; κ. εὐθεῖα, Ac 8²¹; πονηρά, He 3¹²; ἀμετανόητος, Ro 2⁵; εἶναι (ἔχειν) ἐν τῇ κ., II Co 7³, Phl 1⁷; ὀδύνη τῇ κ., Ro 9². 3. Of the central or innermost part of anything (of the pith of wood, Arist.): τ. γῆς, Mt 12⁴⁰ (Cremer, 343 ff.).

*† καρδιο-γνώστης, -ου, ὁ (< καρδ.α, γνώστης), knower of hearts: Ac 1²⁴ 15⁸.†

Κάρπος, -ου, ὁ, Carpus: II Ti 4¹³.†

καρπός, -οῦ, ὁ, [in LXX chiefly for פְּרִי;] fruit: of trees, Mt 12³³ 21¹⁹, Mk 11¹⁴, Lk 6⁴⁴ 13⁶, ⁷; of vines, Mt 21³⁴, Mk 12², Lk 20¹⁰, I Co 9⁷; of fields, Mk 4²⁹ (on καιρός as original reading, v. Turner, SNT, pp. 61 f.), Lk 12¹⁷, II Ti 2⁶, Ja 5⁷; βλαστάνειν, Ja 5¹⁸; ποιεῖν (cf. Heb. עָשָׂה פְּרִי), Mt 3¹⁰ 7¹⁷⁻¹⁹ 13²⁶, Lk 3⁹ 6⁴³ 8⁸ 13⁹, Re 22²; διδόναι, Mt 13⁸, Mk 4⁷, ⁸; φέρειν, Mt 7¹⁸, Jo 12²⁴ 15², ⁴, ⁵, ⁸, ¹⁶; ἀποδιδόναι, Mt 21⁴¹, Re 22²; ὁ κ. τ. κοιλίας פְּרִי בֶטֶן, De 28⁴), Lk 1⁴²; τ. ὀσφύος (Ge 30², al.), Ac 2³⁰. Metaph., (a) of works, deeds: Mt 3⁸ 7¹⁶, ²⁰ 21⁴³, Lk 3⁸, Jo 15⁸, ¹⁶; τ. πνεύματος, Ga 5²²; τ. φωτός, Eph 5⁹; τ. δικαιοσύνης, Phl 1¹¹; σφραγίζεσθαι τὸν κ. (Deiss., BS, 238 f.), Ro 15²⁸; κ. ἀγαθοί, Ja 3¹⁷; (b) of advantage, profit: Phl 1²² 4¹⁷; ἔχειν, Ro 1¹³ 6²¹, ²²; συνάγειν, Jo 4³⁶; κ. τ. δικαιοσύνης, He 12¹¹, Ja 3¹⁸; of praise, καρπὸν χειλέων (Ho 14², al.; cf. Æsch., Eum., 830): He 13¹⁵.†

καρπο-φορέω, -ῶ, [in LXX: Hb 3¹⁷ (פָּרַח), Wi 10⁷ *;] to bear fruit: χόρτον, Mk 4²⁸ (cf. Wi, l.c.). Metaph., of conduct: Mt 13²³, Mk 4²⁰, Lk 8¹⁵, Ro 7⁴, ⁵, Col 1¹⁰; mid., Col 1⁶.†

καρπο-φόρος, -ον (< καρπος, φέρω), [in LXX: Je 2²¹ (זֶרַע), Ps 106 (107)³⁴ 148⁹ (פְּרִי) *;] fruitful: Ac 14¹⁷.†

καρτερέω, -ῶ, [in LXX: Jb 2⁹ (חָזַק hi.), Is 42¹⁴ (פָּעָה), Si 2² 12¹⁵, II, IV Mac ₇ *;] to be steadfast, patient: He 11²⁷ (cf. προσ-καρτερέω).†

κάρφος, -εος (-ους) τό, [in LXX: Ge 8¹¹ (טָרָף) *;] a small dry stalk, a twig; metaph., of a minor fault: Mt 7³⁻⁵, Lk 6⁴¹, ⁴².†

κατά (bef. a vowel κατ', καθ'; on the freq. neglect of elision, v. Tdf., Pr., 95; WH, App., 146ª), prep. c. gen., acc., down, downwards. I. C. gen. (WM, § 47, k; Bl., § 42, 2). 1. C. gen. rei, in local sense; (a) down, down from: Mt 8³², Mk 5¹³, Lk 8³³, I Co 11⁴; (b) through-out (late usage; Bl., l.c.): κ. ὅλης κ.τ.λ., Lk 4¹⁴ 23⁵, Ac 9³¹ 10³⁷; (c) in a peculiar adjectival phrase: ἡ κ. βάθους πτωχεία, deep or extreme poverty, II Co 8². 2. C. gen. pers., usually in hostile sense; (a) against (in cl. only after verbs of speaking, witnessing, etc.): opp. to ὑπέρ, Mk 9⁴⁰; μετά, Mt 12³⁰; after ἐπιθυμεῖν, Ga 5¹⁷; λαλεῖν, Ac 6¹³; διδάσκειν, Ac 21²⁸; ψεύδεσθαι, Ja 3¹⁴; after verbs of accusing, etc., Mt 5²³, Lk 23¹⁴, Ro 8³³, al.; verbs of fighting, prevailing, etc., Mt 10³⁵, Ac 14², I Co 4⁶, al.; (b) of swearing, by: ὄμνυμι κ. (Bl., § 34, 1), He 6¹³, ¹⁶, cf. Mt 26⁶³. II. C. acc. (WM, § 49 d; Bl., § 42, 2). 1. Of motion or direction; (a) through, throughout: Lk 8³⁹ 9⁶ 10⁴, Ac 8¹, ³⁶, al.; (b) to, towards, over against: Lk 10³² (Field, Notes, 62), Ac 2¹⁰ 16⁷, Ga 2¹¹, Phl 3¹⁴, al.; (c) in adverbial phrases, at, in, by, of: κατ' οἶκον, at home, Ac 2⁴⁶; κατ᾽ ἰδίαν (v.s. ἴδιος); καθ᾽ ἑαυτόν, Ac 28¹⁶, Ro 14²², Ja 2¹⁷; c. pron. pers., Ac 17²⁸ 18¹⁵, Ro 1¹⁵, Eph 1¹⁵, al. 2. Of time, at, during, about: Ac 8²⁶ 12¹ 19²³, Ro 9⁹, He 1¹⁰, al. 3. Distributive; (a) of place: κ. τόπους, Mt 24⁷, al.; κ. πόλιν, Lk 8¹·⁴, al.; κ. ἐκκλησίαν, Ac 14²³; (b) of time: κ. ἔτος, Lk 2⁴¹; ἑορτήν, Mt 27¹⁵, al.; (c) of numbers, etc.: καθ᾽ ἕνα πάντες, ι Co 14³¹ (on καθ᾽ εἷς, v.s. εἷς); κ. ἑκατόν, Mk 6⁴⁰; κ. μέρος, He 9⁵; κ. ὄνομα, Jo 10³. 4. Of fitness, reference, conformity, etc.; (a) in relation to, concerning: Ro 1³·⁴ 7²² 9³·⁵, ι Co 1²⁶ 10¹⁸, Phl 1¹²; κ. πάντα, Ac 17²², Col 3²⁰·²², He 2¹⁷ 4¹⁵; (b) according to, after, like: Mk 7⁵, Lk 2²⁷·²⁹, Jo 7²⁴, Ro 8⁴ 14¹⁵, Eph 2², Col 2⁸, Ja 2⁸, al. III. In composition, κ. denotes, 1. down, down from (καταβαίνω, etc.), hence, metaph.; (a) victory or rule over (καταδουλόω, -κυριεύω, etc.); (b) "perfective" action (M, Pr., 111 ff.). 2. under (κατακαλύπτω, etc.). 3. in succession (καθεξῆς). 4. after, behind (καταλείπω). 5. Hostility, against (καταλαλέω).

κατα-βαίνω, [in LXX chiefly for ירד;] to go or come down, descend. 1. Of persons: Mt 3¹⁶ 24¹⁷, Lk 2⁵¹ 6¹⁷ 10³¹ 17³¹ 19⁵·⁶, Jo 4⁴⁷·⁴⁹·⁵¹ 5⁷, Ac 7³⁴ 8¹⁵ 10²⁰ 20¹⁰ 23¹⁰ 24¹·²², Eph 4¹⁰; seq. ἀπό, Mt 8¹ 14²⁹ 27⁴⁰·⁴², Mk 3²² 15³⁰, Lk 10³⁰, Jo 6³⁸, Ac 25⁷, ι Th 4¹⁶; ἐκ, Mt 17⁹; ἐκ τ. οὐρανοῦ, Mt 28², Mk 9⁹, Jo 1³² 3¹³ 6³³·⁴¹·⁴²·⁵⁰·⁵¹·⁵⁸, Re 10¹ 18¹ 20¹; εἰς, Mk 1¹⁰, Lk 10³⁰ 18¹⁴, Jo 2¹², Ac 7¹⁵ 8³⁸ 14²⁵ 16⁸ 18²² 25⁶, Ro 10⁷, Eph 4⁹; ἐπί, c. acc. loc., Jo 6¹⁶; c. acc. pers., Lk 3²², Jo 1³³·⁵²; ἐν, Jo 5⁽⁴⁾; πρός, c. acc pers., Ac 10²¹ 14¹¹, Re 12¹². 2. Of things: σκεῦος, Ac 10¹¹ 11⁵; βροχή, Mt 7²⁵·²⁷; λαῖλαψ, Lk 8²³; seq. ἀπό, Lk 9⁵⁴, Ac 8²⁶, Ja 1¹⁷; ἐπὶ τ. γῆν, Lk 22⁴⁴ (WH, R, mg., reject); ἐκ τ. οὐρανοῦ seq. ἀπό, Re 3¹² 21²·¹⁰; id. seq. εἰς, Re 13¹³; ἐπί, c. acc. pers., Re 16²¹. Fig., κ. ἕως ᾅδου, Mt 11²³, Lk 10¹⁵, WH, txt., Tr., mg. (καταβιβασθήσῃ, T, WH, mg., RV), (cf. συν-καταβαίνω).†

κατα-βάλλω, [in LXX chiefly for נפל hi.;] 1. to cast down, prostrate: metaph., pass., ιι Co 4⁹. 2. to put down, lay down: metaph., mid., c. acc., θεμέλιον, He 6¹.†

*† κατα-βαρέω, -ῶ, to weigh down: metaph., c. acc. pers., ιι Co 12¹⁶.†

† κατα-βαρύνω, [in LXX: ιι Ki 13²⁵ 14²⁶ (כבד), Jl 2⁸, Si 8¹⁵ *;] = καταβαρέω: pass., pres. ptcp., Mk 14⁴⁰.†

κατα-βιβάζω, [in LXX for ירד (hi., etc.): De 21⁴, Ez 31¹⁶, al.;] to cause to go down, cast down: pass., ἕως ᾅδου, Mt 11²³ (WH, R, mg.), Lk 10¹⁵ (WH, mg.).†

** κατα-βολή, -ῆς, ἡ (< καταβάλλω), [in LXX: ιι Mac 2²⁹ *;] 1. a laying down: εἰς κ. σπέρματος, He 11¹¹ (EV, to conceive seed). 2. a foundation (of a house, ιι Mac, l.c.): metaph., ἀπὸ κ. κόσμου, Mt 13³⁵ (LXX) (om. κόσμου WH, R, mg.), ib. 25³⁴, Lk 11⁵⁰, He 4³ 9²⁶, Re 13⁸ 17⁸; πρὸ κ. κόσμου, Jo 17²⁴, Eph 1⁴, ι Pe 1²⁰.†

* κατα-βραβεύω (< βραβεύς, an umpire, cf. βραβεῖον), to give judgment against, condemn (v. Field, Notes, 196; Abbott, Essays, 104 f.): Col 2¹⁸.†

*† καταγγελεύς, -έως, ὁ, a proclaimer, herald (in Inscr., κ. ἀγώνων, Deiss., LAE, 97): c. gen. obj., Ac 17¹⁸.†

κατ-αγγέλλω, [in LXX : Pr 17⁵ A, ii Mac 8³⁶ 9¹⁷ *;] 1. *to proclaim, declare :* c. acc. rei, Ac 3²⁴ 16²¹ 17²³ ; τ. ἀνάστασιν, Ac 4² ; τ. λόγον τοῦ θ., τ. κ., Ac 13⁵ 15³⁶ ; ὁδὸν σωτηρίας, Ac 16¹⁷ ; φῶς, Ac 26²³ ; τ. μυστήριον τοῦ θ., ι Co 2¹ ; τ. εὐαγγέλιον, 9¹⁴ ; τ. θάνατον τοῦ κ., 11²⁶ ; pass., ἄφεσις, Ac 13³⁸ ; ὁ λόγος τοῦ θ., ib. 17¹³ ; ἡ πίστις ὑμῶν, Ro 1⁸ ; c. acc. pers., of Christ, ὅν, Ac 17³, Col 1²⁸ ; τ. Χριστόν, Phl 1¹⁷ ; pass., ib. ¹⁸. 2. *to denounce* (Xen., al.); (for comparison with ἀγγέλλω, ἀναγ-, ἀπαγ-, v. Westc. on ι Jo 1⁵ ; and cf. προ-καταγγέλλω).†

κατα-γελάω, -ῶ, [in LXX chiefly for שׂחק, Jb 5²², Pr 29⁹, al.;] *to deride, laugh scornfully at :* c. gen. pers., Mt 9²⁴, Mk 5⁴⁰, Lk 8⁵³.†

κατα-γινώσκω (v.s. γινώσκω), [in LXX : De 25¹ (רשע hi.), Pr 28¹¹ (חקר), Si 14² 19⁵ *;] *to blame, condemn :* c. gen. pers., ι Jo 3²⁰, ²¹ ; pass., κατεγνωσμένος ἦν (RV, *he stood condemned,* v. Ellic., in l. ; but cf. Field, *Notes,* 188) : Ga 2¹¹.†

κατ-άγνυμι, [in LXX for נחת pi., etc.;] *to break :* c. acc. rei, Mt 12²⁰ (LXX), Jo 19³¹⁻³³.†

κατα-γράφω, [in LXX chiefly for כתב ;] *to trace, draw in outline* (= Att. ἀναγρ-) : Jo 8⁶ (ἔγραφεν, Rec.).†

κατ-άγω, [in LXX chiefly for ירד hi.;] *to bring down :* c. acc. pers., Ac 22³⁰, Ro 10⁶ ; id. seq. εἰς, Ac 9³⁰ 23¹⁵, ²⁰, ²⁸ ; as nautical term, *to bring to land :* τ. πλοῖον ἐπὶ τ. γῆν, Lk 5¹¹ ; pass., seq. εἰς, Ac 27³ 28¹².†

*† κατ-αγωνίζομαι, depon., "perfective" compound (M, *Pr.*, 116); 1. *to struggle against.* 2. *to conquer, overcome :* He 11³³.†

κατα-δέω, -ῶ, [in LXX for חבש, etc.;] *to bind up :* τ. τραύματα (cf. Si 27²¹), Lk 10³⁴.†

* κατά-δηλος, -ον (δ᾽λος), *quite manifest, evident :* He 7¹⁵.†

κατα-δικάζω, [in LXX : Ps 93 (94)²¹ (רשע hi.), La 3³⁶ (עות pi.), Wi 2²⁰, al.;] *to pass sentence upon, condemn ;* in cl., c. gen. pers. (acc. rei); in late writers (so LXX), c. acc. pers. (θανάτῳ, Wi, l.c.) : Mt 12⁷, Ja 5⁶ ; absol. (as Plat., *Legg.*, 958c), Lk 6³⁷ ; pass., Mt 12³⁷, Lk 6³⁷.†

** κατα-δίκη, -ης, ἡ, [in LXX : Wi 12²⁷ *;] *sentence, condemnation :* Ac 25¹⁵. †

κατα-διώκω, [in LXX chiefly for רדף ;] "perfective" compound (M, *Pr.*, 116), *to pursue closely, follow up ;* (a) with hostile intent (Thuc., i, 49, Ge 31³⁶ al.); (b) with kindly intention (Ps 22 (23)⁶, ι Ki 30²², cf. Si 27¹⁷) : Mk 1³⁶.†

κατα-δουλόω, -ῶ, [in LXX chiefly for עבד ;] *to enslave :* ii Co 11²⁰, Ga 2⁴.†

κατα-δυναστεύω, [in LXX for ינה, עשׁק, etc.;] *to exercise power over, oppress :* c. acc. pers. (Xen.; LXX, Mi 2², Wi 2¹⁰, al.); c. gen. pers., Ja 2⁶ (ὑμᾶς, T); pass., Ac 10³⁸ (cf. MM, *Exp.*, xv).†

*† κατά-θεμα, -τος, τό, *a curse* ("perh. somewhat stronger than ἀνάθεμα," Swete, *Re.*, l.c.) : Re 22³ (cf. ἀνάθεμα).†

*† κατα-θεματίζω, *to curse vehemently :* Mt 26⁷⁴ (cf. ἀναθεμ-).†

κατ-αισχύνω, [in LXX chiefly for בּוּשׁ ;] *to disgrace, dishonour, put to shame :* c. acc. rei, ι Co 11⁴, ⁵ ; c. acc. pers., ι Co 1²⁷ 11²² ; pass., *to be ashamed:* Lk 13¹⁷, ɪɪ Co 7¹⁴ 9⁴, ɪ Pe 3¹⁶; as in LXX (Ps 21 (22)⁶ 24 (25)²,³, al.), of unfulfilled hopes: Ro 5⁵; pass., Ro 9³³ 10¹¹, ɪ Pe 2⁶ (LXX).†

κατα-καίω, [in LXX chiefly for שׂרף; in Ex 3² (אכל pu.), distinguished from καίω;] *to burn up, burn completely:* c. acc. rei, Mt 13³⁰, Ac 19¹⁹; pass., ɪ Co 3¹⁵, He 13¹¹, ɪɪ Pe 3¹⁰, Re 8⁷; seq. πυρί, Mt 3¹² 13⁴⁰, Lk 3¹⁷ (cf. Ex 29¹⁴, al.); ἐν πυρί (De 9²¹, al.): Re 17¹⁶ 18⁸.†

κατα-καλύπτω, [in LXX chiefly for כסה pi.;] *to cover up;* mid., *to cover* or *veil oneself:* ɪ Co 11⁶; τ. κεφαλήν, ib. ⁷.†

† κατα-καυχάομαι, -ῶμαι, [in LXX: Za 10¹² (הלך hith.), Je 27 (50)¹¹ (עלז), ib. ³⁸ (הלל)*;] 1. *to boast against, exult over:* c. gen., Ro 11¹⁸, Ja 2¹³; seq. κατά, c. gen., Ja 3¹⁴ (T, om. κατά). 2. seq. ἐν, *to glory in* (Za., l.c., Je 27³⁸).†

κατά-κειμαι, [in LXX: Pr 6⁹ 23³⁴ (שׁכב), Jth 13¹⁵, Wi 17⁷ *;] 1. *to lie down.* 2. *to lie sick:* Mk 1³⁰ 2⁴, Jo 5⁶, Ac 28⁸; seq. ἐπί, c. gen., Ac 9³³; id. c. acc., Lk 5²⁵; ἐν, Jo 5³. 3. *to recline* at meals (cf. ἀνάκειμαι): Mk 14³, Lk 5²⁹; seq. ἐν, Mk 2¹⁵, Lk 7³⁷, ɪ Co 8¹⁰.†

κατα-κλάω, -ῶ, [in LXX: Ez 19¹² (נתש hoph.)*;] *to break up, break in pieces:* Mk 6⁴¹, Lk 9¹⁶.†

κατα-κλείω, [in LXX: Je 39 (32)³ (כלא), Wi 17²,¹⁶, ɪɪ Mac 13²¹, ɪɪɪ Mac 3²⁵ *;] *to shut up:* c. acc. pers., seq. ἐν φυλακῇ (-αῖς), Lk 3²⁰, Ac 26¹⁰.†

† κατα-κληροδοτέω, ῶ, [in LXX: De 1³⁸ 21¹⁶ A (-νομέω, B), ɪ Mac 3³⁶ א R (-νομέω, A)*;] Ac 13¹⁹, Rec., = -νομέω, q.v.†

† κατα-κληρονομέω, -ῶ, [in LXX for נחל, ירשׁ, etc.;] 1. *to distribute by lot* or *as an inheritance* (Nu 34¹⁸, Jos 14¹, al.): Ac 13¹⁹. 2. *to receive by inheritance* (De 1³⁸, al.).†

κατα-κλίνω, [in LXX: Ex 21¹⁸ (נפל), Nu 24⁹, Jg 5²⁷ (כרע), ɪ Ki 16¹¹ (סבב), Jth 12¹⁵, ɪɪɪ Mac 1³ *;] *to lay down, make to lie down,* esp. for meals: c. acc. pers., Lk 9¹⁴,¹⁵; mid., *to recline* at meals: Lk 7³⁶ 24³⁰; seq. εἰς, Lk 14⁸ (cf. Jth, l.c.).†

κατα-κλύζω, [in LXX for שׁטף, Ps 77 (78)²⁰, al.;] *to inundate, deluge:* pass., ɪɪ Pe 3⁶.†

κατα-κλυσμός, -οῦ, ὁ (< κατακλύζω), [in LXX chiefly for מבּול, Ge 6¹⁷, al.; also for שׁטף, Ps 31 (32)⁶, al.;] *a flood, deluge:* Mt 24³⁸,³⁹, Lk 17²⁷, ɪɪ Pe 2⁵.†

† κατ-ακολουθέω, -ῶ, [in LXX: Je 17¹⁶ (רעה), ɪ Mac 6²³, al.;] *to follow after:* Lk 23⁵⁵; c. dat. pers., Ac 16¹⁷.†

κατα-κόπτω, [in LXX for נכה hi., כתת pi., etc.;] *to cut up, cut in pieces* (cf. Is 27⁹, Je 21⁷, ɪɪ Ch 34⁷): ἑαυτὸν λίθοις, Mk 5⁵.†

κατα-κρημνίζω (< κρημνός), [in LXX: ɪɪ Ch 25¹² (שׁלך hi.), ɪɪ Mac 12¹⁵ 14⁴³, ɪᴠ Mac 4²⁵ *;] *to throw over a precipice, cast down headlong:* Lk 4²⁹.†

*† κατά-κριμα, -τος, τό (< κατακρίνω), penalty (RV, condemnation; but cf. Deiss., BS, 264 f.; MM, Exp., xv): Ro 5¹⁶,¹⁸ 8¹.†

κατα-κρίνω, [in LXX: Es 2¹ (גזר ni.), Wi 4¹⁶, Da LXX ᴛʜ Su 53

4³⁴, TH Su ⁴¹, ⁴⁸, ⁵³ * ;] *to give judgment against, condemn :* Ro 8³⁴; c. acc. pers., Mk 14⁶⁴, Jo 8[¹⁰, ¹¹]; disting. fr. κρίνειν, Ro 2¹, I Co 11³²; seq. θανάτῳ (cl. -ον or -ον), Mt 20¹⁸, Mk 10³³; pass., Mt 27³, Mk 16[¹⁶], Ro 14²³, I Co 11³², II Pe 2⁶. Metaph., of condemning through a good example : Mt 12⁴¹, ⁴², Lk 11³¹, ³², Ro 8³, He 11⁷ ⊦

*✝ κατά-κρισις, -εως, ἡ (< κατακρίνω), *condemnation :* II Co 3⁹ 7³ (cf. Deiss., *LAE,* 91 f.).✝

κατα-κύπτω, [in LXX : IV Ki 9³² (שָׁקַף hi.)*;] *to bend down, stoop :* Jo 8[⁸] (κάτω κύψας, Rec., WH, mg.).✝

κατα-κυριεύω, [in LXX : Ge 1²⁸ (כָּבַשׁ), Ps 109 (110)² (רדה), Si 17⁴, al.;] *to gain or exercise dominion (over); (a)* absl. (Arist.) ; *(b)* c. gen. (Arist., al.) : Mt 20²⁵, Mk 10⁴², Ac 19¹⁶, I Pe 5³.✝ *SYN.:* κατεξουσιάζω (v. Swete, *Mk.,* l.c.).

κατα-λαλέω, -ῶ, [in LXX chiefly for דבר ni., pi.;] *to speak evil of, rail at :* in cl., c. acc.; in LXX, *(a)* c. gen., *(b)* seq. κατά, c. gen.; in NT, c. gen. (M, *Pr.,* 65) : Ja 4¹¹, I Pe 2¹²; pass., I Pe 3¹⁶.✝

**✝ κατα-λαλιά, -ᾶς, ἡ (< κατάλαλος), [in LXX: Wi 1¹¹ *;] *evil-speaking, railing :* pl., II Co 12²⁰, I Pe 2¹.✝

*✝ κατά-λαλος, -ον, ὁ, *a railer, defamer :* Ro 1³⁰.✝ *SYN.:* ψιθυριστής, *a whisperer* (v. Tr., *Syn.,* § cvii, 15; Lft., *Notes,* 256).

κατα-λαμβάνω, [in LXX for נשג hi., לכד, etc.;] 1. *to lay hold of, seize, appropriate :* Mk 9¹⁸; c. acc. rei, I Co 9²⁴, Phl 3¹², ¹³. 2. *to overtake :* as correl. of διώκω (Field, *Notes,* 158 f.), Ro 9³⁰; ἡ ἡμέρα, I Th 5⁴; of evils, Jo 1⁵ 12³⁵ (cf. 6¹⁷ T); hence, *to surprise, discover :* Jo 8[³, ⁴]. 3. Of mental action, *to apprehend, comprehend ;* so mid., in NT (M, *Pr.,* 158) : Eph 3¹⁸; seq. ὅτι, Ac 4¹³ 10³⁴; c. acc. et inf., Ac 25²⁵ (MM, *Exp.,* xv).✝

κατα-λέγω, [in LXX : De 19¹⁶ (ענה), II Mac 7³⁰ R *;] 1. *to lay down ;* mid. (in Hom.), *to lie down.* 2. *to narrate* (LXX, ll. c.). 3. *to choose out,* hence, *to enrol* (as of soldiers, Hdt., Thuc., al., v. LS, s.v.) : of widows, pass., I Ti 5⁹ (cf. Ellic.; *CGT,* in l.).✝

✝ κατά-λειμμα, -τος, τό (< καταλείπω), [in LXX for שְׁאָר (Is 10²² 14²²), שְׁאֵרִית, etc.;] *a remnant :* Ro 9²⁷, Rec. (for ὑπόλειμμα, q.v.).✝

κατα-λείπω, [in LXX chiefly for שׁאר, ni., hi., also for עזב, יתר, etc.;] 1. *to leave behind, leave :* c. acc. pers. (rei), Mt 4¹³, Mk 12¹⁹, ²¹, Lk 20³¹, Ac 24²⁷ 25¹⁴, He 11²⁷; of sailing by a place, Ac 21³; ptcp., καταλιπών, redundant (Dalman, *Words,* 21 f.), Mt 16⁴ 21¹⁷; pass., Jo 8[⁹], I Th 3¹; metaph., εὐθεῖαν ὁδόν, II Pe 2¹⁵. 2. *to forsake, abandon :* Mt 19⁵, Mk 10⁷ (LXX) 14⁵², Lk 5²⁸ 15⁴, Ac 6², Eph 5³¹ (LXX). 3. *to leave remaining, reserve :* c. acc. et inf., Lk 10⁴⁰; ἐμαυτῷ, Ro 11⁴ (LXX); pass., He 4¹ (cf. ἐν-κατα-λείπω).✝

*✝ κατα-λιθάζω (= cl. -θόω; cf. -θοβολέω, Ex 17⁴, Nu 14¹⁰), *to cast stones at, to stone :* Lk 20⁶.✝

κατ-αλλαγή, -ῆς, ἡ (< καταλλάσσω), [in LXX : Is 9⁵ ⁽⁴⁾, II Mac 5²⁰ *;] 1. *exchange.* 2. *reconciliation :* Ro 5¹¹; κ. κόσμου, Ro 11¹⁵; διακονία τῆς κ., II Co 5¹⁸; λόγος τῆς κ., ib.¹⁹.✝

κατ-αλλάσσω (Att. -ττω; cf. ἀλλάσσω), [in LXX : Je 31 (48)³⁹ (חתת),
II Mac 1⁵ 7³³ 8²⁹ *;] prop., to change, exchange (esp. of money); hence,
of persons, to change from emnity to friendship, to reconcile (for exx.
in cl., v. Thayer,, LS) : of the reconciliation of man to God (Lft.,
Notes, 288; ICC on Ro, l.c.; DCG, ii, 474, 797), II Co 5¹⁸,¹⁹ ; pass.,
Ro 5¹⁰, II Co 5²⁰; of a woman returning to her husband, I Co 7¹¹ (cf.
ἀπο-καταλλάσσω).†

κατά-λοιπος, -ον, [in LXX for שְׁאָר, שְׁאֵרִית, יֶרֶת, etc.;] left remaining : οἱ κ. τ. ἀνθρώπων, Ac 15¹⁷ (LXX).†

† κατά-λυμα, -τος, τό (< καταλύω), [in LXX : Ex 4²⁴ (מָלוֹן), I Ki
9²² (לִשְׁכָּה), etc.;] 1. = cl. καταγώγιον (cf. πανδοχεῖον), an inn, lodging-
place : Lk 2⁷ (so Ex, l.c., and MGr.). 2. a guest-room (I Ki, l.c.) : Mk
14¹⁴, Lk 22¹¹.†

κατα-λύω, [in LXX for לין, שׁבת, etc.;] 1. to destroy, cast down :
Mt 24², Mk 13², Lk 21⁶ ; τ. ναόν, Mt 26⁶¹ 27⁴⁰, Mk 14⁵⁸ 15²⁹, Ac 6¹⁴ ;
οἰκίαν, II Co 5¹; opp. to οἰκοδομεῖν, Ga 2¹⁸.   Metaph., to overthrow,
annul, abrogate : Ac 5³⁸,³⁹ ; τ. ἔργον τ. θεοῦ, Ro 14²⁰ ; τ. νόμον, Mt 5¹⁷
(II Mac 2²²). 2. to unloose, unyoke (e.g. horses), hence intrans., of
travellers (cf. κατάλυμα), to take up one's quarters, lodge (cl., Ge 19²,
al.) : Lk 9¹² 19⁷.†

κατα-μανθάνω, [in LXX : Ge 34¹ (ראה), Jb 35⁴ (⁵) (שׁוּר), Si 9⁵,⁸, al.;]
to learn thoroughly, observe well, consider carefully (on distinction
bet. κ. and μανθάνω, cf. M, Pr., 117): Mt 6²⁸.†

κατα-μαρτυρέω, -ῶ, [in LXX : Jb 15⁶, Pr 25¹⁸ (ענה), al.;] to bear
witness againt : c. acc. rei et gen. pers., Mt 26⁶² 27¹³, Mk 14⁶⁰.†

κατα-μένω, [in LXX for ישׁב (Nu 20¹, al.), etc.;] to remain
permanently (or temporarily; v. MM, VGT, s.v.), abide, wait: Ac 1¹³ ;
seq. πρός, stay with : I Co 16⁶, WH (παραμ-, T, RV).†

καταμόνας, Rec. for κατὰ μόνας, v.s. μόνος.

† κατ-ανά-θεμα, Rec. for κατάθεμα, q.v.

† κατ-ανα-θεματίζω, Rec. for καταθεματίζω, q.v.

κατ-αν-αλίσκω, [in LXX chiefly for אכל;] 1. to use up, spend.
2. to consume : of fire, ptcp., He 12²⁹ (LXX).†

* κατα-ναρκάω, -ῶ (< ναρκάω, to grow numb, in LXX, in causal
sense, for יקע, Ge 32²⁵ (²⁶); without Heb. equiv., ib.³² (³³), Jb 33¹⁹,
Da LXX 11⁶ *); 1. to cause to grow numb. 2. Intrans., to grow
numb ; hence metaph., to be inactive, be burdensome to · c. gen., II Co
11⁹ 12¹³,¹⁴ ; pass., to be quite numb (Hippocr.).†

* κατα-νεύω, 1. to nod assent. 2. to make a sign by nodding the
head : c. dat. pers., Lk 5⁷.†

κατα-νοέω, -ῶ, [in LXX for נבט hi., ראה, etc.;] to take note of,
perceive, consider carefully : Ac 7³¹,³² ; c. acc. rei, Mt 7³, Lk 6⁴¹
12²⁴,²⁷ 20²³, Ac 11⁶ 27³⁹, Ro 4¹⁹ ; c. acc. pers., He 3¹ 10²⁴, Ja 1²³,²⁴ (on
the distinction bet. κ. and νοέω simplex, v. M, Pr., 117).†

† κατ-αντάω, -ῶ, [in LXX : II Ki 3²⁹ (חול), II Mac 4²¹,²⁴,⁴⁴ 6¹⁴ *;]
to come to, arrive at, come down to (from a higher level), hence reach :
seq. εἰς, c. acc. loc., Ac 16¹ 18¹⁹,²⁴ 21⁷ 25¹³ (v. M, Pr., 132) 27¹² 28¹³ ;

seq. ἀντικρύ, c. gen., Ac 20¹⁵. Metaph., *to descend* by inheritance (MM, *VGT*, s.v.) : sec. εἰς, c. acc. pers., I Co 10¹¹ 14³⁶ ; id. c. acc. rei, *to attain to, reach* (a destination) : Ac 26⁷, Eph 4¹³, Phl 3¹¹ ; cf. MM, *VGT*, s.v.†

† κατά-νυξις, -εως, ή (< κατανύσσω, q.v.), [in LXX : Ps 59 (60)³ (תַּרְעֵלָה), Is 29¹⁰ (תַּרְדֵּמָה) * ;] 1. *a pricking.* 2. (Perhaps through resembl. of κατανύσσω to -νυστάζω), *torpor* of mind, *stupefaction :* Ro 11⁸ (LXX) (v. *ICC,* in l. ; Field, *Notes,* 157).†

† κατα-νύσσω, [in LXX : Ge 34⁷ (עצב) hith.), Le 10³, Ps 4⁴ 29¹², al. (דמם), Da LXX TH Su ¹⁰ (רדם ni.), Si 12¹² 14¹, al. ;] 1. *to strike* or *prick violently.* 2. *to stun.* 3. Of strong emotion, pass., *to be smitten :* τὴν καρδίαν, Ac 2³⁷ (v.s. κατάνυξις).†

** κατ-αξιόω, -ῶ, [in LXX : II Mac 13¹², III Mac 3²¹ 4¹¹, IV Mac 18³ * ;] *to deem worthy :* c. acc. pers. et gen. rei, II Th 1⁵ ; pass. seq. inf., Lk 20³⁵, Ac 5⁴¹.†

κατα-πατέω, -ῶ, [in LXX for דרך, רמס, שאף, etc. ;] *to tread down, trample under foot :* Mt 7⁶, Lk 12¹ ; pass., Mt 5¹³, Lk 8⁵. Metaph., τ. υἱὸν τ. θεοῦ, He 10²⁹.†

κατά-παυσις, -εως, ή (< καταπαύω), [in LXX chiefly for מְנוּחָה, Ps 94 (95)¹¹, Is 66¹, al. ; ἡμέρα τῆς κ., II Mac 15¹ ;] 1. in cl., *a putting to rest, causing to cease.* 2. In LXX and NT, *rest, repose :* Ac 7⁴⁹ (LXX), He 3¹¹, ¹⁸ 4¹, ³, ⁵, ¹⁰, ¹¹.†

κατα-παύω, [in LXX for נוח, שבת, etc. ;] 1. trans., (*a*) *to cause to cease* or *refrain, restrain :* Ac 14¹⁸ ; (*b*) *to cause to rest :* He 4⁸. 2. Intrans., *to rest :* seq., ἀπό, He 4⁴ (LXX), ¹⁰.†

† κατα-πέτασμα, -τος, τό (= cl. παραπέτασμα, *that which is spread out before, a curtain, covering, veil*), [in LXX chiefly for פָּרֹכֶת (the veil of the Holy of Holies), Ex 26³¹, Le 21²³, al. ; also for מָסָךְ (the outer veil), Ex 35¹², Nu 3²⁶, al. (elsewhere κάλυμμα) ;] in NT always the inner *veil* or *curtain* of the Temple (or Tabernacle) : Mt 27⁵¹, Mk 15³⁸, Lk 23⁴⁵, He 6¹⁹ 9³ ; fig., ἡ σὰρξ αἰτοῦ, He 10²⁰.†

κατα-πίνω, [in LXX chiefly for בלע ;] 1. *to drink down, swallow :* Mt 23²⁴, Re 12¹⁶. 2. *to devour :* I Pe 5⁸. Metaph., *to swallow up, consume :* pass., I Co 15⁵⁴ (LXX), II Co 2⁷ 5⁴, He 11²⁹.†

κατα-πίπτω, [in LXX : Ps 144 (145)¹⁴ (נפל), etc. ;] *to fall down :* Ac 28⁶ ; seq. εἰς, Ac 26¹⁴ ; ἐπί, c. acc., Lk 8⁶.†

* κατα-πλέω, -ῶ, *to sail down, sail to land, put in :* εἰς τ. ιχώραν, Lk 8²⁶.†

** κατα-πονέω, -ῶ, [in LXX : II Mac 8² (A), III Mac 2², ¹³ * ;] *to wear down, oppress, treat hardly :* pass., Ac 7²⁴, II Pe 2⁷.†

κατα-ποντίζω, [in LXX for טבע pu., Ex 15⁴ A, בלע pi., שטף, Ps 54 (55)⁹ 68 (69)², al. ;] *to throw into the sea, sink or drown* therein : Mt 14³⁰ ; pass., 18⁶.†

κατ-άρα, -ας, ή, [in LXX chiefly for קְלָלָה ;] *a curse :* Ga 3¹⁰, ¹³, He 6⁸, II Pe 2¹⁴ ; opp. to εὐλογία, Ja 3¹⁰ ; concrete, of Christ, Ga 3¹³ (v. Lft. in l.).†

κατ-αράομαι, -ῶμαι, depon. (< κατάρα), [in LXX chiefly for קָלַל pi. ;] to curse: c. acc., Mk 11²¹; opp. to εὐλογέω, Lk 6²⁶, Ro 12¹⁴, Ja 3⁹; pass. pf. ptcp., accursed, under a curse (v. M, Pr., 221): Mt 25⁴¹.†

κατ-αργέω, -ῶ (< κατά, causative, ἀργός = ἀ-εργός), [in LXX : II Es 4²¹, ²³ 5⁵ 6⁸ (בְּטֵל) *;] to make idle or inactive (χέρας, Eur., Phœn., 753): of soil occupied by an unfruitful tree, Lk 13⁷. Metaph. (Inscr.), to render inoperative or invalid, to abrogate, abolish: Ro 3³, ³¹, I Co 1²⁸ 6¹³ 13¹¹ 15²⁴, Ga 3¹⁷, Eph 2¹⁵, II Th 2⁸, II Ti 1¹⁰, He 2¹⁴; pass., Ro 4¹⁴ 6⁶, I Co 2⁶ 13⁸, ¹⁰ 15²⁶, II Co 3⁷, ¹¹, ¹³, ¹⁴, Ga 5¹¹; seq. ἀπό (of persons), to be separated, discharged or loosed from, Ro 7², ⁶, Ga 5⁴.†

κατ-αριθμέω, -ῶ, [in LXX : II Ch 31¹⁹ (יָחַשׂ hith.), al. ;] to number or count among: seq. ἐν, Ac 1¹⁷.†

κατ-αρτίζω, [in LXX chiefly in Pss (8² al.; כּוּן, etc.) and II Es (בְּלַל) ;] to render ἄρτιος, i.e. fit, complete; (a) to mend, repair: Mt 4²¹, Mk 1¹⁹; (b) to furnish completely, complete, equip, prepare: pass., Lk 6⁴⁰, Ro 9²², He 11³; mid., Mt 21¹⁶ (LXX), He 10⁵ (LXX); (c) in ethical sense, to prepare, complete, perfect: Ga 6¹ (EV, restore), I Pe 5¹⁰; pass., I Co 1¹⁰ (Field, Notes, 167), II Co 13¹¹, He 13²¹ (cf. προ-καταρτίζω).†

*† κατ-άρτισις, -εως, ἡ (< καταρτίζω), a strengthening, making fit: in ethical sense, II Co 13⁹.†

**† καταρτισμός, -οῦ, ὁ, [in Sm. : Is 38¹² *;] = κατάρτισις (but v. ICC, Eph. l.c.): Eph 4¹².†

** κατα-σείω, [in LXX : Da TH Bel ¹⁴ AR, I Mac 6³⁸ *;] 1. to shake down. 2. Of the hand, to shake or wave as a signal: τ. χεῖρα, Ac 19³³; τ. χειρί, Ac 13¹⁶; id. c. dat. pers., ib. 21⁴⁰; seq. inf., ib. 12¹⁷.†

κατα-σκάπτω, [in LXX for נתץ, הרם, etc.;] to dig down: Ro 11³ (LXX).†

κατα-σκευάζω, [in LXX : Is 40¹⁹, ²⁸ (בָּרָא), etc.;] to prepare, make ready: τ. ὁδόν, Mt 11¹⁰, Mk 1², Lk 7²⁷; οἶκον, He 3³, ⁴; σκηνήν, He 9², ⁶; κιβωτόν, He 11⁷, I Pe 3²⁰; pass. pf. ptcp., λαόν κ., Lk 1¹⁷.†

κατα-σκηνόω, -ῶ, [in LXX chiefly for שׁכן;] to pitch one's tent, lodge, dwell: seq. ἐν, Mt 13³², Lk 13¹⁹; ὑπό, c. acc., Mk 4³², ἐπ' ἐλπιδι, Ac 2²⁶ (LXX).†

† κατα-σκήνωσις, εως, ἡ, [in LXX : I Ch 28² (בְּנוֹת), Ez 37²⁷ (מִשְׁכָּן), To 1⁴, Wi 9⁸, II Mac 14³⁵ (R) *;] 1 prop., an encamping, taking up one's quarters (Polyb., al., v. LS; and cf. LXX, ll. c.). 2. a lodging, abode: of birds, Mt 8²⁰, Lk 9⁵⁸.†

* κατα-σκιάζω, to overshadow: c. acc., He 9⁵.†

κατα-σκοπέω, -ῶ, [in LXX : II Ki 10³, I Ch 19³ (רָגַל pi.), I Mac 5³⁸ (A) *;] to view closely, inspect, spy out: c. acc., Ga 2⁴.†

κατά-σκοπος, -ου, ὁ, [in LXX for רָגַל pi. ;] a spy: He 11³¹.†

† κατα-σοφίζομαι, [in LXX : Ex 1¹⁰ (חכם hith.), Jth 5¹¹, 10¹⁹ *;] to deal craftily with, outwit: Ac 7¹⁹ (LXX).†

** κατα-στέλλω, [in LXX : II Mac 4³¹, III Mac 6¹ *;] 1. to let down, lower. 2. to keep down, restrain: c. acc., Ac 19³⁵, ³⁶.†

**✝ κατά-στημα, -τος, τό (καθίστημι), [in LXX: iii Mac 5⁴⁵ (-εμα, A)* ;]
1. *condition, state,* of the body, etc. 2. *demeanour :* Tit 2³ (for exx. v. Field, *Notes,* 220).✝

κατα-στολή, -ῆς, ἡ (< καταστέλλω), [in LXX: Is 61³ (מַעֲטֶה) * ;]
1. *a letting down, checking.* 2. *steadiness, quietness* in demeanour. 3. LXX and NT (cf. Plut., ii, 65 D; -ίζω = *vestire*), *a garment, dress, attire :* i Ti 2⁹ (but v. Ellic., in l., and cf. MM, *VGT,* s.v. for sense of *demeanour*).✝

κατα-στρέφω, [in LXX for הָפַן, etc., Ge 19²¹, Je 20¹⁶, al.;] 1. *to turn down, turn over ;* as, the soil. 2. *to overturn, overthrow :* Mt 21¹², Mk 11¹⁵; pass. pf. ptcp., Ac 15¹⁶ (LXX).✝

*✝ κατα-στρηνιάω, -ῶ, *to wax wanton against :* c. gen., i Ti 5¹¹.✝

κατα-στροφή, -ῆς, ἡ (< καταστρέφω), [in LXX: Jb 21¹⁷, Pr 1²⁷ (אֵיד), al.;] 1. *overthrow :* ii Pe 2⁶ (WH, om.). 2. Metaph., *subversion, upsetting* (cf. καθαίρεσις, ii Co 13¹⁰): ii Ti 2¹⁴.✝

κατα-στρώννυμι, [in LXX: Nu 14¹⁶ (שָׁטַח), Jb 12²³ (שָׁטַח), Jth ₄, ii Mac ₄*;] 1. *to strew* or *spread over.* 2. *to lay low, overthrow :* i Co 10⁵.✝

κατα-σύρω, [in LXX: Je 29 (49)¹⁰ (חָשַׂף), Da LXX, 11¹⁰, ²⁶ (שָׁטַף) *;] 1. *to pull down.* 2. *to drag away :* c. acc. pers., Lk 12⁵⁸.✝

κατα-σφάζω, [in LXX: Za 11⁵ (הרג), Ez 16⁴⁰ (בתק pi.), ii Mac ₈;] *to kill off, slay :* c. acc., Lk 19²⁷.✝

κατα-σφραγίζω, [in LXX: Jb 9⁷ 37⁷ (חתם), Wi 2⁵ *;] *to seal up, secure with a seal :* Re 5¹.✝

✝ κατά-σχεσις, -εως, ἡ (< κατέχω), [in LXX nearly always for אֲחֻזָּה ;] 1. *a holding back.* 2. LXX and NT, *a holding fast, possession :* Ac 7⁵, ⁴⁵ (v. Field, *Notes,* pp. 114, 116).✝

κατα-τίθημι, [in LXX: i Ch 21²⁷ (שׁוּב hi.), Ps 40 (41)⁸ (יָצַק), i Mac 10²³, al.;] *to lay down, deposit, lay by :* Mk 15⁴⁶, T; mid., *to lay up for oneself :* χάριν, to confer a favour with a view to return, *seek favour* (Hdt., al., v. LS; MM, *VGT,* s.v.), c. dat. pers., Ac 24²⁷ 25⁹.✝

**✝ κατα-τομή, -ῆς, ἡ, [in Sm.: Je 48 (31)³⁷ (κατατέμνω is used in LXX of forbidden mutilations : Le 21⁵, al.);] 1. *incision.* 2. *excision, concision, mutilation :* in sarcasm, by paranomasia, in contrast to (true) περιτομή (v³), of Judaizing Christians, Phl 3² (v. Lft., in l.; Cremer, 883).✝

κατα-τοξεύω, [in LXX: Ex 19¹³ (ירה), al.;] *to strike down with an arrow, shoot dead :* He 12²⁰ (LXX) (Rec.; WH, R, om.).✝

κατα-τρέχω, [in LXX: Le 26³⁷, Jg 1⁶ (רדף), al.;] *to run down :* seq. ἐπί, c. acc. pers., Ac 21³².✝

**✝ κατ-αυγάζω, [in LXX: Wi 17⁵, i Mac 6³⁹ *;] (for αὐγάζω, L, mg., Tr., mg.), *to shine down :* ii Co 4⁴.✝

κατα-φάγω, v.s. κατεσθίω.

κατα-φέρω, [in LXX for ירד hi., etc.;] *to bring down :* αἰτιώματα, Ac 25⁷; ψῆφον, *to cast a ballot,* Ac 26¹⁰; pass., *to be borne down :* ὕπνῳ, ἀπὸ τ. ὕ., Ac 20⁹ (v. MM, *VGT,* s.v.).✝

κατα-φεύγω, [in LXX for נוּם, etc.;] *to flee for refuge :* seq. εἰς, Ac 14⁶; metaph., c. inf., He 6¹⁸.✝

κατα-φθείρω, [in LXX chiefly for שָׁחַת hi., Ge 6¹², al.; 1 *to destroy entirely*. 2. In moral sense (as LXX), *to deprave, corrupt*: pass. pf. ptcp., seq. τ. νοῦν, II Ti 3⁸.†

κατα-φιλέω, -ῶ, [in LXX chiefly for נָשַׁק;] *to kiss fervently, kiss affectionately*: Mt 26⁴⁹, Mk 14⁴⁵, Lk 7³⁸, ⁴⁵ 15²⁰, Ac 20³⁷ (but cf. MM, *VGT*, s.v., where the intensive force of this compound is doubted).†

κατα-φρονέω, -ῶ, [in LXX for בָּגַד, בּוּז, etc.,] *to think little of, despise*: c. gen., Mt 6²⁴ 18¹⁰, Lk 16¹³, Ro 2⁴, I Co 11²², I Ti 4¹² (v. MM, *VGT*, s.v.), 6², He 12², II Pe 2¹⁰.†

† κατα-φρονητής, -οῦ, ὁ, [in LXX for בָּגַד, בֹּגְדוֹת, Hb 1⁵ 2⁵, Ze 3⁴*;] *a despiser*: Ac 13⁴¹.†

κατα-χέω, [in LXX for יָצַק, נָטָה, עָטָה hi.;] *to pour down upon*: c. gen. (cl.), Mk 14³; seq. ἐπί, c. gen., Mt 26⁷.†

* κατα-χθόνιος, -ον (< χθών, *the earth*), *subterranean, under the earth* (in cl., of the infernal gods) : of the departed in Hades, opp. to ἐπουράνιος, ἐπίγειος, Phl 2¹⁰.†

** κατα-χράομαι, -ῶμαι, [in LXX : Ep. Je²⁸, III Mac 4⁵ 5²²*;] *to make full use of, use to the uttermost, use up*: I Co 7³¹; c. dat., ib. 9¹⁸ (for other senses, v. LS, s.v.).†

κατα-ψύχω, [in LXX : Ge 18⁴ (שָׁעַן ni.)*;] *to cool*: c. acc., Lk 16²⁴.†

*† κατείδωλος, -ον (< εἴδωλον), *full of idols*: Ac 17¹⁶.†

† κατέναντι, adv., [in LXX chiefly for נֶגֶד (לְ),‎ לִפְנֵי, etc.;] *over against, opposite, before*: ἡ κ. κώμη, Lk 19³⁰; as prep., c. gen., Mt 21² 27²⁴ (ἀπ-, WH, mg.), Mk 11² 12⁴¹ (ἀπ-, WH, mg.) 13³; metaph., *before*, seq. θεοῦ, Ro 4¹⁷, II Co 2¹⁷ 12¹⁹.†

† κατενώπιον, adv. (= Hom., κατένωπα), [in LXX : Ps 43 (44)¹⁵, al.;] *over against, before*: c. gen., τ. δόξης, Ju²⁴; metaph. (cf. κατέναντι, and v. Lft., *Col.*, l.c.), τ. θεοῦ, Eph 1⁴, Col 1²².†

* κατ-εξουσιάζω, *to exercise authority over*: c. gen. pers., Mt 20²⁵, Mk 10⁴².†

SYN.: κατακυριεύω (v. Swete, *Mk.*, l.c.).

κατ-εργάζομαι (emphatic form of ἐργάζομαι), [in LXX for פָּעַל, etc. (9 exx., each for a different Heb. word);] *to effect by labour, achieve, work out, bring about*: c. acc., Ro 4¹⁵ 5³ 7⁸, ¹⁵, ¹⁷, ¹⁸, ²⁰, II Co 7¹⁰, Eph 6¹³, Ja 1³; pass., II Co 12¹²; c. acc. rei et dat. pers., Ro 7¹³, II Co 4¹⁷ 7¹¹ 9¹¹; id. seq. διά, c. gen. pers., Ro 15¹⁸; τ. σωτηρίαν, Phl 2¹²; c. acc. pers. seq. εἰς, II Co 5⁵ (RV, *wrought*); of evil deeds, Ro 1²⁷ 2⁹, I Co 5³, I Pe 4³.†

** κατ-έρχομαι, [in LXX : To 1²² ℵ 2¹, Es 3¹³, Wi 11²², II Mac 11²⁹*;] *to come down, go down*: seq. εἰς, Lk 4³¹, Ac 8⁵ 13⁴ 15³⁰ 19¹, T; ἀπό, Lk 9³⁷, Ac 15¹ 18⁵ 21¹⁰; ἀπό et εἰς, Ac 11²⁷ 12¹⁹; of coming to port by ship, Ac 18²² 21³ 27⁵; seq. πρός, c. acc. pers., Ac 9³²; metaph., of gifts from God, Ja 3¹⁵.†

κατ-εσθίω ("perfective" comp. of ἐσθίω, q.v., and cf. M, *Pr.*, 111), [in LXX chiefly for אָכַל;] *to eat up, devour*: c. acc., of seed, Mt 13⁴, Mk 4⁴, Lk 8⁵; τέκνον, Re 12⁴; βιβλαρίδιον, Re 10⁹, ¹⁰; metaph., οἰκίας, Mt 23¹³, Mk 12⁴⁰, Lk 20⁴⁷; τ. βίον, Lk 15³⁰; c. acc. pers., Jo 2¹⁷ (LXX), ιι Co 11²⁰, Ga 5¹⁵, Re 11⁵ 20⁹.†

κατ-ευθύνω, [in LXX for כּוּן ni., hi., etc.;] to make or keep straight, direct, guide: metaph., τ. ὁδόν, ι Th 3¹¹; τ. πόδας εἰς ὁδὸν εἰρήνης, Lk 1⁷⁹; τ. καρδίας εἰς τ. ἀγάπην, ιι Th 3⁵.†

**† κατ-ευλογέω, -ῶ, [in LXX: To 11¹,¹⁷*;] to bless fervently: Mk 10¹⁶ (v. Swete, in l.).†

*† κατ-εφ-ίστημι, to rise up against: Ac 18¹².†

κατ-έχω, [in LXX for אחז, חזק hi., etc.;] 1. perfective of ἔχω (M, Pr., 116; M, Th., 155), (a) to possess, hold fast: Lk 8¹⁵, Jo 5[⁴], Ro 1¹⁸ (Lft., Notes, 251), ι Co 7³⁰ 11², ιι Co 6¹⁰, ι Th 5²¹, He 3⁶, ¹⁴ 10²³; (b) to lay hold of, get possession of: Lk 14⁹. 2. to hold back, detain, restrain (M, Th., 156 f.): c. acc. seq. τοῦ μή c. inf., Lk 4⁴²; seq. πρός, c. acc., Phm ¹³; absol., τὸ κατέχον (ὁ κ.), ιι Th 2⁶,⁷. 3. Intrans., as nautical term, to put in, make for (LS, s.v.): Ac 27⁴⁰ (for illustrations of various meanings, v. MM, VGT, s.v.).†

κατηγορέω, -ῶ (< κατά, ἀγορεύω), [in LXX: Da LXX 6⁵ ⁽⁶⁾, ι Mac 7⁶, ²⁵, ιι Mac 4⁴⁷ 10¹³,²¹, ιv Mac 9¹⁴*;] to make accusation, accuse, (a) in general: absol., Ro 2¹⁵; c. gen. pers. (cl., WM, 254), Jo 5⁴⁵; irreg. c. acc. pers., Re 12¹⁰; (b) before a judge: absol., Ac 24²,¹⁹; c. gen. pers., Mt 12¹⁰, Mk 3², Lk 6⁷ 11⁵⁴ (WH, txt., R, om.), 23²,¹⁰, Jo 8[⁶], Ac 25⁵ 28¹⁹; id. c. acc. rei (cl., but v. WM, l.c.), Mk 15³,⁴; c. gen. rei (Dem.), Ac 24⁸ 25¹¹; seq. περί, c. gen. rei (Thuc., viii, 85), Ac 24¹³; c. acc. rei, seq. κατά c. gen. pers. (WM, § 28, 1), Lk 23¹⁴. Pass. (Bl., § 54, 3), seq. ὑπό c. gen., Mt 27¹², Ac 22³⁰; ὁ κατηγορούμενος, Ac 25¹⁶.†

* κατηγορία, -ας, ἡ (< κατήγορος), an accusation, charge: c. gen. pers., Jo 18²⁹; seq. κατά, c. id., ι Ti 5¹⁹; c. gen. rei, Tit 1⁶.†

κατήγορος, -ου, ὁ, [in LXX: Pr 18¹⁷ (ריב), ιι Mac 4⁵*;] an accuser: Ac 23³⁰, ³⁵ 24⁸ (WH, R, txt. om.) 25¹⁶,¹⁸.†

*† κατήγωρ, ὁ (Aram. קַטִיגוֹר; Dalman, Gr., 185; but v. Deiss., LAE, 90 f.), a vulgar form (cf. MM, VGT, s.v.), = κατήγορος, an accuser: Re 12¹⁰.†

* κατήφεια, -ας, ἡ (< κατηφής, downcast, Wi 17⁴*), dejection: Ja 4⁹.†

*† κατ-ηχέω, -ῶ, 1. to resound. 2. to teach by word of mouth, instruct, inform (v. Bl., Phil. Gosp., 20, 31): Ga 6⁶; c. acc. pers., ι Co 14¹⁹; pass. c. acc. rei, Lk 1⁴ (ICC, in l.), Ac 18²⁵ 21²⁴ (cf. Lk, i.c.), Ga 6⁶; seq. ἐκ, c. gen. rei, Ro 2¹⁸; περί, c. gen. pers., Ac 21²¹.†

**† κατ-ιόω, -ῶ (intensive of ἰόω; < ἰός), [in LXX: Si 12¹¹*;] to rust over; pass., become rusted over: Ja 5³.†

κατ-ισχύω, [in LXX chiefly for חזק;] to overpower, prevail against, prevail: absol., Lk 23²³; c. inf., Lk 21³⁶; c. gen., Mt 16¹⁸.†

κατ-οικέω, -ῶ, [in LXX very freq. and nearly always for ישׁב;] 1. trans., to inhabit, dwell in: c. acc., Lk 13⁴, Ac 1¹⁹ 2⁹,¹⁴ 4¹⁶ 9³²,³⁵ 19¹⁰,¹⁷, Re 17²; of God, Mt 23²¹. 2. Intrans., to settle, dwell: Ac 22¹²; seq. ἐν (cl.), Ac 1²⁰ (LXX) 2⁵ 7²,⁴,⁴⁸ 9²² 11²⁹ 13²⁷ 17²⁴, He 11⁹, Re 13¹²; seq. εἰς (Bl., § 39, 3; M, Pr., 62 f., 234 f.), Mt 2²³ 4¹³, Ac 7⁴; ἐπὶ τ. γῆς (Nu 13³³, al.), Re 3¹⁰ 6¹⁰ 8¹³ 11¹⁰ 13⁸,¹⁴ 17⁸; ἐπὶ παντὸς προσώπου τ. γ., Ac 17²⁶; ὅπου, Re 2¹³; ἐκεῖ (of demons), Mt 12⁴⁵, Lk 11²⁶. Metaph., of divine indwelling: ὁ Χριστός, Eph 3¹⁷; τ. πνεῦμα, Ja 4⁵ (κατῴκισεν, T, WH, R, txt.); τ. πλήρωμα (τ. θεότητος), Col 1¹⁹ 2⁹; δικαιοσύνη (cf. Wi 1⁴), II Pe 3¹³ (cf. ἐν-κατοικέω).†

κατ-οίκησις, -εως, ἡ (< κατοικέω), [in LXX for יֵשֵׁב, Ge 10³⁰, al.;] *dwelling:* Mk 5³.†

† **κατ-οικητήριον,** -ου, τό (< κατοικέω), [in LXX for מוֹשָׁב, מָעוֹן, etc.;] *a habitation, dwelling-place:* Eph 2²², Re 18².†

† **κατ-οικία,** -ας, ἡ (< κατοικέω), [in LXX chiefly for מוֹשָׁב, Ex 35³, al.;] 1. *a dwelling:* Ac 17²⁶. 2. *a settlement* (Polyb.).†

κατοικίζω, [in LXX for יֵשֵׁב hi., etc.;] *to cause to dwell:* metaph., c. acc., τὸ πνεῦμα, Ja 4⁵ (perh. itacism for Rec., R, mg., κατῴκησεν; but v. MM, *VGT*, s.v.).†

† **κατοπτρίζω** (< κάτοπτρον, *a mirror*), *to show as in a mirror.* Mid., *to see oneself mirrored* (v. MM, *Exp.*, xv); c. acc. rei (R, txt., but v. mg.), *to reflect as a mirror:* II Co 3¹⁸ (cf. Abbott, *Essays*, 94); on R, mg., *to see as in a mirror,* cf. Professor A. E. Brooke in *JThS*, xxiv, p. 98 (Oct., 1922).†

κατόρθωμα, -τος, τό, Rec. for διόρθωμα (q.v.), Ac 24³.†

κάτω, adv. (< κατά), [in LXX for מַטָּה, מִתַּחַת and cogn. forms;] 1. *down, downwards* (with verbs of motion), Mt 4⁶, Lk 4⁹, Jo 8[⁶, ⁸], Ac 20⁹. 2. *below, beneath:* Mk 14⁶⁶, Ac 2¹⁹ (LXX); ἕως κ. (Ez 1²⁷, al.), Mt 27⁵¹, Mk 15³⁸; τὰ κ. (opp. to τ. ἄνω), Jo 8²³. Compar. κατωτέρω: ἀπὸ διετοῦς καὶ κ. (cf. I Ch 27²³), Mt 2¹⁶.†

κατώτερος, -έρα, -ερον (< κάτω), [in LXX for תַּחְתִּי, תַּחְתּוֹן;] *lower;* τὰ κ. τῆς γῆς (v. AR, *Eph.*, l.c; for rendering *this lower earth,* v. ICC, Eph, l.c.), *the lower parts of the earth* (cf. Ps 138 (139)¹⁵; cf. also MGr., ἡ κάτω γῆ, *the underworld,* Thumb, *MGV*, 334): Eph 4⁹.†

κατωτέρω, v.s. κάτω.

Καῦδα (TR, mg., Κλαῦδα; Rec. Κλαύδη), ἡ, *Cauda, Clauda,* an island near Crete: Ac 27¹⁶.†

καῦμα, -τος, τό (< καίω), [in LXX for חֹם, חֹרֶב, etc.;] *heat:* Re 7¹⁶ 16⁹.†

*† **καυματίζω** (< καῦμα), *to burn* or *scorch up:* c. acc. seq. ἐν πυρί, Re 16⁸. Pass., Mt 13¹⁴, Mk 4⁶; seq. καῦμα μέγα, Re 16⁹.†

καῦσις, -εως, ἡ (< καίω), [in LXX for בֵּעֵר pi., etc.;] *burning:* He 6⁸.†

*† **καυσόω,** -ῶ (< καῦσος, *burning heat, fever*), only in pass., 1. *to burn with fever* (Galen., al.). 2. In NT, *to burn with great heat:* II Pe 3¹⁰, ¹² (v. Mayor, in l.).†

*† **καυστηριάζω** (Rec. καυτηρ-, and so usually in Gk. writers, v. Soph., *Lex.,* s.v.), *to mark by branding, brand* (AV, *sear,* but v. *CGT,* in l.): metaph., pass. pf. ptcp., I Ti 4² (cf. καυτήριον, IV Mac 15²²*).†

† **καύσων,** -ωνος, ὁ (< καίω), [in LXX: Ge 31⁴⁰ א (חֹרֶב), Is 49¹⁰ (שָׁרָב), Jb 27²¹, Ho 12¹ ⁽²⁾ 13¹⁵, Jh 4⁸, Je 18¹⁷, Ez 17¹⁰ 19¹² (קָדִים); Je 28 (51)¹, Da TH 3 ⁽⁶⁷⁾, Jth 8³, Si 18¹⁶ 31 (34)¹⁶ 43²² *;] 1. *burning heat* (Ge, Is (?), Jth, ll.c., Si 18¹⁶): Mt 20¹², Lk 12⁵⁵ (Ja 1¹¹, AV). 2. *a hot*

wind from the east (Heb. קָדִים, v. LXX, ll.c.), the modern *sirocco*
(v. *CGT* on Am 4⁹): Ja 1¹¹ (RV, *the scorching wind;* cf. R, mg., *the
hot wind,* Mt, Lk, ll.c.).†

καυτηριάζω, Rec. for καυστηριάζω, q.v.

καυχάομαι, -ῶμαι, [in LXX for הָלַל hith., etc.;] *to boast* or *glory*
(in LXX, of joyous exultation, and so in the NT quotations, infr.; cf.
DB, ii, 790ᵇ; Hort on Ja 1⁹): absol., 1 Co 1³¹ (LXX) 4⁷ 13³, 11 Co
10¹³, ¹⁷ (LXX) 11¹⁶, ¹⁸ 12¹, ⁶, Eph 2⁹, Ja 4¹⁶; c. acc. rei, 11 Co 9² 11³⁰;
seq. ἐν (LXX), Ro 2²³ 5³, 1 Co 3²¹, 11 Co 5¹² 10¹⁵ 11¹² 12⁵, ⁹, Ga 6¹³, ¹⁴,
Ja 1⁹; ἐν (τ.) θεῷ, Ro 2¹⁷ 5¹¹; ἐν κυρίῳ, 1 Co 1³¹ (LXX), 11 Co 10¹⁷ (LXX);
ἐν X. Ἰησοῦ, Phl 3³; seq. ἐπί, c. dat., Ro 5²; περί, c. gen., 11 Co 10⁸;
εἰς, ib. ¹⁶; ὑπέρ, c. gen. pers., 11 Co 7¹⁴ 12⁵; ἐνώπιον τ. θεοῦ, 1 Co 1²⁹
(cf. ἐν-, κατα-καυχάομαι).†

καύχημα, -τος, τό (< καυχάομαι), [in LXX chiefly for תְּהִלָּה,
תִּפְאֶרֶת;] 1. *a boast* (Pind.): 11 Co 5¹² 9³ (Thayer, s.v.; e. contra, 2,
Ellic., Lft., on Ga 6⁴; Lft., *Notes*, 204, 277). 2 *ground* or *matter of
glorying:* Ro 4², 1 Co 5⁶ 9¹⁵, ¹⁶, 11 Co 1¹⁴, Ga 6⁴, Phl 1²⁶ 2¹⁶, He 3⁶
(cf. καύχησις).†

† **καύχησις, -εως, ἡ** (< καυχάομαι), [in LXX for תִּפְאֶרֶת (1 Ch 29¹³,
Ez 16¹², al); *a boasting, glorying:* Ro 3²⁷, 11 Co 11¹⁰, ¹⁷, Ja 4¹⁶; seq.
ὑπέρ, 11 Co 7⁴ 8²⁴; ἐπί, c. gen., 11 Co 7¹⁴; ἔχω τὴν κ. ἐν Χρ. Ἰησ., Ro 15¹⁷;
στέφανος καυχήσεως (Ez. l.c., al.), 1 Th 2¹⁹; of the cause of glorying,
a boast (= καύχημα), 11 Co 1¹².†

Καφαρναούμ (Καπερ-, Rec., v. WH, *App.* 160), ἡ (Heb. כְּפַר נַחוּם,
Nahum's village), *Capernaum:* Mt 4¹³, Mk 1²¹, Jo 2¹², al.

Κεγχρεαί, v.s. **Κενχρεαί.**

κέδρος, -ου, ἡ, [in LXX chiefly for אֶרֶז, Nu 24⁶, al.; χειμάρρους
τῶν Κέδρων, 11 Ki 15²³, 111 Ki 15¹³ (קִדְרוֹן);] *a cedar:* χείμαρρος τῶν Κ.
(as in 11 Ki, 111 Ki, ll. c.), Jo 18¹ (Rec. Tr., WH, R, mg.; τοῦ Κέδρου, T,
WH, mg., v.s. Κεδρών, and cf. Westc., in l.; WH, *App.,* 89 f.; Abbott,
JG, 513 ff.).†

Κεδρών (v.s. κέδρος), ὁ, indecl. (in FlJ, gen. -ῶνος; Heb. קִדְרוֹן), [in
LXX: 11 Ki 15²³, 1V Ki 23⁶, al.;] *Cedron* (OT, *Kidron*): χείμαρρος
τοῦ Κ., Jo 18¹ (L, Tr., mg., R, txt.; cf. Bl., § 10, 5; Lft., *Essays*, 172 ff.).†

κεῖμαι, [in LXX: Je 24¹ (יָעַד hoph.), al.;] used as passive of
τίθημι (LS, s.v.), *to be laid, to lie;* (*a*) of persons: an infant, Lk 2¹², ¹⁶;
a dead body, Mt 28⁶, Lk 23⁵³, Jo 20¹²; (*b*) of things, *to lie, be laid* or
set, stand: Mt 5¹⁴, Jo 2⁶ 19²⁹ 20⁵⁻⁷ 21⁹, Re 4² 21¹⁶; trop., θεμέλιος,
1 Co 3¹¹; seq. prep. c. acc., πρός, Mt 3¹⁰, Lk 3⁹; εἰς, Lk 12¹⁹; ἐπί,
trop., κάλυμμα, 11 Co 3¹⁵. Metaph., ὁ κόσμος ἐν τ. πονηρῷ κ., 1 Jo 5¹⁹;
to be laid down, appointed : of law, c. dat. pers., 1 Ti 1⁹; seq. εἰς
c. acc. (of purpose), Lk 2³⁴, Phl 1¹⁶, 1 Th 3³ (cf. ἀνά-, συν-ανά-, ἀντί-,
ἀπό-, ἐπί-, κατά-, παρά-, περί-, πρό-κειμαι).†

κειρία, -ας, ἡ, [in LXX: Pr 7¹⁶ (מַרְבַדִּים *;] a vernacular word,
1. *a bed-cord* (Aristoph., *Av.*, 816; Pr, l.c.). 2. In pl., *swathings*
(cf. Field, *Notes*, 96 f.): Jo 11⁴⁴.†

κείρω, [in LXX chiefly for גזז, Is 53⁷, al.;] *to cut short the hair,
shear:* a sheep, Ac 8³² (Is, l.c.). Mid., *to have one's hair cut off, be
shorn:* absol., I Co 11⁶; τ. κεφαλήν, Ac 18¹⁸.†

Κείς (Rec. Κίς), ὁ, indecl. (Heb. קִישׁ), *Kish:* Ac 13²¹.†

κέλευσμα, -τος, τό (< κελεύω), [in LXX: Pr 24⁶² (30²⁷) *;] *a call,
summons, shout of command:* I Th 4¹⁶ (v. M, *Th.*, in l.).†

** κελεύω, [in LXX: I Es 9⁵³, To 8¹⁸, al., and freq. in I-IV Mac;]
to urge on, bid by word of mouth, *order, command* (mostly of one in
authority): c. acc. et. inf. aor., Mt 14¹⁹, ²⁸ 18²⁵ 27⁶⁴, Lk 18⁴⁰, Ac 4¹⁵ 5³⁴
8³⁸ 22³⁰ 23¹⁰ 25⁶, ¹⁷; with ellipse of acc., Mt 8¹⁸ 14⁹ 27⁵⁸, Ac 12¹⁹ 21³³;
c. acc. et. inf. pres., Ac 21³⁴ 22²⁴ 23³, ³⁵ 25²¹ 27⁴³; with ellipse of acc.,
Ac 16²²; ptcp. aor., Ac 25²³.†
  SYN.: v.s. ἐντέλλω.

*† κενεμβατεύω (not elsew., but perh. = -έω, Plut., al.), *to tread on
emptiness:* ἑώρα (αἰώρα) κ. (conjec. for ἃ ἑόρακεν ἐμβ., Lft., in l.), Col 2¹⁸
(cf. also *ICC*, in l.), but v. supr., s.v. ἐμβατεύω.†

**† κενοδοξία, -ας, ἡ (< κενόδοξος), [in LXX: Wi 14¹⁴, II Mac 2¹⁵
8¹⁹ *;] 1. *foolish fancy, vain opinion, error* (LXX, ll. c.). 2. *vainglory, groundless conceit:* Phl 2³.†

*† κενόδοξος, -ον (< κενός, δόξα), *vain-glorious:* Ga 5²⁶.†

κενός, -ή, -όν, [in LXX chiefly for רִיק and cognate forms;] *empty*
(Ge 37²⁴, Jg 7¹⁶). Metaph., (*a*) *empty, vain:* λόγοι, Eph 5⁶; ἀπάτη,
Col 2⁸; κήρυγμα, πίστις, I Co 15¹⁴; (*b*) *vain, fruitless:* ἡ χάρις, I Co 15¹⁰;
κόπος, ib. ⁵⁸; ἡ εἴσοδος, I Th 2¹; κενά, Ac 4²⁵ (LXX); εἰς κενόν, *in vain, to
no purpose* (Diod., LXX; cl. διὰ κενῆς), II Co 6¹, Ga 2², Phl 2¹⁶, I Th 3⁵;
(*c*) of persons, *empty-handed:* Mk 12³, Lk 1⁵³ 20¹⁰, ¹¹; *vain,* Ja 2²⁰.†
  SYN.: μάταιος, of the aim or effect of an action, κ. of its quality
(Lft. on Cl. Rom., *I Co.*, § 7; Tr., *Syn.*, xlix).

*† κενοφωνία, -ας, ἡ (< κενός, φωνέω), [cf. κενολογέω (צפה), Is 8¹⁹ *;]
empty talk, babbling: pl., I Ti 6²⁰, II Ti 2¹⁶.†

κενόω, -ῶ (< κενός, q.v.), [in LXX: Je 14² 15⁹ (אמל pu.) *;] *to
empty.* Metaph., *to empty, make empty, vain* or *of no effect:* καύχημα,
I Co 9¹⁵; ἑαυτόν, of Christ, Phl 2⁷ (v Lft.; *ICC*, in l, and esp. Gifford,
Incarn., 54 ff.); pass., πίστις, Ro 4¹⁴; ὁ σταυρός, I Co 1¹⁷; καύχημα,
II Co 9³.†

κέντρον, -ου, τό (< κεντέω, *to prick*), [in LXX: Pr 26³ (מֶתֶג), Ho
13¹⁴ (קֹטֶב), 5¹², Si 38²⁵, IV Mac 14¹⁹ *;] 1. *a sting* (IV Mac, l.c.):
Re 9¹⁰. Metaph. (as Ho 13¹⁴): τ. θανάτου, I Co 15⁵⁵ (LXX), ⁵⁶. 2. *a
goad:* pl., Ac 26¹⁴.†

*† κεντυρίων, -ωνος, ὁ (Lat. *centurio*); *a centurion:* Mk 15³⁹, ⁴⁴, ⁴⁵
(Mt, Lk, use ἑκατόνταρχος (-ης), q.v.).†

Κενχρεαί (Rec. Κεγχ-; v. WH, *App.*, 150), -ῶν, αἱ, *Cenchreæ,* a
port of Corinth: Ac 18¹⁸, Ro 16¹.†

κενῶς, adv., [in LXX: Is 49⁴ (לְרִיק) *;] *in vain, to no purpose*: Ja 4⁵.†

* **κεραία** (WH, κερέα, v. *App.*, 151), -ας, ἡ (< κέρας), *a little horn*: of the *point* or extremity which distinguishes some Heb. letters from others (e.g. ר from ד; *DCG*, ii, 733), Mt 5¹⁸, Lk 16¹⁷.†

κεραμεύς, -εως, ὁ (< κεράννυμι), [in LXX for יֹצֵר, Ps 2⁹, Je 18², al.;] *a potter*: Ro 9²¹; ὁ ἀγρὸς τοῦ κ., Mt 27⁷, ¹⁰ (LXX).†

κεραμικός, -ή, -όν (< κέραμος), [in LXX: Da LXX 2⁴¹ (פֶּחָר) *;] 1. (cl.) *of a potter* (e.g. γῆ). 2. In LXX and NT, = cl., κεραμεοῦς (Plut., κερίμειος, Polyb., -μαῖος, etc.), *earthen*: Re 2²⁷.†

κεράμιον, -ου, τό (< κέραμος), [in LXX: Je 42 (35)⁵ (נֶבֶל), etc.;] *an earthen vessel, a jar* or *jug*: ὕδατος, Mk 14¹³, Lk 22¹⁰.†

κέραμος, -ου, ὁ (< κεράννυμι), [in LXX: II Ki 17²⁸ (כְּלִי יוֹצֵר) *;] 1. *potter's clay*. 2. *an earthen vessel*. 3. *a tile*: Lk 5¹⁹.†

κεράννυμι, [in LXX for מָסַךְ, Is 5²², al.;] *to mix, mingle*, chiefly of the diluting of wine: Re 18⁶; by *oxymoron*, κεκεράσμενος ἄκρατος, Re 14¹⁰.†

SYN.: μίγνυμι. κ. implies "a mixing of two things, so that they are blended and form a compound, as in wine and water, whereas μ. implies a mixing without such composition, as in two sorts of grain" (LS, s.v. κρᾶσις).

κέρας, -ατος (pl. not irreg. as in Attic), τό, [in LXX chiefly for קֶרֶן;] *a horn*: Re 5⁶ 12³ 13¹, ¹¹ 17³, ⁷, ¹², ¹⁶; of the projections at the corners of the altar (Ex 29¹², al.): Re 9¹³. Metaph., as symbol of strength, κ. σωτηρίας (cf. Ps 17 (18)³, al.): Lk 1⁶⁹.†

* **κεράτιον**, -ου, τό (dimin. of κέρας), 1. *a little horn* (Arist.). 2. In pl. (the fruit of the κερατέα), *carob-pods*: Lk 15¹⁶.†

** **κερδαίνω**, [in Sm.: Jb 22³ *;] *to gain*: c. acc., Mt 25¹⁶, ¹⁷, ²⁰, ²²; τ. κόσμον, Mt 16²⁶, Mk 8³⁶, Lk 9²⁵; absol., *to make profit, get gain*: Ja 4¹³. Metaph., c. acc. rei, *to save oneself from, avoid*: Ac 27²¹ (Field, *Notes*, 145); c. acc. pers., *to gain, win*: Mt 18¹⁵, I Co 9¹⁹⁻²², Phl 3⁸; pass., I Pe 3¹.†

** **κέρδος**, -εος (-ους), τό, [in Aq.: Ez 27²⁴; Sm.: Ps 29 (30)¹⁰, al.;] *gain*: Phl 1²¹ 3⁷, Tit 1¹¹.†

κερέα, v.s. κεραία.

* **κέρμα**, -τος, τό (< κείρω), 1. *a slice*, hence, 2. *a small coin*: pl., Jo 2¹⁵.†

*† **κερματιστής**, -οῦ, ὁ (κερματίζω, *to cut small, coin into small money*), *a money changer*: Jo 2¹⁴.†

κεφάλαιος, -α, -ον (< κεφαλή), [in LXX (-αιον, τό) for רֹאשׁ, Nu 4², al.;] *of the head;* metaph., *principal, chief;* mostly as subst., κεφάλαιον, τό; 1. *the chief point*: He 8¹. 2. *the sum total, amount*: Ac 22²⁸ (other meaning, LS, s.v.).†

κεφαλαιόω, -ῶ, v.s. κεφαλιόω.

κεφαλή, -ῆς, ἡ, [in LXX nearly always for רֹאשׁ;] the head : Mt 5[36], Mk 6[4], Re 1[14] 9[7], al. mult.; fig., ἄνθρακες ἐπὶ τὴν κ., Ro 12[20] (LXX); αἷμα, Ac 18[6]; metaph.. of a husband, c. gen., 1 Co 11[3], Eph 5[23]; of Christ, 1 Co 11[3], Eph 4[15] 5[23], Col 1[18] 2[10, 19]; of things, κ. γωνίας, Mt 21[42] (LXX); on the phrase in 1 Co 11[10], v. Peake, Comm., p. 842, Lietzmann, Handbuch, iii, i, p. 128 f., ICC, in l.

** κεφαλιόω (Rec. -αιόω, [so in LXX: Si 35 (32)[8] *]), -ῶ (< κεφάλιον, dimin. of κεφαλή, in late writers); 1. (-αιόω) to sum up (Thuc., al.). 2. (In NT, only) to wound on the head : Mk 12[4] (see further MM, VGT, s.v. -αιόω, Milligan, NTD, 177, n. [1]).†

κεφαλίς, -ίδος, ἡ (dimin. of κεφαλή), [in LXX for מְגִלָּה, זָו, etc.;] 1. a little head. 2. an extremity, capital (of a column). 3. (As in Ez 2[9], Ps 39 (40)[8], ii Es 6[2]) a roll : κ. βιβλίου, He 10[7] (LXX).†

* κημόω, -ῶ (< κημός, a muzzle), to muzzle : 1 Co 9[9] (TTr., WH, mg.) (cf. φιμόω).†

*† κῆνσος, -ου, ὁ (Lat. census), a poll-tax : Mt 17[25] 22[17], Mk 12[14] (WH, mg., ἐπικεφάλαιον); τ. νόμισμα τοῦ κ., Mt 22[19] (v. MM, Exp., xv).† SYN.: τέλος (q.v.), φόρος.

κῆπος, -ου, ὁ, [in LXX for גַּן, גַּנָּה, גִּנָּה, De 11[10], Ca 4[12], al.;] a garden : Lk 13[19], Jo 18[1, 26] 19[41].†

* κηπ-ουρός, -οῦ, ὁ (< κῆπος + οὖρος, a watcher), a gardener : Jo 20[15].†

κηρίον, -ου, τό (< κηρός, wax), [in LXX for נֹפֶת, צוּף, Ps 18 (19)[10] 117 (118)[12], Pr 16[24], al.;] honeycomb : κ. μελίσσιον, Lk 24[42] (Rec.; WH, txt., R, txt., omit).†

κήρυγμα, -τος, τό (< κηρύσσω), [in LXX: ii Ch 30[5] (קוֹל), Jh 3[2] (קְרִיאָה), Pr 9[3], i Es 9[3] *;] in cl., that which is cried by a herald, a proclamation. In NT (v. Lft., Notes, 161), of God's heralds, proclamation, message, preaching (i.e. the substance as distinct from the act which would be expressed by † κήρυξις): Mt 12[41], Mk 16 [alt. ending], Lk 11[32], i Co 1[21], ii Ti 4[17], Tit 1[3]; c. gen. subj., τὸ κ. μου, 1 Co 2[4]; ἡμῶν, ib. 15[14]; ο. gen. obj., Ἰησοῦ Χρ., Ro 16[25].†

κῆρυξ (κήρ-, T), -υκος, ὁ, [in LXX: Da LXX TH 3[4] (כָּרוֹז), Ge 41[43], Si 20[15], iv Mac 6[4] *;] a herald : i Ti 2[7], ii Ti 1[11], ii Pe 2[5].†

κηρύσσω, [in LXX chiefly for קרא;] to be a herald, to proclaim : Mk 1[45] 7[36], Lk 4[18, 19] (LXX) (but v. Field, Notes, 174) 8[39], Ro 2[21], i Co 9[27], Ga 5[11], al.; in NT, chiefly of the proclamation of the Gospel, to proclaim, preach : τὸ εὐαγγέλιον, Mt 4[23] 9[35] 24[14] 26[13], Mk 1[14] 13[10] 14[9] 16[15], Ga 2[2], Col 1[23], i Th 2[9]; seq. εἰς, Mk 1[39] 13[10], Lk 4[44], i Th 2[9]; ἵνα, Mk 6[12]; c. inf., Ro 2[21]; κ. Χριστόν, Ἰησοῦν, Ac 8[5] 9[20] 19[13], i Co 1[23] 15[12], ii Co 1[19] 11[4], Phl 1[15], i Ti 3[16] (cf. προ-κηρύσσω).

κῆτος, -εος (-ους), τό, [in LXX: Jh 2[1, 11] (דָּג), Ge 1[21] (תַּנִּין), etc.;] a huge fish, sea-monster : Mt 12[40] (LXX).†

Κηφᾶς, -ᾶ (v. Bl., § 10, 3), ὁ (Aram. כֵּיפָא), Cephas, i.e. Peter : Jo 1[43], i Co 1[12] 3[22] 9[5] 15[5], Ga 1[18] 2[9, 11, 14].†

κιβωτός, -οῦ, ἡ, [in LXX : Ge 6-9 (תֵּבָה), elsewhere, very freq., as Ex 25⁹ ⁽¹⁰⁾, for אָרוֹן ;] a wooden box or chest : of Noah's ark, Mt 24³⁸, Lk 17²⁷, He 11⁷, 1 Pe 3²⁰ ; of the ark of the covenant, He 9⁴, Re 11¹⁹.†

κιθάρα, -ας, ἡ, [in LXX chiefly for כִּנּוֹר, freq. in Pss (32 (33)², al.) ; and in Da (3⁵, al.) for קִיתָרֹם, itself a transliteration of κίθαρις, the Homeric form of κ. (cf. CB, Dn., lviii) ;] a lyre, harp : 1 Co 14⁷, Re 5⁸ 14² 15².†

κιθαρίζω, [in LXX : Is 23¹⁶ (נגן pi.) * ;] to play upon the lyre or harp : 1 Co 14⁷, Re 14².†

* κιθαρ-ωδός, -οῦ, ὁ (< κιθάρα, ἀοιδός, a singer), one who plays and sings to the lyre, a harper : Re 14² 18²².†

Κιλικία, -ας, ἡ, Cilicia, a province of Asia Minor : Ac 6⁹ 15²³, ⁴¹ 21³⁹ 22³ 23³⁴ 27ᵉ, Ga 1²¹.†

κινάμωμον, v.s. κιννάμωμον.

κινδυνεύω (< κίνδυνος), [in LXX for יקשׁ ni., etc. ;] 1. to be daring, to venture. 2. to be in danger : Lk 8²³, Ac 19²⁷,⁴⁰, 1 Co 15³⁰.†

κίνδυνος, -ου, ὁ, [in LXX : Ps 114 (116)³ (מֵצַר), Si 3²⁶, al. ;] danger, peril : Ro 8³⁵ ; pl., 11 Co 11²⁶.†

κινέω, -ῶ, [in LXX for נוּד hi., רמשׂ, etc. ;] to set in motion, move : Mt 23⁴ ; τ. κεφαλήν (Ps 21 (22)⁸, al.), Mt 27³⁹, Mk 15²⁹ ; pass. (cf. Ge 7²¹), Ac 17²⁸. 2. to remove : Re 2⁵ 6¹⁴. 3. to excite, stir up : Ac 24⁵ ; pass., 21³⁰ (cf. μετα-, συν-κινέω).†

κίνησις, -εως, ἡ (< κινέω), [in LXX : Jb 16⁶ ⁽⁵⁾, (נִיד), al. ;] a moving : Jo 5 ⁽³⁾.†

κιννάμωμον (Rec. κινάμ-), -ου, τό (from the Phœnician, v. LS, s.v., and cf. Heb. קִנָּמוֹן), cinnamon : Re 18¹³.†

Κίς, v.s. Κείς.

κίχρημι, v.s. χράω.

κλάδος, -ου, ὁ (< κλάω), [in LXX for דָּלִית, כַּף, etc. ;] a young tender shoot broken off for grafting ; then, a branch : Mt 13³² 21⁸ 24³², Mk 4³² 13²⁸, Lk 13¹⁹ ; metaph., of descendants (cf. Si 40¹⁵), Ro 11¹⁶⁻¹⁹, ²¹.†

κλαίω, [in LXX chiefly for בכה ;] of any loud expression of pain or sorrow, esp. for the dead, to weep, lament ; (a) intrans. : Mk 5³⁸, ³⁹ 14⁷² (M, Pr., 131) 16⁽¹⁰⁾, Lk 7¹³, ³², ³⁸ 8⁵², Jo 11³¹, ³³ 16²⁰ 20¹¹, ¹³, ¹⁵, Ac 9³⁹ 21¹³, 1 Co 7³⁰, Phl 3¹⁸, Ja 4⁹ 5¹, Re 5⁵ 18¹⁵, ¹⁹ ; πολύ, Re 5⁴ ; πολλά, Ac 8²⁴ (WH, mg.) ; πικρῶς, Mt 26⁷⁵, Lk 22⁶² ; opp. to γελάω, Lk 6²¹, ²⁵ ; χαίρω, Ro 12¹⁵ ; seq. ἐπί, c. acc., Lk 19⁴¹ 23²⁸, Re 18⁹ ; (b) trans., c. acc. pers., to weep or lament for, bewail : Mt 2¹⁸.†

SYN. : v.s. δακρύω.

* κλάσις, -εως, ἡ (< κλάω), a breaking : Lk 24³⁵, Ac 2⁴².†

κλάσμα, -τος, τό (< κλάω), [in LXX for פַּת, פֶּלַח ;] a broken piece, fragment : Mt 14²⁰ 15³⁷, Mk 6⁴³ 8⁸, ¹⁹, ²⁰. Lk 9¹⁷, Jo 6¹², ¹³.†

Κλαῦδα, v.s. Καῦδα.

Κλαυδία, -ας, ή, *Claudia :* II Ti 4²¹.†

Κλαύδιος, -ου, ὁ, *Claudius ;* 1. the Emperor : Ac 11²⁸ 18². 2. A military tribune, *C. Lysias :* Ac 23²⁶.†

κλαυθμός, -οῦ, ὁ (< κλαίω), [in LXX chiefly for בְּכִי ;] *crying, weeping,* Ac 20³⁷ ; κ. καὶ ὀδυρμός, Mt 2¹⁸ (LXX) ; ὁ κ. καὶ ὁ βρυγμός, Mt 8¹² 13⁴², ⁵⁰ 22¹³ 24⁵¹ 25³⁰, Lk 13²⁸.†

κλάω, [in LXX : Je 16⁷ (פרס), al. ;] *to break, break in pieces :* of bread, Mt 14¹⁹ 15³⁶ 26²⁶, Mk 8⁶ 14²², Lk 22¹⁹ 24³⁰, Ac 2⁴⁶ 20⁷, ¹¹ 27³⁵, I Co 10¹⁶ 11²⁴ ; seq. εἰς, c. acc. pers., Mk 8¹⁹ (cf. ἐκ-, κατα-κλάω).†

κλείς, -δός, Att. acc., κλεῖν, later -εῖδα, pl., κλεῖδες, -ας, contr., -εῖς, ή, [in LXX for מַפְתֵּחַ, Is 22²², al. ;] *a key.* Fig., τ. βασιλείας τ. οὐρανῶν, Mt 16¹⁹ ; τ. γνώσεως, Lk 11⁵² ; of David (cf. LXX, l.c.), Re 3⁷ ; τ. θανάτου κ. τ. ᾅδου, Re 1¹⁸ ; τ. ἀβύσσου, Re 20¹ ; τ. φρέατος τῆς ἀ., ib. 9¹.†

κλείω, [in LXX chiefly for סגר ;] *to shut :* θύραν, Mt 6⁶ ; τ. ἄβυσσον, Re 20³ ; pass., θύρα, Mt 25¹⁰, Lk 11⁷ (pf.) Jo 20¹⁹, ²⁶, Ac 21³⁰ ; δεσμωτήριον, Ac 5²³ ; πυλῶνες, Re 21²⁵. Metaph., τ. οὐρανόν, Lk 4²⁵, Re 11⁶ ; τ. σπλάγχνα, I Jo 3¹⁷ ; τ. βασιλείαν, Mt 23¹⁴ ; id. absol., Re 3⁷ ; τ. θύραν, ib. 8. (Cf. ἀπο-, ἐκ-, κατα-, συν-κλείω.) †

κλέμμα, -τος, τό (< κλέπτω), [in LXX : Ge 31³⁹, Ex 22³, ⁴ (2, 3) (גְּנֵבָה, גֶּנֶב*;] 1. *a thing stolen* (Arist., LXX). 2. = κλοπή, *theft* (Plato, al.) : pl., Re 9²¹.†

Κλεόπας, -α (v. Bl., § 7, 2), ὁ, *Cleopas :* Lk 24¹⁸.†

κλέος, -ους, τό, [in LXX : Jb 28²² (שֵׁמַע) 30⁸ *;] 1. *a rumour, report.* 2. *good report, fame, glory :* I Pe 2²⁰.†

κλέπτης, -ου, ὁ, [in LXX for גַּנָּב ;] *a thief :* Mt 6¹⁹, ²⁰ 24⁴³, Lk 12³³, ³⁹, Jo 10¹, ¹⁰ 12⁶, I Co 6¹⁰, I Pe 4¹⁵. Fig., ὡς κ. ἐν νυκτί, I Th 5², ⁴ (κλέπτας, WH, txt., R, mg. ; v. Lft., *Notes,* 73 ; but cf. also M, *Th.,* l.c.), II Pe 3¹⁰, Re 3³ 16¹⁵. Metaph., of false teachers, Jo 10⁸.†

SYN. : λῃστής, *a robber, a brigand* who plunders, openly, with violence ; κ. is *a thief* who steals in secret, by fraud and cunning (Tr., *Syn.,* § xliv).

κλέπτω, [in LXX for גנב ;] *to steal :* absol., Mt 6¹⁹, ²⁰ 19¹⁸, Mk 10¹⁹, Lk 18²⁰, Jo 10¹⁰, Ro 2²¹ 13⁹, Eph 4²⁸ ; c. acc., Mt 27⁶⁴ 28¹³.†

κλῆμα, -τος, τό (< κλάω), [in LXX chiefly for זְמוֹרָה, דָּלִית, Ez 15² 17⁶, ⁷, al.;] *a vine-twig, vine-branch :* Jo 15², ⁴⁻⁶.†

Κλήμης, -εντος, ὁ, *Clement :* Phl 4³.†

κληρονομέω, -ῶ (< κληρονόμος), [in LXX chiefly for ירשׁ, also for נחל, etc.;] 1. *to receive by lot.* 2. *to inherit* (in cl., usually c. gen. rei) : absol., Ga 4³⁰ (LXX) ; in general, *to possess oneself of, receive as one's own, obtain* (as De 4⁵, al., cf. Ps 24 (25)³, Is 61⁷) : c. acc. rei (as generally in late Gk., v. M, *Pr.,* 65), of the Messianic Kingdom (cf. Ps 36 (37)¹¹, Si 4¹³ 37²⁶, and v. Dalman, *Words,* 125 ff.) and its blessings and privileges, τ. γῆν, Mt 5⁵ (cf. LXX); τ. βασιλείαν, β. θεοῦ, Mt 25³⁴, ι Co 6⁹,¹⁰ 15⁵⁰, Ga 5²¹; ζωὴν αἰώνιον, Mt 19²⁹, Mk 10¹⁷, Lk 10²⁵ 18¹⁸; σωτηρίαν, He 1¹⁴; τ. ἐπαγγελίας, He 6¹²; ἀφθαρσίαν, ι Co 15⁵⁰; ὄνομα, He,1⁴; τ. εὐλογίαν, He 12¹⁷, ι Pe 3⁹; ταῦτα, Re 21⁷ (cf. κατα-κληρονομέω).†

κληρονομία, -ας, ἡ (< κληρονόμος), [in LXX chiefly for נַחֲלָה, also for יְרֻשָּׁה, etc.;] prop., an inherited property, an inheritance : Mt 21³⁸, Mk 12⁷, Lk 12¹³ 20¹⁴; in general, a possession, inheritance : Ac 7⁵, He 11⁸; of the Messianic Kingdom and its blessings, Ac 20³², Ga 3¹⁸, Col 3²⁴, Eph 1¹⁴,¹⁸ 5⁵, He 9¹⁵, ι Pe 1⁴.†

κληρονόμος, -ου, ὁ (< κλῆρος, νέμομαι, to possess), [in LXX : Jg 18⁷, ιι Ki 14⁷, Mi 1¹⁵, Je 8¹⁰ (יוֹרֵשׁ), Si 23²² *;] 1. (as in cl.) an heir : Mt 21³⁸, Mk 12⁷, Lk 20¹⁴, Ga 4¹; of those who as sons of God inherit the privileges of the Messianic Kingdom; of Christ himself, He 1²; of Abraham, Ro 4¹³,¹⁴; of Christians, Ro 8¹⁷, Ga 3²⁹, Tit 3⁷, Ja 2⁵. 2. (As in LXX : Jg, Mi, Je, ll. c.) a possessor : He 6¹⁷ 11⁷ (Cremer, 359 f.).†

κλῆρος, -ου, ὁ, [in LXX chiefly for נַחֲלָה, גּוֹרָל;] a lot; (a) that which is cast or drawn : Mt 27³⁵, Mk 15²⁴, Lk 23³⁴, Jo 19²⁴ (LXX), Ac 1²⁶; (b) that which is obtained by casting : Ac 1¹⁷ 8²¹; of a part in the Kingdom of God (cf. Wi 5⁵), Ac 26¹⁸, Col 1¹²; pl. of the "cure" of a presbyter, ι Pe 5³ (v. ICC, in l.).†

κληρόω, -ῶ, [in LXX : ι Ki 14⁴¹ (לכד ni.), Es 4¹¹ A (קרא ni.), Is 17¹¹ *;] 1. to cast lots. 2. to choose by lot. 3. to assign by lot, assign a portion : pass., ἐν ᾧ καὶ ἐκληρώθημεν, Eph 1¹¹ (on the various interpretations, v. ICC; AR; Ellic., in l.).†

κλῆσις, -εως, ἡ (καλέω), [in LXX : Je 38 (31)⁶ (קרא), Jth 12¹⁰ A, ιιι Mac 5¹⁴ *;] a calling, call; in NT, always of the Divine call to salvation : Ro 11²⁹, ι Co 1²⁶ 7²⁰, Eph 1¹⁸ 4¹,⁴, Phl 3¹⁴, ιι Th 1¹¹, ιι Ti 1⁹, He 3¹, ιι Pe 1¹⁰ (Cremer, 332).†

κλητός, -ή, -όν (< καλέω), [in LXX for קרא, מִקְרָא, Ex 12¹⁶, al.;] called, invited (as to a banquet, Æsch., ι Ki 1⁴¹, ιιι Mac 5¹⁴); in NT, always of the Divine call; (a) to some office : κ. ἀπόστολος, Ro 1¹, ι Co 1¹; (b) to salvation : Ro 8²⁸, ι Co 1²⁴, Ju ¹; κ. καὶ ἐκλεκτοὶ κ. πιστοί, Re 17¹⁴; in gosp. (not in pl., v.s. καλέω) disting. fr. ἐκλεκτός, Mt 20¹⁶ (WH, txt., R, omit), 22¹⁴; κ. Ἰησοῦ Χρ., Ro 1⁶; κ. ἅγιοι, saints by calling, Ro 1⁷, ι Co 1².†

κλίβανος, -ου, ὁ (Att., κρίβ-, but κλ- in Ion., Hdt., ii, 92), [in LXX for תַּנּוּר, Ge 15¹⁷, Ho 7⁴,⁶, al.;] 1. in cl., a clibanus, cribanus, an earthen vessel for baking bread. 2. In LXX and NT, a furnace (cf. MM, Exp., xv), an oven : Mt 6³⁰, Lk 12²⁸.†

κλίμα, -τος, τό (< κλίνω), [in LXX : Jg 20² A (פֵּנָּה) *;] 1. an inclination, slope, esp. the slope from the equator to the pole (Arist). 2. a region (Polyb., al.) : pl., Ro 15²³, ιι Co 11¹⁰, Ga 1²¹.†

* κλινάριον, -ου, τό, dimin. of κλίνη, a couch : Ac 5¹⁵ (cf. κλινίδιον).†

κλίνη, -ης, ἡ (< κλίνω), [in LXX chiefly for מִטָּה;] *a bed, couch:* Mt 9², ⁶, Mk 4²¹ 7⁴, ³⁰, Lk 5¹⁸ 8¹⁶ 17³⁴, Re 2²² (cf. MM, *Exp.*, xv).†

* κλινίδιον, -ου, τό, dimin. of κλίνη, *a couch:* Lk 5¹⁹, ²⁴ (cf. κλινάριον).†

κλίνω, [in LXX chiefly for נטה;] 1. *to make to bend, to bow:* τ. κεφαλήν (of one dying), Jo 19³⁰; τ. πρόσωπον (of terrified persons), Lk 24⁵. 2. *to make to lean, to rest:* τ. κεφαλήν (in sleep), Mt 8²⁰, Lk 9⁵⁸. 3. As in Hom., of soldiers, *to turn* (to flight), παρεμβολάς, He 11³⁴. 4. In late Gk. (as mid. in cl.), *to decline:* intrans., ἡ ἡμέρα, Lk 9¹² 24²⁹.†

** κλισία, -ας, ἡ (< κλίιω), [in LXX: iii Mac 6³¹ A *;] 1. *a place for reclining;* hence, (a) *a hut;* (b) *an easy chair;* (c) *a couch.* 2. *a company reclining:* pl., Lk 9¹⁴ (cf. FlJ, *Ant.*, xii, 2, 12).†

κλοπή, -ῆς, ἡ (< κλέπτω), [in LXX for גנב;] *theft:* pl., Mt 15¹⁹, Mk 7²².†

κλύδων, -ω·ος, ὁ (κλύζω, of the sea, *to wash over*), [in LXX: Jh 1⁴, ¹² (סער), al.;] *a billow, surge:* Lk 8²⁴, Ja 1⁶.†
SYN.: κῦμα, *a wave.*

† κλυδωνίζομαι (< κλύδων), [in LXX: Is 57²⁰ (גרש) *;] *to be tossed by waves;* metaph., *to be tossed like waves* (cf. FlJ, *Ant.*, ix, 11, 3): Eph 4¹⁴.†

Κλωπᾶς, -ᾶ, ὁ (Aram.; on the original, v. Lft., *Gal.*, 267 f.), *Clopas:* Jo 19²⁵.†

* κνήθω (late form of κνάω), 1. *to scratch.* 2. *to tickle;* pass., *to itch:* metaph. of eagerness to hear, ii Ti 4³.†

Κνίδος, -ου, ἡ, *Cnidus,* a city (and peninsula) on S.W. coast of Asia Minor: Ac 27⁷.†

*† κοδράντης, -ου, ὁ (Lat. *quadrans,* the fourth part of an *as*), *a quadrans* (AV, farthing): Mt 5²⁶, Mk 12⁴².†

κοιλία, -ας, ἡ (< κοῖλος, *hollow*), [in LXX chiefly for בֶּטֶן, מֵעִים, קֶרֶב, De 7¹³, ii Ki 7¹², Ge 41²¹, al.; also (Jb 3¹¹ 10¹⁸ 31¹⁵ 38⁸) for רֶחֶם;] 1. *the belly* (stomach or intestines or both): Mt 12⁴⁰ 15¹⁷, Mk 7¹⁹, Lk 15¹⁶, Ro 16¹⁸, i Co 6¹³, Phl 3¹⁹, Re 10⁹, ¹⁰. 2. (As often in LXX) *the womb* (cl. μήτρα, q.v.): Lk 1⁴¹, ⁴², ⁴⁴ 2²¹ 11²⁷ 23²⁹, Jo 3⁴; ἐκ κ. μητρός (cf. Ps 21 (22)¹¹, Jb 1²¹, al.), Mt 19¹², Lk 1¹⁵, Ac 3² 14⁸, Ga 1¹⁵. 3. Metaph. (as Heb. בֶּטֶן, cf. Jb 15³⁵, Pr 20²⁷, Si 19¹²), of the *heart:* Jo 7³⁸.†

κοιμάω, -ῶ, [in LXX chiefly for שכב;] *to lull to sleep, put to sleep.* Mid and pass., *to fall asleep* (M, *Pr.*, 162; M, *Th.*, i, 4, 13): Mt 28¹³, Lk 22⁴⁵, Jo 11¹², Ac 12⁶. Metaph., of death: Mt 27⁵², Jo 11¹¹, Ac 7⁶⁰ 13³⁶, i Co 7³⁹ 11³⁰ 15⁶, ¹⁸, ²⁰, ⁵¹, i Th 4¹³⁻¹⁵, ii Pe 3⁴ (cf. Is 14⁸, 43¹⁷, ii Mac 12⁴⁵).†
SYN.: καθεύδω.

** κοίμησις, -εως, ἡ, [in LXX: Si 46¹⁹ 48¹³ *;] *a reclining, resting:* Jo 11¹³.†

κοινός, -ή, -όν, [in LXX: Pr 1¹⁴ (אֶחָד) 21⁹ 25²⁴ (חָבֵר), Wi 7³, al.;]

1. *common* (general; = Lat. *communis*): Ac 2⁴⁴ 4³²; κ. πίστις, Tit 1⁴; σωτηρία, Ju³. 2. *common* (ordinary; = *vulgaris*); hence in LXX (I Mac 1⁴⁷, al.) and NT, *unhallowed, unclean* (cl., βέβηλος, q.v.): Mk 7²,⁵, Ac 10¹⁴,²⁸ 11⁸, Ro 14¹⁴, He 10²⁹, Re 21²⁷.†
κοινόω, -ῶ, [in LXX: IV Mac 7⁶ אR*;] 1. in cl., *to make common.* 2. In LXX, l.c., and NT (as κοινός, 2), *to make ceremonially unclean, to profane* (= cl., βεληλόω): Mt 15¹¹,¹⁸,²⁰, Mk 7¹⁵,¹⁸,²⁰,²³, Ac 21²⁸; pass., He 9¹³. 2. *to count unclean* (cf. δικαιόω): Ac 10¹⁵ 11⁹.†
SYN.: βεβηλόω. Thayer (s.v. κ.) mentions that Winer notes the accuracy whereby the Jews are said to use κ. in addressing Jews, Ac 21²⁸, and β. when speaking to Felix, 24⁶ (Cremer, 362).
κοινωνέω, -ῶ, [in LXX: II Ch 20³⁵, Jb 34⁸, Ec 9⁴ (חבר), Pr 1¹¹, Wi 6²³, Si 13¹, al.;] *to have a share of, go shares in* (something) *with* (some one), *take part in:* c. gen. rei (as usually in cl., so Pr, l.c.), He 2¹⁴; c. dat. rei, Ro 12¹³ 15²⁷, I Ti 5²², I Pe 4¹³, II Jo 11; c. dat. pers., seq. εἰς, Phl 4¹⁵; ἐν, Ga 6⁶ (cf. συν-κοινωνέω).†
κοινωνία, -ας, ἡ (< κοινωνός), [in LXX: Le 6² (5²¹) (תְּשׂוּמֶת יָד), Wi 8¹⁸, III Mac 4⁶*;] 1. *fellowship, communion:* Ac 2⁴², II Co 6¹⁴, Phl 1⁵; τ. υἱοῦ, I Co 1⁹; τ. αἵματος, σώματος Χρ., I Co 10¹⁶; παθημάτων αὐτοῦ, Phl 3¹⁰; τ. πνεύματος, II Co 13¹³, Phl 2¹; δεξιὰς κοινωνίας, Ga 2⁹; τ. πίστεώς σου, Phm⁶; seq. μετά: τ. πατρός, I Jo 1³,⁶; ἡμῶν, ἀλλήλων, ib.³,⁷. 2. *contribution* (as outcome of fellowship): Ro 15²⁶, II Co 8⁴ 9¹³, He 13⁶ (cf. Art. *Communion, DB*, i, 460 ff.; MM, *Exp.*, xv).†
* κοινωνικός, -ή, -όν (< κοινωνία), 1. *sociable.* 2. *ready to communicate* or *impart* (R, mg., *ready to sympathize*, v. Field, *Notes*, 213 f.): I Ti 6¹⁸.†
κοινωνός, -ή, -όν (< κοινός), [in LXX: Pr 28²⁴, Is 1²³ (חָבֵר), Ma 2¹⁴ (חֲבֶרֶת), Es 8¹³, al.;] 1. as adj., = κοινός. 2. As subst., ὁ, ἡ κ., (*a*) *a partner, associate, companion:* II Co 8²³, Phm¹⁷; c. dat. pers., Lk 5¹⁰; c. gen. pers., He 10³³; id. seq. ἐν, Mt 23³⁰; (*b*) *a partaker, sharer:* c. gen. rei, I Co 10¹⁸,²⁰, II Co 1⁷, I Pe 5¹, II Pe 1⁴ (v. Deiss., *BS*, 368 n₂).†
κοίτη, -ης, ἡ (in Hom., κοῖτος), [in LXX chiefly for מִשְׁכָּב, also for שְׁכָבָה, etc.;] *a bed:* Lk 11⁷; esp. *the marriage-bed:* κ. ἀμίαντος, He 13⁴; κ. ἔχειν, of a woman conceiving, Ro 9¹⁰ (cf. peculiar phrases in LXX, Le 15¹⁸, al.); of illicit intercourse, pl., Ro 13¹³.†
κοιτών, -ῶνος, ὁ (< κοίτη; = Att., δωμάτιον, v. Kennedy, *Sources*, 40), [in LXX chiefly for חֶדֶר, II Ki 4⁷, Jl 2¹⁶, I Es 3³, al.;] *a bedchamber;* ὁ ἐπὶ τοῦ κ., *a chamberlain:* Ac 12²⁰.†
† κόκκινος, -η, -ον (< κόκκος, as used of the "berry" of the *ilex coccifera*, v. *DB*, iv, 416), [in LXX for תּוֹלָע, תּוֹלָעָה, שְׁנִי, Ex 25⁴, Ge 38²⁸, Is 1¹⁸, al.;] *scarlet:* Mt 27²⁸, He 9¹⁹, Re 17³; neut., without substantive, of clothing, Re 17⁴ 18¹²,¹⁶.†

κόκκος, -ου, ὁ, [in LXX: La 4⁵ B אּ R (תּוֹלָע), Si 45¹¹ *;] a grain: Mt 13³¹ 17²⁰, Mk 4³¹, Lk 13¹⁹ 17⁶, Jo 12²⁴, ι Co 15³⁷.†

κολάζω (< κόλος, docked), [in LXX: Da 6¹² ⁽¹³⁾ (no Heb.), ι Es 8²⁴, Wi 3⁴ (and freq.), ι Mac 7⁷, al.;] 1. to curtail, dock, prune. 2. to check, restrain. 3. to chastise, correct, punish: pass., ιι Pe 2⁹; mid., cause to be punished (ιιι Mac 7³): Ac 4²¹.†

*κολακία (Rec. -εία), -ας, ἡ (< κολακεύω, to flatter), flattery: ι Th 2⁵ (v. Lft., Notes, 23).†

κόλασις, -εως, ἡ (< κολάζω), [in LXX: Ez 14³⁻⁷ 18³⁰ 44¹² (מִכְשׁוֹל) 43¹¹, λαμβάνειν τὴν κ. (כְּלִם ni.); Wi 11¹³ 16²,²⁴ 19⁴, Je 18²⁰, ιι-ιv Mac₅*;] correction, penalty, punishment: Mt 25⁴⁶, ι Jo 4¹⁸.†

SYN.: τιμωρία, requital. Arist. distinguishes between κ. as that which, being disciplinary, has reference to the sufferer, and τ. as that which, being penal, has reference to the satisfaction of him who inflicts (v. Thayer, s.v. κ., and cf. Tr., Syn., § vii). But in late Gk. especially, the distinction is not always maintained (v. reff. in Thayer).

Κολασσαεύς (Rec. Κολοσ-), -έως, ὁ, a Colossian: pl., Col., tit. (and subscr., Rec., Tr.).†

Κολασσαί, v.s. Κολοσσαί.

*† κολαφίζω (< κόλαφος = Att., κόνδυλοι, the knuckles, the closed fist), to strike with the fist, to buffet: Mt 26⁶⁷, Mk 14⁶⁵, ιι Co 12⁷; pass., ι Co 4¹¹, ι Pe 2²⁰.†

κολλάω, -ῶ (< κόλλα, glue), [in LXX chiefly for דבק;] 1. to glue or cement together. 2. Generally, to unite, to join firmly. Pass., to cleave to, join (oneself to): c. dat. pers., Mt 19⁵ ⁽ᴸˣˣ⁾, Lk 10¹¹ 15¹⁵, Ac 5¹³ (but v. Field, Notes, 118) 9²⁶ 10²⁸ (v. Field, l.c.) 17³⁴; τ. πόρνῃ, ι Co 6¹⁶; τ. Κυρίῳ, ib. ¹⁷; c. dat. rei, ἅρματι, Ac 8²⁹; τ. ἀγαθῷ, Ro 12⁹; of sins joining together, ἄχρι τ. οὐρανοῦ, Re 18⁵, of dust, Lk 10¹¹ (cf. προσ-κολλάω).†

κολλούριον (TTr., κολλύ-, the more usual form), -ου, τό (dimin. of κολλύρα = κόλλιξ, a coarse bread roll), [in LXX: ιιι Ki 12²⁴ ʰⁱˡ B *;] 1. a small bread roll (LXX, ll. c.). 2. (Usually in pl., LS, s.v.) an eye salve shaped like a roll: Re 3¹⁸.†

*† κολλυβιστής, -οῦ, ὁ (< κόλλυβος, a small coin, a rate of exchange), a money-changer: Mt 21¹², Mk 11¹⁵, Jo 2¹⁵ (cf. κερματιστής).†

κολλύριον, v.s. κολλούριον.

κολοβόω, -ῶ (< κολοβός, docked), [in LXX: ιι Ki 4¹² (קָצַץ pi.) *;] to cut off, amputate (LXX), hence, to curtail, shorten: Mt 24²², Mk 13²⁰.†

Κολοσσαεύς, v.s. Κολασσαεύς.

Κολοσσαί (so in cl.; -ασσαί, Rec., LTr.), -ῶν, αἱ, Colossæ, a city on the Lycus in Phrygia: Col 1².†

κόλπος, -ου, ὁ, [in LXX chiefly for חֵיק, חוֹק, חֵק;] 1. prop., the bosom: Jo 13²³; fig., of close association, ἐν (εἰς τὸν) τοῖς κ. Ἀβραάμ, Lk 16²², ²³ (cf. ιv Mac 13¹⁶); ὁ ὢν εἰς τὸν κ. τ. πατρός, Jo 1¹⁸. 2. The bosom or fold of a loose garment falling over a girdle, used as a pocket, hence fig., εἰς τὸν κ. (Is 65⁶, Je 39 (32)¹⁸) :ı Lk 6³⁸. 3. A bosom-like hollow, as *a bay* or *gulf* : Ac 27³⁹.†

** κολυμβάω, -ῶ, [in Al. : Is 25¹¹ * ;] *to dive, plunge into the sea*, hence, *to swim* : Ac 27⁴³ (cf. ἐκ-κολυμβάω).†

κολυμβήθρα, -ας, ἡ (< κολυμβάω), [in LXX for בְּרֵכָה ; ıv Ki 18²⁷, al. ;] *a swimming-pool, pool* : Jo 5² ⁽⁴⁾, ⁷ 9⁷.†

*† κολωνία, (Rec. -ώνια), -ας, ἡ (< Lat. *colonia*), a city settlement of disbanded soldiers, whose inhabitants enjoyed the *jus Italicum* (v. *DB*, s.v. Colony), *a colony* : Ac 16¹² (v. Lft., *Phl.*, 50 f.).†

* κομάω, -ῶ (< κόμη), *to wear long hair* : ı Co 11¹⁴, ¹⁵.†

κόμη, -ης, ἡ, [in LXX : Nu 6⁵, Ez 44²⁰ (פֶּרַע), al. ;] *the hair* : ı Co 11¹⁵.†

κομίζω, [in LXX for נָשָׂא, etc. ;] 1. *to take care of.* 2. *to carry off safe.* 3. *to carry off* as booty. 4. *to bear* or *carry* : Lk 7³⁷. Mid., *to bear for oneself*, hence, (*a*) *to receive* : He 10³⁶ 11¹³, ³⁹, ı Pe 1⁹ 5⁴, ıı Pe 2¹³ ; (*b*) *to receive back, recover* (in cl. so also act.) : Mt 25²⁷, He 11¹⁹ ; metaph., of requital, ıı Co 5¹⁰, Col 3²⁵ ; παρὰ Κυρίου, Eph 6⁸ (cf. ἐκ-, συν-κομίζω).†

* κομψός, -ή, -όν (< κομέω, *to take care of*), *well-dressed, elegant, fine* ; compar. neut., κομψότερον ἔχειν (cf. κόμψως ἔχειν, Epict., and colloq. Eng., "*to be doing finely*") : Jo 4⁵².†

κονιάω, -ῶ (< κονία, *dust, lime*), [in LXX : De 27², ⁴ (שִׂיד), Pr 21⁹ * ;] *to plaster* or *whiten over* : of tombs, Mt 23²⁷ ; fig., of a hypocrite, Ac 23³.†

κονιορτός, -οῦ, ὁ (< κόνις or κονία, *dust, ὄρνυμι, to stir up*), [in LXX for אָבָק, etc. ;] in cl., *dust stirred up* (Ex 9⁹, Is 5²⁴) ; in NT, simply *dust* : Mt 10¹⁴, Lk 9⁵ 10¹¹, Ac 13⁵¹ 22²³.†

κοπάζω (< κόπος), [in LXX : Ge 8¹, Es 2¹ 7¹⁰ (שָׁכַךְ), Ru 1¹⁸, al. (חָדַל), Jh 1¹¹, ¹² (שָׁתַק), al. ;] *to grow weary* : of the wind (Hdt., Jh., l.c.), *to abate, cease raging* : Mt 14³², Mk 4³⁹, 6⁵¹.†

κοπετός, -οῦ, ὁ (< κόπτω, mid.), [in LXX chiefly for מִסְפֵּד ;] = cl. *κομμός, a beating of the head and breast, lamentation* : seq. ἐπί, c. dat. pers., Ac 8².†

κοπή, -ῆς, ἡ (< κόπτω), [in LXX : Ge 14¹⁷, Jos 10²⁰ (נכה hi., מַכָּה), De 28²⁵ (נגף), Jth 15⁷ * ;] 1. in cl., *a stroke, a pounding* (as in a mortar). 2. In LXX, *a smiting* in battle : He 7¹ ⁽ᴸˣˣ⁾.†

κοπιάω, -ῶ (< κόπος), [in LXX chiefly for יָגַע ;] 1. (as in cl.) *to grow weary* : Mt 11²⁸, Jo 4⁶, Re 2³ (cf. Is 40³¹). 2. Hence, in LXX and NT, *to work with effort, to toil* : absol., Mt 6²⁸, Lk 5⁵ 12²⁷, Jo 4³⁸, Ac 20³⁵, ı Co 4¹², Eph 4²⁸, ıı Ti 2⁶ ; c. acc. rei, Jo 4³⁸ ; freq. in *Paul. Epp.*, of ministerial labour : ı Co 15¹⁰ 16¹⁶ ; seq. ἐν, Ro 16¹², ı Th 5¹² (v. M, *Th.*, in l.), ı Ti 5¹⁷ ; εἰς, Ro 16⁶, Ga 4¹¹, Phl 2¹⁶, Col 1²⁹, ı Ti 4¹⁰.†

κόπος, -ου, ὁ (< κόπτω), [in LXX chiefly for עָמָל, also for

אָנֶן, etc.;] 1. *a striking, beating* (in Je 51³³ (45³) = κοπετός). 2. *laborious toil, trouble*: Jo 4³⁸, 1 Co 3⁸ 15⁵⁸, 1 Th 3⁵; κ. τ. ἀγάπης, 1 Th 1³; ἔργα καὶ κ., Re 2²; κ. καὶ μόχθος, 11 Co 11²⁷, 1 Th 2⁹, 11 Th 3⁸; pl., ἐν κ., 11 Co 6⁵ 10¹⁵ 11²³; ἐκ τ. κ., Re 14¹³; κόπους (-ον) παρέχειν (in cl. more freq. π. πράγματα, πόνον), c. dat. pers., Mt 26¹⁰, Mk 14⁶, Lk 11⁷ 18⁵, Ga 6¹⁷.†

SYN.: μόχθος, *labour; πόνος* (q.v.), *toil, painful effort;* in cl., "π. gives prominence to the effort (work as requiring force), κ. to the fatigue, μ. (chiefly poetic) to the hardship" (Thayer, s.v. κ.).

κοπρία, -ας, ἡ, [in LXX chiefly for אַשְׁפֹּת;] *a dung hill* (1 Ki 2⁸ Ps 112 (113)⁷ al.): Lk 14³⁵.†

κόπριον, -ου, τό, [in LXX (pl.): Je 32 (25)³³ (דֹּמֶן), Si 22², 1 Mac 2⁶² *;] = κόπρος, *dung:* pl., Lk 13⁸ (WH, mg., κόφινον κοπρίων).†

κόπτω, [in LXX for כרת, ספד, נכה hi., etc.;] 1. *to strike, smite.* 2. *to cut off:* c. acc. rei, seq. ἀπό, Mt 21⁸; ἐκ, Mk 11⁸. Mid., *to beat one's breast* with grief, *to mourn, bewail:* Mt 11¹⁷ 24³⁰; c. acc. pers., Lk 8⁵² 23²⁷; seq. ἐπί, c. acc., Re 1⁷ 18⁹ (cf. ἀνα-, ἀπο-, ἐκ-, ἐν-, κατα-, προ-, προσ-κόπτω).†

SYN.: θρηνέω, q.v.

κόραξ, -ακος, ὁ, [in LXX for עֹרֵב;] *a raven:* Lk 12²⁴.†

κοράσιον, -ου, τό, (dimin. of κόρη), [in LXX chiefly for נַעֲרָה, Ru 2⁸, al.; in Jl 3 (4)³, Za 8⁵ for וַיַּלְדָּה;] a colloquial word which survives in MGr. (Kennedy, *Sources*, 154), *girl, maiden:* Mt 9²⁴,²⁵ 14¹¹, Mk 5⁴¹,⁴², 6²²,²⁸.†

*† κορβάν (Rec., T, -βᾶν), indecl. (Heb. קָרְבָּן), *an offering, a gift* offered to God: Mk 7¹¹ (cf. κορβανᾶς).†

*† κορβανᾶς, -ᾶ, ὁ (Heb. קָרְבָּן), the Temple *treasury:* Mt 27⁶ (cf. κορβάν).†

Κορέ, indecl. (in FlJ, -έου), ὁ (Heb. קֹרַח), *Korah:* Ju¹¹.†

** κορέννυμι (< κόρος, *surfeit*), [in Sm.: Ps 21 (22)²⁷, Al, 102 (103)⁵ *;] *to satisfy:* pass., τροφῆς, Ac 27³⁸; metaph., of spiritual things, 1 Co 4⁸.†

Κορίνθιος, -α, -ον, *Corinthian;* as subst., ὁ K., *a Corinthian:* Ac 18⁸,²⁷ (WH, txt., R, omit), 11 Co 6¹¹; 1 Co, 11 Co, *tit.*†

Κόρινθος, -ου, ἡ, *Corinth:* Ac 18¹,²⁷ 19¹, 1 Co 1², 11 Co 1¹,²³ 11 Ti 4²⁰.†

Κορνήλιος, -ου, ὁ (Lat.), *Cornelius:* Ac 10¹ ff..†

κόρος, -ου, ὁ (Heb. כֹּר), [in LXX: Le 27¹⁶, Nu 11³², Ez 45¹³ (חֹמֶר); more freq., 11 Ch 27⁵, al. (כֹּר);] *a cor,* a Hebrew measure containing about 15 bushels (AV, RV, *measure*): Lk 16⁷.†

κοσμέω, -ῶ (< κόσμος), [in LXX for עדה, תקן, etc.;] 1. *to order, arrange, prepare* (in Hom. esp. of marshalling armies): Mt 25⁷ (cf.

Si 50⁹, al.). 2. *to adorn, furnish*: οἶκον, pass., Mt 12⁴⁴, Lk 11²⁵; μνημεῖα, Mt 23²⁹; τὸ ἱερόν, pass., Lk 21⁵; θεμέλιοι, Re 21¹⁹; νύμφην, pass., Re 21²; ἑαυτάς, seq. ἐν, 1 Ti 2⁹. Metaph., c. acc. pers., 1 Pe 3⁵; c. acc. rei, Tit 2¹⁰.†

*** κοσμικός, -ή, -όν** (κόσμος), 1. *pertaining to the world* or universe. 2. *of this world, earthly*. He 9¹. 3. In ethical sense, *worldly*: ἐπιθυμίαι, Tit 2¹².†

κόσμιος, -ον (in cl. -α, -ον), (< κόσμος), [in LXX: Ec 12⁹ (תקן)*;] *orderly, decent, modest*: 1 Ti 2⁹ (WH, mg., -ίως, q.v.) 3².†

*** κοσμίως**, adv (< κόσμος), *decently, fittingly*: 1 Ti 2⁹ (WH, mg.).†

*† κοσμοκράτωρ, -ορος, ὁ (< κόσμος, κρατέω), 1. in Orphic hymns, al. (v. AR, *Eph.*, l.c.), *a ruler of the whole world* (and so in Rabbinic writings: קוזמוקרטור). 2. *a ruler of this world* (in contrast to παντοκράτωρ): οἱ κ. τ. σκότους τούτου, *the rulers of this dark world*, Eph 6¹².†

κόσμος, -ου, ὁ [in LXX: Ge 2¹, De 4¹⁹ 17³, Is 24²¹ 40²⁶ (צבא), Ex 33⁵, ⁶, Je 2³² 4³⁰, Ez 7²⁰ 16¹¹ 23⁴⁰ (עדי), Is 61¹⁰ (כלי), al., Wi 2²⁴ and freq., Si 6³⁰, al.;] 1. *order* (Hom., Plat., al.). 2. *ornament, adornment*, esp. of women (Hom., al.): 1 Pe 3³. 3. Later, the *world* or *universe*, as an ordered system (Plat., al.): Ac 17²⁴, Ro 4¹³, 1 Co 3²², Phl 2¹⁵, He 4³, al. 4. In late writers only, *the world*, i.e. *the earth* (= ἡ οἰκουμένη, cf. Mt 4⁸ with Lk 4⁵): Mt 4⁸, Mk 16[¹⁵], Col 2²⁰, 1 Ti 6⁷, al.; hence by meton., (*a*) of the human inhabitants of the world: Mt 5¹⁴ 13³⁸, Mk 14⁹, Jo 1¹⁰ 4⁴² 12⁴⁷, Ro 3⁶, 1 Co 4¹³, 11 Co 5¹⁹, 11 Pe 2⁵, al.; (*b*) of worldly affairs or possessions: Mt 16²⁶, Mk 8³⁶, Lk 9²⁵, 1 Co 7³¹, 1 Jo 2¹⁶, al.; (*c*) in ethical sense, of the ungodly, the world as apart from God and thus evil in its tendency: Jo 7⁷ 14¹⁷, ²⁷, 1 Co 1²¹, Ja 1²⁷, 1 Jo 4⁴, al.; (*d*) metaph.: ὁ κ. τῆς ἀδικίας, Ja 3⁶. *SYN.*: αἰών, q.v. (cf. also Dalman, *Words*, 162 ff.; Tr., *Syn.*, § lix; Westc., additional note on Jo 1¹⁰; *DB*, iv, 938 ff.).

Κούαρτος, -ου, ὁ (Lat.), *Quartus*: Ro 16²³.†

κούμ (Tr., txt., κούμ, Rec. κούμι) (Heb. imperat. masc., used as an interjection: קום), *koum (arise)*: Mk 5⁴¹.†

*† κουστωδία, -ας, ἡ, (Lat. *custodia*), *a guard*: Mt 27⁶⁵, ⁶⁶ 28¹¹.†

κουφίζω (< κοῦφος, *light*), [in LXX: Ex 18²², Jh 1⁵, al. (קלל hi.), Es 5¹, al.;] 1. intrans., *to be light* (poetic chiefly). 2. *to lighten, make light*: c. acc., Ac 27³⁸.†

κόφινος, -ου, ὁ, [in LXX: Jg 6¹⁹ (סל), Ps 80 (81)⁶ (דוד) *;] *a basket*, probably of wicker-work, such as were carried by Jews for food: Mt 14²⁰ 16⁹, Mk 6⁴³ 8¹⁹, Lk 9¹⁷ 13⁸, Jo 6¹³ (cf. σφυρίς).†

**† κράβαττος (Rec. κράββατος), ου, ὁ (a Macedonian word, = Lat. *grabatus*, cl. σκίμπους), [in Aq.: Am 3¹²*;] *a camp bed, pallet*: Mk 2⁴, ⁹, ¹¹, ¹² 6⁵⁵, Jo 5⁸⁻¹¹, Ac 5¹⁵ 9³³ (v. Swete, *Mk.*, 2⁴, and cf. κλίνη).†

κράζω, [in LXX for זעק, צעק, קרא, etc.;] in cl. chiefly poët., 1. prop. onomatop., of the raven, *to croak*, hence generally, of inartic. cries, *to scream, cry out* (Æsch., al.): Mk 5⁵ 9²⁶ 15³⁹ (Rec., R, mg.), Lk 9³⁹, al.; of crying for vengeance (cf. Ge 4¹⁰), Ja 5⁴. 2. *to cry, call* *out* with a loud voice: c. acc. rei, Ac 19³²; seq. orat. dir., Mk 10⁴⁸, Lk 18³⁹, al.; (ἐν) φωνῇ μεγάλῃ, Mk 5⁷, Re 14¹⁵, al.; λέγων, Mt 8²⁹, al.; of public teaching, Jo 1¹⁵, Ro 9²⁷, al.; of importunate prayer (cf. Jb 35¹², Ps 3⁵, al.), Ro 8¹⁵, Ga 4⁶; pf. with pres. sense (vernac.; M, *Pr.*, 147), Jo 1¹⁵.

SYN.: v.s. βοάω.

* κραιπάλη (κρεπάλη, WH), -ης, ἡ (cf. κραιπαλάω for שָׁכַר, Is 24²⁰ 29⁹), *drunken nausea* (EV, *surfeiting*): Lk 21³⁴.†

SYN.: κῶμος, *revelling ;* μέθη, *drunkeness ;* οἰνοφλυγία, *a debauch ;* πότος, *a drinking bout* (v. Tr., *Syn.*, § lxi).

κρανίον, -ου, τό (< κάρα, *the head*), [in LXX : Jg 9⁵³, IV Ki 9³⁵ (גֻּלְגֹּלֶת) *;*] *a skull :* Mt 27³³, Mk 15²², Lk 23³³, Jo 19¹⁷.†

κράσπεδον, -ου, τό, [in LXX : Nu 15³⁸, ³⁹ (צִיצִת), De 22¹², Za 8²³ (כָּנָף) *;*] 1. in cl., *an edge, border.* 2. In LXX (v. supr.) and NT, *a tassel* or *corner :* Mt 9²⁰ 14³⁶ 23⁵, Mk 6⁵⁶, Lk 8⁴⁴.†

κραταιός, -ά, -όν (< κράτος), (in cl. poët. form of κρατερός), [in LXX chiefly for חָזַק and cognates;] *strong, mighty :* I Pe 5⁶.†

† κραταιόω, -ῶ (late form of κρατύνω; < κράτος), [in LXX chiefly for חָזַק;] *to strengthen;* pass., *to wax strong :* Lk 2⁴⁰, I Co 16¹³; πνεύματι, Lk 1⁸⁰; δυνάμει κ. διὰ τ. πνεύματος, Eph 3¹⁶.†

κρατέω, -ῶ (< κράτος), [in LXX chiefly for חָזַק hi., also for אָחַז, etc.;] 1. *to be strong, mighty,* hence, *to rule, be master, prevail* (so chiefly in cl.; in LXX : Es 1¹, I Es 4³⁸, Wi 14¹⁹, al.). 2. *to get possession of, obtain, take hold of* (Hdt., Thuc., al.): c. gen. rei (M, *Pr.*, 65), Ac 27¹³; τ. χειρός, Mt 9²⁵, Mk 1³¹ 5⁴¹ 9²⁷, Lk 8⁵⁴; c. acc. rei, Mt 12¹¹; c. acc. pers., Mt 14³ 18²⁸ 21⁴⁶ 22⁶ 26⁴, ⁴⁸ ff., Mk 3²¹ 6¹⁷ 12¹² 14¹, ⁴⁴ ff., Ac 3¹¹ 24⁶, Re 20² (cf. II Ki 6⁶). 3. *to hold, hold fast* (Æsch., Polyb., al.): c. acc. rei, ἐν τ. δεξιᾷ, Re 2¹. Metaph.: c. acc. pers., pass., Ac 2²⁴; c. acc. rei, Re 2¹³, ²⁵ 3¹¹; τ. κεφαλήν (i.e. Christ), Col 2¹⁹; τ. πα‚άδοσιν (-εις), λόγον, διδαχήν, Mk 7³, ⁴, ⁸ 9¹⁰, II Th 2¹⁵, Re 2¹⁴, ¹⁵; c. gen. rei, He 4¹⁴ 6¹⁸; of sins, *to retain,* Jo 20²³; of restraint, seq. ἵνα μή, Re 7¹; pass., seq. τοῦ μή, Lk 24¹⁶.†

κράτιστος, -η, -ον, superl. of κρατύς (Hom.), 1. *strongest, mightiest* (Hom.). 2. *noblest, best* (cf. κρείσσων), *most excellent* (Pind., Soph., al.): voc., κράτιστε, as title of honour and respect (*DCG*, ii, 727ª), Lk 1³, Ac 23²⁶ 24³ 26²⁵.†

κράτος, -εος (-ους), τό, [in LXX chiefly for עֹז, Jb 12¹⁶, Ps 89 (90)¹¹, al.;] 1. *strength,* esp. as in Hom., of bodily strength. 2. *power, might :* He 2¹⁴; τὸ κ. τῆς ἰσχύος αὐτοῦ, Eph 1¹⁹ 6¹⁰ (Is 40²⁶, Da TH 4²⁷); τ. δόξης αὐτοῦ, Col 1¹¹; κατὰ κράτος, *mightily,* Ac 19²⁰; *a mighty deed, an act of power,* Lk 1⁵¹; in doxologies, I Ti 6¹⁶, I Pe 4¹¹ 5¹¹, Ju ²⁵, Re 1⁶ 5¹³.†

κραυγάζω (< κραυγή), [in LXX : II Es 3¹³ (רוּעַ hi.) *;*] = κράζω, 1. of animals, *to bay, to croak,* etc. 2. Of men, *to cry out, shout :*

Mt 12¹⁹, Jo 12¹³ 19¹⁵, Ac 22²³; seq. λέγων, Jo 18⁴⁰ 19⁶, ¹²; καὶ λέγων, Lk 4⁴¹ (WH, κράζ-); φωνῇ μεγάλῃ, Jo 11⁴³ (cf. Abbott, *JV*, 269 f.).†

κραυγή, -ῆς, ἡ, [in LXX for צְעָקָה, תְּרוּעָה, שַׁוְעָה, etc.;] *crying, outcry, clamour:* Mt 25⁶, Lk 1⁴², Ac 23⁹, Eph 4³¹, He 5⁷, Re 21⁴.†

κρέας, -έως, pl., κρέα, collective, [in LXX for בָּשָׂר (freq.);] *flesh, meat:* Ro 14²¹, 1 Co 8¹³.†

κρείσσων (Epic and old Att.) and **κρείττων** (later Att.), prop. comparat. of κρατύς, *strong*, but in sense often (as in cl., v. LS, s.v.) as comparat. of ἀγαθός, [in LXX chiefly for טוֹב;] *better;* (*a*) as to advantage or usefulness: 1 Co 11¹⁷, He 11⁴⁰ 12²⁴; πολλῷ μᾶλλον κ., Phl 1²³; κρεῖσσον ποιεῖν, 1 Co 7³⁸; ἐστιν, seq. inf., 1 Co 7⁹, 11 Pe 2²¹; (*b*) as to excellence: He 1⁴ 6⁹ 7⁷, ¹⁹, ²² 8⁶ 9²³ 10³⁴ 11¹⁶, ³⁵; κ. ἐστι, seq. inf., 1 Pe 3¹⁷.†

κρέμαμαι, v.s. κρεμάννυμι.

κρεμάννυμι (also κρεμαννύω, κρεμάω; the pres. is not found in NT), [in LXX (where also κρεμάζω, Jb 26⁷) chiefly for תלה;] trans., *to hang, suspend:* c. acc. pers., seq. ἐπὶ ξύλου, Ac 5³⁰ 10³⁹; pass., Lk 23³⁹; seq. περί, Mt 18⁶. Mid., κρέμαμαι, intrans., *to hang:* seq. ἐκ, Ac 28⁴; ἐπὶ ξύλου, Ga 3¹³ (LXX); metaph., seq. ἐι, Mt 22⁴⁰.†

κρεπάλη, v.s. κραιπάλη.

κρημνός, -οῦ, ὁ (< κρεμάννυμι), [in LXX: 11 Ch 25¹² (סֶלַע)*;] *a steep bank:* Mt 8³², Mk 5¹³, Lk 8³³.†

Κρής, ὁ, pl., Κρῆτες, *a Cretan:* Ac 2¹¹, Tit 1¹².†

Κρήσκης, -εντος (Bl., § 10, 4), ὁ (Lat.), *Crescens:* 11 Ti 4¹⁰.†

Κρήτη, -ης, ἡ, *Crete:* Ac 27⁷, ¹², ¹³, ²¹, Tit 1⁵.†

κριθή, -ῆς, ἡ, [in LXX for שְׂעֹרָה;] *barley:* pl. (as usually in cl.), Re 6⁶.†

κρίθινος, -η, -ον (< κριθή), [in LXX for שְׂעֹרָה;] *of barley:* Jo 6⁹, ¹³.†

κρίμα (Bl., § 27, 2), -τος, τό (< κρίνω), [in LXX chiefly for מִשְׁפָּט;] *the issue of a judicial process*, hence, 1. *judgment,* the decision passed on the faults of others: Mt 7²; in forensic sense, c. gen. pun., Lk 24²⁰; esp. of the judgment of God, Ro 2² 5¹⁶ 11³³ (*ICC,* in l.), 11 Pe 2³, Ju⁴; κ. λαμβάνεσθαι, Mt 23¹³ (Rec., R, mg.), Mk 12⁴⁰, Lk 20⁴⁷, Ro 13², Ja 3¹; ἔχειν, 1 Ti 5¹²; βαστάζειν, Ga 5¹⁰; ἐσθίειν ἑαυτῷ, 1 Co 11²⁹; εἰς κ. συνέρχεσθαι, ib. ³⁴; εἶναι ἐν τ αὐτῷ κ., Lk 23⁴⁰; c. gen. obj., Ro 3⁸, 1 Ti 3⁶, Re 17¹; of God's judgment through Christ, Jo 9³⁹; τὸ κ. ἄρχεται, 1 Pe 4¹⁷; τ. κ. τ. μέλλον, Ac 24²⁵; κ. αἰώνιον, He 6²; ἔκρινεν ὁ Θεὸς τ. κ. ὑμῶν, Re 18²⁰; of the right of judgment, Re 20⁴. 2. *a matter for judgment, a law-suit, a case:* 1 Co 6⁷.†

κρίνον, -ου, τό [in LXX chiefly for שׁוֹשָׁן, שׁוֹשַׁנָּה;] *a lily:* Mt 6²⁸, Lk 12²⁷.†

κρίνω, [in LXX chiefly for שׁפט, also for דִּין, רִיב, etc.;] 1. *to* *separate, select, choose* (cl.; in LXX: ii Mac 13¹⁵). 2. *to approve, esteem* : Ro 14⁵. 3. *to be of opinion, judge, think* : Lk 7⁴³, i Co 11¹³; seq. τοῦτο ὅτι, ii Co 5¹⁴; c. acc. et inf., Ac 16¹⁵; c. acc. et pred., Ac 13⁴⁶ 26⁸. 4. *to decide, determine, decree* : c. acc., Ac 16⁴, Ro 14¹³, i Co 7³⁷, ii Co 2¹; c. inf. (Field, *Notes*, 167), Ac 20¹⁶ 25²⁵, i Co 2² 5³, Tit 3¹² (cf. i Mac 11³³, Wi 8⁹, al.); c. acc. et inf., Ac 21²⁵ 27¹. 5. *to judge, adjudge, pronounce judgment* : absol., Jo 8¹⁶,²⁶; seq. κατά, c. acc., Jo 7²⁴ 8¹⁵; κρίσιν κ., Jo 7²⁴; τ. δίκαιον, Lk 12⁵⁷ (Deiss., *LAE*, 118); in forensic sense, Jo 18³¹, Ac 23³, al.; pass., Ro 3⁴ (LXX); of God's judgment, Jo 5³⁰ 8⁵⁰, Ro 2¹⁶ 3⁶, ii Ti 4¹, i Pe 4⁵, al. 6. = κατακρίνω, *to condemn* (cl.): Ac 13²⁷; of God's judgment, Jo 3¹⁸ 5²² 12⁴⁷,⁴⁸, Ac 7⁷, Ro 2¹², i Co 11³², He 10³⁰ (LXX), Ja 5⁹, Re 19², al. 7. As in LXX (for שׁפט), *to rule, govern* (iv Ki 15⁵, Ps 2¹⁰, al.): Mt 19²⁸, Lk 22³⁰, i Co 6³. 8. *to bring to trial* (cl.); mid., *to go to law* : c. dat. pers., Mt 5⁴⁰; seq. μετά, c. gen. pers. (of the opponent), ἐπί, c. gen. (of the judge), i Co 6¹,⁶ (cf. ἀνα-, ἀπο-, ἀντ-απο- (-μαι), δια-, ἐν-, ἐπι-, κατα-, συν-, ὑπο- (-μαι), συν-υπο- (-μαι)).

SYN. : v.s. δικάστης.

κρίσις, -εως, ἡ (< κρίνω), [in LXX chiefly for מִשְׁפָּט, also for רִיב, etc.;] 1. *a separating, selection* (Arist., al.). 2. *a decision, judgment* (cl.): Jo 8¹⁶, i Ti 5²⁴, ii Pe 2¹¹, Ju⁹; κ. κρίνειν, Jo 7²⁴; in forensic sense, Ac 8³³ (LXX) (v. Page, in l.); esp. of the Divine judgment, Jo 3¹⁹ 5²⁴,²⁷,²⁹,³⁰ 12³¹ 16⁸,¹¹, ii Th 1⁵, He 10²⁷, Ja 2¹³ 5¹², ii Pe 2⁴, Re 18¹⁰; pl., Re 16⁷ 19²; of the last judgment, Mt 10¹⁵ 11²²,²⁴ 12³⁶,⁴¹,⁴², Lk 10¹⁴ 11³¹,³², He 9²⁷, ii Pe 2⁹ 3⁷, i Jo 4¹⁷, Ju⁶,¹⁵; ἡ κ. τῆς γεέννης, Mt 23³³. 3. By meton. (as in LXX for מִשְׁפָּט, Is 5⁷, al.; דִּינָא, Da 7¹⁰), of the standard of judgment, *right, justice* : Mt 12¹⁸,²⁰ (LXX, Is 42⁴³) 23²³, Lk 11⁴²; of the tribunal (a local court), Mt 5²¹,²².†

Κρίσπος, -ου, ὁ, *Crispus* : Ac 18⁸, i Co 1¹⁴.†

κριτήριον, -ου, τό (< κριτής), [in LXX: iii Ki 7⁷ (מִשְׁפָּט), Da LXX TH 7¹⁰, TH²⁶ (דִּין), Su⁴⁹, Ex 21⁶, Jg 5¹⁰*;] 1. *a means of judging, test, criterion*. 2. (a) *a tribunal, law-court* : i Co 6²,⁴ (R, mg.), Ja 2⁶ (so in π., and cf. Jg, Da, ll.c.); (b) *a law-case, cause* : i Co, l.c. (R, txt., *matters, things*). But this meaning is doubtful.†

κριτής, -οῦ, ὁ (< κρίνω), [in LXX chiefly for שֹׁפֵט;] *a judge* : Mt 5²⁵, Lk 12¹⁴,⁵⁸ 18², τ. ἀδικίας, Lk 18⁶; c. gen. rei (obj.), Ac 18¹⁵, Ja 4¹¹; (qual.), διαλογισμῶν πονηρῶν, Ja 2⁴; of a Roman procurator, Ac 24¹⁰; of God, He 12²³, Ja 4¹²; Christ, Ac 10⁴², ii Ti 4⁸, Ja 5⁹; of those whose conduct is made a standard for judging, Mt 12²⁷, Lk 11¹⁹; in the OT sense (Jg 2¹⁶, Ru 1¹, al), of a ruler in Israel, Ac 13²⁰.†

SYN. : δικάστης, q.v.

***κριτικός, -ή, -όν** (< κρίνω), *critical, able to discern* or *judge* : c. gen. obj., He 4¹².†

κρούω, [in LXX: seq. ἐπί, Jg 19²² Ca 5² (דפק);] c. acc., τ. αὐλαίαν, Jth 14¹⁴*;] *to strike, knock* : at a door (κόπτειν, in Att.),

Mt 7⁷,⁸, Lk 11⁹,¹⁰ 12³⁶, Ac 12¹⁶, Re 3²⁰; c. acc., τ. θύραν, Lk 13²⁵, Ac 12¹³.†

κρύβω, v.s. κρύπτω.

*†κρύπτη (WH, R; κρυπτή, LT, Tr.; -όν, Rec.), -ης, ἡ, *a crypt, cellar*: Lk 11³³.†

κρυπτός, -ή, -όν (κρύπτω), [in LXX for אטם, מִסְתָּר, etc.;] *hidden, secret*: Mt 10²⁶, Mk 4²², Lk 8¹⁷ 12²; ὁ κ. τῆς καρδίας ἄνθρωπος, 1 Pe 3⁴; neut., ἐν τῷ κ., Mt 6⁴,⁶; ἐν κ., Jo 7⁴,¹⁰ 18²⁰; ὁ ἐν κ. Ἰουδαῖος, Ro 2²⁹; pl., τὰ κ. τ. σκότους, 1 Co 4⁵; τ. ἀνθρώπων, Ro 2¹⁶; τ. καρδίας, 1 Co 14²⁵; τ. αἰσχύνης, 11 Co 4².†

κρύπτω, [in LXX for חבא, טמן, סתר, צפן, etc.;] *to hide, conceal*: c. acc., Mt 13⁴⁴ 25¹⁸; seq. ἐν, ib.²⁵ (pass., Mt 13⁴⁴, Col 3³); pass., Mt 5¹⁴, He 11²³, 1 Ti 5²⁵, Re 2¹⁷; ἐκρύβη (on the tense and its formation, v. M, *Pr.*, 161; Bl., § 19, 3) κ. ἐξῆλθεν, Jo 8⁵⁹; seq. εἰς, Lk 13²¹, Re 6¹⁵; ἀπό (in cl. more freq. dupl. acc.), Re 6¹⁶; pass., Jo 12³⁶, (Bl., § 34, 4). Metaph.: Mt 11²⁵ 13³⁵, Lk 11⁵², WH, mg., 18³⁴ 19⁴², Jo 19³⁸ (cf. ἀπο-, ἐν-, περι-κρύπτω).†

*†κρυσταλλίζω (< κρύσταλλος), *to shine like crystal, be crystal-clear*: Re 21¹¹ (ἅπ. λεγ.).†

κρύσταλλος, -ου, ὁ (< κρύος, *frost*), [in LXX: Jb 38²⁹, Ps 147⁶,⁽¹⁷⁾, Ez 1²² (קֶרַח), etc.;] *crystal*: Re 4⁶ 22¹.†

κρυφαῖος, -αία, -αῖον (< κρύφα = κρυφῇ), [in LXX for מִסְתָּר, Je 23²⁴, al.;] *hidden, secret*: ἐν τῷ κ., Mt 6¹⁸.†

κρυφῇ (prop. -ῇ, Rec.; later spelling is due to assimilation to dat.; cf. εἰκῇ), adv., [in LXX chiefly for סתר;] *secretly, in secret*: Eph 5¹².†

κτάομαι, -ῶμαι, [in LXX chiefly for קנה;] in pres., impf., fut. and aor., *to procure for oneself, get, gain, acquire* (the pf. and plpf., *to have acquired*, hence *to possess*, do not occur in NT): c. acc. rei, Mt 10⁹, Lk 18¹², Ac 8²⁰; c. gen. pret., Ac 22²⁸; ἐκ c. gen. pret., Ac 1¹⁸; τ. ψυχὰς ὑμῶν (MM, xvi), Lk 21¹⁹; τ. ἑαυτοῦ σκεῦος κτᾶσθαι, 1 Th 4⁴ (where if σ. = *body*, κ. must = pf., κέκτημαι; v. MM, xvi; M, *Th.*, in l.; Field, *Notes*, 72 f. But σ. is most freq. taken as = *wife*; v. Thayer, s.v.; Lft., *Notes*, 53 ff.; *ICC*, in l.).†

κτῆμα, -τος, τό (< κτάομαι), [in LXX for כֶּרֶם, etc.;] *a possession, property*: Mt 19²², Mk 10²², Ac 2⁴⁵ 5¹.†

κτῆνος, -ους, τό (< κτάομαι, hence primarily *a possession*), [in LXX chiefly for בְּהֵמָה, Ge 1²⁵, al., also for מִקְנֶה, צֹאן, etc.;] *a beast*, (in late Gk. esp.) *a beast of burden*: Lk 10³⁴; pl. (as chiefly in cl.), Ac 23²⁴, Re 18¹³; of quadrupeds, as opp. to fishes and birds (cf. Ge, l.c.), 1 Co 15³⁹.†

**†κτήτωρ, -ορος, ὁ (κτάομαι), [in Sm.: Jl 1¹¹ *;] *a possessor*: Ac 4³⁴.†

κτίζω, [in LXX chiefly for ברא, Ps 50 (51)¹⁰, al.; also for קנה, Ge 14¹⁹, Pr 8²²; יצר, Is 22¹¹ 46¹¹; Wi 2²³, Si 1⁴,⁹ (and freq.), ι Es 4⁵³, al.;] 1. in cl., *to people* or *found* a region or city (ι Es, l.c.).

2. In LXX and NT, of God, *to create*: Mk 13¹⁹, ι Co 11⁹, Col 1¹⁶ 3¹⁰, Eph 3⁹, ι Ti 4³, Re 4¹¹ 10⁶; ὁ κτίσας, Mt 19⁴ (WH, R, mg.), Ro 1²⁵; of the divine operation on the soul, Eph 2¹⁰, ¹⁵ 4²⁴ (cf. Ps., l.c.).†

κτίσις, -εως, ἡ (< κτίζω), [in LXX: Ps 103 (104)²⁴ (קִנְיָן), Pr 1¹³ A (הוֹן), To 8⁵, Wi 2⁶, Si 16¹⁷, ιιι Mac 2², al.;] 1. *a founding, settling, foundation* (cl.). 2. In LXX and NT, (a) *the act of creating, creation*: Mk 10⁶ (Swete, in l.), 13¹⁹, Ro 1²⁰, ιι Pe 3⁴; (b) *that which has been created, creation*: Ro 1²⁵ 8³⁹, He 4¹³; καινὴ κ., ιι Co 5¹⁷, Gᴀ 6¹⁵; πάσῃ ἀνθρωπίνῃ κ. (Hort., in l.), ι Pe 2¹³; collectively, of the sum of created things (Wi 19⁶, Jth 16¹⁴), Mk 16[¹⁵], Col 1¹⁵, ²³, He 9¹¹, Re 3¹⁴; of the irrational creation, Ro 8¹⁹⁻²².†

** **κτίσμα**, -τος, τό (< κτίζω), [in LXX: Wi 9² 13⁵ 14¹¹, Si 36²⁰ (¹⁷), 38³⁴, ιιι Mac 5¹¹ *;] 1. (cl.) *a colony*. 2. *a created thing, creature*: ι Ti 4⁴, Ja 1¹⁸, Re 5¹³, 8⁹.†

κτίστης, -ου, ὁ (< κτίζω), [in LXX: ιι Ki 22³² (Heb., al.), Jth 9¹², Si 24⁸, ιι, ιν Mac₅*;] 1. (cl.) *a founder*. 2. *a creator*: of God, ι Pe 4¹⁹.†

κυβεία, v.s. κυβία.

κυβέρνησις, -εως, ἡ (< κυβερνάω, Lat. *gubernare, to guide*), [in LXX: Pr 1⁵ 11¹⁴ 24⁶ (תַּחְבֻּלוֹת) *;] 1. *steering, pilotage* (Plat.). 2. Metaph., *government*: pl., ι Co 12²⁸.†

κυβερνήτης, -ου, ὁ (v.s. κυβέρνησις), [in LXX for חֹבֵל, Ez 27⁸, ²⁷, ²⁸, Pr 23²⁴, ιν Mac 7¹*;] 1. *a steersman, pilot*: Ac 27¹¹, Re 18¹⁷. 2. Metaph., *a guide, governor* (Eur., Plat.).†

* **κυβία** (Att. -εία, and so Rec.), -ας, ἡ (< κύβος, *a cube, a die*), *dice-playing*; metaph., *trickery, sleight*: Eph 4¹⁴.†

κυκλεύω (< κύκλος), [in LXX: ιν Ki 3²⁵ B (סבב) *;] 1. *to make a circle, go round*. 2. *to encircle, surround*: c. acc. pers., Jo 10²⁴ (Tr., WH, mg.); c. acc. rei, Re 20⁹.†

κυκλόθεν, adv., (< κύκλος), [in LXX chiefly for מִסָּבִיב, סָבִיב;] *from all sides, round about*: Re 4³, ⁴, ⁸.†

κύκλος, -ου, ὁ, [in LXX chiefly for סָבִיב;] *a ring, circle*. Dat., κύκλῳ, as adverb., *round about, around*: Mk 3³⁴ 6⁶, ³⁶, Lk 9¹², Ro 15¹⁹; c. gen., Re 4⁶ 5¹¹ 7¹¹.†

κυκλόω, -ῶ (< κύκλος), [in LXX chiefly for סבב;] 1. *to move in a circle, revolve*. 2. *to surround, encircle*: c. acc. pers., Jo 10²⁴ (WH, txt., cf. -εύω), Ac 14²⁰; pass., Lk 21²⁰, He 11³⁰ (cf. περι-κυκλόω).†

** ✝ **κύλισμα**, -τος, τό (< κυλίω), [in Sm.: Ez 10¹³ *;] 1. *a roll*. 2. = κυλισμός (q.v.), *a rolling, wallowing* (or, as κυλίστρα, Xen., *Eq.*, v. 3, *a rolling-place*): ιι Pe 2²² (Rec.).†

** ✝ **κυλισμός**, -οῦ, ὁ (< κυλίω), [in Th.: Pr 2¹⁸ *;] = cl. κύλισις, *rolling, wallowing*: ιι Pe 2²² (cf. κύλισμα).†

κυλίω, late form of κυλίνδω, [in LXX: Jos 10¹⁸, ι Ki 14³³, al.

(גָּלַל), iv Ki 9³³ (שָׁמֵם), al. ;] *to roll, roll along.* Pass., *to be rolled;* of persons (in Hom. as sign of grief), *to roll* or *wallow :* Mk 9²⁰.†

* κυλλός, -ή, -όν, 1. *crooked, crippled :* Mt 15³⁰, ³¹ (WH, txt. om.); 2. *maimed :* Mt 18⁸, Mk 9⁴³.†

κῦμα, -τος, τό (< κύω, *to be pregnant, to swell*), [in LXX chiefly for גַּל;] *a wave :* pl., Mt 8²⁴ 14²⁴, Mk 4³⁷ ; κ. θαλάσσης, fig., Ju ¹³.†

SYN. : κλύδων, q.v.

κύμβαλον, -ου, τό (< κύμβη, *a cup*), [in LXX chiefly for מְצֵלֶת;] *a cymbal :* 1 Co 13¹.†

κύμινον, -ου, τό, [in LXX : Is 28²⁵, ²⁷ (כַּמֹּן) * ;] *cummin :* Mt 23²³.†

* κυνάριον, -ου, τό (in Att. also κυνίδιον, dim. of κύων), *a little dog :* Mt 15²⁶, ²⁷, Mk 7²⁷, ²⁸.†

Κύπριος, -α, -ον, *of Cyprus, Cyprian :* Ac 4³⁶ 11²⁰ 21¹⁶.†

Κύπρος, -ου, ἡ, *Cyprus :* Ac 11¹⁹ 13⁴ 15³⁹ 21³ 27⁴.†

κύπτω, [in LXX chiefly for קָדַד;] *to bow the head, stoop down :* Mk 1⁷ ; seq. κάτω, Jo 8 [⁶, ⁸] (cf. ἀνα-, παρα-, συν-κύπτω).†

Κυρηναῖος, -α, -ον (< Κυρήνη), *of Cyrene, a Cyrenæan :* Mt 27³², Mk 15²¹, Lk 23²⁶, Ac 6⁹ 11²⁰ 13¹.†

Κυρήνη, -ης, ἡ, *Cyrene,* a city in Libya : Ac 2¹⁰.†

Κυρήνιος (prop. -ίνιος, v. Bl., 13 ; -ῖνος L, -εῖνος, Tr., WH, mg.), -ου, ὁ, *Quirinus,* prop. *Quirinius :* Lk 2² ; v. reff., s.v. ἡγεμονεύω.†

κυρία (Κυρία, T, WH, mg.), -ας, ἡ, [in LXX chiefly for גְּבֶרֶת;] *a lady :* ii Jo ¹, ⁵ (on the interpretation, v. ICC, 167 ff.).†

**† κυριακός, -ή, -όν (< κύριος), [in LXX : κ. φωνῇ (Συριακή φ., R), ii Mac 15³⁶ A * ;] 1. as freq. in Inscr. (LS, s.v.; Deiss., BS, 217 f.), *of the lord* or *master, imperial.* 2. *of the Lord* (i.e. Christ): δεῖπνον, 1 Co 11²⁰ ; ἡμέρα, Re 1¹⁰. (Cf. λόγια κ., Papias, Eus., HE, iii, 39, 1 ; γραφαὶ κ., Clem. Alex., etc. ; for eccl. usage, cf. Soph., Lex., s.v.) ; on κ. ἡμέρα, Re 1¹⁰, v. ICC, in l., Zahn, Intr., iii, p. 426₁₀, MM, VGT, s.v.†

κυριεύω (< κύριος), [in LXX chiefly for מָשַׁל;] *to be lord* or *master of, to rule* (*over*): c. gen. obj., Lk 22²⁵, Ro 14⁹, ii Co 1²⁴ ; absol., i Ti 6¹⁵ ; metaph., ὁ θάνατος, Ro 6⁹ ; ἡ ἁμαρτία, ib. ¹⁴ ; ὁ νόμος, ib. 7¹ (cf. κατα-κυριεύω).†

κύριος, -α, -ον (also -ος, -ον) [in LXX (subst.) chiefly for יְהֹוָה, also for אָדוֹן, בַּעַל, etc.;] *having power* (κῦρος) or *authority ;* as subst., ὁ κ., *lord, master ;* 1. in general : c. gen. rei, Mt 9³⁸ 20⁸, Mk 12⁹ 13³⁵, Lk 19³³ ; τ. σαββάτου, Mt 12⁸, Mk 2²⁸, Lk 6⁵ ; c. gen. pers., δούλου, etc., Mt 10²⁴, Lk 14²¹, Ac 16¹⁶, al.; absol., opp. to οἱ δοῦλοι, Eph 6⁵, ⁹, al.; of the Emperor (Deiss., LAE, 161), Ac 25²⁶ ; θεοὶ πολλοὶ καὶ κ. πολλοί, i Co 8⁵ ; of a husband, i Pe 3⁶ ; in voc., as a title of respect to masters, teachers, magistrates, etc., Mt 13²⁷ 16²² 27⁶³, Mk 7²⁸, Lk 5¹², Jo 4¹¹, Ac 9⁵, al. 2. As a divine title (freq. in π.; Deiss., LAE, 353 ff.); in NT, (a) of God : ὁ κ., Mt 5³³, Mk 5¹⁹, Lk 1⁶, Ac 7³³, He 8², Ja 4¹⁵, al.; anarth. (Bl., § 46, 6), Mt 21⁹, Mk 13²⁰, Lk 1¹⁷, He 7²¹, i Pe 1²⁵, al.; κ. τ. οὐρανοῦ καὶ τ. γῆς, Mt 11²⁵ ; τ. κυριευόντων, i Ti 6¹⁵ ; κ. ὁ θεός,

Mt 4⁷,¹⁰, al.; id. seq. ὁ παντοκράτωρ, Re 4⁸; κ. σαβαώθ, Ro 9²⁹; (ὁ) ἄγγελος κυρίου, Mt 1²⁰ 2¹³, Lk 1¹¹, al.; πνεῦμα κυρίου, Lk 4¹⁸, Ac 8³⁹; (b) of the Christ: Mt 21³, Mk 11³, Lk 1⁴³ 20⁴⁴, al.; of Jesus after his resurrection (Dalman, Words, 330), Ac 10³⁶, Ro 14⁸, 1 Co 7²², Eph 4⁵, al.; ὁ κ. μου, Jo 20²⁸; ὁ κ. Ἰησοῦς, Ac 1²¹, 1 Co 11²³, al.; id. seq. Χριστός, Eph 1², al.; ὁ κ. ἡμῶν, 1 Ti 1¹⁴, He 7¹⁴, al.; id. seq. Ἰησοῦς, 1 Th 3¹¹, He 13²⁰, al.; Χριστός, Ro 16¹⁸; Ἰ. Χ., 1 Co 1², 1 Th 1³, al.; Ἰ. Χ. (Χ. Ἰ.) ὁ κ. (ἡμῶν), Ro 1⁴, Col 2⁶, Eph 3¹¹, al.; ὁ κ. καὶ ὁ σωτήρ, II Pe 3²; id. seq. Ἰ Χ., ib. ¹⁸; anarth., 1 Co 7²², ²⁵, Ja 5⁴, al.; κ. κυρίων, Re 19¹⁶; c. prep., ἀπὸ (κατὰ, πρὸς, σὺν, etc.) κ., Col 3²⁴, al.

    SYN.: v.s. δεσπότης.

*† κυριότης, -ητος, ἡ (< κύριος), lordship, dominion: Eph 1²¹, II Pe 2¹⁰, Ju⁸; pl., Col 1¹⁶ (cf. Lft., Col.; Mayor, Ju., in ll.; DB, i, 616 f.).†

    κυρόω, -ῶ (< κῦρος, 1. authority. 2. validity), [in LXX for קוּם;] to confirm, ratify, make valid: II Co 2⁸; pass., Ga 3¹⁵ (cf. προ-κυρόω).†

    κύων, κυνός, ὁ, ἡ (in NT masc. only), [in LXX for כֶּלֶב;] a dog: Lk 16²¹, II Pe 2²²; metaph., as a word of reproach, Mt 7⁶, Phl 3², Re 22¹⁵.†

    κῶλον, -ου, τό, a limb, member of a body, [but in LXX (Le 26³⁰, Nu 14²⁹, ³², ³³, 1 Ki 17⁴⁶, Is 66²⁴ *) for פֶּגֶר;] hence, carcase: He 3¹⁷ (LXX).†

    κωλύω (< κόλος), [in LXX for כָּלָא, מָנַע, etc.;] to hinder, restrain, forbid, withhold: c. acc. et inf., Mt 19¹⁴, Lk 23², Ac 8³⁶ 16⁶, 24²³, 1 Th 2¹⁶, He 7²³; inf. om., Mk 9³⁸, ³⁹ 10¹⁴, Lk 9⁴⁹, ⁵⁰ 11⁵² 18¹⁶, Ac 11¹⁷, Ro 1¹³, III Jo ¹⁰; acc. om., 1 Ti 4³; c. acc. pers. et gen. rei, Ac 27⁴³; c. acc. rei, 1 Co 14³⁹, II Pe 2¹⁶; id. seq. τοῦ μή, Ac 10⁴⁷; id. seq. ἀπό (like Heb. מִן כָּלָא, Ge 23⁶, al.), Lk 6²⁹ (cf. δια-κωλύω).†

    κώμη, -ης, ἡ, [in LXX for בַּת, חָצֵר, עִיר, etc.;] a village or country town, prop. as opp. to a walled city: Mt 14¹⁵, Mk 6⁶, al.; πόλεις καὶ κ., Mt 9³⁵, al.; with the name added, Βηθλεέμ, Jo 7⁴²; Βηθανία, ib. 11¹; with the name of the district, τὰς κ. Καισαρίας, Mk 8²⁷; Σαμαρειτῶν, Lk 9⁵², Ac 8²⁵.

*† κωμόπολις, -εως, ἡ, a country town: Mk 1³⁸ (v. Swete, in l.).†

** κῶμος, -ου, ὁ, [in LXX: Wi 14²³, II Mac 6⁴ *;] a revel, carousal: Ro 13¹³, Ga 5²¹, 1 Pe 4³.†

    SYN.: v.s. κραιπάλη.

* κώνωψ, -ωπος, ὁ, a gnat: Mt 23²⁴.†

    Κῶς, gen. Κῶ, ἡ, Cos, an island in the Ægean Sea: acc. Κῶ, Ac 21¹ (Κῶν, Rec.).†

    Κωσάμ, ὁ, Cosam: Lk 3²⁸.†

    κωφός, -ή, -όν (< κόπτω), [in LXX chiefly (Ex 4¹¹, al.) for אִלֵּם; for חֵרֵשׁ, Hb 2¹⁸;] blunt, dull. Metaph., of the senses, esp. (a) of speech, dumb: Mt 9³², ³³ 12²² 15³⁰, ³¹, Lk 1²² 11¹⁴; (b) of hearing, deaf: Mt 11⁵, Mk 7³², ³⁷ 9²⁵, Lk 7²².†

Λ

Λ, λ, λάμβδα, τό, indecl., *lambda*, *l*, the eleventh letter. As a numeral, λ' = 30; λ, = 30,000.

λαγχάνω, [in LXX: I Ki 14⁴⁷ (לכד, v. Th., *Gr.*, 38), Wi 8¹⁹, III Mac 6¹*;] 1. *to obtain by lot, to obtain* (in cl., c. gen.): c. inf. art. (Bl., § 36, 3; 71, 3), Lk 1⁹; c. acc. rei, Ac 1¹⁷, II Pe 1¹. 2. *to draw lots:* seq. περί, Jo 19²⁴.†

Λάζαρος, -ου, ὁ, colloquial abbreviation of Ἐλεαζάρ (-άζαρος), q.v.), *Lazarus;* 1. of Bethany: Jo 11¹ ᶠᶠ· 12¹, ², ⁹, ¹⁰, ¹⁷. 2. The beggar in the parable: Lk 16²⁰, ²³⁻²⁵.†

λάθρα (Att.; in Hom., -ρῃ, Rec. -ρα), adv., [in LXX chiefly for בַּסֵּתֶר;] *secretly:* Mt 1¹⁹ 2⁷, Mk 5³³ (WH, mg.), Jo 11²⁸, Ac 16³⁷.†

λαῖλαψ, -απος, ἡ, [in LXX: Jb 21¹⁸ 27²⁰ א (סוּפָה) 38¹, Je 32 (25)³² (סְעָרָה), סַעַר), Wi 5¹⁴, ²³, Si 48⁹, ¹² *;] *a hurricane, whirlwind:* Mk 4³⁷, Lk 8²³, II Pe 2¹⁷.†

SYN.: θύελλα, q.v., and cf. ἄνεμος.

λακέω, Dor. for ληκέω = λάσκω, q.v.

*λακτίζω (< λάξ, *with the foot*), *to kick:* Ac 26¹⁴.†

λαλέω, -ῶ, [in LXX chiefly for דבר pi., also for אמר, etc. :] 1. cl. (*a*) *to chatter*, of birds, *to chirp; (b) *to utter*, of inanimate things, Re 4¹ 10⁴; metaph., He 11⁴ 12²⁴. 2. *to talk, speak, say:* absol., Mt 9³³ 12⁴⁶, Mk 5³⁵, Lk 8⁴⁹; seq. ὡς, I Co 13¹¹, Re 13¹¹; εἰς, I Co 14⁹; ἐκ, Mt 12³⁴; c. acc. rei, Mt 10¹⁹, Mk 11²³, Jo 8³⁰, al.; c. dat. pers., Mt 12⁴⁶, Lk 24⁶, Ro 7¹, al.; c. acc. rei et dat pers., Mt 9¹⁸, Jo 10⁶, al.; c. prep., πρός, μετά, περί, Mk 6⁵⁰, Lk 1¹⁹ 2³³, al.; ἐν, ἐξ, ἀπό, Mt 13³, Jo 12⁴⁹ 14¹⁰, al.; λ. τ. λόγον, Mk 8³², al.; seq. orat. dir. (not cl.), Mk 14³¹, He 5⁵ 11¹⁸; Hebraistically (Dalman, *Words*, 25 f.), ἐλάλησε λέγων, Mt 14²⁷, Jo 8¹², Ac 8²⁶, al.

SYN.: v.s. λέγω.

λαλιά, -ᾶς, ἡ, [in LXX chiefly for דָּבָר, דִּבְרָה;] 1. *loquacity*. 2. *talk, speech, conversation:* Mt 26⁷³ (cf. Ca 4³), Jo 4⁴² 8⁴³.†

λαμά (Heb. לָמָה, v.l. λεμά = Aram. לְמָא), *why:* Mt 27⁴⁶ (WH, mg., λεμά TTr., WH, txt., λεμά L), Mk 15³⁴ (λεμά LT, λαμμᾶ, Rec.).†

λαμβάνω, [in LXX chiefly for לקח, also for נשׂא, לכד, אחז, etc.;] 1. *to take, lay hold of:* absol., Mt 26²⁶, Mk 14²²; c. acc. rei, Mt 5⁴⁰ 26⁵², al. mult.; c. acc. pers., Mt 21³⁵, Mk 12³, al.; pleonastic λαβών (M, *Pr.*, 230; Bl., § 74, 2), Mt 13³¹ 14¹⁹, al.; so also indic., Mk 7²⁷, Jo 19¹, ⁴⁰, Re 8⁵, al.; metaph., c. acc. rei, ἀφορμήν, Ro 7⁸, ¹¹; ὑπόδειγμα, Ja 5¹⁰; id. c. acc. pers., φόβος, Lk 7¹⁶; πνεῦμα, Lk 9³⁹; πειρασμός, I Co 10¹³; aoristic pf. (M, *Pr.*, 145, 238; Bl., § 59, 4), Re 5⁷ 8⁵, al. 2. *to receive:* absol., opp. to διδόναι, Mt 10⁸, Ac 20³⁵ = παραλαμβάνω (v. ¹¹, the compound being dropped because of repetition; v. M, *Pr.*, p. 115); c. acc. rei, Mt 27⁶, Mk 10³⁰, al. mult.; c. acc. pers., Jo 6²¹ 13²⁰ 19²⁷, II Jo ¹⁰; ῥαπίσμασιν (a vulgarism; Bl., § 38, 3), Mk 14⁶⁵; metaph., τ. λόγον, Mt 13²⁰, Mk 4¹⁶; τ. μαρτυρίαν, Jo 3¹¹; τ. ῥήματα,

Jo 12⁴⁸; πρόσωπον (Heb. נְשִׂיא פָנִים; Dalman, *Words*, 30), Lk 20²¹, Ga 2⁶; ζωὴν αἰώνιον (Dalman, *op. cit.*, 124 f.), Mk 10³⁰ (cf. ἀνα-, ἀντι-, συν-αντι- (-μαι), ἀπο-, ἐπι-, κατα-, μετα-, παρα-, συν-παρα-, προ-, προσ-, νυν-, συν-περι-, ὑπο-λαμβάνω).

λάμεχ, ὁ, indecl. (Heb. לֶמֶךְ), *Lamech* (Ge 5²⁵): Lk 3³⁶.†

λαμμᾶ, v.s. λαμά.

λαμπάς, -άδος, ἡ (< λάμπω), [in LXX for לַפִּיד;] *a torch* (freq. fed, like a lamp, with oil): Mt 25¹ ff., Jo 18³, Ac 20⁸, Re 4⁵ 8¹⁰.† *SYN.*: λύχνος, *lamp*, q.v.; φαιός, *torch* or *lantern; cf.* Rutherford's *NPhr.*, 131 f.; Tr., *Syn.*, § xlvi; *DCG*, s.v. *lamp; DB*, iii, 43 f.

** λαμπρός, -ά, -όν (< λάμπω), [in LXX: To 13¹¹, Wi 6¹² 17²⁰, Si 29²² 33¹³ (30²⁵) 34 (31)²³, Ep. Je ⁶⁰ *;] *bright, brilliant*: ποταμός, Re 22¹ (EV, *clear*); ἀστήρ, ib. ¹⁶; of clothing, *brilliant, splendid*: Lk 23¹¹, Ac 10³⁰, Ja 2², ³, Re 15⁶ 18¹⁴ 19⁸.†

λαμπρότης, -ητος, ἡ, [in LXX: Ps 109 (110)³ (הָדָר), al.;] *brightness, brilliancy*: τ. ἡλίου, Ac 26¹³.†

* λαμπρῶς, adv., *splendidly*: of sumptuous fare (as freq.; cf. ἐδέσματα λαμπρά, Si 29²²), Lk 16¹⁹.†

λάμπω, [in LXX for נגה, etc.;] *to shine*: Mt 5¹⁵, ¹⁶ 17², Lk 17²⁴, Ac 12⁷, II Co 4⁶ (cf. ἐκ-, περι-λάμπω).†

λανθάνω, [in LXX for עלם ni., etc.;] *to escape notice, be hidden (from)*: Mk 7²⁴, Lk 8⁴⁷; c. acc. pers., Ac 26²⁶, II Pe 3⁵, ⁸; as in common cl. idiom, seq. ptcp., ἔλαθον ξενίσαντες, *entertained unawares*. He 13² (cf. ἐκ-, ἐπι-λανθάνω).†

† λαξευτός, -ή, όν (< λαξεύω; < λᾶς, *a stone*, ξέω, *to scrape*), [in LXX: De 4⁴⁹ (פְּסֶגָּה); in Aq.: Nu 21²⁰; Th.: Jg 7¹¹ *;] *hewn* (in stone); Lk 23⁵³ (elsewhere κοινή writers use λατομητός, IV Ki 12¹², al.; cf. λατομέω).†

Λαοδικεία, v.s. Λαοδικία.

Λαοδικεύς, -έως, ὁ, *a Laodicean*: Col 4¹⁶.†

Λαοδικία (Rec. -εία), -ας, ἡ, *Laodicea*, a city on the Lycus in Phrygia: Col 2¹ 4¹³, ¹⁵, ¹⁶, Re 1¹¹ 3¹⁴.†

λαός, -οῦ, ὁ, [in LXX very freq. for עַם, Ge 14¹⁶, al.; occasionally for לְאֹם (Ge 25²³, al.), etc.;] a word rarely found in Att. prose; 1. *the people* at large (Hom., al.), esp. of people assembled: Mt 27²⁵, Lk 1²¹ 3¹⁵ al.; pl. (Hom., al., π.; v. MM, xvi), Ac 4²⁷. 2. *a people*, those of the same race and language (Pind., Æsch., al. in LXX, Ge 26¹¹, Ex 9¹⁶, al.): joined with γλῶσσα, φυλή, ἔθνος, Re 5⁹ 7⁹ 11⁹, al.; pl., Lk 2³¹, Ro 15¹¹; esp. as almost always in LXX, of Israel, Mt 4²³, Mk 7⁶, Lk 2¹⁰, Jo 11⁵⁰, He 2¹⁷, al.; opp. to τ. ἔθνη Ac 26¹⁷, ²³, Ro 15¹⁰; οἱ πρεσβύτεροι (πρῶτοι, etc.) τοῦ λ., Mt 21²³, Lk 19 ʹ, Ac 4⁸, al.; ὁ λ. μου (αὐτοῦ, τ. θεοῦ), Mt 2⁶, Lk 1⁶⁸, He 11²⁵, al.; of the people disting. from the rulers and priests (I Es 1¹⁰, Jth 8⁹, al.), Mt 26ʾ, Lk 20¹⁹, He 5³, al.; of Christians, as the people of God, Ac 15¹⁴, Ro 9²⁵,²⁶, He 4⁹; περιούσιος, Tit 2¹⁴; εἰς περιποίησιν, 1 Pe 2⁹ (LXX).

SYN.: v.s. δῆμος.

λάρυγξ, -γγος, ὁ, [in LXX chiefly for חֵךְ, Jb 6³⁰, al.; Ps 5⁹ (גָּרוֹן);] the *larynx, throat :* metaph., of speech (cf. Si 6⁵), Ro 3¹³ (LXX).†

Λασέα (Rec. -αία), -ας, ἡ, *Lasea,* a city of Crete, otherwise unknown : Ac 27⁸.†

* **λάσκω,** 1. (in cl., poët.) *to clang, crash, crack ;* in late prose, *to crack* or *burst noisily :* Ac 1¹⁸ (ἐλάκησεν, perh., however, from λακέω, q.v.; Bl., in l.). 2. (in cl., prose) *to scream, shout.*†

† **λατομέω,** -ῶ (< λατόμος, a *stonecutter,* iv Ki 12¹², al.; < λᾶς, τέμνω; cf. λαξευτός), [in LXX : 1 Ch 22², al. (חצב); Ex 21³³, Nu 21¹⁸ (כרה);] *to hew, hew out* stones : Mt 27⁶⁰, Mk 15⁴⁶.†

λατρεία, -ας, ἡ (< λατρεύω, q.v.), [in LXX (always of divine service) : Ex 12²⁵,²⁶ 13⁵, Jos 22²⁷, 1 Ch 28¹³ (עֲבֹדָה), 1 Mac 1⁴³ 2¹⁹,²², iii Mac 4¹⁴ *;*] 1. *hired service, service.* 2. (in cl. also) divine *service, worship :* Jo 16², Ro 9⁴ 12¹, He 9¹, ⁶.†

λατρεύω (< λάτρις, a *hired servant*), [in LXX (always, as λατρεία, of the service of God or of heathen divinities) chiefly for עבד, Ex 3¹², al.; in Da LXX TH (3¹², al.) for פְּלַח;] 1. *to work for hire.* 2. *to serve ;* in cl., also of divine service, *to serve, worship,* and so always in NT : c. dat. pers., τ. θεῷ, Mt 4¹⁰, Lk 4⁸ (LXX), Ac 7⁷ 24¹⁴ 27²³, He 9¹⁴, Re 7¹⁵ 22³; of idol worship (cf. Ex 20⁵, Ez 20³²), Ac 7⁴², Ro 1²⁵; τ. θεῷ λ. ἐν τ. πνεύματί μου, Ro 1⁹; id. ἐν καθαρᾷ συνειδήσει, ii Ti 1³; μετ᾽ εὐλαβείας κ. δέους, He 12²⁸; ἐν ὁσιότητι κ. δικαιοσύνῃ, Lk 1⁷⁴; (without θεῷ) νηστείαις κ. δεήσεσι, Lk 2³⁷; πνεύματι θεοῦ, Phl 3³; absol., Ac 26⁷; ὁ λατρεύων, the *worshipper,* He 9⁹ 10²; of ministerial service, c. dat. rei, He 8⁵ 13¹⁰.†

SYN.: λειτουργέω, q.v.

λάχανον, -ου, τό (λαχαίνω, *to dig*), [in LXX : Ge 9³, iii Ki 20 (21)², Ps 36 (37)², Pr 15¹⁷ (יָרָק, יֶרֶק) *;*] a *garden herb, vegetable :* Lk 11⁴²; usually in pl., Mt 13³², Mk 4³², Ro 14².†

SYN.: βοτάνη, q.v.

Λεββαῖος, -ου, ὁ (on the derivation, v. Dalman, *Words,* 50 ; Swete, *Mk.,* l.c.), *Lebbæus :* Mt 10³, Mk 3¹⁸ (WH, mg.; Θαδδαῖος, q.v., Rec., WH, txt., RV, cf. WH, *App.,* 11, 24. In Lk 6¹⁵, Ac 1¹³, he is called Σίμων ὁ Ζηλωτής.)†

† **λεγιών** (Rec. -εών), -ῶνος, ἡ, (Lat. *legio*), a *legion :* Mt 26⁵³, Mk 5⁹, ¹⁵, Lk 8³⁰.†

λέγω, [in LXX very freq., chiefly for אמר; λέγει for נְאֻם, Ge 22¹⁶, al.;] 1. in Hom., *to pick out, gather, reckon, recount.* 2. In Hdt. and Att., *to say, speak, affirm, declare :* absol., Ac 13¹⁵ 24¹⁰; seq. orat. dir., Mt 9³⁴, Mk 3¹¹, Jo 1²⁹, al.; seq. ὅτι recit., Mk 3²¹, Lk 1²⁴, Jo 6¹⁴, al.; acc. et. inf., Lk 11¹⁸, Jo 12²⁹, al.; after another verb of speaking, προσφωνεῖν κ. λέγειν, Mt 11¹⁷, al.; ἀπεκρίθη (ἐλάλησεν) λέγων (καὶ λέγει; Dalman, *Words*, 24 ff.), Mt 25⁹, Mk 3³³ 7²⁸, Lk 24⁶, ⁷, al.; of unspoken thought, λ. ἐν ἑαυτῷ, Mt 3⁹, Lk 3⁸, al.; of writing, II Co 8⁸, Phl 4¹¹, al.; λέγει ἡ γραφή, Ro 4³, Ja 2²³, al.; c. acc. rei, Lk 8⁸ 9³³, Jo 5³⁴, al.; σὺ λέγεις (a non-committal phrase; Swete, *Mk.*, 359, 369 f.), Mt 27¹¹, Mk 15², Lk 23³, Jo 18³⁷; c. dat. pers., seq. orat. dir., Mt 8²⁰, Mk 2¹⁷, al. mult.; id. seq. ὅτι, Mt 3⁹, al.; c. prep., πρός, μετά, περί, etc., Mk 4⁴¹, Jo 11⁵⁶, He 9⁵, al.; *to mean* (cl.), Mk 14⁷¹, Jo 6⁷¹, I Co 10²⁹, al.; *to call, name,* Mk 10¹⁸; pass., Mt 9⁹, Mk 15⁷, al (cf. ἀντι-, δια- (-μαι), προ-, συλ-λέγω).

SYN.: λαλέω, which refers to the utterance, as λέγω to the meaning of what is said, its correspondence with thought (Tr., *Syn.*, lxxvi; Thayer, s.v. λαλέω).

λεῖμμα (WH, λίμμα, v. their *App.*, 154), -τος, τό (< λείπω), [in LXX: IV Ki 19⁴ A (שְׁאָרִית) *;] *a remnant:* Ro 11⁵.†

λεῖος, -εία, -εῖον, [in LXX: Ge 27¹¹, I Ki 17⁴⁰ R (חָלָק, חַלִּיק); ὁδὸς λ., Is 40⁴ A (בִּקְעָה); Pr 2²⁰ 12¹³ 26²³ *;] *smooth:* opp. to τραχύς, Lk 3⁵ (LXX).†

λείπω, [in LXX: Jb 4¹¹, Pr 19¹ ⁽⁴⁾ (פרד), al.;] 1. trans., *to leave, leave behind;* pass., *to be left behind, to lack:* seq. prep. (as more usual in cl.), ἐν, Ja 1⁴; c. gen. rei, ib ⁵ 2¹⁵. 2. Intrans., *to be gone, to be wanting:* c. dat. pers., Lk 18²², Tit 3¹³; τὰ λείποντα, Tit 1⁵ (cf. ἀπο-, δια-, ἐκ-, ἐπι-, κατα-, ἐν-κατα-, περι-, ὑπο-λείπω).†

λειτουργέω, -ῶ (< λειτουργός), [in LXX chiefly for שרת pi., also for עבד, צבא, etc.;] 1. in cl., at Athens, *to supply public offices at one's own cost, render public service to the State,* hence, generally, 2. *to serve the State, do a service, serve* (of service to the Gods, Diod., i, 21): of the official service of priests and Levites (Ex 29³⁰, Nu 16⁹, Si 4¹⁴, I Mac 10⁴², al.; cf. Deiss., *BS*, 140 f.), He 10¹¹; of Christians: c. dat. pers. seq. ἐν, Ro 15²⁷ (cf. Si 10²⁵); τ. κυρίῳ, Ac 13².†

SYN.: λατρεύω (q.v.), prop., *to serve for hire,* LXX (as sometimes in cl.), always of service to the deity on the part of both priests and people (Ex 4³, De 10¹², and similarly in NT). λειτουργέω "is the fulfilment of an office: it has a definite representative character, and corresponds with a function to be discharged". It is therefore used of serving in an office or ministry: in LXX always of priests and Levites, in NT, with its cognates (Ro 13⁶ 15²⁷, are not really exceptions), of services rendered either to God or man by apostles, prophets, teachers, and other officers of the church (cf. Tr., *Syn.*, § xxxv; ICC on Ro 1⁹; Westc., *He.*, 232 ff.).

λειτουργία, -ας, ἡ (< λειτουργέω), [in LXX chiefly for עֲבֹדָה, Nu 4²⁴, I Ch 9¹³, al.;] 1. in cl. (chiefly of Athens), *the discharge of a public office at one's own expense* (v. LS, s.v.), hence, 2. *a service, ministry;* in π. (Deiss., *BS*, 140 f.) and in LXX (though here also of secular service, III Ki 1⁴, al.), of religious service or ministration; and so in NT : of priestly ministrations, Lk 1²³, He 8⁶ 9²¹ ; fig., θυσία καὶ λ. τῆς πίστεως ὑμῶν, Phl 2¹⁷ ; of Christian beneficence, ii Co 9¹², Phl 2³⁰.†

†λειτουργικός, -ή, -όν, [in LXX for עֲבֹדָה, שָׁרֵת ; ἔργα, Nu 7⁵ ; στολαί, Ex 31⁹ ⁽¹⁰⁾ 39¹³ ⁽¹⁾ ; σκευή, Nu 4¹², ²⁶, ii Ch 24¹⁴ * ;] of or for service, ministering : πνεύματα, He 1¹⁴.†

λειτουργός, -οῦ, ὁ (< λαός, ἔργον), [in LXX chiefly for מְשָׁרֵת, Jos 1¹ A, iii Ki 10⁵, Ps 102 (103)²¹, Si 7³⁰, al. ;] 1. in cl., one who discharges a public office at his own expense, then, generally, 2. a public servant, a minister, servant : τ. ἁγίων λ., He 8² (cf. Ne 10³⁹, Si, l.c.) ; Ἰησοῦ Χριστοῦ, Ro 15¹⁶ ; pl., τ. θεοῦ, Ro 13⁶, He 1⁷ ⁽ᴸˣˣ⁾ ; λ. ὑμῶν τ. χρείας μου, Phl 2²⁵.†

SYN.: v.s. διάκονος, λειτουργέω.

λεμά, v.s. λαμά.

*†λέντιον, -ου, τό (Lat. linteum), a linen cloth, towel : Jo 13⁴, ⁵.†

λεπίς, -ίδος, ἡ (< λέπω, to peel), [in LXX chiefly for קַשְׂקֶשֶׂת ;] a scale : Ac 9¹⁸.†

λέπρα, -ας, ἡ (< λεπρός), [in LXX for צָרַעַת ;] leprosy : Mt 8³, Mk 1⁴², Lk 5¹², ¹³.†

λεπρός, -ά, -όν (< λεπίς), [in LXX for צָרוּעַ, מְצֹרָע ;] 1. (in cl.) scaly, rough. 2. leprous ; chiefly as subst., ὁ λ., a leper : Mt 8² 10⁸ 11⁵, Mk 1⁴⁰, Lk 4²⁷ 7²² 17¹² ; of Simon, formerly a leper, Mt 26⁶, Mk 14³.†

*λεπτός, -ή, -όν (λέπω, to peel), 1. peeled. 2. fine, thin, small, light ; hence, in late Gk., as subst. τὸ λ., a small coin (one-eighth of an as, AV, mite) : Mk 12⁴², Lk 12⁵⁹ 21².†

Λευεί (indecl.) and Λευείς (Rec. -υί, -υίς), gen. Λευεί, acc. -είν, ὁ (Heb. לֵוִי), Levi ; 1. the son of Jacob : He 7⁵, ⁹, Re 7⁷. 2. Son of Melchi : Lk 3²⁴. 3. Son of Simeon : Lk 3²⁹. 4. Son of Alphæus (cf. Ματθαῖος) : Mk 2¹⁴ (WH, mg., Ἰάκωβον), Lk 5²⁷, ²⁹.†

Λευείτης (Rec. Λευίτης), -ου, ὁ, [in LXX for לֵוִי ;] a Levite : Lk 10³², Jo 1¹⁹, Ac 4³⁶.†

Λευειτικός (Rec. Λευΐτ-), -ή, -όν, [in LXX : Le, tit. * ;] Levitical : He 7¹¹.†

λευκαίνω (< λευκός), [in LXX : Ps 50 (51)⁷, Is 1¹⁸ (לבן hi.), etc. ;] to whiten, make white : c. acc. rei, Mk 9³, Re 7¹⁴.†

*†λευκο-βύσσινος, -ον (cf. λευκολινής, a robe of white flax, C.I., 155, 17), white linen : Re 19¹⁴ (WH, mg.).†

λευκός, ή, -όν, [in LXX chiefly for לָבָן ;] 1. bright, brilliant : of clothing, Mt 17², Mk 9³ 16⁵, Lk 9²⁹, Ac 1¹⁰, Re 3⁵ 4⁴ 6¹¹ 7⁹, ¹³ 19¹⁴ (cf. Ec 9⁸) ; ὡς χιών, Mt 28³ ; ἐν λ. (sc. ἱματίοις), Jo 20¹², Re 3⁴ ; θρόνος, Re 20¹¹. 2. white : Mt 5³⁶, Re 1¹⁴ 2¹⁷ 4⁴ 6² 14¹⁴ 19¹¹ ; fig., of garments, Re 3¹⁸ ; of ripened grain, Jo 4³⁵.†

λέων, -οντος, ὁ, [in LXX chiefly for אֲרִי, אַרְיֵה, also for כְּפִיר, etc.;] *a lion :* He 11³³, 1 Pe 5⁸, Re 4⁷ 9⁸, ¹⁷ 10³ 13² ; metaph., 11 Ti 4¹⁷, Re 5⁵.†

λήθη, -ης, ἡ (< λήθω = λανθάνω), [in LXX : Le 5¹⁵ (מַעַל), Wi 16¹¹, Si 14⁷, al.;] *forgetfulness :* λ. λαβεῖν (on the phrase, v. Mayor, in l.) : 11 Pe 1⁹.†

λημά, Τ, for λαμά, q.v., in Mt 27⁴⁶.†

λῆμψις (Rec. λῆψις, so in cl.), -εως, ἡ (< λαμβάνω), [in LXX (λῆψ-) : Pr 15²⁹ (16⁸) ; λ. δώρων, Pr 15²⁷ (מַתָּנָה) ; λ. καὶ δόσις, Si 41¹⁹ 42⁷ * ;] *receiving :* δόσις καὶ λ., Phl 4¹⁵.†

ληνός, -οῦ, ἡ (in some MSS., LXX and NT, ὁ), [in LXX chiefly for יֶקֶב, Nu 18²⁷, al. ; also for רֶחָט (Ge 30³⁸, ⁴¹), גַּת (Ne 13¹⁵, al.), etc.;] *a trough* or *vat ;* esp. for the treading of grapes : Mt 21³³, Re 14²⁰ 19¹⁵ ; τὴν λ. . . . τὸν μέγαν (a solecism perhaps inadvertent), Re 14¹⁹ (cf. ὑπολήνιον).†

**λῆρος, -ου, ὁ, [in LXX : iv Mac 5¹⁰ * ;] *silly talk, nonsense :* Lk 24¹¹.†

λῃστής, -οῦ, ὁ (< Ep. λῃίς = λεία, *booty*), [in LXX for גְּדוּד, etc.;] *a robber, brigand :* Mt 21¹³ (LXX) 26⁵⁵ 27³⁸, ⁴⁴, Mk 11¹⁷ 14⁴⁸ 15²⁷, Lk 10³⁰, ³⁶ 19⁴⁶ 22⁵², Jo 10¹, ⁸ 18⁴⁰, 11 Co 11²⁶.†
SYN.: κλέπτης, q.v.

λῆψις, v.s. λῆμψις.

λίαν, adv., [in LXX chiefly for מְאֹד, Ge 1³¹ 4⁵, Je 24³, al. ; To 9⁴, 11 Mac 11¹, al.;] *very, exceedingly :* Mt 2¹⁶ 4⁸ 8²⁸ 27¹⁴, Mk 1³⁵ 6⁵¹ (Rec. λ. ἐκ περισσοῦ) 9³ 16², Lk 23⁸, 11 Ti 4¹⁵, 11 Jo ⁴, 111 Jo ³ (cf. ὑπερλίαν).†

λίβανος, -ου, ὁ (rarely ἡ), (from the Semitic ; cf. the Heb. equiv.), [in LXX for לְבֹנָה, Ex 30³⁴, Is 60⁶ ; Si 24¹⁵, al.;] 1. in cl., *the frankincense-tree.* 2. (Occas. in cl.) *frankincense* (so Le 2¹ ; cf. λιβανωτός) : Mt 2¹¹, Re 18¹³.†

λιβανωτός, -οῦ, ὁ (< λίβανος), [in LXX : 1 Ch 9²⁹ (לְבֹנָה), 111 Mac 5² * ;] 1. in cl. (and LXX), *frankincense,* the gum of the *libanus.* 2. = Late Gk., λιβανωτρίς, *a censer :* Re 8³, ⁵ (the same form appears in Inscr. ; MM, xvi).†

Λιβερτῖνος, -ου, ὁ (Lat. *libertinus*), *a freedman :* ἡ συναγωγὴ ἡ λεγομένη Λιβερτίνων, Ac 6⁹ (Bl. thinks the original reading was Λιβυστίνων, *Phil. Gosp.,* 69 f.).†

Λιβύη, -ης, ἡ, *Libya :* Ac 2¹⁰.†

λιθάζω (< λίθος), [in LXX (seq. ἐν λίθοις) : 11 Ki 16⁶, ¹³ (סָקַל pi.) * ;] 1. *to throw stones* (Arist., Polyb., al.). 2. = λιθοβολέω (LXX, NT), *to pelt with stones, to stone :* c. acc. pers., Jo 8 [5] 10³¹⁻³³ 11⁸, Ac 14¹⁹ ; pass., Ac 5²⁶, 11 Co 11²⁵, He 11³⁷ (v. *DB,* Art., "Crimes and punishments," and cf. κατα-λιθάζω).†

λίθινος, -η, -ον (λίθος), [in LXX for אֶבֶן;] of stone: Jo 2⁶, II Co 3³, Re 9²⁰.†

† λιθο-βολέω, -ῶ (< λίθος, βάλλω), [in LXX for סקל, רגם, Ex 19¹³, Le 20², al.;] to pelt with stones, to kill by stoning, to stone (cf. λιθάζω): c. acc. pers., Mt 21³⁵ 23³⁷, Lk 13³⁴, Ac 7⁵⁸, ⁵⁹ 14⁵; pass., He 12²⁰ (LXX).†

λίθος, -ου, ὁ (and, in Att., of precious stones, ἡ), [in LXX for אֶבֶן, Ge 11³, al.; λ. τίμιος, for פָּז, Ps 18 (19)¹⁰ 20 (21)³, Pr 8¹⁹, al.;] a stone: Mt 4⁶, al.; pl., Mt 3⁹, al.; at the entrance of a tomb, Mt 27⁶⁰, ⁶⁶ 28², Mk 15⁴⁶ 16³, ⁴, Lk 24², Jo 11³⁸, ³⁹, ⁴¹ 20¹; λ. μυλικός, Lk 17², cf. Re 18²¹; of building stones, Mt 21⁴² [⁴⁴], 24², Mk 12¹⁰ 13¹, ², Lk 19⁴⁴ 20¹⁷, ¹⁸ 21⁵, ⁶, Ac 4¹¹, I Pe 2⁷; metaph., of Christ, λ. ἀκρογωνιαῖος, ἐκλεκτός, ἔντιμος, I Pe 2⁶ (LXX); λ. ζῶν, ib. ⁴; προσκόμματος, ib. ⁸, Ro 9³³; of Christians, λ. ζῶντες, I Pe 2⁵; of precious stones, λ. τίμιος, Re 17⁴ 18¹², ¹⁶ 21¹¹, ¹⁹; ἴασπις, Re 4³; ἐνδεδυμένοι λ. καθαρόν, Re 15⁶ (λίνον, Rec., R, mg., v. Swete, in l.); metaph., λ. τίμιοι, I Co 3¹²; of the tables of the law, II Co 3⁷; of idols, Ac 17²⁹.

λιθό-στρωτος, -ον (< στρώννυμι), [in LXX: II Ch 7³, Es 1⁶, Ca 3¹⁰ (רִצְפָה), רָצַף)*;] paved with stones, esp. of tessallated work (Ca, l.c.); as subst., τὸ λ., a tessallated pavement: Jo 19¹³ (cf. Γαββαθᾶ).†

λικμάω, -ῶ (< λικμός = λίκνον, a winnowing-fan), [in LXX chiefly for זרה ni., pi., Ru 3², III Ki 14¹⁵, Is 17¹³, Je 38 (31)¹⁰, Da 2⁴⁴, al.;] 1. in cl., to winnow (so Ru, l.c.). 2. In LXX (ll. c., exc. Ru), to scatter (as chaff or dust): Lk 20¹⁸ (RV, scatter as dust, Deiss., BS, 225 f., quotes ex. in π. which suggests the meaning ruin, destroy; cf. Vg. comminuet, AV, grind to powder; cf. also Kennedy, Sources, 126), Mt 21⁴⁴ [WH], R, txt.†

λιμά, T⁷, for λαμά, q.v.

λιμήν, -ένος, ὁ, [in LXX: Ps 106 (107)³⁰ (מָחוֹז), ib. ³⁵, I Es 5⁵⁵, I, II, IV Mac₇*;] a harbour, haven: Ac 27⁸, ¹² (cf. Καλοὶ Λιμένες).†

λίμμα, v.s. λεῖμμα.

λίμνη, -ης, ἡ, [in LXX: Ps 106 (107)³⁵ 113 (114)⁸ (אֲגַם), Ca 7⁴ (⁵) (בְּרֵכָה), I Mac 11³⁵, II Mac 12¹⁶*;] a lake: of the Sea of Galilee (Mt, Mk, v.s. θάλασσα), Lk 5² 8²², ²³, ³³; λ. Γεννησαρέτ (q.v.), Lk 5¹; λ. τ. πυρός, Re 19²⁰ 20¹⁰, ¹⁴, ¹⁵; καιομένη πυρί, Re 21⁸.†

λιμός, -οῦ, ὁ (so in Att.; in Dor. ἡ, and so sometimes in LXX, v. Th., Gr., 146; in NT: Lk 15¹⁴, Ac 11²⁸; cf. M, Pr., 60), [in LXX chiefly for רָעָב;] hunger, famine: Lk 4²⁵ 15¹⁴, ¹⁷, Ac 7¹¹ (LXX) 11²⁸, Ro 8³⁵, Re 6⁸ 18⁸; λ. καὶ δίψος, II Co 11²⁷; pl., Mt 24⁷, Mk 13⁸, Lk 21¹¹.†

λίνον (Tr. λῖνον), -ου, τό, [in LXX: Ex 9³¹ (פִּשְׁתָּה), al.;] 1. flax: Mt 12²⁰ (LXX). 2. linen: Re 15⁶ (R, mg., v.s. λίθος).†

Λίνος (Rec. Λῖνος), ου, ὁ, Linus: II Ti 4²¹.†

λιπαρός, -ά, -όν (< λίπος, fat), [in LXX: Jg 3²⁹, Ne 9³⁵, Is

30²³ (שָׁמֵן) *;] *oily, fatty;* metaph., of living, *rich, dainty:* τὰ λ. καὶ
τ. λαμπρά, Re 18¹⁴.†

*†λίτρα, -ας, ἡ (cf. Lat. *libra*), 1. a Sicilian coin = Rom. *libra* or
as. 2. In weight, *a pound:* Jo 12³ 19³⁹.†

λίψ, λιβός, ὁ, [in LXX chiefly for נֶגֶב, also for תֵּימָן, מַעֲרָבָה,
etc., Ge 13¹⁴, Nu 2¹⁰, ii Ch 32³⁰, al.;] *the SW. wind:* βλέποντα κατὰ λ.,
Ac 27¹² (v. Page, in l.; Deiss., *BS*, 141).†

λογεία, v.s. λογία.

*†λογία (prop., -εία, v. *BS*, 142 ff.), -ας, ἡ (< λογεύω, *to collect*, a
word found in π., v. Deiss., *BS*, l.c.; *LAE*, 70, 103; MM, xvi), *a
collection:* i Co 16¹, ².†

λογίζομαι (< λόγος), [in LXX chiefly for חָשַׁב;] 1. prop., of
numerical calculation, *to count, reckon:* c. acc. seq. μετά, Mk 15²⁸ (LXX)
(Rec., R, mg.), Lk 22³⁷. 2. Metaph., without reference to numbers,
by a reckoning of characteristics or reasons; (*a*) *to reckon, take into
account:* c. acc. rei, i Co 13⁵; id. seq. dat. pers., Ro 4³ (LXX), 4, 6, 8 (LXX),
ii Co 5¹⁹, ii Ti 4¹⁶; seq. εἰς (cf. Heb. לְ נֶחְשָׁב; Bl., § 33, 3), Ac 19²⁷, Ro
2²⁶ 4³, 5, 9-11, 22-24 9⁸, Ga 3⁶ (LXX), Ja 2²³ (LXX); (*b*) *to consider, calculate:*
c. acc. rei, Phl 4⁸; seq. ὅτι, Jo 11⁵⁰, He 11¹⁹; τοῦτο, ὅτι, ii Co 10¹¹; c. acc.
pers., c. inf., Ro 6¹¹; seq. ὡς, Ro 8³⁶ (LXX); (*c*) *to suppose, judge, deem:*
i Co 13¹¹; ὡς, i Pe 5¹²; οὕτως, i Co 4¹; c. acc. rei, ii Co 3⁵; id. seq.
εἰς, ii Co 12⁶; ὅτι, Ro 8¹⁸; τοῦτο, ὅτι, Ro 2³, ii Co 10⁷; c. inf., ii Co
11⁵; acc. et inf., Ro 3²⁸ 14¹⁴, Phl 3¹³; c. acc. pers. seq. ὡς, ii Co 10²;
(*d*) *to purpose, decide:* c. inf. (Eur., *Or.*, 555), ii Co 10² (cf. ἀνα-, δια-,
παρα-, συλ-λογίζομαι).†

*λογικός, -ή, -όν (< λόγος, *reason*), *reasonable, rational:* λατρεία,
Ro 12¹; τὸ λ. (i.e. *spiritual*) γάλα (v. Hort, in l.; MM, xvi), i Pe 2² (in
support of AV, *milk of the word*, v. *ICC*, in l.).†

λόγιον, -ου, τό (dimin. of λόγος, v. *ICC, Ro.*, 70), [in LXX chiefly
for אִמְרָה, אֵמֶר, Ps 17 (18)³⁰ 18 (19)¹⁴, al.; also for דָּבָר, Is 28¹³,
al.; (cf. λογεῖον (-ιον), for חֹשֶׁן, *the oracular breastplate* of the H.P.,
Ex 28¹⁵, al.);] *an oracle, divine response* or *utterance:* Ac 7³⁸, Ro 3²,
He 5¹², i Pe 4¹¹ (on the eccl., λόγια τ. Κυρίου, v. Lft., *Essay on Sup. Rel.*,
172 ff. and reff. in MM, *VGT*, s.v.).†

*λόγιος, -ον (< λόγος), 1. in cl., *learned* (Ac, l.c., R, txt.). 2. In
late Gk., *eloquent:* Ac 18²⁴ (v. Page, in l.; Field, *Notes*, 129).†

λογισμός, -οῦ, ὁ (< λογίζομαι), [in LXX: Ps 32 (33)¹⁰, ¹¹, Pr 19²¹,
Is 66¹⁸, al. (מַחֲשָׁבֶת);] *a reasoning, thought:* Ro 2¹⁵, ii Co 10⁵.†

*†λογομαχέω, -ῶ (< λόγος, μάχομαι), *to strive with words:* ii Ti 2¹⁴.†
*†λογομαχία, -ας, ἡ (< λογομαχέω), *a strife of words:* pl., i Ti 6⁴.†

λόγος, -ου, ὁ (< λέγω), [in LXX chiefly for דָּבָר, also for
אֵמֶר, מִלָּה, etc.;] I. Of that by which the inward thought is expressed, Lat. *oratio, sermo, vox, verbum.* 1. *a word*, not in the
grammatical sense of a mere name (ἔπος, ὄνομα, ῥῆμα), but a word as

embodying a conception or idea: Mt 8⁸, Lk 7⁷, ı Co 14⁹, ¹⁹, He 12¹⁹, al. 2. *a saying, statement, declaration*: Mt 19²² (T om.), Mk 5³⁶ 7²⁹, Lk 1²⁹, Jo 2²² 6⁶⁰, Ac 7²⁹, al.; c. gen. attrib., Ac 13¹⁵, Ro 9⁹, He 7²⁸, al.; of the sayings, commands, promises, etc., of teachers, Mt 7²⁴ 10¹⁴, Mk 8³³, Lk '9⁴⁴, Jo 14²⁴, al.; λ. κενοί, Eph 5⁶; ἀληθινοί, Re 19⁹; πιστοί, Re 22⁶; esp. of the precepts, decrees and promises of God, ὁ λ. τ. θεοῦ, *the word of God*: Mk 7¹³, Jo 10³⁵, Ro 13⁹, ı Co 14³⁶, Phl 1¹⁴, al.; absol., ὁ λ., Mt 13²¹, ²², Mk 16[²⁰], Lk 1², Ac 6⁴, He 4¹², al. 3. *speech, discourse*: Ac 14¹², ıı Co 10¹⁰, Ja 3²; opp. to ἐπιστολή, ıı Th 2¹⁵; disting. from σοφία, ı Co 2¹; ἀναστροφή, ı Ti 4¹²; δύναμις, ı Co 4¹⁹, ı Th 1⁵; ἔργον, Ro 15¹⁸; οὐδενὸς λ. τίμιον (*not worthy of mention*), Ac 20²⁴; of the faculty of speech, Lk 24¹⁹, ıı Co 11⁶; of the style of speech, Mt 5³⁷, ı Co 1⁵; of instruction, Col 4³, ı Pe 3¹; c. gen. pers., Jo 5²⁴ 8⁵², Ac 2⁴¹, al.; ὁ λ. ὁ ἐμός, Jo 8³¹; c. gen. obj. (τ.) ἀληθείας, ıı Co 6⁷, Col 1⁵, Ja 1¹⁸; τ. καταλλαγῆς, ıı Co 5¹⁹; τ. σταυροῦ, ı Co 1¹⁸; of mere talk, ı Co 4¹⁹, ²⁰, Col 2²³, ı Jo 3¹⁸; of the talk which one occasions, hence, *repute*: Col 2²³. 4. *subject-matter*, hence, *teaching, doctrine*: Ac 18¹⁵, ıı Ti 2¹⁷, al.; esp. of Christian doctrine: Mt 13²⁰⁻²³, Mk 4¹⁴⁻²⁰ 8³², Lk 1², Ac 8⁴, Ga 6⁶, ı Th 1⁶, al.; c. gen. pers., τ. θεοῦ, Lk 5¹, Jo 17⁶, Ac 4²⁹, ı Co 14³⁶, ı Jo 1¹⁰, Re 6⁹, al.; τ. Κυρίου, Ac 8²⁵, ı Th 1⁸, al.; τ. Χριστοῦ, Col 3¹⁶, Re 3⁸; c. gen. appos., Ac 15⁷; c. gen. attrib., He 5¹³. 5. *a story, tale, narrative*: Mt 28¹⁵, Jo 21²³, Ac 1¹ 11²²; seq. περί, Lk 5¹⁵. 6. That which is spoken of (Plat., al.; v. Kennedy, *Sources*, 124), *matter, affair, thing*: Mt 21²⁴, Mk 1⁴⁵ 11²⁹, Lk 20³, Ac 8²¹; of a matter in dispute, as a case or suit at law, Ac 19³⁸; pl. (ı Mac 7³³, al.), Lk 1⁴. II. Of the inward thought itself, Lat. *ratio*. 1. *reason*, (*a*) of the mental faculty (Hdt., Plat., al.): κατὰ λόγον, Ac 18¹⁴; (*b*) *a reason, cause*: τίνι λόγῳ, Ac 10²⁹; παρεκτὸς λόγου πορνείας, Mt 5³² 19⁹, WH, mg., R, mg. 2. *account*, (*a*) *regard*: Ac 20²⁴, Rec.; (*b*) *reckoning*: Phl 4¹⁵, ¹⁷, He 4¹³; συναίρειν (q.v.) λ., Mt 18²⁵ 25¹⁹; in forensic sense, Ro 14¹², He 13¹⁷, ı Pe 4⁵; c. gen. rei, Lk 16²; seq. περί, Mt 12³⁶, Ac 19⁴⁰, ı Pe 3¹⁵. 3. *proportion, analogy*: Phl 2¹⁶ (Field, *Notes*, 193 f.). III. ὁ λ., the Divine *Word* or *Logos*: Jo 1¹, ¹⁴; τ. ζωῆς, ı Jo 1¹; τ. θεοῦ, Re 19¹³ (v. Westc., Swete, *CGT*, in ll.; reff. in Artt., *Logos*, *DB*, *DCG*).

λόγχη, -ης, ἡ, [in LXX for רֹמַח, etc.;] 1. *a spear-head*. 2. *a lance, spear*: Mt 27⁴⁹ (|[WH]|, R, mg.), Jo 19³⁴.†

λοιδορέω, -ῶ (< λοίδορος), [in LXX chiefly for רִיב;] *to abuse, revile*: c. acc. pers., Jo 9²⁸, Ac 23⁴; pass., ı Co 4¹², ı Pe 2²³ (cf. ἀντι-λοιδορέω).†

λοιδορία, -ας, ἡ (< λοιδορέω), [in LXX chiefly for רִיב, מְרִיבָה;] *abuse, railing*: ı Ti 5¹⁴, ı Pe 3⁹.†

λοίδορος, -ον, [in LXX: Pr 25²⁴ 26²¹ 27¹⁵ (מִדְיָן), Si 23⁸ *;] *railing, abusive*; as subst., ὁ λ., *a railer*: ı Co 5¹¹ 6¹⁰.†

λοιμός, -οῦ, ὁ, [in LXX for לוּץ, עָרִיץ, בְּלִיַּעַל, etc.;] *pestilence*:

272 MANUAL GREEK LEXICON OF THE NEW TESTAMENT

pl., Lk 21¹¹; metaph. (as in cl.; LXX: Ps 1¹, Pr 21²⁴, 1 Mac 15²¹, al.), of persons, *a pest*: Ac 24⁵ (also as adj., ἄνδ‚ες λοιμοί, 1 Mac 10⁶¹, al.).†

λοιπός, -ή, -όν (< λείπω), [in LXX chiefly for יֶתֶר, also for שְׁאָר, etc.;] *the remaining, the rest,* 1. pl., οἱ λ.: c. subst., Mt 25¹¹, Ac 2³⁷, Ro 1¹³, al.; absol., Mt 22⁶, Mk 16[¹³], Lk 24¹⁰, al.; οἱ λ. οἱ (Bl., § 47, 8), Ac 28⁹, 1 Th 4¹³, Re 2²⁴; οἱ λ. τ. ἀνθρώπων (LS, s.v., ad. init.), Re 9²⁰; τὰ λ., Mk 4¹⁹, Re 3², al. 2. Neut. sing. (acc. ref.), adverbially, τὸ λ.; (*a*) *for the future, henceforth*: Mk 14⁴¹, 1 Co 7²⁹ (Lft., *Notes*, 232 f.), He 10¹³; anarth. (Deiss., *LAE*, 176₁₆, 188₅,₂₀), Ac 27²⁰, 11 Ti 4⁸; τοῦ λ. (sc. χρόνου; LS, s.v.; M, *Pr.*, 73; Bl., § 36, 13), Ga 6¹⁷, Eph 6¹⁰; (*b*) *besides, moreover, for the rest*: Phl 3¹ 4⁸; anarth., 1 Co 1¹⁶ 4², 1 Th 4¹ (M, *Th.*, in l.; Lft., *Notes*, 51).

Λουκᾶς, -ᾶ, ὁ (prob. an abbreviation of Λουκανός; v. Lft., *Col.*, 240; *ICC, Lk.*, xviii; Bl., § 29; acc. to Ramsay, *Exp.*, Dec., 1912, pp. 502 ff., a by-form of Λούκιος, from Lat. *Lucius*), *Luke*: Lk, *tit.*, Col 4¹⁴, 11 Ti 4¹¹, Phm 24.†

Λούκιος, -ου, ὁ (Lat. *Lucius*), *Lucius*: Ac 13¹, Ro 16²¹.†

λουτρόν, -οῦ, τό (< λούω), [in LXX: Ca 4², 6⁵,(⁶) (רַחְצָה), Si 31 (34)²⁵ *;*] *a washing, bath*: τ. ὕδατος, Eph 5²⁶; τ. παλιγγενεσίας, Tit 3⁵ (v. AR, *Eph.*, l.c.).†

λούω, [in LXX chiefly for רחץ (freq. of ceremonial washing; cf. Deiss., *BS*, 226 f.);] *to bathe, wash* the body: c. acc. pers., Ac 9³⁷ (of a dead body); id. seq. ἀπό (Deiss., *BS*, l.c.), Ac 16³³; pass. ptcp. pf., Jo 13¹⁰, He 10²²; mid., *to wash oneself* (Mayor, in l.; M. *Pr.*, 155 f., 238 f.), 11 Pe 2²²; metaph., Re 1⁵, Rec., R, mg. (cf. ἀπο-λούω).†

SYN.: νίπτω, used of parts of the body—hands, feet, face; πλύνω, of things, as garments, etc. (v. Le 15¹¹; cf. Tr., *Syn.*, § xlv).

Λύδδα, -ας (Ac 9³⁸, -ης Rec.), ἡ and Λύδδα, -ων, τά (ib.³²,³⁵; -αν, Rec.), (Heb. לֹד), *Lydda* (modern *Ludd*): Ac, ll. c.†

Λυδία, -ας, ἡ, *Lydia,* a woman of Thyatira: Ac 16¹⁴,⁴⁰.†

Λυκαονία, -ας, ἡ, *Lycaonia,* a region in Asia Minor: Ac 14⁶.†

Λυκαονιστί, adv., *in Lycaonian* (speech): Ac 14¹¹.†

Λυκία, -ας, ἡ, *Lycia,* a region of Asia Minor: Ac 27⁵.†

λύκος, -ου, ὁ, [in LXX for זְאֵב;] *a wolf*: Mt 10¹⁶, Lk 10³, Jo 10¹²; fig. (as Ez 22²⁷, Ze 3³, Je 5⁶, al.), Mt 7¹⁵, Ac 20²⁹.†

λυμαίνομαι (< λύμη, *outrage*), [in LXX chiefly for שחת pi., hi., also for כָּרְסֵם, etc.;] 1. *to outrage, maltreat*: c. acc., Ac 8³. 2. *to corrupt, defile* (Ez 16²⁵, Pr 23⁸, iv Mac 18⁸, al.).†

λυπέω, -ῶ (< λύπη), [in LXX for חרה, etc.;] *to distress, grieve, cause pain* or *grief*: c. acc. pers., 11 Co 2²,⁵ 7⁸; pass., Mt 14⁹ 17²³ 18³¹ 19²² 26²², Mk 10²² 14¹⁹, Jo 16²⁰ 21¹⁷, Ro 14¹⁵, 11 Co 2⁴, 1 Th 4¹³, 1 Pe 1⁶; λ. καὶ ἀδημονεῖν, Mt 26³⁷; opp. to χαίρειν, 11 Co 6¹⁰; κατὰ θεόν, 11 Co 7⁹,¹¹; τ. πνεῦμα τ. ἅγιον, Eph 4³⁰ (cf. συν-λυπέω).†

SYN.: v.s. θρηνέω.

λύπη, -ης, ἡ, [in LXX for עֶצֶב and cogn. forms, etc.;] *pain* of body or mind, *grief, sorrow*: Jo 16⁶, II Co 2⁷; opp. to χαρά, Jo 16²⁰, He 12¹¹; ἀπὸ τῆς λ., Lk 22⁴⁵; ἐκ λ., II Co 9⁷; ἡ κατὰ θεὸν λ., opp. to ἡ τ. κόσμου λ., II Co 7¹⁰; λ. μοί ἐστιν, Ro 9²; λ. ἔχω, Jo 16²¹, ²²; id. seq. ἀπό, II Co 2³; λ. ἐπὶ λ. ἔχω, Phl 2²⁷; ἐν λ. ἐλθεῖν, II Co 2¹ (to come sad and cause sadness); pl. (cf. Ge 3¹⁶, Pr 15¹³, al.), I Pe 2¹⁹.†

Λυσανίας, -ου, ὁ, *Lysanias*: Lk 3¹.†

Λυσίας, -ου, ὁ, *Lysias (Claudius L.*, Ac 23²⁶), Ac 24⁽⁷⁾, ²².†

λύσις, -εως, ἡ (< λύω), [in LXX: Ec 7³⁰ (8¹) (פֵּשֶׁר), Da LXX 12⁸, Wi 8⁸ *;] *a loosing*: of divorce, I Co 7²⁷.†

**λυσιτελέω, -ῶ (< λυσιτελής, *useful*, prop., τὰ τέλη λύων), [in LXX: To 3⁶, Si 20¹⁰, ¹⁴ 29¹¹ *;] 1. prop., *to indemnify, pay expenses*. 2. *to be useful, to profit*; usually impers., λυσιτελεῖ, *it profits*: c. dat. pers., seq. εἰ . . . ἤ, Lk 17².†

Λύστρα, -ας, ἡ, and (in Ac 14⁸ 16², II Ti, l.c.) -ων, τά (cf. Λύδδα), *Lystra*, a city of Lycaonia: Ac 14⁶, ⁸, ²¹ 16¹, ², II Ti 3¹¹.†

λύτρον, -ου, τό (< λύω), [in LXX (Pent. ₁₅, Pr ₂, Is ₁) for פִּדְיוֹן and cogn. forms, גְּאֻלָּה, כֹּפֶר, מְחִיר;] *a ransom* (as for a life, Ex 21³⁰; for slaves, Le 19²⁰; for captives, Is 45¹³): ἀντὶ πολλῶν, Mt 20²⁸, Mk 10⁴⁵ (v. Swete, in l., and for discussion of λ. and its cognates, Westc., *He.*, 295 f.; Deiss., *LAE*, 331 f.; cf. also ἀντι-λύτρον).†

λυτρόω, -ῶ (< λύτρον, q.v.), [in LXX chiefly for פדה, גאל;] *to release on receipt of ransom*; mid., *to release by paying ransom, to redeem*: in spiritual sense, Tit 2¹⁴; pass., I Pe 1¹⁸; in general sense, *to deliver* (cf. Ex 6⁶, Ps 68 (69)¹⁸, al.): Lk 24²¹.†

†λύτρωσις, -εως, ἡ (< λυτρόω), [in LXX: Le 25²⁹, ⁴⁸, Is 63⁴ (גְּאוּלִים, גְּאֻלָּה), Nu 18¹⁶, Ps 48 (49)⁸ 110 (111)⁹ 129 (130)⁷ (פְּדוּת, פִּדְיוֹם, פָּדָה), Jg 1¹⁵ *;] *a ransoming, redemption* (αἰχμαλώτων, Plut., *Arat.*, 11): of the mediatorial work of Christ, He 9¹²; in general sense, *deliverance* (cf. Ps 48, l.c.): Lk 1⁶⁸ 2³⁸.†

λυτρωτής, -οῦ, ὁ (< λυτρόω), [in LXX: of God, Ps 18 (19)¹⁴ 77 (78)³⁵ (גֹּאֵל) *;] *a redeemer, deliverer*: Ac 7³⁵.†

λυχνία, -ας, ἡ (vulgar form of λυχνίον = λυχνοῦχος; v. Kennedy, *Sources*, 40), [in LXX for מְנוֹרָה (Ex 25³¹ 40⁴, al.);] *a lampstand*: Mt 5¹⁵, Mk 4²¹, Lk 8¹⁶ 11³³; of that in the Tabernacle, He 9²; metaph., of the two witnesses, Re 11⁴; of the seven churches of Asia, Re 1¹², ¹³, ²⁰ 2¹; of the removal of a church from its position, κινεῖν τ. λυχνίαν κ.τ.λ., ib. ⁵.†

λύχνος, -ου, ὁ, [in LXX for נֵר (Ex 25³⁶ ⁽³⁷⁾, al.);] *a lamp* (portable, and usually set on a stand, λυχνία): Mt 5¹⁵, Lk 11³⁶; ἔρχεται ὁ λ., Mk 4²¹; λ. ἅπτειν, Lk 8¹⁶ 11³³ 15⁸; φῶς λύχνου, Re 18²³; id. opp. to φ. ἡλίου, ib. 22⁵; metaph., of the eye, Mt 6²², Lk 11³⁴; of John the

Baptist, Jo 5³⁵; of the Lamb, Re 21²³; of prophccy, ιι Pe 1¹⁹; of spiritual readiness, pl., λύχνοι (as always in LXX; freq. in Att. λύχνα), Lk 12³⁵.†

SYN.: λαμ-άς, q.v.

λύω, [in LXX for פתח, נתר hi., etc.;] 1. *to loose, unbind, release:* of things, Mk 1⁷, Lk 3¹⁶, al.; of beasts, Mt 21², Lk 13¹⁵, al.; of persons, Jo 11⁴⁴, Ac 22³⁰; of Satan, Re 20³, ⁷; metaph., of the marriage tie, ι Co 7²⁷; of one diseased, Lk 13¹⁶; of release from sin, Re 1⁵, WH, R, txt. (v.s. λούω). 2. To resolve a whole into its parts, *loosen, dissolve, break up, destroy:* Jo 2¹⁹, Ac 27⁴¹, Re 5²; metaph., ιι Pe 3¹¹; of an assembly, *to dismiss:* Ac 13⁴³; τ. μεσότοιχον τ. φραγμοῦ, Eph 2¹⁴; τ. στοιχεῖα, ιι Pe 3¹⁰; οὐραν ί, ib. ¹²; τ. ἔργα τ. διαβ ὶλου, ι Jo 3⁸; τ. ὠδῖνας τ. θανάτου, Ac 2²⁴; of laws, etc., *to break, annul, cancel* (MM, xvi): ἐντολήν, Mt 5¹⁹; τ. νόμον, Jo 7²³; τ. σάββατον, Jo 5¹⁸; τ. γραφήν, Jo 10³⁵. (Cf. ἀνα-, ἀπο-, δια-, ἐκ-, ἐπι-, κατα-, παρα-λύω.)

Λωΐς (Rec. Λωΐς), -ίδος, ἡ, *Lois:* ιι Ti 1⁵.†

Λώτ, ὁ (Heb. לוֹט), indecl., *Lot* (Ge 11²⁷, al.): Lk 17²⁸, ²⁹, ³², ιι Pe 2⁷.†

M

M, μ, μῦ, τό, indecl., *mu, m,* the twelfth letter. As a numeral, μ′ = 40, μ, = 40,000.

Μαάθ, ὁ, indecl., *Maath:* Lk 3²⁶.†

Μαγαδάν, *Magadan,* an unidentified place on the coast of the Sea of Galilee: Mt 15³⁹ (Rec. Μαγδαλά; cf. Mk 8¹⁰, where for Δαλμανουθά, D* has Μελεγαδά, D¹ Μαγαιδά, some cursives Μαγαδά, and Euseb. *Onomast.* Μεγαιδάν; cf. *DB,* iii, s.v.).†

Μαγδαλά (Aram. מַגְדְּלָא = Heb. מִגְדֹּל, which in Jos 15³⁷ B is rendered Μαγαδά), *Magdala:* Mt 15³⁹ (Rec. for Μαγαδάν, q.v.).†

Μαγδαληνός, -ά, όν, *Magdalene, of Magdala:* Μαρία (q.v.) ἡ M., Mt 27⁵⁶, ⁶¹ 28¹, Mk 15⁴⁰, ⁴⁷ 16¹ (v. Turner, *SNT,* pp. 60 f.) [⁹], Lk 8² 24¹⁰, Jo 19²⁵ 20¹, ¹⁸.†

Μαγεδών, *Magedon:* Re 16¹⁶ (WH, Ἀρ M. for Ἁρμαγεδών, q.v.).† μαγεία, v.s. μαγία.

* μαγεύω (Eur., Plut., al.), 1. *to be a Magus, or skilled in Magian lore.* 2. *to practise magic:* Ac 8⁹.†

* μαγία (Rec. -εία), -α;, ἡ (< μάγος), 1. *the lore of the Magians* (Plat.). 2. *magic:* pl., *magic arts, sorceries:* Ac 8¹¹.†

μάγος, -ον, ὁ, [in LXX for אַשָּׁף, Da LXX TH 2², ¹⁰, al. (cf. רַב־מַג, *chief magian,* Je 39³, ¹³);] 1. one of the Μάγοι, a Median tribe (Hdt.). 2. *a Magian,* one of a sacred caste, originally Median, who seem to have conformed to the Persian religion, while retaining some of their old beliefs (v. *DB,* ι vol., 565 f.; *DB,* iii, 203 ff.): Mt 2¹, ⁷, ¹⁶. 3. *a wizard, sorcerer:* Ac 13⁶, ⁸ (cf. Wi 17⁷, Ac 8⁹, ¹¹).†

Μαγώγ, ὁ, indecl. (Heb. מָגוֹג, Ge 10², Ez 38², al.), *Magog,* associated with Gog: Re 20⁸ (v. Swete, in l.).†

Μαδιάμ, ὁ, indecl. (Heb. מִדְיָן), *Midian;* 1. son of Abraham (Ge 25²). 2. An Arabian tribe (Ge 36³⁵, Ps 82 (83)⁹, al). 3. γῆ Μ. (Heb. אֶרֶץ מִדְיָן), *the land of Midian* (Ex 2¹⁵, al.) : Ac 7²⁹.†

* **μαζός**, -οῦ, ὁ, *the breast* : Re 1¹³ (L for μαστός, q.v).†

*† **μαθητεύω** (< μαθητής), 1. intrans. (as prop. vb. in -εύω, and so Plut., *mor.* 837 c. and elsew.), *to be a disciple:* c. dat., Mt 27⁵⁷ (Rec., WH, mg.). 2. Trans., *to make a disciple:* c. acc., Mt 28¹⁹, Ac 14²¹; pass., seq. dat., τ. Ἰησοῦ, Mt 27⁵⁷ (WH, R); τ. βασιλείᾳ, Mt 13⁵².†

μαθητής, -οῦ, ὁ (μανθάνω), [in LXX only as v.l. (A) in Je 13²¹ 20¹¹ 26 (46)⁹ *;] *a disciple:* opp. to διδάσκαλος, Mt 10²⁴, Lk 6⁴⁰; Ἰωάννου, Mt 9¹⁴, Lk 7¹⁸, Jo 3²⁵; τ. Φαρισαίων, Mt 22¹⁶, Mk 2¹⁸, Lk 5³³; Μωυσέως, Jo 9²⁸; Ἰησοῦ, Lk 6¹⁷ 7¹¹ 19³⁷, Jo 6⁶⁶ 7³ 19³⁸; esp. the twelve, Mt 10¹ 11¹, Mk 7¹⁷, Lk 8⁹, Jo 2², al.; later, of Christians generally, Ac 6¹, ², ⁷ 9¹⁹, al.; τ. κυρίου, Ac 9¹.

*† **μαθήτρια**, -ας, ἡ (= μαθητρίς, fem. of μαθητής, q.v.), *a female disciple:* Ac 9³⁶.†

Μαθθαθίας, v.s. Ματταθίας.

Μαθθαῖος (Rec. Ματθ-, v. WH, *App.*, 159; Bl., § 3, 11; on the Semitic form, v. Dalman, *Words*, 51; *Gr.*, 142), -ου, ὁ, *Matthew:* Mt *tit.*, 9⁹ 10³, Mk 3¹⁸, Lk 6¹⁵, Ac 1¹³ (cf. Λευεί).†

Μαθθάν (Rec. Ματθ-, v.s. Μαθθαῖος), ὁ, indecl. (Heb. מַתָּן), *Matthan:* Mt 1¹⁵.†

Μαθθάτ (T, -άθ; Rec. Ματθ-, v.s. Μαθθαῖος), ὁ, indecl. (Heb. מַתָּת), *Matthat:* Lk 3²⁹ (cf. Ματθάτ).†

Μαθθίας (Rec. Ματθ-, v.s. Μαθθαῖος), -α, ὁ (Heb. מַתִּיָה), *Matthias:* Ac 1²³, ²⁶.†

Μαθουσάλα (WH, -αλά), ὁ (Heb. מְתוּשֶׁלַח), *Methuselah:* Lk 3³⁷.†

Μαϊνάν, v.s. Μεννά.

μαίνομαι, [in LXX: Je 32 (25)¹⁶ הלל hith.) 36 (29)²⁶ (שׁגע pu.), Wi 14²⁸, al.;] 1. *to rage, be furious.* 2. *to rave, be mad:* Jo 10²⁰, Ac 12¹⁵ 26²⁴, ²⁵, 1 Co 14²³ (cf. ἐμ-μαίνομαι).†

μακαρίζω (< μακάριος), [in LXX for אשר pi., pu.;] *to bless, pronounce blessed* or *happy:* c. acc. pers., Lk 1⁴⁸, Ja 5¹¹.†

μακάριος, -α, -ον (collat. form of poët. μάκαρ, in Hom., Hes., chiefly of the gods and the departed), [in LXX for אַשְׁרֵי;] *blessed, happy* (*DCG*, i, 177, 213): θεός (δυνάστης), 1 Ti 1¹¹ 6¹⁵; ἐλπίς, Tit 2¹³; esp. in congratulations, usually with the omission of the copula (M, *Pr.*, 180; Bl., § 30, 3), μ. ὁ, Mt 5³ ᶠᶠ·, Lk 6²⁰ ᶠ·, Jo 20²⁹, Re 1³, al.; seq. ptcp., Lk 1⁴⁵, al.; ὅς, Mt 11⁶, Lk 7²³, Ro 4⁷, ⁸; ὅτι, Mt 13¹⁶, al.; ἐάν, Jo 13¹⁷, 1 Co 7⁴⁰; compar., μ. . . . μᾶλλον, Ac 20³⁵; -ώτερος, 1 Co 7⁴⁰.

SYN.: εὐλογητός, q.v.

* **μακαρισμός**, -οῦ, ὁ (μακαρίζω), *a declaration of blessedness, felicitation:* Ro 4⁶, ⁹, Ga 4¹⁵ (Plat., Arist.).†

Μακεδονία, -ας, ἡ, *Macedonia* : Ac 16⁹, ¹⁰, ι Co 16⁵, ιι Co 1¹⁶, Phl 4¹⁵, al. ; M. καὶ Ἀχαία, Ac 19²¹, Ro 15²⁶, ι Th 1⁷, ⁸.

Μακεδών, -όνος, ὁ, *a Macedonian* : Ac 16⁹ 19²⁹ 27², ιι Co 9², ⁴.†

† μάκελλον, -ου, τό (Lat. *macellum*), *a meat-market* : ι Co 10²⁵ (v. Deiss., *LAE*, 274 ; MM, xvi).†

μακράν (prop. fem. acc. of μακρός, sc. ὁδόν), adv., [in LXX for רָחוֹק hi., רָחֹק, etc. ;] *a long way, far* : Lk 15²⁰, Ac 22²¹ ; seq. ἀπό, Mt 8³⁰, Lk 7⁶, Jo 21⁸, Ac 17²⁷ ; id. metaph., Mk 12³⁴ ; οἱ εἰς μ., Ac 2³⁹ (cf. Is 2²) ; metaph., οἱ ποτὲ ὄντες μ. (opp. to ἐγγύς), Eph 2¹³ ; οἱ μ., ib. ¹⁷.†

μακρόθεν (< μακρός), adv. (chiefly late), [in LXX for רָחוֹק, מֶרָחוֹק, etc. ;] *from afar, afar* : Lk 18¹³ 22⁵⁴ ; ἀπὸ μ. (Ps 137 (138)⁶, ιι Es 3¹³, al.), Mt 26⁵⁸ 27⁵⁵, Mk 5⁶ 8³ 11¹³ 14⁵⁴ 15⁴⁰, Lk 16²³ 23⁴⁹, Re 18¹⁰, ¹⁵, ¹⁷.†

† μακροθυμέω, -ῶ (< μακρό-θυμος, *long-tempered ;* v.s. *-ία*), [in LXX : Ec 8¹² א², Pr 19¹¹ (אֶרֶךְ, הֶאֱרִיךְ אַף), Jb 7¹⁶, Si 2⁴, al. ;] 1. actively = καρτερέω, *to persevere* (Plut., 2, 593 F). 2. Passively, *to be patient, long-suffering* : absol., ι Co 13⁴, He 6¹⁵, Ja 5⁸ ; seq. ἕως, c. gen., ib. ⁷ ; ἐπί, c. dat., ib. (Si 2⁴) ; πρός, c. acc., ι Th 5¹⁴ ; ἐπί, c. dat., Mt 18²⁶, ²⁹, Lk 18⁷ ; εἰς, ιι Pe 3⁹.†

SYN. : ὑπομένω, q.v.

† μακροθυμία, -ας, ἡ (< μακρό-θυμος), [in LXX : Pr 25¹⁵ (אֹרֶךְ אַפַּיִם), Je 15¹⁵ (אֶרֶךְ אַפַּיִם), Is 57¹⁵, Si 5¹¹, ι Mac 8⁴ * ;] *patience, long-suffering, forbearance* : of men, esp. in experiencing troubles and difficulties, Col 1¹¹, ιι Ti 3¹⁰, He 6¹², Ja 5¹⁰ ; of God's forbearance, Ro 2⁴ 9²². ιι Co 6⁶, Ga 5²², Eph 4², Col 3¹², ι Ti 1¹⁶, ιι Ti 4², ι Pe 3²⁰, ιι Pe 3¹⁵.†

SYN. : ὑπομονή (cf. Lft., *Col.*, 138 ; Tr., *Syn.*, liii).

† μακροθύμως, adv., *with forbearance, patiently* : Ac 26³.†

μακρός, -ά, -όν, [in LXX for אֹרֶךְ, רָחוֹק and cognate forms, etc. ;] 1. of space and time, *long* : μακρὰ προσεύχεσθαι, Mk 12⁴⁰, Lk 20⁴⁷. 2. Of distance, *far, far distant* : χώρα, Lk 15¹³ 19¹².†

μακρο-χρόνιος, -ον (μακρός, χρόνος), [in LXX . μ. γίγνεσθαι, εἶναι (הַאֲרִיךְ יָמִים), Ex 20¹², De 4⁴⁰ 5¹⁶ 17²⁰ * ;] *of long duration, long-lived* : Eph 6³ (LXX).†

μάλα, adv., [in LXX for אֲבָל, ιιι Ki 1⁴³, Da LXX 10²¹, al.; compar. for מִ, Nu 13³² (³¹), al. ; μᾶλλον ἤ (מִ), Ge 19⁹, al.; superlat., ιι Mac 8⁷, ιν Mac 4²² 12⁹ 15⁴ ;] I. Pos., *very, very much, exceedingly* (cl. ; LXX ut supr. ; in NT its place is taken by λίαν, σφόδρα, etc.). II. Compar., μᾶλλον. 1. Of increase, *more ;* with qualifying words : πολλῷ, Mk 10⁴⁸, Lk 18³⁹, Ro 5¹⁵, ¹⁷, Phl 2¹², al. ; πόσῳ, Lk 12²⁴, Ro 11¹², al. ; τοσούτῳ . . . ὅσῳ, He 10²⁵. 2. Of comparison, *the more* : Lk 5¹⁵, Jo 5¹⁸, Ac 5¹⁴, ι Th 4¹, ¹⁰, ιι Pe 1¹⁰ ; ἔτι μ. καὶ μ., Phl 1⁹ ; c. compar., Mk 7³⁶, ιι Co 7¹³ ; πολλῷ μ. κρεῖσσον, Phl 1²³ ; μ. διαφέρειν,

c. gen., Mt 6²⁶; μ. ἤ, Mt 18¹³; c. gen., ι Co 14¹⁸; as periphr. for compar., Ac 20³⁵, ι Co 9¹⁵, Ga 4²⁷; μ. δέ (EV, *yea rather*), Ro 8³⁴. 3. Of preference, *rather, the rather, sooner*: with qualifying words, πολλῷ, Mt 6³⁰, al.: πολύ, He 12²⁵; πόσῳ, Mt 7¹¹, al.; in a question, οὐ μ., ι Co 9¹²; after a neg.. Mt 10⁶, al.; θέλω (εὐδοκῶ) μ., ι Co 14⁵, ιι Co 5⁸; ζηλῶ, ι Co 14¹; c. subst., τ. σκότος ἤ τ. φῶς, Jo 3¹⁹; μ. δέ, Ga 4⁹. III. Superl., μάλιστα, *most, most of all, above all :* Ac 20³⁸ 25²⁶, Ga 6¹⁰, Phl 4²², ι Ti 4¹⁰ 5⁸, ¹⁷, ιι Ti 4¹³, Tit 1¹⁰, Phm ¹⁶, ιι Pe 2¹⁰; μ. γνώστης, Ac 26³.

μαλακία -ας, ἡ (< μαλακός), [in LXX chiefly for חֳלִי, De 7¹⁵ 28⁶¹, Is 38⁹ 53³, al.;] 1. prop., *softness, effeminacy* (Hdt., Thuc., al.). 2. In NT, as in LXX, = ἀσθένεια, *weakness, sickness :* νόσος καὶ μ., Mt 4²³ 9³⁵ 10¹.†

SYN.: v.s. ἀσθένεια.

μαλακός, -ή, -όν, [in LXX: Pr 25¹⁵ (רַךְ) 26²² (כְּמִתְלַהֲמִים) *;] *soft;* 1. prop., to the touch (opp. to σκληρός) : of clothing, pl., Mt 11⁸, Lk 7²⁵. 2. Of persons and their mode of living; (a) *mild, gentle;* (b) *soft, effeminate :* ι Co 6⁹ (prob. in obscene sense, cf. Deiss., *LAE,* 150₄; MM, xvi; Zorell, s.v.).†

Μαλελεήλ (T, Μελ-), ὁ (Heb. מַהֲלַלְאֵל), *Mahalaleel :* Lk 3³⁷.†

μάλιστα, v.s. μάλα.

μᾶλλον, v.s. μάλα.

Μάλχος, -ου, ὁ (Hellenistic form of Heb. מֶלֶךְ), *Malchus :* Jo 18¹⁰.†

** μάμμη, -ης, ἡ (onomatop.), [in LXX: ιν Mac 16⁹ *;] 1. in cl., a child's name for *mother.* 2. In late Gk. (= cl., τήθη), a *grandmother :* (LXX, l.c.), ιι Ti 1⁵.†

*† μαμωνᾶς (Rec. μαμμ-), -ᾶ (Bl., § 7, 4), ὁ (Aram. מָמוֹנָא), *mammon, riches :* Mt 6²⁴, Lk 16⁹, ¹¹, ¹³.†

Μαναήν, ὁ (Heb. מְנַחֵם), *Manaen :* Ac 13¹.†

Μανασσῆς, -ῆ, ὁ (Heb. מְנַשֶּׁה), *Manasseh ;* 1. (a) the first-born son of Joseph; (b) the tribe which bore his name : Re 7⁶. 2. King of Judah : Mt 1¹⁰.†

μανθάνω, [in LXX chiefly for למד] 1. *to learn,* esp. by inquiry : absol., ι Co 14³¹, ι Ti 2¹¹, ιι Ti 3⁷; c. acc. rei, Jo 7¹⁵ (sc. αὐτά), Ro 16¹⁷, ι Co 14³⁵, Phl 4⁹, ιι Ti 3¹⁴, Re 14³; seq. quaes. indir., Mt 9¹³; Χριστόν, Eph 4²⁰ (*ICC,* in l.); seq. ἀπό, c. gen. rei, Mt 24³², Mk 13²⁸; ἀπό, c. gen. pers., Mt 11²⁹, Col 1⁷; παρά, c. gen. pers., ιι Ti 3¹⁴; ἐν, c. dat. pers., ι Co 4⁶; "point" aorist (M, *Pr.,* 117), *to ascertain,* seq. ὅτι, Ac 23²⁷; c. acc. seq. ἀπό, Ga 3². 2. *to learn* by use and practice, *acquire the habit of, be accustomed to :* c. inf. (Bl., § 69, 4), ι Ti 5⁴, Tit 3¹⁴; id. c. nom. in pred. (Bl., § 72, 1), Phl 4¹¹; c. acc. rei seq. ἀπό, He 5⁸; ἀργαὶ μανθάνουσιν (EV, *they learn to be idle ;* Bl., § 73, 5; Field, *Notes,* 210), ι Ti 5¹³.†

μανία, -ας, ή (< μαίνομαι), [in LXX: Ho 9⁷'⁸ מִשְׁטֵמָה), Wi 5⁴; al.;] *frenzy, madness:* Ac 26²⁴.†

μάννα, τό, (in FlJ, also ή), indecl. [in LXX: τὸ μάν, Ex 16³¹ ᶠᶠ·, elsewhere τ. μάννα, Nu 11⁶ ᶠᶠ·, al. (מָן, Aram. מַנָּא);] *manna:* Jo 6³¹' ⁴⁹, He 9⁴; symb., Re 2¹⁷.†

μαντεύομαι (< μαντίς, *a seer, diviner*), [in LXX for קסם, De 18¹⁰, al.;] *to divine, practise divination:* Ac 16¹⁶.τ SYN.: προφητεύω, q.v., in distinction from which μ. is used in LXX and NT only of false prophets and those who practise the heathen arts of divination and soothsaying (cf. 1 Ki 28⁸, and v. Tr., Syn., § vi).

μαραίνω, [in LXX: Jb 15³⁰ (יָבֵשׁ pi.), 24²⁴, Wi 2⁸ 19²¹ *;] in cl., 1. prop., *to quench* fire; pass., of fire, *to die away, go out.* 2. In various relations, *to quench, waste, wear out* (cf. Wi 19²¹); pass., *to waste away;* in later writers (Plut., Luc., al.), of the withering of flowers and herbage (act., Jb 15³⁰; pass., ib 24²⁴, Wi 2⁸): Ja 1¹¹ (cf. ἀμάραντον).†

μαρὰν ἀθά (Rec. μαραναθά; Aram.: on the original form v. Dalman, *Gr.*, § 41, 1; 74, 3; *Words,* 328), *Maran atha,* i.e. *the Lord cometh* (but v. Dalman, ll. c.; Field, *Notes,* 180; *ICC,* in l.): ꞏ Co 16²²; on the division of the words and the sense " our Lord, come !ꞏ v. Peake, *Comm.*, in l., Zahn, *Intr.*, I, pp. 303 ff. ₁₃; MM, *VGT,* s.v.†

***μαργαρίτης,** -ου, ὁ, *a pearl:* Mt 13⁴⁵'⁴⁶, 1 Ti 2⁹, Re 17⁴ 18¹²'¹⁶ 21²¹ (-ῖται, WH); proverbially, Mt 7⁶.†

Μάρθα, -ας (Bl., § 7, 2), ή (Aram. מָרְתָא), *Martha:* Lk 10³⁸'⁴⁰'⁴¹, Jo 11¹' ⁵' ¹⁹ ᶠᶠ. 12².†

Μαρία, -ας (Hellenized form), and **Μαριάμ,** indecl., ή (Aram. מִרְיָם; Heb. (MT) מִרְיָם), *Mary.* In NT; 1. the mother of Jesus: Mt 1¹⁶ ᶠᶠ· 2¹¹ 13⁵⁵, Mk 6³, Lk 1²⁷ ᶠᶠ. 2⁵'¹⁶'¹⁹'³⁴, Ac 1¹⁴. 2. *M. Magdalene* (q.v.). 3. The wife of Clopas (Jo 19²⁵) and mother of James the little, and Joses: Mt 27⁵⁶'⁶¹ 28¹, Mk 15⁴⁰'⁴⁷ 16¹ (v. Turner, *SNT,* pp. 60 f.), Lk 24¹⁰. 4. The sister of Martha and Lazarus: Lk 10³⁹'⁴⁹, Jo 11¹'²'¹⁹ᶠᶠ. 12³. 5. The mother of John Mark: Ac 12¹². 6. A Christian greeted by St. Paul: Ro 16⁶ (on the signification of the name, v. Zorell, s.v.; on the use of the alternative forms in NT, *DB,* iii, 278 bₙ).†

Μάρκος, -ου, ὁ, *Mark:* Mk., *tit.*, Ac 12¹²'²⁵ 15³⁷'³⁹, Col 4¹⁰, II Ti 4¹¹, Phm ²⁴, I Pe 5¹³ (v. Swete, *Mk.*, *Intr.*, xiii ff.; *DB,* iii, 245 ff).†

****μάρμαρος,** -ου, ὁ (< μαρμαίρω, *to glisten*), [in LXX: Ep. Je ⁷² *;] 1. any *crystalline stone* (Hom., Eur., al.). 2. In later writers, *marble:* Re 18¹².†

μάρτυρ, v.s. μάρτυς.

μαρτυρέω, -ῶ (< μάρτυς), [in LXX chiefly for עֵד (Ge 31⁴⁷'⁴⁸, al.), also for עוד hi. (Ge 43³, La 2¹³), ענה (Nu 35³⁰);] (a) prop., *to be a witness, bear witness, testify:* absol. (Pind., al.), Jo 15²⁷, Ac 26⁵; parenthetical (Bl., § 79, 7; MM, xvi), II Co 8³; c. dat. pers. (comm. et incomm.; Bl., § 37, 2), Ac 22⁵, He 10¹⁵; id. seq. ὅτι, Mt 23³¹,

Ro 10², al.; acc. et inf., Ac 10⁴³; c. acc. rei (cl.), Jo 3¹¹, Re 22¹⁶, ²⁰;
c. acc. cogn., seq. περί, Jo 5³², ι Jo 5¹⁰; c. dat. rei, Jo 5³³, Ac 14³, al.;
seq. περί, c. gen. (pers. et rei), Jo 1⁷, ⁸, ¹⁵ 2²⁵ 18²³ 21²⁴, al.; id. seq.
ὅτι, Jo 5³⁶ 7⁷; ὅτι, Jo 1³⁴ 4⁴⁴ al.; ὅτι recit., Jo 4³⁹; κατά seq. ὅτι,
ι Co 15¹⁵; pass., He 7⁸; ptcp., Ro 3²¹; impers., He 7¹⁷; (b) in late
Gk., to witness favourably, give a good report, approve (Bl., § 54, 3;
MM, xvi; Deiss., BS, 265): c. dat. pers., Lk 4²²; seq. ἐπί, c. dat. rei,
He 11⁴; pass., Ac 6³; seq. ἐν, ι Ti 5¹⁰, He 11²; διά, c. gen. rei, He 11³⁹;
ὑπό, c. gen. pers., Ac 10²², al.; impers., ιιι Jo¹² (cf. ἐπι-, συν-επι-,
κατα-, συν-μαρτυρέω).

μαρτυρία, -ας, ἡ (< μαρτυρέω), [in LXX: Ge 31⁴⁷ R (שָׂהֲדוּתָא),
Ex 20¹⁶, De 5²⁰ ⁽¹⁷⁾, Pr 25¹⁸, Ps 18 (19)⁷ (עֵד, עֵדוּת), Pr 12¹⁹, Si
34 (31)²³, ²⁴, ιν Mac 6³² *;] witness, testimony, evidence: Mk 14⁵⁶,
Lk 22⁷¹, Jo 5³⁴ 19³⁵ 21²⁴, ι Ti 3⁷, Tit 1¹³, ιιι Jo¹², Re 11⁷; c. gen.
subj., Mk 14⁵⁹, Jo 8¹⁷ (LXX aliter), ι Jo 5⁹; seq. κατά, c. gen. pers.,
Mk 14⁵⁵; esp. of witness concerning Christ and divine things, Jo 1⁷
3¹¹, ³², ³³ 5³², ³⁶, Re 6⁹; c. gen. subj., Jo 1¹⁹ 5³¹ 8¹³, ¹⁴, Ac 22¹⁸, ι Jo 5⁹⁻¹¹,
Re 12¹¹; c. gen. obj., Re 1², ⁹ 12¹⁷ 19¹⁰, 20⁴; μ. ἔχειν, Re 6⁹ 12¹⁷ 19¹⁰.†

μαρτύριον, -ου, τό (< μάρτυρ), [in LXX chiefly for מוֹעֵד, also for
עֵדָה, עֵדוּת and cogn. forms;] a testimony, witness, proof (Hdt.,
Thuc., al.): c. gen. subj., ιι Co 1¹², ιι Th 1¹⁰; c. gen. obj., Ac 4³³,
ι Co 1⁶ 2¹ (WH, txt., R, txt., μυστήριον); ιι Ti 1⁸; εἰς μ., Mt 8⁴ 10¹⁸
24¹⁴, Mk 1⁴⁴ 6¹¹ 13⁹, Lk 5¹⁴ 9⁵ 21¹³, He 3⁵, Ja 5³; τὸ μ. καιροῖς ἰδίοις
(CGT, in l.), ι Ti 2⁶; ἡ σκηνὴ τοῦ μ. (LXX for אֹהֶל מוֹעֵד), Ac 7⁴⁴,
Re 15⁵.†

** μαρτύρομαι (< μάρτυρ), [in LXX: Jth 7²⁸, ι Mac 2⁵⁶ א *;] to
summon as witness (M, Th., 25 f.; Hort., ι Pe., 53 f.; Lft., Notes, 29;
Ga 203), hence, (a) to protest, affirm solemnly: seq. ὅτι, Ac 20²⁶,
Ga 5³; (b) to adjure, beseech: c. dat. pers., Ac 26²²; c. acc. et inf.,
Eph 4¹⁷; seq. εἰς, ι Th 2¹² (cf. δια-, προ-μαρτύρομαι).†

μάρτυς (Æolic μάρτυρ), -υρος, ὁ (also ἡ), [in LXX for עֵד;] a
witness: Ac 10⁴¹, ι Ti 6¹², ιι Ti 2², He 12¹ (Westc., in l.); in forensic
sense, Mt 18¹⁶ 26⁶⁵, Mk 14⁶³, Ac 6¹³ 7⁵⁸, ιι Co 13¹, ι Ti 5¹⁹, He 10²⁸;
c. gen. obj., Lk 24⁴⁸, Ac 1²² 2³² 3¹⁵ 5³² 10³⁹ 26¹⁶, ι Pe 5¹; c. gen. poss.,
Ac 1⁸ 13³¹, Re 11³; c. dat. pers., Lk 11⁴⁸, Ac 22¹⁵; of Christ, Re 1⁵
3¹⁴; of God, Ro 1⁹, ιι Co 1²³, Phl 1⁸, ι Th 2⁵, ¹⁰; of those who have
witnessed for Christ by their death (in later Xn. lit., martyr: Swete,
Ap., 35), Ac 22²⁰, Re 2¹³ 17⁶.†

μασάομαι (Rec. μασσ-), -ῶμαι (Aristoph. and late writers, but not
in Trag. or in good Att. prose), [in LXX: Jb 30⁴ (לָחַם), Si 19⁹ A *;] to
bite, chew: Re 16¹⁰.†

μασθός, v.s. μαστός.

μαστιγόω, -ῶ (< μάστιξ), [in LXX chiefly for נכה hi.;] to scourge:

c. acc., Mt 10¹⁷ 20¹⁹ 23³⁴, Mk 10³⁴, Lk 18³³, Jo 19¹ ; metaph., He 12⁶ (cf. Pr 3¹², Je 5³, Jth 8²⁷).†

μαστίζω (Ep. and late prose = Att. μαστιγόω), [in LXX : Nu 22²⁵ (נכה hi.), Wi 5¹¹, ii Mac 2²¹ *;] *to whip, scourge :* c. acc., Ac 22²⁵.†

μάστιξ, -ιγος, ἡ, [in LXX for שׁוֹט, etc. ;] *a whip, scourge :* Ac 22²⁴, He 11³⁶ ; metaph., of disease or suffering as a divine chastisement (cf. Ps 88 (89)³³, Pr 3¹², ii Mac 9¹¹), Mk 3¹⁰ 5²⁹, ³⁴, Lk 7²¹.†

μαστός, -οῦ, ὁ, [in LXX chiefly for שַׁד ;] *the breast :* pl., Lk 11²⁷ 23²⁹, Re 1¹³ (T, μασθοῖς ; WH, *App.*, 149 ; L, μαζοῖς).†

† ματαιολογία, -ας, ἡ (< ματαιολόγος), *idle or foolish talk :* i Ti 1⁶.†

† ματαιολόγος, -ον (< μάταιος, λέγω), *talking idly :* Tit 1¹⁰.†

μάταιος, -ον (as in Att., but -αία, -αιον, i Co 15¹⁷, i Pe 1¹⁸ ; < μάτην), [in LXX for שָׁוְא, הֶבֶל, כָּזָב, etc. ;] *vain, useless :* ἀνωφελὴς κ. μ., Tit 3⁹ ; πίστις, i Co 15¹⁷ ; θρησκεία, Ja 1²⁶ ; διαλογισμοί, i Co 3²⁰ (LXX) ; ἀναστροφή, i Pe 1¹⁸ ; of idols and heathen gods, τὰ μ. (Je 2⁵, iv Ki 17¹⁵, al.) : Ac 14¹⁵.

SYN. : κενός, q.v.

† ματαιότης, -ητος, ἡ (< μάταιος), [in LXX for הֶבֶל, Ps 30 (31)⁶ 38 (39)⁵ 61 (62)⁹, al., and nearly 40 times in Ec ; for שָׁוְא, Ps 25⁴, al. ; רִיק, etc. ;] *vanity, emptiness, frailty, folly :* Ro 8²⁰, ii Pe 2¹⁸ ; τ. νοός, Eph 4¹⁷ (elsewhere only in Pollux, 6, 134, and Eccl.).†

† ματαιόω, -ῶ (< μάταιος), [in LXX : iv Ki 17¹⁵, Je 2⁵, al. (הבל), etc. ;] *to make vain, foolish :* Ro 1²¹.†

μάτην (prop. acc. of μάτη, *a fault, folly*), adv., [in LXX for הֶבֶל, שָׁוְא, etc. ;] *in vain, to no purpose :* Mt 15⁹, Mk 7⁷ (LXX).†

Ματθαῖος, -άν, -ίας, v.s. Μαθθ-.

Ματθάτ (v.s. Μαθθάτ), *Matthat :* Lk 3²⁴ (T, Μαθθάθ).†

Ματταθά, ὁ, indecl. (Heb. מַתַּתָּה), *Mattatha :* Lk 3³¹.†

Ματταθίας, -ου, ὁ, *Mattathias* (cf. Μαθθίας) : Lk 3²⁵, ²⁶.†

μάχαιρα, -ης (Att. -ας ; v. WH, *App.*, 156ª ; Bl., § 7, 1), ἡ, [in LXX chiefly for חֶרֶב ; also for מַאֲכֶלֶת, etc. ;] 1. (in Hom., al.) *a large knife or dirk,* for sacrificial purposes (Ge 22⁶, ¹⁰, Jg 19²⁹ A). 2. *a short sword or dagger* (as disting. from ῥομφαία, a large broad sword and ξίφος, a straight sword for thrusting) : Mt 26⁴⁷ ff., Mk 14⁴³, ⁴⁷, ⁴⁸, Lk 22³⁶ ff., Jo 18¹⁰, ¹¹, Ac 16²⁷, He 11³⁷, Re 6⁴ 13¹⁰, ¹⁴ ; στόμα μαχαίρης (as in Heb. פִּי חֶרֶב, Ge 34²⁶, al.), *the edge of the sword :* Lk 21²⁴, He 11³⁴ ; μ. δίστομος, He 4¹² ; ἀναιρεῖν μαχαίρῃ, Ac 12² ; τὴν μ. φορεῖν, Ro 13⁴. Metaph., Mt 10³⁴ (opp. to εἰρήνη), Ro 8³⁵ ; μ. τοῦ πνεύματος, Eph 6¹⁷.†

μάχη, -ης, ἡ (< μάχομαι), [in LXX chiefly for רִיב ;] 1. *a fight.* 2. *a strife, contention, quarrel :* ii Co 7⁵, ii Ti 2²³, Ja 4¹ ; pl., Tit 3⁹.†

μάχομαι, [in LXX chiefly for רִיב, also for נצה ni., etc. ;] 1. *to fight*: Ac 7²⁶. 2. *to quarrel, dispute*: ιι Ti 2²⁴, Ja 4²; πρὸς ἀλλήλους, Jo 6⁵² (cf. δια-μάχομαι).†

μεγαλ-αυχέω, -ῶ (= μεγάλα αὐχέω), [in LXX: Ez 16⁵⁰ (גָּבַהּ), al.;] *to boast great things*: Ja 3⁵ (Rec. for μεγάλα αὐχεῖ, WH).†

μεγαλεῖος, -εία, -εῖον (< μέγας), [in LXX: Ps 70 (71)¹⁹ (גָּדוֹל), al., freq. in Si;] *magnificent, splendid* (Xen., Plut., al.): Ac 2¹¹.†

μεγαλειότης, -ητος, ἡ (< μεγαλεῖος), [in LXX: Je 40 (33)⁹ (תִּפְאָרֶת), Da LXX 7²⁷, ι Es 1⁵ 4⁴⁰*;] *splendour, magnificence*: Lk 9⁴³, Ac 19²⁷, ιι Pe 1¹⁶ (freq. in π. as a ceremonial title, MM, xvi).†

μεγαλοπρεπής, ές (= μεγάλῳ πρέπων), [in LXX: De 33²⁶ (גַּאֲוָה), ιι Mac 8¹⁵ 15¹³, ιιι Mac 2⁹*;] *befitting a great man, magnificent, majestic*: ιι Pe 1¹⁷ (cf. MM, xvi).†

μεγαλύνω (< μέγας), [in LXX chiefly for גָּדַל pi., hi.;] 1. *to make great*: Mt 23⁵, Lk 1⁵⁸. 2. *to declare great, extol, magnify*: Lk 1⁴⁶, Ac 5¹³ 10⁴⁶ 19¹⁷, ιι Co 10¹⁵; pass., seq. ἐν, Phl 1²⁰.†

μεγάλως, adv., [in LXX for גָּדוֹל, etc.;] *greatly*: Phl 4¹⁰.†

† μεγαλωσύνη, -ης, ἡ (< μέγας), [in LXX chiefly for גְּדֻלָּה and cogn. forms, ιι Ki 7²³, Ps 144 (145)³, al.;] *greatness, majesty*: He 1³ 8¹, Ju ²⁵ (elsewhere Eccl. only).†

μέγας, μεγάλη, μέγα, [in LXX chiefly for גָּדוֹל, also for רַב, מֶרְכָּבָה (incl. μείζων), רֹב (μέγιστος);] *great*; 1. of external form, bodily size, measure, extent: λίθος, Mt 27⁶⁰; δράκων, Re 12³; ἰχθῦς, Jo 21¹¹; πόλις, Re 11⁸; μάχαιρα, Re 6⁴, al. 2. Of intensity and degree: δύναμις, Ac 4³³; φόβος, Mk 4⁴¹; ἀγάπη, Jo 15¹³; ἄνεμος, ib. 6¹⁸; κραυγή, Ac 23⁹; φῶς, Mt 4¹⁶; πυρετός, Lk 4³⁸; θλίψις, Mt 24²¹. 3. Of rank; (*a*) of persons: θεός (MM, xvi), Tit 2¹³; Ἄρτεμις, Ac 19²⁷; compar. (v. infr.), Mt 18¹ (cf. Dalman, *Words*, 113 f.); neut. for masc. (Bl., § 32, 1), Mt 12⁶; (*b*) of things: ἁμαρτία, Jo 19¹¹; μυστήριον, Eph 5³²; = μεγίστη (v. infr., and cf. Field, *Notes*, 16 f.), Mt 22³⁶; compar. for superl. (M, *Pr.*, 78), ι Co 13¹³. 4. (*a*) Compar., μείζων: Mt 11¹¹ 23¹⁷, al.; neut. pl., μείζονα, contr. μείζω, Jo 1⁵¹; double compar., μειζότερος (M, *Pr.*, 236; Bl., § 11, 4), ιιι Jo ⁴; (*b*) superl., μέγιστος (Deiss., *BS*, 365), ιι Pe 1⁴.

μέγεθος, -ους, τό (< μέγας), [in LXX chiefly for קוֹמָה;] *greatness*: Eph 1¹⁹ (cf. MM, xvi, s.v. μέγας).†

† μεγιστάν, -ᾶνος, ὁ (< μέγιστος), [in LXX chiefly for שַׂר, Je 24⁸, al.; רַבְרְבָן, Da LXX τη 5²³, al.; freq. in Si (sing., 4⁷);] usually pl., οἱ μ., *the chief men, nobles* (Manetho, FlJ, al.): Mk 6²¹, Re 6¹⁵ 18²³.†

μέγιστος, v.s. μέγας.

**† μεθερμηνεύω, [in LXX: Si prol. ²³*;] *to translate, interpret*: Mt 1²³, Mk 5⁴¹ 15²², ³⁴, Jo 1³⁸, ⁴², Ac 4³⁶ 13⁸ (cf. ἑρμηνεύω).†

μέθη, -ης, ἡ, [in LXX chiefly for שֵׁכָר and cognate forms;] *drunkenness*: Lk 21³⁴; pl., Ro 13¹³, Ga 5²¹.†

SYN.: v.s. κῶμος.

μεθ-ίστημι and (late form, 1 Co 13²) μεθιστάνω, [in LXX for סור hi., etc.;] trans. in pres., impf., fut. and aor. 1, *to change, remove*: c. acc. rei, ὄρη, 1 Co 13² (cf. Is 54¹⁰); c. acc. pers.: seq. εἰς, Col 1¹³; seq. ἐκ, pass., Lk 16⁴; of causing death (cf. similar intrans. sense, Eur., *Alc.*, 21, al.), Ac 13²². Metaph. (cf. τ. καρδίαν μ., Jos 14⁸), c. acc. pers., *to pervert*: Ac 19²⁶.†

*†μεθ-οδία (Rec. -εία; cf. Bl., § 3, 5), -ας, ἡ (< †μεθοδεύω, 1. *to treat by rule*. 2. *to employ craft*: iv Ki 19²⁷*), *craft, deceit*: Eph 4¹⁴ 6¹¹ (not found elsewhere; v. AR, in l.).†

μεθ-όριον, -ου, τό (neut. of μεθόριος, -α, -ον), [in LXX: Jos 19²⁷ A*;] Rec. for ὅριον (q.v.), *a border, boundary*: Mk 7²⁴.†

μεθύσκω, [in LXX: Ps 22 (23)⁵ (רוה), Pr 4¹⁷ (שחה), etc.;] causal of μεθύω, *to make drunk, intoxicate*; pass., *to get drunk*: Lk 12⁴⁵, Eph 5¹⁸, 1 Th 5⁷.†

μέθυσος, -α, -ον (also -ος, -ον; prop., only of women, but in late writers also = μεθυστικός, of men), [in LXX: Pr 23²¹ (סבא) 26⁹ (שכור), Si 19¹ 26⁸, iv Mac 2⁷*;] *drunken*: 1 Co 5¹¹ 6¹⁰.†

μεθύω (< μέθυ, *wine*, cf. μέθη), [in LXX chiefly for שכר, רוה;] *to be drunken*: Mt 24⁴⁹, Jo 2¹⁰, Ac 2¹⁵, 1 Co 11²¹, 1 Th 5⁷; metaph., Re 17²,⁶.†

μεῖγμα, -τος, τό, v.s. μίγμα, and cf. Bl., § 3, 5.

μείγνυμι, v.s. μίγνυμι, and cf. Bl., § 3, 5.

μειζότερος, v.s. μέγας.

μείζων, v.s. μέγας.

μέλαν, τό, v.s. μέλας.

μέλας, -αινα, -αν, gen., -ανος, -αίνης, -ανος, [in LXX: Ca 1⁵, Za 6² (שחר), etc.;] *black*: Re 6⁵, ¹²; opp. to λευκός, Mt 5³⁶; neut., τὸ μ., *ink*: ii Co 3³, ii Jo ¹², iii Jo ¹³.†

Μελεά (Rec. -ᾶς, gen., -ᾶ), indecl., ὁ (Heb. מלאה), *Melea*: Lk 3³¹.†

μέλει, v.s. μέλω.

Μελελεήλ, v.s. Μαλ-.

μελετάω, -ῶ (< μελέτη, *care*), [in LXX chiefly for הגה;] 1. c. gen., *to care for* (Hes.). 2. C. acc. *to attend to, practise*: 1 Ti 4¹⁵ (RV, *be diligent in*; cf. Souter in *Exp.*, viii, vi, 429, but v. infr.). 3. *to study, ponder*: Ac 4²⁵ (LXX), 1 Ti 4¹⁵ (AV, *meditate on*; cf. *CGT*, in l., but v. supr.; cf. προ-μελετάω).†

μέλι, -τος, τό, [in LXX freq. (Ge 43¹¹, al.) for דבש; for נפת, Pr 5³;] *honey*: Re 10⁹, ¹⁰; ἄγριον (q.v.), Mt 3⁴, Mk 1⁶.†

*†μελίσσιος, -α, -ον (elsewhere †-αιος, -ειος; < μέλισσα, *a bee*, cf. μέλι), *made by bees*: Lk 24⁴² (Rec., WH, R, mg.).†

Μελίτη, (Rec., R, txt.), Μελιτήνη (WH, R, mg., v. WH, *App.*, 160), *Melita, Melitene* (mod. *Malta*): Ac 28¹.†

μέλλω, [in LXX: Jb 3⁸ (עתיד) 19²⁵ (אחרון); elsewhere for fut., and freq. in Wi, ii, iv Mac;] *to be about to* be or do; 1. c. inf. (Bl., § 62, 4; 68, 2; M, *Pr.*, 114); (*a*) of intending or being about to do of one's own free will: c. inf. praes., Mt 2¹³, Lk 10¹, Ac 3³ 5³⁵, He 8⁵, II Pe 1¹² (Field, *Notes*, 240), al.; c. inf. aor. (Bl., § 58, 3), Ac 12⁶, Re 3¹⁶; (*b*) of compulsion, necessity or certainty: c. inf. praes., Mt 16²⁷, Lk 9³¹, Jo 6⁷¹, Ro 4²⁴, al.; c. inf. aor., Ro 8¹⁸, Ga 3²³, Re 3² 12⁴. 2. Ptcp., ὁ μέλλων: absol., Ro 8³⁸, I Co 3²²; τὰ μ., Col 2¹⁷; εἰς τὸ μ. (Field, *Notes*, 65); c. subst., Mt 3⁷ 12³² (ὁ αἰὼν ὁ μ.; LXX for עַד), Ac 24²⁵, I Ti 4⁸, He 2⁵, al.

μέλος, -ους, τό, [in LXX chiefly for נתח;] a *member, limb* of the body: I Co 12¹⁴,¹⁹,²⁶, Eph 4¹⁶ (WH, mg.), Ja 3⁵; pl. (as always in cl.), τὰ μ.: Mt 5²⁹,³⁰, Ro 6¹³,¹⁹ 7⁵,²³ 12⁴, I Co 12¹² ff., Col 3⁵, Ja 3⁶ 4¹. Metaph., πόρνης, I Co 6¹⁵; of Christians, μ. ἀλλήλων, Ro 12⁵, Eph 4²⁵; Χριστοῦ, I Co 6¹⁵; σώματος Χριστοῦ, I Co 12²⁷, Eph 5³⁰.†

Μελχεί (Rec. -χί), indecl., ὁ (Heb. מַלְכִּי), *Melchi*: Lk 3²⁴,²⁸.†

Μελχισεδέκ, indecl., ὁ (Heb. מַלְכִּי צֶדֶק), *Melchizedek*: He 5⁶,¹⁰ 6²⁰ 7¹,¹⁰ ¹¹,¹⁵,¹⁷.†

μέλω, [in LXX: Jb 22³ (חָפֵץ), To 10⁵, Wi 12¹³, I Mac 14⁴²,⁴³ *;] 1. intrans., *to be an object of care, be a care* (-ήσω, perh. the true reading in II Pe 1¹²; v. Mayor in l.; Field, *Notes*, p. 240); commonly in third pers.: c. dat. pers., Ac 18¹⁷; very freq. impers., I Co 7³¹; seq. ὅτι, Mk 4³⁸, Lk 10⁴⁰; c. gen. rei (as freq. in Att.), I Co 9⁹; seq. περί, Mt 22¹⁶, Mk 12¹⁴, Jo 10¹³ 12⁶, I Pe 5⁷. 2. Trans., in act. and mid., *to care for* (not in LXX or NT).†

***†μεμβράνα**, -ας, ἡ (Lat. *membrana*), *parchment*: II Ti 4¹³.†

****μέμφομαι**, [in LXX: Si 11⁷ 41⁷, II Mac 2⁷*;] *to blame, find fault*: absol., Ro 9¹⁹; c. acc., αὐτούς (WH, txt.; αὐτοῖς, Rec., WH, mg.; on rendering with αὐτοῖς v. Westc., in l.), He 8⁸.†

***μεμψίμοιρος**, -ον (< μέμφομαι, + μοῖρα, *fate, lot*), *complaining of one's fate, querulous*: Ju 16.†

μέν, conjunctive particle (originally a form of μήν), usually related to a following δέ or other adversative conjunction, and distinguishing the word or clause with which it stands from that which follows. It is generally untranslatable and is not nearly so frequent in NT as in cl. Like δέ, it never stands first in a clause. 1. Answered by δέ or some other particle: μὲν . . . δέ, *indeed . . . but*, Mt 3¹¹, Lk 3¹⁶, al.; with pronouns, ὃς μὲν . . . ὃς δέ, *one . . . another*, Mt 21³⁵, al.; pl., Phl 1¹⁶,¹⁷; ὃ μὲν . . . ὃ δὲ . . . ὃ δέ, *some . . . some . . . some*, Mt 13⁸; τοῦτο μὲν . . . τοῦτο δέ, *partly . . . partly*, He 10³³; μὲν . . . ἔπειτα, Jo 11⁶; μὲν . . . καί, Lk 8⁵. 2. μέν *solitarium*, answered by no other particle: πρῶτον μέν (Bl., l.c.), Ro 1⁸ 3², I Co 11¹⁸; μὲν οὖν in narrative, summing up what precedes or introducing something further (Bl., § 78, 5), *so then, rather, nay rather*: Lk 11²⁸ (WH, μενοῦν), Ac 1⁶ 9³¹, al.; μὲν οὖν γε (Phl 3⁸, WH): v.s. μενοῦνγε.

Μεννά, (L, Μεννᾶς, -ᾶ; Rec. Μαϊνάν) ὁ, *Menna*: Lk 3³¹.†

μεν-οῦν = μὲν οὖν, v.s. μέν.

μεν-οῦν-γε = μὲν οὖν γε, *nay rather*: Ro 9²⁰ 10¹⁸, Phl 3⁸.†

μέν-τοι = μέν τοι, yet, however : Jo 4²⁷, al. ; εἰ μ., Ja 2⁸ (if indeed).
μένω, [in LXX for עָמַד, קוּם, etc.;] to stay, abide, remain.
1. Intrans.; (i) of place : seq. ἐν, Lk 8²⁷, al.; παρά, c. dat. pers., Jo 1⁴⁰,
al.; σύν, Lk 1⁵⁶; καθ᾽ ἑαυτόν, Ac 28¹⁶; c. adv., ἐκεῖ, Mt 10¹¹; ὧδε,
Mt 26³⁸; metaph., ι Jo 2¹⁹; of the Holy Spirit, Jo 1³²,³³ 14¹⁷; of
Christ, Jo 6⁵⁶ 15⁴, al.; ὁ θεός, ι Jo 4¹⁰, conversely, of Christians,
Jo 6⁵⁶ 15⁴, ι Jo 4¹⁵, al.; ὁ λόγος τ. θεοῦ, ι Jo 2¹⁴; ἡ ἀλήθεια, ΙΙ Jo 2, al.
(ii) Of time; (a) of persons : Phl 1²⁵; seq. εἰς τ. αἰῶνα Jo 12³⁴, He 7²⁴,
ι Jo 2¹⁷; ὀλίγον, Re 17¹⁰; ἕως ἔρχομαι, Jo 21²²,²³; (b) of things, lasting
or enduring: cities, Mt 11²³, He 13¹⁴; λόγος θεοῦ, ι Pe 1²³; ἁμαρτία,
Jo 9⁴¹.   (iii) Of condition : c. pred., μόνος, Jo 12²⁴; ἄγαμος, ι Co 7¹¹;
πιστός, ΙΙ Ti 2¹³; ἱερεύς, He 7³; c. adv., οὕτως, ι Co 7⁴⁰; ὡς κἀγώ, ib. ⁸;
seq. ἐν, ib. ²⁰,²⁴. 2. Trans. (Bl., § 34, 1; Field, Notes, 132): c. acc.
pers., Ac 20⁵,²³ (cf. ἀι α-, δια-, ἐν-, ἐπι-, κατα-, παρα-, συν-παρα-, περι-,
προσ-, ὑπο-μένω).

μερίζω (< μέρος), [in LXX chiefly for חלק;] to divide; (a) to
divide into parts : metaph., pass., ι Co 7³⁴ (WH, R, mg.), 34 (Rec., R, txt.) (on
reading and punctuation, v. ICC, in l.); μεμέρισται ὁ Χριστός, ι Co 1¹³;
as in late authors, of factional division (cf. Polyb., viii, 23, 9), καθ᾽
ἑαυτοῦ, Mt 12²⁵; ἐφ᾽ ἑαυτόν, ib. ²⁶, Mk 3²⁴⁻²⁶; (b) to distribute : c. acc.
rei et dat. pers., Mk 6⁴¹; as in later usage (cf. Polyb., xi, 28, 9), to
bestow : Ro 12³, ι Co 7¹⁷, ΙΙ Co 10¹³, He 7²; mid., c. acc. rei seq. μετά,
Lk 12¹³ (cf. δια-, συμ-μερίζω).†

μέριμνα, -ης, ἡ, [in LXX: Ps 54 (55)²² (יְהָב), Jb 11¹⁸, Si 30²⁴,
al;] (in cl. chiefly poët.) care, anxiety : ι Pe 5⁷; pl., Lk 8¹⁴, 21³⁴;
c. gen. obj., Mt 13²², Mk 4¹⁹, ΙΙ Co 11²⁸.†

μεριμνάω, -ῶ (< μέριμνα), [in LXX: Ps 37 (38)¹⁸ (דְּאַג), etc.;]
1. to be anxious : absol., Mt 6²⁷,³¹, Lk 12²⁵; μηδὲν μ., Phl 4⁶; c. dat.
rei, Mt 6²⁵, Lk 12²²; seq. περί, Mt 6²⁸, Lk 10⁴¹ 12²⁶; πῶς, Mt 10¹⁹,
Lk 12¹¹; εἰς τὴν αὔριον, Mt 6³⁴. 2. to care for : c. acc., τὰ τ. κυρίου,
ι Co 7³²⁻³⁴; τὰ τ. κόσμου, ib. ³⁴; τὰ περὶ ὑμῶν, Phl 2²⁰; seq. ὑπέρ,
ι Co 12²⁵; c. gen. (a construction otherwise unknown), ἑαυτῆς (WH;
τὰ ἑ. Rec.; v. Bl., § 36, 7), Mt 6³⁴ (cf. προ-μεριμνάω).†

μερίς, -ίδος, ἡ, [in LXX chiefly for חֵלֶק, חֶלְקָה;] 1. (as in cl.) a
part, portion : Lk 10⁴², Ac 8²¹, ΙΙ Co 6¹⁵, Col 1¹². 2. In later Gk
(v. MM, xvi), as geographical term, a division, district : Ac 16¹².†

μερισμός, -οῦ, ὁ (< μερίζω), [in LXX for מַחְלֹקֶת, מַחְלָקָה, Jos 11²³,
ΙΙ Es 6¹⁸ *;] 1. a dividing, division : ψυχῆς κ. πνεύματος (i.e. between
them or of the things themselves, v. Westc., in l.), He 4¹². 2. a distribution, bestowal (cf. μερίζω, 2); pl., He 2⁴.†

*† μεριστής, -οῦ, ὁ (< μερίζω), a divider : Lk 12¹⁴.†

μέρος, -ους, τό (< μείρομαι), [in LXX chiefly for קָצֶה;] 1. a part,
share, portion : Jo 13⁸, Ac 19²⁷ (Page, in l.), Re 20⁶ 22¹⁹; hence (cl.),
lot, destiny, Mt 24⁵¹, Lk 12⁴⁶, Re 21⁸. 2. a part as opp. to the whole :
Lk 11³⁶, Jo 19²³, Ac 5² 23⁶, Eph 4¹⁶, Re 16¹⁹; c. gen. (of the whole),

MANUAL GREEK LEXICON OF THE NEW TESTAMENT 285

Lk 15¹² 24⁴²; of a party, τ. Φαρισαίων, Ac 23⁹; pl., Jo 21⁶; of the divisions of a province, Mt 2²², Ac 2¹⁰ 19¹ 20²; of the regions belonging to a city, Mt 15²¹ 16¹³, Mk 8¹⁰; c. gen. appos., Eph 4⁹; in adverbial phrases, ἀνὰ (κατὰ) μέρος, 1 Co 14²⁷, He 9⁵; μέρος τι, ἀπὸ μ., in part, Ro 11²⁵ 15¹⁵, ²⁴, 1 Co 11¹⁸, 11 Co 1¹⁴ 2⁵; ἐκ μ., 1 Co 12²⁷, 13⁹, ¹²; τὸ ἐκ μ., ib. ¹⁰. 3. A class or category (in cl. usually ἐν μ. τιθέναι, λαβεῖν, etc.): ἐν μ., in respect of, Col 2¹⁶; ἐν τ. μ. τούτῳ, in this respect, 11 Co 3¹⁰ 9³.†

μεσανύκτιον, v.s. μεσονύκτιος.

μεσημβρία, -ας, ἡ (μέσος, ἡμέρα), [in LXX chiefly for צֹהַר, Ge 3¹⁶, al; also for נֶגֶב, Da LXX 8⁴, ⁹, al.;] 1. noon: Ac 22⁶. 2. the South: Ac 8²⁶.†

*†μεσιτεύω (< μεσίτης), to interpose, mediate, give surety: ὅρκῳ, He 6¹⁷ (MM, ii, iii).†

†μεσίτης, -ου, ὁ (< μέσος), [in LXX: Jb 9³³ (בַּיִן)*;] an arbitrator, mediator: Ga 3¹⁹; c. dupl. gen. pers., θεοῦ κ. ἀνθρώπων, 1 Ti 2⁵; c. gen. rei, διαθήκης, He 8⁶ 9¹⁵ 12²⁴; ὁ δὲ μ. ἑνὸς οὐκ ἔστιν, Ga 3²⁰ (v. Lft., in l.; and for exx. of this word in π., v. MM, xvi).†

μεσο-νύκτιος (on v.l. μεσα-, v. Bl., § 6, 2), -ον (< μέσος, νύξ), [in LXX chiefly for חֲצִי הַלַּיְלָה;] of or at midnight; as subst., neut., τὸ μ., midnight (Arist. and late writers): gen., Lk 11⁵; μέχρι μ., Ac 20⁷; κατὰ τὸ μ., Ac 16²⁵; acc. (Rec., gen.; v. Bl., § 34, 8), Mk 13³⁵.†

Μεσοποταμία, -ας, ἡ (sc. χώρα), Mesopotamia: Ac 2⁹ 7².†

μέσος, -η, -ον, [in LXX chiefly for תָּוֶךְ;] middle, in the middle or midst; 1. prop., as an adj.: Lk 23⁴⁵, Jo 19¹⁸, Ac 1¹⁸; c. gen. pl., Lk 22⁵⁵, Jo 1²⁶; gen. temp. (Bl., § 36, 13), μέσης νυκτός, Mt 25⁶; μ. ἡμέρας, Ac 26¹³. 2. In adverbial phrases, neut., μέσον, τὸ μ., as subst.: ἀνὰ μέσον, c. gen., between (cl.; in LXX: Ge 1⁴, al.), elliptically (but v. M, Pr., 99), 1 Co 6⁵; = ἐν μ., among, in the midst of (Bl., § 39, 2; 40, 8; cf. in LXX: Jos 19¹, Si 27²), Mt 13²⁵, Mk 7³¹, Re 7¹⁷; διὰ μέσου, c. gen., Lk 4³⁰; διὰ μέσον (Rec. -ου, v. Bl., § 42, 1), between, Lk 17¹¹ (ICC, in l.); εἰς τὸ μ. (v.s. εἰς), Mk 3³, Lk 4³⁵ 5¹⁹ 6⁸, Jo 20¹⁹, ²⁶; εἰς μ., Mk 14⁶⁰; ἐν τῷ μ., Mt 14⁶; ἐν μ., Jos 8⁽³, ⁹⁾, Ac 4⁷; c. gen. loc., Mk 6⁴⁷, Lk 21²¹ 22⁵⁵, Ac 17²², He 2¹²(LXX), Re 4⁶ 5⁶ 22²; c. gen. pl., Mt 10¹⁶ 18², ²⁰, Mk 9³⁶, Lk 2⁴⁶ 8⁷ 10³ 22²⁷ 24³⁶, Ac 1¹⁵ 2²² 27²¹, 1 Th 2⁷, Re 1¹³ 2¹ 5⁶ 6⁶; κατὰ μέσον τ. νυκτός, Ac 27²⁷ (Bl., § 47, 6); ἐκ τοῦ μ. (Lft., in l.; Deiss., BS, 252 f.), Col 2¹⁴; ἐκ μ., 11 Th 2⁷; ἐκ τοῦ μ., c. gen., Mt 13⁴⁹, Ac 17³³ 23¹⁰, 1 Co 5², 11 Co 6¹⁷. 3. Neut., μέσον, adverbially, c. gen., in the midst of (v. MM, VGT, s.v.), Mt 14²⁴ (WH, txt., R, mg., aliter), Phl 2¹⁵ (διὰ μέσου—v. supr.—also Jo 8⁵⁹, R, mg.).†

*†μεσότοιχον, -ου, τό (< μέσος, τοῖχος), a partition wall: Eph 2¹⁴ (not elsewhere, but v. LS, s.v. μεσότοιχος).†

*†μεσουράνημα, -τος, τό (< μεσουρανέω, to be in mid-heaven, of the sun at the meridian), the zenith, mid-heaven: Re 8¹³ 14⁶ 19¹⁷.†

μεσόω, -ῶ (< μέσος), [in LXX: μεσούσης τ. νυκτός, Ex 12²⁹ (חָצָה)

etc.;] *to be in the middle*, esp. of time: τ. ἑορτῆς μεσούσης, *in the middle of the feast*, Jo 7¹⁴.†

Μεσσίας, -ου, ὁ (Aram. מְשִׁיחָא = Heb. מָשִׁיחַ = Χριστός, q.v.), *Messiah :* Jo 1⁴² 4²⁵.†

μεστός, -ή, -όν, [in LXX : Na 1¹⁰, Ez 37¹ (מָלֵא), Es 5², Pr 6³⁴ * ;] *full :* c. gen. rei, Jo 19²⁹ 21¹¹, Ja 3⁸ ; metaph., of thoughts and feelings, Mt 23²⁸, Ro 1²⁹ 15¹⁴, II Pe 2¹⁴, Ja 3¹⁷ (cf. Pr, l.c.).†

** μεστόω, -ῶ (< μεστός), [in LXX : III Mac 5¹, ¹⁰ *;] *to fill :* pass., c. gen. rei, Ac 2¹³.†

μετά (before vowel μετ'; on the neglect of elision in certain cases, v. WH, *App.*, 146 ᵇ), prep. c. gen., acc. (in poët. also c. dat.), [in LXX for אֵת, עִם, אַחַר, etc.].

I. C. gen., 1. *among, amid :* Mk 1¹³, Lk 22³⁷ (LXX, ἐν) 24⁵, Jo 18⁵, al.; διωγμῶν, Mk 10³⁰.   2. Of association and companionship, *with* (in which sense it gradually superseded σύν, than which it is much more freq. in NT; cf. Bl., § 42, 3): c. gen. pers., Mt 8¹¹ 20²⁰, Mk 1²⁹ 3⁷, Lk 5³⁰, Jo 3²², Ga 2¹, al. mult.; εἶναι μετά, Mt 5²⁵, Mk 3¹⁴, al.; metaph., of divine help and guidance, Jo 3², Ac 7⁹, Phl 4⁹, al.; opp. to εἶναι κατά, Mt 12³⁰, Lk 11²³ ; in Hellenistic usage (but v. M Pr., 106, 246 f., and cf. M, *Gr.*, II, pp. 466 f.), πολεμεῖν μετά = cl. π., c. dat., *to wage war against* (so LXX for עִם נִלְחַם, I Ki 17³·⁰), Re 2¹⁶, al.; c. gen. rei, χαρᾶς, Mt 13²⁰, Mk 4¹⁶, al. ; ὀργῆς, Mk 3⁵, al.

II. C. acc., 1. of place, *behind, after :* He 9³.   2. Of time, *after :* Mt 17¹, Mk 14¹, Lk 1²⁴, Ac 1⁵, Ga 1¹⁸, al.; μετὰ τοῦτο, Jo 2¹², al.; ταῦτα, Mk 16[¹²], Lk 5²⁷, Jo 3²², al.; c. inf. artic. (Bl., § 71, 5 ; 72, 3), Mt 26³², Mk 1¹⁴, al.

III. In composition, 1. of association or community : μεταδίδωμι, μετέχω, etc.   2. Exchange or transference : μεταλλάσσω, μετοικίζω, etc. 3. *after :* μεταμέλομαι.

** μετα-βαίνω, [in LXX : Wi 7²⁷ 19¹⁹, II Mac 6¹, ⁹, ²⁴ * ;] *to pass over* from one place to another : Mt 17²⁰, Lk 10⁷ ; with reference to the point of departure only, *to withdraw, depart :* Mt 8³⁴ 11¹ 12⁹ 15²⁹, Jo 7³, Ac 18⁷ ; of removal from this life, ἐκ τ. κόσμου πρὸς τ. Πατέρα, Jo 13¹ ; metaph., ἐκ τ. θανάτου εἰς τ. ζωήν, Jo 5²⁴, I Jo 3¹⁴.†

μετα-βάλλω, [in LXX chiefly for הפך ;] *to turn about, change.* Pass. and mid., *to turn oneself about ;* metaph., *to change one's mind :* Ac 28⁶.†

μετ-άγω, [in LXX : III Ki 8⁴⁷, ⁴⁸, II Ch 6³⁷ (שבה) 36³ (סור hi.), I Es 1⁴⁵ 2¹⁰ 5⁶⁹, Es 8¹⁷, Si prol. ¹⁶ 10⁸, II Mac 1³³ * ;] 1. in Xen., Plut., and later writers, *to transfer, transport* (so LXX).   2. In sense otherwise unknown (v. Hort, in l.), *to turn about, direct :* Ja 3³, ⁴.†

μετα-δίδωμι, [in LXX : Pr 11²⁶ (שבר hi.), Wi 7¹³, al.;] *to give a share of, impart :* c. dat. pers. et acc. rei (in cl. more freq., c. gen. part., but acc. of that which is imparted, whether part or whole, so here, v. Bl., § 36, 1), Ro 1¹¹, I Th 2⁸, and (with ellipse of acc.) Lk 3¹¹ ; c. dat. pers., Eph 4²⁸ ; absol., ὁ μεταδιδούς, Ro 12⁸.†

** μετά-θεσις, -εως, ἡ (< μετατίθημι), [in LXX: ιι Mac 11²⁴ *;]
1. *change* of position, *removal*: He 11⁵. 2. *change*, as of that which
has been established: He 7¹² 12²⁷.†

μετ-αίρω, [in LXX: ιν Ki 16¹⁷ 25¹¹, Ps 79 (80)⁸, Pr 22²⁸ (סוּר hi.,
גָּלָה hi., etc.)*;] 1. trans., *to remove* (LXX, ll. c.). 2. (not cl.) *to
depart*: Mt 13⁵³ 19¹ (cf. Aq.: Ge 12⁹).†

μετα-καλέω, -ῶ, [in LXX: Ho 11¹· ² (קָרָא), ι Es 1⁵⁰ *;] *to call
from one plac. to another*. Mid., *to send for*: c. acc., Ac 7¹⁴ 10³²
20¹⁷ 24²⁵.†

μετα-κινέω, -ῶ, [in LXX: De 19¹⁴ (סוּג hi.), Is 54¹⁰ (מוּט), etc.;]
trans., *to move away, remove* (ὅρια, De, l.c.). Mid., *to remove oneself,
remove, shift*: metaph., ἀπὸ τ. ἐλπίδος, Col 1²³.†

** μετα-λαμβάνω, [in LXX: Es 5¹, Wi 18⁹, ιι-ιν Mac₁₂ *;] *to have
or get a share of, partake of*: c. gen. rei, ιι Ti 2⁶, He 6⁷ 12¹⁰ ; τροφῆς,
Ac 2¹⁶ 27³³, ³⁴; c. acc. rei (of the whole), *to get*: καιρόν, Ac 24²⁵
(v. Bl., § 36, 1; MM, xvi).†

* μετά-λημψις (Rec. -ληψις), -εως, ἡ (< μεταλαμβάνω), *participation,
taking, receiving*: of food, ι Ti 4³.†

μετά-ληψις, v.s. μετάλημψις.

μετ-αλλάσσω, [in LXX: Es 2⁷ (מוּר), ib.²⁰, ι Es 1³¹, ιι Mac₉ *;]
1. *to exchange*: τ. ἀλήθειαν . . . ἐν τ. ψεύδει, the truth for a lie (v. Bl.,
§ 36, 8), Ro 1²⁵. 2. *to change*: c. acc. seq. εἰς, Ro 1²⁶ (ἀλλάσσω).†

μετα-μέλομαι, [in LXX chiefly for נחם ni.;] depon., pass., *to
regret, repent one*: Mt 21³⁰, ³² 27³, ιι Co 7⁸, He 7²¹ (LXX).†

SYN.: μετανοέω, *to change one's mind, repent*. On the distinction, difficult to maintain by usage, between these words, v. Thayer,
s.v.; Tr., *Syn.*, § lxix.

**† μετα-μορφόω, -ῶ [in Sm.: Ps 33 (34)¹*;] *to transform, trans-
figure*: pass., of Christ's transfiguration, Mt 17², Mk 9² (cf. Lk 9²⁹);
of Christians, Ro 12², ιι Co 3¹⁸.†

SYN.: μετασχηματίζω, *to change in fashion* or *appearance*, v.s.
μορφή, and cf. Lft., *Phl.*, 125 ff.

μετα-νοέω, -ῶ, [in LXX for נחם ni., ι Ki 15²⁹, Je 4²⁸, al.;] *to
change one's mind* or *purpose*, hence, *to repent*; in NT (exc. Lk 17³· ⁴),
of repentance from sin, involving amendment: seq. ἀπό, Ac 8²²; ἐκ,
Re 2²¹, ²² 9²⁰, ²¹ 16¹¹ (cf. שׁוּב מִן); ἐπί, ιι Co 12²¹; absol., Mt 3² 4¹⁷
11²⁰ 12⁴¹, Mk 1¹⁵ 6¹², Lk 11³² 13³, ⁵ 15⁷, ¹⁰ 16³⁰ 17³, ⁴, Ac 2³⁸ 3¹⁹ 17³⁰ 26²⁰,
Re 2⁵, ¹⁶, ²¹ 3³, ¹⁹; c. inf., Re 16⁹; ἐν σάκκῳ κ. σποδῷ, Mt 11²¹, Lk 10¹³.†

SYN.: μεταμέλομαι, q.v.

μετάνοια, -οίας, ἡ (< μετανοέω), [in LXX: Pr 14¹⁵, Wi 11²³
12¹⁰, ¹⁹, Si 44¹⁶ *;] *after-thought, change of mind, repentance*: He 12¹⁷;
of repentance from sin, Mt 3⁸, ¹¹, Lk 3⁸ 15⁷ 24⁴⁷, Ac 26²⁰, ιι Co 7⁹, ¹⁰;
βάπτισμα (q.v.) μετανοίας, Mk 1⁴, Lk 3³, Ac 13²⁴ 19⁴; ἡ εἰς θεὸν μ.,
Ac 20²¹; μ. ἀπὸ νεκρῶν ἔργων, He 6¹; εἰς μ. καλεῖν, Lk 5³²; id. ἄγειν,
Ro 2⁴; ἀνακαινίζειν, He 6⁶; εἰς μ. χωρῆσαι, ιι Pe 3⁹; μ. δοῦναι, Ac
5³¹ 11¹⁸, ιι Ti 2²⁵.†

μεταξύ (< μετά + ξύν = σύν), [in LXX: Ge 31⁵⁰, Jg 5²⁷, ιιι Ki

15⁶, ³², Wi 4¹⁰ 16¹⁹ 18²³ *;] 1. adv. of place and time (in NT time only); (a) *between*: ἐν τῷ μ. (sc. χρόνῳ), Jo 4³¹; (b) in late writers (FlJ, Plut., al.), like μετά (adv.), *after, afterwards*: τὸ μ. σάββατον, Ac 13⁴² (cf. Cl., *Ro.*, *I Co.*, 44, 2). 2. Prep. c. gen., *between*: of place, Mt 23³⁵, Lk 11⁵¹ 16²⁶, Ac 12⁶; of persons, as to mutual relation, Mt 18¹⁵, Ac 15⁹, Ro 2¹⁵.†

μετα-πέμπω, [in LXX (mid.): Ge 27⁴⁵ (לקח), Nu 23⁷ (נחה hi.), II Mac 15³¹, III Mac 5¹⁸ R, IV Mac 12³, ⁶ *;] *to send after* or *for*: pass., Ac 10²⁹ᵃ. Chiefly in mid., *to send for, summon*   Ac 10⁵, ²², ²⁹ᵇ 11¹³ 20¹ 24²⁴, ²⁶ 25³.†

μετα-στρέφω, [in LXX chiefly for הפך;] *to turn about, turn, change*: pass., Ac 2²⁰ (LXX), Ja 4⁹ (WH, txt., μετατρέπω, q.v.); in evil sense, *to pervert, corrupt* (cf. primary sense *reverse*): Ga 1⁷.†

** **μετα-σχηματίζω**, [in LXX: IV Mac 9²² *;] *to change in fashion* or *appearance*: c. acc. rei, τ. σῶμα, Phl 3²¹; mid., seq. εἰς, II Co 11¹³, ¹⁴; seq. ὡς, ib. ¹⁵; of a rhetorical device, *to transfer by a fiction* or *figure* (cf. J. H. Colson in *JThS*, xvii, pp. 379 ff. (July, 1916); v. also MM, *VGT*, s.v.; Field, *Notes*, in l.), seq. εἰς, 1 Co 4⁶.†

SYN.: μεταμορφόω, q.v.

μετα-τίθημι, [in LXX: Ge 5²⁴ (לקח), De 27¹⁷, al. (סוג hi.), Si 44¹⁶, II Mac 7²⁴, al;] 1. *to transfer* to another place: c. acc., pass., He 11⁵ (LXX); seq. εἰς, Ac 7¹⁶.   2. *to change*: c. acc., pass., He 7¹²; seq. εἰς, fig., i.e. to make one thing a pretext for another, χάριν εἰς ἀσέλγειαν, Ju ⁴. Mid., *to change oneself, pass over*: seq. ἀπό et εἰς, Ga 1⁶ (cf. II Mac, l.c.).†

μετα-τρέπω, [in LXX: IV Mac 6⁵ 7³, ¹² 15¹¹, ¹⁸ *;] *to turn about, turn* (Hom., al., but not found in Att.): c. acc., Ja 4⁹ (WH, txt.; cf. μεταστρέφω).†

** **μετ-έπειτα**, adv., [in LXX: Jth 9⁵, Es 3¹³, III Mac 3²⁴ *;] *afterwards*: He 12¹⁷.†

μετ-έχω, [in LXX: Pr 5¹⁷ (את), 1¹⁸, I Es 5⁴⁰ 8⁷⁰, Si 51²⁸, al.;] *to partake of, share in*: ἐπ᾽ ἐλπίδι τοῦ μετέχειν, I Co 9¹⁰; c. gen. rei, I Co 9¹² 10²¹, ³⁰, He 2¹⁴; in sacramental sense, ἐκ τ. ἑνὸς ἄρτου μ., I Co 10¹⁷ (cf. MM, xvi); metaph., γάλακτος, He 5¹³; of belonging to a tribe, He 7¹³.†

μετ-εωρίζω (< μετέωρος, (a) *in mid air*; (b) *buoyed up*; (c) *in suspense*; Thuc.; in π. opp. to ἀμέριμνος, v. Zorell, s.v.): [in LXX: Ob 1⁴ (גבה hi.), Mi 4¹ (נשא ni.), Ps 130 (131)¹, Ez 10¹⁶, ¹⁷, ¹⁹ (רום), II Mac 5¹⁷, 7³⁴, III Mac 6⁵ *;] *to raise on high* (Thuc., Xen., al.; Ob, Mi, Ez, ll. c.).   Metaph., (a) *to buoy up*; pass., *to be elated, puffed up* (Polyb., al., Ps, II, III Mac, ll. c.); (b) *to be anxious, in suspense* (Polyb., v. 70, 10; FlJ, *BJ*, iv, 2, 5): Lk 12²⁹.†

μετοικεσία, -ας, ἡ (= cl. μετοικία, -κησις; < μετοικέω, *to change one's abode*), [in LXX chiefly for גלה and cogn. forms, Ez 12¹¹, Ob 1²⁰, al.;] *change of abode, migration*: of the Babylonian exile, μ. Βαβυλῶνος, Mt 1¹¹, ¹², ¹⁷.†

μετ-οικίζω (< μέτοικος, an emigrant), [in LXX chiefly for הגלה hi. ;] to remove to a new abode, cause to migrate : Ac 7⁴, ⁴³ (LXX).†

μετοχή, -ῆς, ἡ (< μετέχω), [in LXX : Ps 121 (122)³ א R (חבר pu.) *;] sharing, fellowship : II Co 6¹⁴.†

μέτοχος, -ον (< μετέχω), [in LXX chiefly for חָבֵר;] 1. sharing in, partaking of : c. gen. rei, He 3¹ 6⁴ 12⁸; τ. Χριστοῦ, He 3¹⁴. 2. As subst., ὁ μ., a partner, associate : Lk 5⁷, He 1⁹ (LXX).†

μετρέω, -ῶ (< μέτρον), [in LXX : Ex 16¹⁸, Nu 35⁵, Ru 3¹⁵, Is 40¹², (מדד), Da TH 5²⁶ (מְנָה), Wi 4⁸ *;] 1. to measure, of space, number, value, etc.: c. acc. rei, Re 11² 21¹⁵, ¹⁷; c. dat. instr., Re 11¹ 21¹⁶. Metaph., ἑαυτὸν ἐν ἑαυτῷ, II Co 10¹². 2. to measure out, give by measure : prov., ἐν ᾧ μέτρῳ κ.τ.λ., Mt 7², Mk 4²⁴, Lk 6³⁸ (WH, mg., cf. ἀντι-μετρέω).†

μετρητής, -οῦ, ὁ (< μετρέω), [in LXX : III Ki 18³² (מָאָה), II Ch 4⁵, (בַּת), etc.;] 1. a measurer (Plat.). 2. = ἀμφορεύς, an Attic measure, = 1½ Roman amphoræ or about 9 Eng. gallons : Jo 2⁶.†

*† μετριοπαθέω, -ῶ (< μετριοπαθής, moderating one's passions), to hold one's passions or emotions in restraint; hence, to bear gently with, feel gently towards : He 5².†

** μετρίως, adv. (μέτριος, moderate), [in LXX : II Mac 15³⁸ *;] moderately : litotes, οὐ μ., exceedingly, Ac 20¹².†

μέτρον, -ου, τό, [in LXX chiefly for מִדָּה, also for אֵיפָה, etc.;] 1. that which is used for measuring, a measure; (a) a vessel : fig.; Mt 23³², Lk 6³⁸ ; ἐκ μ., by measure (i.e., in scanty measure), Jo 3³⁴; (b) a rod or rule : Re 21¹⁵, ¹⁷; fig., Mt 7², Mk 4²⁴. 2. That which is measured, measure : c. gen. rei, Ro 12³, II Co 10¹³, Eph 4⁷, ¹³, ¹⁶.†

μέτωπον, -ου, τό (μετά + ὤψ, an eye), [in LXX for מֵצַח;] the forehead : Re 7³ 9⁴ 13¹⁶ 14¹, ⁹ 17⁵ 20⁴ 22⁴.†

μέχρι (bef. consonants, exc. Lk 16¹⁶, μέχρι Ἰωάνου) and μέχρις (bef. vowels, Mk, Ga, ll. c., He 12⁴; v. Bl., § 5, 4), 1. as prep., c. gen., as far as, even to, until ; (a) of place : Ro 15¹⁹; (b) of time : Mt 11²³ 13³⁰ 28¹⁵, Lk 16¹⁶, Ac 10³⁰ 20⁷, Ro 5¹⁴, I Ti 6¹⁴, He 3⁶, ¹⁴ 9¹⁰; (c) of measure or degree : Phl 2⁸, ³⁰, II Ti 2⁹, He 12⁴ (μ. αἵματος, cf. II Mac 13¹⁴). 2. As conjunct. (as long as), until : Eph 4¹³; μ. οὗ (Thuc., iii, 28, but more freq. μ. ἄν; v. Bl., § 65, 10), Mk 13³⁰, Ga 4¹⁹ (μ. is prop. an adv., cf. Lat. usque, seq. prep. or adv.; LS, s.v., and cf. ἄχρι).†

μή, subjective negative particle, used where the negation depends on a condition or hypothesis, expressed or understood, as distinct from οὐ, which denies absolutely. μή is used where one thinks a thing is not, as distinct from an absolute negation. As a general rule, οὐ negatives the indic., μή the other moods, incl. ptcp. [In LXX for אַל, אַיִן, אֵין.]

I. As a neg. adv., *not;* 1. with ref. to thought or opinion : Jo 3¹⁸, Tit 1¹¹, ΙΙ Pe 1⁹. 2. In delib. questions, c. subjc. (M, *Pr.*, 185) : Mk 12¹⁴, Ro 3⁸. 3. In conditional and final sentences, after εἰ, ἐάν, ἄν, ἵνα, ὅπως : Mt 10¹⁴, Mk 6¹¹ 12¹⁹, Lk 9⁵ Jo 6⁵⁰, Ro 11²⁵, al. 4. C. inf. (v. M, *Pr.*, 234 f., 239, 255), (*a*) after verbs of saying, etc. : Mt 2¹² 5³⁴, Mk 12¹⁸, Ac 15³⁸, Ro 2²¹, al.; (*b*) c. artic. inf. : after a prep., Mt 13⁵, Mk 4⁵, Ac 7¹⁹, Ι Co 10⁶, al.; without a prep., Ro 14¹³, ΙΙ Co 2¹, ¹³, Ι Th 4⁶; (*c*) in sentences expressing consequence, after ὥστε : Mt 8²⁸, Mk 3²⁰, Ι Co 1⁷, ΙΙ Co 3⁷, al. 5. C. ptcp. (v. M, *Pr.*, 231 f., 239), in hypothetical references to persons of a certain character or description : Mt 10²⁸ 12³⁰, Lk 6⁴⁹, Jo 3¹⁸, Ro 4⁵, Ι Co 7³⁸, Ι Jo 3¹⁰, al.; where the person or thing being definite, the denial is a matter of opinion : Jo 6⁶⁴, Ι Co 1²⁸ 4⁷, ¹⁸, ΙΙ Co 5²¹, al.; where the ptcp. has a concessive, causal or conditional force, *if, though, because not :* Mt 18²⁵, Lk 2⁴⁵, Jo 7⁴⁹, Ac 9²⁶, Ro 2¹⁴ 5¹³, ΙΙ Co 3¹⁴, Ga 6⁹, Ju ⁵; where the ptcp. has a descriptive force (*being such as*), *not :* Ac 9⁹, Ro 1²⁸, Ι Co 10³³, Ga 4⁸, He 12²⁷, al. 6. μή prohibitive, in indep. sentences, (*a*) c. subjc. praes., 1 pers. pl. : Ga 5²⁶ 6⁹, Ι Th 5⁶, Ι Jo 3¹⁸; (*b*) c. imperat. praes., usually where one is bidden to desist from what has already begun (cf. M, *Pr.*, 122 ff.) : Mt 7¹, Mk 5³⁶, Lk 6³⁰, Jo 2¹⁶ 5⁴⁵, Ac 10¹⁵, Ro 11¹⁸, Ja 2¹, Re 5⁵, al.; (*c*) forbidding that which is still future : c. imperat. aor., 3 pers., Mt 24¹⁸, Mk 13¹⁵, Lk 17³¹, al.; c. subjc. aor., 2 pers., Mt 3⁹ 10²⁶, Mk 5⁷, Lk 6²⁹, Jo 3⁷, Ro 10⁶, al.; (*d*) c. optat., in wishes : ΙΙ Ti 4¹⁶ (LXX); μὴ γένοιτο (v. M, *Pr.*, 194; Bl., § 66, 1), Lk 20¹⁶, Ro 3³, al. ; μή τις, Mk 13⁵, al.

II. As a conj., 1. after verbs of fearing, caution, etc., *that, lest, perhaps* (M, *Pr.*, 192 f.) : c. subjc. praes., He 12¹⁵ ; c. subjc. aor., Mt 24⁴, Mk 13⁵, Lk 21⁸, Ac 13⁴⁰, Ga 5¹⁵, al.; ὅρα μή (v. M, *Pr.*, 124, 178), elliptically, Re 19¹⁰ 22⁹; c. indic. fut. (M, *Pr.*, l.c.), Col 2⁸. 2. *in order that not :* c. subjc. aor., Mk 13³⁶, ΙΙ Co 8²⁰ 12⁶.

III. Interrogative, in hesitant questions (M, *Pr.*, 170), or where a negative answer is expected : Mt 7⁹, ¹⁰, Mk 2¹⁹, Jo 3⁴, Ro 3³ 10¹⁸, ¹⁹, Ι Co 1¹³, al.; μή τις, Lk 22³⁵, al ; seq. οὐ (Ro 10¹⁷, al. in Pl.), expecting an affirm. ans. ; οὐ μή, Lk 18⁷, Jo 18¹¹.

IV. οὐ μή as emphatic negation (cf. M, *Pr.*, 188, 190 ff.; Bl., § 64, 5), *not at all, by no means :* c. indic. fut., Mt 16²², Jo 6³⁵, He 10¹⁷, al.; c. subjc. aor., Mt 24², Mk 13², Lk 6³⁷, Jo 13⁸, Ι Co 8¹³, al.

μήγε, v.s. γε.

μηδαμῶς (= μηδαμῇ, -δαμά, adv. fr. μηδαμός = μηδείς), [in LXX chiefly for חָלִילָה, חֲלִילָה ;] *by no means, not at all . μ.*, Κύριε (sc. τοῦτο γένοιτο), Ac 10¹⁴ 11⁸.†

μηδέ, negative particle, related to οὐδέ as μή to οὐ, 1. as conjc., continuing a negation or prohibition, *but not, and not, nor :* preceded by μή, Mt 6²⁵ 22²⁹, Mk 12²⁴, Lk 14¹², al.; ἵνα μή, Jo 4¹⁵; ὅπως μή, Lk 16²⁶; μηδὲ . . . μηδέ, *neither . . . nor,* Mt 10¹⁰, Ι Co 10⁸, ⁹. 2. As adv., strengthening a negation, *not even :* Mk 2², Ι Co 5¹¹, al.

μηδείς, -δεμία, -δέν (and -θέν, Ac 27³³, a Hellenistic form; v. Bl.,

§ 6, 7; Thackeray, *Gr.*, 58), related to οὐδείς as μή to οὐ, *no, none, no one*; neut., *nothing*: Mt 16²⁰, Mk 5⁴³ 6⁸, Lk 3¹⁴, Ac 8²⁴, Ro 13⁸, al.; c. gen., Ac 4¹⁷ 24²³; neut. acc., μηδέν, adverbially, *in no respect*, Ac 10²⁰ 11¹²; as acc. obj. after verb, βλάπτειν, Lk 4³⁵; ὠφελεῖσθαι, Mk 5²⁶; ὑστερεῖν, II Co 11⁵; μεριμνᾶν, Phl 4⁶; in double negation, strengthening the denial, μηκέτι μ., Mk 11¹⁴, Ac 4¹⁷; μὴ . . . μηδέν (μηδένα, μηδεμίαν), II Co 13⁷, II Th 2³, I Pe 3⁶.

μηδέποτε (μηδέ, ποτέ), adv., *never*: II Ti 3⁷.†

μηδέπω (μηδέ, πώ), adv., *not yet*: He 11⁷.†

Μῆδος, -ου, ὁ, a *Mede, Median*: pl., Ac 2⁹.†

μηθείς, v.s. μηδείς.

μηκέτι (< μή, ἔτι), adv., *no more, no longer*: c. 2 aor. subjc., Mk 9²⁵; οὐ μ., Mt 21¹⁹; c. praes. subjc., Ro 14¹³; c. praes. imperat., Lk 8⁴⁹, Jo 5¹⁴ 8⁽¹¹⁾, Eph 4²⁸, I Ti 5²³; c. optat., Mk 11¹⁴; ἵνα μ., II Co 5¹⁵, Eph 4¹⁴; c. inf., Mk 1⁴⁵ 2², Ac 4¹⁷ 25²⁴, Ro 6⁶, Eph 4¹⁷, I Pe 4²; c. ptcp., Ac 13³⁴, Ro 15²³, I Th 3¹, ⁵.†

μῆκος, -εος (-ους), τό, [in LXX chiefly for אֹרֶךְ;] *length*: Eph 3¹⁸, Re 21¹⁶.†

μηκύνω (< μῆκος), [in LXX: Is 44¹⁴ (גָּדֵל pi.), Ez 12²⁵, ²⁸ (מָשַׁךְ ni.) *;] *to lengthen, extend*: of causing plants to grow, Is, l.c.; pass. (mid., Swete, in l.), *to grow*: Mk 4²⁷.†

μηλωτή, -ῆς, ἡ (< μῆλον, a *sheep* or *goat*), [in LXX for אַדֶּרֶת, III Ki 19¹³, ¹⁹, IV Ki 2⁸, ¹³, ¹⁴ *;] *a sheepskin*: He 11³⁷.†

μήν, a particle of assurance, *verily, truly; εἰ (εἶ) μ. (=* cl., ἦ μ. in LXX and π.), *now verily, full surely*: He 6¹⁴ ⁽ᴸˣˣ⁾.†

μήν, gen., μηνός, ὁ, [in LXX very freq. for חֹדֶשׁ, Ge 7¹¹, al.; a few times for יֶרַח; a *month* (lunar): Lk 1²⁴, ²⁶, ³⁶, ⁵⁶ 4²⁵, Ac 7²⁰ 18¹¹ 19⁸ 20³ 28¹¹, Ja 5¹⁷, Re 9⁵, ¹⁰, ¹⁵ 11² 13⁵ 22²: pl., of the festival of the new moon (cf. Is 66²³), Ga 4¹⁰.†

** **μηνύω,** [in LXX: II Mac 3⁷ 6¹¹ 14³⁷, III Mac 3²⁸, IV Mac 4³ *;] *to disclose, declare, make known*: Lk 20³⁷, I Co 10²⁸; in forensic sense, *to inform, report*: Jo 11⁵⁷; pass., c. dat. pers., Ac 23³⁰.†

μὴ οὐκ, v.s. μή, III.

μήποτε (= μή ποτε, and so written in WH, exc. Mt 25⁹), negative particle, related to οὔποτε as μή to οὐ. 1. As neg. particle, *never*: He 9¹⁷ (R, mg., but v. infr.; WH, txt., μή τότε). 2. As conjc., *lest ever, lest haply* (the idea of chance rather than of time seems to prevail in NT): Mt 4⁶ ⁽ᴸˣˣ⁾ 5²⁵ 7⁶ 13¹⁵ ⁽ᴸˣˣ⁾, ²⁹ 15³² 27⁶⁴, Mk 4¹² ⁽ᴸˣˣ⁾ 14², Lk 4¹¹ 12⁵⁸ 14¹², ²⁹, Ac 28²⁷; after verbs of fearing or taking heed, Lk 21³⁴, He 2¹ 3¹² 4¹; with ellipse of the verb or ptcp., Lk 14⁸, Ac 5³⁹; in later writers (v. M, *Pr.*, 192 f.), *perhaps*, Mt 25⁹. 3. As interrogative; (*a*) in direct questions, like μή, expecting a negative answer: Jo 7²⁶, He 9¹⁷ (R, txt., cf. Westc., in l.; but v. supr.); (*b*) in indirect questions, *whether haply, if haply*: Lk 3¹⁵. II Ti 2²⁵.†

μήπου (WH, μή που), *lest anywhere, lest haply*: Ac 27²⁹.†

*μήπω (μή πω, LTr., in Ro, l.c.), adv., *not yet :* c. ptcp., Ro 9¹¹;
c. acc. et inf., He 9⁸.†

μήπως or μή πως (so WH), negative particle, 1. as conjc., *lest
haply :* in final sentences, I Co 9²⁷, II Co 2⁷ 9⁴; after verbs of fearing
or taking heed, I Co 8⁹, II Co 11³ 12²⁰, Ga 4¹¹; with an ellipse of
ptcp. (sc. φοβούμενος; cf. Bl., § 65, 3; Burton, § 225), I Th 3⁵ (but v.
infr.). 2. As interrogative, *whether haply :* Ga 2², I Th 3⁵ (cf. M,
Th., in l., but v. supr.).†

μηρός, -οῦ, ὁ, [in LXX chiefly for יָרֵךְ;] *the thigh :* Re 19¹⁶.†

μή-τε, negative particle, differing from οὔτε as μή from οὐ, *neither,
nor :* μήτε . . . μήτε, *neither* . . . *nor*, Mt 11¹⁸, Lk 7³³ 9³, Ac 23¹²,²¹
27²⁰, He 7³; μὴ (μηδὲ) . . . μήτε . . μήτε, Mt 5³⁴⁻³⁶, Mk 3²⁰ T, Ac 23⁸,
II Th 2², I Ti 1⁷, Ja 5¹², Re 7¹,³.†

μήτηρ, gen., μητρός, ἡ, [in LXX chiefly for אֵם;] *mother :* Mt 1¹⁸
2¹¹, al.; fig., of one who takes the place of a mother, ἰδοὺ ἡ μ. μου, Mt
12⁴⁹ (cf. ib. ⁵⁰, Mk 3³⁵, Jo 19²⁷, Ro 16¹³, I Ti 5²); of a city, ἥτις ἐστὶν μ.
ἡμῶν, Ga 4²⁶; symbolically of Babylon, ἡ μ. τ. πορνῶν, Re 17⁵.

μή-τι, interrog. particle, expecting a negative answer : Mt 7¹⁶
26²²,²⁵, Mk 4²¹ 14¹⁹, Lk 6³⁹, Jo 8²² 18³⁵, Ac 10⁴⁷, II Co 12¹⁸, Ja 3¹¹; in
hesitant questions (v. M, *Pr.*, 170ₐ), μ. οὗτός ἐστιν, *can this be*, Mt 12²³,
Jo 4²⁹; μ. ἄρα, II Co 1¹⁷; on εἰ μήτι (Lk 9¹³, cf. Bl., § 65, 6), v.s. εἰ.†

μή-τι-γε (μήτι γε, Rec., L; μή τι γε, Tr.), strengthened form of
μήτι, *let alone :* i.e. according to context; (a) *much less ;* (b) *much
more :* I Co 6³.†

μή-τις, Rec. for μή τις (v.s. μή, I, III, and cf. Thayer, s.v. μήτις).

μήτρα, -ας, ἡ (< μήτηρ), [in LXX chiefly for רֶחֶם; *the womb* (elsewhere in NT, κοιλία, q.v.) : Lk 2²³ (LXX), Ro 4¹⁹.†

*μητρολῴας (Rec. -αλῴας, in cl., -αλοίας, v. Bl., § 3, 3; 6, 2), -ου, ὁ
(< μήτηρ + ἀλοιάω, *to smite*); (a) *a matricide :* I Ti 1⁹ (AV, R, txt.,
but v. infr.); (b) *a smiter of his mother :* I Ti 1⁹ (R, mg., cf. Ex 21¹⁵,
and v. Ellic., *CGT*, in l.).†

μητρό-πολις, -εως, ἡ, [in LXX for אֵם, etc.;] *a metropolis, chief
city :* I Ti, subscr. (Rec.).τ

μία, v.s. εἷς.

μιαίνω, [in LXX chiefly for טָמֵא;] 1. *to dye* or *stain.* 2. *to
stain, defile, soil ;* (a) in physical sense; (b) in moral sense : Tit 1¹⁵,
He 12¹⁵, Ju 8; (c) in ritual sense (cf. Le 22⁵, al.) : Jo 18²⁸.†

SYN. : μολύνω, *to besmear*, which also differs from μ. in that it is
never used, as μ. in its primary meaning, in an honourable sense
(cf. Tr., *Syn.*, § xxxi).

μίασμα, -τος, τό (< μιαίνω), chiefly in trag. and late writers;
[in LXX : Le 7⁸ ⁽¹⁸⁾ (מְפֻגָּל), Je 39 (32)³⁴ (שִׁקּוּץ), Ez 33³¹ (בֶּצַע), Jth
9²,⁴ 13¹⁶, I Mac 13⁵⁰ *;] *a stain, defilement :* pl., II Pe 2²⁰.†

**† μιασμός, -οῦ, ὁ (< μιαίνω), [in LXX : Wi 14²⁶, I Mac 4⁴³ *;]

1. prop., *the act of defiling*. 2. = μίασμα (q.v.): ιι Pe 2¹⁰ (cf. Plut., *Mor.*, 393c).†

μίγμα (LT, cl., μῖγμα; on the orthogr., v. Bl., § 3, 5), -τος, τό (< μίγνυμι), [in LXX: Si 38⁸*;] *a mixture*: Jo 19³⁹ (ἕλιγμα, WH, R, mg.).†

μίγνυμι (on the spelling μείγ-, v. Bl., § 3, 5), [in LXX for ערב hith., etc.;] *to mix, mingle*: c. acc. et dat., Re 15²; c. acc. seq. ἐν, Re 8⁷; seq. μετά, Mt 27³⁴, Lk 13¹.†

SYN.: κεράννυμι, q.v.

μικρός, -ά, -όν, [in LXX chiefly for קָטֹן, מָעַט;] *small, little*; 1. of persons; (a) lit., of stature: Mk 15⁴⁰ (MM, iii, xvi; on the view that age is meant, v. Deiss., *BS*, 144), Lk 19³; οἱ μ., *the little ones*, Mt 18⁶,¹⁰,¹⁴, Mk 9⁴²; (b) hence metaph., of rank or influence (cf. Dalman, *Words*, 113 f.): Mt 10⁴², Lk 17², Ac 8¹⁰ 26²², He 8¹¹ (LXX), Re 11¹⁸ 13¹⁶ 19⁵,¹⁸ 20¹²; compar., -ότερος, Mt 11¹¹, Lk 7²⁸ 9⁴⁸. 2. Of things; (a) of size: Mt 13³², Mk 4³¹, Ja 3⁵; (b) of quantity: Lk 12³², ι Co 5⁶, Ga 5⁹, Re 3⁸; (c) of time: Jo 7³³ 12³⁵, Re 6¹¹ 20³. 3. Neut., μικρόν, used adverbially; (a) of distance: Mt 26³⁹, Mk 14³⁵; (b) of quantity: ιι Co 11¹,¹⁶; (c) of time: Jo 13³³ 14¹⁹ 16¹⁶⁻¹⁹, He 10³⁷; μετὰ μ., Mt 26⁷³, Mk 14⁷⁰.†

Μίλητος, -ου, ἡ, *Miletus*, a maritime city of Caria: Ac 20¹⁵,¹⁷, ιι Ti 4²⁰.†

*† **μίλιον**, -ου, τό, *a Roman mile* (1680 yds.): Mt 5⁴¹.†

μιμέομαι, -οῦμαι (< μῖμος, *a mimic, an actor*), [in LXX: Ps 30 (31)⁶, Wi 4² 15⁹, ιν Mac 9²³ 13⁹*;] *to imitate*: ιι Th 3⁷,⁹, He 13⁷, ιιι Jo ¹¹.†

* **μιμητής**, -οῦ, ὁ (< μιμέομαι), in NT always (like the verb) in good sense, *an imitator*: ι Co 4¹⁶ 11¹, Eph 5¹, 1 Th 1⁶ 2¹⁴, He 6¹².†

μιμνήσκω (Bl., -ῄ-, § 3, 3), [in LXX chiefly for זכר;] *to remind*: mid. and pass.; (a) reflexive, *to remind oneself of*, hence, *to remember*: c. gen. rei, Mt 26⁷⁵, Lk 1⁵⁴,⁷² 24⁸, Ac 11¹⁶, ιι Pe 3², Ju ¹⁷; c. neg., of sins, = *to forgive*, He 8¹² 10¹⁷(LXX); c. gen. pers., Lk 23⁴²; seq. ὅτι, Mt 5²³ 27⁶³, Lk 16²⁵, Jo 2¹⁷,²² 12¹⁶; ὡς, Lk 24⁶; pf., μέμνημαι, in pres. sense (cl.), c. gen. pers. (rei), ι Co 11², ιι Ti 1⁴; pres., μιμνήσκομαι (only in late writers), c. gen. pers., in sense of caring for, He 2⁶ (LXX) 13³; (b) in passive sense, *to be remembered*, aor., ἐμνήσθην; seq. ἐνώπιον, c. gen. pers. (cf. Ez 18²²), Ac 10³¹, Re 16¹⁹ (cf. ἀνα-, ἐπ-ανα-, ὑπο-μιμνήσκω. The tenses of this verb are from the older μνάομαι).†

μισέω, -ῶ, [in LXX chiefly for שָׂנֵא;] *to hate*: c. acc. pers., Mt 5⁴³ 24¹⁰, Lk 1⁷¹ 6²²,²⁷, 19¹⁴, Jo 7⁷ 15¹⁸,¹⁹,²³⁻²⁵ 17¹⁴, Tit 3³, ι Jo 2⁹,¹¹ 3¹³,¹⁵ 4²⁰, Re 17¹⁶; pass., Mt 10²² 24⁹, Mk 13¹³, Lk 21¹⁷; c. acc. rei, Jo 3²⁰, Ro 7¹⁵, Eph 5²⁹, He 1⁹, Ju ²³, Re 2⁶; pass., Re 18². As the Heb. שָׂנֵא is sometimes found with the modified sense of indifference to or relative disregard for one thing in comparison with another (cf. Ge 29²⁰,³¹, De 21¹⁵,¹⁶, Ma 1³) so prob. μ. in the foll.: Mt 6²⁴, Lk 14²⁶ 16¹³, Jo 12²⁵, Ro 9¹³ (LXX).†

*† μισθαποδοσία, -ας, ἡ (< μισθός, ἀποδίδωμι; cl. μισθοδοσία), *pay-ment of wages, recompense;* meton., (a) of reward : He 10³⁵ 11²⁶; (b) of punishment : He 2².†

*† μισθ-απο-δότης, -ου, ὁ, (v. supr.), *one who pays wages ;* meton., *a rewarder :* He 11⁶.†

† μίσθιος, -α, -ον (also -ος, -ον), [in LXX : Le 19¹³ A 25⁵⁰, Jb 7¹ (שָׂכִיר), To 5¹¹, Si 7¹⁰ 31 (34)²² 37¹¹ *;] *hired;* as subst., ὁ μ., *a hired servant :* Lk 15¹⁷, ¹⁹, ²¹ (Anth., Plut.).†

μισθός, -οῦ, ὁ, [in LXX chiefly for שָׂכָר;] 1. prop., *wages, hire :* Mt 20⁸, Lk 10⁷, Ro 4⁴, ι Ti 5¹⁸, Ja 5⁴, Ju¹¹; μ. ἀδικίας, Ac 1¹⁸, ιι Pe 2¹³ (but v. Mayor and *ICC*, in l.), ib.¹⁵. 2. Generally, *reward :* Jo 4³⁶, ι Co 9¹⁸; esp. of divine rewards, Mt 5¹² 6¹, ², ⁵, ¹⁶ 10⁴¹, ⁴², Mk 9⁴¹, Lk 6²³, ³⁵, ι Co 3⁸, ¹⁴, ιι Jo⁸, Re 11¹⁸ 22¹²; ἔχειν μ., Mt 5⁴⁶, ι Co 9¹⁷.†

μισθόω, -ῶ (< μισθός), [in LXX (mid.) chiefly for שָׂכַר;] *to let out for hire.* Mid., *to hire :* c. acc., Mt 20¹, ⁷.†

μίσθωμα, -τος, τό (< μισθόω), [in LXX : De 23¹⁸ ⁽¹⁹⁾, Mi 1⁷, Ez 16³¹, ³⁴, ⁴¹ (אֶתְנָה), ib³³ (נֵדֶה, נֶדֶן), ib.³², Pr 19¹³ *;] 1. *price, hire* (cl., and LXX). 2. In sense not found elsewhere, *a hired dwelling :* Ac 28³⁰.†

μισθωτός, -ή, όν, (< μισθόω), [in LXX for שָׂכִיר, Ex 12⁴⁵, al.;] *hired;* as subst., ὁ μ., *a hired servant, hireling :* Mk 1²⁰, Jo 10¹², ¹³.†

Μιτυλήνη, -ης, ἡ (late form — Strab., Plut. — of cl. Μυτιλ-), *Mytilene, Mitylene,* chief city of Lesbos : Ac 20¹⁴.†

Μιχαήλ, ὁ, indecl. (Heb. מִיכָאֵל, *who like God ?*), *Michael,* the Archangel (cf. Da 12¹) : Ju⁹, Re 12⁷.†

μνᾶ, -ᾶς, ἡ (a Semitic word ; cf. Heb. מָנֶה, Aram. מְנָא, *a weight and a sum of money* = 100 shekels, cf. ιιι Ki 10¹⁷), *a mina* (Lat.), *mna,* in Attic a weight and sum of money = 100 δραχμαί (q.v.) : Lk 19¹³, ¹⁶, ¹⁸, ²⁰, ²⁴, ²⁵.†

μνάομαι, v.s. μιμνήσκω.

Μνάσων, -ωνος, ὁ, *Mnason :* Ac 21¹⁶.†

μνεία, -ας, ἡ (< μιμνήσκω), [in LXX for זֵכֶר, its parts and deriva-tives;] *remembrance, mention* (= μνήμη) : Phl 1³ ; μ. ποιεῖσθαι, c. gen. pers., Ro 1⁹, Eph 1¹⁶, ι Th 1², Phm⁴ (cf. Ps 110 (111)⁴) ; μ. ἔχειν, c. gen. pers., ι Th 3⁶, ιι Ti 1³ (on the v.l. in Ro 12¹³, v. *ICC*, in l. ; Field, *Notes*, 163).†

μνῆμα, -τος, τό (< μνάομαι), [in LXX for קֶבֶר, קְבוּרָה;] 1. *a memorial.* 2. *a sepulchral monument, a sepulchre, tomb :* Mk 5³, ⁵ 15⁴⁶ 16² (WH, μνημεῖον), Lk 8²⁷ 23⁵³ 24¹, Ac 2²⁹ 7¹⁶, Re 11⁹.†

SYN. : μνημεῖον.

μνημεῖον, -ου, τό, [in LXX for קֶבֶר, קְבוּרָה;] 1. *a memorial, record* (cl., cf. Wi 10⁷). 2. (a) (cl.) *a monument :* Lk 11⁴⁷ ; (b) *a sepulchre, tomb*

(Ge 23⁶·⁹, Is 22¹⁶, al.): Mt 23²⁹, Mk 5², Lk 11⁴⁴, Jo 5²⁸, and freq. in Gospels, Ac 13²⁹.

SYN.: μνῆμα.

μνήμη, -ης, ἡ (< μνάομαι), [in LXX for זֵכֶר, זִכָּרוֹן;] memory, remembrance, mention: μ. ποιεῖσθαι, c. gen., to remember, ii Pe 1¹⁵ (but in cl., π., μ. π. more freq. = to make mention, and so perh. here, cf. Mayor, in l.; and for ex. from π., v. Zorell, s.v.).†
SYN.: μνεία, q.v.

μνημονεύω (< μνήμων, mindful), [in LXX for זכר;] 1. to call to mind, remember: absol., Mk 8¹⁸; c. gen. pers., Lk 17³², Col 4¹⁸, I Th 1³, He 11ᴸᵗ (but v. infr.) 13⁷; τ. πτωχῶν, Ga 2²⁰; c. gen. rei, Jo 15²⁰ 16⁴·²¹, Ac 20³⁵; c. acc. obj. (as more freq. in cl.), of persons, ii Ti 2⁸; of things, Mt 16⁹, i Th 2⁹, Re 18⁵; seq. ὅτι, Ac 20³¹, Eph 2¹¹, ii Th 2⁵; πόθεν, Re 2⁵; πῶς, ib. 3³. 2. to make mention of: c. gen., He 11¹⁵ (but v. supr., and cf. M, Th., i, 1³); seq. περί, He 11²².†

μνημόσυνον, -ου, τό (< μνήμων, mindful), [in LXX freq. for זֵכֶר, זִכָּרוֹן and cogn. forms;] a memorial: Mt 26¹³, Mk 14⁹, Ac 10⁴ (where cf. Le 2⁹·¹⁶ 5¹², Nu 5²⁶, Si 45¹⁶, al.).†

μνηστεύω, [in LXX for ארשׂ pi., pu.;] 1. to woo and win, espouse. 2. to promise in marriage, betroth; pass., of the woman, to be betrothed: c. dat. pers., Mt 1¹⁸, Lk 1²⁷ 2⁵.†

μογγι-λάλος, v.s. μογιλάλος.

† μογι-λάλος, -ον (< μόγις, λάλος), [in LXX: Is 35⁶ (אִלֵּם) * ;] speaking with difficulty: Mk 7³² (Tr., txt., μογγιλάλος, thick-voiced, v. Swete, in l.).†

** μόγις, adv. (< μόγος, toil), [in LXX: Wi 9¹⁶ א A (μόλις, B), iii Mac 7⁶ * ;] with toil or difficulty, hardly: Lk 9³⁹ (μόλις, WH).†

μόδιος, -ου, ὁ (Lat. modius), a measure (16 sextarii, or about one English peck; EV, bushel; Moffatt, bowl): Mt 5¹⁵, Mk 4²¹, Lk 11³³.†

† μοιχαλίς, -ίδος, ἡ (= Att. μοιχάς, fem. of μοιχός), [in LXX: Pr 18²² 24⁵⁵ (30²⁰), Ez 16³⁸ 23⁴⁵, Ho 3¹, Ma 3⁵ (נֹאָפֶת, מְנָאָפֶת) * ;] an adulteress: Ro 7³; meton., for μοιχεία, ii Pe 2¹⁴. Metaph., of infidelity to God (cf. Ez 16¹⁵ ff., 23⁴³ ff., al.), Ja 4⁴; as an adj., Mt 12³⁹16⁴, Mk 8³⁸.†

μοιχάω, -ῶ (= cl. μοιχεύω), [in LXX (mid., absol. and c. acc., with party of either sex as subj.): Je 3⁸ 5⁷ 7⁹ 9² ⁽¹⁾ 23¹⁴ 36 (29)²³, Ez 16³² 23³⁷·⁴³ (נאף) * ;] to commit adultery with: c. acc. fem. In NT always mid. in same sense; of the man: absol., Mt 5³² 19⁹ (WH, txt., R, mg., om.); seq. ἐπ᾽ αὐτήν, Mk 10¹¹; of the woman: Mk 10¹².†

μοιχεία, -ας, ἡ (< μοιχεύω), [in LXX: Ho 2² ⁽⁴⁾ (נַאֲפוּפִים), 4² (נָאֹף), Je 13²⁷ (נַאֲפִים), Wi 14²⁶ * ;] adultery: Jo 8⁽³⁾; pl. (v. WM, 220; Bl., § 32, 6), Mt 15¹⁹, Mk 7²¹.†

μοιχεύω (< μοιχός), [in LXX: Ex 20¹³, Le 20¹⁰, al. (נאף);] to commit adultery: absol., Mt 5²⁷ 19¹⁸, Mk 10¹⁹, Lk 16¹⁸ 18²⁰, Ro 2²² 13⁹, Ja 2¹¹; c. acc. fem., Mt 5²⁸. Pass., of the woman, Mt 5³² 19⁹ WH, mg.), Jo 8⁽⁴⁾. Metaph., of idolatry (v.s. μοιχαλίς, and cf. Je 3⁹, al.), seq. μετ᾽ αὐτῆς, Re 2²².†

μοιχός, -οῦ, ὁ, [in LXX for נֹאֵף ;] *an adulterer :* Lk 18¹¹, 1 Co 6⁹, He 13⁴.†

μόλις, adv. (< μόλος, *toil*), post-Hom. alternative for μόγις, [in LXX : Pr 11³¹, Wi 9¹⁶, al. ;] *with difficulty, hardly, scarcely :* Lk 9³⁹ (T, μόγις), Ac 14⁸ 27⁷, ⁸, ¹⁶, Ro 5⁷, 1 Pe 4¹⁸ (LXX).†

Μολόχ, ὁ, indecl. (Heb. מֶלֶךְ, prop. מֶלֶךְ, *King,* but vocalized to read בֹּשֶׁת, *shame,* cf. Βάαλ, and v. *DB,* iii, 415 f.), *Moloch,* the god of the Ammonites : Ac 7⁴³ (LXX).†

μολύνω, [in LXX : Ge 37³¹ (טבל), Is 59³ (גאל ni.), Za 14² (שכב ni.), Si 21²⁸, al. ;] *to stain, soil, defile ;* in NT always symb. and fig. : 1 Co 8⁷, Re 3⁴ 14⁴.†

SYN. : μιαίνω, q.v.

† μολυσμός, -οῦ, ὁ (< μολύνω), [in LXX : Je 23¹⁵ (חנֻפָּה), 1 Es 8⁸³, 11 Mac 5²⁷ * ;] *defilement :* c. gen. obj., 11 Co 7¹ (Plut., FlJ).†

* μομφή, ῆς, ἡ (< μέμφομαι), poët. form of μέμψις, *blame, complaint :* Col 3¹³.†

** μονή, -ῆς, ἡ (< μένω), [in LXX : 1 Mac 7³⁸ * ;] 1. in cl., (*a*) *a staying, abiding ;* (*b*) *continuance* (LXX, l.c.). 2 In late Gk., (*a*) *a station* (Paus.) ; (*b*) *an abode :* Jo 14², ²³ ; (*c*) *a monastery* (cf. MM, iii, xvi ; so in MGr.).†

μονογενής, -ές (< μόνος, γένος), [in LXX : Jg 11³⁴, Ps 21 (22)²⁰ 24 (25)¹⁶ 34 (35)¹⁷ (יָחִיד), To 3¹⁵ 6¹⁰, ¹⁴ 8¹⁷, Wi 7²², Ba 4¹⁶ * ;] *only, only begotten* (*DCG,* ii, 281), of sons and daughters : Lk 7¹² 8⁴² 9³⁸, He 11¹⁷ ; of Christ, Jo 3¹⁶, ¹⁸, 1 Jo 4⁹ ; μ. παρὰ πατρός, Jo 1¹⁴ ; μ. θεός, ib. ¹⁸.†

μόνον, v.s. μόνος.

μόνος, -η, -ον, [in LXX chiefly for לְבַד ;] 1. adj., *alone, solitary, forsaken :* c. verb., Mt 14²³, Mk 6⁴⁷, Lk 9³⁶, al. ; c. pron., Mt 18¹⁵, Mk 9², al. ; c. subst., Mk 9⁸, Lk 4⁸, al. ; pleonast., οὐκ . . . εἰ μὴ μ., Mt 12⁴, Lk 6⁴, al. ; attrib., *only,* (ὁ) μ. θεός, Jo 5⁴⁴ 17³, Ro 16²⁷, 1 Ti 1¹⁷, Ju ²⁵. 2. As adv., (*a*) neut., μόνον, *alone, only :* referring to verb or predic., Mt 9²¹, Mk 5³⁶, Ja 1²², al. (v. Bl., § 44, 2) ; οὐ (μὴ) μ., Ga 4¹⁸, Ja 1²² ; οὐ μ. . . . ἀλλά (Bl., § 77, 13₃), Ac 19²⁶, 1 Jo 5⁶, al. ; id. seq. καί (Bl., § 81, 1₂), Ro 5³ 9¹⁰, 11 Co 8¹⁹, al. ; (*b*) κατὰ μόνας, *alone* (Bl., § 44, 1), Mk 4¹⁰, Lk 9¹⁸.

* μον-όφθαλμος, -ον (< μόνος), Ionic and κοινή, *one-eyed, having one eye :* Mt 18⁹, Mk 9⁴⁷.†

** μονόω, -ῶ (< μόνος), [in Aq. : Ge 49⁶ ;] *to leave alone, forsake :* of a childless widow, pf. ptcp. pass., 1 Ti 5⁵.†

μορφή, -ῆς, ἡ, [in LXX : Jg 8¹⁸ A (תֹּאַר), Jb 4¹⁶ (תְּמוּנָה), Is 44¹³ (תַּבְנִית), Da LXX 3¹⁹ (צְלֵם), Da TH 4³³ 5⁶, ⁹, ¹⁰ 7²⁸ (זִיו), To 1¹³, Wi 18¹, IV Mac 15⁴ * ;] *form, shape, appearance* (Hom., Eur., Æsch., al.) ; in philos. lang. the specific character or essential *form* (Arist., v. Gifford, *Inc.,* 26 ff.) : Mk 16[¹²], Phl 2⁶, ⁷.†

SYN. : μόρφωσις, the outline, delineation, semblance of the μορφή, as distinct from the μ. itself (Lft., *Notes*, 262); σχῆμα, *shape, fashion*, disting. from μορφή as the outward and accidental from the inward and essential (cf. Tr., *Syn.*, § lxx; Lft., *Phl.*, 125 ff.; Gifford., *Inc.*, l.c.).

**†μορφόω, -ῶ (< μορφή), [in Aq.: Is 44¹³ *;] *to form*: fig., Ga 4¹⁹ (cf. μετα-, συμ-μορφόω).†

*†μόρφωσις, -εως, ἡ (< μορφόω), 1. *a forming, shaping* (Theophr.). 2. *form, outline, semblance*: Ro 2²⁰; opp. to δύναμις, ιι Ti 3⁵.†
    SYN.: μορφή (q.v.), σχῆμα.

*†μοσχο-ποιέω, -ῶ, *to make a calf* (as an image): Ac 7⁴¹ (LXX, ἐποίησε μόσχον).†

μόσχος, -ου, ὁ, [in LXX chiefly for פַּר, also for שׁוֹר, עֵגֶל, etc.;] 1. *a young shoot or twig*. 2. ὁ, ἡ, μ., *offspring*; (a) of men; (b) of animals; most freq. (as always in LXX), *a calf, bullock, heifer*: Lk 15²³, ²⁷, ³⁰, He 9¹², ¹⁹, Re 4⁷.†

μουσικός, -ή, -όν, [in LXX: Ge 31²⁷, Ez 26¹³ (שִׁיר), Da LXX TH 3⁵ ff. (זְמַר), Si 22⁶, al.;] *skilled in the arts*, esp. *in music*; as subst., ὁ μ., *a minstrel, musician*: Re 18²².†

μόχθος, -ου, ὁ (= Hom. μόγος), in cl. chiefly poët., [in LXX for עָמָל, תְּלָאָה, etc.;] *toil, labour, hardship, distress*: ιι Co 11²⁷, ι Th 2⁹, ιι Th 3⁸.†
    SYN.: κόπος (q.v.), πόνος.

μυελός, -οῦ, ὁ, [in LXX: Ge 45¹⁸ (חֵלֶב), Jb 21²⁴ (מֹחַ) 33²⁴ *;] *marrow*: He 4¹².†

**μυέω, -ῶ (< μύω, *to shut* the mouth), [in LXX: ιιι Mac 2³⁰ *;] *to initiate into the mysteries* (so chiefly in cl.; LXX, l.c.); hence, *to instruct*: pass., Phl 4¹² (RV, *I have learned the secret*).†

**μῦθος, -ου, ὁ, [in LXX: Wi 17⁴ A, Si 20¹⁹ *;] 1. *speech, conversation*. 2. (a) *a story, narrative* (Hom.); (b) later, opp. to λόγος (*a true narrative*) = Lat. *fabula*, *a myth, fable, fiction*: ι Ti 1⁴ 4⁷, ιι Ti 4⁴, Tit 1¹⁴, ιι Pe 1¹⁶.†
    SYN.. λόγος, q.v.

**μυκάομαι, -ῶμαι, in cl. chiefly poët., [in Sm.: Jb 6⁵ *;] prop., of oxen (onomatop.), *to low, bellow*; of a lion, *to roar*: Re 10³.†

μυκτηρίζω (< μυκτήρ, *the nose*), [in LXX: ιv Ki 19²¹, Jb 22¹⁹, Ps 79 (80)⁶, al. (לעג), Pr 1³⁰ (נאץ) 15²⁰ (בזה), ι Mac 7³⁴, al.;] *to turn up the nose* or *sneer at, mock*: pass., Ga 6⁷ (cf. ἐκ-μυκτηρίζω).†

*†μυλικός, -ή, -όν (< μύλη, *a mill*), *of a mill*: λίθος μ., Lk 17².†

*†μύλινος, -η, -ον (< μύλος), 1. *made of mill-stone* (*C.I.* 3371). 2. = μυλικός: Re 18²¹ (μύλον, T).†

†μύλος, -ου, ὁ, [in LXX for רֵחַיִם, Nu 11⁸, De 24⁶, al.;] 1. = μύλη, *a mill* (Strab., Plut., LXX): Mt 24⁴¹, Re 18²². 2. *a mill-stone* (Anth.): Re 18²¹ (T); μ. ὀνικός, Mt 18⁶, Mk 9⁴² (v. Swete, in l.).†

μυλών, -ῶνος, ὁ, [in LXX: Je 52¹¹ *;] *a mill-house*: Mt 24⁴¹ (Rec.; μύλος, WH, R).†

Μύρα, Μύρρα (LT, Tr., WH), -ων, τά, *Myra*, a city of Lycia: Ac 27⁵.†

μυριάς, -άδος, ἡ (< μυρίος), [in LXX chiefly for רְבָבָה;] *ten thousand, a myriad*: pl., Ac 19¹⁹, Re 5¹¹ 9¹⁶; hyperb., of vast numbers, Lk 12¹, Ac 21²⁰, He 12²², Ju ¹⁴.†

* μυρίζω (< μύρον), Ionic and poët. (comic), *to anoint*: Mk 14⁸.†
SYN.: v.s. ἀλείφω, and cf. μύρον.

μυρίος, -α, -ον, 1. *numberless, countless, infinite*: 1 Co 4¹⁵ 14¹⁹. 2. As a definite numeral, in pl., μύριοι, -αι, -α, *ten thousand*: Mt 18²⁴.†

μύρον, -ου, τό, [in LXX chiefly for שֶׁמֶן, Pr 27⁹, Ps 132 (133)², al.;] *ointment*: Mt 26⁷, ¹², Mk 14³⁻⁵, Lk 7³⁷, ³⁸, ⁴⁶ 23⁵⁶, Jo 11² 12³, ⁵, Re 18¹³.†
SYN.: ἔλαιον, q.v.
Μύρρα, v.s. Μύρα.

Μυσία, -ας, ἡ, *Mysia*, a province of Asia Minor: Ac 16⁷, ⁸.†

μυστήριον, -ου, τό (< μυέω), [in LXX: Da LXX TH 2¹⁸ ᶠᶠ. (רָז), To 12⁷, ¹¹, Jth 2², Wi 2²² 6²² 14¹⁵, ²³, Si 3¹⁸ 22²² 27¹⁶, ¹⁷, ²¹, II Mac 13²¹ *;] 1. *that which is known to the μύστης* (*initiated*), a mystery or secret doctrine, mostly in pl., τὰ μ. (Æsch., Hdt., al.). 2. In later writers (Menand., *Incert.*, 168), that which may not be revealed (not, however, as in the modern sense, intrinsically difficult to understand), a *secret* or *mystery* of any kind (To, Jth, II Mac, ll. c.). 3. In NT, of the counsels of God (cf. Th.: Jb 15⁸, Ps 24 (25)¹⁴ for סוֹד), once hidden but now revealed in the Gospel or some fact thereof; (*a*) of the Christian revelation generally: Ro 16²⁵, I Co 2⁷, Col 1²⁶, ²⁷, Eph 3³, ⁹; τ. βασιλείας τ. θεοῦ, Mk 4¹¹; τ. θεοῦ, I Co 2¹, Re 10⁷; τ. θ., Χριστοῦ, Col 2²; τ. Χριστοῦ, Col 4³, Eph 3⁴; τ. θελήματος αὐτοῦ, Eph 1⁹; τ. εὐαγγελίου, Eph 6¹⁹; τ. πίστεως, I Ti 3⁹; τ. εὐσεβείας, ib. ¹⁶; (*b*) of particular truths, or details, of the Christian revelation: Ro 11²⁵, I Co 15⁵¹, Eph 5³², II Th 2⁷, Re 1²⁰ 17⁵, ⁷; pl., τὰ μ., I Co 13² 14²; θεοῦ, I Co 4¹; τ. βασιλείας τ. οὐρανῶν (θεοῦ), Mt 13¹¹, Lk 8¹⁰ (cf. Westc., *Eph.*, 180 ff.; AR, *Eph.*, 234 ff.; Lft., *Col.*, 165 f.; Hatch, *Essays*, 57 f.; DB, iii, 465 ff.; DCG, ii, 213 ff.).†

Μυτιλήνη, v.s. Μιτυλήνη.

*† μυ-ωπάζω (< μύωψ, *closing the eyes, short-sighted*; < μύω, ὤψ), *to be short-sighted*: II Pe 1⁹ (R, mg., *closing his eyes*; v. *ICC*, in l.).†

μώλωψ, -ωπος, ὁ, [in LXX for חַבּוּרָה, Ex 21²⁵, al.;] *a bruise, wound from a stripe*: I Pe 2²⁴ (LXX) (Arist., Plut., al.).†

μωμάομαι, -ῶμαι (< μῶμος), poët. and late prose, [in LXX: Pr 9⁷ (מוּם), Wi 10¹⁴, Si 31 (34)¹⁸ *;] *to find fault with, blame*: II Co 8²⁰; pass., ib. 6³.†

μῶμος, -ου, ὁ, [in LXX, of physical blemishes: Le 21¹⁷ ᶠᶠ., De 15²¹, Ca 4⁷, al. (מוּם); of mental defect, Si 20²⁴, al.;] 1. In cl. poets and late prose, *blame, disgrace.* 2. In LXX, perh. because of resemblance to מוּם, a physical *blemish* (cf. ἄμωμος, I Pe 1¹⁹, and v. Hort., in l.); metaph., of licentious persons, II Pe 2¹³.†

μωραίνω (< μωρός), [in LXX: Is 19¹¹, Je 10¹⁴ 28 (51)¹⁷ (בער ni.), II Ki 24¹⁰, Is 44²⁵ R (סכל ni., pi.)*;] 1. cl., to be foolish, play the fool. 2. LXX and NT, causal, to make foolish: I Co 1²⁰; pass., to become foolish: Ro 1²²; of salt that has lost its flavour, become tasteless: Mt 5¹³, Lk 14³⁴.†

**μωρία, -ας, ἡ (< μωρός), [in LXX: Si 20³¹*;] foolishness: I Co 1¹⁸, ²¹, ²³ 2¹⁴ 3¹⁹.†

*μωρολογία, -ας, ἡ, foolish talking: Eph 5⁴.†

μωρός, -ά, -όν, [in LXX for נָבָל, etc.; freq. in Si.;] 1. prop., of the nerves, dull, sluggish (Hipp., Arist.). 2. Of the mind, dull, stupid, foolish: Mt 5²² (v. Field, Notes, 3 ff.) 7²⁶ 23¹⁷, ¹⁹ (T, WH, txt., R, om.) 25², ³, ⁸, I Co 3¹⁸ 4¹⁰; of things, παράδοσις, Mk 7¹³ (T, WH, txt., R, om.): ζητήσεις, II Ti 2²³, Tit 3⁹; τὸ μ. τ. θεοῦ, I Co 1²⁵; τὰ μ. τ. κόσμου, ib. ²⁷.†

Μωυσῆς (Μωϋσῆς, T; Μωσῆς, Rec.), -έως, dat. -ῆ (as LXX: Ex 5²⁰, al.), and -εῖ, acc. -ῆν (as LXX) and -έα (Lk 16²⁹ only), (Heb. מֹשֶׁה), Moses: Mt 8⁴ 17³, ⁴, al.; νόμος Μωυσέως, Lk 2²² 24⁴⁴, Jo 7²³, Ac 13³⁹ 15⁵ 28²³, I Co 9⁹, He 10²⁸; by meton., of the books of Moses, Lk 16²⁹ 24²⁷, Ac 15²¹, II Co 3¹⁵.

N

N, ν, Νῦ, Nu, n, the thirteenth letter. As a numeral, ν´ = 50, ν, = 50,000.

Ναασσών, ὁ, indecl. (Heb. נַחְשׁוֹן), Naasson: Mt 1⁴, Lk 3³².†

Ναγγαί, ὁ, indecl., Naggai: Lk 3²⁵.†

Ναζαρά (Mt 4¹³—L, -άθ—Lk 4¹⁶), Ναζαρέθ (Mt 21¹¹, Ac 10³⁸), Ναζαρέτ (so always Rec.; WH, in foll. instances, where -έθ, T), ἡ, indecl. (Semitic form uncertain), Nazareth: Mt 2²³, Mk 1⁹, Lk 1²⁶ 2⁴, ³⁹, ⁵¹, Jo 1⁴⁵, ⁴⁶.†

Ναζαρηνός, -οῦ, ὁ, (on the Semitic form, v. Dalman, Gr., 141 n.), a Nazarene: Mk 1²⁴ 10⁴⁷ 14⁶⁷ 16⁶, Lk 4³⁴ 24¹⁹.†

Ναζωραῖος, -ον, ὁ (=-αρηνός, q.v.), a Nazarene: Mt 2²³ (LXX) 26⁷¹, Lk 18³⁷, Jo 18⁵, ⁷ 19¹⁹, Ac 2²² 3⁶ 4¹⁰ 6¹⁴ 22⁸ 24⁵ 26⁹.†

Ναθάμ (Rec. Ναθάν), ὁ, indecl. (Heb. נָתָן), Nathan: Lk 3³¹.†

Ναθαναήλ, ὁ, indecl. (Heb. נְתַנְאֵל), Nathanael, prob. to be identified with Bartholomew (q.v.): Jo 1⁴⁵⁻⁴⁹ 21².†

ναί, particle of affirmation, yea, verily, even so; in answer to a question: Mt 9²⁸ 13⁵¹ 17²⁵ 21¹⁶, Jo 11²⁷ 21¹⁵, ¹⁶, Ac 5⁸ 22²⁷, Ro 3²⁹; seq. λέγω ὑμῖν, Mt 11⁹, Lk 7²⁶; repeated for emphasis, ναὶ ναί (opp. to οὐ οὐ): Mt 5³⁷; ἤτω ὑμῶν τὸ ναὶ ναί, Ja 5¹²; v. καὶ οὔ, II Co 1¹⁸, ¹⁹; ἵνα ᾖ . . . τὸ ναὶ ναί, ib. ¹⁷; τὸ ν., ib. ²⁰; in assent to an assertion: Mt 15²⁷, Mk 7²⁸, Re 14¹³ 16⁷; in confirmation of a previous assertion: Mt 11²⁶, Lk 10²¹ 11⁵¹ 12⁵, Phl 4³, Phm ²⁰; in solemn asseveration: Re 1⁷ 22²⁰.†

Ναιμάν (Rec. Νεεμάν), ὁ, indecl. (Heb. נַעֲמָן), *Naaman :* Lk 4²⁷.†

Ναίν (Rec. Ναΐν), ἡ, indecl. (Heb. נָאִין), *Nain,* a village of Galilee : Lk 7¹¹.†

ναός, -οῦ, ὁ, (Att. νεώς; < ναίω, *to inhabit*), [in LXX (νεώς, II Mac 6², al.) chiefly for הֵיכָל ;] 1. *a temple* (Hom., Pind., al.). 2. The inmost part of a temple, *the shrine* (Hdt., Xen., al.); in NT, (*a*) generally : pl., Ac 17²⁴; of silver models of a heathen shrine, Ac 19²⁴; (*b*) of the *temple* building proper, or *sanctuary*, at Jerusalem, as distinct from τ. ἱερόν (q.v.), the whole temple enclosure : Mt 23¹⁶, ¹⁷, ³⁵ 27⁵, ⁴⁰, Mk 14⁵⁸ 15²⁹, Jo 2¹⁹, ²⁰, Re 11²; (τοῦ) θεοῦ, Mt 26⁶¹ 27⁵¹, Mk 15³⁸, Lk 1⁹, ²¹, ²² 23⁴⁵, I Co 3¹⁷, II Co 6¹⁶, II Th 2⁴, Re 11¹; of the temple in the Apocal. visions, Re 3¹² 7¹⁵ 11¹⁹ 14¹⁵, ¹⁷ 15⁵, ⁶, ⁸ 16¹, ¹⁷ 21²²ᵃ. Metaph., of Christians, I Co 3¹⁶ 6¹⁹, II Co 6¹⁶, Eph 2²¹; of Christ's body, Jo 2²¹ (cf. ib. ¹⁹); ὁ θεὸς ν. αὐτῆς ἐστιν, Re 21²²ᵇ.†
SYN. : ἱερόν.

Ναούμ, ὁ, indecl. (Heb. נַחוּם), *Nahum :* Lk 3²⁵.†

νάρδος, -ου, ἡ (Heb. נֵרְדְּ, both from Sanscrit *narda*, v. Boisacq, s.v.), [in LXX : Ca 1¹² 4¹³, ¹⁴ (נֵרְדְּ) * ;] *nard ;* (*a*) an Indian plant, *the Nardostachys nardus jatamansi,* used for the preparation of a fragrant ointment; (*b*) *ointment of nard :* Mk 14³, Jo 12³.†

Νάρκισσος, -ου, ὁ, *Narcissus :* Ro 16¹¹.†

* **ναυαγέω**, -ῶ (< ναῦς, + ἄγνυμι, *to break*), *to suffer shipwreck :* II Co 11²⁵ ; metaph., seq. περὶ τ. πίστιν, I Ti 1¹⁹.†

* **ναύ-κληρος**, -ου, ὁ (< ναῦς, κλῆρος), *a shipowner, shipmaster :* Ac 27¹¹.†

ναῦς, νεώς, acc. ναῦν, ἡ, [in LXX for אֳנִי, אֳנִיָּה ;] *a ship :* Ac 27⁴¹ (elsewhere in NT always τ. πλοῖον ; v. M, *Pr.,* 25 f. ; Bl., *Gosp.,* 186 f.).†

** **ναύτης**, -ου, ὁ (< ναῦς), [in Aq. : Ez 27⁹ ; Sm. : ib. ²⁹ * ;] *a seaman, sailor :* Ac 27²⁷, ³⁰, Re 18¹⁷.†

Ναχώρ, ὁ, indecl. (Heb. נָחוֹר), *Nahor :* Lk 3³⁴.†

νεανίας, -ου, ὁ (< νεάν = νέος), [in LXX for נַעַר, בָּחוּר ;] *a young man :* Ac 7⁵⁸ 20⁹ 23¹⁷, ¹⁸.†

νεανίσκος, -ου, ὁ (dimin. of νεανίας), [in LXX chiefly for נַעַר, also for בָּחוּר, etc. ;] *a young man, youth :* Mt 19²⁰, ²² Mk 14⁵¹ 16⁵, Lk 7¹⁴, Ac 2¹⁷ (LXX) 23¹⁸, ²², I Jo 2¹³, ¹⁴; of an *attendant* (cf. Ge 14²⁴, al.) : Ac 5¹⁰.†

Νεάπολις, -εως, ἡ, Rec. for Νέα Πόλις (WH), the more freq. form (LS, s.v.), *Neapolis,* a maritime city of Macedonia : Ac 16¹¹.†

Νεεμάν, v.s. Ναιμάν.

νεκρός, -ά, -όν, [in LXX chiefly for מֵת ;] *dead,* I. as adj., 1. prop. : Ac 5¹⁰ 20⁹, Ja 2²⁶, Re 1¹⁸, al. ; ὡσεὶ ν., Mt 28⁴, Mk 9²⁶, Re 1¹⁷;

of that which is subject to death, Ro 8¹⁰. 2. Metaph., (a) of persons : Lk 15²⁴, ³²; of those immersed in worldly cares, Mt 8²², Lk 9⁶⁰; of spiritual death, Jo 5²⁵, Ro 6¹³, Eph 5¹⁴, Re 3¹; τ. παραπτώμασιν, Eph 2¹, ⁵, Col 2¹³; of the opposite condition, ν. τῇ ἁμαρτίᾳ, Ro 6¹¹; (b) of things regarded as inoperative, devoid of power : ἁμαρτία, Ro 7⁸; πίστις, Ja 2¹⁷, ²⁶; ἔργα, He 6¹ 9¹⁴. II. As subst., νεκρός, ὁ (Hom., al.), chiefly in pl. (οἱ) ν., the dead : Mt 11⁵, Mk 12²⁶, Lk 20³⁷, 1 Co 15¹⁵, al.; ἀνάστασις (τ.) νεκρῶν, Mt 22³¹, Ac 17³², al.; ν. . . . . ζῶντες, Mt 22³², Mk 12²⁷, Ac 10⁴², al.; ἀπὸ νεκρῶν, Lk 16³⁰; ἐκ ν., Mk 6¹⁴, Lk 24⁴⁶, Jo 12¹, Ac 13³⁴, Ro 10⁷, al.; πρωτότοκος ἐκ τῶν ν., Col 1¹⁸; ζωὴ ἐκ ν., Ro 11¹⁵; constr. praegn., ἐκ ν. ζῶντες, Ro 6¹³.

*† νεκρόω, ῶ (< νεκρός), to make dead, put to death; pass., to be dead : hyperbolically, of impotent age, He 11¹²; σῶμα, Ro 4¹⁹. Trop., of carnal impulses, τὰ μέλη, Col 3⁵.†

*† νέκρωσις, -εως, ἡ (< νεκρόω), 1. a putting to death. 2. a state of death, death : Ro 4¹⁹, II Co 4¹⁰ (v. Deiss., LAE, 94).†

νεομηνία (Att. contr., νουμ-, Rec.), -ας, ἡ (< νέος, μήν), [in LXX chiefly for חֹדֶשׁ;] new moon : of the Jewish festival, Col 2¹⁶.†

νέος, -α, -ον, [in LXX for נַעַר (Ge 37², Ex 33¹¹, al.), חָדָשׁ (Le 23¹⁶, Nu 28²⁶, al.), etc.; compar. -ώτερος for קָטֹן, צָעִיר, etc.;] 1. young, youthful : Tit 2⁴. 2. new (prop., in respect of time; v.s. καινός) : οἶνος (cf. οἰ. καινός, Mt 26²⁹), Mt 9¹⁷, Mk 2²², Lk 5³⁷⁻[³⁹]; φύραμα (fig.), 1 Co 5⁷; διαθήκη (cf. καινὴ δ., He 9¹⁵), He 12²⁴; metaph., ἄνθρωπος (cf. καινὸς ἀ., Eph 2¹⁵), Col 3¹⁰. 3. Compar., -ώτερος, -α, -ον, younger : Lk 15¹², ¹³ 22²⁶, Jo 21¹⁸; pl., οἱ ν., Ac 5⁶ (Rackham, in l.), 1 Ti 5¹¹, Tit 2⁶; opp. to πρεσβύτεροι, 1 Ti 5¹, 1 Pe 5⁵; αἱ ν., 1 Ti 5², ¹⁴. 4. Νέα Πόλις, Neapolis : Ac 16¹¹ (Rec., Νεάπολις, q.v.).

SYN. : καιιός, q.v.

νεοσσός, v.s. νοσσός.

νεότης, -ητος, ἡ (< νέος), [in LXX chiefly for נְעוּרִים;] youth : Mk 10²⁰, Lk 18²¹, Ac 26⁴, 1 Ti 4¹².†

νεό-φυτος, -ον (< νέος, φύω), [in LXX : Jb 14⁹, Ps 143 (144)¹², Is 5⁷ (נֶטַע), Ps 127 (128)³ (שָׁתִיל) *;] newly-planted (LXX). Metaph., as subst., ὁ ν., a new convert, neophyte, novice : 1 Ti 3⁶.†

Νέρων, -ωνος, ὁ, Nero : II Ti subscr. (Rec.).†

νεύω, [in LXX : Pr 4⁵ 21¹ *;] to nod or beckon, as a sign : c. dat. pers. et inf., Jo 13²⁴, Ac 24¹⁰ (cf. δια-, ἐκ-, ἐν-, ἐπι-, κατα-νεύω).†

νεφέλη, -ης, ἡ (< νέφος), [in LXX chiefly for עָנָן, also for עָב, etc.;] a cloud (single and specific as opp. to νέφος, a great indefinite mass of vapour) : Mt 17⁵ 24³⁰ 26⁶⁴, Mk 9⁷ 13²⁶ 14⁶², Lk 9³⁴, ³⁵ 12⁵⁴ 21³⁷, Ac 1⁹, 1 Th 4¹⁷, Ju ¹², Re 1⁷ 10¹ 11¹² 14¹⁴⁻¹⁶; of the pillar of cloud in the wilderness (Ex 14¹⁹, ²⁰, Ps 104³⁹, al.) : 1 Co 10¹, ².†

Νεφθαλείμ (-λίμ, WH in Re, l.c.), ὁ, indecl. (Heb. נַפְתָּלִי), Naphtali : Mt 4¹³, ¹⁵ (LXX), Re 7⁶.†

νέφος, -ους, τό, [in LXX for עָב, שַׁחַק, עָנָן;] a mass of clouds, a cloud (cf. νεφέλη); metaph. (as in Hom., Hdt., al.), of a dense throng: He 12¹.†

νεφρός, -οῦ, ὁ, [in LXX for כִּלְיָה, Ex 29¹³, al.; metaph., Ps 7⁹, 15 (16)⁷ 25 (26)², Wi 1⁶, al.;] a kidney; pl., the kidneys, reins; metaph., of the will and affections: ν. καὶ καρδίαι (thoughts), Re 2²³.†

* νεω-κόρος, -ου, a temple-keeper; as honorary title given to a city (v. DB, i, 722 b): Ac 19³⁵.†

**† νεωτερικός, -ή, -όν (< νεώτερος), [in LXX: iii Mac 4⁸ *;] = νεανικός, youthful, esp. of qualities: ἐπιθυμίαι, ii Ti 2²² (Polyb.).†

νεώτερος, v.s. νέος.

νή, particle of affirmation employed in oaths, [in LXX: ν. τ. ὑγίειαν, Ge 42¹⁵, ¹⁶ (חֵי) *;] by: c. acc., i Co 15³¹.†

νήθω, [in LXX for טָוָה, שָׁזַר hoph., Ex 26³¹ 35²⁵, al.;] to spin: Mt 6²⁸, Lk 12²⁷.†

* νηπιάζω (< νήπιος), (Hippocr., = νηπιαχεύω, Hom.), to be a babe: i Co 14²⁰.†

νήπιος, -α, -ον, [in LXX chiefly for עוֹלֵל, also for פְּתִי, etc.;] infant; of children and minors: Mt 21¹⁶ (LXX), i Co 13¹¹, Ga 4¹ (v. Lft., in l.).   Metaph., childish, unskilled, simple (Ps 18 (19)⁸, Pr 1³², al.): Mt 11²⁵, Lk 10²¹, Ro 2²⁰, Ga 4³, Eph 4¹⁴, i Th 2⁷ (WH, for ἤπιοι); opp. to τέλειος, He 5¹³; ν. ἐν Χριστῷ, i Co 3¹.†

Νηρεί (Rec. -ρί), ὁ, indecl. (Heb. נֵרִי), Neri: Lk 3²⁷.†

Νηρεύς, -έως, ὁ, Nereus: Ro 16¹⁵.†

*† νησίον, -ου, τό (dimin. of νῆσος), = νησίς (Hdt., Thuc., al.), a small island: Ac 27¹⁶.†

νῆσος, -ου, ἡ, [in LXX for אִי;] an island: Ac 13⁶ 27²⁶ 28¹, ⁷, ⁹, ¹¹, Re 1⁹ 6¹⁴ 16²⁰.†

νηστεία, -ας, ἡ (< νηστεύω), [in LXX for צוֹם;] fasting, a fast; (a) of voluntary abstinence from food: Mt 17²¹ (WH, R, txt., om.), Mk 9²⁹ (WH, txt., R, txt., om.), Lk 2³⁷, Ac 14²³; of the Day of Atonement, Ac 27⁹; (b) of involuntary abstinence: ii Co 6⁵ 11²⁷.†
SYN.: ἀσιτία, q.v.

νηστεύω (< νῆστις), [in LXX for צוּם;] to fast (Arist., Aristoph., al.): Mt 4² 6¹⁶⁻¹⁸ 9¹⁴, ¹⁵, Mk 2¹⁸⁻²⁰, Lk 5³³⁻³⁵ 18¹², Ac 13², ³.†

νῆστις, -ιος, ὁ, ἡ (< νη-, neg. prefix, + ἐσθίω), in cl., chiefly poët., [in LXX: Da LXX 6¹⁸ ⁽¹⁹⁾ (טְוָת) *;] not eating, fasting: Mt 15³², Mk 8³.†

* νηφάλιος (-λεος, Rec., in i Ti, ll. c), -ον (in cl., -α, -ον), (< νήφω), 1. in cl., of drink, not mixed with wine. 2. In later writers (Plut., al.), of persons, sober, temperate: i Ti 3², ¹¹, Tit 2².†

* νήφω, to be sober, abstain from wine; metaph., of moral alert-

ness, *to be sober, calm, circumspect*: 1 Th 5⁶, ⁸, 11 Ti 4⁵ (v. Ellic., in l.), 1 Pe 1¹³ 4⁷ 5⁸ (cf. ἀνα-, ἐκ-νήφω, and v. MM, xvii).†

SYN.: ἀγρυπνέω, γρηγορέω.

Νίγερ, ὁ (Lat. *niger*), *Niger* : Ac 13¹.†

νίζω, v.s. νίπτω.

Νικάνωρ, -ορος, ὁ, *Nicanor* : Ac 6⁵.†

νικάω, -ῶ (< νίκη), [in LXX: Ps 50 (51)⁴ (זכה), Pr 6²⁵ (חמד); freq. in iv Mac;] *to conquer, prevail* : absol., of Christ, Re 3²¹ 6²; c. inf., ib. 5⁵; of Christians, Re 2⁷, ¹¹, ¹⁷, ²⁶ 3⁵, ¹², ²¹ 21⁷; seq. ἐκ (RV, *come victorious from*), Re 15²; as law-term (cl.), Ro 3⁴ ⁽ᴸˣˣ⁾; c. acc. pers., Lk 11²², Re 11⁷ 13⁷ ([WH], R, mg., om.); of Christ, Jo 16³³ (τ. κόσμον), Re 17¹⁴; of Christians, 1 Jo 4⁴; τ. πονηρόν, 1 Jo 2¹³, ¹⁴; αὐτόν (ref. to ὁ κατήγωρ, ib. ¹⁰), Re 12¹¹; c. acc. rei, τὸν κόσμον, Jo 16³³, 1 Jo 5⁴, ⁵; τὸ κακόν, Ro 12²¹; pass., μὴ νικῶ ὑπὸ τ. κακοῦ, ib. (cf. ὑπερ-νικάω).†

νίκη, -ης, ἡ, [in LXX: 1 Ch 29¹¹ (נצח), freq. in i-iv Mac;] *victory*: 1 Jo 5⁴.†

Νικόδημος, -ου, ὁ, *Nicodemus* : Jo 3¹, ⁴, ⁹ 7⁵⁰ 19³⁹.†

Νικολαΐτης, -ου, ὁ, *a Nicolaitan* : pl., Re 2⁶, ¹⁵.†

Νικόλαος, -ου, ὁ, *Nicolaus* : Ac 6⁵.†

Νικόπολις, -εως, ἡ, *Nicopolis*, prob. the city of that name in Epirus (*CGT*, in l.) : Tit 3¹².†

† νῖκος, -ους, τό, late form of νίκη, [in LXX: La 3¹⁸ (נצח), 1 Es 3ᶜ, 11 Mac 10³⁸, iv Mac 17¹²; εἰς ν. (instead of εἰς τέλος, Jb 14²⁰), 11 Ki 2²⁶, Jb 36⁷, Am 1¹¹ 8⁷, Je 3⁵, La 5²⁰ (לנצח, as נ in Syr., = *victory*)*;] *victory*: Mt 12²⁰ (Is 42³, LXX ἀλήθεια), 1 Co 15⁵⁴ (Is 25⁸, Aq., Th.), ib. ⁵⁵ (Ho 13¹⁴, LXX δίκη), ib. ⁵⁷.†

Νινευείτης (Rec. -ευίτης, L, -ίτης), -ου, ὁ, *a Ninevite* : Mt 12⁴¹, Lk 11³⁰, ³².†

Νινευί, ἡ (Heb. נינוה), *Nineveh* : Lk 11³², Rec.†

*† νιπτήρ, -ῆρος, ὁ (νίπτω), *a basin* : Jo 13⁵.†

νίπτω, late form of νίζω, [in LXX chiefly for רחץ;] *to wash*, usually of a part of the body: c. acc. pers., Jo 13⁸; τ. πόδας, Jo 13⁵, ⁶, ⁸, ¹², ¹⁴, 1 Ti 5¹⁰; mid., reflexive, *to wash oneself* : Jo 9⁷, ¹¹, ¹⁵; τ. χεῖρας, Mt 15², Mk 7³; τ. πόδας, Jo 13¹⁰; τ. πρόσωπον, Mt 6¹⁷ (in cl. Att. prose, used only in compounds; cf. ἀπο-νίπτω).†

SYN. : λούω (q.v.), πλύνω.

νοέω, -ῶ (< νοῦς), [in LXX chiefly for בין, also for שכל hi., etc ;] 1. *to perceive* with the mind, *understand* (for the phrase νοῶν κ. φρονῶν, in wills, v. MM, xvii): absol., Mt 16⁹, Mk 8¹⁷; c. acc., Eph 3⁴, 1 Ti 1⁷; c. dat. instr., τ. καρδία, Jo 12⁴⁰; pass., Ro 1²⁰; seq. ὅτι, Mt 15¹⁷ 16¹¹, Mk 7¹⁸; c. acc. et inf., He 11³. 2. *to think, consider* : absol., Mt 24¹⁵, Mk 13¹⁴, Eph 3²⁰; c. acc. rei, 11 Ti 2⁷ (cf. εὐ-, κατα-, μετα-, προ-, ὑπο-νοέω).†

** νόημα, -τος, τό (νοέω), [in LXX: Si 21¹¹, Ba 2⁸, iii Mac 5³⁰ *;] *a* *thought, purpose, design:* ɪɪ Co 2¹¹ 10⁵ 11³, Phl 4⁷. Meton., of the mind, ɪɪ Co 3¹⁴ 4⁴.†

** **νόθος**, -η, -ον, [in LXX: Wi 4³ *;] *a bastard, base born,* i.e. born of a slave or concubine : He 12⁸.†

νομή, -ῆς, ἡ (< νέμω, *to pasture*), [in LXX chiefly for מִרְעֶה, also for נָוֶה, etc.;] 1. *a pasture, pasturage:* fig., Jo 10⁹. 2. *a grazing, feeding;* metaph., of a spreading sore, ɪɪ Ti 2¹⁷ (Polyb.).†

** **νομίζω** (< νόμος), [in LXX: Wi 13² 17³, Si 29⁴, ɪɪ Mac ₄, ɪv Mac ₈ *;] 1. *to practise, hold by custom:* Ac 16¹³ (Rec., but v. infr.). 2. *to deem, consider, suppose:* Mt 5¹⁷ 10³⁴ 20¹⁰, Lk 2⁴⁴ 3²³, Ac 7²⁵ 8²⁰ 14¹⁹ 16¹³, ²⁷ 17²⁹ 21²⁹, ɪ Co 7²⁶, ³⁶, ɪ Ti 6⁵.†

  SYN.: ἡγέομαι, q.v.

** **νομικός**, -ή, -όν (< νόμος), [in LXX: ɪv Mac 5⁴ *;] 1. *relating to law:* μάχαι, Tit 3⁹. 2. *learned in the law;* as subst., ὁ ν. (EV, *lawyer*): Mt 22³⁵, Lk 10²⁵, Tit 3¹³; pl., Lk 7³⁰ 11⁴⁵, ⁴⁶, ⁵² 14³ (cf. MM, xvii).†

  SYN.: γραμματεύς, q.v.

** **νομίμως**, adv. (< νόμιμος, *conformable to law*), [in LXX: ɪv Mac 6¹⁸ *;] *rightly, lawfully:* ɪ Ti 1⁸, ɪɪ Ti 2⁵.†

νόμισμα, -τος, τό (< νομίζω), [in LXX: ɪɪ Es 8³⁶ (דַּת), Ne 7⁷¹ R (דַּרְכְּמוֹן), ɪ Mac 15⁶ *;] 1. *that which is established by usage, a custom.* 2. The *current coin* of a state: Mt 22¹⁹.†

*†**νομο-διδάσκαλος**, -ου, ὁ, *a teacher of the law:* Lk 5¹⁷, Ac 5³⁴, ɪ Ti 1⁷ (NT and eccl. only; cf. νομοδείκτης, -διδάκτης, Plut.).†

  SYN.: γραμματεύς, q.v.

** **νομοθεσία**, -ας, ἡ (< νόμος, τίθημι), [in LXX: ɪɪ Mac 6²³, ɪv Mac 5³⁵ 17¹⁶ *;] *legislation, lawgiving:* Ro 9⁴.†

νομοθετέω, -ῶ, [in LXX for ירה hi.;] 1. intrans., *to make laws;* pass., *to be furnished with laws:* He 7¹¹. 2. Trans., *to ordain by law, enact:* pass., He 8⁶.†

νομο-θέτης, -ου, ὁ (< νόμος, τίθημι), [in LXX: Ps 9²⁰ *;] *a law-giver:* Ja 4¹².†

νόμος, -ου, ὁ (< νέμω, *to deal out, distribute*), [in LXX chiefly for תּוֹרָה, also for חֻקָּה, etc.;] *that which is assigned, hence, usage, custom,* then *law;* in NT (only in Mt, Jo, Ja, and the Lucan and Pauline bks.); 1. of law in general: Ro 3²⁷ 5¹³ᵇ; pl., of divine laws, He 8¹⁰ 10¹⁶; ὁ ν. τ. Χριστοῦ, Ga 6²; (τ.) ἐλευθερίας, Ja 1²⁵ 2¹²; βασιλικός (Hort., in l.; Deiss., *LAE*, 367₃), Ja 2⁸. 2. Of a force or influence impelling to action: Ro 7²¹, ²³ᵃ, ²⁵ 8². 3. Of the Mosaic law: Mt 5¹⁸, Lk 2²⁷, Jo 1¹⁷, Ac 6¹³, Ro 2¹⁵, ɪ Co 9⁸, ɪ Ti 1⁸, He 7¹⁹, al.; ν. Μωυσέως, Lk 2²², Jo 7²³, Ac 15⁵, al.; κυρίου, Lk 2³⁹; κατὰ τὸν ν., Ac 22¹², He 7⁵ 9²². 3. Anarthrous (Bl., § 46, 8; *ICC* on Ro 2¹², ¹³)), νόμος, (*a*) of law in general: Ro 2¹², ¹⁴ᵇ 3²⁰, ²¹ 4¹⁵, al.; (*b*) of the Mosaic law in its quality as law: Ro 2¹⁴ᵃ 5²⁰ 10⁴, Ga 2¹⁹, al.; οἱ ἐκ ν., Ro 4¹⁴; ὑπὸ νόμον, ɪ Co 9²⁰, Ga 4⁵; ν. πράσσειν (πληροῦν), Ro 2²⁵ 13⁸. 4. Of Christian teaching: ν. πίστεως, Ro 3²⁷; τ. Χριστοῦ, Ga 6². 5. By meton., of the books which contain the law; (a) of the Pentateuch: Mt 12⁵, Jo 1⁴⁵, al.; ὁ ν. καὶ οἱ προφῆται, Mt 5¹⁷, Lk 16¹⁶, al.; ὁ ν. καὶ προφῆται κ. ψαλμοί, Lk 24⁴⁴; (b) of the OT Scriptures in general (as Heb. תּוֹרָה): Jo 10³⁴ 12³⁴ 15²⁵, 1 Co 14²¹, al. (v. MM, VGT, s.v.; ICC on Ga, pp. 443 ff.).

νόος, v.s. νοῦς.

** νοσέω, -ῶ (< νόσος), [in LXX (metaph.): Wi 17⁸ *;] to be sick: metaph., of mental ailment, seq. περί, 1 Ti 6⁴ (cf. Plat., Mor., 546 d).†

* νόσημα, -τος, τό (< νοσέω), sickness: Jo 5⁽⁴⁾.†

νόσος, -ου, ἡ, [in LXX for חֳלִי, etc.;] disease, sickness: Mt 4²³, ²⁴ 8¹⁷ (Aq.) 9³⁵ 10¹, Mk 1³⁴, Lk 4⁴⁰ 6¹⁷ 7²¹ 9¹, Ac 19¹².†
SYN.: v.s. ἀσθένεια.

νοσσιά, -ᾶς, ἡ (< νοσσός), late form of cl., νεοσσιά, [in LXX chiefly for קֵן;] 1. a nest of birds. 2. a brood of young birds: Lk 13³⁴.†

νοσσίον, -ου, τό, dimin. of νοσσός, q.v., [in LXX: Ps 83 (84)³ (אֶפְרֹחַ) *;] a young bird: Mt 23³⁷.†

νοσσός (νεοσσός, Rec., as in cl. Att. -ττός; Phryn. rejects the dissyl. form), -οῦ, ὁ (< νέος), [in LXX chiefly for בֵּן;] a young bird: Lk 2²⁴ (LXX).†

νοσφίζω (< νόσφι, apart, aside), [in LXX: Jos 7¹ (לָקַח), 11 Mac 4³² *;] 1. in Hom., as depon., to turn away (from), abandon. 2. After Hom., in act., to set apart, remove. Mid., to set apart for oneself, peculate, purloin: absol., Tit 2¹⁰ (for ex. in π., v. MM, xvii); seq. ἀπό, Ac 5², ³.†

νότος, -ου, ὁ, [in LXX chiefly for נֶגֶב, also for דָּרוֹם, תֵּימָן and קָדִים;] 1. prop., the south wind: Lk 12⁵⁵, Ac 27¹³ 28¹³. 2. South: Lk 13²⁰, Re 21¹³. 3. the South, as a region (cf. נֶגֶב): Mt 12⁴², Lk 11³¹.†

** νουθεσία, -ας ἡ (< νουθετέω), = cl. νουθέτησις; [in LXX: Wi 16⁶ *;] admonition: 1 Co 10¹¹, Eph 6⁴, Tit 3¹⁰ (Aristoph., Diod., al.).†

νουθετέω, -ῶ (< νοῦς, τίθημι, hence, put in mind), [in LXX: 1 Ki 3¹³ (כהה pi.), Jb 8 (יסר pi., בִּין), Wi 11¹⁰ 12², ²⁶ *;] to admonish, exhort: c. acc. pers., Ac 20³¹, Ro 15¹⁴, 1 Co 4¹⁴, Col 1²⁸ 3¹⁶, 1 Th 5¹², ¹⁴, 11 Th 3¹⁵.†

νουμηνία, v.s. νεομηνία.

* νουνεχῶς, adv. (< νοῦς, ἔχω), sensibly, discreetly: Mk 12³⁴.†

νοῦς (contr. from νόος), ὁ, gen., dat., νοός, νοΐ (late forms, = cl., νοῦ, νῷ; Bl., § 9, 3), acc., νοῦν, [in LXX chiefly for לֵב, לֵבָב;] 1. prop., of the ruling faculty, mind, understanding, reason (v. Lft., Notes, 88 f.; Vaughan on Ro 7²³): Lk 24⁴⁵, Ro 1²⁸ 7²³ 12² 14⁵, Eph 4¹⁷, ²³, Phl 4⁷, 11 Th 2², 1 Ti 6⁵, 11 Ti 3⁸, Tit 1¹⁵, Re 13¹⁸ 17⁹; ν. τ. σαρκός (ICC, in l.), Col 2¹⁸; opp. to σάρξ, Ro 7²⁵; to πνεῦμα, 1 Co 14¹⁴, ¹⁵; to γλῶσσα, ib. ¹⁹.

2. By meton., of an act of mind, *a mind, thought, purpose:* Ro 11³⁴ = 1 Co 2¹⁶ (LXX), 1 Co 1¹⁰.†
SYN.: v.s. πνεῦμα.

Νύμφα (Rec., R, txt., Νυμφᾶς, q.v.), -ης, ἡ, *Nympha* (v. M, *Pr.*, 48): Col 4¹⁵, WH, R, mg.†

Νυμφᾶς, -ᾶ, ὁ (WH, R, mg., Νύμφα, q.v.), *Nymphas:* Col 4¹⁵, R, txt. (cf. *ICC*, Lft., in l.).†

νύμφη, -ης, ἡ, [in LXX chiefly for כַּלָּה;] 1. cl., *a bride, young wife, young woman:* Mt 25¹, WH, mg., Jo 3²⁹, Re 18²³ 21², ⁹ 22¹⁷. 2. As freq. in LXX (Ge 38¹¹, al., for כַּלָּה; (a) *bride;* (b) *daughter-in-law*) and in MGr. (νύφφη, νύφη), *a daughter-in-law:* Mt 10³⁵, Lk 12⁵³.†

νυμφίος, -ου, ὁ (<νύμφη), [in LXX for חָתָן;] *a bridegroom:* Mt 9¹⁵ 25¹, ⁵, ⁶, ¹⁰, Mk 2¹⁹, ²⁰, Lk 5³⁴, ³⁵, Jo 2⁹, 3²⁹, Re 18²³.†

**†νυμφών, -ῶνος, ὁ (<νύμφη), [in LXX: To 6¹³, ¹⁶ *;] *the bride-chamber* (Heb. חֻפָּה, LXX, παστός, Ps 18 (19)⁵, Jl 2¹⁶): Mt 22¹⁰ (WH; γάμος, RV); οἱ υἱοὶ τοῦ ν. (cf. cl. νυμφαγωγός, νυμφευτής), the bridegroom's friends who have charge of the nuptial arrangements: Mt 9¹⁵, Mk 2¹⁹, Lk 5³⁴.†

νῦν, adv., [in LXX chiefly for עַתָּה;] 1. prop., of time, *now,* i.e. at the present time: as opp. to past, Jo 4¹⁸, Ac 7⁵², Ro 13¹¹, II Co 7⁹, Col 1²⁴, al.; opp. to fut., Jo 12²⁷, Ro 11³¹, al.; c. art., ὁ (ἡ, τὸ) ν. et subst., *the present:* Ro 3²⁶, Ga 4²⁵, I Ti 6¹⁷, Tit 2¹², al.; ἀπὸ τοῦ ν. (LXX for מֵעַתָּה), Lk 1⁴⁸, Ac 18⁶, al.; ἄχρι τοῦ ν., Ro 8²², Phl 1⁵; ἕως τοῦ ν. (LXX for עַד עַתָּה), Mt 24²¹, Mk 13¹⁹; τὰ ν., as *regards the present,* Ac 5³⁸; νῦν, c. praet., *just now, but now,* Mt 26⁶⁵, Jo 11⁸ 21¹⁰; c. fut., *now, presently,* Jo 12³¹, Ac 20²²; so c. praes., *presently, forthwith,* Jo 12³¹ 17¹³; καὶ ν., Jo 11²² 17⁵, al.; ἀλλὰ ν., Lk 22³⁶; ἔτι ν., I Co 3²; τότε (πότε) . . . ν. (δέ), Ro 6²¹ 11³⁰; ν. ἤδη, I Jo 4³; ν. οὖν, Ac 10³³, al. 2. Of logical sequence (often difficult to disting. from the temporal sense; cf. Lft., *Notes,* 113 f.), *now, therefore, now, however, as it is:* Lk 11³⁹; καὶ ν., Ac 3¹⁷, II Th 2⁶, I Jo 2·⁸; id. seq. δεῦρο, Ac 7³⁴; ν. δέ, Jo 8⁴⁰ 9⁴¹ 15²², ²⁴, 18³⁶, I Co 5¹¹ 7¹⁴ 12²⁰, al. (cf. WM, 579ₙ).

νυνί, an Attic strengthened form of νῦν (in cl. always of time, and most often strictly of the pres.), [in LXX: Jb ₅, Pss ₂, II, IV Mac ₄, Ep. Je *;] *now;* 1. of time: c. praes., Ac 24¹³, Ro 15²³, ²⁵, I Co 13¹³, II Co 8¹¹, ²², Phm ⁹, ¹¹; c. pf., Ro 3²¹; c. pret., Ro 6²² 11³⁰ (WH, mg.) 7⁶, Eph 2¹³, Col 1²¹ 3⁸; ἡ ν. ἀπολογία, Ac 22¹. 2. Of logical sequence (not so in cl.): Ro 7¹⁷, I Co 5¹¹ (νῦν, WH) 12¹⁸ (νῦν, WH, txt.) 15²⁰, He 8⁶ (νῦν, WH, txt.), ib. 9²⁶ (cf. WM, 24, 579ₙ).

νύξ, gen. νυκτός, ἡ, [in LXX chiefly for לַיְלָה;] *night:* Mt 12⁴⁰, Mk 6⁴⁸, Jo 13³⁰, al.; gen. temp. (of the time within which something

happens; M, *Pr.*, 73; Bl., § 36, 13), νυκτός, *by night*, Mt 2¹⁴, Jo 3²,
I Th 5⁷, al.; *v.* κ. ἡμέρας, Mk 5⁵, I Th 2⁹, al.; ἡμέρας κ. ν., Lk 18⁷,
Re 4⁸, al.; μέσης *v.*, Mt 25⁶; dat., νυκτί, in ans. to the question,
"when?" (rare in cl.; Hdt., Soph.), ταύτῃ τ. ν., Lk 12²⁰, al.; ἐκείνῃ,
Ac 12⁶; ἐπιούσῃ, Ac 23¹¹; acc. durat. (Bl., § 34, 8; Kühner³, III, 314 b),
v. κ. ἡμέραν, Lk 2³⁷, Ac 20³¹; τ. νύκτας, Lk 21³⁷; διὰ νυκτός (= cl. νυκτός;
Bl., § 42, 1; 46, 7), Ac 5¹⁹ 16⁹ 17¹⁰ 23³¹; δι᾿ ὅλης ν., Lk 5⁵; κατὰ μέσον
τῆς ν. (Bl., § 47, 6), Ac 27²⁷. Metaph.: Jo 9⁴, Ro 13¹², I Th 5⁵.

**νύσσω (Att. -ττω), [in LXX: Si 22¹⁹, III Mac 5¹⁴*;] *to pierce*:
τ. πλευρὰν λόγχῃ, Jo 19³⁴, [Mt 27⁴⁹], WH.†

νυστάζω (cf. νεύω), [in LXX for נום, etc;] *to nod in sleep, fall
asleep*: Mt 25⁵. Metaph., of negligence or delay, ἡ ἀπώλεια αὐτῶν οὐ
νυστάζει (cf. Ps 120 (121)⁴, Is 5²⁷): II Pe 2³.†

*†νυχθήμερος, -α, -ον (< νύξ, ἡμέρα, v. Bl., § 28, 4), *lasting a night
and a day;* as subst., (τὸ) ν., *a night and a day*: II Co 11²⁵ (pl., *Or. Sib.*,
8, 203).†

Νῶε (as LXX, FlJ, who also gives Νώεος, Νῶχος), ὁ, indecl.
(Heb. נֹחַ), *Noah*: Mt 24³⁷, ³⁸, Lk 3³⁶ 17²⁶, ²⁷, He 11⁷, I Pe 3²⁰, II Pe 2⁵.†

νωθρός, -ά, -όν, [in LXX: Pr 22²⁹ (עָצֵל), Si 4²⁹ 11¹² *;] *sluggish,
slothful*: He 5¹¹ 6¹² (for similar usage in π., v. MM, xvii).†
SYN.: ἀργός (q.v.), βραδύς.

νῶτος, -ου, ὁ, in Att. most freq. τὸ νῶτον, and in pl. always τὰ νῶτα,
[in LXX, ὁ ν., pl., οἱ νῶτοι and τὰ νῶτα, chiefly for כָּתֵף, also for עֹרֶף,
מָתְנַיִם;] *the back*: Ro 11¹⁰ (LXX).†

Ξ

Ξ, ξ, ξῖ, τό, indecl., *Xi*, *x*, the fourteenth letter. As a numeral,
ξ′ = 60, ͵ξ = 60,000.

**ξενία, -ας, ἡ (< ξένος), [in LXX: Si 29²⁷ B¹ *;] *hospitality, enter-
tainment*: Phm ²² (cf. ICC, in l., but v. infr.). By meton., *a place of
entertainment, a lodging-place*: Ac 28²³, and so perh. Phm ²² (Lft., in l.,
Phl., p. 9; but v. supr., and cf. MM, xvii).†

**ξενίζω (< ξένος), [in LXX: Es 3¹³, Si 29²⁵, II Mac 9⁶, III Mac
7³ *;] 1. *to receive as a guest, entertain*: c. acc. pers., Ac 10²³ 28⁷,
He 13²; pass., Ac 10⁶, ¹⁸, ³² 21¹⁶. 2. In late writers (Polyb., al.;
II Mac, l.c.), *to surprise, astonish* by strangeness: Ac 17²⁰; pass.,
I Pe 4⁴, ¹².†

*ξενοδοχέω, late Gk. for -κέω (< ξένος, δέχομαι), *to entertain
strangers*: I Ti 5¹⁰.†

ξένος, -η, -ον, [in LXX chiefly for נָכְרִי;] (*a*) *foreign, alien*:
δαιμόνια, Ac 17¹⁸; διδαχαί, He 13⁹; (*b*) c. gen. rei, *strange to, estranged
from, ignorant of*: Eph 2¹²; (*c*) *strange, unusual*: I Pe 4¹². As subst.,
ὁ ξ., (*a*) *a foreigner, stranger*: Mt 25³⁵, ³⁸, ⁴³, ⁴⁴ 27⁷, Ac 17²¹, III Jo ⁵;
ξένοι κ. πάροικοι (opp. to συμπολῖται, οἰκεῖοι), Eph 2¹⁹; ξ. καὶ παρεπί-

δημοι, He 11¹³ ; (b) one of the parties bound by ties of hospitality; (a) the guest ; (β) the host (= ξενοδόκος, Hom., Il., xv, 532) : Ro 16²³.†

**†ξέστης, -ου, ὁ (a Sicilian corruption of Lat. sextarius), [in Al. : Le 14¹⁰ (לֹג, LXX κοτύλη) *;] 1. a sextarius (about a pint). 2. In NT, a pitcher of wood or stone : Mk 7⁴.†

ξηραίνω (< ξηρός), [in LXX chiefly for יָבֵשׁ;] to dry up, parch, wither : c. acc., τ. χόρτον, Ja 1¹¹ ; pass., to become or be dry or withered : of plants, Mt 13⁶ 21¹⁹, ²⁰, Mk 4⁶ 11²⁰, ²¹, Lk 8⁶, Jo 15⁶, ι Pe 1²⁴; of ripened crops, Re 14¹⁵ ; of liquids, Mk 5²⁹, Re 16¹² ; of members of the body, to waste away, Mk 3¹ (cf. iii Ki 13⁴) 9¹⁸.†

ξηρός, -ά, -όν, [in LXX chiefly for יָבֵשׁ, its parts and derivatives, also for חָרָבָה, etc. ;] dry : metaph. (of a sinner), ξύλον ξ., Lk 23³¹ ; of members of the body shrunken by disease, withered : Jo 5³ ; of the hand, Mt 12¹⁰, Mk 3³, Lk 6⁶, ⁸ ; of the dry land, ἡ ξηρά (sc. γῆ, cf. Ge 1⁹, ¹⁰, Jh 1⁹, al.) : Mt 23¹⁵ ; γῆ, He 11²⁹.†

ξύλινος, -η, -ον (ξύλον), [in LXX chiefly for עֵץ;] wooden : ii Ti 2²⁰, Re 9²⁰ (cf. Ep. Je ⁴ ᶠᶠ.).†

ξύλον, -ου, τό, [in LXX chiefly for עֵץ;] 1. wood : ι Co 3¹², Re 18¹². 2. a piece of wood, hence, anything made of wood, as, (a) a cudgel, staff : pl., Mt 26⁴⁷, ⁵⁵, Mk 14⁴³, ⁴⁸, Lk 22⁵² ; (b) stocks, for confining the feet (Jb 33¹¹, סַד) : Ac 16²⁴ ; (c) a beam to which malefactors were bound (late Gk.), in LXX, of a gibbet (De 21²², ²³), in NT, of the Cross : Ac 5³⁰ 10³⁹ 13²⁹, Ga 3¹³, ι Pe 2²⁴. 3. In late writers (v. MM, xvii), a tree (Ge 1²⁹, Is 14⁸, al.) : Lk 23³¹ ; ξ. τῆς ζωῆς, Re 2⁷ 22², ¹⁴, ¹⁹.†

ξυράω, -ῶ, late form of ξυρέω (q.v.) : ι Co 11⁶ (ξυρᾶσθαι, Rec. and Edd., but v.s. ξύρω).†

ξυρέω, -ῶ (< ξυρόν, a razor), [in LXX (also -άω) chiefly for גָּלַח pi., pu.;] (no ex. of pres. -έω), to shave : pass. and mid., to shave oneself, have oneself shaved, aor., Ac 21²⁴ ; pf. (Att.), ι Co 11⁵.†

ξύρω, rare form of ξυρέω (Veitch, s.v.), aor. mid., ξύρασθαι (Bl., § 24, s.v.; Zorell, s.v., etc.) for -ᾶσθαι (Rec., Edd.) : ι Co 11⁶.†

O

O, ο, ὁ μικρόν, omicron, short o, the fifteenth letter. As a numeral, ο´ = 70, ο, = 70,000.

ὁ, ἡ, τό, the prepositive article (ἄρθρον προτακτικόν), originally a demonstr. pron. (so usually in Hom.), in general corresponding to the Eng. definite article.

I. As demonstr. pron. 1. As freq. in Hom., absol., he (she, it), his (etc.): Ac 17²⁸ (quoted from the poet Aratus). 2. Distributive, ὁ μὲν . . . ὁ δέ, the one . . . the other : ι Co 7⁷, Ga 4²² ; pl., Ac 14⁴ 17³², Phl 1¹⁶, al.; οἱ μὲν . . . ἄλλοι δέ, Mt 16¹⁴, Jo 7¹² ; οἱ μὲν . . . ὁ δέ, He 7²¹,²³. 3. In narration (without ὁ μὲν preceding), ὁ δέ, *but he*: Mt 2¹⁴, Mk 1⁴⁵, Lk 8²¹, Jo 9³⁸, al. mult.

II. As prepositive article, *the*, prefixed, 1. to nouns unmodified: ὁ θεός, τὸ φῶς, etc.; to abstract nouns, ἡ σοφία, etc., to pl. nouns which indicate a class, οἱ ἀλώπεκες, *foxes*, Mt 8²⁰, al.; to an individual as representing a class, ὁ ἐργάτης, Lk 10⁷; c. nom. = voc. in addresses, Mt 11²⁶, Jo 19³, Ja 5¹, al.; to things which pertain to one, ἡ χείρ, *his hand*, Mk 3¹; to names of persons well known or already mentioned; usually to names of countries (originally adjectives), ἡ Ἰουδαία, etc. 2. To modified nouns: c. pers. pron. gen., μοῦ, σοῦ, etc.; c. poss. pron., ἐμός, σός, etc.; c. adj. between the art. and the noun, ὁ ἀγαθὸς ἄνθρωπος, Mt 12³⁵; the noun foll. by adj., both c. art., ὁ ποιμὴν ὁ καλός, Jo 10¹¹ (on ὁ ὄχλος πολύς, Jo 12⁹, v. M, *Pr.*, 84); before adjectival phrases, ἡ κατ᾽ ἐκλογὴν πρόθεσις, Ro 9¹¹. 3. To other parts of speech used as substantives; (*a*) neuter adjectives: τ. ἀγαθόν, etc.; (*b*) cardinal numerals: ὁ εἷς, οἱ δύο, etc.; (*c*) participles: ὁ Βαπτίζων (= ὁ Βαπτιστής, Mt 14²), Mk 6¹⁴; πᾶς ὁ, c. ptcp., *every one who*, etc.; (*d*) adverbs: τὸ πέραν, τὰ νῦν, ὁ ἔσω ἄνθρωπος; (*e*) infinitives: nom., τὸ θέλειν, Ro 7¹⁸, al.; gen., τοῦ, after adjectives, ἄξιον τοῦ πορεύεσθαι, 1 Co 16⁴; verbs, ἔλαχεν τοῦ θυμιᾶσαι, Lk 1⁹; and freq. in a final sense, ἐξῆλθεν ὁ σπείρων τοῦ σπείρειν, Mt 13³ (on the artic. inf., v. Bl., § 71; M, *Gr.*, II, pp. 448 ff.). 4. In the neut. to sentences, phrases or single words treated as a quotation: τὸ Εἰ δύνῃ, Mk 9²³; τὸ ἔτι ἅπαξ, He 12²⁷; τὸ ἀνέβη, Eph. 4⁹ al. 5. To prepositional phrases: οἱ ἀπὸ Ἰταλίας, He 13²⁴; οἱ ἐκ νόμου, Ro 4¹⁴; neut. acc. absol., in adverbial phrases, τὸ καθ᾽ ἡμέραν, *daily*, Lk 11³; τὸ κατὰ σάρκα, *as regards the flesh*, Ro 9⁵. 6. To nouns in the genitive, denoting kinship, association, etc.: ὁ τοῦ, *the son of* (unless context indicates a different relationship), Mt 10², al.; τὰ τοῦ θεοῦ, *the things that pertain to God*, Mt 16²³; τὰ τῆς εἰρήνης, Ro 14¹⁹ (cf. M, *Pr.*, 81 ff.; Bl., §§ 46, 47; M, *Gr.*, II, pp. 430 f.).

ὀγδοήκοντα, *eighty*: Lk 2³⁷ 16⁷.†

ὄγδοος, -η, -ον, *the eighth*: Lk 1⁵⁹, Ac 7⁸(LXX), Re 17¹¹ 21²⁰; *one of eight, with seven others* (usually, in this sense, with αὐτός added, but cf. Plat., *Legg.*, iii, 695 c; Plut., *Pelop.*, 13; II Mac 5²⁷): II Pe 2⁵.†

*ὄγκος, -ου, ὁ, *bulk, mass*; metaph., *an encumbrance*: He 12¹.†
SYN.: βάρος, *a weight*; φορτίον, *a burden*, that which is borne.

ὅδε, ἥδε, τόδε (the old demonstr. pron., ὁ + the enclitic δε), = Lat. *hicce, this* (*here*), referring prop. to what is present, can be seen or pointed out: of a person just named, τῆδε (= ταύτῃ), Lk 10³⁹; neut. pl., τάδε (λέγει), referring to words which follow (so in Att., and v. MM, xvii): Ac 21¹¹, Re 2¹,⁸,¹²,¹⁸ 3¹,⁷,¹⁴; εἰς τήνδε τ. πόλιν (= Att. τῇ καὶ τῇ, Plat., *Legg.*, iv, 721 B), *such and such a city*, Ja 4¹³.†

ὁδεύω (< ὁδός), [in LXX: III Ki 6¹² A (metaph., הלך), To 6⁵, Wi 5⁷ (fig.) *;] *to travel, journey*: Lk 10³³ (cf. δι-, συν-οδεύω).†

ὁδηγέω, -ῶ (< ὁδηγός), [in LXX chiefly for נחה, also for דרך hi., הלך hi., etc.;] *to lead* on one's way, *to guide*: c. acc. pers., Mt 15¹⁴,

Lk 6³⁹; id. seq. ἐπί, Re 7¹⁷. Metaph., *to guide, instruct, teach:* Ac 8³¹; seq. εἰς τ. ἀλήθειαν (ἐν τ. ἀ., WH, mg.), Jo 16¹³ (cf. Ps 24 (25)⁵).†

†ὁδηγός, -οῦ, ὁ (<ὁδός, ἡγέομαι), [in LXX: ii Es 8¹, Wi 7¹⁵ 18³, i Mac 4², ii Mac 5¹⁵*;] *a leader* on the **way, *a guide:* Ac 1¹⁶. Fig., ὁ. τυφλῶν, Ro 2¹⁹; pl., Mt 15¹⁴ 23¹⁶,²⁴.†

*ὁδοιπορέω, -ῶ (<ὁδοιπόρος, *a traveller,* Ge 37²⁵, al.), *to travel, journey:* Ac 10⁹.†

**ὁδοιπορία, -ας, ἡ (v. supr.), [in LXX: Wi 13¹⁸ 18³ 19⁵, i Mac 6⁴¹*;] *a journey:* Jo 4⁶, ii Co 11²⁶.†

ὁδο-ποιέω, -ῶ, [in LXX: Jb 30¹², Ps 67 (68)⁴ (סָלַל) 77 (78)⁵⁰ (פֶּלֶס pi.) 79 (80)⁹, Is 62¹⁰ (פָּנָה pi.)*;] *to make a road* or *path:* Mk 2²³ (WH, mg.).†

ὁδός, -οῦ, ἡ, [in LXX chiefly (very freq.) for דֶּרֶךְ;] 1. *a way, path, road:* Mt 2¹², Mk 10⁴⁶, Lk 3⁵, al.; κατὰ τὴν ὁ., Lk 10⁴, al.; παρὰ τὴν ὁ., Mt 13⁴, al.; c. gen. pers. (subj.), τὴν ὁ. ἑτοιμάζειν (fig.), Mt 3³, Mk 1³, al.; c. gen. term. (obj.), ἐθνῶν, Mt 10⁵; τ. ἁγίων (fig.), He 9⁸; acc., ὁδόν, with force of prep. (like Heb. דֶּרֶךְ; Bl., § 34, 8; 35, 5), ὁ. θαλάσσης, Mt 4¹⁵ (LXX). 2. A traveller's *way, journey:* ἐν τ. ὁ., Mt 5²⁵, Mk 8²⁷, al.; ἐξ ὁ., Lk 11⁶; εἰς ὁ., Mt 10¹⁰; τ. ὁδὸν πορεύεσθαι, Ac 8³⁹; ὁ. ἡμέρας, Lk 2⁴⁴; ὁδὸν ποιεῖν (= cl., ὁ. ποιεῖσθαι; v. Field, *Notes,* 25), *to make* one's *way,* i.e. proceed on one's journey, Mk 2²³. 3. Metaph. (cl.; but esp. freq. in Heb.; v. Cremer, 442 ff.), of a course of conduct, a way of thinking or acting: Ac 14¹⁶, i Co 4¹⁷ 12³¹, Ja 1⁸ 5²⁰; τοῦ Κάϊν, Ju¹¹; τ. Βαλαάμ, ii Pe 2¹⁵; εἰρήνης, Ro 3¹⁷; ζωῆς, Ac 2²⁸; ἡ ὁ. ἡ ἀπάγουσα εἰς τ. ζωήν (Dalman, *Words,* 160), Mt 7¹⁴; τ. δικαιοσύνης, Mt 21³²; σωτηρίας, Ac 16¹⁷; αἱ ὁ. τ. θεοῦ (κυρίου), Ac 13¹⁰, Ro 11³³, Re 15³ (cf. Ho 14⁹, Ps 94 (95)¹⁰, Si 39²⁴, al.); ἡ ὁ. τ. θεοῦ (the way approved by God), Mt 22¹⁶, Mk 12¹⁴, Lk 20²¹; id., of the Christian religion, Ac 18²⁶; so, absol., ἡ ὁ., Ac 9² 19⁹,²³ 24²²; of Christ as the means of approach to God, Jo 14⁶. 4. Ellipsis of ὁ.: ποίας (sc. ὁδοῦ), Lk 5¹⁹; ἐκείνης, ib. 19⁴ (v. Bl., § 36, 13; 44, 1).

ὁδούς, -όντος, ὁ, [in LXX for שֵׁן;] *a tooth:* Mt 5³⁸, Mk 9¹⁸, Ac 7⁵⁴; pl., Re 9⁸; ὁ βρυγμὸς (q.v.) τ. ὁδόντων, Mt 8¹² 13⁴²,⁵⁰ 22¹³ 24⁵¹ 25³⁰, Lk 13²⁸.†

ὁδυνάω, -ῶ (<ὁδύνη), [in LXX: Za 9⁵ (חִיל), 12¹⁰ (מָרַר hi.), La 1¹³ (דָּוָה), Wi 14²⁴, al.;] *to cause pain* or *suffering;* pass. and mid., *to suffer pain, be tormented* or *greatly distressed:* Lk 2⁴⁸ 16²⁴,²⁵ (ὀδυνᾶσαι, v. M, *Pr.,* 53 f.); seq. ἐπί, Ac 20³⁸.†

ὀδύνη, -ης, ἡ, [in LXX for יָגוֹן, מַר, etc. (26 words in all);] *pain, distress,* of body or mind: Ro 9², i Ti 6¹⁰.†

ὀδυρμός, -οῦ, ὁ (<ὀδύρομαι, *to lament*), [in LXX: Je 38 (31)¹⁵ (תַּמְרוּרִים), ii Mac 11⁶*;] *lamentation, mourning:* Mt 2¹⁸ (LXX), ii Co 7⁷.†

'Οζείας (Rec. 'Οζίας), -ου, ὁ (Heb. עֻזִּיָּה), *Uzziah :* Mt 1⁸, ⁹.†

'Οζίας, v.s. 'Οζείας.

ὄζω, [in LXX : Ex 8¹⁴ ⁽¹⁰⁾ (בָּאַשׁ) * ;] *to smell* (i.e. emit a smell): Jo 11³⁹.†

ὅθεν, adv., *whence;* (a) of direction or source : Mt 12⁴⁴, Lk 11²⁴, Ac 14²⁶ 28¹³ ; = ἐκεῖθεν ὅπου, Mt 25²⁴, ²⁶ (cf. Thuc., i, 89, 3); ὅ. γινώσκομεν, ₁ Jo 2¹⁸ ; (b) of cause, *whence, wherefore :* Mt 14⁷, Ac 26¹⁹, He 2¹⁷ 3¹ 7²⁵ 8³ 9¹⁸ 11¹⁹.†

* ὀθόνη, -ης, ἡ (of Semitic origin, cf. Heb. אֵטוּן , *yarn*); 1. *fine linen* (Hom., al.). 2. Later, *a sheet* or *sail :* Ac 10¹¹ 11⁵.†

ὀθόνιον, -ου, τό (dimin. of ὀθόνη, q.v.), [in LXX : Jg 14¹³ (סָדִין), Ho 2⁵ ⁽⁷⁾, ⁹⁽¹¹⁾ (פִּשְׁתָּה) * ;] *a piece of fine linen, a linen cloth :* Lk 24¹² (WH, R, mg., om.), Jo 19⁴⁰ 20⁵, ⁶, ⁷.†

οἶδα, (from same root as εἶδον, q.v.), [in LXX chiefly for יָדַע ;] pf. with pres. meaning (plpf. as impf. ; the cl. forms of pres. pl. indic. and impv. are rare : ἴστε, prob. impv., Eph 5⁵, He 12⁷, Ja 1¹⁹ ; ἴσασι, Ac 26⁴ ; cf. M, *Pr.*, p. 245, and M, *Gr.*, ii, pp. 220 ff.), *to have seen* or *perceived,* hence, *to know, have knowledge of :* c. acc. rei, Mt 25¹³, Mk 10¹⁹, Jo 10⁴, Ro 7⁷, al.; c. acc. pers., Mt 26⁷², Jo 1³¹, Ac 3¹⁶, al. ; τ. θεόν, ₁ Th 4⁵, Tit 1¹⁶, al. ; c. acc. et inf., Lk 4⁴¹, al. ; seq. ὅτι, Mt 9⁶, Lk 20²¹, Jo 3², Ro 2² 11², al. ; seq. quaest. indir., Mt 26⁷⁰, Jo 9²¹, Eph 1¹⁸, al. ; c. inf., *to know how* (cl.), Mt 7¹¹, Lk 11¹³, Phl 4¹², ₁ Th 4⁴, al. ; in unique sense of *respect, appreciate :* ₁ Th 5¹² (but v. also *ICC* on ₁ Th 4⁴).

SYN. : v.s. γινώσκω.

οἰκειακός, v.s. οἰκιακός.

οἰκεῖος, -α, -ον (< οἶκος), [in LXX for דּוֹד , שְׁאֵר , etc.; in Is 58⁷, οἱ. τοῦ σπέρματος for בְּשָׂר ;] *in* or *of the house* (opp. to ξένος, ἀλλότριος) ; (a) of things ; τὰ οἰ., *household affairs* or *goods ;* (b) of persons, *of the same family* or *kin;* as subst., οἱ οἰ., *kinsmen :* ₁ Ti 5⁸ ; c. gen. pers., *of the family of :* metaph., τ. θεοῦ, Eph 2¹⁹ ; τ. πίστεως (Lft., in l.), Ga 6¹⁰.†

SYN. : συγγενής, ἴδιος (v. Cremer, 446 ; Deiss., *BS,* 123).

† οἰκετεία, -ας, ἡ (< οἰκέτης), *a household* (of servants) : Mt 24⁴⁵.†

οἰκέτης, -ου, ὁ (< οἰκέω), [in LXX for עֶבֶד ;] *a house-servant :* Lk 16¹³, Ro 14⁴ ; pl., Ac 10⁷, ₁ Pe 2¹⁸. (In Plat., Hdt., Si 4³⁰ 6¹¹, the pl. includes all the inmates of the house, the *familia,* οἰκετεία.)†

SYN. : v.s. διάκονος.

οἰκέω, -ῶ (< οἶκος), [in LXX chiefly for יָשַׁב ;] (a) trans., *to inhabit :* c. acc., ₁ Ti 6¹⁶ ; (b) intrans., *to dwell :* seq. μετά (of married life), ₁ Co 7¹², ¹³ ; metaph., seq. ἐν : ἀγαθόν, Ro 7¹⁸ ; ἁμαρτία, ib. ²⁰ ; πνεῦμα θεοῦ, Ro 8⁹, ¹¹, ₁ Co 3¹⁶ (cf. ἐν-, κατ-, ἐν-κατ-, παρ-, περι-, συν-οικέω).†

οἴκημα, -τος, τό (< οἰκέω), [in LXX : Ez 16²⁴ (גַּב), To 2⁴, Wi 13¹⁵ * ;] *a dwelling.* As a euphemism for other definite terms (e.g. *brothel :* Hdt., ii, 121; cf. Ez, l.c.), *a prison* (Thuc., iv, 47 f.): Ac 12⁷.†

οἰκητήριον, -ου, τό (< οἰκητήρ = οἰκήτωρ, *an inhabitant*), [in LXX: II Mac 11², III Mac 2¹⁵ *;] *a habitation:* Ju⁶; trop., II Co 5².†

οἰκία, -ας, ἡ (<οἶκος), [in LXX chiefly (very freq.) for בַּיִת;] *a house, dwelling:* Mt 2¹¹ 7²⁴⁻²⁷, Mk 1²⁹, al.; ἐν οἰκίᾳ (= cl. κατ᾽ οἰκίαν), *at home,* Lk 8²⁷; εἰς οἰ., II Jo¹⁰; οἰ., c. gen. pers., usually has the art. (Mt 8¹⁴, al., but cf. οἶκος and v. Bl., § 46, 9); ἡ οἰ. τ. πατρός μου, Jo 14². Metaph., (*a*) of the body as the dwelling of the soul: II Co 5¹; (*b*) of property (as בַּיִת, Ge 45¹⁸, LXX, τ. ὑπάρχοντα; III Ki 13⁸, LXX, οἶκος) = οἶκος (q.v.): Mk 12⁴⁰, Lk 20⁴⁷; (*c*) of the inmates of the dwelling, *the household:* Mt 12²⁵; c. gen. pers., Jo 4⁵³, I Co 16¹⁵.

SYN.: οἶκος, which in Attic law denoted the whole *estate,* ο᾽κία, the *dwelling* only. In cl. poets οἶκος has also the latter sense, but not in prose, except in metaph. usage, where it signifies both *property* and *household.* The foregoing distinction is not, however, consistently maintained in late Greek; cf. MM, ii, xvii, and v. Thayer, s.v. οἰκία.

*† οἰκιακός (in Plut., al., -ειακός), ή, όν (< οἰκία), = οἰκεῖος, *belonging to the household, one's own:* Mt 10³⁶; opp. to οἰκοδεσπότης, ib.²⁵.†

*† οἰκο-δεσποτέω, -ῶ (< οἰκοδεσπότης), *to rule a household:* I Ti 5¹⁴.†

*† οἰκο-δεσπότης, -ου, ὁ (< οἶκος, δεσπότης), *the master of a house, a householder:* Mt 10²⁵ 13²⁷ 20¹¹ 24⁴³, Mk 14¹⁴, Lk 12³⁹ 13²⁵ 14²¹; ἄνθρωπος οἰ., Mt 13⁵² 20¹ 21³³; pleonast., οἰ. τ. οἰκίας, Lk 22¹¹ (v. Bl., § 81, 4).†

οἰκοδομέω, -ῶ (< οἰκοδόμος), [in LXX chiefly for בָּנָה;] *to build a house, to build:* absol., Lk 11⁴⁸ 14³⁰ 17²⁸; οἱ οἰκοδομοῦντες, *the builders* (as Ps 117 (118)²², הַבּוֹנִים), Mt 21⁴², Mk 12¹⁰, Lk 20¹⁷, I Pe 2⁷ (LXX); ἐπ᾽ ἀλλότριον θεμέλιον οἰ., proverb., Ro 15²⁰; c. acc. rei, Ga 2¹⁸; πύργον, Mt 21³³, Mk 12¹, Lk 14²⁸; ἀποθήκας, Lk 12¹⁸; ναόν, Mk 14⁵⁸; pass., Jo 2²⁰; οἰκία, Lk 6⁴⁸; c. acc. rei seq. dat. pers. (cf. Ge 8²⁰, Ez 16²⁴), Lk 7⁵, Ac 7⁴⁷, ⁴⁹; acc. seq. ἐπί, Mt 7²⁴, ²⁶, Lk 6⁴⁹; πόλιν ἐπ᾽ ὄρους, Lk 4²⁹; of rebuilding, or restoring, Mt 23²⁹ 26⁶¹ 27⁴⁰, Mk 15²⁹, Lk 11⁴⁷. Metaph., τ. ἐκκλησίαν, Mt 16¹⁸; of the growth of Christian character (cf. בָּנָה, in Ps 27 (28)⁵, Je 24⁶, al.), *to build up* (AV, *edify*): absol., Ac 20³², I Co 8¹ 10²³; c. acc. pers., I Co 14⁴, I Th 5¹¹; pass., Ac 9³¹, I Co 14¹⁷, I Pe 2⁵; of blameworthy action (AV, *embolden*), I Co 8¹⁰ (cf. ἀν-, ἐπ-, συν-οικοδομέω).†

† οἰκοδομή, -ῆς, ἡ (<οἶκος, + δέμω, *to build*), [in LXX: I Ch 29¹ A (בִּירָה), Ez 17¹⁷ 40² (בִּנְיָה, מִבְנֶה בָּנָה), Si 22¹⁶ 40¹⁹, al.;] = cl. οἰκοδομία (q.v.), -δόμησις (Thuc., Plat.), 1. the act of *building;* in NT always metaph., *building up, edifying:* Ro 14¹⁹ 15², I Co 14²⁶, II Co 10⁸ 13¹⁰, Eph 4²⁹; c. gen. obj., I Co 14¹², II Co 12¹⁹, Eph 4¹², ¹⁶; λαλεῖν, λαβεῖν, οἰ., I Co 14³, ⁵. 2. = οἰκοδόμημα, *a building:* Mt 24¹, Mk 13¹, ²; metaph., I Co 3⁹, II Co 5¹, Eph 2²¹.†

* οἰκοδομία, -ας, ἡ (< οἰκοδομέω), the act of *building:* metaph., I Ti 1⁴ (BE for οἰκονομία, q.v.).†

οἰκο-δόμος, -ου, ὁ (<οἶκος + δέμω, *to build*), [in LXX for בָּנָה, etc.;] *a builder:* Ac 4¹¹.†

οἰκονομέω, -ῶ (< οἰκονόμος), [in LXX: Ps 111 (112)⁵ (כּוּל pilp.), II Mac 3¹⁴*;] *to manage as house-steward, be a steward:* absol., Lk 16²; hence, generally (v.s. οἰκονομία), *to manage, regulate, arrange* (cl., II Mac, l.c., III Mac 3² R).†

οἰκονομία, -ας, ἡ (< οἰκονομέω), [in LXX: Is 22¹⁹, ²¹ (מֶמְשָׁלָה, מַצָּב)*;] 1. prop. (Plat., Arist.), *the office of* οἰκονόμος, *stewardship:* Lk 16²⁻⁴. 2. In later writers (Plut., al.; v. AR on Eph 1¹⁰; MM, xviii), generally, *administration, dispensation:* I Co 9¹⁷, Eph 1¹⁰ 3², ⁹, Col 1²⁵, I Ti 1⁴.†

οἰκονόμος, -ου, ὁ (< οἶκος + νέμω, *to manage*), [in LXX chiefly for עַל־הַבַּיִת;] 1. prop., *the manager of a household or estate, a house-* or *land-steward* (usually a slave or freedman): Lk 12⁴² 16¹, ³, ⁸, I Co 4², Ga 4²; ὁ οἰ. τ. πόλεως (RV, *treasurer;* cf. I Es 4⁴⁹), Ro 16²³. 2. Metaph. (in wider sense; cf. οἰκονομία), *an administrator, a steward:* of Christian ministers, I Co 4¹, Tit 1⁷; of Christians generally, I Pe 4¹⁰.†

οἶκος, -ου, ὁ, [in LXX chiefly for בַּיִת, also for הֵיכָל, אֹהֶל, etc.;] 1. prop., *a house, dwelling:* Ac 2² 19¹⁶; c. gen. poss., Mt 9⁶, ⁷, Mk 2¹¹, Lk 1²³, al.; c. gen. attrib., ἐμπορίου, Jo 2¹⁶; προσευχῆς, Mt 21¹³, al; of a sanctuary (Hdt., Eur.): οἰ. τ. θεοῦ, of the tabernacle, Mt 12⁴, al.; the temple, Mt 21¹³, al.; metaph. of a city: Mt 23³⁸, Lk 13³⁵; of the body, Mt 12⁴⁴, Lk 11²⁴; of Christians, I Pe 2⁵; ἐν οἰ. (M, *Pr.,* 81 f.), *at home,* Mk 2¹, I Co 11³⁴ 14³⁵; so κατ' οἶκον, Ac 2⁴⁶ 5⁴²; οἱ εἰς (= οἱ ἐν; v.s. εἰς) τ. οἰ., Lk 7¹⁰ 15⁶; κατ' οἴκους, *from house to house,* Ac 8³ 20²⁰; εἰς (κατ') οἶκον, c. gen. (Bl., § 46, 9), Mk 8³, Lk 14¹, Ro 16⁵, al. 2. By meton., *a house, household, family:* Lk 10⁵, Ac 7¹⁰, I Co 1¹⁶, I Ti 3⁴, ⁵, al.; of the Church, ὁ οἰ. τ. θεοῦ, I Ti 3¹⁵, He 3², I Pe 4¹⁷; of descendants, οἰ. Ἰσραήλ (Δαυείδ, Ἰακώβ; Bl., § 47, 9), Mt 10⁶, Lk 1²⁷, ³³, al. (cf. Ex 6¹⁴, I Ki 2³⁰, al.).

SYN.: v.s. οἰκία.

οἰκουμένη, -ης, ἡ (fem. pres. pass. ptcp. of οἰκέω; sc. γῆ), [in LXX chiefly for תֵּבֵל, אֶרֶץ;] *the inhabited earth;* (a) in cl., the countries occupied by Greeks, as disting. from barbarian lands (Hdt., Dem., al.); (b) in later writers, the Roman world: Lk 2¹, Ac 11²⁸ 24⁵; by meton., of its inhabitants: Ac 17⁶ 19²⁷; (c) in LXX (Ps 22 (23)¹ 70 (71)⁸, al.) and NT, also of the whole inhabited world: Mt 24¹⁴, Lk 4⁵ 21²⁶, Ro 10¹⁸, He 1⁶, Re 3¹⁰ 16¹⁴; by meton. (ut supr.), Ac 17³¹, Re 12⁹; (d) of the Messianic age, ἡ οἰ. ἡ μέλλουσα = ὁ αἰὼν ὁ μέλλων: He 2⁵.†

†οἰκουργός, -όν (< οἶκος + root of ἔργον), working at home: Tit 2⁵ (Rec. οἰκουρός, q.v.).†

οἰκ-ουρός, -ον (< οἶκος + οὖρος, a keeper); 1. *watching or keeping the house;* as subst., ἡ οἰ., *a housekeeper* (Soph., Eur.; v. LS, s.v.). 2. *keeping at home:* Tit 2⁵, Rec. (v. Field, *Notes,* 220 ff.; *CGT,* in l., and cf. οἰκουργός).†

οἰκτείρω (< οἶκτος, *pity*), [in LXX for רחם pi., חנן, etc.;] *to pity, have compassion on:* c. acc pers., Ro 9¹⁵ (LXX).†

SYN.: ἐλεέω, q.v.

οἰκτιρμός, -οῦ, ὁ (< οἰκτείρω), [in LXX, usually in pl., chiefly for
רַחַם;] compassion, pity: σπλάγχνα οἰκτιρμοῦ, a heart of compassion,
Col 3¹²; in pl. (as LXX for Heb. רַחֲמִים), oἱ. τ. θεοῦ, Ro 12¹, He 10²⁸;
ὁ πατὴρ ἰτῶν οἰ., ΙΙ Co 1³; σπλάγχνα κ. οἰ., Phl 2¹.†
SYN.: ἔλεος, q.v.

οἰκτίρμων, -ον (< οἰκτείρω), in cl. poët. for ἐλεήμων (q.v.), [in LXX
chiefly for רַחוּם;] merciful: Lk 6³⁶, Ja 5¹¹.†

οἶμαι, v.s. οἴομαι.

οἰνο-πότης, -ου, ὁ (< οἶνος + πότης, a drinker), poët. and late
prose, [in LXX: Pr 23²⁰ (סֹבֵא יַיִן) *;] a wine-drinker, wine-bibber:
Mt 11¹⁹, Lk 7³⁴.†

οἶνος, -ου, ὁ, [in LXX chiefly for יַיִן, also for תִּירוֹשׁ, etc.;] wine:
Mt 9¹⁷, Lk 1¹⁵, Jo 2³, al.; οἴνῳ προσέχειν, Ι Ti 3⁸; δουλοῦσθαι, Tit 2³.
Metaph., Re 14⁸, ¹⁰ 16¹⁹ 17² 18³ 19¹⁵. By meton. for ἄμπελος, Re 6⁶.
* οἰνοφλυγία, -ας, ἡ (< φλύω, to bubble up, overflow), cf. -γέω,
De 21²⁰; drunkenness, debauchery: Ι Pe 4³.†
SYN.: v.s. κραιπάλη.

οἴομαι, οἶμαι, [in LXX for הָגָה, Ge 37⁷, al.;] to suppose, expect,
imagine: c. acc. et inf., Jo 21²⁵; c. inf., Phl 1¹⁷; seq. ὅτι, Ja 1⁷.†
SYN.: v.s. ἡγέομαι.

οἷος, -α, -ον, relat. pron., qualitative (related to ὅς as qualis to
qui), what sort or manner of, such as, in NT usually without its
correl. τοιοῦτος : Mt 24²¹, Mk 9³, ΙΙ Co 12²⁰, Ι Th 1⁵, ΙΙ Ti 3¹¹, Re 16¹⁸;
seq. τοιοῦτος, Ι Co 15⁴⁸, ΙΙ Co 10¹¹; id. redundant, Mk 13¹⁹; τ. αὐτὸν
. . . οἷον, Phl 1³⁰; οὐχ οἷον δὲ ὅτι, elliptically, but it is not as though
(RV), Ro 9⁶.†

οἴσω, v.s. φέρω, p. 499.

ὀκνέω, -ῶ (< ὄκνος, shrinking, hesitation), [in LXX: Nu 22¹⁶
(מָנַע ni.), Jg 18⁹ (עָצֵל ni.), To 12⁶, ¹³, Jth 12¹³, Si 7³⁵, iv Mac 14⁴ *;] to
shrink from doing, hesitate to do (Hom., Thuc., al.); hence, to delay:
c. inf., Ac 9³⁸ (cf. Nu, l.c., and v. MM, xviii).†

ὀκνηρός, -ά, -όν (< ὀκνέω), [in LXX for עָצֵל, Pr 6⁶, ⁹ al.;]
shrinking, hesitating, timid: c. dat. (Bl., § 38, 2), Ro 12¹¹; hence,
slothful: Mt 25²⁶. Of things, that which causes shrinking, irksome:
Phl 3¹ (i.e, I do not hesitate).†

*† ὀκταήμερος, -ον (< ὀκτώ, ἡμέρα), of the eighth day, eight days old:
c. dat. ref., περιτομῇ ὀ., Phl 3⁵ (words of this class denote duration,
cf. τεταρταῖος).†

ὀκτώ, οἱ, αἱ, τά, indecl., eight: Lk 2²¹, Jo 5⁵, al.

ὀλεθρεύω, v.s. ὀλοθρεύω.

ὀλέθριος, -ον (also -α, -ον, as in Wi, l.c.), [in LXX: ΙΙΙ Ki 21
(20)⁴² (חֵרֶם), Wi 18¹⁵ *;] destructive, deadly: δίκην, ΙΙ Th 1⁹, L, txt
(for ὄλεθρος, q.v.).†

ὄλεθρος, -ου, ὁ (< ὄλλυμι, to destroy), [in LXX for שׁוֹד, שֹׁדֵד, etc. ;] *ruin, destruction, death:* 1 Th 5³, 1 Ti 6⁹; αἰώνιος, 11 Th 1⁹ (L, txt., ὀλέθριος, q.v.); εἰς ὄ. τῆς σαρκός, for physical discipline, to destroy carnal lusts, 1 Co 5⁵.†

†ὀλιγοπιστία, -ας, ἡ, *little faith* or *trust:* Mt 17²⁰.†

†ὀλιγό-πιστος, -ον, *of little faith* or *trust:* Mt 6³⁰ 8²⁶ 14³¹ 16⁸, Lk 12²⁸.†

ὀλίγος, -η, -ον (on οὐχ ὀλ., v. infr.), [in LXX chiefly for מְעַט ;] of number, quantity, size, *few, little, small, slight:* Mt 9³⁷ 15³⁴, Mk 6⁵ 8⁷, Lk 10² 12⁴⁸ (sc. πληγάς, opp. to πολλάς), 1 Ti 5²³, He 12¹⁰, Re 3⁴ 12¹²; οὐκ ὀ. (in the best uncials written οὐχ ὀ.; v. WH, *App.,* 143; M, *Pr.,* 44; Thackeray, *Gr.,* 126 f.), Ac 12¹⁸ 14²⁸ 15² (c. gen. part.) 17⁴, ¹² 19²³, ²⁴ 27²⁰; pl., absol., Mt 7¹⁴ 20¹⁶ (WH, txt., RV, om.) 22¹⁴, Lk 13²³, 1 Pe 3²⁰. Neut. sing. (τὸ) ὀ.: Lk 7⁴⁷, 11 Co 8¹⁵; πρὸς ὀλίγον, 1 Ti 4⁸, Ja 4¹⁴; ἐν ὀ., Ac 26²⁸, ²⁹ (*with little* effort; v. Page, in l.); id., *in brief,* Eph 3³; adverbially, ὀλίγον, of time, Mk 6³¹, 1 Pe 1⁶ 5¹⁰, Re 17¹⁰; of space, Mk 1¹⁹, Lk 5³; pl., ὀλίγα, Lk 10⁴², Re 2¹⁴; ἐπ' ὀλίγα, Mt 25²¹, ²³; δι' ὀλίγων, *in few words, briefly,* 1 Pe 5¹² (cf. Plat., *Legg.,* vi, 778 c).†

†ὀλιγόψυχος, -ον [in LXX: Is 35⁴ (מהר ni.), etc. ;] *faint-hearted:* 1 Th 5¹⁴.†

ὀλιγωρέω, -ῶ (< ὀλίγος + ὥρα, care), [in LXX: Pr 3¹¹ (מאם)*;] *to esteem lightly, think little of:* c. gen., He 12⁵ (LXX).†

ὀλίγως, adv. (< ὀλίγος), [in Aq.: Is 10⁷*;] *a little, almost, all but:* 11 Pe 2¹⁸.†

†ὀλοθρευτής (Rec. ὀλ-), -οῦ, ὁ (< ὀλοθρεύω), *a destroyer:* 1 Co 10¹⁰ (not elsewhere).†

†ὀλοθρεύω (< ὄλεθρος), late (Alex.) form of ὀλεθρεύω (cf. MGr., ξολοθρεύω), [in LXX for כרת, שׁחת hi., etc. ;] *to destroy:* He 11²⁸ (cf. ἐξ-ολοθρεύω).†

†ὀλοκαύτωμα, -τος, τό (< ὅλος, καίω), [in LXX chiefly for עֹלָה ;] *a whole burnt offering:* Mk 12³³, He 10⁶, ⁸ (LXX) (cf. Kennedy, *Sources,* 113 f.).†

SYN.: v.s. θυσία.

†ὀλοκληρία, -ας, ἡ (< ὁλόκληρος), [in LXX: Is 1⁶ (מְתֹם)*;] *completeness, soundness:* Ac 3¹⁶.†

ὁλό-κληρος, -ον (< ὅλος, κλῆρος, i.e. *with all that has fallen by lot*), [in LXX: Le 23¹⁵, Ez 15⁵ (תָּמִים), De 27⁶, Jos 9² (8³¹) (שָׁלֵם), Za 11¹⁶ (נצב ni.), Wi 15³, 1 Mac 4⁴⁷, 1v Mac 15¹⁷*;] *complete, entire;* in NT in ethical sense (as Wi, 1v Mac, ll. c.), 1 Th 5²³; ὀ. καὶ τέλειοι, Ja 1⁴.†

SYN.: ὁλοτελής (q.v.), τέλειος (Tr., *Syn.,* § xxii).

ὀλολύζω (onomatop.), [in LXX chiefly for ילל hi. ;] (in Hom., of women crying to the gods in prayer or thanksgiving), *to cry aloud:* Ja 5¹.†

ὅλος, -η, -ον, [in LXX chiefly for כֹּל;] of persons and things, *whole, entire, complete;* 1. of indefinite ideas, c. subst. anarth. : Lk 5⁵, Ac 11²⁶ 28³⁰, Tit 1¹¹; ὅλον ἄνθρωπον (*an entire man;* v. Field, *Notes,* 93), Jo 7²³; ὅλη Ἰερουσαλήμ (= πᾶσα Ἰ., Mt 2³; v. Bl., § 47, 9), Ac 21³¹. 2. Definite, c. art.; (*a*) preceding subst.: Mt 4²³, ²⁴, Lk 8³⁹, ι Co 12¹⁷, al.; (*b*) following subst.: Mk 1³³, Lk 9²⁵, Jo 4⁵³, Ac 21³⁰, al.; (*c*) between art. and subst., where subst. is an abstract noun (Plat., al.). 3. Attached to adj. or verb: Mt 13³³, Lk 13²¹, Jo 9³⁴, al.; adverbially, δι' ὅλου (MM, xviii), Jo 19²³.

† ὁλοτελής, -ές (< ὅλος, τέλος), *complete, perfect:* ι Th 5²³.†
SYN.: ὁλόκληρος (q.v.), τέλειος. " As regards meaning, ὁλόκληρος can hardly be distinguished from ὁλοτελής though, in accordance with its derivation, it draws more special attention to the several parts to which the wholeness spoken of extends, no part being wanting or lacking in completeness " (M, *Th.*, 78).

Ὀλυμπᾶς (perh. contr. fr. Ὀλυμπιόδωρος, Bl., § 29), -ᾶ, *Olympas:* Ro 16¹⁵.†

ὄλυνθος, -ου, ὁ, [in LXX: Ca 2¹³ (פַּגָּה)*;] *an unripe fig,* which grows in winter and usually falls off in the spring : Re 6¹³.†

ὅλως, adv. (< ὅλος), *altogether, assuredly, actually* (c. neg., *at all*): Mt 5³⁴, ι Co 5¹ 6⁷ 15²⁹.†

ὄμβρος, -ου, ὁ, [in LXX : De 32² (שָׂעִיר), Wi 16¹⁶, al.;] *a storm of rain, a shower:* Lk 12⁵⁴.†

† ὀμείρομαι (Rec. ὁμ-, v. WH, *App.*, 151), = cl. ἱμείρομαι (but prob. with different derivation, v. Bl., § 6, 4; Zorell, s.v.), [in LXX : Jb 3²¹ (חכה pi.)*;] *to desire earnestly, yearn after:* ι Th 2⁸.†

ὁμιλέω, -ῶ (< ὅμιλος), [in LXX : Pr 5¹⁹ (רוה pi.), al.;] *to be in company with, consort with;* hence, *to converse with:* Ac 20¹¹; c. dat., Ac 24²⁶; seq. πρός, Lk 24¹⁴, ¹⁵.†

ὁμιλία, -ας, ἡ (< ὅμιλος), [in LXX : Ex 21¹⁰ (עֹנָה), al.;] *company, association:* ι Co 15³³.†

** ὅμιλος, -ου, ὁ, [in Aq.: ι Ki 19²⁰ *;] *a crowd, throng:* Re 18¹⁷, Rec.†

ὁμίχλη, -ης, ἡ, [in LXX for עֲרָפֶל, etc.;] *a mist:* ιι Pe 2¹⁷.†
SYN.: νέφος, νεφέλη, both thicker than ὁ.

ὄμμα, -τος, τό, in cl. chiefly poët.; [in LXX for עַיִן (Pr₅, Wi₂, ιν Mac₃)*;] *an eye:* pl., Mt 20³⁴, Mk 8²³.†

ὀμνύω (so Hdt. and some Att. writers) and ὄμνυμι (so generally in Att. prose and always in Trag.; Mk 14⁷¹, -ύναι), [in LXX chiefly for שׁבע ni.;] *to swear, affirm by oath:* Mt 26⁷⁴, Mk 14⁷¹, He 7²¹; seq. εἰ (q.v), He 3¹¹ 4³; c. dat. pers., Mk 6²³; id. c. inf., He 3¹⁸; seq. ὅρκῳ, Ac 2³⁰; ὁ. ὅρκον πρός, c. acc. pers. (cl.), Lk 1⁷³; c. acc. (of that by which one swears; cl., v. MM, xviii), Ja 5¹²; seq. κατά, c. gen. (LXX; Bl., § 34, 1), He 6¹³, ¹⁶; seq. ἐν (εἰς), as in Heb. (Bl., § 39, 4), Mt 5³⁴, ³⁶ 23¹⁶, ¹⁸, ²⁰⁻²², Re 10⁶ (Bl., § 70, 3).†

MANUAL GREEK LEXICON OF THE NEW TESTAMENT 317

ὁμοθυμαδόν (< ὁμός, θυμός), [in LXX for יַחְדָּו, יַחְדָּו (freq. in Jb),
Wi 10²⁰ 18⁵,¹², al.;] *with one mind, with one accord:* Ac 1¹⁴ 2⁴⁶ 4²⁴
5¹² 7⁵⁷ 8⁶ 12²⁰ 15²⁵ 18¹² 19²⁹, Ro 15⁶ (Hatch, *Essays*, 63 f., argues that
the un-cl. sense *together*, which is found in Jb 3¹⁸ 38³³, Nu 24²⁴, Wi
18⁵,¹² (but not 10²⁰), al., should be attached to the NT instances, but
v. Abbott, *Essays*, 96 ; MM, xviii).†
  *†ὁμοιάζω (< ὅμοιος), *to be like:* Mt 23²⁷ (L, Tr., txt., WH, mg.)
26⁷³ (WH, mg.) (not found elsewhere. Cf. παρ-ομοιάζω.) †
  ** ὁμοιοπαθής, -ές (< ὅμοιος, πάσχω), [in LXX : Wi 7³, ιν Mac 12¹³ *;]
of like feelings or affections: c. dat., Ac 14¹⁵, Ja 5¹⁷.†

ὅμοιος, -οία, -οιον, [in LXX for כְּמוֹ, etc.;] *like, resembling, such
as, the same as:* c. dat., of form or appearance, Jo 9⁹, Re 1¹³ (WH, mg.,
R, but v. infr.) ib.¹⁵ 2¹⁸ 4⁶,⁷ 9⁷,¹⁰ (Bl., § 37, 6₂) ib.¹⁹ 11¹ 13²,¹¹; ὁράσει,
Re 4³; of nature, condition, ability, etc., Mt 22³⁹, Ac 17²⁹, Ga 5²¹,
ι Jo 3², Re 13⁴ 18¹⁸ 21¹¹,¹⁸; of comparison in parables, Mt 13³¹ ff. 20¹,
Lk 13¹⁸,¹⁹,²¹; of thinking, acting, etc., Mt 11¹⁶ 13⁵², Lk 6⁴⁷⁻⁴⁹ 7³¹,³²
(T, c. gen.; Bl., § 36, 11) 12³⁶, Jo 8⁵⁵, Ju⁷; c. acc., Re 1¹³ (WH, txt.;
Swete, Hort, in l.) 14¹⁴.†

ὁμοιότης, -ητος, ἡ (< ὅμοιος), [in LXX : Ge 1¹¹,¹² (מִין), Wi 14¹⁹,
ιν Mac 15⁴ *;] *likeness:* καθ᾽ ὁμοιότητα, *in like manner,* He 4¹⁵; id. c.
gen. (MM, xviii), *after the likeness* (of), He 7¹⁵.†

ὁμοιόω, -ῶ (< ὅμοιος), [in LXX chiefly for דָּמָה;] 1. *to make like,*
c. gen. et dat.; pass., *to be made* or *become like:* Mt 6⁸ 13²⁴ 18²³ 22²
25¹, Ac 14¹¹, He 2¹⁷; seq. ὡς (cf. Ez 32², Heb.), Ro 9²⁹. 2. *to liken,
compare:* c. dat., acc., Mt 11¹⁶, Lk 7³¹ 13¹⁸,²⁰; πῶς ὁμοιώσωμεν, Mk 4³⁰;
pass., Mt 7²⁴,²⁶ (cf. ἀφ-ομοιόω).†

ὁμοίωμα, -τος, τό (< ὁμοιόω), [in LXX for תְּמוּנָה, תַּבְנִית, תְּמוּנָה, דְּמוּת,
etc.;] *that which is made like* something; (*a*) concrete, *an image, likeness* (Ps 105 (106)²⁰, Ez 1⁵, ι Mac 3⁴⁸, al.) : Re 9⁷; (*b*) abstract, *likeness, resemblance:* Ro 5¹⁴ 6⁵ 8³, Phl 2⁷; ἐν ὁ. εἰκόνος, Ro 1²³.†
  SYN. : εἰκών (q.v.), ὁμοίωσις.

ὁμοίως (< ὅμοιος), adv., *likewise, in like manner, equally:* Mt 22²⁶,
Mk 4¹⁶, Lk 10³⁷, al.; c. dat., Mt 22³⁹, Lk 6³¹; ὁ. καί, Mt 22²⁶, Mk
15³¹, al.; ὁ. καθώς, Lk 17²⁸; καθὼς . . . ὁ., Lk 6³¹; ὁ. μέντοι καί, Ju⁸.

ὁμοίωσις, -εως, ἡ (ὁμοιόω), [in LXX chiefly for דְּמוּת, Ps 57 (58)⁴,
al.;] 1. *a making like, becoming like* (Plat.). 2. *likeness:* Ja 3⁹ (LXX).†
  SYN.: v.s. ὁμοίωμα, and cf. Tr., *Syn.*, § xv.

ὁμολογέω, -ῶ (< ὁμόλογος, *of one mind:* Da LXX Su⁶⁰*), [in
LXX : Jb 40⁹ (14) (ידה hi.), Je 51 (44)²⁵ (נדר), al.;] 1. *to speak the same
language* (Hdt.). 2. *to agree with* (Hdt., Plat., al.). 3. *to agree,
confess, acknowledge* (Plat., al.) : absol., Jo 1²⁰ 12⁴²; pass., Ro 10¹⁰; seq.
ὅτι, ib., He 11¹³; c. acc. rei, Ac 23⁸, ι Jo 1⁹, Re 3⁵; id. c. dat. pers.,
Ac 24¹⁴; c. acc. cogn., ι Ti 6¹²; c. acc. pers., ι Jo 2²³ 4³; id. seq. pred.
acc. (Bl., § 34, 5; 73, 5), Jo 9²², Ro 10⁹, ι Jo 4²,¹⁵, ιι Jo⁷; c. inf. (M,
Pr., 229), Tit 1¹⁶; c. dat. pers. seq. ὅτι, Mt 7²³; seq. ἐν, c. dat. pers.

(M, *Pr.*, 104; Bl., § 41, 2), Mt 10³², Lk 12⁸. 4. *to agree, promise:* τ. ἐπαγγελίαν, Ac 7¹⁷; c. inf. obj. (Bl., § 61, 3), Mt 14⁷. 5. = ἐξομολογέω, *to praise:* He 13¹⁵ (Westc., in l.). (Cf. ἀνθ-ομολογέομαι, ἐξομολογέω.)†

ὁμολογία, -ας, ἡ (< ὁμολογέω), [in LXX: De 12⁶, ¹⁷, Am 4⁵, Ez 46¹² (נְדָבָה), Le 22¹⁸, Je 51 (44)²⁵ (נֶדֶר), I Es 9⁸ *;] 1. in cl., *an agreement, assent, compact* (in π., of a *contract;* Deis¡., *BS*, 249). 2. *confession* (prob. always in an objective sense): II Co 9¹³, I Ti 6¹², ¹³, He 3¹ 4¹⁴ 10²³.†

** ὁμολογουμένως, adv. (< ὁμολογέω), [in LXX: IV Mac 6³¹ 7¹⁶ 16¹ *;] 1. *as agreed, conformably with.* 2. *confessedly, by common consent :* I Ti 3¹⁶.†

* ὁμότεχνος, -ον (< ὁμός, τέχνη), *practising the same craft, of the same trade:* Ac 18³.†

ὁμοῦ, adv. (< ὁμός), *together;* (a) prop., of place: Jo 21², Ac 2¹; (b) without idea of place: Jo 4³⁶ 20⁴.†

ὁμόω, v.s. ὀμνύω.

* ὁμόφρων, -ον (< ὁμός, φρήν), = ὁμόνοος, *agreeing, of one mind:* I Pe 3⁸.†

ὅμως, adv. (< ὁμός), *yet: ὅ. μέντοι, but yet, nevertheless*, Jo 12⁴²; by hyperbaton, out of its proper position, I Co 14⁷, Ga 3¹⁵ (but v. Bl., § 77, 14).†

* ὄναρ, τό, indecl., used only in nom. and acc. sing. (the other cases are supplied by ὄνειρος), *a dream : κατ᾽ ὄ.* (in later writers only), *in a dream,* Mt 1²⁰ 2¹², ¹³, ¹⁹, ²² 27¹⁹.†

* ὀνάριον, -ου, τό (dimin. of ὄνος), *a young ass:* Jo 12¹⁴.†

ὀνειδίζω (< ὄνειδος), [in LXX chiefly for חרף pi.;] *to reproach, upbraid:* absol., Ja 1⁵; c. acc. pers. (in cl. more freq. c. dat. pers.; Bl., § 34, 2; WM, 278), Mt 5¹¹, Mk 15³², ³⁴, WH, mg., Lk 6²², Ro 15³ (LXX); τ. πόλεις, Mt 11²⁰; pass., I Ti 4¹⁰, WH, mg., I Pe 4¹⁴; c. acc. rei, Mk 16 [14]; c. dupl. acc., Mt 27⁴⁴.†

† ὀνειδισμός, -οῦ, ὁ (ὀνειδίζω), [in LXX chiefly for חֶרְפָּה;] *a reproach :* Ro 15³, He 10³³; εἰς ὄ. ἐμπεσεῖν, I Ti 3⁷; ὁ ὄ. τοῦ Χριστοῦ, He 11²⁶ 13¹³.†

ὄνειδος, -ους, τό, [in LXX chiefly for חֶרְפָּה, also for כְּלִמָּה, etc.;] 1. *reproach, censure, blame.* 2. *matter of reproach, disgrace:* Lk 1²⁵.†

Ὀνήσιμος, -ου, ὁ (i.e. *profitable,* < ὄνησις, *profit*), *Onesimus:* Col 4⁹, Phm ¹⁰ (a common name among slaves; v. MM, iii, xviii).†

Ὀνησίφορος, -ου, ὁ (i.e. *bringing advantage*), *Onesiphorus:* II Ti 1¹⁶ 4¹⁹.†

*† ὀνικός, -ή, -όν (< ὄνος), *of* or *for an ass:* μύλος ὀ., Mt 18⁶, Mk 9⁴² (elsewhere only in π.; v. MM, xviii).†

** ὀνίνημι, [in LXX: To 3⁸, Si 30² *;] *to profit, benefit, help;* mid., *to have profit, derive benefit:* optat. (M, *Pr.*, 195), c. gen., Phm ²⁰.†

ὄνομα, -τος, τό, [in LXX chiefly for שֵׁם;] 1. in general, *the name* by which a person or thing is called: Mt 10², Mk 3¹⁶, Lk 1⁶³, Jo 18¹⁰, al.; ἄνθρωπος (etc.), ᾧ (οὖ) ὅ. (τ. ὅ.), sc. ἦν or ἐστίν (Bl., § 30, 3), Mk 14³², Lk 1²⁶,²⁷; with same ellipsis, καὶ τ. ὅ. αὐτοῦ (ὅ. αὐτῷ), Lk 1⁵, Jo 1⁶, al.; ὀνόματι, seq. nom. prop., Mt 27³², Mk 5²², Lk 1⁵, Ac 5¹, al.; acc. absol. (Bl., § 34, 7), τοὔνομα (= τ. ὄνομα), Mt 27⁵⁷; ὅ. μοι (sc. ἐστίν; cf. Hom., Od., ix, 366), Mk 5⁹ (cf. Lk 8³⁰); ἔχειν ὅ., Re 9¹¹; καλεῖν (ἐπιτιθέναι) ὅ. (Bl., § 33, 1), Mt 1²¹, Mk 3¹⁶; τ. ὅ. ἐν (τ.) βίβλῳ ζωῆς (cf. Deiss., LAE, 121), Phl 4³, Re 13⁸, cf. Lk 10²⁰ (ἐν τ. οὐρανοῖς); ὅ. βλασφημίας, Re 13¹; the name as opp. to the reality, Re 3¹ (cf. Hdt., vii, 138); as a title: Eph 1²¹, Phl 2⁹,¹⁰ (Lft., in l.). 2. By a usage similar to that with ref. to Heb. שֵׁם (Lft., Notes, 106 f.), but also common in Hellenistic (M, Pr., 100; Bl., § 39, 4; Deiss, BS, 146 f., 196 f.; LAE, 123₄), of all that the name implies, of rank, authority, character, etc.: of acting on one's authority or in his behalf, ἐν (εἰς) ὅ., c. gen. pers. (v. reff. supr.), Mt 10⁴¹ 21⁹ 28¹⁹, Mk 11⁹, Lk 13³⁵, Jo 5⁴³, Ac 8¹⁶, ι Co 1¹³; of the name Christian, ι Pe 4¹⁶; esp. of the name of God as expressing the divine attributes: ἁγιάζειν (ἅγιον) τὸ ὅ. (τ. Πατρός, Κυρίου), Mt 6⁹, Lk 1⁴⁹ 11²; ψάλλειν (ὁμολογεῖν) τῷ ὅ., Ro 15⁹, He 13¹⁵; δοξάζειν (φανεροῦν, φοβεῖσθαι) τὸ ὅ., Jo 12²⁸ 17⁶,²⁶, Re 11¹⁸ 15⁴; βλασφημεῖν, Ro 2²⁴, ι Ti 6¹, Re 13⁶; similarly, of the name of Christ: τ. καλὸν ὅ., Ja 2⁷ (Deiss., LAE, 276); πιστεύειν τῷ ὅ., ι Jo 3²³; π. εἰς τ. ὅ. (Bl., § 39, 4), Jo 1¹² 2²³ 3¹⁸; ὀνομάζειν τὸ ὅ., ιι Ti 2¹⁹; κρατεῖν, Re 2¹³; οὐκ ἀρνεῖσθαι, Re 3⁸; ἐν τ. ὅ. (v. reff. supr.), Mk 9³⁸ 16[¹⁷], Lk 10¹⁷, Jo 14¹³ 16²³,²⁴ 20³¹, Ac 3⁶ 4¹², Eph 5²⁰, ι Pe 4¹⁴, al.; εἰς τ. ὅ. συνάγεσθαι, Mt 18²⁰; ἕνεκεν τοῦ ὅ., Mt 19²⁹; διὰ τὸ ὅ., Mt 10²², Mk 13¹³, al.; διὰ τοῦ ὅ., ι Co 1¹⁰; ὑπὲρ τοῦ ὅ., Ac 9¹⁶, Ro 1⁵, al.; id. absol., Ac 5⁴¹, ιιι Jo⁷; πρὸς τὸ ὅ., Ac 26⁹. 3. cause, ground, reason (in cl., usually in bad sense, pretext): Mk 9⁴¹ (Swete, in l.; Dalman, Words, 305 f.). 4. In late Greek (Deiss., BS., 196 f.), an individual, a person: Ac 1¹⁵, Re 3⁴ 11¹³.

ὀνομάζω (< ὄνομα), [in LXX for זכר, נקב, קרא;] 1. to name, mention, or address by name: Ac 19¹³; pass., Ro 15²⁰, Eph 1²¹ 5³; of the use of the Divine name in praise and worship, ιι Ti 2¹⁹ (LXX, Nu 16²⁶; cf. Is 52¹¹, Am 6¹⁰). 2. to name, call, give a name to: Mk 3¹⁴ (T, R, txt. om.), Lk 6¹³,¹⁴; pass., ι Co 5¹¹; seq. ἐξ (cl.), Eph 3¹⁵ (cf. ἐπ-ονομάζω).†

ὄνος, -ου, ὁ, ἡ, [in LXX chiefly for חֲמוֹר, also for אָתוֹן, etc.;] an ass: Mt 21²,⁵ (LXX), Lk 14⁵, Jo 12¹⁵ (LXX); ὁ, Lk 13¹⁵; ἡ, Mt 21⁷.†

ὄντως, adv. (< ὤν, ptcp. of εἰμί, sum), [in LXX: Nu 22³⁷ (אָמְנָה), Je 3²³ (אָכֵן), 10¹⁹ (אַךְ), ιιι Ki 12²⁴, Wi 17¹⁴*;] really, actually, truly: Mk 11³², Lk 23⁴⁷ 24³⁴, Jo 8³⁶, ι Co 14²⁵, Ga 3²¹; ἡ ὅ. ζωή, ι Ti 6¹⁹; ἡ ὅ. χήρα, ib. 5³,⁵,¹⁶.†

ὄξος, -εος (-ους), τό (< ὀξύς), [in LXX: Nu 6³, Ru 2¹⁴, Ps 68 (69)²¹, Pr 25²⁰ (חֹמֶץ)*;] sour wine (posca, vin-de-pays), the ordinary drink of labourers and common soldiers: Mt 27⁴⁸, Mk 15³⁶, Lk 23³⁶, Jo 19²⁹,³⁰.†

ὀξύς, -εῖα, -ύ, [in LXX: Ps 56 (57)⁴, al. (חַד), Am 2¹⁵ (קַל),

Is 5²⁸ (שׁנַן), etc.;] 1. *sharp:* Re 1¹⁶ 2¹² 14¹⁴, ¹⁷, ¹⁸ 19¹⁵. 2. Of motion, *swift:* Ro 3¹⁵ (LXX ταχινός).†

ὀπή, -ῆς, ἡ, [in LXX for חֹר, חֲגוּ, etc.;] *an opening, a hole:* Ja 3¹¹ (cf. Ex 33²²), He 11³⁸ (cf. Ob ³).†

ὄπισθεν, adv. of place, [in LXX chiefly for אַחַר, מֵאַחַר;] *behind, after:* Mt 9²⁰, Mk 5²⁷, Lk 8⁴⁴, Re 4⁶ 5¹. As prep. c. gen.: Mt 15²³, Lk 23²⁶, Re 1¹⁰ (WH, mg.).†

ὀπίσω, adv. of place and time, [in LXX chiefly for אַחַר, אַחֲרֵי, and cogn. forms;] 1. prop., as in cl., adv., (*a*) of time (not in NT); (*b*) of place, *back, behind, after:* Mt 24¹⁸, Lk 7³⁸; τὰ ὀ., Phl 3¹³; εἰς τὰ ὀ., Mk 13¹⁶, Lk 9⁶² 17³¹, Jo 6⁶⁶ 18⁶ 20¹⁴. 2. By a usage not found in cl., and in LXX representing the Heb. prep. אַחֲרֵי (Bl., § 40, 8; Thackeray, *Gr.,* 46 f.), but also prob. general in vernacular (M, *Pr.,* 99), as prep. c. gen.; (*a*) of time, *after:* Mt 3¹¹, Mk 1⁷ Jo 1¹⁵, ²⁷, ³⁰; (*b*) of place, *behind, after:* Mt 4¹⁹ 10³⁸ 16²³, ²⁴, Mk 1¹⁷, ²⁰ 8³³, ³⁴, Lk 9²³ 14²⁷ 19¹⁴ 21⁸, II Pe 2¹⁰, Ju⁷, Re 1¹⁰ 12¹⁵; in constr. praegn. (v. Swete on Re, l.c.), Jo 12¹⁹, Ac 5¹⁷ 20³⁰, I Ti 5¹⁵, Re 13³.†

**ὁπλίζω (< ὅπλον), [in Sm.: Je 52²⁵ *;] *to make ready, equip;* of soldiers, *to arm.* Mid., *to arm oneself;* fig., ἔννοιαν: I Pe 4¹ (cf. θράσος ὁ., Soph., *Elec.,* 995), (cf. καθ-οπλίζω).†

ὅπλον, -ου, τό, [in LXX for מָגֵן, צִנָּה, etc.;] 1. *a tool, implement, instrument:* ὅπλα ἀδικίας (opp. to ὁ. δικαιοσύνης), Ro 6¹³. 2. Freq., in pl., *arms, weapons:* Jo 18³, II Co 10⁴; metaph., τ. φωτός, Ro 13¹²; τ. δικαιοσύνης, II Co 6⁷.†

ὁποῖος, -οία, -οῖον, [in LXX: Ca 5¹⁰, II Mac 11³⁷ *;] *of what sort:* I Co 3¹³, Ga 2⁶, I Th 1⁹, Ja 1²⁴; τοιοῦτος ὁ., *such as,* Ac 26²⁹.†

ὁπότε, *when:* Lk 6³, Rec. (WH, R, ὅτε).†

ὅπου, adv. of place, correlat. of ποῦ (q.v.), *where.* I. Prop., of place, 1. *where;* (*a*) in relative sentences, c. indic: Mt 25²⁴, ²⁶, Mk 2⁴ 4⁵, ¹⁵ 5⁴⁰ 13¹⁴, Jo 3⁸ 6⁶² 7³⁴, ³⁶ 11³² 14³ 17²⁴ 20¹⁹, Ro 15²⁰, Re 2¹³; after nouns of place, for relat. prepositional phrase (ἐν ᾧ, etc.), Mt 6¹⁹, ²⁰ 13⁵ 26⁵⁷ 28⁶, Mk 6⁵⁵ 9⁴⁸, Lk 12³³, Jo 1²⁸ 4²⁰, ⁴⁶ 6²³ 7⁴² 10⁴⁰ 11³⁰ 12¹ 18¹, ²⁰ 19¹⁸, ²⁰, ⁴¹ 20¹², Ac 17¹, Re 2¹³ 11⁸ 20¹⁰; seq. ἐκεῖ, Mt 6²¹, Lk 12³⁴ 17³⁷, Jo 12²⁶; id. pleonast. (= Heb. שָׁם . . . אֲשֶׁר; Aram. תַּמָּן . . דְּ; cf. Ge 13³), ὅ. . . . ἐκεῖ, Re 12⁶, ¹⁴; ὅ. . . . ἐπ᾽ αἰτῶν, ib. 17⁹; ὅ. ἄν, *wherever* (M, *Pr.,* 168), c. impf. indic., Mk 6⁵⁶; c. pres. subjc., Mt 24²⁸; ὅ. ἐάν, ib. 26¹³, Mk 6¹⁰ 9¹⁸ 14⁹, ¹⁴ᵃ; (*b*) in quaest. indir., c. aor. subjc.: Mk 14¹⁴ᵇ, Lk 22¹¹. 2. In late writers (sometimes also in cl.; Bl., § 25, 2), with verbs of motion, = ὅποι, *whither:* c. indic., Jo 8²¹, ²² 13³³, ³⁶ 14⁴ 21¹⁸, He 6²⁰, Ja 3⁴; ὅ. ἄν, *whithersoever,* c. indic. praes. (v.l., subjc.), Re 14⁴; subjc., Lk 9⁵⁷; ὅ. ἐάν, Mt 8¹⁹. II. Without strict local sense, 1. of time or condition: Col 3¹¹, He 9¹⁶ 10¹⁸, Ja 3¹⁶, II Pe 2¹¹. 2. Of cause or reason (AV, *whereas*): I Co 3³.†

†ὀπτάνω, [in LXX: iii Ki 8⁸ (רָאָה ni.), To 12¹⁹*;] late present as from ὤφθην (= ὁρίω); mid., ὀπτάνομαι, to allow oneself to be seen, to appear: c. dat., Ac 1³. (For exx. from π., v. Deiss., *LAE*, 79, 252₅; MM, ii, xviii.) †

†ὀπτασία, -ας, ἡ (< ὀπτάζομαι, Nu 14¹⁴* = ὀπτάνομαι), later form of ὄψις, [in LXX: Ma 3² (רָאָה ni.), Da th 9²³ 10¹, ⁷, ⁸, ¹⁶ (מַרְאֶה), מַרְאָה; LXX, ὅραμα, -σις), Es 4⁷, Si 43², ¹⁶*;] 1. *an appearing, coming into view* (Ma, Es, Si, ll. c.). 2. *a vision:* Lk 1²², 24²³, Ac 26¹⁹, ii Co 12¹ (Da, ll. c., also in MGr.).†

ὀπτός, -ή, -όν, [in LXX: Ex 12⁸, ⁹ (צָלִי)*;] *roasted, boiled:* Lk 24⁴².†

ὄπτω, v.s. ὁράω.

ὀπώρα, -ας, ἡ, [in LXX: Je 31 (48)³² 47 (40)¹⁰, ¹² (קַיִץ)*;] 1. *late summer, early autumn* (the time between the risings of Sirius and Arcturus, i.e. late July, all August and early September). 2. By meton. (as being fruit-time), *ripe fruits:* Re 18¹⁴ (cf. φθινοπωρινά, Ju ¹²).†

ὅπως. I. Relat. adv. of manner, *as, how:* c. indic., Lk 24²⁰. II. Conj., c. subjc. (in cl. also c. opt., indic.: so in Mt 26⁵⁹, LT, Tr.), *in order that, to the end that, that;* 1. final, denoting purpose or design (in which the original idea of modality has been merged): after pres., Mt 6², al.; pf., Ac 9¹⁷, al.; impf., Ac 9²⁴; aor., Ac 9², al.; plpf., Jo 11⁵⁷; fut., Mt 23³⁵; imperat., Mt 2⁸, al.; ὅ. μή (M, *Pr.*, 185), Mt 6¹⁸, Lk 16²⁶, Ac 20¹⁶, i Co 1²⁹; ὅ. πληρωθῇ, Mt 2²³ 8¹⁷ 13³⁵; ὅ. ἄν (Bl., § 65, 2; WM, § 42, 5), Lk 2³⁵, Ac 3¹⁹ 15¹⁷, Ro 3⁴ (cf. Ge 12¹³, Ps 59⁷, i Mac 10³², al.). 2. After verbs of asking, exhorting, etc.: Mt 9³⁸, Lk 7³, Ja 5¹⁶, al. (in late writers its place is often taken by the correl. πῶς, q.v.).

ὅραμα, -τος, τό (< ὁράω), [in LXX for חָזוֹן, מַרְאֶה, etc.;] *that which is seen; (a) a sight, spectacle:* Mt 17⁹, Ac 7³¹; *(b) an appear-ance, vision:* Ac 9¹⁰, ¹² (Rec.) 10³, ¹⁷, ¹⁹ 11⁵ 12⁹ 16⁹, ¹⁰ 18⁹ (cf. ὀπτασία).†

ὅρασις,-εως, ἡ (ὁράω), [in LXX chiefly for מַרְאֶה, חָזוֹן and cognate forms;] 1. in Arist. and later writers, *the act of seeing, the sense of sight*, and by meton., pl., *the eyes*. 2. *appearance* (Nu 24⁴, Ez 1⁵, Si 41²⁰, al.): Re 4³. 3. = ὅραμα, *a vision:* Ac 2¹⁷ (LXX), Re 9¹⁷.†

ὁρατός, -ή, -όν (ὁρίω), *visible:* τὰ ὁ., Col 1¹⁶.†

ὁράω, -ῶ, [in LXX chiefly for חזה, also for חזה, etc.;] in "durative" sense (hence aor. act., εἶδον, pass., ὤφθην, fut., ὄψομαι, from different roots; v. M, *Pr.*, 110 f.; on ὄψησθε, Lk 13²⁸, v. M, *Gr.*, ii, p. 218; on other tense-forms, op. cit., pp. 251 ff., and on relation of ὁράω to βλέπω and εἶδον, pp. 231, 234 ff.), *to see* (in colloq. even the pres. is rare, its place being generally taken by βλέπω, θεωρέω, v. Bl., § 24). 1. Of bodily vision, *to see, perceive, behold:* absol., Mk 6³⁸, al.; ἔρχου καὶ ἴδε, Jo 1⁴⁶, al.; seq. ὅτι, Mk 2¹⁶, al.; c. acc., Mt 2², Mk 1¹⁰ 16⁷, Ga 1¹⁹, al.; θεόν, Jo 1¹⁸, i Jo 4²⁰, al. 2. *to see* with the mind, *perceive, discern:* absol., Ro 15²¹; c. acc. rei., Mt 9² 27⁵⁴, Ac 8²³, Col 2¹⁸, al.

21

3. *to see, take heed, beware:* ὅρα μή, c. aor. subjc., Mt 8⁴ 18¹⁰, Mk 1⁴⁴, ι Th 5¹⁵; id., sc. μὴ ποιήσῃς, Re 19¹⁰ 22⁹ (Bl., § 81, 1); seq. imperat. Mt 9³⁰ 16⁶, Mk 8¹⁵. 4. *to experience:* τ. θάνατον, Lk 2²⁶, He 11⁵; ζωήν, Jo 3³⁶; τ. διαφθοράν, Ac 2²⁷. 5. *to visit:* c. acc. pers., Lk 8²⁰, Jo 12²¹, Ro 1¹¹, al.; c. acc. loc., Ac 19²¹. 6. *to see to, care for:* Mt 27⁴, Ac 18¹⁵ (cf. ἀφ-, καθ-, προ-, συν-οράω).

SYN.: v.s. βλέπω.

ὀργή, -ῆς, ἡ, [in LXX chiefly for אַף, also for חָרוֹן, חֵמָה, קֶצֶף, etc.;] 1. *impulse, propensity, disposition.* 2. *anger, wrath;* (*a*) of men : Mk 3⁵, Eph 4³¹, Col 3⁸, ι Ti 2⁸, Ja 1¹⁹, ²⁰; (*b*) of God; (*a*) that reaction of the divine nature against sin which in anthropomorphic language is called *anger:* Ro 1¹⁸ 9²² 12¹⁹ (*ICC*, in l.), ι Th 1¹⁰ 2¹⁶, He 3¹¹ 4³ (LXX), Re 14¹⁰ 16¹⁹ 19¹⁵; (β) of the effect of God's anger : Mt 3⁷, Lk 3⁷ 21²³, Jo 3³⁶, Ro 2⁵, ⁸ 3⁵ 4¹⁵ 5⁹ 13⁴, ⁵ Eph 5⁶, Col 3⁶, ι Th 5⁹, Ja 1²⁰, Re 6¹⁶, ¹⁷ 11¹⁸; σκεύη ὀργῆς, Ro 9²²; τέκνα ὀργῆς, Eph 2³.†

SYN.: v.s. θυμός.

ὀργίζω (< ὀργή), [in LXX chiefly for חרה, also for קצף, etc.;] *to make angry, provoke to anger ;* in cl. most freq. in pass., and so always in NT, *to be provoked to anger, be angry:* absol., Mt 18³⁴ 22⁷ (v. l. in Mk 1⁴¹, WH, mg.; v. Turner, *SNT,* p. 58), Lk 14²¹ 15²⁸, Eph 4²⁶ (LXX), Re 11¹⁸; c. dat., Mt 5²²; seq. ἐπί, c. dat. (III Ki 11⁹, al.), Re 12¹⁷ (cf. παρ-οργίζω).†

ὀργίλος, -η, -ον (< ὀργή), [in LXX : Pr 22²⁴ 29²² (חֵמָה), etc.;] *inclined to anger, passionate :* Tit 1⁷.†

* ὀργυιά, -ᾶς, ἡ (< ὀρέγω), the length of the outstretched arms, *a fathom :* Ac 27²⁸.†

** ὀρέγω, [in Sm.: Jb 8²⁰, Ez 16⁴⁹ *;] *to reach, stretch out ;* pass. and mid., *to stretch oneself out, reach forth ;* metaph., *to reach after, grasp at, aspire to :* c. gen. rei, ι Ti 3¹, He 11¹⁶; φιλαργυρίας (v. Ellic. and *CGT,* in l.), ι Ti 6¹⁰.†

SYN.: ἐπιθυμέω, to desire (q.v.).

ὀρεινός (WH, ὀριν-; v. MM, xviii,) -ή, -όν (< ὄρος), *mountainous, hilly ;* ἡ ὀ. (sc. χώρα), *the hill-country* (LXX for הַר): Lk 1³⁹, ⁶⁵.†

** ὄρεξις, -εως, ἡ (< ὀρέγομαι), [in LXX : Wi 14² 15⁵ 16², ³, Si 18³⁰ 23⁶, iv Mac 1³³, ³⁵ *;] the most general word for all kinds of *desire, longing, appetite :* of lust, Ro 1²⁷.†

SYN.: v.s. πάθος.

*† ὀρθοποδέω, -ῶ (< ὀρθό-πους, *going straight*), = cl. εὐθυπορέω, *to walk straight :* metaph., Ga 2¹⁴ (not elsewhere).†

ὀρθός, -ή, -όν, [in LXX chiefly for יָשָׁר;] *straight ;* (*a*) in height, straight, upright : Ac 14¹⁰; (*b*) in line, straight, direct : fig., He 12¹³ (LXX).†

† ὀρθοτομέω, -ῶ (< ὀρθός, τέμνω), [in LXX : Pr 3⁶ 11⁵ (יֹשֶׁר pi.) *;] *to cut straight,* as a road (τ. ὁδούς, fig., Pr, ll. c.). Metaph., τ. λόγον τ. ἀληθείας, ιι Ti 2¹⁵ (v. Ellic. and *CGT,* in l.; not found elsewhere).†

† ὀρθρίζω (< ὄρθρος), [in LXX chiefly for שכם hi., Ge 19², al.; also

for שֵׁחֵר pi., Ps 62¹ (63), al., etc.;] = cl. poët., ὀρθρεύω, to rise early : seq. πρός, c. acc. pers. (as Ps, l.c., al.), Lk 21³⁸ (v. Thumb, Hellen., 123).†

† ὀρθρινός, -ή, -όν (< ὄρθρος), [in LXX : Ho 6⁵ ⁽⁴⁾ 13³ (שכם hi.), Hg 2¹⁵ ⁽¹⁴⁾, Wi 11²² *;] late form of ὄρθριος (q.v.), early : Lk 24²².†

ὄρθριος, -α, -ον (< ὄρθρος), [in LXX : I Ki 28¹⁴, Jb 29⁷, III Mac 5¹⁰, ²³ *;] early, in the early morning : Lk 24²², Rec. (v.s. ὀρθρινός).†

ὄρθρος, -ου, ὁ, [in LXX for שֵׁחֵר, בֹּקֶר, etc.;] daybreak, dawn: ὄρθρου βαθέως (M, Pr., 73), at early dawn, Lk 24¹; ὄρθρου, Jo 8⁽²⁾; ὑπὸ τὸν ὄ., Ac 5²¹ (cf. MM, xviii).†

ὀρθῶς, adv. (< ὀρθός), rightly : Mk 7³⁵, Lk 7⁴³ 10²⁸ 20²¹.†

ὁρίζω (< ὅρος, a boundary), [in LXX for אמר, גבל, etc.;] 1. to separate, mark off by boundaries (so Nu 34⁶, Jo 13²⁷). 2. to determine, appoint, designate : of time, c. acc., Ac 17²⁶, He 4⁷; c. acc. pers., Ac 17³¹; c. inf., Ac 11²⁹; pass., Lk 22²², Ac 2²³ 10⁴², Ro 1⁴ (cf. ἀφ-, ἀπο-δι-, προ-ορί ζω).†

ὀρινός, v.s. ὀρεινός.

ὅριον, -ου, τό (< ὅρος, a boundary), [in LXX chiefly for גְּבוּל;] a boundary, bound; chiefly in pl., and so always in NT : Mt 2¹⁶ 4¹³ 8³⁴ 15²², ³⁹ 19¹, Mk 5¹⁷ 7²⁴, ³¹ 10¹, Ac 13⁵⁰.†

ὁρκίζω (< ὅρκος), [in LXX : Ge 24³⁷, al. (שבע hi.);] 1. to make one swear (Xen., Polyb., al.). 2. to adjure : c. dupl. acc., Mk '5⁷, Ac 19¹³ (cf. ἐν-, ἐξ-ορκίζω).†

ὅρκος, -ου, ὁ, [in LXX chiefly for שֶׁבַע, שְׁבֻעָה and cogn. forms;] an oath : Mt 14⁷ 26⁷², Lk 1⁷³, Ac 2³⁰, He 6¹⁶, ¹⁷, Ja 5¹²; pl., Mt 5³³ (LXX) 14⁹, Mk 6²⁶.†

ὁρκωμοσία, -ας, ἡ (< ὅρκος, ὄμνυμι; by metapl. for τὰ ὁρκωμόσια, asseverations on oath ; v. MM, xviii), [in LXX : Ez 17¹⁸, ¹⁹ (אָלָה), I Es 9⁹³ *;] affirmation on oath, an oath : He 7²⁰, ²¹, ²⁸.†

ὁρμάω, -ῶ (< ὁρμή), [in LXX for שׁוּב, etc.;] 1. causal, to set in motion, urge on. 2. Intrans., to hasten on, rush : seq. εἰς, Mt 8³², Mk 5¹³, Lk 8³³, Ac 19²⁹; ἐπί, c. acc., Ac 7⁵⁷.†

ὁρμή, -ῆς, ἡ, [in LXX : Pr 3²⁵ (שֹׁאָה), etc.;] 1. a violent movement, impulse : Ja 3⁴; (b) a hostile movement, onset, assault : Ac 14⁵.†

ὅρμημα, -τος, τό (ὁρμάω), [in LXX : Ho 5¹⁰, Am 1¹¹ (עֶבְרָה), etc.;] a rush : Re 18²¹.†

ὄρνεον, -ου, τό, = ὄρνις, [in LXX chiefly for צִפּוֹר;] a bird : Re 18⁶ 19¹⁷, ²¹ (Hom., al.).†

*† ὄρνιξ (cf. Doric gen., ὄρνιχος, and MGr., ὀρνίχ; v. M, Pr., 45), = ὄρνις : Lk 13³⁴ (T; WH, ὄρνις).†

ὄρνις, -ιθος, ὁ, ἡ, [in LXX : ὄ. ἐκλεκταί, III Ki 3¹ 4²³ (5³) (בַּרְבֻּרִים) *;] a bird ; specif., a cock, a hen : Mt 23³⁷, Lk 13³⁴ (WH).†

*† ὁροθεσία, -ας, ἡ (< ὅρος, a boundary, + τίθημι), a setting of boundaries; in pl., bounds : Ac 17²⁶.†

ὄρος, -ους, τό, [in LXX chiefly, and very freq., for הַר;] a *mountain :* Mt 4⁸ 17¹, Mk 9², Jo 4²⁰, II Pe 1¹⁸, al.; opp. to βουνός, Lk 3⁵ (LXX); ὄ. τ. ἐλαιῶν, Mt 21¹ 24³, al. (v.s. ἐ.); ὄ. Σιών (Σ., prob. in gen. appos.), He 12²², Re 14¹; ὄ. Σινά, Ac 7³⁰, ³⁸, Ga 4²⁴, ²⁵; τὸ ὄ., of the hill district as distinct from the lowlands, esp. the hills above the Sea of Galilee, Mt 5¹ 8¹, Mk 3¹³ 6⁴⁶, al.; τὰ ὄ., Mt 18¹², Mk 5⁵, He 11³⁸, Re 6¹⁴, al.; proverbially (cf. Rabbinic, עָקַר הָרִים), of overcoming difficulties, accomplishing marvels, ὄρη μεθιστάνειν, I Co 13², cf. Mt 17²⁰ 21²¹, Mk 11²³.

ὀρύσσω, [in LXX chiefly for חָפַר, also for כָּרָה, etc.;] *to dig :* c. acc., ληι·όν, Mt 21³³; ὑπολήνιον, Mk 12¹; γῆν, Mt 25¹⁸ (cf. δι-, ἐξ-ορύσσω).†

ὀρφανός, -ή, -όν, [in LXX for יָתוֹם;].1. prop., *orphan, fatherless :* Mk 12⁴⁰, WH, mg, Ja 1²⁷.   2. In a general sense (as also in cl.; v. LS, s.v.; and cf. MM, xviii), *bereft, friendless, desolate :* Jo 14¹⁸.†

ὀρχέομαι, -οῦμαι, [in LXX for רָקַד, etc.;] *to dance ;* Mt 11¹⁷ 14⁶, Mk 6²², Lk 7³².†

ὅς, ἥ, ὅ, the postpositive article (ἄρθρον ὑποτακτικόν).
I. As demonstr. pron. = οὗτος, ὅδε, *this, that,* also for αὐτός, chiefly in nom.: ὃς δέ, *but he* (cf. ἦ δὲ ὅς, freq. in Plat.), Mk 15²³, Jo 5¹¹; ὃς μὲν . . . ὃς δέ, *the one . . . the other,* Mt 21³⁵ 22⁵ 25¹⁵, Lk 23³³, Ac 27⁴⁴, Ro 14⁵, I Co 11²¹, II Co 2¹⁶, Ju ²²; neut., ὃ μὲν . . . ὃ δέ, *the one . . . the other, some . . . some,* Mt 13⁸, ²³, Ro 9²¹; ὃς (ὃ) μὲν . . . (ἄλλος (ἄλλο)) . . . ἕτερος (-ο), Mk 4⁴, Lk 8⁵, I Co 12⁸⁻¹⁰; οὓς μέν, absol., I Co 12²⁸; ὃς μὲν . . . ὁ δέ, Ro 14².
II. As relat. pron., *who, which, what, that ;* 1. agreeing in gender with its antecedent, but differently governed as to case : Mt 2⁹, Lk 9⁹, Ac 20¹⁸, Ro 2²⁹, al. mult.   2. In variation from the common construction; (*a*) in gender, agreeing with a noun in apposition to the antecedent : Mk 15¹⁶, Ga 3¹⁶, Eph 6¹⁷, al.; constr. ad sensum : Jo 6⁹, Col 2¹⁹, I Ti 3¹⁶, Re 13¹⁴, al.; (*b*) in number, constr. ad sensum : Ac 15³⁶, II Pe 3¹; (*c*) in case, by attraction to the case of the antecedent (Bl., § 50, 2) : Jo 4¹⁸, Ac 3²¹, Ro 15¹⁸, I Co 6¹⁹, Eph 1⁸, al.   3. The neut. ὅ with nouns of other gender and with phrases, *which thing, which term :* Mk 3¹⁷ 12⁴², Jo 1³⁹, Col 3¹⁴, al.; with a sentence, Ac 2³², Ga 2¹⁰, I Jo 2⁸, al.   4. With ellipse of a demonstrative (οὗτος or ἐκεῖνος), before or after : before, Mt 20²³, Lk 7⁴³, Ro 10¹⁴, al.; after, Mt 10³⁸, Mk 9⁴⁰, Jo 19²², Ro 2¹, al.   5. Expressing purpose, end or cause : Mt 11¹⁰ (*who = that he may*), Mk 1², He 12⁶, al.   6. C. prep. as periphrasis for conjc. : ἀνθ᾽ ὧν (= ἀντὶ τούτων ὧν), *because,* Lk 1²⁰, al.; *wherefore,* Lk 12³; ἐφ᾽ ᾧ, *since, for that,* Ro 5¹²; ἀφ᾽ οὗ, *since* (temporal), Lk 13²⁵; ἐξ οὗ, *whence,* Phl 3²⁰; etc.   7. With particles : ὃς ἄν (ἐάν), v.s. ἄν, ἐάν; ὃς καί, Mk 3¹⁹, Jo 21²⁰, Ro 5², al.; ὃς καὶ αὐτός, Mt 27⁵⁷.   8. Gen., οὗ, absol., as adv. (v.s. οὗ).   9. Followed by redundant αὐτός (q.v.) : Mk 1⁷ (v. M, *Gr.,* II, p. 434).

ὁσάκις (< ὅσος), relat. adv., *as often as :* seq. ἐάν (q.v.), I Co 11²⁵, ²⁶, Re 11⁶.†

ὅσγε = ὅς γε, v.s. γέ.

ὅσιος, -ον (so sometimes in cl., but most freq. -α, -ον), [in LXX chiefly for חָסִיד, also for מָהוֹר, יָשָׁר, תָּמִים;] *religiously right, right-eous, pious, holy :* of men, Tit 1⁸. He 7²⁶; by meton., ὁ. χεῖρας, ι Ti 2⁸ (cf. De 32⁴); of God, Re 15⁴ 16⁵; as subst., ὁ ὅ., of the Messiah, Ac 2²⁷ 13³⁵ (LXX); τὰ ὅ. Δαυεὶδ τ. πιστά (Field, *Notes,* 121), Ac 13³⁴ (LXX).†

SYN.: v.s. ἅγιος (cf. also *DB,* ii, 399ᵇ; iv, 352ᵇ, and ref. s.v. -ίως).

ὁσιότης, -ητος, ἡ (< ὅσιος), [in LXX: De 9⁵ (יָשָׁר), ι Ki 14⁴¹, ιιι Ki 9⁴ (תֹּם, תָּמִים), Pr 14³², Wi 2²² 5¹⁹ 9³ 14³⁰ *;] *piety, holiness :* assoc. with δικαιοσύνη, Lk 1⁷⁵, Eph 4²⁴.†

SYN.: v.s. ἅγιος.

ὁσίως (< ὅσιος), adv., [in LXX: ιιι Ki 8⁶¹, Wi 6¹⁰ *;] *piously, holily :* ὁ. καὶ δικαίως κ. ἀμέμπτως (on the distinction here between these synonyms, v. M, *Th.,* 24 f.), ι Th 2¹⁰.†

ὀσμή, -ῆς, ἡ (< ὄζω), [in LXX chiefly for רֵיחַ;] *a smell, odour :* Jo 12³; metaph. (EV, *savour*), ιι Co 2¹⁴, ¹⁶; of the effect of sacrifice (cf. רֵיחַ הַנִּיחֹחַ, Ge 8²¹, al., v.s. εὐωδία), ὁ. εὐωδίας, Eph 5², Phl 4¹⁸.†

ὅσον, v.s. ὅσος.

ὅσος, -η, -ον, correlat. of τοσοῦτος, *how much, how many, how great, how far, how long, as much as,* etc. (= Lat. *quantus*); (*a*) of number and quantity: m. pl., Mt 14³⁶, Mk 3¹⁰, Ro 2¹², al.; n. pl., Mt 17¹², Mk 10²¹, Lk 11⁸, al.; πάντες (πάντα) ὅ., Mt 13⁴⁶, Lk 4⁴⁰, al.; seq. οὗτοι (ταῦτα), Ro 8¹⁴, Phl 4⁸; c. indic., Mk 6⁵⁶, Re 3¹⁹; c. subjc., Mk 3²⁸, al.; ὅ. ἄν, Mt 18¹⁸, Jo 11²², al.; (*b*) of measure and degree: Mk 3⁸, Lk 8³⁹, Ac 9¹³; in compar. sent., ὅσον seq. μᾶλλον, Mk 7³⁶; καθ᾽ ὅσον, c. compar., He 3³; seq. τοσοῦτο, He 7²⁰; οὕτως, He 9²⁷; τοσούτῳ, c. compar. seq. ὅσῳ, c. compar., He 1⁴; ἐφ᾽ ὅσον, *inasmuch as,* Mt 25⁴⁰, ⁴⁵, Ro 11¹³; (*c*) of space and time: Re 21¹⁶; ἐφ᾽ ὅσον, *as long as,* Mt 9¹⁵, ιι Pe 1¹³; ἐφ᾽ ὅ. χρόνον, Ro 7¹, ι Co 7³⁹, Ga 4¹; ἔτι μικρὸν ὅσον ὅσον, *yet how very short a time,* He 10³⁷ (LXX).

ὅσπερ, v.s. ὅς.

ὀστέον (Att. contr. ὀστοῦν, -οῦ, and so Jo, l.c.), -ου, τό, [in LXX chiefly for עֶצֶם;] *a bone :* contr., ὀστοῦν (v. supr.), Jo 19³⁶ (LXX); uncontr. (as in Hom., Hdt.), ὀστέα, Lk 24³⁹; ὀστέων, Mt 23²⁷, He 11²².†

ὅστις, ἥτις, ὅ τι (also written ὅ, τι and ὅτι; v. LS, s.v.; WH, § 411; Tdf., *Pr.,* 111), in NT scarcely ever except in nom. (M, *Pr.,* 91), the only instance of the oblique cases being found in ἕως ὅτου (v.s. ἕως), relative of indef. reference (related to simple ὅς as Lat. *quisquis* to *qui*), *whoever, anyone who ;* (*a*) of an indef. person or thing: in general statements, Mt 5³⁹, ⁴¹ 13¹², and freq., Lk 14²⁷, Ga 5⁴, al.; in relative sentences, Mt 7²⁶, Lk 15⁷, Phl 3⁷, al.; πᾶς ὅ., c. indic., Mt 7²⁴ 10³²; ὅ. ἄν (ἐάν), c. subjc., Mt 12⁵⁰ 13¹², Jo 14¹³, ι Co 16², Ga 5¹⁰, al.; (*b*) of a definite person or thing, indicating quality, "either generic, *which, as other like things,* or essential, *which by its very nature*" (Hort on 1 Pe 2¹¹), *who is such as :* Mt 2⁶ 7²⁶, Lk 2¹⁰ 7³⁷ Jo 8⁵³, Ac 7⁵³, Ro 6², 1 Co 3¹⁷, Ga 4²⁴, Eph 1²³, al.; *(c)* where the relative sentence expresses a reason, consequence, etc. (M, *Pr.*, 92), *seeing that he (it, they), and he (it, they)* : Lk 8³ 10⁴², Ac 10⁴⁷ 11²⁸, Phl 4³, al.; *(d)* as in Ionic and late Greek (Bl., § 50, 1; M, *Pr.*, l.c.), differing but little from ὅς : Lk 2⁴ 9³⁰, Ac 17¹⁰, Re 12¹³.

ὀστράκινος -η, -ον (< ὄστρακον, *an earthen vessel* or *potsherd*), [in LXX chiefly for חֶרֶשׂ;] *made of clay, earthen :* 11 Co 4⁷, 11 Ti 2²⁰.†

* ὄσφρησις, -εως, ἡ (ὀσφραίνομαι, *to smell*), *the sense of smell, smelling :* 1 Co 12¹⁷.†

ὀσφύς, -ύος, ἡ, [in LXX chiefly for מָתְנַיִם, also for חָלָץ, etc.;] *the loin :* Mt 3⁴, Mk 1⁶; metaph., περιζώννυσθαι (ἀναζ-) τ. ὀσφύας, Lk 12³⁵, Eph 6¹⁴, 1 Pe 1¹³; regarded, as by the Hebrews, as the seat of generative power, He 7⁵,¹⁰; metaph., καρπὸς τ. ὀσφύος, Ac 2³⁰.†

ὅταν (for ὅτ᾽ ἄν = ὅτε ἄν), temporal particle, with a conditional sense, usually of things expected to occur in an indefinite future; 1. prop., *whenever; (a)* c. subjc. praes.: Mt 6²,⁵, Mk 14⁷, Lk 11³⁶, Jo 7²⁷, Ac 23³⁵, 1 Co 3⁴, al.; ἕως τ. ἡμέρας ἐκείνης, ὅ., Mt 26²⁹, Mk 14²⁵; seq. τότε, 1 Th 5³; *(b)* c. subjc. aor. (M, *Pr.*, 185): Mt 5¹¹, Mk 4¹⁵, Lk 6²², Jo 2¹⁰ 8²⁸ (Field, *Notes,* 94), 10⁴, al.   2. As in Hom. (LS, s.v.), but not in cl. prose, c. indic., *when* (M, *Pr.*, 167 f.; Bl., § 65, 9): c. impf., Mk 3¹¹ (cf. Ge 38⁹, al.); c. praes., Mk 11²⁵; c. fut., Re 4⁹ (Swete, in l.); c. aor., Mk 11¹⁹, Re 8¹ (Swete, in ll.; M, *Pr.*, 168, 248; Field, *Notes,* 35).

ὅτε, temporal particle (correlat. of πότε, τότε), *when;* c. indic. (so generally in cl., but also c. optat., subjc.; LS, s.v.), most freq. c. aor., Mt 9²⁵, Mk 1³², Lk 4²⁵, Jo 1¹⁹, Ac 1¹³, Ro 13¹¹, Ga 1¹⁵, Re 1¹⁷, al.; c. impf., Mk 14¹², Jo 21¹⁸, Ro 6²⁰, 1 Th 3⁴, al.; c. pf., *since, now that,* 1 Co 13¹¹ (B, ἐγενόμην); c. praes., Mk 11¹, Jo 9⁴, He 9¹⁷; c. fut. (Hom.; of a def. fut. as opp. to the indef. fut. of ὅταν c. subjc.), Lk 17²², Jo 4²¹,²³ 5²⁵ 16²⁵, Ro 2¹⁶ (T, txt., WH, mg.), 11 Ti 4³ (in all which instances, and c. praes., Jo, l.c., ὅ. follows a subst. of time, and is equiv. to a rel. phrase, ἐν ᾧ or ᾗ).

ὅτου, v.s. ὅστις.

ὅτι, conjc. (prop. neut. of ὅστις).
   I. As conjc., introducing an objective clause, *that ;* 1. after verbs of seeing, knowing, thinking, saying, feeling: Mt 3⁹ 6³² 11²⁵, Mk 3²⁸, Lk 2⁴⁹, Jo 2²², Ac 4¹³, Ro 1¹³ 8³⁸ 10⁹, Phl 4¹⁵, Ja 2²⁴, al.; elliptically, Jo 6⁴⁶, Phl 3¹², al.   2. After εἶναι (γίνεσθαι): defining a demonstr. or pers. pron., Jo 3¹⁹ 16¹⁹, Ro 9⁶, 1 Jo 3¹⁶, al.; c. pron. interrog., Mt 8²⁷, Mk 4⁴¹, Lk 4³⁶, Jo 4²², al.; id. elliptically, Lk 2⁴⁹, Ac 5⁴,⁹, al.; 3. Untranslatable, before direct discourse (ὅτι *recitantis;* v. MM, *VGT,* s.v.; M, *Gr.,* 11, p. 469): Mt 7²³, Mk 2¹⁶, Lk 1⁶¹, Jo 1²⁰, Ac 15¹, He 11¹⁸, al. (on the pleonastic ὡς ὅτι, v.s. ὡς).
   II. As causal particle, *for that, because :* Mt 5⁴⁻¹², Lk 6²⁰,²¹, Jo 1²⁰ 5²⁷, Ac 1⁵, 1 Jo 4¹⁸, Re 3¹⁰, al. mult.; διὰ τοῦτο ὅτι, Jo 8⁴⁷ 10¹⁷, al.;

answering a question (διὰ τί), Ro 9³², al.; οὐχ ὅτι . . . ἀλλ' ὅτι, Jo 6²⁶ 12⁶. In direct question, = τί: Mk 2¹⁶ (v. Swete in l.; M, *Pr.*, p. 94).

οὖ (prop. gen. of ὅς), adv. of place, *where, whither*; (*a*) in answer *to* the question "where?" (= ubi): Mt 2⁹ 18²⁰, Lk 4¹⁶, ¹⁷ 23⁵³, Ac 1¹³ 2² 7²⁹ 12¹² 16¹³ 20⁶, ⁸ 25¹⁰ 28¹⁴, Ro 9²⁶ (LXX), Col 3¹, He 3⁹ (LXX), Re 17¹⁵; of condition, Ro 4¹⁵ 5²⁰, ii Co 3¹⁷; (*b*) in answer to the question "whither?" (= quo): Mt 28¹⁶, Lk 10¹ 24²⁸; seq. ἐάν, c. subjc., i Co 16⁶.†

οὐ, before a vowel with smooth breathing οὐκ, before one with rough breathing οὐχ (but improperly οὐχ ἰδού, Ac 2⁷, WH, mg.; cf. WH, *Intr.*, § 409; M, *Pr.*, 44, 244), [in LXX for לֹא, אַיִן, אֵין;] neg.

particle, *not, no*, used generally c. indic. and for a denial of fact (cf. μή); 1. absol. (accented), οὔ, *no*: Mt 13²⁹, Jo 1²¹ 21⁵; οὐ οὔ, Mt 5³⁷, Ja 5¹². 2. Most freq. negativing a verb or other word, Mt 1²⁵ 10²⁶, ³⁸, Mk 3²⁵ 9³⁷, Jo 8²⁹, Ac 7⁵, Ro 1¹⁶, Phl 3³, al.; in litotes, οὐκ ὀλίγοι (i.e. *very many*), Ac 17⁴, al.; οὐκ ἄσημος, Ac 21³⁹; πᾶς . . . οὐ, c. verb. (like Heb. לֹא . . . כֹּל), *no, none*, Mt 24²², Mk 13²⁰, Lk 1³⁷, Eph 5⁵, al.; in disjunctive statements, οὐκ . . . ἀλλά, Lk 8⁵², Jo 1³³, Ro 8²⁰, al.; c. 2 pers. fut. (like Heb. לֹא, c. impf.), as emphatic prohibition, Mt 4⁷, Lk 4¹², Ro 7⁷, al. 3. With another negative, (*a*) strengthening the negation: Mk 5³⁷, Jo 8¹⁵ 12¹⁹, Ac 8³⁹, al.; (*b*) making an affirmative: Ac 4²⁰, i Co 12¹⁵. 4. With other particles: οὐ μή (v.s. μή); οὐ μηκέτι, Mt 21¹⁹; with μή interrog., Ro 10¹⁸, i Co 9⁴, ⁵ 11²². 5. Interrogative, expecting an affirmative answer (Lat. *nonne*): Mt 6²⁶, Mk 4²¹, Lk 11⁴⁰, Jo 4³⁵, Ro 9²¹, al.

*†οὐά, interj. of wonder or irony, *ah! ha!*: Mk 15²⁹.†

†οὐαί, interj. of grief or denunciation, [in LXX for הוֹי, אוֹי, etc.;] *alas! woe!* most freq. c. dat. pers., Mt 11²¹ 23¹⁴, Mk 13¹⁷ 14²¹, Lk 6²⁴⁻²⁶, Ju ¹¹, al.; c. vocat. (nom.), Lk 6²⁵, Re 18¹⁰, ¹⁶, ¹⁹ (cf. Is 1²⁴, al.); c. acc., Re 12¹², seq. ἐκ, 8¹³; c. dat. seq. ἀπό (v. M, *Pr.*, 246), Mt 18⁷. As subst., i Co 9¹⁶ (cf. Je 6⁴); ἡ οὐ., Re 9¹² 11¹⁴; pl., Re 9¹²; οὐ., οὐ., οὐ., Re 8¹³.

**οὐδαμῶς (< οὐδαμός, *not even one*), adv., [in LXX: ii-iv Mac₈ *;] *in no wise, by no means*: Mt 2⁶ (OT).†

οὐδέ, negative particle, related to μηδέ as οὐ to μή.

I. As conjc., *and not, also not, neither, nor*: Mt 6¹⁵, Lk 16³¹, Ro 4¹⁵, al.; οὐ . . . οὐδέ, Mt 5¹⁵ 10²⁴, Mk 4²², Lk 6⁴³, ⁴⁴, Jo 6²⁴, Ac 2²⁷, Ro 2²⁸, al. (v. Bl., § 77, 10).

II. As adv., *not even*: Mt 6²⁹, Mk 6³¹, Lk 7⁹, i Co 5¹; οὐδὲ εἷς, Ac 4³², Ro 3¹⁰ (LXX).

οὐδείς, -δεμία, -δέν (also in WH, txt., the Hellenistic forms -θείς, -θέν, Lk 22³⁵ 23¹⁴, Ac 15⁹ 19²⁷ 26²⁶, i Co 13², ii Co 11⁸; cf. Bl., § 6, 7; M, *Pr.*, 56ₙ; Thackeray, *Gr.*, 58), related to μηδείς as οὐ to μή, *no, no one, none*: with nouns, Lk 4²⁴, Jo 10⁴¹, Ro 8¹, al.; absol., Mt 6²⁴, Mk 3²⁷, Lk 1⁶¹, Jo 1¹⁸, Ac 18¹⁰, Ro 14⁷, al. mult.; c. gen. partit., Lk 4²⁶, Jo 13²⁸, al.; neut., οὐδέν, Mt 10²⁶, al.; id. c. gen. partit., Lk 9³⁶, Ac 18¹⁷, al.; οὐδὲν εἰ μή, Mt 5¹³, Mk 9²⁹, al.; c. neg., strengthening the negation, Mk 15⁴, ⁵, Lk 4², Jo 3²⁷, al.; adverbially, Ac 25¹⁰, Ga 4¹², al.

οὐδέ-ποτε, adv., [in LXX: Ex 10⁶ (לֹא), etc.;] *never*: Mt 7²³ 9³³ 26³³, Mk 2¹², Lk 15²⁹, Jo 7⁴⁶, Ac 10¹⁴ 11⁸ 14⁸, ɪ Co 13⁸, He 10¹, ¹¹. Interrog., Mt 21¹⁶, ⁴², Mk 2²⁵.†

οὐδέπω, adv., [in LXX: Ex 9³⁰ (מֶרֶם) *;] *not yet*: Lk 23⁵³, Jo 7³⁹ 19⁴¹ 20⁹, Ac 8¹⁶.†

οὐθείς, v.s. οὐδείς.

οὐκέτι, neg. adv. of time, [in LXX chiefly for עוֹד c. neg., לֹא, etc.;] *no longer, no more*: Mt 19⁶, Mk 10⁸, Lk 15¹⁹, Jo 4⁴², Ro 6⁹, Ga 3²⁵, Eph 2¹⁹, He 10¹⁸, al.; c. neg. (to strengthen the negation), Mt 22⁴⁶, Mk 5³, Ac 8³⁹, al.

οὐκοῦν, adv. (< οὔκουν, *not therefore*), with the negative element lost, *therefore, so then*: Jo 18³⁷.†

οὖν, particle expressing consequence or simple sequence (never standing first in a sentence), *wherefore, therefore, then*: Mt 3¹⁰, Lk 3⁹, Jo 8³⁸, Ac 1²¹, Ro 5⁹, al.; in exhortations, Mt 3⁸, Lk 11³⁵, Ac 3¹⁹, Ro 6¹², al.; in questions, Mt 13²⁸, Mk 15¹², Jo 8⁽⁵⁾, Ro 6¹, al.; continuing a narrative or resuming it after a digression, Mt 1¹⁷, Lk 3¹⁸, Jo 1²² 2¹⁸ (and very freq. in this Gospel), Ac 26²², al.; ἄρα οὖν (v.s. ἄρα); ἐπεὶ οὖν, He 2¹⁴; οὖν c. ptcp. (= ἐπεὶ οὖν), Ac 2³⁰, Ro 5¹, al.; ἐὰν οὖν (where οὖν rather in sense belongs to the apodosis), Mt 5²³, Lk 4⁷, Jo 6⁶², Ro 2²⁶, al.; ὡς οὖν, Jo 4¹, al.

οὔπω, neg. adv. of time, *not yet*: Mt 24⁶, Mk 13⁷, Jo 2⁴ 3²⁴ 6¹⁷, al.; c. neg., Mk 11², Lk 23⁵³; interrog., Mt 16⁹, Mk 4⁴⁰ 8¹⁷, ²¹.

οὐρά, -ᾶς, ἡ, [in LXX for זָנָב;] *a tail*: Re 9¹⁰, ¹⁹ 12⁴.†

οὐράνιος, -ον (cl. usually -α, -ον), [in LXX: De 28¹² A (שָׁמַיִם), etc.;] *of* or *in heaven, heavenly*: Mt 5⁴⁸ 6¹⁴, ²⁶, ³² 15¹³ 18³⁵ 23⁹, Lk 2¹³, Ac 26¹⁹.†

** οὐρανόθεν (< οὐρανός), adv., [in LXX: ɪv Mac 4¹⁰ *;] *from heaven*: Ac 14¹⁷ 26¹³.†

οὐρανός, -οῦ, ὁ, [in LXX chiefly for שָׁמַיִם (hence, often pl., οἱ οὐ., v. infr.);] *heaven*; 1. of the vault or firmament of heaven, the sky and the aerial regions above the earth: opp. to ἡ γῆ, He 1¹⁰, ɪɪ Pe 3⁵, ¹⁰; ὁ οὐ. καὶ ἡ γῆ, i.e. the world, the universe, Mt 5¹⁸, Mk 13³¹, Lk 10²¹, Ac 4²⁴, Re 10⁶, al.; ἀπ᾽ ἄκρων οὐ. ἕως ἄ. αὐτῶν (on the absence of art. aft. prep., v. Bl., § 46, 5), Mt 24³¹; ὑπὸ τὸν οὐ., Ac 2⁵, Col 1²³; ὑψωθῆναι ἕως τοῦ οὐ., fig., Mt 11²³, Lk 10¹⁵; σημεῖον ἐκ τοῦ οὐ., Mt 16¹, Mk 8¹¹, al.; αἱ νεφέλαι τοῦ οὐ., Mt 24³⁰, al.; τὰ πετεινὰ τοῦ οὐ., Mt 6²⁶, Mk 4³², al.; οἱ ἀστέρες τοῦ οὐ., Re 6¹³, al.; pl. (οἱ) οὐ. (Bl., § 32, 5), Mt 3¹⁶, Mk 1¹⁰, Jo 1³², ɪɪ Pe 3⁷, ¹³, al. 2. Of the abode of God and other blessed beings: of angels, Mt 24³⁶, Mk 12²⁵, Ga 1⁸, Re 10¹, al.; of Christ glorified, Mk 16⁽¹⁹⁾, Lk 24⁵¹, Ac 3²¹, Ro 10⁶, al.; of God, Mt 5³⁴, Ro 1¹⁸, al.; ὁ Πατὴρ ὁ ἐν τοῖς οὐ. (Dalman, *Words*, 184 ff.), Mt 5¹⁶ 6¹, al.; θησαυρὸς ἐν οὐ., Mt 6²⁰, Mk 10²¹, al. 3. By meton., (*a*) of the inhabitants of heaven: Re 18²⁰ (cf. ib. 12¹², Jb 15¹⁵, Is 44²³); (*b*) as an evasive reference to God, characteristic of later Judaism (Dalman, *Words,* 204 ff.) : Mt 21²⁵, Mk 11³⁰, Lk 15¹⁸, Jo 3²⁷ al. ; ἡ βασιλεία τῶν οὐ. (= τοῦ Θεοῦ ; v.s. βασιλεία).

Οὐρβανός, -οῦ, ὁ (Lat. *Urbanus*), *Urban :* Ro 16⁹.†

Οὐρίας, -ου, ὁ (Heb. אוּרִיָּה), *Uriah :* Mt 1⁶.†

οὖς, gen., ὠτός, τό, [in LXX chiefly for אֹזֶן;] *the ear :* Mt 13¹⁶, Mk 7³³, Lk 22⁵⁰, 1 Co 2⁹ 12¹⁶, 1 Pe 3¹² ; ἐν τ. ὠσί, Lk 4²¹; εἰς τ. ὦτα ἀκούεσθαι, Ac 7⁵⁷ ; γίνεσθαι, Lk 1⁴⁴ ; εἰσέρχεσθαι, Ja 5⁴ ; εἰς τ. οὖς ἀκούειν, Mt 10²⁷ ; πρὸς τ. οὖς λαλεῖν, Lk 12³ ; τὰ ὦ. συνέχειν (MM, xviii), Ac 7⁵⁷. Metaph., of understanding, perceiving, knowing : Mt 13¹⁶ ; ὁ ἔχων (εἴ τις ἔχει) οὖς ἀκουσάτω, Re 2⁷, ¹¹, ¹⁷, ²⁹ 3⁶, ¹³, ²² 13⁹ ; ὁ ἔχων (ὃς ἔχει, εἴ τις ἔχει) ὦτα (ἀκούειν) ἀκουέτω, Mt 11¹⁵ 13⁹, ⁴³, Mk 4⁹, ²³ 7¹⁶ (R, mg.), Lk 8⁸ 14³⁵ ; τοῖς ὠ. βαρέως ἀκούειν, Mt 13¹⁵, Ac 28²⁷ (LXX) ; ὦ. ἔχοντες οὐκ ἀκούειν, Mk 8¹⁸ ; ὦ. τοῦ μὴ ἀκούειν, Ro 11⁸ ; θέσθε εἰς τὰ ὦ., Lk 9⁴⁴ ; ἀπερίτμητος τοῖς ὠ., Ac 7⁵¹.†

**οὐσία, -ας, ἡ (< οὖσα, fem. part. of εἰμί), [in LXX : To 14¹³, III Mac 3²⁸*;] *substance, property :* Lk 15¹², ¹³.†

οὔτε, negative particle, related to μήτε as οὐ to μή, *and not, neither, nor :* οὐδεὶς . . . οὔτε, Re 5⁴ ; οὐδὲ . . . οὔτε, Ga 1¹² ; οὔτε . . . καί, Jo 4¹¹ ; after a question with μή interrog., Ja 3¹² ; οὔτε . . . οὔτε, *neither . . . nor,* Mt 6²⁰, Mk 12²⁵, Jo 4²¹, Ac 15¹⁰, Ro 8³⁸, ³⁹, Ga 5⁶, al.

οὗτος, αὕτη, τοῦτο, gen., τούτου, ταύτης, τούτου, [in LXX chiefly for זֶה, זֹאת;] demonstr. pron. (related to ἐκεῖνος as *hic* to *ille*), *this ;* 1. as subst., *this one, he ;* (*a*) absol. : Mt 3¹⁷, Mk 9⁷, Lk 7⁴⁴, ⁴⁵, Jo 1¹⁵, Ac 2¹⁵, al. ; expressing contempt (cl.), Mt 13⁵⁵, ⁵⁶, Mk 6², ³, Jo 6⁴², al. ; εἰς τοῦτο, Mk 1³⁸, Ro 14⁹ ; μετὰ τοῦτο (ταῦτα ; v. Westc. on Jo 5¹), Jo 2¹² 11⁷, al. ; (*b*) epanaleptic (referring to what precedes) : Mt 5¹⁹, Mk 3³⁵, Lk 9⁴⁸, Jo 6⁴⁶, Ro 7¹⁰, al. ; (*c*) proleptic (referring to what follows) : seq. ἵνα (Bl., § 69, 6), Lk 1⁴³, Jo 3¹⁹ (and freq.) 15⁸, Ro 14⁹, al. ; seq. ὅτι, Lk 10¹¹, Jo 9³⁰, Ac 24¹⁴, Ro 2³, al. ; ὅπως, Ro 9¹⁷ ; ἐάν, Jo 13³⁵ ; (*d*) special idioms : τοῦτο μὲν . . . τ. δέ (cl), *partly . . . partly,* He 10³³ ; καὶ τοῦτο (τοῦτον, ταῦτα), *and that (him) too,* Ro 13¹¹, 1 Co 2², He 11¹² ; τοῦτ' ἐστιν, *that is to say,* Mt 27⁴⁶. 2. As adj., c. subst.; (*a*) c. art. (*a*) before the art. : Mt 12³², Mk 9²⁹, Lk 7⁴⁴, Jo 4¹⁵, Ro 11²⁴, Re 19⁹, al. ; (β) after the noun : Mt 3⁹, Mk 12¹⁶, Lk 11³¹, Jo 4¹³, Ac 6¹³, Ro 15²⁸, 1 Co 1²⁰, Re 2²⁴, al. ; (*b*) c. subst. anarth. (with predicative force ; Bl., § 49, 4) : Lk 1³⁶ 2² 24²¹. Jo 2¹¹ 4⁵⁴ 21¹⁴, II Co 13¹.

οὕτως, rarely (Bl., § 5, 4 ; WH, *App.,* 146 f.) οὕτω, adv. (< οὗτος), [in LXX chiefly for כֵּן;] *in this way, so, thus ;* 1. referring to what precedes : Mt 5¹⁶ 6³⁰, Mk 10⁴³ 14⁵⁹, Lk 1²⁵ 2⁴⁸ 15⁷, Jo 3⁸, Ro 11⁵, 1 Co 8¹², al. ; οὕτως καί, Mt 17¹², Mk 13²⁹, al.; pleonastically, resuming a ptcp. (cl. ; v. Bl., § 74, 6), Ac 20¹¹ 27¹⁷. 2. Referring to what follows : Mt 1¹⁸ 6⁹, Lk 19³¹, Jo 21¹, 1 Pe 2¹⁵ ; bef. quotations from OT, Mt 2⁵, Ac 7⁶, 1 Co 15⁴⁵, He 4⁴. 3. C. adj. (marking intensity) : He 12²¹, Re 16¹⁸ ; similarly c. adv., Ga 1⁶ (cl.). 4. As a predicate (Bl., § 76, 1) : Mt 1¹⁸ 9³³, Mk 2¹, ² 4²⁶, Ro 4¹⁸ 9²⁰, 1 Pe

2¹⁵; οὔ. ἔχειν (Lat. *sic* or *ita se habere*), Ac 7¹, al.; ἐκαθέζετο οὔ. (as he was, without delay or preparation), Jo 4⁶. 5. In comparison, with correlative adv.: καθάπερ . . . οὔ., Ro 12⁴, ⁵, al.; καθὼς . . . οὔ., Lk 11³⁰, al.; οὔ. . . . καθώς, Lk 24²⁴, al.; ὡς . . . οὔ., Ro 5¹⁵, al.; οὔ. . . . ὡς, Mk 4²⁶, al.; ὥσπερ . . . οὔ., Mt 12⁴⁰, al.; οὔ. . . . οὔ., ι Co 7⁷.

οὐχ, v.s. οὐ.

οὐχί, strengthened form of οὐ, *not;* (*a*) in neg. sentences, *not, not at all :* Lk 1⁶⁰ 12⁵¹, Jo 13¹⁰, al.; (*b*) more freq. in questions where an affirm. ans. is expected (Lat. *nonne*) : Mt 5⁴⁶, ⁴⁷, Lk 6³⁹, Jo 11⁹, al.

*ὀφειλέτης, -ου, ὁ (< ὀφείλω), a *debtor :* c. gen. (of the amount), Mt 18²⁴. Metaph., of obligation or duty in general, with reference to favours received or injury done, etc. : Mt 6¹², Ro 1¹⁴ 8¹² 15²⁷, Ga 5³ ; of sinners, in relation to God (= Heb. חַיָּב; cf. Si (Heb) 8⁵ ⁽⁶⁾), Lk 13⁴.†

*†ὀφειλή, -ῆς, ἡ (< ὀφείλω), a *debt :* Mt 18³² ; metaph., *one's due :* Ro 13⁷, ι Co 7³ (found also in π.; v. Deiss., *BS*, 221 ; MM, xviii).†

ὀφείλημα, -τος, τό (< ὀφείλω), [in LXX : De 24¹⁰ (מַשָּׁאָה), ι Es 3²⁰, ι Mac 15⁸ *;] *that which is owed, a debt :* Ro 4⁴ ; metaph. (as Aram. חוֹב, חוֹבָא), of sin as a debt, Mt 6¹².†

ὀφείλω, [in LXX : De 15², Is 24² (נָשָׁה, נָשָׁא), Ez 18⁷ (חוֹב), Wi 12¹⁵, ²⁰, al.;] *to owe, be a debtor :* c. acc. rei, Mt 18²⁸, Lk 7⁴¹ 16⁷, Phm ¹⁸ ; id. c. dat. pers., Mt 18²⁸, Lk 16⁵. Pass., *to be owed, to be due :* τ. ὀφειλόμενον, Mt 18³⁰, ³⁴. Metaph. : absol. (= Rabbinic חַיָּב; v. McNeile, in l.), Mt 23¹⁶, ¹⁸ ; c. acc. rei et dat. pers., Ro 13⁸ ; c. inf., *to be bound* or *obliged* to do (cf. Westc., *Epp. Jo.*, 50), Lk 17¹⁰, Jo 13¹⁴ 19⁷, Ac 17²⁹, Ro 15¹, ²⁷, ι Co 5¹⁰ 7³⁶ 9¹⁰ 11⁷, ¹⁰, ιι Co 12¹⁴, Eph 5²⁸, ιι Th 1³ 2¹³, He 2¹⁷ 5³, ¹², ι Jo 2⁶ 3¹⁶ 4¹¹, ιιι Jo ⁸ ; ὤφειλον συνίστασθαι, *I ought to have been commended,* ιι Co 12¹¹. In peculiar Aram. sense of having wronged one (v.s. ὀφείλημα; but cf. also Inscr. ἁμαρτίαν ὀφείλω, Deiss., *BS*, 225), c. dat. pers., Lk 11⁴ (cf. προσ-οφείλω).†

ὄφελον, 2 aor. of ὀφείλω, without the augment (v. M, *Pr.*, 201ₙ), used to express a fruitless wish ; [in LXX (with aor. indic.) : Ex 16³ (מִי־יִתֵּן), Nu 14³ ⁽²⁾ 20³ (לוּ), Ps 118 (119)⁵ (אַחֲלַי), etc.;] in cl. with an infin. (chiefly poët.), *would that :* with indic. aor., ι Co 4⁸ ; impf., ιι Co 11¹, Re 3¹⁵ ; fut., Ga 5¹² (a practicable wish, v. Bl., 206 f., 220. The construction with indic. is only found in late writers.)†

ὄφελος, -ους, τό (< ὀφέλλω, *to increase*), [in LXX : Jb 15³ (יַעַל hi.)*;] *advantage, help :* ι Co 15³², Ja 2¹⁴, ¹⁶.†

*†ὀφθαλμο-δουλία (Rec. -εία), -ας, ἡ (< ὀφθαλμός, δοῦλος), *eye-service :* Eph 6⁶, Col 3²² (not found elsewhere).†

ὀφθαλμός, -οῦ, ὁ, [in LXX chiefly for עַיִן ;] *the eye* (as in cl., chiefly pl.) : Mt 5³⁸, Mk 9⁴⁷, Lk 6⁴¹, Jo 9⁶, al.; τοὺς ὀ. ἐξορύσσειν (fig.), Ga 4¹⁵ ; ἐπᾶραι, Lk 6²⁰, Jo 6⁵ ; ἀνοῖξαι, Ac 9⁴⁰ ; id., of restoring sight, Mt 20³³, Jo 9¹⁰, al.; ἐν ῥιπῇ ὀφθαλμοῦ, ι Co 15⁵² ; by anthropom., of

God, He 4¹³, 1 Pe 3¹²; pleonastically (cf. Thackeray, *Gr.*, 42 f.), εἶδον οἱ ὁ. μου, Lk 2³⁰ (similarly, ib. 4²⁰ 10²³, Jo 12⁴⁰, 1 Co 2⁹, 1 Jo 1¹, Re 1⁷). Metaph. (as otherwise in cl.; v. LS, s.v.); (*a*) of ethical qualities: ὁ. πονηρός (meton., for envy; cf. Heb. עַיִן רַע, Pr 28²²; cf. Si 14¹⁰ 34¹³), Mt 6²², ²³, Mk 7²², Lk 11³⁴; ἁπλοῦς, Mt 6²², Lk 11³⁴; ἐπιθυμία (q.v.) ὀφθαλμῶν (cf. Ec 4⁸, Si 14⁹), 1 Jo 2¹⁶; ὁ. μεστοὶ μοιχαλίδος, II Pe 2¹⁴; (*b*) of mental vision : Mt 13¹⁵, Mk 8¹⁸, Lk 19⁴², Jo 12⁴⁰, Ro 11⁸, Ga 3¹, Eph 1¹⁸, al.; ἐν ὀφθαλμοῖς seq. gen. (on the absence of the art., v. Bl., § 46, 9ₙ; M, *Pr.*, 81), Mt 21⁴², Mk 12¹¹.

ὄφις, -εως, ὁ, [in LXX chiefly for נָחָשׁ;] *a serpent, snake :* Mt 7¹⁰, Mk 16¹⁸, Lk 10¹⁹ 11¹¹, Jo 3¹⁴, 1 Co 10⁹, Re 9¹⁹; as typical of wisdom and cunning, Mt 10¹⁶ 23³³, II Co 11³ (cf. Ge 3¹); of Satan (cf. Ge 3¹, Wi 2²³, ²⁴, IV Mac 18⁸), Re 12⁹, ¹⁴, ¹⁵ 20².†

ὀφρύς, -ύος, ἡ, [in LXX : Le 14⁹ (גַּב עַיִן)*;] *an eyebrow,* the *brow* of a hill : Lk 4²⁹.†

** **ὀχετός**, -οῦ, ὁ (< ὀχέω, *to carry*), [in Sm.: Jb 22²⁴, Ps 64 (65)¹⁰, al.;] 1. *a water-pipe, channel.* 2. *the intestinal canal :* Mk 7¹⁹, WH, mg. (for ἀφεδρών).†

** **ὀχλέω**, -ῶ (< ὄχλος), [in LXX : To 6⁷, III Mac 5⁴¹*;] *to move, disturb ;* hence, generally, *to trouble, vex :* pass., Ac 5¹⁶ (act. absol., = pass., *to be in a tumult,* III Mac, l.c.; cf. ἐν-, παρ-εν-οχλέω, and v. MM, xviii).†

*+ **ὀχλο-ποιέω**, -ῶ, *to gather a crowd, make a riot :* Ac 17⁵ (not elsewhere).†

ὄχλος, -ου, ὁ, [in LXX for הָמוֹן (chiefly in Da TH), חַיִל, קָהָל, etc.;] 1. a moving *crowd* or *multitude* of persons, *a throng :* Mt 9²³, Mk 2⁴, Lk 5¹, Jo 5¹³, al.; pl., Mt 5¹, Mk 10¹, Lk 3⁷, and freq.; ὁ. ἱκανός, Mk 10⁴⁶, al.; τοσοῦτος, Mt 15³³; οὐ μετ' ὄχλου, Ac 24¹⁸; ἄτερ ὄχλου, Lk 22⁶; πᾶς ὁ ὁ., Mt 13², Mk 2¹³, al.; ὁ. πολύς (π. ὁ.), Mt 20²⁹, Mk 5²¹, al.; ὁ πολὺς ὁ. (ὁ. π.), *the populace, the common people,* Mk 12³⁷ (Swete, in l.; Field, *Notes,* 37), Jo 12⁹ (Westc., in l.). 2. (As also cl., opp. to δῆμος, q.v., and cf. Tr., *Syn.,* § xcviii), *the populace, the common people* (cf. ὁ πολὺς ὁ., supr.), Mt 14⁵·²¹²⁶, Mk 12¹², Jo 7¹²ᵇ; so with contempt (cl.), Jo 7⁴⁹. In a more general sense, *a multitude :* c. gen., ὀνομάτων (v.s. ὁ.), Ac 1¹⁵; μαθητῶν, Lk 6¹⁷, al.

ὀχύρωμα, -τος, τό (< ὀχυρόω, *to fortify, make firm*), [in LXX for מִבְצָר, etc.;] *a stronghold, fortress* (Ps 88 (89)⁴⁰, Na 3¹², ¹⁴ al.); in LXX and NT, also metaph. of that in which confidence is placed (Pr 10²⁹ 21²², al.) : II Co 10⁴.†

** **ὀψάριον**, -ου, τό (dimin. of ὄψον, (1) *cooked meat ;* (2) *a relish* or *dainty,* esp. *fish,* cf. MGr. τὸ ψάρι, *fish ;* in comic poets and late prose writers only), [in LXX : To 2² א (B, ὄψον)*;] *fish :* Jo 6⁹, ¹¹ 21⁹, ¹⁰, ¹³.†

ὀψέ, adv. of time, [in LXX : Ge 24¹¹, Ex 30⁸ (עֶרֶב), (בֵּין הָעַרְבַּיִם), Je 2²³; τὸ ὁ., Is 5¹¹ (נֶשֶׁף)*;] 1. *long after, late.* 2. *late in the day,* *at evening* (opp. to πρωί); in late writers used almost as an indecl. noun (v. MM, xviii) : Mk 11¹¹, ¹⁹ 13³⁵. 3. C. gen., *late in* or *on;* and, in late writers also *after* (M, *Pr.*, 72 f.), a sense which seems to be required in Mt 28¹.†

** ὀψία, -ας, ἡ, v.s. ὄψιος.

ὄψιμος, -ον (< ὀψέ), [in LXX : De 11¹⁴, Pr 16¹⁵, Ho 6⁴ ⁽³⁾, Jl 2²³, Za 10¹, Je 5²⁴ (מַלְקוֹשׁ), Ex 9³² (אָפִיל) *;] poët. and late for ὄψιος, *late:* ὑετὸς ὄ., *the latter rain* (v. *DB*, s.v. "rain"), with ellipsis of ὑετός (v. WM, 740), Ja 5⁷.†

** ὄψιος, -α, -ον (< ὀψέ), *late:* ἡ ὥρα, Mk 11¹¹ (Rec., WH, mg.). In late writers, ἡ ὀψία (sc. ὥρα), as subst., *evening* [in LXX : Jth 13¹ *] : Mt 8¹⁶ 14¹⁵, ²³ 16² 20⁸ 26²⁰ 27⁵⁷, Mk 1³² 4³⁵ 6⁴⁷ 14¹⁷ 15⁴², Jo 6¹⁶, 20¹⁹.†

ὄψις, -εως, ἡ, [in LXX chiefly for מַרְאֶה;] 1. *the act of seeing, the sense of sight.* 2. *face, countenance:* Jo 11⁴⁴, Re 1¹⁶. 3. *appearance:* κατ᾽ ὄ. κρίνειν (v. MM, xviii), Jo 7²⁴.†

**† ὀψώνιον, -ου, τό (< ὄψον—v.s. ὀψάριον—and ὠνέομαι), [in LXX : I Es 4⁵⁶, I Mac 3²⁸ 14³² *;] 1. *provisions, provision-money, soldiers' pay:* Lk 3¹⁴, I Co 9⁷. 2. Generally, *wages, hire:* II Co 11⁸; ὄ. τῆς ἁμαρτίας, Ro 6²³ (v. Deiss, *BS*, 148, 266).†

Π

Π, π, πῖ, *pi, p,* the sixteenth letter. As a numeral, π' = 80, π, = 80,000.

† παγιδεύω (< παγίς), [in LXX : I Ki 28⁹ (נקשׁ hith.), Ec 9¹² (יקשׁ pu.) *;] *to ensnare:* metaph., c. acc., ἐν λόγῳ, Mt 22¹⁵ (not elsewhere).†

παγίς, -ίδος, ἡ (< πήγνυμι), [in LXX for פח, מוֹקֵשׁ, רֶשֶׁת, etc.;] poët. (Aristoph., al.) and late for πάγη, *a trap, snare;* metaph. (as also in cl.) : Lk 21³⁵, Ro 11⁹ ⁽ᴸˣˣ⁾, I Ti 3⁷ 6⁹, II Ti 2²⁶.†

Πάγος, v.s. Ἄρειος.

* πάθημα, -τος, τό (< πάσχω), like πάθος, 1. *that which befalls one, a suffering, affliction:* pl., Ro 8¹⁸, II Co 1⁶, ⁷, Col 1²⁴, II Ti 3¹¹, He 2¹⁰ 10³², I Pe 5⁹; of Christ's sufferings: τὰ εἰς X., I Pe 1¹¹; τ. Χριστοῦ, I Pe 5¹; id. as shared by Christians, II Co 1⁵, Phl 3¹⁰, I Pe 4¹³. 2. *a passive emotion, affection, passion:* Ga 5²⁴; τ. ἁμαρτιῶν, Ro 7⁵. 3. = τὸ πάσχειν, *an enduring* or *suffering:* c. gen. obj., He 2⁹.†

SYN.: v.s. πάθος.

* παθητός, -ή, -όν (< πάσχω), 1. *one who has suffered.* 2. *subject to suffering* (R, mg., v. M, *Pr.*, 222) or *destined to suffer* (AV, R, txt.) : Ac 26²³.†

πάθος, -ους, τό (< πάσχω), [in LXX : Jb 30³¹ (אֵבֶל), Pr 25²⁰, and very freq. in IV Mac (1¹ ff., al.) *;] like πάθημα; 1. *that which befalls one, that which one suffers.* 2. *a passive emotion* or *affection* (esp. of violent emotion), *a passion, passionate desire;* in NT always in bad sense : Col 3⁵ ; π. ἀτιμίας, Ro 1²⁶ ; π. ἐπιθυμίας, ι Th 4⁵.†

SYN.: π. = πάθημα, exc. that πάθημα is the more concrete and particular. In NT usage, π. represents the passive, ungoverned aspect of evil desire, as opp. to ἐπιθυμία, which is the active and also the more comprehensive term (v. Tr., *Syn.,* lxxxvii) ; cf. also ὄρεξις.

* παιδαγωγός, -οῦ, ὁ (< παῖς, ἄγω), a guide, guardian, trainer of boys, *a tutor* (disting. from διδάσκαλος, Xen., *Lac.,* 3, 1), usually a trusty slave : opp. to πατήρ, ι Co 4¹⁵ ; fig., of the Law, π. εἰς Χριστόν, Ga 3²⁴, ²⁵.†

παιδάριον, -ου, τό, dimin. of παῖς, [in LXX chiefly for נַעַר ;] *a little boy, a lad* (in late and colloq. Gk. the word seems to be used with greater latitude and even to lose its dimin. force entirely ; cf. To 6², ³, and v. MM, xviii) : Jo 6⁹.†

SYN.: v.s. παῖς.

παιδεία (-ία, T), -ας, ἡ (< παιδεύω), [in LXX chiefly for מוּסָר ;] 1. *the rearing of a child* (Æsch.). 2. *training, learning, instruction* (Plat., al.) : Eph 6⁴, ιι Ti 3¹⁶. 3. As in LXX (Pr 3¹¹ 15⁵, al.), *chastening, discipline :* He 12⁵ (LXX), ⁷, ⁸, ¹¹.†

παιδευτής, -οῦ, ὁ (< παιδεύω), [in LXX : Ho 5² (מוּסָר), Si 37¹⁹, ιν Mac 5³⁴ 9⁶ * ;] 1. prop., *a teacher, instructor :* Ro 2²⁰. 2. *a corrector, one who disciplines* (cf. Ho, l.c.) : He 12⁹.†

παιδεύω (< παῖς), [in LXX chiefly for יָסַר] 1. as in cl., *to train children,* hence, generally, *to teach, instruct :* Ac 7²², 22³, ι Ti 1²⁰, Tit 2¹². 2. As in LXX (Ps 6², Pr 19¹⁸, Wi 3⁵, al., and for prob. ex. from π., v. MM, xviii), *to chasten, correct, chastise :* Lk 23¹⁶, ²², ιι Ti 2²⁵, He 12⁷, ¹⁰ ; of divine chastening, ι Co 11³², ιι Co 6⁹, He 12⁶, Re 3¹⁹.†

SYN.: διδάσκω, q.v.

παιδία, v.s. παιδεία.

παιδιόθεν (< παιδίον), adv., [in LXX : Ge 47³ * ;] = cl. ἐκ παιδός, παιδίου, *from childhood :* Mk 9²¹.†

παιδίον, -ου, τό, dimin. of παῖς, [in LXX chiefly for יֶלֶד, also for בֵּן, נַעַר, etc., freq. in To in ref. to full-grown youth ;] *a young child, a little one :* Mt 2⁸, ⁹, ¹¹ ᶠᶠ., Lk 1⁵⁹, ⁶⁶, ⁷⁶, ⁸⁰ 2¹⁷, ²⁷, ⁴⁰, Jo 16²¹, He 11²³ ; of older children, Mt 18², ⁴, ⁵, Mk 5³⁹⁻⁴¹ 7³⁰ 9²⁴, ³⁶, Lk 9⁴⁷, ⁴⁸ 18¹⁷, Jo 4⁴⁹ ; in pl., Mt 11¹⁶ 14²¹ 15³⁸ 18³ 19¹³, ¹⁴, Mk 7²⁸ 10¹³ ᶠᶠ., Lk 7³² 11⁷ 18¹⁶, He 2¹³, ¹⁴. Metaph., ι Co 14²⁰. Colloq. in familiar address (as Eng. colloq., "lads"—v. M, *Pr.,* 170ₙ—and Irish use of "boys") : Jo 21⁵, ι Jo 2¹³, ¹⁸ 37.†

SYN.: v.s. παῖς.

παιδίσκη, -ης, ἡ, dimin. of παῖς, [in LXX for שִׁפְחָה, אָמָה, etc.;] 1. *a young girl, a maiden* (נַעֲרָה, Ru 4¹²). 2. Colloq., *a young female slave, a maid-servant* (v. Kennedy. *Sources,* 40 f. ; Deiss., *LAE,* 186

332₂): Mt 26⁶⁹, Mk 14⁶⁶, ⁶⁹, Lk 12⁴⁵ 22⁵⁶, Jo 18¹⁷, Ac 12¹³ 16¹⁶; of Hagar, Ga 4²², ²³, ³⁰ (LXX); id., metaph., ib. ³¹.†

SYN.: v.s. παῖς.

παίζω (< παῖς), [in LXX: Ge 21⁹ 26⁸, Ex 32⁶ (צחק pi.); and more freq. (Jg 16²⁵, al.) for שׂחק pi.;] prop., *to play as a child,* hence, generally, *to play* (as with singing and dancing): 1 Co 10⁷ (LXX) (cf. ἐμ-παίζω).†

παῖς, gen., παιδός, ὁ, ἡ, [in LXX chiefly for עֶבֶד, also for נַעַר, נַעֲרָה, etc.;] 1. *a child, boy, youth, maiden:* ὁ π., Mt 17¹⁸, Lk 2⁴³ 9⁴², Ac 20¹²; ἡ π., Lk 8⁵¹, ⁵⁴ (on the artic. nom. of address, v. M, *Pr.,* 70 f., 235; Bl., § 33, 4); pl., Mt 2¹⁶ 21¹⁵; of parentage, c. gen., Jo 4⁵¹. 2. Like Heb. עֶבֶד, Lat. *puer,* Fr. *garçon,* Eng. *boy* (Æsch., Aristoph., Xen., al.), *servant, slave, attendant:* Mt 8⁶, ⁸, ¹³, Lk 7⁷ 12⁴⁵ 15²⁶; in late writers (Diod., LXX: Ge 41³⁷, al.), of a king's attendant or minister: Mt 14²; so (= Heb. עֶבֶד יְהֹוָה) π. τ. θεοῦ (Ps 68 (69)¹⁸, Is 41⁸, Wi 2¹³, al.), of Israel, Lk 1⁵⁴; of David, Lk 1⁶⁹, Ac 4²⁵; of Jesus (but v. Dalman, *Words,* 277 f.), Mt 12¹⁸ (LXX), Ac 3¹³, ²⁶ 4²⁷, ³⁰.†

SYN.: 1. τέκνον, *child,* with emphasis on parentage and the consequent community of nature; υἱός, *son,* with emphasis on the privileged position of heirship; π. refers both to age and parentage, but with emphasis on the former. Cf. also παιδάριον, παιδίον, παιδίσκη, and v. Westc. on 1 Jo 3¹. 2. v.s. θεράπων, and cf. Thackeray, *Gr.,* 7 f.

παίω, [in LXX chiefly for נכה hi.;] *to strike, smite:* with the hand or fist, Mt 26⁶⁸, Lk 22⁶⁴; with a sword, Mk 14⁴⁷, Jo 18¹⁰; of a reptile, *to sting:* Re 9⁵ (also perh. in 7¹⁶ for πέσῃ; Swete, *ICC,* in l.).†

Πακατιανή, -ῆς, ἡ, *Pacatiana,* the western part of the Province of Phrygia, as constituted in iv/A.D.: 1 Ti *subscr.* (Rec.).†

πάλαι, adv. of time, [in LXX: Is 48⁵, ⁷ (מֵאָז), etc.;] *long ago, of old, in time past* (denoting past time absolutely, as πρότερον relatively): Mt 11²¹, Lk 10¹³, He 1¹, Ju ⁴; as adj., c. art., II Pe 1⁹; of time just past, Mk 6⁴⁷ (WH, mg.), 15⁴⁴ (WH, mg., R, txt.); c. durat. praes. (RV, *all this time*), II Co 12¹⁹.†

παλαιός, -ά, -όν (< πάλαι), [in LXX: Le 25²² 26¹⁰, Ca 7¹³ (14) (יָשָׁן), Jos 9⁴, ⁵, Je 45 (38)¹¹ (בָּלָה), etc.;] *old, ancient;* opp. to νέος, καινός: οἶνος, Lk 5³⁹; διαθήκη, II Co 3¹⁴; ἐντολή, I Jo 2⁷; ζύμη, I Co 5⁷, ⁸; ὁ π. ἄνθρωπος (for similar phrases, v. Westc., *Eph.,* 68), Ro 6⁶, Eph 4²², Col 3⁹; neut. pl., καινὰ καὶ π., Mt 13⁵²; of things not merely old, but worn by use (as Jo, l.c., LXX), Mt 9¹⁶, ¹⁷, Mk 2²¹, ²², Lk 5³⁶, ³⁷.†

SYN.: v.s. ἀρχαῖος.

*παλαιότης, -ητος, ἡ (< παλαιός), *oldness:* γράμματος, Ro 7⁶.†

παλαιόω, -ῶ (< παλαιός), [in LXX chiefly for בלה pi., in pass. for בָּ qal.;] *to make* or *declare old:* He 8¹³; pass., *to become old:* of things worn out by time and use (cf. Jo 9¹³, Is 50⁹, al., and v.s. παλαιός), Lk 12³³, He 1¹¹ (LXX); τὸ παλαιούμενον, He 8¹³ (where this and the act., v. supr., may have the sense of *abrogate*, v. LS, Zorell, s.v.).†

SYN. : γηράσκω.

* **πάλη**, -ης, ἡ (< πάλλω, to *sway*), *wrestling*, hence, generally, *fight*, *contest* : fig., of the spiritual combat of Christians, Eph 6¹².†
παλιγγενεσία, v.s. παλινγενεσία.

πάλιν, adv., [in LXX for שׁוּב, etc.;] 1. of place, *back*, *backwards* (LS, s.v.). 2. Of time, *again, once more :* Mt 4⁸, Mk 2¹³, Lk 23²⁰, Jo 1³⁵ (and freq.), Ac 17³², Ro 11²³, Ga 1⁹, He 1⁶, al.; pleonastically, π. ἀνακάμπτειν, Ac 18²¹; ὑποστρέφειν, Ga 1¹⁷; εἰς τὸ π., II Co 13²; π. ἐκ τρίτου (Bl., § 81, 4), Mt 26⁴⁴; ἐκ δευτέρου, Mt 26⁴², Ac 10¹⁵; π. δεύτερον, Jo 4⁵⁴ 21¹⁶; π. ἄνωθεν (Wi 19⁶), Ga 4⁹. 3. Rhetorically, *again;* (*a*) *further, moreover :* Mt 5³³, Lk 13²⁰, Jo 12³⁹, al.; (*b*) *in turn, on the other hand* (Soph.; LXX : Wi 13⁸ 16²³, al.) : Lk 6⁴³, I Co 12²¹, II Co 10⁷, I Jo 2⁸.

*† **παλινγενεσία** (Rec. παλιγγ-), -ας, ἡ (< πάλιν, γένεσις), *new birth, renewal, restoration, regeneration;* (*a*) of persons (Plut., Phil., al.), of spiritual regeneration, διὰ λουτροῦ παλινγενεσίας (gen. attr., v. Ellic., in l.), Tit 3⁵; (*b*) of the world, as in Stoics, Jewish Apocal., al. (v. Dalman, *Words*, 177 ff.), Mt 19²⁸.†

παμπληθεί, v.s. πανπληθεί.

** **πάμπολυς**, -πόλλη, -πολυ (< πᾶς, πολύς), [in Sm. : Jb 36³¹, Ps 39 (40)⁶ 88 (89)⁵¹*;] *very much, very great :* Mk 8¹, Rec. (RV, Edd., πάλιν πολλοῦ).†

Παμφυλία, -ας, ἡ, *Pamphylia*, a province of Asia Minor : Ac 2¹⁰ 13¹³ 14²⁴ 15³⁸ 27⁵.†

πανδοκεύς, v.s. πανδοχεύς.
πανδοκίον, v.s. πανδοχεῖον.

* **παν-δοχεῖον** (-δοκίον, T), -ου, τό (< πανδοχεύς), late form of Att. πανδοκεῖον, *an inn (khán, caravanserai)* : Lk 10³⁴.†

* **παν-δοχεύς**, -έως, ὁ (< πᾶς, δέχομαι), late form of the Att. πανδοκεύς (T, in l.), *an innkeeper, host :* Lk 10³⁵.†

πανήγυρις, -εως, ἡ (< πᾶς + ἄγυρα = ἀγορά), [in LXX : Ho 2¹¹ ⁽¹³⁾ 9⁵, Ez 46¹¹ (מוֹעֵד), Am 5²¹ (עֲצָרָה)*;] prop., *a national festal assembly* in honour of a god; hence, generally, *any festal assembly :* He 12²³ (for exx. in π., v. MM, xviii).†

SYN. : ἐκκλησία (q.v.), συναγωγή.

πανοικεί (Rec., LTr., -κί), adv. (< πᾶς, οἶκος), a word rejected by strict Atticists, though found once in Plat. (*Eryx.*, 392 c); [in LXX : Ex 1¹ (בַּיִת), III Mac 3²⁷ (where A in each case reads -κία, the Attic form, cf. Ge 50⁸, al.)*;] *with all the household :* Ac 16³⁴.†

πανοπλία, -ας, ἡ (< πᾶς, ὅπλον), [in LXX : II Ki 2²¹ (חֲלִיצָה), Jb 39²⁰, Jth 14³, Wi 5¹⁷, Si 46⁶, I, II, IV Mac ₆*;] *full armour :* Lk 11²²; metaph. (cf. Wi, l.c.), τ. θεοῦ, Eph 6¹¹, ¹³.†

πανουργία, -ας, ἡ (< πανοῦργος), [in LXX : Jos 9⁴, Pr 1⁴ 8⁵ (עָרְמָה), Nu 24²², Si 19²⁵ 21²² 31 (34)¹⁰ (in all cases in good or indifferent sense)*;] *cleverness*, in cl. nearly always in bad sense, *craftiness, cunning, knavery :* Lk 20²³, ι Co 3¹⁹ (LXX, φρόνησις, for עָרְמָה), ιι Co 4² 11³, Eph 4¹⁴.†

πανοῦργος, -ον, [in LXX chiefly for עָרוּם;] *ready to do anything ;* (a) in cl., chiefly in bad sense, *knavish, crafty :* ιι Co 12¹⁶ ; (b) in good sense, *skilful, clever* (Pr 13¹ 28²).†

*† πανπληθεί (Rec. παμπλ-, v. WH, *App.*, 150), adv. (< πᾶς, πλῆθος), = cl. παμπληθές, *with the whole multitude, all together :* Lk 23¹⁸.†

πανταχῇ (Rec. -χῆ), adv., [in LXX : Is 24¹¹ (בַּחוּצוֹת), Wi 2⁹, ιι Mac 8⁷ *;] *everywhere :* Ac 21²⁸.†

πανταχόθεν, adv., [in LXX : ιv Mac 13¹ 15³² *;] *from all sides :* Mk 1⁴⁵, Rec.†

πανταχοῦ, adv., [in LXX : Is 42²² (כֻּלָּם) *;] *everywhere :* Mk 1²⁸ 16⁽²⁰⁾, Lk 9⁶, Ac 17³⁰ 24³ 28²², ι Co 4¹⁷.†

** παντελής, -ές (< πᾶς, τέλος), [in LXX : ιιι Mac 7¹⁶ A*;] *all-complete, entire, perfect ;* εἰς τ. παντελές, *completely, utterly :* Lk 13¹¹, He 7²⁵ (where perhaps in temp. sense, *finally ;* v. MM, xviii).†

** πάντῃ (Rec. -τη), adv. (< πᾶς), [in LXX : Si 50²², ιιι Mac 4¹ *;] *every way, entirely :* Ac 24³.†

πάντοθεν, adv. (< πᾶς), [in LXX : Je 31 (48)³¹ (כָּלֹה), al.;] *from all sides :* Mk 1⁴⁵, Lk 19⁴³, He 9⁴.†

† παντοκράτωρ, -ορος, ὁ (< πᾶς, κρατέω), [in LXX : freq. in Jb 5⁸,¹⁷, al. (שַׁדַּי), and for צְבָאוֹת, in the phrase θεός (κύριος) π., ιι Ki 5¹⁰, al., and freq. in Am, Za, Ma ; also in Wi 7²⁵, Si 42¹⁷ 50¹⁴,¹⁷, and freq. in Jth, ιι, ιιι Mac;] *almighty :* ιι Co 6¹⁸, Re 1⁸ 4⁸ 11¹⁷ 15³ 16⁷,¹⁴ 9⁶,¹⁵ 21²².†

** πάντοτε, adv. of time (< πᾶς), [in LXX : Wi 11²¹ 19¹⁸ *;] in late writers (once in Arist.) for διαπαντός, ἑκάστοτε, *at all times, always :* Mt 26¹¹, Mk 14⁷, Lk 15³¹, Jo 6³⁴, Ro 1¹⁰, and freq. in Paul. Epp.

πάντως, adv. (< πᾶς), [in LXX : ιv Ki 5¹¹ (v. Thackeray, *Gr.*, 47), To 14⁸, al.;] *altogether, by all means ;* (a) without neg. (from Hdt. on) : ι Co 16¹² ; esp. in strong affirmations, *surely, at all events :* Lk 4²³, Ac 21²² 28⁴, ι Co 9¹⁰; (b) c. neg. (so always in Hom.), in a complete negation : Ro 3⁹ ; in a partial negation (Bl., § 75, 7), ι Co 5¹⁰.†

παρά, prep. c. gen., dat., acc., with radical sense, *beside.*
I. C. gen. pers., *from the side of, from beside, from,* indicating source or origin, [in LXX for מֵאֵצֶל, מִיַּד, מִלִּפְנֵי;] after verbs of motion, Mk 14⁴³, Lk 8⁴⁹, Jo 15²⁶, al; after verbs of seeking, receiving, hearing, etc., Mk 8¹¹ 12², Jo 4⁹,⁵² 10¹⁸, Phl 4¹⁸, ιι Ti 1¹⁸, Ja 1⁷, al.; after passive verbs, of the agent (like ὑπό), Mt 21⁴², Mk 12¹¹, Lk 1³⁷ ; absol., οἱ παρ᾽ αὐτοῦ, *his family, his kinsfolk*, Mk 3²¹ (cf. M, *Pr.*, 106 f. ; Field, *Notes*, 25 f. ; Swete, in l.) ; τὰ παρ᾽ αὐτῆς (αὐτῶν, ὑμῶν), *one's means, wealth*, Mk 5²⁶, Lk 10⁷, Phl 4¹⁸.

II. C. dat. pers. (exc. Jo 19²⁵, π. τ. σταυρῷ), *by the side of, beside, by, with,* [in LXX for אֵצֶל, בְּיַד, בְּעֵינֵי;] Lk 11³⁷ 19⁷, Jo 1³⁹ 4⁴⁰, Ac 28¹⁴, al.; παρ᾽ ἑαυτῷ, *at home,* i Co 16²; c. dat. pl., *among,* Mt 22²⁵, Col 4¹⁶, al.; metaph., Mt 19²⁶, Mk 10²⁷, Lk 1³⁰, Ro 2¹³, Ja 1²⁷, al.

III. C. acc., *of motion by or towards,* [in LXX for אֵצֶל, עַל יַד, בְּעֵבֶר;] 1. *of place, by the side of, beside, by, along:* Ac 10³², He 11¹²; after verbs of motion, Mt 4¹⁸, Mk 4⁴, Lk 8⁵, Ac 4³⁵, al.; after verbs of rest, Mt 13¹, Mk 5²¹, Lk 8³⁵, al. 2. *beside, beyond,* metaph.; (*a*) *beyond, against, contrary to:* Ac 18¹³, Ro 1²⁶ 4¹⁸ 11²⁴, al.; *except,* ii Co 11²⁴; (*b*) *beyond, above, in comparison with:* Lk 3¹³, Ro 12³ 14⁵, He 1⁴, ⁹ 3³, al.; (*c*) *on account of:* i Co 12¹⁵, ¹⁶.

IV. In composition: *beside, to* (παραλαμβάνω, παράγω), *at hand* (πάρειμι), *from* (παραρρέω), *amiss* (παρακούω), *past* (παρέρχομαι), *compared with* (παρομοιάζω), *above measure* (παροργίζω).

παρα-βαίνω, [in LXX for סוּר, עבר, פרר hi., שׂטה, etc.;] 1. in Hom. (twice), *to go by the side of, stand beside.* 2. In Æsch., Herod., Thuc., al., *to go past* or *pass over,* chiefly metaph., *to overstep, violate, transgress* (Jos 7¹¹, Ez 16⁵⁹, Si 40¹⁴, al.): τ. παράδοσιν, Mt 15²; τ. ἐντολήν, ib.³; seq. ἀπό (as סוּר מִן, De 17²⁰, al.), *to turn aside, fall away* (cf. π. τῆς ἀληθείας, Arist., Cael., i, 5, 2): Ac 1²⁵.†

παρα-βάλλω, [in LXX: Pr 2² 4²⁰ 5¹, ¹³ 22¹⁷ (נטה hi.), Ru 2¹⁶ (שׁלל), ii Mac 14³⁸ (elsewhere as v.l. ₄) *;] 1. *to throw to* or *beside,* as fodder to horses (Hom., al.). 2. *to lay beside, compare* (Hdt., Plat., al.): Mk 4³⁰, Rec. 3. Reflexive, *to betake oneself, come near;* of seamen, *to cross over:* εἰς Σάμον, Ac 20¹⁵. 4. In mid. = παραβολεύομαι, q.v.†

παρά-βασις, -εως, ἡ (< παραβαίνω), [in LXX: Ps 100 (101)³ (סֵתִים), iv Ki 2²⁴ A, Wi 14³¹, ii Mac 15¹⁰ *;] 1. *a going aside, a deviation* (Arist.). 2. In later writers, *an overstepping;* metaph., *transgression* (Plut., al.): Ro 4¹⁵ 5¹⁴, He 2² 9¹⁵; τ. νόμου, Ro 2²³; ἐν π., i Ti 2¹⁴; τ. παραβάσεων χάριν, Ga 3¹⁹.

SYN.: v.s. ἁμαρτία.

** παρα-βάτης, -ου, ὁ (< παραβαίνω), [in Sm.: Ps 16 (17)⁴ 138 (139)¹⁹, Je 6²⁸ *;] 1. *one who stands beside, the warrior who stands by the charioteer* (cf. παραβαίνω, 1). 2. *a transgressor* (Æsch., παρβάτης): Ga 2¹⁸, Ja 2⁹; π. νόμου, Ro 2²⁵, ²⁷, Ja 2¹¹.†

† παρα-βιάζομαι, [in LXX: Ge 19⁹, iv Ki 2¹⁷ (פָּצַר בְּ), De 1⁴³ (זוּר hi.), i Ki 28²³ (פָּרַץ בְּ), v.l. ₄ *;] 1. prop., *to force against nature* or *law.* 2. *to compel by force* (Polyb.). 3. *to constrain by entreaty* (Ge, i Ki, ll. c.): Lk 24²⁹, Ac 16¹⁵.†

*† παρα-βολεύομαι = cl. παραβάλλομαι (ii Mac 14³⁸), *to expose oneself to danger, hazard one's life:* c. dat. ref., τ. ψυχῇ (v. M, *Pr.*, 64), Phl 2³⁰ (Rec. παραβουλ-). Cited by Deiss., *LAE,* 84, 120.†

παραβολή, -ῆς, ἡ (< παραβάλλω), [in LXX (cf. McNeile, *Mt.*, 185):
Nu 23⁷, De 28³⁷, Ps 43 (44)¹⁴, Pr 1⁶, Ez 12²², al. (מָשָׁל), Si 47¹⁷ (חִידָה),
al. mult. in Si, Wi 5³;] 1. *a placing beside, juxtaposition* (Polyb., al.).
2. *a comparing, comparison* (Plat., Arist., al.). 3. *a comparison,
illustration, analogy, figure* (Arist., al.): Mt 24³², Mk 3²³ 4³⁰, He 9⁹ 11¹⁹;
specif. of the pictures and narratives drawn from nature and human
life which are characteristic of the synoptic teaching of our Lord,
a parable: Mt 13³, ¹⁰, Mk 4², ¹⁰, Lk 8⁴, ⁹⁻¹¹, al.; c. gen. ref., Mt 13¹⁸, ³⁶.
4. Like Heb. מָשָׁל (ɪ Ki 10¹², Pr 1⁶, Si 3²⁹, al.), = παροιμία, *a proverb*
or gnomic saying: Lk 4²³ 5³⁶ 6³⁹.
    SYN.: παροιμία (v. Abbott, *Essays*, 82 ff.).

*† παρα-βουλεύομαι, *to consult amiss,* or perh. (v. LS, s.v.), a vulg.
form of παρα-βολ- (q.v.): Phl 2³⁰, Rec.†

* παρ-αγγελία, -ας, ἡ (< παραγγέλλω), *an instruction, charge, command:* Ac 5²⁸ 16²⁴, ɪ Th 4², ɪ Ti 1⁵, ¹⁸. (In Xen., Polyb., of a military
order.)†

παρ-αγγέλλω (< παρά, ἀγγέλλω), [in LXX for שמע pi., hi., etc.;]
1. *to transmit a message* (Æsch., Eur.). 2. *to order, command* (Hdt.,
Xen., al.): c. inf., Ac 15⁵; c. acc. rei, ɪ Co 11¹⁷, ɪɪ Th 3⁴, ɪ Ti 4¹¹, 5⁷;
seq. ἵνα (M, *Pr.*, 207; Bl., § 69, 4), Mk 6⁸, ɪɪ Th 3¹²; c. dat. pers.,
Ac 17³⁰ R, txt., ɪ Th 4¹¹; seq. λέγων, Mt 10⁵; c. inf. aor., Mt 15³⁵, Mk 8⁶,
Lk 8²⁹, Ac 10⁴² 16¹⁸ (aoristic pres.; v. M, *Pr.*, 119); id. c. neg., μή,
Lk 5¹⁴ 8⁵⁶, Ac 23²², ɪ Co 7¹⁰; c. inf. pres., Ac 16²³, ɪɪ Th 3⁶; id. c. neg.,
μή, Lk 9²¹, Ac 1⁴ 4¹⁸ 5²⁸, ⁴⁰, ɪ Ti 1³ 6¹⁷; c. acc., τοῦτο, seq. ὅτι (Bl.,
§ 70, 3), ɪɪ Th 3¹⁰; c. acc. et inf., Ac 23³⁰, ɪɪ Th 3⁶, ɪ Ti 6¹³ (Bl., § 72, 5);
ptcp. pf. pass., Mk 16 (alt. ending).†
    SYN.: v.s. ἐντέλλω.

παρα-γίνομαι (Ion. and late for -γίγν-), [in LXX chiefly for בוא;]
1. *to be beside* or *at hand* (Hom., Hdt., al.), hence, *to stand by, support* (Æsch., Thuc., al.): c. dat. pers., ɪɪ Ti 4¹⁶. 2. *to come, come up,
arrive* (Hdt., Xen., al., and freq. in later writers; v. MM, xviii;
Thackeray, *Gr.*, 267₂): absol., Lk 14²¹ 19¹⁶, Jo 3²³, Ac 5²¹, ²², ²⁵ 9³⁹
10³², ³³ 11²³ 14²⁷ 17¹⁰ 18²⁷ 21¹⁸ 23¹⁶, ³⁵ 24¹⁷, ²⁴ 25⁷ 28²¹, ɪ Co 16³; seq. εἰς,
Jo 8², Ac 9²⁶ 15⁴; ἐπί, c. acc., Lk 22⁵²; πρός, c. acc., Lk 7⁴, ²⁰ 8¹⁹, Ac 20¹⁸;
id. seq. ἐκ, Lk 11⁶; παρά, c. gen., Mk 14⁴³; ἀπὸ . . . εἰς, Mt 2¹, Ac 13¹⁴;
ἀπὸ . . . ἐπὶ . . . πρός, Mt 3¹³: of a teacher coming forward in public:
Mt 3¹, Lk 12⁵¹, He 9¹¹.†

παρ-άγω, [in LXX chiefly for עבר;] 1. trans., *to lead by, lead
aside, lead into, lead forward,* etc. 2. Intrans., (*a*) *to pass by:* Mt
9⁹, ²⁷ 20³⁰, Mk 2¹⁴ 15²¹, Jo 8⁵⁹ R, txt., 9¹; seq. παρά, c. acc., Mk 1¹⁶; (*b*) *to
go away, depart;* metaph., *to pass away:* ɪ Co 7³¹; mid., ɪ Jo 2⁸, ¹⁷.†

† παρα-δειγματίζω (< δείκνυμι), [in LXX: Nu 25⁴ (יקע hi.), Je 13²²
(חמס ni.), Ez 28¹⁷ (רָאָה), Es 4¹⁷, Da LXX 2⁵ *;] *to set forth as an
example;* in bad sense, *to put to open shame:* He 6⁶ (Polyb., Plut.,
al.).†

παράδεισος, -ου, ὁ (an Oriental word, first used by Xen. of the
parks of Persian kings and nobles), [in LXX chiefly for גן, Ge 18 ff.,

al.; also for עֵדֶן, Is 51³; פַּרְדֵּם, Ne 2⁸, Ec 2⁵;] 1. *a park, pleasure-ground, garden* (LXX), *an orchard* (in π., v. MM, ii, xviii; Deiss., *BS*, 148). 2. *Paradise*, the abode of the blessed dead : Lk 23⁴³, II Co 12⁴, Re 2⁷.†

παρα-δέχομαι, [in LXX: Ex 23¹ (נִשָׂא), Pr 3¹² (רָצָה), II Mac 4²² R, III Mac 7¹² *;] *to receive, admit;* (a) of things : Mk 4²⁰, Ac 16²¹ 22¹⁸, I Ti 5¹⁹; (b) of persons : Ac 15⁴, He 12⁶ (LXX).†

*† παρα-δια-τριβή, -ῆς, ἡ, *useless wrangling* : v.l. in Rec. for διαπαρατριβή (q.v.), I Ti 6⁵.†

παρα-δίδωμι, [in LXX chiefly for נתן;] correl. to παραδέχομαι, 1. *to give* or *hand over* to another : c. acc. et dat., Mt 11²⁷ 25¹⁴, Lk 4⁶, al.; of being delivered up to a course of teaching, pass. seq. εἰς, Ro 6¹⁷; hence, *to hazard, risk* (cf. π. αὐτὸν τύχῃ, Thuc., 5, 16), Ac 15²⁶. 2. *to commit, commend :* Ac 14²⁶ 15⁴⁰, I Pe 2²³. 3. *to give* or *deliver up* to prison or judgment : c. acc. pers., Mt 4¹², Mk 1¹⁴, Ro 4²⁵, II Pe 2⁴; id. seq. ὑπέρ, Ro 8³²; c. dat., Mt 5²⁵, Mk 15¹, Lk 12⁵⁸, Jo 19¹¹, al.; id. seq. ἵνα, Jo 19¹⁶; c. inf., Ac 12⁴; seq. εἰς, Mt 10¹⁷ 17²² 24⁹, Lk 21¹², Ac 8³, II Co 4¹¹, al.; τ. Σατανᾷ, I Ti 1²⁰; id. seq. εἰς ὄλεθρον σαρκός, I Co 5⁵; with the collat. idea of treachery (= προδίδωμι), c. acc. pers., Mt 26¹⁶, Mk 14¹¹, Jo 6⁶⁴, al.; id. c. dat., Mt 26¹⁵, al.; pres. ptcp., ὁ παραδιδοὺς αὐτόν, Mt 26²⁵, Mk 14⁴², Jo 13¹¹. 4. *to hand down, hand on* or *deliver* verbally (traditions, commands, etc.) : Mk 7¹³, Lk 1², Ac 6¹⁴, I Co 11² 15³; pass., II Pe 2²¹, Ju ³. 5. *to permit* (for exx. in cl., v. LS, s.v.) : Mk 4²⁹.

** παράδοξος, -ον (< παρά, δόξα), [in LXX: Jth 13¹³, Wi 5² 16¹⁷ 19⁵, Si 43²⁵, II-IV Mac ₃ *;] *contrary to received opinion, incredible, marvellous :* pl., Lk 5²⁶.†

SYN. : v.s. δύναμις.

παρά-δοσις, -εως, ἡ (< παραδίδωμι), [in LXX: II Es 7²⁶ (אֱסוּר), Je 39 (32)⁴ (נתן ni.), 41 (34)²*;] 1. *a handing down* or *over, transfer, transmission* (Arist., Polyb., al., LXX). 2. *tradition* of doctrine (Plat., Epict., al.); by meton., of the doctrine itself : Mt 15²,³,⁶, Mk 7³ᶠ., I Co 11², Ga 1¹⁴, Col 2⁸, II Th 2¹⁵ 3⁶.†

† παρα-ζηλόω, -ῶ, [in LXX: De 32²¹, III Ki 14²², Ps 77 (78)⁵⁸ (קָנָא pi., hi.), Ps 36 (37)¹,⁷,⁸ (חרה hith.), Si 30³*;] *to provoke to jealousy :* Ro 10¹⁹ (LXX) 11¹¹,¹⁴, I Co 10²².†

παρα-θαλάσσιος, -α, -ον (< παρά, θάλασσα), [in LXX: Je 29(47)⁷ (חוֹף הַיָּם), etc.;] *by the sea :* Mt 4¹³.†

* παρα-θεωρέω, -ῶ, 1. *to examine side by side, compare.* 2. *to overlook, neglect :* pass., Ac 6¹.†

παρα-θήκη, -ης, ἡ (< παρατίθημι), [in LXX: Le 6², ⁴ (5²¹, ²³) (פִּקָּדוֹן), and in To 10¹³, II Mac 3¹⁰,¹⁵, v.l. for παρακαταθήκη (q.v.) *;] *a deposit* or *trust :* I Ti 6²⁰, II Ti 1¹²,¹⁴ (for exx. of this form, v. MM, *Exp.*, iii, xviii).†

** παρ-αινέω, -ῶ, [in LXX: II Mac 7²⁵,²⁶, III Mac 5¹⁷ 7¹²*;] *to* *exhort, advise :* c. acc. pers. et inf. (v. Bl., § 72, 5; M, *Pr.*, 205), Ac 27²²; absol., seq. λέγων, Ac 27⁹.†

παρ-αιτέομαι, -οῦμαι, [in LXX for בקש pi., etc.;] 1. *to beg of or from* another : Mk 15⁶ (Rec. ὅνπερ ᾐτοῦντο, v. Field, *Notes*, 43). 2. *to deprecate ;* (*a*) prop., c. neg., *to entreat* that *not* (Thuc., al.) : He 12¹⁹; (*b*) *to refuse, decline, avoid :* c. acc., I Ti 4⁷ 5¹¹, II Ti 2²³, Tit 3¹⁰, He 12²⁵ (EV; but v. Field, *Notes*, 234). 3. *to beg off, ask to be excused, excuse* (Polyb., al.) : Lk 14¹⁸, ¹⁹ (He 12²⁵, Field, l.c.).†

*†παρα-καθέζομαι, *to sit down beside :* seq. πρός, Lk 10³⁹ (Plut.).†

παρα-καθίζω, [in LXX : Jb 2¹³ (ישׁב) *;] *to set beside;* act. for mid., *to sit down beside :* Lk 10³⁹, Rec. (for -έζομαι, q.v.).†

παρα-καλέω, -ῶ, [in LXX chiefly for נחם ni., pi.;] 1. *to call to* one, *call for, summon :* Ac 28²⁰ (R, mg.; R, txt., *entreat*) ; hence (of the gods : Dem., Xen., al.), *to invoke, call on, beseech, entreat :* τ. πατέρα μου, Mt 26⁵³; τ. κύριον, II Co 12⁸; in late writers (Polyb., Diod., al.; rarely in LXX; in π., v. Deiss., *LAE*, 176₁₄), also of men . absol., Phm ⁹; c. acc., Mt 8⁵, Mk 1⁴⁰, Ac 16⁹, al.; c. inf., Mk 5¹⁷, Lk 8⁴¹, Ac 8³¹, al.; seq. ἵνα (v. M, *Pr.*, 205, 208), Mt 14³⁶, Mk 5¹⁸, Lk 8³¹, al. 2. *to admonish, exhort :* absol., Lk 3¹⁸, Ro 12⁸, II Ti 4², al.; c. acc., Ac 15³², I Th 2¹¹, He 3¹³, al.; id. seq. inf., Ac 11²³, Ro 12¹, Phl 4², I Th 4¹⁰, al.; seq. ἵνα (v. M, *Pr.*, l.c.), I Co 1¹⁰, II Co 8⁶, I Th 4¹, al. 3. *to cheer, encourage, comfort* (Plut., LXX : Jb 4³, Is 35³, Si 43²⁴, al.) : c. acc., II Co 1⁶, Eph 6²², Col 2², al.; id. seq. ἐν, I Th 4¹⁸; διά, II Co 1⁴; pass., Mt 5⁴, Lk 16²⁵, Ac 20¹².

    SYN. : παραμυθέω (cf. M, *Th.*, 25).

παρα-καλύπτω, [in LXX : Is 44⁸ (פחד), Ez 22²⁶ (עלם hi.) *;] *to cover* by hanging something beside, *to hide :* metaph. (as Plat., al.), Lk 9⁴⁵.†

παρα-κατα-θήκη, -ης, ἡ (< παρακατατίθημι), [in LXX : Ex 22⁸ (⁷), ¹¹ (¹⁰) (מלאכה), and elsewhere as v.l. for παραθήκη, q.v.;] more usual than its variant in Gk. writers for a *trust* or *deposit :* I Ti 6²⁰, II Ti 1¹⁴, Rec.†

**παρά-κειμαι, [in LXX : Jth 3², ³, Si 30¹⁸ 34 (31)¹⁶, Da LXX Bel ¹⁴, II, III Mac₅ *;] *to lie beside, be near, be present :* Ro 7¹⁸, ²¹.†

παρά-κλησις, -εως, ἡ (< παρακαλέω), [in LXX : Jb 21², Ps 93 (94)¹⁹, Ho 13¹⁴, Na 3⁷, Is 57¹⁸ 66¹¹, Je 16⁷ (נחם, its parts and derivatives), ib. 38 (31)⁹ (תנחום), Is 28²⁹ 30⁷, I Mac 10²⁴ 12⁹, II Mac 7²⁴ 15¹¹ *;] 1. *a calling to one's aid, summons* (Thuc.), hence, *appeal, entreaty* (Strab., Plut., al., I Mac 10²⁴; cf. Lft., *Notes*, 20) : II Co 8⁴. 2. *exhortation, encouragement :* Ac 15³¹, Ro 12⁸, I Co 14³, II Co 8¹⁷, Phl 2¹, I Th 2³, I Ti 4¹³, He 12⁵; λόγος (τῆς) π., Ac 13¹⁵, He 13²²; υἱὸς π., Ac 4³⁶. 3. *consolation, comfort* (Phalar., LXX) : Lk 6²⁴, Ac 9³¹, II Co 1⁴⁻⁷ ⁷, ¹³, II Th 2¹⁶, Phm ⁷; τ. γραφῶν, Ro 15⁴; θεὸς τῆς π., Ro 15⁵, II Co 1³; π. τοῦ Ἰσραήλ (v. Dalman, *Words*, 109 f.), Lk 2²⁵.†

**παρά-κλητος, -ον (< παρακαλέω), [in Aq., Th. : Jb 16² *;] *called to one's aid* in a judicial cause (Dion. Cass.) ; hence, most freq. as subst., ὁ π., *an advocate, pleader, intercessor* (Dem., al.; so in Rabbinic lit., (פְּרַקְלִיטָא), "a friend of the accused person, called to speak to his character, or otherwise enlist sympathy in his favour" (Field, *Notes*, 102). In NT, specif., ὁ π., (*a*) of Christ, 1 Jo 2¹ (v. *ICC*, *Jo. Epp.*, 23 ff.); (*b*) of the Holy Spirit (AV, *Comforter;* but v. opp. c.), Jo 14¹⁶, ²⁶ 15²⁶ 16⁷ (cf. also Abbott, *Essays*, 86, 97; Deiss., *LAE*, 339 f.; MM, xviii; Westc., *Jo.*, ii, 188 ff.).†

* παρ-ακοή, -ῆς, ἡ, 1. *a hearing amiss* (Plat.). 2. Later, as following inattention, *disobedience:* Ro 5¹⁹, 11 Co 10⁶, He 2² (cf. παρακούω, and v. Tr., *Syn.*, § lxvi).†

** παρ-ακολουθέω, -ῶ, [in LXX: 11 Mac 8¹¹ 9²⁷ R*;] c. dat., *to follow closely, accompany.* Metaph., in various senses, (*a*) *to result:* Mk 16[17]; (*b*) *to follow up, trace, investigate:* Lk 1³ (so freq. in cl.); (*c*) *to follow* as a standard of conduct: 1 Ti 4⁶, 11 Ti 3¹⁰. (For exx. from π., v. MM, xviii.)†

παρ-ακούω, [in LXX: Es 3³, ⁸ (עבר, עשה, c. neg.) 4¹⁴ 7⁴ (חרש hi.), Is 65¹² (שמע, c. neg.), 1 Es 4¹¹, To 3⁴*;] 1. *to overhear.* 2. *to hear amiss* or *imperfectly.* 3. Later (as in LXX, Polyb., Plut.; also in π., v. MM, xviii), *to hear without heeding, take no heed:* Mk 5³⁶; c. gen., Mt 18¹⁷.†

παρα-κύπτω, [in LXX chiefly for שׁקף ni., hi.;] 1. *to stoop sideways.* 2. *to stoop to look:* Lk 24¹² (R, txt.), Jo 20⁵, ¹¹. Metaph. (v. Hort, *Ja.*, in l.), *to look into:* seq. εἰς, Ja 1²⁵, 1 Pe 1¹².†

παρα-λαμβάνω, [in LXX chiefly for לקח, also for ירשׁ, etc.;] 1. c. acc. rei, like παραδέχομαι, correl. to παραδίδωμι, *to receive* from another: Col 4¹⁷, He 12²⁸; of the mind, 1 Co 11²³ 15¹, ³, Ga 1⁹, Phl 4⁹; c. inf., Mk 7⁴; seq. παρά, c. gen., Ga 1¹², 1 Th 2¹³ 4¹, 11 Th 3⁶; τ. Χριστόν (Lft., in l.), Col 2⁶. 2. C. acc. pers., *to take to* or *with oneself:* Mt 2¹³, ¹⁴, ²⁰, ²¹ 17¹ 26³⁷, Mk 4³⁶ 5⁴⁰ 9² 10³², Lk 9¹⁰, ²⁸ 11²⁶ 18³¹, Jo 19¹⁶, Ac 15³⁰ 23¹⁸; γυναῖκα, Mt 1²⁰, ²⁴; μεθ' ἑαυτοῦ, Mt 12⁴⁵ 18¹⁶, Mk 14³³; seq. εἰς, Mt 4⁵, ⁸ 27²⁷; κατ' ἰδίαν, Mt 20¹⁷; mid., seq. πρὸς ἐμαυτόν, Jo 14³; pass., Mt 24⁴⁰, ⁴¹, Lk 17³⁴⁻³⁶; ptcp., prefixed to other verbs (Bl, § 74, 2), Ac 16³³ 21²⁴, ²⁶, ³²; metaph., Jo 1¹¹.†

* παρα-λέγω, *to lay beside;* mid., (*a*) *to lie beside* (Hom.); (*b*) later, of sailors, *to sail past:* c. acc., Ac 27⁸, ¹³.†

παρ-άλιος, -ον (in cl., chiefly -α, -ον), [in LXX for יָם, הַיָּם, חוֹף, etc., c. prep.;] *by the sea; ἡ π.* (sc. χώρα, in LXX ἡ παραλία, De 1⁷, Jos 9¹, Jth 1⁷, al.), *the sea coast:* Lk 6¹⁷.†

παρ-αλλαγή, -ῆς, ἡ (< παραλλάσσω), [in LXX: 1v Ki 9²⁰ (שִׁגָּעוֹן)*;] in various senses (LS, s.v.), *change:* Ja 1¹⁷.†

παρα-λογίζομαι, [in LXX chiefly for רמה pi.;] 1. *to miscalculate.* 2. *to reason falsely,* hence, *to mislead:* Col 2⁴, Ja 1²².†

*† παρα-λυτικός, -ή, -όν (< παραλύω), *paralytic:* Mt 4²⁴ 8⁶ 9², ⁶, Mk 2³⁻⁵, ⁹, ¹⁰, Lk 5²⁴ (Rec., WH, mg.).†

παρα-λύω, [in LXX: Je 6²⁴ 27⁴³, Ez 21⁷(¹²) (רפה), etc.;] 1. *to loose from the side, set free.* 2. *to weaken, enfeeble;* pass., *to be enfeebled,* esp. by a paralytic stroke: Lk 5¹⁸, ²⁴, Ac 8⁷ 9³³, He 12¹² (LXX).†

παρα-μένω, [in LXX: Pr 12⁷, Da TH 11¹⁷ (עמד), etc.;] *to remain beside* or *near:* He 7²³, Ja 1²⁵; of remaining alive, I Co 16⁶ (WH, κατα-), Phl 1²⁵ (cf. συμ-παραμείω).†

** παρα-μυθέομαι, -οῦμαι, [in LXX: II Mac 15⁹ (Sm.₈)*;] 1. *to encourage, exhort.* 2. *to comfort, console:* c. acc. pers., Jo 11³¹, I Th 2¹¹ 5¹⁴; id. seq. περί, Jo 11¹⁹.†
    SYN.: παρακαλέω.

** παραμυθία, -ας, ἡ (< παραμυθέομαι), [in LXX: Es 8¹³, Wi 19¹² *;] 1. *encouragement, exhortation.* 2. *comfort, consolation:* I Co 14³.†
    SYN.: παράκλησις.

** παραμύθιον, -ου, τό (< παραμυθέομαι), [in LXX: Wi 3¹⁸ *;] 1. *an exhortation, persuasion, encouragement:* Phl 2¹ (cf. Plat., *Legg.*, vi, 773 E, al.; v. Lft. and *ICC, Phl.*, l.c.). 2. *assuagement, abatement,* hence, *consolation* (Wi, l.c., and freq. in cl.).†

παρα-νομέω, -ῶ, [in LXX for חלל, etc., chiefly in Pss and II Mac;] *to be a παράνομος, to transgress the law:* Ac 23³.†

παρανομία, -ας, ἡ, [in LXX: Ps 36 (37)⁷ (מִזִמָה), etc.;] *law-breaking, transgression:* II Pe 2¹⁶.†

† παρα-πικραίνω, [in LXX chiefly for מרה qal., hi., מְרִי, most freq. in Pss and Ez;] *to embitter, provoke:* absol. (yet sc. τ. θεόν, cf. Ps 105 (106)⁷, Ez 2⁵⁻⁸, al., and with τὸν θ. added, Ps 5⁴, Ez 20²¹, al.), He 3¹⁶ (cf. παραπικρασμός).†

† παρα-πικρασμός, -οῦ, ὁ (< παραπικραίνω), [in LXX: Ps 94 (95)⁸ (מְרִיבָה, elsewhere rendered Λοιδόρησις, Ex 17⁷; ἀντιλογία, De 33⁸, al.; λοιδορία, Nu 20²⁴)*;] *provocation:* ἐν τῷ π. (Heb. *at Meribah*), He 3⁸, ¹⁵ (LXX).†

παρα-πίπτω, [in LXX: Ez 14¹³ 15⁸ 18²⁴ 20²⁷ (מעל), 22⁴ (אשם), Es 6¹⁰ (נפל hi.), Wi 6⁹ 12², II Mac 10⁴ A *;] 1. most freq. (Hdt., Thuc., al.), *to fall in one's way, befall.* 2. *to fall into* or *in* (seq. εἰς, Polyb.; c. dat., II Mac, l.c.). 3. *to fall away* (Ez, Wi, ll. c.; in Polyb., c. gen.): absol., He 6⁶. 4. *to fail* (λόγος, Es, l.c.; cf. I Ki 3¹⁹).†

* παρα-πλέω, *to sail by* or *past:* c. acc., Ac 20¹⁶.†

* παρα-πλήσιος, -α, -ον (Hdt., Plat., al.; also -ος, -ον, Thuc., Polyb.), *coming near, nearly resembling.* Neut. -ον, adverbially, = ἴως, *in a way nearly resembling:* c. dat., Phl 2²⁷.†

** παρα-πλησίως, adv. (< παραπλήσιος), [in Quint.: Ho 8⁶ *;] *in like manner:* He 2¹⁴.†

παρα-πορεύομαι, [in LXX chiefly for עבר;] 1. *to go to beside, accompany.* 2. *to go past, pass by:* Mt 27³⁹, Mk 11²⁰ 15²⁹; seq. διά, c. gen., Mk 2²³ 9³⁰ (WH, mg.).†

† παρά-πτωμα, -τος, τό (< παραπίπτω), [in LXX for מעל, פשע, etc.;] 1. *a false step, a blunder* (Polyb.). 2. Ethically, *a misdeed, trespass* (LXX): Mt 6¹⁴,¹⁵, Mk 11²⁵,²⁶, Ro 4²⁵ 5¹⁵ ff. 11¹¹,¹², II Co 5¹⁹, Ga 6¹, Eph 1⁷ 2¹,⁵, Col 2¹³.†
    SYN.: v.s. ἁμαρτία.

παρα-ρέω, [in LXX : Is 44⁴ (יבל), Pr 3²¹ * ;] *to flow by, drift away, slip away :* so in pass., He 2¹.†

παράσημος, -ον (< σῆμα, *a mark*), [in LXX : III Mac 2²⁹ * ;] 1. in cl., *marked amiss, spurious, counterfeit.* Later, 2. *marked at the side, annotated* (Plut.). 3. *marked with a sign* (LXX) ; as subst., *a figure-head :* Ac 28¹¹ (v. MM, xix).†

παρα-σκευάζω, [in LXX : Je 27 (50)⁴² (ערך), etc. ;] *to prepare, make ready :* absol. (sc. τ. δεῖπνον, etc.; cf. Hdt., ix, 82, II Mac 2²⁷), Ac 10¹⁰ ; mid., *to prepare, make preparations :* I Co 14⁸ (cf. Je, l.c.) ; pass., II Co 9², ³.†

παρα-σκευή, -ῆς, ἡ, [in LXX : Ex 35²⁴ 39²²⁽⁴²⁾ (עֲבֹדָה, with v.l., ἀποσκ-, κατασκ-), Jth 2¹⁷ 4⁵, I Mac 9³⁵ א, II Mac 15²¹ * ;] 1. *preparation.* 2. *equipment* (Jth, ll. c.). 3. In Jewish usage, *the day of preparation* for a Sabbath or a feast (= προσάββατον, q.v.) : Mt 27⁶², Mk 15⁴², Lk 23⁵⁴, Jo 19³¹ ; c. gen., τοῦ πάσχα, Jo 19¹⁴ ; τ. Ἰουδαίων, ib. ⁴² (it is the name for *Friday* in MGr.).†

παρα-τείνω, [in LXX : Nu 23²⁸ (שֶׁקֶף ni.), etc. ;] *to extend, prolong :* τ. λόγον, Ac 20⁷.†

παρα-τηρέω, -ῶ, [in LXX : Ps 36 (37)¹² (זמם), 129 (130)³ (שמר), Da TH 6¹¹ ⁽¹²⁾, Su 12, 15, 16 * ;] 1. *to watch closely, observe narrowly :* so mid., τ. πύλας, Ac 9²⁴ ; with evil intent, Mk 3², Lk 20²⁰ (absol., v. Field, *Notes,* 74) ; so mid., Lk 6⁷ 14¹. 2. *to observe scrupulously* (of days and seasons ; cf. Ex 12⁴², Sm.) : mid., Ga 4¹⁰.†

†παρα-τήρησις, -εως, ἡ, [in Aq. : Ex 12⁴² (v.s. παρατηρέω) * ;] *observation :* Lk 17²⁰ (Polyb., Plut., al.).†

παρα-τίθημι, [in LXX chiefly for שׂים ;] I. Act., *to place beside, set before,* c. acc. et dat. : of food, Mk 6⁴¹ 8⁶, ⁷, Lk 9¹⁶ 11⁶ ; τράπεζαν, Ac 16³⁴ ; pass. ptcp., Lk 10⁸, I Co 10²⁷ ; metaph., of teaching, παραβολήν, Mt 13²⁴, ³¹. II. Mid., 1. *to have set before one* (Hom., Thuc., Xen., al.). 2. *to deposit* with another, *give in charge* or *commit to* (Hdt., Xen., Polyb., al.) : c. acc. et dat., Lk 12⁴⁸ 23⁴⁶, Ac 14²³ 20³², I Ti 1¹⁸, II Ti 2², I Pe 4¹⁹. 3. *to bring forward, quote as evidence :* seq. ὅτι, Ac 17³ (v. Page, in l.).†

* παρα-τυγχάνω, *to happen to be near* or *present :* Ac 17¹⁷.†

παρ-αυτίκα, adv. (< πάραυτα = παρ᾿ αὐτά, sc. τὰ πράγματα), [in LXX : Ps 69 (70)³, To 4¹⁴ * ;] 1. *immediately.* 2. C. subst., to express brief duration (cf. ἡ π. λαμπρότης, Thuc., ii, 64), *momentary, for a moment :* II Co 4¹⁷.†

παρα-φέρω, [in LXX : I Ki 21¹³ ⁽¹⁴⁾ (הלל hithpo.), and as v.l. ₂ * ;] 1. *to bring to, set before,* esp. of food (Hdt., al.). 2. *to take* or *carry away :* c. acc. rei, seq. ἀπό, Mk 14³⁶, Lk 22⁴² ; pass., seq. ὑπό, Ju¹² ; metaph., pass., c. dat., He 13⁹.†

παρα-φρονέω (< παρά, φρήν), [in LXX : Za 7¹¹ (סרר) * ;] *to be beside oneself, be deranged :* II Co 11²³.†

*† παρα-φρονία, -ας, ἡ, = cl. παραφροσύνη, *madness :* II Pe 2¹⁶.†

* παρα-χειμάζω, *to winter at a* place : seq. εἰς, Ac 27¹² ; ἐν, ib. 28¹¹ ; πρὸς ὑμᾶς, I Co 16⁶ ; ἐκεῖ, Tit 3¹².†

*† παρα-χειμασία, -ας, ἡ (< παρα-χειμάζω), a wintering : Ac 27¹²
(Polyb., al.).†

παραχρῆμα, adv. (= παρὰ τὸ χρῆμα), [in LXX : . Nu 6⁹ 12⁴, Is 29⁵
30¹³ (פִּתְאֹם), etc. ;] on the spot, forthwith, instantly : Mt 21¹⁹, ²⁰, Lk 1⁶⁴,
4³⁹ 5²⁵ 8⁴⁴, ⁴⁷, ⁵⁵ 13¹³ 18⁴³ 19¹¹ 22⁶⁰, Ac 3⁷ 5¹⁰ 12²³ 13¹¹ 16²⁶, ³³ (on the
usage in Mt, Lk, v. Dalman, Words, 28 f.).†

πάρδαλις, -εως, ἡ, [in LXX for נָמֵר, Ca 4⁸, Ho 13⁷, Is 11⁶, al. ;]
a panther, leopard : Re 13².†

παρ-εδρεύω, [in LXX : Pr 1²¹ 8³ *;] to sit constantly beside, attend
constantly (cf. MM, xix) : τ. θυσιαστηρίῳ, 1 Co 9¹³.†

πάρ-ειμι, [in LXX for בּוֹא, etc. ;] 1. to be by, at hand or present ;
(a) of persons : Re 17⁸; παρών (opp. to ἀπών), 1 Co 5³, 11 Co 10², ¹¹
13², ¹⁰ ; seq. ἐπί, c. gen., Ac 24¹⁹ ; ἐνώπιον, Ac 10³³ ; ἐνθάδε, Ac 17⁶ ;
πρός, c. acc. pers., Ac 12²⁰, 11 Co 11⁸, Ga 4¹⁸, ²⁰ ; (b) of things : of time,
ὁ καιρός, Jo 7⁶ ; τ. παρόν, He 12¹¹ ; ἡ ἀλήθεια, 11 Pe 1¹² ; ταῦτα, ib. ⁹ ;
τ. παρόντα, He 13⁵. 2. to have come or arrived (Hdt., Thuc., al. ; v.
Field, Notes, 65) : Lk 13¹, Jo 11²⁸, Ac 10²¹ ; seq. εἰς, Col 1⁶ ; seq. ἐπί,
c. acc. rei, Mt 26⁵⁰ (cf. συν-πάρειμι).†

* **παρ-εισ-άγω**, 1. to lead in by one's side, bring forward, introduce.
2. In late writers, to introduce or bring in secretly : 11 Pe 2¹.†

*† **παρ-είσ-ακτος**, -ον (< παρεισάγω), brought in secretly (as spies or
traitors) : Ga 2⁴.†

* **παρ-εισ-δύω** (also -δύνω), to slip in secretly, steal in : παρεισεδύησαν
(vulgar aor.; pass. for act., Bl., § 19, 2), Ju ⁴ (cf. also MM, xix).†

* **παρ-εισ-έρχομαι**, 1. to come in beside or by the way : Ro 5²⁰. 2.
to come in secretly, steal in : Ga 2⁴.†

* **παρ-εισ-φέρω**, to bring in or supply besides : σπουδὴν π. (late Gk.
for cl. σ. ποιεῖσθαι ; cf. Deiss., BS, 361), 11 Pe 1⁵.†

† **παρ-εκτός, = cl. παρέκ, -έξ, [in Aq.: De 1³⁶ ; Al., Le 23³⁸ *;] 1. as
adv., besides, in addition : τὰ π. (sc. γινόμενα), 11 Co 11²⁸. 2. As prep.
c. gen., except : Mt 5³² 19⁹ (WH, mg., R, mg.), Ac 26²⁹.†

παρ-εμ-βάλλω, [in LXX freq. and chiefly for חָנָה ;] 1. to put in
beside or between, interpose. 2. In late writers (Polyb., al., LXX) as
technical military term ; (a) of soldiers, to draw up in line (freq. in
1 Mac : 2³², al.); (b) of siege works, to cast up : c. acc. et dat., χάρακά
σοι, Lk 19⁴³.†

παρ-εμ-βολή, -ῆς, ἡ (< παρεμβάλλω), [in LXX chiefly for מַחֲנֶה ;]
1. an insertion, interpolation (Æschin.). 2. In the Macedonian
dialect (Rutherford, NPhr., 473), as a military term ; (a) an army in
battle array : He 11³⁴ (cf. Ex 14¹⁹, ²⁰, Jg 4¹⁶, al. ; freq. in Polyb.) ; (b)
a camp (Ex 29¹⁴, al.) : He 13¹¹, ¹³, Re 20⁹ ; (c) barracks, soldiers'
quarters : Ac 21³⁴, ³⁷ 22²⁴ 23¹⁰, ¹⁶, ³² 28¹⁶ (WH, txt., R, om.).†

παρ-εν-οχλέω, -ῶ (cf. ἐνοχλέω), [in LXX for לאה hi. (Mi 6³), etc. ;]
to annoy concerning a matter (παρά) : c. dat. pers., Ac 15¹⁹.†

† **παρ-επί-δημος**, -ον (v.s. ἐπιδημέω), [in LXX : Ge 23⁴, Ps 38 (39)¹²

(תּוֹשָׁב) *;] *sojourning in a strange place;* as subst., ὁ π., *a sojourner, exile:* of Christians, I Pe 1¹; ξένοι καὶ π., He 11¹³; πάροικοι καὶ π., I Pe 2¹¹ (v. Deiss., *BS*, 149).†

παρ-έρχομαι, [in LXX chiefly for עבר;] 1. *to pass, pass by;* (a) of persons : absol., Lk 18³⁷; c. acc. pers., Mk 6⁴⁸; c. acc. loc., Ac 16⁸; seq. διά, c. gen., Mt 8²⁸; (b) of things : τ. ποτήριον, Mt 26³⁹ (ἀπ' ἐμοῦ), ib. ⁴²; of time, Mt 14¹⁵, Mk 14³⁵, Ac 27⁹, I Pe 4³. Metaph., (a) *to pass away, perish :* Mt 5¹⁸ 24³⁴, ³⁵, Mk 13³⁰, ³¹, Lk 16¹⁷ 21³², ³³, II Co 5¹⁷, Ja 1¹⁰, II Pe 3¹⁰; (b) *to pass by, neglect, disregard :* c. acc. rei, Lk 11⁴² 15²⁹. 2. *to come to, arrive :* Lk 12³⁷ 17⁷, Ac 24⁷, R, mg. (cf. ἀντι-παρέρχομαι).†
SYN. : παραβαίνω.

*πάρεσις, -εως, ἡ (< παρίημι), 1. *a letting go, dismissal.* 2. *prætermission, passing by* (of debt or sin) : Ro 3²⁵.†
SYN.: ἄφεσις, q.v.

παρ-έχω, [in LXX : Ps 29 (30)⁷ (עמד hi.), etc.;] I. Act., 1. *to furnish, provide, supply;* with ref. to incorporeal things, *to afford, show, give, cause :* c. acc., Ac 22², I Ti 1⁴; c. acc. et dat., Mt 26¹⁰, Mk 14⁶, Lk 11⁷ 18⁵, Ac 16¹⁶ 17³¹ 28², Ga 6¹⁷, I Ti 6¹⁷. 2. *to present, offer :* c. acc. et dat., Lk 6²⁹; c. pron. reflex. et acc. pred., *to show* or *present oneself* (v. infr., and cf. Bl., § 55, 1). II. Mid., 1. *to supply, furnish* or *display of one's own part :* c. acc. et dat., Lk 7⁴, Ac 19²⁴, Col 4¹. 2. In late writers, c. pron. reflex. et acc. pred. (= act. ut supr.), *to show* or *present oneself* (Xen., FlJ, al.; cf. M, *Pr.*, 248; Deiss., *BS*, 254) : Tit 2⁷.†

** παρηγορία, -ας, ἡ (< παρηγορέω, *to address, exhort, console*), [in LXX : IV Mac 5¹² 6¹ *;] 1. *an address, exhortation* (LXX, ll. c.). 2. *comfort, consolation :* Col 4¹¹.†

παρθενία, -ας, ἡ (< παρθένος), [in LXX : Je 3⁴ (נְעוּרִים), Si 15² 42¹⁰, IV Mac 18⁸ *;] *virginity :* Lk 2³⁶.†

παρθένος, -ου, ἡ, [in LXX chiefly for בְּתוּלָה, Ex 22¹⁶(¹⁵), Jb 31¹, Is 23⁴, al.; also for נַעַר נַעֲרָה, Ge 24¹⁴, ¹⁶, ⁵⁵ 34³, and for עַלְמָה, Ge 24⁴³, Is 7¹⁴;] *a maiden, virgin :* Mt 1²³ (LXX) 25¹, ⁷, ¹¹, Lk 1²⁷, Ac 21⁹, I Co 7²⁵ ff·, II Co 11²; masc., of chaste persons (*CIG*, 8784 b) : Re 14⁴.†

Πάρθος, -ου, ὁ, *a Parthian :* Ac 2⁹.†

παρ-ίημι, [in LXX : Je 4³¹ (פָּרַשׂ pi.), etc.;] 1. *to pass by* or *over, let alone, disregard :* Lk 11⁴². 2. *to relax, loosen;* pass., *to be relaxed, weakened, exhausted :* παρειμένας χεῖρας, He 12¹² (LXX ἀνειμ-).†

παρ-ιστάνω, v.s. παρίστημι.

παρ-ίστημι, [in LXX for עמד, etc.;] I. Trans. in pres., impf., fut., 1 aor.; 1. *to place beside, present, provide :* c. acc., Ac 9⁴¹ 23²⁴, II Co 4¹⁴, Col 1²⁸; c. acc. et dat., Mt 26⁵³, Lk 2²², Ac 1³ 23³³, I Co 8⁸; seq. acc. pred., Ro 6¹³, ¹⁶ (late pres., παριστάνετε), ib. ¹⁹ 12¹, II Co 11², Eph 5²⁷, Col 1²², II Ti 2¹⁵. 2. *to present to the mind* (cl.) : by argument, *to prove* (Xen., FlJ, al.), c. acc., Ac 24¹³. II. Intrans. in pf., plpf., 2 aor.; 1. *to stand by* or *beside one*: c. dat. pers., Ac 1¹⁰ 9³⁹ 23² 27⁷ ³; ptcp., Mk 14⁴⁷, ⁶⁹, ⁷⁰ 15³⁵, ³⁹, Jo 18²² 19²⁶. 2. *to appear*: c. nom. pred., seq. ἐνώπιον, Ac 4¹⁰; c. dat. pers., Ac 27²⁴; so fut. mid. (cf. LS, s.v., B, ii, 2), Ro 14¹⁰. 3. *to be at hand, be present, have come*: Ac 4²⁶ (LXX); of servants in attendance, ἐνώπιον τ. θεοῦ, Lk 1¹⁹; absol., οἱ παρεστῶτες, Lk 19²⁴; seq. αὐτῷ, Ac 23², ⁴; of time, Mk 4²⁹. 4. *to stand by* for help or defence (Hom., Dem., Xen., al.): c. dat. pers., Ro 16², II Ti 4¹⁷.†

Παρμενᾶς, -ᾶ, ὁ, *Parmenas*: Ac 6⁵.†

πάρ-οδος, -ου, ἡ, [in LXX: Ge 38¹⁴ (דֶּרֶךְ), etc.;] *a passing* or *passage*: ἐν π., *in passing*, I Co 16⁷.†

παρ-οικέω, -ῶ, [in LXX chiefly for גּוּר, also for יָשַׁב, שָׁכַן;] 1. in cl., *to dwell beside* (c. acc.), *among* (c. dat.) or *near by* (absol.). 2. In late writers, *to dwell* in a place *as a* πάροικος (q.v.) or *stranger*: Lk 24¹⁸, He 11⁹.†

† παρ-οικία, -ας, ἡ (< παροικέω, q.v.), [in LXX: II Es 8³⁵ (גֹּלָה), Ps 33 (34)⁴ 54 (55)¹⁵ 118 (119)⁵⁴ 119 (120)⁵, La 2²² (מָגוֹר) and cogn. forms), Hb 3¹⁶, I Es 5⁷, Jth 5⁹, Wi 19¹⁰, Si prol.²⁶ 16⁸ 41⁵ 44⁶, III Mac 6³⁶ 7¹⁹ *;] *a sojourning*: Ac 13¹⁷, I Pe 1¹⁷.†

πάρ-οικος, -ον, [in LXX chiefly for גֵּר, תּוֹשָׁב;] 1. in cl. Attic, *dwelling near, neighbouring*; as subst., *a neighbour*. 2. In late writers (LXX, Philo) and in Inscr. (Deiss., *BS*, 227 f.; Kennedy, *Sources*, 102), *foreign, alien*; as subst., *an alien, a sojourner*: Ac 7⁶ (LXX), ²⁹; metaph., ξένοι καὶ π. (opp. to συμπολίτης), Eph 2¹⁹; π. καὶ παρεπιδήμους (q.v.), I Pe 2¹¹ (v. Lft. on *Clem. Rom., I Co.*, § 1).†

παροιμία, -ας, ἡ (< πάροιμος, *by the way*), [in LXX. Pr tit 1¹ 25¹, (מָשָׁל), subscr., Si 6³⁵ 8⁸ 18²⁹ 39³ 47¹⁷ *;] *a wayside saying* (Hesych.; v. LS, s.v.), *a byword, maxim, proverb*: II Pe 2²². 2. In NT, of figurative discourse (as מָשָׁל, Is 14⁴, al.), *a parable, allegory*: Jo 10⁶ 16²⁵, ²⁹ (v. Abbott, *Essays*, 82 ff.).†

SYN.: παραβολή, q.v.

*† πάρ-οινος, -ον, = cl., παροινικός (παρά, οἶνος), *given to wine, drunken*: I Ti 3³, Tit 1⁷.†

* παρ-οίχομαι, *to have passed by*; of time, *to be gone by*: ἐν τ. παρῳχημέναις γενεαῖς, Ac 14¹⁶.†

*† παρ-ομοιάζω, *to be like*: c. dat., Mt 23²⁷.†

* παρ-όμοιος, -ον (also -η (Hdt.), -α (Arist.), -ον), *much like, like*: Mk 7¹³.†

παρ-οξύνω, [in LXX for נָאַץ, קָצַף, רָנַז, etc.;] 1. primarily, but never so in cl., *to sharpen* (μάχαιραν, De 32⁴¹, שָׁנַן). 2. Metaph., as always in cl., (*a*) *to spur on, stimulate* (Arist., Xen., al.); (*b*) *to provoke, rouse to anger* (De 9⁷, ¹⁸, Ps 105 (106)²⁹, al.): pass., Ac 17¹⁶, I Co 13⁵.†

παροξυσμός, -οῦ, ὁ (< παροξύνω), [in LXX : De 29 (28) 27, Je 39 (32)37 (קֶצֶף) *;] 1. *stimulation, provocation : π. ἀγάπης*, He 10¹⁴. 2. *irritation :* Ac 15³⁹.†

παρ-οργίζω, [in LXX chiefly for כַּעַם hi.;] (in cl., passive only), *to provoke to anger :* Ro 10¹⁹ (LXX), Eph 6⁴.†

† παρ-οργισμός, -οῦ, ὁ (< παροργίζω), [in LXX : III Ki 15³⁰, IV Ki 23²⁶ (כַּעַם) ; IV Ki 19³, Ne 9¹⁸, ²⁶ (נֶאָצָה)); Je 21⁵ A (קֶצֶף) *;] *irritation* ("distinguished from ὀργή as implying a less permanent state"; *ICC*, *Eph.*, 140; and v. Tr., *Syn.*, § xxxvii) : Eph 4²⁶.†

* παρ-οτρύνω, *to urge on, stir up :* c. acc. pers., Ac 13⁵⁰ (Pind., Hipp., and late writers).†

παρ-ουσία, -ας, ἡ, [in LXX : Ne 2⁶ A, Jth 10¹⁸, II Mac 8¹² 15²¹, III Mac 3¹⁷ *;] 1. usually in cl., *a being present, presence :* I Co 16¹⁷, II Co 10¹⁰ ; opp. to ἀπουσία, Phl 2¹² (cf. II Mac 15²¹). 2. *a coming, arrival, advent* (Soph., Eur., Thuc., al., v. LS, s.v.; so Jth, l.c., II Mac 8¹²) : II Co 7⁶, ⁷, Phl 1²⁶, II Th 2⁹ ; in late writers (v. M, *Th.*, 145 ff.; MM, xix; *LAE*, 372 ff.) as technical term for the visit of a king; hence, in NT, specif. of the *Advent* or *Parousia* of Christ : Mt 24³, ²⁷, ³⁷, ³⁹, I Co 15²³, I Th 2¹⁹ 3¹³ 4¹⁵ 5²³, II Th 2¹, ⁸, Ja 5⁷, ⁸, II Pe 1¹⁶ 3⁴, ¹², I Jo 2²⁸.†

* παρ-οψίς, -ίδος, ἡ (< παρά, ὄψον ; v.s. ὀψάριον), 1. *a side-dish of dainties* (Xen., al.). 2. In Comic poets and late prose, *the dish* itself on which the dainties are served : Mt 23²⁵, ²⁶. (In this sense it is condemned by the Atticists ; v. Rutherford, *NPhr.*, 265 f.)†

παρρησία, -ας, ἡ (< πᾶς + ῥῆσις, speech), [in LXX : Le 26¹³ (μετὰ π., קוֹמְמִיּוּת), Pr 1²⁰ 10¹⁰, Wi 5¹, al.;] 1. *freedom of speech, plainness, openness, freedom* in speaking (Eur., Plat., al.) : Ac 4¹³, II Co 3¹² ; παρρησία, adverbially, *freely, openly, plainly*, Mk 8³², Jo 7¹³, ²⁶ 10²⁴ 11¹⁴ 16²⁹ 18²⁰ ; opp. to ἐν παροιμίαις, Jo 16²⁵ ; ἐν π., Eph 6¹⁹ ; μετὰ π., Ac 2²⁹ 4²⁹, ³¹ 28³¹. 2. In LXX (I Mac 4¹⁸, Wi 5¹, al.), FlJ, and NT, also (from the absence of fear which accompanies freedom of speech), *confidence, boldness :* II Co 7⁴, Phl 1²⁰, I Ti 3¹³ ; ἔχειν π., Eph 3¹², Phm ⁸, He 3⁶ 10¹⁹, ³⁵, I Jo 2²⁸ 3²¹ 4¹⁷ 5¹⁴ ; μετὰ π., He 4¹⁶ ; ἐν π., Col 2¹⁵ ; id. (as בְּפַרְהֶסְיָא in Rabbinic lit.; v. Westc., *Jo.*, i, 262), *in public*, Jo 7⁴ and (without ἐν) 11⁵⁴.†

παρρησιάζομαι (< παρρησία), [in LXX : Jb 22²⁶ (עָנַג hithp.), Ps 11 (12)⁵ 93 (94)¹, Pr 20⁹, Ca 8¹⁰, Si 6¹¹ *;] *to speak freely* or *boldly, be bold in speech :* Ac 9²⁷, ²⁹ 13⁴⁶ 14³ 18²⁶ 19⁸ 26²⁶, Eph 6²⁰, I Th 2².†

πᾶς, πᾶσα, πᾶν, gen., παντός, πάσης, παντός, [in LXX chiefly for כֹּל ;] *all, every.*

I. As adj., 1. c. subst. anarth., *all, every, of every kind :* Mt 3¹⁰ 4²³, Mk 9⁴⁹, Lk 4³⁷ Jo 2¹⁰, Ac 27²⁰, Ro 7⁸, Re 18¹⁷, al. mult.; pl., *all*, Ac 22¹⁵, Ro 5¹², He 1⁶, al.; of the highest degree, π. ἐξουσία (προθυμία, χαρά), Mt 28¹⁸, Ac 17¹¹, Phl 2²⁹, al.; also *the whole* (though in this sense more freq. c. art.), Mt 2³, Ac 2³⁶, Ro 11²⁶. 2. C. art.

(before the art., after the noun, or, denoting totality, between the art. and noun), *all, whole*: Mt 8³² 13², Mk 5³³, Lk 1¹⁰, Ac 7¹⁴, Ro 3¹⁹, Ga 5¹⁴, Eph 4¹⁶, al.; pl., Mt 2⁴, Mk 4¹³, Ro 1⁵, al. II. As pron., 1. masc. and fem., *every one*: Mk 9⁴⁹, Lk 16¹⁶, He 2⁹; seq. rel. pron., Mt 7²⁴, Ac 2²¹, Ga 3¹⁰, al.; c. ptcp. (anarth.), Mt 13¹⁹, Lk 11⁴; c. ptcp. (c. art.), Mt 5²², Mk 7⁸, Lk 6⁴⁷, Jo 3⁸, Ro 1¹⁶, al.; pl., πάντες, absol., *all, all men*, Mt 10²², Mk 13¹³, Lk 20³⁸, Jo 1⁷ 3²⁶, I Co 8¹, al.; οἱ π. (collectively, as a definite whole), Ro 11³², I Co 10¹⁷, Eph 4¹³, al.; π. οἱ (ὅσοι), Mt 4²⁴, Mk 1³², Lk 4⁴⁰, al. 2. Neut., (*a*) sing., πᾶν, *everything, all*: πᾶν τό, c. ptcp., I Co 10²⁵,²⁷, Eph 5¹³, I Jo 2¹⁶ 5⁴ (sc. ὄν); πᾶν ὅ, Jo 17², Ro 14²³; collectively, of persons (Westc., in l.), Jo 6³⁷,³⁹; c. prep., in adverbial phrases, διὰ παντός, *always*, Mt 18¹⁰, al.; ἐν παντί, *in everything, in every way*, II Co 4⁸, Phl 4⁶, al.; (*b*) pl., πάντα, *all things*: absol., Jo 1³, I Co 2¹⁰, He 2⁸, al.; of certain specified things, Mk 4³⁴, Lk 1³, Ro 8²⁸, I Th 5²¹, al.; acc., πάντα, adverbially, *wholly, in all things, in all respects*, Ac 20³⁵, I Co 9²⁵, al.; c. art., τὰ π., *all things* (a totality, as distinct from anarth. πάντα, all things severally; cf. Westc., *Eph.*, 186 f.), absol.: Ro 11³⁶, I Co 8⁶, Eph 3⁹, He 1³, al.; relatively, Mk 4¹¹, Ac 17²⁵, Ro 8³², al.; πάντα τά, c. ptcp., Mt 18³¹, al.; πάντα ταῦτα (ταῦτα π.), Mt 6³²,³³, al.; πάντα, c. prep. in adverbial phrases, πρὸ πάντων, *above all things*, Ja 5¹², I Pe 4⁸; ἐν π., *in all things, in all ways*, I Ti 3¹¹, I Pe 4¹¹, al.; κατὰ πάντα, *in all respects*, Ac 17²², al. 3. C. neg., πᾶς οὐ (μή) = οὐδείς, v.s. οὐ and μή, and cf. M, *Pr.*, 245 f., M, *Gr.*, II, pp. 433 f.

† πάσχα, τό, indecl. (Aram. פַּסְחָא), [in LXX for פֶּסַח;] 1. the festival of *the Passover*: Mt 26², Mk 14¹, Lk 22¹, Jo 2¹³,²³ 6⁴ 11⁵⁵ 12¹ 18³⁹ 19¹⁴, Ac 12⁴, He 11²⁸; ἡ ἑορτὴ τοῦ π., Lk 2⁴¹, Jo 13¹. 2. By meton., (*a*) *the paschal supper*: ἑτοιμάζειν τὸ π., Mt 26¹⁹, Mk 14¹⁶, Lk 22⁸,¹³; ποιεῖν τὸ π., Mt 26¹⁸; (*b*) *the paschal lamb*: θύειν τὸ π. (Ex 12²¹), Mk 14¹², Lk 22⁷; of Christ, I Co 5⁷; φαγεῖν τὸ π. (lamb or supper), Mt 26¹⁷, Mk 14¹²,¹⁴, Lk 22¹¹,¹⁵, Jo 18²⁸ (cf. II Ch 30¹⁷).†

πάσχω, [in LXX: Am 6⁶ (חלה ni.), Wi 12²⁷, Si 38¹⁶, al.;] *to suffer, be acted on*, as opp. to acting, often limited by a word expressive of good or evil; (*a*) of misfortunes (most freq. without any limiting word): absol., Lk 22¹⁵ 24⁴⁶, Ac 1³ 3¹⁸ 17³, I Co 12²⁶, He 2¹⁸ 9²⁶ 13¹², I Pe 2¹⁹,²⁰,²³ 3¹⁷ 4¹⁵,¹⁹; seq. ὑπό, c. gen., Mt 17¹²; ὑπέρ, Ac 9¹⁶, Phl 1²⁹, II Th 1⁵, I Pe 2²¹; c. dat. ref., I Pe 4¹; περί, c. gen. (seq. ὑπέρ), I Pe 3¹⁸; διά, c. acc., I Pe 3¹⁴; ὀλίγον (*a little while*), I Pe 5¹⁰; c. acc., Mt 27¹⁹, Mk 9¹², Lk 13² 24²⁶, Ac 28⁵, II Ti 1¹², He 5⁸, Re 2¹⁰; παθήματα, II Co 1⁶; ταῦτα, Ga 3⁴ (EV; cf. Lft., in l., but v. infr.); acc. seq. ἀπό, Mt 16²¹, Lk 9²² 17²⁵; ὑπό, Mk 5²⁶, I Th 2¹⁴; (*b*) of pleasant experiences (but always with qualifying word, εὖ or acc. rei): Ga 3⁴ (cf. Grimm-Thayer, s.v.; *Interp. Com.*, in l., but v. supr.) (cf. προ-, συν-πάσχω).†

Πάταρα, -ων, τά, *Patara*, a maritime city of Lycia: Ac 21¹.†

πατάσσω, [in LXX chiefly and very freq. for נכה hi., also for נגף, etc.;] 1. in Hom., intrans., *to beat* (of the heart). 2. Trans. = πλήσσω, *to strike, smite*: absol., ἐν μαχαίρᾳ, Lk 22⁴⁹; c. acc. pers., Mt 26⁵¹,

Lk 22⁵⁰; c. acc. rei, Ac 12⁷; of a deadly blow, Mt 26³¹, Mk 14²⁷, Ac 7²⁴. Metaph., of disease : Ac 12²³, Re 11⁶ 19¹⁵.†

πατέω, -ῶ, [in LXX for דָּרַךְ, etc.;] 1. intrans., *to tread, walk :* seq. ἐπάνω ὄφεων κ.τ.λ. (fig.), Lk 10¹⁹ (cf. Ps 90 (91)¹³). 2. Tians., *to tread on, trample :* τ. ληνόν, Re 14²⁰ 19¹⁵ (cf. Jg 9²⁷, La 1¹⁵, al.) ; of the desecration of Jerusalem by its enemies, Lk 21²⁴, Re 11² (cf. κατα-, περι-, ἐν-περι-πατέω).†

πατήρ, πατρός, -τρί, -τέρα, [in LXX chiefly and very freq. for אָב;] *a father;* 1. prop., (*a*) of the male parent: Mt 2²², Lk 1¹⁷, Jo 4⁵³; anarth., He 12⁷ (M, *Pr.*, 82 f.); pl., of both parents (cl.), He 11²³; οἱ π.τ. σαρκός, He 12⁹; (*b*) of a forefather or ancestor (in cl. usually in pl. ; Hom., al.) : Mt 3⁹, Lk 1⁷³, Jo 8³⁹, al.; pl., Mt 23³⁰, ³², Lk 6²³, ²⁶, Jo 4²⁰, I Co 10¹, al. 2. Metaph., (*a*) of an author, originator, or archetype (= αἴτιος, ἀρχηγός, etc.; Pind., Plat., al.): Jo 8⁴¹⁻⁴⁴, Ro 4¹¹, ¹², ¹⁶; (*b*) as a title of respect or honour, used of seniors, teachers and others in a position of responsible authority (Jg 17¹⁰, II Ki 2¹², Pr 1⁸, al.): Mt 23⁹ Ac 7² 22¹, I Jo 2¹³. 3. Of God (as in cl. of Zeus) as Father; (*a*) of created things : τ. φώτων, Ja 1¹⁷; (*b*) of all sentient beings : Eph 3¹⁴, ¹⁵, He 12⁹; (*c*) of men, esp. those in covenant relation with Him (freq in OT and later Jewish lit.; v. Dalman, *Words,* 184 ff.) : Mt 6⁴, Lk 6³⁶, Jo 4²¹, Ja 3⁹, al.; ὁ π. ὁ ἐν (τ.) οὐρανοῖς, Mt 5¹⁶, Mk 11²⁵; ὁ π. ὁ οὐράνιος, Mt 6¹⁴ 15¹³; esp. in the Epp., of Christians : Ro 8¹⁵, II Co 6¹⁸, Ga 4⁶, Eph 2¹⁸ 4⁶, I Jo 2¹; c. gen. qual., τ. οἰκτιρμῶν, II Co 1³; τ. δοξῆς, Eph 1¹⁷; (*d*) of Christ (Dalman, *Words,* 190 ff.); (*a*) by our Lord himself : ὁ π., Mt 11²⁵⁻²⁷, Lk 10²¹, ²², Jo 5²⁰⁻²³, al.; ὁ π. μου, Mt 11²⁷, al.; ὁ ἐν τ. οὐρανοῖς, Mt 7¹¹, al.; ὁ οὐράνιος, Mt 15¹³; vocat., Jo 11⁴¹ 12²⁷, ²⁸ 17¹, ⁵, ¹¹, ²⁰, ²⁵ (cf. Abbott, *JG.,* 96 f.); (*β*) by Apostles : Jo 1¹⁴ (anarth.; v. M, *Pr.*, l.c.), Ro 15⁶, II Co 1³ 11³¹, Eph 1³, Col 1³, He 1⁵, I Pe 1³, Re 1⁶ (cf. Westc., *Epp. Jo.*, 27-34).

Πάτμος, -ου, ἡ, *Patmos,* an island in the Ægean Sea : Re 1⁹.†

πατραλῴας, v.s. πατρολῴας.

πατριά, -ᾶς, ἡ (< πατήρ), [in LXX chiefly for אָב, Ex 6¹⁴, al., also for מִשְׁפָּחָה, Ex 6¹⁵, II Ki 14⁷, Ps 21 (22)²⁷, al.;] 1. *lineage, ancestry* (Hdt.). 2. = πάτρα (more common in cl.), *a family or tribe* (so sometimes in Hdt., in LXX of related people, in a sense narrower than φυλή and wider than οἶκος; v. Ex 12³, Nu 32²⁸): Lk 2⁴; in a wider sense (I Ch 16²⁸, Ps 21 (22)²⁷), Ac 3²⁵ (LXX), Eph 3¹⁵.†

†πατριάρχης, -ου, ὁ (< πατριά, ἄρχω), [in LXX: I Ch 24³¹ (אָב), II Ch 19⁸ 26¹² (רֹאשׁ הָאָבוֹת), I Ch 27¹² (שַׂר), II Ch 23²⁰ (שַׂר־הַמֵּאוֹת), IV Mac 7¹⁹ 16²⁵ *;] *a patriarch :* Ac 2²⁹ 7⁸, ⁹, He 7⁴.†

πατρικός, -ή, -όν (< πατήρ), [in LXX for אָב, Ge 50⁸, al.;] *paternal, ancestral :* Ga 1¹⁴.†

πατρίς, -ίδος, ἡ (< πατήρ), [in LXX chiefly for מוֹלֶדֶת;] prop. poët. fem. of πάτρ.ος, *of one's fathers;* as subst., ἡ π. = πάτρα,

fatherland, country, home, native place : Ac 18²⁷, WH, mg., He 11¹⁴;
of one's own town, Mt 13⁵⁴, ⁵⁷, Mk 6¹, ⁴, Lk 4²³, ²⁴, Jo 4⁴⁴.†
Πατρόβας, -â, ὁ, *Patrobas :* Ro 16¹⁴.†
*πατρολῴας (-αλῴας, Rec.; in cl. -αλοίας, v. Bl., § 3, 3; 6, 2, and
cf. μητρολῴας), -ου, ὁ (< πατήρ + ἀλοιάω, *to smite*), (*a*) *a parricide :*
ι Ti 1⁹ (AV, R, txt.); (*b*) *a smiter of his father :* ib. (R, mg.).†
*†πατρο-παρά-δοτος, -ον (< πατήρ, παραδίδωμι), *handed down from
one's fathers, inherited :* ι Pe 1¹⁸ (Diod., al.).†
πατρῷος, -α, -ον (< πατήρ), [in LXX: Pr 27¹⁰ (אָב), ιι Es 7⁵,
ιι-ιv Mac₁₂*;] *of one's fathers, received from one's fathers :* Ac 22³
24¹⁴ 28¹⁷.†
Παῦλος, -ου, ὁ (Lat. *Paulus*), 1. *Sergius Paulus :* Ac 13⁷. 2. *the
Apostle Paul* (cf. Σαῦλος): Ac 13⁹, and freq. throughout Ac., Ro 1¹,
ι Co 1¹, al., ιι Pe 3¹⁵.
παύω, [in LXX for כלה pi., etc.;] *to make to cease, restrain,
hinder :* c. acc. rei, seq. ἀπό, ι Pe 3¹⁰ (LXX). Mid., *to cease, leave off :*
Lk 8²⁴ 11¹, Ac 20¹, ι Co 13⁸; c. ptcp., Lk 5⁴, Ac 5⁴² 6¹³ 13¹⁰ 20³¹ 21³²,
Eph 1¹⁶, Col 1⁹, He 10²; c. gen., ἁμαρτίας, ι Pe 4¹ (WH, mg., R, txt.);
c. dat., ib. (WH, txt., R, mg.).†
Πάφος, -ου, ἡ, *Paphos*, a city in Cyprus : Ac 13⁶, ¹³.†
παχύνω (< παχύς, *thick*), [in LXX: De 32¹⁵, Is 6¹⁰ (שָׁמֵן), al.;]
to thicken, fatten ; pass., *to grow fat.* Metaph., *to make dull* or *stupid*
(τ. ψυχάς, Plut.); pass., *to wax gross :* ἡ καρδία, Mt 13¹⁵, Ac 28²⁷ (LXX).†
πέδη, -ης, ἡ (< πέζα, *the instep*), [in LXX for נְחֹשֶׁת, etc.;]
a fetter : Mk 5⁴, Lk 8²⁹.†
πεδινός, -ή, -όν (< πεδίον, *a plain*), [in LXX chiefly for הַשְּׁפֵלָה
(ἡ π.);] *level, plain :* Lk 6¹⁷.†
*πεζεύω (< πεζός), *to travel on foot* or *by land :* Ac 20¹³.†
πεζῇ, v.s. πεζός.
πεζός, -ή, -όν (< πούς), [in LXX for רַגְלִי;] 1. *on foot :* Mt 14¹³
(WH, mg., R, txt.). 2. Opp. to going by sea, *by land :* Mt 14¹³
(WH, mg., R, mg.). 3. As adv., πεζῇ (sc. ὁδῷ), *on foot* or *by land :*
Mt 14¹³ (WH, txt.), Mk 6³³.†
πειθαρχέω, -ῶ (< πείθομαι, ἀρχή), [in LXX: Da LXX 7²⁷ (שְׁמַע),
Si 30³⁸ (33²⁸), ι Es 8⁹⁴ *;] *to obey one in authority, obey authority, be
obedient :* Tit 3¹; c. dat., Ac 27²¹; θεῷ, Ac 5²⁹, ³².†
*†πειθός (πιθός, WH), -ή, -όν (< πείθω), = cl. πιθανός, *persuasive :*
ι Co 2⁴ (not found elsewhere).†
*Πειθώ, -οῦς, ἡ, 1. *Peitho, Persuasion* (as a goddess). 2. *persuasion :* ἐν πειθοῖ (so Orig., Eus. and some cursives in ι Co 2⁴ for
πειθός, q.v.).†
πείθω, [in LXX chiefly for בטח, its parts and derivatives;]
(i) Active; 1. trans., *to apply persuasion* ("conative" in pres.; v. M,
Pr., 147), *to prevail upon* or *win over, persuade :* absol., Mt 28¹⁴,

Ac 19²⁶; seq. περί, c. gen. rei, Ac 19⁸; c. acc. pers., Ac 12²⁰ 14¹⁹ 18⁴, II Co 5¹¹, Ga 1¹⁰; τ. καρδίας ἡμῶν, I Jo 3¹⁹; c. acc. seq. περί, Ac 28²³; c. acc. et inf., Ac 13⁴³ 26²⁸ (v. Field, *Notes*, 141 ff.); c. acc. seq. ἵνα (Plut.), Mt 27²⁰. 2. Intrans., 2 pf. πέποιθα with pres. sense (v. M, *Pr.*, 147, 154; Bl., § 59, 2): *to trust, be confident, have confidence:* c. acc. et inf., Ro 2¹⁹; c. acc. ref. (v. Ellic., in l.): Phl 1⁶, ²⁵; c. dat., Phl 1¹⁴, Phm²¹; ἑαυτῷ, c. inf., II Co 10⁷; seq. ἐν, Phl 3³, ⁴; ἐν κυρίῳ ὅτι, Phl 2²⁴; ἐπί, c. dat., Mt 27⁴³ (WH, mg.), Mk 10²⁴ (T, WH, R, mg., om.), Lk 11²² 18⁹, II Co 1⁹, He 2¹³; ἐπί, c. acc., Mt 27⁴³ (c. dat., WH, mg.); id. seq. ὅτι, II Co 2³, II Th 3⁴ (v. Lft., *Notes*, 127); εἰς, c. acc. pers. seq. ὅτι, Ga 5¹⁰. (ii) Pass. and mid.; 1. *to be persuaded, believe* (v. M, *Pr.*, 158): absol., Lk 16³¹, Ac 17⁴ 21¹⁴, He 13¹⁸; c. dat., Ac 28²⁴; c. acc. et inf., Ac 26²⁶; so also pf., πέπεισμαι, πεπεισμένος εἰμί: c. acc. ref. seq. περί, He 6⁹; c. acc. et inf., Lk 20⁶; ὅτι, Ro 8³⁸, II Ti 1⁵, ¹²; id. c. ἐν κυρίῳ, Ro 14¹⁴; περί, c. gen. seq. ὅτι, Ro 15¹⁴. 2. *to listen to, obey:* c. dat. pers., Ac 5³⁶, ³⁷, ⁴⁰ 23²¹ 27¹¹, Ro 2⁸, Ga 5⁷, He 13¹⁷, Ja 3³ (cf. ἀνα-πείθω).†

Πειλᾶτος (Rec. Πιλάτος, Tr., -ᾶτος, v. WH, *App.*, 155), -ου, ὁ, *Pontius Pilate:* Mt 27², Mk 15¹, Lk 3¹, Jo 18²⁹, Ac 3¹³, I Ti 6¹³, al

πεῖν = πιεῖν, v.s. πίνω.

πεινάω, -ῶ, [in LXX chiefly for רָעֵב;] *to hunger, be hungry:* Mt 4² 12¹, ³ 21¹⁸ 25³⁵, ³⁷, ⁴², ⁴⁴, Mk 2²⁵ 11¹², Lk 1⁵³ 4² 6³, Ro 12²⁰ (LXX), I Co 4¹¹ 11²¹, ³⁴, Phl 4¹², Re 7¹⁶; metaph., Mt 5⁶, Lk 6²¹, ²⁵, Jo 6³⁵.†

πεῖρα, -ας, ἡ (< πειράω), [in LXX: De 28⁵⁶ (π. λαμβάνειν, נסה pi.) 33⁸ (מַסָּה), Wi 18²⁰, ²⁵, II Mac 8⁹, IV Mac 8¹*;] *a trial, experiment;* π. λαμβάνειν, *to make trial, have experience of:* He 11²⁹, ³⁶ (for exx., v. Field, *Notes*, 232 f.).†

πειράζω, poët. and late prose form of πειράω, q.v., [in LXX for נסה pi.;] 1. *to make proof of* (Hom.). 2. *to try, attempt* (Luc., Polyb., al.): c. inf. (v. M, *Pr.*, 205; Bl., § 69, 4), Ac 9²⁶ 16⁷ 24⁶. 3. In LXX and NT, like Heb. נסה, c. acc. pers., *to test, try, prove;* (a) in a good sense: Jo 6⁶, II Co 13⁵, He 11¹⁷, Re 2²; esp. of trials and afflictions sent or permitted by God (Ge 22¹, Ex 20²⁰, Wi 3⁵, al.), I Co 10¹³, He 2¹⁸ 4¹⁵ 11¹⁷, ³⁷, Re 3¹⁰; (b) in a bad sense (Apoll. Rhod., 3, 10): of the attempts made to ensnare Jesus in his speech, Mt 16¹ 19³ 22¹⁸, ³⁵, Mk 8¹¹ 10² 12¹⁵, Lk 11¹⁶, Jo 8 [6]; of temptation to sin, *to tempt,* Ja 1¹³, ¹⁴ (v. Hort, in l.), Ga 6¹, Re 2¹⁰; esp. of temptations of the devil, Mt 4¹, ³, Mk 1¹³, Lk 4², I Co 7⁵, I Th 3⁵; ὁ πειράζων, *the tempter,* Mt 4³, I Th 3⁵; (c) in bad sense also (Ex 17², ⁷, Nu 14²², al.), of distrustful testing, trying or challenging of God: Ac 15¹⁰, I Co 10⁹ (WH, mg., ἐξεπείρασαν), He 3⁹; τ. πνεῦμα Κυρίου, Ac 5⁹ (cf. ἐκ-πειράζω).†

SYN.: δοκιμάζω, q.v.

†πειρασμός, -οῦ, ὁ (< πειράζω), [in LXX for מַסָּה, עִנְיָן;] 1. = πεῖρα, *an experiment* (Diosc.). 2. *a trial,* of ethical purpose and effect, whether good or evil (v. Hort on Ja 1¹³) (a) in good or neutral sense: Ga 4¹⁴, Ja 1¹², I Pe 4¹²; esp. of afflictions sent by God

(De 7¹⁹, Si 2¹, al.) : 11 Pe 2⁹, Re 3¹⁰ ; pl., Lk 22²⁸, Ac 20¹⁹, Ja 1², 1 Pe 1⁶ ; (b) of trial regarded as leading to sin, *temptation* : Lk 8¹³, 1 Co 10¹³, 1 Ti 6⁹ ; of the temptation of Jesus by the devil, Lk 4¹³ ; εἰσφέρειν (ἔρχεσθαι, εἰσέρχ-) εἰς π., Mt 6¹³ 26⁴¹, Mk 14³⁸, Lk 11⁴ 22⁴⁰·⁴⁶ ; (c) of the testing or challenge of God by man (v.s. πειράζω, 3, c.) : He 3⁸ (LXX : Ps 94 (95)⁹, where κατὰ τ. ἡμέραν πειρασμοῦ = בְּיוֹם מַסָּה, as the day of Massah).†

SYN. : δοκίμιον.

πειράω, more commonly as depon., πειράομαι, [in LXX for נסה ;] to try, attempt : Ac 26²¹.†

*† πεισμονή, -ῆς, ἡ (< πείθω), persuasion : Ga 5⁸.†

** πέλαγος, -ους, τό, [in LXX : 11 Mac 5²¹, 1v Mac 7¹*;] the deep sea, the deep, the sea : Ac 27⁵ ; τὸ π. τῆς θαλάσσης, Mt 18⁶.†

SYN. : θαλάσσα (q.v.) ; and cf. ἄβυσσος.

*† πελεκίζω (< πέλεκυς, a battle-axe), to cut off with an axe, esp. to behead : c. acc., Re 20⁴ (Polyb., al.).†

πέμπτος, -η, -ον, [in LXX for חֲמִישִׁי and cognate forms ;] fifth : Re 6⁹ 9¹ 16¹⁰ 21²⁰.†

πέμπω, [in LXX chiefly for שְׁלֹח ;] to send ; (a) of persons : c. acc., absol., Mt 22⁷, Lk 7¹⁹, Jo 1²², 11 Co 9³, al. ; ptcp. seq. verb., Mt 14¹⁰, Ac 19³¹, al. ; ptcp. seq. διά (= Heb. בְּיֹד, 1 Ki 16²⁰, al.), Mt 11² (cf. Re 1¹) ; of teachers sent by God, Jo 1³³ 4³⁴, Ro 8³, al. ; c. acc. et dat., 1 Co 4¹⁷, Phl 2¹⁹ ; seq. πρός, c. acc., Lk 4²⁶, Jo 16⁷, al. ; seq. λέγων (cf. Heb. שְׁלַח לָאמֹר, Ge 38²⁵, al.), Lk 7⁶·¹⁹ ; seq. εἰς, c. acc. loc., Mt 2⁸, Lk 15¹⁵, al. ; seq. εἰς (of purpose), Eph 6²², Col 4⁸, 1 Pe 2¹⁴ ; c. inf., Jo 1³³, 1 Co 16³, Re 22¹⁶ ; (b) of things : Re 11¹⁰ ; seq. εἰς, Re 1¹¹ ; id., of purpose, Ac 11²⁹, Phl 4¹⁶ ; c. dat. pers., 11 Th 2¹¹ ; π. τ. δρέπανον σου (cf. ἐξαποστείλατε δρέπανα = שִׁלְחוּ מַגָּל, Jl 3 (4)¹³), Re 14¹⁵·¹⁸ (cf. ἀνα-, ἐκ-, μετα-, προ-, συν-πέμπω).

SYN. : ἀποστέλλω, q.v.

πένης, -ητος, ὁ (< πένομαι, to work for one's daily bread), [in LXX for אֶבְיוֹן, עָנִי, דַּל, etc. ;] one who works for his living, a labourer, a poor man : 11 Co 9⁹.†

SYN. : πτωχός, properly a beggar and implying deeper poverty than π. (v. Tr., Syn., § xxxvi ; Abbott, Essays, 78).

πενθερά, -ᾶς, ἡ (fem. of πενθερός), [in LXX for חָמוֹת ;] a mother-in-law : Mt 8¹⁴ 10³⁵, Mk 1³⁰, Lk 4³⁸ 12⁵³.†

πενθερός, -οῦ, ὁ, [in LXX chiefly for חָם, Ge 38¹³, al. ; also for חֹתֵן, Jg 1¹⁶ A ;] a father-in-law : Jo 18¹³.†

πενθέω, -ῶ, [in LXX chiefly for אבל ;] to mourn (for), lament ; (a) intrans. : Mt 5⁴⁽⁵⁾ 9¹⁵, 1 Co 5² ; π. καὶ κλαίειν, Mk16¹⁰, Lk 6²⁵, Ja 4⁹, Re 18¹⁵·¹⁹ ; seq. ἐπί, c. acc., Re 18¹¹ ; (b) trans., c. acc., 11 Co 12²¹.†

SYN. : v.s. θρηνέω.

MANUAL GREEK LEXICON OF THE NEW TESTAMENT 353

πένθος, -ους, τό, [in LXX chiefly for אֵבֶל;] *mourning:* Ja 4⁹, Re 18⁷, ⁸ 21⁴.†

πενιχρός, -ά, -όν (< πένομαι, v.s. πένης), [in LXX: Ex 22²⁵ (עָנִי), Pr 28¹⁵ 29⁷ (רַשׁ) *;] chiefly in Comic poets and late prose (but Plato, Rep., 578 A), = πένης, *needy, poor:* Lk 21² (for ex. in π., v. MM, xix).†

πεντάκις, adv., *five times:* II Co 11²⁴.†

πεντακισ-χίλιοι, -αι, -α, *five thousand:* Mt 14²¹ 16⁹, Mk 6⁴⁴ 8¹⁹, Lk 9¹⁴, Jo 6¹⁰.†

πεντακόσιοι, -αι, -α, *five hundred:* Lk 7⁴¹, I Co 15⁶.†

πέντε, indecl., οἱ, αἱ, τά, *five:* Mt 14¹⁷, al.

πεντε-και-δέκατος, -η, -ον, *the fifteenth:* Lk 3¹.†

πεντήκοντα, indecl., οἱ, αἱ, τά, *fifty:* Lk 7⁴¹ 16⁶, Jo 8⁵⁷ 21¹¹, Ac 13²⁰; ἀνὰ π., Lk 9¹⁴; κατὰ π., Mk 6⁴⁰.†

πεντηκοστή, -ῆς, ἡ, v.s. πεντηκοστός.

πεντηκοστός, -ή, -όν, [in LXX for חֲמִשִּׁים, Le 25¹⁰, ¹¹, IV Ki 15²³, ²⁷; I Mac ₄, II Mac 14⁴; ἡ π., To 2¹, II Mac 12³²*;] *fiftieth.* As subst., ἡ π.; (a) (sc. μερίς), at Athens, a tax of two per cent.; (b) (sc. ἡμέρα, i.e. the fiftieth day after the Passover), *Pentecost,* the second of the three great Jewish feasts (To, II Mac, ll. c.; ἑορτὴ ἑβδομάδων, De 16¹⁰, al.): Ac 2¹ 20¹⁶, I Co 16⁸.†

† πεποίθησις, -εως, ἡ (< πείθω), [in LXX: IV Ki 18¹⁹ (בִּטָּחוֹן) *;] *confidence:* II Co 1¹⁵ 3⁴ 10², Eph 3¹²; seq. εἰς, II Co 8²²; ἐν, Phl 3⁴ (the word is condemned by the Atticists, v. Rutherford, NPhr., 355).†

πέρ (akin to περί), enclitic particle, adding force or positiveness to the word which precedes it: *indeed, by far,* etc. In the NT, it is always affixed to the word to which it relates, v.s. διόπερ, ἐάνπερ, εἴπερ, ἐπείπερ, ἐπειδήπερ, ἥπερ, καθάπερ, καίπερ, ὅσπερ, ὥσπερ.

*περαιτέρω (< πέρα, *beyond*), compar. adv., *beyond:* Ac 19³⁹, L, Tr., WH (T, Rec., R, περὶ ἑτέρων).†

πέραν, adv., [in LXX for עֵבֶר and cognate forms;] *on the other side, across* (usually with the idea of water lying between); (a) as in the older poets, as prep. c. gen.: τ. θαλάσσης, Jo 6¹, ¹⁷, ²², ²⁵; τ. Ἰορδάνου, Mt 4¹⁵ (LXX), ²⁵ 19¹, Mk 3⁸ 10¹, Jo 1²⁸ 3²⁶ 10⁴⁰; τ. χειμάρρου τ. Κέδρων, Jo 18¹; (b) τὸ π., *the region beyond, the other side:* Mt 8¹⁸, ²⁸ 14²² 16⁵, Mk 4³⁵ 5²¹ 6⁴⁵ 8¹³; τ. θαλάσσης, Mk 5¹; τ. λίμνης, Lk 8²².†

πέρας, -ατος, τό (< πέρα, *beyond*), [in LXX chiefly for קֵץ, קָצֶה and cognate forms;] *an end, limit, boundary;* (a) of space: chiefly in pl., τὰ π. τ. γῆς, Mt 12⁴², Lk 11³¹; τ. οἰκουμένης, Ro 10¹⁸ (LXX); (b) (opp. to ἀρχή) *the end:* c. gen., ἀντιλογίας, He 6¹⁶.†

Πέργαμος, -ου, ἡ (so Xen., Paus., al., but -ον, τό in Strabo, Polyb., and most writers, also in Inscr.; in NT the termination is uncertain), *Pergamum,* a city of Mysia: Re 1¹¹ 2¹².†

Πέργη, -ης, ἡ, *Perga,* a city of Pamphylia: Ac 13¹³, ¹⁴ 14²⁵.†

23

περί, prep. c. gen., acc. (in cl. also c. dat.; cf. M, *Pr.*, 105 f.), with radical sense *round about* (as distinct from ἀμφί, *on both sides*). I. C. gen., 1. of place, *about* (poët.). 2. Causal, *about, on account of, concerning, in reference to :* Mt 2⁸, Mk 1⁴⁴, Lk 4³⁸, Jo 16²⁶, Ac 28²¹, al. mult.; τὰ περί, c. gen., *the things concerning* one, one's state or *case :* Mk 5²⁷, Ac 1³ 28¹⁵, Eph 6²², al.; *at the beginning of a sentence*, περί, *regarding, as to*, ι Co 7¹, al.; *in the sense on account of* (Mt 26²⁸, ι Co 1¹³, al.), often with ὑπέρ as variant (cf. M, *Pr.*, 105). II. C. acc., 1. of place, *about, around :* Mt 3⁴, Mk 1⁶, Lk 13⁸, Ac 22⁶, al.; οἱ περί, c. acc. pers., *of one's associates, friends*, etc., Mk 4¹⁰, Lk 22⁴⁹, Jo 11¹⁹, Ac 13¹³; οἱ περὶ τ. τοιαῦτα ἐργάται, Ac 19²⁵; metaph., *about, as to, concerning :* ι Ti 1¹⁹ 6⁴, ιι Ti 2¹⁸ 3⁸, Tit 2⁷; τὰ περὶ ἐμέ, Phl 2²³; αἱ περὶ τ. λοιπὰ ἐπιθυμίαι, Mk 4¹⁹. 2. Of time, in a loose reckoning, *about, near :* Mt 20³, ⁵, ⁶, ⁹ 27⁴⁶, Mk 6⁴⁸, Ac 10³, ⁹ 22⁶. III. In composition : *round about* (περιβάλλω, περίκειμαι), *beyond, over and above* (περιποιέω, περιλείπω), *to excess* (περιεργάζομαι, περισσεύω).

περι-άγω, [in LXX : Am 2¹⁰ (הלך hi.); Is 28²⁷, Ez 47² (סבב hi., ho.); Ez 37² 46²¹ (עבר hi), ιι Mac 4³⁸ 6¹⁰ *;] 1. *to lead about* or *around :* c. acc. pers., ι Co 9⁵. 2. Intrans., *to go about :* Ac 13¹¹; seq. ἐν, Mt 4²³; c. acc. loc. (governed by the περι-, not so in cl., v. Bl., § 34, 1; 53, 1), Mt 9³⁵ 23¹⁵, Mk 6⁶.†

περι-αιρέω, -ῶ, [in LXX chiefly for סור hi.;] *to take away* that which surrounds, *take away, take off* (τείχη, Hdt., Thuc.; χιτῶνα, Plat.; δακτύλιον, Ge 41⁴², cf. σφρηγῖδα, Hdt., ii, 151) : τ. κάλυμμα, pass., ιι Co 3¹⁶ ; as nautical term (RV, *cast off*), ἀγκύρας, Ac 27⁴⁰ ; absol., *to cast loose :* ib. 28¹³. Metaph., *to take away entirely :* ἐλπίς, pass., Ac 27²⁰ ; ἁμαρτίας, He 10¹¹.†

**περι-άπτω, [in LXX : ιιι Mac 3⁷ *;] 1. *to tie about, attach*. 2. In late writers, *to light a fire around, kindle :* πῦρ, Lk 22⁵⁵.†

**†περι-αστράπτω, [in LXX : ιν Mac 4¹⁰ *;] *to flash around :* c. acc., Ac 9³ ; seq. περί, Ac 22⁶ (Eccl. and Byzant.).†

περι-βάλλω, [in LXX chiefly for כסה pi., also for לבש עטה, etc.;] *to throw around* or *over, put on* or *over ; (a)* of siege or defensive works : χάρακά σοι, Lk 19⁴³ (WH, mg.; παρεμβ-, WH, txt.); *(b)* of clothing, *to put on, wrap about, clothe with :* c. acc. rei, Lk 23¹¹; c. acc. pers., Mt 25³⁶, ³⁸, ⁴³ ; c. dupl. acc. (not cl.; Bl., § 34, 4), Jo 19² ; pf. pass., *to have wrapped round* one: c. acc. rei (cl.), Mk 14⁵¹ 16⁵, Re 7⁹, ¹³ 10¹ 11³ 12¹ 17⁴ 18¹⁶ 19¹³ ; c. dat. rei, Re 4⁴ (WH, txt.; seq. ἐν, WH, mg.); fut., seq. ἐν (cf. De 22¹², Ps 44 (45)⁹, ¹³), Re 3⁵. Mid., *to clothe oneself, wrap round* or *put on oneself :* absol., Mt 6²⁹, Lk 12²⁷, Re 3¹⁸ ; c. acc. rei, Mt 6³¹, Ac 12⁸, Re 19⁸.†

περι-βλέπω, [in LXX for שׁוּר, etc.;] *to look around* (*at*). Mid., *to look about* one (*at*) : absol., Mk 9⁸ 10²³ ; c. inf., Mk 5³² ; c. acc. pers., Mk 3⁵, ³⁴, Lk 6¹⁰ ; πάντα, Mk 11¹¹.†

περι-βόλαιον, -ον, τό (< περιβάλλω), [in LXX chiefly for לְבוּשׁ, כְּסוּת and cognate forms;] *that which is thrown around, a covering ;*

in NT, (a) a mantle (Ps 101 (102)²⁷, Is 59¹⁷, al.) : He 1¹² (LXX); (b) a veil : I Co 11¹⁵ (but v. ICC, in l.).†

περι-δέω, [in LXX : Jb 12¹⁶ (אסר) *;] to tie round, bind round : c. acc. et dat., pass., Jo 11⁴⁴.†

** περι-εργάζομαι, [in LXX : Wi 8⁵ א¹, Si 3²³ *;] 1. to waste one's labour about a thing. 2. to be a busybody : II Th 3¹¹ (cf. Plat., Apol., 19 B).†

* περίεργος, -ον, I. of persons; 1. over careful. 2. curious, meddling, a busybody : I Ti 5¹³. II. Of things; 1. over-wrought. 2. superfluous. 3. curious, uncanny ; τὰ π., curious arts, magic : Ac 19¹⁹ (v. Deiss., BS, 323₅.).†

περι-έρχομαι, [in LXX chiefly for סבב;] to go about (as an itinerant) : Ac 19¹³ 28¹³ (περιελόντες, WH, R, mg.), He 11³⁷; τ. οἰκίας, from house to house : I Ti 5¹³.†

περι-έχω, [in LXX for אפף, נקף hi., צפה pi., etc.;] 1. to surround, encompass : Lk 5⁹ (cf. MM, xix). 2. to comprehend, include, contain, esp. of books : c. acc., Ac 23²⁵, Rec.; acc. to a late usage, intrans. (Bl., § 53, 1₃; MM, xix; Hort, in l.), it stands written, I Pe 2⁶.†

περι-ζώννυμι and -ύω (v. Veitch, s.v.), [in LXX chiefly for חגר, also for אזר, etc.;] to gird (c. dupl. acc., as ὁ περιζωννύων με δύναμιν, Ps 17 (18)³²) : pass., αἱ ὀσφύες περιεζωσμέναι, Lk 12³⁵; π. ζώνην χρυσῆν, Re 1¹³ 15⁶ (but v. infr.). Mid., to gird oneself : Lk 12³⁷ 17⁸ (and so perh. Re, ll. c. supr., cf. I Ki 2⁴) ; c. acc. rei (fig.), τ. ὀσφύν, Eph 6¹⁴ (seq. ἐν, cf. I Ch 15²⁷).†

**† περί-θεσις, -εως, ἡ (< περιτίθημι), [in Sm. : Ps 31 (32)⁹ *;] a putting around, putting on : I Pe 3³.†

περι-ίστημι (Rec. -ίστημι), [in LXX : Jos 6³ (סבב), II Ki 13³¹ (נצב ni.), I Ki 4¹⁶, Ep. Je ³⁷, Jth 5²², II Mac 14⁹ *;] 1. to place around. 2. to stand around : Jo 11⁴²; c. acc. pers., Ac 25⁷. Mid. (in late writers), to turn oneself about to avoid, to shun: c. acc. rei, II Ti 2¹⁶, Tit 3⁹.†

† περι-κάθαρμα, -τος, τό (< περικαθαίρω, to purify on all sides or completely, De 18¹⁰, Jos 5⁴, IV Mac 1²⁹ *), [in LXX : Pr 21¹⁸ (כֹּפֶר) *;] 1. a victim, expiation (Pr, l.c). 2. refuse, rubbish : pl., I Co 4¹³ (v. ICC, in l.).†

περι-καθ-ίζω, [in LXX for חנה, לחם ni., etc.;] 1. to invest, besiege (Diod., IV Ki 6²⁴, I Mac 11⁶¹, al.). 2. to sit around : Lk 22⁵⁵, L, txt.†

περι-καλύπτω, [in LXX for כסה pi., שׁבץ pu., etc.;] to cover around, cover up or over . c. acc., Mk 14⁶⁵, Lk 22⁶⁴; pass., seq. χρυσίῳ, He 9⁴.†

** περί-κειμαι, [in LXX : Ep. Je ²⁴, ⁵⁸, IV Mac 12³ *;] 1. to lie round about : μύλος, λίθος (RV, were hanged about), Mk 9⁴², Lk 17²; νέφος μαρτύρων, He 12¹. 2. to have around one, be clothed with : Ac 28²⁰; fig., ἀσθένειαν, He 5².†

† περι-κεφαλαία, -ας, ἡ, [in LXX for כּוֹבַע, קוֹבַע;] a helmet : fig., I Th 5⁸; c. gen. explic., π. τ. σωτηρίου, Eph 6¹⁷ (cf. Is 59¹⁷).†

*† περι-κρατής, -ές, [in LXX: Da TH Su ³⁹ A *;] *having full command of:* Ac 27¹⁶.†

*† περι-κρύβω, v.s. περικρύπτω.

*† περι-κρύπτω, *to conceal entirely, keep hidden:* late 2 aor., περιέκρυβον (but v. Bl., § 17; Soph., *Lex.*, s.v. περικρύβω; M, *Gr.*, II, p. 245, where this word is regarded as prob. impf. of περεκρύβω and not an aor.), Lk 1²⁴.†

περι-κυκλόω, -ῶ, [in LXX chiefly for סבב;] *to encircle, encompass:* of a besieged city, Lk 19⁴³.†

*† περι-λάμπω, *to shine around:* c. acc., Lk 2⁹, Ac 26¹³.†

περι-λείπομαι, depon. mid. and pass., [in LXX: II Ch 34²¹ A (שאר ni.), II Mac 1³¹ 8¹⁴, IV Mac 12⁶ 13¹⁸ *;] *to be left remaining, remain over, survive:* I Th 4¹⁵, ¹⁷.†

περί-λυπος, -ον, [in LXX: Ps 41 (42)⁵, ¹¹, I Es 8⁶⁹, al.;] *very sad, deeply grieved:* Mt 26³⁸, Mk 6²⁶ 14³⁴, Lk 18²³.†

περι-μένω, [in LXX: Ge 49¹⁸ (קוה pi.), Wi 8¹² *;] *to wait for:* c. acc., Ac 1⁴.†

** πέριξ, adv., [in Al.: Le 13³³ *;] *round about:* αἱ π. πολεῖς, Ac 5¹⁶.†

* περι-οικέω, -ῶ, *to dwell round about:* c. acc., Lk 1⁶⁵.†

περί-οικος, -ον, [in LXX for בְּכָר, etc.;] *dwelling around;* as subst., ὁ π., *a neighbour:* Lk 1⁵⁸ (cf. πλησίον).†

† περιούσιος, -ον (< περίειμι, *to be over and above*), [in LXX: Ex 19⁵ 23²², De 7⁶ 14² 26¹⁸ (סְגֻלָּה, עַם) *;] *one's own, of one's own possession:* λαὸς π. (cf. LXX, ll. c.), Tit 2¹⁴.†

περι-οχή, -ῆς, ἡ (< περιέχω), [in LXX for מְצֻדָה, מָצוֹר, etc.;] 1. *compass, circumference.* 2. *a portion circumscribed, a section:* Ac 8³².†

περι-πατέω, -ῶ, [in LXX chiefly for הלך pi., hith.;] *to walk:* absol., Mt 9⁵, Mk 5⁴², Lk 5²³, Jo 1³⁶; c. pred., γυμνός, Re 16¹⁵; ἐπάνω Lk 11⁴⁴; διά, c. gen., Re 21²⁴; ἐν, Mk 11²⁷ 12³⁸, Jo 7¹ 11⁵⁴, Re 2¹, al.; ἐν τ. σκοτίᾳ, fig., Jo 8¹² 12³⁵, I Jo 1⁶, ⁷ 2¹¹; ἐπί, c. gen., Mt 14²⁶; id. c. dat., ib. ²⁵, ²⁹; μετά, Jo 6⁶⁶, Re 3⁴; παρά, c. acc., Mt 4¹⁸. Metaph., of living, passing one's life, conducting oneself (like ἀναστρέφομαι in Xen., Plut., LXX, π.; M, *Pr.*, 11; Deiss., *BS*, 194): ἀκριβῶς, Eph 5¹⁵; ἀτάκτως, II Th 3⁶, ¹¹; εὐσχημόνως, Ro 13¹³, I Th 4¹²; ἀξίως, c. gen., Eph 4¹, Col 1¹⁰, I Th 2¹²; καθώς (ὡς), Eph 4¹⁷ 5⁸, ¹⁵, Phl 3¹⁷, I Th 4¹; οὕτως ὡς, I Co 7¹⁷; seq. nom. qual., Phl 3¹⁸; c. dat., Ac 21²¹, Ro 13¹³, II Co 12¹⁸, Ga 5¹⁶; seq. ἐν, Ro 6⁴, II Co 4² 5⁷ 10³, Eph 2², ¹⁰ 4¹⁷ 5², Col 3⁷ 4⁵, He 13⁹, II Jo ⁴, ⁶, al.; ἐν Χριστῷ, Col 2⁶; κατά, c. acc., Mk 7⁵, Ro 8⁴ 14¹⁵, I Co 3³, II Co 10², II Jo ⁶ (cf. ἐν-περιπατέω).

*† περι-πείρω, *to put on a spit,* hence, *to pierce:* metaph., ἑαυτὸν . . . ὀδύναις, I Ti 6¹⁰.†

περι-πίπτω, [in LXX: Ru 2³, II Ki 1⁶ (קרה), Pr 11⁵ (נפל), Da LXX 2⁹, II Mac 6¹³ 9⁷, ²¹ 10⁴ *;] 1. *to fall around.* 2. *to fall in with, light upon, come across:* c. dat., λῃσταῖς, Lk 10³⁰; πειρασμοῖς, Ja 1²; seq. εἰς, Ac 27⁴¹.†

περι-ποιέω, -ῶ, [in LXX for חיה pi., hi., etc.;] *to make to remain over, preserve.* Mid., (a) *to keep* or *save for* oneself: τ. ψυχήν (cf.

Xen., *Cyr.*, iv, 4, 10; Arist., *Pol.*, v, 11, 30), Lk 17³³; (*b*) *to get or gain for oneself, get possession of* (Thuc., Xen., al.): Ac 20²⁸, ı Ti 3¹³.†

† περι-ποίησις, -εως, ἡ (< περιποιέω), [in LXX: ıı Ch 4¹³ ⁽¹²⁾ (מְחִיָה), Ma 3¹⁷ (סְגֻלָּה), Hg 2¹⁰ ⁽⁹⁾ *;] 1. *preservation:* He 10³⁹ (ıı Ch, l.c.). 2. *acquisition, obtaining:* ı Th 5⁹, ıı Th 2¹⁴ (and so perh. Eph 1¹⁴, v. infr.). 3. *a possession:* Eph 1¹⁴ (but v. supr., and cf. *ICC*, in l.), ı Pe 2⁹ ⁽ᴸˣˣ⁾.†

περι-ραίνω (-ρραίνω, Rec., v. WH, *App.*, 139 f.), [in LXX for נזה hi.;] *to sprinkle around:* Re 19¹³ T (ῥεραντισμένον, WH; ῥε-, R, txt.; βεβαμμένον, Rec., R, mg.).†

** περι-ρήγνυμι (Rec. -ρρ-, v. supr.), [in LXX: ıı Mac 4³⁸ *;] *to break or tear off all around:* freq. of garments, τ. ἱμάτια, Ac 16²².†

περι-σπάω, -ῶ, [in LXX chiefly for ענה;] *to draw around, draw off or away.* Metaph., *to distract:* pass., Lk 10⁴⁰.†

† περισσεία, -ας, ἡ (< περισσεύω), [in LXX: Ec₁₂ (יִתְרוֹן) and cogn. forms, 1³, al.) *;] 1. *abundance, superfluity:* Ro 5¹⁷, ıı Co 8² 10¹⁵, Ja 1²¹ (so also Inscr., v. *LAE*, 80). 2. (*a*) *superiority* (Ec, v. supr.); (*b*) *profit* (ib.).†

† περίσσευμα, -τος, τό (< περισσεύω), [in LXX: Ec 2¹⁵ *;] *that which is over and above, superfluity, abundance:* opp. to ὑστέρημα (q.v.), ıı Co 8¹³,¹⁴; pl., Mk 8⁸; metaph., π. τ. καρδίας, Mt 12³⁴, Lk 6⁴⁵ (cf. Ec, l.c.; Plut., al.).†

περισσεύω (< περισσός), [in LXX: ı Ki 2³³ (מַרְבִּית), ib. ³⁶, Ec 3¹⁹ (יתר) ni., (יוֹתֵר), To 4¹⁶, Si 10²⁷ 11¹² 19²⁴ 30³⁸ (33²⁹), ı Mac 3³⁰ *;] I. Prop., intrans., 1. of things, *to be over and above* the number (Hes.), hence, (*a*) *to be or remain over:* Mt 14²⁰ 15³⁷, Lk 9¹⁷, Jo 6¹²,¹³; (*b*) *to abound, be in abundance:* Mk 12⁴⁴, Lk 12¹⁵ 21⁴, Ac 16⁵, Ro 3⁷ 5¹⁵, ıı Co 1⁵ 8² 9¹², Phil 2⁶. 2. Of persons, (*a*) *to abound in, have in abundance:* ı Co 14¹² 15⁵⁸, Phl 4¹²,¹⁸; c. gen., Lk 15¹⁷ T; (*b*) *to be superior or better, to excel:* absol., ı Co 3⁹ 8⁸; c. dat. ref., ıı Co 3⁹; seq. ἐν, Ro 15¹³, ı Co 15⁵⁸, ıı Co 3⁹ 8⁷, Col 2⁷; μᾶλλον, ı Th 4¹,¹⁰; μ. καὶ μ., Phl 1⁹; πλεῖον, Mt 5²⁰. II. In late writers (Lft., *Notes*, 48 f.), trans., (*a*) *to make to abound:* c. acc. seq. εἰς, ıı Co 4¹⁵ 9⁸, Eph 1⁸; pass., Mt 13¹² 25²⁹; c. gen. rei, Lk 15¹⁷, WH; (*b*) *to make to excel:* c. acc. pers., dat. rei, ı Th 3¹² (cf. ὑπερ-περισσεύω).†

SYN.: πλεονάζω.

περισσός, -ή, -όν, [in LXX for יֶתֶר and cogn. forms;] 1. *more than sufficient, over and above, abundant:* Jo 10¹⁰, ıı Co 9¹; c. gen. (a popular substitute for πλειών, Bl., § 11, 3₄), Mt 5³⁷; id. c. ellips. gen., ib. ⁴⁷ (EV, *more than others;* but v. infr.); ἐκ περισσοῦ, Mk 6⁵¹, Rec., T. (on ὑπὲρ ἐκ π., v.s. ὑπερεκπερισσοῦ). Compar. neut., -ότερον: Lk 12⁴,⁴⁸; c. gen., Mk 12³³; adverbially (cf. περισσῶς), *more abundantly,* ıı Co 10⁸, He 6¹⁷ 7¹⁵; c. gen., π. πάντων, ı Co 15¹⁰; pleonast., μᾶλλον π., Mk 7³⁶. 2. *out of the common, pre-eminent, superior:*

Mt 5⁴⁷ (Thayer, s.v., but v. supr.) ; τὸ π., as subst., Ro 3¹; compar., -ότερος, c. gen., Mt 11⁹, Lk 7²⁶ ; c. subst., Mk 12⁴⁰, Lk 20⁴⁷, ι Co 12²³,²⁴, ιι Co 2⁷.†

περισσότερον, -ως, v.s. περισσῶς.

περισσῶς, adv. (περισός), [in LXX : Ps 30 (31)²³ (עַל־יֶתֶר), Da TH 7⁷, ¹⁹ 8⁹ (יַתִּירָה, יֶתֶר), ιι Mac 8²⁷ 12⁴⁴ A *;] beyond measure, exceedingly, abundantly : Mt 27²³, Mk 10²⁶ 15¹⁴, Ac 26¹¹. Compar., (a) περισσότερον (v.s. περισσός) ; (b) περισσοτέρως : ιι Co 1¹² 2⁴ 7¹⁵ 11²³, Ga 1¹⁴, Phl 1¹⁴, ι Th 2¹⁷, He 2¹ 13¹⁹ ; π. μᾶλλον, ιι Co 7¹³ ; opp. to ἧττον, ιι Co 12¹⁵.†

περιστερά, -ᾶς, ἡ, [in LXX chiefly for יוֹנָה ;] a dove : Mt 3¹⁶ 10¹⁶ 21¹², Mk 1¹⁰ 11¹⁵, Lk 2²⁴ 3²², Jo 1³² 2¹⁴,¹⁶.†

περι-τέμνω, [in LXX chiefly for מוּל ;] (Ion., Epic. and late writers), to cut around (Hdt.), hence, to circumcise (π. τὰ αἰδοῖα, Hdt.) : Lk 1⁵⁹ 2²¹, Jo 7²², Ac 7⁸ 15⁵ 16³ 21²¹. Pass. and mid., to be circumcised, receive circumcision : Ac 15¹, ι Co 7¹⁸, Ga 2³ 5²,³ 6¹²,¹³. Metaph. (cf. De 10¹⁶, Je 4⁴, al.), Col 2¹¹ (v. Deiss., BS, 151 f. ; MM, xix).†

περι-τίθημι, [in LXX for נתן , שׂוּם , etc. ;] to place or put around : c. acc. et dat., Mt 21³³ 27⁴⁸, Mk 12¹ 15³⁶, Jo 19²⁹ ; of garments, etc., to put on : Mt 27²⁸ Mk 15¹⁷ (Si 6³¹). Metaph., like περιβάλλω, to bestow, confer (Thuc., al., Es 1²⁰) : ι Co 12²³.†

† περι-τομή, -ῆς, ἡ (<περιτέμνω), [in LXX : Ge 17¹³, Ex 4²⁵,²⁶ (מוּל ni., מוּלָה), Je 11¹⁶ *;] circumcision ; (a) of the rite itself : Jo 7²²,²³, Ac 7⁸, Ro 4¹¹, Ga 5¹¹, Phl 3⁵ ; (b) of the state of circumcision : Ro 2²⁵⁻²⁸ 3¹, ι Co 7¹⁹, Ga 5⁶ 6¹⁵, Col 3¹¹ ; ἐν π. ὤν, Ro 4¹⁰ ; (c) by meton., ἡ π. = οἱ περιτμηθέντες, the circumcised : Ro 3³⁰ 4⁹,¹² 15⁸, Ga 2⁷⁻⁹, Eph 2¹¹ ; οἱ ἐκ τῆς π., of Jews, Ro 4¹² ; of Jewish Christians, Ac 11², Ga 2¹², Tit 1¹⁰ ; οἱ ἐκ π. πιστοί, Ac 10⁴⁵ ; οἱ ὄντες ἐκ π., Col 4¹¹. Metaph., Ro 2²⁹, Col 2¹¹, Phl 3³.†

** περι-τρέπω, [in LXX : Wi 5²³ *;] to turn about, turn : c. acc. et dat., Ac 26²⁴ (cf. FlJ, Ant., ix, 4, 4).†

περι-τρέχω, [in LXX : Am 8¹², Je 5¹ (שׁוּט pil.) *;] to run about : c. acc. loc., Mk 6⁵⁵.†

περι-φέρω, [in LXX : Ec 7⁸⁽⁷⁾ (הלל po.), al. ;] to carry about : Mk 6⁵⁵, ιι Co 4¹⁰. Pass., metaph. : Eph 4¹⁴.†

** περι-φρονέω, -ῶ, [in LXX : ιv Mac 6⁹ 14¹ *;] 1. to examine on all sides, consider carefully (Aristoph.). 2. = ὑπερφρονέω, to have thoughts beyond, to despise (Thuc., Plut., al. ; ιv Mac, ll. c.) : Tit 2¹⁵.†

περί-χωρος, -ον, [in LXX : chiefly (ἡ π.) for כִּכָּר ;] round about, neighbouring (Dem., Plut., al.). In LXX and NT, as subst., ἡ π. (sc. γῆ), the region round about : Mt 14³⁵, Mk 1²⁸, Lk 4¹⁴,³⁷ 7¹⁷ 8³⁷, Ac 14⁶ ; ἡ π. τοῦ Ἰορδάνου, Lk 3³ ; by meton for the people of the same region, Mt 3⁵.†

**† περί-ψημα, -τος, τό (< περιψάω, to wipe off all round), [in LXX :

To 5¹⁸ *;] *that which is wiped off, offscouring :* metaph. (assoc. with περικάθαρμα, q.v.), ι Co 4¹³ (and so prob., To, l.c., as EV; but v. Thayer, s.v., for the meaning *expiation, ransom,* in To; and cf. LS, s.v. κάθαρμα ; Lft., *Notes,* 200 f., and on Ign., *Eph.,* 8).†

*† περπερεύομαι (< πέρπερος, *vainglorious*), *to boast* or *vaunt oneself :* ι Co 13⁴ (elsewh. only in Antonin.; v. Abbott, *Essays,* 87).†

Περσίς, -ίδος, ή, *Persis :* Ro 16¹².†

*† πέρυσι, adv. (< πέρας), *last year, a year ago : ἀπὸ π.* (as in π., v. Deiss., *BS,* 221; *LAE,* 70), ιι Co 8¹⁰ 9².†

πετάομαι, [in LXX : De 4¹⁷ *;] false form of ποτάομαι, poët., frequentat. of πέτομαι (Aristoph., al.), Rec. for πέτομαι (q.v., cf. Veitch, s.v.).

πετεινός, -ή, -όν (< πέτομαι), [in LXX chiefly for עוֹף ;] in trag., Ion. and late writers, *winged, flying ;* as subst., τὸ π., *a winged fowl, a bird :* pl., Mt 6²⁶ 8²⁰ 13⁴, ³², Mk 4⁴, ³², Lk 8⁵ 9⁵⁸ 12²⁴ 13¹⁹, Ac 10¹², 11⁶, Ro 1²³, Ja 3⁷.†

πέτομαι, [in LXX chiefly for עוּף ;] *to fly :* Re 4⁷ 8¹³ 12¹⁴ 14⁶ 19¹⁷ (Rec. πετάομαι, q.v.).†

πέτρα, -ας, ή, [in LXX chiefly for סֶלַע, צוּר ;] *a rock,* i.e. a mass of live rock as distinct from πέτρος, a detached stone or boulder : Mt 7²⁴, ²⁵ 27⁵¹, ⁶⁰, Mk 15⁴⁶, Lk 6⁴⁸ 8⁶, ¹³ ; of a hollow rock, *a cave,* Re 6¹⁵, ¹⁶ (cf. Is 2¹⁰, al.). Metaph., Mt 16¹⁸ (on the meaning, v. Hort, *Eccl.,* 16 ff , but cf. also *ICC,* in l.), ι Co 10⁴ ; = πέτρος, Ro 9³³, ι Pe 2⁸ (LXX).†

Πέτρος, -ου, ὁ (i.e. *a stone,* v.s. πέτρα, Κηφᾶς), *Simon Peter,* the Apostle : Mt 4¹⁸ 10², Mk 3¹⁶, Lk 5⁸, Jo 1⁴¹, ⁴³, al.

* πετρώδης, -ες (< πέτρα, εἶδος), *rock-like, rocky, stony : τὸ, τὰ π.,* of shallow soil with underlying rock, Mt 13⁵, ²⁰, Mk 4⁵, ¹⁶.†

* πήγανον, -ου, τό, *rue :* Lk 11⁴².†

πηγή, -ῆς, ή, [in LXX chiefly for עַיִן, also for מָקוֹר, etc.;] *a spring, fountain :* Ja 3¹¹, ιι Pe 2¹⁷ ; τ. ὑδάτων, Re 8¹⁰ 14⁷ 16⁴ ; of a well fed by a spring, Jo 4⁶ ; π. τοῦ αἵματος, of a flow of blood, Mk 5²⁹ ; metaph., Jo 4¹⁴, Re 7¹⁷ 21⁶.†

πήγνυμι, [in LXX chiefly for נטה, also for תקע, etc.;] *to make fast, to fix ;* of tents, *to pitch :* He 8² (cf. προσ-πήγνυμι).†

* πηδάλιον, -ου, τό (< πηδός, *the blade of an oar*), *a rudder :* Ja 3⁴ ; pl., Ac 27⁴⁰.†

πηλίκος, -η, -ον, [in LXX : Za 2²⁽⁶⁾ (כַּמָּה), ιν Mac 15²² *;] interrog., *how large, how great ?* (prop., of magnitude, as πόσος of quantity) : in exclamations, = ἡλίκος (v. Bl., § 51, 4), Ga 6¹¹ ; of personal greatness, He 7⁴.†

πηλός, οῦ, ὁ, [in LXX chiefly for חֹמֶר, טִיט ;] 1. *clay,* as used by a potter : Ro 9²¹ (cf. Is 29¹⁶, al.). 2. = βόρβορος, *wet clay, mud :* Jo 9⁶, ¹¹, ¹⁴, ¹⁵.†

** πήρα, -ας, ή, [in LXX : Jth 10⁵ 13¹⁰, ¹⁵ *;] *a leathern pouch* for

victuals, etc., *a wallet* (Deiss. thinks *an alms-bag*, v. *LAE*, 108 ff.) :
Mt 10¹⁰, Mk 6⁸, Lk 9³ 10⁴ 22³⁵,³⁶.†

πῆχυς, -εως, gen. pl., -ῶν (for Att. -εων, v. WH, *App.*, 157 ;
Thackeray, *Gr.*, 151 ; Deiss., *BS*, 153), [in LXX chiefly and freq. for
אַמָּה ;] 1. *the forearm* (Hom.). 2. As a measure of length (in Mt, Lk,
ll.c., prob. of time, v.s. ἡλικία), *a cubit :* Mt 6²⁷, Lk 12²⁵, Jo 21⁸, Re 21¹⁷.†

πιάζω (cf. MGr. πιάνω ; v. Kennedy, *Sources*, 155), Doric and
late Att. for πιέζω in its later senses ; [in LXX : Ca 2¹⁵ (אחז), Si
23²¹ *;] 1. *to lay hold of :* Ac 3⁷ (Theocr.). 2. *to take, capture,
apprehend :* Jo 7³⁰, ³², ⁴⁴ 8²⁰ 10³⁹ 11⁵⁷ 21³, ¹⁰, Ac 12⁴, II Co 11³², Re 19²⁰
(v. MM, xx).†

πιέζω, [in LXX : Mi 6¹⁵ (דרך) *;] 1. *to press, press down* or *together :* Lk 6³⁸ (cl). 2. Later, *to seize* (v.s. πιάζω).†

* πιθανολογία, -ας, ἡ (<πιθανός, *persuasive, plausible*), in cl.
(Plat), *the use of probable arguments*, as opp. to demonstration
(ἀπόδειξις) ; hence, *persuasive speech :* Col 2⁴ (v. *ICC*, in l.).†

πιθός, v.s. πειθός.

πικραίνω (<πικρός), [in LXX for מרר, קצף, etc.;] *to make
bitter :* Re 10⁹; pass., ib. 8¹¹ 10¹⁰; metaph., *to embitter* (LXX) :
pass., seq. πρός, Col 3¹⁹.†

πικρία, -ας, ἡ (<πικρός), [in LXX chiefly for מַר, מָרָה and
cognate forms;] *bitterness ;* (a) of taste (Arist., Je 15¹⁷, al.) ; (b)
metaph., of temper, character, etc. : Ro 3¹⁴ (LXX), Eph 4³¹ ; ῥίζα πικρίας,
He 12¹⁵; χολὴ π., *a malignant disposition*, Ac 8²³.†

πικρός, -ά, -όν (poët. in cl.), [in LXX chiefly for מר ;] 1. *sharp,
pointed.* 2. *sharp* to the senses ; of taste, *bitter :* opp. to γλυκύ,
Ja 3¹¹; metaph., *harsh, bitter :* ib. ¹⁴.†

πικρῶς, adv. (<πικρός), [in LXX for מַר, מרר pi.;] *bitterly :*
metaph., (cf. πικρὸν δάκρυον, Hom.), ἔκλαυσε π., Mt 26⁷⁵, Lk 22⁶² (v.
MM, xviii, s.v. παρακολουθέω).†

Πιλάτος, v.s. Πειλᾶτος.

πίμπλημι, [in LXX chiefly for מלא, also for שׂבע ;] trans. form
in pres. and impf. of πλήθω (intrans. in these tenses), which supplies
the other tense forms ; *to fill :* c. acc., Lk 5⁷; c. acc. et gen., Mt 27⁴⁸;
pass., Mt 22¹⁰, Ac 19²⁹; of that which fills or takes possession of the
mind : pass., c. gen., Lk 1¹⁵, ⁴¹, ⁶⁷ 4²⁸ 5²⁶ 6¹¹, Ac 2⁴ 3¹⁰ 4⁸, ³¹ 5¹⁷ 9¹⁷
13⁹, ⁴⁵. Metaph. (as in LXX for מלא : Ge 29²⁷, Jb 15³²), *to complete,
fulfil :* pass., of prophecy, Lk 21²²; of time, Lk 1²³, ⁵⁷ 2⁶, ²¹, ²² (cf.
ἐμ-πίμπλημι).†

SYN.: πληροφορέω, πληρόω.

πίμπρημι (in cl. prose, rare in the simple form), [in LXX : Nu
5²¹, ²², ²⁷ (צבה) *; 1. *to blow, burn.* 2. Later, *to cause to swell ;* mid.,
of parts of the body, *to become swollen* (LXX) : Ac 28⁶ (cf. ἐμπίπρημι).†

** πινακίδιον, -ου, τό (dimin. of πινακίς, q.v.), [in Sm. : Ez 9² *;] *a
writing tablet :* Lk 1⁶³.†

πινακίς, -ίδος, ή, [in Sm.: Ez 9¹¹*;] = πινάκιον, *a tablet*: Lk 1⁶³, Tr., mg. (v.s. πινακίδιον).†

πίναξ, -ακος, ό, [in LXX: IV Mac 17⁷ R*;] prop., *a board, plank*; hence, of various flat wooden articles; (*a*) *a tablet*; (*b*) *a disc, a dish*: Mt 14⁸, ¹¹, Mk 6²⁵, ²⁸, Lk 11³⁹.†

πίνω, [in LXX chiefly for שתה;] *to drink*: absol., Lk 2¹⁹, Jo 4⁷, al.; c. acc. rei, Mt 6²⁵, ³¹, Mk 14²⁵, al.; of habitual use, Lk 1¹⁵, Ro 14²¹, al.; by meton., τὸ ποτήριον, I Co 10²¹, al.; of the earth absorbing rain (Hdt., al.), He 6⁷; spiritually, of the blood of Christ, Jo 6⁵³, ⁵⁴, ⁵⁶; seq. ἐκ (of the vessel), Mt 26²⁷, al.; id. (of the drink; Bl., § 36, 1), Mt 26²⁹, Jo 4¹³, ¹⁴, Re 14¹⁰, al.; ἀπό, Lk 22¹⁸ (cf. ἀπο-, συν-πίνω; on the form πίεσαι, Lk 17⁸, v. Bl., § 21, 8, and on the contr. aor. πεῖν, M, *Pr.*, 44 f., Thackeray, *Gr.*, 63 f.).

πιότης, -ητος, ή (< πίων, *fat*), [in LXX chiefly for דשׁן;] *fatness*: Ro 11¹⁷.†

πιπράσκω, [in LXX chiefly for מכר ni.;] *to sell*: c. acc. rei, Mt 13⁴⁶ (on this pf., v. Bl., § 59, 5), Ac 2⁴⁵ 4³⁴ 5⁴; c. gen. (of price), Mt 26⁹, Mk 14⁵, Jo 12⁵; c. acc. pers. (of slavery), Mt 18²⁵; hence metaph., Ro 7¹⁴ (cf. IV Ki 17¹⁷, I Mac 1¹⁵, al.).†

πίπτω, [in LXX chiefly for נפל;] *to fall*; 1. of descent, *to fall, fall down* or *from*: seq. ἐπί, c. acc. loc., Mt 10²⁹, al.; εἰς, Mt 15¹⁴, al.; ἐν μέσῳ, c. gen., Lk 8⁷; παρὰ τ. ὁδόν, Mt 13⁴, Mk 4⁴, Lk 8⁵; seq. ἀπό, Mt 15²⁷, al.; ἐκ, Mk 13²⁵, Lk 10¹⁸, Re 8¹⁰ 9¹. Metaph.: ὁ ἥλιος, seq. ἐπί, Re 7¹⁶; ἀχλὺς κ. σκότος, Ac 13¹¹; ὁ κλῆρος, Ac 1²⁶; ὑπὸ κρίσιν, Ja 5¹². 2. Of prostration, (*a*) of persons, *to fall prostrate, prostrate oneself*: χαμαί, Jo 18⁶; seq. ἐπί, c. acc., Mt 17⁶, Ac 9⁴; id. c. gen., Mk 9²⁰; πρὸς τ. πόδας, Ac 5¹⁰, Re 1¹⁷; πεσὼν ἐξέψυξε, Ac 5⁵; of supplication, homage or worship: πρὸς (παρὰ, ἐπὶ) τ. πόδας, Mk 5²², Lk 8⁴¹, Ac 10²⁵, al.; π. καὶ προσκινεῖν, Re 5¹⁴ 19⁴; ptcp. c. προσκυνεῖν, Mt 2¹¹, al.; ἐνώπιον, Re 4¹⁰ 5⁸; ἐπὶ πρόσωπον, Mt 26³⁹, al.; (*b*) of things, *to fall, fall down*: Mt 21⁴⁴, Lk 23³⁰; of falling to ruin and destruction, Mt 7²⁵, Ac 15¹⁶, He 11³⁰; ἔπεσε (timeless aorist; M, *Pr.*, 134), Re 18². Metaph.: Ro 11¹¹; πόθεν πέπτωκας, Re 2⁵; opp. to ἑστάναι, I Co 10¹²; to στήκειν, Ro 14⁴; of virtues, I Co 13⁸; of precepts, Lk 16¹⁷; of the heat of the sun, Re 7¹⁶ (but v.s. παίω, supr.). (Cf. ἀνα-, ἀντι-, ἀπο-, ἐκ-, ἐπι-, κατα-, παρα-, περι-, προσ-, συν-πίπτω.)

Πισιδία, -ας, ή, *Pisidia*, a region of Asia Minor: Ac 14²⁴.†

Πισίδιος, -α, -ον, = Πισιδικός, *of Pisidia*: Ac 13²⁴.†

πιστεύω, [in LXX chiefly for אמן hi.;] 1. intrans., *to have faith* (in), *to believe*; in cl., c. acc., dat., in NT also c. prep. (on the significance of the various constructions, v. M, *Pr.*, 67 f.; Vau. on Ro 4⁵; Ellic. on I Ti 1¹⁶; Abbott, *JV*, 19-80): absol., Mt 24²³, ²⁶, Mk 13²¹, I Co 11¹⁸; c. acc. rei, Ac 13⁴¹, I Co 13⁷; c. dat. pers. (to believe what one says), Mk 16.[¹³, ¹⁴], I Jo 4¹; τ. ψεύδει, II Th 2¹¹; περὶ . . . ὅτι, Jo 9¹⁸; esp. and most freq. with reference to religious belief: absol., Mt 8¹³, Mk 5³⁶, Lk 8⁵⁰, Jo 11⁴⁰, al.; seq. ὅτι, Mt 9²⁸, al.; c. dat. (v. supr., and cf. *DB*, i, 829a), Jo 3¹² 5²⁴ 6³⁰ 8³¹, Ac 16³⁴, Ga 3⁶ (LXX), II Ti 1¹², I Jo 5¹⁰, al.; c. prep. (expressing personal trust and reliance as distinct from mere credence or belief; v. M, *Pr.*, l.c.; *DB*, i, 829 b), *to believe in* or *on* : ἐν (Ps 77 (78)²², al.), Mk 1¹⁵ (v. Swete, in l.); εἰς, Mt 18⁶, Jo 2¹¹ (v. Westc., in l.), and freq., Ac 10⁴³ 19⁴, Ro 10¹⁴, Ga 2¹⁶, Phl 1²⁹, ι Jo 5¹⁰, ι Pe 1⁸; εἰς τ. ὄνομα (v.s. ὄνομα), Jo 1¹² 2²³ 3¹⁸, ι Jo 5¹³; ἐπί, c. acc., Mt 27⁴², Ac 9⁴² 11¹⁷ 16³¹ 22¹⁹, Ro 4⁵; ἐπί, c. dat., Ro 9³³ (LXX) 10¹¹ (ib.), ι Ti 1¹⁶, ι Pe 2⁶ (LXX); ptcp. pres., οἱ π., as subst., Ac 2⁴⁴, Ro 3²², ι Co 1²¹, al.; aor., Mk 16[¹⁶], Ac 4³²; pf., Ac 19¹⁸ 21²⁰ (on Johannine use of the tenses of π., v. Westc., *Epp. Jo.*, 120). 2. Trans., *to entrust* : c. acc. et dat., Lk 16¹¹, Jo 2²⁴; pass., *to be entrusted with* : c. acc., Ro 3², ι Co 9¹⁷, Ga 2⁷, ι Th 2⁴ (v. Lft., *Notes*, 21 f.), ι Ti 1¹¹, Tit 1³, v. *ICC* on Ga, pp. 475 ff.

†πιστικός, -ή, -όν (πίστις), 1. *having the gift of persuasion* (Plat., *Gorg.*, 455 A). 2. (*a*) of persons, *faithful, trusty* (Plut.); (*b*) of things, *trustworthy, genuine* : νάρδος π., Mk 14³, Jo 12³; cf. *EB*, 4750 f.†

πίστις, -εως, ἡ (< πείθω), [in LXX chiefly for אֱמוּנָה;] 1. in active sense, *faith, belief, trust, confidence*, in NT always of religious faith in God or Christ or spiritual things : Mt 8¹⁰, Lk 5²⁰, Ac 14⁹, Ro 1⁸, ι Co 2⁵, ιι Co 1²⁴, ι Ti 1⁵, al.; c. gen. obj., Mk 11²², Ac 3¹⁶, Ro 3²², Ga 2¹⁶, Eph 3¹², Ja 2¹, al.; c. prep., ἐν, Ro 3²⁵, Ga 3²⁶, Eph 1¹⁵, Col 1⁴, ι Ti 1¹⁴ 3¹³, ιι Ti 1¹³ 3¹⁵, ιι Pe 1¹; εἰς, Ac 20²¹ 24²⁴ 26¹⁸, Col 2⁵, ι Pe 1²¹; πρός, ι Th 1⁸, Phm ⁵; ἐπί, c. acc., He 6¹; ἐν τῇ π. στήκειν (εἶναι, μένειν), ι Co 16¹³, ι Co 13⁵, ι Ti 2¹⁵; ὑπακοὴ τῆς π., Ro 1⁵ 16²⁶; ὁ ἐκ π., Ro 3²⁶ 4¹⁶, Ga 3¹²; διὰ (τῆς) π., Ro 3³⁰, Ga 2¹⁶, Phl 3⁹. By meton., objectively, that which is the object or content of belief, *the faith* : Ac 6⁷ 14²², Ga 1²³ 3²³ 6¹⁰, Phl 1²⁵,²⁷, Ju ³,²⁰, and perh. also Ac 13⁸ 16⁵, Ro 1⁵ and 16²⁶ (v. supr.), ι Co 16¹³, Col 1²³, ιι Th 3² (Lft., *Notes*, 125), ι Ti 1¹⁹ 3⁹ 4¹,⁶ 5⁸ 6¹⁰,¹², ιι Ti 3⁸ 4⁷, Tit 1⁴,¹³ 3¹⁵, ι Pe 5⁹. 2. In passive sense, (*a*) *fidelity, faithfulness* : Mt 23²³, Ga 5²²; ἡ π. τοῦ θεοῦ, Ro 3³; (*b*) objectively, *plighted faith, a pledge* of fidelity : ι Ti 5¹². (On the various shades of meaning in which the word is used in NT, v. esp. *ICC* on Ro 1¹⁷, pp. 31 ff.; Lft., *Ga.*, 154 ff.; Stevens, *Th. NT*, 422, 515 ff.; *DB*, i, 830 ff.; Cremer, s.v.), v. *ICC* on Ga, pp. 475 ff.

πιστός, -ή, -όν (< πείθω), [in LXX chiefly for אָמַן;] I. Pass., *to be trusted* or *believed* ; 1. of persons, *trusty, faithful* : Mt 24⁴⁵ 25²¹,²³, Lk 12⁴², Ac 16¹⁵, ι Co 4²,¹⁷ 7²⁵, Eph 1¹ 6²¹, Col 1²,⁷ 4⁷,⁹, ι Ti 1¹², ιι Ti 2², He 2¹⁷ 3²,⁵, ι Pe 5¹², Re 2¹³ 19¹¹; of God, ι Co 1⁹ 10¹³, ιι Co 1¹⁸, ι Th 5²⁴, ιι Th 3³, He 10²³ 11¹¹, ιι Ti 2¹³, ι Jo 1⁹, ι Pe 4¹⁹; seq. ἐν, Lk 16¹⁰⁻¹² 19¹⁷, ι Ti 3¹¹; ἐπί, c. acc., Mt 25²³; ἄχρι θανάτου, Re 2¹⁰; ὁ μάρτυς ὁ π., Re 1⁵; id. καὶ ἀληθινός, Re 3¹⁴. 2. Of things, *trustworthy, reliable, sure* : Ac 13³⁴, ι Ti 1¹⁵ 3¹ 4⁹, ιι Ti 2¹¹, Tit 1⁹ 3⁸, Re 21⁵ 22⁶. II. Act., *believing, trusting, relying* : Ac 16¹, ιι Co 6¹⁵, Ga 3⁹, ι Ti 4¹⁰ 5¹⁶ 6², Tit 1⁶, Re 17¹⁴; pl., Ac 10⁴⁵, ι Ti 4³,¹²; opp. to ἄπιστος, Jo 20²⁷; π. εἰς θεόν, ι Pe 1²¹; π. ποιεῖν, ιιι Jo ⁵. (On the difficulty of choosing in some cases between the active and the passive meaning, v. Lft., *Gal.*, 157.)†

πιστόω, -ῶ (< πιστός), [in LXX chiefly for אמן ni.;] *to make* *trustworthy* (Thuc., III Ki 1³⁶), hence, *to establish* (I Ch 17¹⁴). Pass. and mid., *to be assured of :* c. acc. rei, II Ti 3¹⁴.†

πλανάω, -ῶ (< πλάνη), [in LXX chiefly for תעה ;] *to cause to wander, lead astray.* Pass., *to go astray, wander :* Mt 18¹²,¹³, He 11³⁸, I Pe 2²⁵ (cf. Is 53⁶). Metaph., *to lead astray, deceive :* c. acc. pers., Mt 24⁴,⁵,¹¹,²⁴, Mk 13⁵,⁶, Jo 7¹², II Ti 3¹³, I Jo 1⁸ 2²⁶ 3⁷, Rẹ 2²⁰ 12⁹ 13¹⁴ 19²⁰ 20³,⁸,¹⁰; pass., *to be led astray, to err :* Mt 22²⁹, Mk 12²⁴,²⁷, Lk 21⁸, Jo 7⁴⁷, II Ti 3¹³, Tit 3³, He 5², II Pe 2¹⁵, Re 18²³; τ. καρδία, He 3¹⁰; ἀπὸ τ. ἀληθείας, Ja 5¹⁹; μὴ πλανᾶσθε, I Co 6⁹ 15³³, Ga 6⁷, Ja 1¹⁶ (cf. ἀπο-πλανάω).†

πλάνη, -ης, ἡ, [in LXX: Pr 14⁸ (מִרְמָה), Wi 1¹², al;] *a wandering.* Metaph., *a going astray, an error* (in NT always with respect to morals or religion): Mt 27⁶⁴, Ro 1²⁷, Eph 4¹⁴, I Th 2³, II Th 2¹¹, Ja 5²⁰, II Pe 2¹⁸ 3¹⁷, I Jo 4⁶, Ju¹¹.†

* **πλάνης**, -ητος, ὁ, v.s. πλανήτης.

πλανήτης, -ου, ὁ (< πλανάω), [in LXX: Ho 9¹⁷ (נדד) * ;] = πλάνης, *a wanderer :* ἀστέρες π. (cl. *planets*), *wandering stars,* Ju¹³ (WH, mg., -τες).†

πλάνος, -ον, [in LXX: Jb 19⁴ (מְשׁוּגָה), Je 23³² * ;] 1. *wandering.* 2. *leading astray, deceiving :* πνεύματα π., I Ti 4¹. As subst., ὁ π., *a deceiver, impostor :* Mt 27⁶³, II Co 6⁸, II Jo⁷.†

πλάξ, -ακός, ἡ, [in LXX for לוּחַ ;] *anything flat and broad.* 1. *a plain* (poët.). 2. In late writers (Luc., al.), *a flat stone, a tablet :* II Co 3³, He 9⁴.†

πλάσμα, -τος, τό (< πλάσσω), [in LXX chiefly for יֵצֶר ;] *that which is moulded* or *formed :* Ro 9²⁰ (LXX).†

πλάσσω, [in LXX chiefly for יצר ;] *to form, mould :* Ro 9²⁰ (LXX), I Ti 2¹³.†

* **πλαστός**, -ή, -όν (< πλάσσω), 1. *formed, moulded* (Hes., Plat., al.). 2. Metaph., *made up, fabricated, feigned* (Hdt., Xen., al.) : II Pe 2³.†

πλατεῖα, -ας, ἡ, v.s. πλατύς.

πλάτος, -ους, τό, [in LXX chiefly for רֹחַב ;] *breadth :* Eph 3¹⁸, Re 21¹⁶; τ. π. τῆς γῆς (Hb 1⁶, מֶרְחָב), Re 20⁹.†

πλατύνω (< πλατύς), [in LXX chiefly for רחב hi.;] *to make broad, enlarge, extend :* c. acc. rei, Mt 23⁵. Metaph. (cf. Ps 118 (119)³², al.), pass., ἡ καρδία, II Co 6¹¹; ὑμεῖς, ib.¹³.†

πλατύς, -εῖα, -ύ, [in LXX for רָחָב ;] *broad :* Mt 7¹³. As subst., ἡ π. (sc. ὁδός), in [LXX chiefly for רֹחַב ;] *a street :* Mt 6⁵ 12¹⁹ (LXX), Mk 6⁵⁶, WH, mg., Lk 10¹⁰ 13²⁶ 14²¹, Ac 5¹⁵, Re 11⁸ 21²¹, 22².†

** **πλέγμα**, -τος, τό (< πλέκω), [in Aq., Th.: Is 28⁵ *;] *what is woven* or *twisted* (as basket-work, nets, etc.); *a braiding* (sc. τριχῶν, cf. I Pe 3³): pl., I Ti 2⁹.†

πλεῖστος, πλείων, v.s. πολύς.

πλέκω, [in LXX: Ex 28¹⁴ (עָבַת), Is 28⁵ (צְפִירָה)*;] to plait, twist, weave: Mt 27²⁹, Mk 15¹⁷, Jo 19².†

πλέον, v.s. πολύς.

πλεονάζω (< πλέον), [in LXX for עדף, רבה, etc.;] I. Intrans. 1. Of persons; (a) to abound in (Arist.); (b) to superabound: II Co 8¹⁵ (LXX). 2. Of things, to abound, superabound: Ro 5²⁰ 6¹, II Co 4¹⁵, Phl 4¹⁷, II Th 1³, II Pe 1⁸. II. Trans. (Nu 26⁵⁴, Ps 70 (71)²¹; not cl., v. Lft., Notes, 48 f.), to make to abound: I Th 3¹² (cf. ὑπερ-πλεονάζω).†
SYN.: περισσεύω, q.v.

πλεονεκτέω, -ῶ (< πλεονέκτης, q.v.), [in LXX: Hb 2⁹, Ez 22²⁷ (בצע), Jg 4¹¹ B*;] 1. intrans., to have more, to have an advantage (cl., c. gen. pers.). 2. Trans., in late writers (v. M, Pr., 65), to overreach, defraud: c. acc. pers., II Co 7² 12¹⁷,¹⁸; ἐν τ. πράγματι, I Th 4⁶ (v. M, Th., in l.); pass., II Co 2¹¹ (as also in cl.; v. LS, s.v.).†

** πλεονέκτης, -ου, ὁ (< πλέον, ἔχω), [in LXX: Si 14⁹ *;] = ὁ θέλων πλέον ἔχειν (v. MM, xx), one desirous of having more, covetous: I Co 5¹⁰,¹¹ 6¹⁰, Eph 5⁵.†

πλεονεξία, -ας, ἡ (< πλεονέκτης), [in LXX for בֶּצַע;] the character and conduct of a πλεονέκτης. 1. advantage. 2. desire for advantage, grasping, aggression, cupidity, covetousness: Lk 12¹⁵, Ro 1²⁹, II Co 9⁵, Eph 4¹⁹ (v. ICC, in l.) 5³, Col 3⁵, I Th 2⁵, II Pe 2³,¹⁴; pl. (v. Bl., § 32, 6), Mk 7²².†
SYN.: φιλαργυρία, avarice (v. Tr., Syn., § xxiv).

πλευρά, -ᾶς, ἡ, [in LXX (freq. pl. as in Hom.) chiefly for צֵלָע;] the side: Mt 27⁴⁹ ([[WH]] R, mg.), Jo 19³⁴ 20²⁰,²⁵,²⁷, Ac 12⁷.†

πλέω, [in LXX, seq. εἰς, Jh 1³ (בוא), I Es 4²³, Is 42¹⁰; seq. ἐπί, IV Mac 7³; c. acc. (poët.), Si 43²⁴, I Mac 13²⁹ (cf. Ac 27², Rec.)*;] to sail: Lk 8²³, Ac 27²⁴; seq. εἰς, Ac 21³ 27²,⁶; ἐπί, Re 18¹⁷ (cf. ἀπό-, δια-, ἐκ-, κατα-, παρα-, ὑπο-πλέω).†

πληγή, -ῆς, ἡ (< πλήσσω), [in LXX chiefly for מַכָּה, also for מַגֵּפָה, etc.;] 1. a blow, stripe, wound: pl., Lk 10³⁰ 12⁴⁸, Ac 16²³,³³, II Co 6⁵ 11²³; ἡ π. τ. θανάτου (RV, death-stroke), Re 13³,¹²; τ. μαχαίρας, Re 13¹⁴. 2. Metaph., a calamity, plague: Re 9¹⁸,²⁰ 11⁶ 15¹,⁶,⁸ 16⁹,²¹ 18⁴,⁸ 21⁹ 22¹⁸.†

πλῆθος, -ους, τό, [in LXX chiefly for רֹב, also for הָמוֹן, etc.;] 1. a great number, a multitude; (a) of things: ἰχθύων, Lk 5⁶, Jo 21⁶; φρυγάνων, Ac 28³; ἁμαρτιῶν, Ja 5²⁰, I Pe 4⁸; τ. πλήθει, in multitude, He 11¹²; (b) of persons: Ac 21²² (WH, R, om.); c. gen., Lk 2¹³, Jo 5³, Ac 5¹⁴; π. πολύ (πολὺ π.), Mk 3⁷,⁸; id. c. gen., Lk 6¹⁷ 23²⁷, Ac 14¹ 17⁴. 2. Of persons, c. art., the whole number, the multitude (in Plat., Thuc., Xen., al., = δῆμος, the commons, or—opp. to δῆμος—the populace): Ac 2⁶ 15³⁰ 19⁹ 23⁷; τ. λαοῦ, Ac 21³⁶; τ. πόλεως, Ac 14⁴; πᾶν τὸ π., Ac 15¹²; c. gen., Lk 1¹⁰ 8³⁷ 19³⁷ 23¹, Ac 4³² 5¹⁶ 6²,⁵ 25²⁴.†

πληθύνω (causal of πληθύω, to be full, < πληθύς, Ion. for πλῆθος), [in LXX chiefly for רבה hi. ;] 1. trans., *to increase, multiply :* ΙΙ Co 9¹⁰, He 6¹⁴ (LXX) ; pass., *to be increased, to multiply :* Mt 24¹², Ac 6⁷ 7¹⁷ 9³¹ 12²⁴ ; c. dat. pers. (Da LXX ΤΗ 3³¹ (98), al.), 1 Pe 1², ΙΙ Pe 1², Ju². 2. Intrans., *to be increased, to multiply :* Ac 6¹.†

πλήθω, v.s. πίμπλημι.

** πλήκτης, -ου, ὁ (< πλήσσω), [in Sm.: Ps 34 (35)¹⁵ * ;] *a striker, brawler :* ι Ti 3³, Tit 1⁷ (Arist., Plut., al.).†

† πλήμμυρα, -ης (for Att. -ας, v. Bl., § 7, 1) (< πλήθω), [in LXX: π. γένεσθαι, Jb 40¹⁸ (23) (עָשׁ֫ק נָהָר) * ;] *a flood* (of sea or river) : Lk 6⁴⁸.†

πλήν, adv., [in LXX for רק, לְבַד, אַךְ, etc. ;] 1. introducing a clause (= ἀλλά, δέ; "it is obvious that πλήν was the regular word in the vulgar language": Bl., § 77, 13), *yet, howbeit, only :* Mt 11²², ²⁴ 18⁷ 26³⁹, ⁶⁴ (M, Pr., 86), Lk 6²⁴, ³⁵ 10¹¹, ¹⁴, ²⁰ 11⁴¹ 12³¹ 13³³ 17¹ 18⁸ 19²⁷ 22²¹, ²², ⁴² (WH, mg. om.) 23²⁸, ι Co 11¹¹, Eph 5³³, Phl 3¹⁶ 4¹⁴, Re 2²⁵ ; π. ὅτι (Hdt., Plat., al.), *except that, save that,* Ac 20²³, Phl 1¹⁸. 2. As prep., c. gen., *except, save* (cl.): Mk 12³², Jo 8¹⁰, Ac 8¹ 15²⁸ 27²².†

πλήρης, -ες, [in LXX chiefly for מָלֵא ;] 1. *full, filled :* Mt 14²⁰ 15³⁷ ; c. gen. rei, Mk 8¹⁹ ; λέπρας, Lk 5¹² ; metaph., of the soul : πνεύματος ἁγίου, Lk 4¹, Ac 6³ 7⁵⁵ 11²⁴ ; πίστεως, Ac 6⁶ ; χάριτος, ib. ⁸ ; χ. καὶ ἀληθείας (where π. is indecl.; v. M, Pr., 50 ; Milligan, NTD, 65, with reff. in each), Jo 1¹⁴ ; δόλου, Ac 13¹⁰ ; θυμοῦ, Ac 19²⁸ ; ἔργων ἀγαθῶν, Ac 9³⁶. 2. *full, complete :* μισθός, ΙΙ Jo ⁸ ; σῖτος (π. prob. indecl. here ; v. on Jo 1¹⁴, supr.), Mk 4²⁸.†

† πληροφορέω, -ῶ, [in LXX: Ec 8¹¹ (מָלֵא) * ;] 1. *to bring in full measure,* hence, *to fulfil, accomplish :* Lk 1¹, ΙΙ Ti 4⁵,¹⁷. 2. *to persuade, assure* or *satisfy fully* (so in π.; v. Deiss., LAE, 82 f.; M, Th., 9) : pass., Ro 4²¹ 14⁵, Col 4¹² (v. Lft., in l.). 3. *to fill :* Ro 15¹³, L, mg. (Cl. Ro., ι Co 54) ; metaph., pass., *to be filled with,* hence, *fully bent on* (Ec, l.c.).†

*† πληροφορία, -ας, ἡ (< πληροφορέω), *full assurance, confidence :* ι Th 1⁵ ; τ. συνέσεως, Col 2² ; τ. ἐλπίδος, He 6¹¹ ; πίστεως, He 10²² (cf. Lft. on Col., l.c. ; M, Th., 9).†

πληρόω, -ῶ, [in LXX chiefly for מָלֵא ;] 1. *to fill, make full, fill to the full,* c. acc. ; (a) of things : pass. (σαγήνη, φάραγξ), Mt 13⁴⁸, Lk 3⁵ (LXX) ; fig., Mt 23³² ; but chiefly of immaterial things : πᾶσαν χρείαν, Phl 4¹⁹ ; ἦχος ἐπλήρωσε τ. οἶκον, Ac 2² ; c. gen. rei (cl.), Ac 5²⁸ ; pass., seq. ἐκ, Jo 12³ (cf. Bl., § 36, 4) ; π. τ. καρδίαν, Jo 16⁶, Ac 5³ ; metaph., of the all-pervading activity of Christ, Eph 4¹⁰ ; mid., Eph 1²³ ; (b) of persons : *to fill* with, *cause to abound* in : c. gen. rei (cl.), Ac 2²⁸ (LXX), Ro 15¹³ ; pass., *to be filled* with, *abound* in : Eph 3¹⁹, Phl 4¹⁸ ; c. gen. rei (cl.), Ac 13⁵², Ro 15¹⁴, ΙΙ Ti 1⁴ ; c. dat. (Æsch., al.), Lk 2⁴⁰ (c. gen., T), Ro 1²⁹, ΙΙ Co 7⁴ ; c. acc. (so in π., v. MM, xx), Phl 1¹¹, Col 1⁹ ; seq. ἐν, Eph 5¹⁸, Col 2¹⁰. 2. *to complete ;* (a) *to complete, fulfil :* of number, Re 6¹¹, WH, txt. ; of time (MM, xx), Mk 1¹⁵, Lk 21²⁴, Jo 7⁸,

Ac 7²³, ³⁰ 9²³ 24²⁷ ; ἐνδοκίαν, II Th 1¹¹ ; τ. χαράν, Phl 2² ; pass., Jo 3²⁹ 15¹¹ 16²⁴ 17¹³, I Jo 1⁴, II Jo ¹² ; τ. ἔργα, Re 3² ; ἡ ὑπακοή, II Co 10⁶ ; τ. πάσχα, Lk 22¹⁶ ; (b) to execute, accomplish, carry out to the full : Mt 3¹⁵, Lk 7¹ 9³¹, Ac 12²⁵ 13²⁵ 14²⁶ 19²¹, Ro 8⁴ 13⁸ 15¹⁹, Ga 5¹⁴, Col 1²⁵ 4¹⁷, Re 6¹¹, T, WH, R, mg. ; (c) of sayings, prophecies, etc., to bring to pass, fulfil : Mt 1²² 2¹⁵, ¹⁷, ²³ 4¹⁴ 5¹⁷ 8¹⁷ 12¹⁷ 13³⁵ 21⁴ 26⁵⁴, ⁵⁶ 27⁹, Mk 14⁴⁹ 15²⁸ (WH, R, txt. om.), Lk 1²⁰ 4²¹ 24⁴⁴, Jo 12³⁸ 13¹⁸ 15²⁵ 17¹² 18⁹, ³² 19²⁴, ³⁶, Ac 1¹⁶ 3¹⁸ 13²⁷, Ja 2²³ (cf. Lft., Col., 255 ff.).†

πλήρωμα, -τος, τό (< πληρόω), [in LXX for מְלֹא ;] the result of the action involved in πληρόω (Lft., Col., 255 ff. ; AR, Eph., 255 ff.), hence, 1. in passive sense, that which has been completed, complement, plenitude, fullness (in Xen., Luc., Polyb., al., of a ship's crew or cargo, and by meton. of the ship itself) : Jo 1¹⁶, Ro 11¹², ²⁵ 15²⁹, I Co 10²⁶ (LXX) Eph 1²³ (AR, 42 ff.) 3¹⁹ (ib. 87 ff.) 4¹³, Col 1¹⁹ 2⁹ ; of time, Ga 4⁴, Eph 1¹⁰ ; κοφίνων (σφυρίδων) πληρώματα, basketfuls, Mk 6⁴³ 8²⁰. 2. In active sense (= πλήρωσις, as freq. in words of these formations, cf. κτίσις, and v. MM, xx) ; (a) that which fills up (but v. Lft., l.c.) : Mt 9¹⁶, Mk 2²¹ ; (b) a filling up, completing, fulfilment : Ro 13¹⁰.†

πλησίον, v.s. πλησίος.

πλησίος, -α, -ον (< πέλας, near), near, close by, neighbouring. As adv., πλησίον = πέλας, near : c. gen., Jo 4⁵ ; c. art., ὁ π., one's neighbour [in LXX chiefly for רֵעַ] : Lk 10²⁹, ³⁶, Ac 7²⁷, Ro 13¹⁰ 15², Eph 4²⁵, Ja 4¹² ; ἀγαπήσεις τὸν π. σου ὡς σεαυτόν (Le 19¹⁸, LXX), Mt 5⁴³ 19¹⁹ 22³⁹, Mk 12³¹, ³³, Lk 10²⁷, Ro 13⁹, Ga 5¹⁴, Ja 2⁸ (on the various senses of ὁ π. in OT, NT, v. DB, iii, 511 ; DCG, ii, 240 f.).†

πλησμονή, -ῆς, ἡ (< πίμπλημι), [in LXX chiefly for שֹׂבַע and cognate forms;] a filling up, satiety : πρὸς π. σαρκός (RV, against the indulgence of the flesh ; but ICC, in l., for the full satisfaction of the flesh, op. cit., 276 ff.), Col 2²³.†

πλήσσω, [in LXX chiefly for נכה hi., ho.;] to strike, smite : pass., Re 8¹² (cf. ἐκ-, ἐπι-πλήσσω).†

* πλοιάριον, -ου, τό (dimin. of πλοῖον), a boat : Mk 3⁹, Lk 5² (πλοῖα, WH, txt., R), Jo 6²², ²³ (πλοῖα, WH) ²⁴ 21⁸.†

πλοῖον, -ου, τό (< πλέω), [in LXX chiefly for אֳנִיָּה ;] a boat, also (= obsol. ναῦς) a ship : Mt 4²¹, ²², and freq. in Gosp. and Ac, Ja 3⁴, Re 8⁹ 18¹⁹.

** πλόος, πλοῦς, gen., -όου, -οῦ (and in late writers also πλοός, like νοός from νοῦς), ὁ (< πλέω), [in LXX : Wi 14¹ *;] a voyage : Ac 21⁷ 27⁹, ¹⁰.†

πλούσιος, -α, -ον (< πλοῦτος), [in LXX chiefly for עָשִׁיר ;] rich, wealthy : Mt 27⁵⁷, Lk 12¹⁶ 14¹² 16¹, ¹⁹ 18²³ 19². Substantively, ὁ π., Lk 16²¹, ²², Ja 1¹⁰, ¹¹ ; οἱ π., Lk 6²⁴ 21¹, I Ti 6¹⁷, Ja 2⁶ 5¹, Re 6¹⁵ 13¹⁶ ; anarth., a rich man, Mt 19²³, ²⁴, Mk 10²⁵ 12⁴¹, Lk 18²⁵. Metaph., of God, ἐν ἐλέει (= cl., c. gen., dat.), Eph 2⁴ ; of Christ, II Co 8⁹ ; of Christians, Re 2⁹ 3¹⁷ ; ἐν πίστει, Ja 2⁵.†

*πλουσίως, adv., *richly, abundantly :* Col 3¹⁶, ι Ti 6¹⁷, Tit 3⁶, ιι Pe 1¹¹.†

πλουτέω, -ῶ, [in LXX chiefly for עָשַׁר hi. ;] *to be rich,* aor., *to become rich :* Lk 1⁵³, ι Ti 6⁹; seq. ἀπό (Si 11¹⁸), Re 18¹⁵; ἐκ, Re 18³,¹⁹; ἐν (= cl., c. gen., dat., acc., cf. πλούσιος), ι Ti 6¹⁸. Metaph., π. εἰς θεόν, Lk 12²¹; of God, εἰς πάντας, Ro 10¹²; aor., *I became rich,* ι Co 4⁸, ιι Co 8⁹, Re 3¹⁸; pf., *I have become rich,* Re 3¹⁷.†

πλουτίζω (< πλοῦτος), [in LXX chiefly for עָשַׁר hi. ;] *to make rich, enrich :* c. acc. pers., pass., ιι Co 9¹¹. Metaph., of spiritual riches, c. acc. pers., ιι Co 6¹⁰; seq. ἐν, pass., ι Co 1⁵.†

πλοῦτος, -ου, ὁ and (in ιι Co 8², Eph 1¹⁷ 2⁷ 3⁸,¹⁶, Phl 4¹⁹, Col 1²⁷ 2²; v. WH, *App.,* 158; M, *Pr.,* 60) τό, [in LXX chiefly for עָשַׁר ;] *riches, wealth :* of external possessions, Mt 13²², Mk 4¹⁹, Lk 8¹⁴, ι Ti 6¹⁷, Ja 5², Re 18¹⁶; of moral and spiritual conceptions, Ro 2⁴ 9²³ 11¹²,³³, ιι Co 8², Eph 1⁷,¹⁸ 2⁷ 3⁸,¹⁶, Phl 4¹⁹, Col 1²⁷ 2², He 11²⁶, Re 5¹².†

πλύνω, [in LXX chiefly for כָּבַס pi. ;] *to wash* (inanimate objects, esp. clothing) : τ. δίκτυα, Lk 5². Fig., τ. στολάς, Re 7¹⁴ 22¹⁴ (cf. Ps 50 (51)⁴,⁹ and v.s. ἀπο-πλύνω).†

SYN. : v.s. λούω.

πνεῦμα, -τος, τό (< πνέω), [in LXX chiefly and very freq. for רוּחַ;] 1. of air in motion; (*a*) *wind :* Jo 3⁸; pl., He 1⁷ (LXX); (*b*) *breath :* π. ζωῆς, Re 11¹¹; π. τοῦ στόματος, fig., ιι Th 2⁸ (cf. Ps 32 (33)⁶). 2. Of the vital principle, *the spirit* (Arist., Polyb., al.) : Lk 8⁵⁵, Jo 19³⁰, Ac 7⁵⁹, al.; opp. to σάρξ, Mt 26⁴¹, Mk 14³⁸, ι Co 5⁵, al.; to σῶμα, Ro 8¹⁰, ι Co 6¹⁷ 7³⁴, ι Pe 4⁶; to ψυχή, Phl 1²⁷, He 4¹²; τὸ π. καὶ ἡ ψ. καὶ τ. σῶμα, ι Th 5²³ (M, *Th.,* in l.); dat., τῷ π., *in spirit,* Mk 2⁸ 8¹², Jo 11³³ 13²¹, Ac 18²⁵, Ro 12¹¹, ι Co 7³⁴, ι Pe 3¹⁸, al.; of the human spirit of Christ, Ro 1⁴, ι Ti 3¹⁶. 3. *spirit,* i.e. frame of mind, disposition, influence : Lk 1¹⁷, Ro 8¹⁵, ι Co 4²¹, Gal 6¹, Eph 2², ιι Ti 1⁷, ι Jo 4⁶, al. 4. An incorporeal being, *a spirit :* Lk 24³⁷,³⁹, Ac 23⁸; π. ὁ θεός, *God is spirit,* Jo 4²⁴; πατὴρ τῶν π., He 12⁹; of disembodied human beings, He 12²³, ι Pe 3¹⁹ (*ICC,* in l.; *DB,* iii, 795); of angels, He 1¹⁴; of demons or evil spirits, Mt 8¹⁶, Mk 9²⁰, Lk 9³⁹, al.; π. πύθωνα, Ac 16¹⁶; πνεύματα δαιμονίων, Re 16¹⁴; π. δαιμονίου ἀκαθάρτου, Lk 4³³; π. ἀσθενείας (Bl., § 35, 5), Lk 13¹¹; π. ἀκάθαρτον, Mt 10¹, Mk 1²³, Lk 4³⁶, Ac 5¹⁶; π. ἄλαλον (καὶ κωφόν), Mk 9¹⁷,²⁵; πονηρόν, Lk 7²¹, Ac 19¹², al. 5. Of the Holy Spirit, π. ἅγιον, τὸ ἅ. π., τὸ π. τὸ ἅ., τὸ π., π. (the article as a rule being used when the Spirit is regarded as a Person or a Divine Power, and omitted when the reference is to an operation, influence or gift of the Spirit; v. WM, 151₅; Bl., § 46, 7) : anarth., Mt 1¹⁸ 3¹¹,¹⁶ 4¹, Mk 1⁸ (Swete, in l.), ib.¹⁰, Lk 1¹⁵, Jo 7³⁹, Ac 19², Ro 5⁵, ι Co 2⁴, al.; c. art., Mt 4¹ 12³¹,³², Mk 1¹⁰ 3²⁹, Lk 2²⁶, Jo 7³⁹ 14²⁶, Ac 4³¹ 5³, Ro 8¹⁶, al.; (τὸ) π. (τοῦ) θεοῦ, Mt 3¹⁶, Ro 8⁹, Eph 3¹⁶, ι Jo 4², al.; τὸ π. τ. πατρός, Mt 10²⁰; π. θεοῦ ζῶντος, ιι Co 3³; (τὸ) π. τοῦ κυρίου, Lk 4¹⁸, Ac 5⁹ 8³⁹; τὸ π. Ἰησοῦ, Ac 16⁷; Χριστοῦ, Ro 8⁹; Ἰησοῦ Χριστοῦ, Phl 1¹⁹; τὸ π. τ. ἀληθείας, Jo 15²⁶ 16¹³, ι Jo 4⁶; λέγει (μαρτυρεῖ) τὸ π. (τὸ ἅγιον), Ac 21¹¹ 28²⁵, ι Ti 4¹, He 3⁷ 10¹⁵, Re 14¹³; seq. τ. ἐκκλησίαις,

Re 2⁷, ¹¹, ¹⁷, ²⁹ 3⁶, ¹³, ²² ; ἐν τ. π., Lk 2²⁷ ; κατὰ πνεῦμα, Ro 8⁴, ⁵ ; ἐξ ὕδατος καὶ π., Jo 3⁵ ; διὰ πνεύματος αἰωνίου, He 9¹⁴ ; ἐν ἁγιασμῷ πνεύματος, ιι Th 2¹³, ι Pe 1² ; ἐν π., ι Co 12¹³, Eph 2¹⁸ 4⁴ ; ὁ δὲ κύριος τὸ π. ἐστιν, ιι Co 3¹⁷ ; of that which is effected or governed by the Spirit, opp. to γράμμα, Ro 2²⁹ 7⁶, ιι Co 3⁶. (v. ICC on Ga, pp. 486 ff.)

SYN.: νοῦς, which in NT is contrasted with π. as " the action of the understanding in man with that of the spiritual or ecstatic impulse " (DB, iv, 612); ψυχή—the usual term in cl. psychology—in NT, " expresses man as apart from God, a separate individual. π. expresses man as drawing his life from God " (DB, 1-vol., 872).

* πνευματικός, -ή, -όν (< πνεῦμα), 1. of or caused by the wind, air or breath (Arist., al.). 2. spiritual (opp. to σωματικός, Plut.); (a) of created beings : τὰ π. (RV, the spiritual hosts), Eph 6¹² ; of that which is related to the human spirit, opp. to ψυχικός, ι Co 15⁴⁴, ⁴⁶ ; (b) of that which belongs to or is actuated by the Divine Spirit; (a) of persons : ι Co 2¹³ (R, mg., but v. infr.) 2¹⁵ 3¹ 14³⁷, Ga 6¹ ; οἶκος π., fig., ι Pe 2⁵ ; (β) of things : Ro 1¹¹ 7¹⁴, ι Co 2¹³ (R, txt., but v. supr.) 10³, ⁴ 12¹ 14¹, Eph 1³ 5¹⁹, Col 1⁹ 3¹⁶, ι Pe 2⁵ ; opp. to τ. σαρκικά, Ro 15²⁷, ι Co 9¹¹.†

SYN.: ψυχικός, q.v., and cf. DB, ii, 410, iv, 612.

*† πνευματικῶς, adv. (< πνεῦμα), spiritually; (a) by the aid of the Holy Spirit : ι Co 2¹³ (WH. mg.), ¹⁴ ; (b) in a spiritual sense : Re 11⁸.†

πνέω, [in LXX : Ps 147⁷ (¹⁸) (נשׁב hi.), Is 40²⁴ (נשׁף), Si 43¹⁶, ²⁰, Ep. Je⁶¹, ιι Mac 9⁷ * ;] to breathe, blow : of the wind, Mt 7²⁵, ²⁷, Lk 12⁵⁵, Jo 3⁸ 6¹⁸, Re 7¹ ; τῇ πνεούσῃ (sc. αὔρᾳ), Ac 27⁴⁰ (cf. ἐκ-, ἐν-, ὑπο-πνέω).†

πνίγω, [in LXX : ι Ki 16¹⁴, ¹⁵ (בעת pi.) * ;] to choke : c. acc., Mt 13⁷ (WH, mg.); impf. (conative), Mt 18²⁸ ; of drowning, pass., Mk 5¹³ (cf. ἀπο-, ἐπι-, συν-πνίγω).†

* πνικτός, -ή, -όν (< πνίγω), strangled : Ac 15²⁰, ²⁹ (om. D, Lat. vet., Iren.; v. Turner, SNT, p. 30) 21²⁵ (cf. Le 17¹³, ¹⁴).†

πνοή, -ῆς, ἡ (< πνέω), [in LXX chiefly for נשׁמה ;] 1. a blowing, blast, wind : Ac 2². 2. a breathing, breath : Ac 17²⁵ (Ge 2⁷, al.).†

ποδήρης, -ες (< πούς), [in LXX : Ex 25⁶ (⁷) 35⁹ (חשׁן), 28⁴ 29⁵ (מעיל), 28²⁷ (³¹) (אפוד), Ez 9², ³, ¹¹ (בד), Za 3⁵ (⁴) (מחלצות), Wi 18²⁴, Si 27⁸ 45⁸ * ;] reaching to the feet. of a garment (sc. χιτών, cf. Ex, Ez, ll. c.; Xen., al.), Re 1¹³ (for -η, LT⁷ read -ην ; v. M, Pr., 49).†

SYN.: στολή, v. Tr., Syn., § 1.

πόθεν, adv., whence; (a) of place : Mt 15³³, Lk 13²⁵, ²⁷, Jo 3⁸ 6⁵ 8¹⁴ 9²⁹, ³⁰ 19⁹, Re 7¹³ ; metaph., of condition, Re 2⁵ ; (b) of origin : Mt 13²⁷, ⁵⁴, ⁵⁶ 21²⁵, Mk 6², Lk 20⁷, Jo 2⁹, Ja 4¹ ; of parentage, Jo 7²⁷, ²⁸ ; (c) of cause : Mk 8⁴ 12³⁷, Lk 1⁴³, Jo 1⁴⁹ 4¹¹.†

ποία, -ας, ἡ, Dor. for πόα, [in LXX (with v.l. πόα) : Pr 27²⁵ (אשׁא), and of a kind of soap (Soph., Lex., s.v.), Ma 3², Je 2²² (בּרית) * ;] grass : Ja 4¹⁴ (where, however, it is usually taken to be fem. of ποῖος ; but v. MM, xx).†

ποιέω, -ῶ, [in LXX for a great variety of words, but chiefly for עָשָׂה;] 1. *to make, produce, create, cause* : c. acc. rei, Mt 17⁴, Mk 9⁵, Jo 9¹¹, Ac 9³⁹, Ro 9²⁰, al. ; of God as Creator (c. acc. pers. also), Mt 19⁴, Mk 10⁶, Lk 11⁴⁰, Ac 4²⁴, He 1², al. ; like Heb. עָשָׂה, absol. = ἐργάζομαι, *to work*, Mt 20¹² (cf. Ru 2¹⁹ ; so AV, but v. infr.), Re 13⁵, R, mg. (but v. infr.) ; σκ ίνδαλα, Ro 16¹⁷ ; εἰρήνην, Eph 2¹⁵, Ja 3¹⁸ ; ἐπίστασιν, Ac 24¹² ; συστροφήν, Ac 23¹² ; c. acc. rei et dat. pers., Lk 1⁶⁸, Ac 15³ ; with nouns expressing action or its accomplishment, forming a periphr. for the cogn. verb : ὁδόν π. (cl. ὁ. ποιεῖσθαι), *to go on, advance*, Mk 2²³ ; πόλεμον, Re 11⁷, al. ; ἐκδίκησιν, Lk 18⁷,⁸ ; ἐνέδραν, Ac 25³ ; κρίσιν, Jo 5²⁷, Ju ¹⁵ ; ἔργα, Jo 5³⁶, al. ; σημεῖα (τέρατα καὶ σ.), Jo 2²³ and freq., Ac 2²², al. ; so also mid. ποιεῖσθαι : μονήν, Jo 14²³ ; πορείαν, Lk 13²² ; κοινωνίαν, Ro 15²⁶ ; of food, *to make ready, prepare* : δεῖπνον, Mk 6²¹, al. ; δοχήν, Lk 5²⁹ 14¹³ ; γάμους, Mt 22² ; of time, *to spend* (cl.) : ὥραν, Mt 20¹², RV (but v. supr. and cf. McN, in l.) ; μῆνας, Re 13⁵, R, txt. (cf. Swete, in l. ; but v. supr.) ; ἐνιαυτόν, Ja 4¹³ ; c. acc. seq. ἐκ, Jo 2¹⁵, al. ; c. acc. et acc. pred., Mt 3³ 12¹⁶, Mk 1³ 3¹², Jo 5¹¹, al. ; c. adv., καλῶς, Mk 7³⁷ ; ἑορτὴν π. (Dem., Ex 23¹⁶, al.), Ac 18²¹, Rec. ; πάσχα, Mt 26¹⁸ ; *to make* or *offer* a sacrifice (Plat., Xen., al. ; Jb 42⁸, iii Ki 11³³ ; so some understand τοῦτο ποιεῖτε, Lk 22¹⁹, but v. Abbott, *Essays*, 110 ff.) ; seq. ἵνα (WM, 422 f. ; M, *Pr.*, 228), Jo 11³⁷, Col 4¹⁶, Re 3⁹. 2. *to do, perform, carry out, execute* : absol., c. adv., καλῶς π., Mt 12¹², I Co 7³⁷,³⁸, Ja 2¹⁹ ; id. seq. ptcp. (cl. ; v. M, *Pr.*, 228), Ac 10³³, Phl 4¹⁴, ii Pe 1¹⁹, iii Jo ⁶ ; οὕτως, Mt 24⁴⁶, Lk 9¹⁵, al. ; ὡς (καθώς), Mt 1²⁴ 21⁶, al. ; ὁμοίως, Lk 3¹¹ ; ὡσαύτως, Mt 20⁵ ; c. ptcp., ἀγνοῶν ἐποίησα, I Ti 1¹³ ; c. acc. rei : τί interrog., Mt 12³, Mk 2²⁵, Lk 6², al. ; τοῦτο, Mt 13²⁸, Mk 5³², Lk 22¹⁹ (WH om. ; v. supr., ref. to Abbott, *Essays*), Ro 7²⁰, al. ; with nouns expressing command or regulation : τ. νόμον (not as in cl., *to make* a law), Jo 7¹⁹, Ga 5³ (cf. in LXX, Jos 22⁵, I Ch 22¹², al.) ; τ. ἐντολάς, Mt 5¹⁹ ; similarly with other nouns expressing conduct : τ. δικαιοσύνην, Mt 6¹, al. ; τ. ἀλήθειαν, Jo 3²¹, al., etc. ; c. dupl. acc., Mt 27²², Mk 15¹² ; c. acc. rei et dat. pers. (commod., incomm. ; rare in cl.), Mt 7¹², Mk 5¹⁹,²⁰, Lk 1⁴⁹, Jo 9²⁶, al.

SYN. : πράσσω, q.v. The general distinction between the two words is that between particular action and its habitual performance (cf. Tr., *Syn.*, § xcvi ; Westc. on Jo 3²¹ ; *ICC* on Ro 1³²).

ποίημα, -τος, τό (< ποιέω), [in LXX chiefly for מַעֲשֶׂה (freq. in Ec) ;] *that which is made* or *done, a work* : Ro 1²⁰, Eph 2¹⁰.†

ποίησις, -εως, ἡ (ποιέω), [in LXX chiefly for מַעֲשֶׂה and cognate forms ;] 1. *a making* (Hdt., Thuc., al.). 2. *a doing* (Si 19¹⁸ 51¹⁹) : Ja 1²⁵.†

**ποιητής, -οῦ, ὁ (< ποιέω), [in LXX : I Mac 2⁶⁷ * ;] in cl., 1. *a maker, author*. 2. Esp., *a poet* : Ac 17²⁸. Later, 3. *a doer* : τ. νόμου, Ro 2¹³, Ja 4¹¹ (I Mac, l.c.) ; ἔργου, Ja 1²⁵ ; λόγου, ib. ²²,²³.†

ποικίλος, -η, -ον, [in LXX for נָקֹד, רִקְמָה, etc. ;] *many-coloured,* *variegated.* Metaph., *various, manifold:* Mt 4²⁴, Mk 1³⁴, Lk 4⁴⁰, II Ti 3⁶, Tit 3³, He 2⁴ 13⁹, Ja 1², I Pe 1⁶ 4¹⁰.†

ποιμαίνω (< ποιμήν), [in LXX chiefly for רעה;] *to act as shepherd, tend* flocks : Lk 17⁷; c. acc., πο'μνην, I Co 9⁷. Metaph., *to tend, shepherd, govern:* c. acc., Mt 2⁶ (LXX), Jo 21¹⁶, Ac 20²⁸, I Pe 5², Ju ¹², Re 2²⁷ 7¹⁷ 12⁵ 19¹⁵.†

SYN.: βόσκω, q.v.

ποιμήν, -ένος, ὁ, [in LXX for רעה;] *a shepherd:* Mt 9³⁶ 25³² 26³¹ (LXX), Mk 6³⁴ 14²⁷, Lk 2⁸, ¹⁵, ¹⁸,.²⁰, Jo 10², ¹². Metaph., of Christ; Jo 10¹¹, ¹⁴, ¹⁶, He 13²⁰, I Pe 2²⁵; of Christian pastors, Eph 4¹¹ (cf. Hom., *Il.*, i, 263, ποιμένα λαῶν).†

ποίμνη, -ης, ἡ, [in LXX: Ge 32¹⁶ ⁽¹⁷⁾ (עדר), Za 13⁷ A *;] *a flock,* prop., of sheep : Mt 26³¹, Lk 2⁸, I Co 9⁷. Metaph., of Christ's followers, Jo 10¹⁶.†

ποίμνιον, -ου, τό, = ποίμνη, q.v., [in LXX chiefly for צאן, also for עדר, etc.;] *a flock,* prop., of sheep. Metaph., of Christians : Lk 12³², Ac 20²⁸, ²⁹, I Pe 5³; τ. θεοῦ, ib. ².†

ποῖος, -α, -ον, interrog. pronom. adj. (corresponding to the demonstr. τοῖος and the relat. οἷος), [in LXX chiefly for אי־זה;] *of what quality* or *sort:* absol., n. pl., Lk 24¹⁹; c. subst.; (*a*) prop., in direct questions : Mt 19¹⁸ 21²³ 22³⁶ 24⁴², Mk 11²⁸ 12²⁸, Lk 6³²·³⁴, Jo 10³², Ac 4⁷ 7⁴⁹, Ro 3²⁷, I Co 15³⁵, Ja 4¹⁴ (but v.s. ποία), I Pe 2²⁰; (*b*) in indirect questions = ὁποῖος : Mt 21²⁴, ²⁷ 24⁴³, Mk 11²⁹, ³³, Lk 12³⁹ 20², ⁸, Jo 12³³ 18³² 21¹⁹, Ac 23³⁴, I Pe 1¹¹, Re 3³; ποίας (sc. ὁδοῦ), Lk 5¹⁹.†

πολεμέω, -ῶ (< πόλεμος), [in LXX chiefly for לחם ni.;] *to make war, fight:* Re 12⁷ᵇ 19¹¹; seq. μετά (II Ki 21¹⁵ and v. M, *Pr.*, 106, 247), Re 2¹⁶ 12⁷ᵃ 13⁴ 17¹⁴; hyperb., of private quarrels, Ja 4².†

πόλεμος, -ου, ὁ, [in LXX chiefly for מלחמה;] 1. *war:* Mt 24⁶, Mk 13⁷, Lk 14³¹ 21⁹, He 11³⁴; π. ποιεῖν, seq. μετά, c. gen. (cf. πολεμέω), Re 11⁷ 12¹⁷ 13⁷ 19¹⁹. 2. = μάχη, *a fight, battle:* I Co 14⁸, Re 9⁷, ⁹ 12⁷ 16¹⁴ 20⁸; hyperb., of private quarrels (cf. πολεμέω), Ja 4¹.†

πόλις, -εως, ἡ, [in LXX chiefly and very freq. for עיר;] *a city:* Mt 2²³, Mk 1⁴⁵, Lk 4²⁹, Jo 4⁸, al. mult.; opp. to κῶμαι (κ. καὶ ἀγροί), Mt 9³⁵ 10¹¹, Mk 6⁵⁶, Lk 8¹ 13²²; c. nom. propr. in appos. (cl.), Ac 11⁵ 16¹⁴; c. id. in gen. appos. (Bl., § 35, 5), Ac 8⁵, II Pe 2⁶; gen., of the region, Lk 1²⁶ 4³¹, Jo 4⁵; of the inhabitants, Mt 10⁵, ²³, Lk 23⁵¹, Ac 19³⁵, II Co 11³²; c. gen. pers., of one's residence or native place, Mt 22⁷, Lk 2⁴, ¹¹ 4²⁹ 10¹¹, Jo 1⁴⁵, Ac 16²⁰, Re 16⁹; of Jerusalem : ἡ ἁγία π., Mt 4⁵ 27⁵³, Re 11²; ἡ ἠγαπημένη, Re 20¹⁹; π. τοῦ μεγάλου βασιλέως, Mt 5³⁵ (cf. Ps 47 (48)²); of the heavenly city in the Apocalyptic visions, Re 3¹² 21², ¹⁰, ¹⁴ ff. 22¹⁴, ¹⁹. By meton., of the inhabitants of a city : Mt 8³⁴ 12²⁵ 21¹⁰, Mk 1³³, Ac 14²¹ 21³⁰.

*†πολιτάρχης, -ου, ὁ, = πολίαρχος (Pind., Eur.), *the ruler of a city, a politarch:* Ac 17⁶, ⁸ (v. MM, xx).†

** πολιτεία, -ας, ἡ (< πολιτεύω), [in LXX: ii Mac 4¹¹ 6²³ 8¹⁷ 13¹⁴, iii Mac 3²¹, ²³, iv Mac 3²⁰ 8⁷ 17⁹ *;] 1. *citizenship*: Ac 22²⁸ (iii Mac, ll. c., Hdt., Xen., al.). 2. *government, administration* (Aristoph., Dem., al.). 3. *a commonwealth*: Eph 2¹².†

** πολίτευμα, -τος, τό (< πολιτεύω), [in LXX: ii Mac 12⁷ *;] 1. *an act of administration*. 2. *a form of government*. 3. = πολιτεία, (*a*) *citizenship*: Phl 3²⁰ (R, txt.); (*b*) *community, commonwealth*: Phl, l.c. (R, mg.; for exx. v. MM, *VGT*, s.v.); Moffatt renders *We are a colony of Heaven*.†

** πολιτεύω, more freq. as depon., -ομαι, and so in LXX and NT (< πολίτης), [in LXX: Es 8¹³, ii Mac 6¹ 11²⁵, iii Mac 3⁴, iv Mac₄ *;] *to be a citizen, live as a citizen*: metaph., of conduct as based on heavenly citizenship, Ac 23¹, Phl 1²⁷.†

πολίτης, -ου, ὁ (< πόλις), [in LXX chiefly for רֵעַ;] 1. *a citizen*. c. gen. loc., Lk 15¹⁵, Ac 21³⁹. 2. *a fellow-citizen*: c. gen. pers. Lk 19¹⁴, He 8¹¹ (LXX).†

πολλάκις, adv. (< πολύς), *often*: Mt 17¹⁵, al.

*† πολλαπλασίων, -ον (< πόλυς), = πολλαπλάσιος, *many times more*: Mt 19²⁹, Lk 18³⁰.†

πολυ-εύσπλαγχνος, v.s. πολύσπλαγχνος.

πολυλογία, -ας, ἡ, [in LXX: Pr 10¹⁹ (רֹב דְּבָרִים) *;] *much speaking, loquacity*: Mt 6⁷.†

*† πολυμερῶς, adv. (< πολύς, μέρος), *in many parts or portions*: He 1¹ (Plut., al.).†

* πολυ-ποίκιλος, -ον, 1. *much variegated, of greatly differing colours* (Eur.). 2. *manifold*: Eph 3¹⁰.†

πολύς, πολλή, πολύ, [in LXX chiefly for רַב and cognate forms;] 1. as adj., *much, many, great*, of number, space, degree, value, time, etc.: ἀριθμός, Ac 11²¹; ὄχλος, Mk 5²⁴; θερισμός, Mt 9³⁷; χόρτος, Jo 6¹⁰; χρόνος, Mt 25¹⁹; γογγυσμός, Jo 7¹²; πόνος, Col 4¹³; δόξα, Mt 24³⁰; σιγή, Ac 21⁴⁰; pl., προφῆται, Mt 13¹⁷; ὄχλοι, Mt 4²⁵; δαιμόνια, Mk 1³⁴; δυνάμεις, Mt 7²². 2. As subst., pl. masc., πολλοί, *many* (persons): Mt 7²², Mk 2², al.; c. gen. partit., Mt 3⁷, Lk 1¹⁶, al.; seq. ἐκ, Jo 7³¹, Ac 17¹²; c. art., οἱ π., *the many*, Mt 24¹², Ro 12⁵, i Co 10¹⁷, ³³, ii Co 2¹⁷; opp. to ὁ εἷς (Lft., *Notes*, 291), Ro 5¹⁵, ¹⁹; neut. pl., πολλά: Mt 13³, Mk 5²⁶, al.; acc. with adverbial force, Mk 1⁴⁵, Ro 16⁶ (Deiss., *LAE*, 317; M, *Gr.*, ii, p. 446), i Co 16¹², Ja 3², al.; neut. sing., πολύ: Lk 12⁴⁸; adverbially, Mk 12²⁷, al.; πολλοῦ (gen. pret.), Mt 26⁹; c. compar. (Bl., § 44, 5), π. σπουδαιότερον, ii Co 8²²; πολλῷ πλείους, Jo 4⁴¹.

Compar., πλείων, neut., πλεῖον and πλέον (v. WH, *App.*, 151), pl., πλείονες, -ας, -α, contr., πλείους, -ω (cf. Mayser, 69), *more, greater*; 1. as adj.: Jo 15², Ac 18²⁰, He 3³; seq. παρά, He 11⁴ (cf. Westc., in l Was ΠΛΙΟΝΑ here a primitive error for ΗΔΙΟΝΑ?); pl., Ac 13³¹ al.; c. gen. compar., Mt 21³⁶; c. num. (ἤ of comp. omitted), Ac 4² 24¹¹, al. 2. As subst., οἱ π., *the greater number*: Ac 19³² 27¹², i Co 10⁵ 15⁶; also (Bl., § 44, 3) *others, more, the more*: ii Co 2⁶ 4¹⁵, Phl 1¹⁴; πλείονα, Lk 11⁵³; πλεῖον, πλέον, Mt 20¹⁰, ii Ti 3⁹; c. gen. comp., Mk

12⁴³, Lk 21³; π. Ἰωνᾶ ὧδε, Mt 12⁴¹; ἐπὶ π., adverbially, Ac 4¹⁷ 20⁹ 24⁴. 3. As adv., πλεῖον: seq. ἤ, Lk 9¹³; c. gen. comp., Mt 5²⁰; πλείω: c. num., Mt 26⁵³.

Superl., πλεῖστος, -η, -ον, (a) prop., most: Mt 11²⁰ 21⁸; adverbially, τὸ π., ι Co 14²⁷; (b) elative (M, Pr., 79), very great: ὄχλος π., Mk 4¹.

*† πολύσπλαγχνος, -ον (< πολύς, σπλάγχνον), very pitiful: Ja 5¹¹.†

πολυτελής, -ές (< πολύς, τέλος), [in LXX for יָקָר, etc.;] very costly, very precious, of great value: Mk 14³, ι Ti 2⁹; metaph., ι Pe 3⁴.†

* πολύτιμος, -ον (< πολύς, τιμή), 1. much revered (Menand.). 2. very costly, very precious: Mt 13⁴⁶ 26⁷ (βαρύτιμος, WH), Jo 12³; comparat., ι Pe 1⁷.†

** πολυτρόπως, adv. (< πολύτροπος, 1. much turning. 2. manifold), [in LXX: ιv Mac 3²¹ A*;] in many ways or manners: He 1¹ (Philo).†

πόμα, -τος, τό (< πίνω), late form of Att. πῶμα, [in LXX: Ps 101 (102)⁹ (שִׁקּוּי), al. ₄*;] drink: ι Co 10⁴, He 9¹⁰.†

πονηρία, -ας, ἡ (< πονηρός), [in LXX chiefly for רָעָה;] iniquity, wickedness: Mt 22¹⁸, Lk 11³⁹, Ro 1²⁹, Eph 6¹²; pl. (v. Bl., § 32, 6; WM, 220; Swete, Mk., 153), Mk 7²², Ac 3²⁶; κακία καὶ π., ι Co 5⁸.†

SYN.: v.s. κακία.

πονηρός, -ά, -όν (< πονέω, to toil), [in LXX chiefly for רַע;] 1. (a) of persons, oppressed by toils (Hes.); (b) of things, toilsome, painful (καιρός, Si 51¹²): Eph 5¹⁶ 6¹³, Re 16². 2. bad, worthless; (a) in physical sense: καρπός, Mt 7¹⁷,¹⁸; (b) in ethical sense, bad, evil, wicked; (a) of persons: Mt 7¹¹ 12³⁴,³⁵ 18³² 25²⁶, Lk 6⁴⁵ 11¹³ 19²², Ac 17⁵, ιι Th 3², ιι Ti 3¹³; γενεά, Mt 12³⁹,⁴⁵ 16⁴, Lk 11²⁹; πνεῦμα, Mt 12⁴⁵, Lk 7²¹ 8² 11²⁶, Ac 19¹²,¹³,¹⁵,¹⁶; as subst., οἱ π., opp. to δίκαιοι, Mt 13⁴⁹; to ἀγαθοί, Mt 5⁴⁵ 22¹⁰; οἱ ἀχάριστοι καὶ π., Lk 6³⁵; sing., ὁ π., Mt 5³⁹, ι Co 5¹³; id. esp. of Satan, the evil one, Mt 5³⁷ 6¹³ (v. Lft., Notes, 125 ff.; but cf. McN, in l.) 13¹⁹,³⁸, Lk 11⁴ (WH, R, om.), Jo 17¹⁵, Eph 6¹⁶, ιι Th 3³ (Lft., Notes, l.c.), ι Jo 2¹³,¹⁴ 3¹² 5¹⁸,¹⁹; (β) of things: Mt 5¹¹ 12³⁵ 15¹⁹, Lk 6²²,⁴⁵, Jo 3¹⁹ 7⁷, Ac 18¹⁴ 25¹⁸, Ga 1⁴, Col 1²¹, ι Ti 6⁴, ιι Ti 4¹⁸, He 3¹² 10²², Ja 2⁴ 4¹⁶, ι Jo 3¹², ιι Jo ¹¹, ιιι Jo ¹⁰; ὀφθαλμός (q.v.), Mt 6²³ 20¹⁵, Mk 7²², Lk 11³⁴; as subst., neut., τὸ π., Ac 28²¹, ι Th 5²²; opp. to ἀγαθόν, Lk 6⁴⁵, Ro 12⁹; pl., Mt 9⁴, Mk 7²³, Lk 3¹⁹.†

SYN.: v.s. ἄθεσμος.

πόνος, -ου, ὁ [in LXX for עָמָל, etc.;] 1. labour, toil: Col 4¹³. 2. The consequence of toil, distress, suffering, pain (Xen., al., LXX): Re 16¹⁰,¹¹ 21⁴.†

SYN.: v.s. κόπος.

Ποντικός, -ή, -όν, Pontic, of Pontus: Ac 18².

Πόντιος, -ου, ὁ, Pontius, the praenomen of Pilate (v.s. Πειλᾶτος), Mt 27² (Rec., WH, mg.), Lk 3¹, Ac 4²⁷, ι Ti 6¹³.†

Πόντος, -ου, ὁ, Pontus, a region of Asia Minor, bordering on the πόντος Εὔξεινος: Ac 2⁹, ι Pe 1¹.†

Πόπλιος, -ου, ὁ (Latin), *Publius* : Ac 28⁷, ⁸.†

πορεία, -ας, ἡ (< πορεύω), [in LXX chiefly for הֲלִיכָה and cogn.
forms ;] 1. *a journey* : Lk 13²². 2. *a going* : metaph. (" the rich man
perishes while he is still *on the move*," Hort., in l.), Ja 1¹¹.†

πορεύω, (< πόρος, *a ford, a passage*), [in LXX chiefly for הלךְ ;]
in cl. (the act. becomes obsolete in late Gk. ; v. M, *Pr.*, 162), *to cause
to go over, carry, convey.* Mid. (always in LXX and NT), -ομαι, *to go,
proceed, go on one's way* : c. acc., ὁδόν, Ac 8³⁹ ; seq. ἐκεῖθεν, Mt 19¹⁵ ;
ἐντεῦθεν, Lk 13³¹ ; ἀπό, Mt 25⁴¹, Lk 4⁴² ; εἰς, Mt 2²⁰, Mk 16¹², Lk 1³⁹,
Jo 7³⁵, al. ; εἰς εἰρήνην (cf. ι Ki 1¹⁷), Lk 7⁵⁰ ; ἐν εἰρήνῃ, Ac 16³⁶ ; ἐπί,
c. acc., Mt 22⁹, Ac 25¹², al. ; ἕως, Ac 23²³ ; οὗ, Lk 24²⁸, ι Co 16⁶ ; πρός,
c. acc. pers., Mt 25⁹, Lk 11⁵, al. ; κατὰ τ. ὁδόν, Ac 8³⁶ ; διά, c. gen.,
Mt 12¹, Mk 9³⁰ ; c. inf., Lk 2³, Jo 14² ; σύν, Lk 7⁶, al. ; ἵνα, Jo 11¹¹ ;
absol., Mt 2⁹, Lk 7⁸, Jo 4⁵⁰, Ac 5²⁰, al. ; ptcp., πορευθείς (on the pass.
form of the aor., v. M, *Pr.*, 161 f.), redundant (as in Heb. and Aram. ;
v. M, *Pr.*, 231 ; Dalman, *Words*, 21), Mt 2⁸, Lk 7²², al. Metaph.
(cf. Soph., *O.T.*, 884 ; Xen., *Cyr.*, 2, 2, 24, al.), (*a*) like οἴχομαι in cl.,
as euphemism for θνήσκω (so הלךְ in Ge 15²) ; Lk 22²² and perh. also
13³³ (v. Field, *Notes*, 66) ; (*b*) in ethical sense (De 19⁹, Ps 14², al.,
cf. M, *Pr.*, 11₂ ; Kennedy, *Sources*, 107) : seq. ἐν, Lk 1⁶, ι Pe 4³,
ιι Pe 2¹⁰ ; κατά, c. acc., ιι Pe 3³, Ju¹⁶,¹⁸ ; c. dat. (Bl., § 38, 3), Ac 9³¹
14¹⁶, Ju¹¹ ; (*c*) of disciples or partisans (Jg 2¹², ιιι Ki 11¹⁰, Si 46¹⁰) :
seq. ὀπίσω, c. gen. pers., Lk 21⁸ (cf. δια-, εἰς- (-μαι), ἐκ- (-μαι), ἐν- (-μαι),
ἐπι- (-μαι), παρα- (-μαι), προ-, προσ- (-μαι), συν- (-μαι)).

** πορθέω, collat. form (in cl. chiefly poët.) of πέρθω, [in LXX
ιν Mac 4²³ 11⁴ * ;] *to destroy, ravage* : Ac 9²¹, Ga 1¹³, ²³.†

**† πορισμός, -οῦ, ὁ (< πορίζω, *to procure*), [in LXX : Wi 13¹⁹ 14² * ;]
1. *a providing*. 2. *a means of gain* : ι Ti 6⁵, ⁶ (Polyb., al.).†

Πόρκιος, -ου, ὁ, *Porcius*, prænomen of Porcius Festus (v.s.
Φῆστος) : Ac 24²⁷.†

πορνεία, -ας, ἡ (< πορνεύω), [in LXX for זְנוּנִים, תַּזְנוּת and cogn.
forms ;] *fornication* : Ac 15²⁰, ²⁹ 21²⁵, ι Co 5¹ 6¹³, ¹⁸, ιι Co 12²¹, Ga 5¹⁹,
Eph 5³, Col 3⁵, ιTh 4³ (Lft., *Notes*, 53), Re 9²¹ ; pl. (v. WM, 220 ; Bl., § 32,
6), ι Co 7² ; disting. from μοιχεία, Mt 15¹⁹, Mk 7²¹ ; = μοιχεία (Am 8¹⁷
Si 23²³, al.), Mt 5³² 19⁹. Metaph. (of idolatry : De 23², Ho 1²) : Jo 8⁴¹
(Westc., in l.), and so perh. (Thayer-Grimm, s.v. ; but v. Swete, in ll.),
Re 2²¹ 14¹⁸ 17², ⁴ 18³ 19².†

πορνεύω, [in LXX for זנה ;] 1. *to prostitute* the body for hire.
2. *to commit fornication* : Mk 10¹⁹ (WH, mg.), ι Co 6¹⁸ 10⁸, Re 2¹⁴, ²⁰.
Metaph. (as in LXX : ι Ch 5²⁵, Je 3⁶, Ho 9¹, al.), of idolatry (but v.
Swete, *Ap.*, 180 f.), Re 17² 18³, ⁹ (cf. ἐκ-πορνεύω).†

πόρνη, -ης, ἡ, [in LXX chiefly for זֹנָה ;] *a prostitute, harlot* :
Mt 21³¹, ³², Lk 15³⁰, ι Co 6¹⁵, ¹⁶, He 11³¹, Ja 2²⁵. Metaph. (v. Swete,
Ap., 180 f.), of Babylon (i.e. Rome) : Re 17¹, ⁵, ¹⁵, ¹⁶ 19² (on Re 17⁵ v.s.
πόρνος).†

** πόρνος, -ου, ὁ, [in LXX : Si 23¹⁶⁻¹⁸ * ;] 1. *a male prostitute* (Xen., al.). 2. *a fornicator:* 1 Co 5⁹⁻¹¹ 6⁹, Eph 5⁵, 1 Ti 1¹⁰, He 12¹⁵ 13⁴, Re 21⁸ 22¹⁵ (perh. also 17⁵, where ΠΟΡΝΩΝ, unaccented, may be πόρι ων from πόρνος, not πορνῶν from πόρνη).†

πόρρω, adv. (in older Attic, πρόσω), [in LXX for רָחוֹק, etc.;] *far off:* Mt 15⁸, Mk 7⁶ (LXX), Lk 14³²; comparat., πορρώτερον (-ρω, T), Lk 24²⁸.†

πόρρωθεν, adv. (< πόρρω, q.v.), [in LXX for מֵרָחוֹק and cogn. forms;] *from afar:* Lk 17¹², He 11¹³.†

πορφύρα, -ας, ἡ, [in LXX for אַרְגָּמָן, אַרְגְּוָן;] 1. *the purple-fish* (cf. 1 Mac 4²³). 2. *purple dye.* 3. Later, = πορφυρίς, *a purple garment:* Mk 15¹⁷, ²⁰, Lk 16¹⁹, Re 18¹².†

πορφύρεος, -α, -ον, contr., -οῦς, -ᾶ, -οῦν (< πορφύρα), [in LXX for אַרְגָּמָן;] *purple:* Jo 19², ⁵; as subst., πορφυροῦν (sc. ἱμάτιον), Re 17⁴ 18⁶.†

*† πορφυρόπωλις, -ιδος, ἡ, *a seller of purple fabrics:* Ac 16¹⁴.†

ποσάκις, interrog. num. adv., *how often:* Mt 18²¹ 23³⁷, Lk 13³⁴.†

πόσις, -εως, ἡ (< πίνω), [in LXX: Da, LXX ΤΗ 1¹⁰ (מִשְׁתֶּה) *;] 1. prop., *drinking:* Ro 14¹⁷, Col 2¹⁶ (v. Lft.; *ICC*, in l.). 2. = πόμα, *drink:* Jo 6⁵⁵ (cf. βρῶσις).†

πόσος, -η, -ον, adj. of number, magnitude, degree, etc., *how much how great, how many:* Mt 6²³, II Co 7¹¹; of time, Mk 9²¹; neut., absol., Lk 16⁵, ⁷; dat., πόσῳ, adverbially, *how much,* Mt 12¹²; id. seq. μᾶλλον, Mt 7¹¹ 10²⁵, Lk 11¹³ 12²⁴, ²⁸, Ro 11¹², ²⁴, Phm ¹⁶, He 9¹⁴; π. χείρονος τιμωρίας, He 10²⁹; pl., Mt 15³⁴ 16⁹, ¹⁰ 27¹³, Mk 6³⁸ 8⁵, ¹⁹, ²⁰ 15⁴, Lk 15¹⁷, Ac 21²⁰.†

ποταμός, -οῦ, ὁ, [in LXX chiefly for נָהָר, יְאֹר;] *a river, stream, torrent:* Mt 3⁶ 7²⁵, ²⁷, Mk 1⁵, Lk 6⁴⁸, ⁴⁹, Ac 16¹³, II Co 11²⁶, Re 8¹⁰ 9¹⁴ 12¹⁵, ¹⁶ 16⁴, ¹² 21¹, ². Fig., pl., π. ὕδατος ζῶντος, Jo 7³⁸.†

*† ποταμο-φόρητος, -ον, *carried away by a stream:* Re 12¹⁵ (for two exx. in π., v. MM, xxi).†

** ποταπός (late form of cl. ποδ-), -ή, -όν, [in LXX: Da LXX Su ⁵⁴ *;] 1. (= ποδαπός) *from what country?* 2. In late writers, = ποῖος, *of what sort?:* Mt 8²⁷, Mk 13¹, Lk 1²⁹ 7³⁹, II Pe 3¹¹, 1 Jo 3¹.†

πότε, interrog. adv. of time, *when?:* Mt 25³⁷⁻³⁹, ⁴⁴, Lk 21⁷, Jo 6²⁵; ἕως π., *how long:* Mt 17¹⁷, Mk 9¹⁹, Lk 9⁴¹, Jo 10²⁴, Re 6¹⁰. In indir. questions, = ὁπότε, Mt 24³, Mk 13⁴, ³³, ³⁵, Lk 12³⁶ 17²⁰ (v. Bl., § 25, 4).†

ποτέ, enclitic particle, 1. *once, formerly, sometime:* of the past, Jo 9¹³, Ro 7⁹, 11³⁰, Ga 1¹³, ²³ 2⁶ (Lft., in l.), Eph 2², ³, ¹¹, ¹³ 5⁸, Col 1²¹ 3⁷, 1 Th 2⁵, Tit 3³, Phm ¹¹, 1 Pe 2¹⁰ 3⁵, ²⁰; ἤδη ποτέ, *now at length,* Phl 4¹⁰; of the fut., Lk 22³²; εἴ πως ἤδη ποτέ, *if sometime soon at length,* Ro 1¹⁰. 2. *ever:* after a neg., Eph 5²⁹, II Pe 1¹⁰, ²¹; in a question, τίς π., 1 Co 9⁷, He 1⁵, ¹³. On μή ποτε (μή and ποτε) v.s. μήπτε.

πότερος, -α, -ον, *which of two.* Neut., adverbially, πότερον, *whether:* Jo 7¹⁷.†

ποτήριον, -ου, τό, dimin. of ποτήρ (< πίνω), [in LXX chiefly for כּוֹס ;] *a wine cup*: Mt 23²⁵, ²⁶ 26²⁷, Mk 7⁴ 14²³, Lk 11³⁹ 22¹⁷, ²⁰ᵃ (WH, R, mg., om.), 1 Co 11²⁵, Re 17⁴; πίνειν ἐκ τοῦ π., 1 Co 11²⁸; c. gen. rei, Mt 10⁴², Mk 9⁴¹; τ. εὐλογίας, 1 Co 10¹⁶; by meton., of the contents of the cup, Lk 22²⁰ᵇ (WH, R, mg., om.), 1 Co 11²⁵, ²⁶; c. gen. pers., 1 Co 10²¹, 11²⁷. Metaph., of experience of divine providence; of prosperity (Ps 15 (16)⁵, al.); of adversity (Ps 10 (11)⁶, Is 51¹⁷, al.): of the sufferings of Christ, Mt 20²², ²³ 26³⁹, Mk 10³⁸, ³⁹ 14³⁶, Lk 22⁴², Jo 18¹¹; of divine punishment, Re 14¹⁰ 16¹⁹ 18⁶.†

ποτίζω (< πότος), [in LXX chiefly for שָׁקָה hi.;] *to give to drink*: c. acc. pers., Mt 25³⁵, ³⁷, ⁴² 27⁴⁸, Mk 15³⁶, Lk 13¹⁵, Ro 12²⁰; c. dupl. acc., Mt 10⁴², Mk 9⁴¹; fig., γάλα, 1 Co 3²; ἐκ τ. οἴνου, Re 14³; of plants, *to water* (Xen., Strab., al.; Ge 13¹⁰), fig., 1 Co 3⁶·⁸. Metaph. (cf. Is 29¹⁰, Si 15³), of the Spirit, 1 Co 12¹³.†

Ποτίολοι, -ων, οἱ, *Puteoli* (mod. *Pozzuoli*), a city on the Bay of Naples: Ac 28¹³.†

πότος, -ου, ὁ (< πίνω), [in LXX chiefly for מִשְׁתֶּה ;] *a drinking bout, carousal*: 1 Pe 4³.†
SYN.: v.s. κραιπάλη.

ποῦ, interrog. adv., [in LXX for אַי, אַיֵּה, אָנָה ;] 1. prop., *where ?*: Mt 2² 26¹⁷, Mk 14¹², ¹⁴, Lk 17¹⁷, ³⁷ 22⁹, ¹¹, Jo 1³⁹ 7¹¹ 8[¹⁰], ¹⁹ 9¹² 11³⁴; ποῦ (ἐστιν), indicating that the subject in question is not to be found, Lk 8²⁵, Ro 3²⁷, 1 Co 1²⁰ 12¹⁷, ¹⁹ 15⁵⁵, Ga 4¹⁵, 11 Pe 3⁴; ποῦ φανεῖται, 1 Pe 4¹⁸. 2. = ὅπου (WM, 640; Bl., § 50, 5): c. indic., Mt 2⁴, Mk 15⁴⁷, Jo 1⁴⁰ 11⁵⁷ 20², ¹³, ¹⁵, Re 2¹³; c. subjc., Mt 8²⁰, Lk 9⁵⁸ 12¹⁷. 3. In colloq. (as in Eng.) = ποῖ, *whither*: in direct questions, Jo 7³⁵ 9¹² 13³⁶ 16⁵; in indir. quest., Jo 3⁸ 8¹⁴ 12³⁵ 14⁵, He 11⁸, 1 Jo 2¹¹.†

πού, enclitic particle, 1. *anywhere, somewhere*: He 2⁶ 4⁴. 2. *in some degree, perhaps, about*: Ac 27²⁹ (T, μήπου), Ro 4¹⁹; δή που (T, δήπου), *surely*: He 2¹⁶.†

Πούδης (in π., gen. -εντος, v. Zorell, s.v.), ὁ (Latin), *Pudens*: 11 Ti 4²¹.†

πούς, ποδός, ὁ, [in LXX chiefly for רֶגֶל ;] *a foot*, both of men and beasts: Mt 4⁶ (LXX), Mk 9⁴⁵, Lk 1⁷⁹, Jo 11⁴⁴, Ac 7⁵, al.; ὑπὸ τοὺς π., Ro 16²⁰, 1 Co 15²⁵, ²⁷, Eph 1²², He 2⁸; ὑποκάτω τῶν π., Mt 22⁴⁴ (LXX); πρὸς (παρὰ) τοὺς π., Mk 5²², Lk 8⁴¹, al.; fig., Mt 15³⁰, Lk 10³⁹, Ac 5², al.; ἔμπροσθεν τῶν π., Re 3⁹ 19¹⁰, al.; ἐπὶ τοὺς π., Ac 10²⁵. By meton., of a person in motion (Ps 118 (119)¹⁰¹): Lk 1⁷⁹, Ac 5⁹, Ro 3¹⁵ 10¹⁵, He 12¹³.

πρᾶγμα, -τος, τό (< πράσσω), [in LXX chiefly for דָּבָר ;] 1. that which has been done, a deed, act: Lk 1¹, Ac 5⁴, 11 Co 7¹¹, He 6¹⁸. 2. That which is being done (like Lat. res), hence, a thing, matter, affair: Mt 18¹⁹, Ro 16², 1 Th 4⁶ (v. M, Th., in l.), He 10¹ 11¹, Ja 3¹⁶; in forensic sense (as freq. in π., v. Deiss., BS, 233), a law-suit: 1 Co 6¹.†

πραγματεία, v.s. πραγματία.

πραγματεύομαι (< πρᾶγμα), [in LXX : III Ki 10²² B, 9¹⁹ A (חשק),
Da LXX 8²⁷ (עָשָׂה אֶת־מְלָאכָה) * ;] 1. to busy oneself. 2. to be engaged
in business, esp. to trade : Lk 19¹³ (cf. δια-πραγματεύομαι).†

πραγματία (Rec. -εία, as in cl.), -ας, ἡ (< πραγματεύομαι), [in LXX
for חֵפֶץ, etc. ;] 1. careful application, hard work. 2. business, occupation : pl., II Ti 2⁴.†

*† πραιτώριον, -ου, τό, (Lat. prætorium), 1. headquarters in a Roman
camp. 2. The palace or official residence of the Governor of a
province : Mt 27²⁷, Mk 15¹⁶ (v. Swete, in l.), Jo 18²⁸, ³³ 19⁹ ; τ. π. τ.
Ἡρώδου, Ac 23³⁵. 3. the Prætorian Guard : Phl 1¹³ (v. Lft., in l.;
ICC, 51 f.).†

πράκτωρ, -ορος, ὁ (< πράσσω}, [in LXX : Is 3¹² (נֹגֵשׂ) * ;] 1. (poët.)
one who does or accomplishes. 2. In Athens, one who exacts payment,
a collector ; hence, generally (freq. in π., v. Deiss., BS, 154), a court
officer : Lk 12⁵⁸.†

πρᾶξις, -εως, ἡ (< πράσσω), [in LXX : II Ch 13²² 27⁷ 28²⁶ (דֶּרֶךְ),
Jb 24⁵ A (פֹּעַל), Pr 13¹³, Wi 9¹¹, al. ;] 1. a doing, deed, act : Mt 16²⁷ ;
pl., π. ἀποστόλων, Ac, tit. ; in late writers especially of wicked deeds or
practices (freq. in Polyb.) : Lk 23⁵¹ ; pl., Ro 8¹³, Col 3⁹ ; with ref. to
magic (v. BS, 323₅), Ac 19¹⁸. 2. an acting, action, business, function :
Ro 12⁴.†

πρᾷος, πρᾶος, v.s. πραΰς.

πραότης, πραότης, v.s. πραΰτης.

** πρασιά, -ᾶς, ἡ, [in LXX : Si 24³¹ * ;] a garden-bed ; metaph., of
ranks or orderly groups of persons : Mk 6⁴⁰.†

πράσσω, (Att. -ττω, and so Ac 17⁷ Rec. ; cf. M, Pr., 25, 45), [in
LXX chiefly for עֲשׂוֹת, פָּעַל ;] = Lat agere, as ποιέω (q.v.) = facere, 1.
to do, practise, be engaged in : Ac 19¹⁹, ³⁶, I Co 9¹⁷ ; τ. ἴδια π., to mind
one's own business (τὰ ἑαυτοῦ, Soph., Plat.), I Th 4¹¹ ; intrans., to act,
Ac 17⁷. 2. to achieve, effect, accomplish, perform : Ac 26²⁰, ²⁶, Ro 7¹⁵ 9¹¹,
II Co 5¹⁰, Phl 4⁹ ; νόμον (ICC, in l.), Ro 2²⁵ ; of unworthy acts (for wh.
usually ποιέω in cl.), to commit, do : Lk 22²³ 23⁴¹, Jo 3²⁰ 5²⁹, Ac 3¹⁷
5³⁵ 16²⁸ 25¹¹, ²⁵ 26⁹, ³¹, Ro 1³² (ICC, in l.), 2¹⁻³ 7¹⁹ 13⁴, I Co 5², II Co 12²¹,
Ga 5²¹. 3. to transact, manage, hence, of payment, to exact (cl.) :
Lk 3¹³ 19²³. 4. Reflexively, of state or condition, to do or fare (Æsch.,
Hdt., al.) : Eph 6²¹ ; εὖ π. (v. M, Pr., 228 f.), Ac 15²⁹.†

SYN. : v.s. ποιέω.

*† πραϋπαθία (Rec. -πάθεια), -ας, ἡ (< πραΰς, πάσχω), = πραΰτης,
meekness, gentleness : I Ti 6¹¹ (Philo.).†

πραΰς, -εῖα, -ύ, and πρᾶος (or πρᾷος, v. Bl., § 3, 3), -α, -ον (v. LS,
Thayer, s.v.), [in LXX (always -ΰς, exc. II Mac 15¹², -ᾷος, v. Thackeray,
Gr., 180 f.) for עָנָו עָנָיו, עָנִי ;] gentle, meek : Mt 5⁵ 11²⁹ 21⁵ (LXX),
I Pe 3⁴.†

πραΰτης (Rec. -ότης, exc. Ja, I Pe, ll. c., where πραΰτης), -ητος, ἡ,

late form of πραότης, [in LXX : Ps 44 (45)⁴ 89 (90)¹⁰ 131 (132)¹ (עֻנּוֹתוֹ,
עֲנָוָה), Es 5¹, Si ₆ *;] *gentleness, meekness :* 1 Co 4²¹, 11 Co 10¹, Ga 5²³ 6¹,
Eph 4², Col 3¹² (v. Lft., in l.), 11 Ti 2²⁵, Tit 3², Ja 1²¹ 3¹³, 1 Pe 3¹⁵.†
SYN. : ἐπιείκια, q.v.

πρέπω, [in LXX : Ps 92 (93)⁵ (נָאה pi.), etc.;] 1. *to be clearly
seen.* 2. *to resemble.* 3. *to be fitting* or *becoming, to suit :* c. dat.,
He 7²⁶, 1 Ti 2¹⁰, Tit 2¹; impers., c. dat., Eph 5³; id. seq. inf., He 2¹⁰ ;
πρέπον ἐστίν, c. dat. pers. et inf., Mt 3¹⁵ ; c. acc. et inf., 1 Co 11¹³ (v.
Bl., § 72, 5).†

** πρεσβεία, -ας, ἡ (< πρεσβεύω), [in LXX : 11 Mac 4¹¹ *;] 1. *age,
seniority.* 2. *rank, dignity.* 3. *an embassy;* by meton., of the am-
bassadors, *embassy :* Lk 14³² 19¹⁴.†

* πρεσβεύω (< πρέσβυς), 1. *to be the elder, to take precedence.* 2.
to be an ambassador (v.s. πρεσβύτης) : 11 Co 5²⁰, Eph 6²⁰.†

πρεσβευτής, v.s. πρέσβυς.

πρέσβυς, -εως, ὁ, poët. form of πρεσβύτης (q.v.), [in LXX (=
πρεσβευτής, *an ambassador*) : Nu 21²⁰ ⁽²¹⁾, al. (מַלְאָךְ), Is 13⁸ 57⁹ (צִיר),
1 Mac 9⁷⁰, al.;] *an old man.* Compar., πρεσβύτερος, -α, -ον, [in LXX
chiefly for זָקֵן;] 1. *of age, elder :* ὁ υἱὸς ὁ π., Lk 15²⁵ ; as subst., opp.

to νεανίσκοι, Ac 2¹⁷ ; to νεώτερος, 1 Ti 5¹, ² ; of the religious leaders of the
past, Mt 15², Mk 7³, ⁵, He 11² (= οἱ πατέρες, He 1¹). 2. Of dignity,
rank or office (as found in π. and Inscr. of civil and religious offices,
including priesthood, in Asia Minor and in Egypt; v. Deiss., BS, 154 ff.,
233 ff. ; LAE, 373); (a) among Jews : Mt 16²¹ 26⁴⁷, ⁵⁷ 27³, ¹², ²⁰, ⁴¹ 28¹²,
Mk 8³¹ 11²⁷ 14⁴³, ⁵³ 15¹, Lk 7³ 9²² 20¹ 22⁵², Jo 8⁽⁹⁾, Ac 4⁵, ⁸, ²³ 6¹² 23¹⁴ 24¹ ;
τ. Ιουδαίων, Ac 25¹⁵ ; τ. λαοῦ, Mt 21²³ 26³ 27¹ ; (b) among Christians, *elder*
or *presbyter :* Ac 11³⁰ 14²³ 15², ⁴, ⁶, ²², ²³ 16⁴ 21¹⁸, 1 Ti 5¹⁷, ¹⁹, Tit 1⁵, 11 Jo ¹,
111 Jo ¹, 1 Pe 5¹, ⁵ ; τ. ἐκκλησίας, Ac 20¹⁷, Ja 5¹⁴ ; (c) in the visions of the
Apocalypse : Re 4⁴, ¹⁰ 5⁵, ⁶, ⁸, ¹¹, ¹⁴ 7¹¹, ¹³ 11¹⁶ 14³ 19⁴. (On the NT
use of this word and its relation to ἐπίσκοπος (q.v.), cf. Lft., Phl.,
93 ff., 189 ff. ; CGT, Past. Epp., lvi ff.) †

**† πρεσβυτέριον, -ου, τό (< πρεσβύτερος), [in LXX : Da TH Su ⁵⁰ A *;]
a body of elders, presbytery : of the Sanhedrin (cf. συνέδριον), Lk 22⁶⁶,
Ac 22⁵ ; of Christian presbyters, 1 Ti 4¹⁴.†

πρεσβύτερος, v.s. πρέσβυς.

πρεσβύτης, -ου, prose form of πρέσβυς, q.v., [in LXX chiefly for
זָקֵן, Ge 25⁸, al.; also (= πρεσβευτής), 11 Ch 32³¹ B¹ (מֵלִיץ), 1 Mac 14²² S,
al. (v. Thackeray, Gr., 97);] 1. *an old man :* Lk 1¹⁸, Tit 2², Phm ⁹
(R, txt., but v. infr.). 2. As in LXX, also = πρεσβευτής, *an ambassador :* Phm ⁹ (R, mg., v. Lft. and ICC, in l.).†

** πρεσβῦτις, -ιδος, ἡ, fem. of πρεσβύτης, [in LXX : iv Mac 16¹⁴ *;]
an aged woman : Tit 2³.†

** πρηνής, -ές (in Att. also πρανής), [in LXX : Wi 4¹⁹, 111 Mac 5⁴³, ⁵⁰
6²³ *;] *headlong, prone :* Ac 1¹⁸; for the meaning *swollen up (swelling up,*
Moffatt) from √ found in πίμπρημι, q.v., v. Bp. Chase in JThS, xii, 278
(Jan., 1912), J. R. Harris in AJTh, Jan., 1934.†

πρίζω = πρίω, [in LXX: Am 1³, Da TH Su ⁵⁹*;] to saw, saw asunder (= π. δίχα, Thuc., iv, 100): pass, He 11³⁷ (cf. δια-πρίω).†

πρίν, 1. as adv. of time, before, formerly (cl.; III Mac 5²⁸ 6⁴,³¹). 2. As conjc. (cl.), before; (a) after a positive sentence, c. acc. et inf.: Mt 26³⁴,⁷⁵, Mk 14⁷², Lk 22⁶¹, Jo 4⁴⁹ 8⁵⁸ (where D. om. γενέσθαι and π. becomes prep. c. gen.; v. Bl., § 69, 7) 14²⁹, Ac 2²⁰ (LXX), WH, txt.; πρὶν ἤ (not such good Attic in this construction; v. Bl., l.c.), Mt 1¹⁸, Mk 14³⁰, Ac 2²⁰, WH, mg., 7²; (b) after a negative sentence, πρὶν ἤ: c. subjc. (seq. ἄν, M, Pr., 169), Lk 2²⁶; c. optat., Ac 25¹⁶.†

Πρίσκα, -ας, ἡ (Lat.), and Πρίσκιλλα, -ης, ἡ, Prisca: Ro 16³, I Co 16¹⁹, II Ti 14¹⁹; Priscilla: Ac 18²,¹⁸,²⁶; the wife of Aquila, v.s. 'Ακύλας.†

Πρίσκιλλα, v.s. Πρίσκα.
πρίω, v.s. πρίζω.

πρό, prep. c. gen., [in LXX chiefly for לִפְנֵי;] before; (a) of place: Ac 12⁶,¹⁴ 14¹³, Ja 5⁹; π. προσώπου (= Heb. לִפְנֵי, De 3¹⁸, Ma 3¹, al.; Bl., § 40, 9), Mt 11¹⁰, Mk 1², Lk 1⁷⁶ 7²⁷ 9⁵² 10¹, Ac 14¹³; (b) of time: Mt 8²⁹ 24³⁸, Lk 11³⁸ 21¹², Jo 11⁵⁵ 13¹ 17²⁴, Ac 5³⁶ 21³⁸, I Co 2⁷ 4⁵, Eph 1⁴, Col 1¹⁷, II Ti 1⁹ 4²¹, Tit 1², He 11⁵, I Pe 1²⁰, Ju ²⁵; π. ἐτῶν δεκατεσσάρων, fourteen years ago, II Co 12² ; π. προσώπου (v. supr.), Ac 13²⁴; c. gen. pers., Mt 5¹², Jo 5⁷ 10⁸, Ro 16⁷, Ga 1¹⁷; c. gen. art. inf. (= πρίν; M, Pr., 100; Bl., § 69, 7), Mt 6⁸, Lk 2²¹ 22¹⁵, Jo 1⁴⁹ 13¹⁹ 17⁵, Ac 23¹⁵, Ga 2¹² 3²³; as in late writers (resembling a Latin idiom but independent of it; Bl., § 40, 5; M, Pr., 100 f.; cf. Am ‾' II Mac 15³⁶, and for other exx., Soph., Lex., s.v.), πρὸ ἐξ ἡμέρας τοῦ πάσχα, on the sixth day bef. the Passover, Jo 12¹; (c) of preference: π. πάντων, Ja 5¹², I Pe 4⁸; (d) in compos., (a) c. subst., of position before: προαύλιον, πρόδρομος; priority of rank or order, προπάτωρ; anticipation, πρόγνωσις, πρόνοια; (β) c. adj., intensity, πρόδηλος; (γ) c. verb., of place, προάγω, προβαίνω; of preference, προαιρέομαι.†

προ-άγω, [in LXX: I Ki 17¹⁶ (נגשׁ), Wi 19¹¹, al.;] 1. prop. trans., to lead on, lead forth or forward: c. acc. pers., Ac 16³⁰ 17⁵; of bringing forth to trial, Ac 12⁶ (WH, txt., προσάγ-); seq. ἐπί, c. gen. pers., Ac 25²⁶. 2. Intrans. (Plat., Polyb., and later writers; v. Bl., § 53, 1; MM, xxi); (a) to lead the way, I Ti 1¹⁸ (R, mg.), hence, to go before, precede: Lk 18³⁹; opp. to ἀκολουθέω, Mk 11⁹; seq. εἰς, Mt 14²² Mk 6⁴⁵, I Ti 5²⁴, He 7¹⁸; c. acc. pers., Mt 2⁹ 21⁹, Mk 10³² 14²⁸; seq. εἰς, Mt 21³¹ 26³² 28⁷, Mk 14²⁸ 16⁷; (b) to go on, advance (Si 20²⁷): II Jo ⁹.†

προ-αιρέω, -ῶ, [in LXX: for פשׁה, etc.;] to bring forth or forward. Most freq. in mid., to take by choice, prefer, propose: II Co 9⁷.†

*† προ-αιτιάομαι, -ῶμαι, to accuse or charge beforehand: Ro 3⁹ (not elsewhere).†

* προ-ακούω, to hear beforehand: Col 1⁵ (v. Lft., in l.).†

*† προ-αμαρτάνω, to sin before: II Co 12²¹ 13².†

* προ-αύλιον, -ου, τό (< πρό, αὐλή), a porch, vestibule: 'Mk 14⁶⁸.†

προ-βαίνω, [in LXX chiefly for בוא ;] *to go forwards, go on,*
advance : Mt 4²¹, Mk 1¹⁹. Metaph., of age (Ge 18¹¹, al., Lys., Diod.,
al.), ἐν τ. ἡμέραις, Lk 1⁷, ¹⁸ 2³⁶.†

προ-βάλλω, [in LXX for חזר, מרק, etc.;] 1. *to throw before.*
2. *to put forward :* c. acc., Ac 19³³ ; of trees, *to put forth, produce*
(sc. φύλλα), Lk 21³⁰.†

προβατικός, -ή, -όν (< πρόβατον), [in LXX (π. πύλη): Ne 3¹, ³²
12³⁹ (צאן) * ;] *of sheep :* ἡ π. (sc. πύλη, v. supr.), *the sheep-gate,* Jo 5².†

* προβάτιον, -ου, τό, dimin. of πρόβατον (used as a term of endearment, v. Bl., § 27, 4), *a little sheep :* Jo 21¹⁶, ¹⁷ (πρόβατα, WH, mg.).†

πρόβατον, -ου, τό (< προβαίνω), [in LXX chiefly for צאן, also for
שׂה, more rarely for כֶּשֶׂב (כֶּבֶשׂ), רָחֵל;] 1. in Hom., Hdt., *cattle,*
esp. of small cattle, *sheep* and *goats.* 2. In NT, as in Attic writers
generally (cf. MM, xxi), *a sheep :* Mt 7¹⁵, Mk 6³⁴, al. ; πρόβατα σφαγῆς,
Ro 8³⁶ (LXX). Metaph. (in cl. of timidity, stupidity or idleness), of the
followers of a leader or master, esp. of those who are subject to the
care of the Good Shepherd : Mt 10⁶ 15²⁴ 26³¹ (LXX), Mk 14²⁷ (LXX), Jo
10⁷, ⁸, ¹⁵, ¹⁶, ²⁶, ²⁷ 21¹⁶, ¹⁷ (WH, txt., προβάτια), He 13²⁰ ; opp. to ἐρίφια,
Mt 25³³.

προ-βιβάζω, causal of προβαίνω, [in LXX : Ex 35³⁴ (ירה hi.), De
6⁷ (שנן pi.) * ;] *to lead forward, lead on ;* metaph., *to induce, incite,*
urge : Mt 14⁸.†

† προ-βλέπω, [in LXX : Ps 36 (37)¹³ (ראה) * ;] *to foresee :* mid.,
He 11⁴⁰ (v. Bl., § 24, 55, 1).†

** προ-γίνομαι, [in LXX : Wi 19¹³ אA, ii Mac 14³ 15⁸ * ;] *to happen*
before : pf. pass. ptcp., Ro 3²⁵.†

** προ-γινώσκω, [in LXX : Wi 6¹³ 8⁸ 18⁶ * ;] *to know beforehand,*
foreknow : ii Pe 3¹⁷ ; c. acc. pers., Ac 26⁵ ; of the Divine fore-
knowledge, Ro 8²⁹ 11², i Pe 1²⁰.†

**† πρό-γνωσις, -εως, ἡ (< προγινώσκω), [in LXX : Jth 9⁶ 11¹⁹ * ;] *fore-*
knowledge : Ac 2²³, i Pe 1².†

** πρό-γονος, -ον (< προγίνομαι), [in LXX : Es 4¹⁷, Si 8⁴, al. ;] 1. *born*
before. 2. As subst., in pl., οἱ π., *ancestors, forefathers :* ii Ti 1³ ; of
living parents (so Plat.), i Ti 5⁴.†

προ-γράφω, [in LXX : Da LXX 3³ cod., i Mac10³⁶ * ;] 1. *to write*
before : Ro 15⁴, Eph 3³, Ju ⁴. 2. *to write in public, placard, proclaim*
(Dem., Plut., al.): Ga 3¹ (Lft., in l.). 3. = ζωγραφέω, *to pourtray,*
depict : Ga, l.c. (Syr. Pesh., Chrys.; Field, *Notes,* 189; *CGT,* in l.).†

** πρό-δηλος, -ον, [in LXX : Jth 8²⁹, ii Mac 3¹⁷ 14³⁹ * ;] 1. *evident*
beforehand. 2. *clearly evident :* i Ti 5²⁴, ²⁵, He 7¹⁴.†

προ-δίδωμι, [in LXX : Ez 16³⁴ A (נתן), iv Mac 4¹, al. ;] 1. *to give*
before, give first : Ro 11³⁵ (Jb 41²⁽¹¹⁾, LXX, al.). 2. *to betray*
(iv Mac, l.c.).†

** προ-δότης, -ου, ὁ (προδίδωμι), [in LXX : ii Mac 5¹⁵ 10¹³, ²², iii Mac
3²⁴ * ;] *a betrayer, traitor :* Lk 6¹⁶, Ac 7⁵², ii Ti 3⁴.†

πρό-δρομος, -ον (< προτρέχω), [in LXX : Nu 13²¹ ⁽²⁰⁾, Is 28⁴ (בכר),

Wi 12⁸*;] *running forward, going in advance.* As subst., ὁ π., *an advance guard, forerunner :* He 6²⁰.†

προ-εῖδον, aor. without pres. in use (v.s. προοράω), [in LXX : Ge 37¹⁸ (רָאָה), Ps 138 (139)³ (סָכַן hi.) *;] *to foresee :* Ac 2³¹ (προϊδών ; WH, προιδών), Ga 3⁸.†

** προ-εῖπον, 2 aor. from unused pres. (v.s. εῖπον), and pf., -είρηκα (III Mac 6³⁵*), pass., -είρημαι (II Mac 2³², III Mac 1²⁶, al.), 1. *to say before :* Ga 1⁹, I Th 4⁶ (on the form -αμεν, v. WH, *App.*, 164), He 4⁷ ; seq. ὅτι, II Co 7³ 13², Ga 5²¹ ; of prophecy, Mt 24²⁵, Mk 13²³, Ac 1¹⁶, Ro 9²⁹, II Pe 3², Ju ¹⁷. 2. *to proclaim publicly, declare openly* or *plainly* (cl.) : so R, mg., in II Co 13², Ga 5²¹, I Th 4⁶ (cf. προλέγω ; but v. supr., and cf. M, *Th.*, 38).†

προ-είρηκα, -είρημαι, v.s. προεῖπον.

*† προ-ελπίζω, *to hope before :* seq. ἐν, Eph 1¹².†

*† προ-ενάρχομαι, *to begin before :* II Co 8⁶ ; c. acc., τὸ θέλειν, ib.¹⁰ (not elsewhere).†

*† προ-επ-αγγέλλω, *to announce before.* Mid., *to promise before :* c. acc. rei, Ro 1², II Co 9⁵ (Dio. Cass.).†

προ-έρχομαι, [in LXX : Ge 33³, ¹⁴ R (עָבַר), Jth 2¹⁹, Si 35 (32)¹⁰, al ;] 1. *to go forward, go on, advance :* seq. μικρόν, Mt 26³⁹ and Mk 14³⁵ (WH, mg., προσελθών) : ῥύμην μίαν (cf. Plat., *Rep.*, i, 328e), Ac 12¹⁰. 2. Of relative position, *to go before, precede :* c. gen. (cl. ; Jth, l.c.) ; c. acc. pers. (not cl.), Lk 22⁴⁷ (c. gen., Rec.) ; seq. ἐνώπιον, Lk 1¹⁷ (cf. Ge 33³). 3. Of time, *to go before* or *in advance :* Ac 20⁵, ¹³ (WH, mg., R, mg.), II Co 9⁵ ; c. acc. pers. (= cl. φθάνω), Mk 6³³.†

προ-ερέω, -ῶ, v.s. προεῖπον.

προ-ετοιμάζω, [in LXX : Is 28²⁴ B, Wi 9⁸*;] *to prepare before :* c. acc. rei, Ro 9²³, (οἷς for ἅ by attraction) Eph 2¹⁰.†

*† προ-ευαγγελίζομαι, *to announce glad tidings beforehand :* Ga 3⁸.†

προ-έχω, [in LXX : Jb 27⁶ A (חָזַק hi.) *;] 1. Trans., *to hold before ;* mid., *to hold something before oneself* (Hdt.), hence, metaph., *to excuse oneself :* Ro 3⁹, R, mg. (but v. Field, *Notes*, 152 f. ; Lft., *Notes*, 266 f. ; ICC and Vau., in l.). 2. Intrans. (*a*) *to project ;* (*b*) in running, *to have the start*, hence, metaph., *to excel :* mid., Ro, l.c., R, txt. (v. reff. supr.).†

προ-ηγέομαι, [in LXX : De 20⁹ (בְּרֹאשׁ), Pr 17¹⁴ (לִפְנֵי), II Mac 4⁴⁰, al. ;] 1. *to go before* as leader (in cl., c. gen., dat.) : Ro 12¹⁰ (Chrys. Vg., al. ; v. ICC, in l.). 2. In a sense not elsewhere found, ἀλλήλους προηγούμενοι = ἀ. ἡγούμενοι ὑπερέχοντας : Ro, l.c. (ICC, cf. I Th 5¹³, Phl 2³ and EV "*preferring*").†

πρό-θεσις, -εως, ἡ, [in LXX : Ex 40⁴, ²³ (עֶרֶךְ), I Ch 9³², al. (מַעֲרֶכֶת), II Ch 4¹⁹ (פָּנִים), I Mac 1²², II Mac 3⁸, al. ;] 1. *a setting forth* (Plat., Plut., al.) : οἱ ἄρτοι τῆς π. (cf. LXX, ll. c., elsewhere ἄρτοι ἐνώπιοι, Ex 25²⁹ ; οἱ ἄ. τοῦ προσώπου, Ne 10³³), Mt 12⁴, Mk 2²⁶, Lk 6⁴ ; ἡ π. τῶν ἄρτων, He 9². 2. *a purpose* (Arist., Polyb., al. ; II Mac, l.c.) : Ac 11²³ 27¹³, Ro 8²⁸ 9¹¹, Eph 1¹¹ 3¹¹, II Ti 1⁹ 3¹⁰.†

** προ-θέσμιος, -α, -ον, [in Sm.: Jb 28³, Da 9²⁶ *;] *appointed before-hand.* In Attic law, as subst. (so always in cl.), ἡ π. (sc. ἡμέρα), *a day appointed beforehand, a previously appointed time :* Ga 4².†

** προθυμία, -ας, ἡ (< πρόθυμος), [in LXX: Si 45²³ *;] *eagerness, willingness, readiness :* Ac 17¹¹, II Co 8¹¹,¹²,¹⁹ 9².†

πρόθυμος, -ον, [in LXX: I Ch 28²¹, II Ch 29³¹ (נָדִיב), Hb 1⁸ (חוּשׁ), al.;] *willing, ready :* Mt 26⁴¹, Mk 14³⁸; neut., τὸ π. = ἡ προθυμία (Thuc., al., III Mac 5²⁶), οὕτως τὸ κατ᾽ ἐμὲ (= cl. τὸ ἐμὸν) π., Ro 1¹⁵ (but v. *ICC,* in l.).†

προθύμως, [in LXX: II Ch 29³⁴ (וַיִּשֲׁרֵי לָבָב), To 7⁸, al.;] *eagerly, readily, with a ready mind :* I Pe 5².†

πρόϊμος (Rec. πρώ-, of which προ- is a late form; v. Bl., § 6, 4; WH, *App.,* 152), -ον, [in LXX: De 11¹⁴ (יוֹרֶה), etc.;] = the more common πρώϊος (q.v.), *early :* of rain (as most freq. in LXX), Ja 5⁷.†

προ-ίστημι, [in LXX: II Ki 13¹⁷, Pr 23⁵ 26¹⁷, Is 43²⁴, Am 6¹⁰ (no proper Heb. equiv.), Da LXX Bel⁷, I Mac 5¹⁹, IV Mac 11²⁷ *;] 1. trans. in fut., 1 aor., and mid. 1 aor., *to put before, set over* (Plat., al.). 2. Intrans., in pf., plpf., 2 aor. and mid. pres. and impf.; (a) *to preside, rule, govern :* Ro 12⁸, I Ti 5¹⁷; c. gen., I Th 5¹², I Ti 3⁴,⁵,¹²; (b) *to direct, maintain :* c. gen. rei, καλῶν ἔργων, Tit 3⁸,¹⁴ (on R̄, mg., *profess honest occupations,* v. *CGT,* in l.; Field, *Notes,* 223 f.; *make it their business to do good,* MM, *VGT,* s.v.).†

** προ-καλέω, -ῶ, [in LXX: II Mac 8¹¹ A *;] *to call forth.* Most freq. in mid., (a) *to challenge ;* hence, *to provoke :* Ga 5²⁶; (b) *to invite* (II Mac, l.c.).†

*† προ-κατ-αγγέλλω, *to announce beforehand :* c. acc. et inf., Ac 3¹⁸; seq. περί, Ac 7⁵².†

* προ-κατ-αρτίζω, *to make ready beforehand :* II Co 9⁵.†

πρό-κειμαι, [in LXX: Ex 39¹⁸ ⁽³⁶⁾, Nu 4⁷ (פָּנִים), etc.;] used as pass. of προτίθημι; 1. *to be set before* one, *to be set forth :* He 6¹⁸ 12¹,², Ju⁷. 2. *to present oneself, be present :* II Co 8¹² (v. Mey., in l.).†

* προ-κηρύσσω, 1. *to proclaim by herald.* 2. Of one who acts as a herald, *to proclaim :* Ac 13²⁴.†

**† προ-κοπή, -ῆς, ἡ (< προκόπτω), [in LXX: Si 51¹⁷ II Mac 8⁸ *;] *progress* (prop., on a journey, then generally): Phl 1¹²,²⁵, I Ti 4¹⁵ (condemned by Atticists, v. Rutherford, *NPhr.,* 158).†

** προ-κόπτω, [in Sm.: Ps 44 (45)⁵ *;] *to cut forward* a way, *forward, advance,* in cl. trans. with neut. adj., as οὐδὲν π., τὰ πολλὰ π. In late writers (Polyb., al.), wholly intrans., *to advance, progress :* of time, Ro 13¹². Metaph., Lk 2⁵², Ga 1¹⁴, II Ti 2¹⁶ 3⁹,¹³.†

*† πρό-κριμα, -τος, τό (< cl. προκρίνειν, 1. *to prefer.* 2. *to judge beforehand*), *pre-judging, prejudice :* I Ti 5²¹ (v. Cremer, 378).†

*† προ-κυρόω, -ῶ, *to establish* or *confirm beforehand :* Ga 3¹⁷.†

** προ-λαμβάνω, [in LXX: Wi 17¹¹ א², ib. ¹⁷ א²B *;] 1. *to take beforehand :* c. acc., I Co 11²¹ (but v. infr.). 2. *to be beforehand,* *anticipate* (in cl., c. acc., gen. or dat.) : c. inf. (= cl. φθάνω, v. Bl., § 69, 4; Swete, in l.), Mk 14⁸. 3. *to overtake, surprise :* pass., Ga 6¹ (on the virtual disappearance of the temporal force of the preposition in this compound here and perhaps also in I Co, l.c., v. MM, xxi).†

προ-λέγω, [in LXX : Is 41²⁶ (נגד hi.) *;] 1. *to tell* or *say beforehand :* II Co 13², Ga 5²¹, I Th 3⁴ (R, txt.; cf. προεῖπον, but v. infr.). 2. *to declare, tell plainly :* II Co, Ga, I Th, ll. c. (R, mg.; v. MM, xxi, and cf. Is, l.c.).†

*† προ-μαρτύρομαι, *to protest beforehand* (cf. μαρτύρομαι, and v. Hort, in l.) : I Pe 1¹¹ (elsewhere only in Theod. Met., xiv/AD.).†

* προ-μελετάω, -ῶ, *to premeditate :* Lk 21¹⁴.†

*† προ-μεριμνάω, -ῶ, *to be anxious beforehand :* Mk 13¹¹.†

προ-νοέω, -ῶ, and depon. -έομαι, οῦμαι, [in LXX : Da LXX 11³⁷ (בִּין), Wi 6⁷, al. ;] 1. *to foresee.* 2. *to provide* (RV, *take thought for*) : c. acc. rei, καλά, Ro 12¹⁷ (-ούμενοι), II Co 8²¹ (-οῦμεν). 3. *to provide for* (seq. περί, Wi, l.c.) : c. gen. pers., I Ti 5⁸ (-εῖ, WH, mg., -εῖται).†

πρόνοια, -ας, ἡ (< πρόνοος, *careful*), [in LXX : Da LXX 6¹⁸ (19), Wi 14³ 17², II-IV Mac ₆*;] *foresight, forethought :* Ac 24³; π. ποιεῖσθαι, c. gen. (Dem., 546, 6), *make provision for, show care for :* Ro 13¹⁴.†

προ-οράω, -ῶ, [in LXX : Ps 15 (16)⁸ (שִׁוָּה pi.), I Es 5⁶³ A *;] *to see before* (as to place or time) : c. acc., Ac 21²⁹. Mid., c. acc., seq. ἐνώπιόν μου, Ac 2²⁵ (LXX).†

*† προ-ορίζω, *to predetermine, foreordain :* c. acc., Ro 8³⁰; id. et inf., Ac 4²⁸; id. seq. εἰς, I Co 2⁷, Eph 1⁵; c. dupl. acc., Ro 8²⁹; pass., Eph 1¹¹.†

* προ-πάσχω, *to suffer before :* I Th 2².†

** προ-πάτωρ, -ορος, ὁ (< πατήρ), [in LXX : III Mac 2²¹ A *;] *a forefather :* Ro 4¹.†

** προ-πέμπω, [in LXX : I Es 4⁴⁷, Jth 10¹⁵, Wi 19², I Mac 12⁴, II Mac 6²³ *;] 1. *to send before, send forth.* 2. *to set forward* on a journey, *escort :* c. acc. pers., I Co 16¹¹, Tit 3¹³, III Jo⁶; seq. εἰς, Ac 20³⁸; οὗ, I Co 16⁶; ἕως, Ac 21⁵; pass., Ac 15³, Ro 15²⁴, II Co 1¹⁶.†

προπετής, -ές (< προπίπτω), [in LXX : Pr 10¹⁴ (אֱוִיל) 13³ (פֹּשֵׂק), Si 9¹⁸ *;] *falling forwards, headlong.* Metaph., *precipitate, rash, reckless :* of persons, II Ti 3⁴; of things, Ac 19³⁶.†

προ-πορεύω, [in LXX chiefly for הלך, also for עבר, etc. ;] *to make to go before.* Pass. and mid., *to go before :* Lk 1⁷⁶, Ac 7⁴⁰ (LXX).†

πρός, prep. c. gen., dat., acc.
I. C. gen., of motion from a place, *from the side of,* hence metaph., *in the interests of,* Ac 27³⁴ (cf. Page, in l.).
II. C. dat., of local proximity, *hard by, near, at :* Mk 5¹¹, Lk 19³⁷, Jo 18¹⁶ 20¹¹, ¹², Re 1¹³.
III. C. acc., of motion or direction towards a place or object, *to, towards.* 1. Of place, (*a*) after verbs of motion or of speaking and other words with the idea of direction : ἔρχομαι, ἀναβαίνω, πορεύομαι,

λέγω, ἐπιστολή, etc., Mt 3¹⁴, Mk 6⁵¹, Lk 11⁵, Jo 2³, Ac 9², al. mult.;
metaph., of mental direction, hostile or otherwise, Lk 23¹², Jo 6⁵²,
II Co 7⁴, Eph 6¹², Col 3¹³, al.; of the issue or end, Lk 14³², Jo 11⁴, al.;
of purpose, Mt 26¹², Ro 3²⁶, I Co 6⁵, al.; πρὸς τό, c. inf., denoting
purpose cf. M, Pr., 218, 220; Lft., Notes, 131), Mt 5²⁸, Mk 13²², Eph
6¹¹, I Th 2⁹, al.; (b) of close proximity, at, by, with (v. M, Gr., II, p.
467): Mt 3¹⁰, Mk 11⁴, Lk 4¹¹, Ac 3², al.; after εἶναι, Mt 13⁵⁶, Mk 6³, Jo 1¹, al.
2. Of time, (a) towards (Plat., Xen., LXX: Ge 8¹¹, al.): Lk 24²⁹; (b) for:
πρὸς καιρόν, Lk 8¹³, I Co 7⁵; πρὸς ὥραν, Jo 5³⁵, al.; πρὸς ὀλίγον, Ja 4¹⁴. 3.
Of relation (a) toward, with: Ro 5¹, II Co 1¹², Col 4⁵, I Th 4¹², al.;
(b) with regard to: Mt 19⁸, Mk 12¹², Ro 8³¹, al.; (c) pertaining to, to:
Mt 27⁴, Jo 21²², Ro 15¹⁷, He 2¹⁷ 5¹; (d) according to: Lk 12⁴⁷, II Co
5¹⁰, Ga 2¹⁴, Eph 3⁴ 4¹⁴; (e) in comparison with: Ro 8¹⁸.
IV. In composition: towards (προσέρχομαι), to (προσάγω), against
(προσκόπτω), besides (προσδαπανάω).

• † προ-σάββατον, -ου, τό, [in LXX: Ps 91 (92) tit. א (שַׁבָּת) 92 (93) tit.,
Jth 8⁶ *;] the day before the Sabbath: Mk 15⁴² (L, Tr., txt., πρὸς σ.).†

προσ-αγορεύω, [in LXX: De 23⁶ (7) (דרשׁ), II Es 10¹ B¹ ידה hith.),
Wi 14²², I Mac 14⁴⁰, II Mac 1³⁶ 4⁷ 10⁹ 14³⁷ *;] to address, greet, salute;
hence, to call by name, address, style: c. dupl. acc., pass., He 5¹⁰.†

προσ-άγω, [in LXX chiefly for קרב hi., also for נגשׁ, etc.;] 1.
trans., to bring or lead: c. acc. et dat., Ac 16²⁰; metaph., τ. θεῷ, I Pe
3¹⁸; seq. ὧδε, Lk 9⁴¹; pass., c. dat., Mt 18²⁴ (προσηνέχθη, T); in forensic
sense, to summon: Ac 12⁶ (προαγαγεῖν, T, WH, mg., R). 2. Intrans.,
to draw near, approach (Jos 3⁹, Je 26 (46)³, al.): c. dat., Ac 27²⁷ (WH,
προσαχεῖν).†

* προσ-αγωγή, -ῆς, ἡ, (< προσάγω), 1. a bringing to. 2. approach,
access (v. Lft., Notes, 284; MM, xxi): Ro 5², Eph 2¹⁸ 3¹² (but v. Ellic.,
Eph., 59 f., where the transitive sense "introduction" is advocated).†

προσ-αιτέω, -ῶ, [in LXX: Jb 27¹⁴ *;] 1. to ask besides. 2. to
continue asking; hence, to importune, beg, ask alms: Jo 9⁸.†

*† προσαίτης, -ου, ὁ, a beggar: Mk 10⁴⁶, Jo 9⁸ (= cl. πτωχός,, q.v.).†

προσ-ανα-βαίνω, [in LXX: Ex 19²³, al. (עלה);] 1. to go up
besides. 2. to go up higher: Lk 14¹⁰.†

* προσ-αναλίσκω, to spend besides: Lk 8⁴³ (WH, R, mg., om.).†

** προσ-αναπληρόω, -ῶ, [in LXX: Wi 19⁴ *;] to fill up by adding
to, to supply fully: II Co 9¹² 11⁹.†

* προσ-ανα-τίθημι, to lay on or offer besides; mid., (a) to lay on
oneself in addition, undertake besides; (b) c. gen. pers., of giving or
obtaining information, to consult, communicate: Ga 1¹⁶ 2⁶ (Lft., in l.;
cf. ἀνα-τίθημι).†

* προσ-αν-έχω, to approach: v.l. for προσαχέω, Ac 27²⁷ L.†

** προσ-απειλέω, -ῶ, [in LXX: Si 13³ א *;] to threaten further:
Ac 4²¹.†

*† προσ-αχέω, -ῶ, Doric for προσηχέω, to resound: of land perceived
by the roar of the surf, Ac 27²⁷ (WH, mg., cf. προσάγω).´

*† προσ-δαπανάω, -ῶ, to spend besides : c. acc., Lk 10³⁵.†
SYN. : προϲαναλίϲκω.

προσ-δέομαι, [in LXX: Pr 12⁹ (חָסֵר), Si ₆ *;] to want further, need in addition : Ac 17²⁵.†

προσ-δέχομαι, [in LXX chiefly for רצה;] 1. to receive to oneself, receive favourably, admit, accept : c. acc. pers., Lk 15², Ro 16², Phl 2²⁹; c. acc. rei, Ac 24¹⁵ (R, mg.), He 10³⁴ 11³⁵. 2. to expect, look for, wait for : c. acc. pers., Lk 12³⁶ ; c. acc. rei, Mk 15⁴³, Lk 2²⁵, ³⁸ 23⁵¹, Ac 23²¹, Tit 2¹³, Ju ²¹ (cf. δέχομαι).†

προσ-δοκάω, -ῶ (the simple verb exists only in the forms δοκέω, -εύω), [in LXX : Ps 103 (104)²⁷ (שׂבר pi.), etc. ;] to await, expect : Mt 24⁵⁰, Lk 3¹⁵ 12⁴⁶, Ac 27³³ 28⁶ ; c. acc. pers., Mt 11³, Lk 1²¹ 7¹⁹, ²⁰ 8⁴⁰, Ac 10²⁴ ; c. acc. rei, II Pe 3¹²⁻¹⁴ ; c. acc. et inf., Ac 28⁶ ; c. inf., Ac 3⁵.†

προσδοκία, -ας, ἡ (< προσδοκάω), [in LXX : Ge 49¹⁰ (יִקְּהַת), Ps 118 (119)¹¹⁶ (שׂבר), Wi 17¹³, Si 40², al.;] expectation : c. gen. obj., Lk 21²⁶ ; c. gen. subjc., Ac 12¹¹.†

*† προσ-εάω, -ῶ, to permit further : Ac 27⁷.†

† προσ-εγγίζω, [in LXX chiefly for נגשׁ, קרב ;] 1. trans., to bring near (Luc.). 2. Intrans., to approach : c. dat., Mk 2⁴ (WH, προσενέγκαι).†

** προσεδρεύω (< πρόσεδρος, sitting near), [in LXX : i Mac 11⁴⁰ *;] 1. to sit near. 2. to attend regularly : c. dat., i Co 9¹³, Rec. (v.s. παρεδρεύω).†

* προσ-εργάζομαι, 1. to work or do service besides (Hdt., Plut.). 2. to gain besides, by working or trading : Lk 19¹⁶ (Xen.).†

προσ-έρχομαι, [in LXX for קרב, נגשׁ, etc. ;] to approach, draw near : absol., Mt 4¹¹, Lk 9⁴², al.; c. infin., Mt 24¹, al.; c. dat. loc., He 12¹⁸, ²² ; dat. pers., Mt 5¹, and freq., Jo 12²¹, al.; ptcp., προσελθών, c. indic., Mt 8², and freq., Mk 1³¹, Lk 7¹⁴, al.; π. αὐτῷ, c. indic., Mt 4³, Mk 6³⁵, al. Metaph., (a) of approaching God : absol. (Le 21¹⁷, De 21⁵, al.), He 10¹, ²² ; τ. θεῷ, He 7²⁵ 11⁶ ; τ. θρόνῳ τ. χάριτος, He 4¹⁶ ; πρὸς Χριστόν, I Pe 2⁴ ; (b) in sense not found elsewhere (Field, Notes, 211), to consent to : ὑγιαίνουσι λόγοις, i Ti 6³.†

† προσ-ευχή, -ῆς, ἡ (< προσεύχομαι), [in LXX chiefly for תְּפִלָּה;] 1. prayer to God : Mt 17²¹ (WH, R, txt., om.) 21²², Mk 9²⁹, Lk 22⁴⁵, Ac 3¹ 6⁴ 10³¹, Ro 12¹², i Co 7⁵, Col 4² ; pl., Ac 2⁴² 10⁴, Ro 1¹⁰, Eph 1¹⁶, Col 4¹², i Th 1², Phm 4, ²², i Pe 3⁷ 4⁷, Re 5⁸ 8³, ⁴ ; οἶκος προσευχῆς, Mt 21¹³, Mk 11¹⁷, Lk 19⁴⁶ (LXX) ; π. καὶ δέησις, Eph 6¹⁸, Phl 4⁶ ; pl., i Ti 2¹ 5⁵ ; ἡ π. τοῦ θεοῦ, prayer to God (cf. Wi 16²⁸), Lk 6¹² ; πρὸς τ. θεόν, seq. ὑπέρ, Ac 12⁵ ; pl., Ro 15³⁰ ; Hebraistically (Bl., § 38, 3), προσευχῇ προσεύχεσθαι, Ja 5¹⁷ (EV, prayed fervently). 2. a place of prayer : of a synagogue (iii Mac 7²⁰, v.l.; v. Charles, APOT, i, 173 ; for other exx., v. Kennedy, Sources, 114) ; of a place in the open (FlJ, Ant., xiv, 10, 23), Ac 16¹³, ¹⁶.†
SYN. : v.s. δέησις.

προσ-εύχομαι, [in LXX chiefly for פלל hith.;] *to pray* (always of prayer to God, or in cl., to gods): absol., Mt 6⁵⁻⁷, ⁹ 14²³ 19¹³ 26³⁶, ³⁹, ⁴¹, ⁴⁴, Mk 1³⁵ 6⁴⁶ 11²⁴, ²⁵ 13³³ (WH, R, txt., om.) 14³², ³⁸, ³⁹, Lk 1¹⁰ 3²¹ 5¹⁶ 6¹² 9¹⁸, ²⁸, ²⁹ 11¹, ² 18¹, ¹⁰ 22⁴⁴ (WH, R, mg., om.), Ac 1²⁴ 6⁶ 9¹¹, ⁴⁰ 10⁹, ³⁰ 11⁵ 12¹² 13³ 14²³ 16²⁵ 20³⁶ 21⁵ 22¹⁷ 28⁸, I Co 11⁴, ⁵ 14¹⁴, I Th 5¹⁷, I Ti 2⁸, Ja 5¹³, ¹⁸; seq. λέγων, Mt 26³⁹, ⁴², Lk 22⁴¹; c. dat. instr., I Co 11⁵ 14¹⁴, ¹⁵; μακρά, Mt 23¹⁴ (WH, R, txt., om.), Mk 12⁴⁰, Lk 20⁴⁷; ἐν πνεύματι (ἁγίῳ), Eph 6¹⁸, Ju ²⁰; προσευχῇ π. (a Hebraism, v.s. προσευχή), Ja 5¹⁷; c. acc. rei, Lk 18¹¹, Ro 8²⁶; seq. ἐπί, c. acc. pers., Ja 5¹⁴; c. dat. pers., Mt 6⁶, I Co 11¹³; seq. περί, c. gen., Ac 8¹⁵, Col 1³ 4³, I Th 5²⁵, II Th 1¹¹ 3¹, He 13¹⁸; ὑπέρ, Mt 5⁴⁴ Lk 6²⁸, Col 1⁹, . Ja 5¹⁶; seq. ἵνα, Mt 24²⁰, Mk 13¹⁸ 14³⁵, Lk 22⁴⁶, I Co 14¹³; τοῦτο ἵνα, Phl 1⁹; c. inf., Lk 22⁴⁰; seq. τοῦ, c. inf. (Bl., § 71, 3), Ja 5¹⁷.†

προσ-έχω, [in LXX for קשב hi., שמר ni., etc.;] 1. *to turn to, bring to* (freq. ναῦν, expressed or understood, *to bring to port, land;* Hdt., al.). 2. τ. νοῦν, seq. dat., *to turn one's mind to, attend to;* in Xen. and later writers with νοῦν omitted (Bl., § 53, 1; 81, 1): Ac 8⁶ 16¹⁴, He 2¹, II Pe 1¹⁹; in sense of caring or providing for, Ac 20²⁸; π. ἑαυτῷ, *to give heed to oneself* (M, *Pr.*, 157; cf. Ge 24⁶, Ex 10²⁸, al.): Lk 17³ 21³⁴, Ac 5³⁵; id. seq. ἀπό (M, *Pr.*, 102; Bl., § 34, 1₁; 40, 3; v.s. βλέπω), Lk 12¹; (without dat.) Mt 7¹⁵ 10¹⁷ 16⁶, ¹¹, ¹², Lk 20⁴⁶ (cf. Si 6¹³, al.); seq. μή, c. inf. (M, *Pr.*, 193; Bl., § 69, 4), Mt 6¹. 3. *to attach* or *devote oneself to:* c. dat. pers., Ac 8¹⁰, ¹¹, I Ti 4¹; c. dat. rei, I Ti 1⁴ 3⁸ 4¹³ 6³ T (-ερχ-, WH, R), Tit 1¹⁴, He 7¹³.†

** προσ-ηλόω, -ῶ, [in LXX: III Mac 4⁹ *;] *to nail to:* c. acc. et dat., fig., Col 2¹⁴.†

† προσήλυτος, -ον (< προσέρχομαι; v. M, *Gr.*, II, p. 237), [in LXX for גר;] 1. *one who has arrived, a stranger.* 2. Of converts to Judaism, *a proselyte* (v. DB, s.v.): Mt 23¹⁵, Ac 2¹⁰ 6⁵ 13⁴³.†

** πρόσ-καιρος, -ον, [in LXX: IV Mac 15², ⁸, ²³ *;] 1. *in season.* 2. *for a season, temporary, transient:* II Co 4¹⁸, He 11²⁵; of plants, *short-lived:* Mt 13²¹, Mk 4¹⁷.†

προσ-καλέω, -ῶ, [in LXX chiefly for קרא;] *to call to.* Mid., *to call to oneself* (v. M, *Pr.*, 157): c. acc. pers., Mt 10¹, Mk 3¹³, ²³ 6⁷, Lk 7¹⁹, Ac 5⁴⁰, Ja 5¹⁴, al. Metaph., of the Divine call: Ac 2³⁹; c. inf., Ac 16¹⁰ (v. Bl., § 69, 4); seq. εἰς, Ac 13².†

προσ-καρτερέω, -ῶ (< καρτερός, *strong, stedfast*), [in LXX: Nu 13²¹ (חזק hith.), To 5⁸ א, Da TH Su ⁶ *;] *to attend constantly, continue stedfastly, adhere to, wait on:* c. dat. pers., Mk 3⁹, Ac 8¹³ 10⁷; c. dat. rei, Ac 1¹⁴ 2⁴² 6⁴, Ro 12¹², Col 4²; seq. ἐν, Ac 2⁴⁶; εἰς, Ro 13⁶.†

*† προσ-καρτέρησις, -εως, ἡ (< προσκαρτερέω), *stedfastness, perseverance:* Eph 6¹⁸.†

προσ-κεφάλαιον, -ον, τό, [in LXX: Ez 13¹⁸, ²⁰ (כסת), I Es 3⁸ *;] *a pillow, cushion:* Mk 4³⁸.†

*† προσ-κληρόω, -ῶ, *to allot to, assign to by lot;* pass. (but perh. as mid., EV, *consorted with,* so Syr.): Ac 17⁴ (for exx., v. Cremer, 749).†

πρόσ-κλησις, -εως, ἡ, LTr., mg., for πρόσκλισις, q.v.
** προσ-κλίνω, [in LXX : II Mac 14²⁴ * ;] 1. *to make to lean against.*
2. *to make* the scale *incline* one way or another; hence, metaph., of
persons, *to incline* (sc. ἑαυτόν) *towards :* pass., Ac 5³⁶.†
*† πρόσ-κλισις, -εως, ἡ (< προσκλίνω), *inclination, partiality :* I Ti 5²¹.†
προσ-κολλάω, -ῶ, [in LXX chiefly for דבק ;] *to glue to ;* pass.,
reflexive, *to stick to, cleave to* (Plat.) : metaph. (c. dat., Jos 23⁸, Si 6³⁴
al.), seq. πρός, Mk 10⁷ (R, txt.), Eph 5³¹ (LXX).†
† πρόσ-κομμα, -τος, τό (< προσκόπτω), [in LXX : Ex 23³³ 34¹²
(מוֹקֵשׁ), Is 8¹⁴ (נֶגֶף), Jth 8²², Si 17²⁵, al. ;] (a) a *stumble, stumbling :*
λίθος προσκόμματος (= אֶבֶן נֶגֶף, Is, l.c.), fig., Ro 9³², ³³, I Pe 2⁸ (LXX) ;
(b) = προσκοπή, an occasion of *stumbling, a stumbling-block :* metaph.,
Ro 14¹³, ²⁰, I Co 8⁹ (Plut.).†
SYN. : σκάνδαλον (cf. Cremer, 752 f.).
** προσκοπή, -ῆς, ἡ (< προσκόπτω), [in Gr. Ven. : Pr 16¹⁸ (בִּשָּׁלוֹן) * ;]
an occasion of *stumbling, offence :* II Co 6³.†
προσ-κόπτω, [in LXX for נגף כשל ni., etc. ;] 1. trans., *to strike*
(e.g. hand or foot) *against :* c. acc. seq. πρός, fig., Mt 4⁶, Lk 4¹¹ (LXX).
2. Intrans., *to stumble :* absol. (To 11⁹, Pr 3²³), Jo 11⁹, ¹⁰ ; of wind, *to*
rush against, beat upon : c. dat, Mt 7²⁷. Metaph., in late writers, (a)
to offend (Polyb.) ; (b) *to take offence at, stumble at :* seq. ἐν, Ro 14²¹ ;
c. dat., τ. λόγῳ, I Pe 2⁸ ; τ. λίθῳ τ. προσκόμματος, Ro 9³².†
* προσ-κυλίω, *to roll up, roll to :* c. acc. et dat., Mt 27⁶⁰ ; acc. seq.
ἐπί, Mk 15⁴⁶.†
προσ-κυνέω, -ῶ (< κυνέω, *to kiss*), [in LXX chiefly for שחה hith. ;]
to make obeisance, do reverence to, worship ; (a) prop. (as in cl., of the
gods : Hdt., Æsch., Plat., al.), of God, Christ and supra-mundane
beings : absol., Jo 4²⁰ 12²⁰, Ac 8²⁷ 24¹¹, He 11²¹ (Westc., in l.), Re 11¹ ;
πίπτειν καὶ π., Re 5¹⁴ ; c. dat. (on the significance of this constr. as compared with the usual cl., c. acc., v. Abbott, JG, 78 f. ; JV, 133 ff.),
Jo 4²¹, ²³, Ac 7⁴³, I Co 14²⁵, He 1⁶, Re 4¹⁰ 7¹¹ 11¹⁶ 13⁴, ¹⁵ 14⁷ 16², 19⁴, ¹⁰, ²⁰
22⁸, ⁹ ; c. acc. (v. supr.), Mt 4¹⁰, Lk 4⁸ 24⁵² (WH, R, mg., om.), Jo 4²², ²⁴,
Re 9²⁰ 13⁴, ⁸, ¹² 14⁹, ¹¹ 20⁴ ; seq. ἐνώπιον, Lk 4⁷, Re 15⁴ ; (b) as in cl., of
homage to human superiors (cf. MM, xxi) : absol., Mt 20²⁰, Ac 10²⁵ ;
c. dat. (v. supr.), Mt 2², ⁸ 8², 9¹⁸, 14³³ 15²⁵ 18²⁶ 28⁹, Mk 15¹⁹, Jo 9³³ ; πεσὼν
π., Mt 2¹¹ 4⁹ ; ἐνώπιον τ. ποδῶν, Re 3⁹ ; c. acc., Mk 5⁶ (dat. T).†
*† προσ-κυνητής, -οῦ, ὁ (< προσκυνέω), a *worshipper :* Jo 4²³.†
προσ-λαλέω, -ῶ, [in LXX : Ex 4¹⁶ AB² (דבר pi.), Wi 13¹⁷ * ;] *to*
speak to : Ac 28²⁰ ; c. dat. pers., Ac 13⁴³.†
προσ-λαμβάνω, [in LXX : Ps 17 (18)¹⁶ (משה hi.), 72 (73)²⁴ (לקח),
etc. ;] 1. *to take in addition.* 2. *to take to oneself, take, receive ;* in
NT always mid., -ομαι ; (a) of things : of food, c. acc., Ac 27³³ ; c. gen.
part., ib. ³⁶ ; (b) of persons : c. acc., Mt 16²², Mk 8³² (v. Swete, in l.),
Ac 17⁵ 18²⁶ 28², Ro 14¹, ³ 15⁷, Phm ¹⁷.†
* πρόσ-λημψις (Rec. -ληψις, as in Att.), -εως, ἡ (< προσλαμβάνω),
1. *an assumption* (Plat.). 2. *a receiving* (cf. προσλαμβάνω) : Ro 11¹⁵.†

προσ-μένω, [in LXX: Jg 3²⁵ A (חוּל hi.), To 2² א, Wi 3⁹, III Mac 7¹⁷*;] 1. *to wait longer, continue, remain still :* Ac 18¹⁸; seq. ἐν, I Ti 1³. 2. C. dat., *to remain with :* Mt 15³², Mk 8². Metaph., *to remain attached to, cleave unto, abide in :* τ. κυρίῳ, Ac 11²³ (R, txt.; ἐν τ. κ., R, mg., v. supr.); τ. χάριτι τ. θεοῦ, Ac 13⁴³; τ. δεήσεσιν, I Ti 5⁵.†

* προσ-ορμίζω (< ὅρμος, *an anchorage*), *to bring* a ship *to anchor at ;* usually in mid., *to come to anchor near,* and so pass. in late writers (Ael., Dio Cass.) : Mk 6⁵³.†

* προσ-οφείλω, *to owe besides :* Phm ¹⁹ (v. Field, *Notes*, 225).†

† προσ-οχθίζω, [in LXX: Le 26¹⁵, al. (גָּעַל); ib. 18²⁵, al. (קוֹא), Ps 94 (95)¹⁰, Ez 36³¹ (קוּט), Si 6²⁵, al. (other writers use ὀχθέω, rarely -ίζω) ;] *to be angry with :* c. dat., He 3¹⁰ (LXX), 17.†

προσ-παίω = προσπίπτω, Mt 7²⁵ L (v.s. προσπίπτω).†

*† πρόσπεινος, -ον (< πεῖνα, *hunger*), *hungry :* Ac 10¹⁰.†

* προσ-πήγνυμι, *to fasten to :* absol., *to crucify,* Ac 2²³.†

προσ-πίπτω, [in LXX for נפל, נבע hi., ברע;] 1. *to fall upon, strike against :* c. dat., of wind, Mt 7²⁵. 2. *to fall down at one's feet, fall prostrate before :* absol., seq. πρός, Mk 7²⁵; c. dat. pers., Mk 3¹¹ 5³³, Lk 8²⁸, ⁴⁷, Ac 16²⁹; τ. γόνασιν, Lk 5⁸.†

προσ-ποιέω, -ῶ, [in LXX: I Ki 21¹³ (14) (הלל hithpo.), Jb 19¹⁴, Si 34 (31)³⁰, Da LXX Su ¹¹*;] *to make over to, add* or *attach to.* Mid., *to take to oneself, claim ;* hence, *to pretend ;* c. inf. (cf. Xen., *Anab.*, iv, 3, 20), *to make as if :* Lk 24²⁸.†

προσ-πορεύομαι, [in LXX for קרב, נגש, etc.;] *to come near, approach :* c. dat. pers., Mk 10³⁵.†

**† προσ-ρήγνυμι, [in Aq.: Ps 2⁹*;] *to break against, dash against ;* (a) trans. (παιδία πέτραις, FlJ, *Ant.*, ix, 4, 6); (b) intrans., c. dat. : Lk 6⁴⁸, ⁴⁹ (cf. προσπίπτω).†

προσ-τάσσω, [in LXX chiefly for צוה pi.;] 1. c. acc. pers., *to place at, to attach to.* 2. *to give a command, enjoin, appoint :* Lk 5¹⁴; c. dat. pers., Mt 1²⁴; c. acc. rei, Mt 8⁴, Mk 1⁴⁴; c. acc. et inf., Ac 10⁴⁸; pass., Ac 10³³ 17²⁶.†

* προστάτις, -ιδος, ἡ (fem. of προστάτης), *a patroness, protectress :* Ro 16².†

προσ-τίθημι, [in LXX chiefly for יסף hi., also for אסף ni., etc.;] 1. *to put to.* 2. *to add, join to, give in addition :* c. acc. seq. ἐπί, Mt 6²⁷, Lk 3²⁰ 12²⁵; ἐπὶ τὸ αὐτό, Ac 2⁴⁷; c. acc. et dat., Lk 17⁵, He 12¹⁹ (v. MM, xxi) ; pass., absol., Ac 2⁴¹, Ga 3¹⁹; c. dat., Mt 6³³, Mk 4²⁴, Lk 12³¹, Ac 5¹⁴ 11²⁴; προσετέθη πρὸς τ. πατέρας (cf. Ge 26⁸, Jg 2¹⁰, al.), Ac 13³⁶; c. inf., of repeating or continuing the action signified by the following verb, as in Heb. idiom (Ge 4² 8¹², al.; cf. WM, § 54, 5; Lft. on Clem., I Co., xii; but v. also M, Pr., 67, 233; Deiss., BS, 67₁; MM, VGT, s.v.; M, Gr., II, p. 445), Lk 20¹¹, Ac 12³; similarly ptcp., προσθείς, c. indic. (Ge 38⁵, al.), Lk 19¹¹.†

προσ-τρέχω, [in LXX for רוץ;] *to run to :* Mk 9¹⁵ 10¹⁷, Ac 8³⁰.†

*† προσφάγιον, -ον, τό (< φαγεῖν), Hellenistic for ὄψον (v.s. ὀψάριον), *a relish* or *dainty* (esp. *cooked fish*), *to be eaten with bread :* Jo 21⁵

(*have ye taken any fish*, Field, *Notes*, 109; Abbott, *Essays*, 105; cf. M, *Pr.*, 170ₙ; MM, *Exp.*, xxi).†

πρόσφατος, -ον (on the derivation, v. Boisacq, s.v. and cf. -ως), [in LXX: Nu 6³ (חֵל), De 32¹⁷, Ec 1⁹ (חָדָשׁ), Ps 80 (81)⁹ (זוּר), Si 9¹⁰ *;] 1. originally, *freshly slain*. 2. Generally (from Æsch. on), *new, fresh, recent :* ὁδός, He 10²⁰ (v. MM, *Exp.*, xxi; Rutherford, *NPhr.*, 471 f.).†

προσφάτως, adv. (v.s. πρόσφατος), [in LXX: De 24⁵ (חָדָשׁ), Jth 4³, ⁵, Ez 11³, II Mac 14³⁶ *;] *recently :* Ac 18² (v. MM, *Exp.*, xxi).†

προσ-φέρω, [in LXX chiefly for קרב hi.;] 1. *to bring to, lead to :* c. acc. et dat. pers., Mt 4²⁴ 8¹⁶ 9², ³² 14³⁵ 17¹⁶, Mk 2⁴ (WH, R, txt.; sc. αὐτόν) 10¹³, Lk 18¹⁵, 23¹⁴; pass., Mt 12²² (act., WH, txt.) 18²⁴ (προσήχθη, WH) 19¹³; c. acc. rei, Mt 25²⁰; id. c. dat. pers., Mt 22¹⁹, Lk 23³⁶; τ. στόματι, Jo 19²⁹; metaph., c. dat pers., *to deal with*, He 12⁷ (cl.). 2. *to offer :* Mt 2¹¹, Ac 8¹⁸; esp. (as freq. in LXX; cf. FlJ, *Ant.*, iii, 9, 3) sacrifices, gifts and prayers to God: absol., seq. περί (ὑπέρ), Mk 1⁴⁴, Lk 5¹⁴, He 5¹, ³ 9⁷ 10¹²; pass., Ac 21²⁶; c. acc. rei (δῶρον, θυσίαν, λατρείαν, προσφοράν), Mt 5²³, ²⁴ (aoristic pres.; M, *Pr.*, 247) 8⁴, Jo 16², Ac 7⁴² 21²⁶, He 5¹ 8³, ⁴ 9⁷, ⁹ 10¹, ², ⁸, ¹¹, ¹² 11⁴; δεήσεις τε κ. ἱκετηρίας, He 5⁷; c. acc. pers., He 11¹⁷ (conative impf.; M, *Pr.*, 129); of Christ, He 7²⁷ (ἀνενέγκας, WH, txt.) 9¹⁴, ²⁵, ²⁸.†

** προσφιλής, -ές (< φιλέω), [in LXX: Es 5¹, Si 4⁷ 20¹³ *;] (a) of persons, in both act. and pass. sense (LXX, ll. c.); (b) of things, *pleasing, agreeable* (EV, *lovely*): Phl 4⁸.†

προσ-φορά, -ᾶς, ἡ (< προσφέρω), [in LXX: III Ki 7⁴⁸ (כֵּנִים), Ps 39 (40)⁶ (מִנְחָה), I Es 5⁵², Si 14¹¹, al.;] 1. *a bringing to, offering* (Plat., al.). 2. (Less freq. in cl.), *a present, an offering;* in NT, of sacrificial offerings: Ac 21²⁶ 24¹⁷, Eph 5², He 10⁵, ⁸, ¹⁴; περὶ ἁμαρτίας, He 10¹⁸; c. gen. obj., Ro 15¹⁶, He 10¹⁰.†

προσ-φωνέω, -ῶ, [in LXX: I Es 2²¹ 6⁶, ²², II Mac 15¹⁵ *;] 1. *to address, call to;* in cl., c. acc. pers., c. dupl. acc. (cf. II Mac, l.c.); absol. (Hom., *Od.*, v, 159, al.): Ac 21⁴⁰. In late writers, c. dat. pers.: Mt 11¹⁶, Lk 7³² 13¹² 23²⁰, Ac 22². 2. *to call by name, summon :* c. acc. (as in cl.), Lk 6¹³.†

*† πρόσ-χυσις, -εως, ἡ, *a pouring* or *sprinkling upon :* He 11²⁸.†

* προσ-ψαύω, in poët. and late writers, *to touch :* c. dat., Lk 11⁴⁶.†

*† προσωπολημπτέω (Rec. -ληπτ-), -ῶ (< -λήμπτης, q.v.), *to have respect of persons :* Ja 2⁹.†

*† προσωπο-λήμπτης (Rec. -λήπτης, v. Bl., § 6, 8), -ου, ὁ (< πρόσωπον λαμβάνειν, v.s. πρόσωπον), *a respecter of persons :* Ac 10³⁴ (on this group of cognate forms, v. Mayor, *Ja.*, 78 f.; and cf. Thackeray, *Gr.*, 44).†

*† προσωπολημψία (Rec. -ληψία), -ας, ἡ (< προσωπολήμπτης), *respect of persons :* Ro 2¹¹, Eph 6⁹, Col 3²⁵, Ja 2¹ (v. Mayor, in l.).†

πρόσωπον, -ου, τό (< πρός, ὤψ), [in LXX chiefly and very freq. for פָּנִים;] 1. prop., of persons (so always in cl.); (a) *the face, counte-*

nance : Mt 6¹⁶,¹⁷, Mk 14⁶⁵, Lk 9²⁹, ii Co 3⁷, Re 4⁷, al.; τὸ π. τῆς γενέσεως (EV, *natural face*), Ja 1²³; πίπτειν ἐπὶ (τὰ) π., Mt 17⁶, Lk 5¹², Re 7¹¹, al.; ἀγνοούμενος τῷ π., Ga 1²²; π., οὐ καρδίᾳ, i Th 2¹⁷; κατὰ πρόσωπον (*in front, facing :* Thuc., Xen., al.), *when present, face to face,* Ac 25¹⁶, ii Co 10¹,⁷, Ga 2¹¹; id. c. gen., as compound prep., *in the presence of* (not cl.; v. Bl., § 40, 9; M, *Pr.,* 99 f.; Thackeray, *Gr.,* 43 f.; M, *Gr.,* ii, p. 466), Lk 2³¹, Ac 3¹³; similarly ἀπὸ π. (Heb. מִלִּפְנֵי; v. Dalman, *Words,* 29), *from the presence of,* Ac 3¹⁹ 5⁴¹ 7⁴⁵, ii Th 1⁹, Re 12¹⁴ 20¹¹; πρὸ π. (Heb. לִפְנֵי), *before,* Mt 11¹⁰, Mk 1², Lk 7²⁷ (LXX), al.; in other phrases resembling Heb. idiom (Thackeray,*Gr.,*42), βλέπειν (ὁρᾶν, θεωρεῖν, ἰδεῖν) τὸ π., *to see one's face,* i.e. see him in person, Mt 18¹⁰, Ac 20²⁵,³⁸, i Th 3¹⁰, Re 22⁴; ἐμφανισθῆναι τῷ π. τοῦ θεοῦ, He 9²⁴; ἐν π. Χριστοῦ, ii Co 2¹⁰ 4⁶; μετὰ τοῦ π. σου, *with thy presence,* Ac 2²⁸(LXX); εἰς π. τῶν ἐκκλησιῶν, ii Co 8²⁴; στηρίζειν τὸ π. (Heb. שִׂים פָּנִים : Je 21¹⁰, al.; v. Dalman, *Words,* 30), c. inf., *to set one's face towards,* Lk 9⁵¹; similarly, τὸ π. αὐτοῦ ἦν πορευόμενον (*op. cit.,* 31), ib.⁵³; τὸ π. τοῦ κυρίου ἐπί, i Pe 3¹²(LXX); (*b*) *form, person :* καυχᾶσθαι ἐν π. καὶ μὴ ἐν καρδίᾳ, ii Co 5¹² (cf. i Ki 16⁷); metaph., as in Heb. idiom, of judgment according to appearance,external condition or circumstances (נָשָׂא פָנִים; v. Dalman, *Words,* 30; Thackeray, *Gr.,* 43 f.) : λαμβάνειν π., Lk 20²¹, Ga 2⁶; βλέπειν εἰς π., Mt 22¹⁶, Mk 12¹⁴; θαυμάζειν πρόσωπα, Ju¹⁶.   2. Of things (cf. Dalman, l.c.); (*a*) *face, appearance* (Ps 103 (104)³⁰): Mt 16³ (WH, R, mg., om.), Lk 12⁵⁶, Ja 1¹¹; (*b*) *surface* (Ge 2⁶): Lk 21³⁵, Ac 17²⁶.

** προ-τάσσω, [in LXX: ii Mac 8³⁶ R (A, προστ-)*;] 1. *to place in front.*   2. *to arrange beforehand :* Ac 17²⁶, Rec. (for προστ., Edd.).†

** προ-τείνω, [in LXX: ii Mac ₇, iii Mac 2¹*;] *to stretch out, stretch forth :* of preparations for scourging (v. Field, *Notes,* 136 f.), Ac 22²⁵.†

πρότερος, and πρῶτος, compar. and superl. from πρό, opp. to ὕστερος, ὕστατος.

A. Compar., πρότερος, -α, -ον, [in LXX for לְפָנִים, רִאשׁוֹן, etc.;] *before,* of time, place, rank, etc.; in NT always of Time, *before, former :* Eph 4²². Adverbially, πρότερον, *before, aforetime, formerly :* Jo 7⁵⁰, ii Co 1¹⁵, He 4⁶; opp. to ἔπειτα, He 7²⁷; τὸ π., Jo 6⁶² 9⁸, Ga 4¹³, i Ti 1¹³; αἱ π. ἡμέραι, He 10³²; αἱ π. ἐπιθυμίαι, i Pe 1¹⁴.†

B. Superl., πρῶτος, -η, -ον, [in LXX chiefly for רִאשׁוֹן, also for אֶחָד, etc.;] *first,* 1. of Time or Place; (*a*) absol., as subst., ὁ π., Lk 14¹⁸, Jo 19³², i Co 14³⁰; ὁ π. καὶ ὁ ἔσχατος, Re 1¹⁷ 2⁸ 22¹³; neut., τὸ π., opp. to τ. δεύτερον, He 10⁹; τὰ π., opp. to τ. ἔσχατα, Mt 12⁴⁵, Lk 11²⁶, ii Pe 2²⁰; anarth., Mt 10²; pl., Mt 19³⁰, Mk 10³¹, Lk 13³⁰; ἐν πρώτοις (EV, *first of all*), i Co 15³; (*b*) as adj.: πρώτῃ (sc. ἡμέρᾳ) σαββάτου, Mk 16⁽⁹⁾; φυλακή, opp. to δευτέρα, Ac 12¹⁰; equiv. to adv. in English, Jo 8⁽⁷⁾ 20⁴,⁸, Ac 27⁴³, Ro 10¹⁹, i Ti 1¹⁶, i Jo 4¹⁹; = πρότερος (v. infr.; cf.

M, *Pr.*: 79; Bl., § 11, 5; Thackeray, *Gr.*, 183 f.) : c. gen., π. μου ἦν (*my chief:* Abbott, *Jg.*, 509 ff.; but cf. M, *Pr.*, 245), Jo 1¹⁵, ³⁰; c. art., Mk 14¹², Ac 1¹, al.; seq. ὁ δεύτερος, etc., Mt 22²⁵, Mk 12²⁰, al. 2. Of Rank or Dignity, *chief, principal :* Mt 20²⁷ 22³⁸, Mk 9³⁵, Eph 6², al.; c. gen., Mk 12²⁸, ²⁹, al.; πόλις (Field, *Notes*, 124), Ac 16¹²; c. art., Lk 15²² 19⁴⁷, Ac 13⁵⁰, al. 3. Neut., πρῶτον, as adv., *first, at the first ;* (*a*) of Time : Mt 8²¹, Mk 4²⁸, al.; τὸ π., Jo 10⁴⁰, al.; (*b*) of Order : Ro 3², 1 Co 11¹⁸, al.

προ-τίθημι, [in LXX : Ex 40⁴, ²³, Le 24⁸ (עָרַךְ), Ps 53 (54)³ (שׂוּם), etc.;] 1. *to set before, set forth* publicly; so also in mid.: c. acc. pers., Ro 3²⁵ (for a suggested alt. rend., v. MM, xxii). 2. Mid., *to set before oneself, propose, purpose :* c. inf., Ro 1¹³; c. acc. rei, Eph 1⁹.†

** προ-τρέπω, [in LXX : Wi 14¹⁸, ii Mac 11⁷, iv Mac 12⁷ 15¹² 16¹³ *;] *to urge forwards, exhort, persuade.* Mid., in same sense (as also in cl.) : Ac 18²⁷.†

προ-τρέχω, [in LXX : 1 Ki 8¹¹ (רוּץ לִפְנֵי), Jb 41¹³ ⁽¹⁴⁾ A (דּוּץ), To 11³ (seq. ἔμπροσθεν), 1 Mac 16²¹ *;] 1. *to run forward.* 2. *to run on, run in advance :* Jo 20⁴; seq. εἰς τὸ ἔμπροσθεν, Lk 19⁴.†

** προ-ϋπ-άρχω, [in LXX : Jb 42¹⁸ *;] 1. *to be beforehand in.* 2. *to be before* or *previously :* c. ptcp., Lk 23¹², Ac 8⁹.†

πρό-φασις, -εως, ἡ (< φήμι), [in LXX : Ps 140 (141)⁴ (עֲלִילָה), Da TH 6⁴, ⁵ ⁽⁵, ⁶⁾ (עִלָּה), Pr 18¹, Ho 10⁴ *;] *a pretence, pretext :* Mt 23¹³ (WM, R, txt., om.), Mk 12⁴⁰, Lk 20⁴⁷, Jo 15²², Ac 27³⁰, Phl 1¹⁸, 1 Th 2⁵.†

προ-φέρω, [in LXX : Pr 10¹³ (מוצא ni.), To 9⁵, al.;] *to bring forth :* c. acc. rei, seq. ἐκ, Lk 6⁴⁵.†

† προφητεία, -ας, ἡ (< προφητεύω), [in LXX for נְבוּאָה, חָזוֹן;] the gift (and its exercise) of interpreting the Divine will and purpose, *prophecy, prophesying :* of OT prophecy, Mt 13¹⁴, ii Pe 1²⁰, ²¹; of NT prophecy, Ro 12⁶, 1 Co 12¹⁰ 13² 14⁶, ²², 1 Ti 4¹⁴, Re 11⁶ 22¹⁹; pl., 1 Co 13⁸, 1 Th 5²⁰, 1 Ti 1¹⁸; οἱ λόγοι τῆς π., Re 1³ 22⁷, ¹⁰, ¹⁸; τ. πνεῦμα τῆς π., Re 19¹⁰ (Luc., FlJ, LXX, π.; v. Deiss., *BS*, 235 f.; MM, xxii).†

προφητεύω (< προφήτης), [in LXX chiefly for נבא ni., hith.;] *to be a προφήτης* (q.v.), *to prophesy :* in the primary sense of telling forth the Divine counsels, Mt 7²² 26⁶⁸, Mk 14⁶⁵, Lk 1⁶⁷ 22⁶⁴, Ac 19⁶, 1 Co 11⁴, ⁵ 13⁹ 14¹, ³⁻⁵, ²⁴, ³¹, ³⁹, Re 11³; with the idea of foretelling future events (an idea merely incidental, not essential; v. Lft., *Notes*, 83 f.), Mt 11¹³, Ac 2¹⁷, ¹⁸ ⁽ᴸˣˣ⁾ 21⁹; seq. περί, Mt 15⁷, Mk 7⁶, 1 Pe 1¹⁰; ἐπί, c. dat., Re 10¹¹; λέγων, Ju ¹⁴; ὅτι, Jo 11⁵¹.†

SYN. : μαντεύομαι, q.v.

προφήτης, -ου, ὁ (< πρόφημι, *to speak forth*), [in LXX chiefly for נָבִיא;] one who acts as an interpreter or forth-teller of the Divine will (v. Lft., *Notes*, 83 f.; Tr., *Syn.*, § vi), *a prophet;* 1. in cl. (Æsch., Hdt., Plat., al.), of the interpreters of oracles. 2. In NT, (*a*) of the OT prophets : Mt 5¹², Mk 6¹⁵, Lk 4²⁷, Jo 8⁵², Ro 11³, al.; (*b*) of prophets in general : Mt 10⁴¹ 13⁵⁷ 21⁴⁶, Mk 6⁴, Lk 13³³, al.; (*c*) of John the Baptist : Mt 21²⁶, Mk 6¹⁵, Lk 1⁷⁶; (*d*) of Christ : Mt 21¹¹, Jo 6¹⁴, Ac 3²², ²³ 7³⁷ (LXX); (*e*) of Christian prophets in the apostolic age : Ac 15³², ɪ Co 12²⁸, Eph 2²⁰, al.; (*f*) by meton., of the writings of prophets : Lk 24²⁷, Ac 8²⁸, al.; (*g*) of a poet : Tit 1¹² (on the use of the term in π. and Inscr., v. Deiss., *BS*, 235 f.; MM, xxii).

*† **προφητικός**, -ά, -όν (< προφήτης), *of prophecy, prophetic* : Ro 16²⁶, ɪɪ Pe 1¹⁹.†

προφῆτις, -ιδος, ἡ, fem. of προφήτης, [in LXX : Ex 15²⁰, Jg 4⁴, ɪv Ki 22¹⁴, ɪɪ Ch 34²², Is 8³ (וּבִיאָה) *;] *a prophetess* : Lk 2³⁶, Re 2²⁰.†

προ-φθάνω, [in LXX chiefly for קָדַם pi. ;] c. ptcp. (as in cl., but more freq. the simple φθάνω, q.v.), *to anticipate* : Mt 17²⁵.†

προ-χειρίζω (< πρόχειρος, *at hand*), [in LXX : Ex 4¹³ (שָׁלַח), Jos 3¹² (לָקַח), Da LXX 3²², ɪɪ Mac 3⁷ 8⁹ 14¹² A *;] 1. *to put into the hand, deliver up* : pass., Ac 3²⁰. 2. More freq. as depon., -ομαι, *to take into one's hand;* hence, metaph., *to propose, determine, choose* : c. inf., Ac 22¹⁴ ; c. acc. pers., ib. 26¹⁶.†

* **προ-χειρο-τονέω**, -ῶ (v. χειροτονέω), *to choose or appoint beforehand* : Ac 10⁴¹ (Plat., al.).†

Πρόχορος, -ου, ὁ, *Prochorus* : Ac 6⁵.†

* **πρύμνα**, -ης, ἡ, prop. fem. of adj. πρύμνος, -η, -ον, (sc. ναῦς), *the hindmost part* of a ship, *the stern* : Mk 4³⁸, Ac 27²⁹ ; opp. to πρῷρα, ib. ⁴¹.†

πρωί (Rec. πρωΐ), adv. (< πρό), [in LXX chiefly for בֹּקֶר, בַּבֹּקֶר ;] *in the morning, early* : Mt 16³ (R, txt.) 21¹⁸, Mk 1³⁵ 11²⁰ 13³⁵ 15¹ 16[⁹], Joɪ18²⁸ 20¹ ; λίαν π., Mk 16² ; ἅμα π., Mt 20¹ ; ἀπὸ π. (cf. ἀπὸ πρωΐθεν, Ex 18¹³), Ac 28²³.†

πρωία, v.s. πρώϊος.

πρώϊμος, v.s. πρόϊμος.

† **πρωϊνός** (Rec. -ϊνός, v. WH, *App.*, 152), -ή, -όν (< πρωΐ), [in LXX chiefly for בֹּקֶר ;] = cl. πρώϊος, *at early morn, early* : ἀστήρ, Re 2²⁸ 22¹⁶.†

πρώϊος (Rec. -ϊος), -α, -ον (< πρωΐ), [in LXX for בֹּקֶר, בַּ, בְּ ;] *at early morn, early;* as subst., ἡ π. (sc. ὥρα, cf. ἡ ὥ. ἡ π., ɪɪɪ Mac 5²⁴), *early morning* : Mt 27¹, Jo 21⁴.†

* **πρῷρα** (Rec. incorrectly πρώρα, v. Bl., § 3, 3 ; LS, s.v.), -ης (for Att. -ας, v. Bl., § 7, 1 ; Mayser, 12), ἡ, the forward part of a ship, *the prow* : Ac 27³⁰ ; opp. to πρύμνα, ib. ⁴¹.†

πρωτεύω (< πρῶτος), [in LXX : Es 5¹¹, ɪɪ Mac 6¹⁸ 13¹⁵ *;] *to be first, pre-eminent, have the first place* : Col 1¹⁸.†

*† **πρωτοκαθεδρία**, -ας, ἡ (< πρῶτος, καθέδρα), *the chief seat* : Mt 23⁶, Mk 12³⁹ (v. Swete, in l.), Lk 11⁴³ 20⁴⁶.†

*† **πρωτο-κλισία**, -ας, ἡ, *the chief place* at table (v. Swete, *Mk.*, l.c.) : Mt 23⁶, Mk 12³⁹, Lk 14⁷, ⁸ 20⁴⁶.†

πρῶτον, πρῶτος, v.s. πρότερος.

πρωτοστάτης, -ου, ὁ (< πρῶτος, ἵστημι), [in LXX : Jb 15²⁴ AB *;]
prop., of soldiers, one who stands first, one in the front rank (Thuc.,
Xen.) ; hence, metaph., a leader : Ac 24⁵.†

† πρωτοτόκια, -ων, τά (< πρωτότοκος), [in LXX (with v.l. -εῖα, -εία) :
Ge 25³¹ ⁿ· 27³⁶, De 21¹⁷, ɪ Ch 5¹ (בְּכֹרָה) *;] the rights of the first-born,
birthright (= cl. ἡ πρεσβεία) : He 12¹⁶.†

πρωτότοκος, -ον (< πρῶτος, τίκτω), [in LXX chiefly for בְּכוֹר;]
first-born : Lk 2⁷; pl., He 11²⁸. Metaph., of the priority of Christ
(originally perh. a Messianic title, cf. Ps 88 (89)²⁸, He 1⁶; v. ICC on
Col 1¹⁵) : He 1⁶ ; π. πάσης κτίσεως, Col 1¹⁵ ; ἐν πολλοῖς ἀδελφοῖς, Ro
8²⁹ ; π. (ἐκ) τ. νεκρῶν, Col 1¹⁸, Re 1⁵ ; pl., of the elect, ἐκκλησία πρωτο-
τόκων, He 12²³.†

* πρώτως, adv., first : Ac 11²⁶.†

πταίω, [in LXX chiefly for נגף ni.;] 1. trans., to cause to stumble
(ɪ Ki 4³, cf. Deiss., BS, 68₁). 2. Intrans., to stumble. Metaph., in moral
sense, Ro 11¹¹, Ja 2¹⁰ 3², ɪɪ Pe 1¹⁰.†

πτέρνα, -ης, ἡ, [in LXX for עָקֵב;] the heel : fig., ἐπαίρειν τὴν π.
ἐπί, Jo 13¹⁸ (LXX).†

πτερύγιον, -ου, τό (dimin. of πτέρυξ), [in LXX chiefly for כָּנָף;] 1.
a little wing. 2. Anything like a wing, as a turret, battlement : τ. ἱεροῦ,
Mt 4⁵, Lk 4⁹.†

πτέρυξ, -υγος, ἡ (< πέτομαι), [in LXX chiefly for כָּנָף;] a wing :
of birds, Mt 23³⁷, Lk 13³⁴, Re 12¹⁴ ; of creatures seen in a vision, Re
4⁸ 9⁹.†

** πτηνός, -ή, -όν (< πέτομαι), [in Aq. : Jb 5⁷ *;] winged; as subst.,
τὰ π., birds : ɪ Co 15³⁹.†

πτοέω, -ῶ, [in LXX chiefly for חתת ni.;] to terrify. Pass., to be
terrified : Lk 21⁹ 24³⁷ (WH, mg., θροηθέντες).†

πτόησις, -εως, ἡ (< πτοέω), [in LXX : Pr 3²⁵ (פַּחַד), Si 50⁴ אֲ¹,
ɪ Mac 3²⁵ R *;] a fluttering, excitement, caused by any emotion, but esp.
by fear, hence, terror : φοβεῖσθαι πτόησιν, to be afraid with (cogn. acc.)
or of any terror (v. ICC, in l.) : ɪ Pe 3⁶.†

Πτολεμαΐς, -ΐδος, ἡ, Ptolemais, a maritime city of Phœnicea :
Ac 21⁷.†

** πτύον, -ου, τό, [in Sm. : Is 30²⁴ *;] a winnowing shovel or fan :
Mt 3¹², Lk 3¹⁷.†

* πτύρομαι, depon., to be startled, frightened : Phl 1²⁸. (The active
πτύρω is also found in some late writers.) †

* πτύσμα, -τος, τό, (< πτύω), spittle : Jo 9⁶ (Hipp., Polyb., al.).†

* πτύσσω, to fold; of a scroll, to roll up : βιβλίον, Lk 4²⁰ (cf.
ἀνα-πτύσσω).†

πτύω, [in LXX : Nu 12¹⁴ (ירק), Si 28¹² *;] to spit : Mk 7³³ 8²³.
Jo 9⁶ (cf. ἐκ-, ἐμ-πτύω).†

πτῶμα, -τος, τό (< πίπτω), [in LXX: Jg 14⁸ (מַפֶּלֶת), Jb 16¹⁵ ⁽¹⁴⁾ (פֶּרֶץ), Is 51¹⁹ (שֹׁד), Jth 8¹⁹, Wi 4¹⁸, al.;] 1. *a fall*, metaph., *a mis-fortune, calamity* (Trag., Plat., Polyb., al.; LXX). 2. That which has fallen; (*a*) of buildings, *a ruin* (Polyb.); (*b*) of living creatures, in cl. (poët. only) usually c. gen., νεκρῶν, etc., but also absol., as in late writers and NT, *a fallen body, a carcase, corpse*: Mt 14¹² 24²⁸, Mk 15⁴⁵; π. αὐτοῦ, Mk 6²⁹; αὐτῶν, Re 11⁸, ⁹ (cf. Rutherford, *NPhr.*, 472 f.).†

πτῶσις, -εως, ἡ (< πίπτω), [in LXX chiefly for נֶגֶף, מַפֶּלֶת, and cogn. forms;] *a falling, fall* (Plat., Plut., al.): Mt 7²⁷; metaph., Lk 2³⁴.†

πτωχεία, -ας, ἡ (< πτωχεύω), [in LXX chiefly for עֳנִי;] *beggary, destitution*: ii Co 8², ⁹, Re 2⁹.†

πτωχεύω (< πτωχός), [in LXX: Jg 6⁶, Ps 78 (79)⁸ (דלל); Jg 14¹⁵ A, Pr 23²¹ (ירשׁ); Ps 33 (34)¹⁰ (רושׁ), To 4²¹*;] 1. *to be a beggar, to beg* (so chiefly in cl.). 2. *to be poor as a beggar, to be destitute, poor*: opp. to πλούσιος ὤν, ii Co 8⁹.†

πτωχός, -ή, -όν (< πτώσσω, *to crouch, cower*), [in LXX for עָנִי, דַּל, רָשׁ, etc.;] of one who crouches and cowers, hence, 1. as subst., *a beggar*: Lk 14¹³, ²¹ 16²⁰, ²². 2. As adj., (*a*) prop., *beggarly*: metaph., στοιχεῖα, Ga 4⁹ (v. Lft., in l.); (*b*) in broader sense (opp. to πλούσιος), *poor*: Mt 11⁵ 19²¹ 26⁹, ¹¹, Mk 10²¹ 12⁴², ⁴³ 14⁵, ⁷, Lk 4¹⁸ 7²² 18²² 19⁸ 21³, Jo 12⁵, ⁶, ⁸ 13²⁹, Ro 15²⁶, ii Co 6¹⁰, Ga 2¹⁰, Ja 2², ³, ⁶, Re 13¹⁶; π. τ. κόσμῳ, Ja 2⁵; metaph., Lk 6²⁰, Re 3¹⁷; π. τ. πνεύματι, Mt 5³.†

SYN.: πένης, q.v.; προσαίτης.

πυγμή, -ῆς, ἡ, [in LXX: Ex 21¹⁸, Is 58⁴ (אֶגְרוֹף)*;] *the fist*: πυγμῇ νίψασθαι τ. χεῖρας (T, πυκνά; Vg., Goth., Copt., *crebro*), to wash the hands with the fist (*diligently*, R, txt.; *up to the elbow*, R, mg.; the exact meaning is doubtful; v. Swete, in l.): Mk 7³.†

* πύθων, -ωνος, ὁ, 1. in cl., *Python*, a serpent slain by Apollo, who is hence surnamed the Pythian. 2. In Plut. (ii, 414 E), a name given to ventriloquist soothsayers (ἐγγαστρίμυθοι; cf. Le 19³¹ 20⁶, ²⁷, i Ki 28⁷), and perhaps in this sense πνεῦμα πύθωνα, *a python-spirit*: Ac 16¹⁶.†

πυκνός, -ή, -όν, [in LXX: Ez 31³ A (חֹרֶשׁ), iii Mac 1²⁸ 4¹⁰, iv Mac 12¹²*;] 1. *close, compact, solid*. 2. *frequent*: i Ti 5²³. Neut. pl., πυκνά, as adv., *much, often*: Mk 7³ T (v.s. πυγμή), Lk 5³³. Comparat., πυκνότερον, *very often* or *so much the oftener* (v. Bl., § 44, 3ₙ): Ac 24²⁶.†

* πυκτεύω (< πύκτης, *a pugilist*), *to box*: i Co 9²⁶.†

πύλη, -ης, ἡ, [in LXX chiefly and very freq. for שַׁעַר, sometimes for דֶּלֶת, פֶּתַח;] *a gate*: Lk 7¹², Ac 9²⁴ 12¹⁰ 16¹³, He 13¹²; ἡ Ὡραία Π. τ. ἱεροῦ, Ac 3¹⁰. Metaph., Mt 7¹³, ¹⁴; πύλαι (for conjectural emendation, v. Peake, *Comm.* in l.) ᾅδου (Wi 16¹³, iii Mac 5⁵¹, and cf. κλεῖς ᾅδου, Re 1¹⁸): Mt 16¹⁸.†

πυλών, -ῶνος, ὁ (< πύλη), [in LXX chiefly for שַׁעַר, פֶּתַח;] 1. the porch or vestibule of a house or palace: Mt 26⁷¹, Lk 16²⁰, Ac 10¹ᵀ 12¹³, ¹⁴. 2. The gate-way or gate-tower of a walled town: Ac 14¹³, Re 21¹², ¹³, ¹⁵, ²¹, ²⁵ 22¹⁴.†

πυνθάνομαι, [in LXX for דָּרַשׁ;] 1. to inquire: c. acc. rei, Jo 4⁵², Ac 23²⁰; seq. quæst. indir., Mt 2⁴, Lk 15²⁶ 18³⁶, Ac 10¹⁸ 21³³; quæst. dir., Ac 4⁷ 10²⁹ 23¹⁹; seq. παρά, c. gen. pers., Mt 2⁴, Jo 4⁵². 2. to learn by inquiry: seq. ὅτι, Ac 23³⁴.†

πῦρ, gen., πυρός, τό, [in LXX chiefly and very freq. for אֵשׁ;] fire: Mt 3¹⁰, Mk 9²², Lk 3⁹, Jo 15⁶, Ac 2¹⁹, I Co 3¹³, Ja 3⁵, Re 8⁵, al; π. καὶ θεῖον, Lk 17²⁹; κατακαίειν (ἐν) π., Mt 13⁴⁰, Re 17¹⁶ 18⁸; καίεσθαι πυρί, He 12¹⁸, Re 8⁸ 21⁸; φλὸξ πυρός, Ac 7³⁰, II Th 1⁸, He 1⁷, Re 1¹⁴ 2¹⁸ 19¹²; λαμπάδες πυρός, Re 4⁵; στῦλοι πυρός, Re 10¹; ἄνθρακες πυρός, Ro 12²⁰ (LXX); γλῶσσαι ὡσεὶ πυρός, Ac 2³; δοκιμάζειν (πυροῦσθαι) διὰ πυρός, I Pe 1⁷, Re 3¹⁸; ὡς διὰ π. (Lft., Notes, 193), I Co 3¹⁵. Of the fire of hell (cf. Dalman, Words, 161): Mk 9⁴⁸ (LXX); τὸ π. τὸ αἰώνιον, Mt 18⁸ 25⁴¹ (cf. IV Mac 12¹²); ἄσβεστον, Mk 9⁴³; πυρὸς αἰωνίου δίκην ὑπέχειν, Ju ⁷; γέεννα τοῦ π., Mt 5²² 18⁹; κάμινος τοῦ π., Mt 13⁴², ⁵⁰; ἡ λίμνη τοῦ π., Re 19²⁰ 20¹⁰, ¹⁴, ¹⁵; πυρὶ τηρεῖσθαι, II Pe 3⁷; βασανισθῆναι ἐν π., Re 14¹⁰. Metaph.: βαπτίζειν πυρί, Mt 3¹¹, Lk 3¹⁶; of the tongue, Ja 3⁵; of strife and discord, Lk 12⁴⁹; ἐκ π. ἁρπάζειν, Ju ²³; πυρὶ ἁλίζεσθαι, Mk 9⁴⁹; ζῆλος πυρός, He 10²⁷; of God, π. καταναλίσκον, He 12²⁹ (LXX).

** πυρά, -ᾶς, ἡ (< πῦρ), [in LXX: Jth 7⁵, Wi 17⁶, al.;] a fire: Ac 28², ³.†

πύργος, -ου, ὁ, [in LXX chiefly for מִגְדָּל;] a tower: Lk 13⁴; of a watch-tower in a vineyard (Is 5²): Mt 21³³, Mk 12¹, and prob., Lk 14²⁸.†

* πυρέσσω (< πῦρ), to be ill of a fever: Mt 8¹⁴, Mk 1³⁰.†

πυρετός, -οῦ, ὁ (< πῦρ), [in LXX: De 28²² (קַדַּחַת) *;] a fever: Mt 8¹⁵, Mk 1³¹, Lk 4³⁹, Jo 4⁵², Ac 28⁸; π. μέγας, a high fever: Lk 4³⁸ (on the technical phrase here, v. MM, xxii).†

πύρινος, -η, -ον, [in LXX: Ez 28¹⁴, ¹⁶ (אֵשׁ), Si 48⁹ *;] fiery: Re 9¹⁷.†

πυρόω, -ῶ (< πῦρ), [in LXX chiefly for צָרַף;] to set on fire, burn up. In NT always pass., 1. to be set on fire, to burn: Eph 6¹⁶, II Pe 3¹²; ptcp., glowing, Re 1¹⁵. Metaph., of grief or indignation, II Co 11²⁹; of lust, I Co 7⁹. 2. Of metals (cf. Jo 22²⁵, Ps 11 (12)⁷, Za 13⁹), to be refined or purified by fire: Re 3¹⁸ (and so in RV, ib. 1¹⁵, but v. supr.).†

† πυρράζω (< πυρρός), [in LXX, πυρρίζω: Le 13¹⁹, ⁴² π. 14³⁷ (אָדַם) *;] to be fiery red: Mt 16ǀ[2, 3]ǀ.†

πυρρός, -ά, -όν (< πῦρ), [in LXX for אָדֹם;] fiery red: Re 6⁴ 12³.†

Πύρρος, -ου, ὁ, Pyrrhus: Ac 20⁴.†

πύρωσις, -εως, ἡ (< πυρόω), [in LXX: Pr 27²¹ (כּוּר), Am 4⁹ (שִׁדָּפוֹן) *;] 1. a burning: Re 18⁹, ¹⁸. 2. a refining or trial by fire: metaph., I Pe 4¹².†

πω, enclit. part., *yet*, v.s. μή-πω, μηδέ-πω, ου-πω, ουδέ-πω, πώ-ποτε.
πωλέω, -ῶ, [in LXX chiefly for מכר ;] 1. *to exchange* or *barter*.
2. *to sell* : Lk 17²⁸, Re 13¹⁷ ; οἱ πωλοῦντες, Mt 21¹² 25⁹, Mk 11¹⁵, Lk 19⁴⁵ ; c. acc. rei, Mt 13⁴⁴ 19²¹ 21¹², Mk 10²¹ 11¹⁵, Lk 12³³ 18²² 22³⁶, Jo 2¹⁴, ¹⁶, Ac 5¹ (sc. αὐτά, αὐτόν), ib. 4³⁴, ³⁷. Pass., I Co 10²⁵ ; c. gen. pretii, Mt 10²⁹, Lk 12⁶.†

πῶλος, -ου, ὁ (in cl. also ἡ), [in LXX chiefly for עיר ;] *a foal, colt*, prop., of a horse, then the young of other animals ; in NT of the colt of an ass : Mt 21², ⁵ (LXX), ⁷, Mk 11², ⁴, ⁵, ⁷, Lk 19³⁰, ³³, ³⁵, Jo 12¹⁵ (LXX).†

πώ-ποτε, adv., *ever yet* : Lk 19³⁰, Jo 1¹⁸ 5³⁷ 6³⁵ 8³³, I Jo 4¹².†

πωρόω, -ῶ (< πῶρος, 1. *a stone*. 2. *a callus*), [in LXX : Jb 17⁷ B (כהה), Pr 10²⁰ A *;] *to petrify, harden, form a callus*. Metaph., π. τ. καρδίαν, Jo 12⁴⁰. Pass., Ro 11⁷ ; τ. νοήματα, II Co 3¹⁴ ; ἡ καρδία, Mk 6⁵² 8¹⁷.†

* πώρωσις, -εως, ἡ (< πωρόω), *a covering with a callus, a hardening* : metaph. of dulled spiritual perception, *blindness* (Vg., cf. Gore, *Comm.*, NT, p. 59ᵇ), Mk 3⁵, Ro 11²⁵, Eph 4¹⁸.†

πως, enclit. part., *at all ;* v.s. εἴπως, μήπως.
πῶς, interrog. adv., correl. of ὅπως, 1. prop., in direct questions, *how ?* : c. indic., Mt 12²⁹, Mk 3²³, Lk 11¹⁸, Jo 3⁴, al. ; καὶ π., Mk 4¹³, Lk 20⁴⁴ ; π. οὖν, Mt 12²⁶ ; π. οὐ, Mt 16¹¹, Lk 12⁵⁶ ; in deliberative questions (cf. Bl., § 64, 6), c. subjc., Mt 23³³ 26⁵⁴ ; π. οὖν, Ro 10¹⁴ ; π. δέ, Ro 10¹⁴, ¹⁵ ; seq. ἄν, c. optat., Ac 8³¹. 2. As sometimes in cl. but more freq. and increasingly so in late writers (v. WM, § 57, 2 ; Bl., § 70, 2 ; Thumb, *MGr.*, 192 ; Jannaris, *Gr.*, *App.*, vi, 13 f.), = ὅπως, ὡς ; (*a*) in indirect discourse : c. indic., Mt 6²⁸, Mk 12⁴¹, Lk 8³⁶, Jo 9¹⁵, Ac 9²⁷, al. ; c. subjc., Mk 11¹⁸, Lk 12¹¹ ; (*b*) in exclamations : Mt 21²⁰, Mk 10²³, ²⁴, Lk 12⁵⁰ 18²⁴, Jo 11³⁶.

P

P, ρ, ῥω, τό, indecl., *rho, r*, as initial always ῥ (on the use of the breathing and the reduplication of ρ, v. WH, *App.*, 163 ; Tdf., *Prol.*, 105 f. ; Veitch, s.v. ῥάπτω, etc.), the seventeenth letter. As a numeral, ρ' = 100, ρ, = 100,000.

Ῥαάβ (and Ῥαχόβ, Mt 1⁵ ; Ῥαχάβη, -ης, in FlJ), ἡ, indecl. (Heb. רחב), *Rahab* (LXX, Jos 2¹, al.) : He 11³¹, Ja 2²⁵.†

*† ῥαββεί (Rec. -βί, v. WH, *App.*, 155) (Heb. and Aram. רבּי, *my master ;* v. Dalman, *Words*, 327, 331 ff.), a title of respectful address to Jewish teachers, *Rabbi* : Mt 23⁷, ⁸ ; of John, Jo 3²⁶ ; of Christ, Mt 26²⁵, ⁴⁹, Mk 9⁵ 11²¹ 14⁴⁵, Jo 1³⁹, ⁵⁰ 3² 4³¹ 6²⁵ 9² 11⁸ ; κύριε ῥ., Mk 10⁵¹ (WH, mg., v.s. ῥαββουνεί).†

*† ῥαββουνεί (Rec. -βονί, v.s. ῥαββεί) (Aram. רבּוֹני, later, רבּוֹני, *my master ;* on the Greek vocalization and the relation of the word to ῥαββεί, v. Dalman, *Words*, 324, 340 ; *Gr.*, 140ₙ ; *DB*, iv, 190) ; *Rabboni* : Mk 10⁵¹ (WH, mg., κύριε ῥαββεί), Jo 20¹⁶.†

ῥαβδίζω (< ῥάβδος), [in LXX: Jg 6¹¹ Ru 2¹⁷ (חבט)*;] *to beat with a rod:* Ac 16²², ɪɪ Co 11²⁵.†

ῥάβδος, -ου, ἡ, [in LXX chiefly for מַטֶּה (e.g. Ge 47³¹, MT, מִטָּה, *bed*), also for מַקֵּל, שֵׁבֶט, etc.;] *a staff, rod:* He 9⁴, Re 11¹; in particular, (*a*) *a staff,* such as is used on a journey: Mt 10¹⁰, Mk 6⁸, Lk 9³, He 11²¹ (LXX); (*b*) a ruler's staff, *a sceptre:* He 1⁸ (LXX), Re 2²⁷ 12⁵ 19¹⁵; (*c*) a *rod* for chastisement (cf. ῥαβδίζω): ἐν ῥ. (v.s. ἐν): 1 Co 4²¹.†

* ῥαβδοῦχος, -ου, ὁ (< ῥάβδος, ἔχω), one who carries a rod or staff of office; (*a*) an *umpire* or *judge* (Plat.); (*b*) in late writers, a Roman *lictor:* Ac 16³⁵, ³⁸.†

Ῥαγαύ (Rec. -αύ), ὁ, indecl. (LXX for Heb. רְעוּ, Ge 11¹⁸, al.), *Reu:* Lk 3³⁵.†

* ῥᾳδιούργημα, -τος, τό (< ῥᾳδιουργέω, *to act recklessly* or *wrongly*), 1. *a reckless act.* 2. *crime, villany:* Ac 18¹⁴.†

* ῥᾳδιουργία, -ας, ἡ (v.s. ῥᾳδιούργημα), 1. *ease in doing, facility* (Xen.). 2. *easiness, laziness* (Xen.). 3. *recklessness, wickedness* (of lewdness, Xen.; fraud, Plut.; in π., of theft, MM, xxii): Ac 13¹⁰.†

ῥαίνω, v.s. ῥαντίζω. Pf. ptc. pass. may be original reading in Re 19¹³ (v. M, *Gr.*, ɪɪ, p. 256).

* ῥακά (T, ῥαχά), usually taken to represent the Aram. רִיקָא, a shortened form of רִיקָן, "*empty*," as vocalized in the Galilæan dialect; an expression of contempt, *raca:* Mt 5²² (cf. *DB*, iv, 191 f.; and for other explanations, v. Zorell, s.v.).†

ῥάκος, -ους, τό, [in LXX: Is 64⁶ ⁽⁵⁾ (בֶּגֶד), Je 45 (38)¹¹ (מְחָבָה), Es 4¹⁷ *;] 1. *a ragged garment* (Hom.). 2. *a rag, remnant, piece* of cloth: Mt 9¹⁶, Mk 2²¹.†

Ῥαμά (Rec. -ᾶ), ἡ, indecl. (Heb. רָמָה), *Ramah:* Mt 2¹⁸ (LXX).†

† ῥαντίζω, [in LXX: Le 6²⁷ ⁽²⁰⁾, ɪv Ki 9³³ (נזה), Ps 50 (51)⁷ (חטא pi.) *;] = cl., ῥαίνω, *to sprinkle, besprinkle:* c. acc., He 9¹³, ¹⁹ id. et dat., ib. ²¹; pass., Re 19¹³, WH; of cleansing by sprinkling, He 10²² (v. M, *Gr.*, ii, 100); mid., Mk 7⁴ (WH, txt., R, mg.).†

† ῥαντισμός, -οῦ, ὁ (< ῥαντίζω), [in LXX for נִדָּה;] *sprinkling:* of the ceremonial sprinkling of blood for purification, He 12²⁴, ɪ Pe 1² (v. Hort, *Pe.*, 23 ff.).†

ῥαπίζω (< ῥαπίς, *a rod*), [in LXX: Jg 16²⁵, Ho 11⁴, ɪ Es 4³¹ *;] 1. prop., *to strike with a rod.* 2. In late writers, *to strike* (the face) *with the palm of the hand:* Mt 26⁶⁷; c. acc. pers., seq. εἰς τ. σιαγόνα, Mt 5³⁹ (cf. Field, *Notes*, 40, 105).†

ῥάπισμα, -τος, τό (ῥαπίζω), [in LXX: Isa 50⁶ (מרט) ; *] *a blow* with a stick (R, mg.) or with the palm of the hand (v. Swete on Mk, l.c., and reff. there): Mk 14⁶⁵, Jo 18²² 19³.†

* ῥαφίς, -ίδος, ἡ (ῥάπτω, *to sew*), *a needle:* Mt 19²⁴, Mk 10²⁵ (cf. βελόνη).†

ῥαχά, v.s. ῥακά.

Ῥαχάβ, v.s. Ῥαάβ.

Ῥαχήλ, ἡ, indecl. (Heb. רָחֵל), *Rachel:* Mt 2¹⁸ (LXX).†

ʹΡεβέκκα, -ας (v. Bl., § 7, 2), ἡ (Heb. רִבְקָה), *Rebecca* : Ro 9¹⁰.†

† ῥέδη (v. WH, *App*., 151), -ης, ἡ (a Gallic word), *a chariot* :
Re 18¹³.†

ʹΡεμφάν, ʹΡεφάν, v.s. ʹΡομφά.

ῥέω, [in LXX chiefly for זוּב ;] *to flow* : Jo 7³⁸ (cf. παραρρέω).†

ʹΡήγιον, -ου, τό, *Rhegium*, a town in Sicily : Ac 28¹³.†

ῥῆγμα, -τος, τό (< ῥήγνυμι), [in LXX : III Ki 11³⁰, ³¹ 12²⁴, IV Ki
2¹² (קְרָעִים), Am 6¹²⁽¹¹⁾ A (בָּקְרָע) * ;] 1. cl. (and so in LXX), *a fracture ;*
then by meton., *that which is torn*. 2. In NT, *ruin* : Lk 6⁴⁹.†

ῥήγνυμι and (Mk 9¹⁸) ῥήσσω, [in LXX chiefly for בָּקַע, also for
קָרַע, etc. ;] 1. *to rend, break asunder* : Mt 7⁶, Mk 2²², Lk 5³⁷ ; pass.,
Mt 9¹⁷. 2. Of the voice, c. acc., φωνήν, etc. (Hdt., al.), *to break forth*
into speech : absol., Ga 4²⁷ ⁽ᴸˣˣ⁾. 3. = ῥάσσω (Dem., al.), *to throw* or
dash down : Mk 9¹⁸, Lk 9⁴² (cf. δια-, περι-, προσ-ρήγνυμι).†

SYN. : θραύω, κατάγνυμι.

ῥῆμα, -τος, τό, [in LXX chiefly for דָּבָר, also for פֶּה, and Aram.
פִּתְגָם, etc. ;] 1. prop., of that which is said or spoken, (a) *a word* :
Mt 27¹⁴, II Co 12⁴ ; pl., τὰ ῥ., of speech, discourse, Lk 7¹, Jo 8²⁰, Ac
2¹⁴, Ro 10¹⁸, II Pe 3², al. ; (b) opp. to ὄνομα (a single word), *a saying,
statement, word* of prophecy, instruction or command (in cl., *phrase*) :
Mt 26⁷⁵, Mk 9³², Lk 1³⁸ 2⁵⁰, Ac 11¹⁶, Ro 10⁸, He 11³ ; ῥ. θεοῦ (κυρίου),
Lk 3², Ac 11¹⁶, Eph 6¹⁷, He 6⁵ 11³, I Pe 1²⁵ ⁽ᴸˣˣ⁾ ; τὰ ῥ. τ. θεοῦ, Jo 3³⁴
8⁴⁷ ; ῥ. ἀργόν, Mt 12³⁶ ; ῥ. ἄρρητα, II Co 12⁴. 2. Like Heb. דָּבָר (but
perh. also a Gk. colloquialism, v. Kennedy, *Sources*, 124 ; Thackeray,
Gr., 41), of that which is the subject of speech, *a thing, matter* (Ge
15¹, De 17⁸, al.) : Lk 1³⁷ 2¹⁵, Ac 10³⁷ ; pl., Lk 1⁶⁵ 2¹⁹, ⁵¹, Ac 5³² 13⁴².

ʹΡησά (L, -σᾶ), ὁ, indecl., *Rhesa* : Lk 3²⁷.†

ῥήσσω, v.s. ῥήγνυμι.

* ῥήτωρ, -ορος, ὁ, *a public speaker, an orator* : Ac 24¹.†

*† ῥητῶς, adv. (< ῥητός, *stated, specified*), *in stated terms, expressly* :
I Ti 4¹.†

ῥίζα, -ης, ἡ, [in LXX chiefly for שֹׁרֶשׁ ;] *a root* : Mt 3¹⁰, Lk 3⁹ ;
ἐκ ῥιζῶν, Mk 11²⁰ ; ῥ. ἔχειν, Mt 13⁶, Mk 4⁶ ; id. seq. ἐν ἑαυτῷ, fig., Mt
13²¹, Mk 4¹⁷, Lk 8¹³. Metaph. (as in various senses in cl.), of cause,
origin, source, etc. ; (a) of things, ῥ. πάντων τ. κακῶν (Eur.), I Ti 6¹⁰ ;
(b) of persons : of ancestors, Ro 11¹⁶⁻¹⁸ ; ῥ. πικρίας, He 12¹⁵. Of that
which springs from a root, *a shoot ;* metaph., of offspring, Ro
15¹² ⁽ᴸˣˣ⁾, Re 5⁵ 22¹⁶.†

ῥιζόω, -ῶ (< ῥίζα), [in LXX : Is 40²⁴, Je 12² (שֹׁרֶשׁ), Si 3²⁸
24¹² * ;] *to cause to take root*. Metaph., *to plant, fix firmly, establish* :
pass. (EV, *rooted*), ἐν ἀγάπῃ, Eph 3¹⁸⁽¹⁷⁾ ; ἐν Χριστῷ, Col 2⁷ (cf. ἐκ-
ριζόω).†

* ῥιπή, -ῆς, ἡ (< ῥίπτω), poët. in cl., any rapid movement such as
the *throw* or *flight* of a javelin, the *rush* of wind or flame, the *flapping*
of wings, the *twinkling* of lights ; ῥ. ὀφθαλμοῦ, the *twinkling* of an
eye : I Co 15⁵² (L, mg., ῥοπή, q.v.).†

ῥιπίζω (< ῥιπίς, a fan), [in LXX: Da LXX 2³⁵ (נְשָׁא)*;] primarily, to fan a fire, hence generally, to make a breeze (Plut., al.). In pass. (cf. Philo, de incer. mund., 24), to be tossed or blown by the wind : of waves, ἀνεμιζομένῳ καὶ ῥιπιζομένῳ, blown and raised with the wind (Hort, in l.), Ja 1⁶.†

ῥιπτέω, v.s. ῥίπτω.

ῥίπτω and (Ac 22²³) ῥιπτέω (strengthened form; v. Veitch, s.v. ῥίπτω, fin.), [in LXX chiefly for שָׁלַךְ hi.;] 1. to throw, cast, hurl : c. acc. rei, Mt 27⁵, Ac 27¹⁹,²⁹; c. acc. pers., Mt 15³⁰, Lk 4³⁵; pass., Lk 17²; ptcp., ἐριμμένοι, cast down, prostrate (Polyb., al.): Mt 9³⁶; of garments, to throw off (for flight, Eur., Xen., al.; ὅπλα, ι Mac 5⁴³; so EV in Ac 22²³, but v. infr.). 2. = ῥιπτάζω, to shake, toss, throw about : τ. ἱμάτια, Ac 22²³ (EGT, Page, Rackham, in l.; Field, Notes, 136; but v. supr.).†

Ῥοβοάμ, ὁ, indecl. (Heb. רְחַבְעָם), Rehoboam : Mt 1⁷.†

Ῥόδη, -ης, ἡ, Rhoda : Ac 12¹³.†

Ῥόδος, -ου, ὁ, the island of Rhodes : Ac 21¹.†

* ῥοιζηδόν, adv. (< ῥοῖζος, the whistling of an arrow), with rushing sound (as of roaring flames): ιι Pe 3¹⁰.†

Ῥομφά (-άν, T; Ῥεφάν, LTr.; Ῥεμφάν, Rec.; v. WH, App., 92), [in LXX: Am 5²⁶ (Ῥαιφάν or Ῥεφάν, Heb. כִּיּוּן) *;] Rompha, Rephan (RV), one of the names of Seb, the Egyptian Saturn : Ac 7⁴³ (LXX).†

† ῥομφαία, -ας, ἡ, [in LXX chiefly for חֶרֶב;] a large broad sword, used by the Thracians (v. DB, iv, 634); then generally (in LXX used interchangeably with μάχαιρα, q.v.), a sword : Re 1¹⁶ 2¹²,¹⁶ 6⁸ 19¹⁵,²¹; metaph., Lk 2³⁵.†

ῥοπή, -ῆς, ἡ (< ῥέπω, to incline), [in LXX: Is 40¹⁵ (שַׁחַק), etc.;] inclination downwards, as the turn of the scale : L, mg., for ῥιπή, q.v., ι Co 15⁵² (v. Tdf., in l.).†

Ῥουβήν, ὁ, indecl., (Heb. רְאוּבֵן), Reuben : Re 7⁵.†

Ῥούθ, ἡ, indecl. (Heb. רוּת), Ruth : Mt 1⁵.†

Ῥοῦφος, -ου, ὁ (Lat.), Rufus : Mk 15²¹, Ro 16¹³.†

ῥύμη, -ης, ἡ, [in LXX: Is 15³ (רְחֹב), Pr 31²³ א, To 13¹⁸, Si 97 א¹*;] 1. in cl., the force, rush, swing, of a moving body; esp. of a charge of soldiers. 2. In late Greek (as in Macedonian, v. Kennedy, Sources, 15), a narrow road, lane, street : in Polyb., of a road in camp; in LXX and NT (π. also) of streets in a town, Mt 6², Lk 14²¹ Ac 9¹¹ 12¹⁰ (cf. Rutherford, NPhr., 488).†

ῥύομαι, [in LXX chiefly for נצל hi., also for גאל, פלט pi., etc.;] to draw to oneself, hence, to rescue, deliver : c. acc. pers., Mt 27⁴³, ιι Pe 2⁷; id. seq. ἀπό, Mt 6¹³, Lk 11⁴ (Rec., R, mg.), ιι Ti 4¹⁸; seq. ἐκ, Ro 7²⁴, ιι Co 1¹⁰, Col 1¹³, ι Th 1¹⁰, ιι Ti 3¹¹, ιι Pe 2⁹; absol., ὁ ῥυόμενος, the deliverer, Ro 11²⁶. Passive: seq. ἀπό, Ro 15³¹, ιι Th 3²; seq. ἐκ, Lk 1⁷⁴, ιι Ti 4¹⁷.†

*ῥυπαίνω (< ῥύπος), in Arist., Xen., and later writers, *to make filthy, defile* : pass., in ethical sense (on the tense, v. Swete, in l.)₁ Re 22¹¹ LT, Tr., WH, txt.†

*† ῥυπαρεύομαι = ῥυπαίνομαι, q.v.: Re 22¹¹, WH, mg. (nowhere else).†

*ῥυπαρία, -ας, ἡ (ῥυπαρός), *filthiness* : metaph., of moral defilement, Ja 1²¹.†

ῥυπαρός, -ά, -όν (< ῥύπος), [in LXX: Zā 3⁴, ⁵, (3, 4) (צוֹא) *;] *filthy, dirty* : of old, shabby clothing (Za, l.c.), Ja 2²; metaph., of moral defilement, Re 22¹¹.†

ῥύπος, -ου, ὁ, [in LXX: Is 4⁴ (צֹאָה), Jb 14⁴ (טָמֵא), etc.;] *dirt, filth* : I Pe 3²¹.†

*ῥυπόω, -ῶ (< ῥύπος), *to make filthy* : Re 22¹¹ Rec. (AV, tr. as = ῥυπάω, *to be filthy*).†

ῥύσις, -εως, ἡ (< ῥέω), [in LXX chiefly for זוֹב;] *a flowing, issue* : r. αἵματος, Mk 5²⁵, Lk 8⁴³, ⁴⁴.†

*ῥυτίς, -ίδος, ἡ, *a wrinkle* : Eph 5²⁷.†

Ῥωμαϊκός, -ή, -όν, *Roman, Latin* : Lk 23³⁸ Rec.†

Ῥωμαῖος, -α, -ον, *Roman* : Jo 11⁴⁸, Ac 2¹⁰ (RV, *from Rome*), 16²¹, ³⁷, ³⁸ 22²⁵⁻²⁷, ²⁹ 23²⁷ 25¹⁶ 28¹⁷.†

Ῥωμαϊστί, adv., *in Latin* : Jo 19²⁰.†

Ῥώμη, -ης, ἡ, *Rome* : Ac 18² 19²¹ 23¹¹ 28¹⁴, ¹⁶, Ro 1⁷, ¹⁵, II Ti 1¹⁷.†

ῥώννυμι, [in LXX: II Mac 9²⁰ 11²¹, ²⁸, ³³, III Mac ₆ *;] *to strengthen* ; most freq. in pf., ἔρρωμαι, *to put forth strength, be strong*, hence, often in imperat., ἔρρωσο, ἔρρωσθε, *farewell* (Lat. *vale*): Ac 15²⁹ 23³⁰ Rec., R, mg.†

Σ

Σ, σ, final ς, σίγμα, τό, indecl., *sigma*, the eighteenth letter. As a numeral, σ' = 200, σ, = 200,000.

† σαβαχθανεί (Rec. -νί; ζαφθανεί, Mt, l.c., WH, mg.), (Aram. שְׁבַקְתַּנִי), *sabachthani*, i.e. *thou hast forsaken me* : Mt 27⁴⁶, Mk 15³⁴ (Ps 21 (22)², Heb. עֲזַבְתָּנִי).†

† σαβαώθ, indecl., [in LXX for צְבָאוֹת, chiefly in Isaiah (in other places, the phrase יְהוָה צְ is also rendered by κύριος παντοκράτωρ, κ. τῶν δυνάμεων; v. DB, iii, 137 f.) ;] *Sabaoth*, i.e. *hosts* or *armies* (v. DB, l.c.): Ro 9²⁹ (LXX), Ja 5⁴.†

*† σαββατισμός, -οῦ, ὁ (< σαββατίζω, *to keep the sabbath*, Ex 16³⁰, al.), *a keeping sabbath, a sabbath rest* : metaph., as in Mishna (Zorell, s.v.), He 4⁹.†

† σάββατον, -ου, τό (Aram. שַׁבְּתָא, transliterated σάββατα, and this being mistaken for a pl., the sing. σάββατον was formed from it), and σάββατα, -ων, τά, [in LXX for שַׁבָּת, שַׁבָּתוֹן ;] 1. *the seventh day* of the week, *the sabbath* ; (a) the sing. form -ον, τὸ σ.: Mt 12⁸, Mk 2²⁷, Lk 6⁵,

al.; ἡ ἡμέρα τοῦ σ. (in LXX, Ex 20⁸, al., usually τῶν σ., v. infr.), Lk 13¹⁶ 14⁵; ὁδὸς σαββάτου, Ac 1¹² (cf. Mt 24²⁰); dat., of time (τῷ) σ., Lk 6⁹ 14¹; ἐν (τῷ) σ., Mt 12², Lk 6⁷, Jo 5¹⁶, al.; acc., of duration, τὸ σ., Lk 23⁵⁶; κατὰ πᾶν σ., Ac 13²⁷ 15²¹ 18⁴; pl., σ. τρία, Ac 17² R, txt. (but v. infr.); (b) as most freq. in LXX (v. Swete, Mk., 17; Thackeray, Gr., 35) the pl. form, τὰ σ. (v. supr. on the Aram. form. There is also an analogy in the names of other festivals, τ. ἐγκαίνια, ἄζυμα, etc.) : Mt 28¹, Col 2¹⁶; ἡ ἡμέρα τῶν σ. (Ex 20⁸, al.), Lk 4¹⁶, Ac 13¹⁴ 16¹³; dat. pl. (in LXX -τοις, but I Mac 2³⁸ as in NT) by metaplasmus (Bl., § 9, 3), σάββασι, Mt 12¹, ⁵, ¹⁰⁻¹², Mk 1²¹ 2²³ 3², ⁴, Lk 4³¹ 6². 2. seven days, a week; (a) the sing. form : πρώτη σαββάτου, Mk 16⁹; δὶς τοῦ σ. (Bl., § 35, 4; 36, 13), Lk 18¹²; κατὰ μίαν σαββάτου, I Co 16²; pl., σ. τρία, Ac 17² R, mg. (but v. supr.); (b) the pl. form : ἡ μία τῶν σ. (where the gen. = μετὰ τά; Soph., Lex., 43a), Mt 28¹, Mk 16², Lk 24¹, Jo 20¹, ¹⁹, Ac 20⁷.

σαγήνη, -ης, ἡ, [in LXX chiefly for חֵרֶם;] a drag-net, seine. Mt 13⁴⁷.†

SYN.: ἀμφίβληστρον (q.v.), δίκτυον.

Σαδδουκαῖος, -ου, ὁ (< Heb. צָדוֹק, II Ki 15²⁴, al.), a Sadducee (cf. Swete, Mk., 277): Mt 3⁷ 16¹, ⁶, ¹¹, ¹² 22²³, ³⁴, Mk 12¹⁸, Lk 20²⁷, Ac 4¹ 5¹⁷, 23⁶⁻⁸.†

Σαδώκ, ὁ, indecl. (Heb. צָדוֹק, v. supr., s.v. Σαδδουκαῖος), Sadoc, Zadok : Mt 1¹⁴.†

* σαίνω, 1. prop. (Hom., al.), of dogs, to wag the tail, fawn. 2. Metaph., of persons, c. acc., to fawn upon, flatter, beguile : pass., I Th 3³ (for conjectural emendations of the text, v. ICC, and M, Th., in l.).†

σάκκος, also written σάκος, -ου, ὁ (cf. Heb. שַׂק, which it renders in LXX), 1. a coarse cloth, sackcloth, usually made of hair : Re 6¹². 2. Anything made of sackcloth; (a) a sack (Ge 42²⁵, al.); (b) a garment of sackcloth, expressive of mourning or penitence : Mt 11²¹, Lk 10¹³, Re 11³.†

Σαλά, ὁ, indecl. (Heb. שָׁלַח), Sala, Shalah : Lk 3³² (R, txt., Σαλμών, q.v.), ib. ³⁵.†

Σαλαθιήλ, ὁ, indecl. (Heb. שְׁאַלְתִּיאֵל), Salathiel : Mt 1¹², Lk 3²⁷.†

Σαλαμίς, -ῖνος, ἡ, Salamis, the chief city of Cyprus : Ac 13⁵.†

Σαλείμ, τό, indecl., Salim : Jo 3²³ (v. Westc., in l.; DB, iii, 354).†

σαλεύω (< σάλος), [in LXX for מוֹט , נוּד , etc. ;] prop., of the action of wind, storm, etc., to agitate, shake : of a reed, Mt 11⁷, Lk 7²⁴; a house, Lk 6⁴⁸, Ac 4³¹ 16²⁶; the earth, He 12²⁶; the heavenly bodies, Mt 24²⁹, Mk 13²⁵, Lk 21²⁶; of a vessel shaken in filling, Lk 6³⁸. Metaph., (a) to shake, i.e. to render insecure : τὰ σαλευόμενα, τὰ μὴ σ., He 12²⁷; (b) c. acc. pers., to cast down from a sense of security and happiness :

Ac 2²⁵ (LXX); (c) to *unsettle* or *drive away*: pass., seq. ἀπὸ τ. νοός, ii Th 2²; (d) to *stir up*: τ. ὄχλους, Ac 17¹³.†

Σαλήμ, ἡ (Heb. שָׁלֵם, Ge 14¹⁸), *Salem*: He 7¹⁻²(LXX).†

Σαλμών, ὁ, indecl. (Heb. שַׂלְמוֹן), *Salmon*: Mt 1⁴⁻⁵, Lk 3³² (Σαλά, WH, R, mg.).†

Σαλμώνη, -ης, ἡ, *Salmone*, a promontory of Crete: Ac 27⁷.†

σάλος, -ου, ὁ, [in LXX for מוֹט, etc.;] in poets and late prose, a *tossing*, as of an earthquake; esp. the *tossing*, the *rolling swell* of the sea: Lk 21²⁵.†

σάλπιγξ, -ιγγος, ἡ, [in LXX chiefly for שׁוֹפָר, חֲצֹצְרָה;] a *trumpet*, used in war and in religious ceremonies: 1 Co 14⁸, He 12¹⁹, Re 1¹⁰ 4¹ 8²,⁶,¹³ 9¹⁴. By meton., a *trumpet blast*: μετὰ σ. μεγάλης, Mt 24³¹; ἐν σ. θεοῦ, 1 Th 4¹⁶; ἐν τ. ἐσχάτῃ σ., 1 Co 15⁵².†

σαλπίζω, [in LXX chiefly for תָּקַע;] to *sound a trumpet*: Re 8⁶ᵃ· 9¹,¹³ 10⁷ 11¹⁵; metaph., Mt 6². Impers., the *trumpet sounds*: 1 Co 15⁵².†

*σαλπιστής (so Inscr. and late writers for Att. σαλπιγκτής), -οῦ, ὁ, a *trumpeter*: Re 18²².†

Σαλώμη, -ης, ἡ (< Heb. שָׁלוֹם), *Salome*: Mk 15⁴⁰ 16¹ (v. Turner, SNT, pp. 60 f.).†

Σαλωμών, v.s. Σολομών.

Σαμάρεια, v.s. Σαμαρία.

Σαμαρείτης (-ίτης, T; v. WH, App., 154; Bl., § 3, 4), -ου, ὁ, a *Samaritan*, i.e. an inhabitant of the city or the region of Samaria, in NT always the latter (v.s. Σαμαρία): Mt 10⁵, Lk 9⁵² 10³³ 17¹⁶, Jo 4[9],³⁹,⁴⁰, Ac 8²⁵; as an opprobrious epithet, Jo 8⁴⁸.†

Σαμαρεῖτις (-ῖτις, T, v. supr.), -ιδος, ἡ, 1. in FlJ (*B.J.*, i, 21, 2, al.), the region of *Samaria*. 2. a *Samaritan woman*: Jo 4⁹.†

Σαμαρία (Rec. -άρεια), -ας, ἡ (Heb. שֹׁמְרוֹן; Aram. שָׁמְרָיִן), *Samaria*; (a) the city: Ac 8⁵ (and perhaps also ⁹,¹⁴); (b) the region: Lk 17¹¹, Jo 4⁴,⁵,⁷, Ac 1⁸ 8¹ (and perhaps also ⁹,¹⁴), 9³¹ 15³.†

Σαμοθράκη (-θράκη, BE), -ης, ἡ, *Samothrace*, an island in the Ægean: Ac 16¹¹.†

Σάμος, -ου, ἡ, *Samos*, an island in the Ægean: Ac 20¹⁵.†

Σαμουήλ, ὁ, indecl. (in FlJ, Σαμούηλος; Heb. שְׁמוּאֵל), *Samuel* (1 Ki 1²⁰, al.): Ac 3²⁴ 13²⁰, He 11³².†

Σαμψών, ὁ, indecl. (Heb. שִׁמְשׁוֹן), *Samson* (Jg 13 ff.): He 11³².†

σανδάλιον, -ου, τό (dimin. of σάνδαλον, prob. Persian), [in LXX: Jos 9⁵, Is 20² (נַעַל, elsewhere rendered ὑπόδημα, q.v.), Jth 10⁴ 16⁹ *;] a *sandal*: Mk 6⁹, Ac 12⁸.†

σανίς, -ίδος, ἡ, [in LXX: Ca 8⁹, Ez 27⁵ (לֻחַ) *;] a *board, plank*: Ac 27⁴⁴.†

Σαούλ, ὁ, indecl. (in FlJ, Σάουλος; Heb. שָׁאוּל), *Saul;* (a) the King of Israel : Ac 13²¹; (b) the Jewish name of the Apostle Paul, used in the indecl. form only in address (cf. Σαῦλος) : Ac 9⁴,¹⁷ 22⁷,¹³ 26¹⁴.†

** σαπρός, -ά, -όν, [in Sm. : Le 27¹⁴, ³³ * ;] *rotten, corrupt, bad, worthless :* of trees and fruit (opp. to ἀγαθός, καλός), Mt 7¹⁷,¹⁸ 12³³, Lk 6⁴³; of fish, Mt 13⁴⁸. Metaph., in moral sense : λόγος σ., Eph 4²⁹. "In Hellenistic . . . it became a synonym for αἰσχρός or κακός," MM, xxii.†

Σαπφείρα, -ης (v. Bl., § 3, 4), ἡ (< Aram. שַׁפִּירָא), *Sapphira :* Ac 5¹.†

† σάπφειρος, -ου, ἡ, [in LXX for סַפִּיר;] *sapphire* (perh. = *lapis lazuli*) : Re 21¹⁹.†

* σαργάνη, -ης, ἡ, 1. *a plaited rope* (Æsch.). 2. *a hamper, a basket* made of ropes : ΙΙ Co 11³³.†

Σάρδεις, -εων, αἱ, *Sardis,* the chief city of Lydia : Re 1¹¹ 3¹,⁴.†

σάρδινος, -ου, ὁ, = σάρδιον (q.v.), Re 4³, Rec.†

σάρδιον, -ου, τό, [in LXX for אֹדֶם, Ex 28¹⁷, al.; also for שֹׁהַם;] the *sardian* stone, *sard* (of which *carnelian* is one variety) : Re 4³ 21²⁰.†

* σαρδόνυξ (L, σαρδιόνυξ), -υχος, ὁ (< σάρδιον, ὄνυξ), *sardonyx,* a stone marked by the red of the sard and the white of the onyx : Re 21²⁰.†

Σάρεπτα, -ων (Ob ²⁰), τά (Heb. צָרְפַת), *Sarepta,* a city of Sidon : Lk 4²⁶.†

* σαρκικός, -ή, -όν (< σάρξ) (v.l. for σάρκινος, Arist., *H.A.*, x, 2, 7), = Lat. *carnalis,* i.e. (a) associated with or pertaining to the flesh, *fleshly, carnal :* Ro 15²⁷, ι Co 9¹¹; (b) in a more ethical sense, of the nature of the flesh, under the control of its appetites, *fleshly, carnal, sensual* (but including more than mere sensuality; cf. Hort, *I Pe.,* 133) : ι Co 3³, ΙΙ Co 1¹² 10⁴, ι Pe 2¹¹.†

SYN. : σάρκινος (q.v.), ψυχικός; cf. Tr., *Syn.,* §§ lxxi, lxxii; Lft., *Notes,* 184 f.; Vau. on Ro 7¹⁴.

σάρκινος, -η, -ον (< σάρξ), [in LXX: ΙΙ Ch 32⁸, Ez 11¹⁹ 36²⁶ (בָּשָׂר), Es 4¹⁷, Pr 24²³ (29²⁷) * ;] = Lat. *carneus* (the termination -ινος denoting the substance or material of a thing; v. Tr., *Syn.,* § lxxii; Lft., *Notes,* 184; and for illustrations from π., v. MM, xxii), *of the flesh, of flesh, fleshy* (Plat., Arist., Plut., al.) : Ro 7¹⁴, ι Co 3¹, ΙΙ Co 3³, He 7¹⁶. (Rec. has -ικός in all these passages except ΙΙ Co, l.c., but the evidence is decisive against it.)†

SYN. : σαρκικός, q.v.

σάρξ, σαρκός, ἡ, [in LXX chiefly for בָּשָׂר;] *flesh;* 1. as in cl. generally, (a) prop., of the soft substance of the animal body : ι Co 15³⁹ ΙΙ Co 12⁷, Ga 6¹³, al. ; σ. καὶ αἷμα, Mt 16¹⁷, ι Co 15⁵⁰; σ. καὶ ὀστέα, Lk 24³⁹; pl., of the flesh of many or parts of the flesh of one (cl.), Re 17¹⁶ 19¹⁸; φαγεῖν, Re, ll.c. (cf. κατεσθίειν, ιν Ki 9³⁶, al., and βιβρώσκειν, freq. in cl.) ; metaph., Ja 5³; mystically, φ. (τρώγειν) τὴν σ. τοῦ υἱοῦ τ. ἀνθρώπου,

Jo 6⁵²⁻⁵⁶; (b) of the whole substance of the body, = σῶμα: Ac 2²⁶ (LXX), ³¹, ɪɪ Co 12⁷, Ga 4¹⁴, Eph 5²⁹; μία σ., Mk 10⁸; εἰς σ. μίαν.(Ge 2²⁴), Mt 19⁵, Mk 10⁸, ɪ Co 6¹⁶, Eph 5³¹; hence, of the material as opp. to the immaterial part of man (cf. Lft., Notes, 88): opp. to πνεῦμα, ɪ Co 5⁵, ɪɪ Co 7¹, Col 2⁵, ɪ Pe 3¹⁸ 4⁶; to ψυχή, Ac 2³¹, Rec.; of the present life, ἐν σ., Ro 7⁵, Ga 2²⁰, Phl 1²², ²⁴, ɪ Pe 4²; of Christ's life on earth, αἱ ἡμέραι τ. σαρκὸς αὐτοῦ, He 5⁷; of things pertaining to the body, ἐν (τῇ) σ., Ga 6¹², ¹³, Phl 3³, ⁴. 2. As in Heb. idiom, (a) of a living creature: πᾶσα σ. (Heb. כָּל־בָּשָׂר; cf. Bl., § 47, 9), Mt 24²², Mk 13²⁰, ɪ Pe 1²⁴; esp. of man and his mortality (Ps 55 (56)⁵, Si 28⁵, al.), Jo 1¹⁴; πᾶσα σ. (v. supr.), Lk 3⁶, Jo 17², Ac 2¹⁷; ἐν σ., ɪ Jo 4², ɪ Ti 3¹⁶; (b) of natural origin and relationship (Ge 2²⁴, Is 58⁷, al.): τέκνα τῆς σ., Ro 9⁸; κατὰ σάρκα, ib. ³, ⁵, ɪ Co 10¹⁸, Ga 4²³, ²⁹; ἡ σ. μου, Ro 11¹⁴ (cf. Jg 9², ɪɪ Ki 5¹, al.). 3. Of the physical nature as subject to sensation and desire (Plut.), (a) without any ethical disparagement: Ro 7¹⁸ 13¹⁴; opp. to πνεῦμα, Mt 26⁴¹, Mk 14³⁸; τ. θέλημα τῆς σ., Jo 1¹³; ἡ ἐπιθυμία τῆς σ., ɪ Jo 2¹⁶; pl., ɪɪ Pe 2¹⁸; παθεῖν σαρκί, ɪ Pe 4¹; (b) in ethical sense, esp. in Pauline Epp., of the flesh as the seat and vehicle of sinful desires: opp. to νοῦς, Ro 7²⁵; to πνεῦμα, Ro 8⁴⁻⁹, ¹², ¹³, Ga 5¹⁶, ¹⁷, ¹⁹ 6⁸ (cf. DB, ii, 14 f.; iv, 165 f.; Cremer, 844 ff.); v. ICC on Ga, pp. 486 ff.

Σαρούχ, v.s. Σερούχ.

*σαρόω, -ῶ, late form of σαίρω, to sweep: c. acc., Lk 15⁸; pass., Mt 12⁴⁴, Lk 11²⁵.†

Σάρρα, -as, ἡ (Heb. שָׂרָה, Ge 17¹⁵), Sarah: Ro 4¹⁹ 9⁹, He 11¹¹, ɪ Pe 3⁶.†

Σάρων, -ωνος (acc. -ῶνα, WH), ὁ (Heb. שָׁרוֹן), the plain of Sharon: Ac 9³⁵.†

Σατανᾶς, -ᾶ (so also Si 21³⁰, but in ɪɪɪ Ki 11¹⁴, σατάν indecl.; Heb. שָׂטָן; Aram. סָטָנָא, whence the inflected Gk. form), ὁ, Satan (i.e. the adversary, as in LXX, ll. c.): Mt 4¹⁰ 12²⁶, Mk 1¹³ 3²³, ²⁶ 4¹⁵, Lk 10¹⁸ 11¹⁸ 13¹⁶ 22³, ³¹, Jo 13²⁷, Ac 5³ 26¹⁸, Ro 16²⁰, ɪ Co 5⁵ 7⁵, ɪɪ Co 2¹¹ 11¹⁴, ɪ Th 2¹⁸, ɪɪ Th 2⁹, ɪ Ti 1²⁰ 5¹⁵, Re 2⁹, ¹³, ²⁴ 3⁹ 12⁹ 20², ⁷; addressed in person of Peter, Mt 16²³. Mk 8³³; ἄγγελος Σατανᾶ, ɪɪ Co 12⁷.†

†σάτον, -ου, τό (Aram. סָאתָא = Heb. סְאָה), [in LXX: Hg 2¹⁷ (16) *;] a Hebrew measure (= about a peck and a half): Mt 13³³, Lk 13²¹.†

Σαῦλος, -ου, ὁ (Hellenized form of Σαούλ, q.v.), Saul, the Jewish name of the Apostle Paul: Ac 7⁵⁸ 8¹, ³ 9¹, ⁸, ¹¹, ²², ²⁴ 11²⁵, ³⁰ 12²⁵ 13¹, ², ⁷, ⁹.†

σβέννυμι, [in LXX chiefly for כבה;] of fire or things on fire, to quench: c. acc., Mt 12²⁰, Eph 6¹⁶, He 11³⁴; pass., Mt 25⁸, Mk 9 [⁴⁴, ⁴⁶], ⁴⁸. Metaph. (cf. Ca 8⁷, ɪv Mac 16⁴): τὸ πνεῦμα, ɪ Th 5¹⁹.†

σεαυτοῦ, -ῆς, -οῦ (in NT not contracted, σαυτοῦ, as in Att.), reflex. pron. of 2nd pers. sing., used only in gen., dat. and acc. (of, to) thyself: Mt 4⁶, Jo 8¹³, ɪ Ti 4¹⁶, al. (In Hellenistic, the pl. is ἑαυτῶν (q.v.), not ὑμῶν αὐτῶν as in Attic, v. Bl., § 13, 1.) †

σεβάζομαι (< σέβας, *reverential awe*), [in Aq.: Ho 10⁵ *;]; 1. *to fear* (Hom). 2. In later writers, = σέβομαι, *to worship* : Ro 1²⁵.†

σέβασμα, -τος, τό (< σεβάζομαι), [in LXX : Wi 14²⁰ 15¹⁷, Da τη Bel²⁷*;] *an object of worship* : Ac 17²³, ιι Th 2⁴.†

*σεβαστός, -ή, -όν (σεβάζομαι), 1. *reverend, august*. 2. In late writers, with reference to the Roman Imperial name; (a) ὁ Σ., *Augustus*, i.e. the Roman Emperor : Ac 25²¹, ²⁵; (b) *Augustan* : σπεῖρα σ., Ac 27¹. (See further, Deiss., *BS*, 218.) †

σέβω, [in LXX (chiefly for יָרֵא, Jos 4²⁴, al.) and NT always mid., σέβομαι, exc. ιν Mac 5²⁴;] *to worship* : c. acc. pers., Mt 15⁹, Mk 7⁷, Ac 18¹³ 19²⁷; σεβόμενος τ. θεόν, Ac 16¹⁴ 18⁷; σεβόμενοι (σ. προσήλυτοι, σ. Ἕλληνες), *devout*, Ac 13⁴³, ⁵⁰ 17⁴, ¹⁷ (cf. προσήλυτος).†

σειρά, -ᾶς, ἡ, [in LXX : Jg 16¹³, ¹⁴, ¹⁹ (מַחְלָפוֹת), Pr 5²² (חֶבֶל) *;] 1. (a) a cord; (b) a chain (cf. Pr., l.c.) : σειραὶ ζόφου, ιι Pe 2⁴, Rec., R, mg. (v.s. σειρός). 2. a lock of hair (Jg, ll. c.).†

*σειρός (σιρός, T), -οῦ, ὁ (Rec., R, mg., σειρά, q.v.), = cl. σιρός, a pit for the storage of grain : σειροὶ ζόφου, ιι Pe 2⁴, WH, R., txt. (but v. Mayor, in l.; Field, *Notes*, 241).†

σεισμός, -οῦ, ὁ (< σείω), [in LXX chiefly for רַעַשׁ;] *a shaking, commotion*, as a *tempest* at sea : Mt 8²⁴; esp. *an earthquake* : Mt 24⁷ 27⁵⁴ 28², Mk 13⁸, Lk 21¹¹, Ac 16²⁶, Re 6¹² 8⁵ 11¹³, ¹⁹ 16¹⁸.†

σείω, [in LXX chiefly for רַעַשׁ;] *to shake, move to and fro*: τ. γῆν, He 12²⁶ (LXX); pass., ἡ γῆ, Mt 27⁵¹ (LXX); συκῆ, Re 6¹³. Metaph., *to agitate, stir up*, with fear or some other emotion : Mt 21¹⁰ 28⁴ (cf. ἀνα-, δια-, κατα-σείω).†

Σέκουνδος (Rec. Σεκοῦνδος), -ου, ὁ (Lat.), *Secundus* : Ac 20⁴.†

Σελευκία (Rec. -ύκεια), *Seleucia*, a city of Syria : Ac 13⁴.†

σελήνη, -ης, ἡ, [in LXX chiefly for יָרֵחַ (Ge 37⁹, al.), also for לְבָנָה (Ca 6⁹ (10), Is 24²³ א, 30²⁶);] *the moon*: Mt 24²⁹, Mk 13²⁴, Lk 21²⁵, Ac 2²⁰ (LXX), ι Co 15⁴¹, Re 6¹² 8¹² 12¹ 21²³.†

*†σεληνιάζω (< σελήνη), act. in Manetho (*Carm.*, 4, 81), in NT depon. -ομαι, *to be moonstruck*, i.e. *epileptic* (epilepsy being supposed to be influenced by the moon) : Mt 4²⁴ 17¹⁵.†

Σεμεείν (Rec. Σεμεΐ), ὁ, indecl., *Semein* : Lk 3²⁶.†

σεμίδαλις, -εως, ἡ, [in LXX chiefly for סֹלֶת;] *fine wheaten flour* : Re 18¹³.†

σεμνός, -ή, -όν, (< σέβομαι), [in LXX : Pr 6⁸ 8⁶ 15²⁶ (נֶגֶד, נֹעַם), ιι Mac 6¹¹, ²⁸ 8¹⁵, ιν Mac 5³⁶ 7¹⁵ 17⁵ *;]; 1. *reverend, august, venerable*, in cl. of the gods and also of human beings. 2. *grave, serious;* of persons : ι Ti 3⁸, ¹¹, Tit 2²; of things : Phl 4⁸ (v. Tr., *Syn.*, § xcii; Cremer, 37; MM, xxii).†

σεμνότης, -ητος, ἡ (< σεμνός), [in LXX : ιι Mac 3¹² *;] *gravity* : ι Ti 2² 3⁴ (Vg. *castitas*, cf. Soph., *Lex.*, and Zorell, s.v.), Tit 2⁷.†

Σέργιος, -ου, ὁ, *Sergius*, surnamed Paulus : Ac 13⁷.†

Σερούχ (Rec. Σαρ-), ὁ, indecl. (Heb. שְׂרוּג), *Serug :* Lk 3³⁵.†

Σήθ, ὁ (Heb. שֵׁת), indecl., *Seth* (Ge 4²⁵) : LK 3³⁸.†

Σήμ, ὁ, indecl. (Heb. שֵׁם), *Shem :* Lk 3³⁶.†

σημαίνω (< σῆμα, *a sign*), [in LXX for רדץ hi., תקע, etc. ;] *to give a sign, signify,* indicate : c. acc. rei, Ac 25²⁷, Re 1¹ (cf. MM, xxii) ; c. acc. et inf., Ac 11²⁸ ; seq. quæst. indir., Jo 12³³ 18³² 21¹⁹.†

σημεῖον, -ου, τό, [in LXX chiefly for אוֹת ;] *a sign, mark, token ;* (*a*) of that which distinguishes a person or thing from others : Mt 26⁴⁸ Lk 2¹², II Th 3¹⁷ (cf. Deiss., *LAE,* 153₂) ; seq. gen. epexeg., Ro 4¹¹ ; c. gen. obj., Mt 24³, ³⁰, II Co 12¹² ; c. gen. subj., Mt 16³ ; (*b*) a sign of warning or admonition : Mt 12³⁹ 16⁴ Lk 2³⁴ 11²⁹, ³⁰, I Co 14²² ; (*c*) a sign portending future events (Soph., Plat. al.) : Mk 13⁴, Lk 21⁷, ¹¹, ²⁵, Ac 2¹⁹, Re 12¹, ³ 15¹ ; (*d*) of miracles and wonders (MM, xxii), regarded as signs of a divine authority : Mt 12³⁸, ³⁹ 16¹, ⁴, Mk 8¹¹, ¹², Lk 11¹⁶, ²⁹ 23⁸, Jo 2¹¹, ¹⁸, ²³ 4⁵⁴ 6³⁰ 10⁴¹ 12¹⁸, Ac 4¹⁶, ²² ; pl., Mk 16[¹⁷, ²⁰], Jo 2¹¹, ²³ 3² 6², ¹⁴, ²⁶ 7³¹ 9¹⁶ 11⁴⁷ 12³⁷ 20³⁰, Ac 8⁶, I Co 1²² (Lft., *Notes,* 162) ; the same ascribed to false teachers and demons : Mt 24²⁴, Mk 13²², II Th 2⁹, Re 13¹³, ¹⁴ 16¹⁴ 19²⁰ ; σ. καὶ τέρατα (τ. καὶ σ. ; cf. Tr., *Syn.,* § xci), Mt 24²⁴, Mk 13²², Jo 4⁴⁸, Ac 2¹⁹, ⁴³ 4³⁰ 5¹² 6⁸ 7³⁶ 14³ 15¹², Ro 15¹⁹, II Th 2⁹ ; id. seq. καὶ δυνάμεις, II Co 12¹², He 2⁴ ; σ. καὶ δυνάμεις, Ac 8¹³ ; δ. καὶ τ. καὶ σ., Ac 2²² ; σ. διδόναι, Mt 24²⁴, Mk 13²².†

σημειόω, -ῶ (< σημεῖον), [in LXX : Ps 4⁶ (נשׂא) * ;] *to mark, note.* Mid., *to note for oneself :* II Th 3¹⁴ (freq. in π. ; v. ICC, M, *Th.,* in l.).†

σήμερον (Att. τήμερον), adv., [in LXX for הַיּוֹם ;] *to-day :* Mt 6¹¹, Lk 4²¹, Ac 4⁹, al. ; opp. to αὔριον, Mt 6³⁰, Lk 12²⁸, Ja 4¹³ ; χθὲς καὶ σ. καὶ εἰς τοὺς αἰῶνας, He 13⁸ ; ἡ σ. ἡμέρα, Ac 20²⁶ ; ἕως (ἄχρι) τῆς σ. ἡμέρας, Ro 11⁸, II Co 3¹⁴ ; μέχρι (ἕως) τῆς σ. (sc. ἡμέρας), Mt 11²³ 27⁸ ; as subst., τὸ σ., He 3¹³ ; id. in appos., ὁρίζει ἡμέραν, σ., He 4⁷ R, mg., (v. Westc., in l.).

σήπω, [in LXX : Ps 37 (38)⁵ (מקק ni.), Jb 33²¹ (כלה) 40⁷, Si 14¹⁹, al. ;] *to make corrupt :* 2 pf. act. with mid. sense (v. M, *Pr.,* 154), σέσηπεν, *has perished, become corrupted,* Ja 5².†

σηρικός, v.s. σιρικός.

σής, σητός (late gen. for cl. σεός), ὁ, [in LXX : Jb 4¹⁹, Is 50⁹ (עָשׁ), Is 51⁸ (סָס), al. ;] *a moth, clothes moth :* Mt 6¹⁹, ²⁰, Lk 12³³.†

†σητό-βρωτος, -ον (< σής, βιβρώσκω), [in LXX : Jb 13²⁸ (אָכְלוֹ עָשׁ) * ;] *moth-eaten :* Ja 5².†

***†σθενόω,** -ῶ (< σθένος, *strength*), *to strengthen :* c. acc., I Pe 5¹⁰ (Hesych.).†

σιαγών, -όνος, ἡ, [in LXX for לְחִי ;] *the jawbone, jaw, cheek :* Mt 5³⁹, Lk 6²⁹ (cf. MM, xxii).†

σιγάω, -ῶ (< σιγή), [in LXX for חרשׁ. חשׁה, etc. ;] 1. intrans.,

to be silent, keep silence : Lk 9³⁶ 18³⁹ 20²⁶, Ac 12²⁷ 15¹²,¹³, ι Co
14²⁸,³⁰,³⁴. 2. Trans., to keep secret ; pass., to be kept secret : Ro 16²⁵.†
    SYN.: ἡσυχάζω, σιωπάω.
    ** σιγή, -ῆς, ἡ, [in LXX : Wi 18¹⁴, III Mac 3²³ * ;] silence : Ac 21⁴⁰,
Re 8¹.†
    σιδήρεος, -α, -ον (-οῦς, -ᾶ -οῦν) (< σίδηρος), [in LXX chiefly for
בַּרְזֶל ;] of iron : Ac 12¹⁰, Re 2²⁷ 9⁹ 12⁵ 19¹⁵.†
    σίδηρος, -ου, ὁ, [in LXX chiefly for בַּרְזֶל ;] iron : Re 18¹².†
    Σιδών, -ῶνος, ἡ (Heb. צִידוֹן), Sidon, a maritime city of Phœnicia :
Mt 11²¹,²² 15²¹, Mk 3⁸ 7²⁴,³¹, Lk 6¹⁷ 10¹³,¹⁴, Ac 27³ (on Mk 7²⁴, v. Turner,
SNT, p. 59).†
    Σιδώνιος, -α, -ον (< Σιδών), of Sidon, Sidonian ; (a) the region :
sc. χώρα, Lk 4²⁶ ; (b) the people : Ac 12²⁰.†
    *† σικάριος, -ου, ὁ (Lat.; < sica, a dagger carried under their cloth-
ing by the Sicarii), a bandit, assassin, one of the Sicarii (FlJ, B.J.,
ii, 17, 6, al.) : Ac 21³⁸.†
    †σίκερα, τό, indecl. (Aram. שִׁכְרָא), [in LXX for שֵׁכָר (also
rendered μέθυσμα, Jg 13⁴, Mi 2¹¹), Le 10⁹, al.;] fermented liquor, strong
drink : Lk 1¹⁵.†
    Σίλας, -α (acc. to Bl., § 29, W-Schm., 74, -ᾶς, -ᾶ), ὁ (Aram.
שְׁאִילָא; v. Dalman, Gr., 157₅), Silas (called also Σιλουανός, q.v.) :
Ac 15²²,²⁷,³²,³⁴,⁴⁰ 16¹⁹,²⁵,²⁹ 17⁴,¹⁰,¹⁴,¹⁵ 18⁵.†
    Σιλουανός (in MSS also Σιλβανός, a form freq. in π.), -οῦ, ὁ,
Silvanus, latinized name of Silas : II Co 1¹⁹, I Th 1¹, II Th 1¹
I Pe 5¹².†
    Σιλωάμ (indecl., but in FlJ, gen., -ᾶ, B.J., ii, 16, 2), ὁ (Heb.
שִׁלֹחַ), Siloam (v. DB, iii, 515 f.) : Lk 13⁴, Jo 9⁷,¹¹.†
    *† σιμικίνθιον (also written σημι-), -ου, τό (Lat. semicinctium), a work-
man's apron : Ac 19¹².†
    Σίμων, -ωνος, ὁ, a Greek name (transliterated סִימוֹן in Heb.) used
as a substitute for Συμεών (q.v.), Simon ; 1. Simon Peter : Mt 17²⁵,
Mk 1²⁹, al. 2. Simon the Zealot (v.s. ζηλωτής, Καναναῖος) : Mt 10⁴,
Mk 3¹⁸, Lk 6¹⁵, Ac 1¹³. 3. One of the Brethren of our Lord (v.s.
ἀδελφός) : Mt 13⁵⁵, Mk 6³. 4. The father of Judas Iscariot, himself
surnamed Ἰσκαριώτης (q.v.) : Jo 6⁷¹ 12⁴ (Rec.) 13²,²⁶. 5. Simon the
Cyrenian : Mt 27³², Mk 15²¹, Lk 23²⁶. 6. Simon the Pharisee : Lk
7⁴⁰,⁴³,⁴⁴. 7. Simon of Bethany, surnamed ὁ λεπρός : Mt 26⁶, Mk 14³.
8. Simon Magus, a Samaritan sorcerer : Ac 8⁹,¹³,¹⁸,²⁴. 9. Simon the
tanner, of Joppa : Ac 9⁴³ 10⁶,¹⁷,³².
    Σινά (-ᾶ, Rec.), indecl. (but τὸ Σιναῖον, FlJ, Ant., iii, 5, 1 ; τὸ
Σιναῖον ὄρος, ib. ii, 12, 1), τό (Heb. סִינַי), Sinai (Ex 19¹¹, al.) : Ac 7³⁰,³⁸,
Ga 4²⁴,²⁵.†
    *† σίναπι, -εως, τό (prob. Egyptian), = Attic τὸ νᾶπυ, mustard.
Mt 13³¹ 17²⁰, Mk 4³¹, Lk 13¹⁹ 17⁶.†

σινδών, -όνος, ή, [in LXX: Jg 14¹², ¹³ᴬ, Pr 31²⁴ (סָדִין), 1 Mac 10⁶⁴ A*;]
fine linen cloth ; (*a*) as used for swathing dead bodies (cf. Hdt., ii, 86) :
Mt 27⁵⁹, Mk 15⁴⁶, Lk 23⁵³; (*b*) a garment or wrap of this material (cf.
ICC, Jg, l.c.; *Theology*, Vol. VII, Aug., 1913, p. 90) : Mk 14⁵¹, ⁵².†

*†σινιάζω (< σίνιον, *a sieve*), = σήθω, *to sift, winnow :* fig., Lk
22³¹.†

*σιρικός (by assimilation of vowels, for σηρικός; v. Mayser, 150;
WH, *App.*, p. 158), -ή, όν (< οἱ Σῆρες, a people of India from whom the
ancients got the first silk), *silk, silken ;* as subst., τὸ σ., *silken fabric,
silk :* Re 18¹² (cf. FlJ, *B.J.*, vii, 5, 4).†

σιρός, v.s. σειρός.

σιτευτός, -ή, -όν (< σιτεύω, *to feed, fatten*), [in LXX: III Ki 4²³
(אבם), etc. ;] *fattened :* Lk 15²³, ²⁷, ³⁰.†

σιτίον, -ου, τό (dimin. of σῖτος), [in LXX : Pr 24⁵⁷ (30²²) (לֶחֶם) *;]
1. *corn, grain :* Ac 7¹² (but v. Bl., § 9, 1). 2. Mostly in pl., σιτία,
bread, food, provisions (LXX, l.c., Hdt., al.).†

**†σιτιστός, -ή, -όν (< σιτίζω, *to fatten*), [in Sm.: Ps 21 (22)¹³, Je
46 (26)²¹ *;] = σιτευτός, *fattened ;* as subst., pl., τὰ σ., *fatlings :* Mt
22⁴.†

*†σιτομέτριον, -ου, τό (< σιτομετρέω, Ge 47¹², ¹⁴ *, = Attic τὸν σῖτον
μετρέω), *a measured portion of food :* Lk 12⁴² (for exx. in π., v. Deiss.,
BS, 158; *LAE*, 103₁).†

σῖτος, -ου, ὁ, [in LXX chiefly for דָּגָן;] *wheat, corn :* Mt 3¹²
13²⁵, ²⁹, ³⁰, Mk 4²⁸, Lk 3¹⁷ 12¹⁸ 16⁷ 22³¹, Jo 12²⁴, Ac 27³⁸, 1 Co 15³⁷,
Re 6⁶ 18¹³.†

Σιχάρ, v.s. Συχάρ.

Σιών, indecl., in NT anarth., but in LXX when used of the city
of Jerusalem, ἡ Σ. (Heb. צִיּוֹן), *Zion ;* 1. the mountain : in typical
sense, of the Church, He 12²²; of heaven, Re 14¹. 2. The city, i.e.
Jerusalem ; in poetical sense ; (*a*) of the inhabitants : θυγάτηρ Σ., Mt
21⁵, Jo 12¹⁵ (LXX); (*b*) in wider sense, of Israel : Ro 11²⁶; (*c*) fig. :
τίθημι ἐν Σ. λίθον, Ro 9³³, 1 Pe 2⁶ (LXX).†

σιωπάω, -ῶ (< σιωπή, *silence*), [in LXX for חשה, חרש hi., etc. ;]
to be silent or *still, keep silence :* Mt 20³¹ 26⁶³, Mk 3⁴ 9³⁴ 10⁴⁸ 14⁶¹, Lk 19⁴⁰,
Ac 18⁹; of one dumb, Lk 1²⁰ (cf. IV Mac 10¹⁸) ; addressed rhetorically
to the sea, σιώπα, Mk 4³⁹.†

SYN. : ἡσυχάζω, σιγάω (q.v.).

†σκανδαλίζω (< σκάνδαλον), [in LXX : Da LXX 11⁴¹ (כשל ni.),
Si 9⁵ 35 (32)¹⁵ (יקש ho.) ib. 23⁸ (also in Aq., Sm., Th., and in Ps Sol 16⁷;
not elsewhere, except NT and eccl.) *;] prop., *to put a snare* or
stumbling-block in the way; in NT always metaph. of that which
hinders right conduct or thought, *to cause to stumble :* c. acc. pers.,
Mt 5²⁹, ³⁰ 17²⁷ 18⁶, ⁸, ⁹, Mk 9⁴², ⁴³, ⁴⁵, ⁴⁷, Lk 17², Jo 6⁶¹, 1 Co 8¹³. Pass.,
to be made to stumble, to stumble : Mt 11⁶ 13²¹, ⁵⁷ 15¹² 24¹⁰ 26³¹, ³³, Mk
4¹⁷ 6³ 14²⁷, ²⁹, Lk 7²³, Jo 16¹, Ro 14²¹ (WH, R, txt., om.), II Co 11²⁹.†

†σκάνδαλον, -ου, τό (late form of the˙rare word σκανδάληθρον, v. LS, s.v.), [in LXX chiefly for מוֹקֵשׁ, מִכְשׁוֹל;] prop., the *bait-stick* of a trap, a *snare, stumbling-block* (Le 19¹⁴, Jth 5¹): fig., Ro 9³³, i Pe 2⁸ (Is 8¹⁴; aliter in LXX; στερεὸν σκανδάλου in Aq.). Metaph., of that which causes error or sin; (a) of persons: Mt 13⁴¹ 16²³; Χριστὸς ἐσταυρωμένος, i Co 1²³; (b) of things: Mt 18⁷, Ro 11⁹ (LXX) 14¹³, i Jo 2¹⁰, Re 2¹⁴; τὸ σ. τοῦ σταυροῦ, Ga 5¹¹; pl., Mt 18⁷, Lk 17¹, Ro 16¹⁷.†
  SYN.: πρόσκομμα.

σκάπτω, [in LXX: Is 5⁶ (עדר ni.) *;] to dig: Lk 6⁴⁸ 13⁸ 16³.†

** σκάφη, -ης, ἡ (< σκάπτω), [in LXX: Da LXX Bel ³², TH ib. ³³ *;] anything scooped out, esp. a *light boat, skiff*: Ac 27¹⁶, ³⁰, ³².†

σκέλος, -ους, τό, [in LXX for רֶגֶל, etc.;] the *leg* from the hip downwards: Jo 19³¹⁻³³.†

* σκέπασμα, -τος, τό (< σκεπάζω, to cover), a *covering*, esp. *clothing*: i Ti 6⁸.†

Σκευᾶς, -ᾶ, *Sceva*: Ac 19¹⁴.†

** σκευή, -ῆς, ἡ, [in LXX: iii Mac 5⁴⁵ R *;] *equipment, tackle*: Ac 27¹⁹.†

σκεῦος, -ους, τό, [in LXX chiefly for כְּלִי;] a *vessel, implement* (for exx. in various senses, v. MM, xxii): Mk 11¹⁶, Lk 8¹⁶, Jo 19²⁹, Ac 10¹¹, ¹⁶ 11⁵, Ro 9²¹, Re 18¹²; pl., ii Ti 2²⁰, Re 2²⁷; τὰ σ. τῆς λειτουργίας, He 9²¹; pl., τὰ σ., *utensils, goods*, Mt 12²⁹, Mk 3²⁷, Lk 17³¹; id. of the *tackle* or *gear* of a ship (Xen., Polyb., al.); so in sing., τὸ σ., Ac 27¹⁷. Metaph., of persons: σ. ἐκλογῆς, Ac 9¹⁵; ὀργῆς, Ro 9²²; ἐλέους, ib. ²³; σ. εἰς τιμήν (cf. Ro 9²¹), ii Ti 2²¹; of woman, ἀσθενέστερον σ., i Pe 3⁷; so perh. τ. ἑαυτοῦ σ., i Th 4⁴ (but v. infr.); of the body, ii Co 4⁷; so perh. i Th 4⁴ (but v. supr., and v.s. κτάομαι).†

σκηνή, -ῆς, ἡ, [in LXX chiefly for אֹהֶל, also for מִשְׁכָּן, סֻכָּה, etc.;] a *tent, booth, tabernacle*: Mt 17⁴, Mk 9⁵, Lk 9³³, He 11⁹; αἱ αἰώνιοι σ., Lk 16⁹; of the Mosaic tabernacle, He 8⁵ 9², ³, ⁶, ⁸, ²¹; σ. τ. μαρτυρίου, Ac 7⁴⁴; of its heavenly prototype, He 8² 9¹¹, Re 13⁶ 15⁵ 21³; of the temple, He 13¹⁰; ἡ σ. τοῦ Μολόχ, Ac 7⁴³ (LXX); metaph., ἡ σ. Δαυείδ, Ac 15¹⁶ (LXX).†

σκηνοπηγία, -ας, ἡ (< σκηνή, πήγνυμι), [in LXX for סֻכּוֹת, De 16¹⁶ 31¹⁰, Za 14¹⁶, ¹⁸, ¹⁹; i Es 5⁵¹, i Mac 10²¹, ii Mac 1⁹, ¹⁸ *;] prop., the *setting up of tents* or *dwellings* (Arist.); in LXX and NT, ἡ σ., ἡ ἑορτὴ τῆς σ. (called also ἑορτὴ σκηνῶν, Le 23³⁴, al.; v. Deiss., *LAE*, 116 f.), the feast of Tabernacles: Jo 7².†

*†σκηνοποιός, -όν (< σκηνή, ποιέω), *making tents*; as subst., ὁ σ., a *tent-maker*: Ac 18³.†

** σκῆνος, -ους, τό, [in LXX: Wi 9¹⁵ *;] = σκηνή, a *tent, tabernacle* (*C.I.*, 3071). Metaph., of the body as the tabernacle of the soul: ii Co 5¹, ⁴.†

σκηνόω, -ῶ (< σκηνή), [in LXX chiefly for שָׁכַן;] *to have one's tabernacle, to dwell* (in π. of temporary dwelling, v. MM, *Exp.*, xxii) : seq. ἐπί, c. acc. pers., Re 7¹⁵; seq. ἐν, c. dat. pers., Jo 1¹⁴; id. c. dat. loc., Re 12¹² 13⁶; seq. μετά, c. gen. pers., Re 21³ (cf. ἐπι-, κατα-σκηνόω).†

σκήνωμα, -τος, τό (< σκηνόω), [in LXX chiefly for אֹהֶל;] *a tent, tabernacle* (cf. σκηνή, σκῆνος) : of the temple as God's dwelling (Ps 131 (132)⁵, al.), Ac 7⁴⁶. Metaph., of the body : 11 Pe 1¹³, ¹⁴.†

σκιά, -ᾶς, ἡ, [in LXX chiefly for צֵל, iv Ki 20⁹ ᶠᶠ·, Ps 56 (57)¹, al.; but σ. and σ. θανάτου are also used for צַלְמָוֶת, Jb 3⁵, Ps 22 (23)⁴, Is 9² ⁽¹⁾ (v. *ICC*, in l.), al.;] 1. *shadow, shade,* caused by interception of light : Mk 4³², Ac 5¹⁵; metaph., σ. θανάτου, of ignorance and error, Mt 4¹⁶, Lk 1⁷⁹ (LXX). 2. *a shadow,* the image or outline cast by an object : fig., ὑπόδειγμα καὶ σ., He 8⁵; opp. to σῶμα, Col 2¹⁷; opp. to εἰκών, He 10¹.†

σκιρτάω, -ῶ, [in LXX: Ge 25²² (רצץ hithpo.), Ps 113 (114)⁴, ⁶ (רקד), etc.;] *to leap* : Lk 1⁴¹, ⁴⁴ 6²³.†

† σκληρο-καρδία, -ας, ἡ (< σκληρός, καρδία), [in LXX: De 10¹⁶, Je 4⁴ (עָרְלַת לֵבָב), Si 16¹⁰ (cf. καρδία σκληρά, ib. 3²⁶, ²⁷) *;] *hardness of heart* : Mt 19⁸, Mk 10⁵ 16⁽¹⁴⁾.†

σκληρός, -ά, -όν (< σκέλλω, to dry), [in LXX chiefly for קָשֶׁה;] *hard* to the touch, *rough, harsh,* (opp. to μαλακός) ; metaph., in various uses ; (*a*) of men, *hard, stern, severe* : Mt 25²⁴ ; (*b*) of things, *hard, rough, violent* : σκληρόν σοι (ἐστι), Ac 26¹⁴ ; λόγος, Jo 6⁶⁰ ; ἄνεμος, Ja 3⁴ ; σκληρὰ λαλεῖν, Ju 15.†
SYN. : αὐστηρός, q.v.

σκληρότης, -ητος, ἡ (< σκληρός), [in LXX: De 9²⁷ (קְשִׁי), etc.;] *hardness;* metaph., of stubbornness : Ro 2⁵.†

† σκληρο-τράχηλος, -ον (σκληρός, τράχηλος), [in LXX: Ex 33³, ⁵ (קְשֵׁה־עֹרֶף); etc.;] *stiff-necked* : metaph., Ac 7⁵¹.†

σκληρύνω (< σκληρός), [in LXX chiefly for קָשָׁה hi., also for חזק;] *to harden.* Metaph., *to harden, make stubborn* : c. acc. pers., Ro 9¹⁸ ; τ. καρδίας (Ps 94 (95)⁸), He 3⁸, ¹⁵ 4⁷. Pass., *to become hardened* : Ac 19⁹, He 3¹³.†

σκολιός, -ά, -όν, [in LXX: De 32⁵ (עִקֵּשׁ), Pr 28¹⁸ (σ. ὁδοῖς πορεύεσθαι, for נֶעְקַשׁ דְּרָכַיִם), Is 40⁴ (עָקֹב), etc.;] *curved, bent, winding* (opp. to ὀρθός, εὐθύς) : Lk 3⁵ ⁽ᴸˣˣ⁾. Metaph., *crooked, perverse, unjust* : Ac 2⁴⁰, Phl 2¹⁵, ı Pe 2¹⁸.†

σκόλοψ, -οπος, ὁ, [in LXX: Nu 33⁵⁵ (שֵׂךְ), Ho 2⁶ ⁽⁸⁾ (סִיר), Ez 28²⁴ (סִלּוֹן), Si 43¹⁹ *;] *anything pointed,* esp. 1. in cl., *a stake.* 2. In Hellenistic vernacular, *a thorn* (cf. LXX, ll. c.) : σ. τῇ σαρκί, 11 Co 12⁷ (cf. MM, i, xxiii; *DB*, iii, 700 f.; Deiss., *St. Paul*, 62 f.; Field, *Notes*, 187).†

σκοπέω, -ῶ (< σκοπός), [in LXX: Es 8¹³, ɪɪ Mac 4⁵ * ;] *to look at, behold, watch, contemplate*. Metaph., *to look to, consider :* c. acc. rei, ɪɪ Co 4¹⁸, Phl 2⁴ ; c. acc. pers., Ro 16¹⁷, Phl 3¹⁷ ; seq. μή, Lk 11³⁵ ; σεαυτόν, seq. μή (v. M, *Pr.*, 192), Ga 6¹ (cf. ἐπι-, κατα-σκοπέω).†
SYN. : βλέπω, θεωρέω, ὁράω.

σκοπός, -οῦ, ὁ, [in LXX chiefly for צֹפֶה ;] 1. *a watcher, watchman* (Ez 3¹⁷, al.). 2. *a mark* on which to fix the eye (Wi 5¹², ²¹, al.). Metaph., of an aim or object : Phl 3¹⁴.†

σκορπίζω, [in LXX for פזר hi., etc. ;] in vernac. and in Ion. and late writers for σκεδάννυμι (v. MM, xxiii; Rutherford, *N Phr.*, 295), *to scatter :* ὁ λύκος, Jo 10¹² ; ὁ μὴ συνάγων μετ' ἐμοῦ σκορπίζει, Mt 12³⁰, Lk 11²³ ; pass., seq. εἰς, c. acc. loc., Jo 16³² ; of one who dispenses blessings, ɪɪ Co 9⁹ (ʟxx) (cf. δια-σκορπίζομαι).†

σκορπίος, -ου, ὁ, [in LXX for עַקְרָב ;] *a scorpion :* Lk 10¹⁹ 11¹², Re 9³, ⁵, ¹⁰.†

σκοτεινός (WH. -τινός), -ή, -όν (< σκότος), [in LXX chiefly for חשֶׁךְ and cogn. forms ;] *dark :* opp. to φωτεινός, Mt 6²³, Lk 11³⁴, ³⁶.†

†**σκοτία, -ας, ἡ**, [in LXX: Jb 28³ (אֹפֶל), Mi 3⁶ (חֲשֵׁכָה), Is 16³ * ;] in late writers = σκότος, *darkness :* Jo 6¹⁷ 20¹. Metaph., (*a*) of secrecy (opp. to ἐν τ. φωτί): Mt 10²⁷, Lk 12³ ; (*b*) of spiritual darkness : Mt 4¹⁶, Jo 1⁵ 8¹² 12³⁵, ⁴⁶, ɪ Jo 1⁵ 2⁸, ⁹, ¹¹.†

†**σκοτίζω** (< σκότος), [in LXX for חשֶׁךְ ;] *to darken ;* in NT always pass., -ομαι, *to be darkened :* of the heavenly bodies, Mt 24²⁹, Mk 13²⁴, Lk 23⁴⁵ (Rec., WH, mg.), Re 8¹². Metaph., of the mind, Ro 1²¹ 11¹⁰ (ʟxx) (cf. σκοτόω).†

σκότος, -ου, ὁ, the more usual cl. form (cf.σ., τό), *darkness :* He 12¹⁸, Rec.†

σκότος, -ους, τό, a form rare in cl. (cf. ὁ σ.) but freq. in LXX, [chiefly for חשֶׁךְ ;] *darkness :* Mt 27⁴⁵, Mk 15³³, Lk 22⁵³ 23⁴⁴, Ac 2²⁰, ɪɪ Co 4⁶ ; τὰ κρυπτὰ τοῦ σ., ɪ Co 4⁵ ; of blindness, Mt 6²³, Ac 13¹¹ ; by meton., of a dark place, Mt 8¹² 22¹³ 25³⁰, ɪɪ Pe 2¹⁷, Ju ¹³. Metaph., of moral and spiritual darkness : Lk 11³⁵, Jo 3¹⁹, Ac 26¹⁸, ɪɪ Co 6¹⁴, Eph 6¹², Col 1¹³, ɪ Pe 2⁹ ; by meton., of those who are in spiritual darkness, Eph 5⁸ ; τ. ἔργα τοῦ σ., Ro 13¹², Eph 5¹¹ ; σκότους εἶναι, ɪ Th 5⁵ ; ἐν σ. εἶναι, ib. ⁴ ; οἱ ἐν σ., Lk 1⁷⁹, Ro 2¹⁹ ; ὁ λαὸς ὁ καθήμενος ἐν σ., Mt 4¹⁶ (ʟxx) (WH. σκοτίᾳ) ; ἐν σ. περιπατεῖν, ɪ Jo 1⁶.†

σκοτόω, -ῶ (< σκότος), [in LXX for שׁוחר, קדר, חשׁך ;] *to darken :* Re 9² 16¹⁰. Metaph., of the mind : pass., Eph 4¹⁸ (cf. σκοτίζω).†

σκύβαλον, -ου, τό, [in LXX: Si 27⁴ * ;] *refuse*, esp. *dung* (v. MM, ii, iii, xxiii) : Phl 3⁸.†

Σκύθης, -ου, ὁ, *Scythian*, an inhabitant of Scythia, i.e. Russia and Siberia, a synonym with the Greeks for the wildest of barbarians : Col 3¹¹.†

σκυθρωπός, -όν (also -ή, -όν) (< σκυθρός, *sullen*, + ὤψ), [in LXX : Ge 40⁷ (רַע), etc. ;] *of a gloomy countenance :* Mt 6¹⁶, Lk 24¹⁷.†

*σκύλλω, 1. in cl., *to skin, flay, rend* (Æsch., Anthol.). 2. In Hellenistic writers, *to vex, trouble, annoy :* c. acc. pers., Mk 5³⁵, Lk 8⁴⁹ ; pass., ἐσκυλμένοι, *distressed*, Mt 9³⁶ ; mid., *to trouble oneself, μὴ σκύλλου*, Lk 7⁶ (freq. in π. ; v. MM, i, ii, and cf. M, *Pr.*, 89 ; Abbott, *Essays*, 87 ; Kennedy, *Sources*, 82).†

σκῦλον (Rec. σκύλον), -ου, τό, [in LXX chiefly for שָׁלָל ;] mostly in pl., σκῦλα, *arms stripped from a foe, spoils :* Lk 11²².†

*σκωληκό-βρωτος, -ον (< σκώληξ, βιβρώσκω), *eaten of worms :* Ac 12²³ (cf. ii Mac 9⁹, and v. MM, xxiii).†

σκώληξ, -ηκος, ὁ, [in LXX chiefly for תּוֹלָע and cogn. forms ;] *a worm :* of the kind which preys upon dead bodies, metaph., of fut. punishment, Mk 9⁴⁸ (LXX, Is 66²⁴ ; cf. Si 7¹⁷, Jth 16¹⁷).†

*†σμαράγδινος (< σμάραγδος, q.v.), 1. *of emerald* (Luc., *V.H.*, ii, 11). 2. As in π. (Deiss., *BS*, 267), *emerald-green :* Re 4³ (for the construction, v. Swete, in l. ; Zorell, s.v.).†

σμάραγδος, -ου, ἡ (and in late writers also ὁ), [in LXX : Ex 28⁹ (שֹׁהַם) 36¹⁷ (39¹⁰) (בָּרֶקֶת), Ez 28¹³ (יַהֲלֹם), etc. ;] *emerald* or other transparent green stone (LS, s.v. ; *DB*, iv, 620 ; Swete, *Ap.*, 67, 288) : Re 21¹⁹.†

σμύρνα (in some MSS, ζμ- ; v. Bl., § 3, 9), -ης, ἡ, [in LXX for מֹר, מוֹר ;] *myrrh*, a resinous gum used as an unguent and for embalming : Mt 2¹¹, Jo 19³⁹.†

Σμύρνα (T, Ζμ- ; Bl., § 3, 9), -ας, ἡ, *Smyrna*, an Ionian city on the Ægean : Re 1¹¹ 2⁸.†

Σμυρναῖος, -α, -ον, *of Smyrna :* Re 2⁸, Rec.†

*†σμυρνίζω (< σμύρνα), 1. intrans., *to be like myrrh* (Diosc., i, 79). 2. Trans., *to mingle* or *drug with myrrh :* pass., Mk 15²³.†

Σόδομα, -ων, τά (Heb. סְדֹם), *Sodom* (Ge 13¹⁰, ¹², al.) : Mt 10¹⁵ 11²³, ²⁴, Lk 10¹² 17²⁹, Ro 9²⁹ (LXX), ii Pe 2⁶, Ju ⁷, Re 11⁸.†

Σολομών, -ῶνος (so prop., but Rec. has freq. -ῶν, -ῶντος, as also WH in Ac 3¹¹ 5¹² ; in Ac 7⁴⁷ T has Σαλωμών, as LXX freq., indecl. ; v. Bl., § 10, 1 ; Tdf., *Prol.*, 104, 119 ; WH, *App.*, 158), ὁ (Heb. שְׁלֹמֹה), *Solomon :* Mt 1⁶, ⁷ 6²⁹ 12⁴², Lk 11³¹ 12²⁷, Jo 10²³, Ac 3¹¹ 5¹² 7⁴⁷.†

σορός, -οῦ, ἡ, [in LXX : Ge 50²⁶ (אָרוֹן), Jb 21³²A * ;] (*a*) *a cinerary urn* (Hom.) ; (*b*) *a coffin* (Hdt., i, 68, 3, al.) : Lk 7¹⁴.†

σός, -ή, -όν, possess. pron. of second pers., *thy, thine :* Mt 7³, al. ; as subst., οἱ σοί, *thy kinsfolk, friends*, Mk 5¹⁹ ; τὸ σόν, *what is thine*, Mt 20¹⁴ 25²⁵ ; τὰ σά, *thy goods*, Lk 6³⁰.

*†σουδάριον, -ου, τό (Lat.), *handkerchief, kerchief :* Lk 19²⁰, Ac 19¹² ; used as a head covering for the dead, Jo 11⁴⁴ 20⁷ (cf. Deiss., *BS*, 223).†

Σουσάννα, -ης (cf. Da LXX TH Su, inscr., [2, 7, al.]), ή, Susanna : Lk 8³.†

σοφία, -ας, ή, [in LXX chiefly for חָכְמָה;] skill, intelligence, wisdom, ranging from knowledge of the arts and matters of daily life to mental excellence in its highest and fullest sense; (a) of human wisdom : 1 Co 2[1, 4, 5], Ja 3¹⁵, Re 13¹⁸ 17⁹; σ. Σολομῶνος, Mt 12⁴², Lk 11³¹; Αἰγυπτίων, Ac 7²²; Ἕλληνες σ. ζητοῦσιν, 1 Co 1²²; σ. λόγου, 1 Co 1¹⁷; τ. σοφῶν, ib. ¹⁹ (LXX); τ. κόσμου, ib. ²⁰, ²¹ 3¹⁹; ἀνθρωπίνη, 1 Co 2¹³; σαρκική, 11 Co 1¹²; of wisdom in spiritual things : Lk 21¹⁵, Ac 6³, ¹⁰ 7¹⁰, 1 Co 2⁶, Col 1²⁸ 2²³ 3¹⁶ 4⁵, Ja 1⁵ 3¹³, ¹⁷, 11 Pe 3¹⁵; λόγος σοφίας, 1 Co 12⁸; πνεῦμα σοφίας, Eph 1¹⁷; σ. καὶ φρόνησις, Eph 1⁸; σ. καὶ σύνεσις, Col 1⁹; (b) of divine wisdom : of God, Ro 11³³, 1 Co 1²¹, ²⁴ 2⁷, Re 7¹²; πολυποίκιλος, Eph 3¹⁰; of Christ, Mt 13⁵⁴, Mk 6², Lk 2⁴⁰, ⁵², 1 Co 1³⁰, Col 2³, Re 5¹²; of wisdom personified, Mt 11¹⁹, Lk 7³⁵ 11⁴⁹.†

SYN.: σύνεσις, intelligence; φρόνησις, prudence, which with σ. make up (Arist., N. Eth., i, 13) the three intellectual ἀρεταί. σ. is wisdom primary and absolute; in distinction from which φ. is practical, σύνεσις critical, both being applications of σ. in detail (cf. Lft., and ICC on Col 1⁹; Lft., Notes, 317 f.; Tr., Syn., § lxxv; Cremer, 870 ff.).

σοφίζω (< σοφός), [in LXX chiefly for חכם;] to make wise, instruct : c. acc. pers., 11 Ti 3¹⁵ (cf. Ps 18 (19)⁸ 118 (119)⁹⁸). As depon., -ομαι; (a) intrans., to become wise (111 Ki 4²⁷ (5¹¹), Ec 2¹⁵, and freq. in Si, 7⁵, al.); (b) trans., to invent, devise cleverly : pass., 11 Pe 1¹⁶ (cf. κατα-σοφίζομαι).†

σοφός, -ή, -όν, [in LXX chiefly for חָכָם;] skilled, clever, wise, whether in handicraft, the affairs of life, the sciences or learning : Ro 16¹⁹, 1 Co 3¹⁰; of the learned, Ro 1¹⁴, ²², 1 Co 1¹⁹, ²⁰, ²⁶, ²⁷ 3¹⁸-²⁰; of Jewish teachers, Mt 11²⁵, Lk 10²¹; Christian, Mt 23³⁴; of those endowed with practical wisdom, 1 Co 6⁵, Eph 5¹⁵, Ja 3¹³; of God, Ro 16²⁷; compar., τ. μωρὸν τ. θεοῦ σοφώτερον, 1 Co 1²⁵.†

SYN.: συνετός, φρόνιμος (v.s. σοφία, SYN.).

Σπανία, -ας, ή (= cl. Ἑσπερία or Ἰβηρία; late writers adopted the Roman name, Ἱσπανία (1 Mac 8³) or Σ. as here), Spain : Ro 15²⁴, ²⁸.†

σπαράσσω, [in LXX: 11 Ki 22⁸ B (בעש hith.), Je 4¹⁹ (המה), Da LXX 8⁷ (שלף hi.), 111 Mac 4⁶ *;] 1. to tear, rend, mangle. 2. to convulse : Mk 1²⁶ (v. Swete, in l.) 9²⁶, Lk 9³⁹ (cf. συν-σπαράσσω).†

σπαργανόω, -ῶ (< σπάργανον, a swathing-band), [in LXX: Jb 38⁹, Ez 16⁴ (חתל pu.) *;] to swathe, wrap in swaddling-clothes : Lk 2⁷, ¹² (Hipp., Arist., Plut.).†

†σπαταλάω, -ῶ (< σπατάλη, wantonness, luxury, Si 27¹³ *), [in LXX: Ez 16⁴⁹ (שקט hi.), Si 21¹⁵ *;] to live riotously : 1 Ti 5⁶, Ja 5⁵ (Polyb.).†

SYN.: στρηνιάω, τρυφάω (v. Tr., Syn., § liv).

σπάω, [in LXX chiefly for שלף;] in cl. poët. for ἕλκω; mostly used in mid. (cf. M, Pr., 157), to draw : μάχαιραν, Mk 14⁴⁷, Ac 16²⁷.†

** σπεῖρα, -ης (on this form of gen., v. M, *Pr.*, 38, 48; Bl., § 7, 1; Mayser, 12; Deiss., *BS*, 186), [in LXX : Jth 14¹¹, ΙΙ Mac 8²³ 12²⁰,²² *;] 1. (= Lat. *spira*) *anything wound* or *rolled up, a coil.* 2. As a military term used (by Polyb. and later writers) of a body of soldiers, *a maniple* (third part of a cohort) or *cohort* (v. Swete, *Mk.*, 375; Westc., *Jo.*, 251 f.) : Mt 27²⁷, Mk 15¹⁶, Jo 18³,¹², Ac 10¹ 21³¹ 27¹.†

σπείρω, [in LXX chiefly for זרע;] *to sow* (seed): absol., Mt 6²⁶ 13³, ⁴, ¹⁸ 25²⁴,²⁶, Mk 4³,⁴, Lk 8⁵ 12²⁴, Jo 4³⁶, ΙΙ Co 9¹⁰; c. acc. rei, Mt 13²⁴,²⁷,³⁷,³⁹, Mk 4³², Lk 8⁵, ι Co 15³⁶,³⁷; seq. εἰς, Mt 13²², Mk 4¹⁸; ἐν, Mt 13²⁴,³¹; ἐπί, c. gen., Mk 4³¹; ἐπί, c. acc., Mt 13²⁰,²³, Mk 4¹⁶,²⁰; παρά, c. acc., Mt 13¹⁹. Metaph.: ι Co 9¹¹ 15⁴²⁻⁴⁴, Ga 6⁷,⁸, Ja 3¹⁸; in proverbial sayings, Mt 25²⁴,²⁶, Lk 19²¹,²², Jo 4³⁷, ΙΙ Co 9⁶, Ga 6⁷; in interpretation of parables, Mt 13¹⁹⁻²³, Mk 4¹⁴⁻²⁰.†

*† σπεκουλάτωρ, -ορος (Rec. -ωρος), ὁ (Lat. *speculator*), 1. prop., *a spy* or *scout.* 2. An *executioner :* Mk 6²⁷ (v. Swete, in l.).†

σπένδω, [in LXX chiefly for נסך hi.;] *to pour out* as a drink-offering, *make a libation;* pass., fig., σπένδομαι, *I am poured out* or *offered as a libation* (in the shedding of my life-blood) : Phl 2¹⁷ (v. Lft., in l.), ΙΙ Ti 4⁶ (for exx. from π., v. Milligan, *Selections*, 114 f.; MM, xxiii).†

σπέρμα, -τος, τό (< σπείρω), [in LXX chiefly for זרע;] *seed;* (*a*) of plants: Mt 13²⁴,²⁷,³⁷,³⁸, ΙΙ Co 9¹⁰; pl., Mt 13³², Mk 4³¹, ι Co 15³⁸; metaph., of an escaping remnant (שָׂרִיד, Is 1⁹; cf. Wi 14⁶; Plat., *Tim.*, 23 c; FlJ, *Ant.*, xi, 5, 3), Ro 9²⁹; (*b*) of men (as γονή; Lat. *semen genitale;* so in cl.; cf. in LXX, Le 15¹⁶, al.) : He 11¹¹; metaph., of the divine influence, ι Jo 3⁹; by meton. (as freq. in poets), *seed, offspring, posterity :* Mt 22²⁴,²⁵, Mk 12¹⁹⁻²², Lk 1⁵⁵ 20²⁸(LXX), Jo 7⁴² 8³³,³⁷, Ac 3²⁵ 7⁵,⁶ 13²³, Ro 1³ 4¹³,¹⁸ 9⁷,⁸ 11¹, ΙΙ Co 11²², Ga 3¹⁶,¹⁹, ΙΙ Ti 2⁸, He 2¹⁶ 11¹⁸; pl. (FlJ, *Ant.*, viii, 7, 6; Plat., *Leg.*, ix, 853 c; ιν Mac 18¹; in Ga, l.c., contrasted with sing., v. Lft., in l.; Milligan, *NTD*, 105 f.), Ga 3¹⁶; of spiritual offspring, Ro 4¹⁶,²⁸ 9⁸, Ga 3⁹, Re 12¹⁷; v. ICC on Ga, pp. 505 ff.†

* σπερμολόγος, -ον (< σπέρμα, λέγω), *a seed-picker;* (*a*) prop., of birds (Arist., Aristoph, al.); (*b*) in Attic slang, of an idler who lives on scraps picked up in the agora; hence, as subst., ὁ σ., *an idle babbler :* Ac 17¹⁸.†

σπεύδω, [in LXX chiefly for מהר pi., also for בהל pi., hi., etc.;] 1. most freq. intrans., *to hasten :* c. inf. (as freq. in cl.), Ac 20¹⁶; ptcp. c. indic., Lk 2¹⁶; c. imperat., Lk 19⁵,⁶; σπεῦσον κ. ἔξελθε, Ac 22¹⁸. 2. Trans., c. acc.; (*a*) *to hasten, urge on, accelerate* (as Hom., *Od.*, xix, 137; Eur., *Med.*, 152; Si 33 (36)⁸) : ΙΙ Pe 3¹², R, mg. (cf. Mayor and ICC, in l., but v. infr.); (*b*) *to desire eagerly* (Pind., *Pyth.*, iii, 110; Eur., *Suppl.*, 161; Is 16⁵) : ΙΙ Pe, l.c., R, txt. (but v. supr.).†

σπήλαιον, -ον, τό, [in LXX chiefly for מְעָרָה;] *a cave, cavern :* Jo 11³⁸, He 11³⁸, Re 6¹⁵; σ. (EV, *den*) λῃστῶν (Je 7¹¹), Mt 21¹³, Mk 11¹⁷, Lk 19⁴⁶.†

*σπιλάς, -άδος, ἡ (on the gender in Ju, l.c., v. Mayor, *Ju.*, 41), 1. poët. in cl., a *rock* or *reef* over which the sea dashes (Polyb., FlJ, al.). Metaph., of men whose conduct causes danger to others, Ju¹², R, txt. (but v. infr.). 2. In late writers = σπίλος (q.v.), a *spot, stain;* metaph., Ju, l.c., R, mg. (cf. Mayor, 41, but v. supr.).†

*σπίλος (Rec. σπῖλος), -ου, ὁ, 1. a *rock, cliff* (Arist., al.). 2. In late writers = Att. κηλίς (v. Rutherford, *NPhr.*, 87 f.), a *spot, stain;* metaph., (a) of moral blemish : Eph 5²⁷; (b) of riotous and lascivious persons (cf. Dion. Hal., quoted by Mayor, in l.) : ιι Pe 2¹³.†

**†σπιλόω, [in LXX : Wi 15⁴*;] to *stain, spot, defile :* c. acc., Ja 3⁶, Ju²³.†

σπλαγχνίζομαι (< σπλάγχνον), [in LXX (act., -ίζω): Pr 17⁵ A, ιι Mac 6⁸ (= -εύω)*;] to *be moved as to the σπλάγχνα* (q.v.), hence, to *feel pity* or *compassion :* absol., Lk 10³³ 15²⁰; ptcp., σπλαγχνισθείς, c. indic., Mt 18²⁷ (c. gen. pers.) 20³⁴, Mk 1⁴¹ (v.l. ὀργίζομαι, WH, mg.; v. Turner, *SNT*, p. 58); seq. ἐπί, c. dat. pers., Mt 14¹⁴, Lk 7¹³; ἐπί, c. acc., Mt 15³², Mk 6³⁴ 8² 9²²; περί, Mt 9³⁶. (The word is elsewhere found only in Sm : ι Ki 23²¹, Ez 24²¹, *Test. Zeb.*, 4⁶, ⁷; v. Thayer, s.v.; MM, xxiii quote Thumb, *Hellen.*, 123 as practically confirming Lft. on Phl 1⁸, in the suggestion that the verb was a coinage of the Jewish dispersion.)†

σπλάγχνον, -ου, τό, mostly (in NT always) in pl., σπλάγχνα, -ων, τά, [in LXX : Pr 12¹⁰ (רַחֲמִים, elsewhere rendered by οἰκτιρμοί, Ps 24 (25)⁶ 39 (40)¹² and by ἔλεος, Is 47⁶), Pr 26²² (בֶּטֶן), Wi 10⁵, Si 30⁷, ιι Mac 9⁵, ⁶, al.;] the *inward parts* (heart, liver, lungs, etc.; Lat. *viscera*): Ac 1¹⁸.   Metaph., of the seat of the feelings and of the feelings themselves (in Gk. poets, of anger, anxiety, etc.), the *heart, affections* (the characteristic LXX and NT reference of the word to feelings of kindness, benevolence and pity, is found in π.; v. MM, xxiii; cf. Lft. on Phl 1⁸) : ιι Co 6¹² 7¹⁵, Phm ⁷, ¹², ²⁰, ι Jo 3¹⁷; σ. οἰκτιρμοῦ, Col 3¹²; σ. καὶ οἰκτιρμοί, Phl 2¹; σ. ἐλέους θεοῦ ἡμῶν, Lk 1⁷⁸; σ. Χριστοῦ Ἰησοῦ, Phl 1⁸.†

*σπόγγος, -ου, ὁ, a *sponge :* Mt 27⁴⁸, Mk 15³⁶, Jo 19²⁹.†

σποδός, -οῦ, ὁ, [in LXX chiefly for אֵפֶר;] *ashes :* He 9¹³; ἐν σάκκῳ καὶ σ. (Is 58⁵, Jo 3⁶, Da LXX 9³, al.), Mt 11²¹, Lk 10¹³.†

σπορά, -ᾶς, ἡ (< σπείρω), [in LXX : ιν Ki 19²⁹ (זֶרַע), ι Mac 10³⁰*;] 1. a *sowing.* 2. *seedtime.* 3. *seed* sown (of human offspring, Soph., Tr., 316, 420) : ι Pe 1²³ (cf. σπέρμα, and v. Milligan, *NTD*, 105 f.).†

σπόριμος, -ον (< σπείρω) [in LXX : Ge 1²⁹, Le 11³⁷ (זֶרַע), Si 40²² א¹*;] *fit for sowing, sown;* as subst., τὰ σ., *corn-fields :* Mt 12¹, Mk 2²³, Lk 6¹.†

σπόρος, -ου, ὁ (< σπείρω), [in LXX chiefly for זֶרַע;] = σπορά, 1. *sowing* or *seedtime.* 2. *seed* sown (so usually in late Gk.) : Mk 4²⁶, ²⁷, Lk 8⁵, ¹¹, ιι Co 9¹⁰ᵃ (LTr.); metaph., of almsgiving, ιι Co 9¹⁰ᵇ.†

σπουδάζω (< σπουδή), [in LXX chiefly for בהל ni.;] to *make haste;* hence, to *be zealous* or *eager, to give diligence :* c. inf. (v. M, *Pr.*, 205 f.),

Ga 2¹⁰, Eph 4³, I Ti 2¹⁷, II Ti 2¹⁵ 4⁹, ²¹, Tit 3¹², He 4¹¹, II Pe 1¹⁰ 3¹⁴;
c. acc. et inf. (on this construction v. Mayor in l.; MM, xxiii), II Pe 1¹⁵
(for other constructions v. LS, s.v.).†

σπουδαῖος, -α, -ον (< σπουδή), [in LXX: Ez 41²⁵ *;] *in haste;*
hence, *zealous, eager, diligent, earnest:* seq. ἐν, II Co 8²²; compar.,
-οτερος, ib. ¹⁷ (here in superl. sense, v. Bl., § 44, 3) ²².†

** σπουδαίως, adv. (< σπουδαῖος), [in LXX: Wi 2⁶ *;] 1. *with haste*
or *zeal,* i.e. *earnestly, zealously, diligently:* Lk 7⁴, II Ti 1¹⁷, Tit 3¹³;
compar., -οτέρως, Phl 2²⁸ (RV, Lft., Weymouth, al., but v. infr.). 2.
hastily, speedily: compar., -οτέρως, Phl 2²⁸ (Thayer, Zorell, s.v.; ICC,
in l., al., but v. supr.).†

σπουδή, -ῆς, ἡ (< σπεύδω), [in LXX chiefly for בֶּהָל, its parts and
derivatives;] 1. *haste, speed:* μετὰ σ. (Wi 19²), Mk 6²⁵, Lk 1³⁹. 2.
zeal, diligence, earnestness: Ro 12¹¹, II Co 7¹¹, ¹² 8⁷, ⁸; ἐν σ., Ro 12⁸
(v. M, Pr, 104); seq. ὑπέρ, II Co 8¹⁶; σπουδὴν ἐνδείκνυσθαι, He 6¹¹; σ.
παρεισφέρειν, II Pe 1⁵; πᾶσαν σ. ποιεῖσθαι, Ju ³ (v. MM, xxiii; M, Pr.,
214; Deiss., BS, 361, 364).†

σπυρίς, v.s. σφυρίς.

στάδιον, -ου, τό, pl., στάδια (Jo 6¹⁹, T), and metapl., στάδιοι (v. Bl.,
§ 9, 1), [in LXX: Da LXX 4⁹, Su ³⁷, II Mac 11⁵ 12⁹ ff. *;] *a stadium,*
i.e. 1. a measure of length = 600 Greek feet or ⅛ of a Roman mile:
Mt 14²⁴ (Rec., WH, txt., R, mg.), Lk 24¹³, Jo 6¹⁹ 11¹⁸, Re 14²⁰ 21¹⁶,
and, this being the length of the Olympic course, 2. a race-course:
I Co 9²⁴.†

στάμνος, -ου (ὁ and), ἡ, [in LXX: Ex 16³³ (צִנְצֶנֶת), III Ki 12²⁴
14³ (בַּקְבֻּק), Da LXX Bel ³² *;] prop., *an earthen jar* for racking off
wine, hence, generally, *a jar:* He 9⁴.†

*† στασιαστής (< στασιάζω, to stir up sedition, Jth 7¹⁵, II Mac 4³⁰ 14⁶ *)
= Att. στασιώτης, *a rebel, revolutionist, one who stirs up sedition:*
Mk 15⁷ (FlJ, al.).†

στάσις, -εως, ἡ (< ἵστημι), [in LXX chiefly for עָמַד, its parts and
derivatives, also for רִיב (Pr 17¹⁴), etc. (v. Deiss., BS, 158 f.);] 1. *a
standing, place, status:* σ. ἔχειν (Polyb., v, 5, 3; and cf. Lat. *locum
habere*), He 9⁸. 2. *insurrection, sedition:* Mk 15⁷, Lk 23¹⁹, ²⁵, Ac 19⁴⁰
24⁵. 3. In poets and late prose, *strife, dissension* (cf. MM, xxiii):
Ac 15² 23⁷, ¹⁰.†

στατήρ, -ῆρος, ὁ, [in Aq., Sm., for שֶׁקֶל;] *a stater;* (a) a weight;
(b) a coin (used by late writers of the Greek τετράδραχμον): Mt 17²⁷
26¹⁶, WH, mg.†

* σταυρός, -οῦ, ὁ, 1. an upright *pale* or *stake* (Hom., Hdt., Thuc.,
al.). 2. In late writers (Diod., Plut., al.) of the Roman instrument
of crucifixion, *the Cross:* of the Cross on which Christ suffered,
Mt 27³², ⁴⁰, ⁴², Mk 15²¹, ³⁰, ³², Lk 23²⁶, Jo 19¹⁷, ¹⁹, ²⁵, ³¹, Col 2¹⁴, He 12²;
θάνατος σταυροῦ, Phl 2⁸; τ. αἷμα τοῦ σ., Col 1²⁰. Metaph., in proverbial
sayings: αἴρειν (λαμβάνειν, βαστάζειν) τὸν σ., Mt 10³⁸ 16²⁴, Mk 8³⁴ 10²¹

416   MANUAL GREEK LEXICON OF THE NEW TESTAMENT

15²¹, Lk 9²³ 14²⁷ (for an interesting ex. of metaph. use in π., v. MM, xxiii).   By meton., for Christ's death on the Cross: I Co 1¹⁷, Ga 5¹¹ 6¹², ¹⁴, Eph 2¹⁶, Phl 3¹⁸; ὁ λόγος ὁ τοῦ σ., I Co 1¹⁸.†

σταυρόω, -ῶ (< σταυρός), [in LXX: Es 7⁹ (תלה), 8¹³ * ;] 1. to fence with pales, impalisade (Thuc.). 2. In late writers (Polyb., FlJ; but ἀνασταυρόω is more common) to crucify: c. acc. pers., Mt 20¹⁹ 23³⁴ 26² 27²² ff. 28⁵, Mk 15¹³ ff. 16⁶, Lk 23²¹, ²³, ³³ 24⁷, ²⁰, Jo 19⁶ ff., Ac 2³⁶ 4¹⁰, I Co 1¹³, ²³ 2², ⁸, II Co 13⁴, Ga 3¹, Re 11⁸; metaph., Ga 5²⁴ 6¹⁴.†

σταφυλή, -ῆς, ἡ, [in LXX for עֵנָב ;] a bunch of grapes: Mt 7¹⁶, Lk 6⁴⁴, Re 14¹⁸. " σ. is properly the ripe grape-cluster as opp. to ὄμφαξ, cf. Ge 40¹⁰, Jb 15³³; as contrasted with βότρυς, it describes the grapes rather than the cluster on which they grow" (Swete, Apoc., 187 f.).†

στάχυς, -υος, ὁ, [in LXX chiefly for שִׁבֹּלֶת ;] an ear of corn: Mt 12¹, Mk 2²³ 4²⁸, Lk 6¹.†

Στάχυς, -υος, ὁ, Stachys: Ro 16⁹ (v. Lft., Phl., 174; MM, xxiii).†

στέγη, -ης, ἡ (< στέγω), [in LXX: Ge 8¹³ (מִכְסֶה), etc. ;] a roof: Mk 2⁴; of entering a house, εἰσέρχεσθαι ὑπὸ τὴν σ., Mt 8⁸, Lk 7⁶ (cf. MM, xxiii).†

** στέγω (cf. Lat. tego), [in LXX: Si 8¹⁷ * ;] 1. prop., to cover closely, to protect by covering, esp. to keep water in or out (Soph., Plat., al.). 2. to cover, keep secret, conceal (Si, l.c., Polyb., al.) : I Co 13⁷, R, mg. 3. By covering to ward off, bear up under, endure (for exx., v., Lft., Notes, 40; M, Th., 36): I Co 9¹² 13⁷, I Th 3¹, ⁵.†

στεῖρος, -ον, also -α, -ον, [in LXX for עֲקָרָה, עֲקֶרֶת ;] barren: of a woman, Lk 1⁷, ³⁶ 23²⁹, Ga 4²⁷ (LXX).†

στέλλω, [in LXX (mid.) : Ma 2⁵ (חתת ni.), Pr 31²⁴ (²⁶), Wi 7¹⁴ 14¹, II Mac 5¹, III Mac 1¹⁹ 4¹¹ * ;] 1. prop., to set, place, arrange, fit out; hence, mid., to set oneself for, prepare (Wi, II Mac, ll. c.). 2. to bring together, gather up (in Hom. of furling sails), hence to restrain, check ; mid., to restrain or withdraw oneself, hold aloof, avoid : II Co 8²⁰ ; seq. ἀπό, II Th 3⁶ (cf. ἀπο-, ἐξ-απο-, συν-απο-, δια-, ἐπι-, κατα-, συ(ν)-, ὑπο-στέλλω).†

* στέμμα, -τος, τό (< στέφω, to put around, enwreath), a wreath, garland : as used in sacrifices, Ac 14¹³.†

στεναγμός, -οῦ, ὁ (< στενάζω), [in LXX for נְאָקָה, אֲנָקָה, אֲנָחָה, etc. ;] a groaning : Ac 7³⁴ (LXX κραυγή), Ro 8²⁶.†

στενάζω, [in LXX for אנח ni., אנק, etc. ;] to groan ("the word denotes feeling which is internal and unexpressed," Mayor, Ja., 162) : Mk 7³⁴, II Co 5², ⁴, He 13¹⁷, Ja 5⁹ (EV, murmur) ; ἐν ἑαυτοῖς, Ro 8²² (cf. ἀνα-, συ(ν)-στενάζω).†

SYN. : v.s. κλαίω.

στενός, -ή, -όν, [in LXX for צר, etc. ;] narrow : fig. (v. MM, xxiii), Mt 7¹³, ¹⁴, Lk 13²⁴.†

στενο-χωρέω, -ῶ (< στενός + χῶρος, space), [in LXX: Jos 17¹⁵ (אִיץ), Jg 16¹⁶ (אלץ pi.), Is 28¹⁹ ⁽²⁰⁾ (קצר) 49¹⁹ (צרר), iv Mac 11¹¹ *;] 1. to be straitened (cf. Is 49¹⁹); metaph., to be anxious (Hipp., al.). 2. In late writers, trans., to straiten, compress (LXX, Diod., al.; π. ap. MM, xxiii): pass., trop., ii Co 4⁸, 6¹².†

στενοχωρία, -ας, ἡ (v. supr.), [in LXX for צוּקָה, etc.;] narrowness of space, want of room (Thuc., al.). Metaph. (Xen., Polyb., De 28⁵³, Wi 5³, al.), difficulty, distress: θλίψις καὶ (ἤ) σ., Ro 2⁹ 8³⁵ (EV, anguish); pl. (cf. Bl., § 32, 6; WM, 220), ii Co 6⁴ 12¹⁰.†
Syn.: θλίψις, q.v.

στερεός, -ά, -όν, [in LXX: Nu 8⁴ (מִקְשָׁה); σ. πέτρα, Is 5²⁸ (צַר), etc.;] hard, firm, solid: τροφή, He 5¹², ¹⁴; θεμέλιος, fig., ii Ti 2¹⁹. Metaph., (a) in bad sense, hard, cruel (Hom., al.); (b) in good sense, steadfast, firm: τ. πίστει, i Pe 5⁹.†

στερεόω, -ῶ (< στερεός), [in LXX: Is 42⁵ (רקע), Je 5³ (חזק pi.), etc.;] (a) to make firm or solid; (b) to strengthen, make strong; c. acc. pers., Ac 3¹⁶; τ. βάσεις, pass., ib.⁷. Metaph. (cf. Je, l.c.): τ. πίστει, pass., Ac 16⁵.†

στερέωμα, -τος, τό (< στερεόω), [in LXX: Ge 1⁶ ᶠᶠ, Ps 18 (19)¹, 150¹, Ez 1²²⁻²⁶ 10¹ 13⁵, Da LXX, ΤΗ 3⁽⁵⁶⁾ 12³ (רָקִיעַ), De 33²⁶ (שׁחק), Ps 17 (18)² 70 (71)³ (סֶלַע), Es 9²⁹, i Es 8⁷⁸ ⁽⁸²⁾, Si 43¹, ⁸, i Mac 9¹⁴ *;] a solid body; (a) a support, foundation (Arist., al.); metaph., strength (Ps 17 (18)⁷⁰, i Mac, ll. c.); steadfastness, firmness: τ. πίστεως, Col 2⁵; (b) the dome of heaven (believed to be a solid canopy), the firmament (LXX).†

Στεφανᾶς, -ᾶ, ὁ, Stephanas: i Co 1¹⁶ 16¹⁵, ¹⁷.†

Στέφανος, -ου, ὁ, Stephen: Ac 6⁵, ⁸, ⁹ 7⁵⁹ 8² 11¹⁹ 22²⁰.†

στέφανος, -ου, ὁ (< στέφω, to encircle), [in LXX chiefly for עֲטָרָה;] 1. that which surrounds or encompasses (as a wall, a crowd: Hom., al.). 2. a crown, i.e. the wreath, garland or chaplet given as a prize for victory, as a festal ornament, or as a public honour for distinguished service or personal worth (so to sovereigns, especially on the occasion of a παρουσία, q.v.; cf. Deiss., LAE, 372 ff.; on its use in LXX for the golden crown of royalty (prop., διάδημα, q.v., cf. Hort and Mayor on Ja 1¹²): Mt 27²⁹, Mk 15¹⁷, Jo 19², ⁵, i Co 9²⁵, Re 4⁴, ¹⁰ 6² 9⁷ 12¹ 14¹⁴. Metaph.: Phl 4¹, Re 3¹¹; τ. δικαιοσύνης (cf. Deiss., LAE, 312), ii Ti 4⁸; τ. δόξης, i Pe 5⁴; καυχήσεως, i Th 2¹⁹ (v. M, Th., in l.); τ. ζωῆς (gen. appos.), Ja 1¹², Re 2¹⁰.†

στεφανόω, -ῶ (< στέφανος), [in LXX for עטר;] c. acc. pers., to crown: of a victor, ii Ti 2⁵. Metaph., δόξῃ κ. τιμῇ, He 2⁷, ⁹ (LXX).†

στῆθος, -ους, τό, [in LXX: Ex 28²³, ²⁶ ⁽²⁹, ³⁰⁾ (לֵב), etc.;] the breast: Jo 13²⁵ 21¹⁰, Re 15⁶; as a sign of penitence, τύπτειν (εἰς) τὸ σ., Lk 18¹³ 23⁴⁸.†

27

† στήκω, late pres., formed from perf., ἕστηκα (v. Bl., § 17 ; WH, *Aₚp*., 169 ; Kennedy, *Sources*, 158 ; M, *Pr*., 238 ; MM, xxiii), [in LXX : Ex 14¹³ A, Jg 16²⁶ B, III Ki 8¹¹ B * ;] = ἵστημι, to stand : Mk 3³¹ 11²⁵, Jo 1²⁶, Re 12⁴ (ἕστηκεν, T). Metaph., to stand firm, stand fast : absol., Ga 5¹ (but v. Field, *Notes*, 189 f.), II Th 2¹⁵ ; seq. ἐν, Jo 8⁴⁴ (ἕστηκεν, T, R, mg.), I Co 16¹³, Phl 1²⁷ 4¹ ; c. dat., Ro 14⁴.†

** στηριγμός, -οῦ, ὁ (< στηρίζω), [in Sm. : Is 3¹ * ;] 1. a setting firmly, supporting. 2. fixedness, firmness, steadfastness : II Pe 3¹⁷.†

στηρίζω, [in LXX for סמך, שׂוּם (שׂים), etc. ;] to fix, set fast, make fast : Lk 16²⁶ ; τ. πρόσωπον (Ez 6² 13¹⁷, al. ; v. Dalman, *Words*, 30 f.), Lk 9⁵¹. Metaph., to confirm, establish : c., acc., Lk 22³², Ac 18²³, Ro 1¹¹ 16²⁵, I Th 3², ¹³, II Th 3³, Ja 5⁸, I Pe 5¹⁰, Re 3² ; id. seq. ἐν, II Th 2¹⁷, II Pe 1¹².†

** στιβάς, -άδος, ἡ, [in Aq. : Ez 46²³ (מִירוֹת) * ;] a litter of leaves or rushes : pl., Mk 11⁸ (Rec. στοιβ-).†

στίγμα, -τος, τό (< στίζω, to prick), [in LXX : Ca 1¹¹ (נְקֻדָּה) * ;] a tattoed mark or brand : τὰ σ. τοῦ Ἰησοῦ, Ga 6¹⁷ (v. Lft., in l. ; Deiss., *BS*, 349 ; *LAE*, 303 ; MM, xxiii).†

στιγμή, -ῆς, ἡ (< στίζω, to prick), [in LXX : Is 29⁵ (פֶּתַע), II Mac 9¹¹ * ;] a prick, a point ; metaph., σ. χρόνου, a moment : Lk 4⁵.†

στίλβω, [in LXX : Na 3³ (לָהַב), etc. ;] to shine, glisten : Mk 9³.†

στοά, -ᾶς, ἡ, [in LXX : Ez 40¹⁸ (רִצְפָה), etc. ;] a portico : Jo 5² ; used of the covered colonnade in the Temple (EV, *porch*), Jo 10²³, Ac 3¹¹ 5¹².†

στοιβάς, v.s. στιβάς.

Στοϊκός, v.s. Στωικός.

** στοιχεῖον, -ου, τό, [in LXX : Wi 7¹⁷ 19¹⁸, IV Mac 12¹³ * ;] prop., one of a row (στοῖχος) or series, hence, 1. the shadow-line of a dial (Aristoph.). 2. an elementary sound or letter of the alphabet (Anth., Plut., π.). 3. the elements or rudiments of knowledge (Arist., al.) : He 5¹² ; πτωχὰ σ., Ga 4⁹ ; σ. τοῦ κόσμου, ib. ³ (v. *ICC* on Ga, pp. 510 ff.), Col 2⁸, ²⁰ (but v. infr.). 4. The material elements of the universe (Plat. ; LXX, ll. c.) : II Pe 3¹⁰, ¹². 5. The heavenly bodies (Diog. Laert.). 6. The demons or tutelary spirits of nature (Enoch., Test. Sol., al. ; for this sense in Ga, Col, ll. c., v. *ICC* on Col 2⁸ ; *Enc. Bibl.*, s.v. "Elements").†

στοιχέω, -ῶ (< στοῖχος, a row), [in LXX : Ec 11⁶ (כָּשֵׁר) * ;] to be in rows (of waves, plants, etc., as well as of men), to walk in line (esp. of marching in file to battle ; Xen., *Cyr.*, vi, 3, 34, al.). Metaph., in late writers, to walk by rule : Ac 21²⁴ ; c. dat., to walk by or in (as a rule of life), Ro 4¹² (cf. MM, xxiii), Ga 5²⁵ 6¹⁶, Phl 3¹⁶ (cf. συν-στοιχέω).†

στολή, -ῆς, ἡ (< στέλλω), [in LXX chiefly for בֶּגֶד, also for לְבֻשׁ, etc. ;] 1. an equipment, an armament (Æsch.). 2. Equipment in clothes, *apparel*, esp. *flowing raiment, a festal robe*: (cf. Jh 3⁶, Es 8¹⁵, ɪ Mac 6¹⁵): Mk 12³⁸ 16⁵, Lk 15²² 20⁴⁶, Re 6¹¹ 7⁹, ¹³, ¹⁴ 22¹⁴.†

στόμα, -τος, τό, [in LXX chiefly for פֶּה;] *the mouth*: of man, Mt 15¹¹, Jo 19²⁹, Ac 11⁸, al.; of animals, Mt 17²⁷, ɪɪ Ti 4¹⁷ (fig.), He 11³³, Ja 3³, al.; fig., of inanimate things (ποταμοῦ, Hom.), ἤνοιξεν ἡ γῆ τὸ σ., Re 12¹⁶; σ. μαχαίρας (Heb. פִּי־חֶרֶב, Ge 34²⁶, al.), the *edge* of the sword, Lk 21²⁴, He 11³⁴; esp. of the mouth as the organ of speech: opp. to καρδία, Mt 12³⁴, Ro 10⁸, ¹⁰; in various phrases (some cl., some resembling Hebrew; cf. Bl., § 40, 9): ἀνοίγειν τ. σ. (v.s. ἀνοίγω); σ. πρὸς σ. (פֶּה אֶל־פֶּה, Nu 12⁸; = cl., κατὰ σ., Hdt., al.), *face to face*, ɪɪ Jo ¹², ɪɪɪ Jo ¹⁴; διὰ τοῦ σ. (of the Holy Spirit), Lk 1⁷⁰, Ac 1¹⁶, al.; ἀπὸ (ἐκ) τοῦ σ. (cf. ἀπὸ σ. εἰπεῖν, Plat., al.), of speaking by word of mouth, Lk 22⁷¹, Ac 22¹⁴; δόλος (ψεῦδος) ἐν τ. σ., ɪ Pe 2²², Re 14⁵ (LXX); metaph., ἡ ῥομφαία τοῦ σ., Re 2¹⁶. By meton., for speech (Soph.): Mt 18¹⁶ (LXX), Lk 19²² 21¹⁵, ɪɪ Co 13¹.

*στόμαχος, -ου, ὁ (< στόμα), prop., *a mouth, an opening;* (a) in early Gk. writers, *the throat;* (b) of the opening of the stomach (Arist.); (c) in later writers (Plut., al.), *the stomach*: ɪ Ti 5²³.†

στρατεία (on the orthogr., v. Deiss., *BS*, 181 f.), -ας, ἡ (< στρατεύω), [in LXX chiefly for צָבָא;] *an expedition, a campaign, warfare*: metaph., ɪɪ Co 10⁴ (-τιά, T), ɪ Ti 1¹⁸.†

**στράτευμα, -τος, τό (< στρατεύω), [in LXX: ɪ Mac 9³⁴, ɪɪ Mac 5²⁴ 8²¹ 12³⁸ 13¹³; pl., Jth 11⁸, ɪv Mac 5¹ *;] 1. = στρατεία (Hdt., al.). 2. *an army, a host*: pl., Mt 22⁷, Re 9¹⁶ 19¹⁴, ¹⁹; = *soldiers, company of soldiers*, Ac 23¹⁰, ²⁷; pl., Lk 23¹¹.†

στρατεύω, and depon., -ομαι, so always in NT (< στρατός, *an encamped army*), [in LXX for מהה hith., יצא, צבא; metaph., ɪv Mac 9²³;] used of the general, *to make war, do battle*, and (chiefly) of the soldiers serving under him, *to serve as a soldier*: Lk 3¹⁴, ɪ Co 9⁷, ɪɪ Ti 2⁴. Metaph. (cf. MM, ii, xxiii), of spiritual conflict, *to war, make war*: ɪɪ Co 10³, ɪ Ti 1¹⁸, Ja 4¹, ɪ Pe 2¹¹.†

στρατηγός, -οῦ, ὁ (< στρατός, ἄγω), [in LXX chiefly for סָגָן (always in pl.), שֹׁטֵר;] 1. a military commander, *a general* (Hdt., al.). 2. A civic commander, *a governor, magistrate* (Hdt., Xen., al.): Ac 16²⁰, ²², ³⁵, ³⁶, ³⁸. 3. The commander of the Levitical guard of the Temple, ὁ σ. τ. ἱεροῦ (EV, *captain of the Temple*): Ac 4¹ 5²⁴, ²⁶; pl., Lk 22⁴, ⁵².†

SYN.: ἄρχων (cf. *EGT* on Ac 16²⁰; Ramsay, *St. Paul*, 217).

στρατιά, -ᾶς, ἡ, [in LXX chiefly for צָבָא;] 1. = στρατός, *an army, a host*: of angels (ɪɪɪ Ki 22¹⁹, al.), Lk 2¹³; of the stars of heaven (Je 8², ɪɪ Ch 33³), Ac 7⁴². 2. As sometimes in cl. (poët.), = στρατεία: ɪɪ Co 10⁴, T (WH, RV, στρατεία).†

στρατιώτης, -ου, ὁ, [in LXX: ɪɪ Ki 23⁸ B¹, ɪɪ Mac 5¹² 14³⁹, ɪɪɪ Mac

3¹², ɪᴠ Mac₃*;] *a soldier :* Mt 8⁹, Mk 15¹⁶, Jo 19², Ac 10⁷, al.; metaph., σ. Χριστοῦ Ἰησ., ɪɪ Ti 2³.†

*† στρατολογέω, -ῶ (< στρατός, λέγω), *to levy a troop, enlist soldiers :* ɪɪ Ti 2⁴ (Diod., Plut., al.).†

στρατοπεδάρχης, v.s. στρατοπέδαρχος.

*† στρατοπέδ-αρχος (Rec. -ης), -ου, ὁ (< στρατόπεδον, ἄρχω), a *military commander,* esp. *the Pretorian prefect :* Ac 28¹⁶ (WH, om.).†

στρατό-πεδον, -ου, τό (στρατός + πέδον, a *plain*), [in LXX : Je 41 (34)¹ (חַיִל), ɪɪ Mac 8¹², al.;] (*a*) *a military camp ;* (*b*) *an army :* Lk 21²⁰.†

στρεβλόω, -ῶ (< στρέφω), [in LXX : ɪɪ Ki 22²⁷ (פתל hithp.), ɪɪɪ Mac 4¹⁴, ɪᴠ Mac 9¹⁷ 12⁴, ¹¹ 15¹⁴*;] *to twist, torture.* Metaph. (cf. ɪɪ Ki, l.c.), *to twist* or *pervert* language : ɪɪ Pe 3¹⁶.†

στρέφω, [in LXX chiefly for הפך, also for סבב, etc.;] *to turn :* c. acc. rei dat. pers., Mt 5³⁹ ; = ἀποσ-, *to bring back,* Mt 27³ (cf. Is 38⁸) ; reflexively (WM, § 38, 1), *to turn oneself,* Ac 7⁴² ; c. acc. seq. εἰς, = μετασ-, *to change,* Re 11⁶. Pass., reflexive, *to turn* oneself : seq. εἰς, Jo 20¹⁴, Ac 7³⁹ 13⁴⁶ ; ptcp., στραφείς, c. indic., Mt 7⁶ 9²² 16²³, Lk 7⁹ 9⁵⁵ 14²⁵ 22⁶¹, Jo 1³⁸ 20¹⁶ ; id. seq. πρός, Lk 7⁴⁴ 10²² (WH, R, om.), ib. ²³ 23²⁸ ; metaph., *to change :* absol., Mt 18³, Jo 12⁴⁰ (cf. ἀνα-, ἀπο-, δια-, ἐκ, ἐπι-, κατα-, μετα-, συ(ν)-, ὑπο-στρέφω).†

** στρηνιάω, -ῶ (< στρῆνος, q.v.), [in Sm. : Is 61⁶ (אכל)*;] a word which first appears in the middle comedy (Rutherford, *NPhr.*, 475 f.), *to run riot, wax wanton :* Re 18⁷, ⁹ (cf. κατα-στρηνιάω).†

Syn. : σπαταλάω (q.v.), τρυφάω.

στρῆνος, -ους, τό (cf. Lat. *strenuus*), [in LXX : ɪᴠ Ki 19²⁸ (שָׁאֲנָן*;] *insolent luxury, wantonness :* Re 18³ (a late word, first found in a Comic poet, ʙ.ᴄ. 300, v. Kennedy, *Sources,* 41, cf. στρηνιάω).†

στρουθίον, -ου, τό, [in LXX chiefly for צִפּוֹר;] dimin. of στρουθός, a *sparrow :* Mt 10²⁹, ³¹, Lk 12⁶, ⁷.†

στρωννύω or στρώννυμι (v. Bl., § 23, 1 ; Veitch, s.v.), [in LXX for יצע hoph., etc.;] *to spread :* ἱμάτια ἐν τ. ὁδῷ (εἰς τ. ὁδόν), Mt 21⁸, Mk 11⁸ ; of making a bed, στρῶσον (sc. τ. κλίνην) σεαυτῷ, Ac 9³⁴ ; of furnishing a room, ἐστρωμένον, *spread* with carpets or carpeted couches (cf. Ez 23⁴¹), Mk 14¹⁵, Lk 22¹².†

* στυγητός, -όν (< στυγέω, to hate), *hated, hateful, odious :* Tit 3³.†

† στυγνάζω (< στυγνός, *sombre, gloomy, sullen,* Is 5¹⁷, Wi 17⁵, Da LXX 2¹²*), [in LXX : Ez 27³⁵, 28¹⁹ 32¹⁰ (שָׁמֵם)*;] *to have a sombre, gloomy* appearance : of the human countenance (RV, *his countenance fell*), Mk 10²² ; of the sky (so στυγνότης, Polyb., iv, 21, 1), Mt 16³ (|[WH]|, R, mg., om.).†

στύλος (T, στῦλος, as in cl.), -ου, ὁ, [in LXX chiefly for עַמּוּד, also for קֶרֶשׁ, etc.;] *a pillar,* regarded especially as a support: σ. πυρός, Re 10¹ ; σ. ἐν τ. ναῷ, fig., Re 3¹². Metaph., Ga 2⁹ ; τ. ἀληθείας, ɪ Ti 3¹⁵.†

Στωικός (Rec. -ϊκός, T, Στοϊκός), -ή, -όν, Stoic : Ac 17¹⁸.†

σύ, pron. of 2nd pers., thou, you, gen., σοῦ, dat., σοί, acc., σέ, pl., ὑμεῖς, -ῶν, -ῖν, -ᾶς (enclitic in oblique cases sing., except after prep. (Bl., § 48, 3), though πρὸς σέ occurs in Mt 25³⁹). Nom. for emphasis or contrast : Jo 1³⁰, ⁴² 4¹⁰ 5³⁸, ³⁹, ⁴⁴, Ac 4⁷, Eph 5³²; so also perhaps σὺ εἶπας, Mt 26⁶⁴, al. (M, Pr., 86); before voc., Mt 2⁶, Lk 1⁷⁶, Jo 17⁵, al.; sometimes without emphasis (M, Pr., 85 f.), as also in cl., but esp. as rendering of Heb. phrase, e.g. υἱός μου εἶ σύ (בְּנִי־אַתָּה, Ps 2⁷), Ac 13³³. The gen. (σοῦ, ὑμῶν) is sometimes placed bef. the noun : Lk 7⁴⁸ 12³⁰, al.; so also the enclitic σου, Mt 9⁶; on τί ἐμοὶ κ. σοί, v.s. ἐγώ.

συγγένεια, -ας, ἡ (< συγγενής), [in LXX chiefly for מִשְׁפָּחָה;] 1. kinship. 2. By meton., kinsfolk, kindred : Lk 1⁶¹, Ac 7³, ¹⁴.†

**†συγγενεύς, v.s. συγγενής.

συγγενής, -ές (dat. pl., -εῦσιν, Mk 6⁴, Lk 2⁴⁴, as though from -εύς, v. Swete, Mk., l.c.; Bl., § 8, 6; cf. ι Mac 10⁸⁹ A א² *;) (< σύν, γένος), [in LXX for דּוֹד, דּוֹדָה, מִשְׁפָּחָה;] 1. congenital, natural, innate. 2. akin to; as subst., a kinsman : Mk 6⁴, Lk 1⁵⁸ 2⁴⁴ 14¹² 21¹⁶, Jo 18²⁶, Ac 10²⁴; of tribal kinship, Ro 9³ 16⁷, ¹¹, ²¹.†

Syn. : ἴδιος, οἰκεῖος (q.v.).

*†συγγενίς, -ίδος, ἡ, late fem. form of συγγενής, q.v., a kinswoman : Lk 1³⁶.†

συγγνώμη, v.s. συνγνώμη.

συγκ-, v. passim συνκ-.

** συγκυρία, -ας, ἡ (< συγκυρέω, to happen), [in Sm. : ι Ki 6⁹ (מִקְרֶה) *;] (more freq. in late writers, συγκύρησις, -ημα), chance, coincidence : κατὰ σ. (v. MM, xxiii), Lk 10³¹ (Hippocr., Eccl.).†

συγχ-, v. passim συνχ-.

σύγχυσις, -εως, ἡ (< συγχέω), [in LXX: Ge 11⁹ (בָּבֶל), ι Ki 5⁶, ¹² (¹¹) 14²⁰ (מְהוּמָה) *;] confusion : of a popular uproar, Ac 19²⁹.†

συζ-, v. passim συνζ-.

συκάμινος, -ου, ἡ, [in LXX for שִׁקְמָה (pl.);] the mulberry tree (Lat. morus ; cf. μόρον, ι Mac 6³⁴ *), the sycamine: Lk 17⁶. (In LXX, σ. appears to represent the συκόμορος (v.s. συκομορέα), but St. Luke distinguishes between the two; v. ICC, in l.; DB, iv, 634.) †

συκῆ (contr. fr. συκέα), -ῆς, ἡ (< σῦκον), [in LXX for תְּאֵנָה;] a fig-tree : Mt 21¹⁹⁻²¹ 24³², Mk 11¹³, ²⁰, ²¹ 13²⁸, Lk 13⁶, ⁷ 21²⁹, Jo 1⁴⁹, ⁵¹, Ja 3¹², Re 6¹³.†

*†συκο-μορέα (Rec. -μωραία, L, -μωρέα), -ας, ἡ, more commonly (so Aq., Sm., Ps 77 (78)⁴⁷, Is 9¹⁰ (⁹)) συκόμορος (< σῦκον + μόρον, the black mulberry), a fig-mulberry, a sycamore : Lk 19⁴ (cf. συκάμινος).†

σῦκον, -ου, τό, [in LXX for תְּאֵנָה] a fig : Mt 7¹⁶, Mk 11¹³, Lk 6⁴⁴ Ja 3¹².†

συκοφαντέω, -ῶ (< σῦκον, φαίνω), [in LXX : Ge 43¹⁸ (בָּלַל hithpo.), Le 19¹¹ (שָׁקַר pi.), Jb 35⁹, Ps 118 (119)¹²², Pr 14³¹ 22¹⁶ 28³, Ec 4¹ (עֹשֶׁק) * ;] to act the συκοφάντης (on conjectures as to the origin of the term, v. LS, s.v.), to accuse falsely (Aristoph., Xen., al.) : Lk 3¹⁴ (R, mg.) 19⁸ (RV, exact wrongfully; but cf. Hatch, Essays, 89 ff., v. also Field, Notes, 56 f. ; MM, xxiv).†

**† συλαγωγέω, -ῶ (< σύλη, booty + ἄγω), to carry off as spoil, lead captive (θυγατέρα, Heliod., Aeth., 10, 35) : metaph., Col 2⁸.†

** συλάω, -ῶ, [in LXX : Ep. Je ¹⁸ * ;] c. acc. pers., to strip, plunder, spoil : II Co 11⁸.†

συλλ-, v. passim συνλ-.

συλ-λαμβάνω, [in LXX for תָּפַשׂ, הָרָה, etc. ;] 1. c. acc., to bring together, collect. 2. to seize, take : c. acc. pers., as a prisoner, Mt 26⁵⁵, Mk 14⁴⁸, Lk 22⁵⁴, Jo 18¹², Ac 1¹⁶ 12³ ; pass., Ac 23²⁷ ; mid., in sense of act., Ac 26²¹ ; σ. ἄγραν ἰχθύων, Lk 5⁹. 3. C. dat. pers., to take part with, assist, succour ; mid., in same sense : Lk 5⁷, Phl 4³. 4. Of a woman, to conceive : absol., Lk 1²⁴ ; seq. ἐν γαστρί, Lk 1³¹ ; c. acc., Lk 1³⁶ ; ib. seq. ἐν τ. κοιλίᾳ, Lk 2²¹ ; metaph., of lust producing sin, Ja 1¹⁵.†

συλ-λέγω, [in LXX chiefly for לָקַט ;] to bring together, collect, gather up : c. acc. rei, Mt 13²⁸⁻³⁰ ; pass., ib. ⁴⁰ ; c. acc., seq. ἀπό, Mt 7¹⁶ ; id. seq. ἐκ, Mt 13⁴¹, Lk 6⁴⁴ ; seq. εἰς, Mt 13⁴⁸.†

συλ-λογίζομαι, [in LXX chiefly for חָשַׁב pi. ;] 1. to compute. 2. to reason : Lk 20⁵.†

συμβ-, v. passim συνβ-.

συμ-βαίνω, [in LXX for עָשָׂה, קָרָא, קָרָה, etc. ;] 1. to stand with the feet together. 2. to come together, come to terms. 3. Of events, to come to pass, happen : c. dat. pers., Mk 10³², Ac 3¹⁰ 20¹⁹, I Co 10¹¹, I Pe 4¹², II Pe 2²² ; absol., τὰ συμβεβηκότα, Lk 24¹⁴ (cf. I Mac 4²⁶) ; c. acc. et inf., Ac 21³⁵.†

συμ-βουλεύω, [in LXX chiefly for יָעַץ ;] 1. to advise, counsel : c. dat. pers., Jo 18¹⁴ ; id. seq. inf., Re 3¹⁸. 2. Mid., to take counsel, consult : seq. ἵνα, Mt 26⁴ ("reciprocal middle," v. M, Pr., 157) ; c. inf., Ac 9²³.†

**† συμβούλιον, -ου, τό (< σύμβουλος), [in LXX : IV Mac 17¹⁷ א * ;] a word of the Graeco-Roman period (cf. Lat. consilium, and v. Deiss., BS, 238) = cl. συμβουλία (Arist., Xen.), 1. counsel : σ. λαμβάνειν, Mt 12¹⁴ 22¹⁵ 27¹, ⁷ 28¹² ; διδόναι, Mk 3⁶ (ποιεῖν, Rec.) ; ποιεῖν, Mk 15¹ (ἑτοιμάζειν, WH, mg.). 2. By meton., a council (IV Mac, l.c. א ; συνέδριον, AR) : Ac 25¹² (v. MM, xxiv).†

σύμβουλος, -ου, ὁ (< σύν, βουλή), [in LXX for יוֹעֵץ and cogn. forms ;] a counsellor, adviser : Ro 11³⁴ (LXX).†

Συμεών, ὁ, indecl., (Heb. שִׁמְעוֹן), Simeon (so always AV ; RV in Lk 2²⁵, ³⁴, Re 7⁷), Symeon, a Heb. name for which the Gk. Σίμων, q.v., was also used ; 1. the son of Jacob (Ge 29³³) : Re 7⁷. 2. An ancestor of our Lord : Lk 3³⁰. 3. An aged worshipper in the Temple :

Lk 2²⁵,³⁴. 4. One surnamed *Niger :* Ac. 13¹. 5. The apostle *Peter :* Ac 15¹⁴, II Pe 1¹ (R, txt., WH, txt., Σίμων).†

συμμ-, v. passim συνμ-.

*† **συμ-μορφίζω** (T, συν-), (< σύμμορφος), *to conform to :* pass. ptcp., Phl 3¹⁰ (v. Lft., *Phl.*, 128).†

*† **σύμ-μορφος,** -ον (< σύν, μορφή), 1. absol., *similar* (Luc.). 2. *conformed to :* c. dat., Phl 3²¹; c. gen., Ro 8²⁹ (v. Bl., § 36, 11; 37, 6).†

συμ-μορφόω, -ῶ, Rec. for -ίζω (q.v.), Phl 3¹⁰.†

συμπ-, v. passim συνπ-.

συμπαθής, -ές (< σύν, πάσχω), [in LXX : Jb 29²⁵ A (אָבֵל), IV Mac 5²⁵ א, 13²³ 15⁴*;] 1. *affected by like feelings, sympathetic :* I Pe 3⁸. 2. *exciting sympathy* (Jb, l.c.; Dion. H.).†

συμ-παρα-μένω, Rec. for παρα-μένω (q.v.), Phl 1²⁵.†

συμπόσιον, -ου, τό (< συμπίνω), [in LXX : Es 7⁷ (מִשְׁתֵּה הַיַּיִן) 4¹⁷, I Mac 16¹⁶, II Mac 2²⁷, III Mac 4¹⁶ 5³⁶ 6³³; σ. οἴνου, Si 34 (31)³¹ 35 (32)⁵, 49¹*;] 1. *a drinking-party.* 2. By meton., of the party itself, the guests (Plut.); pl., σ. σ. (colloq.; v. M, *Pr.*, 97), *in parties or companies :* Mk 6³⁹.†

συμφ-, v. passim συνφ-.

συμ-φέρω, [in LXX : Je 33 (26)¹⁴ (טוֹב), Pr 19¹⁰ (נָאוֶה), Si 30¹⁹, al.;] 1. trans. *to bring together :* c. acc. rei, Ac 19¹⁹. 2. Intrans., and mostly impers., συμφέρει, *it is expedient, profitable or an advantage :* I Co 6¹² 10²³, II Co 8¹⁰; c. inf. (M, *Pr.*, 210), Mt 19¹⁰, Jo 18¹⁴; c. dat., seq. ἵνα (Bl., § 69, 5), Mt 5²⁹, ³⁰ 18⁶, Jo 11⁵⁰ 16⁷. Ptcp., συμφέρων, *profitable :* I Co 12⁷; pl., Ac 20²⁰; (οὐ σ. sc. ἐστιν; = οὐ συμφέρει; cf. Thuc., iii, 44, 2), II Co 12¹; as subst., τὸ σ., *profit,* He 12¹⁰.†

** **σύμ-φορος,** -ον (< συμφέρω), [in LXX : II Mac 4⁵*;] *profitable, useful, expedient.* As subst., τὸ σ. (in cl. usually pl., τὰ σ.), *advantage, profit :* c. gen. pers., I Co 7³⁵ 10³³.†

*† **συμ-φυλέτης,** -ου, ὁ (< σύν, φυλή; cf. σύμφυλος, Aq.: Za 13⁷; and v. Rutherford, *NPhr.,* 255 f.), *a fellow-tribesman, fellow-countryman :* I Th 2¹⁴ (v. M, *Th.,* in l., and Intr. liii). Not found elsewhere.†

σύμ-φυτος, -ον (< συμφύω, *to make to grow together*), [in LXX : Za 11² (בֶּצֶר), Es 7⁷, ⁸ א², Am 9¹³, III Mac 3²²*;] 1. *congenital, innate* (Plat., al.; III Mac, l.c.). 2. *grown along with, united with :* τ. ὁμοιώματι* τ. θανάτου αὐτοῦ (v. Field, *Notes,* 155 f.), Ro 6⁵.†

συμ-φωνέω, -ῶ, [in LXX : Ge 14³ (חבר), IV Ki 12⁸⁽⁹⁾ (אות ni.), Is 7² (נוח), IV Mac 14⁶*;] prop., *to agree in sound, be in harmony* (Plat., Arist.). Metaph., (*a*) *to agree with, agree together :* Lk 5³⁶; c. dat. rei, Ac 15¹⁵; seq. περί, Mt 18¹⁹; pass., c. dat. pers., συνεφωνήθη ὑμῖν, Ac 5⁹; (*b*) *to agree* as to a price (Polyb., Diod.): c. dat. pers., gen. praet., Mt 20¹³; seq. μετά . . . ἐκ, ib. ².†

*† **συμ-φώνησις,** -εως, ἡ (< συμφωνέω), *concord, agreement :* seq. πρός, c. acc. pers., II Co 6¹⁵.†

συμφωνία, -ας, ἡ (< σύμφωνος), [in LXX : Da LXX TH 3⁵,¹⁵,

TH ib. [7, 10] (סומפניה), IV Mac 14³ A*;] 1. *symphony, music:* Lk 15²⁵.
2. *a musical instrument* (Polyb., al.; Da, ll. c.; v. MM, xxiv).†

σύμφωνος, -ον (< σύν, φωνή), [in LXX: Ec 7¹⁵ (14) (לְעֻמַּת), IV Mac
7⁷ 14⁷*;] *agreeing in sound.* Metaph., *har 'onious, agreeing:* ἐκ
συμφώνου (for exx. from π., v. Deiss., *BS*, 255), *by agreement*, I Co 7⁵.†
συμψ-, v. passim συνψ-.

συμ-ψηφίζω, [in LXX: Je 29 (49)²⁰ A*;] *to reckon together,*
count up: Ac 19¹⁹.†

σύν (old Att. ξύν), prep. c. dat., expressing association, fellowship and inclusion. It gradually gave way to μετά, c. gen. (cf. LS, s.v.;
Bl., § 41, 3), and is therefore comparatively infrequent in NT, being
rare in Mt₄, Mk₆, Jo₃, and elsewhere (exx. Ja 1¹¹, II Pe 1¹⁸) only in
Lk (Gosp. and Ac) and Paul. *With, together with:* of companionship
and association, Lk 2¹³, Jo 21³, Ac 10²³, al.; εἶναι σύν τινι, Lk 7¹², Ac
4¹³, Phl 1²³, al.; of partisanship, Ac 4¹³; οἱ σύν τινι (ὄντες), of
attendants, companions or colleagues, Mk 2²⁶, Lk 5⁹, Ac 5¹⁷, al.; of
assistance, ἡ χάρις τ. θεοῦ σὺν ἐμοί, I Co 15¹⁰; of two or more things
together, almost = καί, Lk 23¹¹, Ac 3⁴ 10² 14⁵ 23¹⁵, Eph 3¹⁸; σὺν
Χριστῷ ζῆν, II Co 13⁴; *besides* (FlJ, LXX), σὺν πᾶσι τούτοις, Lk 24²¹.
In composition: *with* (συνχαίρω), *together* (συνωδίνω), *altogether*
(συντελέω).

συν-άγω, [in LXX chiefly for אסף, also for קבץ, etc. (cf.
Kennedy, *Sources*, 128);] *to gather* or *bring together:* of things, Jo
6¹², ¹³; seq. εἰς, Mt 3¹², al.; ἐκεῖ, Lk 12¹⁸; ποῦ, Lk 12¹⁷; συναγαγὼν
πάντα (sc. εἰς ἀργύριον; v. Field, *Notes*, 68, MM, xxiv), *having sold off*
all: Lk 15¹³; of persons, Jo 11⁵²; esp. of assemblies, Mt 2⁴, Jo 11⁴⁷,
Ac 14²⁷, al. Pass., *to be gathered* or *come together:* Mt 22⁴¹, Mk 2²,
Lk 22⁶⁶, al.; seq. ἐπί, Mk 5²¹, Ac 4²⁷; πρός, Mt 13², Mk 4¹, al.; εἰς,
Re 19¹⁷; ἐν, Ac 11²⁶ (but v. infr.); μετά, Mt 28¹²; οὖ, Mt 18²⁰; ὅπου,
Mt 26⁵⁷; ἐκεῖ, Jo 18², al. In late writers (v. Kennedy, *Sources*, 128;
cf. De 22², al.), *to receive hospitably, entertain:* Mt 25³⁵, ³⁸, ⁴³ (Ac 11²⁶,
they were guests of the Church: Moffatt), (cf. ἐπι-συνάγω).

συν-αγωγή, -ῆς, ἡ, [in LXX chiefly for עֵדָה, also for קהל, etc.;]
prop., *a bringing together;* 1. of things, (*a*) *a gathering in* of harvest;
(*b*) *a collection* of money. 2. Of persons, (*a*) *a collecting, assembling*
(Polyb.); (*b*) *an assembly* (MM, xxiv; Deiss., *LAE*, 101 ff.): Re 2⁹
3⁹; esp. of a Jewish religious assembly, *a synagogue:* Lk 12¹¹, Ac 9²,
al.; of a Christian assembly, Ja 2². By meton., of the building in
which the assembly is held, *a synagogue:* Mt 10¹⁷, Mk 1²¹, al. (cf.
Cremer, s.v. ἐκκλησία).
Syn.: ἐκκλησία (q.v.).

*συν-αγωνίζομαι, *to strive together with, to help* (prop., of sharing
in a contest): c. dat. pers. et rei, Ro 15³⁰.†

συν-αθλέω, -ῶ, = συναγωνίζομαι: c. dat. commod., Phl 1²⁷; c. dat.
pers., seq. ἐν, Phl 4³.†

συν-αθροίζω, [in LXX chiefly for קבץ;] *to gather together,*
assemble: c. acc. pers., Ac 19²⁵; pass., Ac 12¹².†

συν-αίρω. [in LXX: Ex 23⁵ (עזב)*;] to take up together: σ. λόγον (of which there are several exx. in π.; v. Deiss., LAE, 118 f.; MM, i, xxiv; M, Pr., 160), to settle accounts, Mt 18²³,²⁴; seq. μετά, c. gen. pers., Mt 25¹⁹.†

*† συν-αιχμάλωτος, -ου, ὁ, a fellow-prisoner (prop., of a captive in war, v. Lft., Col., 234): Ro 16⁷, Col 4¹⁰, Phm ²³.†

** συν-ακολουθέω, -ῶ, [in LXX: II Mac 2⁴,⁶*;] to follow along with, accompany: c. dat. pers., Mk 14⁵¹, Lk 23⁴⁹; seq. μετά, c. gen. pers., Mk 5³⁷.†

** συν-αλίζω, [in Al.: Ps 140 (141)⁴*;] to assemble with: Ac 1⁴ (EV, mg., eating with, but on this rendering and on the force of the pres. ptcp. here, v. Field, Notes, 110).†

* συν-αλλάσσω, to reconcile: impf. (conative, v. M, Pr., 129), Ac 7²⁶.†

συν-ανα-βαίνω, [in LXX for עלה;] to go up with: c. dat. pers., seq. εἰς, c. acc. loc., Mk 15⁴¹, Ac 13³¹.†

**† συν-ανά-κειμαι, [in LXX: III Mac 5³⁹*;] to recline with or together at table: Mt 14⁹, Mk 6²², Lk 7⁴⁹ 14¹⁵; c. dat. pers., Mt 9¹⁰, Mk 2¹⁵, Lk 14¹⁰.†

* συν-ανα-μίγνυμι (acc. to Bl., 8, -μείγνυμι), [in LXX: Ho 7⁸ A (בלל) hithpo.), Ez 20¹⁸ A*;] to mix up together; pass., reflex. and metaph., to associate with (Plut., Ath., al.): I Co 5⁹,¹¹, II Th 3¹⁴ (v. M, Th., 117).†

συν-ανα-παύομαι, [in LXX: Is 11⁶ (רבץ)*;] c. dat. pers., to lie down to rest with, sleep with. Metaph., to be refreshed in spirit with: Ro 15³² (L, om.).†

συν-αντάω, -ῶ, [in LXX for פגע, פגש, קרא, קרה, etc.;] to meet with: c. dat. pers., Lk 9¹⁸,³⁷ 22¹⁰, Ac 10²⁵, He 7¹,¹⁰. Metaph., of events, to happen, befall (Diog. L., Plut., al.): Ac 20²².†

συν-άντησις, -εως, ἡ, Rec. for ὑπάντησις (q.v.), Mt 8³⁴.†

† συν-αντι-λαμβάνομαι, [in LXX: Ge 30⁸ R (†), Ex 18²², Nu 11¹⁷ (נשא), Ps 88 (89)²¹ (כון ni.)*;] to take hold with at the side for assistance; hence, to take a share in, help in bearing, and generally, help (with various constructions, v. LXX, ll. c., Deiss., LAE, 83 f.): c. dat., Lk 10⁴⁰, Ro 8²⁶.†

συν-απ-άγω, [in LXX: Ex 14⁶ (לקח)*;] to lead away with or together (Ex, l.c.). Pass., metaph. (as συμπεριφέρομαι, v. LS, s.v.), to be carried away with: c. dat., Ga 2¹³, II Pe 3¹⁷; of accommodating oneself to (EV, condescend to) things or persons (on the meaning, v. ICC, in l.; Field, Notes, 163), Ro 12¹⁶.†

** συν-απο-θνήσκω, [in LXX: Si 19¹⁰*;] to die with or together: Mk 14³¹, II Co 7³ (v. Meyer, in l.), II Ti 2¹¹.†

συν-απ-όλλυμι, [in LXX chiefly for ספה;] to destroy with or together. Mid., to perish together (with): c. dat. pers., He 11³¹.†

συν-απο-στέλλω, [in LXX: Ex 33²,¹² (שלח), I Es 5²*;] to send along with: c. acc., II Co 12¹⁸ (cf. MM, xxiv).†

*† συν-αρμολογέω, -ῶ (< ἁρμός, λέγω), = cl. συναρμόζω, to fit or frame

together : of the parts of a building, Eph 2²¹ ; of the members of the body, Eph 4¹⁶ (Eccl.).†

συν-αρπάζω, [in LXX : Pr 6²⁵ (לָקַח), II Mac 3²⁷ 4⁴¹, IV Mac 5⁴ *;] "perfective" of ἁ‹π›άζω (v. M, *Pr.*, 113), (*a*) *to seize and carry away* (so most commonly): Ac 27¹⁵ ; (*b*) *to seize and hold :* Lk 8²⁹, Ac 6¹² 19²⁹.†

** συν-αυξάνω, [in LXX : II Mac 4⁴, IV Mac 13²⁷ *;] *to cause to increase* or *grow together.* Pass., *to grow together :* Mt 13³⁰ (Xen., al.).†

συν-βάλλω (Rec. συμ-), [in LXX : II Ch 25¹⁹ (גָּרָה hith.), Is 46⁶ (זוּל), Je 50 (43)³ (סוּת hi.), Wi 5⁸, al. ;] *to throw together,* hence, (*a*) of speech (seq. λόγους, Eur., al.), *to discuss, confer* (sc. λόγους): c. dat. pers., Lk 11⁵³, WH, mg., Ac 17¹⁸ ; seq. πρὸς ἀλλήλους, Ac 4¹⁵ ; (*b*) *to reflect, consider, ponder :* ἐν τ. καρδίᾳ, Lk 2¹⁹ ; (*c*) *to meet with, fall in with :* Ac 20¹⁴ ; in hostile sense, εἰς πόλεμον, c. dat. (εἰς μάχην, Polyb.), Lk 14³¹ ; (*d*) mid., *to contribute* (Polyb., al. ; cf. MM, xxiv) : Ac 18²⁷.†

**† συν-βασιλεύω (Rec. συμ-), [in LXX : I Es 8²⁶ A *;] *to reign together* or *with :* metaph., of sharing the glories of the Kingdom of God, I Co 4⁸, II Ti 2¹².†

συν-βιβάζω (Rec. συμ-), [in LXX : Ex 4¹²·¹⁵, Le 10¹¹, Jg 13⁸, Ps 31 (32)⁸ (ירה hi.) ; Ex 18¹⁶, De 4⁹, Is 40¹³ (יָדַע hi.), ib. ¹⁴ (בִּין hi.), Da TH 9²² (שָׂכַל hi.) *;] 1. *to join* or *knit together, unite :* Eph 4¹⁶, Col 2² (but v. infr.), ib. ¹⁹. 2. *to compare, consider, conclude* (Plat.) : Ac 16¹⁰. 3. *to deduce, prove, demonstrate* (Arist.) : Ac 9²². 4. As in LXX ("translation Greek," = ἐμβιβάζω, metaph.), *to teach, instruct :* I Co 2¹⁶ Ac 19³³, R, mg. (also in Vg., Col 2², *instructi,* but v. supr.).†

** συν-γνώμη (Rec. συγγ-), -ης, ἡ (< συγγιγνώσκω, (*a*) *to agree with ;* (*b*) *to pardon*), [in LXX : Si prol. ¹⁴ (B¹א¹ om.) 3¹³, II Mac 14²⁰ *;] 1. *confession.* 2. *fellow-feeling ;* hence, *concession, allowance :* I Co 7⁶ (v. *ICC,* in l.). 3. *pardon.*†

σύν-δεσμος, -ου, ὁ (< συνδέω), [in LXX for קֶשֶׁר , קֶטֶר , etc. ;] *that which binds together, a bond :* of the ligaments of the body, Col 2¹⁹. Metaph., σ. ἀδικίας, Ac 8²³ ; τ. τελειότητος, Col 3¹⁴ ; τ. εἰρήνης, Eph 4³ (v. Lft., *Col.,* ll. c.).†

συν-δέω, [in LXX for שָׁבַץ, etc.;] (*a*) *to bind together ;* (*b*) *to bind together with :* pass., He 13³.†

* συν-δοξάζω, 1. *to join in approving* (Arist.). 2. In NT only, *to glorify together :* pass., Ro 8¹⁷.†

σύν-δουλος, -ου, ὁ, [in LXX : II Es 4⁷·⁹·¹⁷·²³ 5³·⁶ 6⁶·¹³ (כְּנָת) *;] *a fellow-servant :* Mt 18²⁸⁻³³ 24⁴⁹ ; of servants of the same divine Lord, Col 1⁷ 4⁷, Re 6¹¹ ; so of angels, Re 19¹⁰ 22⁹.†

** συνδρομή, -ῆς, ἡ (< συντρέχω), [in LXX : Jth 10¹⁸, III Mac 3⁸ *;] *a concourse,* esp. of a riotous gathering : Ac 21³⁰ (Arist., Polyb., al.).†

συν-εγείρω, [in LXX : Ex 23⁵ B² (עָזַב), Is 14⁹ (עוּר pil.), IV Mac 2¹⁴ *;] *to raise together :* metaph., of the Christian's mystical resurrection with Christ, Eph 2⁶ ; pass., Col 2¹² 3¹.†

συνέδριον, -ου, τό (< σύν + ἕδρα, a seat), [in LXX : Pr 11¹³ 15²², Je 15¹⁷ (סוֹד), Ps 25 (26)⁴ (מַת), Pr 22¹⁰ (דִּין) 26²⁶ (קָהָל) ; Pr 24⁷ 27²² 31²³, ii Mac 14⁵, iv Mac 17¹⁷ * ;]   1. a council (Plat., Xen., al. ; LXX ; in π., σ. τ. πρεσβυτέρων, Deiss., BS, 156) : of a local Jewish tribunal, Mt 10¹⁷, Mk 13⁹.   2. The supreme ecclesiastical court of the Jews, the Sanhedrin (i.e. Talmudic סַנְהֶדְרִין = συνέδριον) : Mt 5²² 26⁵⁹, Mk 14⁵⁵ 15¹, Lk 22⁶⁶, Ac 5²¹, ²⁷, ³⁴, ⁴¹ 6¹², ¹⁵ 22³⁰ 23¹, ⁶, ¹⁵, ²⁰, ²⁸ (WH, R, mg., om.) 24²⁰ ; of a meeting of the Sanhedrin, Jo 11⁴⁷ ; of the place of meeting, Ac 4¹⁵.†

συν-είδησις, -εως, ἡ (< συνεῖδον), [in LXX : Ec 10²⁰ (מַדָּע), Wi 17¹¹, Si 42¹⁸א * ;]   1. consciousness : c. gen. obj., He 10², i Pe 2¹⁹.   2. In ethical sense, innate discernment, self-judging consciousness, conscience (Stoics and late writers) : Ro 2¹⁵ 9¹, i Co 10²⁹, ii Co 1¹² 4² 5¹¹, i Ti 4², He 9¹⁴ ; σ. ἀγαθή, Ac 23¹, i Ti 1⁵, ¹⁹, i Pe 3¹⁶, ²¹ ; ἀσθενής, i Co 8⁷, ¹⁰ ; ἀσθενοῦσα, ib. ¹² ; ἀπρόσκοπος, Ac 24¹⁶ ; καθαρά, i Ti 3⁹, ii Ti 1³ ; καλή, He 13¹⁸ ; πονηρά, He 10²² ; ὁ νοῦς καὶ ἡ σ., Tit 1¹⁵ ; διὰ τὴν σ., Ro 13⁵, i Co 10²⁵, ²⁷, ²⁸ ; κατὰ σ., He 9⁹ ; ὑπὸ (τῆς) σ., Jo 8 [⁹] (Rec.), i Co 10²⁹ (cf. Cremer, 233 ff. ; ICC on Ro 2¹⁵ ; DB, i, 468 ff.).†

** συν-εῖδον, irreg. aor. of συνοράω (v.s. εἶδον), [in LXX : i Mac 4²¹ א, ii Mac 2²⁴ 4⁴, ⁴¹ R 5¹⁷ 7⁴, ²⁰ 8⁸, iii Mac 2⁸ A * ;] ; 1. to see together or at the same time (Arist., Xen.).   2. to see in one view, hence, of mental vision, to comprehend, understand (LXX, Polyb., Plut., al.) : Ac 12¹² 14⁶ (on the related σύνοιδα, v. s.v.).†

* σύν-ειμι (< εἶμι, to go), to come together : Lk 8⁴.†

σύν-ειμι (< εἰμί, to be), [in LXX : Je 3²⁰ (רֵעַ), al. ;]   to be with : Lk 9¹⁸ (WH, mg., συνήντησαν), Ac 22¹¹.†

συν-εισ-έρχομαι, [in LXX : Jb 22⁴ (בּוֹא עִם), etc. ;] to enter together : c. dat. pers., seq. εἰς, c. acc. loc., Jo 6²² 18¹⁵.†

*† συν-έκδημος, -ου, ὁ (< ἔκδημος, abroad), a fellow-traveller : Ac 19²⁹, ii Co 8¹⁹.†

*† συν-εκ-λεκτός, -ή, -όν, chosen together with, co-elect : ἡ ἐν Βαβυλῶνι συνεκλεκτή (on the meaning, v. ICC, in l.), i Pe 5¹³.†

** συν-ελαύνω, [in LXX : ii Mac 4²⁶, ⁴² 5⁵ * ;] to drive together, force together : εἰς εἰρήνην, Ac 7²⁶, Rec. (WH, RV, συνήλλασσεν).†

* συν-επι-μαρτυρέω, -ῶ, to join in attesting, bear witness together with : He 2⁴ (Arist., Polyb., al.).†

συν-επι-τίθημι, [in LXX for שִׁית, etc. ;] to help in putting on. Mid., to join in attacking (Thuc.) : Ac 24⁹ (RV, joined in the charge). †

** συν-έπομαι, [in LXX : ii Mac 15², iii Mac 5⁴⁸ R 6²¹ * ;] to follow with, accompany : c. dat. pers., Ac 20⁴.†

** συνεργέω, -ῶ, [in LXX : i Es 7², i Mac 12¹ * ;] 1. prop., to work together (with) : absol., Mk 16[²⁰], i Co 16¹⁶, ii Co 6¹ ; c. dat., Ja 2²² ; dat. commod., Ro 8²⁸, T, R, txt. (but v. infr.).   2. In Hellenistic writers (M, Pr., 65), trans., to cause to work together (cf. ICC, in l.) : c. acc. rei, Ro 8²⁸ [WH] R, mg. (but v. supr.).†

** συνεργός, -οῦ, [in LXX: ΙΙ Mac 8⁷ 14⁵ *;] *a fellow-worker :* c. gen. pers., Ro 16³, ⁹, ²¹, Phl 2²⁵ 4³, ι Th 3², Rec., Phm ¹, ²⁴ ; θεοῦ (cf. Lft., *Notes*, 41, 188), ι Co 3⁹ (pl.), ι Th 3² [WH] R, mg. (R, txt., διάκοιον τοῦ θ. ; ɔn the original reading, v. *ICC*, in l.) ; τ. χαρᾶς ὑμῶν, ΙΙ Co 1²⁴ ; τ. ἀληθείᾳ, ΙΙΙ Jo ⁸ ; seq. εἰς, ΙΙ Co 8²³, Col 4¹¹.†

συν-έρχομαι, [in LXX for הָלַךְ, בּוֹא, אָסַף ni., etc. ;] 1. (cl.) *to come together, assemble :* Mk 3²⁰ 14⁵³, T, WH, txt., Ac 1⁶ 2⁶ 10²⁷ 16¹³ 19³² 21²² 22³⁰ 28¹⁷, ι Co 14²⁶ ; seq. εἰς, c. acc. loc., Ac 5¹⁶ ; ἐπὶ τ. αὐτό, ɑ Co 11²⁰ 14²³ ; c. dat. pers., Mk 14⁵³, WH, mg., R (πρὸς αὐτόν, v. Field, *Notes*, 40), Jo 11³³ ; ἐν ἐκκλησίᾳ, ι Co 11¹⁸ ; ἐνθάδε, Ac 25¹⁷ ; αὐτοῦ, Mk 6³³, WH, mg. (cf. WH, *Intr.*, 95 ff.) ; ὅπου, Jo 18²⁰ ; c. inf., Lk 5¹⁵ ; εἰς τ. φαγεῖν, ι Co 11³³ ; εἰς τ. ἧσσον, ι Co 11¹⁷, ³⁴ ; of sexual intercourse (Xen., al.; γυναικί or absol.), Mt 1¹⁸. 2. In later-sense (v. exx. in Milligan, *Selections*, 64, 105), *to accompany :* c. dat. pers., Lk 23⁵⁵, Ac 1²¹ 9³⁹ 10²³, ⁴⁵ 11¹² ; seq. σύν, Ac 21¹⁶ ; εἰς, Ac 15³⁸.†

συν-εσθίω, [in LXX : Ge 43³² Ex 18¹² (אכל), ΙΙ Ki 12¹⁷ (ברה), Ps 100 (101)⁵ *;] *to eat with* one : c. dat. pers., Lk 15², Ac 10⁴¹ 11³, ι Co 5¹¹ ; seq. μετά, c. gen. pers., Ga 2¹².†

σύνεσις, -εως, ἡ (< συνίημι), [in LXX for בִּינָה and cogn. forms, חָכְמָה, דַּעַת, מַשְׂכִּיל, etc. ;] 1. *a running* or *flowing together* (Hom.). 2. *(a) understanding :* Lk 2⁴⁷, ι Co 1¹⁹ (LXX), Eph 3⁴, Col 1⁹ 2², ΙΙ Ti 2⁷ ; *(b) the understanding, the mind* or *intelligence :* Mk 12³³.†

SYN. : v.s. σοφία.

συνετός, ή, -όν (< συνίημι), [in LXX for נָבוֹן, חָכָם, etc. ;] *intelligent, sagacious, understanding :* Mt 11²⁵, Lk 10²¹, Ac 13⁷, ι Co 1¹⁹ (LXX).†

** συν-ευ-δοκέω, -ῶ, [in LXX : ι Mac 1⁵⁷ 4²⁸ א¹, ΙΙ Mac 11²⁴, ³⁵ *;] *to join in approving, consent, agree to* or *with :* absol., Ac 22²⁰ ; c. dat. pers., Ro 1³² ; c. dat. rei, Lk 11⁴⁸, Ac 8¹ ; c. inf., ι Co 7¹², ¹³ (chiefly in late writers).†

* συν-ευωχέω, -ῶ, *to entertain together.* Pass., *to fare sumptuously* or *feast together* or *with :* Ju ¹² ; c. dat. pers., ΙΙ Pe 2¹³ (Arist., Luc., al.).†

* συν-εφ-ίστημι, *to place over.* Pass., 1. *to stand over* (Thuc.). 2. *to rise together :* seq. κατά, c. gen. pers. (*against*), Ac 16²².†

συν-έχω, [in LXX for עָצַר, חָבַר, etc.;] 1. *to hold together* (τ. σνι έχον τ. πάντα, Wi 1⁷) : of closing the ears, Ac 7⁵⁷ (τ. στόμα, Is 52¹⁵); *to hem in, press on every side :* Lk 8⁴⁵ 19⁴³. 2. *to hold fast; (a)* of a prisoner, *to hold in charge* (Luc.; cf. exx. in Deiss., *BS*, 160; MM, xxiv) : Lk 22⁶³ ; *(b) to constrain :* ΙΙ Co 5¹⁴ ; pass., Lk 12⁵⁰, Ac 18⁵ (τ. λόγῳ ; cf. Field, *Notes*, 128), Phl 1²³ ; in pass., of ills, *to be seized* or *afflicted by, suffering from :* Mt 4²⁴, Lk 4³⁸ 8³⁷, Ac 28⁸.†

* συν-ζάω (Rec. συζ-), *to live with :* opp. to συναποθανεῖν, ΙΙ Co 7³ ; of life in union with Christ, here and hereafter, Ro 6⁸, ΙΙ Ti 2¹¹.†

συν-ζεύγνυμι (Rec. συζ-), [in LXX : Ez 1¹¹, ²³ (חבר) *;] *to yoke together :* metaph., of union in wedlock, Mt 19⁶, Mk 10⁹.†

MANUAL GREEK LEXICON OF THE NEW TESTAMENT   429

συν-ζητέω (Rec. συζ-), -ῶ, [in LXX : Ne 2⁴ AB¹ (בקשׁ pi.)*;] 1.
to search or *examine together* (Plat.). 2. In NT (and π., v. MM,
xxiii; also in MGr., v. Kennedy, *Sources*, 155), *to discuss, dispute*:
Mk 1²⁷ 12²⁸, Lk 24¹⁵ ; seq. quæst. indir., Mk 9¹⁰ ; c. dat. pers., Mk 8¹¹,
Ac 6⁹ ; seq. πρός, c. acc. pers., Mk 9¹⁴, ¹⁶, Ac 9²⁹; id. seq. quæst.
indir., Lk 22²³.†

*† συν-ζήτησις (Rec. συζ-), -εως, ἡ, *disputation*: Ac 28²⁹ (WH,
R, txt., om.).†

*† συν-ζητητής (Rec. συζ-), -οῦ, ὁ (< συνζητέω), *a disputer, disputant*:
ɪ Co 1²⁰.†

** σύν-ζυγος (Rec. συζ-), or as WH, mg., Σύνζυγος, -ον (< συν-
ζεύγνυμι), [in Aq., Ez 23²¹*;] *a yoke-fellow*. Prob., as proper name,
Σ. γνήσιε, *genuinely Synzygus, S. properly so-called*, Phl 4³ (v. ICC,
Lft., in l.; MM, xxiii).†

*† συν-ζωο-ποιέω (Rec. συζ-), -ῶ, *to make alive* or *quicken together
with*; metaph., of the spiritual life : τ. Χριστῷ, Eph 2⁵; σὺν τ. Χ.,
Col 2¹³.†

* συν-ήδομαι, *to rejoice together*; c. dat., *to rejoice with* or *in*: τ.
νόμῳ τ. θεοῦ, Ro 7²² (v. Lft., *Notes*, 304).†

** συνήθεια, -ας, ἡ (< ἦθος), [in LXX : ɪv Mac 2¹² 6¹³ 13²², ²⁷*;] 1.
intimacy. 2. *habit, custom*: Jo 18³⁹, ɪ Co 11¹⁶; c. gen. obj. (cf.
Æschin., 23, 37, and v. MM, xxiv), *habitual use, force of habit* with
respect to, ɪ Co 8⁷.†

*† συν-ηλικιώτης (< ἡλικία), = συνῆλιξ (Æsch.), *one of the same age,
an equal in age*: Ga 1¹⁴.†

* συν-θάπτω, *to bury together with*: in symbolical sense, of baptism,
αὐτῷ (*with Christ*), Ro 6⁴, Col 2¹².†

συν-θλάω, -ῶ, [in LXX for מחץ , etc. ;] *to crush together, crush*:
Mt 21⁴⁴ ([WH], R, mg., om.), Lk 20¹⁸.†

συν-θλίβω, [in LXX : Ec 12⁶ א A (רצץ), Si 34 (31)¹⁴, ɪ Mac
15¹⁴ A *;] *to press together, press on all sides*: Mk 5²⁴, ³¹.†

*† συν-θρύπτω, *to break in pieces, crush*: metaph., τ. καρδίαν,
Ac 21¹³.†

συν-ίημι and συνίω (v. Bl., § 23, 7), [in LXX chiefly for בין hi.,
שׂכל hi. ;] 1. *to bring* or *set together*. 2. Metaph., *to perceive, understand* (to know by perception, to join the perception with the thing perceived): Mt 13¹³⁻¹⁵ (LXX), ¹⁹ 15¹⁰, Mk 4⁹ (WH, mg.), ¹² 7¹⁴ 8¹⁷, ²¹, Lk 8¹⁰, Ac
7²⁵ 28²⁶, ²⁷, Ro 15²¹ (LXX), ɪɪ Co 10¹² ; c. acc. rei, Mt 13²³, ⁵¹, Lk 2⁵⁰ 18³⁴
24⁴⁵ ; seq. ὅτι, Mt 16¹² 17¹³ ; seq. quæst. indir., Eph 5¹⁷ ; ἐπὶ τ. ἄρτοις,
Mk 6⁵² ; as subst., συνίων (ὁ σ., WH, mg.), *a man of understanding*,
i.e. in moral and religious sense, Ro 3¹¹ (LXX).†

συνιστάνω and συνιστάω, v.s. συνίστημι.

συν-ίστημι, [in LXX for צוה pi., קהל ni., etc. ; ɪ Mac 12⁴³, ɪɪ Mac
4²⁴, ɪɪɪ Mac 1¹⁹ (and freq. in these books) ;] 1. trans., (*a*) *to commend,
recommend*: c. acc. pers., ɪɪ Co 3¹ 6⁴ 10¹², ¹⁸ ; id. c. dat., Ro 16¹ (as
freq. at the beginning of a letter; Deiss., *LAE*, 226), ɪɪ Co 5¹² ; seq.
πρός, ɪɪ Co 4² ; pass., seq. ὑπό,, ɪɪ Co 12¹¹ ; (*b*) *to show, prove, establish*:
c. acc., Ro 3⁵ 5⁸, ɪɪ Co 6⁴ ; dupl. acc., Ga 2¹⁸ ; acc. et inf., ɪɪ Co 7¹¹

2. Intrans., pf., συνέστηκα (as also 2 aor. and plpf.); (a) to stand with or near : Lk 9³²; (b) to be composed of, consist, cohere : Col 1¹⁷ (v. Lft., in l.), ii Pe 3⁵.†

συν-κάθημαι (Rec. συγκ-), [in LXX : Ps 100 (101)⁶ (ישב) *;] to sit together or with : c. dat., Ac 26³⁰; seq. μετά, c. gen., Mk 14⁵⁴.†

συν-καθίζω (Rec. συγκ-), [in LXX for ישב, רבץ;] 1. trans., to make to sit together : c. acc. pers., seq. ἐν, Eph 2⁶. 2. Intrans. = mid., to sit together : Lk 22⁵⁵.†

*† συν-κακοπαθέω (Rec. συγκ-), -ῶ, to bear evil treatment along with, take one's share of ill-treatment : ii Ti 2³; c. dat. commod., τ. εὐαγγελίῳ, ib. 1⁸.†

*† συν-κακουχέομαι (Rec. συγκ-), -οῦμαι, pass., to endure adversity with : c. dat. pers., He 11²⁵. Not elsewhere.†

συν-καλέω (Rec. συγκ-), -ῶ, [in LXX for קרא;] to call together : c. acc., Mk 15¹⁶, Lk 15⁶, ⁹ (v.l. -εῖται, v. Bl., § 55, 1), Ac 5²¹. Mid., to call together to oneself : Lk 9¹ (and v.l. in 15⁶, ⁹, v. supr.) 23¹³, Ac 10²⁴ 28¹⁷.†

συν-καλύπτω (Rec. συγκ-), [in LXX chiefly for כסה pi.;] to veil or cover completely : c. acc., pass., Lk 12².†

συν-κάμπτω (Rec. συγκ-), [in LXX : Ps 68¹⁰, ²³ (מעד hi.), etc. ;] to bend completely, bend together : τ. νῶτον, fig., Ro 11¹⁰ (LXX).†

συν-κατα-βαίνω (Rec. συγκ-), [in LXX : Ps 48 (49)¹⁷ (ירד), Wi 10¹³, Da LXX TH 3 (49) * ;] to go down with : Ac 25⁵. In late writers also metaph. (Wi, l.c.), to condescend, on wh. v. Rutherford, NPhr., 485 f.†

*† συν-κατά-θεσις (Rec συγκ-), -εως, ἡ (< συνκατατίθημι), concord, agreement : ii Co 6¹⁶ (Polyb., Plut., al.).†

*† συν-κατα-νεύω, to agree, consent to : Ac 18²⁷, WH, mg. (Polyb.).†

συν-κατα-τίθημι (Rec. συγκ-), [in LXX : Ex 23¹ (שית יד), ib. ³² (כרת), Da TH Su ²⁰ * ;] to deposit together. Mid., to deposit one's vote with, hence, to agree with, assent to : c. dat., Lk 23⁵¹.†

*† συν-κατα-ψηφίζω (Rec. συγκ-), 1. to condemn with or together (Plut., Themist., 21). 2. to vote one a place among : pass., Ac 1²⁶. Not elsewhere.†

συν-κεράννυμι (Rec. συγκ-), [in LXX : Da LXX 2⁴³ (ערב ithpa.), ii Mac 15³⁹ *;] to mix or blend together, compound : c. acc., i Co 12²⁴; ptcp. pf. pass., He 4², T, WH, mg., R, mg.; id., of persons, c. dat. instr., to be united with, agree with, ib., WH, txt., R, txt. (v. Westc., in l.).†

* συν-κινέω (Rec. συγκ-), -ῶ, to move together. Metaph., to excite, stir up : τ. λαόν, Ac 6¹² (Arist., Polyb., al.).†

συν-κλείω (Rec. συγκ-), [in LXX chiefly for סגר;] to shut together, enclose, shut in on all sides : of a catch of fish, Lk 5⁶; metaph. (Ps 30 (31)⁹, al.), Ro 11³², Ga 3²², ²³.†

*† συν-κληρο-νόμος (Rec. συγκ-), -α, -ον, as subst., ὁ, a co-inheritor, fellow-heir : Ro 8¹⁷, Eph 3⁶; c. gen. rei, He 11⁹, i Pe 3⁷ (for exx., v. Deiss., LAE, 88 f.).†

*συν-κοινωνέω (Rec. συγκ-), -ῶ, *to have fellowship with* or *in* (in cl., c. gen. rei, dat. pers.): c. dat. rei, Eph 5¹¹, Re 18⁴; id. c. gen. pers., Phl 4¹⁴.†

*†συν-κοινωνός (Rec. συγκ-), -όν, *partaking jointly of:* c. gen. rei, Ro 11¹⁷, 1 Co 9²³; id. c. gen. pers., Phl 1⁷; seq. ἐν, Re 1⁹.†

συν-κομίζω (Rec. συγκ-), [in LXX: Jb 5²⁶ (עלה) *;] 1. *to bring together, collect* (Hdt., Xen., al.). 2. *to take up* a body for burial (Soph., *Aj.*, 1048): Ac 8² (v. Field, *Notes*, 116).†

συν-κρίνω (Rec. συγκ-), [in LXX chiefly for פתר;] 1. *to compound, combine:* 1 Co 2¹³, R, mg.₁ (Lft., *Notes*, 180 f.). 2. In Arist. and later writers (Wi 7²⁹, al.) = παραβάλλω, *to compare:* 1 Co, l.c., R, txt. (Field, *Notes*, 168), 11 Co 10¹². 3. In LXX, of dreams, *to interpret* (Ge 40⁸, al.): 1 Co, l.c., R, mg.₂ (but v. reff. supr.).†

συν-κύπτω (Rec. συγκ-), [in LXX: Jb 9²⁷ (עזב), Si 12¹¹ 19²⁶ *;] 1. *to bend forwards* (Arist., al.). 2. *to be bowed down:* Lk 13¹¹.†

συν-λαλέω (Rec. συλλ-), -ῶ, [in LXX for דבר pi., שׂיח;] *to talk with* or *together:* c. dat. pers., Mk 9⁴, Lk 9³⁰ 22⁴; seq. μετά, c. gen., Mt 17³, Ac 25¹²; πρός, c. acc., Lk 4³⁶.†

συν-λυπέω (Rec. συλλ-), -ῶ, [in LXX: Ps 68 (69)²⁰, Is 51¹⁹ (נחד) *;] *to make to grieve with* (Arist.). Pass., *to be moved to grief* by sympathy: seq. ἐπί, c. dat., Mk 3⁵.†

*συν-μαθητής (Rec. συμμ-), -οῦ, ὁ, *a fellow-disciple:* Jo 11¹⁶ (on the use of συν- in such compounds as this, v. Rutherford, *NPhr.*, 255 f.).†

*συν-μαρτυρέω (Rec. συμμ-), -ῶ, *to bear witness with:* Ro 2¹⁵; c. dat., Ro 8¹⁶; seq. ὅτι, Ro 9¹.†

†συν-μερίζω (Rec. συμμ-), [in LXX: Pr 29²⁴ א² (חלק) *;] *to distribute in shares.* Mid., *to have a share in:* 1 Co 9¹³ (Diod., al.).†

*συν-μέτοχος (Rec. συμμ-), -ον, *partaking together with;* as subst., ὁ σ., *a joint partaker* (c. dat. pers. et gen. rei, FlJ, *BJ*, i, 24, 6): c. gen. rei, Eph 3⁶; c. gen. pers., ib. 5⁷ (Arist.).†

*†συν-μιμητής (Rec. συμμ-), -οῦ, ὁ, *a fellow-imitator:* c. gen. obj., Phl 3¹⁷ (v. *ICC*, in l.). Not elsewhere.†

συν-μορφίζω, v.s. συμμορφίζω.

†συν-οδεύω, [in LXX: Za 8²¹ א¹(הלך), To 5¹⁶ א, Wi 6²³ *;] *to journey with:* c. dat. pers., Ac 9⁷ (Plut., al.).†

συνοδία, -ας, ἡ, [in LXX: Ne 7⁵, ⁶⁴ (יחשׂ) *;] 1. *a journey in company* (Plut., al.). 2. By meton., a *company* of travellers, a *caravan:* Lk 2⁴⁴.†

σύν-οιδα, pf. with pres. meaning (v.s. οἶδα), [in LXX: Le 5¹ (ידע), Jb 27⁶; ptcp., 1 Mac 4²¹ A, 11 Mac 4⁴¹ A, 111 Mac 2⁸ R *;] 1. *to share the knowledge of, be privy to* (Hdt., Thuc., al.): ptcp., Ac 5². 2. C. pron. reflex., *to be conscious of* (Eur., Plat., al.), esp. of guilty consciousness: οὐδὲν γὰρ ἐμαυτῷ σ., *for I know nothing against myself,* 1 Co 4⁴.†

συν-οικέω, -ῶ, [in LXX for בעל, etc.;] *to dwell together:* of man and wife (Hdt., al.), c. dat. pers., 1 Pe 3⁷.†

** συν-οικοδομέω, -ῶ, [in LXX : 1 Es 5⁶⁸ * ;] to build together or with (c. dat. pers., 1 Es, l.c.).   2. Of various materials, to build up together (Thuc., al.) : metaph., of Christians, Eph 2²².†

* συν-ομιλέω, -ῶ, to converse with (absol., FlJ, BJ, v, 13, 1; seq. μετά, Cebes, 13) : c. dat. pers., Ac 10²⁷.†

*† συν-ομορέω, -ῶ, to border on : c. dat., Ac 18⁷ (Byz.).†

συν-οράω, v.s. συνεῖδον.

συν-οχή, -ῆς, ἡ (< συνέχω), [in LXX : Jg 2³ (?), Jb 30³ (שׁוֹאָה), ib. 38²⁸ A; Mi 5¹ (4¹⁴), Je 52⁵ (מָצוֹר) * ;] 1. a holding or being held together.   2. a narrow place (Hom., al.).   Metaph., straits, distress : Lk 21²⁵ ; καρδίας, II Co 2⁴.†

** συν-παθέω (Rec. συμπ-), -ῶ, [in LXX : iv Mac 5²⁵ AR 13²³ * ;] to have a fellow-feeling for or with, sympathize with or in : c. dat. rei, He 4¹⁵ ; dat. pers., ib. 10³⁴ (Arist., Plut., al.).†

συν-παρα-γίνομαι (Rec. συμπ-), [in LXX : Ps 82 (83)⁸ (לוה ni.) * ;] 1. to come up or be present together : seq. ἐπί, Lk 23⁴⁸.   2. to come up to assist (Thuc., al. ; II Ti 4¹⁶, Rec.).†

* συν-παρα-καλέω (Rec. συμπ-), -ῶ, to call upon or exhort together (Plat.).   Pass., to be strengthened or comforted with and among : Ro 1¹².†

συν-παρα-λαμβάνω (Rec. συμπ-), [in LXX : Ge 19¹⁷ (מסה ni.), Jb 1⁴ (שׁלח), III Mac 1¹ * ;] to take along with : as a companion, c. acc., Ac 12²⁵ 15³⁷, ³⁸ (on the tenses, v. M, Pr., 130), Ga 2¹.†

συν-πάρειμι (Rec. συμπ-), [in LXX : To 12¹² AB, Pr 8²⁷ (?), Wi 9¹⁰ * ;] to be present together or with : c. dat. pers., Ac 25²⁴.†

** συν-πάσχω (Rec. συμπ-), [in Al. : 1 Ki 22⁸ * ;] 1. to suffer together or with : Ro 8¹⁷, I Co 12²⁶.   2. to sympathize with (Plat., Arist.).†

* συν-πέμπω (Rec. συμπ-), to send together with : c. acc. et dat., II Co 8²² ; id. seq. μετά, c. gen., ib. ¹⁸.†

συν-περι-λαμβάνω (Rec. συμπ-), 1. to enclose (Ez 5³ (צרר) *).   2. to embrace : c. acc. pers., Ac 20¹⁰.†

συν-πίνω (Rec. συμπ-), [in LXX : Es 7¹ (שָׁתָה עִם) ;] to drink with : c. dat. pers., Ac 10⁴¹.†

συν-πίπτω (Rec. συμπ-), [in LXX for נפל, etc. ;] to fall together, fall in, etc. : of a house (cf. MM, xxiv), Lk 6⁴⁹.†

συν-πληρόω (Rec. συμπ-), -ῶ, [in LXX : Je 25¹² (מָלֵא) * ;] 1. to fill up completely (Thuc., of manning ships) : of a ship filling with water, and by meton., of those on board, Lk 8²³.   2. to complete, fulfil : of time (Je, l.c., and v. MM, xxiv), Lk 9⁵¹, Ac 2¹ (on the "durative inf.," v. M, Pr., 233).†

* συν-πνίγω (Rec. συμπ-), to choke : of thronging by a crowd, Lk 8⁴². Fig., of seed, τ. λόγον, Mt 13²², Mk 4⁷, ¹⁹, Lk 8¹⁴.†

* συν-πολίτης (Rec. συμπ-), -ου, ὁ, a fellow-citizen : pl., σ. τ. ἁγίων, opp. to ξένοι κ. πάροικοι, Eph 2¹⁹ (Eur. ; C.I., 6446; condemned by Atticists; v. Rutherford, NPhr., 255 f.).†

συν-πορεύομαι (Rec. συμπ-), [in LXX chiefly for הָלַךְ;] 1. *to journey together* (Plat., al.) : c. dat. pers., Lk 7¹¹ 14²⁵ 24¹⁵. 2. *to come together*: Mk 10¹ (Plut., al.).†

*† συν-πρεσβύτερος (Rec. συμπ-), -ου, ὁ, *a fellow-elder*: 1 Pe 5¹ (Eccl.).†

συνσ-, v. passim συσσ-.

*† σύν-σωμος (Rec. συσσ-), -ον (< σῶμα), *of the same body*: Eph 3⁶ (Eccl.).†

* συν-σταυρόω (Rec. συσ-), -ῶ, *to crucify together with*: pass., c. dat., Jo 19³²; id. seq. σύν, Mt 27⁴⁴, Mk 15³². Metaph., of the mystical death of the Christian with Christ: Ro 6⁶, Ga 2²⁰ (Eccl.).†

συν-στέλλω (Rec. συσ-), [in LXX: Jg 8²⁸ 11³³ (כָּנַע ni.), Si 4³¹, al. ;] 1. *to draw together, contract, shorten*: of time, 1 Co 7²⁹. 2. *to wrap up*: of enshrouding a body for burial (Eur.), c. acc., Ac 5⁶.†

* συν-στενάζω (Rec. συσ-), *to groan together* or *with*: Ro 8²² (c. dat. pers., Eur., *Ion.*, 935).†

*† συν-στοιχέω (Rec. συσ-), -ῶ, *to stand in the same rank* or *line* (Polyb). Metaph., *to correspond to*: Ga 4²⁵ (v. Lft., in l.).†

* συν-στρατιώτης (Rec. συσ-), -ου, ὁ, *a fellow-soldier* (Plat., Xen., al.). Metaph., of fellowship in Christian service: Phl 2²⁵, Phm 2.†

* συν-σχηματίζω (Rec. συσ-), (< σχῆμα), *to conform to* (Arist.). Pass., *to be conformed to, conform oneself to*: Ro 12², 1 Pe 1¹⁴.†

συν-τάσσω, [in LXX chiefly for צָוָה pi.;] *to prescribe, ordain, arrange*: c. dat. pers, Mt 21⁶ 26¹⁹ 27¹⁰ (LXX).†

συντέλεια, -ας, ἡ (< συντελέω), [in LXX chiefly for כָּלָה and (in Da) for קֵץ;] 1. in cl., *a joint payment* or *contribution* for public service; hence, generally, *joint action* (Plat.). 2. In late writers (Polyb., al.), *consummation, completion*: σ. τ. αἰῶνος, -ων (cf. Da LXX τη 12¹³, al.), Mt 13³⁹, ⁴⁰, ⁴⁹ 24³ 28²⁰, He 9²⁶.†

συν-τελέω, -ῶ, [in LXX chiefly for כָּלָה pi., also for עָשָׂה, תָּמַם, etc. ;] "perfective" of τελέω (cf. M, *Pr.*, 118), 1. *to complete, finish, bring to an end*: Lk 4¹³; pass., ib. ², Jo 2³, WH, mg., Ac 21²⁷. 2. *to effect, accomplish, bring to fulfilment* (cf. MM, xxiv) : Mk 13⁴, Ro 9²⁸, He 8⁸.†

συν-τέμνω, [in LXX chiefly for חָרַץ;] 1. *to cut in pieces*. 2. *to cut down, cut short*: metaph., λόγον, Ro 9²⁸ (LXX) (Hdt., Plat., Eur., al.).†

συν-τηρέω, -ῶ, [in LXX: Ez 18¹⁹ (שָׁמַר), Da τη 7²⁸ A (נְטַר), Si 13¹² and freq., To 1¹¹, II Mac 12⁴², al. ;] "perfective" of τηρέω (v. M, *Pr.*, 113, 116), 1. *to preserve, keep safe, keep close*: c. acc. pers., Mk 6²⁰; c. acc. rei, Mt 9¹⁷; ἐν τ. καρδίᾳ, Lk 2¹⁹ (Arist. and later writers; cf. MM, xxiv).†

συν-τίθημι, [in LXX: 1 Ki 22¹³ (קָשַׁר), etc. ;] *to place* or *put together*, in various senses. Mid., (*a*) *to observe, perceive;* (*b*) *to determine, agree, covenant*: c. inf., Lk 22⁵; seq. τοῦ, c. inf., Ac 23²⁰; seq. ἵνα, Jo 9²².†

συν-τόμως, adv. (< συντέμνω), [in LXX: Pr 13²³ (בְּלֹא מִשְׁפָּט) 23²⁸,

28

III Mac 5²⁵ * ;] *concisely, briefly :* Mk 16 [alt. ending], Ac 24⁴ (for a similar ex., v. MM, xxiv).†

συν-τρέχω, [in LXX : Ps 49 (50)¹⁸ (עָם רָצָה), II Mac ₂, Jth ₄ * ;] *to run together or with :* seq. ἐκεῖ, Mk 6³³ ; πρός, c. acc., Ac 3¹¹ ; metaph., I Pe 4⁴.†

συν-τρίβω, [in LXX chiefly for שׁבר ;] *to shatter, break in pieces :* Mt 12²⁰ (LXX), Mk 5⁴ 14³, Jo 19³⁶ (LXX), Re 2²⁷ ; of persons and parts of the body, *to break, crush, bruise :* Lk 9³⁹ ; fig., Ro 16²⁰.†

σύν-τριμμα, -τος, τό (< συντρίβω), [in LXX (Le 21¹⁹, al.) chiefly for שֶׁבֶר ; also for שׁד (Is 59⁷), etc. ;] *a fracture* (Arist. ; Le, l.c., al.). Metaph., *calamity, destruction* (Is, l.c., Wi 3³, al.) : Ro 3¹⁶ (LXX).†

σύν-τροφος, -ον, ὁ (< συντρέφομαι, *to be brought up together*), [in LXX : III Ki 12²⁴, I Mac 1⁶ R, II Mac 9²⁹ * ;] 1. prop., *one nourished or brought up with, a foster-brother :* Ac 13¹ EV. 2. In Hellenistic usage, as a court term, *an intimate friend* of a king (v. Deiss., *BS*, 305, 310 f.) : Ac 13¹ (cf. also MM, xxiv).†

** συν-τυγχάνω, [in LXX : II Mac 8¹⁴ * ;] *to meet with, fall in with :* c. dat. pers., Lk 8¹⁹.†

Συντύχη (T, -τυχή), -ης, ἡ, *Syntyche :* Phl 4².†

*† συν-υπο-κρίνομαι, *to play a part with, dissemble with :* c. dat., Ga 2¹³ (Polyb.).†

* συν-υπουργέω, -ῶ, *to help together, join in serving :* c. dat. instr., II Co 1¹¹.†

* σύν-φημι (Rec. συμ-), *to consent, confess :* c. dat., seq. ὅτι, Ro 7¹⁶.†

** συν-φύω (Rec. συμ-), [in LXX : Wi 13¹³ * ;] *to cause to grow together.* Pass., *to grow together or with* (Plat. al.) : Lk 8⁷.†

συν-χαίρω (Rec. συγ-), [in LXX : Ge 21⁶ (צָחַק), III Mac 1⁸ R * ;] 1. *to rejoice with :* c. dat pers., Lk 1⁵⁸ 15⁶, ⁹, Phl 2¹⁷, ¹⁸, EV ; c. dat. rei, I Co 12²⁶ 13⁶. 2. *to congratulate* (Æschin., Polyb., al.) : Phl, l.c. (Lft., in l. ; cf. MM, xxiv).†

συν-χέω (Rec. συγ-), [in LXX for בָּלַל, רנן, etc. ;] *to pour together, commingle, confuse ;* metaph., *confound, throw into confusion, stir up, trouble :* Ac 21²⁷ (cf. συν-χύννω).†

**† συν-χράομαι (Rec. συγ-), -ῶμαι, [in Al. : I Ki 30¹⁹ * ;] *to use together with.* Metaph., c. dat. pers., *to associate with :* Jo 4⁹ (Polyb., al.).†

*† συν-χύννω (Rec. συγ- ; and in Ac 9²² with LTr., as in late writers generally, -χύνω), Hellenistic form of -χέω (q.v.) : Ac 2⁶ 9²² 19³² 21³¹.†

*† σύν-ψυχος (Rec. συμ-), -ον (< ψυχή), *of one mind :* Phl 2².†

* συν-ωδίνω, *to be in travail together* (Arist.) : metaph. (Eur.), Ro 8²².†

** συνωμοσία, -ας, ἡ (συνόμνυμι, *to conspire*), [in Sm. : Ez 22²⁵ * ;] *a conspiracy :* Ac 23¹³.†

Συράκουσαι, -ῶν, αἱ, *Syracuse :* Ac 28¹².†

Συρία, -ας, ἡ, *Syria :* Mt 4²⁴, Lk 2², Ac 15²³, ⁴¹ 18¹⁸ 20³ 21³, Ga 1²¹.†

Σύρος, -ου, ὁ, fem. Σύρα, *a Syrian :* Lk 4²⁷, Mk 7²⁶, WH, mg.†

Συροφοινίκισσα (Rec. -φοίνισσα), -ης, ἡ, *a Syrophœnician* woman : Mk 7²⁶, WH, txt., RV (cf. ἡ Φοινίκη Συρία, Diod., 19, 93).†

Σύρτις (L, σύρτις), -εως, acc. -ιν, ή, *Syrtis*, the name of two large sand-banks on the Libyan coast : Ac 27¹⁷.†

σύρω, [in LXX : II Ki 17¹³ (מחב), IV Mac 6¹, al. ;] *to draw, drag :* c. acc. rei, Jo 21⁸, Re 12⁴ ; c. acc. pers., of taking to trial or punishment, Ac 8³ ; ἔξω τ. πόλεως, Ac 14¹⁹ ; ἐπὶ τ. πολιτάρχας (cf. IV Mac, l.c.), Ac 17⁶ (cf. κατα-σύρω).

συσ-, v. passim *συνσ-.*

***†συ-σπαράσσω**, *to convulse completely :* c. acc. pers., Mk 9²⁰, Lk 9⁴² (cf. σπαράσσω).†

†**σύσ-σημον** (T, συν-), -ου, τό (< σῆμα), [in LXX : Jg 20³⁸, ⁴⁰ (מֵשְׂאֵת), Is 5²⁶ 49²² 62¹⁰ (נֵס) *;] *a fixed sign* or *signal :* Mk 14⁴⁴. (Strab., Plut., al. ; condemned by Atticists, v. Rutherford, *NPhr.*, 492 f.) †

***†συ-στασιαστής**, -οῦ, ὁ, *a fellow-rioter :* Mk 15⁷, Rec.†

*** συ-στατικός** (Ti. συν-), -ή, -όν (< συνίστημι), 1. *for putting together, constructive.* 2. *for bringing together, introductory, commendatory :* ἐπιστολή (Arist., Diog. L., al. ; and v. MM, xxiv), II Co 3¹.†

συ-στρέφω, [in LXX chiefly for קשר ;] 1. *to twist together :* c. acc. rei, Ac 28³. 2. Pass., of persons, *to gather themselves together :* Mt 17²² (WH, R, mg.).†

συ-στροφή, -ῆς, ή (< συστρέφω), [in LXX : Ho 4¹⁹ 13¹² (צרר) ; σ. ποιεῖσθαι, Am 7¹⁰ (קשׁר), etc. ;] 1. *a twisting together* (Plat.). 2. *a concourse, a riotous gathering* (Polyb.) : Ac 19⁴⁰ ; σ. ποιεῖσθαι (Am, l.c.), *to make a compact* (RV, *banded themselves together*) : Ac 23¹².†

Συχάρ (E, Σιχάρ), indecl., ή, *Sychar*, a town of Samaria : Jo 4⁵.†

Συχέμ, indecl. (Heb. שְׁכֶם), *Shechem ;* 1. the son of Hamor (Ge 33¹⁹) : Ac 7¹⁶b, Rec. 2. A city of Samaria (AV, *Sychem ;* in LXX also sometimes Σίκιμα, -ων, as in FlJ) : Ac 7¹⁶a,b.†

σφαγή, -ῆς, ή (< σφάζω), [in LXX for טֶבַח, הֲרֵגָה, etc. ;] *slaughter :* Ac 8³² (LXX) ; πρόβατα σφαγῆς, Ro 8³⁶ (LXX) ; ἡμέρα σφαγῆς, Ja 5⁵.†

σφάγιον, -ου, τό (< σφαγή), [in LXX : Am 5²⁵ (זֶבַח), Ez 21¹⁰, ¹⁵, ²⁸ (טֶבַח), Le 22²³ (נְדָבָה) *;] *a victim* for slaughter : Ac 7⁴² (LXX).†

σφάζω, [in LXX chiefly for שׁחט ;] *to slay, slaughter* (esp. of victims for sacrifice) : ἀρνίον, Re 5⁶, ¹² 13⁸ ; of persons, I Jo 3¹², Re 5⁹ 6⁴, ⁹ 18²⁴ ; ἐσφαγμένη εἰς θάνατον (RV, *smitten unto death*), Re 13³ (cf. κατα-σφάζω).†

σφόδρα, adv. (prop. neut. of σφοδρός, *excessive, violent*), [in LXX chiefly for מְאֹד ;] *very, very much, exceedingly :* with verbs, Mt 17⁶, ²³ 18³¹ 19²⁵ 26²² 27⁵⁴, Ac 6⁷ ; with adjectives, Mt 2¹⁰, Mk 16⁴, Lk 18²³, Re 16²¹.†

σφοδρῶς, adv., *exceedingly :* Ac 27¹⁸.†

σφραγίζω, [in LXX chiefly for חתם (De 32³⁴, al.), also for סתם (Da TH 8²⁶) ;] *to seal,* (a) *for security :* Mt 27⁶⁶, Re 20³ ; τ. καρπὸν τοῦτον, fig. (cf. Deiss., *BS*, 238 f. ; MM, xxiv ; *DB*, iv, 427a), Ro 15²⁸ ; (b) *for concealment,* hence, metaph., *to hide* (Da TH 9²⁴, Jo 14¹⁷) :

Re 10⁴ 22¹⁰; (c) for distinction, Re 7³⁻⁸; metaph., Eph 1¹³ 4³⁰; mid., ɪɪ Co 1²²; (d) for authentication (Es 8⁸): Jo 3³³ 6²⁷ (cf. κατα-σφραγίζω).†

σφραγίς, -ίδος, ἡ, [in LXX: Ex 28¹¹, al. (םֹתֵח) 35²² (חָם), Si 17²², al.;] 1. a seal, signet: Re 7². 2. The impression of a seal or signet, a seal (on its various purposes, v.s. σφραγίζω): on a book or roll, Re 5¹, ², ⁵, ⁹ 6¹, ³, ⁵, ⁷, ⁹, ¹² 8¹; metaph., Ro 4¹¹, ɪ Co 9², ɪɪ Ti 2¹⁹, Re 9⁴.†

*† σφυδρόν, -οῦ, τό, = σφυρόν, the ankle: Ac 3⁷ (v. Bl., § 6, 8).†

* σφυρίς (T, Rec. σπυρίς, v. WH, App., 148; Bl., § 6, 7), -ίδος, ἡ, a flexible mat-basket for carrying provisions: Mt 15³⁷ 16¹⁰, Mk 8⁸, ²⁰, Ac 9²⁵ (v.s. κόφινος).†

σφυρόν, -οῦ, τό, [in LXX: Jb 41²⁰ ⁽²¹⁾ (תוֹחָה) *;] the ankle: Ac 3⁷, Rec. (T, WH, σφυδρόν; v. Bl., § 6, 8).†

** σχεδόν, adv. (< ἔχω), [in LXX: ɪɪ Mac 5², ɪɪɪ Mac 5¹⁴, ⁴⁵ *;] 1. of place, near. 2. Of degree, almost, nearly: Ac 13⁴⁴ 19²⁶, He 9²².†

σχῆμα, -τος, τό (< ἔχω), [in LXX: Is 3¹⁷ (חֹפ) *;] figure, fashion: ɪ Co 7³¹, Phl 2⁸.†

SYN.: v.s. μορφή.

σχίζω, [in LXX chiefly for עקב;] to cleave, rend: Mt 27⁵¹, Mk 1¹⁰ 15³⁸, Lk 5³⁶ 23⁴⁵, Jo 19²⁴ 21¹¹; metaph., in pass., to be divided into factions, Ac 14⁴ 23⁷.†

* σχίσμα, -τος, τό (< σχίζω), a rent (Arist., al.): Mt 9¹⁶, Mk 2²¹. Metaph., a dissension, division: Jo 7⁴³ 9¹⁶ 10¹⁹, ɪ Co 1¹⁰ 11¹⁸ 12²⁵.†

SYN.: v.s. αἵρεσις.

σχοινίον, -ου, τό (dimin. of σχοῖνος, a rush), [in LXX chiefly for חֶבֶל;] a rope (prop., one made of rushes): Jo 2¹⁵, Ac 27³².†

σχολάζω (< σχολή), [in LXX: Ex 5⁸, ¹⁷, Ps 45 (46)¹⁰ (רפה ni., hi.) *;] to be at leisure, hence, to have time or opportunity for, to devote oneself to, be occupied in: ɪ Co 7⁵; of things, to be unoccupied, empty (Plut., Eur., al.): οἶκος, Mt 12⁴⁴, Lk 11²⁵ (T [WH], R, om.).†

σχολή, -ῆς, ἡ, [in LXX: Ge 33¹⁴ (κατὰ σ., לְאִטִּי), Pr 28¹⁹, Si 38²⁴ *;] 1. leisure. 2. Later (from Plato on), (a) that for which leisure is employed, a disputation, lecture; (b) the place where lectures are delivered, a school: Ac 19⁹ (for the later sense of employment, v. MM, xxiv).†

σώζω (on the more accurate σῴζω, v. WH, Intr., § 410; Bl., § 3, 1-3), [in LXX chiefly for ישׁע hi., also for מלט ni., נצל ni., etc.;] to save from peril, injury or suffering: Mt 8²⁵, Mk 13²⁰, Lk 23³⁵, al.; τ. ψυχήν, Mt 16²⁵, al.; seq. ἐκ, Jo 12²⁷, He 5⁷, Ju ⁵; of healing, restoring to health: Mt 9²², Mk 5³⁴, al. In NT, esp. of salvation from spiritual disease and death, in which sense it is "spoken of in Scripture as either (1) past, (2) present, or (3) future, according as redemption, grace, or glory is the point in view. Thus (1) Ro 8²⁴, Eph 2⁵, ⁸, ɪɪ Ti 1⁹, Tit 3⁵; (2) Ac 2⁴⁷, ɪ Co 1¹⁸ 15², ɪɪ Co 2¹⁵; (3) Mt 10²², Ro 13¹¹, Phl 2¹², He 9²⁸ " (Vau. on Ro 5⁹). Seq. ἀπό, Mt 1²¹, Ac 2⁴⁰, Ro 5⁹; ἐκ, Ja 5²⁰, Ju ²³ (cf. Cremer, 532 ff.).

σῶμα, -τος, τό, [in LXX for בָּשָׂר, גְּוִיָּה, etc., and for Aram. נְבֵלָה;] a body. 1. Prop., of the human body, (a) as always in Hom. (opp. to δέμας), of the dead body: Mt 27⁵⁸, ⁵⁹, Mk 15⁴³, al.; (b) of the living body: Lk 11³⁴, ι Co 6¹³, al.; ἐν σ. εἶναι, He 13³; as the instrument of the soul, τὰ διὰ τοῦ σ., ιι Co 5¹⁰; opp. to πνεῦμα, Ro 8¹⁰, ι Co 5³ 7⁴, Ja 2²⁶; to ψυχή, Mt 6²⁵ 10²⁸, Lk 12²² (cf. Wi 1⁴, al.); to τὸ π. καὶ ἡ ψ., ι Th 5²³; σ. ψυχικόν, opp. to σ. πνευματικόν, ι Co 15⁴⁴; ὁ ναὸς τοῦ σ. αὐτοῦ (gen. epexeg.), Jo 2²¹; τὸ σ. τ. ταπεινώσεως ἡμῶν (Hebraistic "gen. of definition"; M, Pr., 73 f.; Bl., § 35, 5), opp. to τὸ σ. τ. δοξῆς αὐτοῦ, Phl 3²¹; similarly, τὸ σ. τ. σαρκός, Col 1²²; σ. τοῦ θανάτου (subject to death), Ro 7²⁴; σ. τ. ἁμαρτίας, Ro 6⁶; (c) periphr., ἀνθρώπου σ., then absol., σῶμα (Soph., Xen., al.), a person, and in later writers (Polyb., al.), a slave: Re 18¹³ (cf. MM, i, ii, xxiv; Deiss., BS, 160). 2. Of the bodies of animals: living, Ja 3³; dead, He 13¹¹ (Ex 29¹⁴, al.). 3. Of inanimate objects (cf. Eng. "heavenly bodies"): ι Co 15³⁷, ³⁸, ⁴⁰ (Diod., al.). 4. Of any corporeal substance (Plat., al.): opp. to σκιά, Col 2¹⁷. Metaph., of a number of persons united by a common bond; in NT, of the Church as the spiritual body of Christ: Ro 12⁵, ι Co 10¹⁶, ¹⁷ 12¹³, ²⁷, Eph 1²³ 2¹⁶ 4⁴, ¹², ¹⁶ 5²³, ³⁰, Col 1¹⁸, ²⁴ 2¹⁹ 3¹⁵; ἕν σ. κ. ἕν πνεῦμα, Eph 4⁴.

**σωματικός, -ή, -όν (< σῶμα), [in LXX: ιν Mac 1³² 3¹*;] (a) of or for the body, bodily: γυμνασία, ι Ti 4⁸; (b) (opp. to ἀσώματος) bodily, corporeal: εἶδος, Lk 3²².†

*σωματικῶς, adv., bodily, corporeally: Col 2⁹ (v. ICC, Lft., in l.).†

Σώπατρος, -ου, ὁ, Sopater: Ac 20⁴.†

σωρεύω, [in LXX: Pr 25²² (חתה), Jth 15¹¹*;] (a) to heap on: c. acc. seq. ἐπί c. acc., Ro 12²⁰ (LXX) (Arist., al.); (b) to heap with: c. acc. et dat., metaph., ἁμαρτίαις, ιι Ti 3⁶ (overwhelmed with, Field, Notes, 217) (Polyb.).†

Σωσθένης, -ους, ὁ, Sosthenes; (a) a Jewish ruler: Ac 18⁷; (b) a Christian: ι Co 1¹.†

Σωσίπατρος, -ου, ὁ, Sosipater: Ro 16²¹.†

σωτήρ, -ῆρος, ὁ (< σώζω), [in LXX for יֵשַׁע and cognate forms;] saviour, deliverer, preserver, a freq. epithet of kings in the Ptolemaic and Rom. periods (Deiss., BS, 83; LAE, 368 f.; MM, xxiv), in NT, (a) of God (as LXX: Ps 23 (24)⁵, Is 12², al.): Lk 1⁴⁷, ι Ti 1¹ 2³ 4¹⁰, Tit 1³ 2¹⁰ 3⁴, Ju 2⁵; (b) of Christ: Lk 2¹¹, Ac 5³¹ 13²³, Phl 3²⁰; τ. κόσμου, Jo 4⁴², ι Jo 4¹⁴ (for the general use of the word, v. Westc., in l.); ἡμῶν, ιι Ti 1¹⁰, Tit 1⁴ 3⁶; θεὸς (κύριος) καὶ σ. (v. Deiss., LAE, 348₄; M, Pr., 84), Tit 2¹³, ιι Pe 1¹, ¹¹ 2²⁰ 3², ¹⁸; σ. τοῦ σώματος (i.e. of the Church; v.s. σῶμα, 5), Eph 5²³.†

σωτηρία, -ας, ἡ (< σωτήρ), [in LXX for יֶשַׁע, יְשׁוּעָה, תְּשׁוּעָה, פְּלֵיטָה, etc.;] deliverance, preservation, salvation, safety (Lat. salus): Ac 7²⁵ 27³⁴, He 11⁷; ἐξ ἐχθρῶν, Lk 1⁷¹. In NT esp. of Messianic and spiritual salvation (v.s. σώζω): Mk 16 [alt. ending], Lk 19⁹, Jo 4²², Ac 4¹²

13⁴⁷, Ro 11¹¹, ΙΙ Th 2¹³, ΙΙ Ti 3¹⁵, He 2³ 6⁹, ΙΙ Pe 3¹⁵, Ju ³ ; opp. to ἀπώλεια, Phl 1²⁸ ; αἰώνιος σ., He 5⁹ ; ὁ λόγος (τὸ εὐαγγέλιον) τῆς σ., Ac 13²⁶, Eph 1¹³ ; ὁδὸς σωτηρίας, Ac 16¹⁷; κέρας σωτηρίας, Lk 1⁶⁹; ἡμέρα σωτηρίας, ΙΙ Co 6²(LXX); κατεργάζεσθαι τὴν ἑαυτοῦ σ., Phl 2¹²; κληρονομεῖν σ., He 1¹⁴; ὁ ἀρχηγὸς τῆς σ., He 2¹⁰ ; εἰς σ., Ro 1¹⁶ 10¹,¹⁰, ι Pe 2² ; σ. as a present possession (v.s. σώζω), Lk 1⁷⁷, ΙΙ Co 1⁶ 7¹⁰, Phl 1¹⁹, ΙΙ Ti 2¹⁰; as more fully realized in the future : Ro 13¹¹, ι Th 5⁸, ⁹, He 9²⁸, ι Pe 1⁵, ⁹, ¹⁰, Re 7¹⁰ 12¹⁰ 19¹.†

σωτήριον, v.s. σωτήριος.

σωτήριος, -ον (< σωτήρ), [in LXX for יְשׁוּעָה, שֶׁלֶם, etc. ;] saving, bringing salvation, in NT always in spiritual sense (v.s. σώζω, σωτηρία) : ἡ χάρις ἡ σ., Tit 2¹¹. Neut., τὸ σ., as subst. (cl.), salvation : Lk 2³⁰ ; τ. σ. τ. θεοῦ, Lk 3⁶, Ac 28²⁸ ; περικεφαλαίαν τοῦ σ., Eph 6¹⁷.†

* σωφρονέω, -ῶ (< σώφρων), (a) to be of sound mind or in one's right mind, sober-minded : Mk 5¹⁵, Lk 8³⁵ ; opp. to ἐκστῆναι, ΙΙ Co 5¹³ (Hdt.) ; (b) to be temperate, discreet, self-controlled (opp. to μαίνεσθαι, ὑβρίζειν, etc. ; Æsch., Thuc., al.) : Tit 2⁶ ; opp. to ὑπερφρονεῖν, Ro 12³ ; σ. καὶ νήφειν, ι Pe 4⁷.†

** σωφρονίζω, [in Aq. : Is 38¹⁶ * ;] to make σώφρων, recall one to his senses, admonish, control (RV, train) : c. acc. pers., Tit 2⁴.†

*† σωφρονισμός, -οῦ, ὁ (< σωφρονίζω), (a) an admonishing (FlJ, Plut., al.) ; (b) self-control, self-discipline : ΙΙ Ti 1⁷ (on the reflexive meaning here, v. Ellic., in l.).†

** σωφρόνως, adv., [in LXX : Wi 9¹¹ * ;] with sound mind, prudently, soberly : Tit 2¹².†

** σωφροσύνη, -ης, ἡ, [in LXX : Es 3¹³, Wi 8⁷, ΙΙ Mac 4³⁷, ιν Mac ₆* ;] (a) soundness of mind, good sense, sanity (opp. to μανία, Xen.) : Ac 26²⁵ ; (b) self-control, sobriety : ι Ti 2⁹ (v. Tr., Syn., § xx), ib. ¹⁵.†

** σώφρων, -ον, [in LXX : ιν Mac ₉* ;] (a) of sound mind, sane, sensible ; (b) self-controlled, sober-minded : ι Ti 3², Tit 1⁸ 2², ⁵ (Arist.).†

T

T, τ, ταῦ, τό, indecl., tau, t, the nineteenth letter. As a numeral, τ′ = 300, τ, = 300,000.

Ταβειθά (Rec. Ταβιθά), ἡ (Aram. טַבְיְתָא or טְבִיתָא), Tabitha : Ac 9³⁶, ⁴⁰ (cf. Δορκάς).†

*† ταβέρνη (Lat. taberna), v.s. Τρεῖς Ταβέρναι.

Ταβιθά, v.s. Ταβειθά.

τάγμα, -τος, τό (< τάσσω), [in LXX chiefly for דֶּגֶל, also for חַיָּה, רַגְלִי ;] that which has been arranged or placed in order ; esp. as military term, a company, troop, division, rank : metaph., ι Co 15²³ (v. ICC, in l.).†

τακτός, -ή, -όν (< τάσσω), [in LXX : Jb 12⁵ (שַׁאֲנָן) * ;] ordered, fixed, stated : ἡμέρα, Ac 12²¹.†

ταλαιπωρέω, -ῶ (< ταλαίπωρος), [in LXX chiefly for שָׁדַד pu. ;] *to do hard labour, suffer hardship or distress;* mid., *distress yourselves:* Ja 4⁹. 2. In cl. occasionally trans., *to weary, distress* (so Ps 16 (17)⁹, Is 33¹).†

ταλαιπωρία, -ας, ἡ (< ταλαίπωρος), [in LXX chiefly for שֹׁד;] 1. *hard work* (Hippocr.). 2. *hardship, suffering, distress:* Ro 3¹⁶(LXX); pl., Ja 5¹ (v. Bl., § 32, 6; WM, 220; Swete, *Mk.*, 153). (Hdt., Thuc., al.; and cf. MM, xxiv.)†

ταλαίπωρος, -ον, [in LXX: Ps 136 (137)⁸ (שְׁדוּדָה), Is 33¹ (ποι ῖν τ., שָׁדַד), To 13¹⁰, Wi 3¹¹, al.;] *distressed, miserable, wretched:* Ro 7²⁴, Re 3¹⁷.†

*ταλαντιαῖος, -α, -ον (< τάλαντον), (a) *worth a talent;* (b) *of a talent's weight:* Re 16²¹.†

τάλαντον, -ου, τό, [in LXX for כִּכָּר;] 1. *a balance* (Hom.). 2. *that which is weighed, a talent;* (a) a talent in weight (in Hom. always of gold); (b) a sum of money, whether gold or silver, equivalent to a talent in weight (v. *DB*, iii, 418 ff.): Mt 18²⁴ 25¹⁵ ff.†

ταλειθά (Rec. ταλιθά), (Aram. טְלִיתָא, v. Dalman, *Gr.*, 150), *talitha,* i.e. *maiden:* Mk 5⁴¹.†

ταμεῖον (late syncopated form of cl. ταμιεῖον; v. M, *Pr.*, 44 f.; Bl., § 6, 5; Thackeray, *Gr.*, 63 ff.; Deiss., *BS*, 182 f.), -ου, τό, [in LXX chiefly for חֶדֶר;] 1. *a treasury* (Thuc., al). 2. *a store-chamber* (Arist., Xen.; De 28⁸): Lk 12²⁴. 3. *an inner chamber* (Xen., *Hell.*, v, 4, 5; Is 26²⁰, al.): Mt 6⁶ 24²⁶, Lk 12³.†

τάξις, -εως, ἡ (< τάσσω), [in LXX: Jb 38¹² (מָקוֹם), Ps 109 (110)⁴ (דִּבְרָה), ΙΙ Mac 9¹⁸, al.;] 1. *an arranging,* hence, in military sense, *disposition* of an army, *battle array* (Thuc., al.). 2. *arrangement, order* (Plat., al.): Lk 1⁸. 3. *due order:* Col 2⁵ (*ICC*, in l.); κατὰ τάξιν, ι Co 14⁴⁰. 4. *office, order* (for exx., v. MM, xxiv): He 5⁶ (LXX), 10 6²⁰ 7¹¹, 17 (LXX).†

ταπεινός, -ή, -όν, [in LXX for שָׁפָל, עָנָו, עָנִי, etc.;] *low-lying;* metaph., (a) *lowly, of low degree, brought low:* Ja 1⁹, ΙΙ Co 7⁶ (cf. Si 25²³); οἱ τ., opp. to δυνάσται, Lk 1⁵²; τ. ταπεινοῖς (neut., R, txt.; masc., R, mg.; v. *ICC*, in l.), Ro 12¹⁶; (b) *lowly in spirit, humble,* in cl. usually in a slighting sense (v. Tr., *Syn.*, § xlii; but v. also Abbott, *Essays*, 81), in NT in an honourable sense: ΙΙ Co 10¹; seq. τ. καρδίᾳ, Mt 11²⁹ (cf. Ps 33 (34)¹⁹); opp. to ὑπερήφανος, Ja 4⁶, ι Pe 5⁵ (LXX).†

*† ταπεινοφροσύνη, -ης, ἡ (< ταπεινόφρων), *lowliness of mind, humility:* Ac 20¹⁹, Eph 4², Phl 2³, Col 3¹², ι Pe 5⁵; *of a false humility,* Col 2¹⁸, 23 (rare outside of NT, but found in bad sense in FlJ, *BJ*, iv, 9, 2; also in Epictet., v. Tr., *Syn.*, § xlii).†

† ταπεινόφρων, -ον (< ταπεινός, φρήν), [in LXX: Pr 29²³ (שְׁפַל רוּחַ)*;] *humble-minded:* ι Pe 3⁸ (in bad sense, Plut., 2, 336 E, cf. Deiss., *LAE*, 72₃).†

ταπεινόω, -ῶ (< ταπεινός), [in LXX chiefly for ענה, also for שפל, כנע, etc. ;] *to make low: ὄρος (βουνόν)*, Lk 3⁵ (LXX). Metaph., *to humble, abase:* Mt 18⁴ 23¹², Lk 14¹¹ 18¹⁴, II Co 11⁷ 12²¹, Phl 2⁸; pass., Mt 23¹², Lk 14¹¹ 18¹⁴, Phl 4¹²; id. with mid. sense, Ja 4¹⁰, I Pe 5⁶.†

ταπείνωσις, -εως, ἡ (< ταπεινόω), [in LXX chiefly for עֳנִי;] *abasement, humiliation, low estate :* Lk 1⁴⁸, Ac 8³³ (LXX), Phl 3²¹, Ja 1¹⁰ (Plat., Arist., and later writers).†

ταράσσω, [in LXX for בהל, רגז, etc., forty-six words in all ;] *to disturb, trouble, stir up:* primarily in physical sense (Hom., Eur.) : τ. ὕδωρ, Jo 5 [4], ⁷. Metaph., of the mind (Æsch., Plat., al.), *to trouble, disquiet, perplex:* Ac 15²⁴, Ga 1⁷ 5¹⁰; ἑαυτόν (*troubled himself;* Westc., in l.), Jo 11³³; of a crowd, *to stir up,* Ac 17⁸, ¹³; pass., Mt 2³ 14²⁶, Mk 6⁵⁰, Lk 1¹² 24³⁸, Jo 12²⁷ (Ps 5 (6)⁴) 14¹, ²⁷, I Pe 3¹⁴ (LXX); τ. πνεύματι, Jo 13²¹ (cf. δια-, ἐκ-ταράσσω).

ταραχή, -ῆς, ἡ (< ταράσσω), [in LXX for הְלָחָה, הַלְחָלָה, מְהוּמָה, etc. ;] *trouble, disturbance: τ. ὕδατος,* Jo 5 [4]. In pl. (as in cl.), *tumults:* Mk 13⁸, Rec.†

τάραχος, -ου, ὁ (< ταράσσω), [in LXX for מְהוּמָה, etc. ;] later form of ταραχή (Xen., al.; v. Thackeray, *Gr.,* 159): Ac 12¹⁸ 19²³.†

Ταρσεύς, -έως, ὁ (< Ταρσός), *of Tarsus:* Ac 9¹¹ 21³⁹.†

Ταρσός, -οῦ, *Tarsus,* a city of Cilicia : Ac 9³⁰ 11²⁵ 22³.†

*†ταρταρόω, -ῶ (< Τάρταρος, a Greek name for the under-world, esp. the abode of the damned), *to cast into hell :* II Pe 2⁴ (v. Mayor, in l.).†

τάσσω, [in LXX chiefly for שֹוּם, also for צוה pi., נתן, etc. ;] primarily, in military sense, then generally, *to draw up in order, arrange* in place, *assign, appoint, order:* c. dat. (acc.) et inf. (Bl., § 72, 5), Ac 15² 18² (διατ-, WH) 22¹⁰; ἑαυτούς, I Co 16¹⁵; pass., Mt 8⁹ (T [WH], R, txt., om.), Lk 7⁸, Ro 13¹; ὅσοι ἦσαν τεταγμένοι εἰς ζωὴν αἰώνιον (perh. in mid. sense; v. *EGT* and Page, in l.), Ac 13⁴⁸; mid., *to appoint* for oneself or by one's own authority, Mt 28¹⁶, Ac 28²³.†

ταῦρος, -ου, ὁ, [in LXX chiefly for שֹור ;] *a bull :* Mt 22⁴, Ac 14¹³, He 9¹³ 10⁴.†

ταφή, -ῆς, ἡ (< θάπτω), [in LXX chiefly for קֶבֶר and cognate forms;] *burial:* Mt 27⁷ (Hdt., al.; for other meanings, v. LS, s.v., Deiss., *BS,* 355 f., MM xxiv).†

τάφος, -ου, ὁ (< θάπτω), [in LXX chiefly for קֶבֶר;] 1. *a burial* (Hom., al.). 2. *a grave, tomb* (Hes., Hdt., al.) : Mt 23²⁷, ²⁹ 27⁶¹, ⁶⁴, ⁶⁶ 28¹, Ro 3¹³ (LXX).†

**τάχα (< ταχύς), adv., [in LXX : Wi 13⁶ 14¹⁹ *;] (a) (chiefly poët.), *quickly, presently ; (b) perhaps :* Ro 5⁷, Phm 15.†

τάχειον, v.s. ταχύ.

ταχέως (< ταχύς), adv., [in LXX chiefly for מְהֵרָה and cognate forms;] *quickly, hastily :* Lk 14²¹ 16⁶, Jo 11³¹, ɪ Co 4¹⁹, Phl 2¹⁹, ²⁴, ɪɪ Ti 4⁹; with suggestion of rashness, Ga 1⁶, ɪɪ Th 2², ɪ Ti 5²².†

ταχινός, -ή, -όν, [in LXX: Pr 1¹⁶, Hb 1⁶, Is 59⁷ (מֲהֵר), Wi 13², Si 11²² 18²⁶*;] poët. and late for ταχύς, *swift :* of swift approach, ɪɪ Pe 1¹⁴ 2¹.†

τάχιστα, v.s. ταχύ.

τάχος, -ους, τό, [in LXX chiefly for parts and derivatives of מֲהֵר;] *swiftness, speed.* Adverbially, ἐν τ. (= ταχέως), *quickly, speedily, soon :* Lk 18⁸, Ac 12⁷ 22¹⁸ 25⁴, Ro 16²⁰, ɪ Ti 3¹⁴, Re 1¹ 22⁶.†

ταχύ (neut. of ταχύς), adv., [in LXX chiefly for מֲהֵר pi.;] *quickly, speedily, forthwith :* Mt 5²⁵ 28⁷, ⁸, Mk 9³⁹, Lk 15²², Jo 11²⁹, Re 2¹⁶ 3¹¹ 11¹⁴ 22⁷, ¹², ²⁰. Compar., τάχειον (T, Rec. τάχιον), = cl. θᾶσσον, θᾶττον (Att.), (v. Bl., § 44, 3) : Jo 13²⁷ 20⁴, ɪ Ti 3¹⁴ (T, Rec.), He 13¹⁹, ²³. Superl., τάχιστα : ὡς τ., *as quickly as possible* (Bl., § 11, 3), Ac 17¹⁵.†

ταχύς, -εῖα, -ύ, [in LXX chiefly for מֲהֵר pi.;] *quick, swift, speedy :* opp. to βραδύς, Ja 1¹⁹.†

τέ, enclitic copulative particle (= Lat. *-que* as καί = *et, ac, atque*), not very freq. in NT, more than two-thirds of the occurrences being in Ac. 1. τέ solitarium, *and,* denoting a closer affinity than καί between words and sentences which it connects (Bl., § 77, 8) : Mt 28¹², Jo 4⁴², Ac 2³³, ³⁷, ⁴⁰ 10²² 11²¹, al. 2. Denoting a closer connection than simple καί, τὲ . . . καί, τὲ καί, τὲ . . . τέ (Ac 26¹⁶ Ro 14⁸), *as well . . . as also, both . . . and :* Lk 12⁴⁵, Ac 1¹ 15⁹, 21³⁰, al.; τὲ . . . δέ, *and . . . and,* Ac 19²; τὲ γάρ . . . ὁμοίως δὲ καί, Ro 1²⁶, ²⁷.

τεῖχος, -ους, τό, [in LXX chiefly for חוֹמָה;] *a wall,* esp. that about a town : Ac 9²⁵, ɪɪ Co 11³³, He 11³⁰, Re 21¹²⁻¹⁹.†

**τεκμήριον, -ου, τό (< τέκμαρ, *a mark, sign*), [in LXX: Wi 5⁴ 19¹³, ɪɪɪ Mac 3²⁴*;] *a sure sign, a positive proof :* Ac 1³ (for exx., v. MM, xxiv).†

Syn. : ἔνδειγμα, q.v.

*†τεκνίον, -ου, τό (dimin. of τέκνον), *a little child :* as a term of endearment, in voc. pl., Jo 13³³, Ga 4¹⁹, ɪ Jo 2¹, ¹², ²⁸ 3⁷, ¹⁸ 4⁴ 5²¹.†

*†τεκνογονέω, -ῶ, *to beget* or *bear children :* ɪ Ti 5¹⁴ (Anthol.).†

* τεκνογονία, -ας, ἡ, *child-bearing :* ɪ Ti 2¹⁵ (Arist.).†

τέκνον, -ου, τό (< τίκτω), [in LXX chiefly for בֵּן, also for יֶלֶד, etc.;] that which is begotten, born (cf. Scottish *bairn*), *a child* of either sex : Mk 13¹², Lk 1⁷, Ac 7⁵; pl., Mt 7¹¹, Mk 7²⁷, Lk 1¹⁷, Eph 6¹, al.; τέκνα ἐπαγγελίας, Ro 9⁸; τ. τῆς σαρκός, ib.; in a wider sense (as Heb. בָּנִים), of posterity, Mt 2¹⁸, Lk 3⁸, al.; specif., of a male child, Mt 21²⁸, Ac 21²¹, al.; in voc. as a form of kindly address from an elder to a junior or from a teacher to a disciple, Mt 9² 21²⁸, Mk 2⁵, Lk 2⁴⁸; τ. μου (= cl. τ. μοι; v. Bl., § 37, 5), Ga 4¹⁹ (τεκνία, WH, txt.), ɪɪ Ti 2¹. Metaph., (*a*) of disciples (apart from direct address, v. supr.) : Phm ¹⁰, ɪ Ti 1², Tit 1⁴, ɪɪɪ Jo ⁴; (*b*) with reference to the Fatherhood of God (v.s. πατήρ, γεννάω), τέκνα τ. θεοῦ (cf. Is 30¹, Wi 16²¹) : Ro 8¹⁶, Eph 5¹, Phl 2¹⁵; and esp. in Johannine bks. (cf. Westc., *Epp. Jo.,* 94, 120),

Jo 1¹², 1 Jo 3¹, al.; (c) of those who imitate others and are therefore regarded as the spiritual offspring of their exemplars : Mt 3⁹, Lk 3⁸ Jo 8³⁹, Ro 9⁷, 1 Pe 3⁶; τ. διαβόλου, 1 Jo 3¹⁰; (d) as in Heb. (LXX, Jl 2²³, Ps 149², 1 Mac 1³⁸), of the inhabitants of a city : Mt 23³⁷, Lk 13³⁴ 19⁴⁴, Ga 4²⁵; (e) with an adjectival gen., freq. rendering a Heb. expression, adopted from LXX or formed on the analogy of its language, but sometimes with parallels in Gk. writers (v. Deiss., BS, 161 ff.) : τέκνα φωτός, Eph 5⁸; τ. ὑπακοῆς 1 Pe 1¹⁴; κατάρας, 11 Pe 2¹⁴; ὀργῆς, Eph 2³ (v. M, Gr., 11, p. 441).

SYN.: v.s. παῖς.

*τεκνο-τροφέω, -ῶ, to rear young (of bees, Arist.), to bring up children : 1 Ti 5¹⁰.†

τέκτων, -ονος, ὁ, [in LXX chiefly for חָרָשׁ;] an artificer in wood, stone or metal, but esp. a carpenter (v. MM, xxiv) : Mt 13⁵⁵, Mk 6³.†

τέλειος, -a, -ον (< τέλος), [in LXX chiefly for שָׁלֵם, תָּמִים and cogn. forms;] having reached its end, finished, mature, complete, perfect; 1. of persons, primarily of physical development, (a) full-grown, mature : He 5¹⁴; ethically : Phl 3¹⁵; opp. to νήπιος (-άζειν), 1 Co 2⁶ 14²⁰, Eph 4¹³; τ. καὶ πεπληροφορημένοι, Col 4¹²; τ. ἐν Χριστῷ, Col 1²⁸; (b) complete, perfect (expressing the simple idea of complete goodness, without reference either to maturity or to the philosophical idea of a τέλος; v. Hort on Ja 1⁴) : Mt 5⁴⁸ 19²¹, Ja 1⁴ 3²; of God, Mt 5⁴⁸. 2. Of things, complete, perfect : Ro 12²; ἔργον, Ja 1⁴; νόμος, ib. ²⁵; δώρημα, ib. ¹⁷; ἀγάπη, 1 Jo 4¹⁸; τὸ τ., 1 Co 13¹⁰; compar., τελειοτέρα (σκηνή), He 9¹¹. (There is probably no reference in St. Paul's usage to the use of this term in the ancient mysteries; cf. ICC on Col 1²⁸; but v. also Lft., in l., and Notes, 173 f.) †

SYN.: v.s. ὁλόκληρος (and cf. Rendall, He., 158 ff.).

τελειότης, -ητος, ἡ (< τέλειος), [in LXX : Jg 9¹⁶, ¹⁹ (תָּמִים), Pr 11³ (תֻּמָּה), Wi 6¹⁵ 12¹⁷, Je 2²*;] perfection, completeness : Col 3¹⁴, He 6¹.†

τελειόω, -ῶ (< τέλειος), [in LXX : Ex 29⁹, Le 4⁵, al. (τ. χεῖρας, מלא pi.), 11 Ki 22²⁶, al. (תמם), Wi 4¹³, al. (cf. Westc., He., 64);] 1. to bring to an end, finish, accomplish, fulfil : Jo 4³⁴, Ac 20²⁴; of time, Lk 2⁴³, Jo 5³⁶ 17⁴; pass., ἡ γραφή, Jo 19²⁸. 2. to bring to maturity or completeness, to complete, perfect; (a) of things : He 7¹⁹, Ja 2²², 1 Jo 2⁵ 4¹², ¹⁷; (b) of persons, in ethical and spiritual sense : He 2¹⁰ 9⁹ 10¹, ¹⁴; pass., Lk 13³², Jo 17²³, Phl 3¹², He 5⁹ 7²⁸ 11⁴⁰ 12²³, 1 Jo 4¹⁸ (for a different view of the meaning in He 2¹⁰, al., v. Rendall, in l.).†

**τελείως (< τέλειος), adv., [in LXX : Jth 11⁶, 11 Mac 12⁴², 111 Mac 3²⁶ 7²², R*;] completely, perfectly : 1 Pe 1¹³.†

τελείωσις, -εως, ἡ (< τελειόω), [in LXX chiefly for מִלְאִים, Ex 29²², al.;] fulfilment, completion, perfection : Lk 1⁴⁵, He 7¹¹.†

*†τελειωτής, -οῦ, ὁ (< τελειόω), a consummator, finisher : He 12² (nowhere else).†

**τελεσφορέω, -ῶ (< τέλος, φέρω), [in LXX : iv Mac 13²⁰ *;] (a) of plants, *to bring fruit to perfection* (Theophr.) : Lk 8¹⁴ ; (*b*) of females, *to bear perfect offspring* (Artemid. ; iv Mac, l.c.).†

τελευτάω, -ῶ (< τελευτή), [in LXX chiefly for מוּת ;] 1. trans., *to complete, finish;* esp. τ. τ. αἰῶνα, τ. βίον, *to complete life, to die* (Æsch., Hdt., al.). 2. Intrans., *to come to an end,* hence, *to die* (Hdt., al.) : Mt 2¹⁹ 9¹⁸ 22²⁵, Mk 9⁴⁸, Lk 7², Jo 11³⁹, Ac 2²⁹ 7¹⁵, He 11²² ; Hebraistically, θανάτῳ τελευτάτω (מוֹת יוּמָת, Ex 21¹⁷), Mt 15⁴, Mk 7¹⁰ (LXX).†

τελευτή, -ῆς, ἡ (< τελέω), [in LXX chiefly for מָוֶת, מוּת ;] 1. *a finishing.* 2. *an end :* τ. βίου (Hdt., al.) : also without βίου, *the end of life, death* (Hdt., Plat., al.) : Mt 2¹⁵.†

τελέω, -ῶ (< τέλος), [in LXX for כלה, pi., etc. ;] 1. *to bring to an end, complete, finish :* τ. δρόμον, II Ti 4⁷ ; τ. λόγους, Mt 7²⁸ 19¹ 26¹ ; τ. παραβολάς, Mt 13⁵³ ; τ. πόλεις, Mt 10²³ : pass., Re 15⁸ 20³, ⁵, ⁷ ; c. ptcp., Mt 11¹. 2. *to execute, perform, complete, fulfil :* Lk 2³⁹, Ac 13²⁹, Ro 2²⁷, II Co 12⁹, Ga 5¹⁶, Ja 2⁸, Re 11⁷ ; pass., Lk 12⁵⁰ 18³¹ 22³⁷, Jo 19²⁸, ³⁰, Re 10⁷ 15¹ 17¹⁷. 3. *to pay* (freq. in cl.) : Mt 17²⁴, Ro 13⁶ (cf. ἀπο-, δια-, ἐκ-, ἐπι-, συν-τελέω).†

τέλος, -ους, τό, [in LXX for קֵץ, etc. ; εἰς τὸ τ., chiefly for לָנֶצַח and cognate forms ;] 1. *end :* most freq. of the termination or limit of an act or state (in NT also of the end of a period of time, cl. τελευτή), Lk 1³³, I Co 10¹¹, II Co 3¹³, I Pe 4⁷ ; by meton., of one who makes an end, Ro 10⁴ ; ἕως (ἄχρι, μέχρι) τέλους, I Co 1⁸, II Co 1¹³, He 3¹⁴ 6¹¹, Re 2²⁶ ; εἰς τ., *to or at the end,* Mt 10²², Mk 13¹³, Lk 18⁵, Jo 13¹ (or here, *to the uttermost,* v. Westc., in l.) ; τ. ἔχειν, Lk 22³⁷ ; adverbially, τὸ δὲ τέλος, *finally,* I Pe 3⁸ (so perh. I Co 15²⁴, v. Burkitt in *JThS,* xvii, p. 384 f.) ; of the last in a series, Re 21⁶ 22¹³ ; of the issue, fate or destiny, Mt 26⁵⁸ ; c. gen. rei, Ro 6²¹, al. ; c. gen. pers., II Co 11¹³, al. ; of the aim or purpose, I Ti 1⁵. 2. *toll, custom, revenue :* Ro 13⁷ ; pl., as most usually, Mt 17²⁵ (cf. κῆνσος, φόρος. For this meaning in I Co 10¹¹, v. MM, *VGT,* s.v. κατανταω).

*τελώνης, -ου, ὁ (< τέλος, ὠνέομαι), 1. *a farmer of taxes* (Lat. *publicanus*). 2. A subordinate of the former, who collected taxes or tolls in a particular district, *a tax-gatherer* (EV, *publican*) : Mt 5⁴⁶ 10³, Lk 3¹² 5²⁷, ²⁹ 7²⁹ 18¹⁰, ¹¹, ¹³ ; pl., τ. κ. ἁμαρτωλοί, Mt 9¹⁰, ¹¹ 11¹⁹, Mk 2¹⁵, ¹⁶, Lk 5³⁰ 7³⁴ 15¹ ; τ. κ. πόρναι, Mt 21³¹, ³² ; ὁ ἐθνικὸς κ. ὁ τ., Mt 18¹⁷ (cf. *DB,* iv, 172 ; *ext.,* 394 f. ; MM, xxiv).†

*†τελώνιον, -ου, τό (< τελώνης), *a custom house* (so in MGr.), *toll-house, place of toll :* Mt 9⁹, Mk 2¹⁴, Lk 5²⁷.†

τέρας, -ατος, τό, [in LXX chiefly for מוֹפֵת ;] *a wonder, marvel :* in NT always pl., τ. κ. σημεῖα, Mt 24²⁴, al. (v.s. σημεῖον).

Τέρτιος, -ου, ὁ, *Tertius :* Ro 16²².†

Τέρτυλλος, -ου, ὁ, *Tertullus :* Ac 24¹, ².†

τέσσαρες (and Ion. and late -ερες and late acc. -ες ; v. WH, *App.,* 150 ; M, *Pr.,* 36, 45 f.), οἱ, αἱ, -αρα, τά, gen., -ων, *four :* Mt 24³¹, Mk 2³, Lk 2³⁷, Jo 11¹⁷ 19²³, Ac 10¹¹, Re 4⁴, ⁶, al.

τεσσαρεσ-και-δέκατος, -η, -ον, *fourteenth :* Ac 27²⁷, ³³.†

τεσσεράκοντα, (Rec. τεσσαρ-, v. WH, *App.*, 150; M, *Pr.*, 45 f.; Thackeray, *Gr.*, 62 f., 73 f.), οἱ, αἱ, τά, indecl., *forty* : Mt 4², Mk 1¹³, Lk 4², Jo 2²⁰, Ac 1³, al.

*τεσσερακονταετής (T, -έτης; Rec. τεσσαρ-, v. supr.), -ές, *of forty years, forty years old* : Ac 7²³ 13¹⁸.†

τεταρταῖος, -α, -ον (< τέταρτος), [in LXX : II Ki 3⁴ A (רְבִיעִי) *;] *of* or *on the fourth day* : τ. εἶναι (Hdt., τ. γενέσθαι), *to be four days dead*, Jo 11³⁹.†

τέταρτος, -η, -ον, [in LXX chiefly for רְבִיעִי;] *fourth* : Mt 14²⁵, Mk 6⁴⁸, Ac 10³⁰. Re 4⁷ 6⁷, ⁸ 8¹² 16⁸ 21¹⁹.†
*† τετρααρχέω (Rec. τετραρχ-; v. WH, *App.*, 145; v. M, *Gr.*, II, p. 276), -ῶ (< τετραάρχης), *to be tetrarch* : c. gen., Lk 3¹ (FlJ, *BJ*, iii, 10, 7).†
*† τετραάρχης (Rec. τετράρχης, v. supr.), -ου, ὁ (< τετρα- in comp. = τέτορα, Doric for τέσσαρα, + ἄρχω), one of four rulers, a *tetrarch*, i.e. (*a*) prop., the governor of a fourth part of a region (Strab.); (*b*) any petty ruler (Plut.) ; in NT, of Herod Antipas : Mt 14¹, Lk 3¹⁹ 9⁷, Ac 13¹.†

τετράγωνος, -ον (< τετρα-, v. supr., + γωνία), [in LXX for רָבוּעַ and cogn. forms;] *square* : Re 21¹⁶ (Hdt., Plat., al.).†
*† τετράδιον, ου, τό, *a quaternion, a group of four* : στρατιωτῶν, Ac 12⁴ (Philo).†

τετρακισ-χίλιοι, -αι, -α, *four thousand* : Mt 15³⁸ 16¹⁰, Mk 8⁹,²⁰, Ac 21³⁸.†

τετρακόσιοι, -αι, -α, *four hundred* : Ac 5³⁶ 7⁶ (LXX) 13²⁰, Ga 3¹⁷.†

τετράμηνος, -ον, [in LXX (neut.) : Jg 19² A 20⁴⁷ A (עַרְבָּעָה חֳדָשִׁים) *;] *of four months, four months;* as subst., τ. (sc. ὥρα, but neut. in Rec.), Jo 4³⁵ (Thuc., al.).†

*τετρα-πλόος, -η, -ον (-οῦς, -ῆ, -οῦν), *fourfold* : Lk 19⁸.†

τετρά-πους, -ουν, [in LXX chiefly for בְּהֵמָה;] *four-footed* : of beasts, neut. pl., Ac 10¹² 11⁶, Ro 1²³.†

τετραρχέω, -αρχής, v.s. τετρααρχέω, -αρχής.

τεύχω, v.s. τυγχάνω.

*τεφρόω, -ῶ (< τέφρα, *ashes;* Wi 2³, al.), *to burn to ashes:* II Pe 2⁶.†

τέχνη, -ης, ἡ, [in LXX for חָכְמָה, מַעֲשֶׂה, עֲבוֹדָה;] *art, craft, trade* : Ac 17²⁹ 18³, Re 18²² (WH, R, mg., om.).†

τεχνίτης, -ου, ὁ (< τέχνη), [in LXX for חָרָשׁ, etc. ;] *a craftsman, artificer* : Ac 19²⁴, ³⁸, Re 18²²; of God (Wi 13¹), He 11¹⁰.†
SYN. : δημιουργός, q.v., and cf. Tr., *Syn.*, § cv.

τήκω, [in LXX for מסס ni., מקק ni., מוג ni., etc. ;] trans., *to melt, melt down;* pass., *to melt, melt away* : II Pe 3¹².†

*τηλαυγῶς, adv. (< τῆλε, *afar,* + αὐγή, *radiance*), poët. and in late prose, *at a distance clearly* : Mk 8²⁵ (WH, mg., δηλαυγῶς).†
** τηλικοῦτος, -αύτη, -οῦτο (altern. of τηλικόσδε, -ήδε, -όνδε, strengthened form of τηλίκος), [in LXX : II Mac 12³, III Mac 3⁹, IV Mac 16⁴ *;]

1. of persons, (a) *of such an age, so old;* (b) *so young.* 2. Of things, *so great:* II Co 1¹⁰, He 2³, Ja 3⁴, Re 16¹⁸.†

τηρέω, -ῶ, [in LXX for שָׁמַר, נָצַר, etc.;] 1. *to watch over, guard, keep, preserve:* Mt 27³⁶, Ac 16²³, al.; ἑαυτόν, II Co 11⁹, I Ti 5²², Ja 1²⁷, Ju ²¹; seq. εἰς, Jo 12⁷, Ac 25²¹, I Pe 1⁴, II Pe 2⁴,⁹ 3⁷, Ju ⁶; ἐν, Jo 17¹¹,¹², Ju ²¹; ἐκ, Jo 17¹⁵, Re 3¹⁰; τ. πίστιν, II Ti 4⁷, Re 14¹²; τ. ἑνότητα τ. πνεύματος, Eph 4³. 2. *to watch, give heed to, observe:* τ. σάββατον, Jo 9¹⁶; τ. ἐντολήν (-άς), Mt 19¹⁷, Jo 14¹⁵ 15¹⁰, I Ti 6¹⁴, I Jo 2³,⁴ 3²²,²⁴ 5³, Re 12¹⁷ 14¹²; τ. λόγον (-ους), Jo 8⁵¹,⁵²,⁵⁵ 14²³,²⁴ 15²⁰ 17⁶ I Jo 2⁵, Re 3⁸,¹⁰, 22⁷,⁹; τ. νόμον, Ac 15⁵, Ja 2¹⁰; τ. παράδοσιν, Mk 7⁹; τ. ἔργα, Re 2²⁶; τ. γεγραμμένα, Re 1³ (cf. δια-, παρα-, συν-τηρέω).

SYN.: φυλάσσω, implying custody and protection: τ. expresses the idea of watchful care and "may mark the result of which φ. is the means" (Thayer s.v.).

** τήρησις, -εως, ἡ (< τηρέω), [in LXX: Wi 6¹⁸, Si 35 (32)²³, I Mac 5¹⁸, II Mac 3⁴⁰, III Mac 5⁴⁴ *;] 1. *a watching,* hence, *imprisonment, ward* (v. Deiss., *BS*, 267): Ac 4³ 5¹⁸. 2. *a keeping:* τ. ἐντολῶν (cf. Si, Wi, ll. c., and v. Westc. on I Jo 7¹⁹.†

Τιβεριάς, -άδος, ἡ (< Τιβέριος), *Tiberias,* a city of Galilee: Jo 6²³; θάλασσα τῆς Τ., Jo 6¹ 21¹ (cf. Γεννησαρέτ, Γαλιλαία).†

Τιβέριος, -ου, ὁ, the Emperor *Tiberius:* Lk 3¹.†

τίθημι, [in LXX for שׂוּם, נתן, שׁית, etc.;] 1. causative of κεῖμαι, (a) *to place, lay, set:* Lk 6⁴⁸, Ro 9³³, al.; of laying the dead to rest, Mk 15⁴⁷, Lk 23⁵⁵, Jo 11³⁴, Ac 7¹⁶, al.; seq. ἐπί, c. gen., Lk 8¹⁶, Jo 19¹⁹, al.; id. c. acc., Mk 4²¹, II Co 3¹³, al.; ὑπό, Mt 5¹⁵, al.; παρά, Ac 4³⁵,³⁷. Mid., *to have put* or *placed, to place for oneself:* of putting in prison, Ac 4³, 5¹⁸,²⁵, al.; of giving counsel, βουλήν, Ac 27¹²; of laying up in one's heart, Lk 1⁶⁶ 21¹⁴ (I Ki 21¹²); (b) *to put down, lay down:* of bending the knees, τ. γόνατα, *to kneel,* Mk 15¹⁹, Ac 7⁶⁰, al.; of putting off garments, Jo 13⁴; of laying down life, τ. ψυχήν, Jo 10¹¹,¹⁵,¹⁷,¹⁸ 13³⁷,³⁸ 15¹³ I Jo 3¹⁶; of laying by money, παρ' ἑαυτῷ, I Co 16²; of setting on food, Jo 2¹⁰; metaph., of setting forth an idea in symbolism, Mk 4³⁰. 2. *to set, fix, establish:* ὑπόδειγμα, II Pe 2⁶. 3. *to make, appoint:* Mt 22⁴⁴, Mk 12³⁶, Lk 20⁴³, Ac 2³⁵, Ro 4¹⁷, al. Mid., *to make, set* or *appoint for oneself:* Ac 20²⁸, I Co 12²⁸, I Th 5⁹, I Ti 1¹², al.; seq. ἵνα, Jo 15¹⁶ (cf. ἀνα-, προσ-ανα-, ἀπο-, δια-, ἀντι-δια-, ἐκ-, ἐπι-, συν-επι-, κατα-, συν-κατα-, μετα-, παρα-, περι-, προ-, προσ-, συν-, ὑπο-τίθημι).

τίκτω, [in LXX chiefly for יָלַד;] prop., of parents, *to beget, bring forth,* but esp. the latter, and so always in NT: absol., Lk 1⁵⁷ 2⁶, Jo 16²¹, Ga 4²⁷ (LXX) (v. M, *Pr.,* 127), Re 12²,⁴; c. acc., Re 12¹³, υἱόν, Mt 1²¹,²³,²⁵, Lk 1³¹ 2⁷, Re 12⁵; pass., Mt 2², Lk 2¹¹. Metaph., of the earth, βοτάνην, He 6⁷ (Æsch., al.); of lust, ἁμαρτίαν, Ja 1¹⁵.†

τίλλω, [in LXX: II Es 9³, Is 18⁷, Da LXX 7⁴ (מְרַט) *;] *to pluck, pluck off:* στάχυας, Mt 12¹, Mk 2²³, Lk 6¹.†

Τιμαῖος, -ου, ὁ (Aram. טָמֵי (?), v. Zorell, s.v.), *Timæus:* Mk 10⁴⁶.†

τιμάω, -ῶ (< τιμή), [in LXX for כָּבֵד pi., עָרַךְ hi., etc.;] 1. *to*

fix the value, price: c. acc. pers., of Christ, Mt 27⁹ (LXX). 2. *to honour:*
c. acc. pers., Mt 15⁴ (LXX), 5, 8 (LXX) 19¹⁹ (LXX), Mk 7⁶,¹⁰ 10¹⁹, Lk
18²⁰ (LXX), Jo 5²³ 8⁴⁹ 12²⁶, Eph 6² (LXX), I Ti 5³, I Pe 2¹⁷; πολλαῖς τιμαῖς,
Ac 28¹⁰.†

τιμή, -ῆς, ἡ, [in LXX for עֵרֶךְ, יְקָר, etc.;] *a valuing,* hence,
objectively; 1. a *price* paid or received: c. gen. pers., Mt 27⁹; c. gen.
rei, Ac 5², ³; pl., Ac 4³⁴ 19¹⁹; τ. αἵματος, Mt 27⁶; ἠγοράσθητε τιμῆς,
I Co 6²⁰ 7²³; ὠνεῖσθαι τιμῆς ἀργυρίου, Ac 7¹⁶. 2. *esteem, honour:* Ro
12¹⁰ 13⁷, I Co 12²³, I Ti 5¹⁷ 6¹, He 5⁴, I Pe 2⁷ (R, txt., *preciousness,* cf.
Hort, in l.), 3⁷; τ. διδόναι, I Co 12²⁴; ἔχειν, Jo 4⁴⁴, He 3³; τ. καὶ δόξα (δ.
κ. τ.), Ro 2⁷, ¹⁰, I Ti 1¹⁷, He 2⁷ (LXX), ⁹, I Pe 1⁷, II Pe 1¹⁷, Re 4⁹, ¹¹ 5¹², ¹³
7¹² 21²⁶; τ. καὶ κράτος, I Ti 6¹⁶; εἰς τ., Ro 9²¹, II Ti 2²⁰, ²¹; ἐν τ., Col 2²³,
I Th 4⁴; by meton., of marks of honour, Ac 28¹⁰.†

τίμιος, -α, -ον (< τιμή), [in LXX chiefly for יָקָר;] *valued,* hence,
(*a*) *precious, costly, highly valued:* primarily, of money value, λίθος,
Re 17⁴ 18¹², ¹⁶ 21¹⁹; pl., I Co 3¹²; compar., -ώτερος, I Pe 1⁷, Rec.; superl.,
-ώτατος, Re 18¹² 21¹¹; in extended sense, καρπός, Ja 5⁷; αἷμα, I Pe 1¹⁹;
ἐπαγγέλματα, II Pe 1⁴; (*b*) *held in honour, honoured, esteemed worthy:*
c. dat., Ac 5³⁴; ὁ γάμος, He 13⁴; ψυχή, Ac 20²⁴ (where τ. is pleonastic,
v. Page, in l.).†

*τιμιότης, -ητος, ἡ (< τίμιος), *preciousness, worth:* Re 18¹⁹ (cf.
Hort on τιμή, I Pe 2⁷).†

Τιμόθεος, -ου, ὁ, *Timothy:* Ac 17¹⁴, ¹⁵ 18⁵, Ro 16²¹, al.

Τίμων, -ωνος, ὁ, *Timon:* Ac 6⁵.†

τιμωρέω, -ῶ (< τιμή + οὖρος, *a guardian*), [in LXX: Ez 5¹⁷ 14¹⁵
(שׂכל pi), Wi 12²⁰ 18⁸, al.;] 1. *to help.* 2. *to avenge;* mid., *to avenge
oneself on, punish* (Hdt., Eur., al.): act. in this sense, Ac 22⁵ 26¹¹
(v. MM, xxiv).†

τιμωρία, -ας, ἡ (< τιμωρέω), [in LXX: Pr 24²² (פִּיד), etc.;]
1. *help, assistance.* 2. *vengeance, punishment:* He 10²⁹.†
SYN.: κόλασις, q.v., and cf. MM, xxiv.

τίνω, [in LXX: Pr 27¹² (τ. ζημίαν, for עָנַשׁ ni.), etc.;] *to pay:*
τ. δίκην (cf. Pr, l.c.), *to pay penalty,* II Th 1⁹ (v. M, *Th.,* in l.).†

τίς, neut., τί, gen., τίνος, interrog. pron., [in LXX for מִי, מָה;] in
masc. and fem., *who, which, what?;* in neut., *which, what?,* used both
in direct and in indirect questions. I. As subst., 1. masc., fem.: τίς;
who, what?, Mt 3⁷ 26⁶⁸, Mk 11²⁸, Lk 9⁹, al. mult.; c. gen. partit., Ac 7⁵²,
He 1⁵, al.; seq. ἐκ (= gen. partit.), Mt 6²⁷, Lk 14²⁸, Jo 8⁴⁶; = ποῖος,
Mk 4⁴¹ 6², Lk 19³, Ac 17¹⁹, al.; = πότερος (M, *Pr.,* 77), Mt 21³¹ 27¹⁷,
Lk 22²⁷, al.; = ὅς or ὅστις (rare in cl.; cf. Bl., § 50, 5; M, *Pr.,* 93).
Mt 10¹⁹ 15³², Mk 6³⁶ 8¹, ², Lk 17⁸, Jo 13¹⁸, Ac 13²⁵. 2. Neut.: τί; *what?,*
Mt 5⁴⁷ 11⁷, Mk 10³, al.; χάριν τίνος, I Jo 3¹²; διὰ τί, Mt 9¹¹, al.; εἰς τί,
Mt 14³¹, al.; elliptically, ἵνα τί (sc. γένηται), *why,* Mt 9⁵, al.; τί οὖν, Ro 3⁹
6¹, ¹⁵, I Co 14¹⁵, al.; τί γάρ, Ro 3³, Phl 1¹⁸; τί ἐμοὶ (ὑμῖν) καὶ σοί, v.s. ἐγώ.
II. As adj.: *who? what? which?,* Mt 5⁴⁶, Lk 14³¹, Jo 2¹⁸, al. III. As

adv. : = διὰ τι (τί ὅτι), *why*, Mt 6²⁸, Mk 4⁴⁰, Lk 6⁴⁶, Jo 18²³, al. ; in rhet. questions, = a negation, Mt 27⁴, Jo 21²², ²³, I Co 5¹² 7¹⁶, al. ; in exclamations (like Heb. מָה), *how* (II Ki 6²⁰, Ps 3², al.), Lk 12⁴⁹.

τις, neut., τι, gen., τινός, enclitic indefinite pron., related to interrog. τίς as πού, πως, ποτέ to πού, πῶς, πότε. I. As subst., 1. *one, a certain one* : Lk 9⁴⁹, Jo 11¹, Ac 5²⁵, al. ; pl., τίνες, *certain, some* : Lk 13¹, Ac 15¹, Ro 3⁸, al. 2. *someone, anyone, something, anything* : Mt 12²⁹, Mk 9³⁰, Lk 8⁴⁶, Jo 2²⁵, Ac 17²⁵, Ro 5⁷, al. ; = indef., *one* (French *on*), Mk 8⁴, Jo 2²⁵, Ro 8²⁴, al. ; pl., τίνες, *some*, Mk 14⁴, al. II. As adj., 1. *a certain* : Mt 18¹², Lk 1⁵ 8²⁷, Ac 3², al. ; with proper names, Mk 15²¹, Lk 23²⁶, al. ; c. gen. partit., Lk 7¹⁹, al. 2. *some* : Mk 16[¹⁸], Jo 5¹⁴, Ac 17²¹ 24²⁴, He 11⁴⁰, al.

Τίτιος, -ου, ὁ, *Titius*, surnamed Justus : Ac 18⁷, T, WH (RV., Τίτος).†

**† τίτλος, -ου, ὁ, (Lat. *titulus*), [in Aq., Sm., Th. : Je 21⁴ * ;] *a title, inscription* : Jo 19¹⁹, ²⁰ (in Christian Inscr., *epitaph*, v. MM. xxiv).†

Τίτος, -ου, ὁ, *Titus* ; 1. St. Paul's disciple and companion : II Co 2¹³ 7⁶, ¹³, ¹⁴ 8⁶, ¹⁶, ²³ 12¹⁸, Ga 2¹, ³, II Ti 4¹⁰, Ti 1⁴, subscr., Rec. (Τίτος). 2. One surnamed Justus : Ac 18⁷, RV (T, WH, Τίτιος).†

τοι-γαρ-οῦν, an inferential particle, [in LXX : Jb 22¹⁰ 24²² (עַל־כֵּן), Si 41¹⁶, al.;] *wherefore then, so therefore :* I Th 4⁸, He 12¹ (Hdt., Plat., al.).†

τοί-νυν, an inferential particle, [in LXX : Is 3¹⁰ 5¹³ 27⁴, Wi 1¹¹ 8⁹, al. * ;] *accordingly, therefore :* as in cl., after the first word in a sentence, I Co 9²⁶ ; acc. to later usage, at the beginning, Lk 20²⁵, He 13¹³.†

τοιόσδε, -άδε, -όνδε, *such :* II Pe 1¹⁷.†

τοιοῦτος, -αύτη, -οῦτο (as usually in Att. prose. Ep. and Ion. neut. -οῦτον in Al., Ac 21²⁵, Rec. only), correlat. of οἷος, ὁποῖος, ὥς, etc., *such as this, of such a kind, such :* Mt 9⁸ 18⁵, Mk 4³³ 6² 7¹³ 9³⁷ (T, τούτων), Jo 9¹⁶, Ac 16²⁴, I Co 5¹ 11¹⁶, II Co 3⁴, ¹² 12³, He 7²⁶ 8¹ 12³ 13¹⁶, Ja 4¹⁶ ; οἷος . . . τ., I Co 15⁴⁸, II Co 10¹¹ ; id. pleonast. (v. Bl., § 50, 4), Mk 13¹⁹ ; seq. ὁποῖος, Ac 26²⁹ ; ὥς, Phm ⁹. As subst., anarth. : pl., Lk 9⁹ ; c. art., ὁ τ., *such a one* (Bl., § 47, 9 ; Ellic. on Ga 5²¹) : Ac 22²², I Co 5⁵, al. ; pl., Mt 19¹⁴, Mk 10¹⁴, al. ; neut. pl., Ac 19²⁵, Ro 1³², al.

τοῖχος, -ου, ὁ, [in LXX chiefly for קִיר ;] *a wall*, esp. of a house : fig., Ac 23³ (cf. τεῖχος).†

τόκος, -ου, ὁ (< τίκτω), [in LXX for נֶשֶׁךְ, etc. ;] *(a) a bringing forth, birth* ; *(b) offspring*. Metaph., of the produce of money lent out, *interest, usury* (cf. *Merch. of Venice*, I, iii, " a breed of barren metal ") : Mt 25²⁷, Lk 19²³ (Soph., Plat., al.).†

τολμάω, -ῶ, [in LXX : Jb 15¹² (לקח), Es 1¹⁸ 7⁵ (מָלְאוֹ לֵב), Jth 14¹³, II Mac 4², III Mac 3²¹ R, IV Mac 8¹⁸ * ;] *to have courage, to venture, dare, be bold :* absol., II Co 11²¹ ; seq. ἐπί, II Co 10² ; c. inf.

(Bl., § 69, 4), Mt 22⁴⁶, Mk 12³⁴, Lk 20⁴⁰, Jo 21¹², Ac 5¹³ 7³², Ro 15¹⁸, I Co 6¹, II Co 10¹², Phl 1¹⁴, Ju ⁹; *to submit to* (in cl. usually absol. in this sense), Ro 5⁷ (v. Field, *Notes*, 155); τολμήσας εἰσῆλθεν, took courage and went in (v. Field, *op. cit.*, 44), Mk 15⁴³ (cf. ἀπο-τολμάω).†

*τολμηρῶς, adv., (< τολμηρός, bold, daring), boldly : compar., -οτέρως ('I', Rec. -ότερον), Ro 15¹⁵.†

*τολμητής, -οῦ, ὁ, (< τολμάω), a bold, daring man : II Pe 2¹⁰ (Thuc.).†

*τομός, -ή, -όν (< τέμνω), sharp: compar., -ώτερος, metaph., He 4¹².†

τόξον, -ου, τό, [in LXX chiefly for קֶשֶׁת ;] a bow : Re 6².†

† τοπάζιον, -ου, τό (and τόπαζος, ὁ), [in LXX : Ex 28¹⁷ 36¹⁷ (39¹⁰), Jb 28¹⁹, Ez 28¹³ (פִּטְדָה), Ps 118 (119)¹²⁷ (פַּז) * ;] topaz : Re 21²⁰ (v. Swete, in l.).†

τόπος, -ου, ὁ, [in LXX chiefly for מָקוֹם ;] place : Lk 4³⁷ 10¹, ³², Jo 5¹³ 6¹⁰, Ac 12¹⁷, I Co 1², al. ; τ. ἅγιος (cf. Is 60¹³), Mt 24¹⁵ ; ἔρημος, Mt 14¹³, al. ; πεδινός, Lk 6¹⁷ ; ἄνυδρος (pl.), Mt 12⁴³, Lk 11²⁴ ; κατὰ τόπους (EV, in divers places), Mt 24⁷, Mk 13⁸ ; τραχεῖς τ., Ac 27²⁹ ; τ. διθάλασσος (q.v.), ib. ⁴¹ ; ἑτοιμάζειν τ., Jo 14², ³ ; ἔχειν, Re 12⁶ ; διδόναι, Lk 14⁹ ; c. gen. defin., τ. βασάνου, Lk 16²⁸ ; τ. καταπαύσεως, Ac 7⁴⁹ ; κρανίου, Mt 27³³, Mk 15²², Jo 19¹⁷ ; seq. οὗ, Ro 9²⁶ ; ὅπου, Mt 28⁶, Mk 16⁶, Jo 4²⁰ 6²³ 10⁴⁰ 11³⁰ 19⁴¹ ; ἐν ᾧ, Jo 11⁶ ; ἐφ' ᾧ, Ac 7³³ ; of a place which a person or thing occupies, Re 2⁵ 6¹⁴ 12⁸ ; τ. μαχαίρας, Mt 26⁵² ; ὁ ἴδιος τ., Ac 1²⁵ ; of a place in a book, Lk 4¹⁷ (cf. Clem. Rom. I Co., 8, 4). Metaph., of condition, station, occasion, opportunity or power : Ac 25¹⁶, Ro 12¹⁹ 15²³, Eph 4²⁷ (cf. Si 38¹²).

SYN.: χώρα (extensive), region ; χωρίον (enclosed), a piece of ground. τ. is "a portion of space viewed in reference to its occupancy, or as appropriated to a thing" (Grimm-Thayer, s.v.).

τοσοῦτος, -αύτη, -οῦτο (He 7³²) and (elsewhere, as usually in Attic) -οῦτον, correlat. of ὅσος, of quantity, size, number, so great, so much, pl., so many : Mt 8¹⁰ Lk 7⁹, He 12¹, Re 18⁷, ¹⁶ ; of time, so long, χρόνος, Jo 14⁹, He 4⁷ ; pl., Lk 15²⁹ (ἔτη), Jo 12³⁷ 21¹¹, I Co 14¹⁰ ; seq. ὥστε, Mt 15³³ ; absol.: pl., Jo 6⁹, Ga 3⁴ ; of price, τοσούτου, Ac 5⁸ ; dat., τοσούτῳ κρείττων, He 1⁴ ; τ. μᾶλλον ὅσῳ, He 10²⁵ ; καθ' ὅσον . . . κατὰ τ., He 7²².†

τότε, demonstr. adv. of time, correlat. of ὅτε, then, at that time ; (a) of concurrent events : Mt 2¹⁷ 3⁵ and freq., Ro 6²¹ ; seq. ptcp., Mt 2¹⁶, Ga 4⁸ ; opp. to νῦν, Ga 4²⁹, He 12²⁶ ; ὁ τ. κόσμος, II Pe 3⁶ ; (b) of consequent events, then, thereupon : Mt 2⁷ 3⁵ 4¹ and freq., Lk 11²⁶ ; τ. οὖν, Jo 11¹⁴ 19¹, ¹⁶ 20⁸ ; εὐθέως τ., Ac 17¹⁴ ; ὅτε . . . τ., Mt 13²⁶ 21¹, Jo 12¹⁶ ; ἀπὸ τ., Mt 4¹⁷ 16²¹ 26¹⁶, Lk 16¹⁶ ; (c) of things future : Mt 24²³, ⁴⁰ 25¹, ³¹ ff. ; opp. to ἄρτι, I Co 13¹² ; καὶ τ., Mt 7²³, Mk 13²¹, Lk 21²⁷, I Co 4⁵, al. ; ὅταν . . . τ., Mt 9¹⁵, Mk 2²⁰, Lk 5³⁵, I Th 5³, al. (more freq. in Mt than in the rest of the NT).

τοὐναντίον, by crasis for τὸ ἐναντίον, neut. acc. used adverbially, *on the contrary, contrariwise :* II Co 2⁷, Ga 2⁷, I Pe 3⁹.†

τοὔνομα, by crasis for τὸ ὄνομα, acc. absol., *by name :* Mt 27⁵⁷.†

τουτέστι = τοῦτ᾽ ἔστι.

τράγος, -ου, ὁ, [in LXX chiefly for עַתּוּד, also for צָפִיר, תַּיִשׁ;] *a he-goat :* He 9¹², ¹³, ¹⁹ 10⁴.†

τράπεζα, -ης, ἡ, [in LXX chiefly for שֻׁלְחָן, also for לֶחֶם, etc.;] 1. *a table, dining-table :* Mt 15²⁷, Mk 7²⁸, Lk 16²¹ 19²³ 22²¹, ³⁰; of the table of shewbread, He 9². By meton., of food provided (v. *DB*, iv, 670 a): Ac 16³⁴, Ro 11⁹ (LXX), I Co 10²¹; διακονεῖν ταῖς τ., Ac 6² (cf. Page, in l., but v. infr.). 2. *A money-changer's table, a bank* (Dem., Arist., al.) : Mt 21¹², Mk 11¹⁵, Lk 19²³, Jo 2¹⁵ ; so also acc. to Dr. Field (*Notes*, 113), Ac 6² (but v. supr.).†

*τραπεζείτης (Rec. -ζίτης, as in cl.), -ου, ὁ (< τράπεζα), *a money-changer, banker :* Mt 25²⁷ (Dem., Plut., al.).†

τραῦμα, -τος, τό, [in LXX for פֶּצַע, חָלָל, etc.;] *a wound :* Lk 10³⁴.†

τραυματίζω (< τραῦμα), [in LXX chiefly for חלל;] *to wound :* Lk 20¹², Ac 19¹⁶.†

*†τραχηλίζω (< τράχηλος), prop., of wrestlers, *to take by the throat,* hence (Philo), *to prostrate, overthrow.* Metaph., but in what sense and from what age it is doubtful (v. Westc., Rendall, on He, l.c.; *DB*, iii, 625 n), τραχηλισμένα, *laid open* (RV, Westc.; *downcast,* Rendall) : He 4¹³.†

τράχηλος, -ου, ὁ, [in LXX chiefly for צַוָּאר, also for עֹרֶף, etc.;] *the neck :* Mt 18⁶, Mk 9⁴², Lk 17² ; ἐπιπεσεῖν ἐπὶ τὸν τ., to embrace (Ge 46²⁹), Lk 15²⁰, Ac 20³⁷. Metaph., ὑποθεῖναι τὸν ἑαυτοῦ τ. (for similar phrase in π., v. Zorell, s.v.), Ro 16⁴ ; ἐπιθεῖναι ζυγὸν ἐπὶ τὸν τ., Ac 15¹⁰.†

τραχύς, -εῖα, -ύ, [in LXX : Is 40⁴ (רֶכֶס), etc.;] *rough :* ὁδοί (Is, l.c.), Lk 3⁵ (LXX); τοποί (i.e. rocky), Ac 27²⁹.†

Τραχωνῖτις, -ιδος, ἡ (< τραχύς), *Trachonitis,* a rough region S. of Damascus (in FlJ, sometimes ἡ Τ., sometimes ὁ Τράχων) : ἡ Τ. χώρα, Lk 3¹.†

τρεῖς, οἱ, αἱ, τρία, τά, *three :* Mt 12⁴⁰, al.; μετὰ τ. ἡμέρας = τῇ τρίτῃ ἡ., Mk 10³⁴, al. (cf. Field, *Notes,* 11 ff.).

Τρεῖς Ταβέρναι (v.s. ταβέρνη), *Three Taverns* (Lat. *Tres Tabernae*), a halting place on the Appian Way : Ac 28¹⁵ (v. *DB*, iv, 690).†

τρέμω, *to tremble,* esp. with fear : Mk 5³³, Lk 8⁴⁷ ; c. ptcp. (in cl. more freq. c. inf.), II Pe 2¹⁰.†

τρέφω, [in LXX for חיה hi., בדל pi., אכל hi., etc.;] 1. *to make to grow, bring up, rear* (cl.; I Mac 3³³ 11³⁹): Lk 4¹⁶ (T, WH, mg., ἀνατ-). 2. *to nourish, feed :* Mt 6²⁶ 25³⁷, Lk 12²⁴, Ac 12²⁰, Re 12⁶, ¹⁴; of a mother, *to give suck,* Lk 23²⁹ ; of animals, *to fatten* (Je 26 (46)²¹), fig., Ja 5⁵ (cf. ἀνα-, ἐκ-, ἐν-τρέφω).†

29

τρέχω, [in LXX chiefly for רוּץ;] *to run* : Mk 5⁶, Jo 20²,⁴, ι Co 9²⁴,²⁶ ; c. inf., Mt 28⁸ ; seq. ἐπί, Lk 24¹² [T ‖[WH]‖ R, mg., om.] ; εἰς, Re 9⁹ ; ptcp., δραμών, c. indic., Mt 27⁴⁸, Mk 15³⁶, Lk 15²⁰. Metaph., from runners in a race, of swiftness or of effort to attain an end : Ro 9¹⁶, Ga 2² 5⁷, Phl 2¹⁶ ; τ. ἀγῶνα (Hdt., Eur., al.), He 12¹ ; ὁ λόγος τ. κυρίου (cf. Ps 147⁴ (146¹⁵), ἕως τάχους δραμεῖται ὁ λ. αὐτοῦ), ιι Th 3¹ (cf. εἰς-, κατα-, περι-, προ-, προσ-, συν-, ἐπι-συν-, ὑπο-τρέχω).†

* τρῆμα, -τος, τό, *a perforation, hole* : ῥαφίδος, Mt 19²⁴, WH, txt. ; βελόνης, Lk 18²⁵ (Aristoph., Plat., al.).†
SYN. : τρυμαλιά, τρύπημα.

τριάκοντα, οἱ, αἱ, τά, indecl. (< τρεῖς), *thirty* : Mt 13⁸, al.

τριακόσιοι, -αι, -α, *three hundred* : Mk 14⁵, Jo 12⁵.†

τρίβολος, -ου, ὁ, [in LXX : Ge 3¹⁸, Ho 10⁸ (דַּרְדַּר), ιι Ki 12³¹ (חָרִיץ), Pr 22⁵ (צֵן)*;] *a thistle* : Mt 7¹⁶, He 6⁸.†

τρίβος, -ου, ἡ (< τρίβω), [in LXX for מְסִלָּה, נָתִיב, etc. ;] *a beaten track, a path* : Mt 3³, Mk 1³, Lk 3⁴ (LXX).†

* τριετία, -ας, ἡ (< τρεῖς, ἔτος), *a period of three years* : Ac 20³¹.†

** τρίζω, [in Aq. : Am 2¹³ ; Sm. : Is 38¹⁴ *;] 1. prop., of sounds by animals, to cry, chirp, etc.   2. Of other sounds, e.g., trans., τ. ὀδόντας, *to gnash* or *grind the teeth* : Mk 9¹⁸.†

τρίμηνος, -ον (< τρεῖς, μήν), [in LXX (neut.) : Ge 38²⁴, ιν Ki 23³¹ B 24⁸, ιι Ch 36²,⁹ (שְׁלֹשָׁה הַ)חֳדָשִׁים)*;] *of three months* ; as subst., τὸ τ (= cl. ἡ τ.), *a space of three months* (Polyb., al. ; LXX) : He 11²³.†

τρίς (< τρεῖς), adv., *thrice* : Mt 26³⁴,⁷⁵, Mk 14³⁰,⁷², Lk 22³⁴,⁶¹, Jo 13³⁸, ιι Co 11²⁵ 12⁸ ; ἐπὶ τ., Ac 10¹⁶ 11¹⁰.†

**† τρίστεγος, -ον (τρεῖς, στέγη), [in Sm. : Ge 6¹⁷ (16), Ez 42⁶ *;] *of three stories* : τὸ τ. (sc. οἴκημα), *the third story*, Ac 20⁹ (Dion., FlJ, al.).†

τρισ-χίλιοι, -αι, -α, *three thousand* : Ac 2⁴¹.†

τρίτος, -η, -ον, *the third* : Mt 22²⁶, Mk 12²¹ 15²⁵, Lk 24²¹, Ac 2¹⁵, al. ; τῇ τ. ἡμέρᾳ (i.e. *the next day but one* : Xen., al. ; v. Field, *Notes*, 11 ff.), Mt 16²¹, Lk 24⁴⁶, al. ; substantively, acc. masc., τρίτον, *a third* (servant), Lk 20¹² ; neut., τὸ τ., c. gen., *the third part of* : Re 8⁷⁻¹² 9¹⁵,¹⁸ 12⁴. As adv., τὸ τ., *the third time* : Mk 14⁴¹, Jo 21¹⁷ ; anarth., τρίτον. *a third time*, Lk 23²², Jo 21¹⁴, ιι Co 12¹⁴ 13¹ ; in enumerations, *thirdly*, ι Co 12²⁸ ; ἐκ τ., *a third time*, Mt 26⁴⁴.

τρίχινος, -η, -ον (< θρίξ), [in LXX : Za 13⁴ (שֵׂעָר), Ex 26⁷ *;] *of hair* : σάκκος, Re 6¹² (Xen., Plat., al.).†

τρόμος, -ου, ὁ (< τρέμω), [in LXX for רְעָדָה, רַעַד, פַּחַד, etc. ;] *trembling, quaking*, esp. from fear : Mk 16⁸ ; φόβος κ. τ. (as in Ge 9², Ex 15¹⁶, De 2²⁵, Is 19¹⁶, al.), ι Co 2³, ιι Co 7¹⁵, Eph 6⁵, Phl 2¹².†

τροπή, -ῆς, ἡ (< τρέπω), [in LXX : De 33¹⁴, Jb 38³³, Wi 7¹⁸, al. ;] *a turning* : esp. of the revolution of heavenly bodies, fig., Ja 1¹⁷ (v.s. ἀποσκίασμα).†

τρόπος, -ου, ὁ (< τρέπω), [in LXX chiefly (ὃν τ.) for כַּאֲשֶׁר;] 1. *a way, manner, fashion* : Mt 23³⁷, Lk 13³⁴, Ac 1¹¹ 7²⁸, II Ti 3⁸, Ju⁷; καθ᾽ ὃν τ., Ac 15¹¹ 27²⁵ (cf. MM, xxv); κατὰ πάντα τ., Ro 3²; κατὰ μηδένα τ. (IV Mac 4²⁴, al.), II Th 2³; (ἐν) παντὶ τ., Phl 1¹⁸, II Th 3¹⁶. 2. Of persons, *manner of life, character* (Hdt., Æsch., al.) : He 13⁵.†

†τροπο-φορέω, -ῶ, [in LXX : De 1³¹ B¹ (נָשָׂא) *;] 1. *to bear another's manners* (R, txt., *suffered he their manners*) : c. acc. pers., Ac 13¹⁸ (Rec., WH, R, txt.; ἐτροφο-, T, R, mg.). 2. = τροφοφορέω (q.v.), (v. Kühner³, I, 276; Jackson and Lake, *Beginnings*, Vol. IV, in l.): Ac, l.c.†

τροφή, -ῆς, ἡ (< τρέφω), [in LXX for לֶחֶם, מָזוֹן, אֹכֶל, etc.;] *nourishment, food* : Mt 3⁴ 6²⁵ 10¹⁰ 24⁴⁵, Lk 12²³, Jo 4⁸, Ac 2⁴⁶ 9¹⁹ 14¹⁷ 27³³, ³⁴, ³⁶, ³⁸, Ja 2¹⁵. Metaph.: He 5¹², ¹⁴.†

Τρόφιμος, -ου, ὁ, *Trophimus* : Ac 20⁴ 21²⁹, II Ti 4²⁰.†

τροφός, -οῦ, ἡ (< τρέφω), [in LXX : Ge 35⁸, IV Ki 11², II Ch 22¹¹, Is 49²³ (מֵינֶקֶת) *;] *a nurse* : I Th 2⁷.†

†τροφο-φορέω, -ῶ, [in LXX : De 1³¹ (נָשָׂא), II Mac 7²⁷ *;] *to nourish* (Hesych.), *bear like a nurse* (R, mg., *bare he them as a nursing-father*) : c. acc. pers., Ac 13¹⁸, T, Tr., R, mg. (WH, R, txt., τροποφορέω, q.v.).†

τροχιά, -ᾶς, ἡ (< τροχός), [in LXX : Pr 2¹⁵ 4¹¹, ²⁶, ²⁷ 5⁶, ²¹ (מַעְגָּל), Ez 27¹⁹ A *;] *the track of a wheel*, hence, *a track, path* : fig., He 12¹³ (LXX).†

τροχός, -οῦ, ὁ (< τρέχω), [in LXX chiefly for אוֹפָן;] *a wheel* : Ja 3⁶ (v. Mayor, Hort, in l.).†

τρύβλιον (Rec. τρυβλίον), -ου, τό, [in LXX chiefly for קְעָרָה;] *a bowl, dish* : Mt 26²³, Mk 14²⁰ (Hippocr., Aristoph., Plut., al.).†

τρυγάω, -ῶ, [in LXX for קצר, בצר, etc.;] *to gather in* : c. acc., (*a*) of the fruit, Lk 6⁴⁴, Re 14¹⁸; (*b*) of that from which it is gathered, Re 14¹⁹.†

τρυγών, -όνος, ἡ (< τρύζω, *to murmur, coo*), [in LXX for תּוֹר, תֹּר;] *a turtle-dove* : Lk 2²⁴.†

†τρυμαλιά, -ᾶς, ἡ (< τρύω, *to wear away*), [in LXX : Je 13⁴ (נָקִיק), etc.;] = τρύμη, *a hole* : τ. ῥαφίδος, *eye of a needle*, Mk 10²⁵.†
SYN.: τρῆμα, τρύπημα.

*τρύπημα, -τος, τό (< τρυπάω, *to bore*), *a hole* : τ. ῥαφιδος, *eye of a needle*, Mt 19²⁴ (WH, txt., τρῆμα).†
SYN.: τρῆμα, τρυμαλιά.

Τρύφαινα, -ης, ἡ, *Tryphæna* : Ro 16¹² (v. Lft., *Phl.*, 175 f.; MM, xxv).†

τρυφάω, -ῶ (< τρυφή), [in LXX : Ne 9²⁵ (עדן hithp.), Is 66¹¹ (ענג hithp.), Si 14⁴ *;] *to live daintily, luxuriously, to fare sumptuously* : Ja 5⁵ (cf. ἐν-τρυφάω).†
SYN.: σπαταλάω (q.v.), στρηνιάω.

τρυφή, -ῆς, ἡ [in LXX chiefly for עֵדֶן ;] *softness, daintiness, luxuriousness :* Lk 7²⁵, ii Pe 2¹³.†

Τρυφῶσα, -ης, ἡ, *Tryphosa :* Ro 16¹² (v. Lft., *Phl.*, 175 f.).†

Τρῳάς (Rec. Τρω-), -άδος, ἡ, *Troas,* a city near the Hellespont: Ac 16⁸, ¹¹ 20⁵, ⁶, ii Co 2¹², ii Ti 4¹³.†

Τρωγύλλιον (also written -γύλιον, -γίλιον, -ία, v. Bl., § 6, 3), -ου, τό, *Trogyllium,* a city of Ionia : Ac 20¹⁵ (WH, txt., R, txt., om.).†

* τρώγω, 1. prop., of animals, *to gnaw, munch, crunch* (Hom., al.). 2. Of men, to *eat* raw food, as vegetables, nuts, etc. (Hdt., al.). 3. In late vernacular, simply *to eat* (= ἐσθίω): Mt 24³⁸, Jo 6⁵⁴, ⁵⁶, ⁵⁷, ⁵⁸ 13¹⁸ (LXX ἐσθίων) (v. Kennedy, *Sources,* 82, 155; MM, xxv).†

τυγχάνω, [in LXX : De 19⁵ (מָצָא), Jb 3²¹ 7² 17¹, Pr 24⁵⁸ (30²³) (without definite Heb. equiv.), Wi 15¹⁹, i Mac 11⁴², iii Mac 3⁷, al.;] I. Trans. 1. *to hit* (opp. to ἁμαρτάνω, *to miss the mark :* Hom., Xen., al.). 2. *to hit upon, light upon ;* (a) of persons, *to meet with, fall in with :* absol., ptcp., ὁ τυχών, *a chance person, anyone* (Lat. *quivis*), οὐ τυχών, *not common* or *ordinary,* Ac 19¹¹ 28²; (b) of things, *to reach, get, obtain :* c. gen. rei. Lk 20³⁵, Ac 24³ 26²² 27³, ii Ti 2¹⁰, He 8⁶ 11³⁵. II. Intrans., *to happen ;* of things, *to happen, chance, befall :* impers., εἰ τύχοι, *it may be, perhaps,* i Co 14¹⁰ 15³⁷; so ptcp., τυχόν (old acc. absol.; v. M, *Pr.,* 74), i Co 16⁶ (cf. ἐν-, ὑπερ-εν-, ἐπι-, παρα-, συν-τυγχάνω).†

τυμπανίζω (< τύμπανον, *a kettle-drum*), [in LXX: i Ki 21¹³ ⁽¹⁴⁾ (תָּוָה pi ?) * ;] 1. *to beat a drum.* 2. *to torture by beating, beat to death* (cf. Westc. on He, l.c.) : pass., He 11³⁵.†

*† τυπικῶς, adv. (< τύπος), (a) *typically* (Greg. Naz.); (b) *by way of example :* i Co 10¹¹.†

τύπος, -ου, ὁ (< τύπτω), [in LXX: Ex 25³⁹ ⁽⁴⁰⁾ (תַּבְנִית), Am 5²⁶ (צֶלֶם), iii Mac 3³⁰, iv Mac 6¹⁹ * ;] 1. the *mark* of a blow: τῶν ἥλων, Jo 20²⁵. 2. An *impression, impress,* the *stamp* made by a die; hence, *a figure, image :* Ac 7⁴³ ⁽ᴸˣˣ⁾. 3. *form* (Plat.) : Ro 6¹⁷ ; the sense or substance of a letter (iii Mac, l.c.), Ac 23²⁵. 4. *an example, pattern :* Ac 7⁴⁴, He 8⁵ ⁽ᴸˣˣ⁾; in ethical sense, i Co 10⁶, Phl 3¹⁷, i Th 1⁷, ii Th 3³, i Ti 4¹², Tit 2⁷, i Pe 5³; in doctrinal sense, *type* (v. *ICC,* in l.), Ro 5¹⁴.†
SYN. : v.s. ὑποτύπωσις.

τύπτω, [in LXX chiefly for נכה hi.;] *to strike, smite, beat :* c. acc., Mt 24⁴⁹, Mk 15¹⁹, Lk 12⁴⁵, Ac 18¹⁷ 21³² 23², ³; of mourners, τὰ στήθη, Lk 18¹³ 23⁴⁸; ἐπὶ τ. σιαγόνα, Lk 6²⁹; εἰς τ. κεφαλήν, Mt 27³⁰. Metaph., of God inflicting evil: Ac 23³ (cf. Ex 8², Ez 7⁹, al.); of disquieting conscience, i Co 8¹².†

Τύραννος, -ου, ὁ, *Tyrannus :* Ac 19⁹.

* τυρβάζω, *to disturb, trouble :* pass., Lk 10⁴¹, Rec. (WH, R, θορυβάζω).†

Τύριος, -ου, ὁ, ἡ, *a Tyrian :* Ac 12²⁰.†

Τύρος, -ου, ἡ, *Tyre,* a maritime city of Phœnicia : Mk 7³¹, Ac 21³, ⁷; T. κ. Σιδών, Mt 11²¹, ²² 15²¹, Mk 3⁸ 7²⁴, Lk 6¹⁷ 10¹³, ¹⁴.†

τυφλός, -ή, -όν, [in LXX for עִוֵּר ;] blind : as subst., ὁ τ., Mt 9²⁷, Mk 8²², Lk 4¹⁸ (LXX), Jo 5³, al. Metaph. : Mt 15¹⁴ 23¹⁶⁻²⁶, Jo 9³⁹⁻⁴¹, Ro 2¹⁹, ii Pe 1⁹, Re 3¹⁷.

τυφλόω, -ῶ (< τυφλός), [in LXX: Is 42¹⁹ (עָוֵר), To 7⁷ א, Wi 2²¹ א *;] to blind, make blind : metaph., Jo 12⁴⁰ (LXX, καμμύω), ii Co 4⁴, i Jo 2¹¹.†

* τυφόω, -ῶ (< τῦφος, smoke; metaph., conceit), prop., to wrap in smoke; used only metaph., to puff up, becloud with pride : pass., i Ti 3⁶ 6⁴, ii Ti 3⁴ (Dem., Arist., al.).†

* τύφω (< τῦφος, smoke), to raise a smoke; pass., to smoke: Mt 12²⁰ (LXX, καπνιζόμενον).†

*† τυφωνικός, -ή, -όν (< τυφῶν, a hurricane, typhoon), tempestuous : Ac 27¹⁴.†

Τύχικος (T, Rec., Τυχικός), -ου, ὁ, Tychicus : Ac 20⁴, Eph 6²¹, Col 4⁷, ii Ti 4¹², Tit 3¹².†

τυχόν, adv., v.s. τυγχάνω.

Υ

Υ, υ, ὖ ψιλόν, τό, indecl., upsilon, u, the twentieth letter. As a numeral, υ′= 400, υ, = 400,000. At the beginning of a word, υ is always aspirated.

ὑακίνθινος, -η, -ον (< ὑάκινθος), [in LXX for תַּחַשׁ, תְּכֵלֶת ;] of hyacinth, hyacinthine (v.s. ὑάκινθος), "doubtless meant to describe the blue smoke of a sulphurous flame" (Swete) : Re 9¹⁷ (Hom., Eur., al.).†

ὑάκινθος, -ου, ὁ, [in LXX chiefly for תְּכֵלֶת ;] hyacinth; (a) in cl., a flower, prob. the dark blue iris; (b) in late writers, a precious stone of the same colour, perhaps the sapphire : Re 21²⁰ (Phil., FlJ, al.).†

* ὑάλινος, -η, -ον (< ὕαλος), of glass, glassy : Re 4⁶ 15².†

ὕαλος, -ου, ὁ, [in LXX: Jb 28¹⁷ (זְכוֹכִית) *;] 1. (Hdt.) a clear transparent stone. 2. (from Plat. on) glass : Re 21¹⁸, ²¹.†

ὑβρίζω (< ὕβρις), [in LXX for גאה, etc.;] 1. intrans., to wax wanton, run riot. 2. Trans., to outrage, insult, treat insolently : c. acc. pers., Mt 22⁶, Lk 11⁴⁵ 18³², Ac 14⁵, i Th 2².†

ὕβρις, -εως, ἡ, [in LXX chiefly for גָּאוֹן and cogn. forms;] 1. wantonness, insolence. 2. = ὕβρισμα, an act of wanton violence, an outrage, injury : ii Co 12¹⁰; metaph., of a loss by sea (Pind.), Ac 27¹⁰, ²¹ (v. MM, xxv).†

ὑβριστής, -οῦ, ὁ (< ὑβρίζω), [in LXX chiefly for גֵּאֶה ;] a violent, insolent man : Ro 1³⁰, i Ti 1¹³ (EV, injurious).†
SYN. : ἀλαζών, ὑπερήφανος, v. Tr., Syn., § xxix.

ὑγιαίνω (< ὑγιής), [in LXX chiefly for שָׁלוֹם, and freq. in To;] *to be sound, healthy, in good health* : Lk 5³¹ 7¹⁰ 15²⁷, III Jo ². In Past. Epp. (as also in cl.) metaph., ὑ. ἐν τ. πίστει, Tit 1¹³; τ. πίστει, τ. αγάπῃ, τ. ὑπομονῇ, Tit 2²; ἡ ὑγιαίνουσα διδασκαλία, I Ti 1¹⁰, II Ti 4³, Tit 1⁹ 2¹; λόγοι ὑγιαίνοντες, I Ti 6³, II Ti 1¹³.†

ὑγιής, -ές, acc., ὑγιῆ (Attic usually -ιᾶ), [in LXX for חַי, etc.;] *sound, whole, healthy* : Mt 12¹³ 15³¹, Jo 5[4], 6, 9, 11, 14, 15 7²³, Ac 4¹⁰; seq. ἀπό, Mk 5³⁴; of words, opinions, etc. (as in cl.), metaph., λόγος, Tit 2⁸.†

ὑγρός, -ά, -όν, [in LXX : Jg 16⁷, ⁸ (לַח), Jb 8¹⁶ (רָטֹב), Si 39¹³ אA *;] *wet, moist*, opp. to ξηρός : of wood, *sappy, green* : Lk 23³¹.†

ὑδρία, -ας, ἡ (< ὕδωρ), [in LXX for כַּד;] 1. prop., *a water-pot* or *jar* : Jo 2⁶, ⁷ 4²⁸. 2. More freq. in Attic = ἄγγος, *a pot, urn* or *jar* of any kind, as for holding wine, coins, etc. (v. Rutherford, *NPhr.*, 23; MM, xxv).†

ὑδροποτέω, -ῶ (< ὕδωρ, πίνω), [in LXX : Da LXX 1¹² (שָׁתָה מַיִם) *;] *to drink water*, opp. to οἴνῳ χρῆσθαι : I Ti 5²³ (Hdt., i, 71; Plat., *Rep.*, 561 c, al.).†

*ὑδρωπικός, -ή, -όν (ὕδρωψ, *dropsy*), *dropsical, suffering from dropsy* : Lk 14².†

ὕδωρ, gen., ὕδατος, τό, [in LXX chiefly for מַיִם;] *water* : Mt 3¹⁶, Mk 1¹⁰, Lk 7⁴⁴, Jo 4⁷, Ja 3¹², Re 8¹⁰, al.; pl., Mt 14²⁸, ²⁹, Jo 3²³, Re 1¹⁵, al.; βαπτίζειν (ἐν) ὕδατι, Mt 3¹¹, Mk 1⁸, Jo 1²⁶, al.; τ. λουτρὸν τοῦ ὕ., Eph 5²⁶; opp. οἶνος, Jo 2⁹ 4⁴⁶; αἷμα, Jo 19³⁴, He 9¹⁹, I Jo 5⁶, ⁸; πῦρ, Mt 17¹⁵ Mk 9²²; πνεῦμα, Jo 1²⁶, ³¹, ³³; πνεῦμα καὶ πῦρ, Mt 3¹¹, Lk 3¹⁶; ἐξ ὕ. κ. πνεύματος γεννηθῆναι, Jo 3⁵; metaph., of divine truth and grace (τ.) ὕ. (τ.) ζῶν, Jo 4¹⁰, ¹¹ (cf. ib. ¹³⁻¹⁵); τ. ὕ. τ. ζωῆς, of spiritual refreshment, Re 21⁶ 22¹, ¹⁷.

ὑετός, -οῦ, ὁ (< ὕω, *to rain*), [in LXX chiefly for מָטָר, גֶּשֶׁם;] *rain* : Ac 14¹⁷ 28², He 6⁷, Ja 5¹⁸, Re 11⁶; ὄψιμος (q.v.), sc. ὑ., Ja 5⁷.†

*† υἱοθεσία, -ας, ἡ (cf. the cl. phrases, υἱὸν τίθεσθαι, θετὸς υἱός), freq. in Inscr. (v. Deiss., *BS*, 239), *adoption* of a son (or daughter); metaph., of God's relation established (a) with Israel : Ro 9⁴; (b) with Christians : Ro 8¹⁵, Ga 4⁵, Eph 1⁵; of its consummation, Ro 8²³.†

υἱός, -οῦ, ὁ, [in LXX very freq. and nearly always for בֵּן, Ge 4¹⁷, al.; for בַּר, Da LXX Th 7¹³, al.; etc.;], *a son*; 1. in the ordinary sense : Mt 10³⁷, Mk 9¹⁷, Lk 1¹³, al. mult.; omitted with the art. of origin (WM, § 30, 3; Bl., § 35, 2), τὸν τοῦ Ἰεσσαί, Ac 13²² (LXX); also c. gen. anarth. (cl.), Σώπατρος Πύρρου Βεροιαῖος, Ac 20⁴; c. adj., πρωτότοκος, Lk 2⁷; μονογένης, Lk 7¹²; opp. to νόθος, He 12⁸ (in Mt 21³, *a foal of an ass*) ; in a wider sense, of posterity : ὁ υἱ. Δαυίδ, of the Messiah (cf. Dalman, *Words*, 316 ff.; *DCG*, ii, 653 f.), Mt 22⁴², ⁴⁵, Mk 12³⁵, ³⁷,

Lk 20⁴¹, ⁴⁴, al.; υἱοὶ Ἰσραήλ (cf. υἷες Ἀχαιῶν, Hom., Il., i, 162, al.), Mt 27⁹, Ac 9¹⁵, al. 2. Metaph.; (a) as belonging to, being connected with or having the quality of that which follows (a usage mainly due to translation from a Semitic original; cf. Deiss., BS, 161 ff.; Dalman, Words, 115 f.; DCG, ii, 652 f.; M, Gr., II, p. 441): τ. πονηροῦ (διαβόλου), Mt 13³⁸, Ac 13¹⁰; τ. νυμφῶνος (v.s. νυμφών), Mt 9¹⁵, Mk 2¹⁹, al.; τ. φωτός (Lft., Notes, 74), Lk 16⁸, Jo 12³⁶, I Th 5⁵; τ. εἰρήνης, Lk 10⁶; γεέννης, Mt 23¹⁵; τ. ἀπωλείας, Jo 17¹², II Th 2³; τ. αἰῶνος τούτου, Lk 16⁸ 20³⁴; τ. ἀπειθείας, Eph 2² 5⁶; βροντῆς, Mk 3¹⁷; τ. ἀναστάσεως, Lk 20³⁶; παρακλήσεως, Ac 4³⁶; τ. προφητῶν κ. τ. διαθήκης, Ac 3²⁵; (b) υἱός τ. θεοῦ (cf. Dalman, Words, 268 ff.; Deiss., BS, 166 f.; DB, iv, 570 ff.; DCG, ii, 654 ff.), of men, as partakers of the Divine nature and of the life to come: Mt 5⁹, Lk 20³⁶, Ro 8¹⁴ 9²⁶, al.; υἱοὶ (κ. θυγατέρες) τ. ὑψίστου, Lk 6³⁵, II Co 6¹⁸; in an unique sense of Jesus, Mt 4³ 8²⁹ 28¹⁹, Mk 3⁴, Lk 4⁴¹, Jo 9³⁵ 11²⁷, al.; ὁ Χριστὸς ὁ υἱ. τ. θεοῦ ζῶντος (τ. εὐλογητοῦ), Mt 16¹⁶, Mk 14⁶¹; (c) (ὁ) υἱὸς τοῦ ἀνθρώπου (in LXX for Heb. אָדָם בֶּן, Aram. בַּר אֱנָשׁ; cf. Dalman, Words, 234 ff.; DB, iv, 579 ff.; DCG, ii, 659 ff.; Westc., St. John, i, 74 ff.; other reff. in Swete, Mk, 2¹⁰), based on the Aram. of Da 7¹³, where the phrase, like the corresponding Heb. (as in Ps 8⁵), means a man, one of the species, and indicates the human appearance of the person in question. It is used of the Messiah in Enoch, c. 46, § 1-4, also in II Es 13³, ¹², al.. Our Lord first makes the phrase a title, using the def. art. It seems to combine the ideas of his true humanity and representative character. Exc. in Ac 7⁵⁶ and (anarth.) Re 1¹³ 14¹⁴, it is used of Jesus only by himself: Mt 8²⁰, Mk 2¹⁰, Lk 5²⁴, Jo 1⁵², al.

ὕλη, -ης, ἡ, [in LXX: Jb 19²⁹ (†) 38⁴⁰ (סְכָה), Ps 68 (69)² B¹ א (יַעַר), Is 10¹⁷ (שָׁמִיר), Wi 11¹⁷ 15¹³, Si 28¹⁰, II Mac 2²⁴, IV Mac 1²⁹ *;] 1. wood, forest, woodland (Thuc., Xen., al.; for sense of forest in Ja, l.c., v. ICC, in l.). 2. wood, timber, fuel (Hom., Hdt., Thuc., al.): Ja 3⁵ (v. Hort, Ja., 70, 104 f.). 3. = Lat. materia, esp. in Philosophy, matter (Arist. and later writers; Wi, II. c.).†

Ὑμέναιος, -ου, ὁ, Hymenæus: I Ti 1²⁰, II Ti 2¹⁷.†

ὑμέτερος, -α, -ον, poss. pron. of second pers. pl. (= emphasized gen., ὑμῶν), your, yours: Jo 7⁶ 8¹⁷ 15²⁰, Ac 27³⁴, Ro 11³¹, I Co 16¹⁷, II Co 8⁸, Ga 6¹³; as pred., Lk 6²⁰; τὸ ὑ., as subst., opp. to τ. ἀλλότριον, Lk 16¹² (WH, txt., R, mg., ἡμέτερον); objectively, ὑ. καύχησις, my glorying in you, I Co 15³¹.†

ὑμνέω, -ῶ (< ὕμνος), [in LXX for הלל pi., שִׁיר, ידה hi., etc.;] 1. trans., c. acc. pers. (in cl. also c. acc. rei), to sing to, laud, sing to the praise of: Ac 16²⁵, He 2¹². 2. Intrans., to sing: in LXX and NT, of singing hymns and praises to God (Ps 64 (65)¹³, al.), Mt 26³⁰, Mk 14²⁶ (v. Swete, in l.).†

ὕμνος, -ου, ὁ, [in LXX for תְּהִלָּה, נְגִינָה, שִׁיר, etc.;] a hymn; (a) in cl. a festal song in praise of gods or heroes; (b) in LXX and NT a song of praise addressed to God: Eph 5¹⁹, Col 3¹⁶.†

Syn.: ψαλμός, that which is sung to a musical accompaniment; ᾠδή, the generic term for song (cf. Tr., *Syn.*, § lxxviii; Lft. on Col 3¹⁶).

ὑπ-άγω, [in LXX: Ex 14²¹ (הֵלֵךְ hi.), elsewhere only as v.l., To 8²¹, al.;] a word of the vulgar language, in pres. and impf. only (Bl., § 53, 1). I. Trans. 1. *to lead* or *bring under, subdue* (Hom., Hdt., al.; Ex, l.c.). 2. *to lead on slowly* (Hdt., Xen., al.). II. Intrans., *to go slowly away, withdraw oneself, depart* (so less freq. in cl.; Thuc., Eur., al.): absol., Mt 8³² 13⁴⁴, Mk 6³³, Lk 8⁴² 17¹⁴, Jo 6⁶⁷ 8² 11⁴⁴ 14⁵, ²⁸ 18⁸; οἱ ἐρχόμενοι κ. οἱ ὑπάγοντες, Mk 6³¹; ὑπῆγον κ. ἐπίστευον, Jo 12¹¹; ἵνα ὑπάγητε κ. καρπὸν φέρητε, Jo 15¹⁶; opp. to ἔρχεσθαι, Jo 3⁸ 8¹⁴; imperat., ὕπαγε, Mt 4¹⁰ 8¹³ 20¹⁴, Mk 2⁹ T, 7²⁹ 10⁵²; εἰς εἰρήνην (ἐν εἰ.), Mk 5³⁴, Ja 2¹⁶; id. prefixed to another imperat. (Bl., § 79, 4), Mt 5³⁴ 8⁴ 18¹⁵ 19²¹ 21²⁸ 27⁶⁵ 28¹⁰, Mk 1⁴⁴ 10²¹ 16⁷, Jo 4¹⁶ 9⁷, Re 10⁸; with καί inserted, Re 16¹; euphemistically, of death, Mt 26²⁴, Mk 14²¹; c. adv.: ποῦ (q.v.), Jo 12³⁵ 14⁵ 16⁵, ι Jo 2¹¹; ὅπου (q.v.), Jo 8²¹, ²² 13³³, ³⁶ 14⁴, Re 14⁴; ἐκεῖ, Jo 11⁸; c. prep.: πρός, Jo 7³³ 13³ 16⁵, ¹⁰, ¹⁷; εἰς, Mt 9⁶ 20⁴, ⁷, Mk 2¹¹ 11² 14¹³, Lk 19³⁰, Jo 6²¹ 7³ 9¹¹ 11³¹, Re 13¹⁰ 17⁸, ¹¹; εἰς ... πρός, Mt 26¹⁸, Mk 5¹⁹; ἐπί, Lk 12⁵⁸; μετά, Mt 5⁴¹; ὀπίσω, Mt 16²³, Mk 8³³; c. inf., Jo 21³.†

† ὑπακοή, -ῆς, ἡ (< ὑπακούω), [in LXX: ιι Ki 22³⁶ (עֲנָוָה); in Aq.: ib. 23²³ *;] *obedience* (opp. to παρακοή); 1. in general, absol., εἰς ὑ., Ro 6¹⁶; c. gen. subj., ιι Co 7¹⁵ 10⁶, Phm ²¹; c. gen. obj., Ro 1⁵ (Lft, *Notes*, 246) 16²⁶, ι Pe 1²²; τ. Χριστοῦ, ιι Co 10⁵. 2. Of obedience to God's commands: absol., ι Pe 1²; opp. to ἁμαρτία, Ro 6¹⁶; τέκνα ὑπακοῆς, ι Pe 1¹⁴; c. gen. subj., Ro 15¹⁸ 16¹⁹. 3. Of Christ's obedience: absol., He 5⁸; c. gen. subj., Ro 5¹⁹. (The word is not found except in LXX, NT and eccl.).†

ὑπακούω, [in LXX: chiefly for שָׁמַע;] *to listen, attend*, hence, (*a*) *to answer* a knock at a door (Plat., Xen., al.): Ac 12¹³; (*b*) *to attend to, submit to, obey* (Hdt., Thuc., al.): absol., Phl 2¹²; c. inf., He 11⁸; c. dat. pers. (Plat., al.; but more freq. c. gen.), Mt 8²⁷, Mk 1²⁷ 4⁴¹, Lk 8²⁵ 17⁶, Ro 6¹⁶, Eph 6¹, ⁵, Col 3²⁰, ²², He 5⁹, ι Pe 3⁶; c. dat. rei, Ac 6⁷, Ro 6¹² 10¹⁶, ιι Th 1⁸ 3¹⁴; seq. εἰς (by attraction, for dat.; v. *ICC*, in l.), Ro 6¹⁷.†

† ὑπανδρος, -ον, [in LXX: Nu 5²⁰, ²⁹ (תַּחַת אִישׁ), Pr 6²⁴, ²⁹, Si 9⁹, 41²¹ *;] *under* or *subject to a man, married*: γυνή, Ro 7² (Polyb., Diod., al.).†

ὑπ-αντάω, -ῶ, [in LXX: Da LXX 10¹⁴ (קְרָה), Si 9³, al.;] *to go to meet, meet*: c. dat. pers. (v. M, *Pr.*, 64), Mt 8²⁸ 28⁹, Mk 5², Lk 8²⁷ 17¹² (ἀπ-, WH, txt.), Jo 4⁵¹ 11²⁰, ³⁰ 12¹⁸, Ac 16¹⁶; of meeting in battle, Lk 14³¹.†

† ὑπ-άντησις, -εως, ἡ (< ὑπαντάω), [in LXX: Jg 11³⁴, εἰς ὑ. (לִקְרַאת), etc.;] *a going to meet*: εἰς ὑ. (v. M, *Pr.*, 14ₙ), Mt 8³⁴ 25¹, Jo 12¹³.†

ὕπαρξις, -εως, ἡ (< ὑπάρχω), [in LXX for רְכוּשׁ, הוֹן, etc.;] 1.

subsistence, existence (Arist., al.). 2. In late writers, = τὰ ὑπάρχοντα, *substance, property* : He 10³⁴ ; pl., Ae 2⁴⁵.†

ὑπάρχω, [in LXX for היה, ישׁ, לין, etc. ; τ. ὑπάρχοντα for מִקְנֶה, רכושׁ, etc. ;] 1. *to begin, make a beginning* (Hom., Hdt., al.). 2. *to be in existence, be ready, be at hand* (Hdt., Thuc., al.) : Ac 19⁴⁰ 27¹², ²¹ ; seq. ἐν, Ac 28¹⁸. 3. *to be*, prop. expressing continuance of an antecedent state or condition (cf. Gifford, *Incarnation*, 11 ff.; MM, xxv) : c. nom. pred., Lk 8⁴¹ 9⁴⁸, Ac 4³⁴ 7⁵⁵ 8¹⁶ 16³ 19³⁶ 21²⁰, I Co 7²⁶ 12²², Ja 2¹⁵, II Pe 3¹¹ ; ptcp. c. pred., Lk 16¹⁴ 23⁵⁰, Ac 2³⁰ 3² 17²⁴ 22³, Ro 4¹⁹, I Co 11⁷, II Co 8¹⁷ 12¹⁶, Ga 1¹⁴ 2¹⁴ ; pl., Lk 11¹³, Ac 16²⁰, ³⁷₁17²⁹, II Pe 2¹⁹ ; seq. ἐν, c. dat. rei, Lk 7²⁵ 16²³, Ac 5⁴ 10¹², I Co 11¹⁸, Phl 3²⁰ ; ἐν μορφῇ θεοῦ ὑπάρχων (R, mg., *being originally*), Phl 2⁶ ; ἐν, c. dat. pers., (*among*), I Co 11¹⁸ ; μακρὰν ἀπό, Ac 17²⁷ ; πρὸς τ. σωτηρίας, Ac 27³⁴. 4. *to belong to* (Thuc., Xen., al.) : c. dat. pers., Ac. 3⁶ 4³⁷ 28⁷, II Pe 1⁸ ; τὰ ὑπάρχοντα, one's *belongings, possessions* : c. dat. pers., Lk 8³ 12¹⁵, Ac 4³² ; c. gen. pers., Mt 19²¹ 24⁴⁷ 25¹⁴, Lk 11²¹ 12³³, ⁴⁴ 14³³ 16¹ 19⁸, I Co 13³, He 10³⁴ (cf. προ-υπάρχω).†

** ὑπ-είκω, [in LXX : IV Mac 6³⁵ * ;] 1. *to retire, withdraw.* 2. *to yield, submit* : metaph., He 13¹⁷.†

ὑπ-εναντίος, -α, -ον, [in LXX for אִיב, צָר, etc. ;] *set over against, opposite.* Metaph. (Plat., Arist., al.), *opposed to, contrary to* : c. dat. pers., Col 2¹⁴ ; absol., as subst., ὁ ὑ., He 10²⁷ (cf. Is 26¹¹).†

ὑπέρ (when following subst.—poët.—ὕπερ ; so as adv., II Co 11²³), prep. c. gen., acc.

I. C. gen., primarily of place (rest or motion), *over, above, across, beyond*, hence, metaph., 1. *for, on behalf of* : of prayer, Mt 5⁴⁴, Ac 8²⁴, Ro 10¹, Ja 5¹⁶, al. ; of laying down life, Jo 10¹¹, Ro 9³, al. ; esp. of Christ giving his life for man's redemption, Mk 14²⁴, Jo 10¹⁵, Ac 21¹³, Ro 5⁶⁻⁸, al. ; opp. to κατά, Mk 9⁴⁰, Lk 9⁵⁰, Ro 8³¹. 2. Causal, *for, because of, for the sake of* : c. gen. pers., Ac 5⁴¹, Ro 1⁵, Phl 1²⁹, II Co 12¹⁰, al. ; c. gen. rei, Jo 11⁴ Ro 15⁸, II Co 1⁶, al. 3. = ἀντί (v. M, *Pr.*, 105), *for, instead of, in the name of* : I Co 15²⁹, II Co 5¹⁵, ²¹, Ga 3¹³, Col 1⁷, Phm 1³ (cf. Field, *Notes*, 225). 4. In more colourless sense, = περί (M, *Pr.*, l.c.), *for, concerning, with regard to* : Ro 9²⁷, II Co 1⁶ 8²³ 12⁸, Phl 1⁷, II Th 2¹, al.

II. C. acc., primarily of place, *over, beyond, across*, hence, metaph., of measure or degree in excess, *above, beyond, over, more than* : Mt 10²⁴, ³⁷, Lk 6⁴⁰, Ac 26¹³, I Co 10¹³, II Co 1⁸, Eph 1²² 3²⁰, Phm ¹⁶, al. ; after comparatives = *than* (Jg 11²⁵, al.), Lk 16⁸, He 4¹².

III. As adv. (v. supr. ad init.), *more* : ὑπὲρ ἐγώ, *I more*, II Co 11²³ ; in compounds, v.s. ὑπεράνω, ὑπερλίαν, ὑπερπερισσῶς.

IV. In composition : *over* (ὑπεραίρω), *beyond* (ὑπερβάλλω), *more* (ὑπερνικάω), *on behalf of* (ὑπερεντυγχάνω).

ὑπερ-αίρω, [in LXX : II Ch 32²³ (נשׂא ni.), etc. ;] *to lift or raise over.* Mid., *to uplift oneself* : II Co 12⁷ ; seq. ἐπί, c. acc. pers., II Th 2⁴ (cf. II Mac 5²³).†

*† ὑπέρακμος, -ον, *past the bloom of youth :* 1 Co 7³⁶ (Eustath.). Lft. prefers tr. *of full age.* See also reff. supr., s.v. γαμίζω.†

ὑπερ-άνω, compound adv., [in LXX for עַל, מֵעַל, etc. ;] *above :* as prep. c. gen., Eph 1²¹ 4¹⁰, He 9⁵.†

*ὑπερ-αυξάνω, *to increase beyond measure :* 11 Th 1³ (v. Lft., *Notes,* 98).†

ὑπερ-βαίνω, [in LXX for עבר, etc. ;] 1. trans., *to step over, transgress* (R, *overreach :* 1 Th 4⁶). 2. Intrans., *to transgress :* metaph., 1 Th 4⁶ (R, txt.; v. M, *Th.,* in l.).†

ὑπερβαλλόντως, [in LXX : Jb 15¹¹ א B (†) * ;] *above measure :* 11 Co 11²³.†

ὑπερ-βάλλω, [in LXX : Jb 15¹¹ A (†), Si 5⁷ 25¹¹, al. ;] 1. trans., *to throw over or beyond.* 2. Intrans., *to run beyond.* In both senses, metaph., *to exceed, surpass, transcend :* 11 Co 3¹⁰ 9¹⁴, Eph 1¹⁹ 2⁷; c. gen. obj., Eph 3¹⁹.†

** ὑπερ-βολή, -ῆς, ἡ (< ὑπερβάλλω), [in LXX : καθ' ὑ., iv Mac 3¹⁸ * ;] *a throwing beyond.* Metaph., *excess, superiority, excellence :* 11 Co 4⁷ 12⁷; καθ' ὑπερβολήν, *beyond measure, exceedingly,* Ro 7¹³, 1 Co 12³¹, 11 Co 1⁸, Ga 1¹³; κ. ὑ. εἰς ὑ., *beyond all measure,* 11 Co 4¹⁷.†

ὑπερ-εῖδον, aor., [in LXX for עלם hi., מֵעַל, etc. ;] *to overlook :* c. acc. rei, Ac 17³⁰.†

*† ὑπερ-έκεινα, comp. adv. (v. Bl., § 28, 2; M, *Pr.,* 99), *beyond :* as prep. c. gen., τὰ ὑ. ὑμῶν, 11 Co 10¹⁶ (Byz. and eccl.).†

*† ὑπερ-εκ-περισσοῦ, comp. adv. (v. supr.), *superabundantly, exceeding abundantly :* 1 Th 3¹⁰ 5¹³; seq. ὑπέρ, Eph 3²⁰ (not elsewhere).†

*† ὑπερ-εκ-περισσῶς, comp. adv. (v. supr.), *beyond measure, exceedingly :* 1 Th 5¹³, WH, mg. (cf. ἐκπερισσῶς).†

*† ὑπερ-εκ-τείνω, *to stretch out overmuch :* metaph., ἑαυτούς, 11 Co 10¹⁴.†

*†|ὑπερ-εκ-χύννω (Rec. -ύνω), late form of -χέω, *to pour out over.* Pass., *to overflow, run over :* Lk 6³⁸ (not elsewhere).†

*† ὑπερ-εν-τυγχάνω, *to intercede* or *make petition for* (v. Deiss., *BS,* 121 f.) : seq. ὑπέρ, Ro 8²⁶.†

ὑπερ-έχω, [in LXX : Ge 25²³ (אָמֵץ), Ex 26¹³ (עָדַף), Si 36⁷, al. ;] 1. trans., *to hold over or above.* 2. Intrans. (when a noun follows, the case is governed by the prep.; v. Bl., § 34, 1 ; 36, 8), *to rise above, overtop;* metaph., (a) *to be superior* in rank, etc. : Ro 13¹, 1 Pe 2¹³ (cf. Wi 6⁶); (b) *to be superior, excel, surpass :* c. gen. (cl.; v. supr.), Phl 2³; c. acc. (cl.; v. supr.), Phl 4⁷; as subst., τ. ὑπερέχον, *the excellency, the surpassing* worth, Phl 3⁸.†

ὑπερηφανία, -ας, ἡ (< ὑπερήφανος, q.v.), [in LXX chiefly for גָּאוֹן and cogn. forms ;] *haughtiness, arrogance, disdain :* Mk 7²² (Plat., Xen.).†

ὑπερήφανος, -ον (< ὑπέρ, φαίνομαι, c. η pleonast., v. Kühner ³, I, 189), [in LXX for זֵד, גֵּאֶה, לֵץ, etc. ;] *showing oneself above others;* (a) in good sense (Plat., al.), *pre-eminent, splendid;* (b) more freq. in bad sense, and so always in Scr., *arrogant, haughty, disdainful* (v. Westc.,

Epp. Jo., 65ᵇ) : Ro 1³⁰, ɪɪ Ti 3² ; διανοίᾳ καρδίας, Lk 1⁵¹ ; opp. to ταπεινός (as in Pr 3³⁴), Ja 4⁶, ɪ Pe 5⁵ (LXX).†
SYN.: ἀλαζών, ὑβριστής, v. Tr., *Syn.*, § xxix.

*† ὑπερλίαν (Rec. ὑπὲρ λίαν, v. WM, § 50, 7ₙ ; Bl., § 4, 1), adv., *exceedingly, pre-eminently :* ɪɪ Co 11⁵ 12¹¹.†

**† ὑπερ-νικάω, -ῶ, [in LXX : Da ᴛʜ 6³ ; in Sm. : Ps 42 (43)¹ * ;] *to be more than conqueror :* Ro 8³⁷ (eccl.).†

ὑπέρ-ογκος, -ον, [in LXX : De 30¹¹ (נִפְלֵאת), etc. ;] *of excessive weight or size ;* metaph., *excessive, immoderate,* in late writers, of arrogant speech (v. Mayor on Ju, l.c.) : n. pl., ɪɪ Pe 2¹⁸, Ju ¹⁶.†

ὑπερ-οράω, v.s. ὑπερεῖδον.

ὑπεροχή, -ῆς, ἡ (< ὑπερέχω), [in LXX : Je 52²² (קוֹמָה), ɪɪ Mac 3¹¹, al. ;] *a projection, eminence,* as the peak of a mountain. Metaph. (Arist.), *excellence, pre-eminence :* λόγου ἢ σοφίας, ɪ Co 2¹ ; οἱ ἐν ὑ. (for a parallel to this phrase, v. Deiss., *BS*, 255, and cf. ɪɪ Mac, l.c.), ɪ Ti 2².†

*† ὑπερ-περισσεύω, *to abound more exceedingly :* Ro 5²¹. Mid., in same sense (RV, *overflow*) : c. dat. rei, ɪɪ Co 7⁴.†

*† ὑπερ-περισσῶς, adv., *beyond measure, exceedingly :* Mk 7³⁷.†

*† ὑπερ-πλεονάζω, *to abound exceedingly :* ɪ Ti 1¹⁴ (Ps Sol 5¹⁹ ; Herm., *Mand.,* v, 2, 5).†

† ὑπερ-υψόω, -ῶ, [in LXX : Ps 36 (37)³⁵ (עָרִיץ) 96 (97)⁹ (עלה ni.), Da ᴛʜ 4³⁴ 11¹² (רוּם), ib. LXX ᴛʜ 3⁵² ᵃ. * ;] 1. *to exalt beyond measure, exalt to the highest place :* Phl 2⁹. 2. *to extol* (Da, ll. c.).†

** ὑπερ-φρονέω, -ῶ, [in LXX : ɪv Mac 13¹ 14¹¹ 16² * ;] 1. *to be overproud, high-minded* (Æsch.) : μὴ ὑ. παρ' ὃ δεῖ φρονεῖν (on the paranom., v. Vau., in l.), Ro 12³. 2. *to overlook, think slightly of* (Thuc., Plat.).†

ὑπερῷον, -ου, τό (neut. of ὑπερῷος, *above*, < ὑπέρ), [in LXX for עֲלִיָּה and cogn. forms ;] 1. in cl., *the upper story* or *upper rooms* where the women resided (Hom., al.). 2. In LXX and NT, *an upper chamber, roof-chamber,* built on the flat roof of the house (v. *DB*, iii, 674ᵃ) : Ac 1¹³ 9³⁷, ³⁹ 20⁸ (cf. ɪv Ki 23²²).†

ὑπ-έχω, [in LXX : Ps 88 (89)⁵⁰ (נשׂא), La 5⁷ (סבל), Wi 12²¹, ɪɪ Mac 4⁴⁸ * ;] *to hold* or *put under.* Metaph., *to undergo, suffer :* δίκην, Ju ⁷ (Soph., Eur., al.).†

ὑπήκοος, -ον (< ὑπακούω), [in LXX : Jo 17¹³ (לָמַס), Pr 21²⁸ (שׁוֹמֵעַ), etc. ;] *giving ear, obedient, subject :* Phl 2⁸ ; c. dat. pers., Ac 7³⁹ ; εἰς πάντα, ɪɪ Co 2⁹.†

** ὑπηρετέω, -ῶ (< ὑπηρέτης), [in LXX : Wi 16²¹, ²⁴, ²⁵ 19⁶, Si 39⁴ * ;] prop., *to serve as rower* on a ship (Diod., al.). In cl. always metaph., *to minister to, serve :* c. dat. pers., Ac 13³⁶ 20³⁴ 24²³.†

ὑπηρέτης, -ου, ὁ (< ὑπό + ἐρέτης, *a rower*), [in LXX : Pr 14³⁵ (עֶבֶד), Wi 6⁴, al. ;] prop., *an under rower ;* hence, generally, *a servant, attendant, minister :* of a magistrate's attendant, Mt 5²⁵ ; of officers of the Synagogue or Sanhedrin, Mt 26⁵⁸, Mk 14⁵⁴, ⁶⁵, Lk 4²⁰, Jo

7³²,⁴⁵,⁴⁶ 18³,¹²,²² 19⁶, Ac 5²²,²⁶; of the attendants of kings, οἱ ὖ. οἱ ἐμοί, Jo 18³⁶; of Christian ministers, Ac 13⁵ 26¹⁶; ὑπηρέται λόγου, Lk 1²; Χριστοῦ, ɪ Co 4¹; δοῦλοι κ. ὖ., Jo 18¹⁸.†

SYN.: v.s. διάκονος.

ὕπνος, -ου, ὁ, [in LXX for שֵׁנָה, חֲלוֹם, etc.;] *sleep:* Mt 1²⁴, Lk 9³², Jo 11¹³, Ac 20⁹; metaph., Ro 13¹¹.†

ὑπό (before smooth breathing ὑπ᾽, Mt 8⁹ᵇ, Lk 7⁸ᵇ; before rough breathing ὑφ᾽, Ro 3⁹; on the neglect of elision in Mt, Lk, ll. c.ᵃ, Ga 3²², v. WH, *App.*, 146; Tdf., *Pr.*, iv), prep. c. gen., dat. (not in NT), acc.
I. C. gen., primarily of place, *under*, hence, metaph., of the efficient cause, *by:* after passive verbs, c. gen. pers., Mt 1²², Mk 1⁵, Lk 2¹⁸, Jo 14²¹, Ac 4¹¹, ɪ Co 1¹¹, He 3⁴, al.; c. gen. rei, Mt 8²⁴, Lk 7²⁴, Ro 3²¹, al.; with neut. verbs and verbs with pass. meaning, Mt 17¹², Mk 5²⁶, ɪ Co 10⁹,¹⁰, ɪ Th 2¹⁴, al.
II. C. acc., *under;* 1. of motion: Mt 5¹⁵ 8⁸, Mk 4²¹, Lk 13³⁴; hence, metaph., of subjection, Ro 7¹⁴, ɪ Co 15²⁷, Ga 3²², ɪ Pe 5⁶, al. 2. Of position: Jo 1⁴⁹, Ac 4¹², Ro 3¹³, ɪ Co 10¹, al.; hence, metaph., *under, subject to,* Mt 8⁹, Ro 3⁹, ɪ Co 9²⁰, Ga 4⁵, al. 3. Of time, *about:* Ac 5²¹.
III. In composition: *under* (ὑποδέω), hence, of *subjection* (ὑποτάσσω), *compliance* (ὑπακούω), *secrecy* (ὑποβάλλω), *diminution* (ὑποπνέω).

**ὑπο-βάλλω, [in LXX: Da ᴛʜ 3⁹ A, ɪ Es 2¹⁸*;] *to throw* or *put under.* Metaph., (*a*) *to subject, submit;* (*b*) *to suggest, whisper, prompt;* (*c*) *to suborn* (v. Field, *Notes*, 113), *instigate:* c. acc. pers., Ac 6¹¹.†

**†ὑπογραμμός, -οῦ, ὁ (< ὑπογράφω, (*a*) *to write under;* (*b*) *to trace letters for copying*), [in LXX: ɪɪ Mac 2²⁸*;] 1. *a writing-copy,* hence, 2. *an example:* ɪ Pe 2²¹ (Philo).†

ὑπό-δειγμα, -τος, τό (< ὑποδείκνυμι), [in LXX: Ez 42¹⁵, Si 44¹⁶, ɪɪ Mac 6²⁸,³¹, ɪᴠ Mac 17²³*;] used by later writers (Xen. onwards) for παράδειγμα (v. Rutherford, *NPhr.*, 62), (*a*) *a figure, copy:* He 8⁵, 9²³; (*b*) *an example:* for imitation, Jo 13¹⁵, Ja 5¹⁰; for warning, He 4¹¹, ɪɪ Pe 2⁶.†

SYN.: ὁμοίωμα, τύπος, ὑποτύπωσις (v. *DB*, iii. 696ᵇ).

ὑπο-δείκνυμι, [in LXX for ירה hi., etc.;] 1. *to show secretly.* 2. *to show by tracing out;* hence, generally, *to teach, make known:* c. dat. pers., Lk 6⁴⁷ 12⁵, Ac 9¹⁶; id. c. inf., Mt 3⁷, Lk 3⁷; seq., ὅτι, Ac 20³⁵.†

**ὑπο-δέχομαι, [in LXX: To 7⁸,⁹, Jth 13¹³ A, ɪ Mac 16¹⁵, ɪᴠ Mac 13¹⁷*;] *to receive under one's roof, receive as a guest, entertain hospitably:* c. acc. pers., Lk 19⁶, Ac 17⁷, Ja 2²⁵; εἰς τ. οἶκον, Lk 10³⁸ (v. MM, xxv).†

ὑπο-δέω, [in LXX: ɪɪ Ch 28¹⁵, Ez 16¹⁰ (נעל)*;] *to bind under,* esp. of foot gear. Most freq. in mid. and pass. c. acc.; (*a*) of the foot, ὑποδησάμενοι τ. πόδας, *your feet shod:* Eph 6¹⁵; (*b*) of that which is put on, σανδάλια: Mk 6⁹, Ac 12⁸.†

ὑπόδημα, -τος, τό (< ὑποδέω), [in LXX for נַעַל;] a sole bound under the foot, a sandal : Mt 3¹¹ 10¹⁰, Mk 1⁷, Lk 3¹⁶ 10⁴ 15²² 22³⁵, Jo 1²⁷; τ. ποδῶν, Ac 7³³ (LXX) 13²⁵.†
    SYN. : σανδάλιον, q.v.

*ὑπόδικος, -ον, brought to trial, answerable to : c. dat. pers., τ. θεῷ, Ro 3¹⁹ (v. MM, xxv).†

ὑπο-ζύγιος, -α, -ον, [in LXX for חֲמוֹר;] under the yoke; as subst., τὸ ζ. (Hdt., al.), a beast of burden; colloq., an ass (v. Deiss., BS, 160 f.), and so always in LXX and NT : Mt 21⁵ (LXX), II Pe 2¹⁶.†

**ὑπο-ζώννυμι, [in LXX : II Mac 3¹⁹*;] to undergird (Hdt., al.; ὑπὸ τ. μάστους, II Mac, l.c.); of a ship, to undergird or frap : Ac 27¹⁷ (v. DB, ext. 367ᵃ).†

ὑπο-κάτω, comp. adv. (v. M, Pr., 99), [in LXX chiefly for תַּחַת;] below, under : as prep. c. gen., Mt 22⁴⁴, Mk 6¹¹ 7²⁸ 12³⁶ (Rec., R, txt., ὑποπόδιον, as in LXX), Lk 8¹⁶, Jo 1⁵¹, He 2⁸ (LXX), Re 5³, ¹³ 6⁹ 12¹.†

ὑπο-κρίνομαι, [in LXX : Jb 39³² (40²) אֵל (AB אֵל² ἀπο-, עָנָה), Si 1²⁹ 35 (32)¹⁵ 36 (33)², II Mac 5²⁵ 6²¹, ²⁴, IV Mac 6¹⁵, ¹⁷*;] 1. = Att. ἀποκρίνομαι (q.v.), to answer, reply (Hom., Hdt., al.). 2. to answer on the stage, play a part (Arist., al.). Metaph., to feign, pretend (Demos., Polyb.) : c. acc. et inf., Lk 20²⁰ (cf. Ps Sol 4²²).†

**ὑπό-κρισις, -εως, ἡ (< ὑποκρίνομαι, q.v.), [in LXX : II Mac 6²⁵*;] 1. a reply, answer (Hdt.). 2. play-acting (Arist., Polyb., al.). Metaph., pretence, hypocrisy : Mt 23²⁸, Mk 12¹⁵, Lk 12¹, Ga 2¹³, I Ti 4², I Pe 2¹ (Polyb., Pss Sol 4⁷).†

ὑπο-κριτής, -οῦ, ὁ (< ὑποκρίνομαι, q.v.), [in LXX : Jb 34³⁰ 36¹³ (חָנֵף) *;] 1. one who answers, an interpreter (Plat.). 2. a stage-player, actor (Plut., Xen., al.). Metaph. (in LXX and NT), a pretender, dissembler, hypocrite : Mt 6², ⁵, ¹⁶ 7⁵ 15⁷ 22¹⁸ 23¹³⁻¹⁵ 24⁵¹, Mk 7⁶, Lk 6⁴² 12⁵⁶ 13¹⁵.†

ὑπο-λαμβάνω, [in LXX : Jb 2⁴ 4¹ and freq. (עָנָה), Ps 47 (48)⁹ (דָּמָה pi.), To 6¹⁷, Wi 17², III Mac 3⁸, ¹¹, al.;] 1. to take or bear up (by supporting from beneath) : c. acc. pers., Ac 1⁹. 2. to receive, welcome, entertain (Xen.) : III Jo ⁸. 3. to catch up in speech (Hdt., al.; Jb, ll. c.) : Lk 10³⁰. 4. Of mental action, to assume, suppose (Xen., al.; To, Wi, III Mac, ll. c.) : Ac 2¹⁵; seq. ὅτι (v. Bl., § 70, 2), Lk 7⁴³.†

*†ὑπολαμπάς, -άδος, ἡ, a window : Ac 20⁸ D (for λαμπάς; v. MM, xxv).†

ὑπό-λειμμα (WH, -λιμμα, v. their App., 154), -τος, τό, [in LXX chiefly for שְׁאֵרִית;] a remnant : Ro 9²⁷ (Arist., al.; cf. κατάλειμμα).†

ὑπο-λείπω, [in LXX chiefly (pass.) for יתר ni., שאר ni.;] to leave remaining (Hom., Thuc., al.) : pass., of survivors, Ro 11³.†

†ὑπολήνιον, -ον, τό (< ὑπό, ληνός), [in LXX : Jl 3 (4)¹³, Hg 2¹⁷ (¹⁶), Za 14¹⁰, Is 16¹⁰ (יֶקֶב) *;] a vessel or trough beneath a winepress to

receive the juice (RV, *a pit for the winepress*) : Mk 12¹ (v. Swete, in l., and cf. ληνός).†

ὑπό-λιμμα, v.s. *ὑπόλειμμα*.

*†ὑπο-λιμπάνω, collat. form of *ὑπολείπω, to leave behind :* 1 Pe 2²¹.† **ὑπο-μένω**, [in LXX chiefly for קוה, also for יחל hi., etc.;] 1. intrans., *to stay behind :* seq. *ἐν*, Lk 2⁴³; *ἐκεῖ*, Ac 17¹⁴. 2. Trans., *(a)* c. acc., *to await, wait for :* Ro 8²⁴ (Hom., Hdt., Xen., al.); *(b)* of things, *to bear patiently, endure :* absol., Mt 10²² 24¹³, Mk 13¹³, II Ti 2¹², Ja 5¹¹, 1 Pe 2²⁰; *τ. θλίψει* (dat. of circumstance), Ro 12¹²; seq. *εἰς*, He 12⁷; c. acc. rei, 1 Co 13⁷, II Ti 2¹⁰, He 10³² 12²,³, Ja 1¹².†

SYN. : μακροθυμέω (v.s. *ὑπομονή*).

ὑπο-μιμνήσκω, [in LXX: III Ki 4³ B (זכר hi.), Wi 12¹ 18²², IV Mac 18¹⁴ *;] *to cause one to remember, put one in mind or remind one of :* c. acc. rei, II Ti 2¹⁴, III Jo ¹⁰; c. dupl. acc. (Thuc., al.), Jo 14²⁶; c. acc. pers., seq. *περί*, II Pe 1¹²; id., seq. *ὅτι*, Ju ⁵; c. inf., Ti 3¹; pass., c. gen. rei, Lk 22⁶¹.†

ὑπό-μνησις, *-εως, ἡ* (*ὑπομιμνήσκω*), [in LXX: Ps 70 (71)⁶ א (תְּהִלָּה), Wi 16¹¹, II Mac 6¹⁷ *;] *a reminding, reminder : ἐν ὑ.,* II Pe 1¹³ 3¹; c. gen., II Ti 1⁵.†

ὑπο-μονή, *-ῆς, ἡ* (*ὑπομένω*), [in LXX for מִקְוֶה and cogn. forms; freq. in IV Mac;] 1. *a remaining behind* (Arist.). 2. *patient enduring, endurance :* Lk 8¹⁵ 21¹⁹, Ro 5³,⁴ 15⁴,⁵, II Co 6⁴ 12¹², Col 1¹¹, II Th 1⁴, 1 Ti 6¹¹, II Ti 3¹⁰, Tit 2², He 10³⁶, Ja 1³,⁴ 5¹¹, II Pe 1⁶, Re 2²,³,¹⁹ 13¹⁰ 14¹²; *δι' ὑπομονῆς,* Ro 8²⁵, He 12¹; c. gen. pers., II Th 3⁵ (*ICC,* in l.), Re 3¹⁰; c. gen. rei, Ro 2⁷, II Co 1⁶, 1 Th 1³; seq. *ἐν*, Re 1⁹.†

SYN. : v.s. *μακροθυμία,* and cf. Hort on Ja 1³.

**ὑπο-νοέω, *-ῶ*, [in LXX: Da TH 7²⁵ (סבר), To 8¹⁶, Jth 14¹⁴, Si 23²¹ *;] *to suspect, conjecture :* Ac 25¹⁸; c. acc. et inf., Ac 13²⁵ 27²⁷.†

ὑπόνοια, *-ας, ἡ* (< *ὑπονοέω*), [in LXX: Da LXX 4¹⁶,³² 5⁶ (רַעְיוֹן), Si 3³⁴ *;] *a suspicion :* 1 Ti 6⁴.†

*ὑπο-πιάζω, later form of *ὑποπιέζω, to press slightly ;* metaph., *to repress :* 1 Co 9²⁷ T⁷ for *ὑπωπιάζω,* q.v.†

*†ὑπο-πλέω, *to sail under,* i.e. *under the lee of :* c. acc., Ac 27⁴,⁷.†

*ὑπο-πνέω, 1. *to blow underneath* (Arist.). 2. *to blow gently :* Ac 27¹³.†

†ὑποπόδιον, *-ου, τό* (< *ὑπό, πούς*), [in LXX: Ps 98 (99)⁵ 109 (110)¹, Is 66¹, La 2¹ (הֲדֹם)*;] *a footstool* (= cl. *θρᾶνος*) : Ja 2³; metaph., Mt 5³⁵, Mk 12³⁶ (*ὑποκάτω,* WH, R, mg.), Lk 20⁴³, Ac 2³⁵ 7⁴⁹, He 1¹³ 10¹³ (all, except Mt, l.c., from LXX, Ps 109 (110)¹, Is 66¹) (for exx., v. Deiss., *BS,* 223).†

ὑπο-στασις, *-εως, ἡ* (< *ὑφίστημι, to set under, stand under, support*), [in LXX for מַצָּב (I Ki 13²³ 14⁴ B), תִּקְוָה (Ru 1¹², Ez 19⁵), etc., also in Wi 16²¹;] 1. *a support, base* or *foundation* (in various senses). 2. *substance* (Arist., al.; opp. to *φαντασία, ἔμφασις*): He 1³. 3. *steadiness,* *firmness* (Polyb., al.), hence, *assurance, confidence :* II Co 9⁴ 11¹⁷, He 3¹⁴ 11¹ (here perhaps *title-deed*, as that which gives reality or guarantee; v. MM, xxv).†

ὑπο-στέλλω, [in LXX : De 1¹⁷ (נוּר), Jb 13⁸ (פָּנִים נָשָׂא), Hb 2⁴ (עפל pu.), Hg 1¹⁰ (כלא), Ex 23²¹, Wi 6⁷, III Mac 5²⁰ * ;] 1. *to draw in, let down* (ἱστίον, οὐράν, etc.). 2. *to draw back, withdraw :* ἑαυτόν, Ga 2¹² (Polyb., al.; v. Lft., in l.). Mid., *to shrink* or *draw back :* He 10³⁸ (LXX) ; seq. τοῦ μή, c. inf., Ac 20²⁰, ²⁷ ; οὐδέν, ib. ²⁰.†

*† ὑπο-στολή, -ῆς, ἡ (< ὑποστέλλω), 1. *a letting down, lowering* (Plut.). 2. *a shrinking back* (Hesych.) : οὐκ ἐσμὲν ὑποστολῆς (on the gen., v. Bl., § 35, 2), He 10³⁹.†

ὑπο-στρέφω, [in LXX chiefly for שׁוּב], 1. trans., *to turn back* or *about* (Hom.). 2. Intrans., *to turn back, return :* Lk 2²⁰, ⁴³ 8³⁷, ⁴⁰ 9¹⁰ 10¹⁷ 17¹⁵ 19¹² 23⁴⁸, ⁵⁶, Ac 8²⁸ ; c. inf., Lk 17¹⁸ ; seq. διά, Ac 20³ ; εἰς, Lk 1⁵⁶ 2⁴⁵ 4¹⁴ 7¹⁰ 8³⁹ 11²⁴ 24³³, ⁵², Ac 1¹² 8²⁵ 13¹³, ³⁴ 14²¹ 21⁶ 22¹⁷ 23³², Ga 1¹⁷ ; ἀπό, Lk 4¹ 24⁹, He 7¹ ; ἐκ, Ac 12²⁵, II Pe 2²¹.†

ὑπο-στρωννύω, [in LXX : Is 58⁵ (יצע hi.), etc. ;] late form of ὑπο-στορέννυμι, *to spread* or *strew under :* c. acc. rei, Lk 19³⁶.†

** ὑπο-ταγή, -ῆς, ἡ, [in LXX : Wi 18¹⁶ A * ;] *subjection :* II Co 9¹³, Ga 2⁵ I Ti 2¹¹ 3⁴.†

ὑπο-τάσσω, [in LXX for דבר hi., דמם, שׁוּם, שׁית, etc. ;] 1. as a military term, *to place* or *rank under* (Polyb.). 2. *to subject, put in subjection :* I Co 15²⁷, Phl 3²¹, He 2⁵, ⁸ ; pass., Ro 8²⁰, I Co 15²⁷, ²⁸, I Pe 3²², Eph 1²². Mid., *to subject oneself, obey :* absol., Ro 13⁵, I Co 14³⁴ ; c. dat. pers., Lk 2⁵¹ 10¹⁷, ²⁰, Ro 8⁷ 10³ 13¹, I Co 14³² 15²⁸ (ὑποταγήσεται ; cf. M, *Pr.,* 163), ib. 16¹⁶, Eph 5²¹, ²² (T, WH, txt., R, om.), ib. ²⁴, Col 3¹⁸, Tit 2⁵, ⁹ 3¹, He 12⁹, I Pe 2¹⁸, 3¹, ⁵ 5⁵ ; imperat., Ja 4⁷, I Pe 2¹³ 5⁵.†

ὑπο-τίθημι, [in LXX for שׁוּם, etc. ;] *to place under, lay down.* Metaph., τ. τράχηλον ὑποθεῖναι, *to risk one's life* (v. Deiss., *LAE,* 119 f.) : Ro 16⁴ ; mid., *to suggest :* I Ti 4⁶.†

* ὑπο-τρέχω, *to run in under ;* of navigators, *to run in the lee of :* c. acc. (v. M, *Pr.,* 65), Ac. 27¹⁶.†

*† ὑπο-τύπωσις, -εως, ἡ (< ὑποτυπόω, *to delineate*), *an outline, sketch.* Metaph., *a pattern, example :* I Ti 1¹⁶, II Ti 1¹³.†
    SYN. : ὁμοίωμα, τύπος, ὑπόδειγμα (v. *DB,* iii, 696ᵇ).

ὑπο-φέρω, [in LXX for נשׂא, etc. ;] *to bear by being under.* Metaph., *to endure :* c. acc. rei, I Co 10¹³, II Ti 3¹¹, I Pe 2¹⁹.†

ὑπο-χωρέω, [in LXX : Jg 20³⁷ B (—), Si 13⁹, II Mac 12¹² * ;] *to go back, retire :* seq. ἐν, Lk 5¹⁶ ; seq. εἰς, Lk 9¹⁰.†

* ὑπωπιάζω (< ὑπώπιον, (a) *the part of the face below the eyes ;* (b) *a blow on the face*), *to strike under the eye, give a black eye :* metaph., (a) of persistent annoyance (RV, *wear out*), Lk 18⁵ ; (b) of severe self-discipline (R, txt. *buffet,* mg. *bruise*), I Co 9²⁷ (v. Field, *Notes,* 71, 174).†

ὗς, ὑός, ὁ, ἡ, [in LXX for חֲזִיר ;] *swine :* fem. (*sow*), II Pe 2²².†

*† ὑσσός, -οῦ, ὁ, *a javelin* (v. ref. s.v. ὕσσωπος).

†ὕσσωπος, -ου, ἡ, [in LXX for אֵזוֹב;] *hyssop*, of which a bunch was used in ritual sprinklings: He 9¹⁹; of a branch or rod (?) of hyssop, Jo 19²⁹ (but v. Field, *Notes*, 106 ff., for suggestion to substitute ὑσσῷ here).†

ὑστερέω, -ῶ (< ὕστερος), [in LXX for חָסֵר, חָדֵל, etc.;] *to come late, be behind* (opp. to προτερέω, φθάνω; c. gen. rei, *for;* c. gen. pers., *later than*). Metaph., 1. of persons, (*a*) absol., *to come short, fail:* He 4¹; seq. ἀπό, 12¹⁵.; (*b*) c. gen. pers., *to come short of, be inferior to:* II Co 11⁵; οὐδέν (in nothing, in no respect), ib. 12¹¹; (*c*) with reference to things, *to come short (of), be in want (of):* c. acc. rei, Mt 19²⁰ (Si 51²⁴); c. gen. rei, Lk 22³⁵; so mid. (Diod., FlJ), Ro 3²³; absol., *to be in want, suffer want,* Lk 15¹⁴, I Co 8⁸, II Co 11⁸, He 11³⁷ (Si 11¹¹); opp. to περισσεύειν, Phl 4¹²; seq. ἐν, I Co 1⁷. 2. Of things, (*a*) *to fail, be lacking:* Jo 2³; c. acc. pers. (v. Swete, in l.; Mozley, *Ps.*, 42), Mk 10²¹; (*b*) *to be inferior:* mid., I Co 12²⁴ (cf. ἀφ-υστερέω).†

†ὑστέρημα, -τος, τό (< ὑστερέω), [in LXX: Jg 18¹⁰ 19¹⁹, ²⁰, Ps 33 (34)⁹ (מַחְסוֹר), Ec 1¹⁵ (חֶסְרוֹן), II Es 6⁹ (ὁ. εἶναι, חֲשַׁח) *;*] (*a*) *that which is lacking, deficiency, shortcoming:* c. gen. poss. (pron. poss.), I Co 16¹⁷, Phl 2³⁰; c. gen. rei, Col 1²⁴, I Th 3¹⁰; (*b*) *need, want, poverty* (Ps 33 (34)¹⁰, Jg 18¹⁰, al.): Lk 21⁴, II Co 9¹² 11⁹; opp. to περίσσευμα, II Co 8¹³,¹⁴ (eccl.).†

**†ὑστέρησις, -εως, ἡ (< ὑστερέω), [in Aq.: Jb 30³ *;] *need, want:* opp. to τὸ περισσεῦον, Mk 12⁴⁴; καθ᾽ὑ., Phl 4¹¹ (eccl.).†

ὕστερος, -α, -ον, [in LXX for אַחֲרוֹן and cogn. forms;] *latter, later:* ἐν ὑ. καιροῖς, I Ti 4¹ (on the reading ὁ ὕ., WH, for ὁ πρῶτος, v. WH, *App.*, in l.). Neut., -ον, used adverbially instead of ὑστέρως, *afterwards, later:* Mt 4² 21²⁹ (30), ³², ³⁷ 25¹¹ 26⁶⁰, Mk 16[14], Lk 20³², Jo 13³⁶. He 12¹¹; c. gen., Mt 22²⁷.†

ὑφαίνω, [in LXX for ארג, etc.;] *to weave:* Lk 12²⁷, T, WH, mg.†

ὑφαντός, -ή, -όν (< ὑφαίνω), [in LXX chiefly for חֹשֵׁב;] *woven:* Jo 19²³.†

ὑψηλός, -ή, -όν, [in LXX chiefly for במה, also for נטה, רום, etc.;] *high, lofty:* ὄρος, Mt 4⁸ 17¹, Mk 9², Re 21¹⁰; τεῖχος, ib. ¹²; μετὰ βραχίονος ὑ., fig., Ac 13¹⁷ (cf. Ex 6⁶, al); pl., ὑψηλά, of heaven (Ps 92 (93)⁴, Is 33⁵, al.), He 1³; compar., ὑψηλότερος τ. οὐρανῶν, He 7²⁶. Metaph: Lk 16¹⁵; ὑψηλὰ φρονεῖν, Ro 11²⁰ 12¹⁶, I Ti 6¹⁷ (WH, txt., ὑψηλοφρονεῖν).†

*†ὑψηλο-φρονέω, -ῶ, = μεγαλοφρονεῖν (Xen., Plat., al.), *to be high-minded:* I Ti 6¹⁷ (WH, mg., ὑψηλὰ φρονεῖν).†

ὕψιστος, -η, -ον, superlat., without positive in use, in cl. chiefly poët. (Æsch., Soph., al.), [in LXX chiefly for עֶלְיוֹן, also for מָרוֹם, etc.;] *highest, most high:* of place, τὰ ὕ. (of the heavens), Mt 21⁹, Mk 11¹⁰, Lk 2¹⁴ 19³⁸ (cf. Jos 16¹⁹, Is 57¹⁵); of God (in cl., of Zeus; Pind., Æsch., al.), ὕ., Lk 1³², ³⁵, ⁷⁶ 6³⁵ (as freq. in Si 4¹⁰, al.); ὁ ὕ., Ac ⁱ⁸; ὁ θεὸς ὁ ὕ., Mk 5⁷, Lk 8²⁸, Ac 16¹⁷, He 7¹ (cf. Ge 14¹⁸).†

ὕψος, -ους, τό, [in LXX for קוֹמָה, מָרוֹם, etc.;] *height*: Eph 3¹⁸, Ja 1⁹, Re 21¹⁶; of heaven (EV, *on high*), ἐξ ὕ., Lk 1⁷⁸ 24⁴⁹; εἰς ὕ., Eph 4⁸(LXX).†

ὑψόω, -ῶ (< ὕψος), [in LXX chiefly for רוּם, also for גָּבַהּ, נָשָׂא, etc.;] *to lift or raise up :* c. acc., Jo 3¹⁴ 8²⁸ 12³²,³⁴; ἕως τ. οὐρανοῦ, fig., pass., Mt 11²³, Lk 10¹⁵. Metaph., *to exalt, uplift :* Ac 2³³ 5³¹ 13⁴⁷, II Co 11⁷, Ja 4¹⁰, I Pe 5⁶; opp. to ταπεινῶ, Lk 1⁵²; ἑαυτόν, Mt 23¹², Lk 14¹¹ 18¹⁴ (cf. ὑπερ-υψόω).†

ὕψωμα, -τος, τό, [in LXX: Jb 24²⁴ (†), Jth 10⁸ 13⁴ 15⁹*;] (a) *height :* Ro 8³⁹; (b) *that which is lifted up, a barrier :* II Co 10⁵.†

Φ

Φ, φ, φῖ, τό, indecl., *phi, ph,* the twenty-first letter. As a numeral, φ′ = 500, φ, = 500,000.

φάγομαι, Hellenistic for cl. ἔδομαι, v.s. ἐσθίω.

*† φάγος, -ου, ὁ (< φαγεῖν, v.s. ἐσθίω), *a glutton :* Mt 11¹⁹, Lk 7³⁴.†

φαιλόνης, v.s. φελόνης.

φαίνω, [in LXX for אוֹר hi., רָאָה ni., etc.;] I. Act., 1. *to bring to light, cause to appear* (so most freq. in cl.). 2. Absol., *to give light, shine* (Hom., Plat., al.): Jo 1⁵ 5³⁵, II Pe 1¹⁹, I Jo 2⁸, Re 1¹⁶ 8¹² 18²³ 21²³. II. Pass., *to come to light, appear, be manifest :* Mt 2⁷ 13²⁶ 24²⁷,³⁰, Lk 9⁸, Phl 2¹⁵, He 11³, I Pe 4¹⁸(LXX); opp. to ἀφανίζεσθαι, Ja 4¹⁴; c. dat. pers. (Bl. § 54, 4), Mt 1²⁰ 2¹³,¹⁹, Mk 16[⁹]; c. nom. pred., Mt 23²⁷,²⁸, Ro 7¹³, II Co 13⁷; id. c. dat. pers., Mt 6⁵,¹⁶,¹⁸ (seq. nom. ptcp., but not as in cl.; v. Bl., § 73, 4); impers., Mt 9³³; of the mind and judgment (= δοκεῖ, q.v.), Mk 14⁶⁴ (cf. I Es 2²¹), Lk 24¹¹.†

SYN.: v.s. δοκέω.

Φάλεκ (T, Rec. Φαλέκ, L, mg., Φάλεγ), ὁ, indecl. (Heb. פֶּלֶג, Ge 11¹⁶), *Peleg :* Lk 3³⁵.†

φανερός, -ά, -όν (< φαίνομαι), [in LXX: De 29²⁹⁽²⁸⁾ (גָּלָה ni.), Pr 14⁴, Si 6²², al.;] *open to sight, visible, manifest :* Ga 5¹⁹; seq. ἐν, Ro 1¹⁹, I Jo 3¹⁰; c. dat. pers., Ac 4¹⁶ 7¹³, I Ti 4¹⁵; φ. γίνεσθαι (in LXX for בְחֹן ni., Ge 42¹⁶), Mk 6¹⁴, Lk 8¹⁷, I Co 3¹³ 14²⁵; id. seq. ἐν, I Co 11¹⁹, Phl 1¹³; φ. ποιεῖν, Mt 12¹⁶, Mk 3¹²; εἰς φ. ἐλθεῖν (cf. Bl., § 47, 2), Mk 4²², Lk 8¹⁷; ἐν τῷ φ. (opp. to ἐν τ. κρυπτῷ), Ro 2²⁸.†

SYN. : v.s. δῆλος.

φανερόω, -ῶ, [in LXX: Je 40 (33)⁶ (גָּלָה pi.)*;] *to make visible, clear, manifest or known :* c. acc. rei, Jo 2¹¹ 17⁶, Ro 1¹⁹, I Co 4⁵, II Co 2¹⁴ 11⁶, Col 4⁴, Tit 1³; pass., Mk 4²², Jo 3²¹ 9³, Ro 3²¹ 16²⁶, II Co 4¹⁰,¹¹, Eph 5¹³, Col 1²⁶, II Ti 1¹⁰, He 9⁸, I Jo 3² 4⁹, Re 3¹⁸ 15⁴; c. acc. pers., of Christ, Jo 7⁴ 21¹; pass., II Co 3³ 5¹⁰,¹¹, I Jo 2¹⁹; of Christ, Mk 16[¹²,¹⁴], Jo 1³¹ 21¹⁴, Col 3⁴, I Ti 3¹⁶, He 9²⁶, I Pe 1²⁰ 5⁴, I Jo 1² (ἡ ζωή; v. Westc., in l.) 2²⁸ 3²,⁵,⁸.†

SYN. : v.s. ἀποκαλύπτω.

**φανερῶς, adv. (< φανερός), [in LXX : ιι Mac 3²⁸ *;] (a) manifestly, openly : Mk 1⁴⁵; opp. to ἐν κρυπτῷ,, Jo 7¹⁰; (b) clearly : Ac 10³ (ιι Mac 3²⁸).†

†φανέρωσις, -εως, ἡ (< φανερόω), [in LXX as v.l. for δήλωσις (אוּרִים), Le 8⁸, Cod. Ven. (Thayer, s.v.) *;] manifestation : ι Co 12⁷, ιι Co 4².†

*φανός, -οῦ, ὁ (< φαίνω), a torch or lantern (v. Rutherford, NPhr., 131 f.) : Jo 18³.†
    Syn. : v.s. λαμπάς.

Φανουήλ, ὁ, indecl. (Heb. פְּנוּאֵל), Phanuel : Lk 2³⁶.†

**φαντάζω (< φαίνω), [in LXX : Wi 6¹⁶, Si 31 (34)⁵ *;] to make visible. In cl. used in pass. only, = φαίνομαι, to become visible, appear : ptcp., He 12²¹.†

φαντασία, -ας, ἡ (< φαντάζω), [in LXX : Za 10¹ (חָזָיוֹן), Hb 2¹⁸, ¹⁹ 3¹⁰, Wi 18¹⁷ *;] 1. as philos. term, (a) imagination ; (b) = φάντασμα (Plat., Arist.). 2. In later writers (Polyb., al.), show, display : Ac 25²³.†

φάντασμα, -τος, τό (< φαντάζω), [in LXX : Jb 20⁸ A (חִזָּיוֹן), Is 28⁷ A, Wi 17¹⁵ *;] = φάσμα, an appearance, apparition (Æsch., al.) : Mt 14²⁶, Mk 6⁴⁹ (v. DCG, i, 111b).†

φάραγξ, -αγγος, ἡ, [in LXX chiefly for נַחַל, also for גַּיְא, etc. ;] a chasm, ravine : Lk 3⁵ (LXX) (v. DB, iv, 845 f.).†

Φαραώ, ὁ, indecl. (in FlJ, Ant., viii, 6, 2, Φαραών, -ῶνος), (Heb. פַּרְעֹה), Pharaoh, the general title of the kings of Egypt : Ac 7¹³, ²¹, Ro 9¹⁷, He 11²⁴ ; Φ. βασιλεὺς Αἰγύπτου, Ac 7¹⁰.†

Φαρές, ὁ, indecl. (Heb. פֶּרֶץ, Ge 38²⁹), Peres : Mt 1³, Lk 3³³.†

Φαρισαῖος, -ου, ὁ (Aram. פְּרִישָׁא; v. Dalman, Gr., 157n, Words, 2n), a Pharisee : Mt 23²⁶, Phl 3⁵ ; usually in pl., Mt 9¹¹, Mk 2¹⁸, al.; Φ. κ. γραμματεῖς, Mt 5²⁰, Mk 2¹⁶, Lk 5²¹, al.; Φ. κ. Σαδδουκαῖοι, Mt 16¹, Ac 23⁶, ⁷, al.; ἀρχιερεῖς κ. Φ., Mt 21⁴⁵, Jo 7³², al. (v. DB, iii, 826b).

φαρμακεία, v.s. φαρμακία.

*φαρμακεύς, -έως, ὁ (< φάρμακον), a sorcerer : Re 21⁸, Rec.†

φαρμακία (Rec. -εία), -ας, ἡ (< φαρμακεύω, to administer drugs), poët. and late prose form of φαρμακεία, [in LXX : Ex 7¹¹, ²² 8⁷, ¹⁸ (3, 14) (לָט, לָהָטִים), Is 47⁹, ¹² (כֶּשֶׁף), Wi 12⁴ 18¹³ *;] 1. generally, the use of medicine, drugs or spells (Xen.). 2. (a) poisoning (Plut., Polyb.) ; (b) sorcery, witchcraft : Ga 5²⁰ (v. Lft., in l.), Re 9²¹ (WH, txt., φαρμάκων) 18²³ (cf. LXX, ll. c.).†

φάρμακον, -ου, τό, [in LXX for כֶּשֶׁף;] (a) a drug ; (b) an incantation, enchantment : Re 9²¹, Tr., mg., WH, txt. (RV, sorceries).†

φαρμακός, -ή, -όν, [in LXX for מְכַשֵּׁף, etc. ;] devoted to magical arts. As subst., ὁ φ. = φαρμακεύς, a magician, sorcerer : Re 21⁸ 22¹⁵.†

φάσις, -εως, ἡ (< φαίνω), [in LXX: ii Es 4¹⁷, Da τη Su ⁵⁵, iv Mac 15²⁵ א¹*;] *information*, esp. against fraud or other crime: Ac 21³¹.†

φάσκω, [in LXX: Ge 26²⁰ (אמר), Da LXX Bel ⁸, ii Mac 14²⁷, ³², iii Mac 3⁷*;] *to affirm, assert:* c. acc. et inf., Ac 24⁹ 25¹⁹; c. inf. et nom., Ro 1²².†

φάτνη, -ης, ἡ, [in LXX for אבוס, etc.;] *a manger:* Lk 2⁷, ¹², ¹⁶ 13¹⁵ (v. *DB*, iii, 234 ª, *DCG*, ii, 111 ª).†

φαῦλος, -η, -ον, [in LXX: Pr 22⁸ (עֲוָלָה) 29⁹ (אֱבִיל), etc.;] *slight, worthless*, of no account, both of persons and things in various shades of meaning (v. LS, s.v.), in NT, as freq. in cl., always with distinct moral reference (v. Ellic., *Past. Epp.*, 203; Hort, *Ja.*, 85; Tr., *Syn.*, § lxxxiv), *worthless, bad :* Jo 3²⁰, Tit 2⁸, Ja 3¹⁶; opp. to ἀγαθός (q.v.), Jo 5²⁹, Ro 9¹¹, ii Co 5¹⁰.†
   Syn. : v.s. ἄθεσμος.

φέγγος, -ους, τό, [in LXX chiefly for נֹגַהּ;] *light, brightness*, usually c. gen. of something that shines or reflects: of the moon, Mt 24²⁹, Mk 13²⁴; of a lamp, Lk 11³³ (WH, RV, φῶς).†
   Syn. : αὐγή, q.v.

φείδομαι, [in LXX for חמל, חוס, חשׂך, etc.;] *to spare :* ii Co 13²; c. gen. pers., Ac 20²⁹, Ro 8³² 11²¹, i Co 7²⁸, ii Co 1²³, ii Pe 2⁴, ⁵; c. inf., *to forbear*, ii Co 12⁶.†
   † φειδομένως, adv. from ptcp. (v. Bl., § 25, 1), *sparingly :* ii Co 9⁶ (Plut.).†

† φελόνης (Rec. φαιλ-), -ου, ὁ, by metath. for φαινόλης (also φενόλης, φαινόλιον; Lat. *pænula*), *a cloak* (v. *DCG*, i, 338; on the idea that the meaning here is *book-cover*, v. *CGT*, in l.; Milligan, *NTD*, 20; Field, *Notes*, 217 f., where the view that the φ. here is an eccl. vestment is discussed): ii Ti 4¹³.†

φέρω, [in LXX chiefly for בוא hi., also for נשׂא, etc.;] *to bear ;* 1. *to bear, carry :* c. acc., Lk 23²⁶ 24¹, Jo 19³⁹, He 1³ (v. Westc., in l.) ; pass., Ac 2² 27¹⁵, ¹⁷, He 6¹, ii Pe 1¹⁷, ¹⁸; of the mind, ib. ²¹. 2. *to bear, endure:* c. acc. rei, He 12²⁰ 13¹³; c. acc. pers., Ro 9²². 3. *to bring, bring forward :* c. acc. pers., Ac 5¹⁶; id. seq. πρός, Mk 1³² 2³ 9¹⁷, ¹⁹, ²⁰; ἐπί, Lk 5¹⁸; c. dat., Mk 7³² 8²²; c. acc. rei, Mk 6²⁷ 11² 12¹⁵, Lk 15²³, Ac 4³⁴, ³⁷ 5², ii Ti 4¹³; id. seq. πρός, Mk 11⁷; εἰς, Re 21²⁴, ²⁶; ἐπί, Mt 14¹¹, Mk 6²⁸; ἀπό, Jo 21¹⁰; c. dat., Mk 12¹⁵, Jo 2⁸; id. seq. ὧδε, Mt 14¹⁸ 17¹⁷; seq. φαγεῖν (sc. τι), Jo 4³³; τ. δάκτυλον (χεῖρα), Jo 20²⁷; pass., ἡ χάρις, i Pe 1¹³; διδαχήν, ii Jo ¹⁰; θάνατον (cf. Field, *Notes*, 230), He 9¹⁶; κρίσιν, ii Pe 2¹¹; κατηγορίαν, Jo 18²⁹; αἰτίαν, Ac 25¹⁸; αἰτιώματα, ib. ⁷, Rec. 4. *to bear, produce, bring forth:* καρπόν, Mt 7¹⁸, Mk 4⁸, Jo 12²⁴ 15², ⁴, ⁵, ⁸, ¹⁶. 5. *to bring, lead :* Mk 15²², Jo 21¹⁸, Ac 14¹³; metaph., of a gate (ὁδός, cl.), seq. εἰς, Ac 12¹⁰ (cf. ἀνα-, ἀπο-, δια-, εἰσ-, παρ-εισ-, ἐκ-, ἐπι-, κατα-, παρα-, περι-, προ-, προσ-, συν-, ὑπο-φέρω).†
   Syn. : φορέω, which expresses habitual and continuous bearing

as distinct from (φέρω) that which is accidental and temporary (cf. Mt 11⁸, al., s.v. φορέω, and v. Tr., *Syn.*, § lviii).

φεύγω, [in LXX chiefly for נוּס, also for בּרח, etc.;] *to flee from or away, take flight :* absol., Mt 8³³ 26⁵⁶, Mk 5¹⁴ 14⁵⁰, Lk 8³⁴, Jo 10¹², Ac 7²⁹; seq. εἰς, Mt 2¹³ 10²³ 24¹⁶ (WH, txt.), Mk 13¹⁴, Lk 21²¹, Re 12⁶; ἐπί, c. acc. loc., Mt 24¹⁶ (WH, mg.); ἐκ, Ac 27³⁰; ἀπό, c. gen. loc. (cl.), Mk 16⁸; id. c. gen. pers. (as in Heb.), Jo 10⁵, Ja 4⁷. Metaph.: absol., Re 16²⁰; c. acc. rei, ɪ Co 6¹⁸, He 11³⁴ (v. M, *Pr.*, 116); opp. to διώκειν, ɪ Ti 6¹¹, ɪɪ Ti 2²²; seq. ἀπό, c. gen. pers., Re 9⁶; ἀπὸ τ. προσώπου, Re 20¹¹; c. gen. rei, Mt 3⁷ (M, *Pr.*, l.c.) 23³³, Lk 3⁷, ɪ Co 10¹⁴ (cf. ἀπο-, δια-, ἐκ-, κατα-φεύγω).†

Φῆλιξ (L, Φή-), -ικος, ὁ, *Felix,* procurator of Judæa : Ac 23²⁴, ²⁶ 24³, ²², ²⁴, ²⁵, ²⁷ 25¹⁴.†

φήμη, -ης, ἡ (< φημί), [in LXX : Pr 16² (15³⁰) (שְׁמוּעָה), ɪɪ Mac 4³⁹, ɪɪɪ Mac 3², ɪv Mac 4²² * ;] *a saying* or *report :* Mt 9²⁶, Lk 4¹⁴.†

φημί, [in LXX chiefly for נאם, also for אמר; freq. in ɪɪ-ɪv Mac ;] *to declare, say :* freq. in quoting the words of another, Mt 13²⁹ 26⁶¹, Lk 7⁴⁰ 22⁵⁸, Jo 1²³, al. ; interjected into the recorded words (cl.), Mt 14⁸, Ac 23³⁵, al. ; φησί, impersonal (Bl., § 30, 4), ɪ Co 6¹⁶ (Lft., *Notes*, 217 ; but cf. Bl., l.c.), ɪɪ Co 10¹⁰ (WH, mg., φασίν), He 8⁵; joined with synon. verb (cf. LS, s.v., ɪɪ, 2), ἀποκριθεὶς αὐτῷ ἔφη, Lk 23³ ; seq. πρός, Lk 22⁷⁰, al. ; c. acc. rei, ɪ Co 10¹⁵, ¹⁹; acc. et inf., Ro 3⁸; seq. ὅτι (Bl., § 70, 3), ɪ Co 10¹⁹ 15⁵⁰ (cf. σύν-φημι).

* φημίζω (< φήμη), *to spread a report :* Mt 28¹⁵, T, WH, mg. (v. δια-φ.).†

Φῆστος, -ου, ὁ (Porcius), *Festus,* procurator of Judæa : Ac 24²⁷ 25¹ ᶠᶠ· 26²⁴, ²⁵ ³².†

φθάνω, [in LXX for נבע hi., מטא, etc. ;] 1. *to come before* another, *anticipate* (cl.): c. acc. pers., ɪ Th 4¹⁵. 2. In late writers and MGr. (v. Kennedy, *Sources*, 156 ; Lft., *Notes*, 35), *to come, arrive :* Ro 9³¹ ; seq. εἰς, Phl 3¹⁶ ; ἄχρι, ɪɪ Co 10¹⁴ ; ἐπί (cf. Da ᴛʜ 4²¹, and v. Dalman, *Words*, 107), Mt 12²⁸, Lk 11²⁰, ɪ Th 2¹⁶ (cf. προ-φθάνω).†

φθαρτός, -ή, -όν (φθείρω), [in LXX : Le 22²⁵ (מָשְׁחָת), Is 54¹⁷ A אֵ³, Wi 9¹⁵ 14⁸, ɪɪ Mac 7¹⁶ * ;] *perishable, corruptible :* ἄνθρωπος, Ro 1²³ (opp. to ἄφθαρτος θεός) ; στέφανος, ɪ Co 9²⁵ (opp. to ἄφθαρτος) ; σπορά, ɪ Pe 1²³ (opp. to ἄφθ.) ; neut., τὸ φ. τοῦτο, ɪ Co 15⁵³, ⁵⁴; pl., ɪ Pe 1¹⁸.†

φθέγγομαι, [in LXX for ענה, נבע hi., etc.;] of men or animals, *to utter* a sound or voice : absol., Ac 4¹⁸ ; seq. ἐν φωνῇ, ɪɪ Pe 2¹⁶ ; c. acc., ὑπέρογκα, ib. 18.†

φθείρω, [in LXX chiefly for שׁחת hi., pi., also for חבל, etc. ;] *to destroy, corrupt, spoil* (on the varied usage and distinctive meaning of the word, v. Mayor on ɪɪ Pe, *App.*, 175 ff.) : c. acc., ɪ Co 3¹⁷ 15³³, ɪɪ Co 7² ; seq. ἀπό, ɪɪ Co 11³ ; ἐν, ɪɪ Pe 2¹², Ju ¹⁰, Re 19² ; κατά, Eph 4²² (cf. δια-, κατα-φθείρω).†

* φθιν-οπωρινός, -ή, -όν (< φθινόπωρον, *late autumn*), *autumnal :* δένδρα φ., *autumn trees* (said to be without fruit therefore at a time when fruit might be expected; v. Mayor's elaborate note, *Ep. Ju.*, 55-59, and reff. there) : Ju ¹².†

φθόγγος, -ου, ὁ (< φθέγγομαι), [in LXX : Ps 18(19)⁴ (קַו), Wi 19¹⁸ *;] *a sound:* Ro 10¹⁸ (LXX), 1 Co 14⁷.†

** **φθονέω**, -ῶ (< φθόνος), [in LXX : To 4⁷, ¹⁶ AB *;] *to envy:* c. dat. (L, txt., Tr., mg., WH, mg., acc.), as in cl., Ga 5²⁶.†

** **φθόνος**, -ου, ὁ, [in LXX : Wi 2²⁴ 6²³, 1 Mac 8¹⁶, III Mac 6⁷ *;] *envy:* Ro 1²⁹, Ga 5²¹, 1 Ti 6⁴, Tit 3³, 1 Pe 2¹; διὰ φθόνον, Mt 27¹⁸, Mk 15¹⁰, Phl 1¹⁵; πρὸς φθόνον ἐπιποθεῖ τ. πνεῦμα (on the meaning, v. R, txt., mg. ₁, ₂; Hort, *Ja.*, 93 f.), Ja 4⁵.†

φθορά, -ᾶς, ἡ (< φθείρω), [in LXX for שַׁחַת, חֶבֶל, etc.;] *destruction, corruption, decay* (v. Mayor on II Pe, *App.*, 175 ff.) : Ro 8²¹, 1 Co 15⁴², Col 2²², II Pe 2¹²; opp. to ζωὴ αἰώνιος, Ga 6⁸; by meton., of that which is subject to corruption, 1 Co 15⁵⁰; of moral decay, II Pe 1⁴ 2¹², ¹⁹ (cf. Wi 14¹²).†

φιάλη, -ης, ἡ, [in LXX chiefly for מִזְרָק;] a shallow *bowl* (= Lat. *patera*), used for pouring libations, etc. : Re 5⁸ 15⁷ 16¹⁻¹⁷ 17¹ 21⁹.†

** **φιλ-άγαθος**, -ον, [in LXX : Wi 7²² *;] *loving that which is good, loving goodness :* Tit 1⁸ (Arist., Polyb., al.).†

Φιλαδελφία (Rec. -έλφεια), -ας, ἡ, *Philadelphia*, a city of Lydia : Re 1¹¹ 3⁷.†

φιλαδελφία, -ας, ἡ (< φιλάδελφος), [in LXX : IV Mac 13²³, ²⁶ 14¹ *;] *the love of brothers, brotherly love :* of Christians' mutual love as brethren (v.s. ἀδελφός), Ro 12¹⁰, 1 Th 4⁹, He 13¹, 1 Pe 1²², II Pe 1⁷.†

** **φιλ-άδελφος**, -ον, [in LXX : II Mac 15¹⁴, IV Mac 13²¹ 15¹⁰ *;] *loving one's brother, loving like a brother* (Soph., Xen., al.) : of Christians' love for one another (EV, *loving as brethren*), 1 Pe 3⁸.†

* **φίλανδρος**, -ον, 1. *loving men* (Æsch.). 2. Of a wife, *loving her husband* (freq. in epitaphs, v. LS, s.v., Deiss., *BS*, 255) : Tit 2⁴.†

** **φιλανθρωπία**, -ας, ἡ (< φιλάνθρωπος, *humane*), [in LXX : Es 8¹³, II Mac 6²² 14⁹, III Mac 3¹⁵, ¹⁸ *;] *humanity, kindness* (v. Field, *Notes*, 147 f.) : Ac 28², Tit 3⁴ (cf. also *DCG*, ii, 356 ff.).†

** **φιλανθρώπως**, adv., [in LXX : II Mac 9²⁷, III Mac 3²⁰ *;] *humanely, kindly :* Ac 27³.†

** **φιλαργυρία**, -ας, ἡ (< φιλάργυρος), [in LXX : IV Mac 1²⁶ 2¹⁵ א¹ *;] *love of money, avarice :* 1 Ti 6¹⁰.†

SYN. : πλεονεξία, *covetousness* (v. Tr., *Syn.*, § xxiv).

** **φιλ-άργυρος**, -ον, [in LXX : IV Mac 2⁸ *;] *loving money, avaricious :* Lk 16¹⁴, II Ti 3².†

* **φίλ-αυτος**, -ον, *loving oneself* (Arist.) ; in bad sense (ib.), *selfish :* II Ti 3².†

SYN. : αὐθάδης (v. Tr., *Syn.*, § xciii).

φιλέω, -ῶ (< φίλος), [in LXX : Ge 27⁴, ⁹, al. (אהב), ib. ²⁷, al. (נשׁק), La 1² (רֵעַ), Wi 8², al. ;] 1. *to love* (with the love of emotion and friendship, Lat. *amare;* v. SYN.) : c. acc. pers., Mt 10³⁷, Jo 5²⁰

11³, ³⁶ 15¹⁹ 16²⁷ 20² 21¹⁵⁻¹⁷, ι Co 16²², Re 3¹⁹; ἐν πίστει, Tit 3¹⁵; c. acc. rei, Mt 23⁶, Lk 20⁴⁶, Jo 12²⁵, Re 22¹⁵; c. inf. (Is 56¹⁰; cf. Bl., § 69, 4), Mt 6⁵. 2. *to kiss:* c. acc. pers., Mt 26⁴⁸, Mk 14⁴⁴, Lk 22⁴⁷ (cf. κατα-φιλέω).†

SYN. : ἀγαπάω (q.v.), the love of duty and respect.

φίλη, ἡ, v.s. φίλος.

*† **φιλήδονος**, -ον (φίλος, ἡδονή), *loving pleasure:* II Ti 3⁴ (Polyb., Plut., al.).†

φίλημα, -τος, τό (< φιλέω), [in LXX: Pr 27⁶, Ca 1² (נְשִׁיקָה) *;] *a kiss:* Lk 7⁴⁵ 22⁴⁸; as a token of Christian brotherhood, φ. ἅγιον, Ro 16¹⁶, ι Co 16²⁰, II Co 13¹², ι Th 5²⁶; φ. ἀγάπης, ι Pe 5¹⁴ (v. Lft., *Notes*, 90; *DB, DCA*, s.v. "Kiss").†

Φιλήμων, -ονος, ὁ, *Philemon:* Phm ¹.†

Φίλητος (T, Φιλητός), -ου, ὁ, *Philetus:* II Ti 2¹⁷.†

φιλία, -ας, ἡ (< φίλος), [in LXX chiefly for אַהֲבָה ;] *friendship:* c. gen. obj., Ja 4⁴.†

Φιλιππήσιος, -ου, ὁ (for other forms in use, v. Lft., in l.), *a Philippian:* Phl. 4¹⁵.†

Φίλιπποι, -ων, οἱ (on the pl., v. WM, § 27, 3), *Philippi:* Ac 16¹² 20⁶, Phl 1¹, ι Th 2².†

Φίλιππος, -ου, ὁ, *Philip;* 1. the husband of Herodias: Mt 14³, Mk 6¹⁷. 2. The tetrarch: Mt 16¹³, Mk 8²⁷, Lk 3¹. 3. The apostle: Mt 10³, Mk 3¹⁸, Lk 6¹⁴, Jo 1⁴⁴⁻⁴⁹ 6⁵, ⁷ 12²¹, ²² 14⁸, ⁹, Ac 1¹³. 4. The deacon and evangelist: Ac 6⁵ 8⁵⁻⁴⁰ 21⁸.†

* **φιλό-θεος**, -ον, *loving God* (Arist.): II Ti 3⁴.†

Φιλόλογος, -ου, ὁ, *Philologus:* Ro 16¹⁵.†

** **φιλονεικία**, -ας, ἡ (< φιλόνεικος), [in LXX: II Mac 4⁴, IV Mac 1²⁶ 8²⁶ *;] *love of strife, rivalry, emulation* (Plat., al.), but mostly in bad sense (Thuc., al.), *contentiousness, contention:* Lk 22²⁴ (but v. Field, *Notes*, 75 f.).†

φιλό-νεικος, -ον (< νεῖκος, *strife*), [in LXX: Ez 3⁷ (חֲזַק־מֵצַח) *;] *fond of strife, contentious:* ι Co 11¹⁶.†

* **φιλο-ξενία**, -ας, ἡ (< φιλόξενος), *love of strangers, hospitality:* Ro 12¹³, He 13².†

* **φιλό-ξενος**, -ον, *loving strangers, hospitable:* ι Ti 3², Tit 1⁸, ι Pe 4⁹.†

*† **φιλο-πρωτεύω** (< φιλόπρωτος, Plut., al.), *to strive to be first:* III Jo ⁹ (eccl.).†

φίλος, -η, -ον, [in LXX chiefly for רֵעַ, אֹהֵב ;] 1. pass., *beloved, dear* (Hom., Eur., al.). 2. Act., *loving, friendly* (in cl. less freq. and only in poets): Ac 19³¹. As subst., *a friend;* (a) masc., ὁ φ.: Lk 7⁶ 11⁵ 14¹⁰ 15⁶ 16⁹ 21¹⁶ 23¹², Ac 27³, III Jo ¹⁵; opp. to δοῦλος, Jo 15¹⁵; φ. ἀναγκαῖοι, Ac 10²⁴; c. gen. subj., Mt 11¹⁹, Lk 7³⁴ 11⁶, ⁸ 12⁴ 14¹² 15²⁹, Jo 11¹¹ 15¹³, ¹⁴; ὁ φ. τοῦ νυμφίου, Jo 3²⁹; τ. Καίσαρος (v. Deiss., *BS* 167; *LAE*, 382 f.), Jo 19¹²; θεοῦ (v. Hort, in l.), Ja 2²³; c. gen. rei, τ. κόσμου, Ja 4⁴; (b) fem., ἡ φ., Lk 15⁹.†

** φιλο-σοφία, -ας, ή (< φιλόσοφος), [in LXX: IV Mac 1¹ 5¹⁰, ²¹ 7⁹, ²¹ *;] the love and pursuit of wisdom ; hence, philosophy, investigation of truth and nature : of the so-called philosophy of false teachers, Col 2⁸ (v. Lft., ICC, in l.).†

φιλό-σοφος, -ον, ό, [in LXX: Da LXX 1²⁰ (אָשַׁף), IV Mac 1¹ 5³⁵ 7⁷ *;] a philosopher : Ac 17¹⁸.†

** φιλόστοργος, -ον (< στοργή, family affection), [in LXX: IV Mac 15¹³ *;] tenderly loving, affectionate (Xen., Plut., al.) : of Christians, Ro 12¹⁰.†

** φιλότεκνος, -ον (< φίλος, τέκνον), [in LXX: IV Mac 15⁴˙⁶ *;] loving one's children (Hdt., Arist., Plut., al.) : of women, joined with φίλανδρος, q.v., Tit 2⁴.†

** φιλοτιμέομαι, -οῦμαι (< φίλος, τιμή), [in LXX: IV Mac 1³⁵ A;] to love or seek after honour, hence, to be ambitious, emulous (Plat., Plut., al.) : c. inf., Ro 15²⁰, II Co 5⁹, I Th 4¹¹.†

** φιλοφρόνως (< φιλόφρων), adv., [in LXX: II Mac 3⁹, IV Mac 8⁵ *;] kindly, with friendliness : Ac 28⁷.†

* φιλόφρων, -ον (< φίλος, φρήν), friendly, kind . I Pe 3⁸, Rec.†

φιμόω, -ῶ (< φιμός, a muzzle), [in LXX: De 25⁴ (חסם), Da LXX Su ⁶¹, IV Mac 1³⁵ אָ R *;] to muzzle : I Co 9⁹, I Ti 5¹⁸ (LXX); metaph., to put to silence : c. acc. pers., Mt 22³⁴, I Pe 2¹⁵ ; pass., to be silenced, silent : Mt 22¹², Mk 1²⁵ 4³⁹, Lk 4³⁵.†

Φλέγων, -οντος, ό, Phlegon : Ro 16¹⁴.†

φλογίζω (< φλόξ), [in LXX : Ex 9²⁴ (לקח hith.), Nu 21¹⁴ (†), Ps 96 (97)³ (להט pi.), Da TH 3²⁷ ⁽⁹⁴⁾ (חֲרַךְ ithp.), Si 3³⁰, I Mac 3⁵ *;] to set on fire, burn, burn up : fig., Ja 3⁶ (on the meaning of the sentence, v. Hort, in l.).†

φλόξ, gen., φλογός, [in LXX chiefly for לַהַב, לֶהָבָה;] a flame : Lk 16²⁴ ; φ πυρός, Ac 7³⁰, II Th 1⁸, He 1⁷ (LXX), Re 1¹⁴ 2¹⁸ 19¹².†

* φλυαρέω, -ῶ (< φλύαρος), to talk nonsense : c. acc. pers., ἡμᾶς (EV, prating against us), III Jo ¹⁰.†

** φλύαρος, -ον (< φλύω, to babble), [in LXX : IV Mac 5¹⁰*;] babbling, garrulous : I Ti 5¹³ (EV, tattlers; of things, φιλοσοφία, IV Mac, l.c.).†

φοβερός, -ά, -όν (< φοβέω), [in LXX chiefly for נוֹרָא, also for דָּחַל, אָיֹם;] fearful, whether act. or pass.; 1. act., = δεινός, causing fear, terrible (LXX): He 10²⁷, ³¹ 12²¹. 2. Pass., = δειλός, feeling fear, timid (cl. in both senses).†

φοβέω, ῶ (< φόβος), [in LXX chiefly for ירא;] 1. in Hom., to put to flight. Pass., to be put to flight, to flee affrighted. 2. to terrify, frighten (Wi 17⁹; Hdt. and Att.). Pass. (so always in NT; cf. M, Pr., 162), to be seized with fear, be affrighted, fear : Mt 10³¹ 14²⁷, Mk 5³³ 6⁵⁰, Lk 1¹³ 8⁵⁰, Jo 6¹⁹ 12¹⁵, Ac 16³⁸, al.; opp. to ὑψηλοφρονεῖν, Ro 11²⁰ ; σφόδρα, Mt 17⁶ 27⁵⁴; c. cogn. acc., φόβον μέγαν, Mk 4⁴¹, Lk 2⁹ (I Mac 10⁸); φόβον αὐτῶν (obj. gen., but cf. ICC, in l.), I Pe 3¹⁴; πτόησιν, I Pe 3⁶; c. acc. pers., Mt 10²⁶, Mk 11¹⁸, Lk 19²¹, Jo 9²², Ac 9²⁶,

Ro 13³, al.; seq. ἀπό (like Heb. מן יָרֵא, Je 1⁸, al.; cf. M, *Pr.*, 102, 104ₙ), Mt 10²⁸, Lk 12⁴; seq. μή (cl.; Bl., § 65, 3; M, *Pr.*, 184 f.), Ac 23¹⁰ 27¹⁷; μήπως, Ac 27²⁹, II Co 11³ 12²⁰, Ga 4¹¹; μήποτε, He 4¹; c. inf. (Bl., § 69, 4; M, *Pr.*, 205), Mt 1²⁰, Mk 9³², al.; of reverential fear: Mk 6²⁰, Eph 5³³; τ. θεόν, Lk 1⁵⁰, Ac 10², I Pe 2¹⁷, Re 14⁷, al.; r. κύριον, Col 3²², Re 15⁴; τ. ὄνομα τ. θεοῦ (v.s. ὄνομα), Re 11¹⁸; οἱ φοβούμενοι τ. θεόν, of proselytes, Ac 13¹⁶,²⁶ (cf. ἐκ-φοβέω).

φόβητρον (LTr., WH, -θρον), -ου, τό (< φοβέω), [in LXX: Is 19¹⁷ (חָגָּא)*;] that which causes fright, a *terror*: pl. (as always, exc. Is, i.c.), Lk 21¹¹ (Hipp., Plat.).†

φόβος, -ου, ὁ, [in LXX chiefly for יָרֵא, also for פַּחַד, אֵימָה, etc.;] 1. in Hom., *flight*. 2. That which causes flight, *fear, dread, terror*: Lk 1¹², Ac 5⁵, I Ti 5²⁰, I Jo 4¹⁸, al.; cogn. acc., φοβεῖσθαι φ., Mk 4⁴¹, Lk 2⁹; c. gen. obj., Jo 7¹³ 19³⁸ 20¹⁹, He 2⁵, I Pe 3¹⁴ (but cf. *ICC*, in l.); ἀπὸ (τοῦ) φ., Mt 14²⁶, Lk 21²⁶; εἰς φ., Ro 8¹⁵; μετὰ φόβου, Mt 28⁸; φ. καὶ τρόμος (Lft., *Notes*, 172), I Co 2³, II Co 7¹⁵, Eph 6⁵, Phl 2¹²; by meton., of that which causes fear, Ro 13³; of reverential fear, Ro 13⁷, I Pe 1¹⁷ 2¹⁸ 3²,¹⁵; τ. κυρίου, Ac 9³¹, II Co 5¹¹ (v. Field, *Notes*, 183); Χριστοῦ, Eph 5²¹; θεοῦ, Ro 3¹⁸, II Co 7¹.
SYN.: v.s. δειλία (and cf. *DCG*, i, 381).

Φοίβη, -ης, ἡ, *Phœbe*, a deaconess of Cenchræa: Ro 16¹.†

Φοινίκη, -ης, ἡ, *Phœnicia*: Ac 11¹⁹ 15³ 21² (v. *DB*, iii, 856ᵇ, 857ᵃₙ).†

Φοινίκισσα (on the ending, v. Bl., § 27, 4, and cf. Φοῖνιξ), a *Phœnician woman*: Σύρα Φ., Mk 7²⁶, WH, mg., for Συροφοινίκισσα, q.v.†

Φοῖνιξ, -ικος, ο, ἡ, (a) a *Phœnician* (also with fem., Φοίνισσα, Hom., al.); (b) *Phœnix*, a city of Crete: Ac 27¹².†

φοῖνιξ (on the accent, v. Bl., § 4, 2; WM, § 6, 1c), -ικος, ὁ, [in LXX for תָּמָר, תֹּמֶר, תִּמֹרָה;] the *date-palm, palm*: τὰ βαΐα τῶν φ., Jo 12¹³; of palm branches, φοίνικες (as Arist., II Mac 10⁷, al.), Re 7⁹.†

** φονεύς, -έως, ὁ (φόνος), [in LXX: Wi 12⁵*;] a *murderer*: Mt 22⁷, Ac 7⁵² 28⁴, I Pe 4¹⁵, Re 21⁸ 22¹⁵; ἀνὴρ φ., Ac 3¹⁴.†
SYN.: ἀνθρωποκτόνος.

φονεύω (< φονεύς), [in LXX chiefly for רצח;] to *kill, murder*: absol., Mt 5²¹, Ja 4²; μὴ (οὐ) φονεύσῃς (-εις), Mt 5²¹ 19¹⁸, Mk 10¹⁹, Lk 18²⁰, Ro 13⁹, Ja 2¹¹ (all from Ex 20¹³,¹⁴); c. acc., Mt 23³¹,³⁵, Ja 5⁶.†

φόνος, -ου, ὁ, [in LXX for דָּם, פֶּה, etc.;] *murder, slaughter*: Mk 15⁷, Lk 23¹⁹,²⁵, Ac 9¹, Ro 1²⁹; φ. μαχαίρης (cf. Ex 17¹³, al.), He 11³⁷; pl., Mt 15¹⁹, Mk 7²¹, Re 9²¹.†

φορέω,-ῶ, [in LXX: Pr 16²³ (יסם hi.), Si 11⁵, al.;] frequent. of φέρω, denoting repeated or habitual action (cf. Tr.,*Syn.*, §lviii), most commonly used of clothing, weapons, etc., to *bear constantly, wear*: Mt 11⁸, Jo 19⁵, Ro 13⁴, I Co 15⁴⁹, Ja 2³.†

*† φόρον, -ου, τό (Lat. *forum*): Ἀππίου Φ., v.s. Ἄππιος.

φόρος, -ου, ὁ (< φέρω), [in LXX chiefly for מַם, also for מִדָּה,

etc.;] *tribute* paid by a subject nation (cf. I Mac 10³³): φ. δοῦναι (I Mac 8⁴'⁷), Lk 20²² 23²; ἀποδοῦναι, Ro 13⁷; τελεῖν, Ro 13⁶ (Hdt., al.).†
Syn.: κῆνσος, τέλος (q.v.).

φορτίζω (< φόρτος), [in LXX: Ez 16³³ (שׁחד)*;] *to load: c.* dupl. acc., Lk 11⁴⁶; pass., *to be laden:* metaph. (EV, *heavy laden*), Mt 11²⁸.†

φορτίον, -ου, τό (dimin. of φόρτος), [in LXX chiefly for מַשָּׂא;] *a burden, load:* of the cargo of a ship (Hdt., al.), Ac 27¹⁰; metaph., Mt 11³⁰ 23⁴, Lk 11⁴⁶, Ga 6⁵.†
Syn.: βάρος (q.v.), ὄγκος.

*φόρτος, -ου, ὁ (< φέρω), *a load:* esp. of a ship's cargo (Hom., Hdt., and late prose writers), Ac 27¹⁰, Rec.†

Φορτούνατος (Rec. Φουρ-, v. Mayser, 116 f.), -ου, ὁ (Lat.), *Fortunatus:* I Co 16¹⁷ (v. Lft., Cl. Ro., I Co., 59).†

*†**φραγέλλιον**, -ου, τό (Lat. *flagellum*), *a scourge:* Jo 2¹⁵.†

*†**φραγελλόω**, -ῶ (< φραγέλλιον, q.v.), *to scourge:* c. acc., Mt 27²⁶, Mk 15¹⁵ (eccl.).†

φραγμός, -οῦ, ὁ (< φράσσω), [in LXX chiefly for גְּדֵרָה, גָּדֵר, also for פֶּרֶץ, etc.;] 1. prop., *a fencing in* (Soph., OT, 1387). 2. = φράγμα, *a fence:* Mt 21³³, Mk 12¹, Lk 14²³. Metaph., μεσότοιχον (q.v.) τοῦ φ., gen. epexeg., Eph 2¹⁴ (v. Ellic., in l.).†

φράζω, [in LXX: Jb 6²⁴ (בִּין hi.) 12⁸ (ירה hi.), Da LXX 2⁴ (חֲוָה pa.)*;] *to show forth, tell, declare, explain:* Mt 13³⁶ (WH, RV, διασάφησον) 15¹⁵.†

φράσσω, [in LXX: Jb 38⁸ (סכך hi.), Ho 2⁶ ⁽⁸⁾ (שׂוּךְ), Pr 21¹³ (אטם), etc.;] *to fence in, stop, close:* στόματα λεόντων, He 11³³; στόμα, metaph., Ro 3¹⁹; pass., καύχησις, II Co 11¹⁰.†

φρέαρ, -ατος, τό, [in LXX chiefly for בְּאֵר;] *a well:* Lk 14⁵, Jo 4¹¹'¹²; φ. τῆς ἀβύσσου, Re 9¹'².†

*†**φρεν-απατάω**, -ῶ (< φρεναπάτης), *to deceive one's mind* (Lft., *deceive by fancies*, v. Ga., l.c.): c. acc. pers., Ga 6³.†

*†**φρεναπάτης**, -ες (< φρήν, ἀπάτη), *self-deceiving, conceited* (M, Gr., II, p. 275): Tit 1¹⁰; as subst., ὁ, *a deceiver* (Bl., *deceiver of his own mind*, § 28, 5₂): Tit, l.c. (eccl.).†

φρήν, gen., φρενός, ἡ, [in LXX most freq. in Pr (6³², al.) and chiefly for לֵב; also III Mac 4¹⁶ 5⁴⁷;] chiefly in Hom. and Trag., but also in Plat., al., both sing. and pl.; 1. in physical sense, the parts about the heart, *midriff*. 2. *heart, mind, thought:* pl., I Co 14²⁰ (v. Edwards, *Eng.-Gr. Lex.*, App., 1).†

φρίσσω (Att. -ττω, and so IV Mac 14⁹ 17⁷), [in LXX: Jb 4¹⁵ (סמר pi.), etc.;] 1. *to be rough, bristle.* 2. *to shiver, shudder, tremble*, from fear: Ja 2¹⁹ (v. Hort, in l.).†

φρονέω, -ῶ (< φρήν), [in LXX: De 32²⁹, Za 9² (חכם), Ps 93 (94)⁸ (שׂכל hi.), Is 44¹⁸ (בִּין) ib. ²⁸, Es 8¹³, Wi 1¹ 14³⁰, I Mac 10²⁰, II Mac 9¹²

14⁸,²⁶*;] 1. *to have understanding* (Hom., al.). 2. *to think, to be
minded* in a certain way: ὡς νήπιος, 1 Co 13¹¹; c. acc. (usually neut.,
adj., or pron., as freq. in cl.), ὃ δεῖ, Ro 12³; ἅ, Ac 28²²; τοῦτο, Phl 3¹⁵;
τι ἑτέρως, ib.; οὐδὲν ἄλλο, Ga 5¹⁰; τ. αὐτὸ φ. (Deiss., *BS*, 256), *to be of the
same mind*, 11 Co 13¹¹, Phl 2² 4²; id. seq. εἰς (ἐν) ἀλλήλους(οις), Ro 12¹⁶
15⁵; τ. ἐν φ., Phl 2² (Lft., in l.); seq. ὑπέρ, Phl 1⁷. 3. *to have in mind,
be mindful of, think of* (Hdt., Xen., al.; Es, 1 Mac, ll. c.): τὰ τ. θεοῦ,
opp. to τ. τ. ἀνθρώπων, Mt 16²³, Mk 8³³; τὰ τ. σαρκός, opp. to τ. τ.
πνεύματος, Ro 8⁵; τ. ἐπίγεια, Phl 3¹⁹; τὰ ἄνω, opp. to τ. ἐπὶ τ. γῆς, Col
3²; τοῦτο φρονεῖτε (RV, *have this mind in you*), Phl 2⁵; ὑψηλά, Ro 12¹⁶;
φ. ἡμέραν (to *observe* a day), Ro 14⁶; seq. ὑπέρ, Phl 4¹⁰ (cf. κατα-, παρα-,
περι-, ὑπερ-φρονέω).†

**φρόνημα, -τος, τό (< φρονέω), [in LXX: 11 Mac 7²¹ 13⁹*;] that
which is in the mind (the content of φρονεῖν, *ICC*, *Ro.*, 8⁶), *the thought*:
Ro 8⁶,⁷,²⁷.†

φρόνησις, -εως, ἡ (< φρονέω), [in LXX for בִּינָה, תְּבוּנָה, חָכְמָה,
etc.;] *understanding, practical wisdom, prudence*: Lk 1¹⁷, Eph 1⁸.†
SYN.: v.s. σοφία, and cf. Lft., *Notes*, 317.

φρόνιμος, -ον (< φρονέω), [in LXX for נָבוֹן, חָכָם etc.;] *practically wise, sensible, prudent*: Mt 10¹⁶ 24⁴⁵, Lk 12⁴², 1 Co 10¹⁵; opp. to
μωρός, Mt 7²⁴ 25²,⁴,⁸,⁹, 1 Co 4¹⁰; to ἄφρων, 11 Co 11¹⁹; φ. παρ' ἑαυτῷ
(EV, *wise in one's own conceit*), Ro 11²⁵ 12¹⁶ (cf. Pr 3⁷); compar.,
-ώτερος, Lk 16⁸.†
SYN.: v.s. σοφός.

φρονίμως, adv., *sensibly, prudently*: Lk 16⁸.†

φροντίζω (< φροντίς, *thought*), [in LXX: 1 Ki 9⁵ (דָּאַב), Ps 39
(40)¹⁷ (חָשַׁב), al.;] *to give heed, take thought* (in cl. usually absol., c
acc., c. gen.), c. inf., Tit 3⁸ (v. Bl., § 69, 4; M, *Pr.*, 206 f.).†

**φρουρέω, -ῶ (< φρουρός, *a guard*), [in LXX: 1 Es 4⁵⁶, Jth 3⁶, Wi
17¹⁶, 1 Mac 11³*;] *to guard, keep under guard, protect* or *keep* by
guarding: 11 Co 11³²; metaph., Ga 3²³, Phl 4⁷, 1 Pe 1⁵.†

†φρυάσσω (so Ps, l.c., NT; elsewhere depon., φρυάσσομαι, Att.
-ττ-), [in LXX: Ps 2¹ (רָגַשׁ), 11 Mac 7³⁴ R, 111 Mac 2²*;] prop., of
horses, *to neigh, whinny* and *prance* (Plut., al.). Metaph., *to be
wanton, insolent*: Ac 4²⁵ (LXX).†

φρύγανον, -ου, τό (< φρύγω, *to parch*), [in LXX chiefly for
קַשׁ, also for הָרוּל, etc.;] *a dry stick*: pl., *brushwood*: Ac 28³.†

Φρυγία, -ας, ἡ (prop., the adj., Φρύγιος, -α, -ον; sc. γῆ, χώρα),
Phrygia, a region of Asia Minor: Ac 2¹⁰; Φ. καὶ Γαλατικὴ χώρα (Γ. χ.
κ. Φ.), Ac 16⁶ 18²³ (on these phrases v. *DB*, i, 89 f.; *CGT, Gal.*,
xxii f.).†

Φύγελος (Rec. -λλος), -ου, ὁ, *Phygelus*: 11 Ti 1¹⁵.†

φυγή, -ῆς, ἡ (< φεύγω), [in LXX chiefly for מָנוֹס and cogn.
forms;] *flight*: Mt 24²⁰.†

φυλακή, -ῆς, ἡ (< φυλάσσω), [in LXX chiefly for מִשְׁמֶרֶת and cogn. forms, also for כְּלָא, etc.;] (a) actively, a guarding, guard, watch (Hom., Plat., Xen., al.): cogn. acc., φυλάσσειν φυλακάς, to keep watch, Lk 2⁸; (b) of those who keep watch (as also Lat. custodia), a guard; pl., sentinels, a guard (Hom., al.): Ac 12¹⁰; (c) of the place where persons are kept under guard, a prison (Hdt., Thuc., al.): Mt 14¹⁰, Mk 6¹⁷, Lk 3²⁰, Ac 5¹⁹, π Co 6⁵, ι Pe 3¹⁹, Re 18², al.; (d) of the time during which guard was kept by night (Lat. vigilia; Anthol.), a watch: Mt 14²⁵ 24⁴³, Mk 6⁴⁸, Lk 12³⁸.

**†φυλακίζω, [in LXX: Wi 18⁴*;] to imprison: Ac 22¹⁹.†

*φυλακτήριον, -ου, τό, 1. an outpost, fortification (Thuc., al.). 2. a safeguard (Plat.). 3. an amulet (Plut., al.); in NT for the Talmudic תְּפִלִּין, a prayer-fillet, a phylactery, a small strip of parchment on which portions of the law were written and worn on the forehead and next the heart (cf. Ex 13¹⁶): Mt 23⁵.†

φύλαξ, -ακος, ὁ (< φυλάσσω), [in LXX for שֹׁמֵר, צֻר;] a guard, keeper: Ac 5²³ 12⁶, ¹⁹.†

φυλάσσω, [in LXX chiefly and very freq. for שָׁמַר, also for נָצַר, etc.;] to guard, watch; (a) to guard or watch: c. cogn. acc., φυλακάς, Lk 2⁸; c. acc. pers., Ac 12⁴ 28¹⁶; pass., Lk 8²⁹, Ac 23³⁵; c. acc. rei, Ac 22²⁰; (b) to guard or protect: c. acc., Lk 11²¹, Jo 12²⁵ 17¹², π Th 3³, ι Ti 6²⁰, π Ti 1¹², ¹⁴, π Pe 2⁵; ἑαυτὸν ἀπό, ι Jo 5²¹ (Westc., in l.); metaph. of law, precept, etc., to keep, preserve, observe: Mt 19²⁰, Lk 11²⁸ 18²¹, Jo 12⁴⁷, Ac 7⁵³ 16⁴ 21²⁴, Ro 2²⁶, Ga 6¹³, ι Ti 5²¹. Mid., to be on one's guard (against), keep oneself from, beware of: c. acc., Ac 21²⁵, π Ti 4¹⁵; seq. ἀπό, Lk 12¹⁵; ἵνα μή, π Pe 3¹⁷; as in LXX (Ex 12¹⁷, Le 18⁴, al.), of laws, etc., to keep, observe: ταῦτα πάντα, Mk 10²⁰ (cf. δια-φυλάσσω).†

SYN.: τηρέω, q.v.

φυλή, -ῆς, ἡ, [in LXX chiefly for מַטֶּה, also for שֵׁבֶט, מִשְׁפָּחָה, etc.;] a body of men united by kinship or habitation, a clan or tribe: of the tribes of Israel, Mt 19²⁸, Lk 2³⁶ 22³⁰, Ac 13²¹, Ro 11¹, Phl 3⁵, He 7¹³, ¹⁴, Ja 1¹, Re 5⁵ 7⁴⁻⁸ 21¹²; of the tribes of the earth, the peoples and nations, Mt 24³⁰, Re 1⁷ 5⁹ 7⁹ 11⁹ 13⁷ 14⁶.†

φύλλον, -ου, τό, [in LXX chiefly for עָלֶה;] a leaf: Mt 21¹⁹ 24³², Mk 11¹³ 13²⁸, Re 22².†

φύραμα, -τος, τό (< φυράω, to mix), [in LXX: Ex 8³ (7²⁸) 12³⁴ (מִשְׁאֶרֶת), Nu 15²⁰, ²¹ (עֲרִיסָה)*;] that which is mixed or kneaded, a lump: of dough, Ro 11¹⁶, ι Co 5⁶, ⁷, Ga 5⁹; of clay, Ro 9²¹.†

'φυσικός, -ή, -όν (< φύσις), natural; (a) produced by nature, innate (Xen., Arist., al.); (b) according to nature (Arist., Diod., al.): opp. to παρὰ φύσιν, Ro 1²⁶, ²⁷; (c) governed by mere natural instinct (cf. Plut., Mor., 706 A): ζῷα γεγεννημένα φ. (RV, born mere animals; Mayor, born creatures of instinct; ICC, animals born of mere nature), π Pe 2¹².†

* φυσικῶς, adv., *naturally, by nature:* Ju¹⁰.†

*† φυσιόω, -ῶ (< φῦσα, *bellows*), = cl. φυσάω, *to puff* or *blow up,
inflate.* Metaph., *to puff up, make proud :* 1 Co 8¹. Pass., *tc be puffed
up* with pride : 1 Co 4¹⁸, ¹⁹ 5² 13⁴; seq. ὑπό, Col 2¹⁸; seq. ὑπὲρ . . . κατά,
1 Co 4⁶ (on the form of the subjc., v. M, *Pr.*, 54; Bl., § 22, 3).†

** φύσις, -εως, ἡ (< φύω), [in LXX : Wi 7²⁰ 13¹ 19²⁰ אA, iii Mac 3²⁹,
iv Mac 1²⁰ 5⁷, ⁸, ²⁵ 13²⁷ 15¹³, ²⁵ 16³ *;] *nature,* i.e., (*a*) the *nature*
(natural powers or constitution) of a person or thing : Ja 3⁷, ii Pe 1⁴;
τέκνα φύσει ὀργῆς, Eph 2³; (*b*) *origin, birth* (Soph., Xen., al.) : Ro 2²⁷,
Ga 2¹⁵; (*c*) *nature,* i.e. the regular order or law of nature : 1 Co 11¹⁴;
dat., φύσει adverbially, *by nature,* Ro 2¹⁴, Ga 4⁸; παρὰ φύσιν, *against
nature,* Ro 1²⁶ 11²⁴; κατὰ φ., *according to nature, naturally,* Ro 11²¹, ²⁴.†

*† φυσίωσις, -εως, ἡ (< φυσιόω), *a puffing up, swelling* with pride :
pl., ii Co 12²⁰.†

φυτεία, -ας, ἡ (< φυτεύω), [in LXX : iv Ki 19²⁹ (נטע), Mi 1⁶,
Ez 17⁷ (מטע) *;] 1. *a planting* (Xen., al.; LXX). 2. = φύτευμα,
that which is planted, a plant (Inscr.) : Mt 15¹³.†

φυτεύω (< φυτόν, *a plant,* < φύω), [in LXX chiefly for נטע, also
for שׁתל, etc. ;] *to plant :* Lk 17²⁸, 1 Co 3⁶⁻⁸; c. acc., φυτείαν, Mt 15¹³;
ἀμπελῶνα, Mt 21³³, Mk 12¹, Lk 20⁹, 1 Co 9⁷; pass., seq. ἐν, Lk 13⁶ 17⁶.†

φύω, [in LXX : Pr 26⁹, Ez 37⁸ (עלה), etc. ;] 1. trans., *to bring
forth, produce* (of men, *to beget*); pass., *to spring up, grow :* Lk 8⁶, ⁸.
2. Intrans., in 2 aor., pf., plpf., and rarely in pres. (v. LS, s.v., A, ii.),
to spring up : He 12¹⁵.†

* φωλεός, -οῦ, ὁ, *a hole, den, lair :* Mt 8²⁰, Lk 9⁵⁸.†

φωνέω, -ῶ (< φωνή), [in LXX for קרא (Je 17¹¹, al.), etc. ;] I.
Intrans. 1. Of persons, *to call out, cry out, speak aloud :* Lk 8⁸;
φωνῇ μεγάλῃ, Mk 1²⁶, Ac 16²⁸; ἐφώνησε (φωνῇ μεγάλῃ) λέγων, Lk 8⁵⁴,
Re 14¹⁸; φωνήσαντες ἐπύθοντο, Ac 10¹⁸. 2. Of the cries of animals
(rarely in cl.; Is 38¹⁴, Je, l.c.) : of a cock, *to crow,* Mt 26₃, Mk 14₄, Lk 22₃,
Jo 13³⁸ 18²⁷. II. Trans. (in cl. chiefly poët.), c. acc. pers., *to call,
summon, invite :* Mt 20³² 27⁴⁷, Mk 9³⁵ 10⁴⁹ 15³⁵, Lk 14¹² 16² 19¹⁵, Jo 1⁴⁹
2⁹ 4¹⁶ 10³ 11²⁸ 12¹⁷ 18³³, Ac 9⁴¹ 10⁷; *to address, call* by name (Soph.),
Jo 13¹³ (cf. ἀνα-, ἐπι-, προσ-, συν-φωνέω).†

φωνή, -ῆς, ἡ, [in LXX chiefly and very freq. for קול ;] *a voice;* (*a*)
prop., of persons, Mt 2¹⁸ (LXX), al.; φ. αἴρειν (ἐπαίρειν), Lk 17¹³, Ac 2¹⁴,
al.; φ. μεγάλη εἰπεῖν (λέγειν, φωνεῖν, etc.), Lk 8²⁸, Ac 7⁵⁷, Re 5¹², al.;
γίνεται (ἔρχεται) φ. ἐκ τ. οὐρανῶν (ἐξ οὐρανοῦ), Mk 1¹¹, Lk 3²², Jo 12²⁸, al.
(cf. *DCG,* ii, 810*; Dalman, *Words,* 204 f.) ; ἀκούειν φωνήν (-ῆς; v.s.
ἀκούω), Ac 9⁴, ⁷, al.; φ. βοῶντος, Mt 3³, Mk 1³, Lk 3⁴, Jo 1²³ (LXX);
τ. θεοῦ, Jo 5³⁷, He 3⁷, al. By meton., (*a*) of the speaker, βλέπειν τὴν φ.,
Re 1¹²; (*β*) *speech, language* (Ge 11¹, iv Mac 12⁷, al.) : 1 Co 14¹⁰; (*b*)
of inanimate things : Mt 24³¹, Jo 3⁸, Ac 2⁶, Re 1¹⁵ᵇ 9⁹ 14², al. (cf. Tr.,
Syn., § lxxxix).

φῶς (Att. contr. from φάος; < φάω), gen., φωτός, τό, [in LXX
chiefly for אור ;] *light* (opp. to τὸ σκότος, ἡ σκοτία) : Mt 17², ⁵, Jo 11⁹, ¹⁰,
ii Co 4⁶; ἡλίου, Re 22⁵; of a lamp, Lk 8¹⁶ 11³³, Jo 5³⁵, Re 18²³; of a

supernatural heavenly light, Ac 9³ 12⁷ 22⁶, ⁹, ¹¹ 26¹³; hence, ἄγγελος φωτός, II Co 11¹⁴; ὁ κλῆρος τ. ἁγίων ἐν τ. φ., Col 1¹²; of the divine glory, Re 21²⁴; by meton., of that which gives light: of fire, Mk 14⁵⁴, Lk 22⁵⁶ (cl.; I Mac 12²⁹; cf. DCG, i, 595); pl., of a lamp or torch, Ac 16²⁹; of heavenly bodies, Ja 1¹⁷. Metaph., (a) of God: I Jo 1⁵, ⁷; φῶς οἰκῶν ἀπρόσιτον, I Ti 6¹⁶; (b) of spiritual truth and its effects on the lives of men: Mt 4¹⁶ 5¹⁶, Jo 1⁴, ⁵ 3¹⁹⁻²¹, Ac 26¹⁸, ²³, II Co 6¹⁴, Eph 5¹³, I Pe 2⁹, I Jo 2⁸; τ. φ. τ. ζωῆς, Jo 8¹²; τ. ὅπλα τοῦ φ., Ro 13¹²; καρπὸς τοῦ φ., Eph 5⁹; ἐν τ. φ. περιπατεῖν (εἶναι, μένειν), I Jo 1⁷ 2⁹, ¹⁰; υἱοὶ (τέκνα) τοῦ φ., Lk 16⁸, Jo 12³⁶, Eph 5⁸, I Th 5⁵; by meton., of one from whom truth shines forth: Ac 13⁴⁷ (LXX), Ro 2¹⁹; esp. of Christ, Lk 2³², Jo 1⁷, ⁸ 12³⁵, ³⁶, ⁴⁶; τ. φ. τ. κόσμου, Jo 8¹² 9⁵; τ. φ. τ. ἀληθινόν, Jo 1⁹; of Christians, Mt 5¹⁴, Eph 5⁸; (c) of the spiritual under-standing: τ. φ. τὸ ἐν σοί, Mt 6²³, Lk 11³⁵; (d) adverbially, of that which is open to view (opp. to ἐν τ. σκοτίᾳ): ἐν τ. φ., Mt 10²⁷, Lk 12³.†

Syn.: v.s. φέγγος.

φωστήρ, -ῆρος, ὁ (< φῶς), [in LXX: Ge 1¹⁴,¹⁶ (מָאוֹר), Da LXX 12³ (זֹהַר), I Es 8⁷⁹, Wi 13², Si 43⁷ *;] a luminary, light: Phl 2¹⁵, Re 21¹¹.†

Syn.: φέγγος, φῶς.

*φωσ-φόρος, -ον (< φῶς, φέρω), light-bringing; as subst., ὁ φ., the morning star (Plat., al.; cf. ἑωσφόρος, Is 14¹², Jb 3⁹, Ps 110³): metaph., II Pe 1¹⁹ (v. Mayor, in l.).†

**φωτεινός (WH, φωτινός), -ή, -όν (< φῶς), [in LXX: Si 17³¹ 23¹⁹ *;] bright, light: νεφέλη, Mt 17⁵; opp. to σκοτεινός, Mt 6²², Lk 11³⁴, ³⁶.†

φωτίζω (< φῶς), [in LXX for אוֹר hi., ירה hi., etc.;] 1. intrans., to shine, give light (Arist., Plut., al.): seq. ἐπί, Re 22⁵. 2. Trans. (a) to illumine, enlighten (Diod., Plut., al.): c. acc., Lk 11³⁶, Re 21²³; pass., Re 18¹. Metaph., of spiritual enlightenment (Ps 118 (119)¹³⁰, Si 45¹⁷, al.): Jo 1⁹, Eph 1¹⁸ 3⁹, R, txt., He 6⁴ 10³²; (b) to bring to light, make known (Polyb.): I Co 4⁵, Eph 3⁹, R, mg., II Ti 1¹⁰ (cf. Kennedy, Sources, 107 f.).†

φωτισμός, -οῦ, ὁ (φωτίζω), [in LXX: Jb 3⁹, Ps 26 (27)¹, 43 (44)³, 77 (78)¹⁴, 138 (139)¹¹ (אוֹר), 89⁸ (מָאוֹר) *;] illumination, light: metaph., II Co 4⁴, ⁶.†

X

X, χ, χῖ, τό, indecl., chi, ch, the twenty-second letter. As a numeral, χ′ = 600, χ͵ = 600,000; but in Inscr., X = 1000.

χαίρω, [in LXX for שָׂמַח (Ge 45¹⁶, al.), גִּיל (Pr 2¹⁴, al.), etc.; inf., as greeting (v. infr.), Is 48²² 57²¹ (שָׁלוֹם), I Mac 10¹⁸, II Mac 1¹ and freq. in these books;] 1. to rejoice, be glad: Mk 14¹¹, Lk 15⁵, ³² 19⁶, ³⁷ 22⁵ 23⁸, Jo 4³⁶ 8⁵⁶ 20²⁰, Ac 5⁴¹ 8³⁹ 11²³ 13⁴⁸, II Co 6¹⁰ 7⁷ 13⁹, Phl 2¹⁷, ²⁸,

Col 2⁵, ι Th 5¹⁶, ι Pe 4¹³, ιιι Jo ³; χ. καὶ ἀγαλλιᾶσθαι, Mt 5¹²; κ. σκιρτᾶι Lk 6²³; opp. to κλαίειν, Ro 12¹⁵, ι Co 7³⁰; to κλαίειν κ. θρηνεῖν, Jo 16²⁰; to λύπην ἔχειν, ib. ²²; c. cogn. acc., χ. χαρὰν μεγάλην, Mt 2¹⁰; χαρᾷ χ. (Bl., § 38, 3; Dalman, *Words*, 34 f.), Jo 3²⁹; ἡ χαρὰ ᾗ χαίρομεν, ι Th 3⁹; c. prep. (Bl., § 38, 2), ἐπί, c. dat. (simple dat. in cl.), Mt 18¹³, Lk 1¹⁴ 13¹⁷, Ac 15³¹, Ro 16¹⁹, ι Co 13⁶ 16¹⁷, ιι Co 7¹³, Re 11¹⁰; διά, Jo 3²⁹ 11¹⁵, ι Th 3⁹; ἐν, Phl 1¹⁸; ἀπό, ιι Co 2³; c. acc. (Dem.), Phl 2¹⁸; seq. ὅτι, Jo 14²⁸, ιι Co 7⁹,¹⁶, ιι Jo ⁴; ἐν τούτῳ ὅτι, Lk 10²⁰; c. dat., Ro 12¹²; ἐν κυρίῳ, Phl 4¹⁰. 2. In salutations, imperat., χαῖρε, χαίρετε, (*a*) at meeting, *hail*: Mt 26⁴⁹ 27²⁹, Mk 15¹⁸, Lk 1²⁸, Jo 19³; pl., Mt 28⁹; so χαίρειν λέγω, to *give greeting*, ιι Jo ¹¹; in letters, χαίρειν (sc. λέγει; Bl., § 81, 1), *greeting*: Ac 15²³ 23²⁶ Ja 1¹; (*b*) at parting, *farewell*: ιι Co 13¹¹; (*c*) on other occasions, *be of good cheer*: ἐν κυρίῳ, Phl 3¹ 4⁴ (cf. συν-χαίρω).†

χάλαζα, -ης, ἡ [in LXX chiefly for בָּרָד;] *hail*: Re 8⁷ 11¹⁹ 16²¹.†

χαλάω, -ῶ, [in LXX: Je 45 (38)⁶ (שלח pi.), etc.;] (*a*) *to slacken, loosen;* (*b*) *to let loose, let go;* (*c*) *to lower, let down*: c. acc. rei, Mk 2⁴, Lk 5⁴,⁵, Ac 9²⁵ 27¹⁷,³⁰; c. acc. pers. (cf. Je, l.c.), pass., ιι Co 11³³.†

Χαλδαῖος, -ου, ὁ, *a Chaldæan*: γῆ Χαλδαίων, Ac 7⁴.†

χαλεπός, -ή, -όν, [in LXX: Is 18² (נוֹרָא), Wi 3¹⁹, Si 3²¹, al.;] *hard;* (*a*) *hard to do* or *deal with, difficult;* (*b*) *hard to bear, painful, grievous:* καιροί, ιι Ti 3¹; (*c*) of persons, *hard to deal with, harsh, fierce, savage:* Mt 8²⁸.†

*†χαλιναγωγέω, -ῶ (< χαλινός, ἄγω), *to lead with a bridle;* metaph., *to bridle, restrain:* c. acc., γλῶσσαν, Ja 1²⁶; σῶμα, 3².†

χαλινός, -οῦ, ὁ, [in LXX chiefly for מֶתֶג;] *a bridle:* Ja 3³, Re 14²⁰.†

χάλκεος, -έα, -εον (-οῦς, -ῆ, -οῦν), (< χαλκός), [in LXX chiefly for נְחֹשֶׁת;] *brazen* (i.e. *of copper*): Re 9²⁰.†

χαλκεύς, -έως, ὁ (< χαλκός), [in LXX for חָרָשׁ, etc.;] *a worker in metal*, esp. *a copper-smith:* ιι Ti 4¹⁴.†

*†χαλκηδών, -όνος, ὁ, *chalcedony,* "supposed to denote a green silicate of copper found in the mines near Chalcedon" (Swete): Re 21¹⁹.†

χαλκίον, -ου, τό (< χαλκός), [in LXX: Jb 41²²⁽²³⁾ (סִיר), etc.;] *a brazen (copper) vessel:* Mk 7⁴.†

*†χαλκο-λίβανον, -ου, τό (or -ος, ἡ; cf. Swete on Re 1¹⁵; Thayer, s.v.; LS, s.v.), *chalcolibanus,* probably "a mixed metal of great brilliance" (Swete): Re 1¹⁵ 2¹⁸ (RV, *burnished brass*).†

χαλκός, -οῦ, ὁ, [in LXX chiefly for נְחֹשֶׁת;] *copper:* ι Co 13¹, Re 18¹²; by meton., of copper coin, Mt 10⁹, Mk 6⁸ 12⁴¹.†

χαμαί, adv., *on* or *to the ground:* Jo 9⁶ 18⁶.†

Χαναάν, ἡ, indecl. (Heb. כְּנַעַן), *Canaan:* Ac 7¹¹; γῆ Χ., Ac 13¹⁹.†

Χαναναῖος, -α, -ον, *Canaanite:* γυνή, Mt 15²².†

χαρά, -âς, ἡ (< χαίρω), [in LXX for שִׂמְחָה, שָׂשׂוֹן, etc. ;] joy,
delight : Lk 1¹⁴ 15⁷, ¹⁰, Jo 15¹¹ 16²², ²⁴ 17¹³, Ac 8⁸, II Co 1²⁴ 7¹³ 8², Ga 5²²,
Col 1¹¹, Phl 2², I Jo 1⁴, II Jo ¹²; opp. to κατήφεια, Ja 4⁹; to λύπη, Jo 16²⁰;
χ. τῆς πίστεως, Phl 1²⁵; ἀγαλλιᾶσθαι (χαίρειν, q.v.), χαρᾷ, Jo 3²⁹, I Pe 1⁸;
χ. ἔχειν, Phm ⁷; πληροῦν (-οῦσθαι) χαρᾶς, Ac 13⁵², Ro 15¹³, II Ti 1⁴; ποιεῖν
χ. μεγάλην, Ac 15³; ἀπὸ τῆς χ., Mt 13⁴⁴, Lk 24⁴¹, Ac 12¹⁴; ἐν χ., Ro 15³²;
μετὰ χαρᾶς, Mt 13²⁰ 28⁸, Mk 4¹⁶, Lk 8¹³ 10¹⁷ 24⁵², Phl 1⁴ 2²⁹, He 10³⁴
13¹⁷; id. seq. πνεύματος ἁγίου, I Th 1⁶; χ. ἐν π. ἁ., Ro 14¹⁷; χ. ἐπί,
II Co 7⁴; διά, I Th 3⁹; ὅτι, Jo 16²¹; ἵνα, III Jo ⁴.   By meton., of the
cause or occasion of joy : Lk 2¹⁰, II Co 1¹⁵, WH, txt., R, mg., Phl 4¹,
I Th 2¹⁹, ²⁰, He 12², Ja 1²; ἡ χ. τ. κυρίου, Mt 25²¹, ²³.†

*χάραγμα, -τος, τό (< χαράσσω, to engrave), (a) a stamp, impress,
mark : Re 13¹⁶, ¹⁷ 14⁹, ¹¹ 16² 19²⁰ 20⁴ (v. Deiss., BS, 240 ff.); (b) a thing
graven : Ac 17²⁹.†

χαρακτήρ, -ῆρος, ὁ (< χαράσσω, to engrave), [in LXX: Le 13²⁸
(צָרֶבֶת), II Mac 4¹⁰, IV Mac 15⁴ א R *;] 1. a tool for graving.   2. a
stamp or impress : as on a coin or seal; metaph., χ. τ. ὑποστάσεως,
He 1³.†

χάραξ, -ακος, ὁ (< χαράσσω), [in LXX for מְצוֹר, צֹר, מִלְלָה, etc.;] 1.
a pointed stake.   2. a palisade or rampart : Lk 19⁴³.†

χαρίζομαι (< χάρις), [in LXX: Es 8⁷ (נתן), Ca 1⁴ א, Si 12³,
II-IV Mac₉*;] 1. to show favour or kindness : c. dat. pers., Ga 3¹⁸.   2. to
give freely, bestow : c. acc. et dat., Lk 7²¹, Ac 3¹⁴ 25¹¹, ¹⁶ 27²⁴, Ro 8³²,
I Co 2¹², Phl 1²⁹ 2⁹, Phm ²².   3. In late Gk. (= Lat. condonare), to grant
forgiveness, forgive freely : of debt, Lk 7⁴², ⁴³ (EGT, in l.); of sin,
II Co 2⁷, ¹⁰ 12¹³, Eph 4³², Col 2¹³ 3¹³ (cf. DB, ii, 57ᵃ).†

χάριν, acc. of χάρις, used adverbially, seq. gen. (Hom., al.; I Ma 9¹⁰,
al.), in favour of, for the pleasure of ; (b) = ἕνεκα (cf. Lat. gratiá, causá), as
prep. c. gen. (which in NT it always follows, except in I Jo 3¹²), because
of, on account of, for the sake of : Lk 7⁴⁷, Ga 3¹⁹, Eph 3¹, ¹⁴, Tit 1⁵, ¹¹, Ju ¹⁶.†

χάρις, -ιτος, acc., χάριν (χάριτα in Ac 24²⁷, Ju ⁴; v. WH, App., 157),
[in LXX chiefly for חֵן;] 1. objectively, that which causes favourable
regard, gracefulness, grace, loveliness of form, graciousness of speech (cl.,
Ec 10¹², Si 21¹⁶, al.) : Col 4⁶; λόγοι τ. χάριτος (gen. qual.), Lk 4²².   2.
Subjectively, (a) on the part of the giver, grace, graciousness, kindness,
goodwill, favour : Lk 2⁵², Ac 7¹⁰, al.; esp. in NT of the divine favour,
grace, with emphasis on its freeness and universality : Lk 1³⁰, Ac 14²⁶,
Ro 1⁷, I Co 1³, al.; opp. to ὀφείλημα, Ro 4⁴, ¹⁶; to ἔργα, Ro 11⁶; (b) on
the part of the receiver, a sense of favour received, thanks, gratitude :
Ro 6¹⁷ 7²⁵, al.; χ. ἔχειν, to be thankful, Lk 17⁹, I Ti 1¹², al.   3. Objectively, of the effect of grace, (a) a state of grace : Ro 5², II Ti 2¹, I Pe
5¹², II Pe 3¹⁸; (b) a proof or gift of grace (cl., a favour) : Jo 1¹⁶, Ac 6⁸,
Ro 1⁵, I Co 3¹⁰, II Co 9⁸, Ga 2⁹, Eph 3², I Pe 5⁵, ¹⁰, al.   (For fuller
treatment of the NT usage, v. AR, Eph., 221 ff.; DB, ii, 254 ff.; DCG,
i, 686 ff.; Cremer, s.v.; ICC on Ga, pp. 423 ff.).

†χάρισμα, -τος, τό (< χαρίζομαι), [in LXX: Si 7³³ א (AB, χάρις) 38³⁰ B¹ (א AB²R, χρῖσμα) *;] *a gift of grace, a free gift,* esp. of extraordinary operations of the Spirit in the Apostolic Church, but including all spiritual graces and endowments (Lft., *Notes,* 148 f.): Ro 1¹¹ 5¹⁵,¹⁶ 6²³ 11²⁹ 12⁶, I Co 1⁷ 7⁷ 12⁴,⁹,²⁸,³⁰,³¹, II Co 1¹¹, I Ti 4¹⁴, II Ti 1⁶, I Pe 4¹⁰.†

†χαριτόω, -ῶ (< χάρις), [in LXX: Si 18¹⁷ (ἀνδρὶ κεχαριτωμένῳ; Vg., *justificato;* Syr., *saintly*) *;] *to endow with* χάρις (q.v.), i.e. 1. (*a*) *to make graceful;* (*b*) *to make gracious* (Si, l.c.). 2. In Hellenistic writings (for exx., v. AR, *Eph.,* 227; Lft., *Notes,* 315), (*a*) *to cause to find favour;* (*b*) *to endue with grace* (i.e. divine favour): Lk 1²⁸, Eph 1⁶.†

Χαρράν, indecl. (in FlJ., *Ant.,* i, 16, 1, Κάρρα, -ας, ib. 6, 5, Χαρρά, -ᾶς; so LXX: Ge 29⁴ E, Ez 27²³ B, elsewhere -άν—Heb. חָרָן), *Haran,* a town in N.W. Mesopotamia: Ac 7²,⁴.†

χάρτης, -ου, ὁ, [in LXX: Is 8¹ A, Je 43 (36)²,⁶,²³ (מְגִלָּה)*;] a sheet of *paper,* made of papyrus strips (v. Kennedy, *Sources,* 42; Milligan, *NTD,* 10-12; *DB,* iv, 945 f.): II Jo¹² (Plat., Inscr.).†

χάσμα, -τος, τό (< χάσκω, *to yawn*), [in LXX: II Ki 18¹⁷ (פַּחַת) *;] *a chasm, wide space:* Lk 16²⁶.†

χεῖλος, -ους, τό, gen. pl., -εων (v. Bl., § 8, 4; Thackeray, *Gr.,* I, 151), [in LXX chiefly for שָׂפָה;] *a lip* (as in Heb., of the lip as the organ of speech): Mt 15⁸, Mk 7⁶, Ro 3¹³, I Co 14²¹, He 13¹⁵, I Pe 3¹⁰ (LXX). Metaph., of things, *an edge, brink,* etc. (Hom., Hdt., al.): of the seashore, He 11¹².†

χειμάζω (< χεῖμα, *winter cold*), [in LXX: Pr 26¹⁰ (†) *;] 1. *to expose to winter cold, go into winter quarters.* 2. *to drive with storm;* pass., *to be driven with storm, tempest-tossed:* Ac 27¹⁸.†

χείμαρρος (shortened form of the more usual -οος, Attic contr., -ους), -ον (< χεῖμα, ῥέω), [in LXX chiefly for נַחַל;] *winter-flowing;* as subst., ὁ χ. (sc. ποταμός), *a torrent:* Jo 18¹.†

χειμών, -ῶνος, ὁ, [in LXX for גֶּשֶׁם, סְתָיו;] 1. *winter:* Jo 10²², II Ti 4²¹; gen., χειμῶνος, *in winter,* Mt 24²⁰, Mk 13¹⁸. 2. Prop., *a winter storm,* hence, generally, *a storm, tempest:* Mt 16³ (T, WH, R, mg., om.), Ac 27²⁰.†

χείρ, gen., χειρός (acc., χεῖραν, I Pe 5⁶ T), ἡ, [in LXX chiefly for יָד;] *the hand:* Mt 3¹², Mk 3¹, Lk 6⁶, al. mult.; ἡ χ., as acting subject, Lk 22²¹; pl., Ac 17²⁵ 20³⁴, I Jo 1¹; τ. ἔργα τῶν χ., Ac 7⁴¹, Re 9²⁰; ὁ ἀσπασμὸς τ. ἐμῇ χ., I Co 16²¹, Col 4¹⁸, II Th 3¹⁷; prepositional phrases, esp. those without art., similar to Heb. constructions (Bl., § 32, 4; 40, 9; 46, 9), ἐν χ., c. gen. (Lft., in l.), Ga 3¹⁹; σὺν χ. ἀγγέλου, Ac 7³⁵; διὰ (τῶν) χειρῶν (διὰ χειρός), Mk 6², Ac 5¹² 7²⁵, al.; ἐπὶ χειρῶν, Mt 4⁶, Lk 4¹¹; ellipse of χ. (ἡ δεξιά, ἀριστερά; Bl., § 44, 1), Mt 6³, al. By meton., for the power or activity of an individual, Mt 17²², Mk 9³¹, Lk 9⁴⁴, Jo 10³⁹,

Ac 12¹¹, al.; metaph., of the activity or power of God: Lk 1⁶⁶ 23⁴⁶, Jo 10²⁹, Ac 11²¹ 13¹¹, al.

χειραγωγέω, -ῶ (< χειραγωγός), [in LXX: Jg 16²⁶ A (מַחֲזִיק בְּיָד), To 11¹⁶ א *;] to lead by the hand: Ac 9⁸ 22¹¹.†

* χειρ-αγωγός, -όν (< χείρ, ἄγω), leading by the hand. As subst., ὁ χ., one to lead by the hand, a guide: Ac 13¹¹.†

**† χειρόγραφος, -ον (< χείρ, γράφω), [in LXX: To 5³ 9², ⁵ *;] written with the hand. As subst., τὸ χ., a handwriting (Inscr., Polyb., al.): metaph., Col 2¹⁴.†

χειρο-ποίητος, -ον (< χείρ, ποιέω), [in LXX (of idols) for אֱלִיל;] made by hand (i.e. of human handiwork): of temples, Mk 14⁵⁸, Ac 7⁴⁸ 17²⁴, He 9¹¹, ²⁴; of circumcision, Eph 2¹¹.†

* χειρο-τονέω, -ῶ (< χείρ, τείνω), 1. to vote by stretching out the hand in the Athenian ἐκκλησία (Luc., Plut.). 2. to appoint: (a) by vote, II Co 8¹⁹; (b) without vote, Ac 14²³ (v. Rackham, in l.) (cf. προ-χειροτονέω).†

χείρων, -ον, compar. of κακός, [in LXX: I Ki 17⁴³ B, Wi 15¹⁸ 17⁶, III Mac 5²⁰ *;] worse: Mt 9¹⁶ 12⁴⁵ 27⁶⁴, Mk 2²¹, Lk 11²⁶, Jo 5¹⁴, I Ti 5⁸, He 10²⁹, II Pe 2²⁰; εἰς (ἐπὶ) τὸ χεῖρον, Mk 5²⁶, II Ti 3¹³.†

† Χερουβείν (Rec. -βίμ), τά (Heb. כְּרוּבִים), Cherubim: He 9⁵ (cf. Ex 25¹⁷ ⁽¹⁸⁾, al.; v. DB, i, 377 ff.).†

-χέω, -χύννω (ἐκ-, συν-), v. M, Gr., II, 195, 214 f., 265.

χήρα, -ας, ἡ, [in LXX chiefly for אַלְמָנָה;] a widow: Mt 23¹³ (Rec., R, mg.), Mk 12⁴⁰⁻⁴³, Lk 2³⁷ 4²⁵ 7¹² 18³, ⁵ 20⁴⁷ 21², ³, Ac 6¹ 9³⁹, ⁴¹, I Co 7⁸, I Ti 5³⁻⁵, ¹¹, ¹⁶, Ja 1²⁷; γυνὴ χ., Lk 4²⁶; of one of an ordo viduarum (v. CGT, in l.), I Ti 5⁹; metaph., of a city forsaken, Re 18⁷.†

χθές, v.s. ἐχθές.

χιλίαρχος (in Hdt., al., -ης), -ου, ὁ (< χίλιοι, ἄρχω), [in LXX chiefly for שַׂר אֶלֶף;] a chiliarch, the commander of a thousand, esp. a Roman military tribune, the commander of a cohort: Jo 18¹², Ac 21³¹⁻³³, ³⁷ 22²⁴⁻²⁹ 23¹⁰, ¹⁵, ¹⁷⁻¹⁹, ²² 24⁷, ²² 25²³; more generally, of officers of similar rank, Mk 6²¹, Re 6¹⁵ 19¹⁸ (v. DB, i, 352 ᵇ; DCG, i, 271ᵃ, 307ᵃ).†

χιλιάς, -άδος, ἡ (< χίλιοι), [in LXX for אֶלֶף;] the number one thousand, a thousand: Lk 14³¹, Ac 4⁴, I Co 10⁸, Re 5¹¹ 7⁴⁻⁸ 11¹³ 14¹, ³ 21¹⁶.†

χίλιοι, -αι, -α, a thousand: II Pe 3⁸ ⁽ᴸˣˣ⁾, Re 11³ 12⁶ 14²⁰ 20²⁻⁷.†

Χίος, -ου, ἡ, Chios, an island in Ægean Sea: Ac 20¹⁵.†

χιτών, -ῶνος, ὁ, [in LXX chiefly for כֻּתֹּנֶת:] the garment worn next the skin (though two tunics were sometimes worn, v. Swete, Mk., 117), a tunic: Mt 10¹⁰, Mk 6⁹ 14⁶³, Lk 3¹¹ 9³, Ju ²³; disting. from ἱμάτιον (q.v.), Mt 5⁴⁰, Lk 6²⁹, Jo 19²³, Ac 9³⁹ (v. DCG, i, 338ᵃ, 340ᵃ, 499ᵃ).†

31

χιών, -όνος, ἡ, [in LXX chiefly for שֶׁלֶג, also (in Da) for תְּלַג;] snow : Mt 28³, Re 1¹⁴.†

** χλαμύς, -ύδος, ἡ, [in LXX : II Mac 12³⁵ * ;] a chlamys, or short cloak worn over the χιτών (q.v.) : Mt 27²⁸, ³¹ (v. Tr., Syn., § 1).†

** χλευάζω (< χλεύη, a jest), [in LXX : Wi 11¹⁴, II Mac 7²⁷ IV Mac 5²² * ;] to jest, mock, jeer : Ac 17³².†

* χλιαρός, -ά, -όν (< χλίω, to become warm), warm, tepid; metaph., of persons, luke-warm : Re 3¹⁶.†

Χλόη, -ης, ἡ (i.e. tender foliage), Chloe : I Co 1¹¹.†

χλωρός, -ά, -όν (< χλόη), [in LXX for יָרָק, etc. ;] (a) pale green : χόρτος, Mk 6³⁹, Re 8⁷ ; πᾶν χ., Re 9⁴ ; (b) pale : ἵππος, Re 6⁸.†

χξς´ (on ς, v.s. Z), in T, Tr., Rec. for ἑξακόσιοι ἑξήκοντα ἕξ, six hundred and sixty-six (L, mg., R, mg., six hundred and sixteen), the mystical number of the Beast : Re 13¹⁸ (on the interpretation, v. Swete, Ap., 172 f. ; ICC, in l., Deiss., LAE, p. 277₁).†

*† χοϊκός, -ή, -όν, (< χοῦς), earthy, made of dust : I Co 15⁴⁷⁻⁴⁹ (v. Field, Notes, 179 f.).†

χοῖνιξ, -ικος, ἡ, [in LXX : Ez 45¹⁰, ¹¹ (בַּת) * ;] a chœnix, a dry measure of rather less than a quart : Re 6⁶ (EV, measure).†

** χοῖρος, -ου, ὁ, [in Sm. : Is 65⁴ 66³ ;] a swine : pl., Mt 7⁶ 8³⁰⁻³², Mk 5¹¹⁻¹³, ¹⁶, Lk 8³², ³³ 15¹⁵, ¹⁶.†

** χολάω, -ῶ (< χολή), [in LXX : III Mac 3¹ R * ;] 1. to be melancholy mad (Aristoph.). 2. = χολοῦμαι, to be angry : c. dat. pers., Jo 7²³.†

χολή, -ῆς, ἡ, [in LXX for רֹאשׁ, לַעֲנָה, מְרֵרָה ;] gall : Mt 27³⁴ (here prob. = myrrh, cf. Mk 15²³, v. Swete, in l.; DCG, i, 634ª); metaph., Ac 8²³.†

χόος, v.s. χοῦς.

Χοραζείν (Rec. -ζίν), ἡ, Chorazin, a town of Galilee : Mt 11²¹, Lk 10¹³.†

χορηγέω, -ῶ (< χορός, ἡγέομαι), [in LXX for כּוּל pilp. ;] 1. to lead a χορός (v. LS, s.v.). 2. to defray the cost of a χορός. 3. In late writers, metaph., c. acc. (v. M, Pr., 65), to supply, furnish abundantly : II Co 9¹⁰, I Pe 4¹¹ (Polyb., al.).†

χορός, -οῦ, ὁ, [in LXX chiefly for מָחוֹל, מְחֹלָה ;] a dance : pl., Lk 15²⁵.†

χορτάζω, (< χόρτος), [in LXX for שָׂבַע, Ps 16 (17)¹⁴, al.;] (a) prop., of animals (v. Lft. on Phl 4¹²), to feed, fatten : Re 19²¹ ; (b) in late Gk. (Kennedy, Sources, 82, 156), of persons, to fill or satisfy with food : c. acc. pers., Mt 15³³ ; pass., Mt 14²⁰ 15³⁷, Mk 6⁴² 7²⁷ 8⁸, Lk 9¹⁷, Jo 6²⁶, Ja 2¹⁶ ; opp. to πεινᾶν, Phl 4¹² ; c. gen. rei, Mk 8⁴ ; ἀπό, Lk 16²¹ ; ἐκ, Lk 15¹⁶, WH, txt., ; metaph., Mt 5⁶, Lk 6²¹.†

† χόρτασμα, -τος, τό (< χορτάζω), [in LXX : Ge 24²⁵, ³² 42²⁷ 43²⁴, Jg 19¹⁹ (מִסְפּוֹא), De 11¹⁵ (עֵשֶׂב), Si 30³³ (33²⁴) 38²⁶ * ;] fodder (Polyb., Plut., al.) : pl., Ac 7¹¹ (RV, sustenance).†

χόρτος, -ου, ὁ, [in LXX chiefly for עֵשֶׂב, also for חָצִיר, etc.;]
1. *an enclosure, a feeding place* (Hom.). 2. *food*, esp. for cattle, *grass*:
Mt 13²⁶ 14¹⁹, Mk 4²⁸ 6³⁹, Lk 12²⁸, Jo 6¹⁰, ι Co 3¹², Ja 1¹⁰, ¹¹, ι Pe 1²⁴ (LXX),
Re 9⁴; χ. χλωρός, Mk 6³⁹, Re 8⁷.†

Χουζᾶς, -ᾶ, ὁ, *Chuzas* (EV, *Chuza*): Lk 8³.†

χοῦς, -οός, acc., οὖν, ὁ, (contr. from χόος), [in LXX chiefly for
עָפָר;] 1. *earth, soil*. 2. In later writers (Plut., LXX), = κονιορτός,
dust: Mk 6¹¹, Re 18¹⁹.†

χράομαι, χρῶμαι (< χρή), [in LXX for עשׂה, etc.;] *to use, make
use of:* c. dat. (cf. M, *Pr.*, 64, 158), Ac 27¹⁷, ι Co 9¹²,¹⁵, ι Ti 1⁸ 5²³;
μᾶλλον χρῆσαι (i.e. the opportunity; v. M, *Pr.*, 247), ι Co. 7²¹; as sometimes in late writers (cf. M, *Pr.*, 64; Lft., *Notes*, 233), c. acc., ι Co 7³¹;
of feelings, etc., *to exercise, shew:* ιι Co 1¹⁷ 3¹²; c. adv., ἀποτόμως, *to
deal sharply*, ιι Co 13¹⁰; c. dat. pers. (cl.), *to treat, deal with*, Ac 27³;
for the form χρήομαι, v. M, *Gr.*, ιι, p. 265.†

χράω, κίχρημι, [in LXX for לוה, etc.;] *to lend:* Lk 11⁵.†

χρεία, -ας, ἡ, [in LXX: ιι Ch 2¹⁶ (15) (צֹרֶךְ), ιι Es 7²⁰ (חַשְׁחוּת);
freq. in Si, ι-ιι Mac;] 1. *need, necessity:* Ac 28¹⁰, Tit 3¹⁴; πρὸς
οἰκοδομὴν τῆς χ. (RV, txt., *for edifying as the need may be;* but v. Field,
Notes, 192), Eph 4²⁹; ἔστι χ., Lk 10⁴², He 7¹¹; χ. ἔχειν, c. gen., Mt 6⁸
21³, Mk 11³, Lk 9¹¹ 15⁷ 19³¹, ³⁴ 22⁷¹, Jo 13²⁹, ι Co 12²¹, ²⁴, ι Th 4¹²,
He 10³⁶, Re 21²³ 22⁵; seq. τοῦ, c. inf. (Bl., § 71, 3), He 5¹²; absol. (sc.
gen.), Ac 2⁴⁵ 4³⁵; c. gen. pers., Mt 9¹² 26⁶⁵, Mk 2¹⁷ 14⁶³, Lk 5³¹; c. inf.
(Bl., § 69, 5), Mt 3¹⁴ 14¹⁶, Jo 13¹⁰, ι Th 1⁸ 4⁹; seq. ἵνα, Jo 2²⁵ 16³⁰,
ι Jo 2²⁷; absol., Mk 2²⁵, Eph 4²⁸, ι Jo 3¹⁷; οὐδὲν χ. ἔχειν, Re 3¹⁷; ἡ χ.,
c. gen. subjc., Phl 2²⁵ 4¹⁶,¹⁹; pl., Ac 20³⁴, Ro 12¹³. 2. *matter, business*
(so esp. in late writers, Polyb., al.; ι Mac 12⁴⁵, al.): Ac 6³.†

†χρεοφειλέτης (Rec. χρεω-, WH, χρεοφιλ-; v. WH, *App.*, 152, 154),
-ου, ὁ, (< χρέος, *a debt*, + ὀφειλέτης), [in LXX: Jb 31³⁷, Pr 29¹³ *;]
a debtor: Lk 7⁴¹ 16⁵.†

* χρή, impers. (< χράω, v. LS, s.v.), *it is necessary, fitting:* Ja 3¹⁰
(cf. δεῖ.).†

χρῄζω (< χρή), [in LXX: Jg 11⁷, ι Ki 17¹⁸ A*;] *to need, have need of:*
c. gen. rei, Mt 6³², Lk 11⁸ 12³⁰, ιι Co 3¹; c. gen. pers. seq. ἐν, Ro 16².†

χρῆμα, -τος, τό (< χράομαι), [in LXX: Jo 22⁸, ιι Ch 1¹¹, ¹² (נְכָסִים),
Jb 27¹⁷ (בְּקֶהַ), etc.; freq. in Si (5¹, ⁸, al.), ιι and ιv Mac;] *a thing that
one uses* or *needs* (and generally, *a matter, event, business*); hence in
pl., (a) *wealth, riches:* οἱ τὰ χ. ἔχοντες, Mk 10²³, ²⁴, Lk 18²⁴; (b) *money*.
Ac 8¹⁸, ²⁰ 24²⁶; sing. (rare in cl.) of a special sum of money, Ac 4³⁷.†

χρηματίζω (< χρῆμα), [in LXX: Je 33 (26)² 36 (29)²³ 37 (30)²
43 (36)², ⁴ A (דבר pi.), 32¹⁶ (25³⁰) (שׁאג), ιιι Ki 18²⁷, Jb 40³ (⁸) *;] 1. *to
transact business*, hence, *to consult, deliberate* (Thuc., Dem., al.);
hence in later writers, 2. *to make answer* (esp. of official pronounce-
ments by magistrates, etc.; in π. of the royal reply to an ἔντευξις, q.v.;
cf. Deiss., *BS*, 122); of an answer by an oracle (Diod., Plut., al.); in
FlJ, LXX and NT, of divine communications, *to instruct, admonish*,

warn: pass. (Bl., § 54, 3), Mt 2²², He 8⁵ 11⁷ 12²⁵; c. inf. (Bl., § 69, 4; 70, 3; 72, 5), Mt 2¹², Lk 2²⁶, Ac 10²². "Two entirely distinct words, the former from χρήματα, 'business' . . ., the latter from an equivalent of χρησμός, 'oracle,'" M, *Gr.*, π, ii, p. 265. 3. *to assume a name* (as in business), *be called* (Polyb., al.): Ac 11²⁶, Ro 7³ (gnomic fut.; cf. Burton, § 69).†

χρηματισμός, -οῦ, ὁ (< χρηματίζω, q.v.), [in LXX: Pr 24⁶⁹ (31¹) (מִשָּׂא), π Mac 2⁴ 11¹⁷ *;] *a divine response, an oracle*: Ro 11⁴ (Xen., Plat., al.).†

χρήσιμος, -η, -ον (< χράομαι), [in LXX: Ge 37²⁶ (בֶּצַע), etc.;] *useful*: π Ti 2¹⁴.†

χρῆσις, -εως, ἡ (< χράομαι), [in LXX: ι Ki 1²⁸ (שָׁאַל), Si 18⁸, al.;] *use*: in a sexual sense, Ro 1²⁶; c. gen. obj., θηλείας, ib.²⁷ (for exx., v. Thayer, s.v.).†

*† χρηστεύομαι (< χρηστός), *to be kind*: ι Co 13⁴ (eccl.).†

*† χρηστολογία, -ας, ἡ (χρηστός, λέγω), *fair speaking*: in bad sense, Ro 16¹⁸ (in good sense also, eccl.).†

χρηστός, -ή, -όν (< χράομαι), [in LXX chiefly for טוֹב (freq. of God: Ps 24 (25)⁸, al.), also for יָקָר (Ez 27²² 28¹³), יָשָׁר (Pr 2²¹ א A);] *serviceable, good*; (a) of things, *good, pleasant*: of food (as often in cl.), οἶνος, Lk 5³⁹; ζυγός, Mt 11³⁰ (EV, *easy*); in ethical sense, ἤθη, ι Co 15³³; (b) of persons, *good, kind, gracious*: Eph 4³²; of God, Lk 6³⁵, ι Pe 2³; τ. χρηστὸν (= ἡ χρηστότης) τοῦ θεοῦ, Ro 2⁴.†

χρηστότης, -ητος, ἡ (< χρηστός), [in LXX for טוֹב and cogn. forms;] 1. *goodness, excellence, uprightness*: Ro 3¹² (LXX). 2. *goodness of heart, kindness*: Ro 2⁴, π Co 6⁶, Ga 5²², Col 3¹², Tit 3⁴; seq. ἐπί, c. acc. pers., Eph 2⁷; id., opp. to ἀποτομία, Ro 11²².†

SYN.: v.s. ἀγαθωσύνη.

χρίσμα (T, χρῖσμα, as in cl.; v. Tdf., *Pr.*, 102; Bl., § 4, 2), -τος, τό (< χρίω), later form of χρῖμα (Æsch., al.), [in LXX for מִשְׁחָה and cogn. forms (Ex 29⁷, al.);] *an anointing, unction* (the result of the action χρίειν; *ICC*, in l.; but cf. Westc., in l., for the view that the *oil*, not the act, is meant): ι Jo 2²⁰, ²⁷.†

Χριστιανός (D, Χρεισ-; on the form Χρησ-, v. Bl., § 3, 6; 27, 4; on the ending, -ανος, v. Bl., ll. c.; Deiss., *LAE*, 382), -οῦ, ὁ, *a Christian*, the name first given to the disciples by pagan gentiles at Antioch: Ac 11²⁶ 26²⁸, ι Pe 4¹⁶ (v. reff. in Thayer, s.v.; also *DB*, i, 384).†

χριστός (Χρ-), -ή, -όν (< χρίω), [in LXX for מָשִׁיחַ and cogn. forms;] 1. as adj., (a) of things, *anointing, to be used as ointment* (Æsch., Eur., al.; τ. ἔλαιον τὸ χ., Le 21¹⁰); (b) of persons, *anointed* (ὁ ἱερεὺς ὁ χ., Le 4⁵; οἱ χ. ἱερεῖς, π Mac 1¹⁰): ὁ χ. τοῦ κυρίου or θεοῦ (ι Ki 2¹⁰, Ps 2², al.), of the Messiah (Aram., מְשִׁיחָא; cf. Dalman, *Words*, 289 ff.), Lk 2¹¹, ²⁶, Jo 1⁴¹, Ac 2³⁶ 4²⁶, al. 2. As subst., ὁ Χριστός, *the Messiah, the Christ*: Mt 2⁴, Mk 8²⁹, Lk 2¹¹, Jo 1²⁰, Ac 2³¹, Ro 7⁴, al.; Ἰησοῦς Χ., Mk 1¹, Jo 1¹⁷, Ac 2³⁸, al.; Χ. Ἰησοῦς, Mt 1¹⁸, WH, mg.,

Ac 5⁴², Ro 6³, al.; X. κύριος, Lk 2¹¹; Ἰησοῦς X. ὁ κύριος, Ac 15²⁶, Ro 1⁷, al.

χρίω, *to anoint* (Hom., al.); [in LXX chiefly for מָשַׁח, of consecration to a sacred office: priest, Ex 28⁴¹; prophet, III Ki 19¹⁶; king, I Ki 10¹; of things, Ex 40⁹, Le 8¹⁰, al.]. In NT, metaph., of God's anointing, (a) Christ: Ac 4²⁷; c. inf., Lk 4¹⁸ (LXX); c. dupl. acc. (v. Bl., § 34, 4), He 1⁹ (LXX); πνεύματι ἁγίῳ, Ac 10³⁸; (b) Christians: II Co 1²¹ (cf. Westc., *Epp. Jo.*, 73) (cf. ἐν-, ἐπι-χρίω).†
SYN.: v.s. ἀλείφω.

χρονίζω (< χρόνος), [in LXX chiefly for אָחַר pi.;] *to spend* or *take time, to tarry, linger, delay*: Mt 24⁴⁸ 25⁵, He 10³⁷; seq. ἐν, c. dat. loc., Lk 1²¹; c. inf., Lk 12⁴⁵.†

χρόνος, -ου, ὁ, [in LXX chiefly for יוֹם, also for עֵת, etc.;] *time* (a space of time, whether long or short; cf. Lft., *Notes*, 70): Mt 2⁷, Mk 9²¹, Lk 1⁵⁷, Ac 3²¹ 7¹⁷,²³ 13¹⁸ 17³⁰ 27⁹, He 11³², I Pe 1¹⁷ 4³, Re 10⁶ (R, mg., *delay*); στιγμὴ χρόνου, Lk 4⁵; πλήρωμα τοῦ χ., Ga 4⁴; ποιεῖν χ., Ac 15³³ 18²³; βιῶσαι, I Pe 4²; διδόναι, Re 2²¹; pl., χ. καὶ (ἡ) καιροί (Lft. l.c.), Ac 1⁷, I Th 5¹; ἐπ᾽ ἐσχάτου τῶν χ. (χρόνου), I Pe 1²⁰, Ju ¹⁸; c. prep., ἄχρι, Ac 3²¹; διὰ τὸν χ., He 5¹²; ἐν χ., Ac 1⁶,²¹; ἐπὶ (πλείονα) χ., Lk 18⁴, Ac 18²⁰; ἐφ᾽ ὅσον χ., Ro 7¹, I Co 7³⁹, Ga 4¹; κατὰ τὸν χ., Mt 2¹⁶; μετὰ πολὺν (τοσοῦτον) χ., Mt 25¹⁹, He 4⁷; πρὸ χ. αἰωνίων, II Ti 1⁹, Tit 1²; instr. dat. of extension of time (v. M, *Pr.*, 75, 148; Deiss., *LAE*, 206), Lk 8²⁷,²⁹, Jo 14⁹, Ac 8¹¹, Ro 16²⁵; acc., of duration of time, Mk 2¹⁹, Lk 20⁹, Jo 5⁶ 7³³ 12³⁵ 14⁹, Ac 14³,²⁸ 19²² 20¹⁸, I Co 16⁷, Re 6¹¹.†
SYN.: v.s. καιρός.

*χρονοτριβέω, -ῶ (< χρόνος, τρίβω), *to spend time*: Ac 20¹⁶.†

χρύσεος, -εα, -εον (-οῦς, -ῆ, -οῦν; on acc. sing. fem., -ᾶν, Re 1¹³ and gen. pl. uncontr., -εων, Re 2¹, LTr., v. M, *Pr.*, 48 and cf. Thackeray, *Gr.*, I, 172 f.) (< χρυσός), [in LXX chiefly for זָהָב;] *golden*, i.e. made or overlaid with gold: II Ti 2²⁰, He 9⁴, Re 1¹²,¹³,²⁰ 2¹ 4⁴ 5⁸ 8³ 9¹³,²⁰ 14¹⁴ 15⁶,⁷ 17⁴ 21¹⁵.†

χρυσίον, -ου, τό (dimin. of χρυσός, q.v.), [in LXX chiefly for זָהָב;] *a piece of gold, gold*: I Co 3¹², He 9⁴, I Pe 1⁷, Re 3¹⁸ 21¹⁸,²¹; of golden ornaments, I Ti 2⁹ (WH, txt., RV), I Pe 3³, Re 17⁴ 18¹⁶ (WH, txt., R); of gold coin, money, Ac 3⁶ 20³³, I Pe 1¹⁸.†

*†χρυσο-δακτύλιος, -ον, *with a gold ring*: Ja 2².†

χρυσό-λιθος, -ου, ὁ, [in LXX: Ex 28²⁰ 36²⁰ (39¹³), Ez 28¹³ (תַּרְשִׁישׁ) *;] *a chrysolite* (on its identification, v. Swete, *Ap.*, 288 f.; *DB*, iv, 620): Re 21²⁰.†

*†χρυσό-πρασος, -ου, ὁ, *a chrysoprase* (v. Swete, *Ap.*, 289): Re 21²⁰.†

χρυσός, -οῦ, ὁ, [in LXX chiefly for זהב;] *gold*: Mt 2¹¹, Re 9⁷; of golden ornaments, Mt 23¹⁶,¹⁷, I Ti 2⁹ (Rec., WH, mg.), Ja 5³, Re 17⁴ (Rec., WH, mg.) 18¹²,¹⁶ (Rec., WH, mg.); of images, Ac 17²⁹; of gold coin, Mt 10⁹.†

χρυσοῦς, v.s. χρύσεος.

χρυσόω, -ῶ (< χρυσός), [in LXX chiefly for צפה pi.;] *to gild, cover with gold*: pass., c. dat., χρυσίῳ (pleonast., cf. Ex 26³⁷), Re 17⁴ 18¹⁶.†

χρώς, gen., χρωτός, ὁ, [in LXX chiefly for בָּשָׂר;] in cl. rare in prose, *the surface of the body, skin*: Ac 19¹².†

χωλός, -ή, -όν, [in LXX for פִּסֵּחַ;] *lame, halt, maimed*: Mt 11⁵ 15³⁰, ³¹ 18⁸ 21¹⁴, Mk 9⁴⁵, Lk 7²² 14¹³, ²¹, Jo 5³, Ac 3² 8⁷ 14⁸, He 12¹³.†

χώρα, -ας, ἡ, [in LXX for אֶרֶץ, מְדִינָה, etc.;] 1. most freq. in cl., *a space, place*. 2. *land*, i.e. (*a*) *a land, country, region*: Mt 12², Mk 5¹⁰ 6⁵⁵, Lk 2⁸ 15¹³⁻¹⁵ 19¹², Jo 11⁵⁴, Ac 13⁴⁹ 27²⁷; χ. Γαλατική, Ac 16⁶ 18²³; Τραχωνίτιδος, Lk 3¹; τ. Ἰουδαίας, Ac 26²⁰; τ. Ἰουδαίων, Ac 10³⁹; pl., τῆς Ἰουδαίας κ. Σαμαρείας, Ac 8¹; Γεργεσηνῶν (Γερασηνῶν, Γαδαρηνῶν), Mt 8²⁸, Mk 5¹, Lk 8²⁶; ἐν χ. καὶ σκιᾷ θανάτου, Mt 4¹⁶; (*b*) *land, property*: Lk 12¹⁶; (*c*) *the country*, opp. to the town; so in pl., Lk 21²¹, Jo 4³⁵, Ja 5⁴.†

SYN.: ἀγρός, τόπος (cf. DCG, i, 591ª; LS, s.v. χώρα, ad init.).

Χωραζίν, v.s. Χοραζείν.

χωρέω, -ῶ, [in LXX: Ge 13⁶ (נשׂא), iii Ki 7²⁶, ³⁸ (כּוּל hi.), ii Ch 4⁵ (חזק hi.), Wi 7²³, ²⁴, al.;] I. Intrans., 1. *to make room, give way, retire, pass*: seq. εἰς, Mt 15¹⁷; metaph. (EV, *come*), εἰς μετάνοιαν, ii Pe 3⁹. 2. *to go forward, advance, progress* (Plat., Polyb., al.) · ὁ λόγος ὁ ἐμὸς οὐ χωρεῖ ἐν ὑμῖν, Jo 8³⁷ (R, txt., *hath not free course;* R, mg., *hath no place*, for wh. cf. Field, *Notes*, 94 f.). II. Trans., *to have space for holding, to hold*: Mk 2² (cf. Ge, l.c.), Jo 21²⁵; of measures (iii Ki, ii Ch, ll. c.), Jo 2⁶. Metaph., of having or making room in mind or heart: Mt 19¹¹, ¹² (EV, *receive*), ii Co 7² (R, txt., *open your hearts;* mg., *make room*) (cf. ἀνα-, ἀπο-, ἐκ-, ὑπο-χωρέω).†

χωρίζω, [in LXX: ii Ch 12⁸, al. (בדל ni., etc.), Wi 1³, ii Mac 5²¹, al.;] 1. *to separate, divide, put asunder*: c. acc. rei, opp. to συζεύγνυμι, Mt 19⁶, Mk 10⁹; c. acc. pers., seq. ἀπό (Wi 1³), Ro 8³⁵, ³⁹; pf. pass. ptcp., He 7²⁶. 2. In late writers, mid. and 1 aor pass., *to separate oneself, depart*: Phm ¹⁵; seq. ἀπό, Ac 1⁴, ἐκ, Ac 18¹, ²; of divorce (Polyb., al.), i Co 7¹⁰, ¹¹, ¹⁵ (cf. ἀπο-, δια-χωρίζω).†

χωρίον, -ου, τό (dimin. of χώρα, χῶρος), [in LXX: i Ch 27²⁷ (כֶּרֶם), ii Mac 11⁵ 12⁷, ²¹, iv Mac 15²⁰*;] 1. *a place, region*. 2. *an estate, property, piece of land*: Mt 26³⁶, Mk 14³², Jo 4⁵, Ac 1¹⁸, ¹⁹ 4³⁴ 5³, ⁸, 28⁷.†

χωρίς, adv., 1. *separately, apart*: Jo 20⁷. 2. As prep., c. gen., (*a*) *separate from, apart from, without* (practically equiv. to ἄνευ; v. Field, *Notes*, 103): Mt 13³⁴, Mk 4³⁴, Lk 6⁴⁹, Jo 1³ 15⁵, Ro 3²¹, ²⁸ 4⁶ 7⁸, ⁹ 10¹⁴, i Co 4⁸ 11¹¹, ii Co 12³, Eph 2¹², Phl 2¹⁴, i Ti 2⁸ 5²¹, Phm ¹⁴, He 4¹⁵ 7⁷, ²⁰ 9⁷, ¹⁸, ²², ²⁸ 10²⁸ 11⁶, ⁴⁰ 12⁸, ¹⁴ (οὗ χωρίς; v. Bl., § 82, 3), Ja 2¹³, ²⁰, ²⁶; (*b*) *besides*: Mt 14²¹ 15³⁸, ii Co 11²⁸.†

*†χῶρος, -ου, ὁ (Lat. *corus*), *the N.W. wind*: Ac 27¹².†

Ψ

Ψ, ψ, ψῖ, τό, indecl., *psi, ps,* the twenty-third letter. As a numeral, ψ′ = 700, ψ, = 700,000.

ψάλλω, [in LXX chiefly for זמר pi. (Jg 5³, Ps 7¹⁷, al.), also for נגן pi. (ι Ki 16¹⁶ ᶠᶠ·, al.) ;] 1. *to pull, twitch, twang* (as a bowstring, etc. ; Æsch., Eur., al.), hence, 2. absol., *(a) to play* a stringed instrument with the fingers (Hdt., Plat., al.) ; *(b)* later, *to sing to a harp, sing psalms* (LXX) ; in NT, *to sing a hymn, sing praise :* Ja 5¹³ ; c. dat. pers., Ro 15⁹ ⁽ᴸˣˣ⁾, Eph 5¹⁹ ; dat. instr., ι Co 14¹⁵.†

ψαλμός, -οῦ, ὁ (< ψάλλω), [in LXX chiefly for מִזְמוֹר ;] 1. *a striking, twitching* with the fingers (Eur., al.), hence, *a striking* of musical strings (Æsch., al.), and hence in later writers, 2. *a sacred song* sung to musical accompaniment, *a psalm* (LXX) : ι Co 14²⁶, Eph 5¹⁹, Col 3¹⁶ ; of OT psalms, Lk 24⁴⁴, Ac 13³³ ; βίβλος ψαλμῶν, Lk 20⁴², Ac 1²⁰.†

SYN. : v.s. ὕμνος.

*† ψευδ-άδελφος, -ου, ὁ, *a false brother :* of professing Christians, ιι Co 11²⁶, Ga 2⁴.†

*† ψευδ-απόστολος, -ου, ὁ, *a false apostle :* ιι Co 11¹³.†

ψευδής, -ές (< ψεύδομαι), [in LXX for שֶׁקֶר, שָׁוְא, כָּזָב ; etc. ;] *lying, false, untrue* (of persons and things) : Re 2² ; μάρτυρες, Ac 6¹³ ; as subst., ὁ ψ., *a liar :* Re 21⁸.†

*† ψευδο-διδάσκαλος, -ου, ὁ, *a false teacher :* ιι Pe 2¹.†

* ψευδο-λόγος, -ον (< ψευδής, λέγω), *speaking falsely, lying :* ι Ti 4² (Aristoph., Polyb., al.).†

ψεύδομαι, v.s. ψεύδω.

ψευδο-μαρτυρέω, -ῶ, [in LXX : Ex 20¹⁶, De 5²⁰ ⁽¹⁷⁾ (ענה), Da ᵀᴴ Su ⁶¹ AB²R (v. ψευδομάρτυς) * ;] *to bear false witness :* Mt 19¹⁸, Mk 10¹⁹, Lk 18²⁰⁽ᴸˣˣ⁾ ; seq. κατά, c. gen. pers., Mk 14⁵⁶, ⁵⁷ (Xen., Plat., al.).†

* ψευδο-μαρτυρία, -ας, ἡ, *false witness :* Mt 15¹⁹ 26⁵⁹.†

**† ψευδο-μάρτυς, -υρος, ὁ, [in LXX : Da LXX Su ⁶⁰, ᵀᴴ ib. ⁶¹ B¹ * ;] *a false witness :* Mt 26⁶⁰ ; c. gen. obj. (v. WM, § 30, 1ᵃ), ι Co 15¹⁵.†

† ψευδο-προφήτης, -ου, ὁ, [in LXX : Za 13², Je ₉ (6¹³, al.) (נָבִיא * ;] *a false prophet* (= cl. ψευδόμαντις) : Mt 7¹⁵ 24¹¹, ²⁴, Mk 13²² (v. Swete, in l.), Lk 6²⁶, Ac 13⁶, ιι Pe 2¹, ι Jo 4¹, Re 16¹³ 19²⁰ 20¹⁰.†

ψεῦδος, -εος (-ους), τό, [in LXX chiefly for שֶׁקֶר, also for כָּחַשׁ, כָּזָב ;] *a falsehood, untruth, lie :* Re 14¹⁵ ; opp. to ἡ ἀλήθεια, Jo 8⁴⁴, Ro 1²⁵, Eph 4²⁵, ιι Th 2¹¹, ι Jo 2²¹ ; to τὸ ἀληθές, ib. ²⁷ ; ποιεῖν ψ., Re 21²⁷ 22¹⁵ ; ἐν πάσῃ δυνάμει κ. σημείοις κ. τέρασιν ψεύδους (gen. qual., v. M, Th., 104 ; and on the meaning and construction, v. also ICC, in l.), ιι Th 2⁹.†

*† ψευδό-χριστος, -ου ὁ, *a false Christ or Messiah,* "a pretender to the

Messianic office" (Swete, *Mk.*, 309; cf. also Tr., ´*Syn.*, § xxx) : Mt 24²⁴, Mk 13²² (cf. ἀντίχριστος).†

ψεύδω, *to deceive by lies;* more freq. in the depon. mid. form ψεύδομαι (so always in NT), [in LXX chiefly for בּזָה pi. ;] 1. absol., *to lie:* Mt 5¹¹, He 6¹⁸, 1 Jo 1⁶, Re 3⁹; οὐ ψεύδομαι, Ro 9¹, 11 Co 11³¹, Ga 1²⁰, 1 Ti 2⁷ : c. dat. pers. (Ps 17 (18)¹⁵, Je 5¹², al.), Ac 5⁴; seq. εἰς, Col 3⁹; κατά, Ja 3¹⁴ (Hort, in l.). 2. Like act., c. acc., *to deceive by lies* (Æsch., al.) : Ac 5³.†

* ψευδώνυμος, -ον (< ψευδής, ὄνομα), *under a false name, falsely called:* 1 Ti 6²⁰ (Æsch., Plut., al.).†

** ψεῦσμα, -τος, τό (< ψεύδω), [in Aq., Th. : Jb 34⁶, Pr 23³; in Sm. : Jb 13⁴, al.;] *a lie, falsehood:* Ro 3⁷ (Plat., Plut. al.).†

ψεύστης, -ου, ὁ (< ψεύδω), [in LXX : Ps 115² (116¹¹) (בּזָב), Pr 19²² A א² (בְּזָב), Si 15⁸ 25²*;] *a liar:* Jo 8⁴⁴, ⁵⁵, Ro 3⁴, 1 Ti 1¹⁰, Tit 1¹², 1 Jo 1¹⁰ 2⁴, ²² 4²⁰ 5¹⁰.†

ψηλαφάω, -ῶ (< ψάω, *to touch*), [in LXX for מוּשׁ, מָשַׁשׁ pi., etc. ;] 1. *to feel or grope about;* c. acc., *to feel about for, search after :* metaph., of seeking God, Ac 17²⁷. 2. *to feel, touch, handle :* c. acc. pers., Lk 24³⁹, 1 Jo 1¹; προσεληλύθατε ψηλαφωμένῳ (ὄρει ?), He 12¹⁸ (R, txt., a mount *that might be touched;* mg., *a palpable and kindled fire;* v. Westc., in l.).†

ψηφίζω (< ψῆφος), [in LXX : 111 Ki 3⁸ 8⁵ A (סָפַר ni.)*;] *to count* (prop., with pebbles), *reckon, calculate :* τ. δαπάνην, Lk 14²⁸; τ. ἀριθμόν (i.e. calculate the number's meaning), Re 13¹⁸ (in cl. chiefly mid., *to vote* by casting a pebble; cf. συγ-κατα-, συμ-ψηφίζω).†

ψῆφος, -ου, ἡ (< ψάω, *to rub*), [in LXX : Ex 4²⁵ (צֹר), La 3¹⁶ (חָצָץ), Ec 7²⁶ ⁽²⁵⁾ (חֶשְׁבּוֹן), 1v Ki 12⁴ ⁽⁵⁾ A, Si 18¹⁰, 1v Mac 15²⁶*;] 1. *a small smooth stone, a pebble:* ψ. λευκή (for suggestions as to the meaning, v. Swete, in l.), Re 2¹⁷. 2. From the use of pebbles in voting, *a vote :* Ac 26¹⁰.†

† ψιθυρισμός, -οῦ, ὁ (< ψιθυρίζω, *to whisper*), [in LXX : Ec 10¹¹ (לַחַשׁ)*;] *a whispering;* (*a*) of secret slander, 11 Co 12²⁰ (Plut.); (*b*) of a murmured enchantment, Ec, l.c.†

* ψιθυριστής, -οῦ, ὁ (v. supr.), *a whisperer* (as epithet of Hermes, Dem., 1358, 6) : in bad sense, Ro 1³⁰.†

SYN. : κατάλαλος, q.v.

*† ψιχίον, -ου, τό, dimin. of ψίξ, *a crumb :* Mt 15²⁷, Mk 7²⁸.†

ψυχή, -ῆς, ἡ, [in LXX very freq. for נֶפֶשׁ, sometimes for לֵב, לֵבָב, etc.;] 1. *breath* (Lat. *anima*), *breath of life, life* (Hom., al.; in Arist., of *the vital principle*) : Mt 6²⁵, Mk 3⁴ 10⁴⁵, Lk 12²², Jo 10¹¹, Ac 20¹⁰, ²⁴, 11 Co 1²³, Phl 2³⁰, 1 Th 2⁸, al. 2. *the soul,* (*a*) as the seat of the will, desires and affections : Mt 26³⁸, Mk 12³⁰ ⁽ᴸˣˣ⁾ 14³⁴, Lk 1⁴⁶, Jo 10²⁴, Ac 14², Phl 1²⁷, al. ; ἐκ ψυχῆς, *from the heart, heartily :* Eph 6⁶, Col 3²³; (*b*) as a periphrasis for person or self (freq. in translation from Semitic originals, v. M, *Pr.*, 87; Robinson, *Gospels*, 113 ff.; but also freq. in cl., v. LS, s.v. ii, 2; Edwards, *Lex.*, App. A.): Mt 11²⁹, Mk 8³⁶, Ac 2⁴¹, Ro 2⁹, 1 Pe 3²⁰, al.; πᾶσα ψ., Ac 2⁴³ 3²³ (LXX), Ro 13¹; ψ. ζῶσα (ζωῆς), 1 Co 15⁴⁵, Re 16³; (c) as the object of divine grace and eternal salvation: He 13¹⁷, Ja 1²¹ 5²⁰, 1 Pe 1⁹, ²² 2¹¹ 4¹⁹, iii Jo ².

SYN.: v.s. νοῦς, πνεῦμα, ψυχικός, and cf. *ICC* on 1 Th 5²³, Lft., *Notes*, 88 f.

** ψυχικός, -ή, -όν (< ψυχή), [in LXX: iv Mac 1³² *;] *of the ψυχή* (as the lower part of the immaterial in man), EV, *natural*: opp. to πνευματικός, 1 Co 2¹⁴ 15⁴⁴, ⁴⁶; πνεῦμα μὴ ἔχοντες (EV, *sensual*; R, mg., *natural* or *animal;* better perhaps, *of the mind;* v. infr.), Ju ¹⁹; with ἐπίγειος, δαιμονιώδης, opp. to ἄνωθεν κατερχομένη (σοφία), *of the mind* (Hort, in l.), Ja 3¹⁵.†

ψύχος (LT, ψῦ-, as in cl.), -εος (-ους), τό (< ψύχω), [in LXX: Ge 8²² (קֹר), Jb 37⁹, Ps 147⁶ ⁽¹⁷⁾ (קָרָה), Za 14⁶, Da LXX TH 3⁶⁷, ⁶⁹ *;] *cold:* Jo 18¹⁸, Ac 28², ii Co 11²⁷.†

ψυχρός, -ά, -όν (< ψύχω), [in LXX: Pr 25²⁵ (קַר), Si 43²⁰, iv Mac 11²⁶ *;] *cold:* sc. ὕδωρ (cf. Theogn., 263; Hdt., ii, 37), Mt 10⁴²; metaph., of indifferent persons, Re 3¹⁵, ¹⁶.†

ψύχω, [in LXX for קוּר, שׁמַח;] *to breathe, blow;* hence, *to make cool.* Pass., *to grow cool:* metaph., Mt 24¹².†

ψωμίζω (< ψωμός, *a morsel*), [in LXX chiefly for אכל hi.;] *to feed with morsels* (as children or the sick; Hippocr.), hence, generally, in late writers, *to feed, nourish:* c. acc. pers., Ro 12²⁰ (LXX); c. acc. rei, *to give out for food,* 1 Co 13³ (cf. WM, § 32, 4aₙ; for dupl. acc., cf. Nu 11⁴, Si 15³, al.).†

*† ψωμίον, -ου, τό, dimin. of ψωμός, *a fragment, morsel:* Jo 13²⁶, ²⁷, ³⁰.†

*† ψώχω (< ψώω, collat. form of ψάω, *to rub*), *to rub:* Lk 6¹.†

Ω

Ω, ω, ὦ μέγα (cf. ὁ μικρόν), *omega*, ō, the twenty-fourth and last letter. As a numeral, ω' = 800, ω, = 800,000. As a symbol of *the last* (= τὸ τέλος), τὸ Ὦ (Rec. Ω, L, ῶ, T, ω), *the Omega:* Re 1⁸ 21⁶ 22¹³ (cf. Ἄλφα).†

ὦ, interj., c. vocat., *O;* (a) in simple address (less freq. than in cl.; M, *Pr.*, 71); Ac 1¹ 18¹⁴ 27²¹, Ro 2¹, ³ 9²⁰, 1 Ti 6²⁰; expressing reproof, Ja 2²⁰; (b) in exclamations of surprise, etc.: Mt 15²⁸, Lk 24²⁵, Ac 13¹⁰, Ro 11³³, Ga 3¹; c. nom. (Bl., § 33, 4), Mt 17¹⁷, Mk 9¹⁹, Lk 9⁴¹.†

Ὠβήδ, v.s. Ἰωβήδ.

ὧδε, adv., [in LXX for הִנֵּה, פֹּה, הֲלֹם, etc.;] 1. prop., of manner, *so* (Hom., al.). 2. In poets (rarely) and late writers, of place, (a) *hither* (Bl., § 25, 2): Mt 8²⁹, Mk 11³, Lk 9⁴¹, Jo 6²⁵, al.; ἕως ὧδε,

Lk 23⁵; (b) *here :* Mt 12⁶, Mk 9¹, Lk 9³³, Jo 6⁹, al.; τὰ ὧδε, Col 4⁹;
opp. to ἐκεῖ, He 7⁸; ὧδε . . . ἢ ὧδε (ἐκεῖ), Mt 24²³, Mk 13²¹; metaph.,
here (i.e. in this circumstance or connection), ι Co 4², Re 13¹⁰, ¹⁸ 14¹²
17⁹.

ᾠδή, -ῆς, ἡ, [in LXX chiefly for שִׁיר;] *a song, ode,* whether sad
or joyful; in LXX and NT always in praise of God or Christ: Re 5⁹
14³ 15³; ᾠ. πνευματικαί, Eph 5¹⁹, Col 3¹⁶.†

ὠδίν (late form of ὠδίς), -ῖνος, ἡ, [in LXX for חֵבֶל (and wrongly
for חֶבֶל, cf. Ac, l.c.), חִיל, etc.;] *a birth-pang, travail-pain :* ι Th 5³;
metaph., of extreme suffering, Mt 24⁸, Mk 13⁸; ὠδῖνες θανάτου (Ps
17 (18)⁴ חֶבְלֵי מָוֶת), Ac 2²⁴.†

ὠδίνω, [in LXX chiefly for חוּל, also for חבל pi., etc.;] *to have
birth-pangs, to travail :* Ga 4²⁷ ⁽ᴸˣˣ⁾, Re 12²; metaph., Ga 4¹⁹ (cf.
συν-ωδίνω).†

ὦμος, -ου, ὁ, [in LXX chiefly for שְׁכֶם, כָּתֵף;] *the shoulder :*
Mt 23⁴, Lk 15⁵.†

* ὠνέομαι, -οῦμαι, *to buy :* ὠνήσατο (= cl. ἐπρίατο; v. Rutherford,
NPhr., 210 ff.; Veitch, s.v.), c. gen. pret., Ac 7¹⁶.†

ᾠόν (Rec. ὠόν), -οῦ, τό, [in LXX for בֵּיצָה;] *an egg :* Lk 11¹².†

ὥρα, -ας, ἡ, [in LXX chiefly for עֵת and in Da for שָׁעָה;] 1. any
time or *period* fixed by nature, esp. a *season* (Hom., Hdt., Plat., al.).
2. A part of the day, and esp. a twelfth part of day or night, *an
hour :* Mt 24³⁶, Mk 13³², Ac 10³, al.; accus. in ans. to "when"? (M,
Pr., 63, 245; Bl., § 34, 8), Jo 4⁵², Ac 10³, ³⁰, ι Co 15³⁰, Re 3³; acc. of
duration, Mt 20¹² 26⁴⁰, Mk 14³⁷; inexactly, πρὸς ὥραν, *for a season, for
a time,* Jo 5³⁵, ιι Co 7⁸, Ga 2⁵; πρὸς καιρὸν ὥρας, *for a short season* (*ICC,*
in l.), ι Th 2¹⁷.   3. A definite point of time, *time, hour :* Mt 26⁴⁵; c.
gen. rei, Lk 1¹⁰ 14¹⁷, Re 3¹⁰, al.; c. gen. pers., Lk 22⁵³, Jo 2⁴ 7³⁰, al.;
ἡ ἄρτι ὥρα, ι Co 4¹¹; ἐσχάτη ὥ., ι Jo 2¹⁸; seq. ὅτε, Jo 4²¹, ²³ 5²⁵ 16²⁵; ἵνα,
Jo 12²³, al.; c. acc. et inf., Ro 13¹¹ (cf. *DB, ext.,* 475ᵇ, 476ᵇ).

ὡραῖος, -α, -ον, (< ὥρα), [in LXX for נָאָה, טוֹב, יָפֶה, etc.;]
seasonable, timely, esp. of ripe fruits; hence, *blooming, beautiful* (both
of things and persons): Mt 23²⁷, Ac 3², ¹⁰, Ro 10¹⁵ (LXX, ὡρα).†

ὠρύομαι, depon., [in LXX for שָׁאַג;] of animals (also of men,
Hdt., al.), *to roar, howl :* λέων, ι Pe 5⁸.†

ὡς, adverbial form of the relative pron. ὅς, ἥ, ὅ.
I. As relat. adv. of manner, *as, like as, just as, even as ;* 1. with
a demonstrative, like οὕτως, expressed or understood : οὕτως . . . ὡς,
Mk 4²⁶, ι Co 3¹⁵, Eph 5²⁸, Ja 2¹², al.; ὡς . . . οὕτως, Ac 8³², ι Co 7¹⁷,
al.; elliptically (sc. οὕτως, οὕτω), c. nom., Mt 6²⁹, al.; c. acc., Mt 19¹⁹,
Mk 12³¹, al.; c. prep., Mt 26⁵⁵, Mk 14⁴⁸, Lk 22⁵², Jo 7¹⁰, al.; c. verb.,
Jo 15⁶, ιι Co 3¹, Eph 2³, ι Th 5⁶, al.; c. ptcp. (the ptcp. however not
having the special force wh. it has in cl.; v. Bl., § 73, 5; 74, 6),
Mt 7²⁹, Mk 1²², He 13¹⁷, al.; freq. implying opinion or belief, Ro 9³²;

so esp. c. gen. absol., I Co 4¹⁸, II Co 5²⁰, I Pe 4¹², II Pe 1³. 2. Before numerals, *about, nearly :* Mk 5¹³, Jo 1⁴⁰, Ac 5⁷, al. ' 3. Before adjectives and adverbs, *how :* Ro 10¹⁵ 11³³, I Th 2¹⁰ ; c. superl., ὡς τάχιστα, *as quickly as possible,* Ac 17¹⁵.
II. As conjunction; 1. temporal, (a) *as, when, since :* Mk 9²¹ 14⁷², Lk 1²³, Jo 2⁹, al. ; (b) *while, when, as long as :* Lk 12⁵⁸, Jo 12³⁶, Ga 6¹⁰ (Field, *Notes,* 191); ὡς ἄν (M, *Pr.,* 167, and v.s. ἄν), Ro 15²⁴, I Co 11³⁴, Phl 2²³. 2. Final, *in order that;* c. inf., *in order to* (M, *Pr.,* 204ₙ), Lk 9⁵², Ac 20²⁴, He 7⁹.

*†ὡσαννά (T, ὡσ-), (Heb. הוֹשַׁעְנָא; v. Dalman, *Words,* 220 ff.; *Gr.,* 249), *hosanna :* Mt 21⁹, Mk 11⁹, ¹⁰, Jo 12¹³ ; τ. υἱῷ Δαυείδ, Mt 21⁹, ¹⁵ ; the Heb. means "save, we pray" (Ps 118²⁵ ; LXX, σῶσον δή). Cf. Swete on Mk, l.c.†

ὡσαύτως, adv., strengthened for ὡς (in Hom. at the beginning of a clause, in the form ὡς δ᾽ αὔτως, later in one word), *in like manner, just so, likewise :* Mt 20⁵ 21³⁰, ³⁶ 25¹⁷, Mk 14³¹, Lk 13⁵ 20³¹, Ro 8²⁶, I Ti 5²⁵, Tit 2⁶ ; with verb to be supplied from context, Mk 12²¹, Lk 22²⁰, I Co 11²⁵, I Ti 2⁹ 3⁸, ¹¹, Tit 2³.†

ὡσεί, adv., (a) *as if, as it were, like as, like :* Mt 3¹⁶ 9³⁶, Ac 2³ 6¹⁵, Ro 6¹³, He 1¹² ; γίνεσθαι (φαίνεσθαι) ὡσεί, Mk 9²⁶, Lk 22⁴⁴ (∥[WH]∥ R, mg., om.), 24¹¹ ; (b) in calculation, and with numbers, *about :* Mt 14²¹, Lk 3²³ 9¹⁴, ²⁸ 22⁴¹, ⁵⁹ 23⁴⁴, Ac 2⁴¹ 10³ 19⁷; ὡσεὶ λίθου βολήν, Lk 22⁴¹.†

Ὠσηέ (TTr., Ὠσ-), ὁ, (Heb. הוֹשֵׁעַ), *Hosea :* Ro 9²⁵.†

ὥσ-περ, adv., *just as, even as :* Mt 6² 20²⁸, Ac 3¹⁷, I Co 8⁵, I Th 5³, al. ; in protasis, with οὕτως (καί) in apodosis : Mt 12⁴⁰, Lk 17²⁴, Jo 5²¹, Ro 5¹⁹, Ga 4²⁹, Ja 2²⁶, al.

* ὥσ-περ-εί, adv., *as, as it were :* I Co 15⁸.†

ὥσ-τε, consecutive particle, 1. c. infin., expressing result, *so as to :* Mt 8²⁴, 12²², Mk 1²⁷, Lk 5⁷, Ac 1¹⁹, Ro 7⁶, I Co 1⁷, He 13⁶, al. ; of a designed result, Mt 10¹, Lk 4²⁹, al.; preceded by οὕτως, Ac 14¹; by τοσοῦτος, Mt 15³³. 2. C. indic., (a) *so that :* Ga 2¹³, preceded by οὕτως, Jo 3¹⁶ ; (b) *so then, therefore :* Mt 12¹², Mk 2²⁸, Ro 7⁴, I Co 3⁷, Ga 3⁹, al. 3. *so then, therefore :* c. subjc., I Co 5⁸; c. imperat., I Co 3²¹ 4⁵, Phl 2¹², I Th 4¹⁸, 1 Pe 4¹⁹, al.

*† ὠτάριον, -ου, τό, = ὠτίον (q.v.), *the ear :* Mk 14⁴⁷, Jo 18¹⁰.†

† ὠτίον, -ου, τό, dimin. of οὖς, [in LXX for אֹזֶן ;] *an ear :* Mt 26⁵¹, Lk 22⁵¹, Jo 18²⁶.†

ὠφέλεια (WH, -λία), -ας, ἡ, [in LXX for יַעַל hi., בֶּצַע, etc.;] 1. *assistance, help* (Thuc., Plat., al.). 2. *profit, advantage, benefit* (Hdt., Plat., al.) : Ro 3¹, Ju ¹⁶.†

ὠφελέω, -ῶ (< ὄφελος), [in LXX chiefly for יַעַל hi. ;] *to help, benefit, do good, profit :* absol., Ro 2²⁵ ; οὐδέν (*do no good;* v. Field, *Notes,* 21), Mt 27²⁴, Jo 6⁶³ 12¹⁹ ; c. acc. pers., He 4² ; c. dupl. acc., Mk 8³⁶, I Co 14⁶, Ga 5² ; pass., He 13⁹; c. acc., Mt 15⁵ 16²⁶, Mk 5²⁶ 7¹¹, Lk 9²⁵, I Co 13³.†

* ὠφέλιμος, -ον (< ὠφελέω), *useful, serviceable, profitable :* c. dat. commod., Tit 3⁸; seq. πρός, c. acc., I Ti 4⁸, II Ti 3¹⁶.†

ADDENDUM

(See p. 135)

ἐκ, before a vowel ἐξ, prep. c. gen., of motion outwards, separation from (opp. to εἰς; = Lat. *e*, *ex*), *from out of, from among, from.* I. Of Place, 1. of motion, *out of, forth from, off from :* Jo 6³¹, Ac 9³, Ga 1⁸, al.; esp. after verbs of motion, Mt 8²⁸ 17⁹, Mk 1²⁵ 7²⁸, Jo 1³³ 20¹, Ac 12⁷· ¹⁷ 27³⁰, al.; constr. præg., σώζειν (διασ.) ἐκ, Ju⁵, Ac 28⁴. Metaph., Mt 7⁴· ⁵, 1 Pe 2⁹; ἐκ τ. χειρός (-ῶν), seq. gen. pers., Lk 1⁷⁴, Jo 10²⁸· ²⁹· ³⁹, Ac 12⁴ 24⁷, Re 19²; πίνειν (q.v.) ἐκ; of the place from which an action proceeds, Lk 5³ (cf. 12³⁶, Jo 13⁴, 11 Co 2⁴). 2. Of change from one place or condition to another: Jo 8⁴², Ro 6¹³ 13¹¹, Re 7¹⁴, al.; c. ellips. of verb of motion, 11 Ti 2²⁶, 11 Pe 2²¹, Re 2²¹, al. 3. Of separation or distinction from a number, before collective or pl. nouns: Mt 13⁴⁷· ⁴⁹, Jo 12¹, Ac 3¹⁵, 1 Pe 1³, al.; after εἷς, Mt 10²⁹, Lk 17¹⁵, al.; οὐδείς, Jo 7¹⁹, al.; πολλοί, Jo 11¹⁹, al.; τις, Lk 11¹⁵, al.; τίς, Mt 6²⁷, al.; in partitive phrase as subject of sentence, Jo 16¹⁷; Hebraistically, ἐκ μέσου seq. gen., = ἐκ (Heb. מִתּוֹךְ), Mt 13⁴⁹, al.

4. Of position or direction (so in cl. = ἔξω): ἐκ δεξιῶν (v.s. δεξιός); ἐξ ἐναντίας, Mk 15³⁹ (metaph., Tit 2⁸); ἐκ ῥιζῶν (i.e., *utterly*), Mt 11²⁰. II. Of Time, 1. of the point of time from which, *from, since :* ἐκ γενετῆς, Jo 9¹, cf. Mk 10²⁰, Lk 23⁸, Ac 24¹⁰, al. 2. Of succession in time: ἐκ δευτέρου, *a second time*, Mk 14⁷², al., cf. Mt 26⁴⁴; ἡμέραν ἐξ ἡμέρας, *from day to day*, 11 Pe 2⁸. III. Of Origin, 1. of nativity, lineage, race: κοίτην (ἐν γαστρί) ἔχειν ἐκ, Ro 9¹⁰, Mt 1¹⁸; γεννᾶν ἐκ, Mt 1³ ᶠᶠ·; γεννᾶσθαι (γίνεσθαι) ἐκ, Jo 3⁶ 8⁴¹, Ga 4⁴; ἐκ πνεύματος (θεοῦ), Jo 1¹³ 3⁵ ᶠᶠ·, al.; ἔρχεσθαι, εἶναι, etc., ἐκ: τ. πόλεως, Jo 1⁴⁴; φυλῆς, Lk 2³⁶, al.; τ. ἐξουσίας Ἡρῴδου, Lk 23⁷; ὁ ὢν ἐκ τ. γῆς, Jo 3³¹. 2. Of the author, occasion or source: Mt 5³⁷, Jo 2¹⁶, Ro 2²⁹, 1 Co 8⁶, Ga 5⁸, al.; ἐκ (τ.) θεοῦ, 1 Co 7⁷, 11 Co 5¹, 1 Jo 4⁷; ἐκ τ. πατρός, Jo 6⁶⁵, al.; ἐκ τ. γῆς ἐστιν, λαλεῖ, Jo 3³¹; ἐκ καρδίας, Ro 6¹⁷, cf. Mk 12³⁰, 1 Ti 1⁵; ἐκ ψυχῆς, Eph 6⁶, Col 3²³; ἐκ πίστεως, Ro 14²³; κρίνειν ἐκ, Lk 19²², Re 20¹². 3. Of the agent, after passive verbs: Mt 15⁵, Mk 7¹¹, 11 Co 2², al.; freq. in Re after ἀδικεῖσθαι (2¹¹), etc. 4. Of cause, dependence, source of supply: τ. πόνου (-ων), Re 16¹⁰· ¹¹; τ. φωνῶν, Re 8¹³; ἐκ τούτου, Jo 6⁶⁶ 19¹² (but v. Meyer, in ll.); ἐκ θεοῦ λαλεῖν, 11 Co 2¹⁷; ἐκ τ. ἀληθείας εἶναι, Jo 18³⁷, 1 Jo 3¹⁹; ὁ ἐκ πίστεως, Ro 3²⁶ 4¹⁶; οἱ (ὄντες) ἐκ περιτομῆς, Ac 11², Ro 4¹², Ga 2¹², Col 4¹¹; πίνειν ἐκ, Mt 26²⁹, Mk 14²⁵, Jo 4¹³, al.; θερίζειν, Ga 6⁸; μετέχειν ἐκ (= partit. gen.), 1 Co 10¹³; c. inf., ἐκ τοῦ ἔχειν, 11 Co 8¹¹. 5. Of material: Mt 27²⁹, Jo 2¹⁵ 19², Ro 9²¹, 1 Co 11¹², Re 18¹², al.; allied to which is its use of price (= cl. gen.): Mt 27⁷, cf. ib. 20², Ac 1¹⁸. IV. By attraction = ἐν (cl.): τὰ ἐκ τ. οἰκιας, Mt 24¹⁷; τ. ἐξ αὐτοῦ δύναμιν, Mk 5³⁰ (v. Field, in l.); ὁ πατὴρ ὁ ἐξ οὐρανοῦ, Lk 11¹³. V. Adverbial phrases: ἐξ ἀνάγκης, 11 Co 9⁷, He 7¹²; ἐξ ἰσότητος, 11 Co 8¹³; ἐκ μέρους, 1 Co 12²⁷ 13⁹⁻¹²; ἐκ μέτρου, Jo 3³⁴; ἐκ συμφώνου, 1 Co 7⁵. VI. In composition, ἐκ signifies, 1. procession, removal: ἐκβαίνω, ἐκβάλλω. 2. Opening out, unfolding: ἐκτείνω; metaph., ἐξαγγέλλω. 3. Origin: ἔκγονος. 4. Completeness: ἐξαπορέω (v. M, *Pr.*, 237), ἐκπληρόω, ἐκτελέω.

APPENDIX A

THE IRREGULAR VERBS OF THE GREEK NEW TESTAMENT

The student is referred to the grammars for the tenses of the regular verbs. The following list comprises those verbs which do not conform to the regular types, with their principal parts and other tenses which occur in the NT, including some which are of regular formation. The list is confined, as a rule (but cf. ἀνοίγω, οἴγω), to simple verbs, from which the form of the compound may usually be determined without difficulty. When a tense occurs only in a compound, the simple form is preceded by a hyphen. Compare a similar list, with helpful notes, which has appeared since this was sent to press, in Moulton's *Grammar*, Vol. II, pt. ii, pp. 225 ff.

(a. = active ; m. = middle ; p. = passive. Alternative forms are enclosed in brackets.)

ἀγγέλλω, fut. -ἀγγελῶ, pf. ἤγγελκα, p. -ἤγγελμαι, 1 aor. ἤγγειλα, m. -άμην, 2 aor. p. (Bl., § 19, 3) ἠγγέλην.

-ἄγνυμι, fut. -εάξω, 1 aor. -έαξα, 2 aor. p. -εάγην, with irreg. use of augment (Bl., § 15, 2) in fut. κατεάξω and 2 aor. subjc. p. κατεαγῶ.

ἄγω, fut. ἄξω, pf. p. ἦγμαι, 2 aor. ἤγαγον, 1 aor. a. -ῆξα, p. ἤχθην, 1 fut. p. ἀχθήσομαι, impf. m. ἠγόμην.

αἰνέω, fut. αἰνέσω (-αινέσω, II Co 11²², aor. subjc. ?), 1 aor. ᾔνεσα.

αἱρέω, fut. αἱρήσω (the simple verb m. only, -ομαι, in NT), ἑλῶ (late Gk., LXX), p. -αἱρεθήσομαι, pf. ᾕρηκα, ᾕρημαι, 2 aor. εἷλον (and -λα, a hybrid form with ending of 1 aor., Bl., § 21, 1 ; inf. ἑλεῖν), 1 aor. p. ᾑρέθην, 2 aor. m. εἱλόμην.

αἴρω, fut. ἀρῶ, pf. ἦρκα, ἦρμαι, 1 aor. a. ἦρα (inf. ἆραι), p. ἤρθην, 1 fut. p. ἀρθήσομαι.

αἰσθάνομαι, 2 aor. ᾐσθόμην.

αἰσχύνομαι (p.), f. αἰσχυνθήσομαι, 1 aor. ᾐσχύνθην (-αισχύνθην).

ἀκούω, fut. ἀκούσω, -ομαι (Bl., § 18, 3), pf. ἀκήκοα, 1 aor. a. ἤκουσα, p. ἠκούσθην, 1 fut. p. ἀκουσθήσομαι.

ἀλείφω, fut. ἀλείψω, 1 aor. a. ἤλειψα, p. inf. ἀλιφθῆναι.

-ἀλλάσσω, fut. ἀλλάξω, 1 aor. a. -ἤλλαξα, pf. p. -ἤλλαγμαι, 2 aor. ἠλλάγην, 2 fut. p. ἀλλαγήσομαι.

ἅλλομαι, 2 aor. -ἡλόμην, a form -ἡλάμην (v.s. αἱρέω).

ἁμαρτάνω, fut. ἁμαρτήσω, pf. ἡμάρτηκα, 2 aor. ἥμαρτον, 1 aor. ἡμάρτησα.

ἀμφιέννυμι (-έζω, -άζω), pf. ἠμφίεσμαι.

ἀναλίσκω (-όω), fut. ἀναλώσω, 1 aor. a. ἀνήλωσα, p. ἀνηλώθην.

ἀνοίγω (v. Bl., § 24, s.v. οἴγω), fut. ἀνοίξω, pf. ἀνέῳγα (M, *Pr.*, 154), -γμαι, ἠνέῳγμαι, ἤνοιγμαι (M, *Pr.*, l.c.), 2 aor. ἠνοίγην (M, *Pr.*, 56), 1 aor. a. ἤνοιξα, ἀνέῳξα, ἠνέῳξα, p. ἠνοίχθην, ἀνεῴχθην, ἠνεῴχθην (inf. ἀνεῳχθῆναι, Lk 3²¹), 1 fut. p. ἀνοιχθήσομαι, 2 ἀνοιγήσομαι.

ἀπο-καθ-ίστημι (v.s. ἵστημι), 1 aor. p. ἀπεκατεστάθην (double augment).

ἀρέσκω, fut. ἀρέσω, 1 aor. a. ἤρεσα.

(493)

ἀρκέω, fut. ἀρκέσω, 1 aor. a. ἤρκεσα, 1 fut. p. ἀρκεσθήσομαι.
ἁρπάζω, fut. ἁρπάσω (M, Pr., 155), pf. ἥρπακα, 2 aor. p. ἡρπάγην (Bl., § 19, 3),
    1 aor. a. ἥρπασα, p. ἡρπάσθην, 2 fut. p. ἁρπαγήσομαι, plpf. a. -ηρπάκειν.
αὐξάνω (αὔξω, v. Bl., § 24), fut. αὐξήσω, 1 aor. a. ηὔξησα, p. ηὔξήθην.
ἀφίημι (-ιέω, -ίω, -έω ; v.s. ἵημι), impf. ἤφιον, pf. p. 3 pl. ἀφέωνται (cf. M, Pr.,
    38, 119).
ἀφοράω (v.s. ὁράω), 2 aor. subjc. ἀφίδω.

-βαίνω, fut. -βήσομαι, pf. -βέβηκα, 2 aor. -ἔβην (M, Pr., 110).
βάλλω, fut. βαλῶ, pf. βέβληκα, -μαι, 2 aor. ἔβαλον (a form -αν, Ac 16³⁷), 1 aor. p.
    ἐβλήθην, 1 fut. p. βληθήσομαι, plpf. p. ἐβεβλήμην.
βδελύσσομαι, pf. ἐβδέλυγμαι.
βιβρώσκω, pf. βέβρωκα.
βλαστάνω (-άω), 1 aor. a. ἐβλάστησα (Bl., § 19, 1 ; 24).
βούλομαι, 1 aor. p. depon. ἐβουλήθην (v.l. ἠβ-).

γαμέω (Bl., § 24), pf. γεγάμηκα, 1 aor. a. ἐγάμησα, ἔγημα, p. ἐγαμήθην.
γελάω, fut. γελάσω.
γηράσκω, 1 aor. a. ἐγήρασα.
γίνομαι (cl. γίγν-), fut. γενήσομαι, pf. γέγονα, γεγένημαι, 2 aor. ἐγενόμην, 1 aor.
    p. ἐγενήθην.
γινώσκω (cl. γιγν-), fut. γνώσομαι, pf. ἔγνωκα, p. ἔγνωσμαι, 2 aor. ἔγνων (subjc.
    γνῷ, γνοῖ ; Bl., § 23, 4 ; M, Pr., 55, 196), 1 aor. p. ἐγνώσθην, 1 fut. p.
    γνωσθήσομαι.
γνωρίζω, fut. γνωρίσω, -ιῶ, 1 aor. a. ἐγνώρισα, p. ἐγνωρίσθην.
γράφω, fut. γράψω, pf. γέγραφα, γέγραμμαι, 1 aor. a. ἔγραψα, 2 aor. p. ἐγράφην.

δεῖ (impers.), subjc. δέῃ, inf. δεῖν, ptcp. neut. δέον (pl. δέοντα), impf. ἔδει.
δείκνυμι (-ύω), fut. δείξω, pf. δέδειγμαι, 1 aor. a. ἔδειξα, p. ἐδείχθην.
δέομαι, 1 aor. p. ἐδεήθην.
δέρω, 1 aor. a. ἔδειρα, 2 fut. p. δαρήσομαι.
δέχομαι, fut. δέξομαι, pf. δέδεγμαι, 1 aor. m. ἐδεξάμην, p. -εδέχθην.
δέω, fut. δήσω, pf. δέδεκα, δέδεμαι, 1 aor. a. ἔδησα, p. ἐδέθην.
διακονέω, impf. διηκόνουν, fut. διακονήσω, 1 aor. διηκόνησα, p. (inf.) διακονη-
    θῆναι.
διδάσκω, fut. διδάξω, 1 aor. a. ἐδίδαξα, p. ἐδιδάχθην.
δίδωμι (-όω ; Bl., § 23, 3, 4 ; M, Pr., 55, 196), fut. δώσω, pf. δέδωκα, δέδομαι,
    2 aor. a. (pl.) ἔδομεν, m. -εδόμην, 1 aor. a. ἔδωκα (subjc. 3 s. δώσῃ), p. ἐδόθην,
    1 fut. p. δοθήσομαι.
δοκέω (-ῶ), 1 aor. a. ἔδοξα.
δραμεῖν, v.s. τρέχω.
δύναμαι, fut. δυνήσομαι, 1 aor. p. ἠδυνήθην, ἠδυνάσθην (Bl., § 24 ; M, Gr., II, 188,
    234).
δύνω (δύω ; Bl., § 24), pf. -δέδυμαι, 2 aor. ἔδυν, 1 aor. ἔδυσα, m. -εδυσάμην.

ἐάξω (fut.), etc., v.s. ἄγνυμι.
ἐάω, fut. ἐάσω, 1 aor. εἴασα, impf. εἴων.
ἐγγίζω, fut. ἐγγίσω (Ja 4⁸ A), -ιῶ, pf. ἤγγικα, 1 aor. a. ἤγγισα.
ἐγείρω, fut. ἐγερῶ, pf. ἐγήγερμαι, 1 aor. a. ἤγειρα, p. ἠγέρθην, 1 fut. p. ἐγερ-
    θήσομαι, impf. unaugmented διεγείρετο, Jo 6¹⁸.
ἐδαφίζω, fut. ἐδαφιῶ.
ἐθίζω, pf. εἴθισμαι.
ἔθω, pf. εἴωθα, q.v.
εἶδον, v.s. ὁράω.

εἰμί (to be), fut. ἔσομαι, impf. ἤμην (cl. ἦν), imperat. ἴσθι, pl. ἔστε, 3 pers. ἔστω (ἤτω), pl. ἔστωσαν, subjc. pres. ὦ, optat. εἴην, inf. εἶναι, ἔσεσθαι, ptcp. ὤν, ἐσόμενος.
εἶμι (to go; in NT, compound only), pres. 3 pl. -ἴασι(ν), impf. -ᾐειν, pl. -ᾐεσαν, inf. -ιέναι, ptcp. -ιών.
εἶπον (2 aor.), εἴρηκα, etc., v.s. λέγω.
εἴωθα (pf.; pres. obsolete), plpf. 3 pl. εἰώθεσαν.
ἐλαύνω, pf. ἐλήλακα, 1 aor. -ἤλασα.
ἐλεῖν, v.s. αἱρέω.
ἐλήλυθα (pf.), ἐλθεῖν (2 aor.), v.s. ἔρχομαι.
ἐλκόω, pf. εἴλκωμαι.
ἑλκύω (ἕλκω), fut. ἑλκύσω, 1 aor. εἴλκυσα, impf. εἶλκον.
ἐλλογάω (-έω), impf. p. unaugmented.
ἐλπίζω, fut. ἐλπιῶ, pf. ἤλπικα, 1 aor. a. ἤλπισα.
ἐμέω, 1 aor. ἤμεσα.
ἐνεγκεῖν, v.s. φέρω.
ἕννυμι, v.s. ἀμφιέννυμι.
ἔοικα (pf.; pres. obsolete).
-ἔπομαι, impf. -εἱπόμην.
ἐργάζομαι, pf. εἴργασμαι, 1 aor. p. -εἰργάσθην, m. ἠργασάμην (εἰργ-).
ἑρμηνεύω, not augmented.
ἔρχομαι, fut. ἐλεύσομαι, pf. ἐλήλυθα, 2 aor. ἦλθον (a form, 1 pl., -αμεν; inf. ἐλθεῖν), (M, Pr., 154; Bl., § 24, s.v.).
ἐρῶ (fut.), v.s. λέγω.
ἐσθίω (ἔσθω; Bl., § 24, s.v.; M, Pr., 54, 111, 155), fut. φάγομαι (2 sing. -εσαι in NT), 2 aor. ἔφαγον.
εὐαγγελίζω, augmented εὐηγ-.
εὐαρεστέω, pf. εὐαρέστηκα (εὐηρ-), 1 aor. inf. εὐαρεστῆσαι.
εὐδοκέω, 1 aor. εὐδόκησα (ηὐ-).
εὑρίσκω, fut. εὑρήσω, pf. εὕρηκα, 2 aor. εὗρον (and -α, v.s. αἱρέω), m. εὑρόμην (ptcp. εὑράμενος, He 9¹²; M, Pr., 51ₙ), 1 aor. p. εὑρέθην, 1 fut. p. εὑρεσθήσομαι.
ἐφίστημι (v.s. ἵστημι), 3 sing. m. ἐπίσταται.
ἐφοράω (v.s. ὁράω), 2 aor. imperat. ἔφιδε.
ἔχω, fut. ἕξω, pf. ἔσχηκα, 2 aor. ἔσχον (inf. σχεῖν), impf. εἶχον (a forms in pl.).

ζάω (Bl., § 24, s.v.; M, Pr., 54), fut. ζήσω (-ομαι), impf. ἔζην, 1 aor. ἔζησα.
ζέω, does not contract, -έω, -εο-.
ζωγρέω, pf. ἐζώγρημαι.
ζώννυμι (-ύω), fut. ζώσω, pf. p. -ἔζωσμαι, 1 aor. -έζωσα, m. ἐζωσάμην.

ἡττάω (ἡσσάω; Bl., § 24, s.v.), pf. ἥττημαι, 1 aor. p. ἡσσώθην.

θάπτω, 1 aor. ἔθαψα, 2 aor. p. ἐτάφην.
θέλω (cl. also ἐθέλω), fut. θελήσω, 1 aor. a. ἠθέλησα, impf. ἤθελον.
θήσω, v.s. τίθημι.
θιγγάνω, 2 aor. ἔθιγον.
θλάω, 1 fut. p. -θλασθήσομαι.
-θνήσκω (θνῄσκω), fut. -θανοῦμαι, pf. τέθνηκα, 2 aor. -ἔθανον.
θραύω, pf. τέθραυσμαι.
θρεψω, etc., v.s. τρέφω.
θύω, pf. τέθυμαι, 1 aor. ἔθυσα, p. ἐτύθην.

ἰδεῖν, v.s. ὁράω.
ἰέναι, v.s. εἶμι.

-ἵημι (cf. ἀφίημι), fut. -ἥσω, pf. -ἕωμαι (ptcp. -εἱμένος), 2 aor. inf. -εἶναι, 1 aor. a.
-ἧκα, p. -ἕθην, 1 fut. p. -ἐθήσομαι.
-ἱκνέομαι, 2 aor. -ἱκόμην.
ἱλάσκομαι, 1 aor. p. ἱλάσθην.
-ἵστημι (-άνω, -άω), fut. στήσω, -ομαι, pf. ἕστηκα (inf. ἑστάναι, ἑστακέναι, ptcp.
-ἑστώς, -ἑστηκώς), plpf. ἱστήκειν (also εἱσ-, ἑσ-), 1 aor. a. ἕστησα, p. ἐστάθην,
1 fut. p. σταθήσομαι.

καθαίρω, 1 aor. a. ἐκάθαρα, pf. p. κεκάθαρμαι.
καθαρίζω (-ερίζω), ſut. καθαριῶ, pf. κεκαθέρισμαι, 1 aor. a. ἐκαθέρισα, p. ἐκαθέ-
ρισθην (augm. and redupl. forms show ε in best NT MSS.).
καθέζομαι, augmented ἐκ-, as if not a compound.
καθεύδω,   „   „   „   „
κάθημαι,   „   „   „   „
καθίζω,   „   „   „   „
καίω, fut. καύσω, pf. κέκαυμαι, 2 aor. p. -ἐκάην, 1 aor. ἕκαυσα, p. ἐκαύθην, 1 fut. p.
καυθήσομαι, 2 fut. p. -καήσομαι.
καλέω, fut. καλέσω, pf. κέκληκα, -μαι, 1 aor. a. ἐκάλεσα, p. ἐκλήθην, 1 fut. p.
κληθήσομαι.
κάμνω, 2 aor. ἕκαμον.
κεῖμαι, impf. ἐκείμην, inf. κεῖσθαι, ptcp. κείμενος.
κείρω, 1 aor. ἕκειρα, m. ἐκειράμην.
-κέλλω, 1 aor. -ἕκειλα.
κεράννυμι, pf. κεκέρασμαι, κέκραμαι, 1 aor. a. ἐκέρασα.
κερδαίνω, fut. κερδανῶ, κερδήσω, 1 aor. a. ἐκέρδανα, ἐκέρδησα, 1 fut. p. κερδη-
θήσομαι.
κίχρημι (cf. χράω), 1 aor. ἕχρησα.
κλαίω, fut. κλαύσω, 1 aor. ἕκλαυσα.
κλάω, 1 aor. a. ἕκλασα, p. ἐκλάσθην.
κλείω, fut. κλείσω, pf. κέκλεισμαι, 1 aor. -ἕκλεισα, p. -ἐκλείσθην.
κλίνω, fut. κλινῶ, pf. κέκλικα, 1 aor. a. ἕκλινα, p. ἐκλίθην, 1 fut. p. κλιθήσομαι.
κομίζω, fut. κομίσομαι, -ιοῦμαι, 1 aor. ἐκόμισα, m. ἐκομισάμην.
κόπτω, fut. κόψω, 2 aor. -ἐκόπην, 1 aor. ἕκοψα, 2 fut. p. κοπήσομαι.
κορέννυμι, pf. κεκόρεσμαι, 1 aor. p. ἐκορέσθην.
κράζω, fut. κράξω, κεκράξομαι, pf. κέκραγα, 2 aor. ἕκραγον, 1 aor. a. ἕκραξα,
ἐκέκραξα.
κρεμάννυμι (κρέμαμαι, and once impf. ἐκρέμετο from -ομαι), 1 aor. a. ἐκρέμασα,
p. ἐκρεμάσθην.
κρίνω, fut. κρινῶ, pf. κέκρικα, -μαι, 1 aor. a. ἕκρινα, p. ἐκρίθην, m. ἐκρινάμην,
1 fut. p. κριθήσομαι.
κρύβω, impf. ἕκρυβον.
κρύπτω, fut. κρύψω, pf. κέκρυμμαι, p. ἐκρύβην, 1 aor. ἕκρυψα.
-κτείνω (-κτέννω, -ννυμι), f. -κτενῶ, 1 aor. a. -ἕκτεινα, p. -ἐκτάνθην.
κτίζω, pf. ἕκτισμαι, 1 aor. a. ἕκτισα, p. ἐκτίσθην.
-κνέω (κύω), 1 aor. a. -ἐκύησα.
-κυλίω, fut. -κυλίσω, pf. -κεκύλισμαι, 1 aor. -ἐκύλισα.

λαγχάνω, 2 aor. ἕλαχον.
λαμβάνω, fut. λήμψομαι (cl. λήψ-), pf. εἵληφα, p. εἵλημμαι, 2 aor. ἕλαβον (2 pl.
ἐλάβατε), p. ἐλαβόμην, 1 aor. p. ἐλήμφθην (cl. ἐλήφ-), 1 fut. p. -λημφθήσομαι
(cl. ληφ-).
λανθάνω, fut. -λέλησμαι, 2 aor. ἕλαθον.
λάσκω (or λακέω), 1 aor. ἐλάκησα.
λέγω (to say), fut. ἐρῶ (cf. Bl., § 24), pf. εἵρηκα, 2 aor. εἶπον, 1 aor. m. -ελεξά-
μην, p. -ελέχθην.

λέγω (to gather, in NT only in comp.), fut. -λέξω, pf. λέλεγμαι, 1 aor. -ἔλεξα,
m. -ἐλεξάμην.
λείπω (λιμπάνω), fut. λείψω, pf. λέλειμμαι, λέλιμμαι, 2 aor. -ἔλιπον, 1 aor.
ἔλειψα, p. ἐλείφθην.
λούω, pf. λέλουμαι, λέλουσμαι, 1 aor. a. ἔλουσα, m. ἐλουσάμην.

μακαρίζω, fut. μακαριῶ.
μανθάνω, pf. μεμάθηκα, 2 aor. ἔμαθον.
μαραίνω, 1 fut. p. μαρανθήσομαι.
μαρτύρομαι, 1 aor. m. ἐμαρτυράμην.
μεθύω (-ύσκομαι), 1 aor. p. ἐμεθύσθην.
μέλλω, fut. μελλήσω, impf. ἔμελλον (ἤμ-).
μέλω, fut. -μελήσομαι, 1 aor. p. -ἐμελήθην, 1 fut. p. -μεληθήσομαι.
μένω, fut. μενῶ, pf. μεμένηκα, 1 aor. ἔμεινα.
μιαίνω, pf. μεμίαμμαι (cl. usually -ασμαι), 1 aor. p. ἐμιάνθην.
-μίγνυμι, pf. μέμιγμαι, 1 aor. a. ἔμιξα.
μιμνήσκω, fut. -μνήσω, pf. μέμνημαι, 1 aor. a. -ἔμνησα, p. ἐμνήσθην, 1 fut. p.
μνησθήσομαι.
μνηστεύω, pf. ἐμνήστευμαι (v.l. μεμ-; Bl., § 15, 6), 1 aor. p. ἐμνηστεύθην.
μωραίνω, 1 aor. ἐμώρανα, p. ἐμωράνθην.

-νέμω, 1 aor. p. -ἐνεμήθην.
νυστάζω, 1 aor. a. ἐνύσταξα.

ξηραίνω, pf. ἐξήραμμαι, 1 aor. a. ἐξήρανα, p. ἐξηράνθην.
ξυράω (cl. -έω), fut. ξυρήσομαι, pf. ἐξύρημαι.

-οἴγω, v.s. ἀνοιγω, an irregular compound.
οἶδα (pf. ; pres. obsolete), alternative form of 2nd pers. pl. ἴστε (cl.) and of
3rd pl. ἴσασι(ν), fut. εἰδήσω, plpf. ᾔδειν, imperat. ἴσθι, ἴστω, ἴστε, ἴστωσαν,
subjc. εἰδῶ, inf. εἰδέναι, ptcp. εἰδώς.
οἰκτείρω, fut. οἰκτειρήσω.
οἴομαι, contr. οἶμαι.
οἴσω, v.s. φέρω.
-οἴχομαι, pf. -ῴχημαι.
-ὀκέλλω, 1 aor. -ὤκειλα.
-ὄλλυμι (-ύω), fut. -ὀλέσω, -ὀλῶ, -οῦμαι, pf. -ὄλωλα, 2 aor. -ὠλόμην, 1 aor. a. -ὤλεσα.
ὄμνυμι (-ύω), 1 aor. ὤμοσα.
ὀνίνημι, 2 aor. (a form ; v.s. αἱρέω), ὠνάμην (opt. ὀναίμην).
ὁράω (Bl., § 24), fut. ὄψομαι, pf. ἑώρακα (ἑόρ-), 2 aor. εἶδον (ἴδον in Re ; inf.
ἰδεῖν), impf. ἑώρων (but cf. προ-ορώμην), 1 aor. m. ὠψάμην, p. ὤφθην,
1 fut. p. ὀφθήσομαι.
ὀρίζω, fut. -ὁριῶ, -ὁρίσω, pf. ὥρισμαι, 1 aor. a. ὥρισα, p. ὡρίσθην.
-ὀρύσσω, 2 aor. -ὠρύγην, 1 aor. a. ὤρυξα, p. -ὠρύχθην.
ὀφείλω, 2 aor. ὄφελον (used as a particle ; cl. ὤφ-), 1 aor. ὤφειλα.

παίζω, fut. -παίξω, 1 aor. -ἔπαιξα, p. -ἐπαίχθην, 1 fut. p. -παιχθήσομαι.
πάσχω, pf. πέπονθα, 2 aor. ἔπαθον.
παύω, fut. -παύσω, παύσομαι, pf. πέπαυμαι, 1 aor. a. ἔπαυσα, m. ἐπαυσάμην,
2 fut. p. -παήσομαι.
πείθω, fut. πείσω, pf. πέποιθα, πέπεισμαι, 1 aor. ἔπεισα, p. ἐπείσθην, 1 fut. p.
πεισθήσομαι.
πεινάω, fut. πεινάσω, 1 aor. ἐπείνασα.
πήγνυμι, 1 aor. a. ἔπηξα.

πικραίνω, fut. πικρανῶ, 1 aor. ἐπίκρανα, p. ἐπικράνθην.
-πίμπλημι, pf. πέπλησμαι, 1 aor. a. ἔπλησα, p. ἐπλήσθην, 1 fut. p. πλησθήσομαι.
πίμπρημι (πίπρημι, πρήθω), 1 aor. -ἔπρησα.
πίνω, fut. πίομαι, pf. πέπωκα, 2 aor. ἔπιον (inf. πιεῖν, πεῖν ; Bl., § 6, 5), 1 aor.
   p. ἐπόθην.
πιπράσκω, pf. πέπρακα, -αμαι, 1 aor. p. ἐπράθην.
πίπτω, fut. πεσοῦμαι, pf. πέπτωκα, 2 aor. ἔπεσον (on a forms, v.s. αἱρέω).
πλάσσω, 1 aor. a. ἔπλασα, p. ἐπλάσθην.
πλατύνω, pf. πεπλάτυμμαι, 1 aor. p. ἐπλατύνθην.
πλέκω, 2 aor. p. -ἐπλάκην, 1 aor. ἔπλεξα.
πλέω (does not contract εο or εω), 1 aor. ἔπλευσα.
-πλήσσω, 2 aor. p. ἐπλήγην (in comp. ἐξ-επλάγην), 1 aor. a. -ἔπληξα.
πνέω (does not contract εο, εω, εη), 1 aor. ἔπνευσα.
πνίγω, 2 aor. p. -ἐπνίγην, 1 aor. ἔπνιξα.
πρίω (πρίζω), 1 aor. p. ἐπρίσθην.
πυνθάνομαι, 2 aor. ἐπυθόμην.

-ῥαίνω, pf. -ῥέραμμαι.
ῥαντίζω, pf. ῥεράντισμαι (v.l. ἐρρ- ; Bl., § 15, 6), 1 aor. a. ἐρράντισα (εραν-).
ῥέω, fut. ῥεύσω, 2 aor. p. ἐρρύην (ἐρυ-).
ῥηθείς, v.s. λέγω.
ῥήσσω (ῥήγνυμι ; Bl., § 24), fut. ῥήξω, 1 aor. ἔρηξα (ἔρρ-).
ῥίπτω (-έω), pf. p. ἔρριμαι (ἔρ-), 1 aor. ἔριψα.
ῥύομαι, fut. ῥύσομαι, 1 aor. m. ἐρυσάμην (ἐρρ-), p. ἐρύσθην (ἐρρ-).
ῥώννυμι, pf. ἔρρωμαι (in imper. ἔρρωσο, farewell).

σβέννυμι (-ύω), fut. σβέσω, 1 aor. a. ἔσβεσα.
σείω, fut. σείσω, 1 aor. a. ἔσεισα, p. ἐσείσθην.
σήπω, 2 pf. σέσηπα.
σκύλλω, pf. ἔσκυλμαι.
σπάω, fut. -σπάσω, pf. -ἔσπασμαι, 1 aor. a. -ἔσπασα, m. ἐσπασάμην, p. -ἐσπάσθην.
σπείρω, pf. ἔσπαρμαι, 2 aor. p. ἐσπάρην, 1 aor. ἔσπειρα.
-στέλλω, fut. -στελῶ, pf. -ἔσταλκα, -μαι, 2 aor. p. -ἐστάλην, 1 aor. -ἔστειλα.
στήκω, impf. ἔστηκον (late pres. and impf. = ἵστημι).
στηρίζω, fut. στηρίξω, -ίσω, pf. ἐστήριγμαι, 1 aor. a. ἐστήριξα (-ισα), p. ἐστηρίχθην.
στρέφω, fut. -στρέψω, pf. ἔστραμμαι (-εμμαι), 2 aor. ἐστράφην, 1 aor. ἔστρεψα,
   2 fut. p. -στραφήσομαι.
στρώννυμι (-ύω), pf. ἔστρωμαι, 1 aor. a. ἔστρωσα, p. -ἐστρώθην.
σφάζω, fut. σφάξω, pf. ἔσφαγμαι, 2 aor. ἐσφάγην, 1 aor. ἔσφαξα.
σώζω (σώζω ; Bl., § 3, 3), fut. σώσω, pf. σέσωκα, -σμαι, 1 aor. a. ἔσωσα, p.
   ἐσώθην, 1 fut. p. σωθήσομαι.

τάσσω, fut. -τάξομαι, pf. τέταχα, -γμαι, 2 aor. -ἐτάγην, 1 aor. a. ἔταξα, p. ἐτάχθην,
   m. ἐταξάμην, 2 fut. p. -ταγήσομαι.
-τείνω, fut. -τενῶ, 1 aor. -ἔτεινα.
τελέω, fut. -τελέσω, pf. τετέλεκα, -εσμαι, 1 aor. a. ἐτέλεσα, p. ἐτελέσθην, 1 fut. p.
   τελεσθήσομαι.
-τέλλω, fut. -τελοῦμαι, pf. -τέταλκα, -μαι, 1 aor. a. -ἔτειλα, m. -ἐτειλάμην.
-τέμνω, pf. -τέτμημαι, 2 aor. -ἔτεμον, 1 aor. p. -ἐτμήθην.
τήκω, 2 fut. p. τακήσομαι.
τίθημι (-έω), fut. θήσω, pf. τέθεικα, -μαι, 2 aor. m. ἐθέμην, 1 aor. a. ἔθηκα,
   p. ἐτέθην, 1 fut. p. ·τεθήσομαι.
τίκτω, fut. τέξομαι, 2 aor. ἔτεκον, 1 aor. p. ἐτέχθην.
τίνω, fut. τίσω.

APPENDIX A 499

-τρέπω, pf. -τέτραμμαι, 2 aor. p. -ἐτράπην, 1 aor. a. -ἔτρεψα, m. ἐτρεψάμην, 2 fut. p. -τραπήσομαι.
τρέφω (root θρεφ), pf. τέθραμμαι, 2 aor. -ἐτράφην, 1 aor. a. ἔθρεψα, m. -ἐθρεψάμην
τρέχω, 2 aor. ἔδραμον.
-τρίβω, fut. -τρίψω, pf. -τέτριμμαι, 1 aor. -ἔτριψα, 2 fut. p. -τριβήσομαι.
τυγχάνω, pf. τέτυχα (-ευχα), 2 aor. ἔτυχον.

φαγεῖν, v.s. ἐσθίω.
φαίνω, fut. φανοῦμαι, 2 aor. p. ἐφάνην, 1 aor. ἔφανα, 2 fut. p. φανήσομαι.
φαύσκω (φώσκω), fut. -φαύσω.
φέρω (defective ; M, Pr., 1, 10), fut. οἴσω, pf. -ἐνήνοχα, 2 aor. ἤνεγκον (inf. ἐνεγκεῖν), 1 aor. a. ἤνεγκα, p. ἠνέχθην.
φεύγω, fut. φεύξομαι, pf. πέφευγα, 2 aor. ἔφυγον.
φημί, impf. ἔφην.
φθάνω, pf. ἔφθακα, 1 aor. a. ἔφθασα.
φθείρω, fut. φθερῶ, pf. -ἔφθαρμαι, 2 aor. ἐφθάρην, 1 aor. a. ἔφθειρα, 2 fut. p. φθαρήσομαι.
φορέω, fut. φορέσω, 1 aor. ἐφόρεσα.
φράσσω, 2 aor. p. ἐφράγην, 1 aor. ἔφραξα, 2 fut. p. φραγήσομαι.
φύω, 2 aor. p. ἐφύην.
φώσκω, v.s. φαύσκω.
φωτίζω, fut. φωτίσω (-ιῶ), pf. πεφώτισμαι, 1 aor. a. ἐφώτισα, p. ἐφωτίσθην.

χαίρω, 2 aor. ἐχάρην, 2 fut. p. χαρήσομαι.
χαλάω, fut. χαλάσω, 1 aor. a. ἐχάλασα, p. ἐχαλάσθην.
-χέω (-χύννω, -χύνω), fut. -χεῶ, pf. -κέχυμαι, 1 aor. a. -ἔχεα, p. -ἐχύθην, 1 fut. p. -χυθήσομαι.
χράομαι (-ῶμαι), pf. κέχρημαι, 1 aor. m. ἐχρησάμην.
χράω, v.s. κίχρημι.
χρίω, fut. χρίσω, 1 aor. a. ἔχρισα, m. ἐχρισάμην.
χρονίζω, fut. χρονιῶ (v.l. -ίσω).

ψάλλω, fut. ψαλῶ.
-ψύχω, 1 aor. -ἔψυξα, 2 fut. p. ψυγήσομαι.

-ὠθέω, 1 aor. a. -ὦσα (-ἔωσα), 1 aor. m. -ὠσάμην.
ὠνέομαι, aor. ὠνησάμην (Attic ἐπριάμην).

APPENDIX B

ALPHABETICAL LIST OF VERBAL FORMS

(The list includes only such forms as might reasonably cause the beginner some difficulty. Where several such forms belonging to the same verb occur, a selection only is given. The others will be recognized by their similarity to those in the list and can be found in Appendix A. Those which can be traced by the cross references in the previous list and in the body of the Lexicon are, as a rule, omitted here. The present tense, enclosed in brackets, is that to which, in the Lexicon, a given form belongs.)

ἀγάγετε (ἄγω), 2 aor. impv. a.
ἀγάγῃ (id.), 2 aor. subjc. a.
ἁγνίσθητι (ἁγνίζω), 1 aor. impv. p.
αἴσθωνται (αἰσθάνομαι), 2 aor. subjc.
αἰτείτω (αἰτέω), pres. impv.
ἀκήκοα (ἀκούω), 2 pf. a.
ἀλλαγήσομαι (ἀλλάσσω), 2 fut. p.
ἀλλάξαι (id.), 1 aor. inf. a.
ἁμαρτήσῃ (ἁμαρτάνω), 1 aor. subjc. a.
ἀμησάντων (ἀμάω), 1 aor. ptcp. a., gen. pl.
ἀνάβα, -ηθι (ἀναβαίνω), 2 aor. impv.
ἀναβέβηκα (id.), pf. a.
ἀναγαγεῖν (ἀνάγω), 2 aor. inf. a.
ἀναγνούς (ἀναγινώσκω), 2 aor. ptcp. a.
ἀναγνῶναι (id.), 2 aor. inf. a.
ἀναγνωσθῇ (id.), 1 aor. subjc. p.
ἀνακεκύλισται (ἀνακυλίω), pf. p.
ἀναλοῖ (ἀναλόω, v.s. -ίσκω), pres. ind. a.
ἀναλωθῆτε (id.), 1 aor. subjc. p.
ἀναμνήσω (ἀναμιμνήσκω), fut.
ἀναπαήσομαι (ἀναπαύω), fut. m.
ἀνάπεσαι (ἀναπίπτω), 1 aor. impv. m.
ἀνάπεσε (id.), 2 aor. impv. a.
ἀνάστα, -στηθι (ἀνίστημι), 2 aor. impv. a.
ἀνατεθραμμένος (ἀνατρέφω), pf. ptcp. p.
ἀνατείλῃ (ἀνατέλλω), 1 aor. subjc. a.
ἀνατέταλκεν (id.), pf. a.
ἀναφάναντες (ἀναφαίνω), 1 aor. ptcp. a.
ἀναφανέντες (id.), 2 aor. ptcp. p.
ἀναχθέντες (ἀνάγω), 1 aor. ptcp. p.
ἀνάψαντες (ἀνάπτω), 1 aor. ptcp. a.

ἀνέγνωτε (ἀναγινώσκω), 2 aor. a.
ἀνεθάλετε (ἀναθάλλω), 2 aor. a.
ἀνεθέμην (ἀνατίθημι), 2 aor. m.
ἀνέθη (ἀνίημι), 1 aor. p.
ἀνεθρέψατο (ἀνατρέφω), 1 aor. m.
ἀνείλατο (ἀναιρέω), 2 aor. m.
ἀνείλατε, -εῖλαν (id.), 2 aor. a. (v.s. αἱρέω, App. A).
ἀνειχόμην ⟨ἀνέχω), impf. m.
ἀνελεῖ (ἀναιρέω), fut. a.
ἀνελεῖν (id.), 2 aor. inf. a.
ἀνενέγκαι (ἀναφέρω), 1 aor. inf. a.
ἀνενεγκεῖν (id.), 2 aor. inf. a.
ἀνέντες (ἀνίημι), 2 aor. ptcp. a.
ἀνέξομαι (ἀνέχω), fut. m.
ἀνέπεσεν (ἀναπίπτω), 2 aor. a.
ἀνέσεισα (ἀνασείω), 1 aor. a.
ἀνεστράφημεν (ἀναστρέφω), 2 aor. p.
ἀνεσχόμην (ἀνέχω), 2 aor. m.
ἀνέτειλα (ἀνατέλλω), 1 aor. a.
ἀνετράφη (ἀνατρέφω), 2 aor. p.
ἀνεῦραν (ἀνευρίσκω), 2 aor. a.
ἀνέῳγα (ἀνοίγω), 2 pf. a.
ἀνέῳξα (id.), 1 aor. a.
ἀνεῳχθῆναι (id.), 1 aor. inf. p.
ἀνήγαγον (ἀνάγω), 2 aor. a.
ἀνήγγειλα (ἀναγγέλλω), 1 aor. a.
ἀνηγγέλην (id.), 2 aor. p.
ἀνήνεγκεν (ἀναφέρω), 1 (2) aor. act.
ἀνῃρέθην (ἀναιρέω), 1 aor. p.
ἀνήφθη (ἀνάπτω), 1 aor. p.
ἀνήχθην (ἀνάγω), 1 aor. p.
ἀνθέξεται (ἀντέχω), fut. m

ἀνθέστηκε (ἀνθίστημι), pf. ind. a.
ἀνθίστανται (id.), pres. m.
ἀνιέντες (ἀνίημι), pres. ptcp. a.
ἀνοιγήσεται (ἀνοίγω), 2 fut. p.
ἀνοιγῶσιν (id.), 2 aor. subjc. p.
ἀνοῖξαι (id.), 1 aor. inf. a.
ἀνοίσω (ἀναφέρω), fut. a.
ἀνοιχθήσεται (ἀνοίγω), 1 fut. p.
ἀνταποδοῦναι (ἀνταποδίδωμι), 2 aor.
  inf. a.
ἀνταποδώσω (id.), fut. a.
ἀντέστην (ἀνθίστημι), 2 aor. a.
ἀντιστῆναι (id.), 2 aor. inf. a.
ἀνῶ (ἀνίημι), 2 aor. subjc. a.
ἀπαλλάξῃ (ἀπαλλάσσω), 1 aor. subjc. a.
ἀπαρθῇ (ἀπαίρω), 1 aor. subjc. p.
ἀπαρνησάσθω (ἀπαρνέομαι), 1 aor.
  impv. m.
ἀπαρνήσῃ (id.), fut. 2 s.
ἀπατάτω (ἀπατάω), pres. impv. act.
ἀπατηθεῖσα (id.), 1 aor. ptcp. p.
ἀπέβησαν (ἀποβαίνω), 2 aor. a.
ἀπέδειξεν (ἀποδείκνυμι), 1 aor. a.
ἀπέδετο (ἀποδίδωμι), 2 aor. m.
ἀπεδίδουν (id.), impf. a.
ἀπέδοτο, -δοσθε (id.), 2 aor. m.
ἀπέδωκεν (id.), 1 aor. a.
ἀπέθανεν (ἀποθνήσκω), 2 aor. a.
ἀπειπάμεθα (ἀπεῖπον), 1 aor. m.
ἀπεῖχον (ἀπέχω), impf. a.
ἀπεκατεστάθην (ἀποκαθίστημι), 1 aor.
  p.
ἀπεκατέστην (id.), 2 aor. a.
ἀπεκρίθην (ἀποκρίνω), 1 aor. p.
ἀπεκτάνθην (ἀποκτείνω), 1 aor. p.
ἀπεληλύθεισαν (ἀπέρχομαι), plpf.
ἀπελθών (id.), 2 aor. ptcp. a.
ἀπενεγκεῖν (ἀποφέρω), 2 aor. inf. a.
ἀπενεχθῆναι (id.), 1 aor. inf. p.
ἀπεπνίγη (ἀποπνίγω), 2 aor. p.
ἀπέπνιξαν (id.), 1 aor. a.
ἀπεστάλην (ἀποστέλλω), 2 aor. p.
ἀπέσταλκα (id.), pf. a.
ἀπέστειλα (id.), 1 aor. a.
ἀπέστη, -ησαν (ἀφίστημι), 2 aor. a.
ἀπεστράφησαν (ἀποστρέφω), 2 aor. p.
ἀπετάξατο (ἀποτάσσω), 1 aor. m.
ἀπῄεσαν (ἄπειμι), impf.
ἀπήλασεν (ἀπελαύνω), 1 aor. a.
ἀπηλγηκότες (ἀπαλγέω), pf. ptcp. a.
ἀπῆλθαν (ἀπέρχομαι), 2 aor. a.
ἀπηλλάχθαι (ἀπαλλάσσω), pf. inf. p.
ἀπηρνησάμην (ἀπαρνέομαι), 1 aor.
ἀπησπασάμην (ἀπασπάζομαι), 1 aor.

ἀποβάντες (ἀποβαίνω), 2 aor. ptcp. a.
ἀποβήσεται (id.), fut. 3 s.
ἀποδεδειγμένον (ἀποδείκνυμι), pf. ptcp.
  p.
ἀποδεικνύντα (id.), pres. ptcp. a.
ἀποδεῖξαι (id.), 1 aor. inf. a.
ἀποδιδόναι (ἀποδίδωμι), pres. inf. a.
ἀποδιδοῦν (id.), pr. ptcp. a. neut. s.
ἀποδοθῆναι (id.), 1 aor. inf. p.
ἀποδοῖ (id.), v.s. -δῶ.
ἀπόδος, -δοτε (id.), 2 aor. impv. a.
ἀποδοῦναι, -δούς (id.), 2 aor. inf.
  (ptcp.) a.
ἀποδῷ (id.), 2 aor. subjc. a. 3 s.
ἀποθανεῖν (ἀποθνήσκω), 2 aor. inf. a.
ἀποκαθιστάνει (ἀποκαθιστάνω), pres. a.
ἀποκατηλλάγητε (ἀποκαταλλάσσω) 2
  aor. p.
ἀποκατιστάνει = ἀποκαθιστάνει.
ἀποκριθείς (ἀποκρίνω), 1 aor. ptcp. p.
ἀποκτανθείς (ἀποκτείνω), 1 aor. ptcp. p.
ἀποκτέννυντες (ἀποκτείνω), pres. ptcp.
  a.
ἀποκτενῶ (id.), fut. a.
ἀπολέσαι (ἀπόλλυμι), 1 aor. inf. a.
ἀπολοῦμαι (id.), fut. m.
ἀπολῶ (id.), fut. a.
ἀπόλωλα (id.), 2 pf. a.
ἀπορίψαντας (ἀπορίπτω), 1 aor. ptcp. a.
ἀποσταλῶ (ἀποστέλλω), 2 aor. subjc. p.
ἀποστείλας (id.), 1 aor. ptcp. a.
ἀποστῇ (ἀφίστημι), 2 aor. subjc. a.
ἀπόστητε, -στήτω (id.), 2 aor. impv. a.
ἀποστραφῇς (ἀποστρέφω), 2 aor. subjc.
  p.
ἀπόστρεψον (id.), 1 aor. impv. a.
ἀποταξάμενος (ἀποτάσσω), 1 aor. ptcp.
  m.
ἅπτου (ἅπτω), pres. impv. m.
ἀπώλεσα (ἀπόλλυμι), 1 aor. a.
ἀπωλόμην (ἀπόλλυμι), 2 aor. m.
ἀπωσάμενος (ἀπωθέω), 1 aor. ptcp. m.
ἆραι (αἴρω), 1 aor. inf. a.
ἄρας (id.), 1 aor. ptcp. a.
ἀρέσει (ἀρέσκω), fut. a.
ἄρῃ (αἴρω), 1 aor. subjc. a.
ἀρθῇ, -θῶσιν (id.), 1 aor. subjc. p.
ἄρθητι (id.), 1 aor. impv. p.
ἀρκέσῃ (ἀρκέω), 1 aor. subjc. a.
ἄρον (αἴρω), 1 aor. impv. a.
ἁρπαγέντα (ἁρπάζω), 2 aor. ptcp. p.
ἁρπαγησόμεθα (id.), 2 fut. p.
ἀρῶ, -οῦσιν (αἴρω), fut. a.
αὐξηθῇ (αὐξάνω), 1 aor. subjc. p.

ἀφέθην (ἀφίημι), 1 aor. p.
ἀφεῖλεν (ἀφαιρέω), 2 aor. a.
ἀφεῖναι (ἀφίημι), 2 aor. inf. a.
ἀφεῖς (id.), pres. ind. a. 2 s.
ἀφείς (id.), 2 aor. ptcp. a.
ἀφελεῖ (ἀφαιρέω), fut. a.
ἀφελεῖν (id.), 2 aor. inf. a.
ἄφες (ἀφίημι), 2 aor. impv. a.
ἀφέωνται (id.), pf. pass.
ἀφῇ (id.), 2 aor. subjc. a.
ἀφῆκα (id.), 1 aor. a.
ἀφίενται and -ονται (id.), pres. p.
ἀφίκετο (ἀφικνέομαι), 2 aor.
ἀφίστασο (ἀφίστημι), pres. impv. m.
ἀφίστατο (id.), impf. m.
ἀφοριεῖ, -οῦσιν (ἀφορίζω), fut. a.
ἀφῶμεν (ἀφίημι), 2 aor. subjc. a.
ἀφωμοιωμένος (ἀφομοιόω), pf. ptcp.
  pass.
ἀχθῆναι (ἄγω), 1 aor. inf. p.
ἀχθήσεσθε (id.), 1 fut. pass.
ἄψας (ἅπτω), 1 aor. ptcp. a.
ἄψῃ (id.), 1 aor. subjc.

βαλῶ (βάλλω), fut. a.
βάλω, -η (id.), 2 aor. subjc. a.
βαρείσθω (βαρέω), pres. impv. p.
βάψῃ (βάπτω), 1 aor. subjc. a.
βεβαμμένον (id.), pf. ptcp. p.
βέβηκα (βαίνω), pf. a.
βέβληκεν (βάλλω), pf. a.
βέβρωκα (βιβρώσκω), pf. a.
βληθείς (βάλλω), 1 aor. ptcp. p.
βλήθητι (id.), 1 aor. impv. p.

γαμησάτωσαν (γαμέω), 1 aor. impv. a.
γεγένημαι (γίνομαι), pf. pass.
γεγέννημαι (γεννάω), pf. pass.
γέγοναν (γίνομαι), 2 pf. a.
γεγόνει (id.), plpf. a. 3 s.
γενάμενος (id.), 2 aor. ptcp. m.
γενέσθω (id.), 2 aor. impv. 3 s.
γένησθε (id.), 2 aor. subjc. m.
γένωνται (id.), 2 aor. subjc. m.
γήμας (γαμέω), 1 aor. ptcp. a.
γήμῃς (id.), 1 aor. subjc. a.
γνοῖ = γνῷ.
γνούς (γινώσκω), 2 aor. ptcp. a.
γνῶ, γνῷ (id.), 2 aor. subjc. a. 1 and 3 s.
γνῶθι (id.), 2 aor. impv. a.
γνωριοῦσιν (γνωρίζω), fut.
γνωσθῇ (γινώσκω), 1 aor. subjc. p.
γνωσθήσεται (id.), 1 fut. p.
γνώσομαι (id.), fut. a.
γνώτω (id.), 2 aor. impv. a.

δαρήσομαι (δέρω), 2 fut. p.
δέδεκται (δέχομαι), pf.
δεδεκώς (δέω), pf. ptcp. a.
δέδεμαι (id.), pf. p.
δεδιωγμένος (διώκω), pf. ptcp. p.
δέδοται (δίδωμι), pf. p.
δεδώκεισαν (id.), plpf. a.
δέῃ (δέω), pres. subjc.
δεθῆναι (δέω), 1 aor. inf. p.
δείραντες (δέρω), 1 aor. ptcp. a.
δέξαι (δέχομαι), 1 aor. impv.
δέξηται, -ωνται (id.), 1 aor. subjc.
δῆσαι (δέω), 1 aor. inf.
δήσῃ (id.), 1 aor. subjc. 3 s.
διαβάς (διαβαίνω), 2 aor. ptcp. a.
διαβῆναι (id.), 2 aor. inf. a.
διάδος (διαδίδωμι), 2 aor. impv. a.
διακαθᾶραι (διακαθαίρω), 1 aor. inf. a.
διαλλάγηθι (διαλλάσσω), 2 aor. impv. p.
διαμείνῃ (διαμένω), 1 aor. subjc. a.
διαμεμενηκότες (id.), pf. ptcp. a.
διαμένεις (id.), pres. ind. a.
διαμενεῖς (id.), fut. ind. a.
διανοίχθητι (διανοίγω), 1 aor. impv. p.
διαρήξας (διαρήσσω), 1 aor. ptcp. a.
  (also -ρρ-).
διασπαρέντες (διασπείρω), 2 aor. ptcp.
  p.
διασπασθῇ (διασπάω), 1 aor. subjc. p.
διαστάσης (διίστημι), 2 aor. ptcp. a.
διαστρέψαι (διαστρέφω), 1 aor. inf. a.
διαταγείς (διατάσσω), 2 aor. ptcp. p.
διαταχθέντα (id.), 1 aor. ptcp. p.
διατεταγμένος (id.), pf. ptcp. p.
διατεταχέναι (id.), pf. inf. a.
διδόασιν (δίδωμι), pres. a.
διέβησαν (διαβαίνω), 2 aor. a.
διεγείρετο (διεγείρω), impf. p. (unaugmented).
διεῖλον (διαιρέω), 2 aor. a.
διενέγκῃ (διαφέρω), 1 or 2 aor. subjc. a.
διέρηξεν (διαρήσσω), 1 aor. a. (also
  -ρρ-).
διερήσσετο (id.), impf. p.
διεσάφησαν (διασαφέω), 1 aor. a.
διεσπάρησαν (διασπείρω), 2 aor. p.
διεσπᾶσθαι (διασπάω), pf. inf. p.
διεστειλάμην (διαστέλλω), 1 aor. m.
διέστη (διίστημι), 2 aor. a.
διεστραμμένος (διαστρέφω), pf. ptcp. a.
διέταξα (διατάσσω), 1 aor. a.
διεφθάρην (διαφθείρω), 2 aor. p.
διεφθαρμένος (id.), pf. ptcp. p.
διηκόνουν (διακονέω), impf. a.
διήνοιγεν (διανοίγω), impf. a.

διήνοιξεν (id.), 1 aor. a.
διηνοίχθησαν (id.), 1 aor. p.
διορυγῆναι (διορύσσω), 2 aor. inf. p.
διορυχθῆναι (id.), 1 aor. inf. p.
διώδευε (διοδεύω), impf. a.
διωξάτω (διώκω), 1 aor. impv. a.
διώξητε (id.), 1 aor. subjc. a.
διωχθήσονται (id.), 1 fut. p.
δοθεῖσαν (δίδωμι), 1 aor. ptcp. p.
δοθῇ (id.), 1 aor. subjc. p.
δοῖ (id.), 2 aor. subjc. a.
δός, δότε, δότω (id.), 2 aor. impv. a.
δοῦναι (id.), 2 aor. inf. a.
δούς (id.), 2 aor. ptcp. a.
δύνῃ (δύναμαι), pres. ind.
δῶ, δώῃ (δίδωμι), 2 aor. subjc. a.
δῴη (id.), 2 aor. opt. a.
δῶμεν, δῶτε (id.), 2 aor. subjc. a.
δώσῃ, -σωμεν (id.), 1 aor. subjc. a.

ἔβαλαν (βάλλω), 2 aor. a.
ἐβάσκανε (βασκαίνω), 1 aor. a.
ἐβδελυγμένος (βδελύσσω), pf. ptcp. p.
ἐβέβλητο (βάλλω), plpf. p.
ἐβλήθην (id.), 1 aor. p.
ἔγγισαν (ἐγγίζω), 1 aor. a.
ἐγεγόνει (γίνομαι), plpf. a.
ἔγειραι (ἐγείρω), 1 aor. impv. m.
ἐγείραι (id.), 1 aor. inf. a.
ἐγείρου (id.), pres. impv. p.
ἐγενήθην (γίνομαι), 1 aor. p.
ἐγεννήθην (γεννάω), 1 aor. p.
ἐγερεῖ (ἐγείρω), fut. a.
ἐγερθείς (id.), 1 aor. ptcp. p.
ἐγερθήσεται (id.), 1 fut p.
ἐγέρθητι (id.), 1 aor. impv. p.
ἐγήγερμαι (id.), pf. p.
ἔγημα (γαμέω), 1 aor. a.
ἔγνωκαν (γινώσκω), pf. a.
ἐγνωκέναι (id.), pf. inf. a.
ἔγνων (id.), 2 aor. a.
ἔγχρισαι (ἐγχρίω), 1 aor. impv. m.
ἐγχρῖσαι (id.), 1 aor. inf. a.
ἔγχρισον (id.), 1 aor. impv. a.
ἐδαφιοῦσιν (ἐδαφίζω), fut. a.
ἐδέετο, -εῖτο (δέομαι), impf.
ἐδεήθην (id.), 1 aor.
ἔδει (impers. δεῖ), impf.
ἔδειραν (δέρω), 1 aor. a.
ἔδησα (δέω), 1 aor. a.
ἐδίωξα (διώκω), 1 aor. a.
ἐδολιοῦσαν (δολιόω), late impf.
ἔδραμον (τρέχω), 2 aor. a.
ἔδυ, ἔδυσεν (δύνω), 2 and 1 aor. a. 3 s.

ἔζησα (ζάω), 1 aor. a.
ἐζῆτε, ἔζων (id.), impf. a.
ἐθέμην (τίθημι), 2 aor. m.
ἔθηκα (id.), 1 aor. a.
ἔθου (id.), 2 aor. m.
ἔθρεψα (τρέφω), 1 aor. a.
εἶα (ἐάω), impf. a.
εἴασα (id.), 1 aor. a.
εἶδα = εἶδον (ὁράω, q.v.), 2 aor.
εἰθισμένον (ἐθίζω), pf. ptcp. p.
εἵλατο (αἱρέω), 2 aor. m.
εἴληπται (λαμβάνω), pf. p.
εἴληφα (id.), pf. a.
εἷλκον (ἕλκω), impf. a.
εἵλκυσε, -αν (ἑλκύω), 1 aor. a.
εἱλκωμένος (ἑλκόω), pf. ptcp. p.
εἴξαμεν (εἴκω), 1 aor. a.
εἰσδραμοῦσα (εἰστρέχω), 2 aor. ptcp.
εἰσελήλυθα (εἰσέρχομαι), pf.
εἰσῄει (εἴσειμι), impf.
εἰσίασιν (id.), pres. ind.
εἱστήκεισαν (ἵστημι), plpf. a.
εἶχαν, -οσαν (ἔχω), impf.
εἴων (ἐάω), impf.
ἐκαθάρισεν, -ερ- (καθαρίζω, -ερ-), 1 aor. act.
ἐκαθαρίσθη, -ερ- (id.), 1 aor. p.
ἐκδώσεται (ἐκδίδωμι), fut. m.
ἐκέκραξα, ἔκραξα (κράζω), 1 aor. a.
ἐκέρασα (κεράννυμι), 1 aor. a.
ἐκέρδησα (κερδαίνω), 1 aor. a.
ἐκκαθάρατε (ἐκκαθαίρω), 1 aor. impv.
ἐκκαθάρῃ (id.), 1 aor. subjc. a.
ἐκκεχυμένος (ἐκχέω), pf. ptcp. p.
ἐκκοπήσῃ (ἐκκόπτω), 2 fut. p.
ἔκκοψον (id.), 1 aor. impv. a.
ἔκλασα (κλάω), 1 aor. a.
ἔκλαυσα (κλαίω), 1 aor. a.
ἐκλέλησθε (ἐκλανθάνω), pf. m.
ἐκλήθην (καλέω), 1 aor. p.
ἐκόψασθε (κόπτω), 1 aor. m.
ἐκπλεῦσαι (ἐκπλέω), 1 aor. inf. a.
ἔκραξα (κράζω), 1 aor. a.
ἐκρύβη (κρύπτω), 2 aor. p.
ἐκσῶσαι (ἐκσώζω), 1 aor. inf. a.
ἐκτενεῖς (ἐκτείνω), fut. a.
ἐκτησάμην (κτάομαι), 1 aor.
ἔκτισται (κτίζω), pf. p.
ἐκτραπῇ (ἐκτρέπω), 2 aor. subjc. p.
ἐκφύῃ (ἐκφύω), pres. or 2 aor. subjc. a.
ἐκχέαι (ἐκχέω), 1 aor. inf. a.
ἐκχέετε (id.), pres. or 2 aor. impv. a.
ἐλάβετε (λαμβάνω), 2 aor. a.
ἐλάκησεν (λάσκω or λακέω), 1 aor. a.

504 APPENDIX B

ἔλαχε (λαγχάνω), 2 aor. a.
ἐλήσον (ἐλεέω), 1 aor. impv. a.
ἐλεύσομαι (ἔρχομαι), fut.
ἐληλακότες (ἐλαύνω), pf. ptcp. a.
ἐλήλυθα (ἔρχομαι), pf.
ἐλιθάσθησαν (λιθάζω), 1 aor. p.
ἐλκύσαι (ἐλκύω), 1 aor. inf. a.
ἑλόμενος (αἱρέω), 2 aor. ptcp. m.
ἐλπιοῦσιν (ἐλπίζω), fut. 3 pl.
ἔμαθον (μανθάνω), 2 aor. a.
ἐμασῶντο (μασάομαι), impf.
ἐμβάς (ἐμβαίνω), 2 aor. ptcp. a.
ἐμβάψας (ἐμβάπτω), 1 aor. ptcp. a.
ἐμβῆναι (ἐμβαίνω), 2 aor. inf. a.
ἔμιξε (μίγνυμι), 1 aor. a.
ἐμπεπλησμένος (ἐμπίμπλημι), pf. ptcp. p.
ἐμπλησθῶ (id.), 1 aor. subjc. p.
ἐμώρανα (μωραίνω), 1 aor. a.
ἐνεδυναμοῦτο (ἐνδυναμόω), impf. p.
ἐνείλησα (ἐνειλέω), 1 aor. a.
ἐνεῖχεν (ἐνέχω), impf. a.
ἐνένευον (ἐννεύω), impf. a.
ἐνέπλησεν (ἐμπίμπλημι), 1 aor. a.
ἐνέπρησε (ἐμπίπρημι, ἐμπρήθω), 1 aor. a.
ἐνέπτυον, -σαν (ἐμπτύω), impf. and 1 aor. a.
ἐνεστηκότα (ἐνίστημι), pf. ptcp. a.
ἐνεστῶτα, -ῶσαν, -ῶτος (id.), pf. ptcp. a.
ἐνετειλάμην (ἐντέλλω), 1 aor. m.
ἐνετύλιξα (ἐντυλίσσω), 1 aor. a.
ἐνεφάνισαν (ἐμφανίζω), 1 aor. a.
ἐνεφύσησεν (ἐμφυσάω), 1 aor. a.
ἐνεχθείς (φέρω), 1 aor. ptcp. p.
ἐνήργηκα (ἐνεργέω), pf. a.
ἐνκρῖναι (ἐνκρίνω), 1 aor. inf. a.
ἐνοικοῦν (ἐνοικέω), pres. ptcp. a.
ἐντελεῖται (ἐντέλλω), fut. m.
ἐντέταλται (id.), pf. m.
ἐντραπῇ (ἐντρέπω), 2 aor. subjc. p.
ἐντραπήσονται (id.), 2 fut. p.
ἔνυξε (νύσσω), 1 aor. a.
ἐνύσταξαν (νυστάζω), 1 aor. a.
ἐνῴκησεν (ἐνοικέω), 1 aor. a.
ἐξαλειφθῆναι, -λιφ- (ἐξαλείφω), 1 aor. inf. p.
ἐξαναστήσῃ (ἐξανίστημι), 1 aor. subjc.
ἐξανέστησαν (id.)., 2 aor. a.
ἐξάρατε (ἐξαίρω), 1 aor. impv. a.
ἐξαρεῖτε (id.), fut. a.
ἐξαρθῇ (id.), 1 aor. subjc. p.

ἐξέδετο (ἐκδίδωμι), 2 aor. m.
ἐξείλατο (ἐξαιρέω), 2 aor. m.
ἐξεκαύθησαν (ἐκκαίω), 1 aor. p.
ἐξέκλιναν (ἐκκλίνω), 1 aor. a.
ἐξεκόπης (ἐκκόπτω), 2 aor. p.
ἔξελε (ἐξαιρέω), 2 aor. impv. a.
ἐξελέξω (ἐκλέγω), 1 aor. m. 2 s.
ἐξέληται (ἐξαιρέω), 2 aor. subjc. m.
ἐξενέγκαντες (ἐκφέρω), 1 aor. ptcp. a.
ἐξενεγκεῖν (id.), 2 aor. inf. a.
ἐξένευσεν (ἐκνεύω), 1 aor. a.
ἐξεπέτασα (ἐκπετάννυμι), 1 aor. a.
ἐξεπλάγησαν (ἐκπλήσσω), 2 aor. p.
ἐξέπλει (ἐκπλέω), impf. a.
ἐξεστακέναι (ἐξίστημι), pf. inf. a.
ἐξέστραπται (ἐκστρέφω), pf. p.
ἐξετάσαι (ἐξετάζω), 1 aor. inf. a.
ἐξετράπησαν (ἐκτρέπω), 2 aor. p.
ἐξέχεε (ἐκχέω), 1 aor. a.
ἐξεχύθησαν (id.), 1 aor. p.
ἐξέωσεν = ἐξῶσεν.
ἐξήεσαν (ἔξειμι), impf.
ἐξηραμμένος (ξηραίνω), pf. ptcp. p.
ἐξήρανα, -ράνθην (id.), 1 aor. a. and p.
ἐξήρανται (id.), pf. p. 3 s.
ἐξηραύνησα (ἐξεραυνάω), 1 aor. a.
ἐξηρτισμένος (ἐξαρτίζω), pf. ptcp. p.
ἐξήχηται (ἐξηχέω), pf. pass.
ἐξιέναι (ἔξειμι), pres. inf.
ἐξιστάνων (ἐξίστημι, q.v.), pres. ptcp.
ἐξοίσουσι (ἐκφέρω), fut. a.
ἐξῶσαι (ἐξωθέω), 1 aor. inf. a.
ἐξῶσεν (id.), 1 aor. a.
ἑόρακα (ὁράω), pf. a.
ἐπαγαγεῖν (ἐπάγω), 2 aor. inf. a.
ἔπαθεν (πάσχω), 2 aor. a.
ἐπαισχύνθην (ἐπαισχύνομαι), 1 aor.
ἐπαναπαήσεται (ἐπαναπαύω), fut. m.
ἐπάξας (ἐπάγω), 1 aor. ptcp. a.
ἐπάρας (ἐπαίρω), 1 aor. ptcp. a.
ἐπεῖδεν (ἐπεῖδον), 3 s.
ἐπειράσω (πειράζω), 1 aor. m.
ἐπειρᾶτο, -ρῶντο (πειράω), impf. m.
ἔπεισα (πείθω), 1 aor. a.
ἐπείσθησαν (id.), 1 aor. p.
ἐπεῖχεν (ἐπέχω), impf. a.
ἐπεκέλλω (ἐπικέλλω), 1 aor. a.
ἐπεκέκλητο (ἐπικαλέω), plpf. p.
ἐπελάθετο, -οντο (ἐπιλανθάνομαι), 2 aor.
ἐπέλειχον (ἐπιλείχω), impf. a.
ἔπεσα (πίπτω), 2 aor. a.
ἐπέστησαν (ἐφίστημι), 2 aor. a.
ἐπέσχεν (ἐπέχω), 2 aor. a.

ἐπετίμα (ἐπιτιμάω), impf.
ἐπετράπη (ἐπιτρέπω), 2 aor. p.
ἐπεφάνη (ἐπιφαίνω), 2 aor. p.
ἐπέχρισεν (ἐπιχρίω), 1 aor. a.
ἐπηκροῶντο (ἐπακροάομαι), impf.
ἐπήνεσεν (ἐπαινέω), 1 aor. a.
ἔπηξεν (πήγνυμι), 1 aor. a.
ἐπῆρα (ἐπαίρω), 1 aor. a.
ἐπήρθη (id.), 1 aor. p.
ἐπῆρκεν (id.), pf. a.
ἐπίασα (πιάζω), 1 aor. a.
ἐπίβλεψαι (ἐπιβλέπω), 1 aor. impv. m.
ἐπιβλέψαι (id.), 1 aor. inf. a.
ἔπιδε (ἐπεῖδον), impv.
ἐπίθες (ἐπιτίθημι), 2 aor. impv. a.
ἐπικέκλησαι (ἐπικαλέω), pf. m.
ἐπικέκλητο (id.), plpf. p.
ἐπικληθέντα (ἐπικαλέω), 1 aor. ptcp. p.
ἐπικράνθησαν (πικραίνω), 1 aor. p.
ἐπιλελησμένος (ἐπιλανθάνομαι), pf. ptcp. p.
ἐπιμελήθητι (ἐπιμελέομαι), 1 aor. impv. p.
ἔπιον (πίνω), 2 aor. a.
ἐπιπλήξῃς (ἐπιπλήσσω), 1 aor. subjc. a.
ἐπιποθήσατε (ἐπιποθέω), 1 aor. impv. a.
ἐπιστᾶσα (ἐφίστημι), 2 aor. ptcp. a.
ἐπίσταται (id.), pres. ind. m.
ἐπίσταται (ἐπίσταμαι), pres. ind.
ἐπίστηθι (ἐφίστημι), 2 aor. impv. a.
ἐπιστώθης (πιστόω), 1 aor. p.
ἐπιτεθῇ (ἐπιτίθημι), 1 aor. subjc. p.
ἐπιτιθέασι (id.), pres. a.
ἐπιτίθει (id.), pres. impv. a.
ἐπιτιμάσαι (ἐπιτιμάω), 1 aor. opt. a.
ἐπιφᾶναι (ἐπιφαίνω), 1 aor. inf. a.
ἐπλανήθησαν (πλανάω), 1 aor. p.
ἐπλάσθη (πλάσσω), 1 aor. p.
ἐπλήγη (πλήσσω), 2 aor. p.
ἔπλησαν (πίμπλημι), 1 aor. a.
ἐπλήσθη, -θησαν (id.), 1 aor. p.
ἐπλουτήσατε (πλουτέω), 1 aor. a.
ἐπλουτίσθητε (πλουτίζω), 1 aor. p.
ἔπλυναν (πλύνω), 1 aor. a.
ἔπνευσαν (πνέω), 1 aor. a.
ἐπνίγοντο (πνίγω), impf. p.
ἔπνιξαν (id.), 1 aor. a.
ἐπράθη (πιπράσκω), 1 aor. p.
ἔπραξα (πράσσω), 1 aor. a.
ἐπρίσθησαν (πρίζω), 1 aor. p.
ἐπροφήτευσα (προφητεύω), 1 aor. a.
ἔπτυσε (πτύω), 1 aor. a.
ἐράντισεν (ῥαντίζω), 1 aor. a.
ἐράπισαν (ῥαπίζω), 1 aor. a.

ἐρριζωμένοι (ῥιζόω), pf. ptcp. p.
ἐριμμένοι (ῥίπτω), pf. ptcp. p.
ἔρριπται (id.), pf. p.
ἔριψαν (id.), 1 aor. a.
ἔρρωσο, -ωσθε (ῥώννυμι), pf. impv. p.
ἐρύσατο (ῥύομαι), 1 aor. m. (ἐρρ-).
ἐρύσθην (id.), 1 aor. p.
ἐσάλπισε (σαλπίζω), 1 aor. a.
ἔσβεσαν (σβέννυμι), 1 aor. a.
ἐσείσθην (σείω), 1 aor. p.
ἐσήμανεν (σημαίνω), 1 aor. a.
ἐσκυλμένοι (σκύλλω), pf. ptcp. p.
ἐσπαρμένος (σπείρω), pf. ptcp. p.
ἐστάθην (ἵστημι), 1 aor. p.
ἑστάναι (id.), pf. inf. a.
ἑστήκασιν (ἵστημι), pf. a.
ἕστηκεν (στήκω), impf.
ἑστηκώς (ἵστημι), pf. ptcp. a.
ἔστην (id.), 2 aor. a.
ἐστηριγμένος (στηρίζω), pf. ptcp. p.
ἐστήρικται (id.), pf. p.
ἔστησαν (ἵστημι), 1 or 2 aor. 3 pl.
ἐστρωμένον (στρώννυμι), pf. ptcp. p.
ἔστρωσαν (id.), 1 aor. a.
ἔστωσαν (εἰμί), impv.
ἐσφαγμένος (σφάζω), pf. ptcp. p.
ἐσφραγισμένος (σφραγίζω), pf. ptcp. p.
ἔσχηκα (ἔχω), pf.
ἐσχηκότα (id.), pf. ptcp. a.
ἔσχον (id.), 2 aor. a.
ἐτάφη (θάπτω), 2 aor. p.
ἐτέθην (τίθημι), 1 aor. p.
ἐτεθνήκει (θνήσκω), plpf. a.
ἔτεκεν (τίκτω), 2 aor. a.
ἐτέχθη (id.), 1 aor. p.
ἐτίθει (τίθημι), impf. a.
ἐτύθη (θύω), 1 aor. p.
εὐαρεστηκέναι, εὐηρ- (εὐαρεστέω), pf inf. a.
εὐξάμην (εὔχομαι), 1 aor.
εὕραμεν, εὗραν (εὑρίσκω), 2 aor. a.
εὑρέθην (id.), 1 aor. p.
εὑρηκέναι (id.), pf. inf. a.
εὐφράνθητι (εὐφραίνω), 1 aor. impv. p.
ἔφαγον (ἐσθίω), 2 aor. a.
ἐφαλόμενος (ἐφάλλομαι), 2 aor. ptcp.
ἐφάνην (φαίνω), 2 aor. p.
ἔφασκεν (φάσκω), impf. a.
ἐφείσατο (φείδομαι), 1 aor.
ἐφεστώς (ἐφίστημι), pf. ptcp. a.
ἔφθακα, -σα (φθάνω), pf. and 1 aor. a.
ἐφθάρην (φθείρω), 2 aor. p.
ἐφίλει (φιλέω), impf. a.
ἐφίσταται (ἐφίστημι), pres. m.

ἔφραξαν (φράσσω), 1 aor. a.
ἐφρύαξαν (φρυάσσω), 1 aor. a.
ἔφυγον (φεύγω), 2 aor. a.
ἐχάρην (χαίρω), 2 aor. p.
ἔχρισα (χρίω), 1 aor. a.
ἐχρῶντο (χράομαι), impf.
ἐψεύσω (ψεύδομαι), 1 aor. m.
ἑώρακα (ὁράω), pf. a.
ἑωράκει (id.), plpf. a.
ἑώρων (id.), impf. a.

ζβέννυτε = σβ- (σβέννυμι), pres.
ζῇ, ζῆν or ζῆν, ζῆς, ζῶ (ζάω).
ζῶσαι (ζώννυμι), 1 aor. impv. m.
ζώσει (id.), fut. a.

ἠβουλήθην (βούλομαι, q.v.), 1 aor. p.
ἤγαγον (ἄγω), 2 aor. a.
ἠγάπα (ἀγαπάω), impf. a.
ἠγαπηκόσι (ἀγαπάω), pf. ptcp. a.
ἤγγειλαν (ἀγγέλλω), 1 aor. a.
ἤγγικα, -σα (ἐγγίζω), pf. and 1 aor. a.
ἤγειρεν (ἐγείρω), 1 aor. a.
ἠγέρθην (id.), 1 aor. p.
ἤγετο, -οντο (ἄγω), impf. p.
ἤγημαι (ἡγέομαι), pf.
ἠγνικότες (ἁγνίζω), pf. ptcp. a.
ἠγνισμένος (id.), pf. ptcp. p.
ἠγνόουν (ἀγνοέω), impf. a.
ᾔδεισαν (οἶδα), plpf.
ἠδυνήθη, -άσθη (δύναμαι), 1 aor.
ἤθελον (θέλω), impf.
ἤκασι (ἥκω), pf. a.
ἠκολουθήκαμεν (ἀκολουθέω), pf. a.
ἥλατο (ἅλλομαι), 1 aor. 3 s.
ἠλάττωσας (ἐλαττόω), 1 aor. ptcp. a.
ἠλαύνετο (ἐλαύνω), impf. p. 3 s.
ἠλεήθην (ἐλεέω), 1 aor. p.
ἠλεημένος (id.), pf. ptcp. p.
ἠλέησα (id.), 1 aor. a.
ἤλειψα (ἀλείφω), 1 aor. a.
ἦλθον (ἔρχομαι), 2 aor. a.
ἠλκωμένος (ἑλκόω), pf. ptcp. p.
ἤλλαξαν (ἀλλάσσω), 1 aor. a.
ἤλπικα, -σα (ἐλπίζω), pf. and 1 aor. a.
ἡμάρτηκα (ἁμαρτάνω), pf. a.
ἥμαρτον (id.), 2 aor. a.
ἤμεθα, ἤμεν (εἰμί), impf.
ἤμελλον (μέλλω), impf.
ἤμην (εἰμί), impf.
ἠμφιεσμένος (ἀμφιέννυμι), pf. ptcp. p.
ἤνεγκα (φέρω), 1 aor. a.
ἠνέχθην (id.), 1 aor. p.
ἠνεῳγμένος (ἀνοίγω), pf. ptcp. p.
ἠνέῳξα (id.), 1 aor. a.

ἠνεῴχθην (id.), 1 aor. p.
ἠνοίγην (id.), 2 aor. p.
ἤνοιξα (id.), 1 aor. a.
ἠνοίχθην (id.), 1 aor. p.
ἥξει (ἥκω), fut. a.
ἠξίου (ἀξιόω), impf. a.
ἠξίωται (id.), pf. p.
ἠπατήθη (ἀπατάω), 1 aor. p.
ἠπείθησαν (ἀπειθέω), 1 aor. a.
ἠπείθουν (id.), impf. a.
ἤπειλει (ἀπειλέω), impf. a.
ἠπίστουν (ἀπιστέω), impf. a.
ἠπόρει (ἀπορέω), impf. a.
ἥπτοντο (ἅπτω), impf. m.
ἦρα (αἴρω), 1 aor. a.
ἠργαζόμην, -σάμην (ἐργάζομαι), impf. and 1 aor.
ἠρέθισα (ἐρεθίζω), 1 aor. a.
ἤρεσα (ἀρέσκω), 1 aor. a.
ἤρεσκον (ἀρέσκω), impf. a.
ἠρημώθη (ἐρημόω), 1 aor. p.
ἤρθην (αἴρω), 1 aor. p.
ἦρκεν (id.), pf. a.
ἠρμένος (id.), pf. ptcp. p.
ἠρνεῖτο (ἀρνέομαι), impf.
ἤρνημαι (id.), pf. pass.
ἠρνησάμην (id.), 1 aor.
ἠρξάμην (ἄρχω), 1 aor. m.
ἡρπάγη (ἁρπάζω), 2 aor. p.
ἥρπασε (id.), 1 aor. a.
ἡρπάσθη (ἁρπάζω), 1 aor. p.
ἠρτυμένος (ἀρτύω), pf. ptcp. p.
ἤρχοντο (ἔρχομαι), impf.
ἠρώτων (ἐρωτάω), impf. a.
ἦς, ἦσθα (εἰμί), impf.
ἤσθιον (ἐσθίω), impf. a.
ἡσσώθητε (ἡττάω), 1 aor. p.
ᾐτήκαμεν (αἰτέω), pf. a.
ᾔτησα, -σάμην (id.), 1 aor. a. and m.
ἠτίμασα (ἀτιμάζω), 1 aor. a.
ἠτίμησα (ἀτιμάω), 1 aor. a.
ἡτοίμακα (ἑτοιμάζω), pf. a.
ᾐτοῦντο (αἰτέω), impf. m.
ἡττήθητε (ἡττάω), 1 aor. p.
ἥττηται (id.), pf. p.
ᾔτω (εἰμί), pres. impv.
ηὐδόκησα (εὐδοκέω), 1 aor. a.
ηὐδοκοῦμεν (id.), impf. a.
ηὐκαίρουν (εὐκαιρέω), impf.
ηὐλήσαμεν (αὐλέω), 1 aor. a.
ηὐλόγει (εὐλογέω), impf. a.
ηὐλόγηκα, -σα (id.), pf. and 1 aor. a.
ηὔξησα (αὔξανω), 1 aor. a.
ηὐπορεῖτο (εὐπορέω), impf. m.

ηὑρίσκετο (εὑρίσκω), impf. p.
ηὕρισκον (id.), impf. a.
ηὐφόρησεν (εὐφορέω), 1 aor. a.
ηὐφράνθη (εὐφραίνω), 1 aor. p.
ηὐχαρίστησαν (εὐχαριστέω), 1 aor. a.
ηὐχόμην (εὔχομαι), impf.
ἤφιε (ἀφίημι), impf.
ἤχθην (ἄγω), 1 aor. p.
ἠχρειώθησαν (ἀχρειόω), 1 aor. p.
ἠψάμην (ἅπτω), 1 aor. m.

θάψαι (θάπτω), 1 aor. inf. a.
θεῖναι, θείς (τίθημι), 2 aor. inf. and ptcp. a.
θέμενος (id.), 2 aor. ptcp. m.
θέντες (id.), 2 aor. ptcp. a. nom. pl. mas.
θέσθε (id.), 2 aor. impv. m.
θέτε (id.), 2 aor. impv. a.
θίγῃς, θίγῃ (θιγγάνω), 2 aor. subjc. a.
θῶ (τίθημι), 2 aor. subjc. a.

ἰάθη (ἰάομαι), 1 aor. p.
ἴαται (id.), pf. p.
ἰᾶτο (id.), impf.
ἴδον = εἶδον.
ἴσασι (οἶδα), 3 pl.
ἴσθι (εἰμί), impv.
ἰστάνομεν, ἰστῶμεν (ἵστημι, q.v.).
ἴστε (οἶδα), ind. or impv.
ἱστήκειν (ἵστημι), plpf. a.
ἰώμενος (ἰάομαι), pres. ptcp.

καθαριεῖ (καθαρίζω), fut.
καθαρίσαι (id.), 1 aor. inf. a.
καθεῖλε (καθαιρέω), 2 aor. a.
καθελῶ (id.), fut. a.
κάθῃ (κάθημαι), pres. ind.
καθῆκαν (καθίημι), 1 aor. a.
καθήσεσθε (κάθημαι), fut.
καθῆψε (καθάπτω), 1 aor. a.
κάθου (κάθημαι), pres. impv.
καλέσαι (καλέω), 1 aor. inf. a.
κάλεσον (id.), 1 aor. impv. a.
κάμητε (κάμνω), 2 aor. subjc. a.
κατάβα, κατάβηθι (καταβαίνω), 2 aor. impv. a.
καταβέβηκα (id.), pf. a.
καταβῇ (id.), 2 aor. subjc. a.
κατακαήσομαι (κατακαίω), 2 fut. p.
κατακαῦσαι (id.), 1 aor. inf. a.
κατακαυχῶ (κατακαυχάομαι), pres. impv.

καταλάβῃ (καταλαμβάνω), 2 aor. subjc. a.
καταπίῃ (καταπίνω), 2 aor. subjc. a.
καταποθῇ (id.), 1 aor. subjc. p.
καταρτίσαι (καταρτίζω), 1 aor. inf. or opt. a.
κατασκηνοῖν, -οῦν (κατασκηνόω), pres. inf. a.
κατάσχωμεν (κατέχω), 2 aor. subjc. a.
κατεαγῶσιν (κατάγνυμι), 2 aor. subjc. p.
κατέαξα (id.), 1 aor. a.
κατεάξει (id.), fut. a.
κατέβη (καταβαίνω), 2 aor. a.
κατεγνωσμένος (καταγινώσκω), pf. ptcp. p.
κατειλημμένος (καταλαμβάνω), pf. ptcp. p.
κατειληφέναι (id.), pf. inf. a.
κατεκάη (κατακαίω), 2 aor. p.
κατέκλασε (κατακλάω), 1 aor. a.
κατέκλεισα (κατακλείω), 1 aor. a.
κατενεχθείς (καταφέρω), 1 aor. ptcp. p.
κατενύγησαν (κατανύσσω), 2 aor. p.
κατεπέστησαν (κατεφίστημι), 2 aor. a.
κατέπιε (καταπίνω), 2 aor. a.
κατεπόθην (id.), 1 aor. p.
κατεσκαμμένος (κατασκάπτω), pf. ptcp. p.
κατεστραμμένος (καταστρέφω), pf. ptcp. p.
κατεστρώθησαν (καταστρώννυμι), 1 aor. p.
κατευθῦναι (κατευθύνω), 1 aor. inf. a.
κατευθύναι (id.), 1 aor. opt. a.
κατέφαγον (κατεσθίω), 2 aor. a.
κατήγγειλα (καταγγέλλω), 1 aor. a.
κατηγγέλη (id.), 2 aor. p.
κατήνεγκα (καταφέρω), 1 aor. a.
κατήντηκα, -σα (καταντάω), pf. and 1 aor. a.
κατηράσω (καταράομαι), 1 aor.
κατήργηται (καταργέω), pf. p.
κατηρτισμένος (καταρτίζω), pf. ptcp. p.
κατηρτίσω (id.), 1 aor. m. 2 s.
κατησχύνθην (καταισχύνω), 1 aor. p.
κατήχηνται (κατηχέω), pf. p.
κατηχήσω (id.), 1 aor. subjc. a.
κατίωται (κατιόω), pf. p.
κατώκισεν (κατοικίζω), 1 aor. a.
κανθήσομαι (καίω), 1 fut. p.
καυχᾶσαι (καυχάομαι), pres. ind.
κεκαθαρισμένος (καθαρίζω), pf. ptcp. p.
κεκαθαρμένος (καθαίρω), pf. ptcp. p.
κεκαλυμμένος (καλύπτω), pf. ptcp. p.

508　　APPENDIX B

κεκαυμένος (καίω), pf. ptcp. p.
κεκερασμένος (κεράννυμι), pf. ptcp. p.
κέκλεισμαι (κλείω), pf. p.
κέκληκα (καλέω), pf. a.
κέκληται (id.), pf. p.
κέκλικεν (κλίνω), pf. a.
κέκμηκας (κάμνω), pf. a.
κεκορεσμένος (κορέννυμι), pf. ptcp. p.
κέκραγε (κράζω), 2 pf. a.
κεκράξονται (id.), fut. m.
κεκρατηκέναι (κρατέω), pf. inf. a.
κεκράτηνται (id.), pf. p.
κεκρίκει (κρίνω), plpf. a.
κέκριμαι (id.), pf. p.
κεκρυμμένος (κρύπτω), pf. ptcp. p.
κεράσατε (κεράννυμι), 1 aor. impv. a.
κερδανῶ, κερδήσω (κερδαίνω), fut. a.
κερδάνω (id.), 1 aor. subjc. a.
κεχάρισμαι (χαρίζομαι), pf.
κεχαριτωμένος (χαριτόω), pf. ptcp. p.
κέχρημαι (χράομαι), pf.
κεχωρισμένος (χωρίζω), pf. ptcp. p.
κηρύξαι, -ῦξαι (κηρύσσω), 1 aor. inf. a
κλάσαι (κλάω), 1 aor. inf. a.
κλαύσατε (κλαίω), 1 aor. impv. a.
κλαύσω, -ομαι (id.), fut.
κλεισθῶσιν (κλείω), 1 aor. subjc. p.
κληθῇς (καλέω), 1 aor. subjc. p.
κλῶμεν (κλάω), pres. ind. a.
κλώμενος (id.), pres. ptcp. p.
κλῶντες (id.), pres. ptcp. a.
κοιμώμενος (κοιμάω), pres. ptcp. p.
κολλήθητι (κολλάω), 1 aor. impv. p.
κομιεῖται (κομίζω), fut. m.
κομίσασα (id.), 1 aor. ptcp. a.
κορεσθέντες (κορέννυμι), 1 aor. ptcp. p.
κόψας (κόπτω), 1 aor. ptcp. a.
κράξας (κράζω), 1 aor. ptcp. a.
κράξουσιν (id.), fut. a.
κράτει (κρατέω), pres. impv.
κριθήσεσθε (κρίνω), 1 fut. p.
κριθῶσιν (id.), 1 aor. subjc. p.
κρυβῆναι (κρύπτω), 2 aor. inf. p.
κτήσασθε (κτάομαι), 1 aor. impv. m.
κτήσησθε (id.), 1 aor. subjc. m.

λάβε, -βη (λαμβάνω), 2 aor. impv. and
　subjc. a.
λαθεῖν (λανθάνω), 2 aor. inf. a.
λαχοῦσι (λαγχάνω), 2 aor. ptcp. a.
λάχωμεν (id.), 2 aor. subjc. a.
λελουμένος, -σμένος (λούω), pf. ptcp. p.
λέλυσαι (λύω), pf. pass.
λημφθῇ (λαμβάνω), 1 aor. subjc. p.

λήμψομαι (id.), fut.
λίπῃ (λείπω), 2 aor. subjc. a.

μάθετε (μανθάνω), 2 aor. impv. a.
μάθητε (id.), 2 aor. subjc. a.
μαθών (id.), 2 aor. ptcp. a.
μαρανθήσομαι (μαραίνω), 1 fut. p.
μακαριοῦσι (μακαρίζω), fut.
μακροθύμησον (μακροθυμέω), 1 aor.
　impv. a.
μεθιστάναι (μεθίστημι), pres. inf. a.
μεθυσθῶσιν (μεθύω), 1 aor. subjc. p.
μεῖναι (μένω), 1 aor. inf.
μείναντες (id.), 1 aor. ptcp.
μείνατε, μεῖνον (id.), 1 aor. impv.
μείνῃ, -ητε, -ωσιν (id.), 1 aor. subjc.
μελέτα (μελετάω), pres. impv. a.
μεμαθηκώς (μανθάνω), pf. ptcp. a.
μεμενήκεισαν (μένω), plpf. a.
μεμιαμμένος (μιαίνω), pf. ptcp. p.
μεμίανται (id.), pf. pass.
μεμιγμένος (μίγνυμι), pf. ptcp. p.
μέμνησθε (μιμνήσκω), pf. m.
μεμύημαι (μυέω), pf. p.
μενεῖτε (μένω), fut. ind.
μένετε (id.), pres. ind. or impv.
μετάβα, -βηθι (μεταβαίνω), 2 aor.
　impv. a.
μετασταθῶ (μεθίστημι), 1 aor. subjc. p.
μεταστραφήτω (μεταστρέφω), 2 aor.
　impv. p.
μετέθηκεν (μετατίθημι), 1 aor. a.
μετέστησεν (μεθίστημι), 1 aor. a.
μετέσχηκεν (μετέχω), pf. a.
μετετέθησαν (μετατίθημι), 1 aor. p.
μετήλλαξαν (μεταλλάσσω), 1 aor. a.
μετῆρεν (μεταίρω), 1 aor. a.
μετοικιῶ (μετοικίζω), fut. a.
μετῴκισεν (id.), 1 aor. a.
μιανθῶσιν (μιαίνω), 1 aor. subjc. p.
μνησθῆναι (μιμνήσκω), 1 aor. inf. p.
μνήσθητι, -τε (id.), 1 aor. impv. p.
μνησθῶ, -θῇς (id.), 1 aor. subjc. p.

νενίκηκα (νικάω), pf. a.
νενομοθέτηται (νομοθετέω), pf. pass.
νήψατε (νήφω), 1 aor. impv.
νόει (νοέω), pres. impv. a.
νοούμενα (id.), pres. ptcp. p.

ὀδυνᾶσαι (ὀδυνάω), pres. ind. m.
οἴσω (φέρω), fut. a.
ὀμνύναι, -ύειν (ὄμνυμι, -ύω), pres. inf. a.
ὀμόσαι (id.), 1 aor. inf. a.

ὁμόσῃ (id.), 1 aor. subjc. a.
ὀναίμην (ὀνίνημι), 2 aor. opt. m.
ὁρῶσαι (ὁράω), pres. ptcp. a.
ὀφθείς (id.), 1 aor. ptcp. p.
ὄψει, -η (id.), fut.
ὄψησθε (id.), 1 aor. subjc. m.

παθεῖν (πάσχω), 2 aor. inf. a.
πάθῃ (id.), 2 aor. subjc. a.
παίσῃ (παίω), 1 aor. subjc. a.
παραβολευσάμενος (παραβολεύομαι), 1 aor. ptcp.
παραβουλευσάμενος (παραβουλεύομαι),1 aor. ptcp.
παραδεδώκεισαν (παραδίδωμι), plpf.
παραδιδοῖ, -δῷ (παραδίδωμι), pres. subjc.
παραδιδούς, παραδούς (id.), pres. and 2 aor. ptcp.
παραδῶ, -δοῖ (id.), 2 aor. subjc. a.
παραθεῖναι (παρατίθημι), 2 aor. inf. a.
παράθου (id.), 2 aor. impr. m.
παραθῶσιν (id.), 2 aor. subjc. a.
παραιτοῦ (παραιτέομαι), pres. impv.
παρακεκαλυμμένος (παρακαλύπτω), pf. ptcp. p.
παρακεχειμακότι (παραχειμάζω), pf. ptcp. a.
παρακληθῶσιν (παρακαλέω), 1 aor. subjc. p.
παρακύψας (παρακύπτω), 1 aor. ptcp. a.
παραλημφθήσεται (παραλαμβάνω), 1 fut. p.
παραπλεῦσαι (παραπλέω), 1 aor. inf. a.
παραρυῶμεν (παραρέω), 2 aor. subjc. p.
παραστῆσαι (παρίστημι), 1 aor. inf. a.
παραστῆτε (id.), 2 aor. subjc. a.
παρασχών (παρέχω), 2 aor. ptcp. a.
παρατιθέσθωσαν (παρατίθημι), pres. impv. 3 pl.
παρεδίδοσαν (παραδίδωμι), impf. 3 pl.
παρέθεντο (παρατίθημι), 2 aor. m.
πάρει (πάρειμι), pres. ind.
παρειμένος (παρίημι), pf. ptcp. p.
παρεῖναι (παρίημι), 2 aor. inf. a.
παρεῖναι (πάρειμι), pres. inf.
παρεισάξουσιν (παρεισάγω), fut. a.
παρεισεδύησαν (παρεισδύω), 2 aor. p.
παρεισέδυσαν (id.), 1 aor. a.
παρεισενέγκαντες (παρεισφέρω), 1 aor. ptcp. a.
παρειστήκεισαν (παρίστημι), plpf. a.
παρεῖχαν (παρέχω), impf.

παρειχόμην (id.), impf. m.
παρέκυψεν (παρακύπτω), 1 aor. a.
παρελάβοσαν (παραλαμβάνω), 2 aor. a.
παρελεύσονται (παρέρχομαι), fut.
παρεληλυθέναι (id.), pf. inf. a.
παρελθάτω (id.), 2 aor. impr. a.
παρενεγκεῖν (παραφέρω), 2 aor. inf.
παρέξει, -η (παρέχω), fut. a. and m.
παρεπίκραναν (παραπικραίνω), 1 aor. a
παρεσκεύασται (παρασκευάζω), pf. p.
παρεστηκότες, -εστῶτες (παρίστημι), pf. ptcp. a.
παρέτεινε (παρατείνω), 1 aor. a.
παρετήρουν (παρατηρέω), impf. a.
παρήγγειλαν (παραγγέλλω), 1 aor. a.
παρηκολούθηκας (παρακολουθέω), pf. a.
παρήνει (παραινέω), impf. a.
παρῃτημένος (παραιτέομαι), pf. ptcp. p.
παρῴκησεν (παροικέω), 1 aor. a.
παρώξυντο (παροξύνω), impf. p.
παρώτρυναν (παροτρύνω), 1 aor. a.
παρῳχημένος (παροίχομαι), pf. ptcp.
παυσάτω (παύω), 1 aor. impv. a.
πεῖν (πίνω), 2 aor. inf. a.
πείσας (πείθω), 1 aor. a.
πέπαυται (παύω), pf. m.
πεπειραμένος (πειράω), pf. ptcp. p.
πεπειρασμένος (πειράζω), pf. ptcp. p.
πέπεισμαι (πείθω), pf. p.
πεπιεσμένος (πιέζω), pf. ptcp. p.
πεπιστευκόσι (πιστεύω), pf. ptcp. a.
πεπλάνησθε (πλανάω), p. p.
πεπλάτυνται (πλατύνω), pf. p.
πεπληρωκέναι (πληρόω), pf. inf. a.
πέποιθα (πείθω), 2 pf.
πέπονθα (πάσχω), 2 pf.
πεπότικεν (ποτίζω), pf. a.
πέπρακε (πιπράσκω), pf. a.
πέπραχα (πράσσω), pf. a.
πέπτωκα (πίπτω), pf. a.
πεπυρωμένος (πυρόω), pf. ptcp. a.
πέπωκε (πίνω), pf. a.
πεπωρωμένος (πωρόω), pf. ptcp. p.
περιάψας (περιάπτω), 1 aor. ptcp. a.
περιδραμών (περιτρέχω), 2 aor. ptcp. a.
περιεδέδετο (περιδέω), plpf. p.
περιεζωσμένος (περιζώννυμι), pf. ptcp. p.
περιέκρυβον (περικρύπτω), 2 aor. a.
περιελεῖν (περιαιρέω), 2 aor. inf. a.
περιέπεσον (περιπίπτω), 2 aor. a.
περιεσπᾶτο (περισπάω), impf. p.
περιέσχον (περιέχω), 2 aor. a.
περιέτεμον (περιτέμνω), 2 aor. a.

περίζωσαι (περιζώννυμι), 1 aor. impv. m.

περιηρεῖτο (περιαιρέω), impf. p.

περιθέντες (περιτίθημι), 2 aor. ptcp. a.

περιΐστασο (περιΐστημι), pres. m. or p.

περιπέσητε (περιπίπτω), 2 aor. subjc. a.

περιρεραμμένος (περιραίνω), pf. ptcp. p.

περιρήξαντες (περιρήγνυμι), 1 aor. ptcp. a.

περισσεῦσαι, -εύσαι (περισσεύω), 1 aor. inf. and opt. a.

περιτετμημένος (περιτέμνω), pf. ptcp. p.

περιτμηθῆναι (περιτέμνω), 1 aor. inf. p.

πεσεῖν (πίπτω), 2 aor. inf. a.

πέτηται (πέτομαι), pres. subjc.

πετώμενος (πετάομαι), pres. ptcp.

πεφανέρωται (φανερόω), pf. p.

πεφίμωσο (φιμόω), pf. impv. p.

πιάσαι (πιάζω), 1 aor. inf. a.

πίε, πιεῖν (πίνω), 2 aor. impv. and inf. a.

πικρανεῖ (πικραίνω), fut. a.

πλάσας (πλάσσω), 1 aor. ptcp. a.

πλέξαντες (πλέκω), 1 aor. ptcp. a.

πλεονάσαι (πλεονάζω), 1 aor. opt. a.

πληθυνθῆναι (πληθύνω), 1 aor. inf. p.

πληρωθῇ (πληρόω), 1 aor. subjc. p.

πλήσας, -σθείς (πίμπλημι), 1 aor. ptcp. a. and p.

ποιήσειαν (ποιέω), 1 aor. opt.

ποιμανεῖ (ποιμαίνω), fut. a.

πραθείς (πιπράσκω), 1 aor. ptcp. p.

προβάς (προβαίνω), 2 aor. ptcp. a.

προβεβηκυῖα (id.), pf. ptcp. a.

προγεγονώς (προγίνομαι), pf. ptcp. a.

προεβίβασαν (προβιβάζω), 1 aor. a.

προεγνωσμένος (προγινώσκω), pf. ptcp. p.

προελεύσεται (προέρχομαι), fut.

προενήρξατο (προενάρχομαι), 1 aor.

προεπηγγείλατο (προεπαγγέλλω), 1 aor. m.

προεστῶτες (προΐστημι), pf. ptcp. a.

προέτειναν (προτείνω), 1 aor. a.

προεφήτευον (προφητεύω), impf. a.

προέφθασεν (προφθάνω), 1 aor. a.

προεωρακότες (προοράω), pf. ptcp. a.

προῆγεν (προάγω), impf. a.

προηλπικότας (προελπίζω), pf. ptcp. a.

προημαρτηκώς (προαμαρτάνω), pf. ptcp. a.

προητιασάμεθα (προαιτιάομαι), 1 aor.

προητοίμασα (προετοιμάζω), 1 aor. a.

προκεκηρυγμένος (προκηρύσσω), pf. ptcp. p.

προκεχειρισμένος (προχειρίζω), pf ptcp. p.

προκεχειροτονημένος (προχειροτονέω), pf. ptcp. p.

προοράωμην (προοράω), impf. m.

προσανέθεντο (προσανατίθημι), 2 aor. m.

προσειργάσατο (προσεργάζομαι), 1 aor.

προσεκλίθη (προσκλίνω), 1 aor. p.

προσεκολλήθη (προσκολλάω), 1 aor. p.

προσεκύνουν (προσκυνέω), impf. a.

προσενήνοχεν (προσφέρω), pf. a.

προσέπισεν (προσπίπτω), 2 aor. a.

προσέρηξεν (προσρήγνυμι), 1 aor. a.

προσέσχηκα (προσέχω), pf. a.

προσεφώνει (προσφωνέω), impf. a.

προσεῶντος (προσεάω), pres. ptcp. a.

προσήνεγκα (προσφέρω), 1 aor. a.

προσηργάσατο (προσεργάζομαι), 1 aor.

προσηύξατο (προσεύχομαι), 1 aor.

πρόσθες (προστίθημι), 2 aor. impv. a.

προσλαβοῦ (προσλαμβάνω), 2 aor. impv. m.

προσμεῖναι (προσμένω), 1 aor. inf. a.

προσπήξας (προσπήγνυμι), 1 aor. ptcp. a.

προστῆναι (προΐστημι), 2 aor. inf. a.

προσωρμίσθησαν (προσορμίζω), 1 aor. p.

προσώχθισα (προσοχθίζω), 1 aor. a.

προτρεψάμενος (προτρέπω), 1 aor. ptcp. m.

προϋπῆρχον (προϋπάρχω), impf. a.

πταίσητε (πταίω), 1 aor. subjc. a.

πτοηθῆτε (πτοέω), 1 aor. subjc. p.

πτύξας (πτύσσω), 1 aor. ptcp. a.

πτύσας (πτύω), 1 aor. ptcp. a.

πυθόμενος (πυνθάνομαι), 2 aor. ptcp.

ῥαντίσωνται (ῥαντίζω), 1 aor. subjc. m.

ῥεύσουσιν (ῥέω), fut.

ῥῆξον (ῥήγνυμι), 1 aor. impv. a.

ῥίψας (ῥίπτω), 1 aor. ptcp. a.

ῥυπανθήτω (ῥυπαίνω), 1 aor. impv. p.

ῥυπαρευθήτω (ῥυπαρεύομαι), 1 aor. impv. p.

ῥῦσαι (ῥύομαι), 1 aor. impv. m.

σβέσαι (σβέννυμι), 1 aor. inf. a.

σέσηπε (σήπω), 2 pf. a.

σεσιγημένος (σιγάω), pf. ptcp. p.

σέσωκα (σώζω), pf. a.

σημᾶναι (σημαίνω), 1 aor. inf. a.

σθενώσει (σθενόω), fut. a.

σπαρείς (σπείρω), 2 aor. ptcp. p.

σπεῦσον (σπεύδω), 1 aor. impv. a.
σταθῇ, στάς, etc. (ἵστημι), 1 and 2
aor.
στηρίξαι (στηρίζω), 1 aor. inf. a.
στήσῃ (ἵστημι), 1 aor. subjc. a.
στραφείς (στρέφω), 2 aor. ptcp. p.
στρῶσον (στρώννυμι), 1 aor. impv. a.
συγκ-, v.s. συνκ-.
συλλαβοῦσα (συλλαμβάνω), 2 aor. ptcp.
a.
συλλήμψῃ (id.), fut.
συμπ-, v.s. συνπ-.
συναγάγετε (συνάγω), 2 aor. impv. a.
συνανέκειντο (συνανάκειμαι), impf.
συναπαχθέντες (συναπάγω), 1 aor.
ptcp. p.
συναπέθανον (συναποθνήσκω), 2 aor. a.
συναπήχθη (συναπάγω), 1 aor. p.
συναπώλετο (συναπόλλυμι), 2 aor. m.
συνᾶραι (συναίρω), 1 aor. inf. a.
συναχθήσομαι (συνάγω), 1 fut. p.
συνδεδεμένος (συνδέω), pf. ptcp. p.
συνέζευξεν (συνζεύγνυμι), 1 aor. a.
συνέθεντο (συντίθημι), 2 aor. m.
συνειδυίης (συνεῖδον), pf. ptcp. a.
συνειληφυῖα (συλλαμβάνω), pf. ptcp. a.
συνείπετο (συνέπομαι), impf.
συνείχετο (συνέχω), impf. p.
συνεκόμισαν (συνκομίζω), 1 aor. a.
συνεληλυθώς (συνέρχομαι), pf. ptcp.
συνεπέστη (συνεφίστημι), 2 aor. a.
συνέπιον (συνπίνω), 2 aor. a.
συνεσπάραξεν (συσπαράσσω), 1 aor. a.
συνεσταλμένος (συστέλλω), pf. ptcp. p.
συνεστῶσα (συνίστημι), pf. ptcp.
συνέταξα (συντάσσω), 1 aor. a.
συνετάφημεν (συνθάπτω), 2 aor. p.
σύνετε (συνίημι), 2 aor. a.
συνετέθειντο (συντίθημι), plpf. m.
συνετήρει (συντηρέω), impf. a.
συνεφαγές (συνεσθίω), 2 aor. a.
συνέχεον (συνχέω), impf. or 2 aor.
συνηγέρθητε (συνεγείρω), 1 aor. p.
συνηγμένος (συνάγω), pf. ptcp. p.
συνήθλησαν (συναθλέω), 1 aor. a.
συνηθροισμένος (συναθροίζω), pf. ptcp.
p.
συνῆκαν (συνίημι), 1 aor. a.
συνήλασεν (συνελαύνω), 1 aor. a.
συνήλλασσεν (συναλλάσσω), impf. a.
συνήντησεν (συναντάω), 1 aor. a.
συνήργει (συνεργέω), impf. a.
συνηρπάκει, -ήρπασαν (συναρπάζω),
plpf. and 1 aor.

συνῆσαν (σύνειμι), impf.
συνήσθιεν (συνεσθίω), impf.
συνῆτε (συνίημι), 2 aor. subjc. a.
συνήχθη (συνάγω), 1 aor. p.
συνιδών (συνεῖδον), ptcp.
συνιείς (συνίημι), pres. ptcp.
συνιόντος (σύνειμι), pres. ptcp. gen. s.
συνιστάνειν (συνίστημι), pres. inf.
συνίωσι (συνίημι), pres. subjc.
συνκατατεθειμένος (συνκατατίθημι), pf.
ptcp. m.
συνκεκερασμένος (συνκεράννυμι), pf.
ptcp. p.
συνπαρακληθῆναι (συνπαρακαλέω), 1
aor. inf. p.
συνόντων (σύνειμι), ptcp. gen. pl.
συνταφέντες (συνθάπτω), 2 aor. ptcp.
p.
συντελεσθείς (συντελέω), 1 aor. ptcp. p.
συντετμημένος (συντέμνω), pf. ptcp. p.
συντετριμμένος (συντρίβω), pf. ptcp. p.
συντετρίφθαι (id.), pf. inf. p.
συνυπεκρίθησαν (συνυποκρίνομαι), 1
aor. p.
συνφύεισαι (συνφύω), 2 aor. ptcp. p.
συνῶσι (συνίημι), 2 aor. subjc. a.
σωθῇ (σώζω), 1 aor. p.
σῶσαι (id.), 1 aor. inf. a.

τακήσεται (τήκω), fut. p.
ταραχθῆναι (ταράσσω), 1 aor. inf. p.
τεθέαται (θεάομαι), pf.
τέθεικα (τίθημι), pf. a.
τεθεμελίωτο (θεμελιόω), plpf. p.
τεθῇ (τίθημι), 1 aor. subjc. p.
τεθλιμμένος (θλίβω), pf. ptcp. p.
τεθνάναι (θνήσκω), pf. inf. a.
τεθνηκέναι (id.), pf. inf. a.
τεθραμμένος (τρέφω), pf. ptcp. p.
τεθραυσμένος (θραύω), pf. ptcp. p.
τεθυμένα (θύω), pf. ptcp. p.
τεθῶσιν (τίθημι), 1 aor. subjc. p.
τέκῃ (τίκτω), 2 aor. subjc. a.
τελεσθῶσιν (τελέω), 1 aor. subjc. p.
τέξῃ (τίκτω), fut.
τεταγμένος (τάσσω), pf. ptcp. p.
τέτακται (id.), pf. p.
τεταραγμένος (ταράσσω), pf. ptcp. p.
τετάρακται (id.), pf. p.
τεταχέναι (id.), pf. inf. a.
τετέλεσται (τελέω), pf. p.
τέτευχα (τυγχάνω), pf. a.
τετήρηκαν (τηρέω), pf. a.
τετιμημένος (τιμάω), pf. ptcp. p.

τετραχηλισμένος (τραχηλίζω), pf. ptcp. p.
τετύφωται (τυφόω), pf. p.
τέτυχα (τυγχάνω), pf. a.
τεχθείς (τίκτω), 1 aor. ptcp. p.
τίσουσιν (τίνω), fut. a.

ὑπέδειξα (ὑποδείκνυμι), 1 aor. a.
ὑπέθηκα (ὑποτίθημι), 1 aor. a.
ὑπέλαβεν (ὑπολαμβάνω), 2 aor. a.
ὑπελείφθην (ὑπολείπω), 1 aor. p.
ὑπέμεινα, -μενον (ὑπομένω), 1 aor. and impf.
ὑπεμνήσθην (ὑπομιμνήσκω), 1 aor. p.
ὑπενεγκεῖν (ὑποφέρω), 2 aor. inf. a.
ὑπενόουν (ὑπονοέω), impf. a.
ὑπέπλευσα (ὑποπλέω), 1 aor. a.
ὑπεριδών (ὑπερεῖδον), ptcp.
ὑπέστρεψα (ὑποστρέφω), 1 aor. a.
ὑπεστρώννυον (ὑποστρώννυμι), impf.
ὑπετάγη (ὑποτασσω), 2 aor. p.
ὑπέταξα (id.), 1 aor. a.
ὑπῆγον (ὑπάγω), impf. a.
ὑπήκουον (ὑπακούω), impf. a.
ὑπήνεγκα (ὑποφέρω), 1 aor. a.
ὑπῆρχον (ὑπάρχω), impf. a.
ὑποδέδεκται (ὑποδέχομαι), pf.
ὑποδεδεμένος (ὑποδέω), pf. ptcp. p.
ὑποδῆσαι (id.), 1 aor. impv. m.
ὑποδραμόντες(ὑποτρέχω), 2 aor. ptcp. a.
ὑπομείνας, -μεμνηκὼς (ὑπομένω), 1 aor. and pf. ptcp. a.
ὑπομνῆσαι (ὑπομιμνήσκω), 1 aor. inf. a.
ὑποπνεύσας (ὑποπνέω), 1 aor. ptcp. a.
ὑποστείληται (ὑποστέλλω), 1 aor. subjc. m.
ὑποταγῇ (ὑποτάσσω), 2 aor. subjc. p.
ὑποτάξαι (id.), 1 aor. inf. a.
ὑποτέτακται (id.), pf. p.
ὑστερηκέναι (ὑστερέω), pf. inf. a.
ὑψωθῶ (ὑψόω), 1 aor. subjc. p.

φάγεσαι (ἐσθίω), fut. 2 s.
φάνῃ (φαίνω), 1 aor. subjc. a.

φείσομαι (φείδομαι), fut.
φεύξομαι (φεύγω), fut.
φθαρῇ (φθείρω), 2 aor. subjc. p.
φθάσωμεν (φθάνω), 1 aor. subjc.
φθερεῖ (φθείρω), fut. a.
φιμοῖν, -οῦν (φιμόω), pres. inf. a.
φραγῇ (φράσσω), 2 aor. subjc. p.
φράσον (φράζω), 1 aor. impv.
φυείς, φύς (φύω), 2 aor. p. and a.
φύλαξον (φυλάσσω), 1 aor. impv. a.
φυτεύθητι (φυτεύω), 1 aor. impv. p.
φωτιεῖ, -τίσει (φωτίζω), fut.

χαλῶσιν (χαλάω), pres. a. 3 pl.
χαρῆναι (χαίρω), 2 aor. inf. p.
χαρήσομαι (id.), fut.
χρῆσαι (χράομαι), 1 aor. impv. m.
χρῆσον (κίχρημι), 1 aor. impv. a.
χρονίσει (χρονίζω), fut.
χρῶ (χράομαι), pres. impv.
χωρῆσαι (χωρέω), 1 aor. inf. a.
χωρίσαι (χωρίζω), 1 aor. inf. a.
χωροῦσαι (χωρέω), pres. ptcp. a.

ψηλαφήσειαν (ψηλαφάω), 1 aor. opt.
ψυγήσεται (ψύχω), 2 fut. p.
ψωμίσω (ψωμίζω), 1 aor. subjc. a.

ᾠκοδόμουν (οἰκοδομέω), impf.
ὡμίλει (ὁμιλέω), impf.
ὡμολόγουν (ὁμολογέω), impf.
ὤμοσα (ὄμνυμι), 1 aor. a.
ὠνείδισα (ὀνειδίζω), 1 aor. a.
ὠνόμασα (ὀνομάζω), 1 aor. a.
ὤρθριζεν (ὀρθρίζω), impf.
ὥρισα (ὁρίζω), 1 aor. a.
ὥρμησα (ὁρμάω), 1 aor. a.
ὤρυξεν (ὀρύσσω), 1 aor. a.
ὠρχήσασθε (ὀρχέομαι), 1 aor.
ὤφειλον (ὀφείλω), impf.
ὤφθην (ὁράω), 1 aor. p.

PRINTED IN GREAT BRITAIN AT THE UNIVERSITY PRESS, ABERDEEN